SAP PRESS e-books

Cloud Integration with SAP® Integration Suite

John Bilay, Shashank Singh, Swati Singh, Peter Gutsche,
Mandy Krimmel

Cloud Integration with SAP® Integration Suite

The Comprehensive Guide

Editor Rachel Gibson
Acquisitions Editor Hareem Shafi
Copyeditor Julie McNamee
Cover Design Graham Geary
Photo Credit iStockphoto: 504400037/© zhangguifu
Layout Design Vera Brauner
Production Kyrsten Coleman
Typesetting SatzPro, Germany
Printed and bound in the United States of America, on paper from sustainable sources

ISBN 978-1-4932-2471-5

4th edition 2024

Library of Congress Cataloging-in-Publication Data
Names: Bilay, John Mutumba, author.
Title: Cloud integration with SAP Integration suite : the comprehensive guide / John Bilay, Shashank Singh, Swati Singh, Peter Gutsche, Mandy Krimmel.
Other titles: SAP HANA cloud integration
Description: 4th edition. | Bonn ; Boston : Rheinwerk Publishing, 2024. | An earlier edition of this work published as: SAP HANA cloud integration / John Mutumba Bilay, Peter Gutsche, Volker Stiehl. 2016.
Identifiers: LCCN 2024015320 | ISBN 9781493224715 (hardcover) | ISBN 9781493224722 (ebook)
Subjects: LCSH: Cloud computing. | SAP HANA (Electronic resource)
Classification: LCC QA76.585 .B55 2024 | DDC 004.67/82--dc23/eng/20240409
LC record available at https://lccn.loc.gov/2024015320

Contents at a Glance

Contents

12 Special Topics in Cloud Integration 857

13 Summary and Outlook 881

Foreword by Andreas Quenstedt

Your interest in the fourth edition of this book indicates that you work in one of the crucial topics of information technology: business process integrations in heterogenous system environments. You enable your business users to run processes across system and organizational boundaries. By mediating interfaces, you contribute significantly to the customer value your organization creates. You might not always think about your daily work that way—but you truly can and should.

Business processes change permanently for a long list of valid reasons. One top of mind example is supply chain refinements to increase resilience against geopolitical challenges. The time and resources required to implement these changes are competitive dimensions in all industries. Your business users will look up to you to get related process integrations adopted fast.

On the other hand, technology evolutions also drive change. These days, everybody follows the innovation curve of generative AI, which is helping to improve the efficiency of daily work. The transformation and modernization of existing system environments (and their integrations) towards cloud services is in full swing. Modern approaches like event-driven architecture (EDA) and application programming interface (API)-led integrations are in large scale adoption, and the enterprise automation domain is rising.

Your topic of interest is not only crucial but also challenging and interesting. Your work will never be boring!

SAP has supported its customers for decades to master their process integration challenges. Since the third edition of this book was published, we combined a set of integration services (including Cloud Integration) into one coherent offering: SAP Integration Suite. Our suite is a market-leading enterprise integration platform as a service (EIPaaS). It is adopted as a strategic, general purpose EIPaaS to integrate heterogenous customer landscapes, including all non-SAP systems. Hundreds of prebuilt integrations at SAP Business Accelerator Hub expedite implementations, while our low-code tools support efficient custom development, testing, and maintenance.

The ongoing cloud adoption demands integration modernization. As not all systems, processes, and data will move to cloud, there is a need for ground-to-ground integrations. SAP Integration Suite offers an optional, hybrid runtime called Edge Integration Cell to serve this demand. Our new API artifact for Edge Integration Cell provides you with an innovative, coherent experience when combining API management and mediation for API-led integrations. For customers implementing EDA, we added SAP Integration Suite, advanced event mesh to our portfolio.

The focus of this book is Cloud Integration. It's a great asset for beginners to get a comprehensive introduction as well as for experts looking for specific details. If you are already an expert in Cloud Integration, I encourage you to also explore other SAP Integration Suite capabilities—it will be easy and interesting learning for you.

Thank you for your interest in SAP Integration Suite. Happy integrating!

Andreas Quenstedt
Chief Product Owner, SAP Integration Suite
Walldorf, March 2024

Preface

The IT landscapes in today's companies are getting more complex every day. With the advent of cloud computing, the need for integration between on-premise applications and cloud solutions, or between cloud applications, becomes apparent. By reading this book, you will learn how Cloud Integration can help you solve your integration challenges.

Enterprise application integration (EAI) has a long history. The need for easy data exchange came up early, with the first computer systems. Whether it was the transfer of master data, such as customer or product data, or the transmission of transactional data, such as orders or invoices, systems of importance always required some sort of communication and integration. Interestingly, this communication wasn't restricted to systems and applications *within one company*. The demand for inter-company data transfer increased the integration challenge even further.

With the arrival of cloud computing, we face a new dimension to the integration domain, as on-premise and cloud applications need to work seamlessly with each other. Companies selling standard software for both worlds, on-premise and on-demand, face an additional challenge: their customers expect seamless data exchange between their applications out of the box. SAP had already gathered experience in building integration software with SAP Process Integration. However, for the era of cloud computing that has evolved in the recent years, the good old SAP Process Integration solution wasn't suitable, as it didn't support typical cloud qualities such as multi-tenancy, data isolation, rolling software updates, zero downtime, or cloud elasticity. Instead of further investing in SAP Process Integration and trying to make it "cloud-ready," SAP delivered a separate integration solution called Cloud Integration. Cloud Integration was developed from scratch on top of the SAP Business Technology Platform (SAP BTP), with typical cloud integration scenarios in mind, and has become a mature constituent of SAP Integration Suite. With this approach, SAP is combining the best of both worlds: on-premise integration with its rock-solid SAP Process Integration product and cloud-based integration with Cloud Integration. With this separation, customers have the freedom of choice when considering their particular needs.

Structure of the Book

This book introduces Cloud Integration and covers a wide range of topics. We will begin with **Chapter 1** and a discussion of how Cloud Integration, as the prime integration point between disparate cloud and on-premise systems, fits into SAP's overall strategy to become *the* cloud-company for business software. In addition, we will present the main use cases of Cloud Integration, such as cloud-to-cloud or cloud-to-on-premise integration. Chapter 1 closes with an explanation of Cloud Integration's major capabilities.

As we wanted to deliver a practical book with lots of examples, **Chapter 2** dives directly into the hands-on experience. After introducing the architecture of Cloud Integration and the new vocabulary you need to get used to, we guide you step-by-step through a very simple scenario. You will work with the *Web UI* as the central Cloud Integration tool used to model, deploy, run, and monitor your integration scenarios, or *integration flows* in Cloud Integration's nomenclature. This chapter lays the foundation upon which all further chapters and exercises will be built.

Besides modeling integration scenarios from scratch, Cloud Integration also comes with prepackaged integration content. Remember, SAP's customers expect a smooth message exchange between SAP's on-premise and cloud solutions, as a single vendor ships both types of products. This data exchange can only work if SAP delivers preconfigured integration content running on top of Cloud Integration out-of-the-box. The delivered integration flows seamlessly glue the systems together without running costly integration projects, which were once a necessity. This prepackaged integration content is already available in the *integration content catalog*. **Chapter 3** explains how you can benefit from the integration content catalog and describes in detail, for example, the integration content for seamlessly connecting SAP SuccessFactors and SAP ERP Human Capital Management. At the end of the chapter, we will also explain how you can develop your own integration content and make it available in the integration content catalog—an offering that is of special interest for SAP's partner ecosystem.

Chapter 4, **Chapter 5**, and **Chapter 6** focus on developing custom integration flows in case the prepackaged content provided in the integration content catalog isn't sufficient for your business needs. In particular, we'll use step-by-step guides on how to apply the various step types that are part of Cloud Integration's web-based modeling environment. Over the course of these three chapters, you will learn how to:

- Work with Cloud Integration's data model.
- Enrich incoming data with data from an external OData source.
- Map data between different message interfaces.
- Route messages to the right receiver depending on the message's content (i.e., *content-based routing*).
- Influence the evaluation sequence of conditions for the content-based router.
- Handle messages comprising a list of items (such as order items); splitting and merging the individual list items are of particular interest in this section.
- Influence the execution of synchronous and asynchronous scenarios.

- Use Java Message Service (JMS) queues to temporarily store messages on the cloud integration platform and, that way, to asynchronously decouple inbound from outbound communication.
- Use the SAP Integration Suite, advanced event mesh adapter for event-driven integration patterns.
- Schedule timer-based integration flows, which run at pre-defined times and/or at pre-defined intervals.
- Dynamically configure integration flow parameters using headers and properties.
- Structure large integration scenarios based on modularization and the usage of local integration flows.
- Exchange data between parent and child integration flows.
- Directly connect integration flows by using the ProcessDirect adapter.
- Connect Cloud Integration with a database system using the JDBC adapter.
- Connect Cloud Integration with an AS2 server using an AS2 adapter.
- Understand advanced message mapping concepts.
- Understand the versioning concept of the cloud-based integration flow modeler and migrate integration flows to another version.
- Simulate integration flow processing.
- Transport integration content across tenants.
- Develop your own adapters by using the *Adapter Development Kit* (ADK).

Last but not least, you'll get an overview of guidelines for integration flow design to make sure to optimize reliability and performance of message processing.

Chapter 7 continues our journey with the operational aspects of Cloud Integration. As the previous chapters have shown you how to design integration flows to cover use cases with increasing complexity, you—the integration developer—will need to monitor how these integration flows actually process messages on your Cloud Integration. Monitoring messages is one task. But there are additional tasks you can accomplish using the **Monitor** section of the Web UI, such as managing security artifacts (for example, the keys and certificates contained in the tenant keystore) and data storages on your tenant. This chapter covers all these aspects in detail.

So far, we have described in detail how people can work with the user interface of Cloud Integration (basically, the Web UI) to perform tasks such as integration flow development or monitoring messages. However, Cloud Integration provides also the option to access integration-related artifacts based on an application programming interface (API). The available APIs are described in detail in **Chapter 8**. This chapter also shows you how you can use Cloud Integration APIs together with API Management, a dedicated service of SAP Integration Suite that helps you to develop, manage, and publish your own APIs.

SAP Integration Suite also comes with Open Connectors, which extends the connectivity capabilities and options of SAP Integration Suite. In **Chapter 9**, we explore how you can leverage the capabilities of Open Connectors and enable Cloud Integration to connect to more than 160 SaaS applications in a uniform and simplified manner.

So far, we have completely left out security aspects from our discussion. However, when it comes to cloud computing, security is one of the top-ranked requirements from customers, whether they are addressing the service provider hosting Cloud Integration or the integration developer running scenarios on top of it. We have decided to collect all security-relevant topics in one chapter, rather than spread them across the book. Therefore, **Chapter 10** will be your one-stop shop for all security-related questions. The chapter summarizes the measures taken by SAP to protect your data at the highest level and shows what you can do to maximize the security level of your integration scenarios. Keeping with our habit of providing hands-on examples, this chapter also contains guides that show you how to build simple integration flows that contain features such as digital encryption or authentication.

We now approach the end of the book. **Chapter 11** looks at already-running productive scenarios using Cloud Integration. We will mainly focus on the specifics of the following scenarios:

- Integration of SAP Cloud for Customer and SAP ERP
- Integration of SAP Cloud for Customer with SAP S/4HANA Cloud
- Integration of SAP Marketing Cloud and various applications
- Integration of SAP SuccessFactors and SAP ERP
- Integration of SAP applications with the Ariba Network
- Integration with German Tax Authority using the ELSTER adapter
- Integration of SAP S/4HANA with Salesforce

Once finished with this chapter, you'll understand how SAP Cloud for Customer plays a crucial role as part of SAP's classical and new business applications.

Chapter 12 covers special topics related to Cloud Integration. In this chapter, we focus on advanced topics like the Edge Integration Cell, migration from the SAP BTP, Neo environment to the SAP BTP, Cloud Foundry environment, and migration from SAP Process Orchestration to Cloud Integration.

Finally, **Chapter 13** concludes the book with an outlook comprising the roadmap for Cloud Integration. By reading this chapter, you will receive an impression of how of Cloud Integration will evolve over time and how Cloud Integration grows even more important for SAP's overall company strategy.

Sample Applications

Over the course of this book, we will be developing many sample applications that demonstrate the key concepts of SAP Integration. Some of these applications require certain artifacts such like files that contain web service descriptions. To make it easy for you to set up these applications, we provide these files ready-to-download in the supplemental materials of this book. You can download them at *www.sap-press.com/5760*.

You can generally find instructions for installing and deploying these applications within the chapters that cover them. If you run into any problems with the examples, you can email the authors directly at: *john.bilay@rojoconsultancy.com, shashank.singh@rojoconsultancy.com, swati.singh@rojoconsultancy.com, mandy.krimmel@sap.com* and *peter.gutsche@sap.com*.

The downloaded archive—when unpacked—will have a directory structure which is oriented along the chapters where the associated files are required:

- Chapter 4: The file *GetOrderShipDetails_Sync.wsdl* contains the Web Services Description Language (WSDL) file that defines an input message (synchronous interface) used in a sample integration flow.
- Chapter 5: The following files are provided:
  - The file *SendOrderList_Async.wsdl* contains the Web Services Description Language (WSDL) file that defines an input message (asynchronous interface) used in a sample integration flow.
  - The two files *SalesOrder.json* and *SalesOrderConsumed.json* contain the definition of the events used in the event-driven messaging scenario.
- Chapter 7: The following files are required to set up the B2B scenario:
  - The archive *EDI to SAP IDoc - Inbound.zip* is the template to be used to create the integration flow.
  - The folder *ASC_X12_to_SAP_IDOC_Purchase_Order* contains *.xsd and *.xsl files generated from Integration Advisor.
  - The file *GroovyScript.txt* contains the coding for the groovy script flow step to retrieve configuration data from partner directory.
  - File *850 – Purchase Order.txt* contains the test payload for the scenario.
  - File *850 – Purchase Order – Technically incorrect.txt* contains an incorrect payload for the scenario to test the error case.
- Chapter 10: The following files are required to set up one tutorial showing how to implement message-level security:
  - The file *secrettext.txt* contains a secret text that is decrypted by an integration flow.
  - The file *tenantkey_secret.gpg* contains the PGP secret key that is used by the integration flow to decrypt the secret text.

- The file *secretkey_passphrase.txt* contains the passphrase required to deploy the secret key on the tenant.
- The file *calculator.wsdl* is required to call a web service that provides functions to calculate integers (used to illustrate how to invoke a SOAP-based web service).

Who This Book Is For

This book addresses a broad audience, from integration architects, integration consultants, and integration developers, to technical-oriented business users, project leaders, and managers who want to understand how Cloud Integration can support either their journey into the cloud or how it can solve integration challenges related to integrating cloud solutions (on-premise-to-cloud or cloud-to-cloud). The reader, ideally, should be familiar with basic concepts regarding enterprise application integration and messaging, as this book will not cover those concepts. In addition, a basic understanding of Java, scripting languages, and enterprise integration patterns is beneficial. However, note that no knowledge of Cloud Integration or SAP Process Integration is required. You will receive everything you need to begin productive work with Cloud Integration, from designing and running a simple integration flow, up to implementing complex integration patterns from this book.

Now that you have an understanding of the book's contents, and for whom the book was written, we don't want to lose any more time getting started. We wish you an enjoyable ride!

Acknowledgments

Writing a book is always a challenging task, and it would be close to impossible without the help of many good friends and colleagues. This chapter is for those who supported us in one way or another.

We would like to start by thanking the team at Rheinwerk Publishing for all their support throughout the project. We are very thankful for your support and your team spirit. You have made it all possible. We would like, in particular, to thank Hareem Shafi for encouraging us to take up the task of writing a fourth edition of the book and for helping us set up the project. We would like to sincerely thank Rachel Gibson for accompanying us throughout the whole project. Rachel was always there when we needed support and quickly answered our many questions. Without her help during the whole writing process, it would not have been possible to bring the project to a successful end. Thank you for that!

We would like to thank Andreas Quenstedt for recognizing this book with his foreword.

We would like also to thank Volker Stiehl, Peter Gutsche, and Mandy Krimmel, the coauthors of the first few editions of this book, for their dedication in shaping the book's initial content and for their insights into the topic of integration. Unfortunately, they couldn't join us in working on this latest edition, but their contributions were invaluable in making the book what it is today.

We would also like to sincerely thank all the people who have contributed and reviewed different chapters of this book. We would also like to acknowledge the many others that we did not mention by name for their direct and indirect support on and interest in the book.

John Mutumba Bilay

I have enjoyed the teamwork and collaborative spirit during this book project. It has been an honor to work alongside Swati and Shashank, as well as with Peter, Mandy, and Volker for the previous editions. Your detailed and critical look at every topic made a difference. Thank you for that.

I would like to personally thank and express my gratitude to the many people who contributed to this book in different ways:

- Udo Paltzer, for his support with questions related to SAP Integration Suite. Your contribution is highly appreciated.
- The entire team of Rojo Consultancy B. V., for their help and consideration during the book writing process.

Finally, a big thank you to my wife, Hermien, and my boys, Ralph, Luc, Ruben, and Finn, for their loving support, patience, and encouragement. You have made me stronger, better, and more fulfilled than I could have ever imagined. During the process of writing this book, you have allowed me to skip some playtime to work on the book instead! I love you all to the moon and back.

Shashank Singh

The journey of writing this book has been an exciting and challenging one. I am grateful to all those who supported me along the way.

First and foremost, I would like to express my gratitude towards my parents. Thank you for giving all the love and support. It would not be possible without your blessings.

I would like to thank John for guiding and mentoring me during the writing process. You made it look so easy. Thanks to Swati for your support in reviewing the chapters. I am grateful to all my colleagues at Rojo Integrations for their help and support during this process.

Finally, thanks to my wife, Madhuri, for the support and encouragement throughout the process. I couldn't have completed the journey without you being on my side. Thank you for believing in me and being my source of strength.

Swati Singh

As an integration consultant, it is a pleasure to share my knowledge about Cloud Integration with you. The process of writing the book has been an intense and rewarding exercise. I enjoyed the process tremendously, as I was not only trying to solve a specific integration challenge but I was looking at the platform holistically and identifying the sheer number of ways that it supports organizations in their integration journey. I also appreciated the quality of work that our colleagues at SAP do, and therefore would like to extend my gratitude to the whole development team at SAP for developing a platform that can support customers in creating and managing data integrations.

John and Shashank have been perfect co-authors. Thanks for all the late-evening calls to review and brainstorm various topics. My journey as an author would be impossible without the support of my talented colleagues at Rojo Consultancy B.V. Thanks for answering my endless questions about your experiences on various topics.

Anything in life is difficult if you do not have the right support system. I would like to express my gratitude to my parents, Anju and Gyan, for your endless support and love.

I want to thank my husband, Sharique, for being my pillar of strength and encouraging me to undertake this project. Thanks for standing with me and being my sounding board through this journey. In the end, I would like to thank my little girl, Sarah, for bringing so much joy and love to our lives.

Chapter 1
Introduction to Cloud Integration

This chapter explains how Cloud Integration, as part of SAP Integration Suite, fits into SAP's overall cloud strategy and describes its main use cases.

It's not a secret anymore—the world is going digital! The convergence of trends such as artificial intelligence (AI), cloud computing, social networks, mobility, the Internet of Things (IoT), blockchain, Hashgraph, and the resulting big data is changing how we conduct business. We're increasingly experiencing this change in our personal lives, but these trends are quickly moving into the enterprise world as well. Just look at how software is consumed today: more and more businesses are choosing software delivered as a service and hosted in huge data centers. While on-premise environments aren't going anywhere soon, the industry is definitely seeing a shift to increased cloud adoption. Subscription-based licensing and central hosting are simply how people want to receive software these days. In this changing world of software delivery, the importance of simplicity can't be understated. All these converging technological forces are creating a much more complex world. Thus, the drive to simplify experiences for software users is of paramount importance.

SAP, the world's largest provider of business software, recognized the technological shift and continuously expands its offering of cloud-based software. However, SAP customers who have invested in on-premise landscapes in recent years can't be expected to immediately abandon their current solutions and move to the cloud. This is where Cloud Integration comes into play, as the solution of choice for companies looking to bring their cloud and on-premise technologies together.

Cloud Integration is now offered as part of SAP Integration Suite—which includes a set of services supporting application integration, as shown in Figure 1.1.

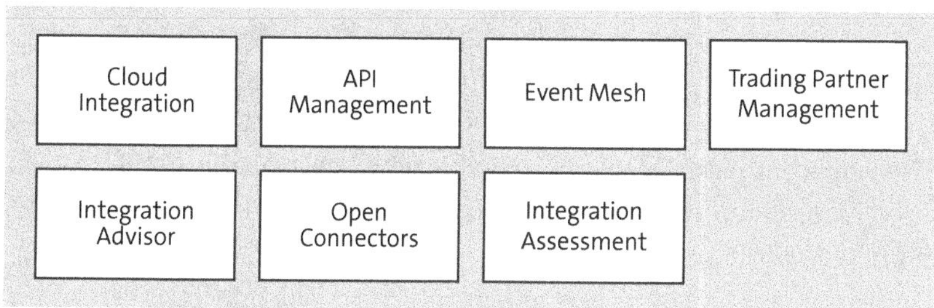

Figure 1.1 SAP Integration Suite Components

SAP Integration Suite is a modular integration platform as a service (iPaaS) to connect the intelligent enterprise. As shown in Figure 1.1, SAP Integration Suite includes the following components:

- **Cloud Integration**
  Seamlessly integrates anything, anywhere, in application-to-application (A2A) and business-to-business (B2B) scenarios in real time. Cloud Integration is the main topic of this book.
- **API Management**
  Enables an enterprise to expose their data processes as application programming interfaces (APIs). This solution further helps in managing these APIs in terms of governance and lifecycle. API Management will be discussed in Chapter 8, Section 8.6.
- **Integration Advisor**
  Enables an enterprise to accelerate the implementation and maintenance of B2B scenarios. The Integration Advisor won't be discussed in this book.
- **Open Connectors**
  Supports easier connectivity with a large number of third-party applications by providing standard connectors. Open Connectors will be discussed in Chapter 9.
- **Integration Assessment**
  Define, document, and govern your integration strategy powered by SAP Integration Solution Advisory Methodology (ISA-M).
- **Event Mesh**
  Enables customers to achieve an event-based architecture integration by using one or more event brokers that allow your applications to communicate asynchronously, in real time, and reliably at scale. Event Mesh will be discussed in Chapter 5.
- **Trading Partner Management**
  A microservice to facilitate your B2B data exchange by providing individual definition and configuration of specific electronic exchange of business data between you and your trading partners. This includes the company profile, trading partner profile, and trading partner agreement template.

For a full description of the capabilities included in SAP Integration Suite, visit *http://s-prs.co/v576002*.

This book will focus primarily on Cloud Integration. Previously, Cloud Integration was only available for the SAP Business Technology Platform (SAP BTP), Neo environment, which contains SAP proprietary runtime components and is operated in SAP data centers. Building on SAP's multicloud strategy, while you can still run Cloud Integration in the SAP BTP, Neo environment, Cloud Integration is now also available in the SAP BTP, Cloud Foundry environment. We'll further elaborate on both environments and their differences in Chapter 2, Section 2.1.

Cloud Foundry is the industry-standard, open-source cloud application platform supported by the most important cloud providers (e.g., Google, Amazon, Microsoft, etc.). Therefore, Cloud Foundry is the best basis for a multicloud architecture for SAP BTP. Note that that SAP Integration Suite is only available on Cloud Foundry.

Throughout this book, we'll mostly focus on and assume that you're running Cloud Integration in the Cloud Foundry environment. However, major differences may arise depending on the environment in which you're running Cloud Integration; we'll briefly elaborate on these differences in separate discussions.

Let's turn now to the role Cloud Integration can play in your company's cloud strategy. We'll also discuss the main use cases of Cloud Integration and introduce you to its various capabilities in this chapter.

1.1 The Role of Cloud Integration in a Cloud-Based Strategy

As SAP moves to the cloud, hybrid deployments will play an increasingly major role in businesses. Most customers who run businesses today must maintain existing IT landscapes. The idea that cloud deployments will completely replace current environments is simply unreasonable. Consequently, successful companies find solutions to help them combine their current environments, which are typically on-premise with cloud-based applications where it makes sense. Hybrid deployments will be the solution of choice for most companies in the years to come. As the market heads in this direction, hybrid deployments are where SAP sees investments in IT moving to the cloud. However, hybrid landscapes automatically mean integration needs: on-premise systems and cloud applications need to exchange data with each other. An integration platform such as Cloud Integration is designed to fill the gap by being responsible for reliable message exchanges between systems. However, before we dive into Cloud Integration and its strategic role in SAP's future plans more deeply, let's explore what motivates a company to implement a cloud-based strategy.

The move to the cloud can be made for many good reasons. Figure 1.2 summarizes the key business benefits of cloud computing, categorized into four major pillars.

When we talk about the cloud, we're actually thinking about the benefits shown in Figure 1.2. First and foremost, cloud-based strategies are all about faster deployments. By deployment, we mean the first setup and customizing of a software to make the solution ready for productive usage. Deployment in the old days used to take months, even years. With cloud-based solutions, deployment time has been reduced drastically, sometimes to weeks or days. This trend is accompanied by a mobile user experience. The cloud is consumer-grade and is beautiful and flexible. Today's users expect to access software instantly and to easily adapt to new solutions without the long training sessions and expensive courses of yesterday.

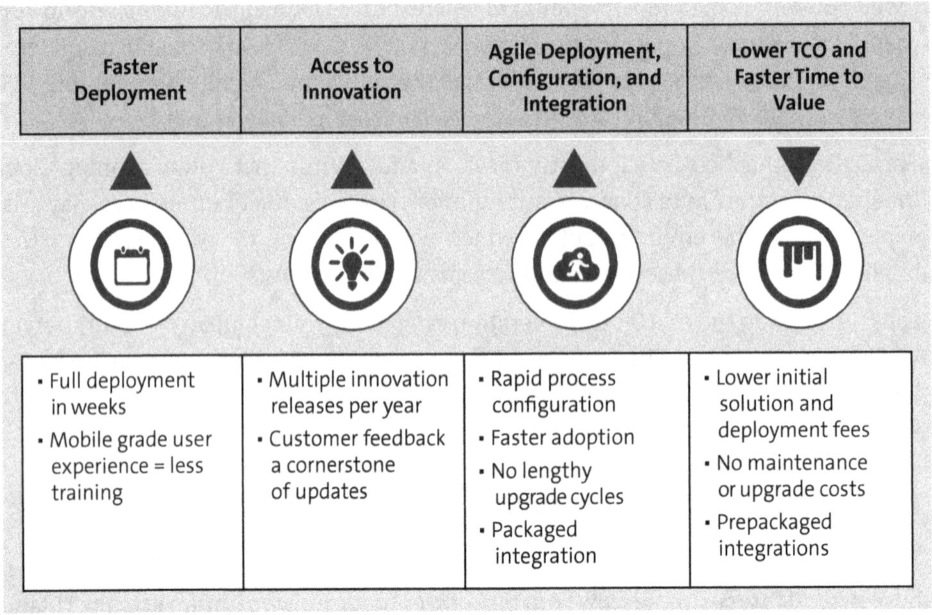

Faster Deployment	Access to Innovation	Agile Deployment, Configuration, and Integration	Lower TCO and Faster Time to Value
▲	▲	▲	▼
• Full deployment in weeks • Mobile grade user experience = less training	• Multiple innovation releases per year • Customer feedback a cornerstone of updates	• Rapid process configuration • Faster adoption • No lengthy upgrade cycles • Packaged integration	• Lower initial solution and deployment fees • No maintenance or upgrade costs • Prepackaged integrations

Figure 1.2 Business Benefits of Cloud Computing

Access to innovation, the second pillar shown in Figure 1.2, is another important benefit of cloud computing. We're moving away from upgrade cycles that once took years, to at least quarterly upgrade cycles with most of today's software as a service (SaaS) offerings. For many solutions, the innovation cycle may even be reduced to a monthly or even biweekly update. Regular, scheduled innovations are thus delivered to all users of a solution at the same time, which means the software can always be up to date. Consequently, all users will be working with the latest version of the software.

This consistency leads directly to the next advantage of cloud computing: because all users are working with the same software at the same time, a short feedback cycle is ensured. Potentially millions of people are working with the software, and these users can report their experiences directly to the vendor. This regular feedback cycle helps the software become better and better each day because the vendor can react to issues almost immediately. Compare this cycle to the old days: after a vendor sold a solution, its deployment, as well as its future upgrades, depended on the customer's planning, and the vendor never really received feedback about the software's usage. Today, cloud solutions allow innovations to be implemented faster, driving the quality of the software forward.

In summary, deployment and upgrade processes are becoming more and more agile, resulting in rapid configurations for faster adoption of the software without lengthy upgrade cycles. However, one problem must be solved in this new world of cloud-based software delivery: How do the systems residing in the cloud and on-premise talk to each other? Fortunately, prepackaged integration content comes to the rescue. Because the vendors of these solutions know their software best, they also know how to best connect them with each other. This connectivity is the home turf of Cloud Integration, as you'll see in a moment. Integrations between cloud systems, or between cloud-based and on-premise systems, are increasingly being delivered prepackaged. Thus, in essence, how those systems communicate and exchange data with each other can be defined in advance by the software vendor so that you, the consumer, only needs to complete a few configuration steps to make the solution executable—plug and play at its best. Customers can also choose to only move certain functionalities to the cloud. Out-of-the-box integrations can then be used to facilitate the smooth transition from the on-premise world to the cloud-based world according to the customer's pace.

Finally, you've probably heard a lot about the lower total cost of ownership (TCO) and faster time to value resulting from cloud-based solutions. These benefits result from the advantages mentioned earlier: You won't have to spend money on hardware and software hosted in your own data centers anymore. You can now outsource these tasks to a solution provider. You can optimize your TCO through lower fees for the initial solution and for its deployment, and you no longer need to shoulder maintenance and upgrade costs. Thus, focusing on TCO, typically, cloud solutions do quite well in this regard.

The obvious benefits of cloud deployments include freeing up time, money, and energy that can instead be spent on new innovations and new engagement models with your customers, partners, suppliers, and employees. You can now dedicate more time to serving your customers best. So, remember, when thinking about the cloud, consider not only its functional benefits but also the further innovations that are made possible because you have more resources to dedicate to what really matters for your business.

Now that you understand the advantages that a cloud-based solution can bring to the table, the need for an integration platform to weave together the loose ends between various combinations of cloud-based and on-premise solutions becomes even more obvious. Cloud Integration is itself a cloud-based solution in SAP BTP. Thus, Cloud Integration benefits from all the advantages just outlined and manages reliable message exchanges between all participants. Whether we're talking about SAP applications on-premise or in the cloud, non-SAP solutions, or B2B integrations, Cloud Integration is the solution of choice to connect them. Cloud Integration is therefore SAP's strategic integration platform to help companies successfully move to the cloud. An organization's cloud strategy must include Cloud Integration.

Cloud Integration has another big advantage when compared to the competition: Because SAP knows its own applications better than any other vendor, Cloud Integration is shipped with preconfigured integration content that just needs a few configuration steps to become productive for most businesses. This approach reduces time and money for integration projects to the absolute minimum.

But what does a typical integration scenario look like? To sharpen the picture of this universal integration platform, let's look at some concrete use cases.

1.2 Use Cases

Business processes, in many cases, require different applications and software systems to exchange data with each other. For example, clicking on the **Buy** button on a seller's website typically triggers subsequent processes that involve complex data flows in a landscape of software systems, often distributed across the boundaries of different organizations. Such landscapes are usually heterogeneous in the sense that the systems that communicate with each other often use different technical communication protocols and store data in different individual formats and data structures.

An integration expert who is in charge of implementing such complex, distributed processes faces the challenge of cross-linking a large number of systems and data sources in the right way and of ensuring that the relevant data is exchanged correctly during the operation of a business process.

In the following sections, we'll first discuss how such integration challenges can be addressed by Cloud Integration. In this context, we'll introduce you to the concept of mediated communication. We'll then describe the various use cases covered by Cloud Integration in general. Over the course of this discussion, we'll also briefly touch on a new capability of SAP Integration Suite to run integration scenarios within their private landscape—Edge Integration Cell.

1.2.1 Point-to-Point versus Mediated Communication

Let's first assume that our integration expert solves our integration challenge by implementing direct connections between each of the components that should exchange data with each other. The resulting method these components use to exchange data with each other is referred to as *point-to-point communication*.

For example, if the components are different SAP systems, *point-to-point connections* can be implemented by remote function calls (RFCs). In this case, all components are tightly coupled with each other, as shown in Figure 1.3, on the left. This setup has a number of disadvantages. For example, if one component, let's say component A, is upgraded, all connections where A is involved also must be adapted. In the case of a large number of components, upgrades and maintenance tasks could easily spiral out of control because the number of connections grows exponentially by the number of components.

A more reliable and efficient approach to solving this integration challenge is to use a central *integration platform*—or an *integration bus*—that is interconnected between the involved systems. This setup is shown in Figure 1.3, to the right. All integration-related tasks are managed by the integration bus. This approach, called *mediated communication*, ensures that the number of connections (and their arrangement) remains manageable.

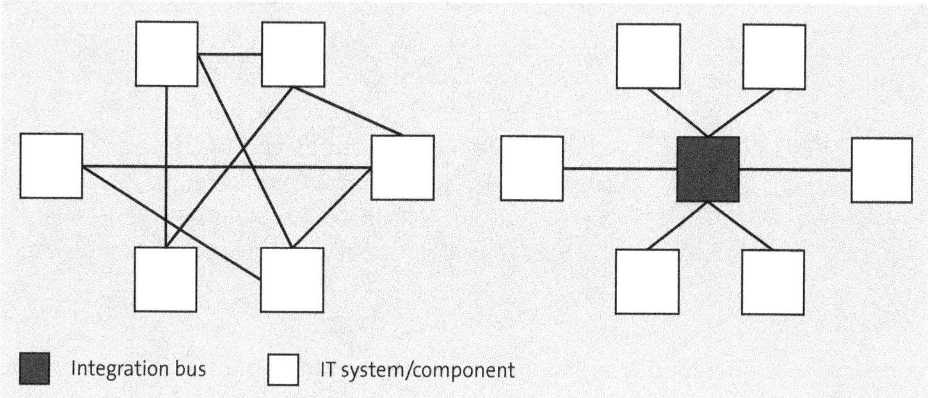

Figure 1.3 Point-to-Point Communication (Left) with a "Spaghetti-Like" Arrangement of Connections Compared to Mediated Communication (Right)

1.2.2 Message-Based Process Integration

Mediated communication is typically based on the exchange of messages. Let's examine this concept through a few simple examples.

The integration bus ensures, for example, that a message sent from system A to system B in a certain process step is transformed in a way that system B can interpret and further process the data contained in the message. If a message is to be forwarded from system A to more than one receiver, the integration platform manages the proper routing of the message. Other process steps, in turn, might require that messages be split into smaller chunks, each of which might be forwarded to a different receiver, and so forth.

The integration bus approach ensures that integration-related information and processes are centrally maintained and that tasks such as maintaining and updating the integration software are kept separate from the integrated business applications themselves.

An additional paradigm is to design the integration in such a way that the integrated applications are loosely coupled with each other; that is, each individual application runs independently. This approach makes the overall business process less error-prone and reduces dependencies.

By addressing such integration challenges and approaches, Cloud Integration enables you to integrate processes that span different applications, organizations, and enterprises. This reach includes systems and applications of any kind, including non-SAP systems.

Of course, different kinds of business processes will require different means of exchanging messages between connected components. Cloud Integration supports a large number of these enterprise integration patterns.

Note

The term *enterprise integration pattern*—also referred to as *messaging pattern*—was popularized by Gregor Hohpe and Bobby Woolf in their book *Enterprise Integration Patterns* (Addison-Wesley, 2004). The book defines and documents a number of integration patterns and how robust integration solutions can be designed. Each of the 65 patterns are illustrated in an intuitively understandable visual notation. The descriptions are general enough to facilitate implementation with many different integration technologies.

A key capability of Cloud Integration—if not the most important—is that it supports the implementation of enterprise integration patterns. As we'll describe in detail in Chapter 2, Cloud Integration uses the Apache Camel integration framework for implementing enterprise integration patterns.

Enterprise Integration Pattern Examples

One example of an enterprise integration pattern is a *content-based router*. Imagine that a sender is connected to multiple receiver systems, and the business process requires that a message from the sender is forwarded to a particular receiver system depending on the content of the message (e.g., a customer ID). The content-based router makes such forwarding possible.

Another example is a *splitter*, which defines how a single message is split into multiple partial messages that can be processed individually.

To support different integration patterns, Cloud Integration offers a wide range of integration capabilities and connectivity options, as described in Section 1.3. However, let's first explore some use cases supported by Cloud Integration.

1.2.3 Cloud-to-Cloud Integration

Cloud Integration is a cloud-based integration platform that provides on-demand process integration services, as shown in Figure 1.4. You can use the platform's resources flexibly by paying a monthly fee. You don't need to install any integration middleware in your own landscape. All software processes that deal with message exchange run either on the SAP BTP, Neo environment, or in the SAP BTP, Cloud Foundry environment.

To run an integration scenario that requires message exchange between the three IT systems shown in Figure 1.4, connections between these systems and Cloud Integration are required. All integration-related processes run either in SAP BTP, Neo environment, or SAP BTP, Cloud Foundry environment.

Figure 1.4 doesn't show which kinds of components or systems can be connected with each other. In our example, let's assume that component A belongs to the system landscape of the customer. The other components to be connected aren't further specified.

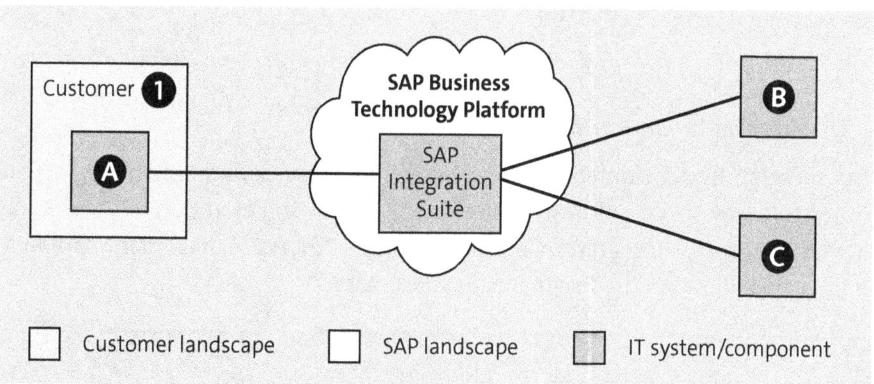

Figure 1.4 Cloud Integration as the Integration Platform Based on SAP BTP

Components or applications subject to an integration scenario can, in principle, be differentiated according to the following criteria:

- **On-premise**
  The component or application is installed and maintained on the premises, or locally, in the customer landscape.
- **Cloud**
  The component or application runs in the cloud—for example, in SAP's cloud—and can be used by the customer on demand.

Cloud Integration is primarily suitable for the integration of cloud applications, that is, for cloud-to-cloud integration.

1.2.4 Cloud-to-On-Premise Integration

More and more cloud applications on the market replace, in part, applications that until recently have only been available as on-premise solutions. However, large enterprises may have invested heavily in their on-premise landscapes and want to keep this investment. In this case, the company may only want to source out part of their business into the cloud. Thus, these enterprises look for integration solutions that support the integration of their existing on-premise applications with new cloud-based applications.

Cloud Integration also supports this cloud-to-on-premise integration use case, whether you're using SAP or non-SAP systems.

Predefined Integration Content

SAP allows Cloud Integration customers to quickly implement a range of integration solutions out of the box. You can choose from among a set of predefined integration packages published on the SAP Business Accelerator Hub. The available integration packages cover integration scenarios with a number of SAP solutions. We'll go into more detail on this topic in Chapter 3.

1.2.5 On-Premise-to-On-Premise Integration

SAP has successfully distributed SAP Process Orchestration for a number of years and continues to support the solution today. SAP Process Orchestration is a combined package of SAP Process Integration and SAP Business Process Management (SAP BPM) capabilities that allow you to design business processes.

Note

Refer to *SAP Process Orchestration: The Comprehensive Guide* (SAP PRESS, 2017) for a comprehensive introduction to SAP Process Orchestration.

The SAP Process Integration part of SAP Process Orchestration is an on-premise integration middleware that, like Cloud Integration, can be used as an integration bus and that addresses the integration challenges mentioned in Section 1.2.1 and Section 1.2.2. In this context, we'll only refer to these integration bus capabilities and therefore don't consider the overall SAP Process Orchestration solution.

In past years, SAP Process Integration has been the recommended solution for pure on-premise-to-on-premise integrations. It's important to note that SAP will discontinue the maintenance of SAP Process Integration in 2027. Cloud Integration is the future solution of choice not only for cloud-based integrations but also for on-premise-to-on-premise integrations.

The newly released Edge Integration Cell is a hybrid solution offered with SAP Integration Suite that provides the flexibility for customers to have a runtime deployed on their private cloud or on-premise landscape. The Edge Integration Cell also offers a migration path for SAP Process Integration customers, to move to SAP Integration Suite, and still be able to run scenarios within their private landscapes.

To have this capability, it's important to subscribe to the SAP Integration Suite application and enable the Edge Integration Cell runtime. This topic will be further discussed in Chapter 12.

Figure 1.5 shows the differences between a cloud-based integration solution and an on-premise integration solution through a high-level comparison of the general technical landscapes for Cloud Integration with and without the Edge Integration Cell. In our example, two customers run integration scenarios that involve message exchanges between three IT systems (A, B, and C), where system A is part of the customer's landscape. Systems B and C aren't further specified. On the left side of Figure 1.5, Edge Integration Cell is installed in the landscape of customer 1. As a result, at runtime, the message exchange among systems A, B, and C is performed by an integration bus hosted *within* the customer's landscape. On the right side of Figure 1.5, customer 2 is using Cloud Integration (without Edge Integration Cell) as an integration bus to facilitate message exchange among IT systems A, B, and C. In this case, Cloud Integration is outside the customer's landscape (i.e., in the cloud and without Edge Integration Cell).

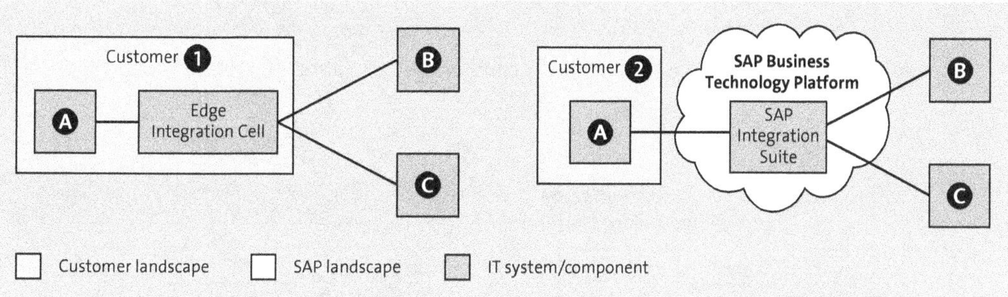

Figure 1.5 General Use Case and Component Setup for Edge Integration Cell (Left) and for Cloud Integration without Edge Integration Cell (Right)

1.2.6 Hybrid Usage of Cloud and On-Premise Integration Solutions

From a use-case perspective, Cloud Integration is suitable for business cases where you would like to outsource your integration-related processes—or parts of them—into the cloud. Obviously, Cloud Integration is the solution of choice when you need to integrate processes that run within a landscape of cloud-based applications. As such, Cloud Integration has been a complementary solution to SAP Process Integration. In many cases, customers have used a strategy that combines the use of Cloud Integration with an already existing SAP Process Integration installation. For example, let's assume that you, the customer, have already invested in an *on-premise integration solution* (e.g., SAP Process Integration) and would like to keep these investments. Thus, you decide to outsource only parts of your integration-related processes to the cloud. Figure 1.6 shows schematically how the landscape of such a hybrid scenario could appear. To connect Cloud Integration with SAP Process Integration, you can use the SAP Connectivity service, which we'll describe in more detail in Section 1.3.3.

However, given that SAP will discontinue the maintenance of SAP Process Integration in 2027, as mentioned in Section 1.2.5, Figure 1.7 presents an alternative architecture that purely uses Cloud Integration without SAP Process Integration.

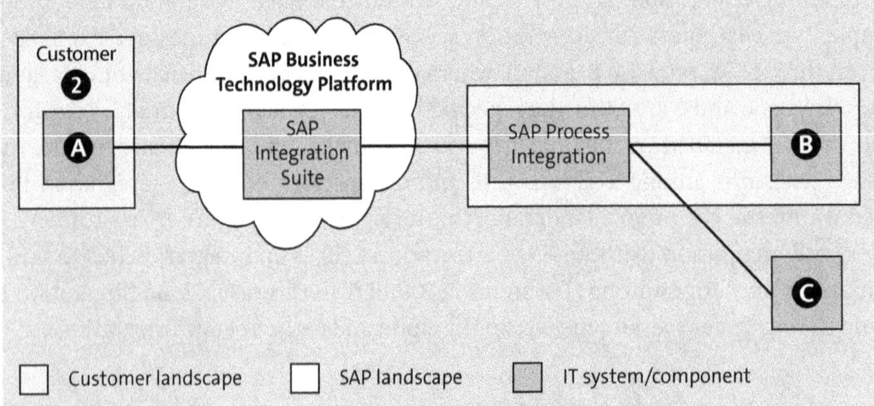

Figure 1.6 Hybrid Use Case Using Both Cloud Integration and SAP Process Integration

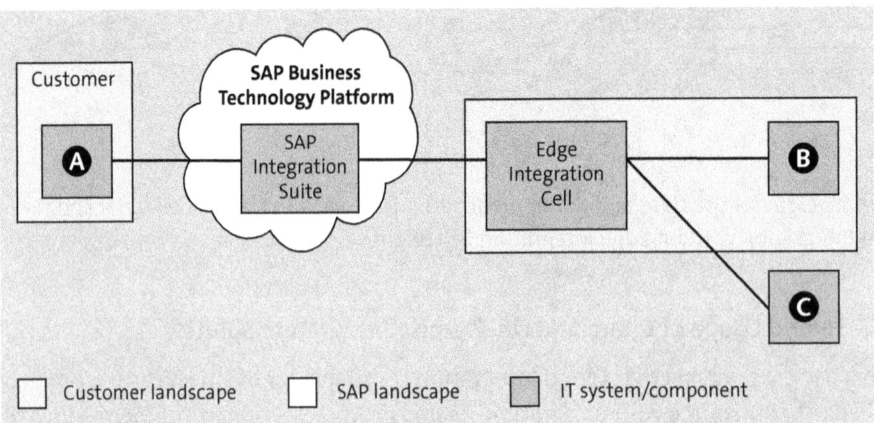

Figure 1.7 Hybrid Use Case Only Using Cloud Integration

In this section, we provided an overview of the general use cases that Cloud Integration can address. To show you how these use cases are implemented in practice, Chapter 11 will describe a few examples of how Cloud Integration can be used in real life.

1.2.7 Usage in Different Cloud Environments

As modern enterprises expand their IT infrastructures into the cloud, they can choose a cloud platform that best suits their strategic needs. Today, cloud platform choices are expanding and include SAP data centers, Amazon Web Services (AWS), Microsoft Azure, Alibaba, private clouds, and so on—just to name a few.

Within this context, SAP strives to give businesses using Cloud Integration the freedom to choose their underlying cloud infrastructure provider. Additionally, SAP also provides the flexibility to co-locate new cloud applications alongside existing investments while meeting regulatory and compliance requirements.

As mentioned earlier, today Cloud Integration runs on both the SAP BTP, Neo environment, and SAP BTP, Cloud Foundry environment. The capability to operate SAP BTP in the Cloud Foundry environment supports openness, as well as the following benefits:

- Ability to choose a cloud provider that best meets the organization's requirements
- Easier entry into new regions and markets while meeting local compliance regulations
- Reduced vendor lock-in through the adoption of portable applications

SAP BTP gives you the ability to centrally manage multicloud application deployments in a single cockpit. While enterprises may choose a public cloud infrastructure to run SAP Integration Suite, such as AWS or Microsoft Azure, SAP takes care of the complexity of managing and operating the underlying infrastructure accounts—thus enabling easier customer adoption. Cloud Foundry also enables you to leverage several advantages, such as centralized logging, autoscaling, and dynamic routing. Some high-level differences between the SAP BTP, Neo environment, and the SAP BTP, Cloud Foundry environment, are shown in Figure 1.8.

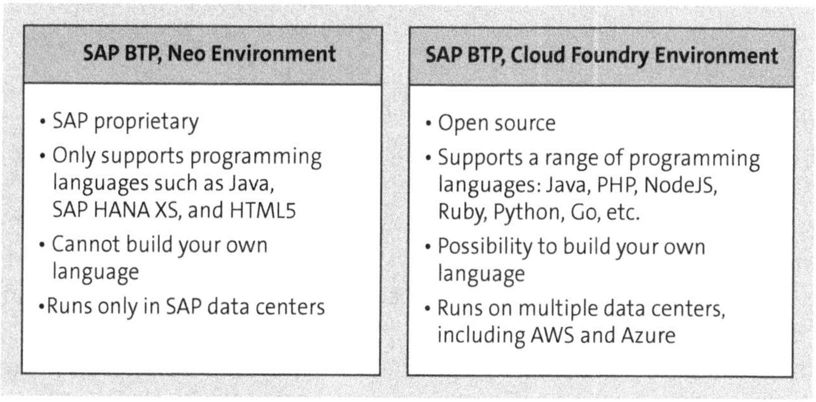

SAP BTP, Neo Environment	SAP BTP, Cloud Foundry Environment
• SAP proprietary • Only supports programming languages such as Java, SAP HANA XS, and HTML5 • Cannot build your own language •Runs only in SAP data centers	• Open source • Supports a range of programming languages: Java, PHP, NodeJS, Ruby, Python, Go, etc. • Possibility to build your own language • Runs on multiple data centers, including AWS and Azure

Figure 1.8 Differences between the SAP BTP, Neo Environment, and the SAP BTP, Cloud Foundry Environment

Note

For more information on the differences between the SAP BTP, Neo environment, and the SAP BTP, Cloud Foundry environment, check out the documentation on the SAP Help Portal at *http://s-prs.co/v576001*.

Based on your specific use cases and the differences shown in Figure 1.8, you have several options to choose the most suitable SAP BTP environment.

In this book, we'll primarily focus on the usage of Cloud Integration in the SAP BTP, Cloud Foundry environment. When relevant differences arise because of differences in environment, we'll explicitly mention these differences.

In Chapter 2, we'll walk you through an architecture overview of Cloud Integration in the SAP BTP, Cloud Foundry environment. The management of user roles and the technical system landscape will be discussed in Chapter 10.

Note that, at the time of this writing, not all features available in the SAP BTP, Neo environment, for Cloud Integration are available in the SAP BTP, Cloud Foundry environment. These features will be continuously enhanced in the coming months. To read about current limitations in running Cloud Integration in the SAP BTP, Cloud Foundry environment, check out SAP Note 2752867.

You can provision your SAP Integration Suite tenant in SAP BTP, Cloud Foundry, via the self-service provided by SAP. You'll find detailed documentation on the SAP Help Portal at *http://s-prs.co/507704*.

You can test out a trial account for the SAP BTP, Cloud Foundry environment. We provide references on how to set up a trial account in Chapter 2, Section 2.3. We recommend that you sign up for a trial account so you can walk through the scenarios in this book, which are based on the SAP BTP, Cloud Foundry environment.

1.3 Capabilities

Now that you understand how Cloud Integration can be used to benefit your business, let's dive more deeply into the solution's capabilities. In this section, we'll provide a high-level overview of Cloud Integration's main features. We'll briefly touch on how Cloud Integration can serve as an integration platform operating in the cloud and summarize the benefits of this setup. We'll then provide an overview of the different ways messages can be processed by Cloud Integration and describe the connectivity options supported by the platform. We'll also succinctly discuss integration content, security, and availability. Finally, we'll introduce you to the tools that come with Cloud Integration and review the different editions of the software available for purchase.

In subsequent chapters of the book, all of these features will be discussed at length.

1.3.1 Integration Platform as a Service

As mentioned at the beginning of the chapter, Cloud Integration is designed as an integration platform as a service (iPaaS). What does that mean? First, Cloud Integration helps you integrate multiple independent applications with each other in the context of a business process. This aspect is how the solution serves as an integration platform or an integration bus, as discussed previously.

Cloud Integration allows you to integrate processes based on the exchange of messages. Similar to SAP Process Integration—the integration bus part of SAP Process Orchestration—Cloud Integration acts as an integration bus connecting components in the context of a business process. All processes that manage data transfer and message routing run on the integration platform. Cloud Integration supports various methods for processing messages and offers many connectivity options that allow several software systems and applications to communicate with each other. These capabilities are described in more detail in Section 1.3.2 and Section 1.3.3.

Second, in contrast to SAP Process Integration, Cloud Integration provides integration services in the cloud. This is the *integration as a service (IaaS)* aspect. The resources of the integration platform can be used on demand. Furthermore, you can flexibly adapt resource consumption to meet changing business requirements. The latter capability is also referred to as *horizontal scaling*—whenever you require more processing capacity, additional resources can be allocated quickly.

With Cloud Integration, you won't need to deal with the upgrades or the maintenance of the integration software. SAP provides monthly updates of the software without any need to schedule downtime for business processes based on Cloud Integration.

A key characteristic of a cloud-based integration platform is its *multitenancy*; that is, although different components and organizations (participants) connected to Cloud Integration share the same physical resources, these resources are strictly isolated by participant. As a result, data owned by a participant is strictly separated from data owned by other participants.

1.3.2 Message Processing Step Types (Integration Capabilities)

Cloud Integration supports various integration patterns, or ways to integrate applications with each other. Each pattern requires a specific set of processing steps. At the time of this writing, Cloud Integration supports the following types of message processing steps:

- **Participants**
  Contains objects that represent participants of an integration scenario, for example, a sender system and a receiver system.
- **Mapping**
  Contains mapping steps that transform the data structure or format used by the sender into a structure or format the receiver can consume.
- **Message transformers**
  Transforms the content of a message. Such transformation steps include content modifiers, converters, encoders, and many others.
- **Persistence**
  Stores the message content in the database. Storage steps may be required when the message content is needed for later processing steps or if the message content should be analyzed in a later step.
- **Security elements**
  Includes steps that enable you to digitally encrypt and/or sign the content of a

message to ensure maximum protection of the exchanged data. You can also decrypt signed messages. Cloud Integration supports a number of security standards, which we'll describe in detail in Chapter 10.

- **Message routing**
  Forwards a message to multiple receivers. Routing can also be defined to depend on the content of the message, also known as content-based routing.
- **Events**
  Contains different types of events, including end events, end messages, error end events, and many others.
- **Process**
  Enables you to define subprocesses and exception processes.
- **Call**
  Enables you to perform calls to local or external services.
- **Message validator**
  Contains the eXtensible Markup Language (XML) validator (at the time of writing), which enables you to validate an XML message based on a specific XML schema.

We'll discuss the complete list of integration patterns and involved processing steps in Chapter 2 and Chapter 5.

1.3.3 Connectivity Options

The variety of integration scenarios that can be designed and operated with Cloud Integration depends on the kinds of systems that can be technically connected to it. These *connectivity options* are implemented by Cloud Integration adapters. Figure 1.9 shows various connectivity options.

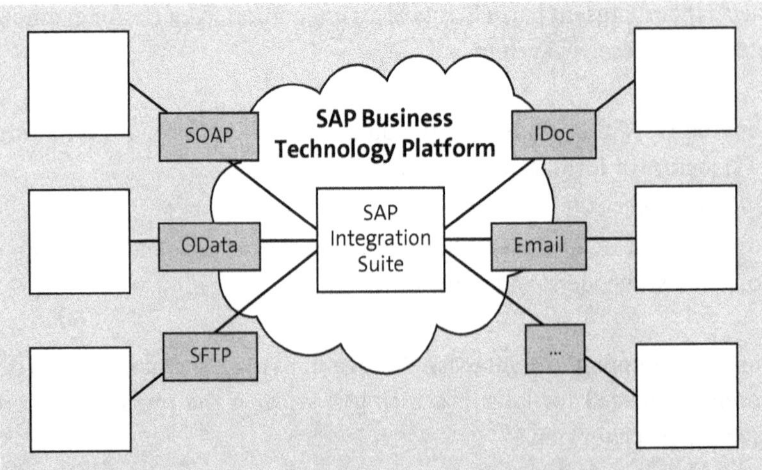

Figure 1.9 Connectivity Options for Integrating Systems with Different Technical Characteristics

At the time of this writing, the adapter types listed in Table 1.1 are available for use.

Adapter Type	Description
SOAP	Allows you to connect Cloud Integration to a system that communicates based on the Simple Object Access Protocol (SOAP). Currently, two flavors of this adapter are available: ▪ SOAP (SAP RM) adapter: Connects Cloud Integration to systems based on SAP Reliable Messaging (SAP RM), which is a simplified communication protocol for asynchronous, one-way communication. ▪ SOAP 1.x adapter: Connects Cloud Integration to systems based on SOAP 1.1.
IDoc (SOAP)	Allows systems to exchange an IDoc through Cloud Integration.
HTTP	Allows you to connect Cloud Integration to receiver systems using HTTP.
HTTPS	Enables the exposure of integration flows (iFlow) in Cloud Integration to external systems in a secure manner. Note that this is only available as a sender adapter.
Mail	Allows you to connect Cloud Integration to mail servers and to send out encrypted emails or poll for newly received mails from mail servers.
SFTP	Allows you to connect Cloud Integration to a system through the Secure Shell (SSH) File Transfer Protocol (SFTP).
FTPS	Allows Cloud Integration to transfer files from and to file servers. This protocol is an extension of File Transfer Protocol (FTP).
SAP Success-Factors	Allows you to connect Cloud Integration to an SAP SuccessFactors system through the SOAP, Representational State Transfer (REST), or OData message protocol.
SAP Ariba	Allows you to connect Cloud Integration to the SAP Business Network.
OData	Allows you to connect Cloud Integration to OData service providers.
Twitter	Allows you to connect Cloud Integration to Twitter and to extract Twitter content.
Facebook	Allows you to connect Cloud Integration to Facebook and to extract Facebook content.
ODC	Enables you to connect Cloud Integration to an SAP Gateway OData channel. Note that this adapter uses HTTPS. The following operations are currently supported: create (`POST`), read (`GET`), update (`PUT`), delete (`DELETE`), merge (`MERGE`), and query (`GET`).

Table 1.1 Cloud Integration Adapter Types

Adapter Type	Description
AS2	Allows you to exchange business-specific data securely and reliably with a partner through the Applicability Statement 2 (AS2) protocol. Security is achieved using digital certificates and encryption.
AS4	Allows you to exchange business-specific data securely and reliably with a trading partner through the Applicability Statement 4 (AS4) protocol. Security is achieved using digital certificates and encryption.
JMS	Allows you to exchange asynchronous messaging using message queues with the Java Message Service (JMS). Note that a license for SAP BTP Enterprise Agreement comes equipped with this feature. However, you can also purchase Event Mesh separately and add it to any Cloud Integration license. See Chapter 5 for more details.
RFC	Enables you to connect Cloud Integration to an SAP ABAP system using an RFC destination.
LDAP	Connects Cloud Integration to a Lightweight Directory Access Protocol (LDAP) directory service (through TCP/IP).
XI	Enables connectivity to handle communication using the SAP Process Integration protocol.
JDBC	Enables you to connect Cloud Integration to a database system operated on SAP BTP and execute various SQL operations.
AMQP	Allows SAP BTP developers to connect to an Advanced Message Queuing Protocol (AMQP) server or messaging systems. The AMQP adapter is available for both sender and receiver. This adapter also supports both TCP and WebSocket transport protocols. See Chapter 5, Sections 5.4 and 5.5, for more details.
ELSTER	Allows you to easily exchange data with the German online tax office system using Cloud Integration. (ELSTER [*ELektronische STeuerERklärung* = electronic tax declaration] is a German online tax system designed by the Federal Central Tax Office [*Bundeszentralamt für Steuern*] to enable anyone to submit their tax returns online.)
Open Connectors	Includes a unified API layer and standards-based implementation with a large number of connectors. The catalog of more than 160 connectors for non-SAP cloud applications allows Cloud Integration to easily connect to most popular SaaS applications, such as Salesforce, Jira, Google, and so on. Open Connectors will be discussed in detail in Chapter 9.

Table 1.1 Cloud Integration Adapter Types (Cont.)

Adapter Type	Description
AdvancedEvent-Mesh	Allows Cloud Integration to connect to an SAP Integration Suite, advanced event mesh broker. It's then possible to retrieve data from a queue or subscribe to a topic. Using its receiver adapter, it's also possible to write data to queues or publish messages to topics.
Data Store	Allows you to consume messages from the Cloud Integration data store. This feature helps you enable asynchronous decoupling of inbound and outbound processing by using the data store as temporary storage.
AzureStorage	Enables you to connect Cloud Integration to different types of Azure storage, including Blob Storage, Files Storage, Queue Storage, and Table Storage.
Dropbox	Allows you to connect Cloud Integration to Dropbox. It can then be used to read files from and write files to Dropbox.
Kafka	Allows Cloud Integration to connect to an external Kafka broker via the Kafka protocol to retrieve and send Kafka records.
MDI	Enables a customer to connect Cloud Integration to SAP Master Data Integration for any scenario that requires master data synchronization.
Microsoft Share-Point	Allows you to connect Cloud Integration to Microsoft SharePoint. It can then be used to create folders, manage lists, download or upload files, and retrieve site information.
RabbitMQ	Enables you to access the features supported by RabbitMQ storage. You can leverage the RabbitMQ adapter to consume and publish messages between the RabbitMQ server and SAP Integration Suite. The adapter is available only for certain service plans of SAP Integration Suite.
Slack	Allows you to connect Cloud Integration to post messages to Slack.
Splunk	Enables you to monitor, search, analyze, and visualize machine-generated data in real time. It performs capturing, indexing, and correlating of the real time data in a searchable container and produces graphs, alerts, dashboards, and visualizations between Splunk and SAP Integration Suite.
Salesforce	Enables a customer to connect their Cloud Integration tenant to Salesforce and exchange data with it. The adapter supports a multitude of features, including create, read, update, and delete (CRUD) operations of Salesforce objects and the retrieval of events from Salesforce (PushTopic events, Generic events, Platform events, and Change Data Capture events).

Table 1.1 Cloud Integration Adapter Types (Cont.)

Adapter Type	Description
Microsoft Dynamics CRM	Enables a customer to connect their Cloud Integration tenant to Microsoft Dynamics CRM and exchange data with it. The adapter supports a multitude of features, including CRUD operations of Microsoft Dynamics CRM entities.
Sugar CRM	Enables a customer to connect their Cloud Integration tenant to Sugar CRM and exchange data with it. The adapter supports a multitude of features, including CRUD operations of Sugar CRM objects.
Amazon Web Services	Enables a customer to connect their Cloud Integration tenant to AWS via various services: ■ Amazon Simple Storage Service (S3) ■ Amazon Simple Queue Service (SQS) ■ Amazon Simple Notification Service (SNS) ■ Amazon Simple Workflow Service (SWF) Note that S3 and SQS are also supported by the sender adapter.
ServiceNow	Enables a customer to connect their Cloud Integration tenant to ServiceNow and exchange data with it. The adapter supports a multitude of features, including CRUD operations of ServiceNow tables.
Workday	Enables a customer to connect their Cloud Integration tenant to Workday and exchange data with it. The adapter supports a multitude of features, including the create, read, update, delete, assign, manage, and import operations of Workday entities.

Table 1.1 Cloud Integration Adapter Types (Cont.)

We should mention that additional adapters for Cloud Integration are also provided by different SAP partners. An up-to-date list of these adapters can be found in the **Discover** page of the web UI of Cloud Integration. Note that some adapters are only available for one side of the communication, either to connect to a sender system or to a receiver system. For the actual available capabilities, refer to the Cloud Integration product documentation.

Several adapter types (e.g., the HTTP adapter and the OData adapter) support the SAP Connectivity service (SAP Connectivity), which can be used as a link between SAP BTP components and on-premise landscapes. SAP Connectivity supports the simple configuration of on-premise systems that are to be connected with SAP BTP. Table 1.2 lists the different protocols supported by SAP Connectivity for the SAP BTP, Neo environment, and the SAP BTP, Cloud Foundry environment.

Protocols	SAP BTP Environment	Description
HTTP	Cloud Foundry and Neo	HTTPS isn't needed because the tunnel used by SAP Connectivity is Transport Layer Security (TLS)-encrypted.
RFC	Cloud Foundry and Neo	Facilitates the communication with SAP systems.
TCP	Cloud Foundry and Neo	Used for communication with any client that supports SOCKS5 proxies. SOCKS5 is an internet protocol used to exchange network packets between server and client via a proxy server. It also restricts access to authorized users only by providing an authentication mechanism.
LDAP	Neo only	Used to communicate with an LDAP server within your network.

Table 1.2 List of Protocols Supported by the SAP Connectivity Service

For more details about the protocols supported by the SAP Connectivity service, refer to the documentation on the SAP Help Portal at *http://s-prs.co/507705*.

You can also build your own adapters using the Adapter Development Kit (ADK), which we'll describe in detail in Chapter 6, Section 6.10.

A concrete integration scenario is specified by combining a set of processing steps and adapters from Table 1.1 in this section. For more information, see Chapter 2.

1.3.4 Prepackaged Integration Content

SAP provides predefined integration content that allows you to implement a number of integration scenarios out of the box.

Integration Content and Integration Packages

The term *integration content* represents iFlows, interfaces, mapping programs, and other objects that define how messages are exchanged through Cloud Integration in the context of an integration scenario. A collection of such objects that addresses the integration challenges of a specific business case is referred to as an *integration package*.

For a more precise definition of an iFlow, see Chapter 2.

From the SAP Business Accelerator Hub (*https://api.sap.com*), you can select integration packages that facilitate the integration of applications with SAP SuccessFactors applications, SAP Cloud for Customer, and SAP Business Network. This list of integration packages within the SAP Business Accelerator Hub is also sometimes referred to as the SAP Integration Content Catalog. For more information on the available integration content in the SAP Business Accelerator Hub, see Chapter 3.

1.3.5 Security Features

Cloud Integration is designed to ensure the maximum protection of customer data during the operation of an integration scenario. Physical protection of relevant data is ensured by the fact that Cloud Integration is hosted in SAP data centers or in hyperscale infrastructure provider the data centers such as from Google or Amazon, which provide a maximum level of protection through various state-of-the-art security technologies.

Although different participants connected to Cloud Integration share the same physical resources, data that is processed and stored on the platform is strictly separated by participant (multitenancy). Each customer can define dedicated permissions for different people working on the customer-related account and tenant.

The connections between Cloud Integration and other components can be secured using standard transport-level security options, such as HTTPS and SSH. On top of that, Cloud Integration provides many options to protect exchanged messages with digital signatures and encryption.

We've only touched on a few key security features. More details on this topic can be found in Chapter 10, which thoroughly describes the security features available in Cloud Integration.

1.3.6 High Availability

Cloud Integration is available to process messages at any time, and productive business processes that use Cloud Integration as their integration bus will continue operations even if one component of the integration platform fails. Cloud Integration's architecture supports horizontal scaling in the sense that additional runtime components can be flexibly added when required (e.g., in the case of component failure). Regular health checks are also performed to make sure that exceptions are detected quickly and that the responsible administrator at SAP can take immediate measures to resolve the issue.

In addition, the Cloud Integration platform is hosted redundantly in different data centers at different locations, and SAP provides monthly software updates without any downtime of productive scenarios. All of these measures ensure that Cloud Integration customers aren't left in the lurch should a component ever fail.

1.3.7 Integration Design and Monitoring Tools

Customers using Cloud Integration have the option to design or enhance integration content themselves and to monitor message exchanges at runtime. The following tools are available:

- The Web UI browser-based web application is provided for these design and monitoring tasks and will be the central tool you'll use throughout this book.
- Various Eclipse add-ons are available for adapter developments.
- The SAP BTP cockpit can be used to perform user management tasks.

1.4 Editions

Cloud Integration is included in SAP Integration Suite. However, depending on the edition of SAP Integration Suite you've selected, different components and core capabilities are included. You can find the different editions and their descriptions in Table 1.3.

Note that, on top of SAP Integration Suite, premium edition, additional instances may be added if needed. Refer to the Agreements or Service Description Guide for more up-to-date and complete information at *http://s-prs.co/507706*.

Edition	Description
SAP Integration Suite, basic edition	This edition is the entry-level version of SAP Integration Suite and includes the following capabilities: ■ One instance of Cloud Integration ■ Application-to-application integration ■ Data integration
SAP Integration Suite, standard edition	This standard edition is a general-purpose integration platform and includes most capabilities available in SAP Integration Suite: ■ One instance of Cloud Integration ■ Application-to-application integration ■ Data integration ■ Integration Advisor ■ API Management ■ Open Connectors ■ JMS/asynchronous queues/events ■ Edge Integration Cell

Table 1.3 Cloud Integration Editions for Cloud Foundry

Edition	Description
SAP Integration Suite, premium edition	This version is a fully featured version of SAP Integration Suite and includes the following capabilities: ▪ Three instances of Cloud Integration ▪ Application-to-application integration ▪ Data integration ▪ Integration Advisor ▪ API Management ▪ Open Connectors ▪ JMS/asynchronous queues/events ▪ Alert Notification Service ▪ SAP Transportation Management ▪ Edge Integration Cell

Table 1.3 Cloud Integration Editions for Cloud Foundry (Cont.)

For more details on the number of connections, messages, and included components in the editions listed in Table 1.3, go to *http://s-prs.co/v576070*.

Note that the SAP Integration Suite editions listed in Table 1.3 are related to the SAP BTP, Cloud Foundry environment, and aren't available in the SAP BTP, Neo environment.

Note

Customers with an existing SAP BTP, Neo environment, can renew their licenses; however, all new Cloud Integration subscriptions will need to be based on the SAP Integration Suite editions listed in Table 1.3.

For each edition listed in Table 1.3, SAP remains fully in charge of providing, maintaining, and upgrading Cloud Integration on a regular basis. SAP sets up the account and tenant for the customer and operates the customer-specific integration runtime. In general, however, you would be responsible for integration content design and deployment on the tenant as well as for monitoring the message exchange at runtime.

1.5 Summary

In this chapter, we introduced Cloud Integration as the integration solution of choice for supporting companies on their digital transformation journeys. We've shown that Cloud Integration's use cases cover both cloud-to-cloud and cloud-to-on-premise integration and that Cloud Integration can also be used for pure on-premise-to-on-premise integrations. This is enabled by the new Edge Integration Cell extension of Cloud Integration. Edge Integration Cell is the new flexible hybrid integration runtime, offered as an optional extension to SAP Integration Suite.

Finally, we provided you with an overview of the product's capabilities and introduced the available editions of Cloud Integration.

In the next chapter, we'll set our focus even more on Cloud Integration, introduce you to its main concepts, and describe the architecture and setup of components. Furthermore, we'll show how you can quickly set up and run your first integration scenario.

Chapter 2
Getting Started

This chapter introduces you to the main concepts and the architecture of SAP Integration Suite. In addition, we'll walk through a tutorial to show you how to set up and run a simple integration scenario.

In this chapter, we'll answer three main questions:

- How does SAP Integration Suite work?
- What are its building blocks?
- How do you get started using Cloud Integration?

Section 2.1 allows you to look behind the scenes of Cloud Integration with a detailed discussion of the solution's architecture. We'll also explain the main components of SAP Integration Suite and how they interact with each other. We're assuming that you're running Cloud Integration in the SAP BTP, Cloud Foundry environment. However, if major differences arise that depend on the environment in which you're running Cloud Integration, we'll briefly elaborate on these differences. We'll then discuss the basic mechanisms in action when a cloud-based integration scenario is executed. Section 2.2 outlines the typical sequence and the main phases of an integration project and points out how the tools provided by Cloud Integration fit into the sequence. Finally, Section 2.3 describes, step-by-step, how to set up and run your first integration scenario.

By the end of this chapter, you'll have the foundational knowledge needed to start working with Cloud Integration.

2.1 Architecture Overview

In this section, we'll show you how Cloud Integration's architectural design makes it a cloud-based integration platform that can be shared by many participants, allows for flexible resource allocation for different participants, and ensures that resources belonging to different participants are strictly separated from each other.

Let's begin with the following questions:

- What are the runtime components in charge of message processing during the operation of an integration scenario?
- Which components are in action when messages are passed through Cloud Integration?

We'll then see how the integration platform is structured in more detail and, finally, provide a complete bird's-eye view of the solution's architecture.

2.1.1 Containerized and Clustered Integration Platform

As discussed in Chapter 1, Cloud Integration is a cloud-based integration platform that allows you to integrate processes by enabling processes to exchange messages with each other. This integration is built on SAP Business Technology Platform (SAP BTP).

SAP Business Technology Platform (SAP BTP)

SAP Business Technology Platform (SAP BTP) is SAP's platform as a service (PaaS) offering that provides a development environment in the cloud to enable you to develop, deploy, and manage applications. SAP BTP offers users the ability to turn data into business value, compose end-to-end business processes, and build and extend SAP applications quickly.

For more information and a summary of the most important concepts and terms, check out the documentation on SAP Help Portal at *https://help.sap.com/docs/btp*.

Cloud Integration is designed as a containerized and clustered integration platform in the cloud. In this context, *containerized* means that the fundamental entities of the integration platform are containers, rather than physical or virtual machines. *Clustered* means that the platform is modularized and composed of smaller, more or less independent entities that, as a whole, make up a cluster.

To illustrate these concepts, consider a simple landscape with only a few IT systems participating in an integration scenario with Cloud Integration connecting them, as shown in Figure 2.1. Let's further assume that, in a dedicated process step within the integration scenario, data is sent from system Ⓐ to system Ⓒ. Another process step triggers system Ⓑ to send data to system Ⓓ and perhaps other systems not specified. Whether system Ⓐ and Ⓑ belong to the same organization or not, or whether the two process steps are part of the same integration scenario or not, aren't important with Cloud Integration.

Figure 2.1 shows several aspects of Cloud Integration: First, all systems (or participants) connected to Cloud Integration share the same physical resources of SAP BTP. You can assume that the required hardware that processes the messages is located on one or several data centers of the relevant cloud infrastructure provider.

Difference between SAP BTP, Cloud Foundry Environment, and SAP BTP, Neo Environment

Note that, when talking about Cloud Integration in the SAP BTP, Cloud Foundry environment, such a data center can be part of the hyperscale infrastructure of companies such as Amazon or Microsoft. When talking about Cloud Integration in the SAP BTP, Neo environment, the hardware that processes the messages is located on one or several SAP data centers. The feature set offered by Cloud Integration is—apart from a few exceptions—identical in both environments.

Throughout this book, we'll assume that you're using Cloud Integration in the SAP BTP, Cloud Foundry environment. When differences exist because of choice of environment, we'll explicitly call your attention to these differences. For more detailed information, see also Section 2.1.7.

Second, each participant can access and use only a part of the commonly shared resources. Furthermore, the resources allocated to individual participants are strictly separated from each other.

As shown in Figure 2.1, a common resource assigned to participant Ⓐ processes messages received by Ⓐ and forwards them to participant Ⓒ, whereas a resource assigned to another participant processes messages from that participant.

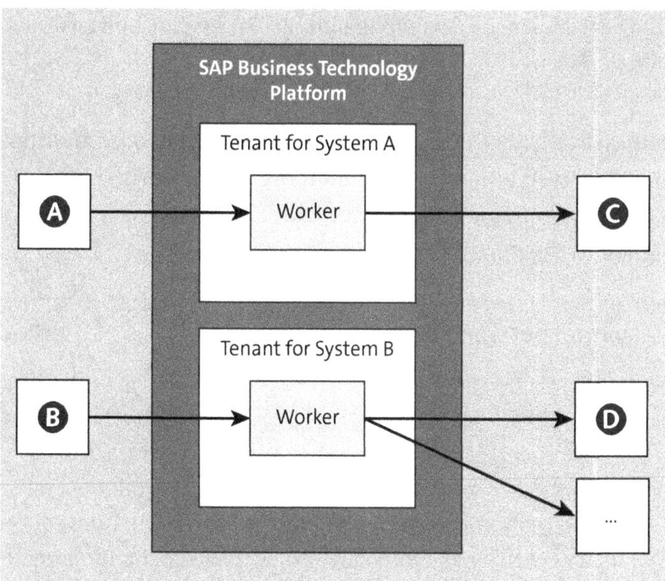

Figure 2.1 Partitioning the Cloud Integration Runtime into Individual Containerized Environments

To explore resource isolation, let's first discuss the terms *account* and *tenant*.

Account

An *account*, the basic point of entry to SAP BTP, represents a hosted environment provided by SAP and defines a set of authorizations and platform resources allocated to the customer. Two types of accounts exist in SAP BTP: global accounts and subaccounts.

- A *global account* represents the functional scope of the platform you're entitled to use based on your license. This account can contain one or more subaccounts.
- A *subaccount* is associated with a certain physical location where applications, data, or services are hosted.

Tenant

A *tenant* is a logical entity that represents the physical resources that SAP BTP has allocated to a specific participant within an application context. Cloud Integration is multitenant-capable, meaning that, although all customers using Cloud Integration share the same physical resources, their tenants can't interfere with each other. Tenants are isolated from each other with regard to memory, data storage, and CPU. Tenant isolation means that physical resources allocated by tenant Ⓐ can't be accessed by tenant Ⓑ.

Although different tenants of Cloud Integration might physically share a single common database, different logical databases per tenant are used. This distinction ensures that data is strictly separated by tenant.

The tenant is the foundational entity of Cloud Integration and will be an important topic throughout this book. For each tenant, a separate integration runtime operates. Messages sent from one participant to Cloud Integration are processed on a worker. A *worker* is a container assigned to the tenant.

Cloud Infrastructures, Environments, and Regions

As already described in Chapter 1, Cloud Integration can be deployed in two different environments: SAP BTP, Neo environment, and SAP BTP, Cloud Foundry environment.

SAP BTP, Cloud Foundry environment, is the industry-standard, open-source cloud application platform. By deploying your software in the SAP BTP, Cloud Foundry environment, not only can Cloud Integration be used on SAP-owned infrastructures (and operated physically in SAP data centers only) but it can also be deployed in infrastructures operated by companies such as Amazon, Alibaba, or Microsoft.

Depending on the environment, Cloud Integration is hosted in different regions, such as Europe (Frankfurt) or US East (Ashburn). The regions indicate the physical location of the data center where the service is operated.

Note that Cloud Integration is one of many services offered in SAP BTP. To find out which services are available in which regions, visit *http://s-prs.co/v576071*.

To recap, the Cloud Integration runtime is designed as a containerized platform. Messages received from different connected participants are processed on separate runtime containers on the platform. The organizing entity is the tenant. All containers belonging to different tenants are isolated from each other with regard to memory, data storage, and CPU.

Figure 2.2 shows a more detailed view of Figure 2.1, including all the entities that come into play during the runtime of SAP BTP and how these entities relate to each other.

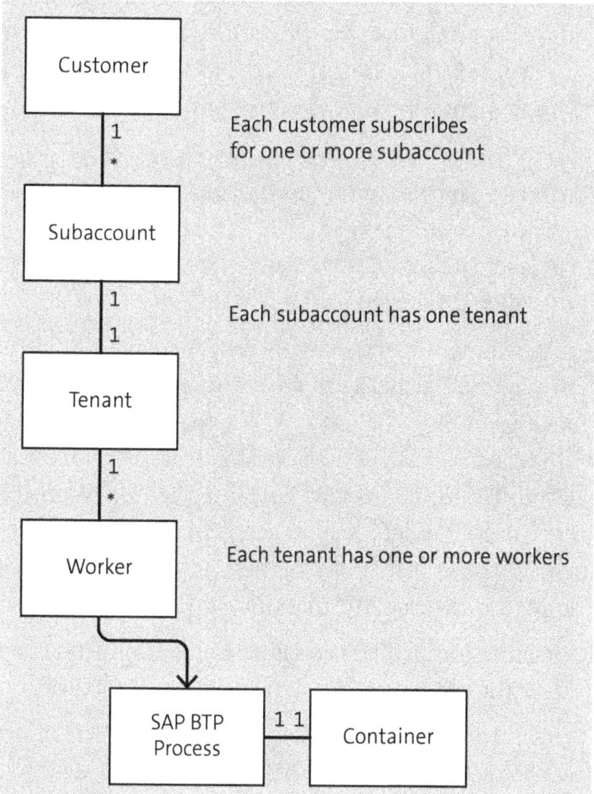

Figure 2.2 Entity Diagram for the Cloud Integration Runtime

As shown in Figure 2.2, on the left, notice that each customer subscribes to one or more subaccounts in SAP BTP. For customers subscribed to Cloud Integration, exactly one tenant is assigned to each subaccount. For each tenant, one or more workers can be started. Each worker is defined as a container, which is an instance of a virtual process running on SAP BTP.

For readers familiar with operating Cloud Integration in the SAP BTP, Neo environment, note that the component denoted as a worker is known as a *runtime node* or a *worker node* in the SAP BTP, Neo environment. For more details, refer to Section 2.1.7.

Note that the 1:*n* relationship of tenant to worker is the basis for the platform to activate and use platform resources flexibly and to ensure efficient load balancing. When hundreds of integration flows (iFlows) are deployed on a customer tenant, resources can be distributed to the available workers flexibly during runtime.

2.1.2 Basic Constituents of the Cloud Integration

To dive more deeply into the technical details, let's further discuss some of the basic constituents of the integration platform (which aren't shown in Figure 2.2). The Cloud Integration runtime environment is based on a *Java Virtual Machine (JVM)*, specified by the Java Platform, Standard Edition (Java SE). In this context, the term *virtual machine* is used in the sense of a software implementation that executes programs in the same way as a physical computer.

A JVM is a virtual environment for executing Java applications. For each tenant, one or more workers are operated. Each worker running on SAP BTP is realized as a JVM and can execute applications written in Java. The actual processing of messages at runtime is accomplished on a Java instance, which is referred to as a JVM instance.

An expert—such as an integration developer—can specify the way messages should be processed on a tenant in an intuitive manner using a graphical editor. The corresponding models are referred to as *integration flows* (iFlows). We'll explain this term and related concepts in more detail in Section 2.1.5. Right now, we simply want to point out that an iFlow is deployed on a JVM in Cloud Integration, enabling the JVM to process messages exactly as specified by the iFlow model. As soon as a JVM instance (the runtime process) has started, and an iFlow has successfully been deployed on it, the JVM instance is ready to process incoming messages in the intended way.

JVM instances constitute the basic *parts* into which the Cloud Integration runtime is split. As we'll describe in this section, the platform is implemented as a cluster of such virtual processes.

Note that each such virtual process doesn't just live during the time a message is being processed. Virtual processes are ready to process incoming messages from the moment a process has been started by an administrator of Cloud Integration and continues to live until the process is stopped either by failure or manually by the administrator.

Note that the resources provided by one JVM aren't restricted to one iFlow. An integration developer can deploy multiple iFlows on the same JVM.

Figure 2.3 shows how a tenant is related to the sender and receiver systems, which are exchanging messages through that tenant (when the sender connects to Cloud Integration through HTTPS).

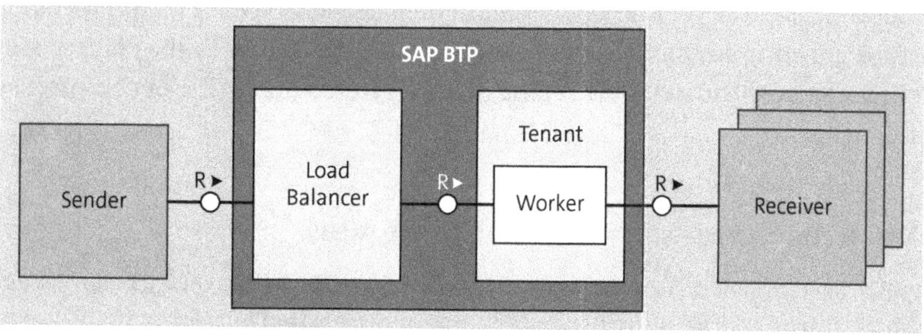

Figure 2.3 Incoming Messages Processed by the Tenant and Forwarded to One or More Receivers

The processing of a sender's message is performed on a worker (i.e., in a container instance on the tenant, as described later in this chapter). Note, however, that the sender isn't directly connected to the tenant. A *load balancer* is connected that intercepts all inbound requests and dispatches each request to the right tenant.

HTTPS is often used as the transport protocol for remote connections, which implies Transport Layer Security (TLS) mechanisms. We'll go into more detail about the security aspects of Cloud Integration in Chapter 10. At this stage, we only want to point out that the load balancer, as shown in Figure 2.3, terminates the inbound TLS connection and establishes a new connection to call the tenant.

If routing steps are specified, the message is forwarded to multiple receiver systems, as shown in Figure 2.3.

You may have noticed the **R>** notation shown in Figure 2.3. This notation will also occur in many other figures throughout this book. **R>** indicates the direction of a request. As shown in Figure 2.3, a sender system sends a message to Cloud Integration, where the message is processed and forwarded to a receiver system. In other words, the direction of the message flow is from the sender to the receiver. In this same example (and in many other cases), the direction of the message flow is identical to the direction of the request. For the sake of simplicity, we'll assume that the sender initiates the message flow by sending a request message to Cloud Integration. Note, however, in other cases, the directions of the request and of the message flow might be opposites (e.g., when a receiver or tenant sends a request to a server to read, or *pull*, data from it). Cloud Integration provides several adapters that also support the pull communication mode, for example, the mail sender adapter. Using this adapter, Cloud Integration can read messages from an email server. We'll show you how this adapter works in Section 2.3.4.

In the previous section, you learned that each Cloud Integration tenant comprises a cluster of workers. We've outlined in detail all the different entities that make up the Cloud Integration runtime.

In the following section, we'll provide a more holistic view of the Cloud Integration architecture, covering additional aspects such as how user access to the platform fits into the architecture picture and what kind of data is stored during the operation of an integration scenario.

2.1.3 Architecture: User Access and Data Storage Areas

In previous sections, we described how Cloud Integration can act as a message exchange platform and showed its underlying architecture. Up to this point, we've ignored two important aspects: how users fit into the picture, and what data is stored on the platform.

While covering these topics, we'll focus on Cloud Integration's main task: integrating processes across different systems. Therefore, regarding user access, we'll focus on the most important persona, the *integration developer*. The entire book in your hands is tailored to the needs of the integration developer who—in a nutshell—interacts with the platform to design, deploy, and test integration scenarios. By reading this book, you'll get to know all aspects of the integration developer's task area in detail.

Figure 2.4 shows the architecture of Cloud Integration, pointing out the main data storage areas and user access points. The architecture discussion in this section assumes that we're talking about running Cloud Integration in the SAP BTP, Cloud Foundry environment—the standard access mode. Note that, on any given level of detail, most aspects we discuss will be valid for both cases (running in the SAP BTP, Cloud Foundry environment, versus in the SAP BTP, Neo environment). When going further into the details, however, some differences will be noticeable. As long as these differences are relevant to understanding the topic at hand, we'll briefly elaborate on these environment-specific aspects. Section 2.1.7 provides a summary of some key architectural differences.

Beginning on the right side of the diagram shown in Figure 2.4, we can connect to the discussion we started in Section 2.1.1. The architecture diagram includes the components shown in Figure 2.3, but with additional components now added. Let's walk through this diagram step-by-step.

At runtime, remote systems (from the perspective of Cloud Integration either acting as a sender or a receiver of messages) interact with the Cloud Integration runtime. This runtime is technically realized as a set of workers (shown also in Figure 2.1 and Figure 2.3 earlier). When describing Figure 2.3, we also showed you how messages received from a sender system are guided through a load balancer before finally reaching the Cloud Integration runtime. This detail is also shown in Figure 2.4 in the **Load Balancer** shape. Note that, consequently, this shape comes in between the sender and the worker, not between the receiver and the worker.

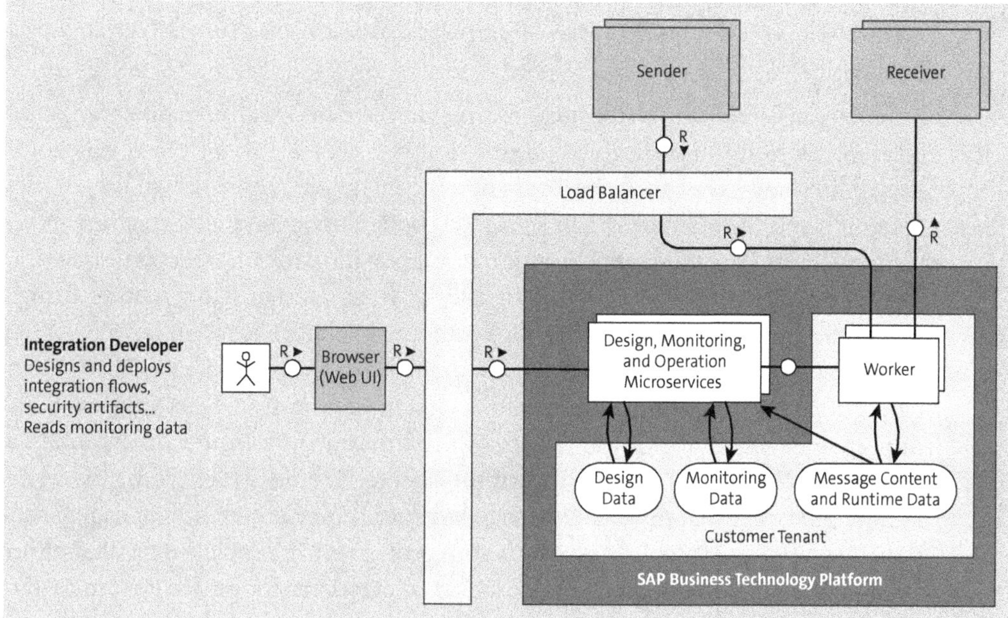

Figure 2.4 Architecture Diagram Indicating the Data Storage Areas and User Access Points

The runtime component processes messages that are exchanged through Cloud Integration. How messages are processed is specified in iFlows deployed on the workers. Multiple workers are shown in Figure 2.4 because technically the responsible integration content is flexibly deployed on multiple such worker components to balance loads. The workers interact with the external systems and the load balancer. For the sake of simplicity (and not shown in Figure 2.4), note that SAP BTP can host multiple customer tenants, each showing the same internal structure as shown in this example for a single tenant.

However, you must understand that the workers responsible for dedicated scenarios are strictly separated by customer tenant. Each customer-specific set of workers exists only on its customer-specific tenant.

When processing messages, Cloud Integration can also temporarily store data. Different kinds of data can be stored, for example, message content and monitoring data. Note that data belonging to different customer tenants is strictly isolated from each other. For more information on the kinds of data stored during runtime, see Table 2.1 later in this section. The workers assigned to a certain tenant store this data in a logical database that can be accessed *only* by this specific tenant. Logical databases from different customer tenants are strictly separated from each other so that the data is protected.

Now, let's look on the left side of the diagram shown in Figure 2.4. Note that we added the most important human agent associated with an integration project—the integration developer. In the context of IT, such human agents are often differentiated according to their typical tasks. In these cases, these human agents are also referred to as *personas*.

For now, you'll need to understand how a human agent fits into the architecture. A user accesses the platform through an internet browser with the Web UI tool, which we'll explain in detail later. The Web UI supports the integration developer in his key task: designing and testing integration scenarios. Designing integration scenarios means defining how Cloud Integration's runtime components should process messages. To define this process, the integration developer would design iFlow models using a graphical editor. In Section 2.1.5, we'll go into more detail about what an iFlow is. For now, all you need to know is that an iFlow defines how messages are processed by the Cloud Integration runtime. The resulting design data is stored per customer in a respective database by a set of agents, which are shown in Figure 2.4, indicated as **Design, Monitoring, and Operation Microservices**. We'll come to these components in a minute. First, note that the Web UI is also the central point of entry for managing additional artifacts, for example, digital keys and certificates to be deployed for configuring secure communication paths between Cloud Integration and remote systems, which we'll explain in detail in later chapters. When the integration developer has finished designing the iFlow, he deploys the corresponding artifacts, and the system distributes the corresponding software packages on the active workers. We'll explain in more detail later how this deployment works and which entities come into play during this phase.

During the testing phase of an integration scenario, the integration developer can use the Web UI to monitor the flow of messages and to perform error analysis if a message exchange fails.

The architectural components of Cloud Integration accessed by the human agent are the **Design, Monitoring, and Operation Microservices**. The name highlights the key tasks relevant for the context of the book. Technically, these microservices are responsible for a variety of tasks, including several already mentioned, such as managing design-time artifacts (iFlows) and reading the data required for monitoring. Nevertheless, this component is also responsible for many other tasks not covered by the name, such as managing security-related artifacts (e.g., key pairs). We won't go into further detail on this topic now, but subsequent chapters will.

These microservices act as agents between human users and the runtime environment (consisting of workers) in Cloud Integration. As you'll learn in Section 2.3, a user accesses the **Design, Monitoring, and Operation Microservices** (using the Web UI) via a URL that follows this format: *https://<Cloud Integration Management Host Address>/shell/design*.

Additionally, the monitoring microservice (from the **Design, Monitoring, and Operation Microservices**) reads the required monitoring data from the database during the operation phase of an integration scenario.

API-Based Access

Not shown in Figure 2.4 is another way of accessing Cloud Integration: application programming interface (API)-based access using the Cloud Integration API. You can enhance the architecture shown in Figure 2.4 by thinking of another connection between any technical component outside of SAP BTP and the **Design, Monitoring, and Operation Microservices** shape.

The Cloud Integration API is accessible through an HTTP call with a URL that follows this format:

https://<Cloud Integration Management Host Address>/api/v1

All of Chapter 8 is dedicated to discussing the Cloud Integration API in detail.

Additional Personas

As shown in Figure 2.4, our example Cloud Integration environment has been set up for a dedicated customer. Everything is up and running so that our integration experts can do their work, and the platform can process messages at runtime.

In our architectural diagram, we excluded a few additional roles important to the context of the architecture discussion early on, when Cloud Integration is being set up for a customer. To jump right in on these additional roles, we elaborate on this topic in detail in Section 2.1.6.

Persistence

During the processing of a message (by a worker), various steps may also store the data in a database, as indicated by the rounded rectangles shown in Figure 2.4.

Table 2.1 summarizes the various kinds of data that can be stored at runtime.

Type of Stored Data	Description
Monitoring data	Monitoring data is data recording what happens to a message during its processing. In particular, all involved processing steps are stored in a structure called a *message processing log (MPL)*. This feature enables integration developers to monitor the message flow during the testing of an integration scenario, which we'll describe in more detail in Chapter 7.

Table 2.1 Different Kinds of Data Stored at Runtime

Type of Stored Data	Description
Monitoring data (Cont.)	During the processing of a message, the worker fires events to the monitoring microservice (part of the **Design, Monitoring, and Operation Microservices** shape shown in Figure 2.4). This microservice aggregates these events and writes the resulting MPL into the database (as indicated by the **Monitoring Data** shape shown in Figure 2.4). This data can be requested by a human agent through the Web UI or through the OData API (as described later in Chapter 8, Section 8.5).
Message content and runtime data	The data storage indicated by the **Message Content and Runtime Data** shape shown in Figure 2.4 stands for technical information generated at runtime and stored on the tenant as well as message content processed by the tenant and stored temporarily. Message content contains business data (in the payload of the message) and the message header. This data can be stored on the tenant if you've activated the **Trace** log level for message monitoring (see Chapter 7, Section 7.2.2). In this case, the content of the message is stored on the tenant so that during monitoring, you can analyze how the message has been transformed step-by-step during the message processing run. Other options are available for storing message content temporarily at specific discrete steps within an integration scenario. The storage duration is 90 days by default. You can configure, per scenario, where in the processing sequence this data should be stored. Message content can be stored temporarily for other purposes such as error analysis, audit logging, and archiving. You must understand that the worker has read and write access to such data. Obviously, the worker stores the message content to the tenant database at specific discrete steps. In certain cases, when configured explicitly within an integration scenario, using the data store **Write** step (Section 2.3.4) or the **Write Variables** step (as described later in Chapter 6, Section 6.4.3), message content stored temporarily can also be made available for later processing steps in the context of the same message processing sequence (or by another iFlow deployed on the same tenant). In other words, message content can also be read by the worker during message processing. In most cases, the data can be stored encrypted. While the worker has read and write access to this kind of data, the monitoring microservice (indicated under the **Design, Monitoring, and Operation Microservices** shape shown in Figure 2.4) only has read access to this data (as expressed by the one-way arrow ending at the **Design, Monitoring, and Operation Microservices** shape).

Table 2.1 Different Kinds of Data Stored at Runtime (Cont.)

Type of Stored Data	Description
Message content and runtime data (Cont.)	For the sake of completeness, we'd like to point out that this storage also comprises further technical data stored temporarily, for example, data used by the system to document that a certain file has already been processed, such as in scenarios where the Secure Shell (SSH) File Transfer Protocol (SFTP) adapter is used. **Java Message Service Queues** A specific, temporary persistence option is storing messages in Java Message Service (JMS) queues. You can use this option to asynchronously decouple inbound from outbound processing in scenarios where you'd like the integration platform (rather than the sender system) to retry message processing when an error occurs. When an iFlow has been configured to use JMS resources, the runtime component also temporarily stores the message content in JMS queues. Note that this option is only available if you've purchased SAP Integration Suite or SAP BTP Enterprise Agreement. As shown in Figure 2.4, message content is stored and accessed in the database and in JMS queues by the worker during message processing. For monitoring purposes, message content is read by the monitoring microservice.

Table 2.1 Different Kinds of Data Stored at Runtime (Cont.)

Note that the separation of data belonging to different customers is achieved by using different logical databases (e.g., JMS instances when JMS queues are used) for each tenant.

For the sake of completeness, as shown in Figure 2.4, the storage indicated by **Design Data** represents all data stored at design time (e.g., iFlow models).

An additional, permanent storage option related to the usage of Cloud Integration is worth mentioning: You also have the option of installing a separate database system available as a service of SAP BTP. Cloud Integration comes with a dedicated adapter, the Java Database Connectivity (JDBC) adapter, for performing SQL database operations on such a database system. In this way, you can permanently store business data in database tables when processing a message, and the persistence layer is part of SAP BTP. We'll elaborate on this topic in detail in Chapter 6, Section 6.5, which includes a tutorial showing you how to use this option. Note that this storage option isn't shown in Figure 2.4 because this storage isn't an inherent part of a Cloud Integration tenant as this storage relies on a separate database system installed independently of the individual Cloud Integration tenant.

Software Updates

The software running on the various subsystems of Cloud Integration is updated monthly by SAP in a process that doesn't require any downtime of productive scenarios running on Cloud Integration.

2.1.4 Secure Communication

A fundamental requirement for a cloud-based integration platform is that the data exchanged through the platform is protected from misuse. To that end, the remote systems and workers of an integration platform should only communicate with each other through secure channels.

Various options are available for setting up secure connections between Cloud Integration and the remote systems involved. A common security measure is to use HTTPS and to enforce mutual authentication of the communicating components based on digital certificates.

On top of transport-level security (e.g., HTTPS), Cloud Integration allows you to set up scenarios so that exchanged messages are digitally encrypted and signed for increased security. We'll describe all of these security options in detail in Chapter 10.

At this point, note that each security option requires the implementation of digital keys of a certain kind as well as the setup of storage locations for digital keys. To activate a certain security option for a tenant (and the integration scenarios deployed on it), these keys and key storage areas must be deployed on the tenant as *integration artifacts*. In Chapter 10, you'll learn about the complete set of security-related integration artifacts. Nevertheless, at the end of this chapter, you'll get a glimpse of this topic when we show you how to upload digital certificates to the tenant keystore so that Cloud Integration can communicate with an email server (Section 2.3.6).

Using this terminology, iFlows, which we introduced in Section 2.1.1 and will describe in more detail in Section 2.1.5, constitute a specific kind of integration artifact that can be deployed on a tenant.

2.1.5 Implementation of Message Flows

In this section, we'll discuss how Cloud Integration is enabled to process messages as defined in an iFlow.

We'll also briefly touch on additional, specific approaches supported by Cloud Integration, namely, specifying integration content for business-to-business (B2B) scenarios using the Integration Advisor and designing OData service artifacts. These options are also described in detail in dedicated chapters (Chapter 7 and Chapter 4, respectively).

An iFlow, however, is the basic design artifact for defining message flows, which is a fundamental concept you must understand about iFlows before we move on to more sophisticated integration design tasks. Therefore, we'll focus on the basics of iFlow design in this section.

Integration Flows as Models to Specify Message Flows

An integration developer can intuitively define the way a message should be processed in a graphical modeling environment. The corresponding models are iFlows. These models follow a notation related to Business Process Model and Notation (BPMN).

Figure 2.5 shows a schematic of an iFlow model where message routing has been configured.

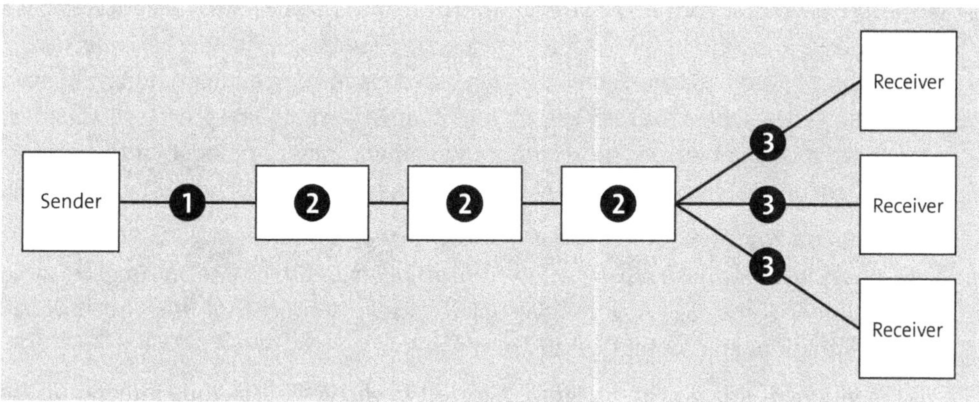

Figure 2.5 Schematic Illustration of the iFlow Elements

First, in an iFlow, you'll specify the sender and receiver systems of a message flow. The details of the technical connection between a sender/receiver and the tenant are configured within a *channel*. A channel allows you to specify an *adapter*, according to the technical protocol of the connected sender or receiver. As shown in Figure 2.5, a sender channel ❶ specifies a connection between a sender and Cloud Integration, whereas a receiver channel ❸ specifies a connection between Cloud Integration and a receiver.

The way a message is processed by the integration platform and how the message is transformed, routed, or enriched with additional data (just a few examples) are all specified within different *iFlow steps* ❷.

iFlow

An iFlow specifies how a message should be processed by Cloud Integration. This BPMN-like model can be intuitively specified by an integration developer as a graphical model. To make an iFlow available for the worker (which oversees processing the message at runtime), the model must be deployed on the corresponding tenant.

OData Services

A specific modeling option is provided by *OData service* artifacts. You can use these artifacts to expose various data sources as OData endpoints. This approach is a simple and intuitive way for converting different kinds of protocols to the OData protocol. In technical terms, when an OData service is created, the system generates an iFlow out of the OData service, which contains an OData sender adapter by default. For more information, check out the "Basic Artifact Types" information box in Section 2.3.4 and learn more in Chapter 4, Section 4.5.

Apache Camel as an Integration Framework

The information specified by an integration developer in an iFlow is made accessible to the worker, who is in charge of actually processing a message, via Apache Camel (*http://camel.apache.org*). Apache Camel is a Java-based, open-source integration framework that allows developers to easily specify how a message should be processed. Chapter 4 provides a detailed introduction to Apache Camel's message model. In this section, we'll focus on aspects required for a basic understanding of the concepts behind iFlows.

An elementary sequence of message processing steps is implemented as a *Camel route*. A Camel route specifies a message flow from one source endpoint to one or more target endpoints. The message flow can be subject to several processing steps such as data transformations and content-based routing.

As mentioned earlier, as an integration expert in charge of designing integration scenarios, you don't need any Java programming skills or knowledge about Apache Camel to get the full functionality out of iFlows. You'll simply design the iFlow with a graphical tool and then deploy the flow on your tenant with a single click. In this way, you'll trigger a process that generates the corresponding Apache Camel objects out of the iFlow and makes these objects available for the workers associated with the tenant.

How the Integration Framework Relates to the Virtual Runtime

In Section 2.1.1, you learned how the containerized runtime of Cloud Integration is structured and about some of its properties. In this section, we introduced you to the Apache Camel integration framework and its associated design-time models, known as iFlows. Now, let's discuss how the entities of the integration framework relate to the entities of the runtime.

For this purpose, we've enhanced the diagram shown earlier in Figure 2.2 by adding entities to define how message processing is implemented on the runtime components. Figure 2.6 shows the result.

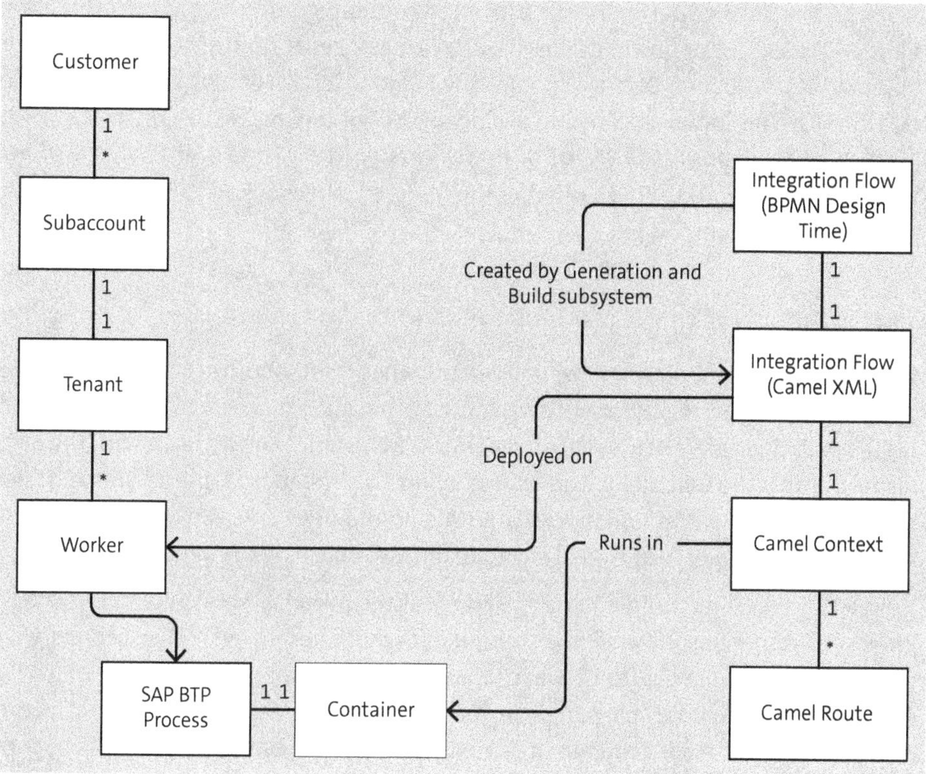

Figure 2.6 Runtime Resources and Artifacts That Define a Message Flow

We described the entities (also shown earlier in Figure 2.2) on the left in Section 2.1.1. These entities make up the containerized runtime.

The right side of Figure 2.6 shows each entity relevant to specifying a message flow. The iFlow is a BPMN-like model created or edited by an integration developer with the support of a graphical tool. With iFlow models, you can fully specify how a message should be processed by the Cloud Integration runtime. When the integration developer has finished modeling and deploys the iFlow on a tenant, the model is transformed into an XML structure, which is compatible with the Apache Camel specification. This XML structure is deployed on all workers assigned to the tenant.

Turning to how message flows are implemented in Java, a Camel context defines a set of Apache Camel components for a specific iFlow. Depending on the complexity of the iFlow, for each Camel context, one or more Camel routes are specified. A Camel route defines (on the level of the Java programming model) a message flow from one source endpoint to one or more target endpoints. In many cases, one iFlow leads to exactly one Camel route. However, complex iFlows can result in multiple Camel routes.

When you've finished designing the iFlow, and your integration scenario is up and running, you can monitor how the iFlow processes messages at runtime with the monitoring application. Chapter 8 covers monitoring in more detail. For now, note that you can also monitor the status of all iFlows deployed on your tenant. We can refer to an iFlow as one kind of *integration artifact*, a term we introduced earlier in Section 2.1.4. With the Web UI, you can quickly check whether the required iFlows are available for your integration runtime components.

2.1.6 Architecture Summary

So far, in the preceding sections, you learned that the Cloud Integration runtime is designed as a clustered, containerized platform. Messages received from different connected participants are processed on separate JVM instances on the platform. The organizing entity is the tenant. All workers belonging to different tenants are isolated from each other with regard to memory, data storage, and CPU. You also learned how message flows can be designed by a user and made available to the platform.

Now, let's pause for a moment and again look at the overall architecture of Cloud Integration to remember how all the components described in previous sections work together. As shown in Figure 2.7, we're using nearly the same setup from Figure 2.4 but enriched with two additional personas. We won't repeat in detail the internal structure of SAP BTP. In this step, we're moving one level higher to show a bird's-eye view, complemented by an additional role, the administrator.

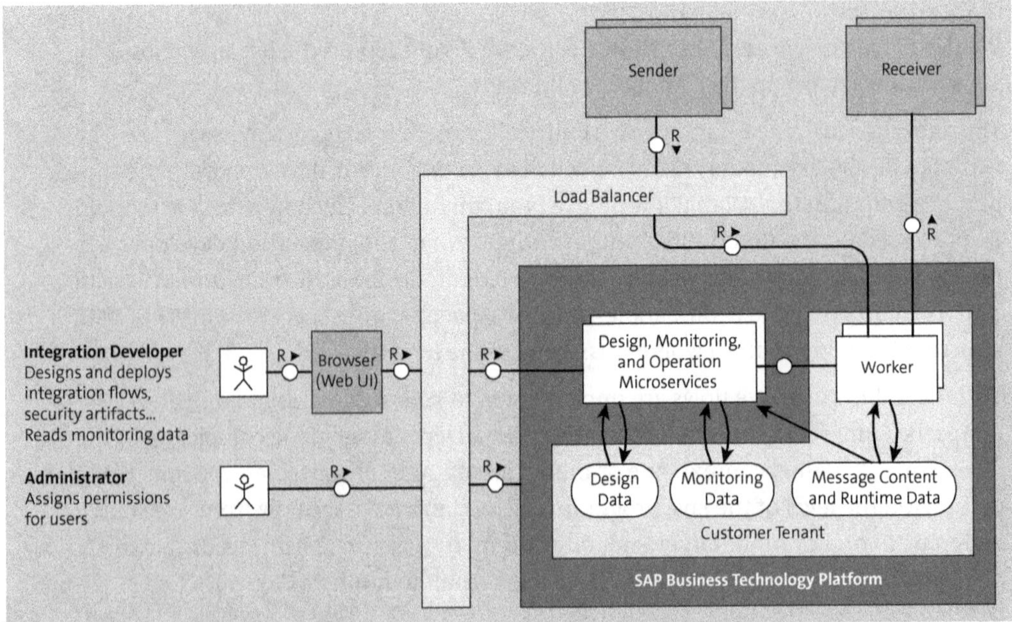

Figure 2.7 Bird's-Eye View of the Cloud Integration Architecture

Recall from Chapter 1 how Cloud Integration can be deployed in two different environments: SAP BTP, Cloud Foundry environment, and SAP BTP, Neo environment. Figure 2.7 shows the architecture of Cloud Integration when operating in the SAP BTP, Cloud Foundry environment, but the aspects we discuss in this chapter are valid generally (for some environment-specific differences, refer to Section 2.1.7).

The basic cloud infrastructure is either being provided by SAP (when Cloud Integration runs on SAP BTP, Neo environment) or by another organization such as Microsoft or Amazon (when Cloud Integration runs on SAP BTP, Cloud Foundry environment). The infrastructure provider (not shown in Figure 2.7) is the persona responsible for making the corresponding software in the related cloud infrastructure available for a customer (of Cloud Integration).

When a customer has been provided access to a corresponding SAP BTP account (with the SAP Integration Suite service activated), a dedicated person on the customer side will first get access to the account as an administrator.

The administrator receives the initial information about how to access Cloud Integration from the infrastructure provider. Using the required URLs and further information provided by the infrastructure provider, the administrator accesses the subaccount through the SAP BTP cockpit. The first task for this persona is to specify which users should get access to the relevant subaccount as an administrator. Second, the administrator will grant permissions to users in charge of dedicated tasks as part of the integration project. In this second task, the administrator defines authorizations for all additional users of the subaccount. These additional users represent people—on the customer side—involved in tasks such as iFlow design or monitoring. In larger organizations, these tasks are typically performed by different persons who have separate permissions.

An administrator comes into the game at the beginning when a customer first sets up the Cloud Integration environment, and this person is responsible for defining the permissions of all persons who will interact with the Cloud Integration.

After these permissions have been set up, the integration team (for the sake of simplicity, represented by the integration developer) can start working. At this point, a third human agent, shown in Figure 2.7, comes into play. With permissions defined, additional enabled users can start working with Cloud Integration. The role in focus is the integration developer.

Finally, everything in Cloud Integration works as described earlier in Section 2.1.3.

Microservices

Before we wrap up this detailed walkthrough of the architecture of Cloud Integration, we need to point out that its cluster architecture implements the concept of microservices to a large extent.

A *microservice*, within a complex architecture, is considered a small and decoupled part of a software or service that covers a specific task or a specified set of tasks. In other words, microservices allow you to modularize complex applications and helps you avoid monolithic systems by decomposing a complex architecture into smaller, independent services. Microservices are small, easy to replace, organized around capabilities, and complete.

The cluster design we've described in this chapter implements this microservice pattern, which is designed in such a way that different kinds of components or services are responsible for different tasks. Tasks related to message processing are accomplished by a worker, whereas tasks related to the design and operation of a cluster and monitoring the message processing are accomplished by microservices, which are represented by the **Design, Monitoring, and Operation Microservices** shape shown in Figure 2.7. Microservices are independent in that the availability of one microservice or worker doesn't impact the availability of other microservices. Therefore, for example, tasks such as monitoring are still possible when an associated worker (container) fails.

High Availability

As shown in Figure 2.4 and Figure 2.7, multiple workers can be put in place to take over the task of processing messages. Operating multiple workers supports failover scenarios where, if a worker fails, other workers can take over its tasks. In this way, high availability is supported by the architecture of Cloud Integration.

This architecture ensures that Cloud Integration is highly available; integration scenarios can be operated without the risk of downtime.

Integration Advisor

If you've purchased SAP Integration Suite or SAP BTP Enterprise Agreement, you'll additionally get access to the Integration Advisor. This application allows you to easily specify integration content for B2B scenarios in an intuitive way (see also Section 2.2.1). The Integration Advisor comes with additional components and a database that stores the required B2B content.

In this chapter, we'll focus on the basic building blocks of Cloud Integration to introduce you to key principles. Therefore, we didn't add the additional components related to the Integration Advisor in the architecture overview shown in Figure 2.7.

2.1.7 Environment-Specific Aspects of the Architecture

For the sake of completeness, we'll shed some more light on some environment-specific aspects of the Cloud Integration architecture that may arise as we dive more deeply.

As mentioned in the previous section (and shown earlier in Figure 2.4), human agents are connected to Cloud Integration through a set of components called **Design, Monitoring, and Operation Microservices**. One detail level further, this application is composed of a set of microservices, each responsible for a task. A key characteristic of these microservices is that they are multitenant capable. In other words, each microservice can be accessed by different tenants of SAP BTP in different ways. Nevertheless, on the application level, both data and user access are strictly separated by customer. When a user connects to Cloud Integration, or similarly when the platform is called by an API, the identity of the caller is checked by the associated identity provider. The identity provider then issues a token that enables access to the relevant tenant-specific data (e.g., when a user monitors messages processed on a certain customer-specific tenant).

Going back to the architecture shown earlier in Figure 2.7, notice that, when Cloud Integration operates in the SAP BTP, Cloud Foundry environment, its workers and their connected data storage areas are strictly separated by tenant. Nevertheless, based on the authentication mechanism described earlier, the platform ensures that a user connecting to Cloud Integration through **Design, Monitoring, and Operation Microservices** can only access the tenant he is permitted to access.

The architecture of Cloud Integration when used in the SAP BTP, Neo environment, is slightly different. In this setup, each customer tenant contains both the **Design, Monitoring, and Operation Microservices** part as well as the runtime part. Readers familiar with earlier versions of Cloud Integration will notice the term *tenant cluster*, which is composed of one or more tenant management nodes, each associated with one or more runtime nodes. The tenant management node in the SAP BTP, Neo environment, is responsible for tasks that, in the SAP BTP, Cloud Foundry environment, are performed by the **Design, Monitoring, and Operation Microservices**. On the other hand, the runtime nodes in the SAP BTP, Neo environment, correspond to the workers shown earlier in Figure 2.7.

For more information on the architecture of Cloud Integration in the SAP BTP, Neo environment, check out the Cloud Integration documentation on SAP Help Portal at *http://s-prs.co/v576003*. Search for "Security in the Neo Environment," and check out **Technical Landscape, Neo Environment**.

Now that you're familiar with the architecture of Cloud Integration, let's look at the tools you'll use to interact with Cloud Integration and the processes relevant to integration developers.

2.2 Tools and Processes

In this section, we'll provide an overview of the available tools and the main processes required to set up and run an Cloud Integration scenario.

2.2.1 Tools

Different tools are available for different kinds of user interaction in Cloud Integration.

SAP BTP Cockpit

This application provides access to SAP BTP and allows administrators to perform user management tasks for the account and tenant. The administrator can specify individual permissions for people who are supposed to work on the Cloud Integration tenant in different roles, such as integration developers.

Customers who have purchased SAP Integration Suite or SAP BTP Enterprise Agreement will also be able to subscribe to the Integration Advisor and set up a JMS message broker for scenarios using JMS queues. Figure 2.8 shows one page of the SAP BTP cockpit for a trial account.

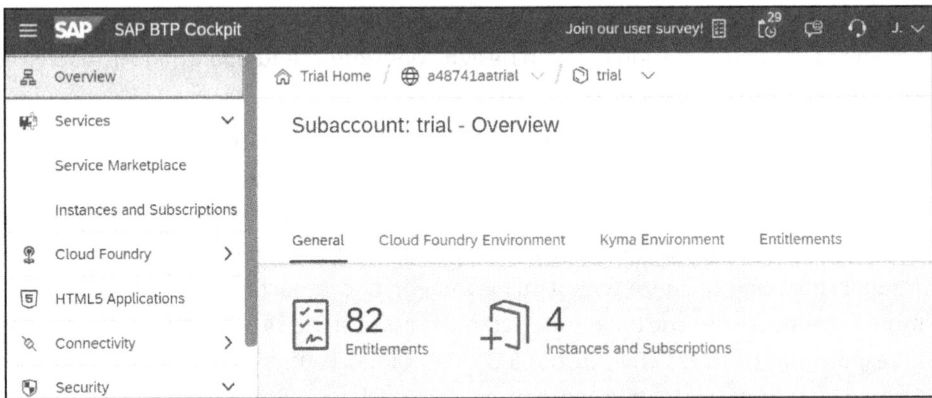

Figure 2.8 SAP BTP Cockpit

SAP Business Accelerator Hub

SAP Business Accelerator Hub, discussed in more detail in Chapter 8, is the central location where SAP publishes APIs and other content. You can also access predefined integration packages provided by SAP that can be used out of the box. As shown in Figure 2.9, you can browse through the content at *https://api.sap.com/*.

These packages are stored in read-only mode. To use an integration package, you'll need to copy it into your own design workspace before you can start modifying it according to your requirements. For more information on the predefined integration content provided by SAP, see Chapter 3.

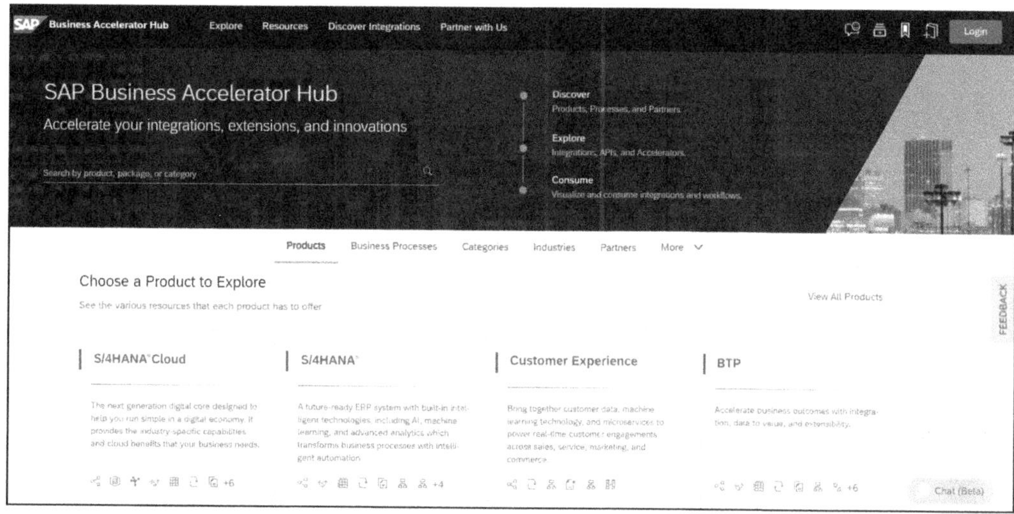

Figure 2.9 Integration Content Published on SAP Business Accelerator Hub

Integration Advisor

As mentioned earlier in Section 2.1.6, Integration Advisor is available if you've purchased SAP Integration Suite or SAP BTP Enterprise Agreement. Integration Advisor facilitates the development of B2B scenarios by allowing you to easily design interfaces, referred to as *message implementation guidelines* (MIGs), that best fit to your own and your partners' business requirements. Additionally, the tool allows you to create *mapping guidelines* (MAGs) to define the transformations between those interfaces. A key feature of the Integration Advisor is that it assists users in defining message implementation guidelines and mappings by adopting an intelligent, crowd-based machine learning approach.

When you've finished specifying the message implementation guidelines and mappings, runtime artifacts are generated out of these objects that you can use in iFlows. Further coverage of B2B is a vast topic that is outside the scope of this book.

Web UI for Integration Design and Monitoring

The Web UI is the most important tool used by integration developers. You can open the Web UI through a URL found in the SAP BTP cockpit.

The Web UI is organized into five pages: **Discover**, **Design**, **Monitor**, **Inspect**, and **Settings**. Figure 2.10 shows how to access the Web UI's pages when Cloud Integration is used in trial mode (as described further in Section 2.3).

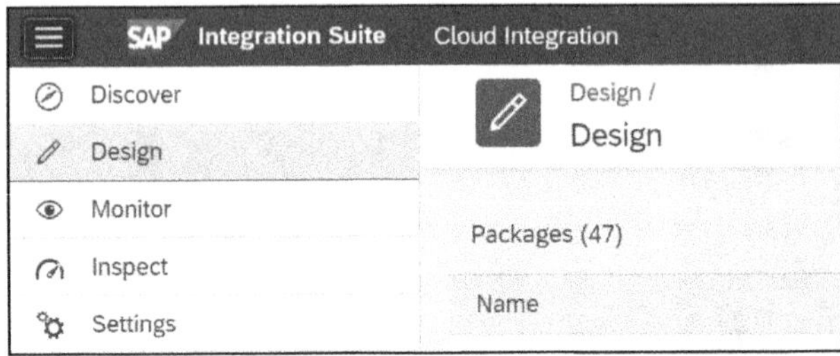

Figure 2.10 Pages in the Web UI with the Design Menu Item Selected

Table 2.2 provides an overview of the task areas covered by each page. For more information, refer to Section 2.3.4, especially the "Basic Artifact Types" information box in that section.

Page	Allows You To . . .
Discover	Access predefined integration content provided by SAP. Under this page of the Web UI, you'll select already available integration content published on SAP Business Accelerator Hub and add this content to your own workspace where you can further edit and adapt the content to meet your own integration challenges. This page also includes a detailed list of third-party adapters provided by SAP partners. We'll discuss predefined integration content further in Chapter 3.
Design	Design the following kinds of artifacts: ■ **Integration Flow** This artifact is the key topic of this book. In Section 2.3, you'll learn how to create and run your first iFlow. Subsequent chapters cover various aspects of integration content design in detail: ■ **OData Service** We'll introduce this design option in Chapter 4, Section 4.3. ■ **Value Mapping** We'll briefly touch on this topic in Chapter 4, Section 4.4. ■ **Integration Adapter** We'll introduce this design option in Chapter 6, Section 6.10. For more information on these artifact types, see the "Basic Artifact Types" information box in Section 2.3.4.
Monitor	Monitor the message flow at runtime, and check the status of deployed artifacts. Under this page, also referred to as the *operations view*, you can also create and deploy security-related artifacts, such as user credentials, keys, and certificates as well as manage message stores and locks. We'll cover this page in detail in Chapter 8.

Table 2.2 Main Pages of the Cloud Integration Web UI

Page	Allows You To . . .
Inspect	Each Cloud Integration tenant comes with certain physical resources that are consumed by iFlows at runtime. Examples of such integration resources are the available database connections. On this page, you can inspect consumption of integration resources, identify those iFlows that contribute significantly to integration-resource exhaustion, and perform steps to resolve critical situations. Based on the insights, you can, for example, optimize iFlow design to overcome integration resource bottlenecks. At the time this book is published, it's possible to inspect the following artifacts: ■ **Data store usage** Using the **Inspect Data Store Usage** tile, you can inspect resource usage of the tenant database caused by iFlows using data store operations steps. ■ **Database connections** Using the **Inspect Database Connections** tile, you can inspect resource usage of the database connections caused by iFlows. ■ **Transactions** Using the **Transactions** tile, you can inspect resource usage of the database transactions caused by iFlows. ■ **Monitoring** Using the **Monitoring Storage** tile, you can inspect resource usage of the monitoring database storage caused by iFlows.
Settings	Configure personal settings. In particular, this page allows you to select a *product profile*. But what are product profiles good for? In this book, we'll only cover scenarios where integration content designed with the Web UI is executed using the cloud-based Cloud Integration runtime. However, you might decide that your integration content must be executed, for example, on an on-premise integration bus of SAP Process Integration (the integration bus that is available as part of SAP Process Orchestration). Because the features supported by the SAP Process Integration runtime (of a specific release) differ slightly from those supported by the Cloud Integration runtime, the Web UI also provides a slightly different set of iFlow design features in case you select a product profile related to a target runtime that uses SAP Process Integration. In other words, a product profile defines the target integration platform for the content designed with the Web UI. Whether or not you have several profiles present on the **Settings** page depends on the basic configuration of your tenant provided initially by the Cloud Integration operations team. Select the profile for which you intend to develop iFlows. Chapter 6, Section 6.7.3, will touch on this topic.

Table 2.2 Main Pages of the Cloud Integration Web UI (Cont.)

Figure 2.11 shows an example iFlow opened in the **Design** page of the Web UI.

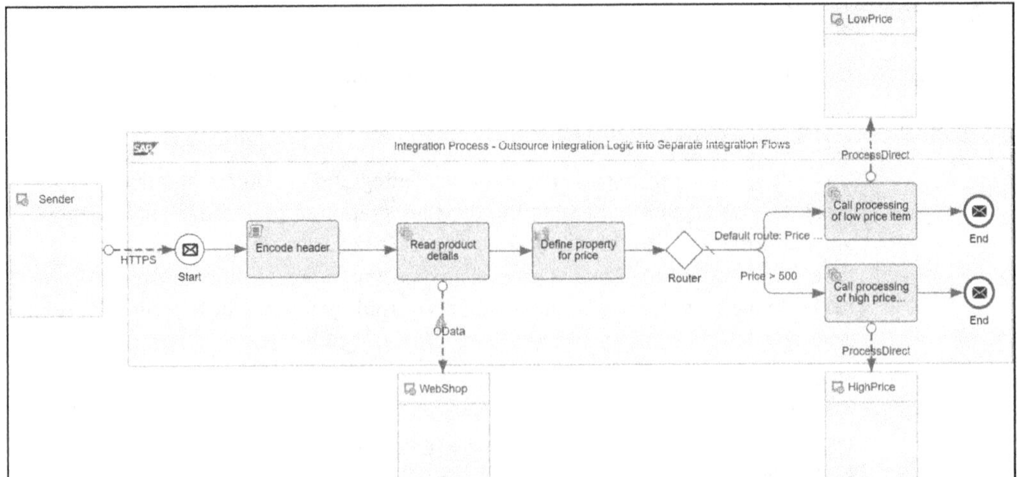

Figure 2.11 An Example iFlow Model Open on the Design Page of the Web UI

When designing an iFlow, you'll add elements (e.g., iFlow steps) and integrate them in a specific order to specify how messages should be processed on the tenant. We provide an overview of the elements that you can add to an iFlow later in Table 2.3.

> **Note**
> When designing OData services, the procedure is slightly different. We'll introduce this option in Chapter 4, Section 4.3.

Figure 2.12 shows the **Monitor** page, which can be accessed from the menu shown earlier in Figure 2.10.

The monitoring application is divided into the following main sections (not all are shown in Figure 2.12):

- **Monitor Message Processing**
  This section allows you to monitor the messages exchanged by your tenant based on the iFlows that are deployed.
- **Manage Integration Content**
  This section allows you to monitor the status of deployed integration content artifacts (iFlows, value mappings, and OData services).
- **Manage Security**
  This section allows you to manage the artifacts required when setting up secure connections between your tenant and remote systems. The **Security Material** tile allows you to manage specific security-related artifacts such as user credentials, Pretty Good Privacy (PGP) key rings, known hosts (required when using SFTP), or OAuth credentials. The **Keystore** tile allows you to manage keys and certificates required when using TLS. Using this tile, you can also manage the lifecycle of keys (renewing

expired keys). The **User Roles** tile allows you create and manage roles to authorize sender systems to place inbound requests at Cloud Integration. You'll use this tile to configure role-based inbound authentication. Two options are available: You can define a role for a sender system authenticating itself with user credentials (the *basic authentication* option), or you can map a digital client certificate (used by the sender for authentication) to a user (for which you can then define permissions based on user roles). For more information on the concepts behind these artifact types and how to use them, go to Chapter 10. Finally, the **Connectivity Tests** tile allows you to test outbound connections for different protocols such as TLS, SSH, Simple Mail Transfer Protocol (SMTP), Internet Message Access Protocol (IMAP), and Post Office Protocol version 3 (POP3). We'll briefly use this tool in Section 2.3.6 but explain it in detail in Chapter 7, Section 7.3.8.

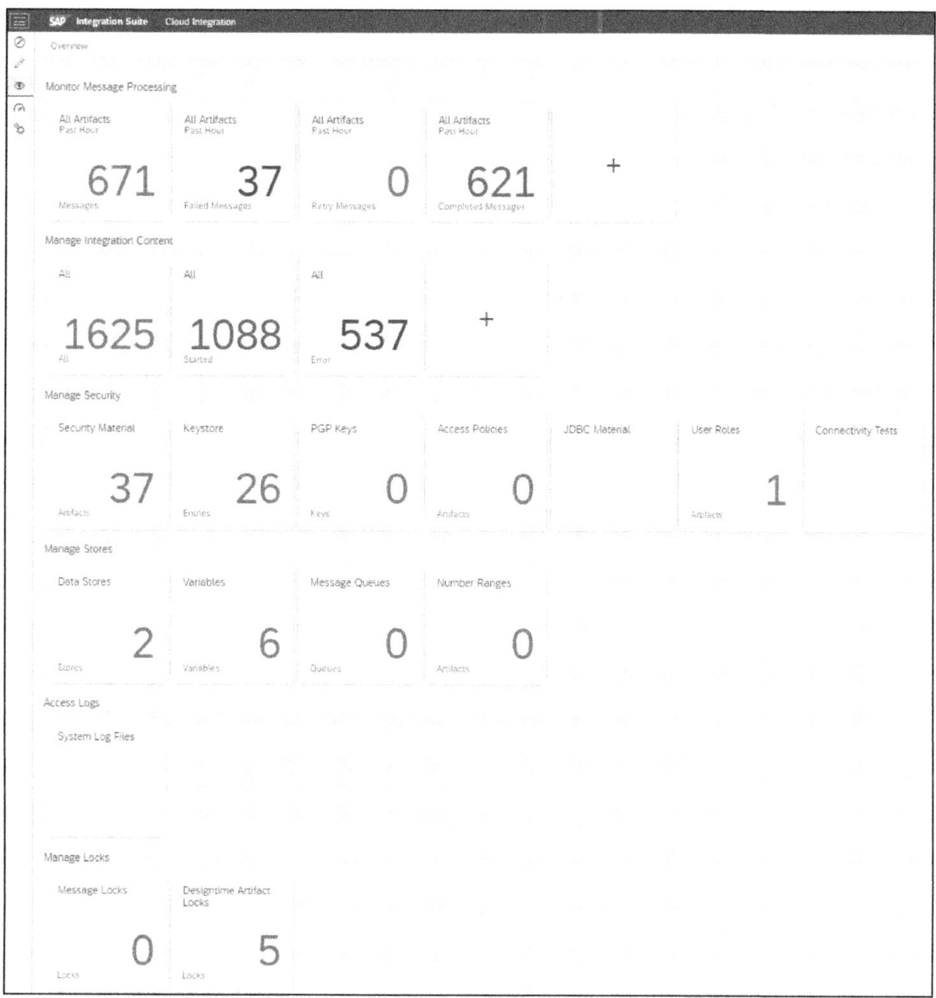

Figure 2.12 The Monitor Page of the Web UI

- **Manage Stores**
  This section allows you to handle storage on the tenant used to temporarily persist data during message processing (as indicated by the message content storage pools shown earlier in Figure 2.7). The **Data Stores** tile allows you to manage data stored temporarily by an iFlow (to make this data available for later processing steps). You can view the content of the data store or delete entries. The **Variables** tile allows you to monitor the variables used in iFlows.

  This section also shows a **Message Queues** tile, which allows you to monitor queues that are relevant when using the JMS adapter or the Applicability Statement 2 (AS2) adapter. (For more information on the JMS adapter, go to Chapter 5, Section 5.4.) For the different kinds of data stored during message processing, see Table 2.1.

  Finally, the **Number Ranges** tile allows you to get an overview of number ranges relevant when running B2B scenarios. In scenarios using Electronic Data Interchange (EDI) messages, a unique interchange number is added to each business document. The **Number Ranges** tile allows you to configure and monitor the interchange number. (This feature is only available if you've purchased SAP Integration Suite or SAP BTP Enterprise Agreement.)

- **Manage Locks**
  This section allows you to manage lock entries to prevent the same message from being processed more than once in parallel. In certain situations (e.g., when a runtime node shuts down unexpectedly), the system tries to reprocess a message; however, a lock entry exists in the database and blocks the processing of subsequent messages. The **Manage Locks** section enables you to resolve such situations.

Note that we've focused on the UI of the **Monitoring** page as it appears when using Cloud Integration in the SAP BTP, Cloud Foundry environment. This page is slightly different in the SAP BTP, Neo environment. However, we won't elaborate more on this topic now. For more information on capabilities found on the **Monitor** page, see Chapter 7.

In Section 2.3, we'll introduce use the Web UI to show you how to create your first iFlow.

Eclipse Tools

The Web UI is the central tool supporting developers throughout the integration project lifecycle. However, over the course of this book, we'll also talk about an additional Cloud Integration–specific tool that requires an Eclipse installation. You'll need this tool to develop adapters (as described later in Chapter 6, Section 6.10).

2.2.2 Processes

In this section, we'll provide a brief overview of the main phases of an integration project before walking you through your first integration project in Section 2.3. The main phases of any Cloud Integration project are as follows:

1. **Browsing predefined integration content**
   First-time users and decision-makers can browse SAP Business Accelerator Hub to explore integration scenarios that can be used out of the box with minimal implementation effort. We'll provide more details on this topic in Chapter 3.
2. **Requesting a tenant and administering the account**
   Customers intending to use Cloud Integration must register at SAP BTP. After you've been provided with an account and a tenant, an administrator on the customer's side can use the SAP BTP cockpit to perform user management tasks on the account. In this phase, the administrator defines which users are allowed to work on the account and defines permissions for individual users.
3. **Provisioning a JMS message broker**
   If you want to use JMS queues, you'll need to perform an additional step to set up a JMS message broker, which is only for users of SAP BTP Enterprise Agreement. This provisioning is also performed in the SAP BTP cockpit.
4. **Setting up secure connections between remote systems and the tenant**
   In this phase, secure communications with Cloud Integration are enabled for sender/receiver systems. This phase is divided into the following tasks (typically performed by different people):
   - **Configuring the sender/receiver systems**
     This task is usually performed by administrators of the sender/receiver system and comprises all steps for setting up the technical connection between the sender/receiver system and Cloud Integration.
   - **Configuring the tenant**
     Users performing this task enable the tenant to securely communicate with the related sender and receiver systems.

   In Chapter 10, we'll show you how to set up a secure connection between Cloud Integration and remote systems.
5. **Designing iFlows**
   In this phase, an integration developer designs iFlows to specify how messages should be processed on the tenant. When the design has been finished, the iFlows are deployed on the tenant.

   To perform these tasks, an integration developer uses the **Discover** and **Design** pages of the Web UI (refer to Figure 2.10).

   Designing iFlows is the core topic of this book. After you've learned how to create, deploy, and run your first iFlow, you can find more details on iFlow design in Chapters 4 through 6. Chapters 7 and 10 also contain tutorials on developing specific iFlows.

   The process of designing an OData service is described in Chapter 4, Section 4.3.

6. **Operating and monitoring Cloud Integration**
   In this phase, you'll monitor the integration artifacts deployed on the tenant cluster and the messages processed by your iFlows. To perform these tasks, an integration developer uses the **Monitor** page of the Web UI.

For more details on these phases, consult Chapter 8.

2.3 Running Your First Integration Scenario

In this section, we'll show you how to set up and run a simple iFlow. By following these steps, you'll learn how to use the Web UI to design, deploy, and test your first iFlow.

2.3.1 Demo Scenario and Landscape

For the sake of illustration, let's build a simple iFlow. As our sender system, we'll use an HTTP client program available for free online (Postman), which you can install with a few clicks on your computer. To keep it simple, in the first part of the tutorial, no receiver system will be connected. Instead of sending a message from the HTTP client to a receiver, the message should be stored in the temporary database of the tenant (in a storage location referred to as a *data store*). After you've executed the iFlow, you can simply check whether the database entry has been created and contains the expected message. Figure 2.13 shows a simple visualization of the required components in our demo scenario.

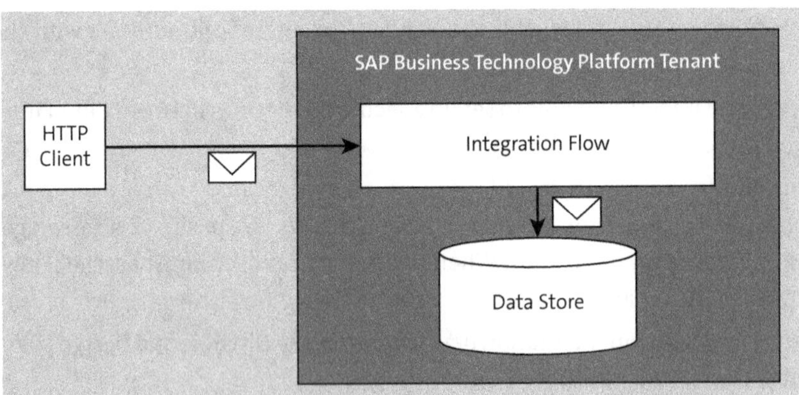

Figure 2.13 Schematic Illustration of the iFlow Developed in This Tutorial

To round out this tutorial, we'll show you how you can add a receiver component to the scenario. To use a system available to everyone, we'll add a connection to an email server. The final setup step enables Cloud Integration to forward messages received from the HTTP client (on your computer) to a private email account. Figure 2.14 shows the final iFlow design.

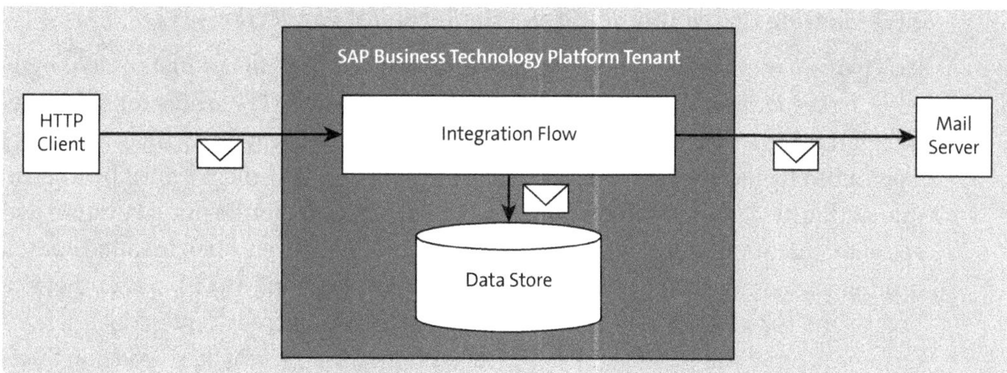

Figure 2.14 Enhancement of the Tutorial iFlow: Adding an Email Server as a Receiver

To set up the second part of the tutorial, you'll only need a publicly accessible email account (from Yahoo!, Google, or any other email provider). The tutorial shows a basic capability of Cloud Integration: exchanging messages between different systems. Cloud Integration supports connectivity with many different systems, as shown in Section 2.3.3. A connected system can be, for example, a complex SAP business system, a file system, or (as in our first example) an HTTP client and an email server, to mention just a few examples.

For simplicity, in this first tutorial, we'll mainly cover the connectivity aspect of Cloud Integration. The iFlow won't perform any complex processing of the message in SAP Integration Suite, except for a step that writes the message content to the tenant database (the **Data Store Write** step). Chapter 4 and subsequent chapters will then successively show you how a message can further be processed in various ways on its path between sender and receiver. We'll show you how to add the different available process step types chapter by chapter.

Let's get started!

2.3.2 Prerequisites

Our first step is to make sure that the following prerequisites are met:

- Subscribe to an SAP BTP trial account at *http://s-prs.co/v576004*, and enable Cloud Integration on this trial account.
- Install Postman from *www.postman.com*. This step is required for setting up the sender component.
- Register an email account. For simplicity, we recommend using Yahoo! mail, and, in this tutorial, we'll show how to connect your tenant to a Yahoo! mail server.

  This step is required for the optional second part of the tutorial, as shown in Figure 2.14.

2.3.3 Setting Up the Landscape and the Technical Connections

Let's pause a moment to consider the security settings used in our first tutorial in the book. To keep it simple, we assume that, in the tutorial, the HTTP sender calls the Cloud Integration system using basic authentication (with user credentials). In this way, you won't need to generate and install client certificates or have them signed by a certificate authority (CA), a process explained in Chapter 10. Nevertheless, a keystore with specific content must be deployed on the tenant because, even when inbound authentication is accomplished based on a user name and password, a TLS-based authentication of the server (Cloud Integration in our case) is enforced (as described later in Chapter 10). SAP will provide the required keystore with the tenant, so you don't need to perform any additional steps related to this topic. If you want to finish the tutorial by adding an email receiver (refer to Figure 2.14), then, depending on the mail server to be used as receiver, you might need to import additional certificates into the keystore, as described later in Section 2.3.6.

Assigning a Role for Inbound Call to Worker

The following scenario uses basic authentication as a simple option for authenticating the sender of the message (i.e., the HTTP client configured with Postman in the second part of the tutorial). The Cloud Integration runtime evaluates the authorization of the sending system (the HTTP client) based on permissions defined for the role associated with the sender. The permission to process messages on SAP Integration Suite is defined in role `ESBMessaging.send`. You'll encounter this role several times in this book.

Before we move on, we also assume that you've followed all steps in the tutorial mentioned earlier. At this point, you've set up a trial account and provisioned a tenant. After you've accomplished these initial steps, you'll also find the address for accessing the Web UI in SAP BTP cockpit. This address ends with */shell/design*. We recommend that you bookmark this address, as this location is the central point of entry for most activities related to your integration projects. You'll need that information in a minute.

Note that an important part of the initial setup as described in the tutorial mentioned earlier is to grant sender systems permissions to call an iFlow endpoint. This step is important because, in the setup shown earlier in Figure 2.14 (and in many tutorials in the following chapters), a sender system (e.g., an HTTP client) triggers message processing by calling an iFlow endpoint. We'll come back to this important topic in Chapter 10, Section 10.3.3. For more information on the technical details of this topic, check out the online documentation on SAP Help Portal at *http://s-prs.co/507713.*

Now, to give you a basic idea of the development process, we'll summarize the most important steps briefly:

1. You'll create an SAP BTP service instance to assign SAP's predefined role (`ESBMessaging.send`), which enables a remote component (a calling application) to access the iFlow endpoint.

A service instance defines how a certain service can be called. More precisely, an OAuth client is defined. (OAuth is a specific authentication mechanism we'll explain in detail in Chapter 10, Section 10.4.3.) When defining a service instance, you'll associate a role with it (in our case, `ESBMessaging.send`).

2. You'll create an SAP BTP service key to generate the credentials required by the sender system to call the service instance.

In Chapter 10, Section 10.4.4, we'll explain the service instance and service key entities in more detail and use them in the context of communication security.

Note that this task, as well as all tasks associated with user and role management, significantly differ in the SAP BTP, Neo environment. For more information on how you can define the required permissions for a sender system to call an iFlow endpoint, check out the online documentation on SAP Help Portal at *https://help.sap.com/docs/cloud-integration*. Search for "Get Started with Cloud Integration."

2.3.4 Developing the Integration Flow

After the initial setup, you're ready to start developing your first iFlow. You'll begin by creating an iFlow, after which you'll design the iFlow using a number of available elements. For an overview of the system landscape relevant for your scenario, refer to Figure 2.13 and Figure 2.14 and the related explanations.

Let's start by creating an integration package, which is a prerequisite to creating any iFlow. An integration package is the fundamental entity used to group iFlows.

Creating an Integration Flow

To create an iFlow, follow these steps:

1. Open the Web UI using the Web UI URL, which we recommended bookmarking earlier.
2. In the Web UI, choose the **Design** page (refer to Figure 2.10).
3. Choose **Create** to create a new integration package, as shown in Figure 2.15 on the top right.

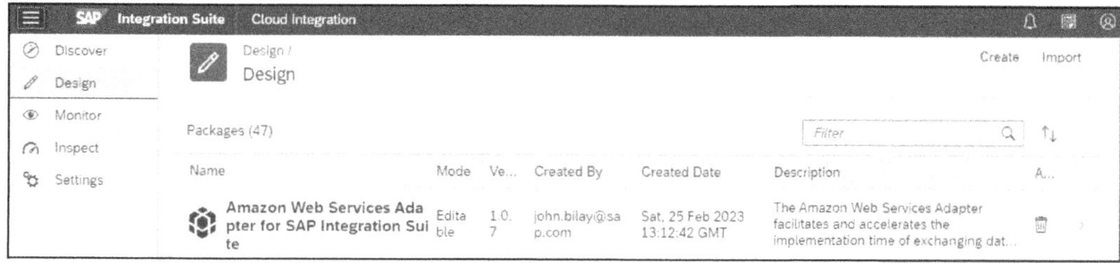

Figure 2.15 Create Button for Integration Packages

4. In the next dialog box, shown in Figure 2.16, provide a name for the integration package and a short description.

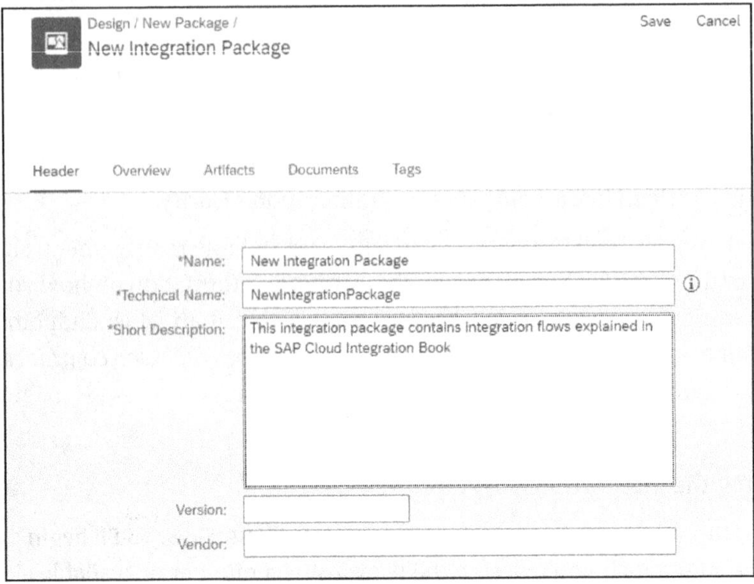

Figure 2.16 Specifying a Name for the New Integration Package

5. Select the **Artifacts** tab, click on **Add**, and select **Integration Flow**, as shown in Figure 2.17. The **Add Integration Flow** dialog box shown later in Figure 2.18 will open.

Figure 2.17 Selectable Artifact Types When Creating Integration Content

This selection step ensures that, in the following steps, you can create and edit the iFlow. Before proceeding, we recommend reviewing the various artifact types you can create in the "Basic Artifact Types" information box.

Basic Artifact Types

Let's briefly talk about the options you'll encounter when adding an artifact to an integration package:

- **Integration Flow**
  This option allows you to create iFlows that integrate business processes across the boundaries of organizations or enterprises. An iFlow does exactly what is required for such scenarios: specifies how messages are exchanged within such a process integration scenario. iFlow design will be covered in detail in this book.
- **SOAP API**
  This option allows you to create iFlows that expose a SOAP API. It also already uses the SOAP sender adapter but has an empty integration logic. You simply need to add your integration logic.
- **Value Mapping**
  This option allows you to define value mappings. If you're already familiar with SAP Process Orchestration or SAP Process Integration, you'll know this function well. If you're not yet familiar with value mappings, the basic idea is that data to be exchanged isn't always represented in the same manner in the sender and receiver systems involved in an integration scenario. System X could be using values such as "male" and "female" to represent an employee's gender, whereas system Y could be using numeric values instead, such as "1" for male and "2" for female. Typically, when a message containing employee data needs to be exchanged between systems X and Y, these two ways of representing the same data must be translated. The value of "male" from the source system will need to become "1" in the target system. This form of translation is called *value mapping*. For more information, see Chapter 4, Section 4.4.4.
- **OData API**
  This option allows you to develop an OData service from an existing data source, for instance, from a SOAP Web Services Description Language (WSDL) file. OData is an open standard that allows service providers to specify HTTP-based data access in a standardized manner. You can choose the **OData API** artifact, for example, when you want to expose data through OData for consumption by a frontend application. Note that you also have the option of creating an **Integration Flow** artifact with an OData sender channel. In this case, however, you can only expose one OData entity and operation at a time, whereas an **OData API** artifact allows you to expose multiple entities and operations at a time. The topic of OData is covered several times within this book, for example, in the context of the SAP Integration Suite APIs (Chapter 8) or when describing scenarios involving an OData adapter (see Chapter 4, Section 4.3). We'll introduce you to the topic of OData service design in Chapter 4, Section 4.5.2.
- **Script Collection**
  This option can be used to create a collection of reusable scripts. Multiple scripts can be added to the collection and can be referenced from various iFlows.

- **API**
  This option is available for tenant having an API Management service activated. The option allows you to create a SOAP or REST API.
- **REST API**
  This option allows you to create iFlows that exposes a REST API. It also already uses the HTTPS sender adapter but has an empty integration logic. You simply need to add your integration logic.
- **Message Mapping**
  This option allows you to create a message mapping as artifact. The message mapping as artifact can be reused by reference across different iFlows. This approach can be better than manually uploading a message mapping every time and avoids duplicates. Maintenance is also simplified because you only have to edit the artifact from a single place.
- **Function Libraries**
  Function libraries are objects used in SAP Process Orchestration in the Enterprise Services Repository (ESR). These functions are normally used in mappings and represent mapping logic in Java. They are also known as User-Defined Functions (UDFs). Note that typically these UDFs can be imported and reused from an SAP Process Orchestration system.
- **Integration Adapter**
  This option allows you to deploy a newly developed adapter type on your tenant. We'll explain adapter development in detail and how to deploy new adapter types in Chapter 6, Section 6.10. This artifact type is only available in the SAP BTP, Cloud Foundry environment. In the dialog box shown in Figure 2.18, make sure the **Create** radio button has been selected, and enter a name for the iFlow in the **Name** field. The **Upload** option (next to the **Create** option) allows you to upload an iFlow file from your computer to the Web UI.

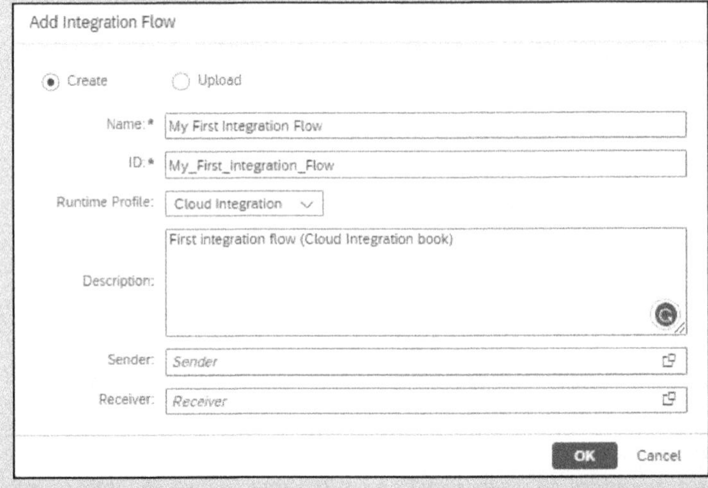

Figure 2.18 Creating an iFlow

- **Data Type**
  This object contains the structure of data that defines the message in the ESR. The date type can be imported and reused from an SAP Process Orchestration system. Note that the data type artifact is generally used by a message type resource, which can be further used in the iFlow and message mapping step.
- **Message Type**
  A message type comprises a data type that describes the structure of a message. It's contained in the ESR. The message type can be imported and reused from an SAP Process Orchestration System. Note that the message type artifact is added as a referenced resource in the iFlow and can further be used in the message mapping step.

6. Click **OK**. The specified iFlow is listed as a new artifact in your integration package, as shown in Figure 2.19.

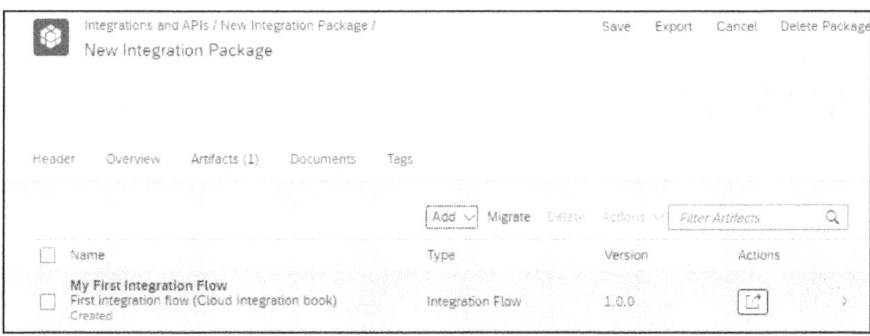

Figure 2.19 Newly Created iFlow Listed as a New Artifact

7. Click the **Save** button (located above the **Artifacts** list) to save the integration package.
8. Now, under the **Artifacts** tab, when you click the name of an iFlow, the editor opens and displays a template where you can begin modeling, as shown in Figure 2.20.

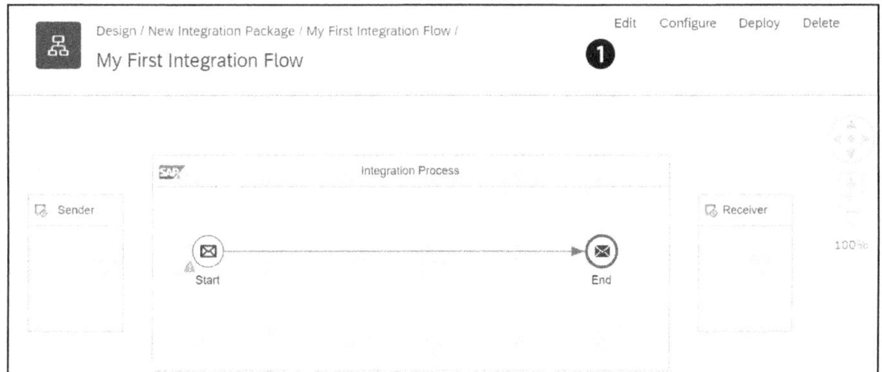

Figure 2.20 iFlow Template to Start Modeling with Edit Button Highlighted

9. Click the **Edit** button ❶ to start modeling the iFlow. Notice that a palette becomes visible on the left side of the editing area. Using this palette, you can select elements to be added to an iFlow. Before we continue, let's briefly discuss the palette and the available modeling elements.

The Palette: Elements of an Integration Flow

The iFlow modeler's palette icons are shown in Table 2.3, with a summary of the modeling elements available at the time of this writing, sorted by group.

Group	Description
	Contains elements that represent the connected participants of an integration scenario, for instance, a **Sender** and a **Receiver**.
	Contains elements that can be used as containers for a whole iFlow (**Integration Process**), a subprocess (**Local Integration Process**), or a subprocess that handles exceptions that occur during message processing (**Exception Subprocess**). You can use **Local Integration Process** elements to source out parts of the process logic, which are invoked from the main process, into smaller chunks. In this way, you can keep larger iFlows at a reasonable size. Local integration processes and exception subprocesses are introduced in Chapter 6, Section 6.3.
	Contains event elements to define the beginning or the end of message processing. You can select from the following step types: **End Message, End Event, Error End Event, Error Start Event, Escalation End Event, Start Message, Start Event, Terminate Message**, and **Timer** (see Chapter 6, Section 6.1).
	Contains connector arrow shapes you can use to connect iFlow components with each other.
	Allows you to delete one or more selected shapes from the graphical editor.
	Allows you to insert a **Mapping** step to transform a source message into a target message. You can select from the following step types: **Message Mapping, ID Mapping, Operation Mapping**, and **XSLT Mapping** (see Chapter 4, Section 4.4).
	Contains elements to modify the message content by applying different operations, such as encoding (e.g., using Base64), conversion (e.g., from comma-separated values [CSV] to XML), or script functions. You can select from the following step types: **Content Modifier** (see the steps in Chapter 4, Section 4.1), **Converter, Decoder, EDI Extractor, Encoder, Filter, Message Digest**, or **Script**.

Table 2.3 iFlow Modeling Elements Offered in the Palette

Group	Description
	Contains elements to enable the tenant to call an external source or a local integration process: ■ **External Call** Enables the tenant to call an external source (e.g., to retrieve data from external sources, such as SOAP or OData, and to enrich the message with it). You can select from the following step types: **Content Enricher**, **Request Reply**, or **Send** (see Chapter 5, Section 5.3.3). ■ **Local Call** Calls a local integration process either once (**Process Call**) or in a loop (**Looping Process Call**) (see Chapter 6, Section 6.3.2).
	Contains elements to forward the message to different receivers, to split larger messages, or to combine multiple messages into a larger one. You can select from the following step types: **Gather** (see Chapter 5, Section 5.2.1), **Router** (see Chapter 5, Section 5.3.3), **Splitter** (see Chapter 5, Section 5.2.1), **Join**, **Multicast** (see Chapter 5, Section 5.3.3), or **Aggregator**.
	Contains elements to decrypt/verify incoming messages or to encrypt/sign outbound messages. You can select from the following step types: **Decryptor**, **Encryptor**, **Signer**, or **Verifier** (see Chapter 10).
	Contains elements to store message content at specific steps within the message processing. You can select from the following step types: **Data Store Operations**, **Persist Message**, or **Write Variables**.
	Allows you to add an **XML Validator** step.

Table 2.3 iFlow Modeling Elements Offered in the Palette (Cont.)

Designing the Integration Flow

Let's start designing our first iFlow by following these steps:

1. Position your cursor over the **Sender** shape, and click the shape. Notice that an information icon, a recycle bin symbol, and an arrow icon will appear, as shown in Figure 2.21.

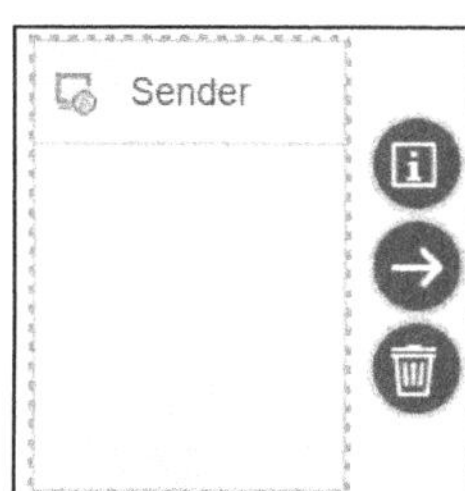

Figure 2.21 Information, Arrow, and Recycle Bin Icons for an Element

The arrow icon is used to connect elements of an iFlow (as shown in the next step). The recycle bin symbol is self-explanatory.

Information Icon

The information icon shows technical information about the selected iFlow element, namely, the ID and the version of the element. The ID is important for relating to the information provided in the MPL (see Chapter 8, Section 8.2) to a certain iFlow shape (when monitoring the iFlow); you'll learn more about the element versions in Chapter 6, Section 6.7.

2. Select, drag, and drop the arrow icon onto the iFlow **Start** shape. A dashed orange line will track your path, as shown in Figure 2.22.

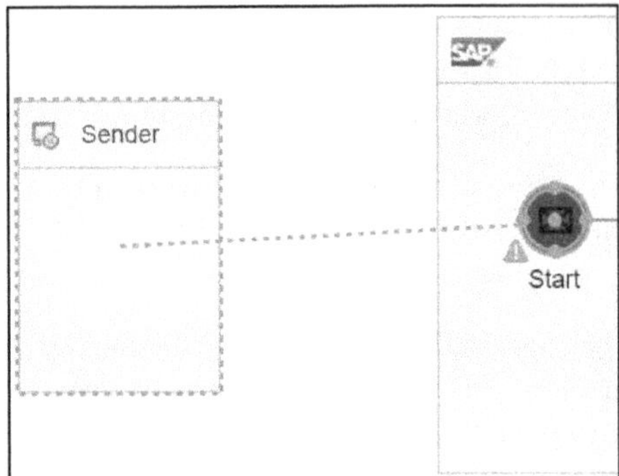

Figure 2.22 Connecting the Sender Shape with the Start Event

3. A dialog box opens where you can select the sender **Adapter Type**, as shown in Figure 2.23. For our example, select **HTTPS**.

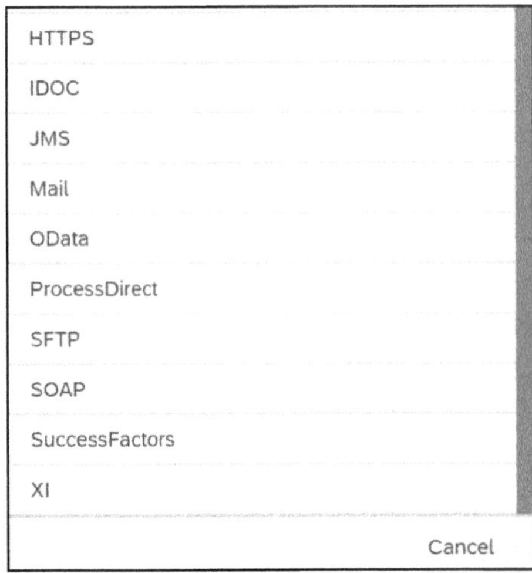

Figure 2.23 Sender Adapter Types (Part of the Selection)

After this step, in the section below your model, a sheet appears where you'll specify the adapter's properties by maintaining the various tabs.

4. Leave the default settings under the **General** tab, and click the **Connection** tab. Under this tab, you'll maintain several settings, shown in Figure 2.24, including the following:
   - **Address**: This value is the specified string (including the forward slash at the beginning) necessary to generate the endpoint URL required by SoapUI. For our example, enter "/myfirstFlow" in this field.
   - **Authorization**: This setting ensures that, for the user associated with the calling sender, permissions are checked based on user-to-role assignments by the Cloud Integration framework. Keep the setting **User Role**. In the **User Role** field, keep the entry **ESBMessaging.send**. This role is predefined by SAP for authorizing a sender (the HTTP client) to call your tenant. Remember that you created the required service key before using the SAP BTP cockpit. The **Select** option allows you to select a custom role if you've defined one (see Chapter 10, Section 10.3.3, for more details).

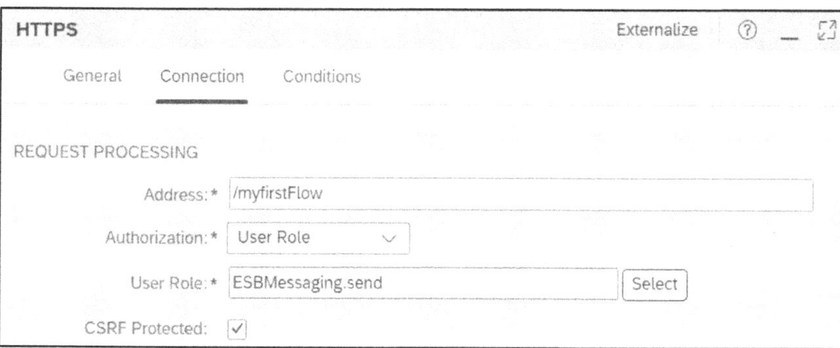

Figure 2.24 Connection Settings of HTTPS Sender Adapter

User Role Authorization

The **User Role** authorization option can be used along with basic authentication (among other authentication options, see the following "Inbound Authorization Options" information box). Using this authentication option, Cloud Integration expects credentials (user name and password) to authenticate the user associated with the incoming call.

Inbound Authorization Options

Different options are available for combining inbound *authorization* with *authentication* methods. The two authorization options offered in the HTTPS sender adapter (as well as in most HTTP-based adapters) can be combined with authentication in the following way:

- **User Role (authorization)**
  The permissions of the caller are checked based on roles defined for the user associated with the inbound call. Thus, different *authentication options* are possible (explained in detail in Chapter 10, Section 10.4.3). Note that, for the tutorials in this book, we recommend that you use basic authentication (using user credentials provided in the HTTP header of the call). However, in productive scenarios, basic authentication isn't acceptable, so, we recommend that you use client certificate authentication instead (as described later in Chapter 10, Section 10.4.3).
- **Client Certificate (authorization)**
  Using this option, the permissions of the caller are checked by evaluating the distinguished name (DN) of the client certificate provided by the caller. The caller is then authenticated based on the client certificate.

This topic is covered in detail in Chapter 10.

5. Now, let's add a step to the model that creates a database entry. Click the **Persistence** group icon in the palette, as shown in Table 2.3.
6. Select the **Data Store Operations** submenu, as shown in Figure 2.25.

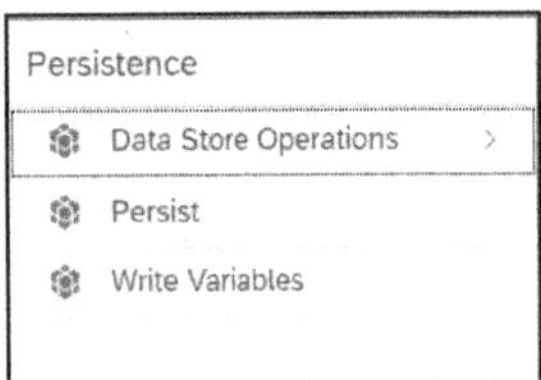

Figure 2.25 Step Types in the Persistence Group of the Palette

This submenu provides access to steps related to the data store of the tenant database. As we'll explain further, the submenu provides access to step variants that perform write and read actions on the database. You can use the steps in this submenu, for example, to write message content to the tenant database at one step and then to read the content from the database either during a later step in the same iFlow or in another iFlow deployed on the same tenant.

Before we explain the available step variants in detail, let's briefly elaborate on the additional steps available next to the **Data Store Operations** submenu. The other two features are also related to temporary data storage:

- **Persist**: With this step, you can also store the message content in the temporary tenant storage. However, in contrast to **Data Store Operations**, no option exists for accessing this database content during message processing. Furthermore, no dedicated UI can access this storage (which is referred to as the *message store*). But you can use the OData API to access message store entries created during iFlows (more information on this API can be found in Chapter 8).

- **Write Variables**: With this step, you can write a variable (e.g., a timestamp) to the tenant database and use this variable at a later step in the same iFlow or in a step in another iFlow deployed on the same tenant. For example, in one iFlow, you might generate a timestamp and store this value in a variable. In another iFlow (deployed on the same tenant), you can access this variable and use it, for example, to query data from an external source newer than the timestamp. We'll provide an example of how to use this feature in Chapter 6, Section 6.4.3.

7. Click **Write**, as shown in Figure 2.26.

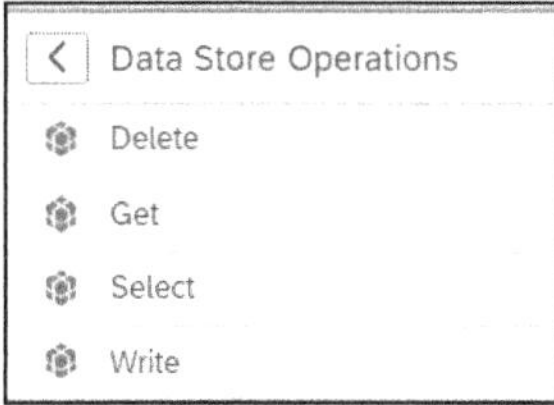

Figure 2.26 Write: One Of Four Operations Supported for the Data Store

As mentioned earlier, several read and write operations are available related to the data store. In total, four operations are available:

- **Delete**: Delete an existing data store entry from the database.
- **Get**: Read a specific entry from a data store.
- **Select**: Select multiple entries from a data store.
- **Write**: Create a data store entry (as we'll do in this tutorial).

Using the **Data Store Operations** step types, you can, for example, configure scenarios that support the push-pull pattern, which is also explained in Chapter 5, Section 5.4.1. However, in this first tutorial, we'll use this step type merely to create a data store entry without accessing the data store at a later step during message processing. Instead, we'll show you how to download and check the content of the data store after the message has been processed.

8. Place the **Write** shape in your model within the **Integration Process** shape, to the right of the **Start** shape.

The iFlow model should now look like the diagram shown in Figure 2.27.

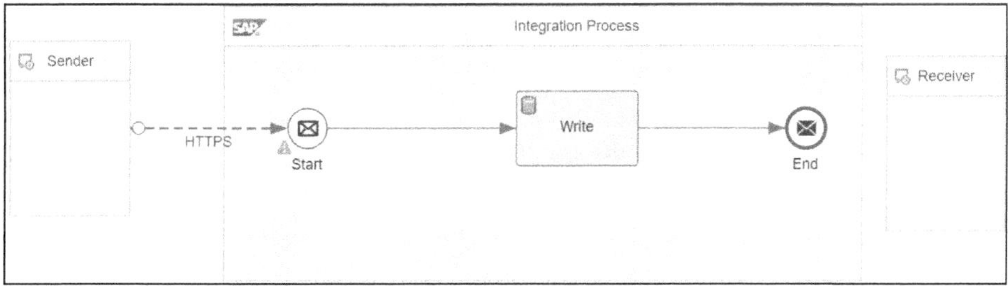

Figure 2.27 Data Store Write Step Placed to the Right of the Start Event

9. Finally, remove the **Receiver** shape from the model by clicking the shape and selecting the recycle bin icon, shown in Figure 2.28. Note that, in the first part of this tutorial, no receiver is required.

Figure 2.28 Removing the Receiver Shape

Your iFlow model should now look like the diagram shown in Figure 2.29. (Compare this diagram with the model shown earlier in Figure 2.13.)

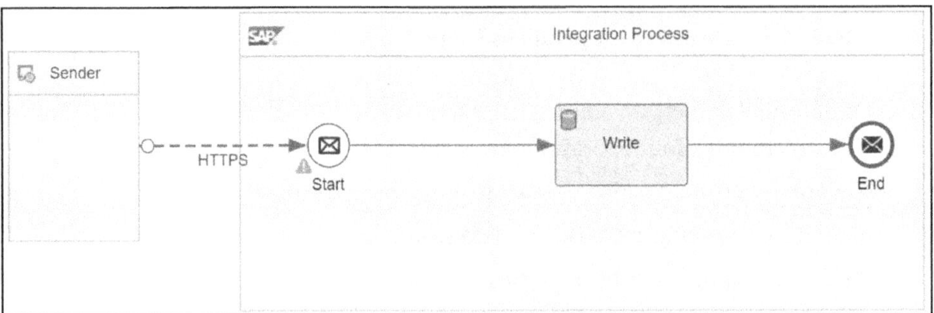

Figure 2.29 Final iFlow Model

10. Go back and click the **Write** shape to inspect the properties of this step type (displayed below the model).

    The **General** tab contains the name of the shape, which you can change, but for our example, we'll keep the default name **Write**.

11. Go to the **Processing** tab, and configure the attributes as shown in Figure 2.30.

    Let's quickly review the properties of this step type:

    - **Data Store Name**: This attribute defines the name of the data store on the tenant; for our example, enter "SimulatedReceiver" to highlight the fact that, within this scenario, the data store entry is used to simulate or replace a receiver system.
    - **Visibility**: This attribute determines whether the data store can be used exclusively by the iFlow that contains the related data store operation (if you select **Integration Flow**, which is the default setting) or if the data store can be shared by all iFlows deployed on the tenant (if you select **Global**). If many iFlows are used to define a complex scenario, selecting the **Global** option might make sense so that a data store can be shared across several iFlows.

- **Entry ID**: This attribute specifies the ID of the data store entry. If you leave this field blank, Cloud Integration generates a unique identifier for this attribute. For our tutorial, we'll enter "MessageContent" to highlight the fact that the data store entry contains the message generated by this first iFlow.
- **Retention Threshold for Alerting (in D)**: This attribute specifies the time period (in days) within which the content must be read from the data store before the corresponding entry in the data store monitor (in the **Monitoring** application under **Manage Stores**) is changed to the **Overdue** status. Before that time period has passed, the entry is in the **Waiting** status.
- **Expiration Period (in D)**: By default, 90 days is the duration of the expiration period. Data store entries are kept in the database for a maximum of 180 days. Note that the data store is a temporary storage option provided by the tenant database (refer to the earlier diagram in Figure 2.7).
- **Encrypt Stored Message**: With this option, you can decide whether or not the data store entry should be stored encrypted on the database.
- **Overwrite Existing Messages**: If a data store entry with the same name exists, the existing entry will be overwritten by the actual step. By default, this option is deselected. In contrast, for our case, we'll select this option because we'll process the iFlow multiple times after each other. If you don't allow existing messages to be overwritten in our case, an error will be raised at the start of the second message processing run.
- **Include Message Headers**: With this option, you can decide whether or not the message header is included in the stored data store entry.

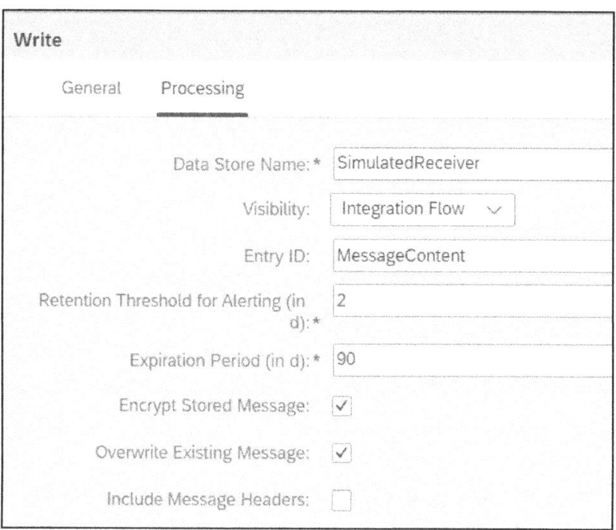

Figure 2.30 Attributes of the Data Store Write Step (Processing Tab)

12. Click **Save** to save the iFlow (see Figure 2.31 ❶). You've now finished designing the iFlow for the first part of this tutorial.
13. Click **Deploy** ❷. On the subsequent **Do you want to deploy?** screen, click **Yes.**
14. On the following screen, which indicates that the iFlow has been triggered for deployment, click **OK**.

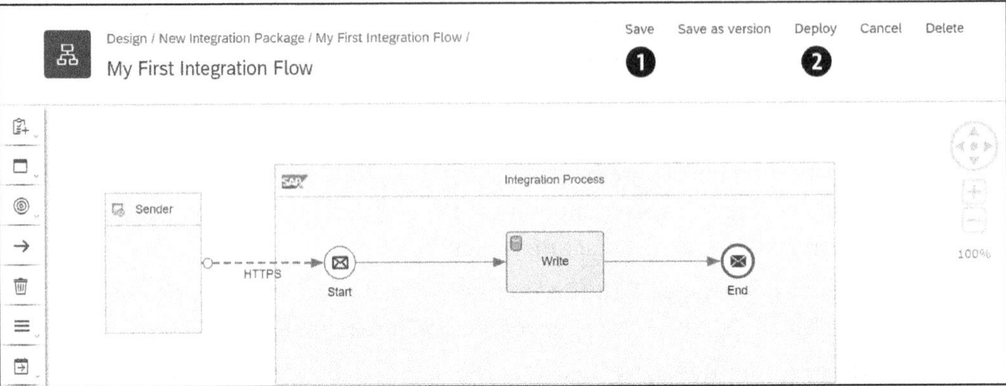

Figure 2.31 Location of the Save and Deploy Buttons for the iFlow

Checking for the Deployed Integration Flow

To check the deployment status of your iFlow, follow these steps:

1. On the **Monitor** page of the Web UI (compare to Figure 2.10), select a tile under **Manage Integration Content** (compare with Figure 2.12). You'll find your iFlow listed.

   Immediately after you've triggered the deployment of the iFlow, its status will be **Starting**, as shown in Figure 2.32.

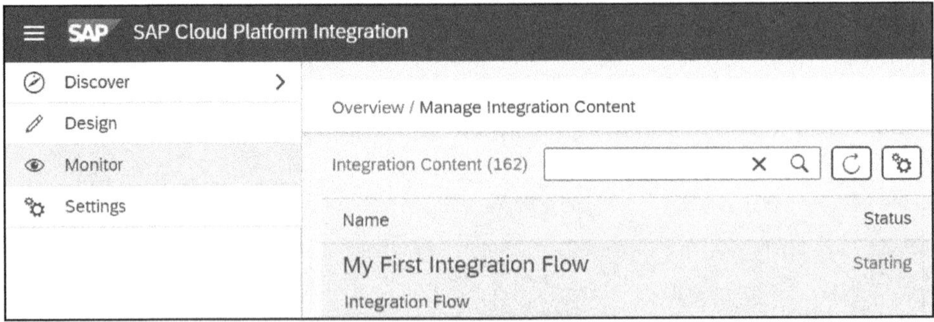

Figure 2.32 iFlow Triggered for Deployment in Starting Status

2. After a short time, refresh the page. The status should have changed to **Started**. If not, refresh the page every so often until the status has changed.
3. Click the iFlow name (in this case, **My First Integration Flow**) to display more details on the right, as shown in Figure 2.33.

To initiate message processing, you'll need to send an HTTP request to Cloud Integration with Postman.

First, you'll need to determine the endpoint address of the iFlow. When viewing the details of the deployed iFlow, as shown in Figure 2.33, under the **Endpoints** tab, you'll find a URL that ends with **/myfirstFlow**. This string was specified earlier as a relative address of the HTTPS sender adapter (refer to Figure 2.24). The complete URL of the endpoint is composed of the **Cloud Integration Runtime Address** for your tenant (see Figure 2.33 ❶); the string **/http** (for the adapter type); and the relative address **/myfirstFlow**, which you specified earlier when configuring the adapter.

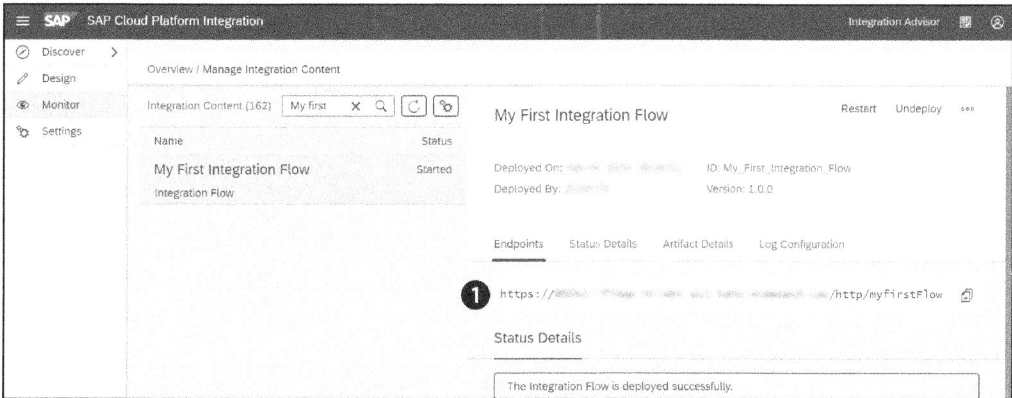

Figure 2.33 Details of the Deployed iFlow

Copy the URL found in the **Endpoint** field. You can click the **Copy entry point URL to clipboard** button to the right of the endpoint address.

Note that the base address in the endpoint URL (which we've called the **Cloud Integration Runtime Address** earlier) is a different base address than the base address contained in the URL of the Web UI (ending with */shell/design*). If you refer to Figure 2.7 earlier, notice that the iFlow is processed by a worker, whereas access to Cloud Integration through the Web UI is routed through another component (indicated by the **Design, Monitoring, and Operation Microservices** shape shown in Figure 2.7).

Processing the Integration Flow

To execute the iFlow, follow these steps:

1. Open Postman, and paste the endpoint address into the address field of the request, as shown in Figure 2.34 ❶.
2. Select the **Authorization** tab.
3. In the **Type** dropdown list, select **Basic Auth** to open the screen shown in Figure 2.35.

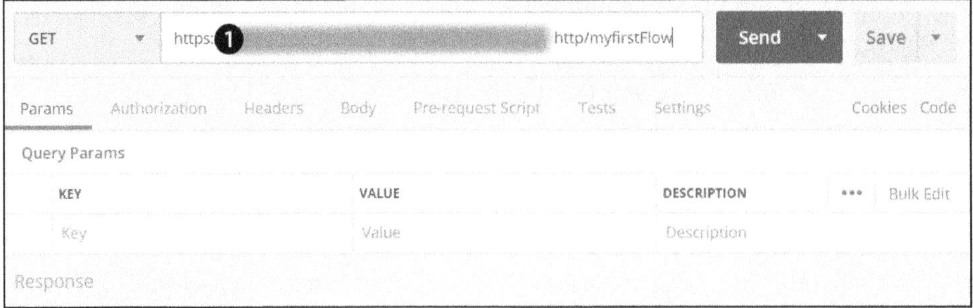

Figure 2.34 Postman UI with Address Field for the Call, Highlighting the Tenant-Specific Cloud Integration Runtime Address

4. To specify the settings for **Username** and **Password**, you now need the values of the parameters `clientid` and `clientsecret`, which were generated when you created the service key on the tenant:
   - In the **Username** field ❶, paste the `clientid` value.
   - In the **Password** field ❷, paste the `clientsectret` value.

   For more information on the technical details, check out the online documentation on SAP Help Portal at *http://s-prs.co/507715.*

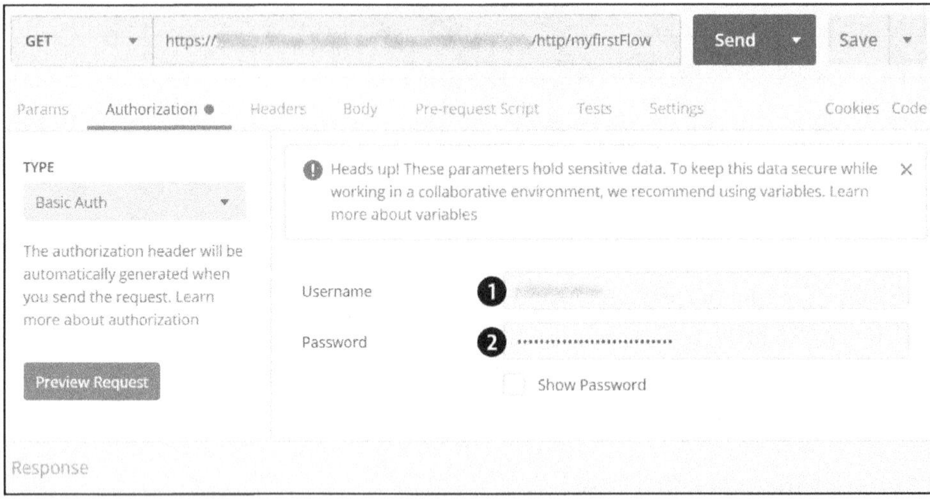

Figure 2.35 Authorization Settings in Postman

5. To specify a message body, select the **Body** tab.
6. As shown in Figure 2.36, select **raw**, and enter a text, for example, "Message from HTTP client".
7. Click **Send**.
8. In Postman, you should get a response, as shown in Figure 2.37.

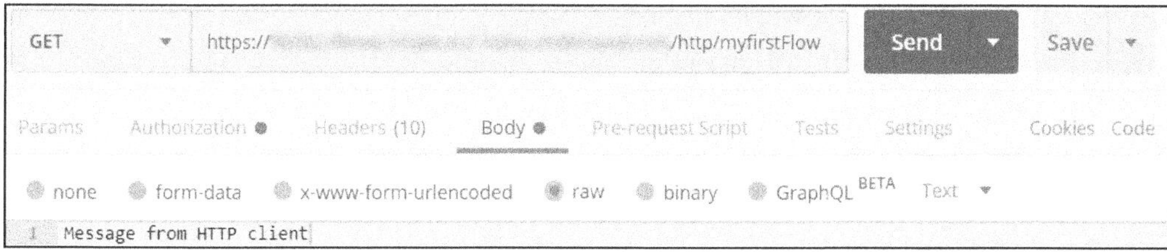

Figure 2.36 Body Tab of Postman for Specifying Message Content

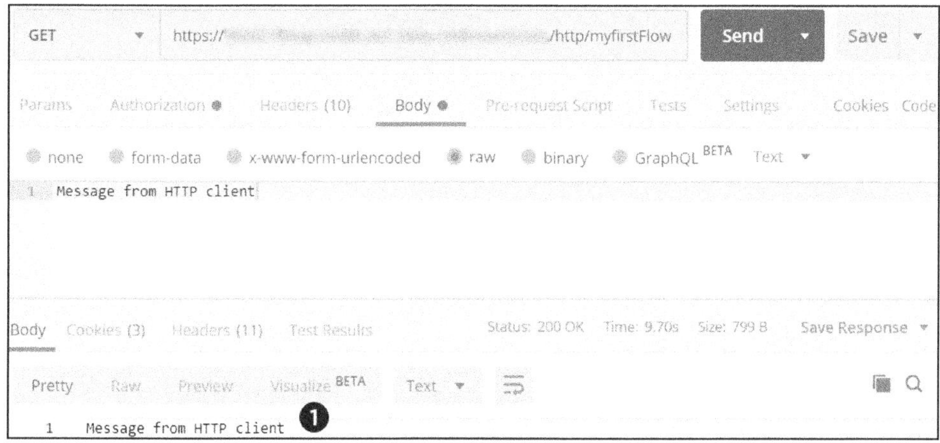

Figure 2.37 Response Shown in Postman

Monitoring Integration Flow Processing

Now let's check how the successful processing of the message is made transparent on the Web UI and determine if the message has been stored on the tenant database as designed. Follow these steps:

1. Go to the **Monitor** page of the Web UI (compare to Figure 2.10).
2. To check for a message that you've just sent, select a tile with suitable filter criteria under **Monitor Message Processing**, as shown in Figure 2.38.

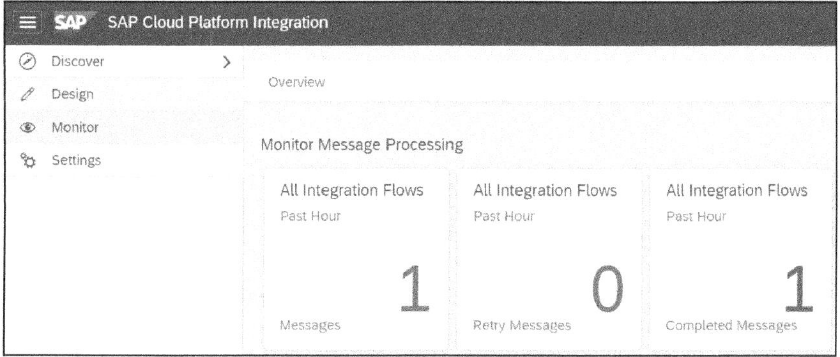

Figure 2.38 Tiles Available under Monitor Message Processing

A list of messages will be displayed. As shown in Figure 2.38, you can see that one iFlow has been processed successfully on your tenant within the last hour.

3. Click the corresponding tile (with a number not equal to 0).

   Details about the processed message (for which the row is selected at the left side) are shown on the right side of the window, as shown in Figure 2.39. Notice that the message associated with your iFlow (**My First Integration Flow** ❶) has been processed successfully (as indicated by the **Completed** status).

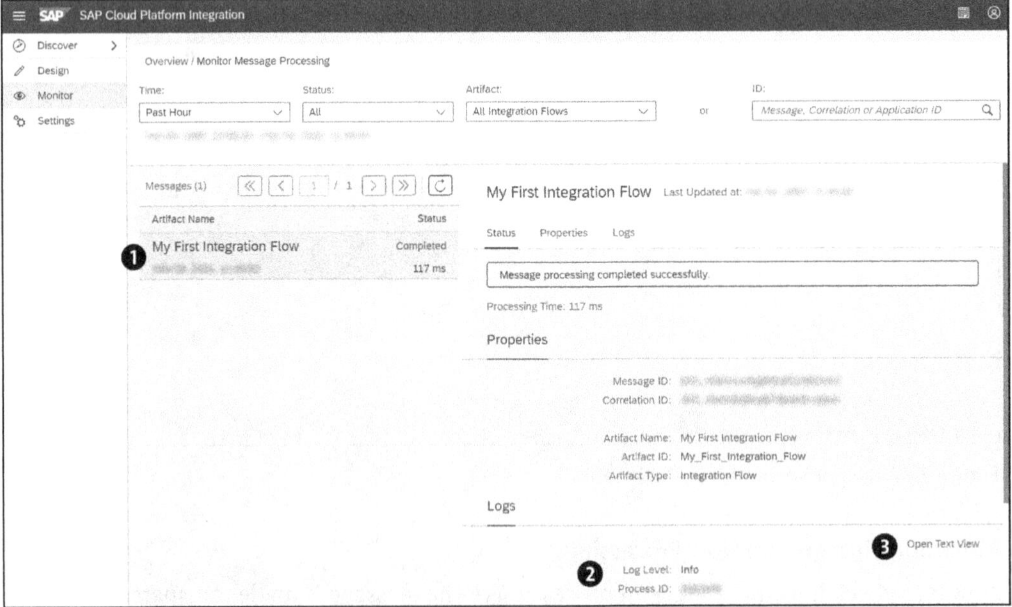

Figure 2.39 Details of the Processed iFlow

4. The **Logs** tab shows a link to the MPL, which provides information on the processing of the message. To display more information on the processing steps of the iFlow, you can click **Open Text View** ❸.

Note that an option is available where, before processing an iFlow, you can configure different log levels to display information about the processing of the message on different detail levels. Notice that log level **Info** has been set ❷, which is the default log level. For more information, see Chapter 8.

Message monitoring indicates that everything went well and that the message has been processed in the expected way without any issues.

Let's now check for the data store entry:

1. On the **Monitor** page of the Web UI, go to the **Manage Stores** section, as shown in Figure 2.40 (compare to Figure 2.12).

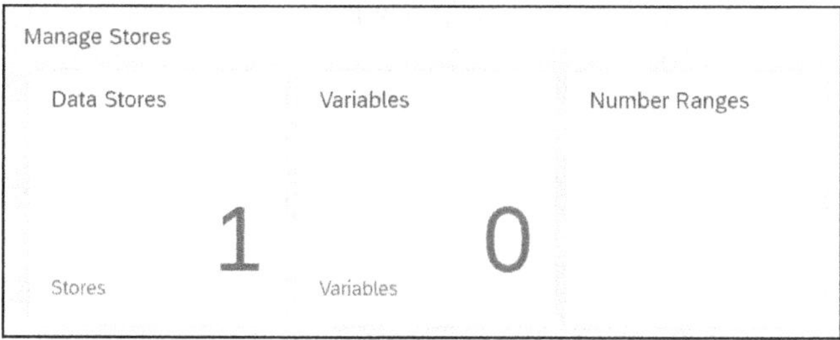

Figure 2.40 Access to the Temporary Tenant Database

Notice that different kinds of storage are accessible through the Web UI (refer to Figure 2.12.) You also might notice that one storage option isn't shown here, **Message Queues**, that was shown earlier in Figure 2.12. We haven't yet activated the required runtime component for the JMS message broker for the trial account. This component ensures the handling of messages in JMS queues. We'll come back to this topic in Chapter 5.

2. Select the **Data Stores** tile to open the screen shown in Figure 2.41.

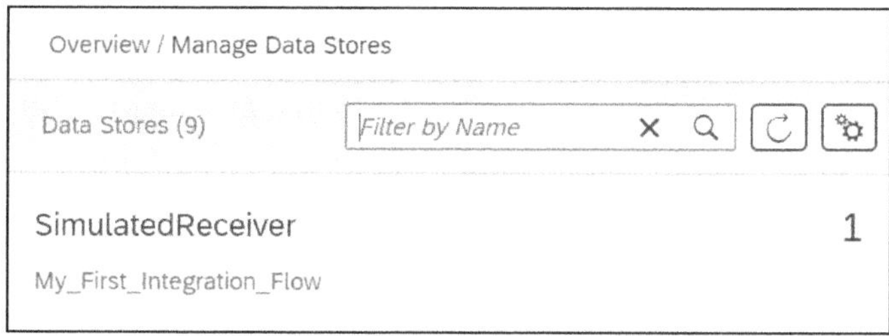

Figure 2.41 One Data Store Available on the Tenant

As you run your first iFlow, you'll find only one data store. Notice that the name of the data store (**SimulatedReceiver**) corresponds to the name you specified when configuring the data store **Write** step of the iFlow (compare to Figure 2.30).

3. By clicking the data store's name (on the left), its entry will be shown in the right, as shown in Figure 2.42.

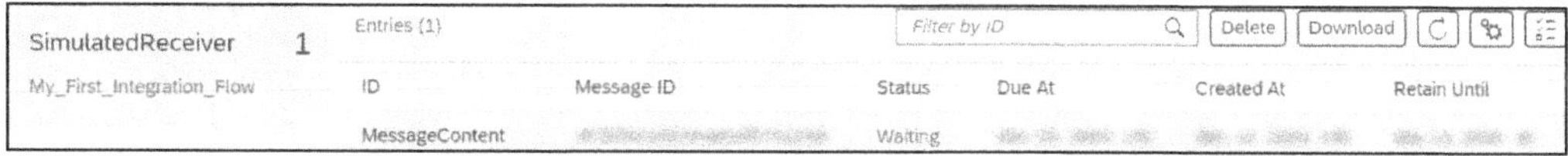

Figure 2.42 Detail Screen for the Data Store

One entry is available. Notice that the ID of the entry (**MessageContent**) corresponds to the ID you specified when configuring the data store **Write** step of the iFlow (compare to Figure 2.30).

4. By selecting the data store entry, the **Download** button will be activated, as shown in Figure 2.43.

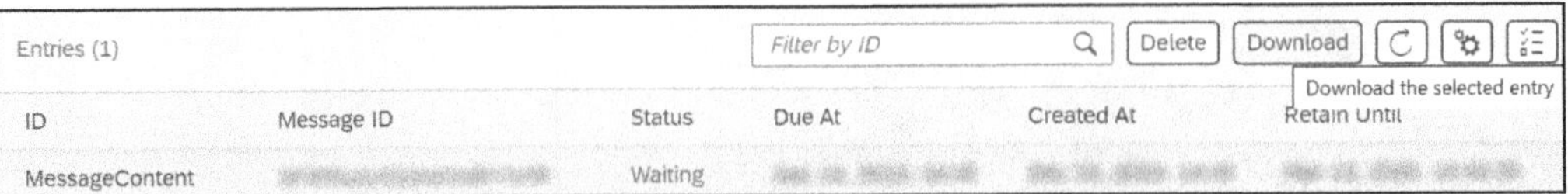

Figure 2.43 Download Option for the Data Store Entry

5. On clicking **Download**, a compressed file called *MessageContent.zip* will be downloaded to the default download directory of your computer. Remember that the file name corresponds to the configured entry ID (refer to Figure 2.30).

When you extract the file and open the contained *body* text file in a text editor (e.g., Notepad), you'll see the following content:

```
Message from HTTP client
```

Note that if you activated the **Include Message Headers** option for the data store **Write** step (refer to Figure 2.30), the downloaded *.zip* file will also contain a *headers.prop* file. When you run the iFlow of this tutorial, this file will only contain the data store name as a header (`SapDataStoreId=MessageContent`) and a timestamp that indicates the time when you downloaded the data store entry. As the first iFlow doesn't set any other headers, no other entries are contained in this file.

Congratulations! You've successfully executed your first iFlow. The result proves that your HTTP client was connected to the tenant and that the data has been transferred as designed.

After sending another HTTP request to trigger the iFlow a second time, you'll find a data store entry with an updated timestamp (in the **Created At** column). Because you selected the **Overwrite Existing Message** option in the data store **Write** step (refer to Figure 2.30), with each message processing run, the data store entry will be overwritten. You've now successfully sent a message from the *outside* to Cloud Integration.

In some cases, you won't be allowed to download the data store entry. When you try to download the entry, you may receive the error message shown in Figure 2.44.

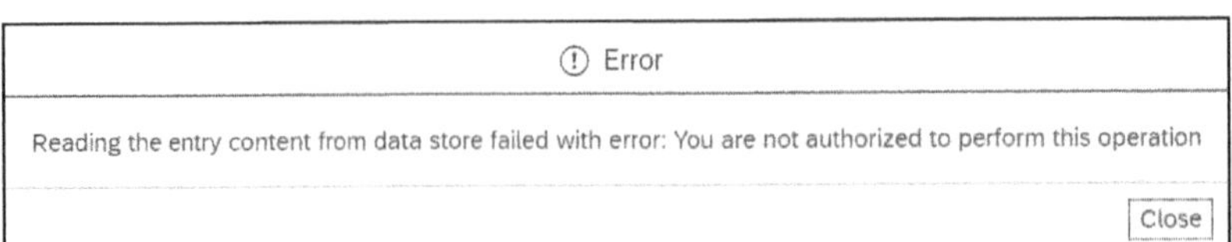

Figure 2.44 Error Message When Trying to Download the Data Store Entry

In this case, check the authorizations configured when onboarding to Cloud Integration. To permit a user to display and download data store entries, role collection

PI_Business_Expert must be assigned to it.. We'll provide more information on the important topic of user management in Chapter 10, Section 10.3.

To round out this tutorial, we'll now show you how to add a real receiver system to the iFlow.

Adding and Configuring the Mail Adapter

We assume that you've already registered an email account. In this section, we'll show how to set up a connection with a Yahoo! email account. But the steps performed with the Cloud Integration Web UI are valid for other email providers as well.

To add and configure the mail receiver adapter, follow these steps:

1. Add a **Receiver** shape. Click the **Participants** icon of the palette, and select **Receiver**, as shown in Figure 2.45.

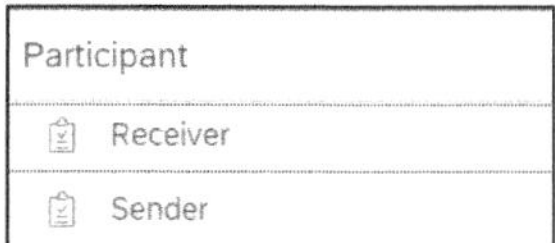

Figure 2.45 Receiver Shape in the iFlow Model Palette

2. Place the **Receiver** shape to the right of the **Integration Process** shape.
3. Click the **End** event so that the context buttons (information, arrow, and recycle bin icons) appear next to the shape, as shown in Figure 2.46. Position the cursor on the arrow button.

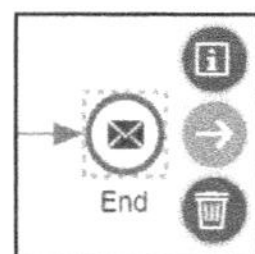

Figure 2.46 Context Buttons for the End Event; Cursor Positioned on Arrow Button

4. Connect the **End** event with the **Receiver** pool by clicking the arrow icon, dragging the cursor to the target shape (the **Receiver** pool in this case), and then releasing the mouse button (drop), as shown in Figure 2.47.

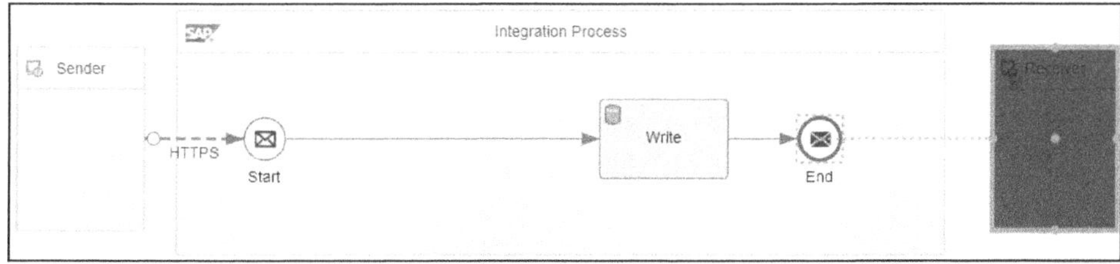

Figure 2.47 Connecting the End Event with the Receiver Pool

5. After releasing the mouse button, the **Adapter Type** dialog box will appear where you'll select the connection type you desire, as shown in Figure 2.48.

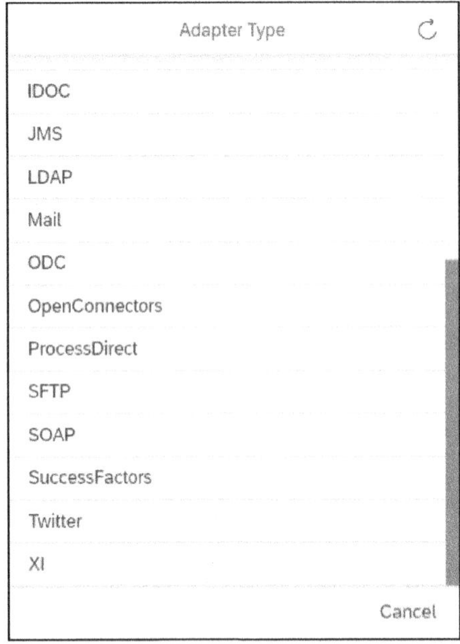

Figure 2.48 Section of the Receiver Adapter Type Selection

6. In the **Adapter Type** dialog box, click on the **Mail** entry.

   In the section below your model, a sheet will appear where you'll specify the properties of the mail adapter by maintaining various tabs.

   Under the **General** tab, you'll find the basic settings for your mail receiver:

   - Under **Channel Details**, you'll find information on the direction of the channel (in this case, from Cloud Integration to a receiver system) as well as the name of the connected system (**Receiver**).
   - Under **Adapter Details**, the adapter type (**Mail**) is again shown as well as the supported transport protocol. For a mail receiver adapter, only SMTP is supported.

   You don't have to change anything under this tab.

7. Click the **Connection** tab, and configure the adapter according to your email account. The values shown in Figure 2.49 fit a Yahoo! email account. We'll briefly explain these parameters.

8. In the **Address** field, specify the address of your mail server, in this case, of Yahoo! Mail. To find this information, you'll need to refer to the support information provided for Yahoo! at the email provider's website. In this field, you'll also need to add the port, separated from the address by a colon. Which port to use depends on other settings, which we'll describe briefly next.

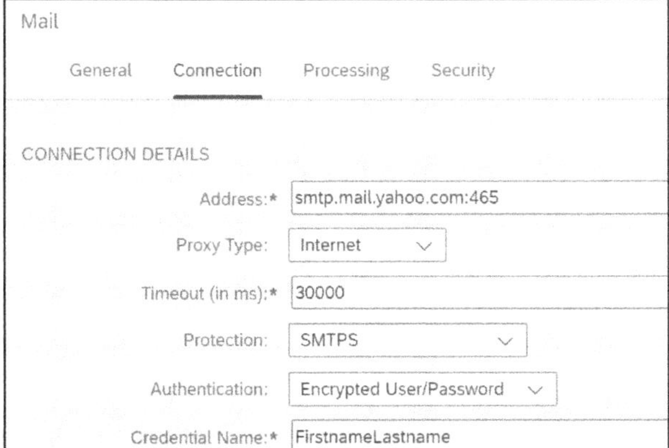

Figure 2.49 Configuring the Mail Adapter: Connection Tab/Connection Details

Allowed Ports for the Mail Receiver Adapter

Note that certain restrictions exist regarding the supported ports for the mail receiver adapter. In particular, you can use the following ports (for different **Protection** settings of the mail receiver adapter):

- 587 for SMTP+STARTTLS
- 465 for SMTPS

Because we want to choose **SMTPS** in the **Protection** dropdown list, port **465** must be also specified in the **Address** field, as shown in Figure 2.49.

Leave the **Proxy Type** parameter with its default setting **Internet**. With this parameter, you're specifying whether the mail adapter connects to a system on the internet or to an on-premise system (hosted behind the firewall of another organization) using SAP Connectivity service. In the latter case, you'll need to choose the **On-Premise** option for the **Proxy Type** field. Then, you'll also maintain the **Location ID** parameter with a value that fits to the location ID defined in the SAP Connectivity configuration. The **Proxy Type** parameter can be configured with other adapters as well, for example, the Advanced Message Queuing Protocol (AMQP) adapter (see Chapter 5, Section 5.6). For now, however, keep the setting **Internet**.

Leave the default value (**30000**) for the **Timeout (in ms)** setting for this connection.

Furthermore, keep the default setting for the **Authentication** parameter (**Encrypted User/Password**). This setting ensures that the credentials (user name and password) with which Cloud Integration authenticates itself against the email server are transformed into a hash value before being sent to the server, which increases security. Other options for this parameter include the following:

- **Plain User/Password**: Credentials are sent to the server in plain text.
- **None**: No authentication is applied at all.

The **Credential Name** field contains a simple string that refers to a deployed credentials artifact on the Cloud Integration server. You can't define the user name and password directly on the configuration screen of the mail adapter; instead, you must deploy the credentials containing the user name and password on the server explicitly. This step is necessary for connections with basic authentication, as is the case for this email connection. When deploying credentials on the server, you must provide a unique name (e.g., **FirstnameLastname** in our case) for reference purposes. This name is the exact name you must enter into the **Credential Name** field. If you have the required rights for deploying (ask your tenant administrator), you can execute the steps described in Section 2.3.5.

9. On the **Processing** tab, under **Mail Attributes**, most settings are self-explanatory, as shown in Figure 2.50. You'll specify the sender mail address (**From** field) and receiver address (**To** field). Optionally, you can specify the mail's carbon copy (**Cc** field) and blind carbon copy (**Bcc** field) as well. Furthermore, you can add a text string to be written into the mail subject line (**Subject** field).

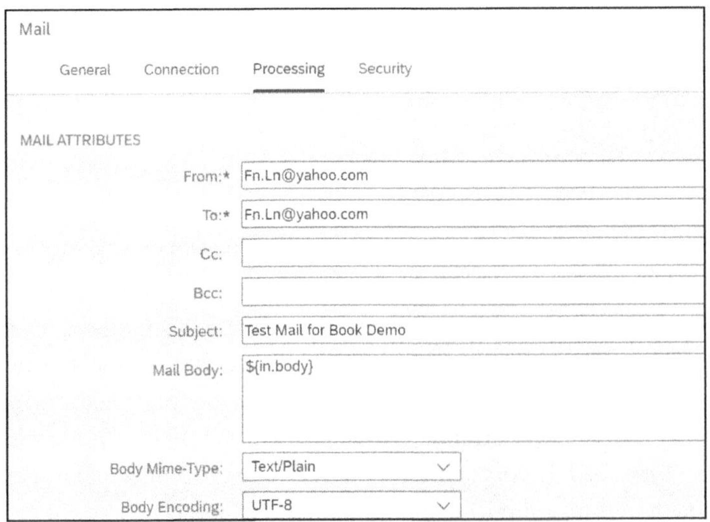

Figure 2.50 Configuring the Mail Adapter: Processing Tab/Mail Attributes

Note

The default definition of the **Mail Body** field (**${in.body}**) makes use of Apache Camel's Simple Expression Language. We're explicitly accessing the `in` message of the exchange and taking its body, which contains nothing but the message's payload, which is exactly what we want to see in our email. The Apache Camel data model is described in more detail in Chapter 4, Section 4.1.

With the **Body Mime-Type** setting, you'll specify the internet media type of the message body, that is, the kind of data transferred with the message. Keep the default value

Text/Plain because no other data format other than plain text (with the XML describing the message structure) is forwarded directly from the HTTP client. **Body Encoding** allows you to specify the character encoding of the incoming data. To ensure that data is passed unmodified, keep the default value **UTF-8** (Unicode encoding).

Under **Attachments** (not shown in Figure 2.50), you can specify that the received mail should contain the outbound message as an attachment. However, we won't define any attachment settings for our first iFlow.

Finally, notice the additional tab labeled **Security**, as shown in Figure 2.49 and Figure 2.50. When you click this tab, you'll access options for digitally signing and encrypting the outbound email. As this topic is beyond the scope of this chapter, we won't elaborate further. For more information, check out the SAP Community blog at *http://s-prs.co/507708*.

For more details on configuring the mail adapter, check out the online documentation for Cloud Integration at *http://s-prs.co/507709*.

The final scenario should look similar to the iFlow shown in Figure 2.51. You can easily identify the sender on the left (connected to the **Integration Process** shape by an HTTPS channel) and the final receiver on the right (connected with the **Integration Process** shape by the mail channel configured just in the previous steps). That's the advantage of using a graphical environment to design iFlows. You can clearly and intuitively describe how a message arrives at a server, how the message is handled within the Cloud Integration server, and to which systems using which channels the message is then forwarded.

In our first iFlow, the message invoked by the HTTP client, which simulates our sender system, is passed on without any further changes to the mail adapter. The data store **Write** step is kept in the model, which means that a data store entry is created with each message processing run, but the message content nevertheless is passed on to the email account.

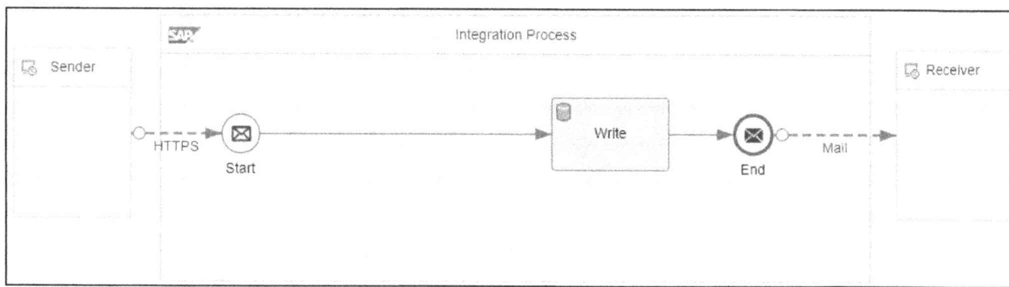

Figure 2.51 The Final iFlow

Finally, save the iFlow, and click **Deploy**.

2.3.5 Creating and Deploying a User Credentials Artifact

To enable the tenant to connect to the email receiver using the credentials of the email account owner, you needed to add a **Credential Name** in the mail adapter of your iFlow, which at this point is little more than a placeholder for an artifact.

In this artifact, you'll now specify the user name of the email account as well as a password. Note that you can use the mail receiver adapter to connect to different email providers, and, in most cases, you'll need to specify the personal password of your account when defining the artifact (as shown in the next steps). However, note that many email providers have introduced a certain security level by restricting access to the email account initiated by applications rather than dialog users. To enable Cloud Integration to connect to a Yahoo! email account, you'll need to generate an app password and use this password (instead of your personal account password) when defining the artifact later on.

To generate an app password with Yahoo!, follow these steps:

1. Go to the **Account security** settings for your Yahoo! account, as shown in Figure 2.52.

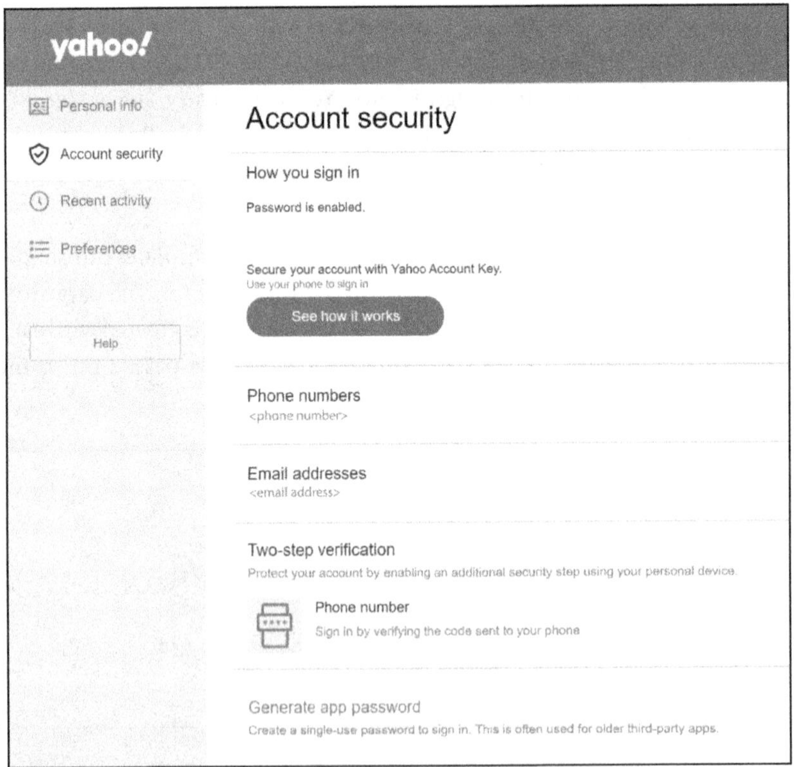

Figure 2.52 Example Security Settings for Yahoo! Mail

2. Click **Generate app password**.
3. On the next screen, open the dropdown menu, and select **Other app**.

4. Specify any name for the app, and click **Generate**.
5. On the next screen, a password will be displayed, as shown in Figure 2.53.
6. Copy this password ❶ to the clipboard or into a text editor. You'll need this password in a few steps when we define the artifact.
7. Click **Done**.

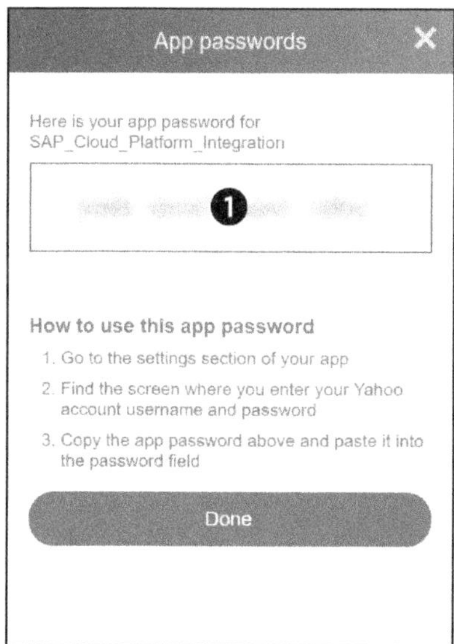

Figure 2.53 App Password Generated for a Yahoo! Email Account

Note that these instructions only apply for Yahoo! and are valid at the time of this writing only. We can't predict if Yahoo! will change this procedure in the future. Therefore, if you run into any issues, check out the newest guidelines on the internet, and modify the configuration procedure if required. See also the information box at the end of this section, which provides information about using a Google mail account.

Create the artifact using the following steps:

1. Choose the **Monitor** page of the Web UI, and select the **Security Material** tile under **Manage Security**, as shown in Figure 2.54.

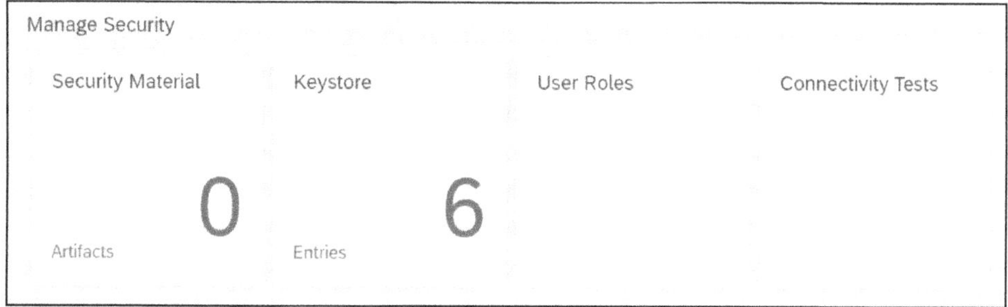

Figure 2.54 Manage Security Section of the Web UI Monitoring Application

2. Choose **Add • User Credentials**, as shown in Figure 2.55.

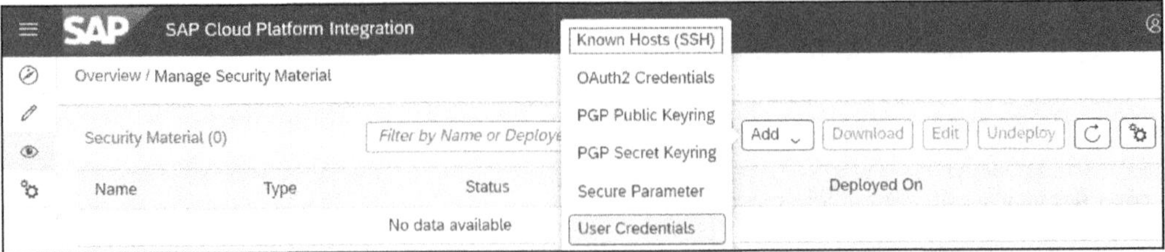

Figure 2.55 Adding a User Credentials Artifact

3. As shown in Figure 2.56, specify the properties of the **User Credentials** artifact. For the **Name** field, enter the value that you entered in the **Credential Name** field in the mail adapter (refer to Figure 2.49). For the **User** field, enter your email account user name, and for the **Password/Repeat Password** fields, enter the app password we just generated (compare to Figure 2.53).

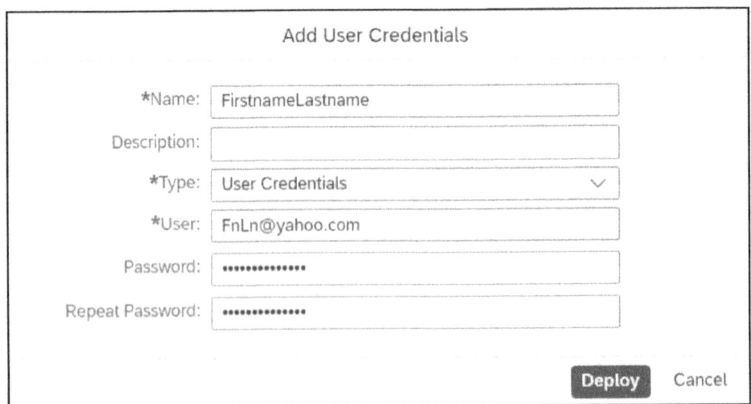

Figure 2.56 Add User Credentials: Properties of a User Credentials Artifact

4. Click the **Deploy** button. If you don't have deployment rights, ask the tenant administrator to take over the process for you.

How Secure Are Your User Credentials?

You've now defined an artifact that contains the credentials used by the tenant to connect to your email account using the mail adapter. While configuring this integration scenario, you didn't have to share these credentials (user name and password) with anyone. In the mail adapter settings, only an alias (**Credential Name**) is specified, which the other participants of your integration team sharing the same tenant can see without any risk of a security leak.

Another artifact type, handled in the same way, is the secure parameter artifact required for scenarios that include social media adapters (for the Twitter adapter, see

Chapter 10, Section 10.4.5) and when you use the Adapter Development Kit (ADK) (see Chapter 6, Section 6.10).

We've almost reached the end of our first tutorial. However, one additional task must be completed before you can successfully run your scenario and send the message: importing certificates.

2.3.6 Importing Certificates Required by the Mail Server into a Keystore

The mail receiver adapter that we configured specifies an outbound connection to an email server. To increase security, connections between an Cloud Integration tenant and remote systems can be protected by various methods, as you'll learn in Chapter 10. In our example iFlow, the tenant (as client) authenticates itself against the email server with the credentials (user and password). You specified the required settings in the **User Credentials** artifact in the steps described in the previous section.

However, in the other direction, Cloud Integration also needs to establish a trust relationship to the email server. When establishing the connection, the email server needs to authenticate itself against Cloud Integration to prove its trustworthiness, usually through a *digital server certificate*. Cloud Integration can only confirm the trustworthiness of the email server when the keystore owned by Cloud Integration (deployed on the tenant) contains a root certificate that is also trusted by the email server. (For more information about certificates, see Chapter 10, Section 10.4.1.)

In this section, we'll show you how to get the required certificate into the tenant keystore (if not already part of it). Although you can find out which certificate must be in the tenant keystore from the website of the organization that runs the email server (Yahoo!, in our example), a smarter way, without needing to search on the internet for the right information, is to use the outbound connectivity test tool. This tool is part of the **Monitor** application, which we'll describe in detail in Chapter 7, Section 7.3.2. Therefore, we'll keep our descriptions short in this section.

To use the outbound connectivity test tool, follow these steps:

1. On the **Monitor** page of the Web UI, click the **Connectivity Tests** tile under **Manage Security**.
2. On the **Overview/Test Connectivity** screen, choose the **SMTP** tab to open the test options for the (outbound) connection to the email receiver, as shown in Figure 2.57.
3. For the **Host** field, enter "smtp.mail.yahoo.com", and for the **Port** field, select **465 (SMTPS)**. (These settings were also specified in the mail receiver adapter previously in Figure 2.49.)
4. For the **Authentication** field, select **None**.
5. Deselect the **Validate Server Certificate** checkbox.

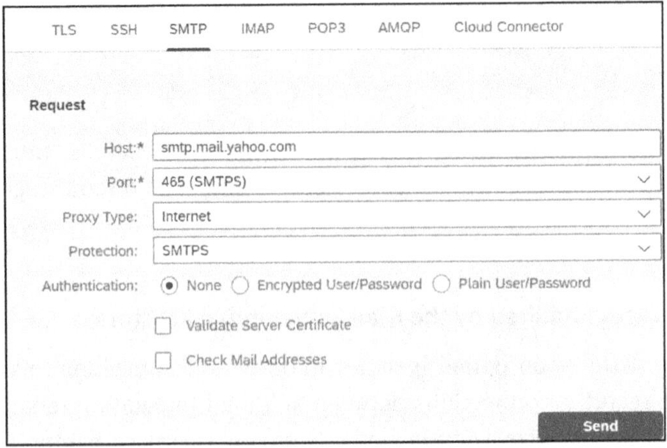

Figure 2.57 SMTP Outbound Connectivity Test

6. Click **Send**.
7. As a response, you'll receive the message: **Successfully reached host at smtp.yahoo.com:465**. Details of the server certificate will also be displayed, as shown in Figure 2.58.
8. Click the **Download server certificates** ⤓ icon ❶. The certificates are downloaded as a compressed file to your computer (*certificates.zip*).
9. Extract the file in a directory.

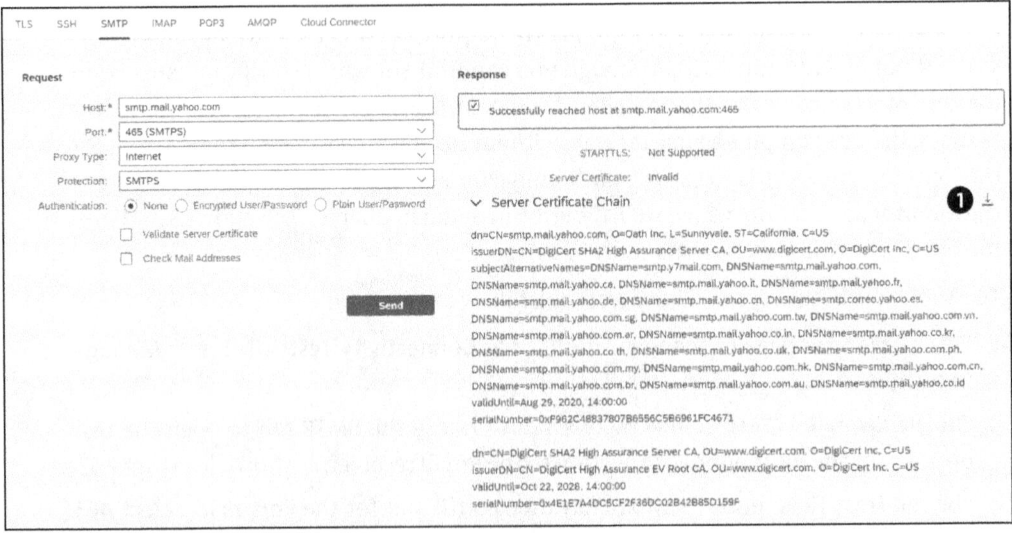

Figure 2.58 Results Page of the Outbound Connectivity Test Displaying the Required Server Certificates

For our example email provider, Yahoo!, at the time of this writing, you'll get the two certificates shown in Figure 2.59 (files with extension *.cer*).

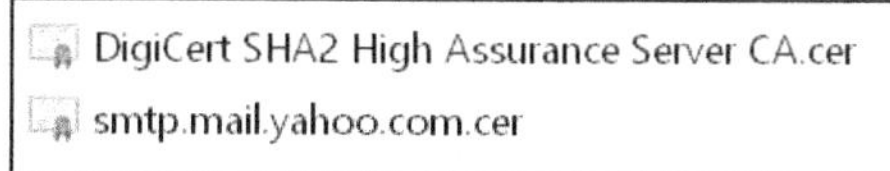

Figure 2.59 Yahoo! Server Certificates Downloaded from the Outbound Connectivity Test Tool

Next, you'll import these certificates into the tenant keystore by following these steps:

1. On the **Monitor** page of the Web UI, under **Manage Security**, click the **Keystore** tile. All certificates already contained in the tenant keystore will be displayed in a table, as shown in Figure 2.60. These certificates are predelivered by SAP and are already in place when you set up your trial tenant. In Chapter 7 and Chapter 10, we'll provide more information on the tenant keystore and its content.

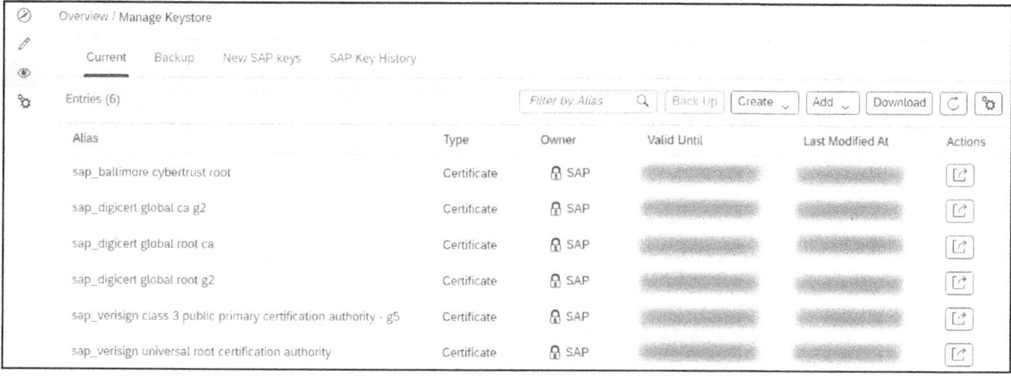

Figure 2.60 Content of Tenant Keystore Prior to Upload of the Yahoo! Certificates

2. Click **Add**, and then select **Certificate**, as shown in Figure 2.61.

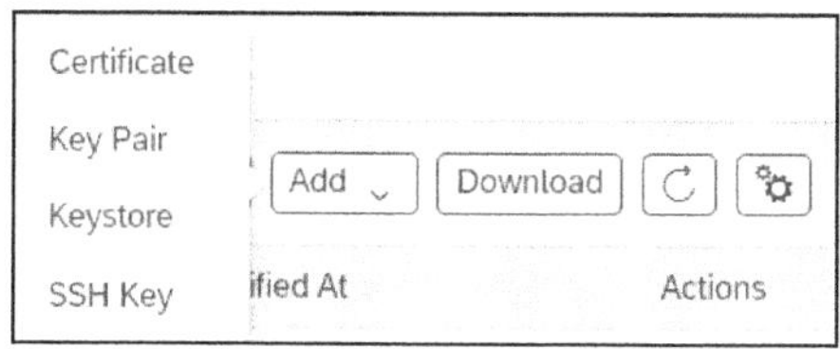

Figure 2.61 Uploading Certificates in the Tenant Keystore

3. Browse for and select one of the extracted certificates from your computer, as shown in Figure 2.62.
4. Click the **Deploy** button.

   On the next screen, details of the certificate are displayed; for more information on these specific details, refer to Chapter 10.
5. As in the previous step, upload the second certificate.

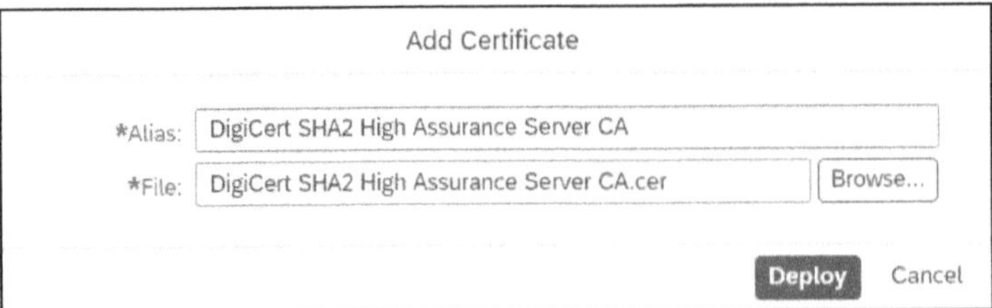

Figure 2.62 Add Certificate Dialog for Certificate Alias and File Name

6. When you click the **Manage Keystore** breadcrumb link, the whole keystore content is displayed again. The list of certificates in the keystore monitor is refreshed and should display the two additional imported certificates (see Figure 2.63 ❶).

Overview / Manage Keystore

Current Backup New SAP keys SAP Key History

Entries (8) Filter by Alias Back Up Create Add Download

Alias	Type	Owner	Valid Until	Last Modified At	Actions
digicert sha2 high assurance server ca	Certificate	Tenant Administrator			
smtp.mail.yahoo.com	Certificate	Tenant Administrator			
sap_baltimore cybertrust root	Certificate	SAP			
sap_digicert global ca g2	Certificate	SAP			
sap_digicert global root ca	Certificate	SAP			
sap_digicert global root g2	Certificate	SAP			
sap_verisign class 3 public primary certification authority - g5	Certificate	SAP			
sap_verisign universal root certification authority	Certificate	SAP			

Figure 2.63 Content of Tenant Keystore after Uploading Two Additional Yahoo! Certificates

That's it! You can now again trigger the iFlow by sending an HTTP request. The message will be delivered to your email account. You should receive an email like the one shown in Figure 2.64.

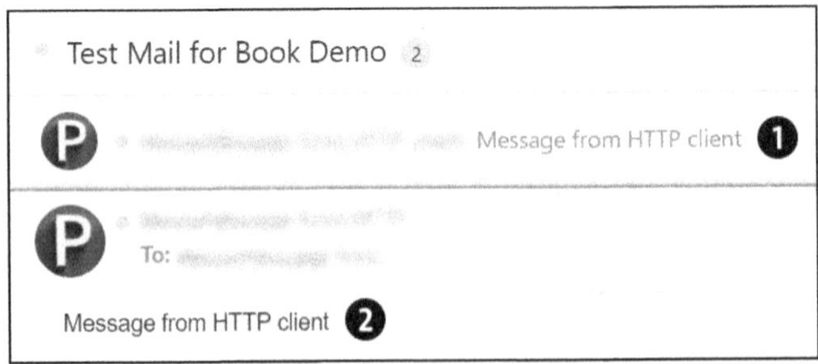

Figure 2.64 Received Email Containing Message Content Sent by HTTP Client (Postman)

The email you received is the best proof that the integration across different systems works as expected: You'll notice the same email subject in Figure 2.64 ❶ as configured in the mail adapter of Cloud Integration (compare to Figure 2.50), whereas the email content ❷ is given by the text string that you've specified as the HTTP request body in your HTTP client (Postman).

You can again monitor the message processing by opening the **Monitor** application as described earlier in Section 2.3.4 and shown in Figure 2.38.

Following is a brief remark about the kind of message content we used in this tutorial: To keep it simple, we used a simple message (`Message from HTTP client`). A plain text was sent to Cloud Integration using an HTTP client. In real life, messages processed by Cloud Integration typically are structured and comply with a dedicated format such as XML. We'll introduce working with more structured messages in Chapter 4.

Troubleshooting

In this chapter, we've shown you how to set up a connection between Cloud Integration and a Yahoo! email account. In this specific case, you may need to change some of the security settings for your email account. In particular, we generated an app password and used this password to define the tenant's **User Credentials** artifact.

When connecting to accounts of other email providers, you'll typically need to use your personal email account password when defining the **User Credentials** artifact. However, email providers typically require that you configure the email account in such a way that access by third-party apps is allowed. Check for related information on the website of the email provider.

We'll close this discussion with some information related to Gmail accounts with Google. If you're using a Google email account, consider the following:

- You might need to temporarily allow less secure apps to access your account. Otherwise, Google email will refuse your connection attempt via Cloud Integration. Note that this temporary change is just for test purposes. You should revert the settings in your Google email account after you've verified the sending of emails via Cloud Integration. More details can be found by searching for "Less secure apps & your Google account" or by directly navigating to *https://support.google.com/accounts/answer/6010255*.
- If you receive an error message, such as **javax.net.ssl.SSLHandshakeException: unable to find valid certification path to requested target**, the reason is a missing certificate. You'll have to add the Google certificate to your keystore on your tenant (as described in this section).

Mail Sender Adapter

Cloud Integration also offers the option of connecting an email sender using a mail sender adapter. An iFlow with this adapter can read emails from a specified email account and further process these messages.

You can enhance your iFlow by replacing the HTTPS sender channel with a mail sender channel and trying out this feature. For simplicity, use the same Yahoo! account and email address specified for the mail receiver adapter. In this way, you use Cloud Integration to send yourself an email.

Quickly set up this scenario by following these steps:

1. Remove the HTTPS channel between the **Sender** and **Start** event (by clicking the connection and selecting the **recycle bin** icon).
2. Create a new channel, and select adapter type **Mail**. On the following screen, select **IMAP4**.
3. Under the **Connection** tab of the mail sender adapter, specify the following settings:
   - **Address**: Enter "imap.gmail.com:993." For more information on the allowed ports for the sender mail adapter, refer to the online documentation for Cloud Integration. For your convenience, we appended the list of allowed ports to the bottom of this box.
   - **Authentication**: To keep it simple, choose **Plain User/Password**, and use the same **Credential Name** as for the mail receiver adapter (i.e., **FirstnameLastname**).
4. Under the **Processing** tab, we recommend the following settings:
   - **Selection**: Choose **Only Unread**; otherwise, the adapter would pick up all mails from the specified folder.
   - **Folder**: Specify a certain folder in your email account (other than the Inbox) so that Cloud Integration will take unread messages from the Inbox and copy them to the specified folder.
   - **Post-Processing**: Specify what should happen with a message once it has been processed by Cloud Integration.
5. Be careful with the settings under the **Scheduler** tab so you don't spam your own inbox after having deployed the iFlow. But as you've specified that only unread mails will be processed (for **Selection**, you've chosen **Only Unread**), you might be safe.

Be aware of certain security risks when using mail sender channels because Cloud Integration can't authenticate the sender of an email. For more information, check out the Cloud Integration online documentation, particularly the mail adapter section.

Allowed Ports for Mail Sender Adapter

You can use the following ports for different **Protection** settings of the mail sender adapter:

- 143 for **IMAP+STARTTLS**
- 993 for **IMAPS**
- 110 for **POP3+STARTTLS**
- 995 for **POP3S**

The tutorial described in this chapter was designed to start simple, and with each part, more complexity was added. At the end of the third part of the tutorial, you were able to operate a scenario where a sender system (realized as an HTTP client on your computer) sends a message to Cloud Integration (residing in the cloud), and this message is then forwarded to a third system, an email server. In particular, when configuring connections to email servers, some steps were required to enable Cloud Integration to securely send a message to this system. For instance, you needed to add certain certificates to the tenant's keystore and to find out specific security settings for the remote system (in particular, to allow Cloud Integration to call Yahoo!'s email server through an app password). Through this first exercise, you already learned some key facts about Cloud Integration security, a topic that we'll discuss in great detail in Chapter 10.

SFTP Adapter

In addition to the mail sender adapter, Cloud Integration provides another polling adapter, the SFTP sender adapter. Note that an iFlow with a sender adapter such as the HTTPS sender is triggered by a sender component sending a message to the iFlow endpoint. In contrast to that, a *polling* adapter is triggered by a scheduler and actively reads content from the connected (sender component).

You can modify this scenario by replacing the sender email server with an SFTP server. In this case, you'll need to store a file on the SFTP server with the encrypted message so that the SFTP sender adapter can poll it. For more information on setting up a secure connection using SFTP, read the SAP Community blog at *http://s-prs.co/507710*.

2.4 Summary

In this chapter, we provided you with a detailed introduction to the architecture of Cloud Integration. We explained its main components and showed you how messages are processed by the virtual runtime environment. We also introduced you to the available tools and processes, and we then finished up the chapter with a brief tutorial on how to design and run your first, relatively simple, iFlow. The tutorial showed you how to send a message to Cloud Integration from a locally installed HTTP client. The tutorial was rounded out by adding an email receiver to the scenario. Using an email server as the receiver system allowed you to set up a simple system landscape without further technical prerequisites to meet.

Without further detail, this tutorial already touched on such topics as security (you needed to get the server certificates from the email provider and upload them into the tenant keystore) and temporary storage options on the tenant (the iFlow stored the message content using a data store **Write** step).

The integration scenario developed in this tutorial, however, didn't impose any further processing of the message. If you can't wait to start modifying messages during processing, you can proceed with Chapter 4 where step-by-step methods for processing a message will be introduced.

However, now that you're equipped with the basic knowledge required to dive further into the world of integration patterns, you might first want to find out what integration scenarios are provided by SAP out of the box. In the next chapter, we'll provide you with an overview of the predefined integration content provided by SAP and made available on SAP Business Accelerator Hub.

Chapter 3
SAP Integration Content Catalog

SAP provides prepackaged integration content to enable the quick implementation of integration scenarios. These packages are found in SAP Integration Content Catalog. In this chapter, we'll dive into SAP Integration Content Catalog, present its available features, and explore the prepackaged integration content currently available.

In Chapter 1, we discussed the role that SAP Integration Suite plays within SAP's cloud strategy. We also discussed SAP Integration Suite's positioning within the SAP landscape and presented a number of use cases.

As the adoption of cloud-based applications keeps growing, the likelihood that more customers will need to build the same integration scenarios will continue to increase. Why not build these common integration scenarios in advance and reduce implementation costs for customers? With this approach, customers simply need to reuse existing integration scenarios, rather than build their own.

This standardization and reuse capability is exactly what SAP has made available through its SAP Integration Content Catalog. In this chapter, we'll introduce you to SAP Integration Content Catalog and walk you through the steps required to consume prepackaged, SAP-provided content. We'll explore available prepackaged content and discuss some use cases. You'll also learn about creating your own content package and using adapters to third-party applications.

3.1 Introduction to SAP Integration Content Catalog

Since the introduction of cloud computing technologies, organizations have shifted investments in software licenses. Organizations have rapidly moved from the concept of software ownership to software rental. As a result, SAP is also growing its cloud-based portfolio with standardized products in HR (with SAP SuccessFactors), marketing, sales, service, procurement, supply chain management, and finance. We're convinced that this portfolio will continue to grow.

Most customers may find themselves needing to integrate cloud-based applications with other on-premise or cloud-based applications to cover the total end-to-end business process. As described in previous chapters, Cloud Integration is well positioned as the integration platform for such use cases.

Most capabilities provided by these cloud-based applications are standardized in terms of protocols, endpoints, and message structures. Therefore, integration scenarios built over Cloud Integration for these cloud-based applications have a good chance of being implemented and reused by many other customers and partners. This reusability is exactly what SAP provides with its prepackaged integration content for the most frequently used SAP cloud-based applications. This integration content is available in SAP Integration Content Catalog.

The catalog includes templates with prebuilt integration flows (iFlows), value mappings, and other integration artifacts that you can reuse, thus significantly reducing implementation time, cost, and risk. The catalog presents and categorizes content in a simple manner, allowing you to browse and discover content that might be relevant for your scenarios. SAP Integration Content Catalog content is bundled in packages. Each package contains artifacts and objects that logically belong together and support a particular integration scenario. The artifacts and objects bundled in a package can be organized into four categories: data integration, iFlow, OData service, or value mapping (see the information box on basic artifact types in Chapter 2, Section 2.3.4).

When dealing with SAP Integration Content Catalog, you'll need to understand the different roles involved in consuming and publishing content. We generally distinguish among the following roles:

- **Integration developer**
  A member of the partner or customer organization responsible for consuming the prepackaged content available in SAP Integration Content Catalog.
- **Content publisher**
  The person responsible for building and making the integration package available in SAP Integration Content Catalog.
- **Content reviewer**
  The person responsible for reviewing and ensuring the quality of the content delivered in SAP Integration Content Catalog by the publisher.

Separating roles during the publication process helps improve the correctness of the content published in the catalog. Note that, at the time of this writing, only SAP can publish content packages. Consequently, the content publisher and reviewer roles aren't yet relevant to customers. This chapter will therefore primarily focus on the role of the *integration developer*, which is the role that you, as a reader of this book, will most likely play.

You can access SAP Integration Content Catalog in two different ways:

- **Via a publicly accessible URL**
  You can access the publicly (and freely) available SAP Integration Content Catalog web-based application at *https://api.sap.com*. The landing page for SAP Integration Content Catalog is shown in Figure 3.1.

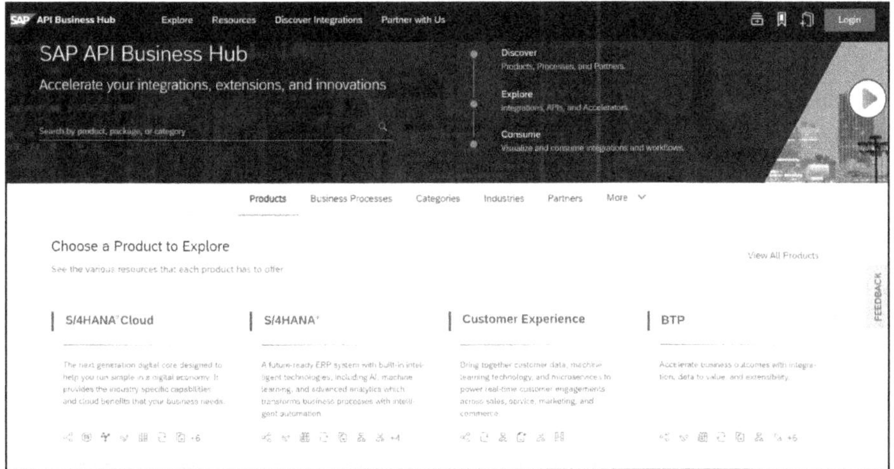

Figure 3.1 Publicly Accessible SAP Integration Content Catalog

Note that SAP Integration Content Catalog is published on SAP Business Accelerator Hub. You don't need a Cloud Integration tenant to use this web application. From this publicly available URL, only read access is available. If you need to reuse this content or have access to other features, you must access a Cloud Integration tenant.

- **Via your own tenant**

  You can access SAP Integration Content Catalog via your own Cloud Integration tenant at *http://<server>:<port>/itspaces*.

  As shown on the left side of Figure 3.2, the Cloud Integration Web UI consists of four main pages:

  - **Discover**
  - **Design**
  - **Monitor**
  - **Settings**

  Refer to Chapter 2, Section 2.2.1, for more details about each section.

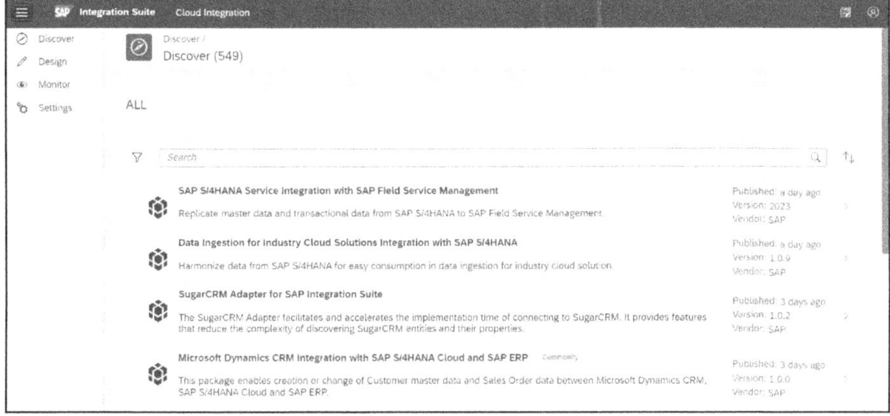

Figure 3.2 Landing Page of the Web UI

As shown in Figure 3.2, the **Discover** page can be used to browse through SAP Integration Content Catalog. Let's dive more deeply into how to consume the available integration content.

3.2 Terms and Conditions of Using Prepackaged Integration Content

Terms and conditions, within the context of Cloud Integration, refer to usage restrictions that affect prepackaged content. The publisher of the content can determine what content in their packages can be used and how. The terms and conditions mainly affect three aspects (at the time of this writing):

- **Quick configure versus content edit**
  Conditions the publisher applies that influence how the content can be consumed.
- **Notify about update (manual update)**
  Related to updating the prepackaged content included in SAP Integration Content Catalog.
- **Automatic update**
  Related to consumed prepackaged content automatically being updated.

We'll discuss these three aspects in the following sections.

3.2.1 Quick Configure versus Content Edit

One of the conditions that a publisher can apply to prepackaged content is the *quick configure versus content edit* condition. Quick configure or content edit conditions are used during the publication process to restrict the usage of the content. Let's explore these two conditions:

- **Quick configure (also called configure-only)**
  The user of the package can only configure the options already made available by the package artifacts. Depending on the specifics of the concerned package, this condition usually only includes configuring the different adapters used in the iFlow. The configure-only option also means that the integration content itself (e.g., the steps in an iFlow) can't be changed and are therefore use-only. This option is somewhat restrictive because you must stick to the provided content. However, one of the advantages of this approach is that managing the various versions of the content is easier for the content publisher, who can also be certain that the content is being used in the intended way. For example, you're usually allowed to adjust the adapter's specific settings, including connection parameters and user name/password, but you wouldn't be allowed to change the adapter type from, for instance, Simple Object Access Protocol (SOAP) to Java Message Service (JMS). The impact of new versions is, therefore, controllable and predictable. If your integration content has quick

configure terms and conditions, the configure-only approach of configuration will apply, which we'll discuss further in Section 3.3.3.

- **Content edit**
  Under this condition, you're free to modify the content as needed, and thus, this approach provides a lot of flexibility; however, with great power comes great responsibility, as they say. With content editing open to the user, integration developers can change the content and fully deviate from the original intention of the content. For example, an integration developer might decide to add new steps to an iFlow or change the type of adapter used to communicate with the sender or receiver system. The changes made to the content by its consumer might make future updates to the content more difficult. The resulting conflicts will need to be manually resolved. At the time of this writing, no automatic conflict resolution solution is available. Therefore, as the consumer, you must consider the impact of the changes you make to prepackaged content with regard to future updates of the content package. If your integration content uses the content edit terms and conditions, the content edit approach of configuration will apply, which we'll discuss further in Section 3.3.3.

Note that currently these options are only available to SAP because only SAP publishes content to SAP Integration Content Catalog.

3.2.2 Notify about Update (Manual Updates)

During the publishing process, the **Notify about Update** checkbox is available. If this option is selected, you'll be notified of any updates made to the integration package. Notifications are sent automatically to consumers using the integration content. As shown in Figure 3.3, a green **Update Available** link accompanies all updatable artifacts in the prepackaged content. In this way, the consumer is made aware that his content has an update available and can decide whether to perform the update.

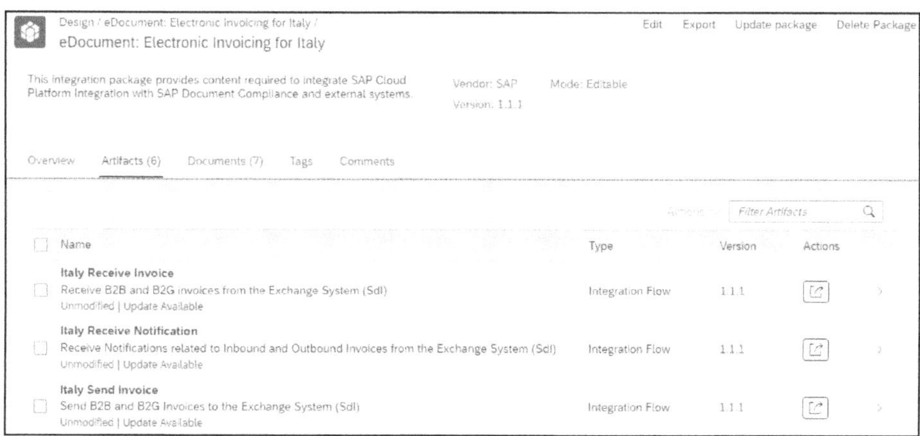

Figure 3.3 Notification of Updated Content in the Catalog

> **Note**
>
> This type of notification is also called *manual update*. With manual update, the customer has the option of implementing the update whenever they like or perhaps even decide not to implement the changes at all. Not updating the content package doesn't run the risk that the deployed artifact will stop working. But the customer will obviously not benefit from the newly added features. Furthermore, reverting back to an older version if necessary is also possible.

As a consumer, you can update your entire content package using the **Update package** button in the top-right corner of the screen shown in Figure 3.4. You can also update individual objects in a package instead of the entire package by following these steps:

1. Select the content package containing the object you would like to update.
2. Under the **Artifacts** tab of the package, select the artifacts that you want to update by selecting the relevant checkboxes. This tab lists all artifacts contained in the package and indicates which artifacts can be updated with the **Update Available** link, as shown previously in Figure 3.3.
3. Click on the **Update package** button, as shown in Figure 3.4.

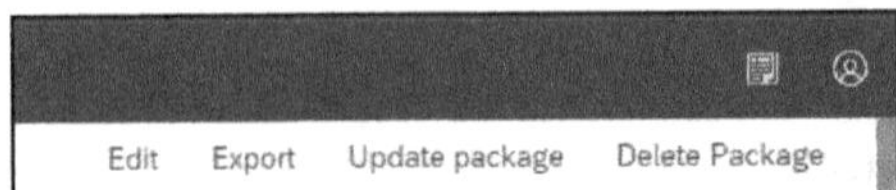

Figure 3.4 Updating Selected Items of the Content Package

Note that you can also update a single iFlow by selecting the **Update** option from the **Actions** menu, as shown in Figure 3.5.

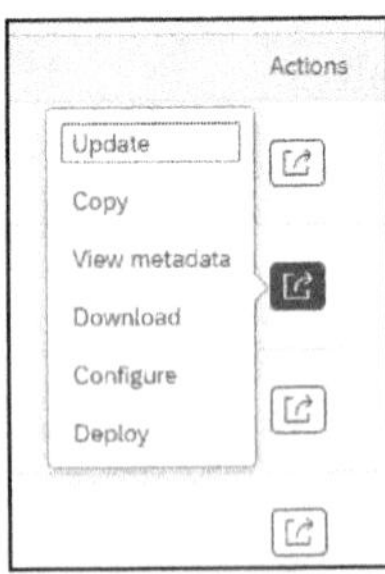

Figure 3.5 Updating a Particular Item of the Content Package

> **Note**
>
> If a consumer modifies integration content in the modifiable mode, a notification won't be sent when the content is updated by the publisher. The notification is only sent in the following cases:

- The consumed prepackaged content is in configure-only mode.
- The consumed prepackaged content is in modifiable mode but has only been configured and not modified. In other words, the package is being used as if it were a configure-only package.

3.2.3 Automatic Updates

Instead of being notified of an update and being free to choose if/when to perform the actual update (as discussed in Section 3.2.2), in some cases, the publisher of the prepackaged content chooses automatic updating. The main difference is that, for manual update, the user explicitly must perform the update operation, whereas no user interaction is required for automatic updates. The updated content is automatically pushed to the tenant, and the deployed content is updated in one of two ways:

- **Immediate**
  With this approach, customers have a window of up to 12 hours before the update is automatically applied to the corresponding deployed artifacts.
- **Scheduled**
  With this approach, the corresponding artifacts are marked with the date when the automatic update will be applied, for example, the artifact marked with the message **Will be updated on . . .**, as shown in Figure 3.6.

SFSF_EC_to_S4HANA_Availability
Availability data replication from SAP SuccessFactors Employee Central to SAP S/4HANA
Unmodified | Will be updated on 07/04/2018

Figure 3.6 Artifact with Automatic Update Scheduled

Note

Irrespective of whether the automatic update is immediate or scheduled, the customer has the option of applying the update before the update is automatically performed.

An automatic update will always be applied, leaving the consumer without control.

Up to this point, you've learned the steps involved in finding and consuming prepackaged content in general. Let's now explore some of the content packages in SAP Integration Content Catalog at the time of this writing.

3.3 Consuming Prepackaged Content

We touched on the role of an integration developer in Section 3.1. In most cases, the integration developer is a member of the partner or customer organization and has been tasked with developing well-defined integration scenarios. Figure 3.7 shows the steps involved in consuming prepackaged content from the catalog.

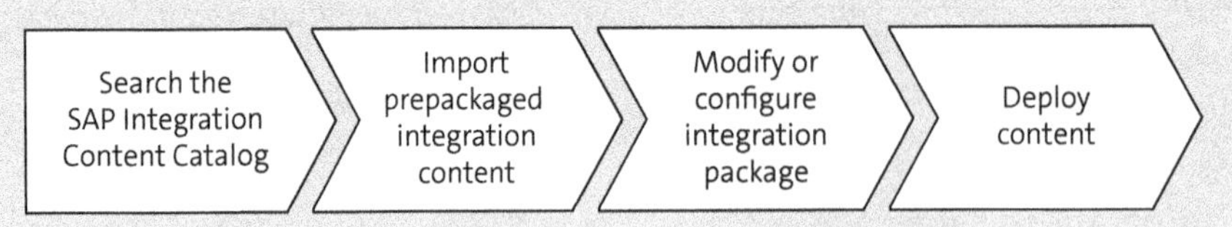

Figure 3.7 Process of Consuming Prepackaged Integration Content

We'll discuss these tasks in more detail in this section with a hands-on, step-by-step guide.

3.3.1 Searching SAP Integration Content Catalog

A good practice is to search through SAP Integration Content Catalog for existing content before attempting to develop your own content from scratch. To search the catalog, follow these steps:

1. Navigate to your Cloud Integration tenant using the link provided by SAP on your browser. The link follows the format *http://<server>:<port>/itspaces*.
2. Select the **Discover** menu item on the left side of the page to access SAP Integration Content Catalog, as shown in Figure 3.8.

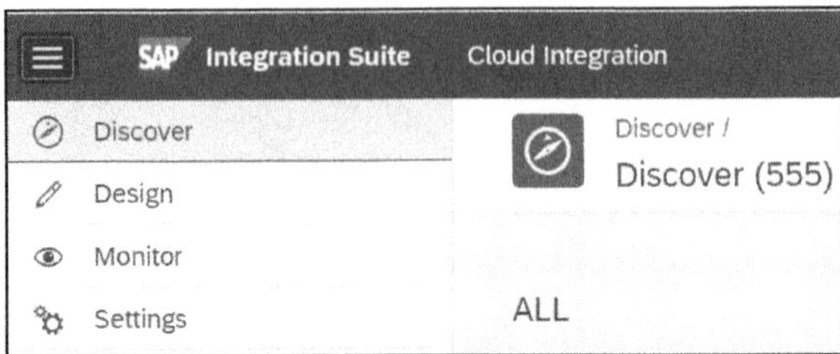

Figure 3.8 Accessing the SAP Integration Content Catalog Main Page

3. In SAP Integration Content Catalog, you'll see a list of integration packages to choose from. By default, only the latest packages are listed. To view all existing packages, click on the **ALL** link in the top left of the page shown in Figure 3.9. You'll then see a page similar to the page shown in Figure 3.10.
4. A new screen will appear offering a variety of filtering categories. You can apply filters using categories such as **Line of Business**, **Products**, **Countries**, **Supported Platforms**, **Vendor**, **Industries**, and **Keywords**, as shown in Figure 3.10. Note that you can also perform a keyword search on this screen.

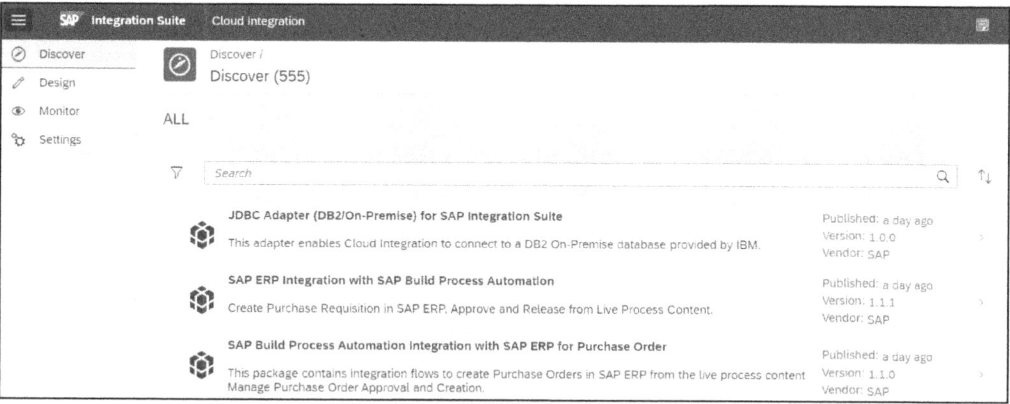

Figure 3.9 Discover Landing Page

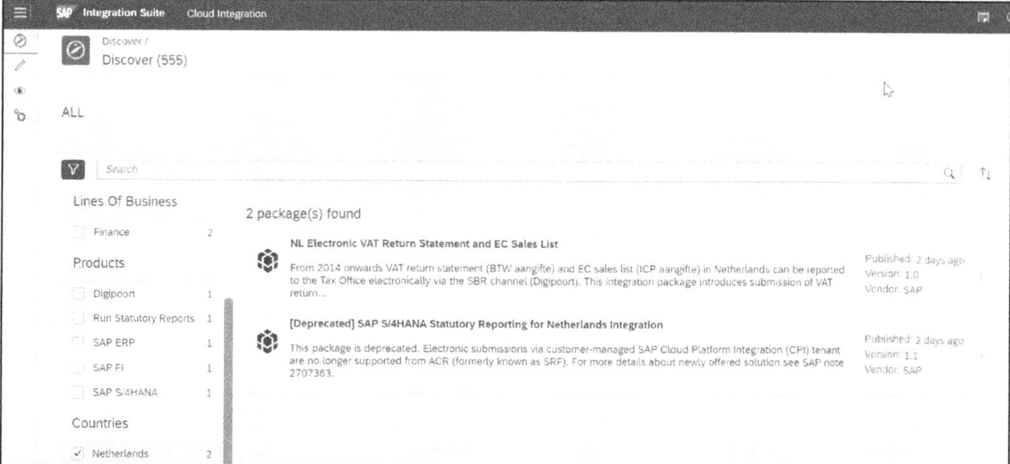

Figure 3.10 Filtering or Searching SAP Integration Content Catalog

The resulting list provides the name, high-level description of the package, published date, vendor, and version. Additionally, a user rating of the integration content is also available.

To view details about a particular package, select the package from the list. As a result, you'll see a page similar to that shown in Figure 3.11.

This integration content detail page contains the following tabs:

- **Overview**
  Contains the description of the package and scenarios it covers.
- **Artifacts**
  Includes a list of iFlows, data iFlows, and other integration artifacts that make up the bundle.

- **Documents**
  Includes guides and links to provide more documentation and information about the integration content to assist the user further. Commonly, integration guides are included among these documents. An integration guide provides step-by-step guidelines on how to set up and configure the integration scenario. Note that the corresponding contacts or components are mentioned in the release notes of the content. This information is useful if issues with the artifacts arise, and you want to report the issue to SAP.
- **Tags**
  Provides different metadata to help classify content. The list of metadata includes industry, line of business, keywords, supported platforms, and so on.
- **Ratings**
  Contains details about consumer ratings as well as the logged-in user's own ratings.

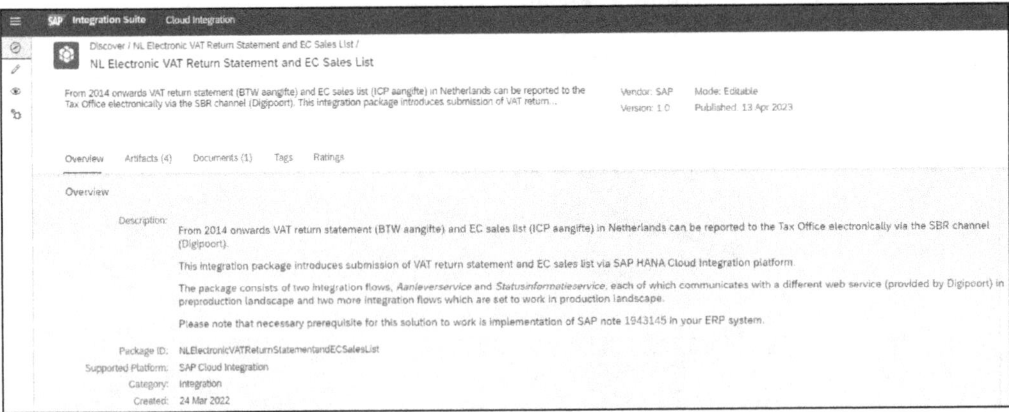

Figure 3.11 Viewing Details of an Integration Package

The items listed under the **Artifacts** tab, as shown in Figure 3.12, can be clicked to view further information. For instance, you can click on an iFlow's name to display more details about the iFlow, as shown in Figure 3.13.

After browsing around and finding the integration package that fits your needs, you're now ready to further modify and configure it according to your requirements. Note that whether you can configure or modify the integration package depends on the mode of the prepackaged content, as we'll discuss in Section 3.3.3.

In the next section, we'll show you how to consume the content by copying it into your customer workspace.

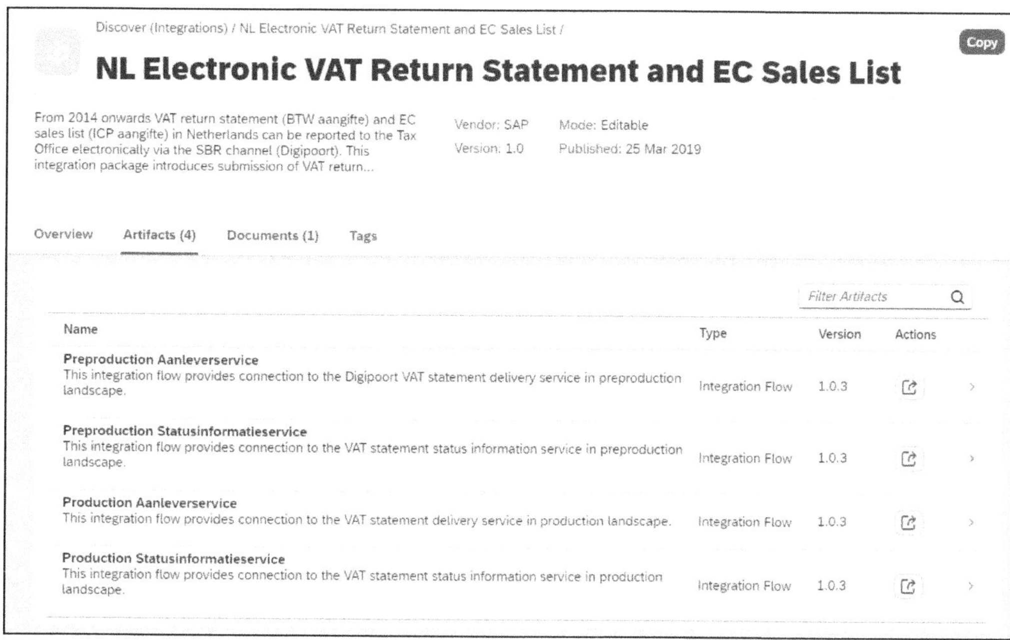

Figure 3.12 List of Artifacts in an Integration Package

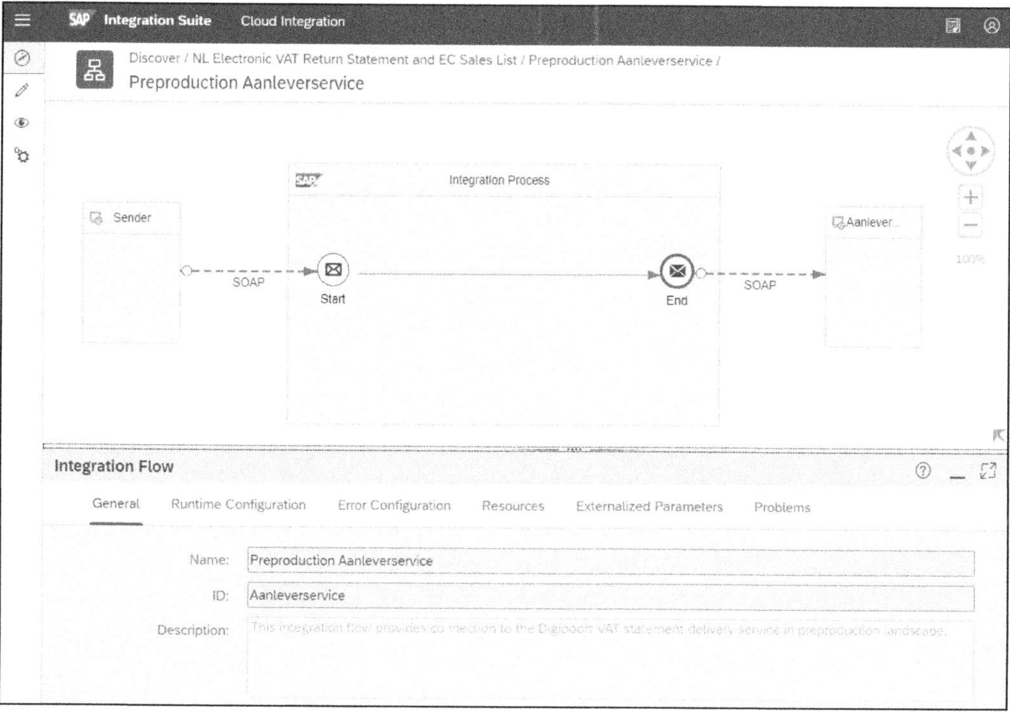

Figure 3.13 Details of the iFlow: Preproduction Delivery Service

3.3.2 Importing Prepackaged Integration Content

You can copy the content available in SAP Integration Content Catalog into your own design workspace for further customer-specific configuration and enhancements. You can use the template contained in the package as the basis upon which to make changes to suit your specific business requirements. To copy an integration package, perform the following steps:

1. After selecting the package that you want to copy (in our example, the **NL Electronic VAT Return Statement and EC Sales List** integration package), a **Copy** link will appear in the top-right corner, as shown in Figure 3.14. Clicking this **Copy** link enables you to copy the integration package to your own customer workspace.

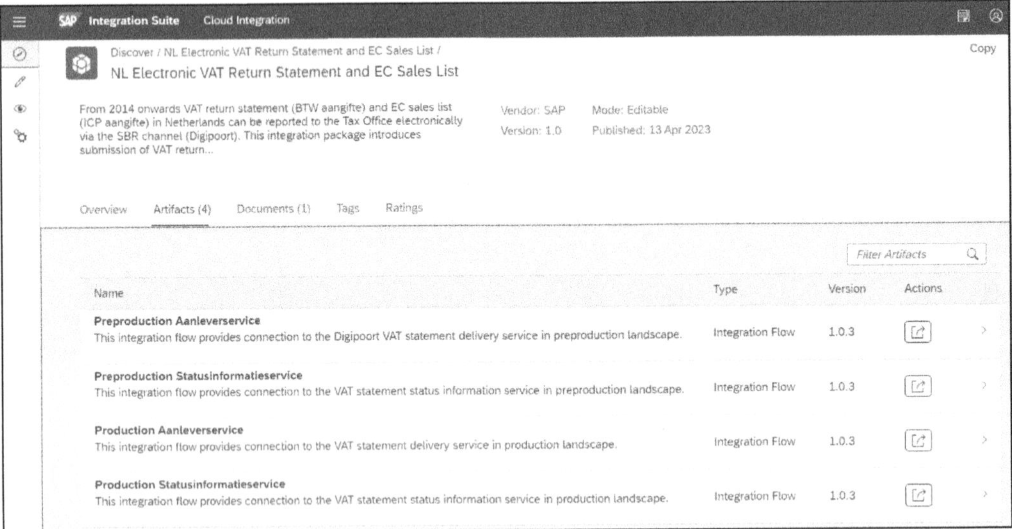

Figure 3.14 Copying Templates to Your Own Workspace

2. After performing the copy action, the copied package and its artifacts are displayed in your own design workspace. Click on the **Design** menu item (refer to Figure 3.8) to further enhance the copied content. Figure 3.15 shows that the copied package is now available in the customer's workspace, on the left.

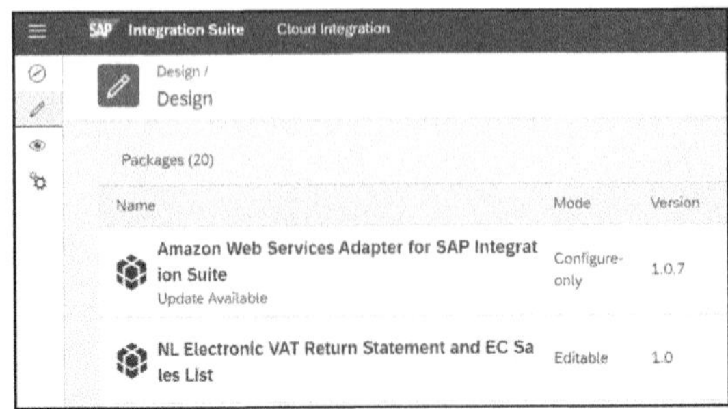

Figure 3.15 Design Component with Copied Templates

Note

Once you've copied a package from the **Discover** view to the **Design** view, a subscription is created in the background for each artifact contained in the package. Having a subscription means that Cloud Integration knows you're interested in any changes or planned updates to the concerned prepackaged integration content.

When anything changes on the package, you're informed via a tag next to the concerned artifacts. This subject was mentioned earlier in Section 3.3.1, and we'll revisit tags in Section 3.5.

3.3.3 Modifying or Configuring the Integration Package

The content copied in the previous step is now ready for configuration. Such configuration steps might include configuring adapter-specific endpoints. Depending on your requirements, you can also remodel and completely change the content. As mentioned earlier, there are two approaches to configuring integration packages: content edit and configure-only. Let's explore each approach in a bit more detail.

Content Edit Approach

This approach allows you to perform configuration steps to remodel and change the package content.

Note

The ability to completely remodel and change the content of a copied package can be restricted by the terms and conditions of the integration package. When the package is restricted, use the configure-only approach. The subject of terms and conditions was also discussed in Section 3.2.

The integration package copied to your tenant can be modified and configured to your own needs by following these steps:

1. Click on the desired package's name from the list of packages displayed in the screen, as shown in Figure 3.15.
2. A new page, similar to the page shown earlier in Figure 3.12, will load. The page should display the full list of objects contained in the integration package. Note that the artifacts can be a mixture of iFlows, data integration, OData services, and value mappings. Furthermore, the **Documents** tab can contain files and URLs.
3. To display an iFlow, click on its name. You'll then see a detailed view of the flow, as shown in Figure 3.16.
4. To change an iFlow, click the **Edit** button in the upper-right corner of the screen. Note that, when in edit mode, the integration package editor locks the object and prevents any other user from changing it.

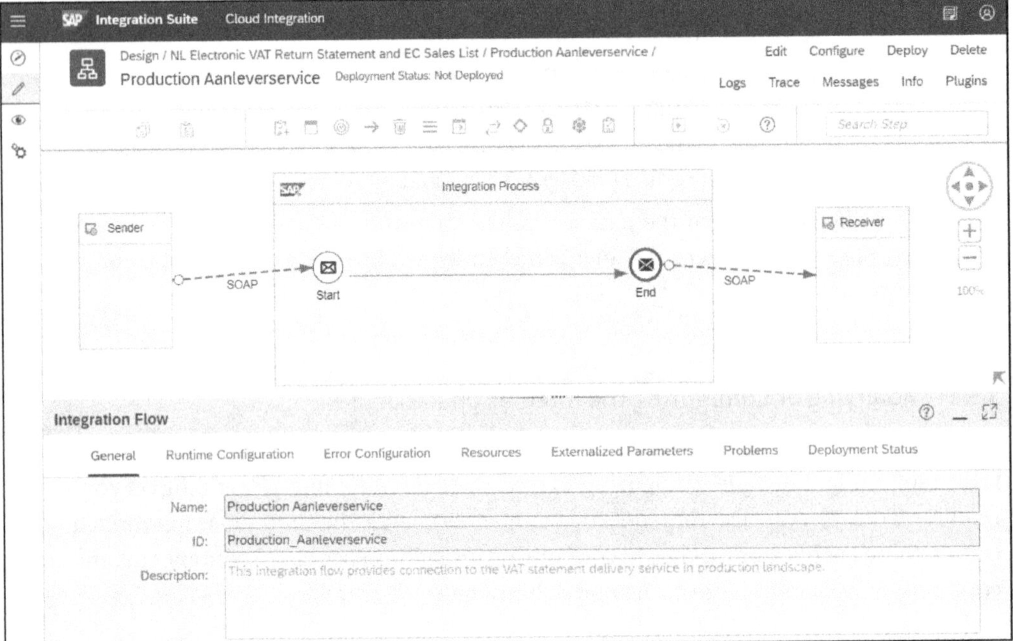

Figure 3.16 Details of the iFlow

5. For most iFlows, connectivity details on the sender and receiver side will need to be changed. Figure 3.17, for instance, shows that the SOAP receiver connection details can be filled in by selecting the relevant connector and specifying the properties under the **Connection** tab.
6. After you've made the desired changes, click on the **Save** button in the top-right corner of the page, as shown in Figure 3.17. Alternatively, click **Save as version** to save a new version of the iFlow. You'll then be asked to provide a comment for the new version. Note that the version number is automatically incremented.
7. After saving your work in the previous step, you can now choose to deploy the iFlow on the tenant by using the **Deploy** option (shown previously in Figure 3.16). If you attempt to deploy without saving, a popup message will warn you that unsaved changes exist. You'll also be asked whether you want to save the iFlow and deploy at the same time.

The iFlow can now be used at runtime to process actual messages. Figure 3.18 shows how you can download the content of an iFlow.

The content is downloaded to your local machine in an archive file (e.g., ZIP file) containing the entire iFlow project. The iFlow's project ZIP file can then be imported into another package or deployed to run on an SAP Process Orchestration server, as described in Chapter 17 of *SAP Process Orchestration: The Comprehensive Guide* (SAP PRESS, 2017).

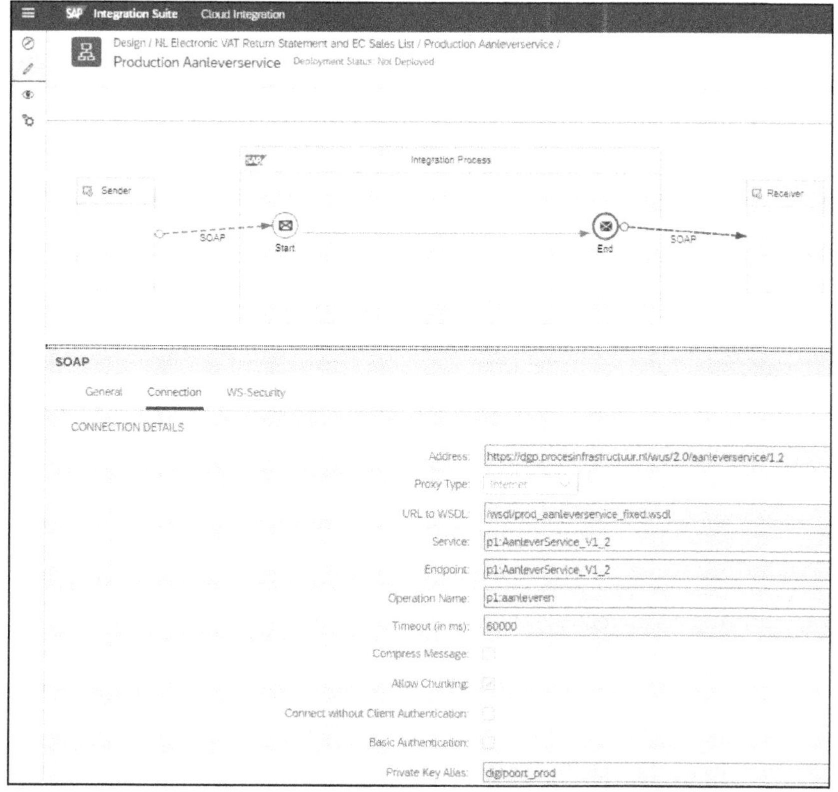

Figure 3.17 Adding Different Items to an Existing iFlow Template

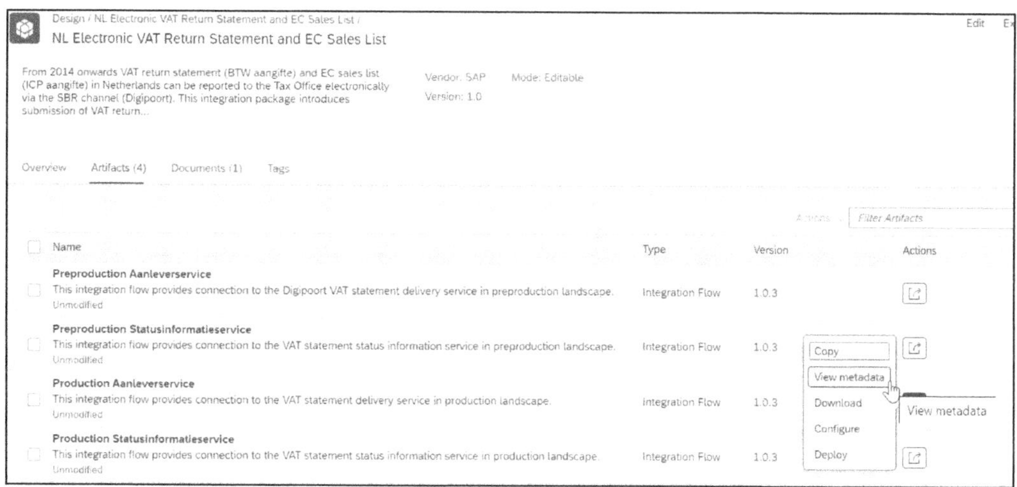

Figure 3.18 Overview of Updated Package

As shown in Figure 3.18, every iFlow contains a version number. After consuming a particular version of the iFlow, you have the option of reverting to an older version by performing the following steps:

1. Under the **Artifacts** tab shown in Figure 3.18, click on the **Version** number of the iFlow. Note that this step works in design mode only.
2. The next screen displays the history of the various versions of the iFlow, as shown in Figure 3.19.

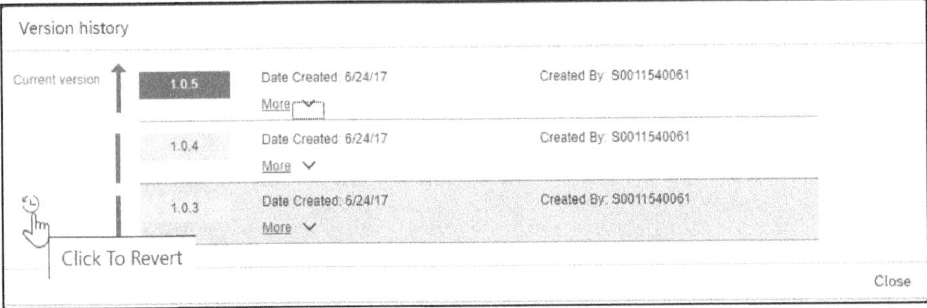

Figure 3.19 Reverting to a Different Version in the Version History

3. Hover over the version that you want to revert to, and click on the clock-like icon on the left side of the **Version history** screen, as shown in Figure 3.19.
4. A new screen pops up, from which you'll need to confirm your action by clicking the **OK** button.

Now that the consumed prepackaged content is configured to suit your needs, it's time to deploy the content and make it available in your tenant's runtime. We'll discuss this next step in Section 3.3.4.

Configure-Only Approach

The configure-only option provides an easy-to-use method of quickly adapting an iFlow to meet your requirements. You can perform only configuration activities, such as adding adapter-specific endpoints and assigning values to externalized parameters.

If you want to modify the content of the integration package, such adding an extra step to the iFlow, you should use the content edit approach discussed earlier.

The following steps are performed when using the configure-only approach:

1. Navigate to your design workspace by selecting the **Design** page (refer to Figure 3.8).
2. Click on the package's name (refer to Figure 3.15). The next screen displays a list of artifacts contained in the package, under the **Artifacts** tab.
3. Select the **Action** button on the row corresponding to the iFlow that you want to configure, and then choose **Configure** from the dropdown menu, as shown in Figure 3.20.

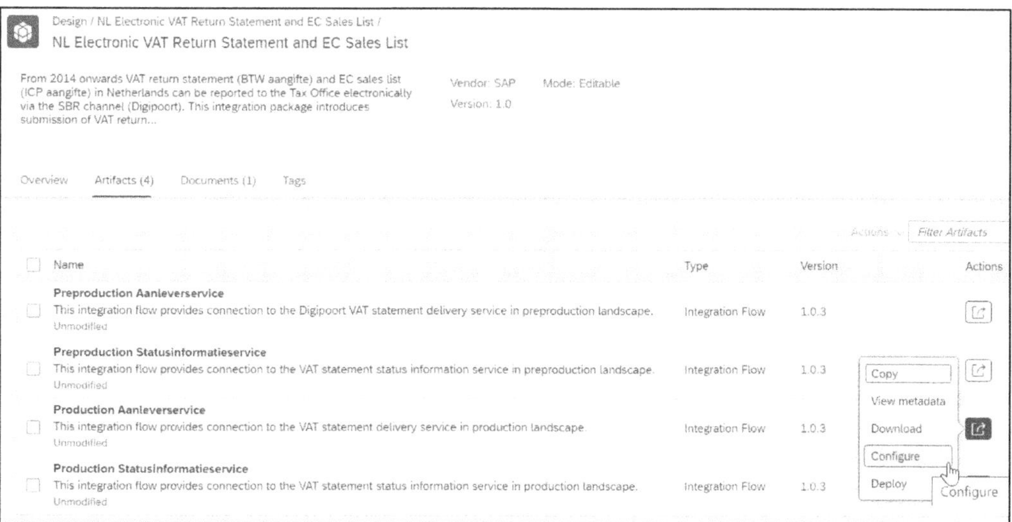

Figure 3.20 Accessing the Configure-Only Option

If the iFlow lacks configurable attributes, a warning message pops up, as shown in Figure 3.21.

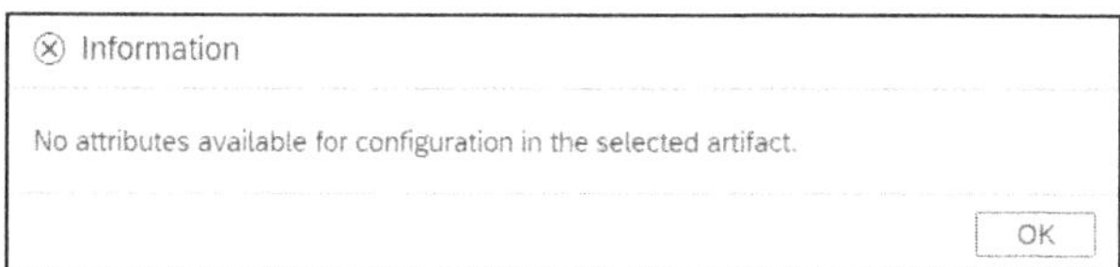

Figure 3.21 Warning for Missing Attributes in the Configure-Only Approach

4. If the iFlow does have configurable attributes, configure the details of each tab shown in Figure 3.22. Notice that, on this screen, only the **Sender**, **Receiver**, and **More** tabs are displayed, but the **Timer** tab is also available. All four configuration tabs and their descriptions are listed in Table 3.1.

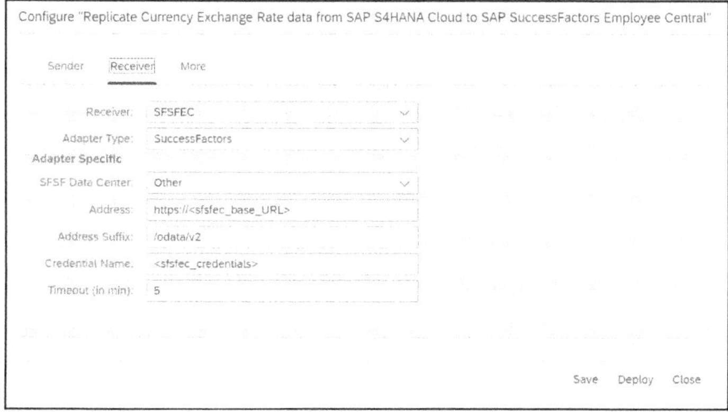

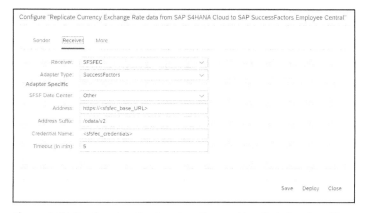

Figure 3.22 Configuring the Receiver Connection Details of an iFlow

Configuration Tab	Description
Timer	If the iFlow uses a scheduler (a timer start event), its settings can be configured under this tab. Possible options include **Run once**, **Schedule on Day**, or **Schedule to Recur**. We'll cover how you can use a timer start event in an iFlow in Chapter 6, Section 6.1.2.
Sender	Configure the connectivity details of the sender adapter.
Receiver	Configure the connectivity details of the receiver adapter. See the example shown in Figure 3.22.
More	Provide a configuration feature for externalized parameters. Note that, at the time of this writing, all string fields can be externalized in all flow steps. Externalized parameters allow you to define variables and use them in an iFlow. The values of these variables can be assigned later in the configuration process. Parameters and externalization are further discussed in Chapter 4, Section 4.2.

Table 3.1 Available Configuration Tabs for the Configure-Only Approach

5. After you've made the desired changes in the previous step, click on the **Save** button (shown earlier in Figure 3.22).
6. Deploy the iFlow on the tenant by using the **Deploy** button (shown earlier in Figure 3.22).

Note

Note that the four tabs listed in Table 3.1 are available after you've clicked on the **Configure** option. However, the tabs are only populated with configurable properties under the following conditions:

- The presence of a sender adapter in the iFlow (**Sender** tab)
- The presence of a receiver adapter in the iFlow (**Receiver** tab)
- The presence of a timer start event (**Timer** tab)
- When you've externalized any string fields in any flow step (**More** tab)

For instance, when you have an iFlow beginning with a timer start event (i.e., no sender system is involved), the **Sender** tab won't be populated. If nothing has been externalized in the entire flow, you'll receive an error message stating, **No attributes available for quick configuration in the selected artifact**.

We'll explore the subject of externalizing parameters further in Chapter 4, Section 4.2.

3.3.4 Deploy Content

Your iFlow is now configured and ready to be deployed. You can deploy the iFlow by following these steps:

1. From within your customer workspace, on the **Design** page, select the iFlow that you configured in Section 3.3.3.
2. Click on the **Deploy** button, shown in the top-right corner of Figure 3.23.

The deployed iFlow is now ready to reliably connect systems with each other through message exchange. Congratulations—you just learned how to consume prepackaged integration content! Imagine how much time you would've needed to figure out the mapping requirements and build this entire iFlow from scratch.

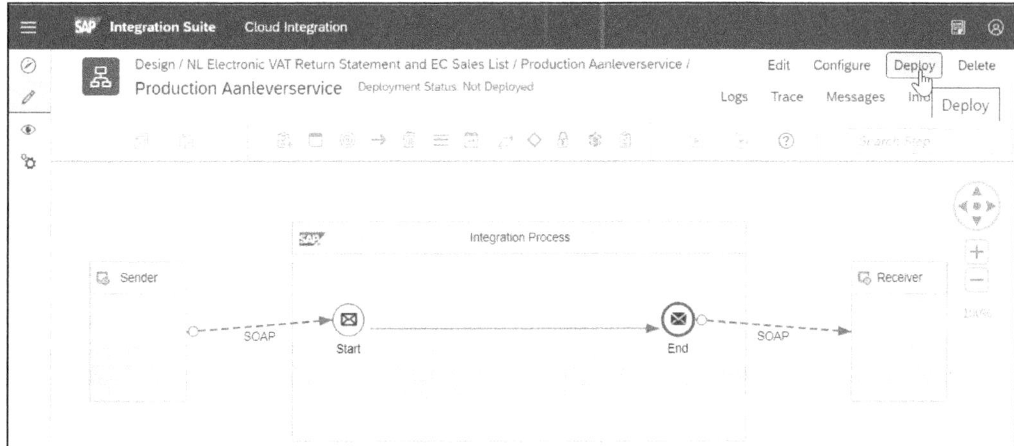

Figure 3.23 Deploying an iFlow

Now, let's explore the wide range of prepackaged integration content available for you to use in your integration scenarios.

3.4 Prepackaged Content Provided by SAP

Let's showcase the available content in SAP Integration Content Catalog, which includes integration scenarios for the most commonly used cloud-based applications from SAP:

- SAP SuccessFactors
- SAP Cloud for Customer
- SAP Ariba
- SAP Customer Experience
- Content for globalization scenarios

- Content for ELSTER (Elektronische Steuererklärung) integration for German tax requirements
- Adapters to third-party applications for SAP Integration Suite

For each category, we'll explore the provided content and specify their use cases in this section.

3.4.1 Content for SAP SuccessFactors

SAP SuccessFactors is a cloud-based human capital management (HCM) solution that integrates onboarding, social business and collaboration tools, a learning management system (LMS), recruiting software, performance management, succession planning, applicant tracking software, talent management, and HR analytics to deliver business strategy alignment, team execution, and maximum people performance. SAP has another HR product called SAP ERP Human Capital Management (SAP ERP HCM), which provides an integrated set of modules to help an organization manage its people. SAP ERP HCM is effectively an on-premise HCM product.

Some customers have opted for a hybrid approach, where SAP ERP HCM (on-premise) and SAP SuccessFactors (in the cloud) work in tandem. In these cases, customers must decide which part of the end-to-end HCM process runs on which system. One popular approach is to use SAP ERP HCM for core HR processes and use SAP SuccessFactors for one or more talent management processes. With such a division of responsibilities between two HCM systems, integration plays a critical part in linking and synchronizing them.

For the sake of illustration, Figure 3.24 shows a common onboarding process between SAP ERP HCM and SAP SuccessFactors. This process shows a requirement to export an employee's prehire data (information about the candidate before they become an employee) from SAP ERP HCM to SAP SuccessFactors Onboarding. Moreover, when the process is completed in SAP SuccessFactors Onboarding, you can export the employee data from SAP SuccessFactors Onboarding back to SAP ERP HCM and create employee master data. The complete use case is shown in Figure 3.24.

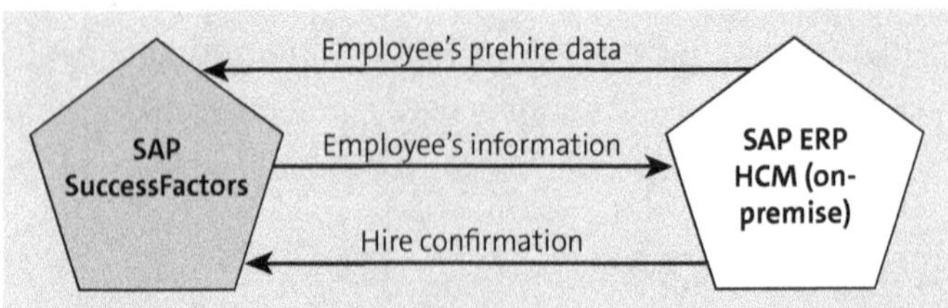

Figure 3.24 Use Case Integrating SAP SuccessFactors Onboarding and SAP ERP HCM

By integrating and combining the functionalities of these two platforms, you can achieve a better end-to-end process result. SAP Integration Content Catalog provides a variety of packages to cover different integration scenarios, including for the use case shown in Figure 3.24. Refer to SAP Integration Content Catalog for the most up-to-date list of SAP SuccessFactors–related packages.

To discover all packages related to SAP SuccessFactors, you'll need to apply a filter on the main page of SAP Integration Content Catalog by selecting any entry with the word **SuccessFactors** as the value of the **Products** dropdown list. This filtering exercise is shown in Figure 3.25.

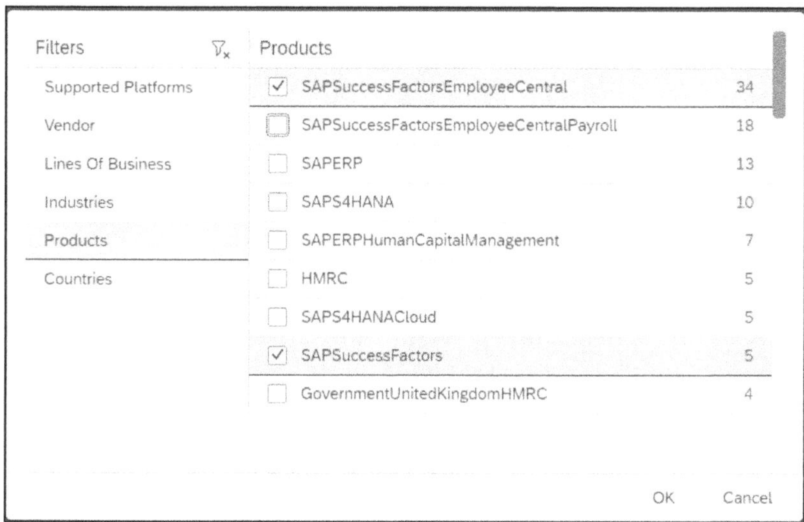

Figure 3.25 Filtering SAP SuccessFactors Packages

Most packages are self-explanatory. In addition, you can further explore and consume their content as already discussed in Section 3.2.

SAP SuccessFactors Adapter

Most iFlows included in this package make use of SAP SuccessFactors adapter for Cloud Integration. This special adapter was developed to connect solely to SAP SuccessFactors applications. Refer to Chapter 1, Section 1.3.3, to read more about Cloud Integration's connectivity options.

3.4.2 Content for SAP Cloud for Customer

SAP Cloud for Customer is SAP's cloud customer relationship management (CRM) solution, which brings marketing, sales, commerce, and customer service together.

As a cloud-based CRM system, SAP Cloud for Customer needs to interact with a number of other systems to ensure that accounts, materials, price conditions, and other master data are in sync.

Currently, SAP Integration Content Catalog provides three main content packages related to SAP Cloud for Customer. These packages include content that supports the following use cases:

- SAP Cloud for Customer integration with SAP ERP
- SAP Cloud for Customer integration with SAP CRM
- SAP Cloud for Customer integration with SAP Marketing Cloud

To further illustrate how the integration packages for SAP Cloud for Customer can be used, let's dig a bit deeper into a use case for integrating SAP Cloud for Customer with SAP ERP.

SAP Cloud for Customer Integration with SAP ERP

As mentioned earlier, SAP Cloud for Customer must exchange master and transactional data with SAP ERP. In terms of master data, in most use cases, SAP ERP acts as the master system. As a result, master data is synchronized one way—from SAP ERP to SAP Cloud for Customer. In addition, transactional data, such as opportunity, pricing, and quotes, is also exchanged between these platforms. An overview of the data exchanged between these two systems is shown in Figure 3.26.

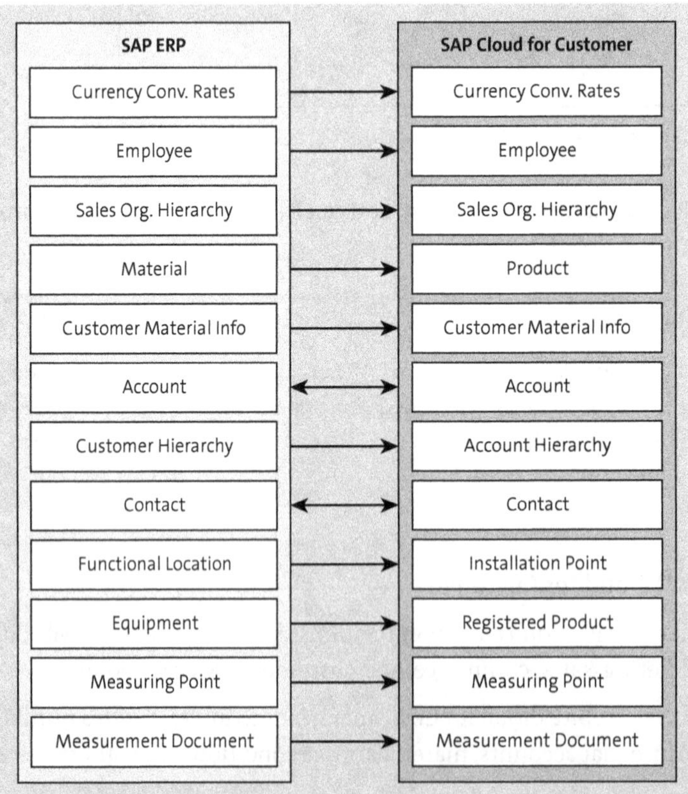

Figure 3.26 Master Data Synchronization between SAP Cloud for Customer and SAP ERP

Through SAP Integration Content Catalog, SAP provides the needed iFlows to synchronize your on-premise SAP ERP and SAP Cloud for Customer systems. The iFlows cover the scope of business objects shown in Figure 3.26.

SOAP Adapter

From a technical perspective, the SOAP adapter is used to integrate Cloud Integration and SAP Cloud for Customer. The consumer of the integration package needs to perform configuration tasks under the **Adapter Specific** tab of the concerned iFlow, as explained in Section 3.3.3. Refer to Chapter 1, Section 1.3.3, to read more about Cloud Integration connectivity options.

To discover SAP Cloud for Customer–related integration packages, you'll need to apply a filter on the main page of SAP Integration Content Catalog by selecting the **SAP Hybris Cloud for Customer** entry from the **Product** dropdown list.

3.4.3 Content for Integrating with SAP Customer Experience

SAP Customer Experience is a family of cloud-based solutions that includes the following products:

- SAP Commerce Cloud
- SAP Customer Data Cloud
- SAP Sales Cloud
- SAP Service Cloud
- SAP Marketing Cloud

Among this list of products, SAP Sales Cloud and SAP Service Cloud are included under the umbrella of SAP Cloud for Customer. The integration content for SAP Cloud for Customer was already covered in Section 3.4.2. In this section, we'll explore the content provided for SAP Commerce Cloud, SAP Marketing Cloud, SAP Subscription Billing, and SAP Billing and Revenue Innovation Management (formerly SAP Hybris Revenue and SAP Hybris Billing).

Note

For the most up-to-date information about the current integration packages for SAP Commerce Cloud, SAP Subscription Billing (or SAP Billing and Revenue Innovation Management), and SAP Marketing Cloud, refer to the **Documents** tab within each package, which generally contains integration guides and various informative documents. You can also refer to the SAP Community site for more information. Note that while the billing and revenue functionality was part of the old SAP Hybris suite, this functionality isn't part of the new SAP Customer Experience suite.

SAP Commerce Cloud

The integration content for SAP Commerce Cloud/SAP Cloud for Customer enables you to perform the following activities:

- Synchronize customer data from SAP Commerce Cloud to SAP Cloud for Customer.
- Synchronize customer service ticket data between the two systems to more efficiently connect customers with service or sales agents.

After SAP Commerce Cloud and SAP Cloud for Customer are connected, customer service representatives (agents) can provide service through the ticket or directly over the phone, all while accessing the same storefront as the customer, through the Assisted Service Module (ASM) for SAP Commerce Cloud for exceptional service and sales assistance on the spot.

At the time of this writing, the SAP Customer Engagement Center Integration with SAP Commerce integration package is an example package used to synchronize data between SAP Commerce Cloud and SAP Customer Engagement Center integration. To illustrate some common use cases, the following business objects are exchanged:

- Customer address replication from SAP Commerce Cloud to SAP Customer Engagement Center
- Customer replication from SAP Commerce Cloud to SAP Customer Engagement Center
- Basic sales order details replication from SAP Commerce Cloud to SAP Customer Engagement Center for indexing

SAP Subscription Billing and SAP Billing and Revenue Innovation Management

At the time of this writing, the Integration with SAP Subscription Billing integration package is an example package that provides capabilities for processing bills originating from SAP Subscription Billing in SAP S/4HANA for billing and revenue innovation management. Common use cases include the following:

- Extracting billing documents from SAP Subscription Billing to SAP S/4HANA
- Sending back customer IDs from SAP S/4HANA to SAP Subscription Billing when customers are created or updated
- Extracting customers from SAP Subscription Billing and then replicating them to SAP S/4HANA
- Replicating customers from SAP S/4HANA to SAP Subscription Billing

SAP Marketing Cloud

At the time of this writing, the available integration content covers many integration scenarios for SAP Marketing Cloud, including the following:

- **Master data and basic replication**
  The accounts, contacts, individual customers, leads activities, and opportunities are replicated from SAP Cloud for Customer to SAP Marketing Cloud.
- **Call center scenarios**
  This scenario creates a call center campaign in SAP Marketing Cloud and executes the campaign in SAP Cloud for Customer.
- **Lead management scenarios**
  Any lead that is converted into an opportunity further creates an opportunity interaction in SAP Marketing Cloud. These leads and opportunities in SAP Cloud for Customer also contain information about the corresponding campaigns from SAP Marketing Cloud.

Furthermore, several integration packages cover a number of use cases with SAP Marketing:

- SAP S/4HANA Enterprise Management on-premise – SAP Marketing Cloud integration
- SAP Marketing Cloud – SAP Customer Relationship Management (SAP CRM) integration
- SAP Cloud for Customer – SAP Marketing integration
- SAP Marketing Cloud – SAP Customer Attribution integration
- SAP Marketing Cloud – SAP ERP order and business partner integration
- SAP Marketing Cloud – Twitter integration
- SAP Marketing Cloud – Content Management System integration
- SAP Marketing – Google AdWords Paid Search integration
- SAP Marketing Cloud – Twitter integration admin
- SAP Marketing Cloud – Facebook integration admin
- SAP Marketing Cloud – Facebook integration
- SAP Marketing – Google Analytics integration

3.4.4 Content for Integrating with SAP Business Network

SAP Business Network is a cloud-based procurement solution that allows you to locate new suppliers, streamline transaction processes, and save costs. One of the largest trading partner communities, SAP Business Network provides connectivity and online services to organizations engaged in business-to-business (B2B) e-commerce.

With SAP Business Network, buyers and suppliers can conduct business with each other over the internet and access each other's services. SAP Business Network contains additional functionalities such as directory services, reporting tools, supplier tools, payment processing, and sourcing.

To illustrate a common use case, customers can create purchase orders, goods receipts, invoices, and so on through SAP Business Network and have these transactions synchronized back to their own (on-premise) SAP Business Suite operational purchasing or supplier-side processes. An overview of these common use cases between SAP ERP Materials Management (MM) and SAP Supplier Relationship Management (SAP SRM) is shown in Figure 3.27.

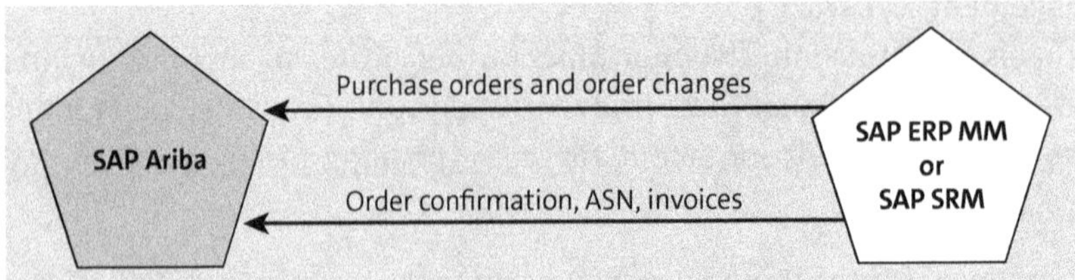

Figure 3.27 Integration Use Cases between SAP Ariba and SAP ERP or SAP SRM

Currently, one package is available to cover the need for integrating SAP Business Network with your existing SAP ERP using Cloud Integration. This content package integrates and automates your SAP Business Suite operational purchasing processes or supplier-side processes with SAP Business Network.

For buyers, the scope of this mediated connection based on the SAP Business Network integration for SAP Business Suite Add-On 1.0 includes the following capabilities:

- Purchase order and invoice automation for MM and SAP SRM classic
- Discount management integration (optional)

The scope supports selected aspects of the following procure-to-pay end-to-end business scenarios:

- Self-service and indirect procurement
- Direct procurement
- Service procurement
- Invoice management
- Collaborative Supply Chain 1.0 with schedule agreement release order processing

For suppliers, the scope of this mediated connection, based on the SAP Business Network integration with SAP Business Suite Add-On 1.0, includes the following:

- Sales order and billing integration with SAP Business Network for SAP ERP Sales and Distribution (SAP SD)

Note

From a technical perspective, the SOAP adapter is used to integrate Cloud Integration with SAP Ariba. The consumer of the integration package must perform several configuration tasks under the **Adapter Specific** tab of the concerned iFlow. Refer to Chapter 1, Section 1.3.3, to read more about the Cloud Integration connectivity options.

To discover SAP Ariba–related integration packages, you'll need to apply a filter on the main page of SAP Integration Content Catalog by selecting **SAP Business Network with SAP Business Suite** from the **Product** dropdown list.

3.4.5 Content for Globalization Scenarios

Recently, many government agencies have moved from traditional paper-based documents to digital or electronic documents. As such, businesses dealing with these government agencies (e.g., the tax office) must quickly adapt their internal processes to comply.

For multinational companies that must, for instance, report their taxes in many countries, one challenge will be sending documents to the necessary tax offices, all in different countries with different formats and standards, from the same source application (SAP ERP system). Another aspect to consider, in most cases, is that the transmission of these government-related documents requires a high level of security.

The mapping of the source application's messages to the required government formats, and the transmission of these message is a classic integration scenario. The need to transfer electronic documents to government agencies around the world is a use case Cloud Integration covers with its integration content for globalization. This content is also known as the eDocument Framework.

The eDocument Framework provides a generic approach for creating, processing, and managing electronic documents. The framework supports handling country-specific requirements for electronic documents with regard to the format of messages, security requirements, and processing steps in end-to-end integration scenarios. The source data for the documents may originate in any application that implements the web services available in the iFlows. At the time of this writing, a number of integration packages are provided in Cloud Integration to support the eDocument Framework for Chile, Italy, Spain, Peru, The Netherlands, Great Britain, Colombia, Germany, India, Mexico, the United States, and Hungary.

With these packages, you won't need to spend time trying to figure out how to perform mappings or finding which security levels are required to comply with government-specific electronic document formats. You can simply reuse the provided integration content to reduce implementation time and costs.

To find a particular eDocument Framework package for a specific country, you'll need to apply a filter on the main SAP Integration Content Catalog page by selecting a country (e.g., **Netherlands**) from the **Country** dropdown list.

3.4.6 Content for ELSTER Integration

ELSTER (i.e., electronic tax declaration) is a German online tax office system designed by the Federal Central Tax Office (Bundeszentralamt für Steuern) to enable anyone to submit their tax returns online.

A number of businesses are also obliged to use ELSTER to submit their monthly employee tax statements and value-added tax (VAT) returns. As discussed in Section 3.4.5, submitting documents to governmental institutions electronically is more effective than traditional documents and is a growing trend around the world. ELSTER is the German tax equivalent for this growing electronic document trend.

Because most businesses typically use an ERP system (e.g., SAP) to maintain sales information as well as HR data, automatically retrieving the relevant data from the ERP system and submitting this data to the German tax authorities makes sense. You'll need to establish an integration from the ERP system on one side and the tax authority's system on the other. Given that many businesses use SAP both for finance- and HR-related processes, Cloud Integration provides standard content to help SAP customers easily integrate with the German tax authorities and therefore save costs. Cloud Integration provides integration content that cover the following areas:

- Sending HR tax data
- Sending finance tax data
- Sending tax data to the German tax office

You can find all ELSTER-relevant packages in Cloud Integration on the **Discover** page by selecting **ELSTER** in the **Products** filter, as shown in Figure 3.28.

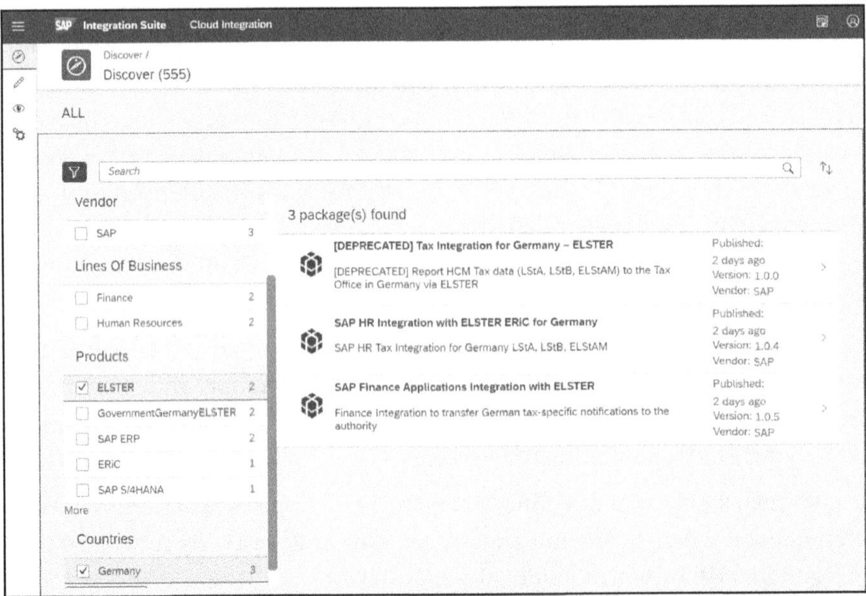

Figure 3.28 Integration Content Packages for ELSTER

We'll discuss the two packages shown in Figure 3.28 further in this section. Note that all these iFlows make use of the ELSTER adapter, mentioned in Chapter 1, which was specially developed for this purpose.

> **Note**
>
> To establish a connection between Cloud Integration and the tax agency's servers, you must obtain several certificates and then deploy these certificates to the Cloud Integration tenant.

Sending HR Tax Data

The first iFlow shown in Figure 3.28 is for exchanging HR notifications with the tax authority in Germany. To exchange tax notifications, ELSTER Rich Client (ERiC) components are used for signing, encryption, and transport.

For the transfer, the integration package applies specific requirements for message security, which are set by the German authorities. Therefore, the integration package uses the mandatory ERiC Libraries. The functionality is valid for German customers only. As a prerequisite, at a minimum, you must have an SAP ERP 6.00 on-premise system and Employee Central Payroll (ECP). As shown in Figure 3.29, this flow uses the ELSTER adapter to send data to the tax authority.

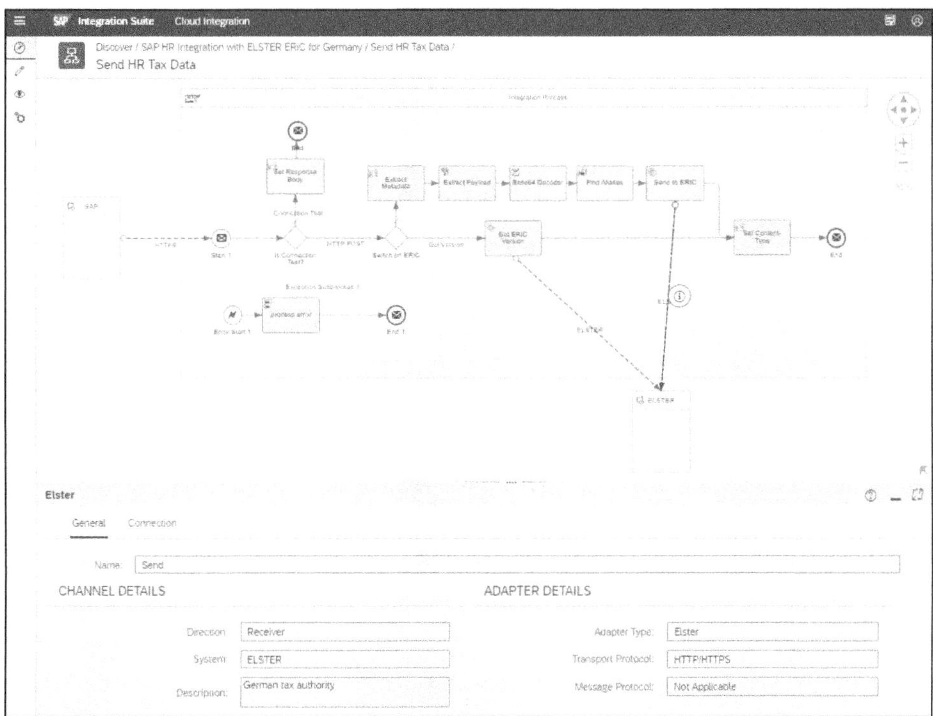

Figure 3.29 Sending Data to the Tax Authority Using the ELSTER Adapter

Transferring Tax Notifications to the German Tax Office

This integration package enables you to transfer German tax-specific notifications to the tax authority. To transfer this data, the related iFlow applies specific requirements for message-level security, which are set by German authorities using ELSTER. The package uses a mandatory ERiC (Elster Rich Client Development Toolkit) Library.

This package includes a single iFlow for exchanging finance notifications with the tax German tax office using ELSTER. As shown in Figure 3.30, this flow doesn't use the ELSTER adapter to send data to the tax authority; instead, a plain HTTP adapter is used (with HTTPS as a transport protocol).

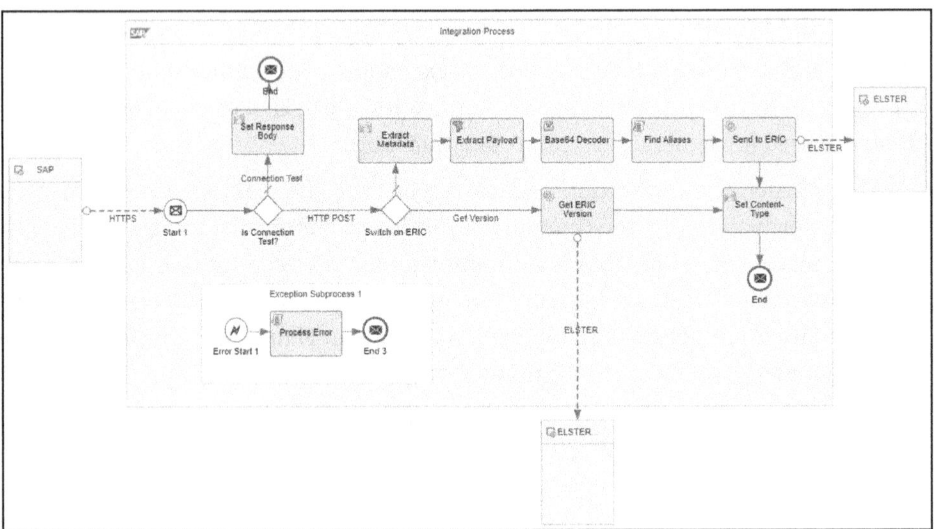

Figure 3.30 Sending Data to the Tax Authority Using the HTTP Adapter

3.4.7 Content for Salesforce Integration

Salesforce is a cloud-based customer relationship management (CRM) solution that provides applications focused on sales, customer service, marketing automation, e-commerce, analytics, and application development.

Several businesses use both SAP ERP and Salesforce for their day-to-day activities. In such cases, the business processes span across SAP and Salesforce. To ensure the good execution of these processes, integration needs to be developed to exchange and synchronize data between SAP S/4HANA, SAP S/4HANA Cloud, or SAP ERP, and Salesforce. There are some packages in SAP Integration Content Catalog that can be reused for this purpose. At the time of publication, the following packages are available:

- SAP ERP Integration with Salesforce
- SAP S/4HANA Cloud Integration with Salesforce
- SAP S/4HANA Integration with Salesforce

Example packages are shown in Figure 3.31.

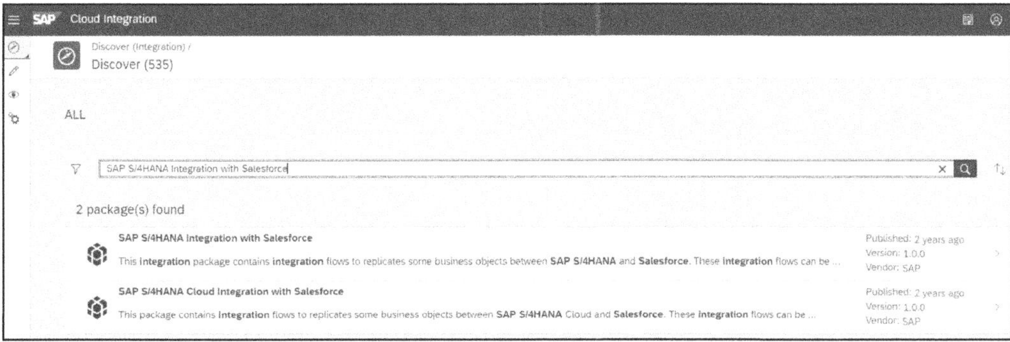

Figure 3.31 Integration Content Packages for Integrating with Salesforce.

Let's look into these packages to get an idea of the included use cases.

SAP ERP Integration with Salesforce

This package supports the integration of some business processes between your Salesforce and your SAP ERP applications. The included iFlows can be used as a starting point to accelerate your integration journey between SAP ERP and Salesforce. It supports the following business transactions:

- **Receive Product Availability from SAP ERP**
- **Receive Sales Order History from SAP ERP**
- **Replicate Account from SAP ERP to Salesforce**
- **Replicate Product from SAP ERP to Salesforce**
- **Replicate Sales Contract from Salesforce to SAP ERP**
- **Replicate Sales Order from Salesforce to SAP ERP**
- **Replicate Sales Order from SAP ERP to Salesforce**
- **Replicate Sales Prices from SAP ERP to Salesforce**
- **Update Account from Salesforce to SAP ERP**

SAP S/4HANA Cloud Integration with Salesforce

This package supports the integration of some business processes between your Salesforce and your SAP S/4HANA Cloud applications. The included iFlows can be used as a starting point to accelerate your integration journey between SAP S/4HANA Cloud and Salesforce. It supports the following business transactions:

- **Replicate sales orders from Salesforce to SAP S/4HANA Cloud**
- **Replicate sales contract from Salesforce to SAP S/4HANA Cloud**
- **Receive sales order history from SAP S/4HANA Cloud**

- **Update account from Salesforce to SAP S/4HANA Cloud**
- **Receive sales pricing from SAP S/4HANA Cloud**
- **Receive availability information from SAP S/4HANA Cloud**
- **Replicate sales orders from SAP S/4HANA Cloud to Salesforce**
- **Replicate account from SAP S/4HANA Cloud to Salesforce**
- **Replicate product master data from SAP S/4HANA Cloud to Salesforce**

SAP S/4HANA Integration with Salesforce

This package supports the integration of some business processes between your Salesforce and your SAP S/4HANA applications. The included iFlows can be used as a starting point to accelerate your integration journey between SAP S/4HANA and Salesforce. It supports the following business transactions:

- **Replicate sales orders from Salesforce to SAP S/4HANA**
- **Replicate sales contract from Salesforce to SAP S/4HANA**
- **Receive sales order history from SAP S/4HANA**
- **Update account from Salesforce to SAP S/4HANA**
- **Receive sales pricing from SAP S/4HANA**
- **Receive availability information from SAP S/4HANA**
- **Replicate sales orders from SAP S/4HANA to Salesforce**
- **Replicate account from SAP S/4HANA to Salesforce**
- **Replicate product master data from SAP S/4HANA to Salesforce**

3.5 Creating Your Own Content Package

In the previous section, you learned about the prepackaged content delivered by SAP in SAP Integration Content Catalog. In this section, we'll cover how you can create your own content. If the existing prepackaged content doesn't meet your business needs, you can create your own package that can be used and reused specifically by team members within your organization.

The first step to publishing your own content is to create the desired integration content. The process of creating your own content was discussed when creating your first iFlow in Chapter 2. Furthermore, Chapter 4 will walk you through the process of creating different integration content artifacts. Therefore, we won't go into the development details in this section and instead focus on creating an integration package.

To create an integration package, follow these steps:

1. Open the **Design** page (refer to Figure 3.8).
2. Select the **Create** option to create an integration package, as shown in Figure 3.32.

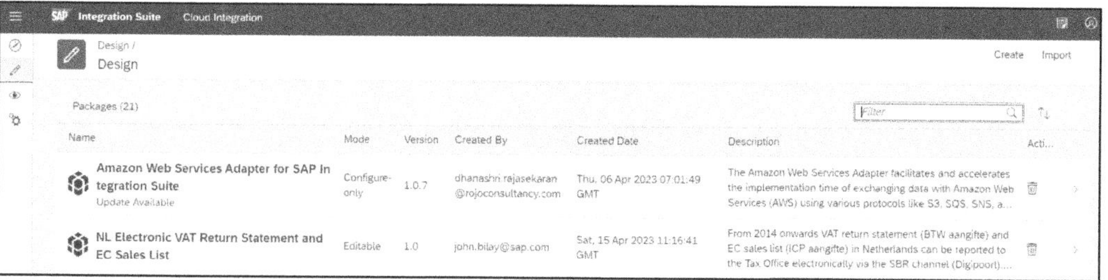

Figure 3.32 Creating an Integration Package

3. On the next screen, specify the name for the new integration package. Additional metadata details, such as the version, owner, mode, description, tags, products, industries, line of business, country, and keywords, can be provided. Some of this metadata is shown in Figure 3.33. You can maintain this metadata in several tabs such as the **Overview** and **Tags** tabs. Keep in mind that this metadata is important to better classify content and allow consumers to find content easily. Therefore, providing as much detail as possible is important.

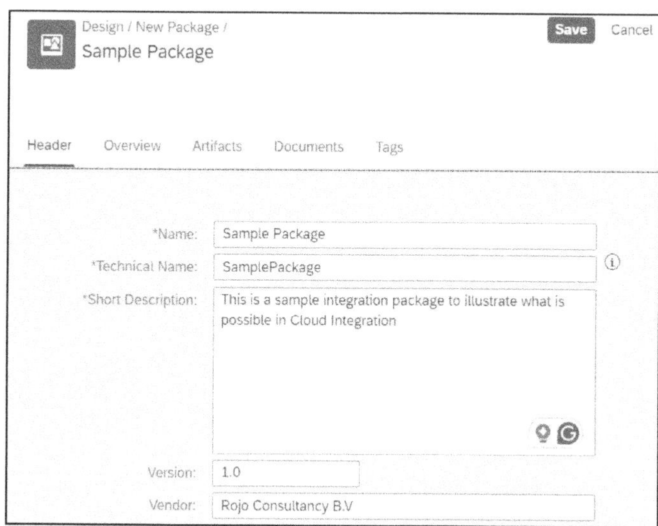

Figure 3.33 Specifying Details in the New Integration Package

4. Save the package by clicking the **Save** button, as shown in Figure 3.33.
5. Under the **Artifacts** tab, click **Add** and choose an artifact of type **Integration Flow**, **REST API**, **Message Mapping**, **SOAP API**, **Value Mapping**, **OData API**, **Script Collection**, or **Integration Adapter** to add it to the integration package, as shown in Figure 3.34.
6. Artifacts can be added to the newly created package by creating them from scratch if they don't already exist. Alternatively, existing artifacts can also be imported. These two options are made possible using the **Create** or **Upload** radio buttons, as shown in Figure 3.35.

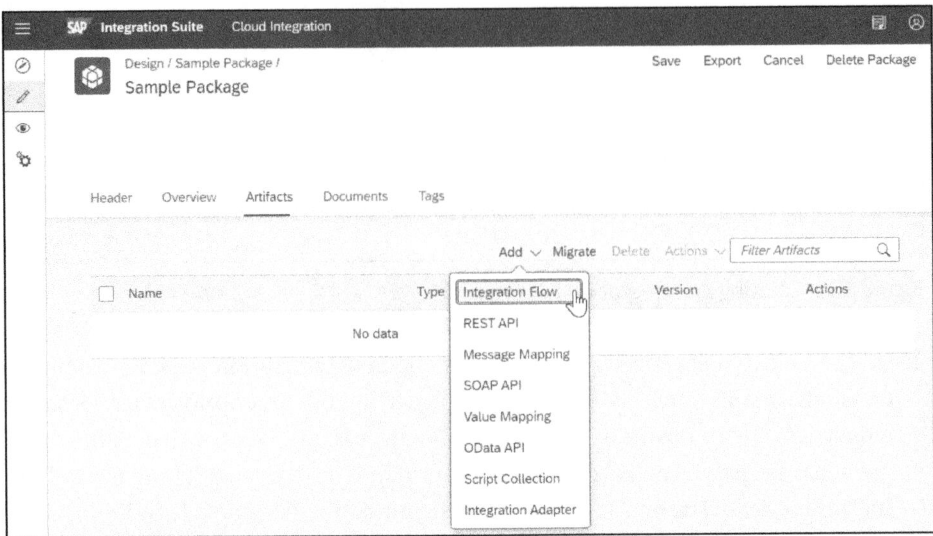

Figure 3.34 Adding Artifacts to an Integration Package

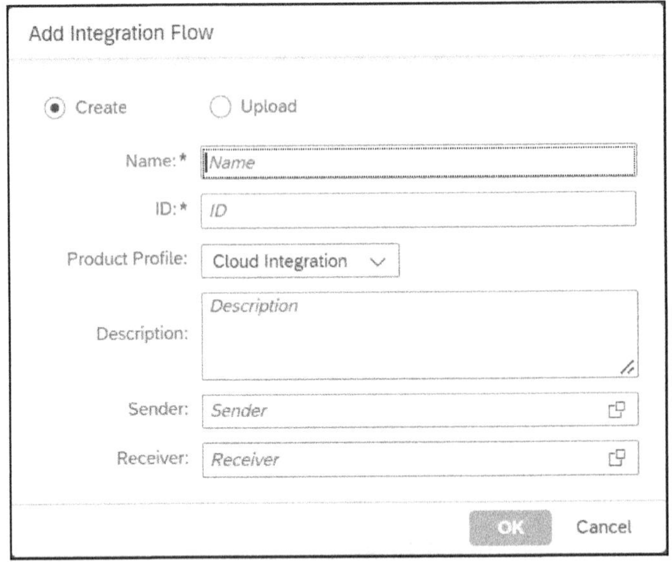

Figure 3.35 Creating or Importing a Process Integration Artifact

7. To provide documentation for the integration package, click on **Add** under the **Documents** tab, as shown in Figure 3.36. Documents of type **File** or **URL** can be added to this tab.

After packaging and saving the integration content, this integration package will be available in your own design space and can therefore be used by team members of your organization.

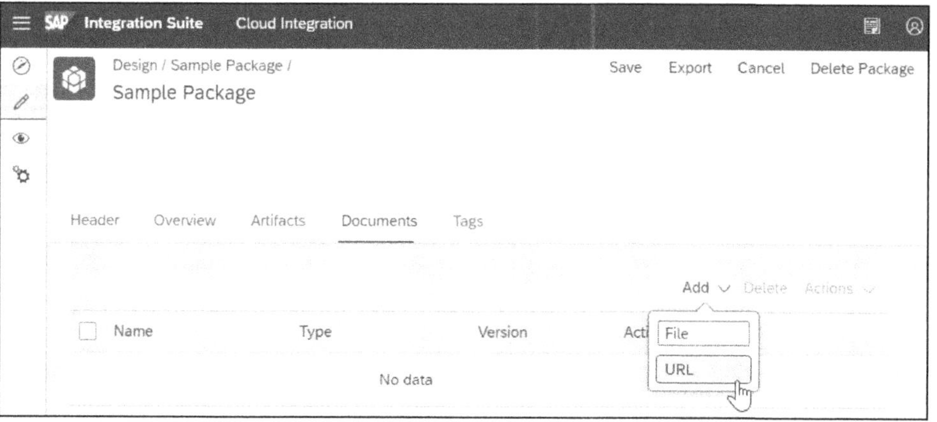

Figure 3.36 Adding a File or URL to a Content Package

> **Note**
>
> A content package is automatically locked against modification from other users when someone is in the process of editing the package. The package is only released for modification after the content package has been saved. If the session times out, or if the browser closes while you're still working on your integration package, the content package will remain locked until saved, canceled, or deleted by the lock owner.

Currently, only SAP is allowed to publish data to SAP Integration Content Catalog, so packages created by customers or partners are for internal use only and can't be directly leveraged by other customers. Different SAP Partners have listed their prepackaged integration content on SAP Integration Content Catalog, but you'll need to contact the specific SAP Partner to purchase and obtain an archive of the package.

3.6 Adapters to Third-Party Applications for SAP Integration Suite

Most customers may find themselves needing to integrate to non-SAP cloud-based applications. Cloud Integration has various adapters for third-party applications. At the time of publication, the following adapters are included:

- Salesforce Adapter for SAP Integration Suite
- Microsoft Dynamics CRM Adapter for SAP Integration Suite
- Amazon Web Services Adapter for SAP Integration Suite
- Workday Adapter for SAP Integration Suite
- ServiceNow Adapter for SAP Integration Suite
- Splunk Adapter for SAP Integration Suite
- Azure Adapter for SAP Integration Suite

- SugarCRM Adapter for SAP Integration Suite
- Slack Adapter for SAP Integration Suite

Note that depending on the type of Cloud Integration license used by the customer, some of these adapters might not be included or might need to be purchased separately.

Furthermore, this list is growing rapidly and provides an alternative to Open Connectors (discussed in Chapter 9). These adapters can also be found in SAP Integration Content Catalog. To illustrate its usage, we'll use the Salesforce Adapter for SAP Integration Suite.

As shown in Figure 3.37, this package contains details about the functionality and capabilities of the Salesforce adapter. It also describes how to download the adapter and deploy it to your Cloud Integration content. The package contains a link that redirects the user to SAP Service Marketplace (see Figure 3.38).

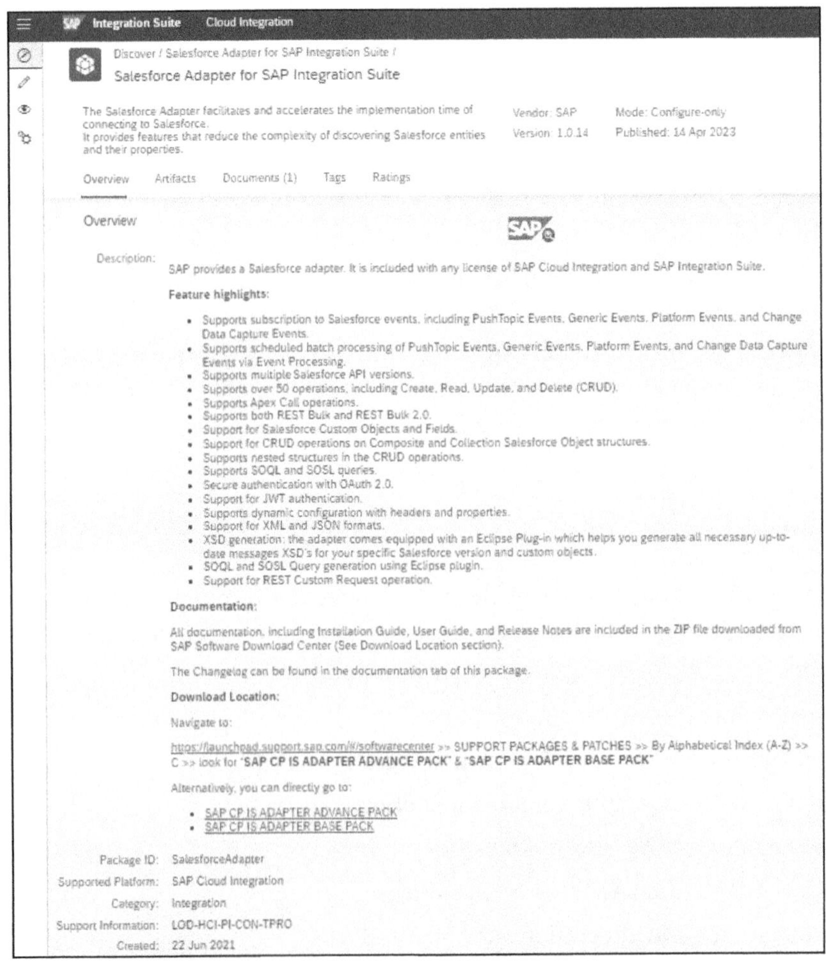

Figure 3.37 Package for the Salesforce Adapter for SAP Integration Suite

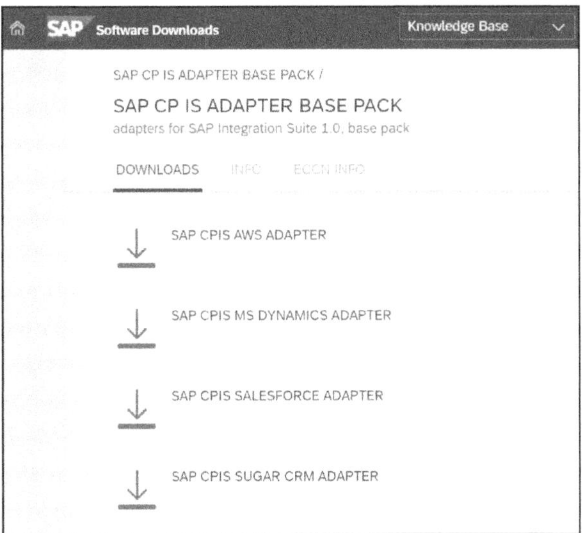

Figure 3.38 SAP Service Marketplace Page to Download Adapters

After downloading the adapter's ZIP file, the adapter files and various documents that describe the installation steps can be extracted. Figure 3.39 shows the extracted adapter file name **salesforce.esa**. This file can be imported into your Integration package as one of the artifacts.

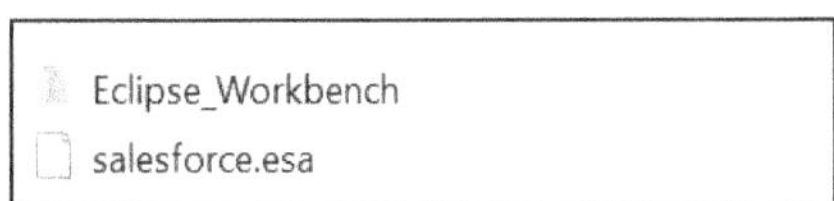

Figure 3.39 The Adapter File to Be Installed in Cloud Integration

The following lists the steps to be to install the adapter:

1. Open an integration package in Cloud Integration.
2. Under the **Artifacts** tab, click **Add**, and choose an artifact of type **Data Integration** to add the adapter to the integration package, as shown in Figure 3.40.
3. Navigate to the location where the adapter file was extracted on your local system, and select the file named **salesforce.esa**.
4. After the adapter has been added to Cloud Integration, it becomes available to be used by any iFlow. It's important, however, to deploy the adapter before it can be used in runtime. For that, select the **Deploy** option, as shown in Figure 3.41, before the adapter can be used in runtime.

After a successful installation and deployment of the adapter, you can use it in any of your own iFlows or any integration content related to Salesforce. These integration packages can also be found in SAP Integration Content Catalog, as we discussed in Section 3.4.7.

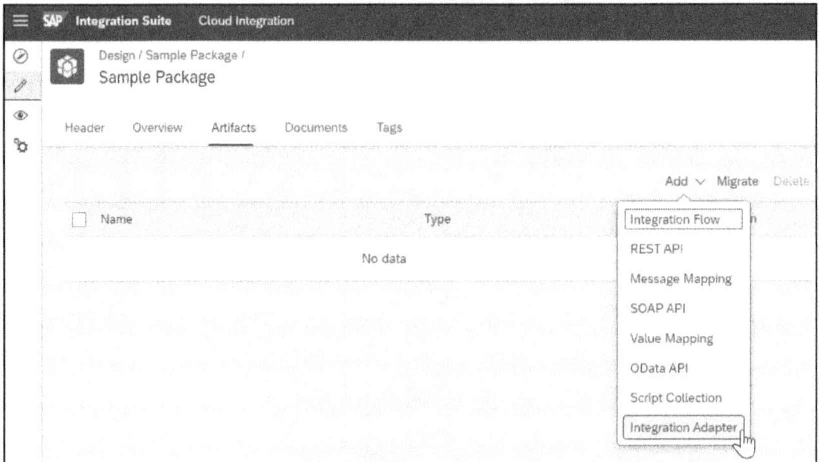

Figure 3.40 Adding an Adapter to Cloud Integration

Figure 3.41 Deploy the Salesforce Adapter to Cloud Integration

3.7 Summary

In this chapter, we introduced you to the capabilities and features of SAP Integration Content Catalog in Cloud Integration. A systematic guide was used to demonstrate how to consume the contents of the catalog. You also learned about how terms and conditions can affect and restrict the way prepackaged content is consumed.

This chapter then explored the prepackaged content that SAP delivers in SAP Integration Content Catalog to speed up implementation time and save costs related to performing integration with SAP's most-used cloud-based applications. SAP Integration Content Catalog is expected to grow and have new packages added on a regular basis. Therefore, be sure to first check SAP Integration Content Catalog before developing your own integration scenarios from scratch to save time and costs.

In the next chapter, we'll further explore how Cloud Integration empowers developers to create their own basic integrations when prepackaged content won't suffice.

Chapter 4
Basic Integration Scenarios

If the prepackaged integration content won't suffice, developers can use Cloud Integration to create their own integrations. This chapter explores these capabilities by taking a closer look at several common concrete integration challenges and showing you how to solve them.

In the previous chapter, you learned how to access prepackaged integration content. However, in many cases, you may have individual integration needs that simply can't be fulfilled by an already existing package, or too much effort might be required to adjust a predelivered scenario to the required functionality. Fortunately, Cloud Integration comes with a web-based development environment that allows you to model unique scenarios from scratch. We'll explore the options for developing your own custom integration scenarios in this chapter, followed by three more chapters drilling into more specialized topics. In this chapter, we'll look closely at Cloud Integration 's data model, how content enrichment works by invoking OData services, and how to add mappings and routers to an integration flow (iFlow).

4.1 Working with Cloud Integration's Data Model

Before we dive into a concrete modeling exercise, let's briefly discuss some terms and fundamental concepts behind Cloud Integration's development and runtime environment. Figure 4.1 shows a basic iFlow in Cloud Integration's web-based environment where a message is being transferred from a sender to a receiver via Cloud Integration. In this case, you'll see the sender component ❶, the Simple Object Access Protocol (SOAP) channel ❷, the Apache Camel (where message processing is performed) ❸, the Secure Shell File Transfer Protocol (SFTP) channel ❹, and the receiver component ❺.

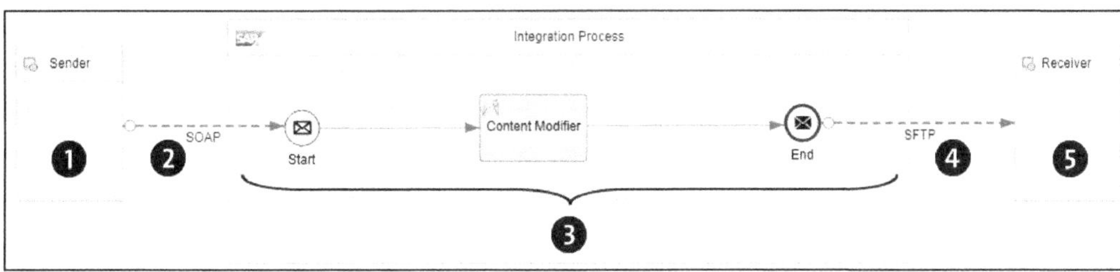

Figure 4.1 A Basic iFlow

The overall representation of iFlows is based on Business Process Model and Notation (BPMN), a widely adopted Object Management Group (OMG) standard for graphically depicting processes. Although the roots of BPMN are in the business process domain (as the name indicates), the language is expressive enough to be useful for integration processes as well. Thus, SAP relies on BPMN as the lingua franca for describing all kinds of processes. BPMN is broadly used in SAP systems—for example, in SAP Solution Manager, SAP Process Integration, and SAP Business Process Management (SAP BPM), to name a few.

On the left side of Figure 4.1, you'll see the sender component representing the sender of a message. The receiver is shown on the far right. Both sender and receiver are represented by pools (the rectangles labeled **Sender** and **Receiver**, respectively). A *pool* is a term adopted from the BPMN standard and typically represents a participant in collaborative scenarios in which several processes work together to fulfill a certain goal. A third pool, labeled **Integration Process**, shown in the middle of Figure 4.1, represents the Cloud Integration server where message processing happens.

The **Sender/Receiver** pools are connected via dashed arrows, or *message flows*, representing the technical connectivity between the respective participants. A dedicated label details how the two are connected: the sender and the iFlow via SOAP and the iFlow with the receiver via SFTP. Dedicated channels take over the responsibility of implementing and "speaking in" the desired protocols.

What's left is the integration process in the middle, which contains details about the message processing steps. The circle on the left of the flow containing a white envelope is a *start event* (again, BPMN nomenclature). This event expresses the start of the message processing sequence. The envelope indicates that the start of the process is caused by the reception of a message. After the flow has received the message, the system continues with the content modifier step because they are connected with a directed solid arrow, also known as a *sequence flow*. The arrow indicates the sequence in which steps are executed.

The rounded rectangle step is called a *task*, which is a type of activity that is executed during runtime. In our example, the content modifier changes the message content, as you'll see later in this chapter. After the task has finished its modifications, the process continues downstream. Again, just follow the sequence flow to the circle on the right, which contains a black envelope and represents an *end event* (circles denote events in BPMN).

Black symbols and white symbols in events have special meanings: white means waiting for the event to happen, and black means that the process itself initiates the event specified by the symbol inside the circle and immediately continues. In this example, the process waits for an incoming message at the beginning (white envelope) and sends a message after the process has reached the end of the flow (black envelope). The sent message is then transported via SFTP to the receiver. This process is expressed by the message flow from the end event to the **Receiver** pool, as shown in Figure 4.1.

4.1.1 Message Processing: The Apache Camel Framework

Let's concentrate on the message processing part of Cloud Integration for a moment. As you now know, from a modeling perspective, the flow is based on BPMN. But how is the iFlow interpreted and executed during runtime? For this purpose, Cloud Integration relies on an open-source integration framework called Apache Camel. To understand the inner workings of Cloud Integration, you should be familiar with the inner workings of Apache Camel. Notice the additional names for message processing shown in Figure 4.1: In Apache Camel, the analogous terms for the handling of messages are *route* or *processor chain*. We won't go into the complete details of the Apache Camel framework in this book. In this chapter, we'll only concentrate on the functions and features of Apache Camel that are relevant for the scenario we're going to discuss. However, Claus Ibsen and Jonathan Anstey have written an excellent book about Apache Camel called *Camel in Action, Second Edition* (Manning Publications, 2018). This book is a helpful reference for all detailed Apache Camel questions you might have. Another valuable source of information for the Apache Camel framework is the online documentation found at *http://s-prs.co/v576005*.

Note

Cloud Integration is currently based on Apache Camel version 3.0. Be aware that you can't just use any Apache Camel feature, property, or header in Cloud Integration. You should only use the features, properties, and headers that are explicitly supported by Cloud Integration, as described in the documentation found at *http://s-prs.co/v576006*.

So, what exactly is Apache Camel? A message routing and mediation engine, Apache Camel is payload agnostic, which means you can feed the engine any data, in any format, and Apache Camel will forward the data to the right receivers depending on the modeled route. As long as you don't need to access the message's content (e.g., for routing or transformation), Apache Camel can handle any message format. However, messages must follow a basic structure to be usable by Apache Camel, as shown in Figure 4.2.

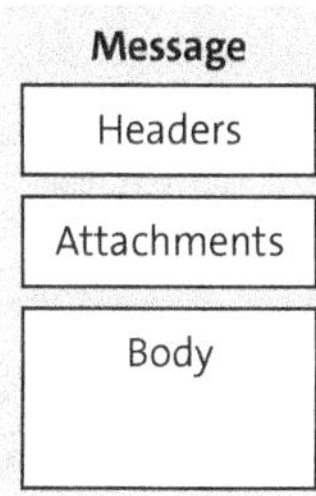

Figure 4.2 Apache Camel Message Model

Apache Camel messages consist of headers, a body containing the raw data (the payload), and (optional) attachments. Messages are uniquely identified by an identifier of the type `java.lang.String` (not shown in Figure 4.2). Headers contain additional values associated with the message, such as the sender identifier, hints about content encoding, and authentication information. This information is included in the form of name-value pairs and is stored in the message as a map. The header name is a unique, case-insensitive string, whereas the value is of the type `java.lang.Object`. Almost anything can be added as an object to the header. The same is applicable for the body, which is also of the type `java.lang.Object`. Attachments are typically used for web services and email components and can transport additional data as separate items, if necessary.

During message processing, Apache Camel requires a dedicated container for the message. This container, called an *exchange*, holds additional data besides the message. The exchange is passed along, step by step, in the processor chain, and every step has access to all the information the exchange carries. Consider an exchange as a kind of global storage for the message's route while the message is being processed. The structure of an exchange is shown in Figure 4.3.

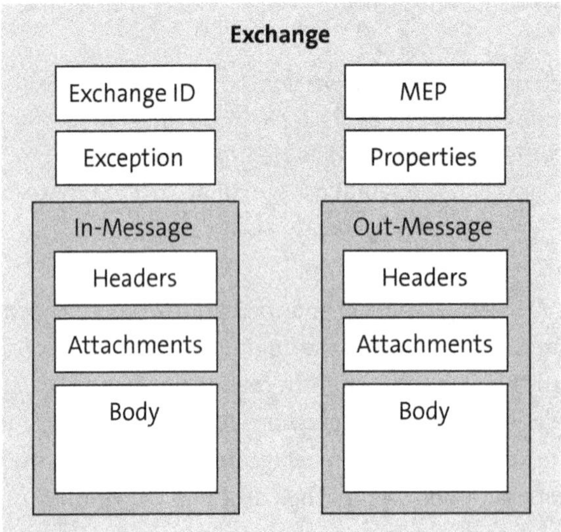

Figure 4.3 An Exchange

Let's briefly review the parts that make up an exchange:

- **Exchange ID**
  A unique ID that identifies the exchange.
- **MEP**
  This field refers to the message exchange pattern (MEP), which is used to differentiate between request-response and one-way messaging between the systems. It can contain one of two possible values: **InOnly** and **InOut**.

  - **InOnly**: The route handles a one-way message where the sender doesn't wait for a reply from the receiver. Thus, the exchange carries an *in* message *only*. A scenario where a message travels in one direction only and where no response message is expected during the communication is also known as *asynchronous message handling*.
  - **InOut**: The route handles a request-response message. The sender expects a reply from the route, which will be stored as an out-message in the exchange. This behavior is also known as *synchronous message handling*. We'll revisit asynchronous and synchronous message handling in Chapter 5, Section 5.3.

- **Exception**
  If an error occurs during message processing, the reason for the error is stored in the **Exception** field of the exchange.
- **Properties**
  A form of temporary storage where process steps can store data in addition to the header area in the message. Properties can contain global-level information. Developers can store and retrieve properties at any point during the lifetime of an exchange.

Difference between Headers and Properties

Note that headers are part of a message and are propagated or transferred to a receiver. On the other side, properties last for the entire duration of an exchange but aren't transferred to a receiver.

A big difference regarding message handling within Cloud Integration, when compared to SAP Process Integration, is the flexible pipeline concept, which is the foundation of Apache Camel. In SAP Process Integration, you basically have three fundamental steps:

1. Receiver determination
2. Interface determination
3. Mapping

In addition, the sequence of these three steps is fixed; you can't have, for example, a mapping step before an interface determination step. The result is a rather static message-processing environment. With Cloud Integration, this message processing changes significantly. You have many more steps at your disposal, and you can use them in (almost) any sequence that your scenario requires. We'll demonstrate the benefits of this flexibility in later chapters when we address more complex integration scenarios.

As described earlier in Chapter 2, Section 2.1, the Apache Camel framework fits into the overall architecture of Cloud Integration (see also Figure 4.6 in Chapter 2, Section 2.1.5).

4.1.2 Working with Apache Camel's Message Model

Now that you have a basic understanding of the data and message models used within Apache Camel and Cloud Integration, let's see how you can benefit from this knowledge during message processing. To demonstrate how to access properties and headers when building a response message and to illustrate the consequences of storing data in the two locations, we'll use a simple scenario. In this example, we take an XML input message and store parts of the message in the properties/header area of the message model. To build the reply, you'll access this stored data from the properties/header areas and construct a response message.

Let's get started by following these steps:

1. Create a new package for our exercise. After you connect to your Cloud Integration tenant with your internet browser, switch to the **Design** view, as shown in Figure 4.4.

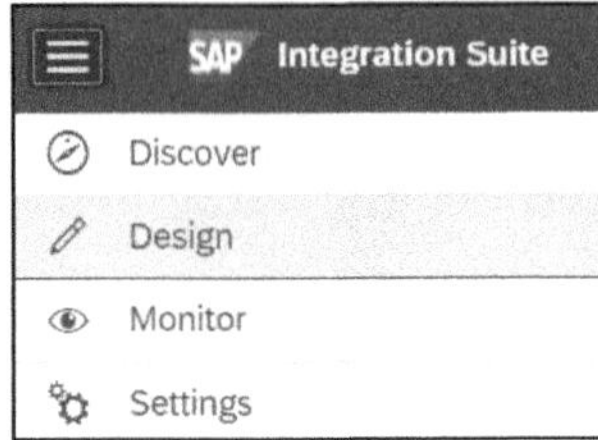

Figure 4.4 Switching to the Design View

2. You'll see a list of available packages. Create a new package by clicking the **Create** button located beneath the package list. The **New Package** dialog box will open, as shown in Figure 4.5.

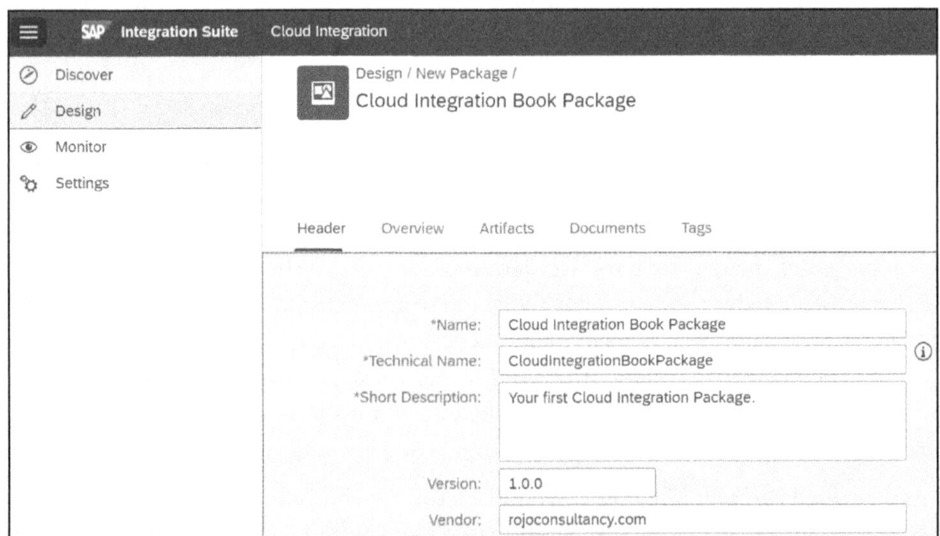

Figure 4.5 Creating a New Integration Package

3. Provide some basic information about the package, such as its name, version, and creator. Save the package by clicking the **Save** button.
4. From the resulting page, navigate to the **Artifacts** tab, and add an iFlow to your package by choosing **Integration Flow** from the **Add** dropdown list, as shown in Figure 4.6.

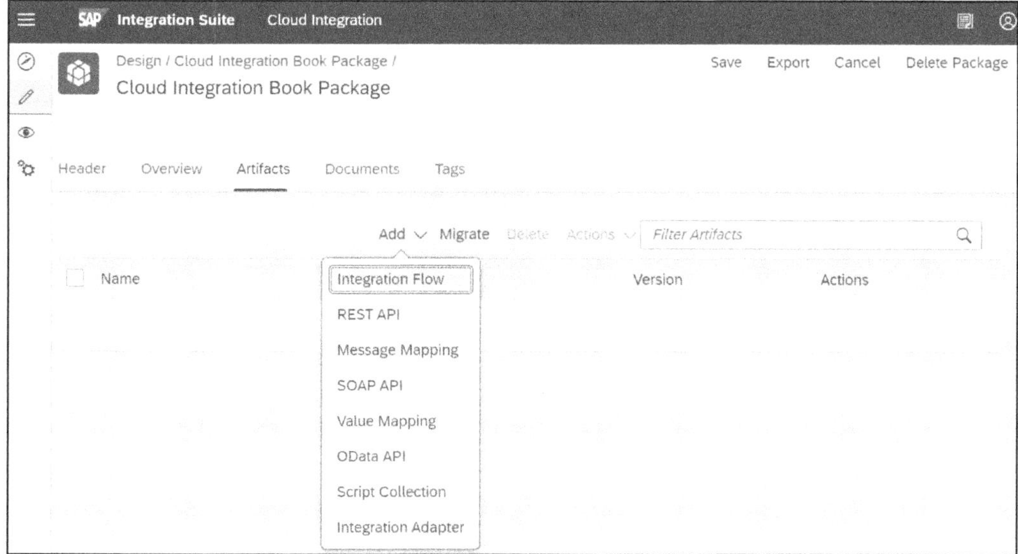

Figure 4.6 Adding an iFlow to the Newly Created Package

Another dialog box opens where you'll maintain some basic information about the iFlow, as shown in Figure 4.7.

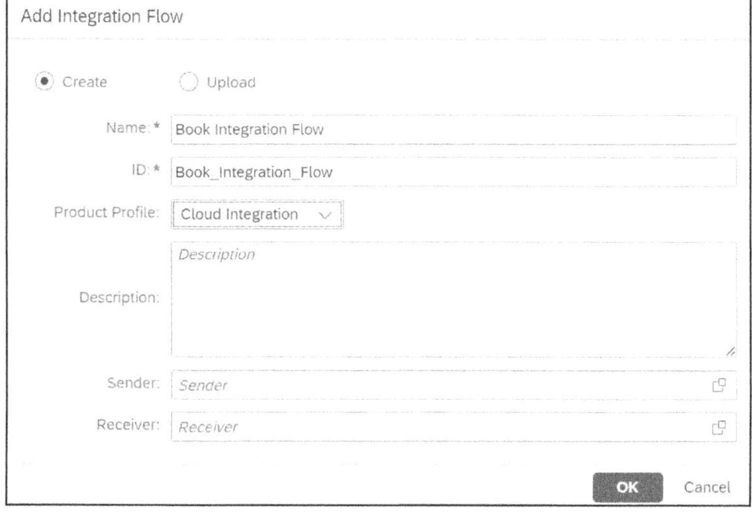

Figure 4.7 Creating an iFlow

5. Confirm the new iFlow by clicking the **OK** button, and then store the new package by clicking on **Save**.
6. You've now created a package and an associated iFlow. Open the iFlow, which should look like the process shown in Figure 4.8.

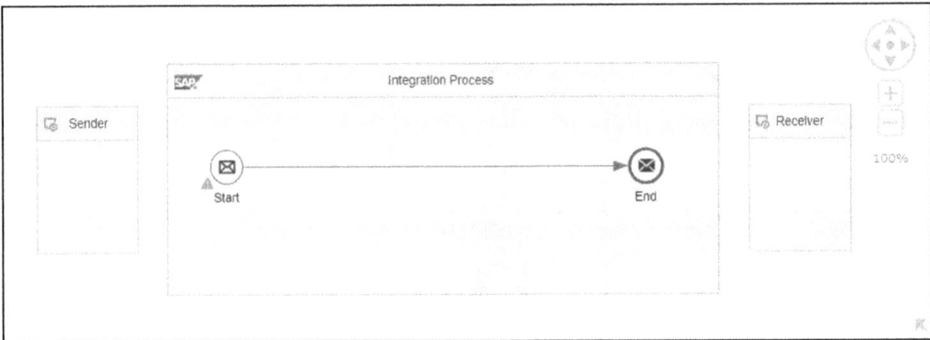

Figure 4.8 An Empty iFlow as a Starting Point for the Exercise

4.1.3 Connecting and Configuring a Sender with an Integration Flow

Switch to edit mode (by clicking the **Edit** button in the top-right corner of the iFlow screen), and delete the **Receiver** pool, as we don't need it for this exercise. Start modeling the connection between the **Sender** pool on the left and the **Start** event by dragging a connection from the pool to the **Start** event via context buttons. Every time you select a shape in the model, context buttons appear on the right side of the shape to indicate what can be done with the shape at this moment. So, if you select the **Sender** pool, the context buttons shown in Figure 4.9 will appear.

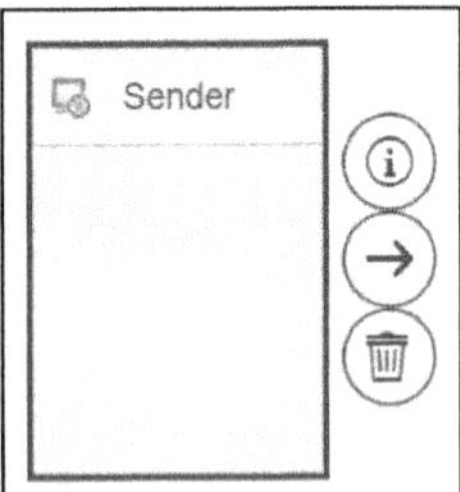

Figure 4.9 Context Buttons Next to the Selected Shape

Next, click the connector icon →, drag the cursor to the target shape (the **Start** event in this case), and then release the mouse button (drop), as shown in Figure 4.10.

After dropping the cursor on the **Start** event, a dialog box opens automatically that allows you to pick the connection type you want between the **Sender** and the Cloud Integration server. In this case, the connection should be a SOAP adapter and the message protocol SOAP 1.x. Simply pick the respective entries from the dialog boxes.

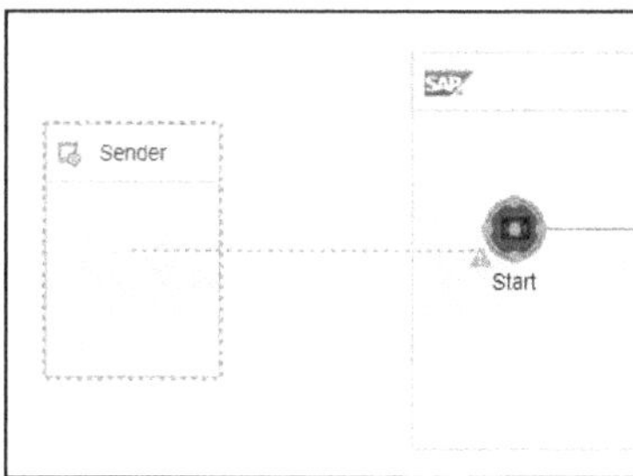

Figure 4.10 Connecting the Sender Pool with the Start Event

Note

According to Wikipedia's definition, SOAP is a messaging protocol specification for exchanging structured information in the implementation of web services in computer networks. Its purpose is to provide extensibility, neutrality, verbosity, and independence. SOAP uses XML as the message format and relies on HTTP as the application layer protocol. You can read more about the SOAP specification at *www.w3.org/TR/soap/*.

The SOAP sender adapter is used to enable Cloud Integration to accept an incoming SOAP message and process it. Similarly, a receiver SOAP adapter can be used to send a SOAP message to another system.

Finally, you must maintain one parameter of the SOAP adapter: the address under which the service will be accessible. For this step, select the message flow between the **Sender** component and the **Start** event so that it appears in orange (see the dotted line shown in Figure 4.11).

Beneath the process model, you should see the properties of the connection (in this case, the details of the channel). A typical workflow for using the Cloud Integration modeling environment is to select shapes in the graphical model and then adjust properties in the area beneath the process model. The properties change depending on the component selected in the main area. In our example, click the **Connection** link, and add "/CI_Book_Demo" as the address in the **Address** field.

When you're exposing an iFlow in Cloud Integration with a SOAP endpoint, you would often have a Web Services Definition Language (WSDL) file or URL, which will define the structure of the request and response messages along with some additional information. You can find a detailed explanation of the components of a WSDL at *www.w3.org/TR/wsdl20/*. For this exercise, you can download the WSDL document named *GetOrderShipDetails_Sync.wsdl* from this book's webpage at *https://www.sap-press.com/5760*.

From the **Service Definition** dropdown, select the value **WSDL**. In Figure 4.12 notice some additional configuration settings such as **URL to WSDL**, **Service**, and **Endpoint**. Click on the **Select** button next to the **URL to WSDL** text box, as shown in Figure 4.12.

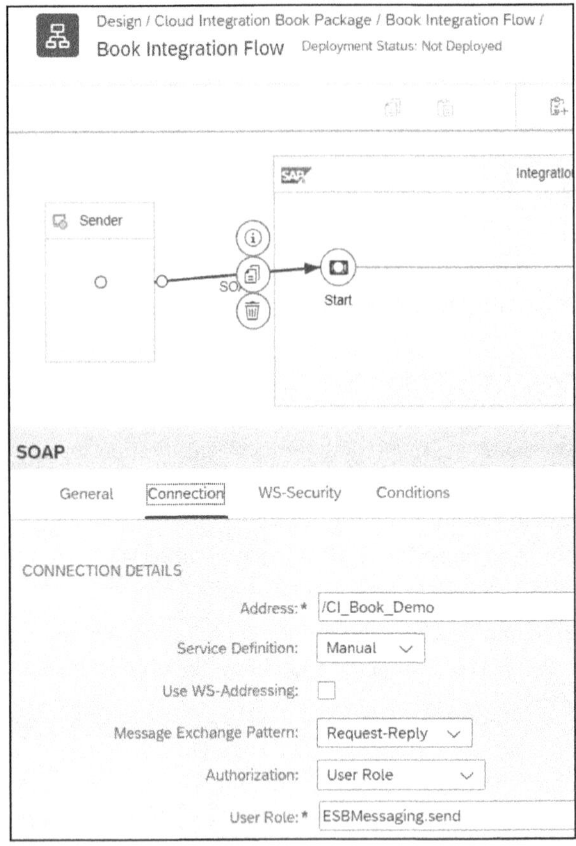

Figure 4.11 Configuration of the SOAP Channel

SOAP
Externalize

General | Connection | WS-Security | Conditions

CONNECTION DETAILS

Address: * /CI_Book_Demo

Service Definition: WSDL

Use WS-Addressing:

URL to WSDL: * Select

Service:

Endpoint:

Processing Settings: Robust

Authorization: User Role

User Role: * ESBMessaging.send Select

Figure 4.12 Configuration of Service Definition in the SOAP Channel

To upload the WSDL document, click on the **Upload from File System** link, and select the file *GetOrderShipDetails_Sync.wsdl* using the file picker, as shown in Figure 4.13.

Select WSDL Resource

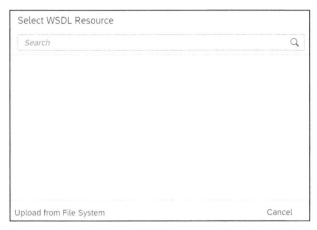

Search

Upload from File System

Cancel

Figure 4.13 Uploading a WSDL Document from the File System

Once the file is uploaded successfully, the value for **Service** and **Endpoint** will be automatically populated, as shown in Figure 4.14.

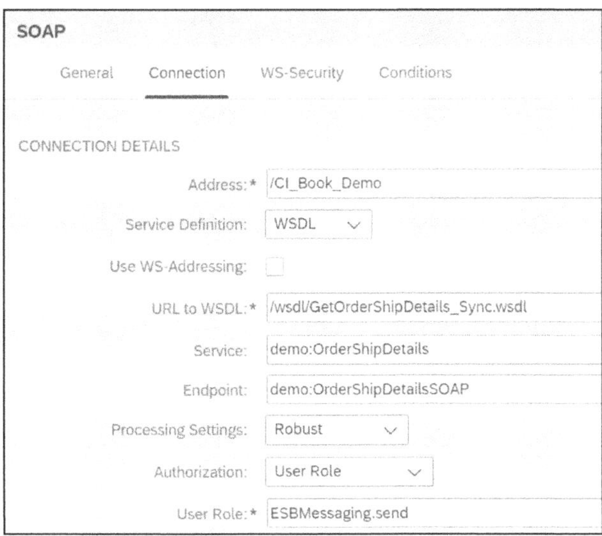

Figure 4.14 Setting the Authentication Type to Basic Authentication

You also must define the authentication type for the communication between the sender and the Cloud Integration server. We chose the SOAP adapter for our connection, so the most convenient authentication type is basic authentication, which only requires the user's user name and password. In Cloud Integration, user role authorization can use either user name/password credentials or a client certificate. The default setting of the SOAP channel for **Authorization** is **User Role**, as shown in Figure 4.14.

As shown in Figure 4.14, the default value for the **User Role** is **ESBMessaging.send**. This role authorizes a sender system to process messages on a tenant. For now, we'll leave the rest of the settings as default.

4.1.4 Adding and Configuring Steps in the Integration Flow

Now, let's add and configure the steps of our iFlow. We'll add two **Content Modifier** steps in this model, which you'll find in the palette on the left, as shown in Figure 4.15.

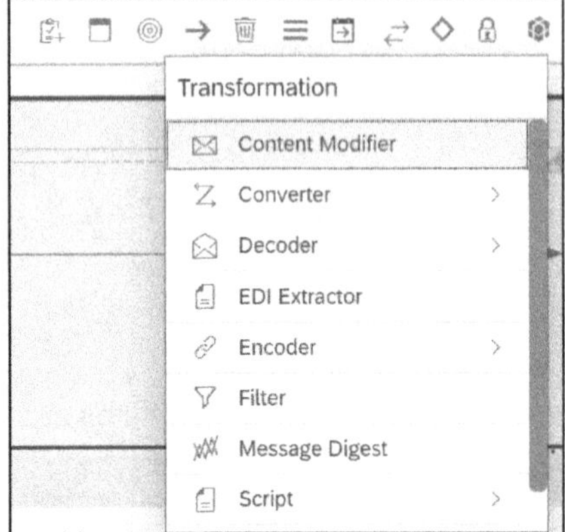

Figure 4.15 Selecting Content Modifier Steps from the Palette

Click the transformer icon in the palette, which will open a submenu. Click the **Content Modifier** shape (black envelope), and move your mouse pointer to the **Integration Process** pool. Click again to position the shape in the pool. Repeat the previous steps so that two **Content Modifier** shapes are added to the process model, as shown in Figure 4.16.

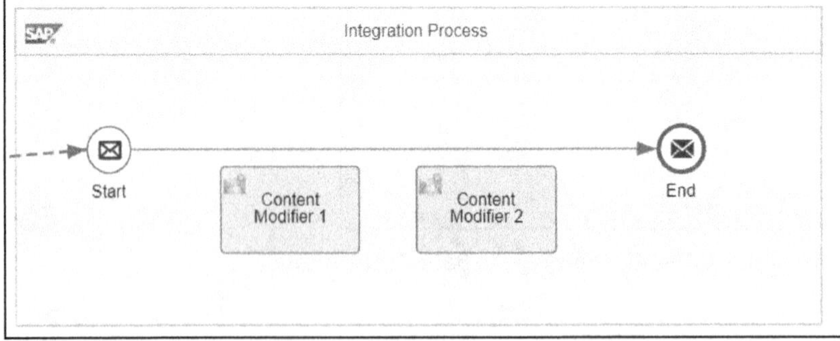

Figure 4.16 Process Model after Adding Two Content Modifier Steps

Let's configure the first **Content Modifier** step. Our goal is to write data with the first **Content Modifier** into the header of the message and the properties area of the exchange. The second **Content Modifier** step retrieves the previously stored data from their respective locations and creates a new result message. In this way, we'll prove that data can be stored in different locations and be available during future steps within the route.

To retrieve data from the message, the structure of the incoming messages must be known. We've defined the message structure used in this example for you, using a simple WSDL document called *GetOrderShipDetails_Sync.wsdl*. An example message following the WSDL's structure is shown in Figure 4.17.

Params Authorization Headers (10) Body ● Pre-request Script Tests Settings

none form-data x-www-form-urlencoded raw binary GraphQL XML

```
<?xml version="1.0" encoding="utf-8"?>
<soap:Envelope xmlns:soap="http://schemas.xmlsoap.org/soap/envelope/">
  <soap:Header/>
  <soap:Body>
    <OrderNumber_MT xmlns="http://ci.sap.com/demo">
      <orderNumber>10249</orderNumber>
    </OrderNumber_MT>
  </soap:Body>
</soap:Envelope>
```

Figure 4.17 Example Message

Our first **Content Modifier** step should retrieve the order number from the message and store this value in the header of the message. In addition, this step should take the complete message's body (the part between the Body tags shown in Figure 4.17) and store this text in the properties area. In this step, we're demonstrating two important features:

- Single fields can be accessed, selectively retrieved, and stored in the header area.
- Complete complex structures, such as complete messages, can be retrieved and stored as properties.

Select the first **Content Modifier** on the left by clicking it once so that its properties can be configured. Note that the configuration parameters of the **Content Modifier** distinguish between three locations: **Message Header**, **Exchange Property**, and **Message Body**, as shown in Figure 4.18.

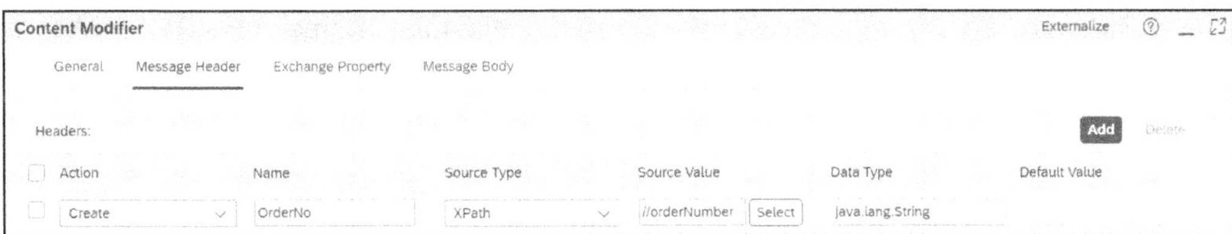

Figure 4.18 Writing Data into the Message's Header Area

The first **Content Modifier** uses the **Message Header** and the **Exchange Property** areas to write the data. The second **Content Modifier** uses the **Message Body** to create the response message. By selecting the appropriate link shown at the top of Figure 4.18, you'll always select the location where data is being stored. Figure 4.18 shows the correct configuration of the **Content Modifier** for writing data into the message's header.

Select the **Message Header** link in the top row. Continue by clicking the **Add** button to create a new row in the table underneath. Next, define the name under which the data should be stored in the message header. In our example, the name is **OrderNo**. You can later access this value by using this exact name.

Now, you'll need to tell the integration engine how to access the value in the message and the type of data to retrieve. We chose **XPath** from the dropdown list because we want to navigate inside an XML document, and XML Path Language (XPath) is the way to retrieve data from an XML document. The XPath expression is simply `//orderNumber`, which is the information we're interested in, and the retrieved value is of type `String`. At this point, a valid Java data type must be assigned—hence, the entry `java.lang.String`. Now, the order number will be stored in the message's header.

Figure 4.19 shows the configuration of the first **Content Modifier** step for writing the complete body of a message into the property area of the exchange. Notice that you can have two (or more) `write` operations configured in a single **Content Modifier** step.

To achieve the result shown in Figure 4.19, click the **Exchange Property** link in the top row. Add a new row in the **Properties** table. The message will be stored under the name (`msg`) in the exchange's property area. This time, we want to store the complete message. Therefore, we aren't accessing a single field but the whole body. For this purpose, Apache Camel provides the Simple Expression Language, which includes predefined variables as shortcuts that allow convenient access to certain parts of a message.

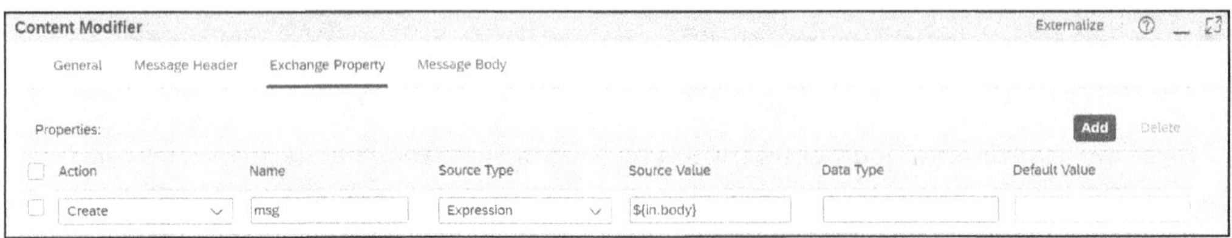

Figure 4.19 Writing Data into the Exchange's Property Area

In our case, we want to access the body of the incoming original message. The Apache Camel variable to do so is `in.body`, as shown in Figure 4.19. The syntax requires a dollar sign and curly brackets to access the variable's content. In the **Content Modifier** screen, choose **Expression** from the **Source Type** dropdown list, and add "${in.body}" to the **Source Value** field.

With that task, you've completed the configuration of the first **Content Modifier** step. To learn more about Apache Camel's expression language, we recommend checking out the Simple Expression Language documentation at *http://camel.apache.org/simple.html.*

We'll continue with the configuration of the second **Content Modifier** step, which is responsible for setting the body of the result message. The correct configuration is shown in Figure 4.20.

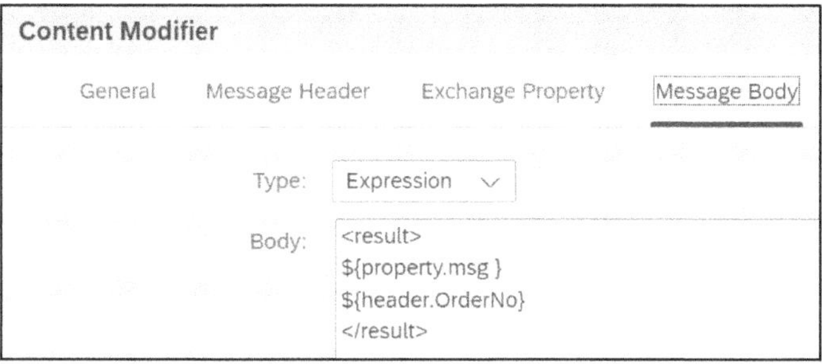

Figure 4.20 Defining the Content of the Reply Message as the New Message Body

Select the **Message Body** link in the top row of the **Content Modifier** screen. Next, fill the **Body** input field, as shown in Figure 4.20. Note that you'll need to set the value of the **Type** dropdown to **Expression**. We defined a new opening and closing tag named `result`. In between those tags, we placed the contents of the two variables defined during the configuration of the first **Content Modifier**. Notice how you can access the different storage areas: the properties in the exchange are accessible via the predefined Apache Camel variable `property`, and the data is stored in the message's header via the predefined Apache Camel variable `header`. In both cases, the actual data is accessed by adding the custom declared variable's name, separated by a dot; for instance, `property.msg` refers to the complete message, and `header.OrderNo` refers to the order number.

Now that you've configured both **Content Modifier** shapes, you can add them to your model by dragging and dropping them onto the sequence flow. Once the sequence flow changes its color to orange, as shown in Figure 4.21, you can release the mouse button, and the shape will be inserted correctly. After adding both shapes, the result should look like the screen shown in Figure 4.22. Finally, save your changes, and deploy the iFlow on your tenant.

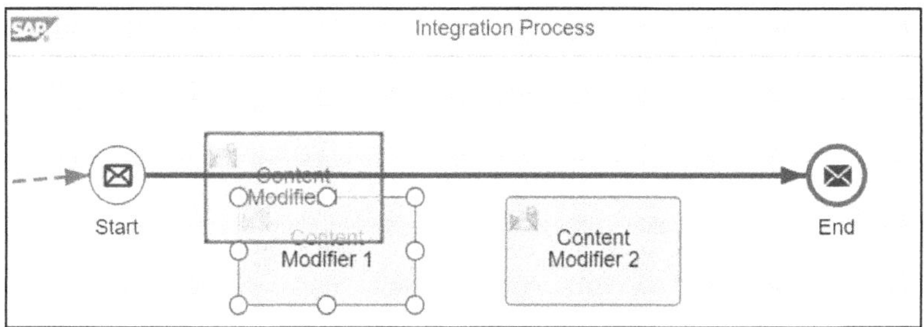

Figure 4.21 Adding the Content Modifier to Your Model

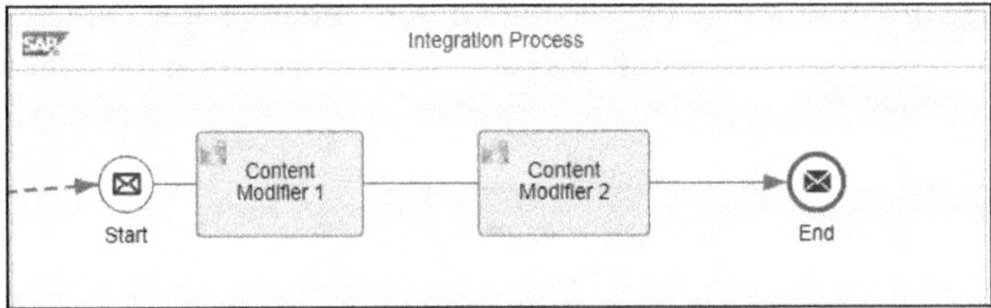

Figure 4.22 The Final Result of the Created iFlow

4.1.5 Checking Configuration Using the Problems Tab

Cloud Integration supports the development process by performing validation checks each time you open, save, and deploy an iFlow. If these checks fail, warnings or problems are detected in the iFlow, and the concerned problematic step is visually marked with a red ⊗ icon (for an error) or a yellow icon ⚠ (for a warning). Figure 4.23 shows that the iFlow model didn't pass the validation check and that there is a problem with the sender connector—as indicated by the red icon ⊗ on the iFlow.

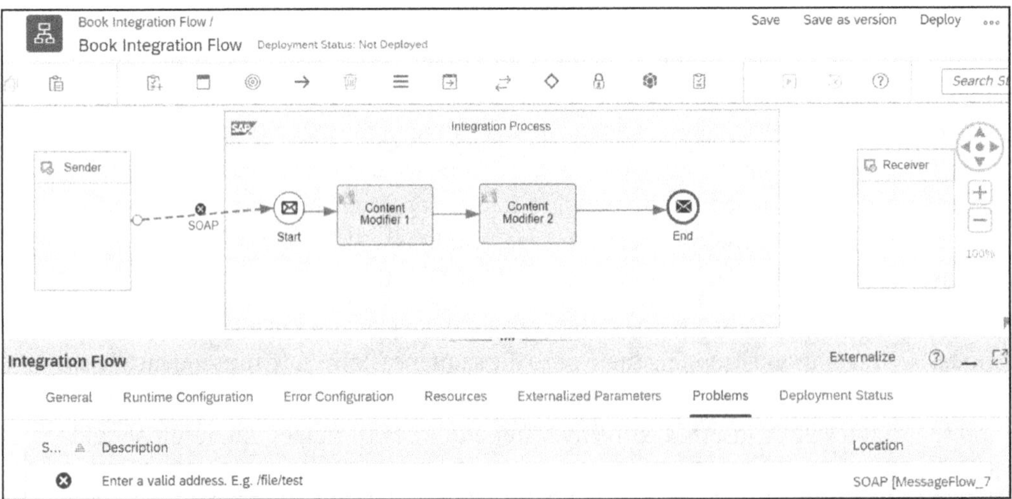

Figure 4.23 Overview of the Problems Tab

As a developer of the iFlow, you can rely on two options to determine the exact problem causing the error:

- Hover your mouse over the error or warning icon in the iFlow to get a tooltip that describes the issue.
- Use the **Problems** tab to obtain details about the error or warning.

The **Problems** tab helps you manage issues and problems in your iFlow by giving you specific details of the problem's root cause. This tab displays all design-time issues related to integration components and resources.

Note

When a validation check is performed on the iFlow, both warnings and errors can be detected and visually shown in the iFlow model under the **Problems** tab. Errors are flagged by a red icon, whereas warnings are flagged with a yellow icon.

Table 4.1 describes the columns available under the **Problems** tab.

Column Name	Description
Severity	The severity status of an issue. This column is populated by icons that represent errors or warnings.
Description	A description of the problem. This column also often presents a tip or example of how to solve the issue.
Location	The location of the integration component or resource with the issue. The location is the name of the concerned integration component or resource, followed by the ID displayed in brackets. You can also click the location ID to be redirected to the concerned step in the iFlow or the affected resource.

Table 4.1 Attributes Available under the Problems Tab

The visual representation of the warnings and errors can get quite cluttered if you have a lot of issues in the iFlow. Furthermore, having to hover over each problem icon before knowing the issues isn't always handy. Compared to the visual representation, the **Problems** tab provides a better overview and a consolidated list of issues in one glance. You can also filter or sort the list of problems according to the columns listed in Table 4.1.

4.1.6 Running the Integration Flow

After a successful deployment, you'll need the endpoint of your iFlow to actually invoke the iFlow via a SOAP client. For the sake of simplicity, let's use SoapUI as our SOAP client and simulate a SOAP sender. The SoapUI software allows you to set up a SOAP client and send a SOAP message to an endpoint with a few clicks. You'll need to download SoapUI from *www.soapui.org* and install it on your computer.

The next step is to retrieve the endpoint address of your iFlow. You can find the endpoint's address using Cloud Integration's monitoring environment. Click the **Monitor** menu item (three-bar navigation icon in the upper-left corner), as shown in Figure 4.24.

A screen with several tiles should appear. Click the **Started** tile, which is beneath the **Manage Integration Content** heading, as shown in Figure 4.25. From this tile, you can navigate to all the already-started iFlows for your tenant.

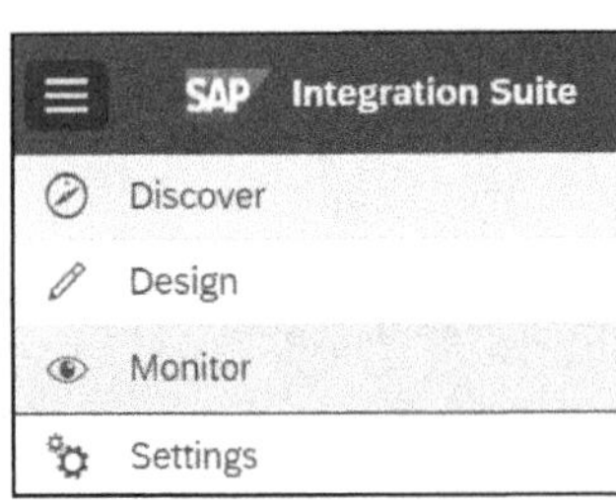

Figure 4.24 Switch to the Monitoring Environment of Cloud Integration

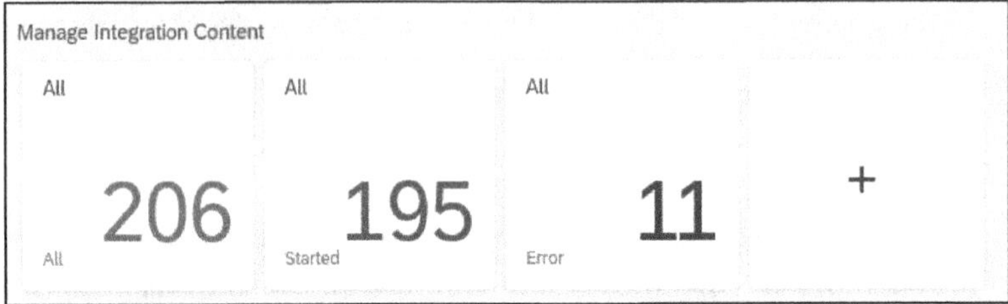

Figure 4.25 Tile for Already-Started iFlows on Your Tenant

From the list of deployed and started integration content, find your newly deployed iFlow, and click its entry row, as shown in Figure 4.26. You'll now see details about this particular iFlow.

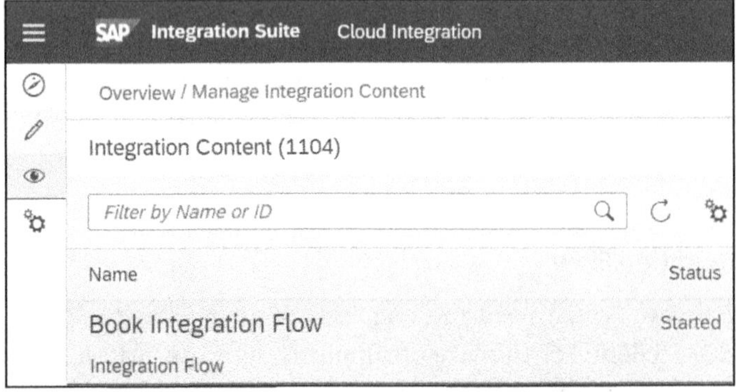

Figure 4.26 Navigating to the Details of a Selected iFlow

Besides other useful information, such as the iFlow's version number, the deployed state, and the deployment date/time, the endpoint's URL is of particular interest. This URL is how the iFlow is invoked. Select the URL, and copy the address by clicking on the **Copy** icon shown in Figure 4.27. Save this URL because you'll need it later. Additionally, download the WSDL via one of these options: **WSDL** or **WSDL without policies**. We'll need to invoke the iFlow via SoapUI.

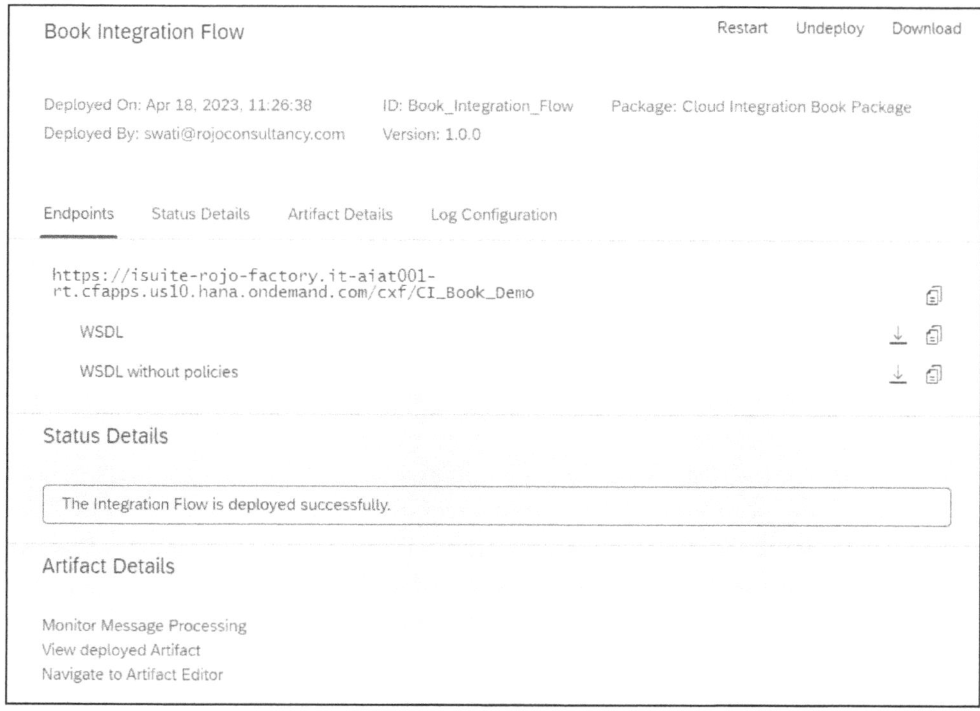

Figure 4.27 Copying the Endpoint URL into the Clipboard

At this point, you've downloaded the WSDL file and have all the information needed to run the iFlow. Using SoapUI, perform the following steps:

1. Open SoapUI, and create a new SOAP project by clicking on **File** and then selecting **New SOAP Project** in the menu.
2. Specify a **Project Name**, and click on the **Browse** button, located to the right of the **Initial WSDL** field (Figure 4.28). Then, click **OK**.

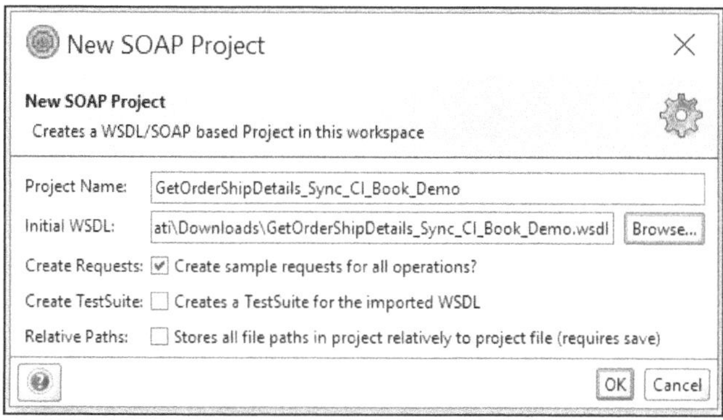

Figure 4.28 Creating a SoapUI project

3. You're then presented with a page similar to the one shown in Figure 4.29. Note that the page already contains a skeleton of the **Request** message to be sent to Cloud Integration, and the correct endpoint is also present. This endpoint must match the one that you noted earlier. If not, change it accordingly.

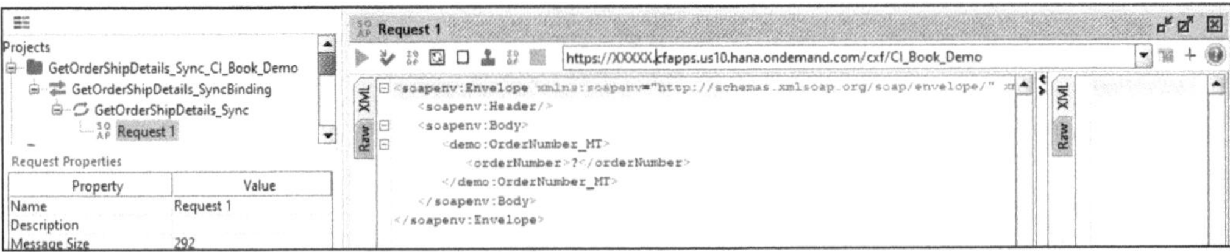

Figure 4.29 Empty Request Message

4. On the left side of the screen, prepare a message that looks similar to the one shown in Figure 4.30. Set the **Order Number** field accordingly (e.g., with **10249**) and don't forget to set the correct authentication type in SoapUI (in this case, **Basic Authentication** with the user name and password provided by SAP for your Cloud Integration instance). You can see the **Username** and **Password** fields on the lower-left side of Figure 4.30.

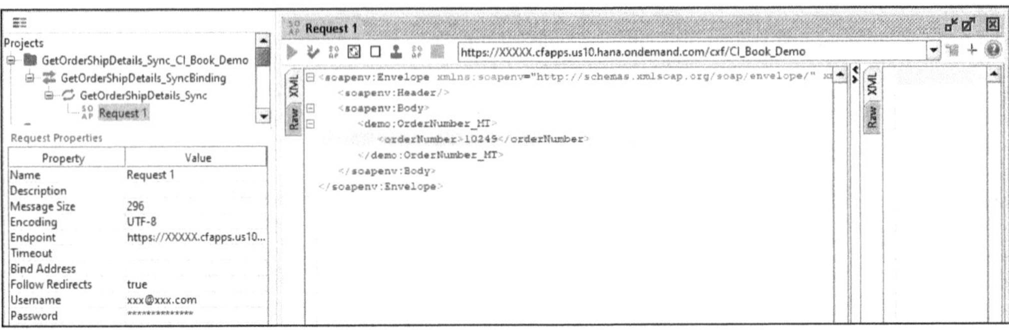

Figure 4.30 Request Message to Invoke the iFlow

Finally, invoke the iFlow by clicking on the submit request icon ▶. As a result, you should receive an output comparable to the screen shown in Figure 4.31.

```
<soap:Envelope xmlns:soap="http://schemas.xmlsoap.org/soap/envelope/">
   <soap:Header/>
   <soap:Body>
      <result>
         <demo:OrderNumber_MT xmlns:demo="http://ci.sap.com/demo" xmlns:soapenv="http://schemas.xmlsoap.org/soap/envelope/">
            <orderNumber>10249</orderNumber>
         </demo:OrderNumber_MT>
         10249
      </result>
   </soap:Body>
</soap:Envelope>
```

Figure 4.31 Response after Invocation of iFlow

Note

Be aware that the user specified in SoapUI must have the `ESBMessaging.send` role assigned for the service call to be authorized.

As shown in Figure 4.31, the returned response isn't a valid XML message because the **10249** is outside the tag. This result occurred because of the way we populated the response in the **Message Body** section in the **Content Modifier** screen (shown earlier in Figure 4.20 and section inflow's Section 4.1.4).

Earlier in Section 4.1.1, we mentioned an important difference between storing data in the message's header and storing it in the exchange's property area: The data stored in the message's header will be forwarded to the receiver of the message, whereas the data in the exchange's properties area won't reach the receiver. How can you verify that? In your SOAP client tool, look at the headers of your response message. In the screenshot shown in Figure 4.32, we've used SoapUI to view the headers.

Header	Value
date	Wed, 19 Apr 2023 09:38:05 GMT
content-length	334
sap_messageprocessinglogid	AGQ_tn1Y-jck4_QuiMcyquXuSam9
server	SAP
expires	0
orderno	10249
x-frame-options	DENY
x-vcap-request-id	7a1dc470-2105-48e9-418d-966cea0d02e0
pragma	no-cache
strict-transport-security	max-age=31536000; includeSubDomains; preload;
x-content-type-options	nosniff
x-xss-protection	1; mode=block
x-correlationid	7a1dc470-2105-48e9-418d-966cea0d02e0
content-type	text/xml;charset=UTF-8
#status#	HTTP/1.1 200 OK
cache-control	no-cache, no-store, max-age=0, must-revalidate

Figure 4.32 Header Fields of the Response Message

In row 6 of the table shown in Figure 4.32, you can identify the **orderno** field that was set during message processing. The value of the **orderno** field reached the receiver, but as you can see, the data stored in the exchange's properties area didn't.

The fact that the data stored as header fields are returned in the message response means that you need to carefully use header fields. Storing large messages in header fields can require a lot of resources and create performance issues.

4.1.7 Troubleshooting

As with every development and runtime environment, errors can occur in Cloud Integration, and you can expect two main types of errors: errors that occur during deployment and errors that occur during message handling. In both cases, the starting point for the error's root cause analysis is Cloud Integration's monitoring environment (refer to Figure 4.24 for details on how to open the monitoring environment). The monitoring environment's homepage consists of several areas, including **Message Processing Monitor**, **Integration Content Monitor**, **Manage Security**, **Manage Stores**, **Access Logs**, and **Manage Locks**. Some of these monitors are shown in Figure 4.33. We'll discuss monitoring functionalities in more detail in Chapter 7.

When faced with deployment errors, you'll find appropriate entries in the **Integration Content Monitor** area; the **Error** tile provides an overview by displaying the number of erroneous artifacts. Click on the tile to learn more about the root cause of each error.

For runtime issues during message processing, the **Message Processing Monitor** section has the appropriate tiles to further analyze these errors. However, these tiles are useful for more than erroneous message handling routes; they also reveal a lot about the exact message processing steps within Apache Camel for successfully completed messages. To further illustrate this transparency, perform the following steps:

1. Click on the **Completed Messages** tile in the **Monitor Message Processing** section, as shown in Figure 4.33. Note that the tiles can be personalized and configured to your liking. If the tile has been modified in your tenant, it may behave differently than described in this section.

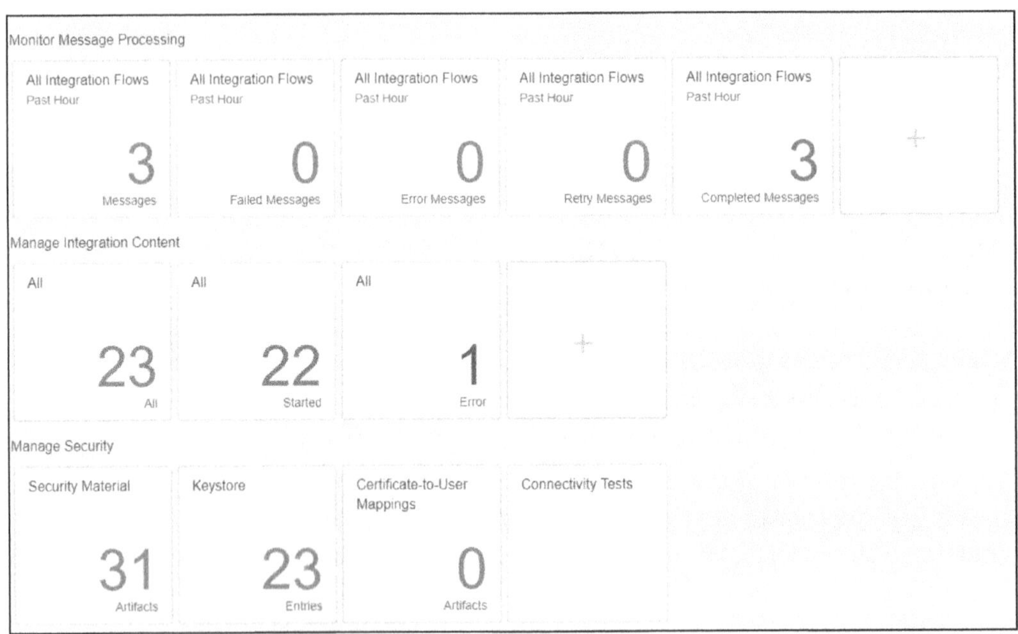

Figure 4.33 Monitoring Homepage

2. From the subsequent monitoring page, click on the concerned iFlow on the left, as shown in Figure 4.34. Then, select the **Logs** tab on the right to view a page similar to the page shown in Figure 4.34.

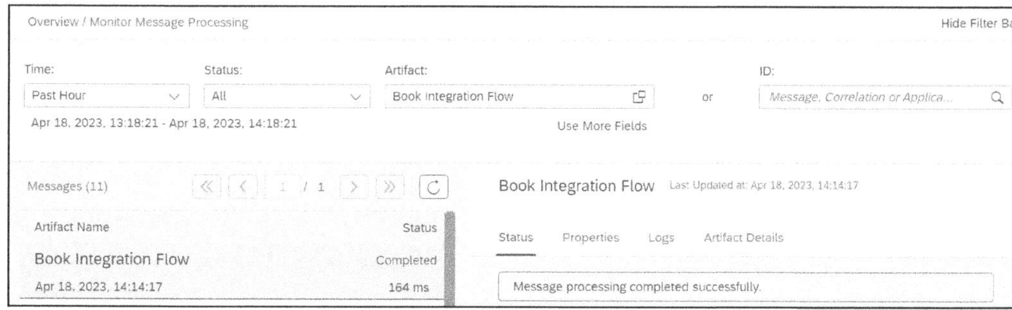

Figure 4.34 Details about Successfully Completed Messages

> **Note**
> Chapter 7, Section 7.2, discusses the various monitors in more detail.

In this section, you learned a lot about the inner workings of Cloud Integration. Although we implemented a relatively simple scenario, doing so revealed many details about message handling within the underlying Apache Camel integration framework, including error analysis. This knowledge can help you work more consciously with messages, headers, and attachments. In the next section, we'll discuss how to use externalization in your iFlow.

4.2 Using Externalization to Enable Easy Reuse of Integration Flows

When designing an integration scenario, considering reusability is important. Some advantages brought about by reusability include the following:

- Reduces the overall cost of software development
- Reduces risks
- Saves time and cost while developing and testing interfaces
- Speeds delivery of software

With regard to Cloud Integration, reusability means in practice that, for every step of your iFlow, you ask yourself the following questions:

- Is the concerned step likely to be repeated several times in your iFlow?
- Are there other steps in the iFlow that will reuse the same data?
- Does the step need a dynamic input coming from a variable or another step in the iFlow?
- Does the concerned iFlow need to be deployed in different tenants in the landscape, and do some steps need to be configured differently in other environments?

- Do any of the values to be used in the adapter depend on the tenant on which the iFlow is running? (For example, the endpoint of a connected backend system might depend on whether you configure an iFlow on a test or on a productive tenant.)

Note that more questions potentially fit into this category, but these questions are posed for the sake of simplicity. If the answer to any of these questions is yes, consider generalizing the concerned step by making it more generic and configurable.

While working with Cloud Integration, one way to generalize and increase the reusability of data within an iFlow is known as *externalization*. In the following sections, we'll discuss externalization and show you how to use externalization in an iFlow. We'll also discuss how to configure the parameters used for externalization.

4.2.1 Externalizing

If the same integration content will be used across multiple landscapes or environments (e.g., development, test, acceptance, production), you can assume that the endpoints of the iFlow for each landscape will differ. In this scenario, you can use externalizing parameters to declare a parameter as a variable at design time. This parameter can then be used later during configuration time to customize the attributes on the sender and receiver side or for a step in the iFlow.

Externalizing a parameter helps you avoid hard-coded values in your iFlow, thus providing the flexibility to change parameter values at configuration time. *Configuration time* refers to the moment after an iFlow has been transported or imported in a tenant in your landscape (test, acceptance, or production). During this time, users might need to adapt some aspects of an iFlow, such as adding adapter-specific endpoints and assigning values to externalized parameters. The good news is that assigning a value to an externalized parameter during configuration doesn't involve changing the iFlow.

Let's now look at a practical use case extending the iFlow we implemented in Section 4.1. We've built an iFlow that accepts a SOAP call. Imagine that you, as the integration developer, decide to use different addresses for calling the iFlow in different environments (development, test, and production). As shown earlier in Figure 4.11, we configured the flow to be called via the SOAP address */CI_Book_Demo*. To externalize the address and make it configurable for each environment, follow these steps:

1. Open the concerned iFlow (in the Web UI design environment), click **Edit**, and select the SOAP adapter line, as shown in Figure 4.35.
2. Click on the **Externalize** button (on the right side of Figure 4.35).
3. The **Externalization** editor, shown in Figure 4.36, will pop up. Note that the **Externalization** editor presents all possible configurations of the component that is selected. Let's now create a new parameter on the **Address** field. Select the **Connection** tab, and remove the existing `/CI_Book_Demo` value.

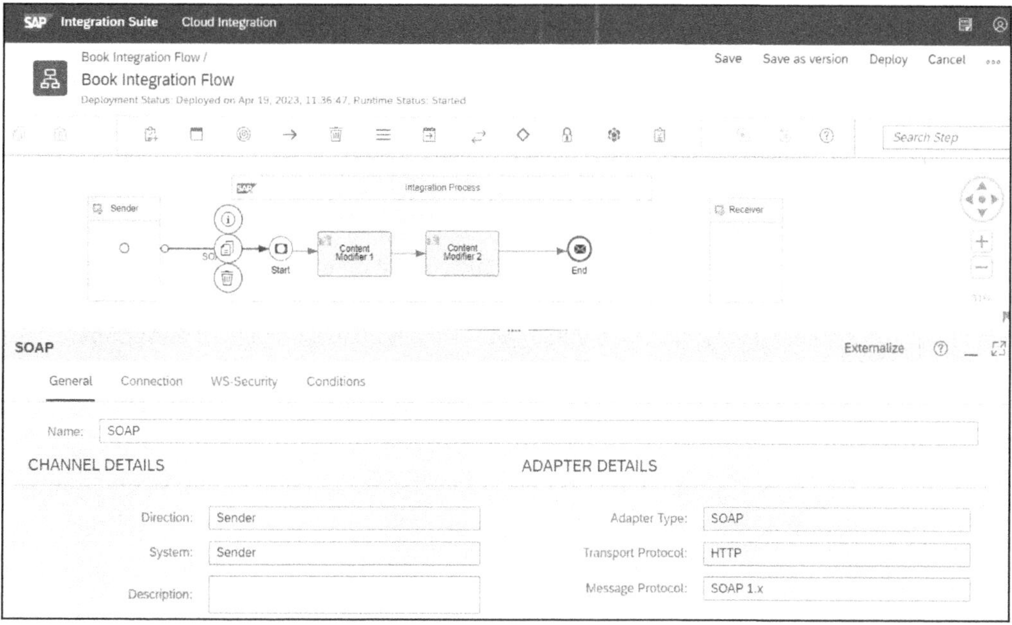

Figure 4.35 Selecting the SOAP Connector and the Externalize Button

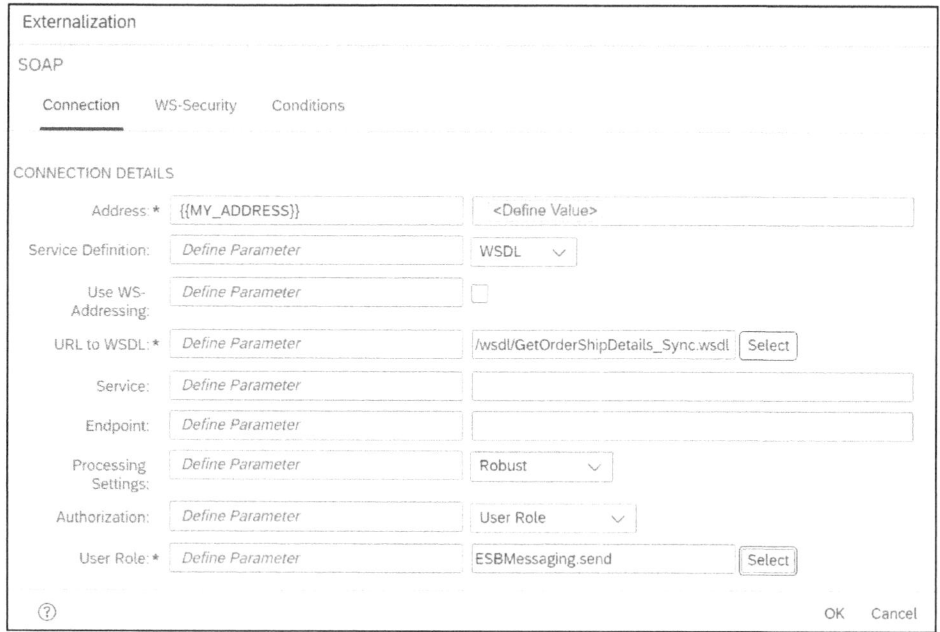

Figure 4.36 Creating a New Parameter in the Externalization Editor

4. The parameter is defined using the format `{{<parameter>}}`. In our case, add a new parameter with the name `{{MY_ADDRESS>}}`, as shown in Figure 4.36.

Note

Not all components can be externalized. After selecting the component in the iFlow, the **Externalize** button only appears if the component contains at least one attribute that can be externalized.

Note that the feature to create a parameter is only enabled when the iFlow is in edit mode. As soon as a parameter is created, it becomes available for various components (e.g., sender channel, receiver channel, timer, etc.) within the same iFlow. Furthermore, existing parameters can always be recalled by typing the double curly brackets "{{" in the parameter column. Cloud Integration will automatically suggest a list of parameters available in the iFlow.

5. The next step is to create a value for the externalized parameter by clicking on the <Define Value> tag, shown in Figure 4.36. The **Define Value** option will appear once you've created an externalizable parameter. A new popup screen will then open where you can define a value for the {{MY_ADDRESS>}} externalized parameter, as shown in Figure 4.37. For our example, enter "/CI_Book_Demo" as its new value.
6. Click the **OK** button to return to the **Externalization** editor.
7. Once back in the **Externalization** editor, select **OK** again to return to the iFlow.

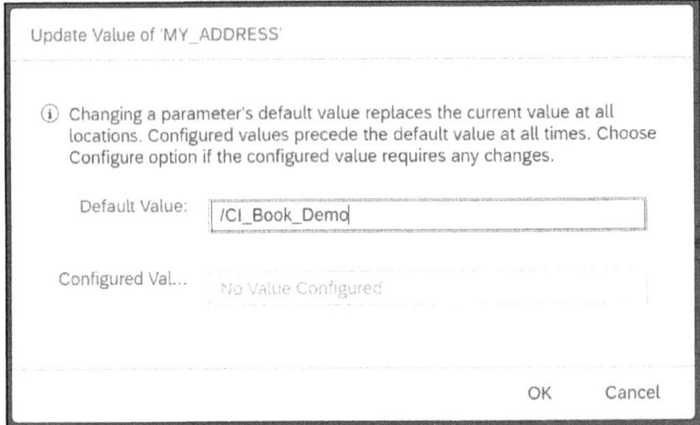

Figure 4.37 Defining a Value for an Externalized Parameter

Note

For some fields in Cloud Integration, you can externalize many parameters at the same time and combine them together to fulfill your requirements. Figure 4.38 shows multiple concatenated strings.

However, you should pay special attention when modifying a parameter value because this change might change the configuration of other iFlow components that use the same parameter.

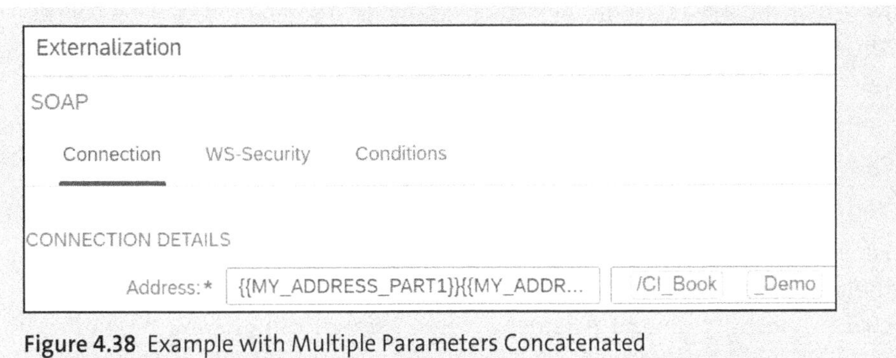

Figure 4.38 Example with Multiple Parameters Concatenated

You can also cancel the externalizing of a field by deleting it. Removing the externalization from a particular field doesn't remove the parameter from the iFlow, however, because the parameter might be used in another component, step, or adapter. The parameter can completely be removed using the **Externalized Parameters** tab, which enables you to manage all externalized parameters of the concerned iFlow.

Follow these steps to manage externalized parameters under the **Externalized Parameters** tab:

1. Click outside the iFlow model area to see the **Externalized Parameters** tab.
2. Open the iFlow in edit mode, and select the **Externalized Parameters** view, as shown in Figure 4.39.

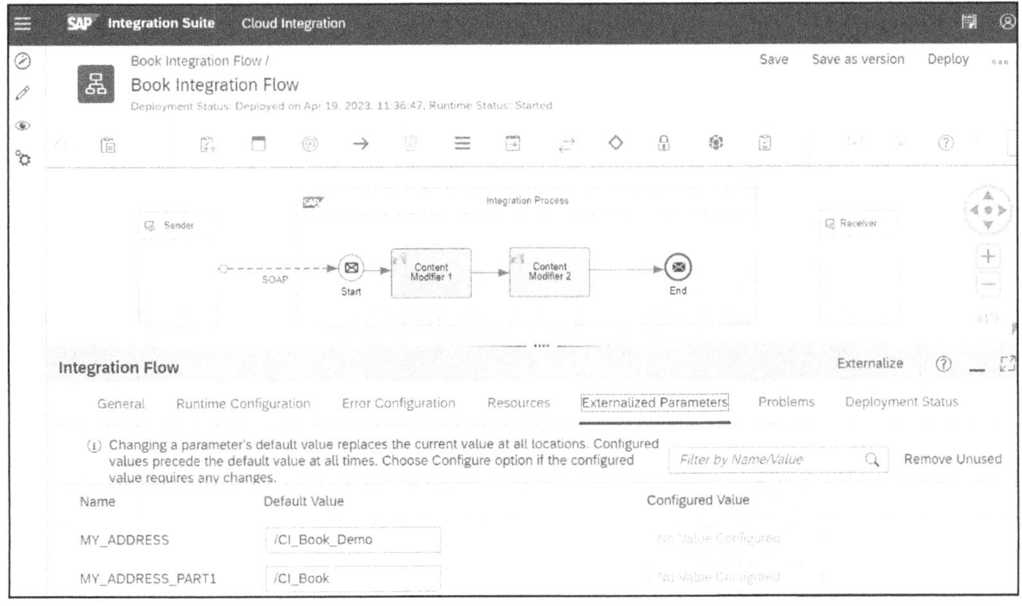

Figure 4.39 Externalized Parameters View in Design Time

Note that you'll see a list of all existing externalized parameters in the whole iFlow. These parameters aren't necessary for our example exercise; they've been added for the sake of illustration.

3. In this view, you can also filter the parameters using their names or values via the **Filter by Name/Value** field (on the right side of Figure 4.39).
4. You can also update and adjust the values of any parameters from this central view.
5. Finally, you can remove unused parameters by clicking the **Remove Unused** link on the right, as shown in Figure 4.39. With this option, Cloud Integration performs a check to identify unused parameters, and a screen will ask you to confirm the removal of unused fields, as shown in Figure 4.40. Upon confirmation, all unused parameters will be removed.

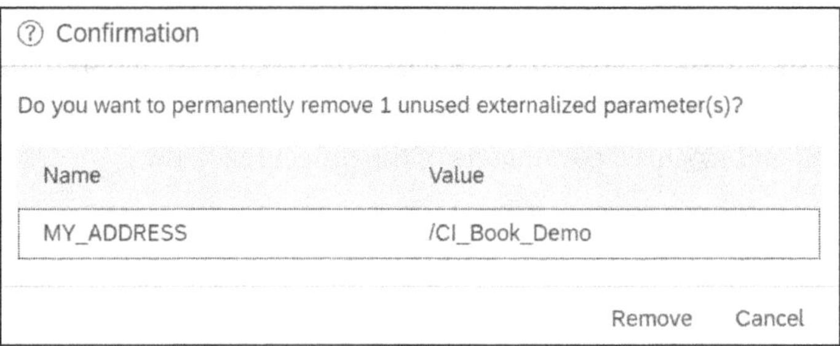

Figure 4.40 Removing Unused Externalized Parameters

6. Save and deploy the iFlow.

Now that you know how to add and manage externalized parameters, let's discuss how externalized parameters can be configured and used for runtime.

4.2.2 Configuring and Running the Scenario

As discussed in the previous section, externalization enables you to create a parameter in design time that can later be changed during configuration time, without the need to change the iFlow. Now that you've successfully developed your iFlow and imported it across other tenants in the landscape (e.g., test, acceptance, production), it's time to learn how to adapt the values of its existing externalized parameters to fit the requirements of the actual environment. Note that an iFlow can be transported across other tenants in the landscape (as we'll address in Chapter 6, Section 6.9).

In the example case we've been building since Section 4.1, we added a parameter to specify a different SOAP address for each environment (Section 4.2.1). To change the SOAP address, proceed as follows:

1. Transport the iFlow to the other tenant where you'll run the iFlow with different parameters.

2. Go to the desired tenant, navigate to the **Design** page, and open the concerned iFlow.
3. Click on the **Configure** link in the top-right corner, as shown in Figure 4.41.

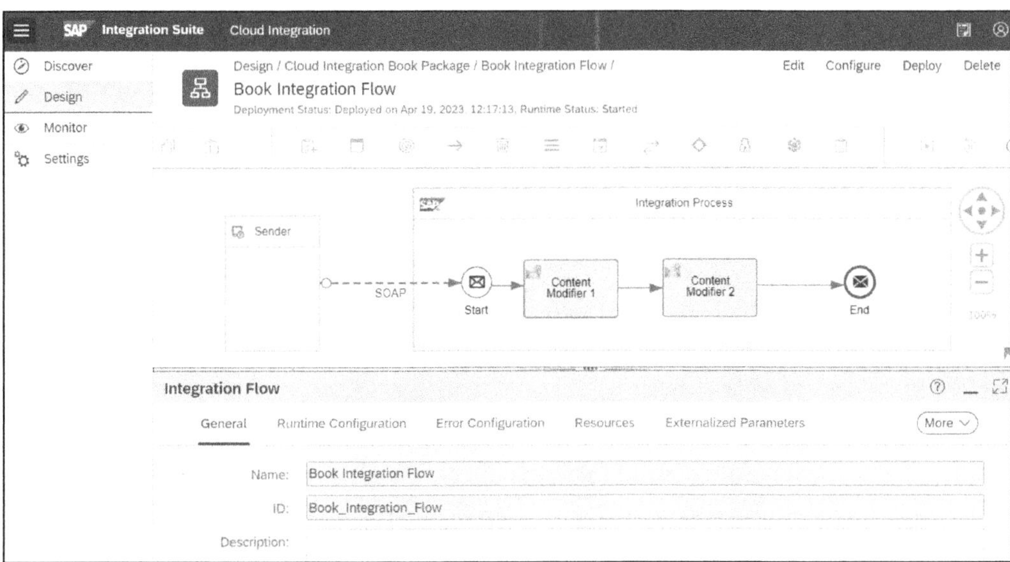

Figure 4.41 Configuring an iFlow

4. The **Configure** view allows you to the maintain values of your externalized parameters. In our case, replace the value of the **MY_Address_PART2** field with a new value. As shown in Figure 4.42, enter the value "_Demo_Test."
5. Click **Save** and then **Deploy** (both buttons are located in the bottom-right corner, as shown in Figure 4.42).

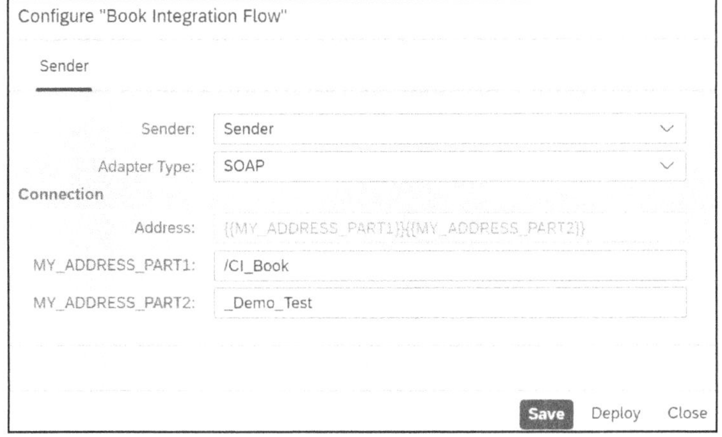

Figure 4.42 Changing an Externalized Parameter Value

Now that our updated iFlow is deployed, we're ready to test the iFlow using SoapUI, which we already described in Section 4.1.6. The main difference in this case is that you should now use the new invocation address instead. This new invocation address or endpoint can be found in the **Manage Integration Content** monitor, as shown in Figure 4.43.

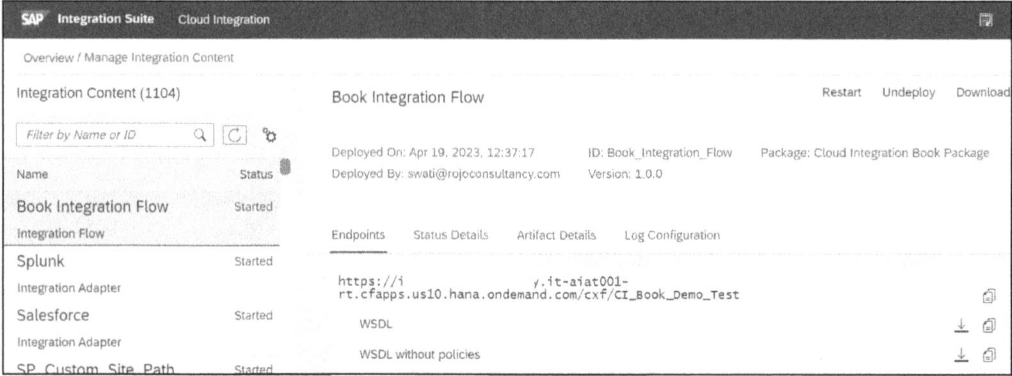

Figure 4.43 Finding the New Endpoint Address after Externalizing the SOAP Address

Congratulations, you're now equipped to define, manage, and configure externalized parameters.

4.3 Calling External Systems by Invoking an OData Service

Cloud Integration allows you to develop sophisticated integration scenarios. In this section, we'll provide an example of such a scenario: a synchronous call to an Open Data Protocol (OData) service to retrieve the details of an order for a given order number. The client sends the order number to Cloud Integration using a standard SOAP call.

Our example dives deeply into communication with external data sources, as well as how to use these data sources in synchronous scenarios. Finally, we explain the Query Editor, which is a tool for generating the sometimes quite complex Representational State Transfer (REST) Uniform Resource Identifiers (URIs) required for actually invoking the external OData sources.

Note

URI is a generic term to identify the name of a resource uniquely over the network. A URL is a concrete URI for a web address. In this book, when we talk about the OData service, we'll use the term URI. When talking about the invocation of the iFlow, which is reachable via SOAP using a concrete web address, we'll use the term URL.

4.3.1 The Target Scenario

The integration scenario shown in Figure 4.44 is the integration scenario we'll build in the next section.

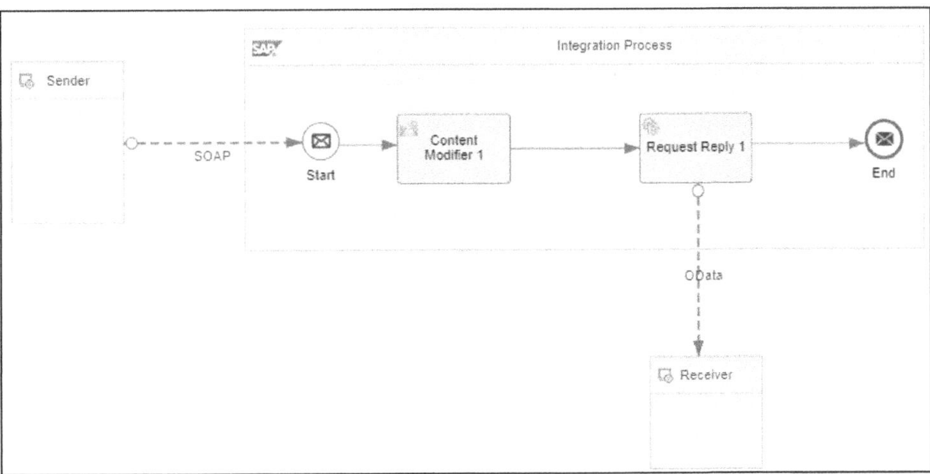

Figure 4.44 Invoking an OData Service

In this scenario, our iFlow covers the following steps:

- Sending a SOAP request containing an order number from the **Sender** participant to Cloud Integration
- Retrieving the order number from the incoming message and storing it in the message's header field for later reference using the **Content Modifier** step
- Invoking an OData service to retrieve the details of that particular order, implementing a **Request Reply** pattern scenario
- Returning the received data to the client

The incoming message's structure is the same as the structure shown earlier in Figure 4.17. This structure contains the order number for which additional data should be retrieved from an external OData service. You can reuse most of the steps from the previous exercise to create this new iFlow. The **Sender** pool is configured with the **User Role** from the **Authorization** dropdown list and with **ESBMessaging.send** as the value for the user role (under the **Connection** tab).

For the message flow between the **Sender** pool and the **Start** event, the adapter-specific attribute **Address** should be set to **/CI_Book_Demo_OData** (to define a different endpoint compared to the previous exercise). This string is later part of the URL through which the iFlow will be invoked. The **Content Modifier** step is responsible for storing the incoming order number in the message's header area. As a reminder, its configuration was shown earlier in Figure 4.18. The **OrderNo** name was chosen as the name to store the value for later access. So far, the message has arrived at the iFlow, and an important piece of information, the order number, has been stored for later reference. Now, we're ready to configure the call to the OData service.

4.3.2 Invoking an OData Service

The modeling environment in Cloud Integration provides a dedicated shape (or step) for accessing external sources synchronously. This shape is the **Request Reply** step, located in the submenu of the **Call** icon ⇄ on the editor's palette, as shown in Figure 4.45.

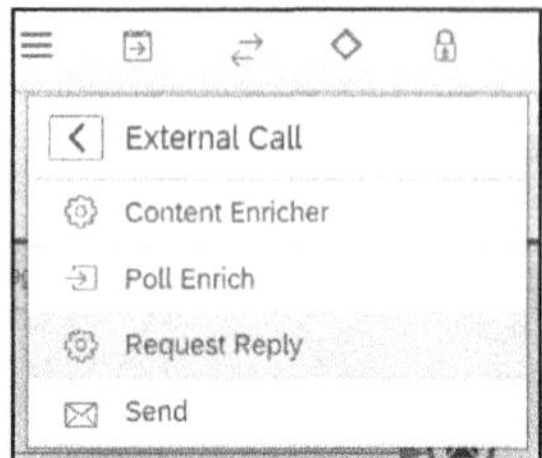

Figure 4.45 Modeling the Request Reply Step

In the submenu, click the **External Call** entry, and then select the **Request Reply** entry. Move your cursor over the **Integration Process** pool, and click again to position the step on the canvas. Figure 4.46 shows the result.

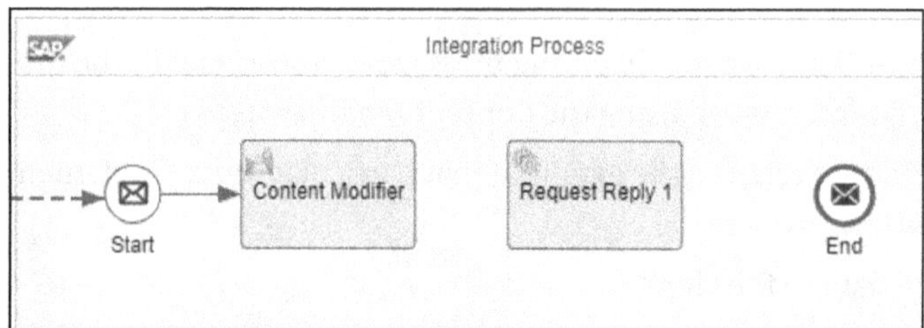

Figure 4.46 The Integration Process Pool with the Request Reply Entry Added

Because the **Request Reply** step must access an additional system, you'll add the target system as an additional pool in the process model. You can find the **Receiver** shape in the submenu of the palette's main entry, **Participant**. Figure 4.47 shows more details.

This next step is important. You must position **Receiver1** outside the **Integration Process** pool close to the **Request Reply** step, as shown in Figure 4.48.

Next, connect the **Request Reply** step with the **Receiver1** pool by using the connection icon → from the **Request Reply** step's context buttons. After dragging the connection to the **Receiver1** pool, a dialog box automatically opens, asking you for the **Adapter Type**. Choose **OData**, and you should see a screen similar to the one shown in Figure 4.49.

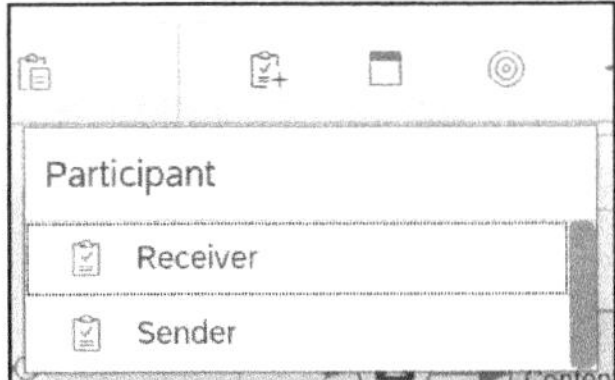

Figure 4.47 Picking an Additional Receiver from the Palette

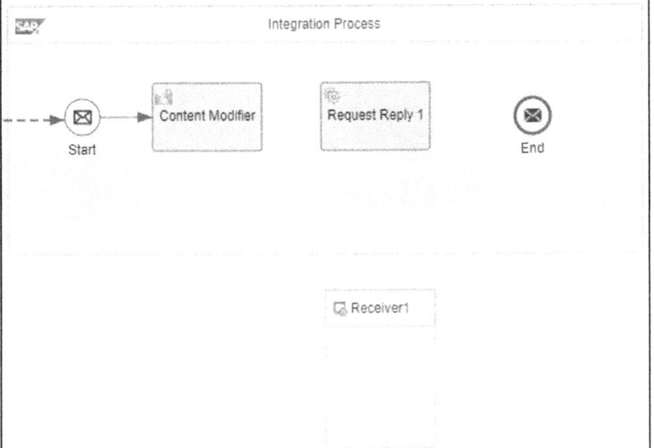

Figure 4.48 Positioning the Receiver1 Pool Close to the Request Reply Step but Outside the Integration Process Pool

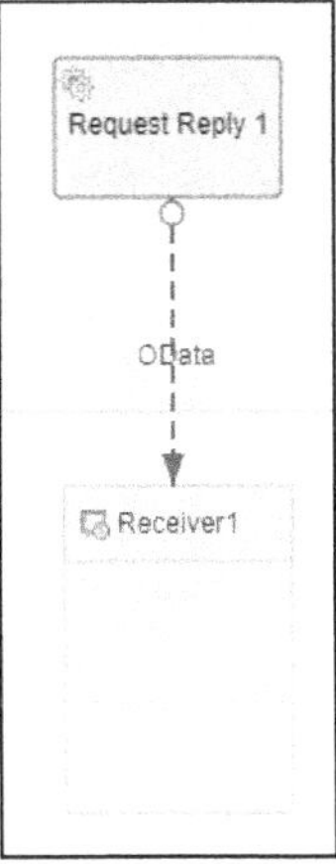

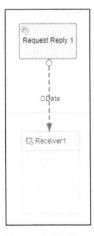

Figure 4.49 Connecting the Request Reply Step with the Receiver1 Pool

4.3.3 Configuring the OData Connection

To invoke an external OData source, you'll need to configure several parameters. After selecting the message flow between the **Request Reply** step and the **Receiver1** pool (the connection's color should switch from blue to blue with dotted orange), the parameters are shown beneath the process diagram. Figure 4.50 shows the details for the connection parameters, and Figure 4.51 shows the details for the processing parameters.

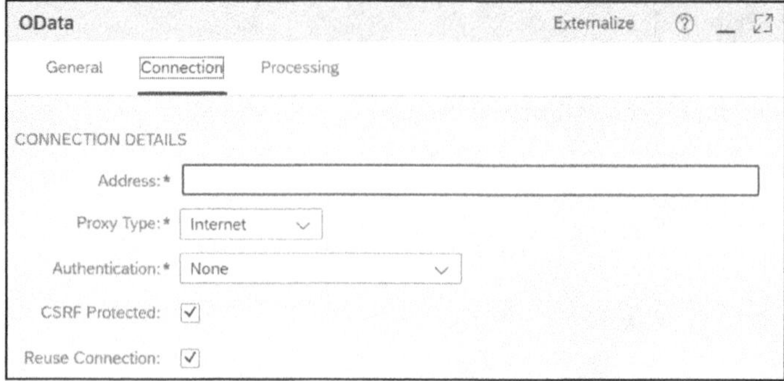

Figure 4.50 Connection Parameters of the OData Connection to the External Source

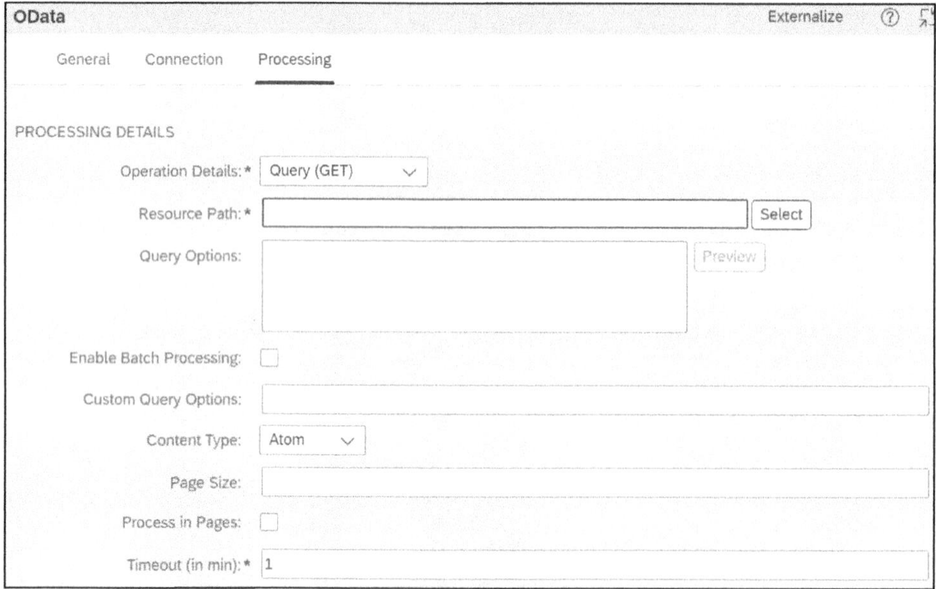

Figure 4.51 Processing Parameters of the OData Connection to the External Source

Let's walk through the configuration fields under the **Connection** tab (shown in Figure 4.50) one by one:

- **Address**
  This field contains the service's root URI of the OData service provider to which you want to connect. In our example, we're connecting to a publicly available service on the internet: one of the OData demo services available for trying out OData connectivity and learning more about how to work with OData services. This service is reachable through the URI *http://services.odata.org/Northwind/Northwind.svc*.

- **Proxy Type**
  This field defines whether you're connecting to a cloud system (**Internet**) or to an on-premise system via the SAP Connectivity services (**On-premise**). Because we're connecting to a cloud-based OData service, we'll leave the field as the **Internet**.
- **Authentication**
  Depending on the OData service, you can choose different authentication types from the dropdown list. **Basic**, **Client Certificate**, **Principal Propagation** (only available for the **On-premise** proxy type), and **None** are currently supported. For our example, select **None** because no authentication is required for the test service.

Let's now walk through the configuration fields under the **Processing** tab (shown in Figure 4.51) one by one:

- **Operation Details**
  OData is based on HTTP, which supports the following main operations: `GET`, for querying a set of entities or for reading one concrete entity (business object); `PUT`, for updating an entity; `POST`, for inserting data, `Merge` to merge entities; and `Delete`, for deleting an entity. Our requirement is to read exactly one order, so we're fine with the **GET** operation for this field.
- **Resource Path**
  In this field, you'll specify the URI that is appended to the OData service endpoint when connecting to the service provider. You may know this extension by heart, which is rarely the case because of the strict syntax you must follow and the lengthiness of the string, but letting the SAP system's built-in Query Editor do the dirty work of creating the resource path for you is easier. Later in this chapter, we'll explain how you can work with the Query Editor to create the correct resource path.
- **Page Size**
  This final field specifies the total number of records that should be returned in the response from the OData service provider. We're leaving this field empty because we're defining a query that returns only one entry, so no limitation of the response is necessary.

From the preceding description, you can understand the importance of the **Resource Path** entry compared to the other fields under the **Processing** tab. This importance is why SAP provides the Query Editor to accurately formulate the string representing the resource path.

4.3.4 Creating the Resource Path Using the Query Editor

Click the **Select** button next to the **Resource Path** input field shown in Figure 4.51 to start the Query Editor. A wizard dialog box opens, asking you for details of the OData service provider to which the Query Editor should connect. Ensure that the **Connect to System** step is populated, as shown in Figure 4.52.

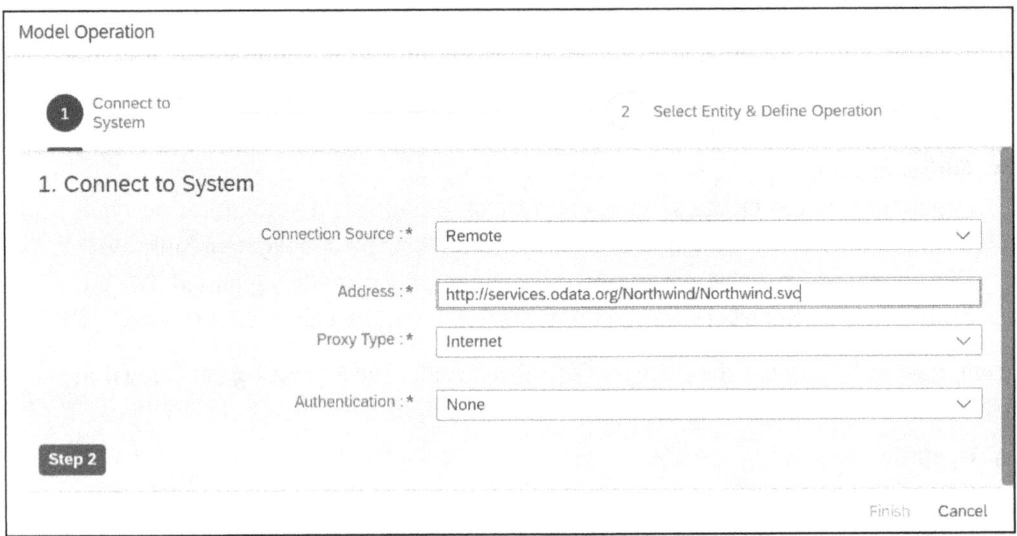

Figure 4.52 Providing Details about the OData Service Provider

Click on the **Step 2** button shown at the bottom of Figure 4.52 to proceed to the next step of the wizard.

The Query Editor connects to the service and retrieves its metadata information, as shown in Figure 4.53. Thus, this tool knows exactly which entities can be accessed and how.

Let's start with the entity and the operation. Because the Query Editor has read details about all the available entities, the tool can list them as options in the **Select Entity** dropdown list, as shown in Figure 4.53. To read exactly one concrete order, pick **Orders** from the list. For the **Operation** dropdown list, stick with the **Query (GET)** operation. Next, specify the fields that should be returned from the service. As you can imagine, an order can consist of hundreds of fields, but most likely, you only need a handful for your concrete scenario. Therefore, pick just the fields relevant to you.

From the **Fields** table list shown in Figure 4.53, specify the required fields by selecting their respective checkboxes. This information is again retrieved from the service's metadata information. For the sake of simplicity, choose the following fields: **OrderID**, **ShippedDate**, **ShipName**, **ShipAddress**, **ShipCity**, **ShipPostalCode**, and **ShipCountry**. After finishing your selections, the result should look like the output shown in Figure 4.53.

Note the string being created for you above the circular icons and beneath the **Query Editor** title:

```
Orders?$select=ShippedDate, OrderID, ShipCountry, ShipPostalCode, ShipCity,
ShipAddress, ShipName
```

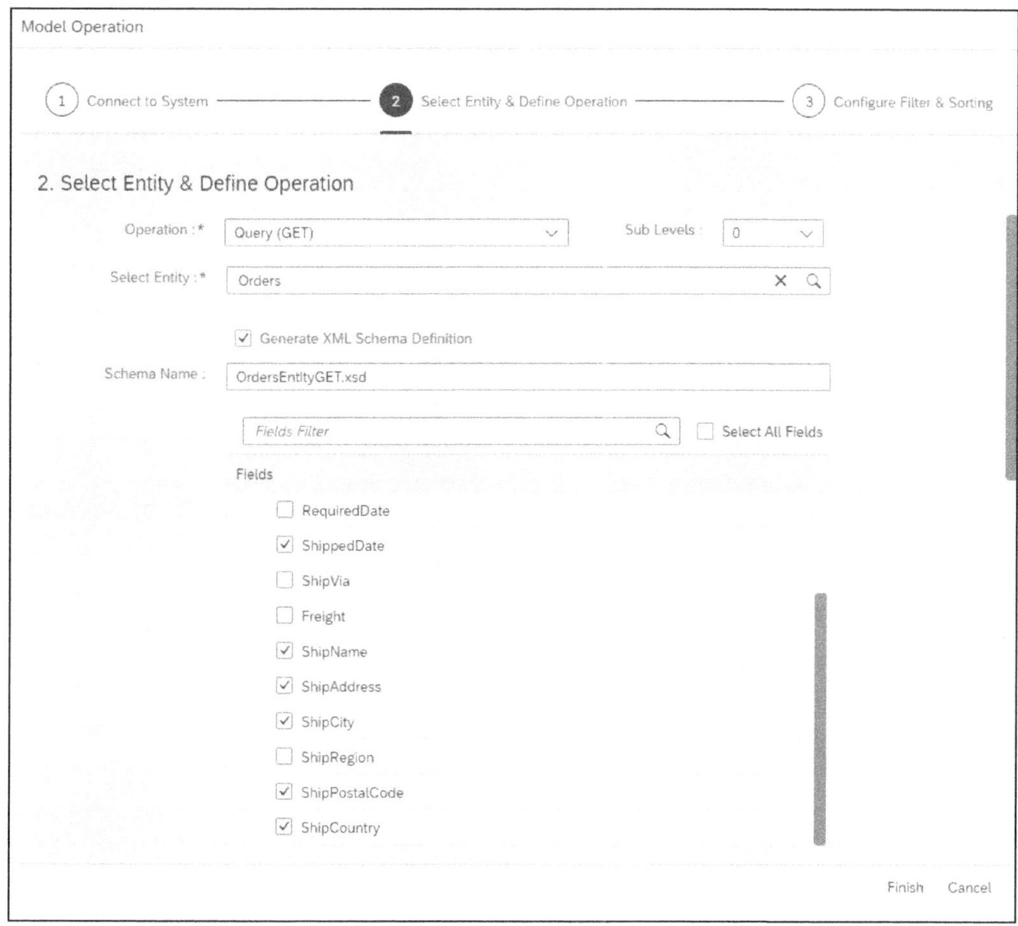

Figure 4.53 Defining the Entity, Operation, and Fields

Then, click on the **Step 3** button shown at the bottom of Figure 4.53 to proceed to the next step of the wizard.

As shown in Figure 4.54, the next screen is where you'll configure how the data should be filtered and sorted:

- The `filter by` condition represents a condition to be used to select the entries that you're interested in. It works similarly to a `WHERE` clause in an SQL statement.
- The `order by` condition is used to sort data based on a particular field in ascending or descending order.

To both filter by and order by area, as shown in Figure 4.54, you'll add as many entries as required to specify your desired selection criteria. In our example, we just need one line because we're searching for an order with a concrete, well-defined order number. Check the **OrderID** field within the **Orders** object. This entry is the exact entry you'll find in the **Filter By** column of the screen shown in Figure 4.54.

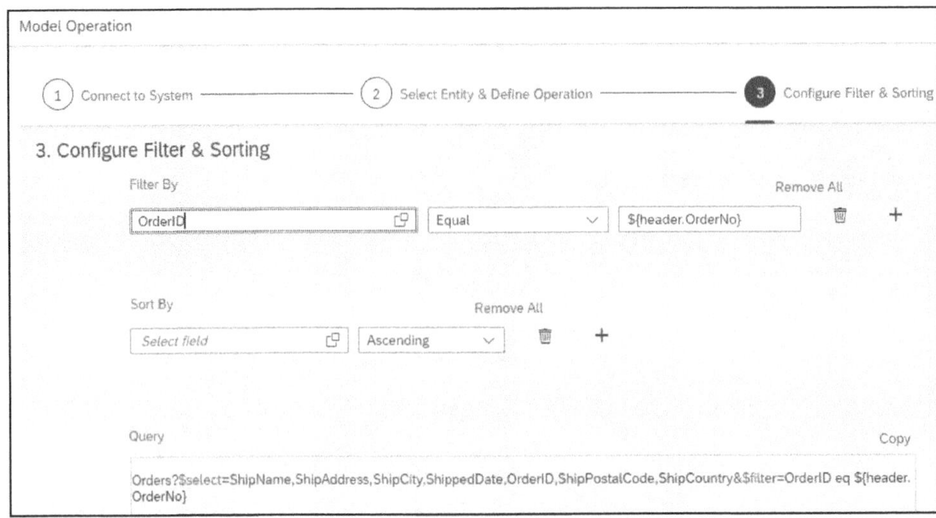

Figure 4.54 Defining the WHERE Clause in the Query Editor

Next, let's define the operator. Several logical operators are possible, but you only need the **eq** (equals) operator. Next, you'll need to decide which value to compare the entity's **OrderID** field against to find the right order. In our scenario, we want to find the order whose number was received in the original incoming message, which we stored in the header area of the message under the variable name **OrderNo** (shown earlier in Figure 4.18).

In this case, set the value to `${header.OrderNo}` to point to the value of **OrderNo**, which was stored in the header attributes. Now, hopefully, you understand why we had to store the number in the message header and how to retrieve that number for the `where` clause. Notice, also, the additional string appended to the previous **Resource Path**. The Query Editor uses the Simple Expression Language to access Apache Camel variables in the header area (`${header.OrderNo}`), which we introduced in Section 4.1. Depending on your scenario, you can also complete the **Resource Path** by using the `Order By` condition.

The configuration is fairly straightforward: Enter the field's name by which the found entries should be sorted. Again, the Query Editor narrows down the fields after you start typing. You want a list, which later actually consists of exactly one entry, to be sorted by the **OrderID**. You could also define whether the list should be in ascending or descending order by selecting **Ascending** or **Descending** in the dropdown menu, but this option doesn't play a role in our scenario.

After finishing this step, you've finally completed the configuration of the OData channel. Click the **Finish** button to close the Query Editor. You'll then see the message shown in Figure 4.55.

This message informs you that two files have been automatically created: an Entity Data Model Designer (EDMX) file and an XML Schema Definition (XSD) file. The EDMX file contains the Entity Data Model (EDM), which stores the schema of the entities encapsulated in the OData service, including their fields and relationships (e.g., one-to-one, one-to-many, etc.). In our example, we selected an entity earlier in Figure 4.53 for a dropdown field named **Select Entity**.

EDMX File services_odata_org_Northwind_Northwind_svc is created.
File OrdersEntityGET0.xsd is created.

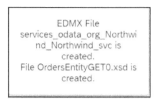

Figure 4.55 Query Editor Confirming the Automatic Creation of the EDMX and XSD Files

But what is the XSD file good for? The OData service returns the found entity in the Atom format. However, Cloud Integration continues working with the result in the XML format. Thus, the runtime requires a description of the resulting XML message that fits the returned values of the newly configured query. Because the Query Editor knows all the details about the selected fields, as well as the format of each field (thanks to the EDMX file), this tool can generate an associated XSD file representing the returned data of the service in the XML format. In the end, this file helps the engine map the returned Atom format to the XML format.

The generated **Resource Path** is added to the channel configuration of the **Query Options** field. The completed configuration of the connection to the OData service is shown in Figure 4.56 for the **Processing** tab and Figure 4.57 for the **Connection** tab.

Figure 4.56 Completed Processing Tab Configuration of the OData Channel

All that's left is to complete the iFlow itself by positioning the **Request Reply** step in between the **Start** and **End** events. Figure 4.58 shows the final result.

OData Externalize

General | Connection | Processing

CONNECTION DETAILS

Address:* http://services.odata.org/Northwind/Northwind.svc

Proxy Type:* Internet

Authentication:* None

CSRF Protected: ✓

Reuse Connection: ✓

Figure 4.57 Completed Connection Tab Configuration of the OData Channel

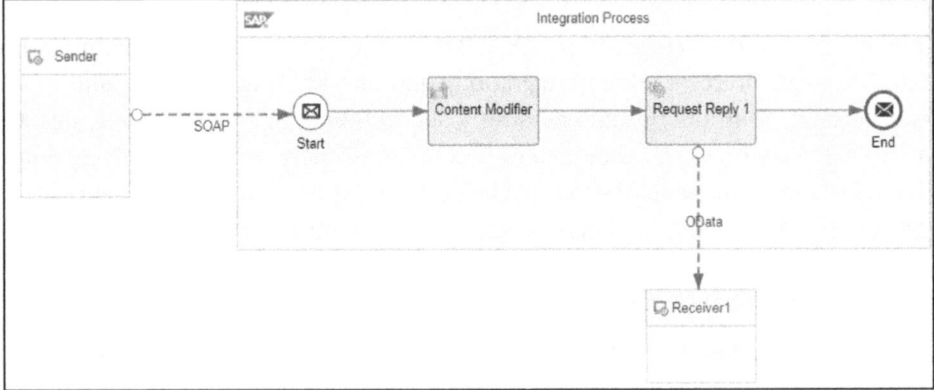

Figure 4.58 Completed Configuration of the iFlow

Now, save and deploy your iFlow. After successful deployment, retrieve the iFlow's endpoint URL, and invoke it (with the order number 10249) via a SOAP client, such as SoapUI. (For a detailed description of the invocation of iFlows, refer to Section 4.1.6.) As a result, you should see the response message shown in Figure 4.59.

```
<soap:Envelope xmlns:soap="http://schemas.xmlsoap.org/soap/envelope/">
    <soap:Header/>
    <soap:Body>
        <Orders>
            <Order>
                <ShipName>Toms Spezialitäten</ShipName>
                <ShippedDate>1996-07-10T00:00:00.000</ShippedDate>
                <ShipCity>Münster</ShipCity>
                <ShipAddress>Luisenstr. 48</ShipAddress>
                <ShipPostalCode>44087</ShipPostalCode>
                <ShipCountry>Germany</ShipCountry>
                <OrderID>10249</OrderID>
            </Order>
        </Orders>
    </soap:Body>
</soap:Envelope>
```

Figure 4.59 Response Message from the OData Service Formatted in XML

4.3.5 Using the Content Enricher Step

An interesting variant of this scenario is the use of the **Content Enricher** step inside the route, instead of the **Request Reply** step. (As shown earlier in Figure 4.45, you can select the **Request Reply** step from the palette.) Above the **Request Reply** entry, you'll find the **Content Enricher** step. In contrast to the **Request Reply** activity, which simply returns the response message from the external data source to the caller, the **Content Enricher** merges the content of the returned external message with the original message. In other words, this step converts the two separate messages into a single enhanced payload. You can try this scenario out yourself because this configuration is pretty straightforward. All you need to do is replace the **Request Reply** step with the **Content Enricher** step, shown in Figure 4.60, and ensure that the OData adapter is selected.

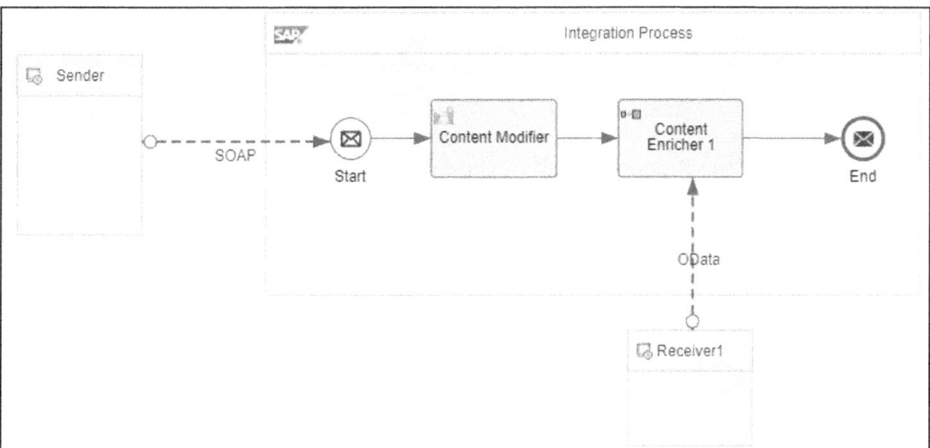

Figure 4.60 Replacing the Request Reply Step with the Content Enricher Step

Note one little, but important, deviation from the configuration of the connection between the **Receiver1** pool and the **Content Enricher** activity: the arrow points from the **Receiver1** pool to the **Content Enricher** step. This direction is the opposite direction of the connection between the **Request Reply** step and the **Receiver1** pool (shown earlier in Figure 4.58). Ensure that you don't mix up the direction of the arrows. The **Content Enricher** step also includes a **Processing** tab with an **Aggregation Algorithm** field that should be left with its default value, namely, **Combine**. We'll revisit the **Aggregation Algorithm** field later in this section.

Once deployed, you can run the same input message against the newly configured iFlow. As a result, you'll see the output shown in Figure 4.61.

You can identify the original input message at the top of the reply, followed by the returned detailed message coming from the external OData call. Thus, you can choose the pattern that best fits your needs.

```xml
<soap:Envelope xmlns:soap="http://schemas.xmlsoap.org/soap/envelope/">
    <soap:Header/>
    <soap:Body>
        <multimap:Messages xmlns:multimap="http://sap.com/xi/XI/SplitAndMerge">
            <multimap:Message1>
                <demo:OrderNumber_MT xmlns:demo="http://cpi.sap.com/demo" xmlns:soapenv="http://schemas.xmlsoap.org/soap/envelope/">
                    <orderNumber>10249</orderNumber>
                </demo:OrderNumber_MT>
            </multimap:Message1>
            <multimap:Message2>
                <Orders>
                    <Order>
                        <ShipName>Toms Spezialitäten</ShipName>
                        <ShippedDate>1996-07-10T00:00:00.000</ShippedDate>
                        <ShipCity>Münster</ShipCity>
                        <ShipAddress>Luisenstr. 48</ShipAddress>
                        <ShipPostalCode>44087</ShipPostalCode>
                        <ShipCountry>Germany</ShipCountry>
                        <OrderID>10249</OrderID>
                    </Order>
                </Orders>
            </multimap:Message2>
        </multimap:Messages>
    </soap:Body>
</soap:Envelope>
```


Figure 4.61 Output after Running the iFlow with the Content Enricher Step

Let's now revisit the **Processing** tab of the **Content Enricher** step, as shown in Figure 4.62.

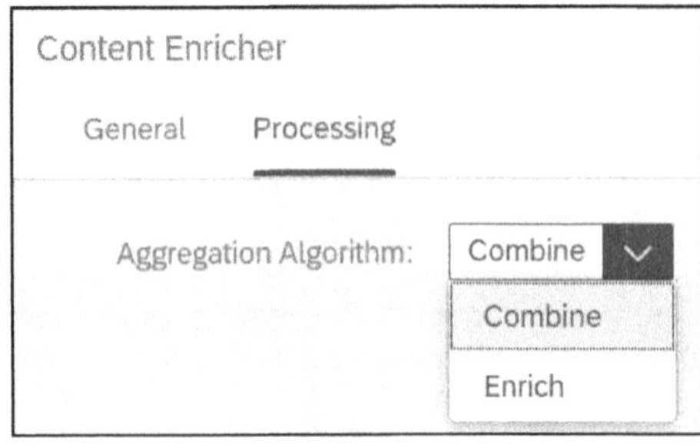

Figure 4.62 Processing Tab of the Content Enricher

As shown in Figure 4.62, the **Content Enricher** step has two different aggregation algorithms that it uses to combine two payloads into a single message: the **Combine** and **Enrich** aggregation algorithms. The following sections discuss both algorithms.

Combine

The **Combine** aggregation algorithm simply creates a new target message by adding two original messages next to each other. You don't have control over how messages should be combined. This algorithm was used in our previous example, which produced the response message shown in Figure 4.61. To better illustrate how the **Combine** algorithm differs from the **Enrich** algorithm, let's use a completely different example message (doesn't relate to the example shown earlier in Figure 4.61). Consider the original message shown in Figure 4.63.

```
<StudentCollection>
        <Student>
                <id>100</id>
                <firstname>John</firstname>
                <lastname>Smith</lastname>
                <score_refid>all</score_refid>
        </Student>
        <Student>
                <id>101</id>
                <firstname>Satoshi</firstname>
                <lastname>Nakamoto</lastname>
                <score_refid>al2</score_refid>
        </Student>
</StudentCollection>
```

Figure 4.63 Example of the Original Message

In addition, consider that the message shown in Figure 4.64 represents the response of the service called by the **Content Enricher** step. Note that this message is also sometimes referred to as a *lookup message* within the context of the **Content Enricher** step.

```
<StudentScores>
        <Score>
                <id>all</id>
                <course>Mathematics</course>
                <score>70</score>
                <year>2018</year>
                <passed>true</passed>
        </Score>
        <Score>
                <id>al2</id>
                <course>Mathematics</course>
                <score>40</score>
                <year>2018</year>
                <passed>false</passed>
        </Score>
</StudentScores>
```

Figure 4.64 Example of the Response Message of the Content Enricher Step (Lookup Message)

Using the **Content Enricher** algorithm, the combination of the two messages shown in Figure 4.63 and Figure 4.64 results in a message similar to the message shown in Figure 4.65. Notice from Figure 4.65 that each of the two messages have been wrapped by the nodes `message1` and `message2`, respectively. Another node named `messages` is used as the root of the message.

Let's next look at how the result would have looked differently with the **Enrich** aggregation algorithm.

```
<multimap:messages xmlns:multimap="http://sap.com/xi/XI/SplitAndMerge">
  <message1>
    <StudentCollection>
        <Student>
                <id>100</id>
                <firstname>John</firstname>
               <lastname>Smith</lastname>
                <score_refid>all</score_refid>
        </Student>
        <Student>
                <id>101</id>
                <firstname>Satoshi</firstname>
              <lastname>Nakamoto</lastname>
                <score_refid>al2</score_refid>
        </Student>
    </StudentCollection>
  </message1>
  <message2>
    <StudentScores>
        <Score>
                <id>all</id>
                <course>Mathematics</course>
                <score>70</score>
                <year>2018</year>
                <passed>true</passed>
        </Score>
        <Score>
                <id>al2</id>
                <course>Mathematics</course>
                <score>40</score>
                <year>2018</year>
                <passed>false</passed>
        </Score>
    </StudentScores>
  </message2>
</multimap:messages xmlns:multimap="http://sap.com/xi/XI/SplitAndMerge">
```

Figure 4.65 Enriched Message Using the Content Enricher Combined Algorithm

Enrich

The **Enrich** algorithm provides more control over how the original message and the resulting message returned by the **Content Enricher** (lookup message) should be merged. You can specify the path to the node and key element based on which the original message will be enriched with the lookup message.

Looking at the message shown earlier in Figure 4.63, note that the element `<score_refid>` represents the reference ID to be used as a link to the lookup message (shown earlier in Figure 4.64). While using the **Enrich** algorithm, you need a way to specify how the correct record should be retrieved from the lookup message. This specification is created with the help of the fields listed in Table 4.2. Note that these fields appear on the screen as soon as you select the **Enrich** value from the **Aggregator Algorithm** dropdown menu, as shown in Figure 4.66.

Figure 4.66 Example Fields Required for the Enrich Algorithm

Category	Field	Description	Example
Original Message	**Path to Node**	Path to the reference node in the original message	**StudentCollection/ Student**
	Key Element	Key element in the original message	**score_refid**
Lookup Message	**Path to Node**	Path to the reference node in the lookup message	**StudentScores/Score**
	Key Element	Key element in the lookup message	**Id**

Table 4.2 Properties Available for the Enrich Aggregator Algorithm

If you configure the **Enrich** properties with the values listed in Table 4.2 ("Example" column), you'll get a result similar to the output shown in Figure 4.67.

Notice how the resulting message from using the **Enrich** algorithm (see Figure 4.67) is different from the resulting message from the **Combine** algorithm (shown earlier in Figure 4.65). Our discussion on using the **Content Enricher** step is now complete.

In this section, we showed you how to configure a connection to an external OData-based service provider, how to use the Query Editor to construct the sometimes complex string for the resource path to retrieve the data you're interested in, and how to add a **Request Reply** (or **Content Enricher**) step to your message processing pipeline. In the next section, we'll explain how to format the message to a target format of your choice by using mappings.

```
<StudentCollection>
        <Student>
                <id>100</id>
                <firstname>John</firstname>
                <lastname>Smith</lastname>
                <score_refid>all</score_refid>
                <Score>
                        <id>all</id>
                        <course>Mathematics</course>
                        <score>70</score>
                        <year>2018</year>
                        <passed>true</passed>
                </Score>
        </Student>
        <Student>
                <id>101</id>
                <firstname>Satoshi</firstname>
                <lastname>Nakamoto</lastname>
                <score_refid>al2</score_refid>
                <Score>
                        <id>al2</id>
                        <course>Mathematics</course>
                        <score>40</score>
                        <year>2018</year>
                        <passed>false</passed>
                </Score>
        </Student>
</StudentCollection>
```

Figure 4.67 Enriched Message Using the Content Enricher's Enrich Algorithm

4.3.6 Using the Poll Enrich Step

So far, you've seen how Cloud Integration facilitates data enrichment by calling synchronous services hosted by external systems. There is one typical scenario that can't be achieved by the **Request Reply** or **Content Enricher** palette shapes: reading a file from an SFTP server during the execution of an iFlow. Connection with the SFTP server is achieved by using the sender SFTP adapter and the receiver SFTP adapter. The Sender SFTP adapter is used to read a file from the SFTP server, and the receiver SFTP adapter is used to write a file to the SFTP server. A sender adapter is used at the beginning of the iFlow with the intention of triggering the iFlow execution. There is one exception to this scenario, and it's the **Poll Enrich** palette shape. **Poll Enrich** is used to connect to an SFTP server to read a file in the middle of a message execution. Let's look at a sample scenario to explain the working of **Poll Enrich**. We'll use the same scenario as explained in Section 4.3.1, but instead of invoking an OData service, we'll be reading a file from an SFTP server. The scenario looks like Figure 4.68.

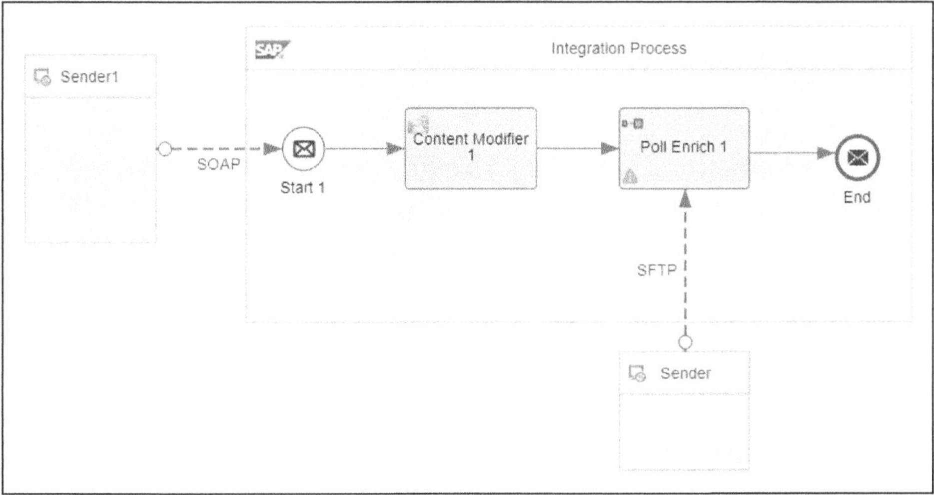

Figure 4.68 iFlow with Poll Enrich

In this scenario, our iFlow covers the following steps:

1. Sending a SOAP request containing an order number from the **Sender** participant to Cloud Integration.
2. Retrieving the order number from the incoming message and storing it in the message's header field for later reference using the **Content Modifier** step.
3. Connecting to an SFTP adapter to retrieve a file that contains the details of that particular order, implementing a **Poll Enrich** pattern scenario.
4. Returning the received data to the client.

The configuration of the SOAP channel is the same as the previous exercise. Update the address field to create a new endpoint: `/CI_Book_Demo_Poll_Enrich`.

Now let's focus on the configuration of **Poll Enrich** by following these steps:

1. After the content modifier, add the **Poll Enrich** palette step from the **External Call** submenu option as shown in Figure 4.69.

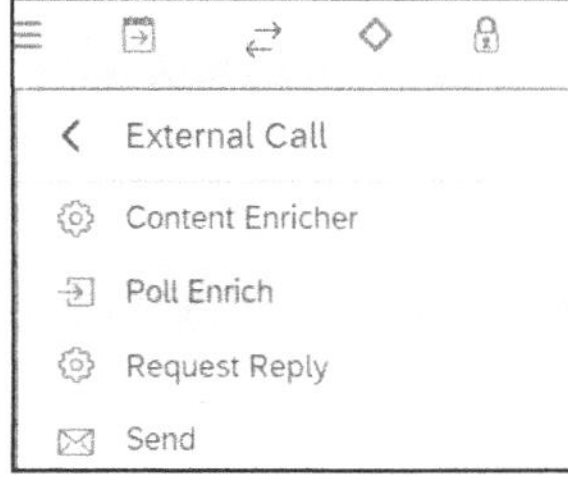

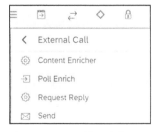

Figure 4.69 Poll Enrich Step under the External Call Submenu

2. As the **Poll Enrich** step is specifically designed to poll messages from external systems such as an SFTP server, a **Sender Participant** shape is required. Add the **Sender** shape to the canvas from the submenu of the palette's main entry, **Participant** via .
3. Connect the **Sender2** step with the **Poll Enrich** step by using the connection icon from the **Sender2** step's context buttons. After dragging the connection to the **Sender2** pool, a dialog box automatically opens, asking you for the **Adapter Type**. Select the adapter as **SFTP**.

The next step is to configure the SFTP adapter, as shown in Figure 4.70:

1. Provide the folder location from which the file is to be picked up in the **Directory** field. As we need to poll the file based on the order number from the incoming message, configure the **File Name** parameter to read the value from the header called **OrderNo**, which was created in the content modifier. Provide the hostname of your SFTP server in the **Address** field.

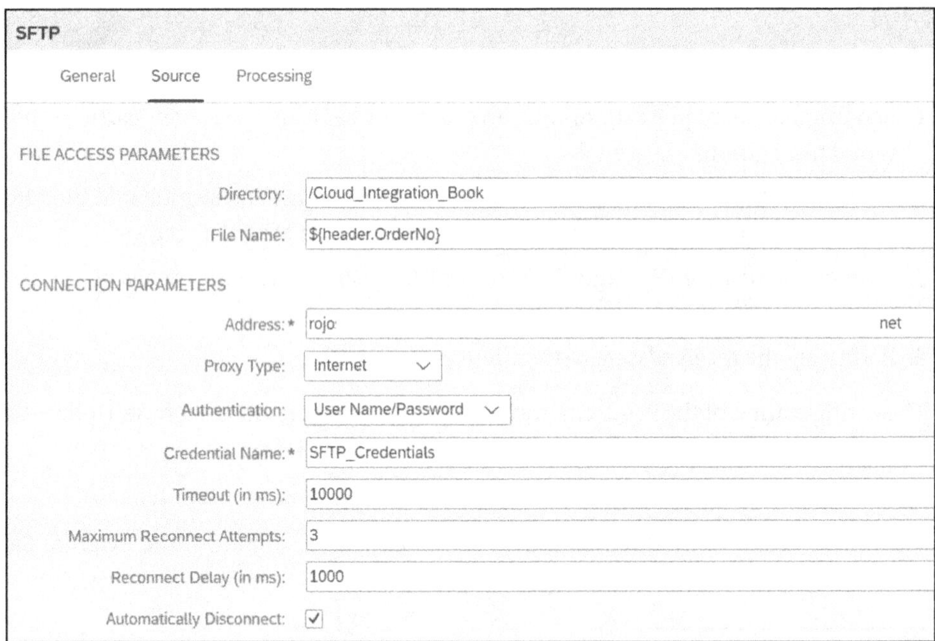

Figure 4.70 Sender SFTP Adapter Configuration

2. To connect to the SFTP server in general you need to follow a certain authentication mechanism. The SFTP server that we're connecting to in this example supports user name/password authentication, so we've selected the corresponding entry from the **Authentication** dropdown. Cloud Integration provides a secure store to save all the credentials and security material to ensure reuse across iFlows. Chapter 10 will cover the various security materials in depth. For this exercise, navigate to **Monitor** and under **Manage Security**, click on the **Security Material** tile, as shown in Figure 4.71.

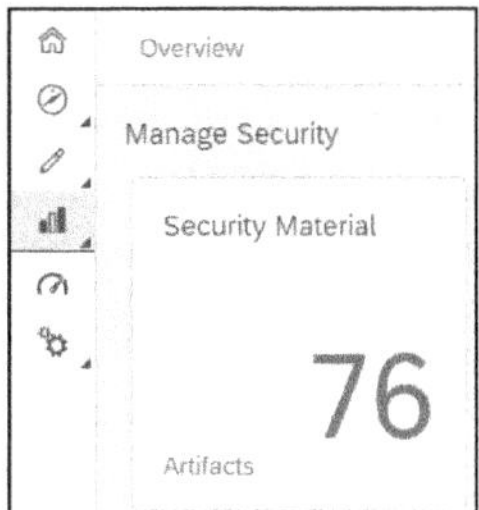

Figure 4.71 Security Material Tile under the Manage Security Section

3. Click on **Create**, and select **User Credentials** from the list, as shown in Figure 4.72.

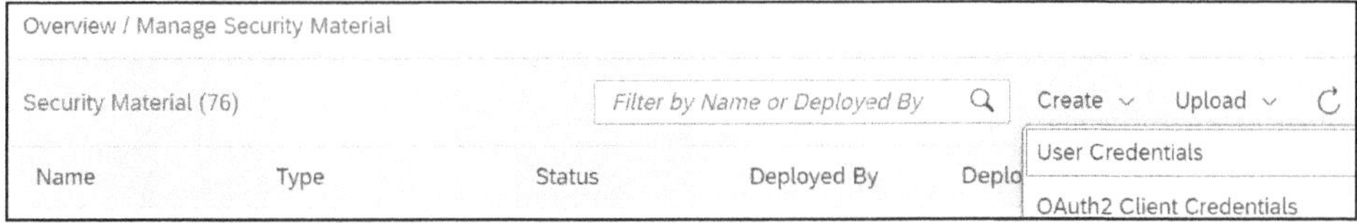

Figure 4.72 Creating a User Credential

4. This will open a popup window, as shown in Figure 4.73. Enter the **Name** of the credential as "SFTP_Credentials", select the **Type** as **User Credentials**, and fill in your SFTP User and Password in the corresponding text boxes. Click on **Deploy** to deploy the user credentials to the Cloud Integration runtime.

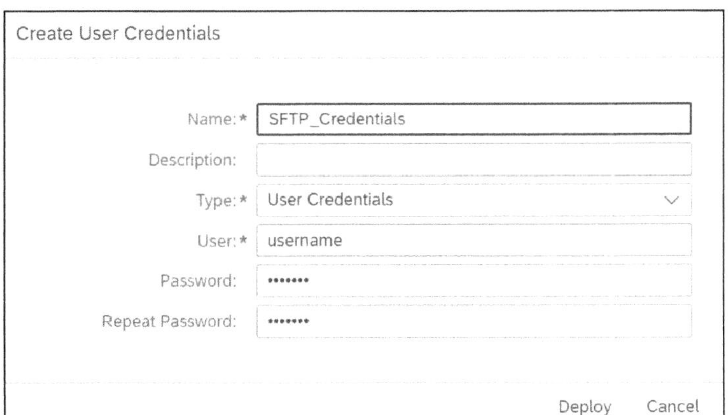

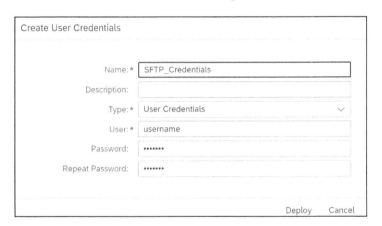

Figure 4.73 User Creation Settings

5. Leave the rest of the configurations as default for the SFTP adapter. The final configuration should look similar to Figure 4.70, shown earlier.
6. Navigate to the **Processing** tab of **Poll Enrich**, and leave the **Aggregation Algorithm** with the default setting of **Replace**. We'll discuss the various possible aggregation algorithms later in this section.
7. The configuration of your iFlow is now complete. Deploy the iFlow as usual.

Next, let's test this iFlow:

1. Once the iFlow is deployed, download the WSDL, and import it in SoapUI. Because **Poll Enrich** is configured to read a file from an SFTP server, you need to first create a file and place it in the source directory, */Cloud_Integration_Book*. For testing, we'll use order number **10249** and create a file with this name with the content specified in Figure 4.74.

```
<Orders>
<Order>
<ShipName>Toms Spezialitäten</ShipName>
<ShippedDate>1996-07-10T00:00:00.000</ShippedDate>
<ShipCity>Münster</ShipCity>
<ShipAddress>Luisenstr. 48</ShipAddress>
<ShipPostalCode>44087</ShipPostalCode>
<ShipCountry>Germany</ShipCountry>
<OrderID>10249</OrderID>
</Order>
</Orders>
```

Figure 4.74 File Content for Testing the iFlow

2. You can use any standard SFTP client to connect to an SFTP server. In this exercise, we'll use an open source FTP client called FileZilla. To connect to the server, provide the host, user name, password, and port (should be **22**), and click on **Quickconnect**. This will make a connection with the server and open the default folder. For this example, the folder used is */Cloud_Integration_Book*. Now upload the file *10249* under this location by navigating to the local folder where this file is stored and double-clicking on the file to initiate transfer, as shown in Figure 4.75.

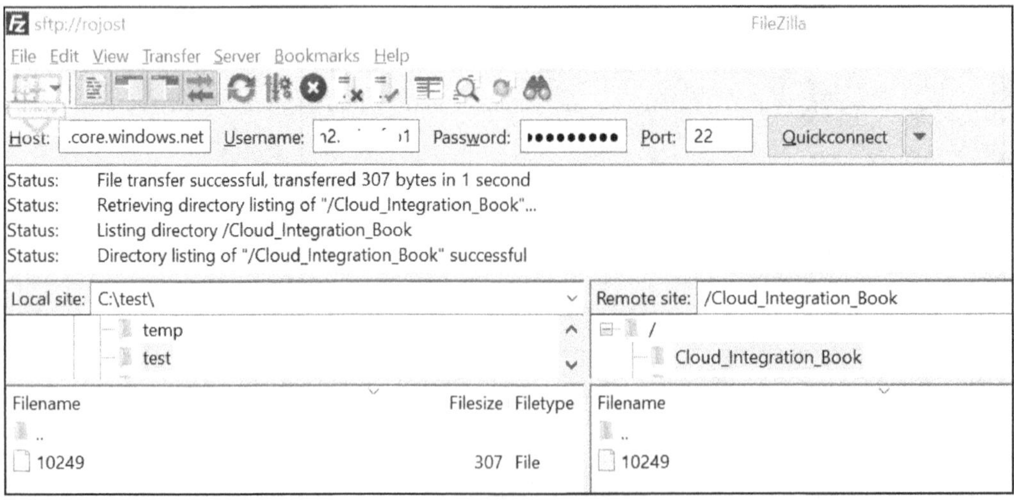

Figure 4.75 FileZilla Tool to Place Test File in the SFTP Server

3. Navigate back to the SoapUI project, and execute the request with `orderNumber` 10249. Your response should look as depicted in Figure 4.76.

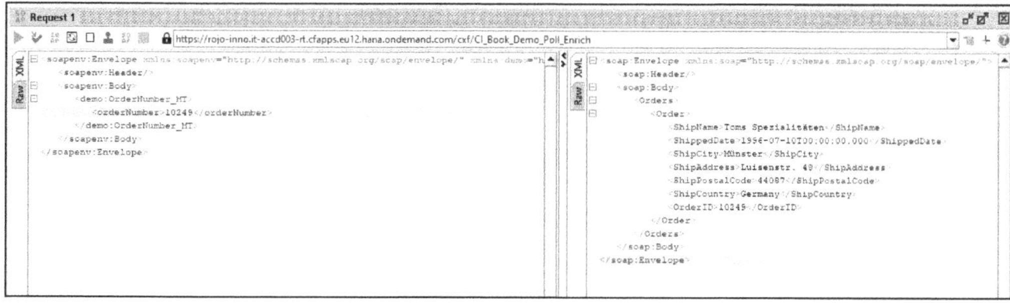

Figure 4.76 SoapUI Request and Response of the Poll Enrich iFlow

Let's explore the features of the **Poll Enrich** shape. Navigate to the **Processing** tab of **Poll Enrich**. You'll notice the **Aggregation Algorithm** dropdown list. Similar to the **Content Enricher**, **Poll Enrich** also provides you with multiple possibilities to combine the `$in.body` (exchange body) data with the polled data. Let's look at each possibility with an example:

- **Replace**
  As the name suggests, this configuration will replace the content of `$in.body` with the content polled from the Sender system. The scenario explained earlier is an example of replace configuration. In Figure 4.76, you'll observe that the response only contains XML segments polled from the file. In this case, the request message is lost or replaced.
- **Combine XML**
  The combine XML strategy combines the `$in.body` content with the polled content under a multimap Messages segment. The incoming message becomes Message1, and the response of the poll becomes Message2. This results in a well-formed XML document if both incoming and polled messages are well-formed XMLs. See a sample response of the scenario with the combine XML setting in Figure 4.77.

```
<soap:Envelope xmlns:soap="http://schemas.xmlsoap.org/soap/envelope/">
  <soap:Header/>
  <soap:Body>
    <multimap:Messages xmlns:multimap="http://sap.com/xi/XI/SplitAndMerge">
      <multimap:Message1>
        <demo:OrderNumber_MT xmlns:demo="http://ci.sap.com/demo" xmlns:soapenv="h
          <orderNumber>10249</orderNumber>
        </demo:OrderNumber_MT>
      </multimap:Message1>
      <multimap:Message2>
        <Orders>
          <Order>
            <ShipName>Toms Spezialitäten</ShipName>
            <ShippedDate>1996-07-10T00:00:00.000</ShippedDate>
            <ShipCity>Münster</ShipCity>
            <ShipAddress>Luisenstr. 48</ShipAddress>
            <ShipPostalCode>44087</ShipPostalCode>
            <ShipCountry>Germany</ShipCountry>
            <OrderID>10249</OrderID>
          </Order>
        </Orders>
      </multimap:Message2>
    </multimap:Messages>
  </soap:Body>
</soap:Envelope>
```

Figure 4.77 Enriched Message Using the Combine XML Algorithm

- **Concatenate**
  Now the combined XML aggregation algorithm only works for well-formed XML. What if you're dealing with non-XML data? In that case, you can use the concatenate option. This will ensure that the incoming and polled data is simply concatenated without any parsing. Figure 4.78 illustrates how the data would be combined to create a target message.

```
<demo:OrderNumber_MT xmlns:demo="http://ci.sap.com/demo" xmlns:soapenv="http://schemas.xmls
        <orderNumber>10249</orderNumber>
      </demo:OrderNumber_MT><Orders>
<Order>
<ShipName>Toms Spezialitäten</ShipName>
<ShippedDate>1996-07-10T00:00:00.000</ShippedDate>
<ShipCity>Münster</ShipCity>
<ShipAddress>Luisenstr. 48</ShipAddress>
<ShipPostalCode>44087</ShipPostalCode>
<ShipCountry>Germany</ShipCountry>
<OrderID>10249</OrderID>
</Order>
</Orders>
```

Figure 4.78 Enriched Message Using the Concatenate Algorithm

In this section, you learned the configurations of the **Poll Enrich** palette shape in Cloud Integration to connect to an SFTP server from the middle of an iFlow. Now let's deep dive into the world of data transformation using mappings in Cloud Integration.

4.4 Working with Mappings

Typically, integration projects require mapping functionality because of the many different message formats used by the systems that need to be connected. Thus, integration solutions such as Cloud Integration must provide capabilities to solve this problem elegantly. In this section, you'll learn how to apply mappings in your iFlows. We'll explain the configuration of the mapping step in detail. In addition, we'll show you how message processing in Cloud Integration differs from message processing in SAP Process Integration and the consequences of this difference on the mapping's configuration.

In every integration scenario, mapping between different data formats of the participating systems is a hot topic. In fact, mappings may be one of the most important tasks you must complete for every integration project, and mappings always require a certain amount of effort to implement. Supporting the modeler with a convenient mapping environment and a performance mapping engine is of the highest importance for every integration framework.

SAP has experience in building a mapping engine through its SAP Process Integration product. From the beginning, SAP Process Integration included a Java-based mapping engine. Consequently, SAP Process Integration became an obvious place to include the same mapping engine in Cloud Integration as well. This stable and reliable mapping engine has been in productive use for many years. In addition, because of this reuse, you can also reuse your SAP Process Integration mappings in Cloud Integration, which saves your investment in mapping logic that you've already developed.

This section, however, isn't about the mapping engine itself, the functionality it provides, or how to solve certain mapping challenges because a plethora of material is already publicly available, either in SAP's online documentation for SAP Process Integration or on the SAP Community site. Instead, we'll address the question of how to apply the mapping engine within Cloud Integration so that you know how to use a mapping step in your message processing chain correctly.

Mapping is of particular importance because Cloud Integration is based on the Apache Camel integration framework, which can handle almost any message format. As a payload-agnostic routing and mediation engine, Apache Camel doesn't follow the interface concept from SAP Process Integration, where you would precisely define XML-based inbound and outbound interfaces in the Enterprise Services Repository (ESR) before you can start modeling an integration scenario.

The overhead of defining interfaces before modeling the integration isn't necessary for Cloud Integration. You can push anything to Cloud Integration, and, as long as you don't need access to the actual payload (e.g., for routing purposes), Cloud Integration forwards the message to the receivers as is. However, the mapping engine has the same history as SAP Process Integration with its XML background. Therefore, the mapping engine works on XML transformations only, which requires a conversion to XML before invoking the mapping engine in Cloud Integration. As such, you must provide the XML schema of the source and the target message by uploading respective XSD or WSDL files to Cloud Integration. Let's explore these concepts in a concrete example.

4.4.1 The Scenario

In this section, we'll continue from where we left off in Section 4.3. In that section, you learned how to invoke an OData service to retrieve order details for a given order number. The scenario was shown earlier in Figure 4.58.

As part of the configuration of the OData connection to the receiver, the Query Editor is used to model access to the OData source. The editor allows you, for example, to define the entities for which a query should search, the individual fields of the entity you're interested in, the filter criteria of the query, and the `order by` condition for sorting the retrieved entities accordingly.

An important part of configuring the connectivity to the OData service provider by the Query Editor is the automatic generation of an XSD file representing the return message of the service in XML format. (See the confirmation message in Cloud Integration's graphical modeling environment after finishing the configuration of the connection's properties with the Query Editor shown earlier in Figure 4.55.)

This file is generated even though an OData service typically returns its results in either JavaScript Object Notation (JSON) or Atom format. The **Request Reply** step shown earlier in Figure 4.58 implicitly invokes a mapping from JSON/Atom to XML so that the message processing chain can continue working on XML in the following steps. But what if the current format within the route isn't in XML? In these cases, you must explicitly call a transformation step. Currently, Cloud Integration supports steps for converting comma-separated values (CSV) and JSON to XML, and vice versa. SAP BTP Enterprise Agreement is additionally equipped with an Electronic Data Interchange (EDI)-to-XML converter. In the web-based modeling environment of Cloud Integration, you'll find the available converters beneath the **Converters** icon, as shown in Figure 4.79.

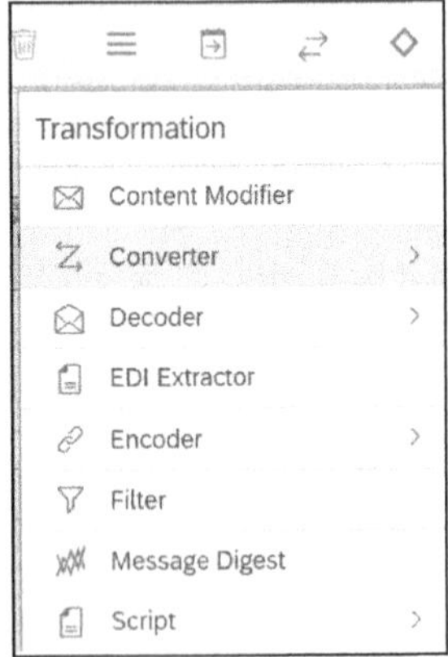

Figure 4.79 Picking a Converter Step from the Palette

The goal for our example scenario is to map the returned entity into an XML format of our choice. The business scenario behind this assumption is that, quite frequently, data must be returned to a consumer in a specific XML format. You'll need to convert the automatically generated XML format of the **Request Reply** step in your route to the target format the consumer expects.

Typically, the required target format is defined either by an XSD or a WSDL file. If you have an SAP Process Integration background, you can also easily define these files using the Enterprise Services Builder—the tool SAP Process Integration provides for designing interfaces in the ESR. Any other XML tool works as well. For our example, we created such an XML file, called *GetOrderShipDetails_Sync.wsdl*, which we used for our first exercise in Section 4.1. For your convenience, you'll find an example message matching the WSDL's description, as shown in Figure 4.80.

To summarize, the source message for the mapping step is the structure defined in the automatically generated XSD file *OrdersEntityGET.xsd* (shown earlier in Figure 4.55), and the target message is the response part of the synchronous service interface described in *GetOrderShipDetails_Sync.wsdl*.

```
<soapenv:Envelope xmlns:soapenv="http://schemas.xmlsoap.org/soap/envelope/"
   <soapenv:Header/>
   <soapenv:Body>
      <demo:OrderNumber_MT>
         <orderNumber>10249</orderNumber>
      </demo:OrderNumber_MT>
   </soapenv:Body>
</soapenv:Envelope>
```

Figure 4.80 Example Message

Before diving more deeply into the mapping topic, let's first import the *GetOrderShip-Details_Sync.wsdl* file into our iFlow via the **References** tab in the next section.

4.4.2 Adding and Using Resources via the References Tab

A typical integration scenario uses a variety of resources, such as mappings, archives, scripts, and schemas, in its steps. Any external file or artifact that can be imported or referred to for the purpose of being used in the iFlow can be considered as a resource. Let's first start by exploring the features of the iFlow. Later in this section, we'll discuss how to extend our example iFlow by adding a WSDL file under the **References** tab.

The resources are typically grouped under the different categories listed in Table 4.3.

Category	Type	Supported Extensions	Source
Archives	Archive	*.jar*	Can be added from the file system
Mappings	Operation mapping	*.opmap*	Can be added from the ESR
	Message mapping	*.mmap*	
	XSLT mapping	*.xslt* *.xsl*	Can be added from the file system or another iFlow
Schemas	WSDL	*.wsdl*	Can be added from the file system or another iFlow
	XSD	*.xsd*	
	EDMX	*.edmx*	
	JSON	*.json*	
Scripts	Groovy script	*.gsh* *.gy* *.groovy*	Can be added from the file system or another iFlow
	JavaScript	*.js*	

Table 4.3 Types of Files Supported by the References Tab

The columns used in Table 4.3 are as follows:

- **Category**
  A grouping under which the different resources can be classified.
- **Type**
  The types of resource files that can be added for each category.
- **Supported Extensions**
  The supported file extensions for each resource type.
- **Source**
  The source from which resources can be added. Some resources can be uploaded from your local file system. You can also add some resources from another existing iFlow. This reuse of resources from another iFlow prevents the duplication of resources.

The **References** tab is where all the artifacts listed in Table 4.3 can be centrally managed. From this view, resources can be opened in their respective editors, downloaded, and deleted. After opening an iFlow, click on the area outside the iFlow model for the **References** tab to appear at the bottom of the screen, as shown in Figure 4.81.

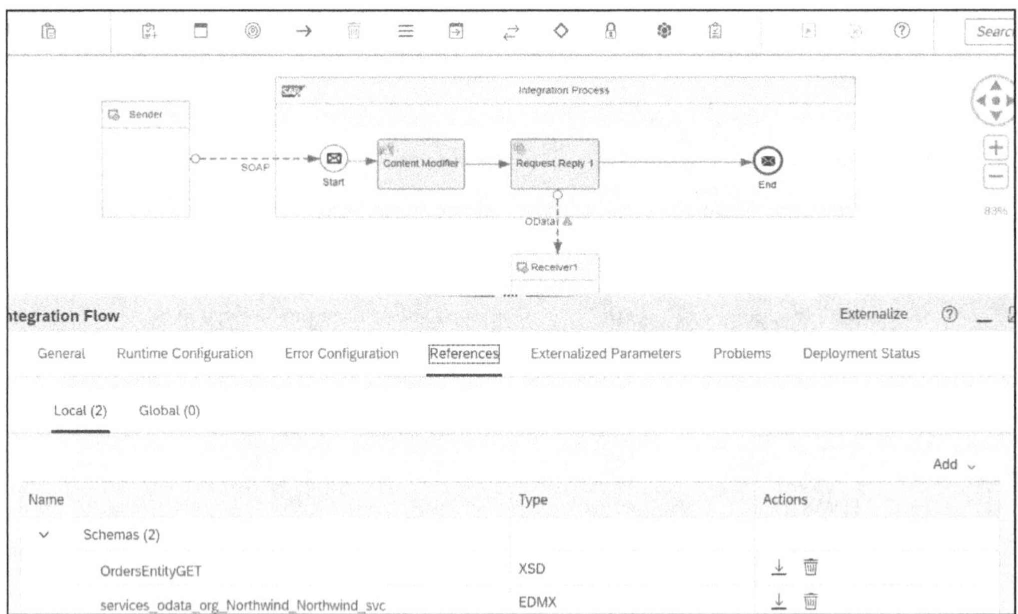

Figure 4.81 The References View Tab

Looking at the scenario we started implementing in Section 4.1.4, the iFlow must be enriched by adding the WSDL resource that will be used to perform some mapping later in Section 4.4.3. In Section 4.1.4, we downloaded the WSDL file named *GetOrder ShipDetails_Sync.wsdl*. You can now import this file by following these steps:

1. Click **Edit**, and then click the area outside the iFlow model.
2. Select the **References** tab at the bottom section of the iFlow, as shown in Figure 4.81.
3. Click the **Add** button, and a menu will appear. Select **Schema** and then **WSDL**, as shown in Figure 4.82.

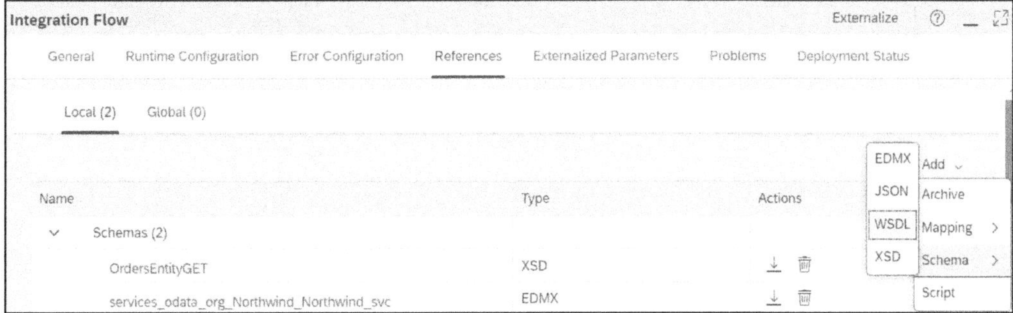

Figure 4.82 Adding an Object in the References View

4. You'll be redirected to a page where you can browse your local file system for the WSDL file and upload it. As a result, the WSDL file is now added to the **References** tab, as shown in Figure 4.83.

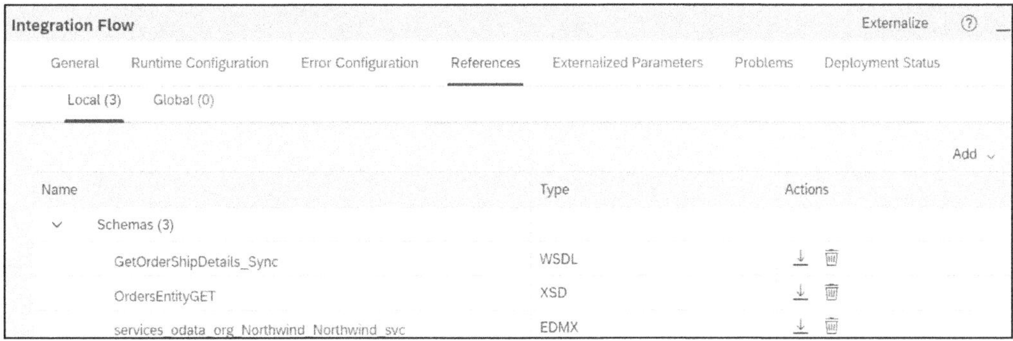

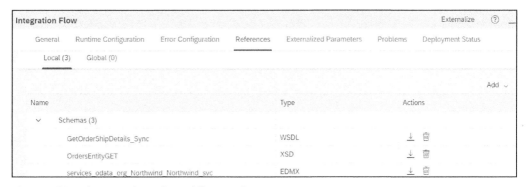

Figure 4.83 Reference View after Adding a WSDL

Note

Because the WSDL can be categorized as a schema (as listed in Table 4.3), note that this file is placed under the **Schemas** node element shown in Figure 4.83.

Hovering over the name of a resource shown in the **References** tab will show you its access path. Alternatively, you can click on a resource name to view the resource details via its editor.

Several actions can be performed on the uploaded resources, including the following actions, shown in Figure 4.83:

- **Delete**
  Click the delete icon 🗑 to delete a resource from the **References** tab.
- **Download**
  Click the download icon ⤓ to download a resource from the **References** tab.

Click on the name of the WSDL file resource, shown in Figure 4.83, and the WSDL file will be loaded into a special view, as shown in Figure 4.84.

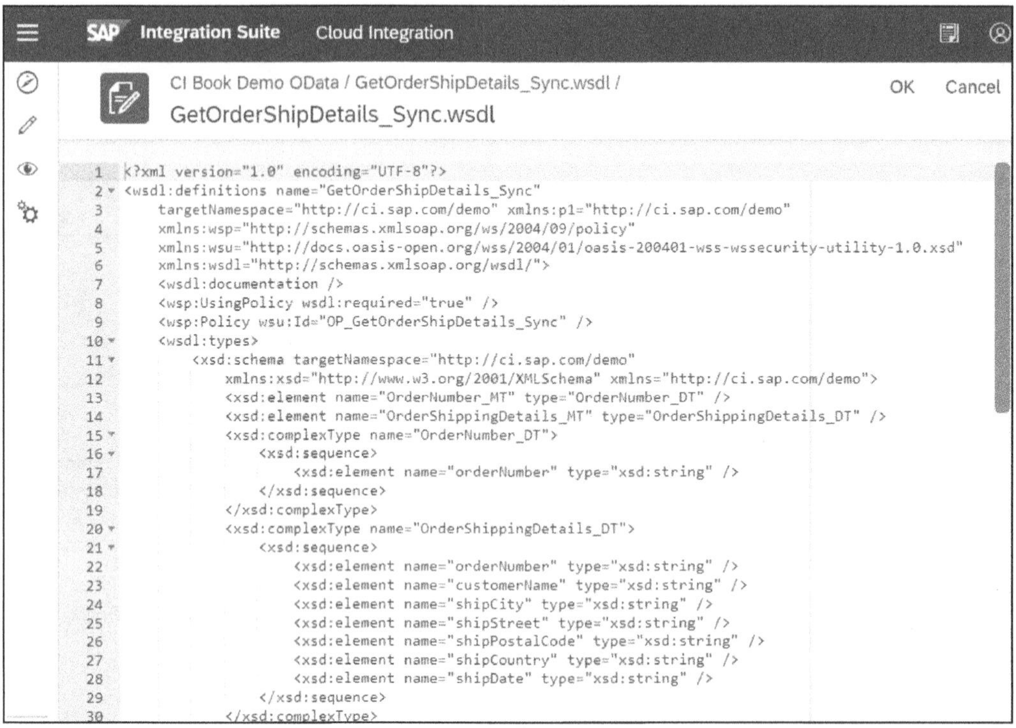

SAP Integration Suite Cloud Integration

CI Book Demo OData / GetOrderShipDetails_Sync.wsdl /
GetOrderShipDetails_Sync.wsdl

OK Cancel

```
<?xml version="1.0" encoding="UTF-8"?>
<wsdl:definitions name="GetOrderShipDetails_Sync"
    targetNamespace="http://ci.sap.com/demo" xmlns:p1="http://ci.sap.com/demo"
    xmlns:wsp="http://schemas.xmlsoap.org/ws/2004/09/policy"
    xmlns:wsu="http://docs.oasis-open.org/wss/2004/01/oasis-200401-wss-wssecurity-utility-1.0.xsd"
    xmlns:wsdl="http://schemas.xmlsoap.org/wsdl/">
    <wsdl:documentation />
    <wsp:UsingPolicy wsdl:required="true" />
    <wsp:Policy wsu:Id="OP_GetOrderShipDetails_Sync" />
    <wsdl:types>
        <xsd:schema targetNamespace="http://ci.sap.com/demo"
            xmlns:xsd="http://www.w3.org/2001/XMLSchema" xmlns="http://ci.sap.com/demo">
            <xsd:element name="OrderNumber_MT" type="OrderNumber_DT" />
            <xsd:element name="OrderShippingDetails_MT" type="OrderShippingDetails_DT" />
            <xsd:complexType name="OrderNumber_DT">
                <xsd:sequence>
                    <xsd:element name="orderNumber" type="xsd:string" />
                </xsd:sequence>
            </xsd:complexType>
            <xsd:complexType name="OrderShippingDetails_DT">
                <xsd:sequence>
                    <xsd:element name="orderNumber" type="xsd:string" />
                    <xsd:element name="customerName" type="xsd:string" />
                    <xsd:element name="shipCity" type="xsd:string" />
                    <xsd:element name="shipStreet" type="xsd:string" />
                    <xsd:element name="shipPostalCode" type="xsd:string" />
                    <xsd:element name="shipCountry" type="xsd:string" />
                    <xsd:element name="shipDate" type="xsd:string" />
                </xsd:sequence>
            </xsd:complexType>
```

Figure 4.84 Viewing the Contents of the WSDL File

Now that you've successfully imported the WSDL file under the **References** tab, let's see how this WSDL file can be useful to your iFlow by using it in the **Sender** channel.

You'll need to select the Sender channel, which will display its details at the bottom of the screen, as shown in Figure 4.85.

Now, click on the **Select** button (see Figure 4.85), and you'll be presented with a new screen where you can select a WDSL file, as shown in Figure 4.86. Select the **GetOrderShipDetails_Sync** row.

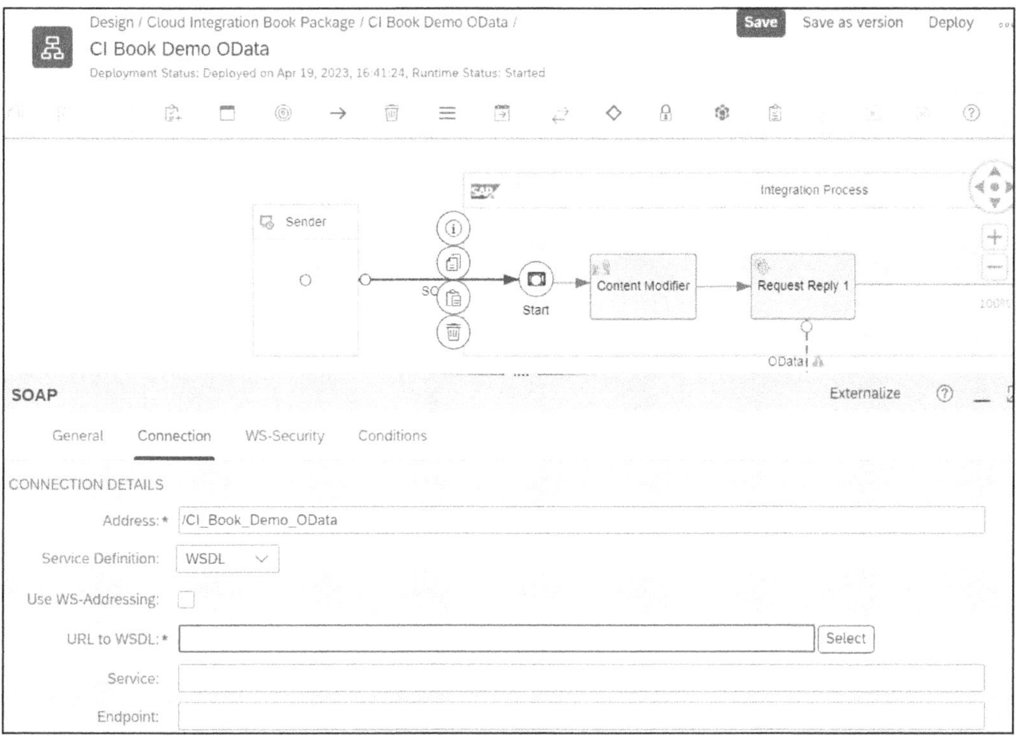

Figure 4.85 Adding a WSDL File to the Sender Channel

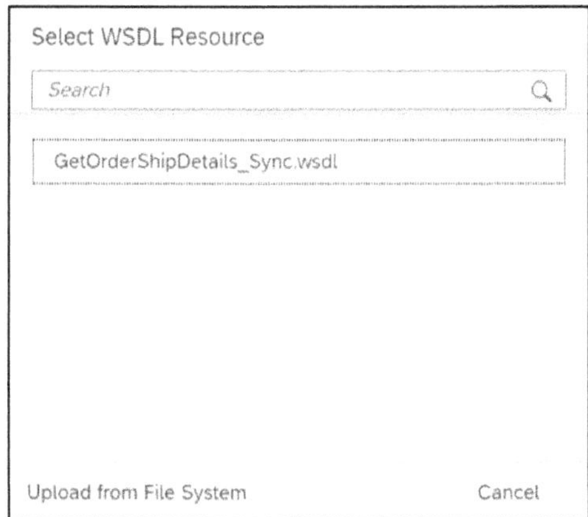

Figure 4.86 Selecting the WSDL File to Be Used in the Sender Channel

The screen is now populated with WSDL file details, as shown in Figure 4.87.

You can now save and deploy your iFlow. We'll discuss the mapping step next.

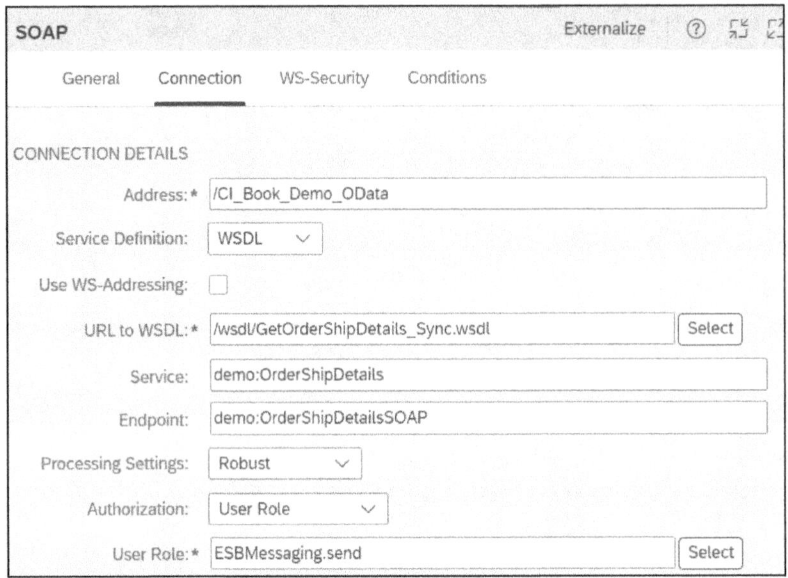

Figure 4.87 Sender Channel Populated with WSDL Details

4.4.3 Applying the Mapping Step in the Message Processing Chain

To use the mapping engine in the route, select the **Message Mapping** palette entry to open the submenu, as shown in Figure 4.88. You first must position the mapping step in the iFlow pool. In the palette, a dedicated mapping icon is available, as shown in Figure 4.88.

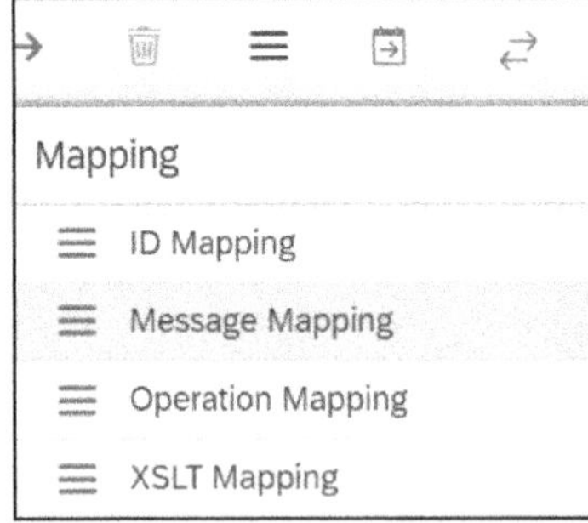

Figure 4.88 Selecting the Mapping Step from the Palette

Click the icon and then move the mouse pointer (which has changed to three parallel horizontal bars) into the **Integration Process** pool, as shown in Figure 4.89. Now, select the step from the iFlow, and click on the (+) icon to create a message mapping, as shown in Figure 4.90. At this point, you must name the message mapping, as shown in Figure 4.91, and then click on the **Create** button.

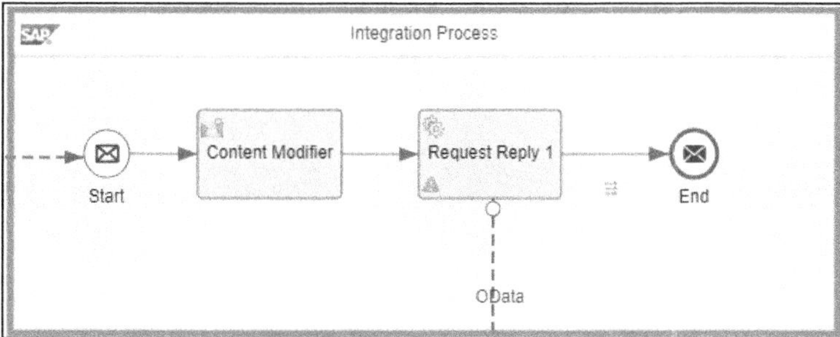

Figure 4.89 Positioning the Mapping Step in the iFlow (Mouse Pointer Changed to Three Horizontal Bars)

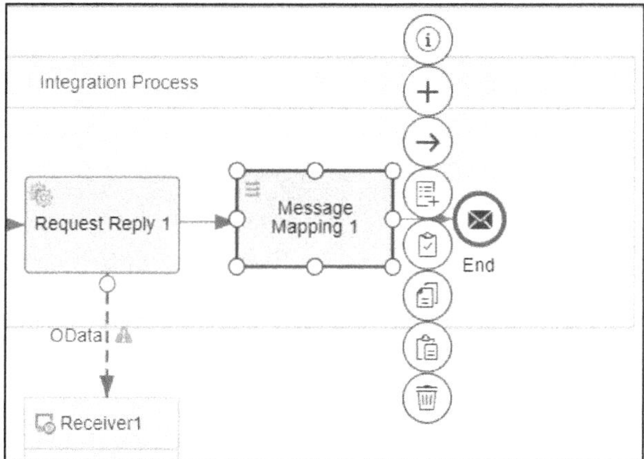

Figure 4.90 Creating a New Message Mapping

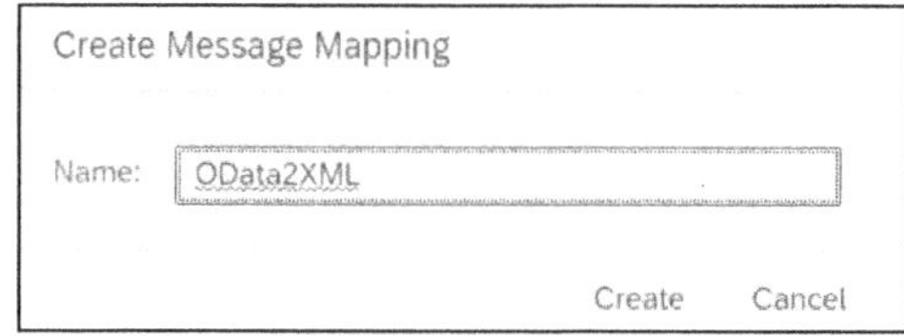

Figure 4.91 Naming the Message Mapping

After clicking on the **Save** button, the mapping editor opens immediately, as shown in Figure 4.92.

Notice that both the source and the target messages are missing. Next, we'll describe how to use either the generated XSD file or a self-developed WSDL file for the definition of source and target messages. We'll start with the assignment of the source message. Click the **Add source message** link shown in Figure 4.92 to open the **Select source message** dialog box shown in Figure 4.93.

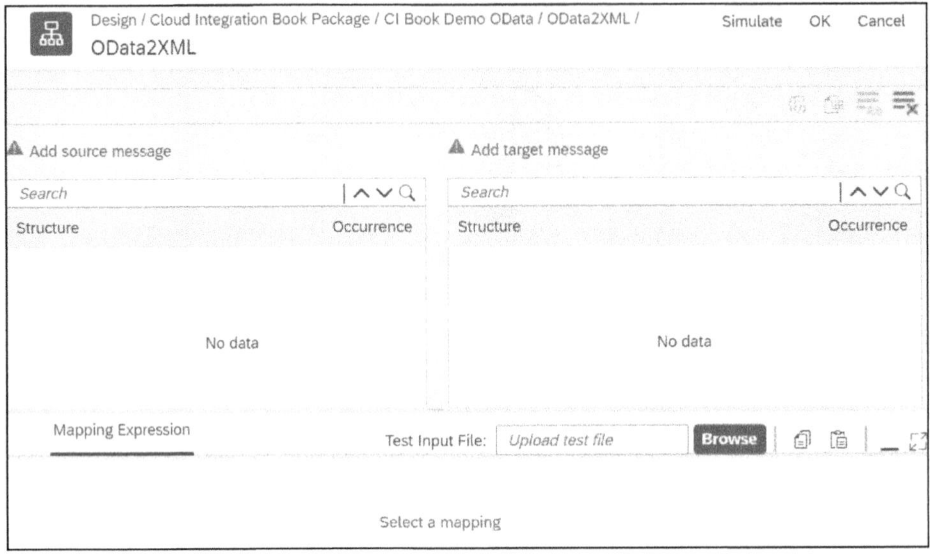

Figure 4.92 Mapping Editor Open after Positioning the Mapping Task

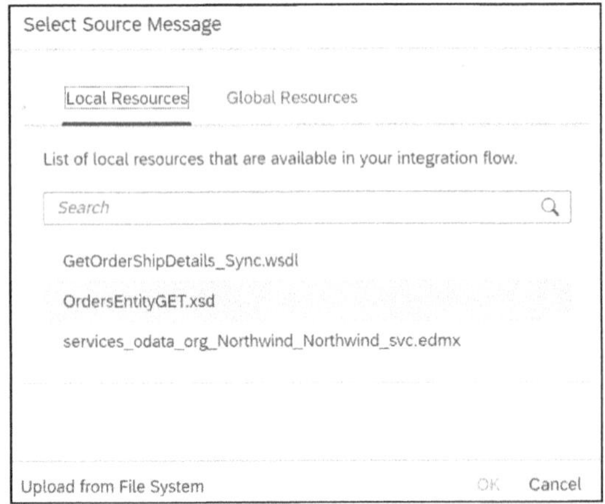

Figure 4.93 Dialog Box for Selecting the Target Message

The dialog box lists all the files that either have already been generated or have been uploaded from the file system. In our example, the file describing the OData service, as well as the file that was automatically generated by the Query Editor, are listed. Recall from the previous section that the *OrdersEntityGETO.xsd* file describes the source message. Click this file once. You'll immediately return to the mapping editor, which shows the **Structure** of the source message on the left side of the screen, as shown in Figure 4.94.

Next, assign the target message by clicking the **Add target message** link in the upper-right corner of the mapping editor. Again, the dialog box for assigning the appropriate file will open, as shown in Figure 4.95.

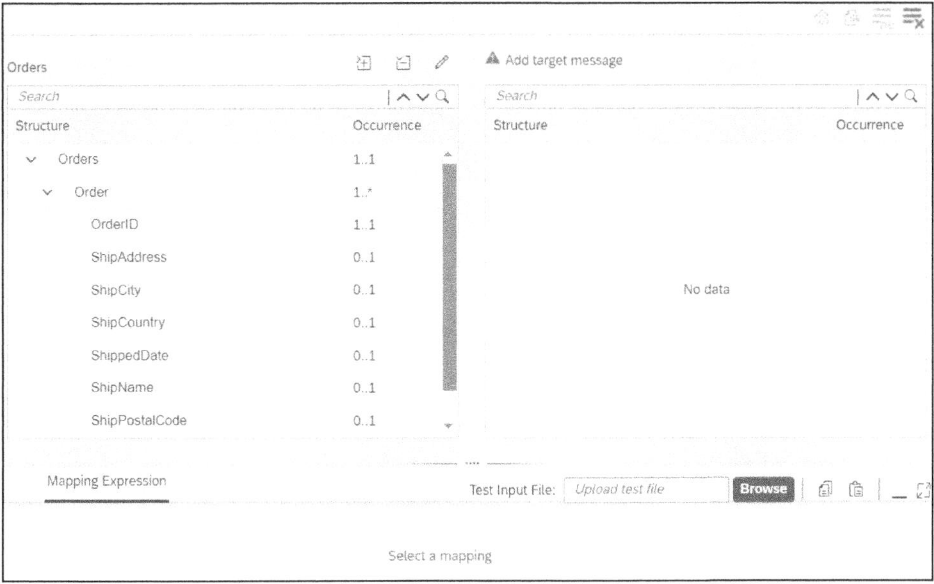

Figure 4.94 Mapping Editor Displaying the Structure of the Source Message after Assigning the XSD File

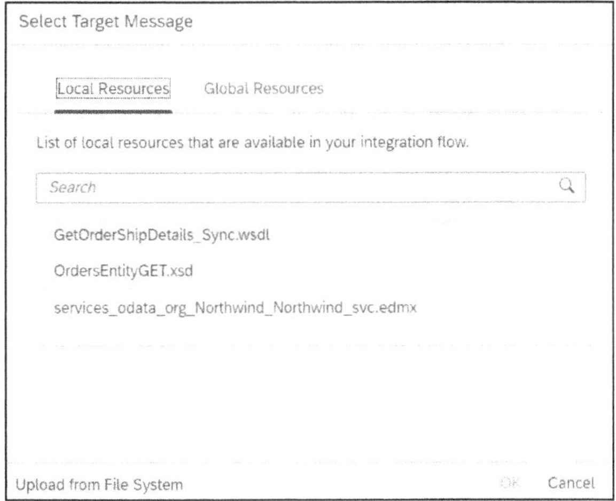

Figure 4.95 Selecting the Target Message's Structure

Note that the WSDL that we need is already available (*GetOrderShipDetails_Sync.wsdl*) because we imported it under the **References** tab in Section 4.4.2. Because the WSDL file contains a description of a synchronous interface, another dialog box for selecting an element opens, as shown in Figure 4.96.

This second dialog box appears because synchronous interfaces consist of two parts: a request and a response. Typically, these two structures are completely different.

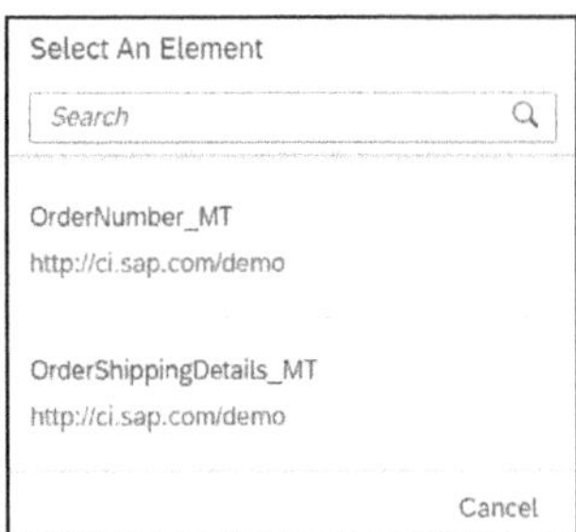

Figure 4.96 Selecting the Correct Target Structure from a Synchronous Interface

In our scenario, we're retrieving details for an order based on an order number coming in via the request message, so the request message contains just one field, the order number. The response message, on the other hand, contains details about the order and thus is comprised of several fields. As shown in Figure 4.96, the first entry, **Order Number_MT**, reflects the request message containing just the order number as the only field. The second entry, **OrderShippingDetails_MT**, stands for the response message and contains all the details that make up the order.

Note

SAP Process Integration specialists will recognize the message type (MT) suffix (the string _MT after the data type's name) for both elements. You'll be used to this naming convention when you create message types in the ESR. And, yes, we've created the synchronous interface in the ESR. In this way, the interoperability between SAP Process Integration and Cloud Integration on a data level is ensured.

You must pick the second entry from the list to specify your target message structure. Click the entry once, and the user interface (UI) immediately returns to the mapping editor. The mapping editor analyzes the structure of the response message and visualizes the structure accordingly. Figure 4.97 shows the result on the right side of the screen.

The mapping editor itself should look familiar if you've worked with SAP Process Integration before. You can now assign field mappings by simply dragging and dropping source fields from the left to the corresponding target fields on the right. For our simple scenario, the result is also shown in Figure 4.97.

You can also benefit from several predefined functions included with the mapping editor, which are listed in the **Functions** area shown in Figure 4.97.

If you're dealing with complex mapping and the predefined functions don't cover your needs, you can also build your own custom Java functions using User-Defined Functions (UDFs), which are discussed in detail in Chapter 8, Section 8.3. An alternative is to build an Extensible Stylesheet Language Transformation (XSLT) mapping.

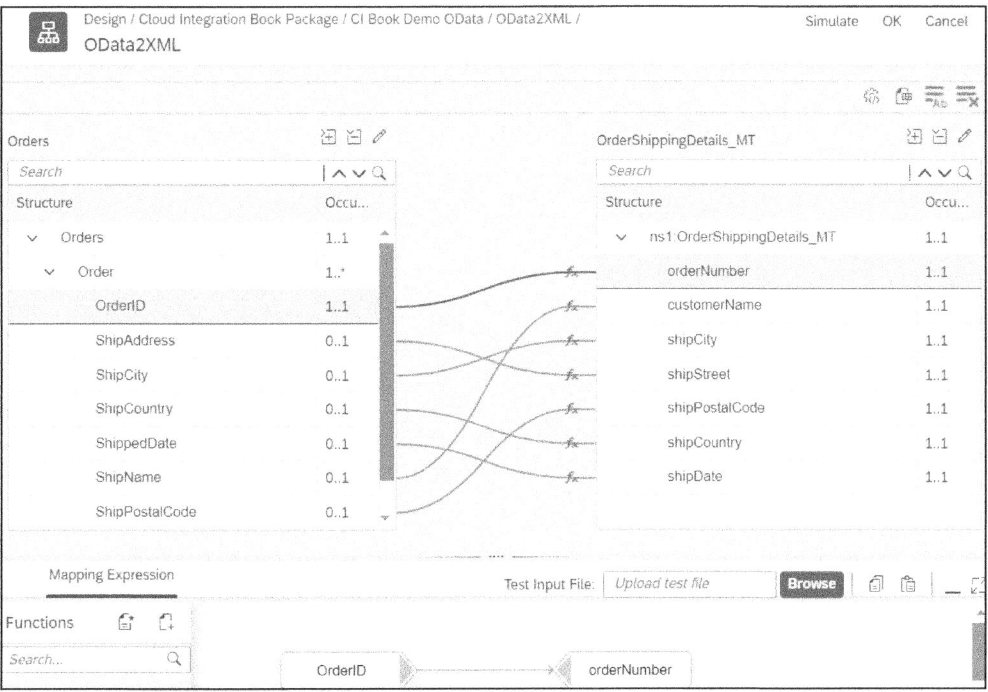

Figure 4.97 The Mapping Editor after Opening Both Structures and after Finishing the Mapping Exercise

As mention earlier, for highly complex mappings, you'll find plenty of material in SAP Community and in the SAP Process Integration online help (*http://s-prs.co/v576007*). You'll probably find the handling of the graphical mapper intuitive and convenient. Defining a mapping between two structures shouldn't be a problem, even when mappings are complex.

To check your mapping for accuracy by uploading an example message to the mapping editor, click the **Simulate** button in the top-right corner of the mapping editor. This quick simulation can help achieve short turnaround cycles between development and test.

After you're done creating your mappings, click the **OK** button (also located in the top-right corner of the mapping editor), and now, you're back in the UI for modeling your iFlow.

Finally, drag the mapping step on the arrow connecting the **Request Reply** step to the **End** event shown earlier in Figure 4.58 to position the mapping activity between the two. The result of your process model is shown in Figure 4.98.

That's it! You've finished configuring the mapping activity and can now save, deploy, and run your new iFlow. Use the SOAP tool of your choice (e.g., SoapUI) and invoke your solution. An appropriate request message might look like the request shown in Figure 4.99.

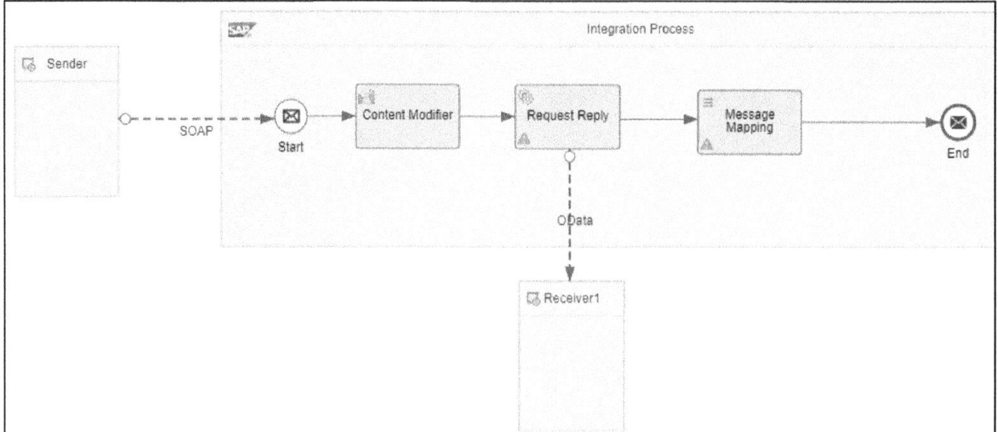

Figure 4.98 The Final Result of the Process Model after Positioning the Mapping Step before the End Event

```
<soapenv:Envelope xmlns:soapenv="http://schemas.xmlsoap.org/soap/envelope/"
   <soapenv:Header/>
   <soapenv:Body>
      <demo:OrderNumber_MT>
         <orderNumber>10249</orderNumber>
      </demo:OrderNumber_MT>
   </soapenv:Body>
</soapenv:Envelope>
```

Figure 4.99 Example Request Message

After passing through the iFlow, the result message should look similar to the message shown in Figure 4.100.

```
<soap:Envelope xmlns:soap="http://schemas.xmlsoap.org/soap/envelope/">
   <soap:Header/>
   <soap:Body>
      <ns1:OrderShippingDetails_MT xmlns:ns1="http://ci.sap.com/demo">
         <orderNumber>10249</orderNumber>
         <customerName>Toms Spezialitäten</customerName>
         <shipCity>Münster</shipCity>
         <shipStreet>LUISENSTR.48_10249</shipStreet>
         <shipPostalCode>44087</shipPostalCode>
         <shipCountry>Germany</shipCountry>
         <shipDate>1996-07-10T00:00:00.000</shipDate>
      </ns1:OrderShippingDetails_MT>
   </soap:Body>
</soap:Envelope>
```

Figure 4.100 Reply Message after Successful Invocation of the iFlow, Including the Mapping Step

To summarize, mappings are an important aspect of every integration project. Cloud Integration benefits from reuse of the mapping engine originally developed for SAP Process Integration. In this section, you learned how the mapping engine is integrated into Cloud Integration and how you can invoke it in your iFlows by applying the mapping activity. You've also seen how the message processing in Cloud Integration differs from SAP Process Integration (Cloud Integration engages in payload-agnostic behavior) and how this difference requires the explicit definition of message structures by using either XSD or WSDL files to configure the mapping step. With this knowledge, you're now well-equipped to tackle even more sophisticated integration challenges.

4.4.4 Using Value Mappings to Enhance Your Scenario

Value mappings represent multiple values of an object. To better illustrate this concept, let's say that the consumer of our service (the entity that receives the returned response, shown in Figure 4.100) doesn't accept country names in the `shipCountry` field but instead prefers International Organization for Standardization (ISO) country codes. As a result, for example, instead of returning the value `Germany`, the consumer prefers the value `DE`. This use case is quite common in integration scenarios. The country object can be represented in many ways (in our case, either a name or an ISO code). In these cases, value mappings come to the rescue.

Let's now extend the example shown in Figure 4.98 to return an ISO code in the field `shipCountry` instead of the country name. To achieve this goal, you'll need to create a **Value Mapping** artifact by following these steps:

1. Go to the **Design** page of Cloud Integration, and open your package in edit mode.
2. From your package, click on the **Add** button and select **Value Mapping** from the resulting menu, as shown in Figure 4.101.

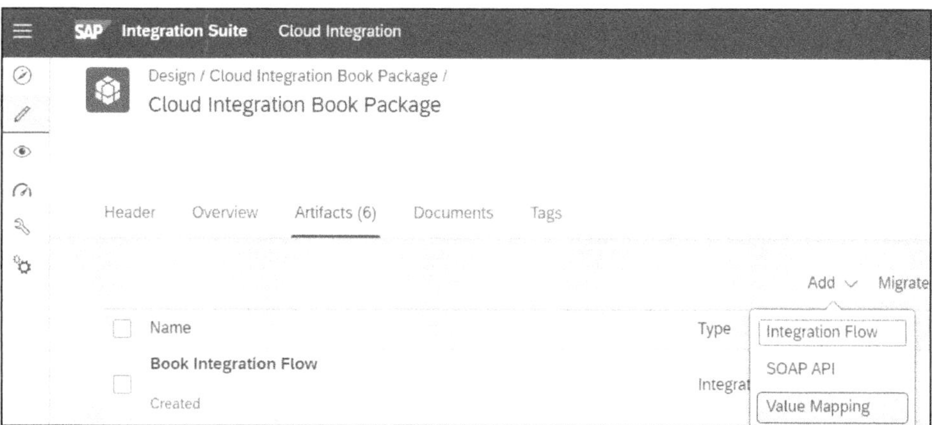

Figure 4.101 Creating a Value Mapping Artifact

3. Provide a name for the value mapping and click **Add**, as shown in Figure 4.102.
4. Navigate to the correct package, and open the value mapping that we created in the previous step. The value mapping editor will open, as shown in Figure 4.103.

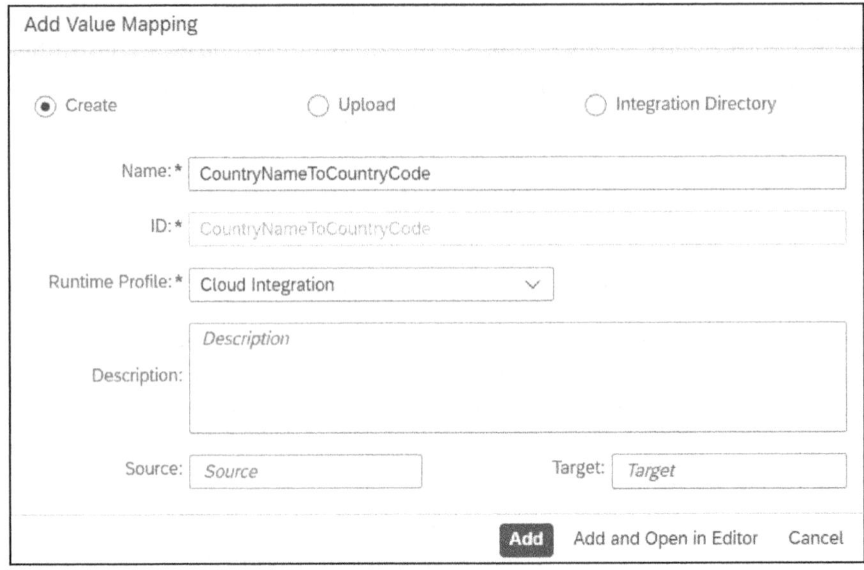

Figure 4.102 Naming the Value Mapping Artifact

5. Click on **Edit** to switch to edit mode.
6. Click on the **Add** button shown in Figure 4.104. You'll see a list of fields (listed in Table 4.4). For the sake of simplicity, fill in the columns with the details shown in Figure 4.104.

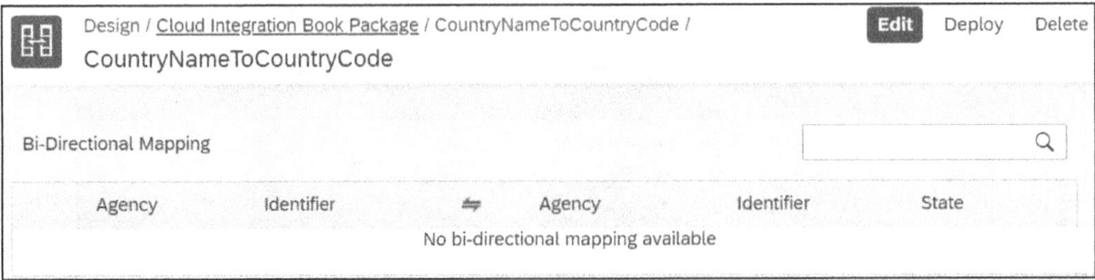

Figure 4.103 Value Mapping Editor

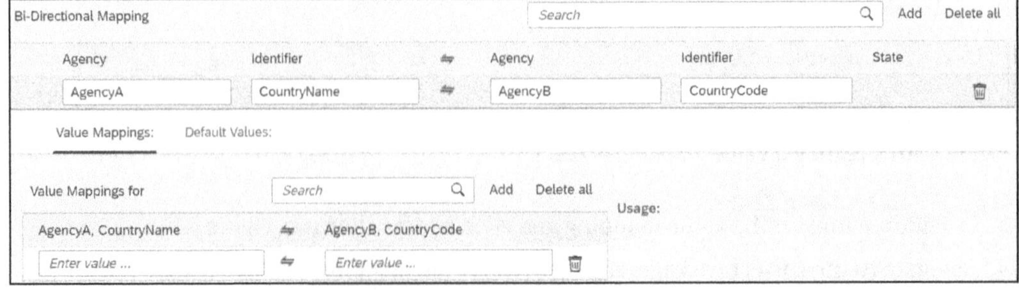

Figure 4.104 Adding Values to the Value Mapping

Column Name	Description
Agency	Represents the organization/scheme responsible for managing and issuing an identifier, for example, a company. Agency A is a country that is responsible for issuing the identifier "passport number" as a way to identify a person. At the same time, Agency B might represent a company that identifies the same person using the identifier "employee number."
Identifier	A unique value issued by an agency, for example, a passport number.

Table 4.4 Columns of the Value Mapping

7. Now, we'll add a list of values for the source and target systems to provide a mapping of values between source and target. Click on the **Add** button at the bottom of the screen shown earlier in Figure 4.104.
8. You'll see another screen similar to the screen shown in Figure 4.105. After populating the value mapping with all required country names and country code values, click on the **Save** button to persist the changes.
9. Finally, click on **Deploy** in the top-right corner of the screen shown in Figure 4.105.

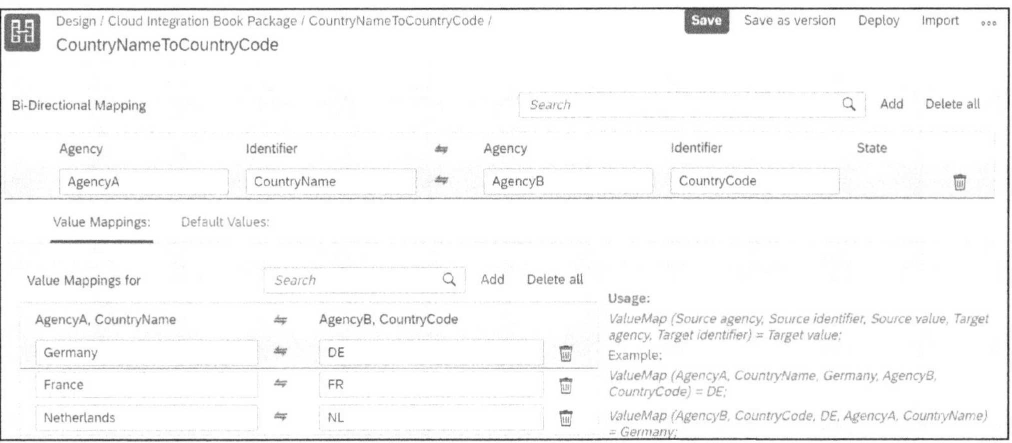

Figure 4.105 Populating the Value Mapping

Now that our value mapping is deployed, let's use it in our mapping. For that, we'll need to open the mapping that we developed earlier in Figure 4.81 (refer also to Figure 4.97).

To open the mapping, follow these steps:

1. Open the iFlow, click the **Edit** button, and select the **Mapping** step, as shown in Figure 4.106. The property of the mapping appears on the bottom section.
2. Select the **Processing** tab, and click on the mapping name next to the resource field (in our case, **/ODate2XML.mmap**) to navigate to the mapping editor.

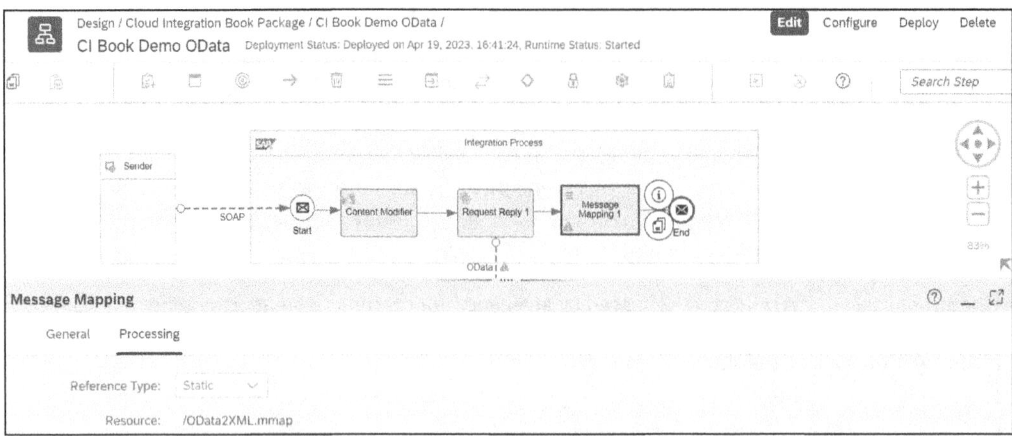

Figure 4.106 Overview of the iFlow

3. You'll be redirected to the mapping editor. Select the **shipCountry** field on the target structure (on the right).
4. Select the **valueMapping** function under the **Conversions** function category, as shown in the bottom-left corner of Figure 4.107.

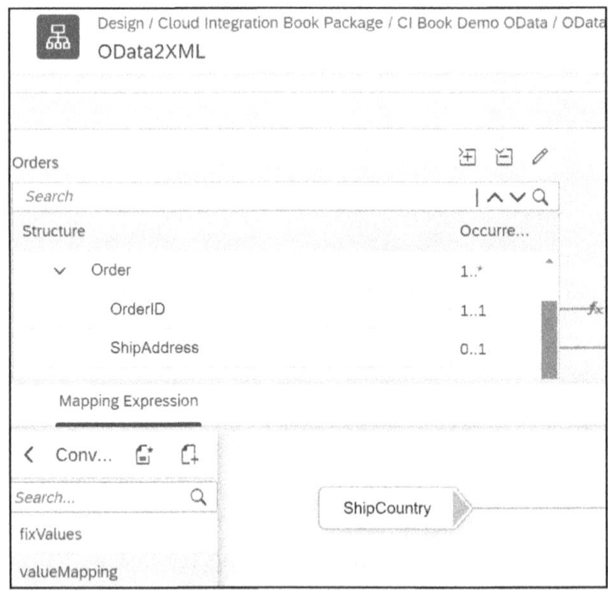

Figure 4.107 Adding a Value Mapping Function in the Mapping Logic

5. Place the **valueMapping** function on the screen. For the input fields **Source Agency**, **Source Identifier**, **Target Agency**, and **Target Identifier**, use the values shown earlier in Figure 4.105. At the end, the configuration should look like the screen shown in Figure 4.108.

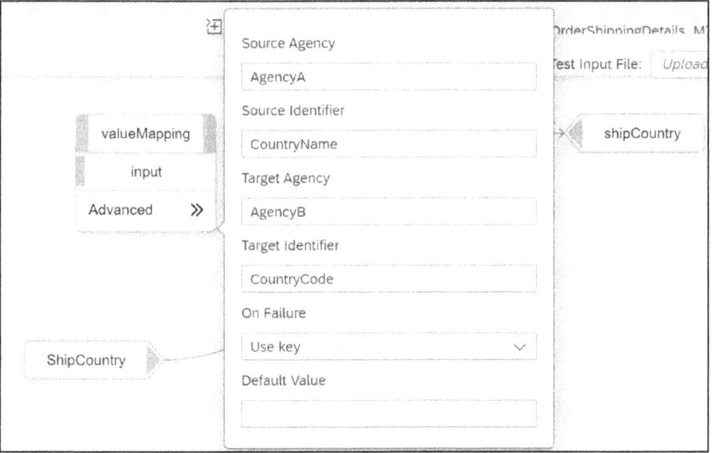

Figure 4.108 Configuring the Value Mapping Function

Note

By using the **Default Value** field shown in Figure 4.108, you can specify a default value to be used if no matches are found for the incoming value. But for this functionality to work, you'll need to select **Use Default Value** from the **On Failure** dropdown list.

The **On Failure** dropdown list includes the following options:

- **Use key**
  If no match can be found, the incoming value will simply be passed to the target value without translation.
- **Throw exception**
  If no match can be found, an exception will be thrown by the mapping framework.
- **Use default value**
  If no match can be found, the default value (specified in the **Default Value** field) will be assigned to the target value.

6. After configuring the value mapping function, place the function between the two **ShipCountry** fields to generate to the final result, which should be similar to the screen shown in Figure 4.109.

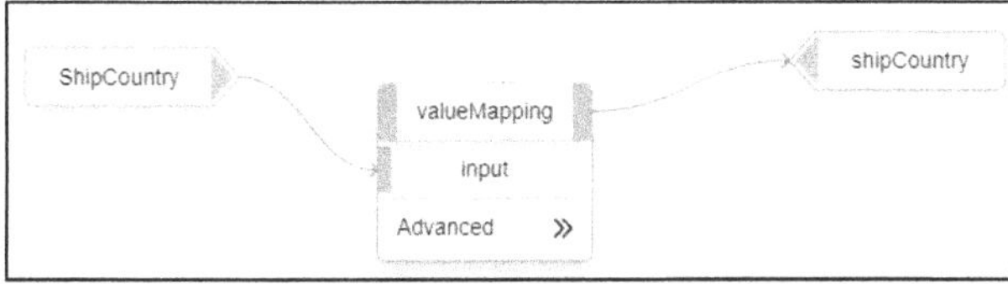

Figure 4.109 Performing a Value Mapping Translation

7. Save and deploy the iFlow.

Congratulations! You can now retest the service using SoapUI. The returned response is shown in Figure 4.110. Note that the value of `ShipCountry` is no longer `Germany` but `DE`, as configured in our value mapping.

```
<soap:Envelope xmlns:soap="http://schemas.xmlsoap.org/soap/envelope/">
   <soap:Header/>
   <soap:Body>
      <ns1:OrderShippingDetails_MT xmlns:ns1="http://ci.sap.com/demo">
         <orderNumber>10249</orderNumber>
         <customerName>Toms Spezialitäten</customerName>
         <shipCity>Münster</shipCity>
         <shipStreet>Luisenstr. 48</shipStreet>
         <shipPostalCode>44087</shipPostalCode>
         <shipCountry>DE</shipCountry>
         <shipDate>1996-07-10T00:00:00.000</shipDate>
      </ns1:OrderShippingDetails_MT>
   </soap:Body>
</soap:Envelope>
```

Figure 4.110 Updated Response of the Service after Using Value Mapping

4.5 Defining and Provisioning API-based Integration

In Section 4.3, we showed you how to consume an external OData service from Cloud Integration. In that case, we used a receiver OData adapter to call the external OData service. In some cases, as an integration developer, you may be asked to provide an API service in Cloud Integration. Cloud Integration provides the developers with the possibility to expose three types of APIs: REST, SOAP, and OData.

In this section, we'll explore how you can provide various API services from Cloud Integration. Let's start by presenting the target scenario that we'll use to explore API provisioning capabilities.

4.5.1 The Target Scenario

In this section, we'll use a publicly available SOAP web service, available at *http://s-prs.co/v576008*, to provision an OData, a SOAP and a REST service in Cloud Integration. We chose this service just for the sake of illustration; you can use any web service of your choosing.

The first step is to download the suggested WSDL file available at *http://s-prs.co/v576009*. Save this file to your local computer. In the following section, let's use this web service to provision an OData API in Cloud Integration.

4.5.2 Providing an OData Service

Cloud Integration facilitates the provision of an OData service with a powerful wizard that automatically generates an iFlow in the background. While using the wizard, the following main steps are involved:

- **Import from Data Source**
  Enables you to create or update an OData model by importing its definition from a SOAP, OData, or OData channel data source.
- **Edit OData Model**
  Enables you to create or update an OData model using the OData Model Editor.
- **Bind to Data Source**
  Supports binding entity sets and function imports to a data source such as SOAP, OData, or OData channel endpoints.
- **Edit Integration Flow**
  Changes and customizes the generated iFlows with additional business logic.
- **Deploy OData Service**
  Deploys and starts using your OData service when the service is ready.

The iFlow in Figure 4.111 shows the integration scenario we'll build in this section.

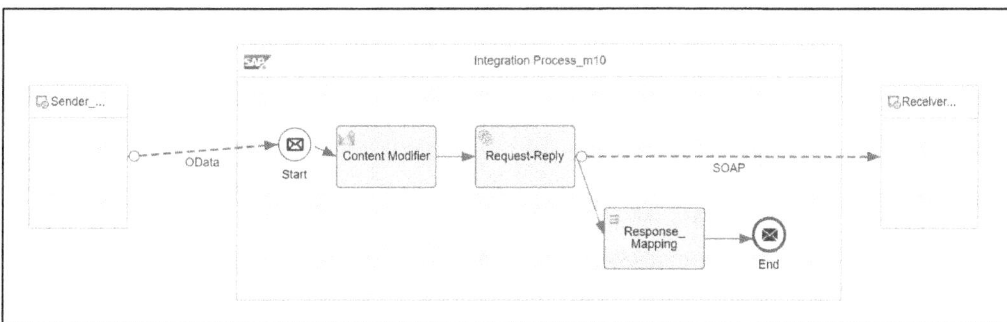

Figure 4.111 OData iFlow

Before exploring each of these steps in detail, let's first create the project by following these steps:

1. From the **Design** page of your Cloud Integration tenant (shown in Figure 4.112 on the left), select the relevant package, and switch to edit mode.

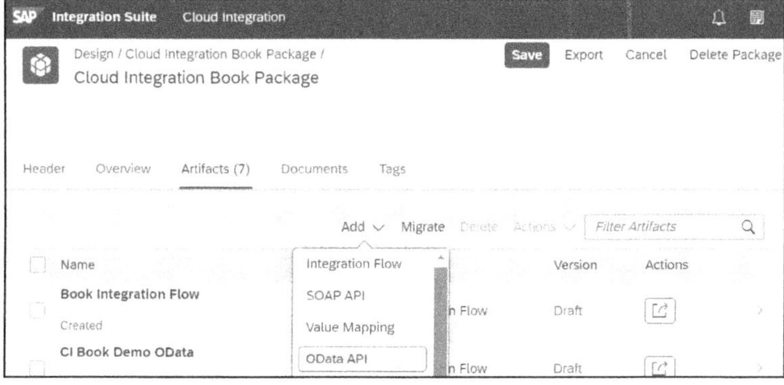

Figure 4.112 Creating an OData Service Artifact

2. Click the **Add** button, and then click **OData API** from the resulting dropdown menu, as shown in Figure 4.112.
3. Give the artifact a suitable name, such as "Country_OData_Service", and leave the other fields with their default values. Note that, by default, the **Namespace** is set with the value **SAP**, as shown in Figure 4.113. Click the **Create** button.

Add OData API

Create Using Wizard | Create Using Template | Upload

Name: * Country_OData_Service

Namespace: * SAP

ID: * Country_OData_Service_SAP_1

Description: <Description>

OData Version: OData V2

Create | Cancel

Figure 4.113 Details of the OData Service Artifact

You'll now be redirected to a page that looks like the pages shown in Figure 4.114 and Figure 4.115. Note that both of these figures are part of the same page and that Figure 4.115 is positioned in the bottom of Figure 4.114. This landing page is the main place where you'll perform all the tasks related to defining and provisioning the OData API.

As shown in Figure 4.114 and Figure 4.115, you'll see the activities that must be performed to define an OData service. These activities were also listed in the beginning of Section 4.5.2. We'll explore these activities in detail next.

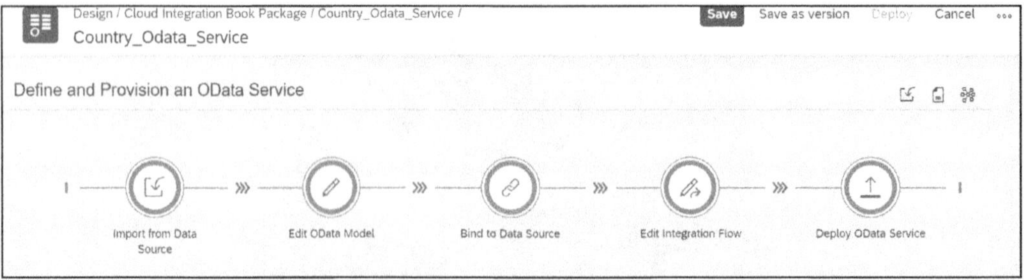

Figure 4.114 Main Landing Page to Define and Provision OData Service A

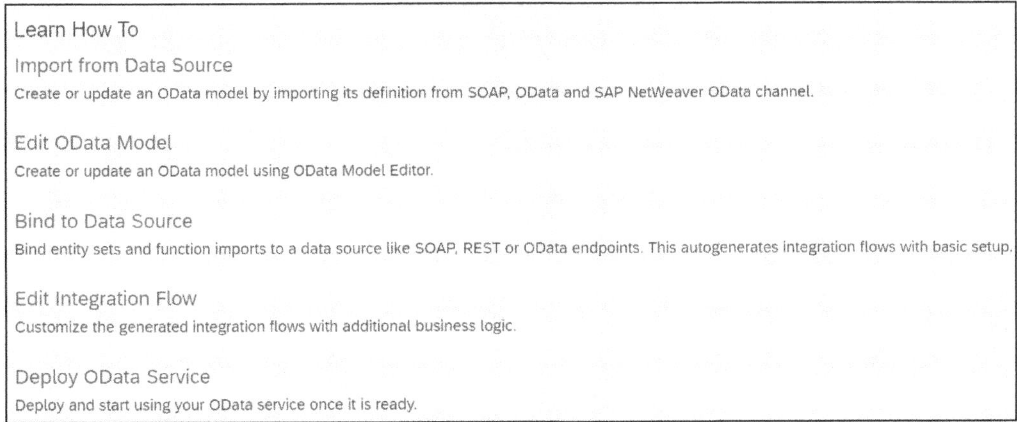

Figure 4.115 Main Landing Page to Define and Provision OData Service B

Importing from a Data Source

The first step is to import the definition of an existing service (data source), which we'll use as the basis for our OData model. At the time of this writing, you could import definitions from SOAP, OData, or OData channel (provided by SAP Gateway) data sources. For simplicity, we'll illustrate the provisioning of an OData service using the import of an existing SOAP web service—the WSDL that we downloaded in Section 4.5.1. To import the WSDL data source, follow these steps:

1. Click the import model wizard button shown in the right-top corner of Figure 4.115.
2. Select **SOAP** from the **Data Source Type** dropdown list, and click on the **Browse** button to select the WSDL file that you downloaded in Section 4.5.1, as shown in Figure 4.116.

Figure 4.116 Importing a WSDL Data Source

3. Click on the **Step 2** button to proceed with the wizard.

4. Select the needed element from the data source. Note that we'll use the `CountryISO-Code` operation. Therefore, select its request and response structures, as shown in Figure 4.117.

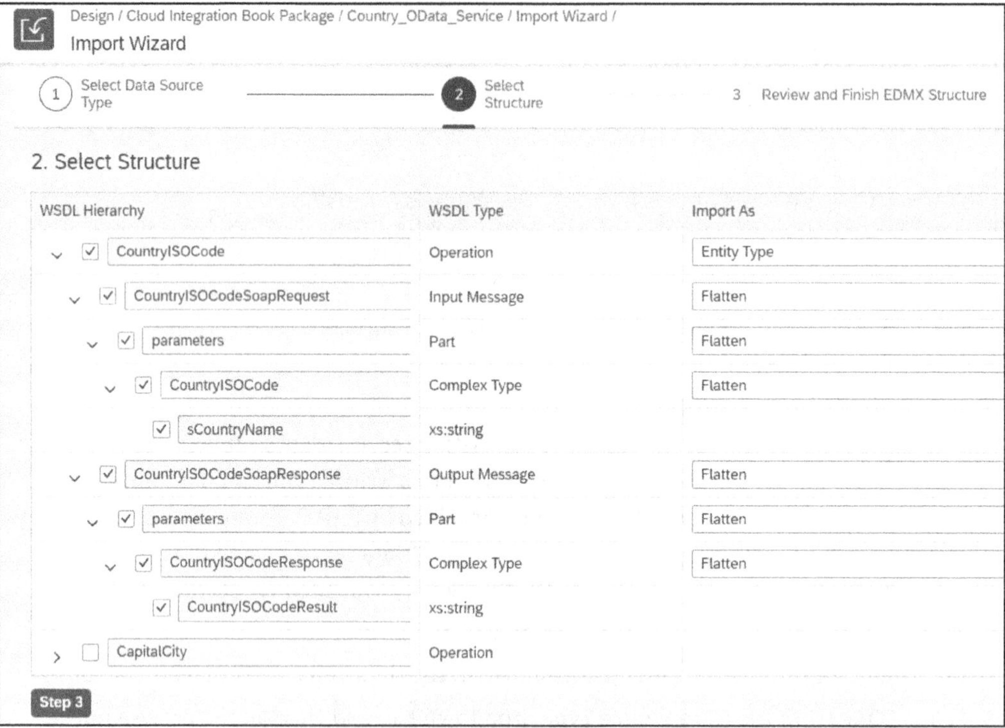

Figure 4.117 Selecting the Desired Request and Response Structures from the Data Source

5. Click on the **Step 3** button.
6. You'll be redirected to the next page in the wizard where you can review the generated EDMX structure. You can change the names or EDM types of any element and add comments and descriptions for each element using the **Documentation** field, as shown in Figure 4.118. Be aware that selecting one of these elements as the primary key is mandatory. When done, click on the **Finish** button.
7. Now that you've imported the WSDL model, you'll be redirected to the **Define and Provision an OData Service** view, shown in Figure 4.119. This view presents the various operations possible in an OData service, including **Query**, **Create**, **Read**, **Update**, and **Delete** operations, as shown in Figure 4.119.

Let's now explore how to edit the OData model generated in the preceding steps.

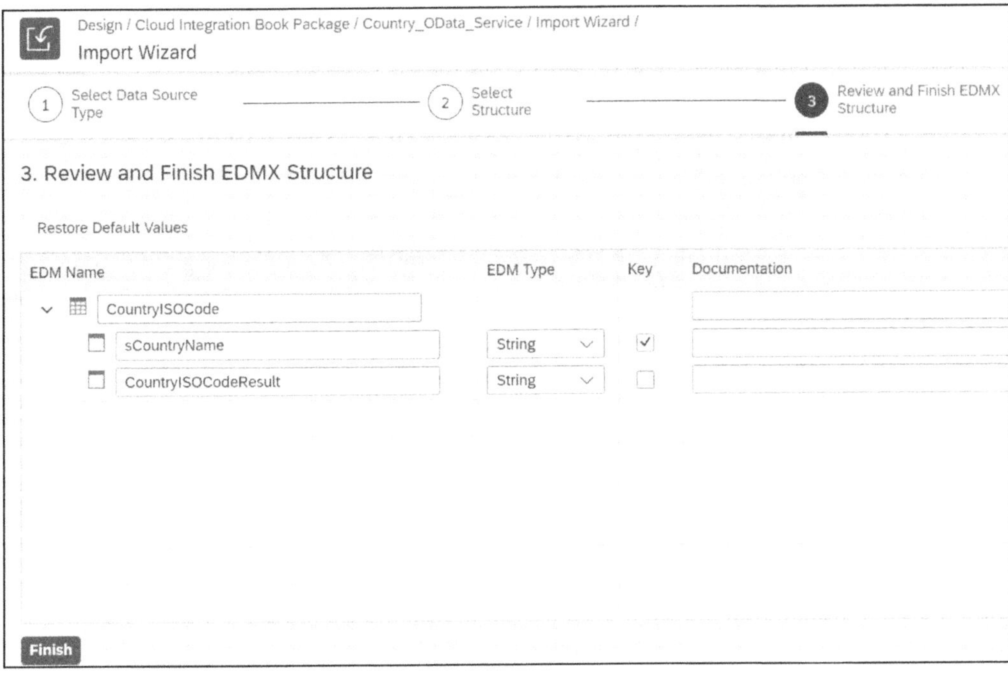

Figure 4.118 Reviewing the EDMX Structure

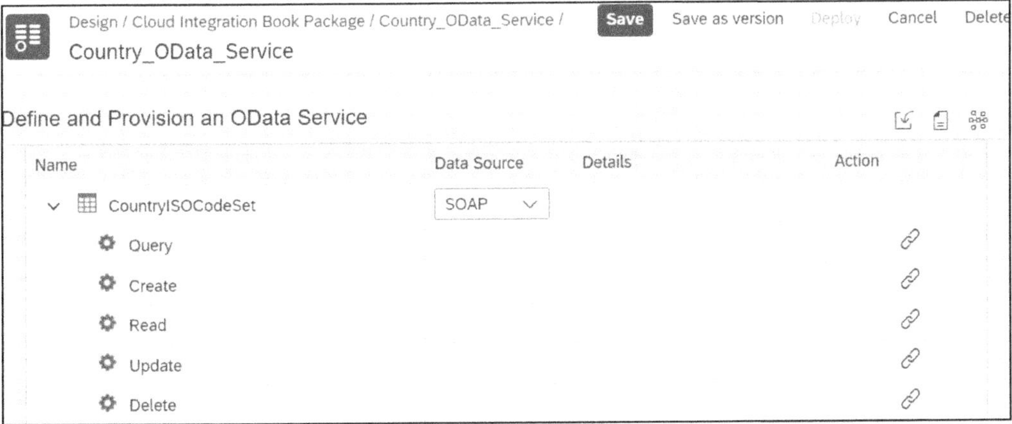

Figure 4.119 Defining and Provisioning an OData Service View

Note

In the step shown in Figure 4.118, you must select a primary key that represents a unique identifier for the OData model. Without selecting a primary key, you'll be confronted with an error, and you won't be able to proceed to the next step of the wizard.

Editing the OData Model

After importing a model based on a WSDL data source as discussed in the previous section, let's look at how you can modify the generated OData model. Return to the **Define and Provision an OData Service** view (shown in Figure 4.119), and follow these steps:

1. On the right of the screen shown previously in Figure 4.119, click on the OData Model Editor icon . The OData Model Editor will open, as shown in Figure 4.120.
2. If you're comfortable with OData models, you can edit and change the model to fit your requirements. The editor features an autocomplete function to help you while editing the model. Press Ctrl+Spacebar to get suggestions, as shown in Figure 4.120. Save the final result by clicking the **OK** button.

Design / Cloud Integration Book Package / Country_OData_Service / Edmx Editor /

Edmx Editor

```
<edmx:Edmx
    xmlns:edmx="http://schemas.microsoft.com/ado/2007/06/edmx"
    xmlns:sap="http://www.sap.com/Protocols/SAPData" Version="1.0">
    <edmx:DataServices
        xmlns:m="http://schemas.microsoft.com/ado/2007/08/dataservices/metadata" m:DataServiceVersion="2.0">
        <Schema
            xmlns="http://schemas.microsoft.com/ado/2008/09/edm" Namespace="S1">
            <EntityContainer Name="EC1" m:IsDefaultEntityContainer="true">
            Edm.Double  Double                                  yType="S1.CountryISOCode"></EntitySet>
            Edm.Int32  Int32
            Edm.String  String
            Edm.Time  Time
            EntityContainer Name="" m:IsDefaultEntityC          opertyRef>
            EntityType Name="">—<Key>——<PropertyRef
            Function Name=""></Function>  Function              tring" Nullable="false"></Property>
                                                                e="Edm.String" Nullable="true"></Property>
            Property Name="" Type="" Nullable="true"><
        </Schema>
    </edmx:DataServices>
</edmx:Edmx>
```

Figure 4.120 OData Model Editor

You can return to the main page (shown in Figure 4.119) by clicking on the OData service name shown at the top of Figure 4.120. In our example, click on **Country OData Service**.

Note that you can view a graphical representation of the generated model. The graphical representation can be accessed by clicking the button shown in the top-right corner of Figure 4.119. You should see a screen similar to the screen shown in Figure 4.121.

At this point, our model is ready, so we'll bind it to the SOAP web service.

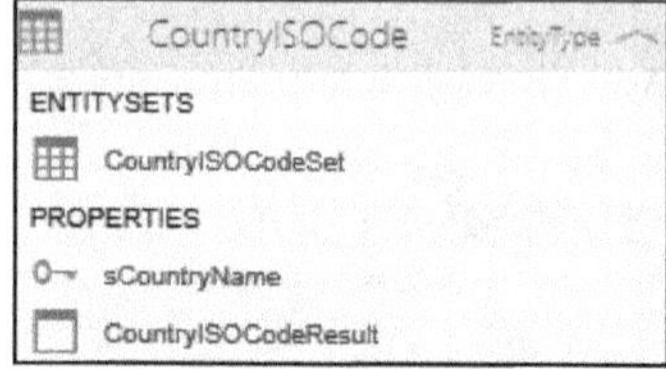

Figure 4.121 Graphical Model Viewer

Binding to the Data Source

Binding a model means that you'll need to link entity sets and function imports to a data source such as SOAP, REST, or OData endpoints. To perform the binding, return to the **Define and Provision an OData Service** view, and then follow these steps:

1. Click on the bind icon on the same row as the desired operation. For now, let's do that for the **Query** operation (shown earlier in Figure 4.119). You'll then be redirected to a page similar to the page shown in Figure 4.122.

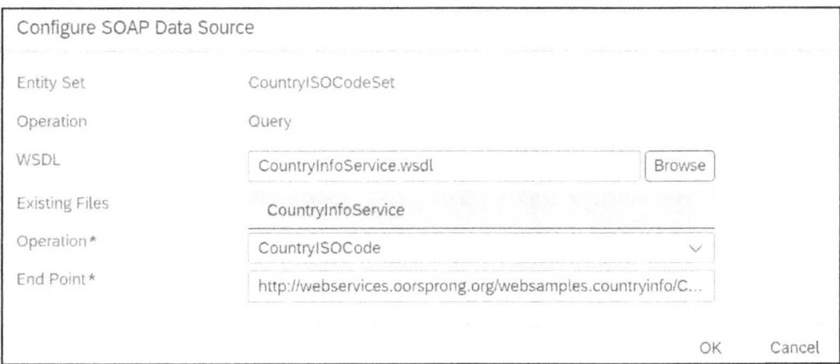

Figure 4.122 Binding an Operation to a Data Source

2. On this page, you can specify the operation to which the **Query** operation should be bound. As shown in Figure 4.122, choose **CountryISOCode** from the **Operation** drop-down list for the SOAP service. Note that the **End Point** text box is automatically filled in with the correct value.
3. Click on the **OK** button to return to the **Define and Provision an OData Service** view, as shown in Figure 4.123. Note that, during this step, an iFlow is automatically generated in the background.

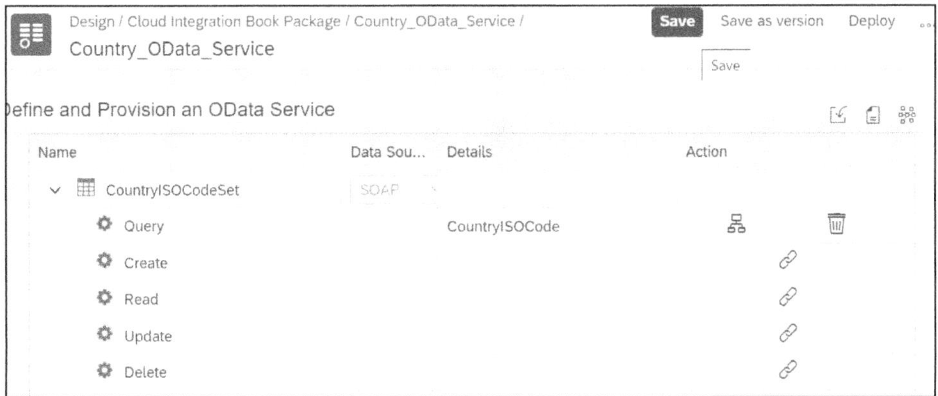

Figure 4.123 Defining and Provisioning an OData Service View after Binding an Operation

4. Click on the **Save** button shown in Figure 4.123 to persist your changes.

5. Let's now navigate to the iFlow editor by clicking on the icon on the same row as the **Query** operation, as shown in Figure 4.123.

You'll be redirected to the iFlow editor. Now, you'll enhance the generated iFlow, which we'll describe in the next section.

Editing the Integration Flow

As shown in Figure 4.124, you'll be presented with the iFlow that was automatically generated based on the actions performed in the previous sections. The generated iFlow has a basic setup with **Sender** and **Receiver** channels already configured automatically.

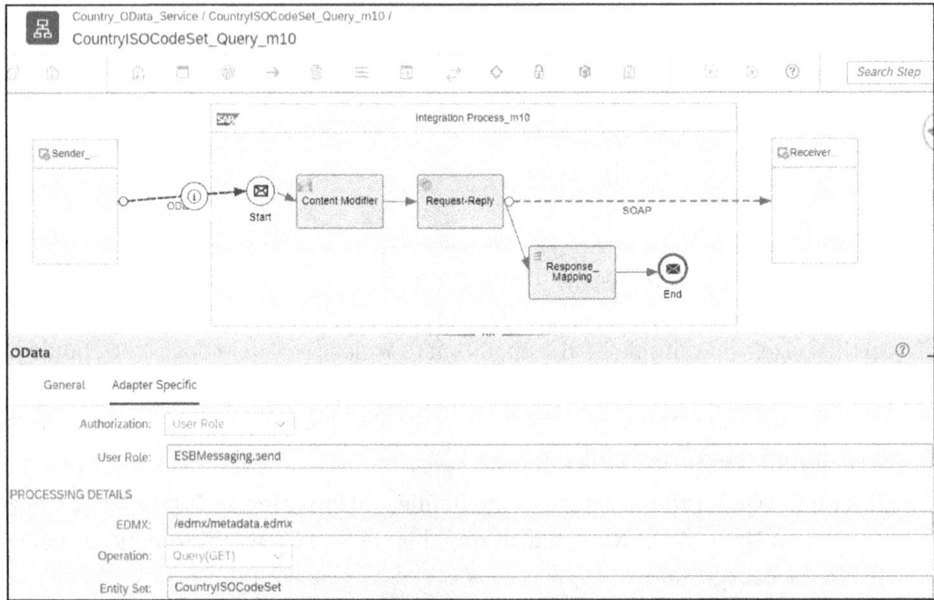

Figure 4.124 Generated iFlow for the OData Service

Look under the **References** tab, shown in Figure 4.125, which shows that a number of artifacts have been automatically included:

- **Response_Mapping1**
  The message mapping artifact used in the **Message Mapping** step named **Response_ Mapping**, shown in Figure 4.124.
- **CountryInfoService**
  WSDL of the SOAP service that we're consuming in our iFlow.
- **Error**
  XSD representing an error, which can be used to throw an exception.
- **Metadata**
  The EDM file that was automatically added by the OData service generation.

Integration Flow

General | Runtime Configuration | Error Configuration | **References** | Problems

Local (5) | Global (0)

Name	Type	Actions
Mappings (1)		
Response_Mapping1	Message Mapping	⤓ 🗑
Schemas (4)		
CountryInfoService	WSDL	⤓ 🗑
Error	XSD	⤓ 🗑
metadata	EDMX	⤓ 🗑

Figure 4.125 Overview of the Resources View

Let's now enhance the iFlow to suit our needs. A good start is to replace the **Content Modifier** with a **Message Mapping** step. We discussed how to use a **Message Mapping** step earlier in Section 4.3.6. As a result, we won't repeat every step in detail. Follow these steps:

1. After opening the iFlow, click on the **Edit** button.
2. Remove the **Content Modifier** step, and replace this step with a **Message Mapping** step, as shown in Figure 4.126.
3. Create a message mapping, assign the EDMX structure on the source message, and assign the XSDL on the target message. In our case, the EDMX file is called *metadata.edmx*, and the WSDL file is called *CountryInfoService.wsdl*, as shown earlier in Figure 4.125. The end result of the newly created message mapping is shown in Figure 4.127. Note that, in the target message, the **CountryISOCode** message structure must be selected.

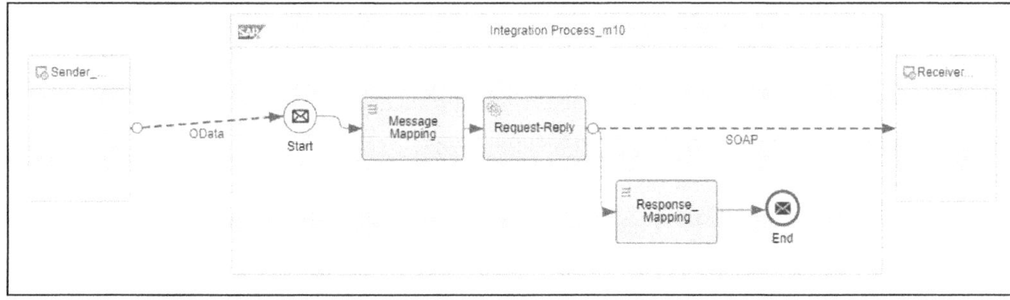

Figure 4.126 iFlow with Message Mapping Instead of Content Modifier

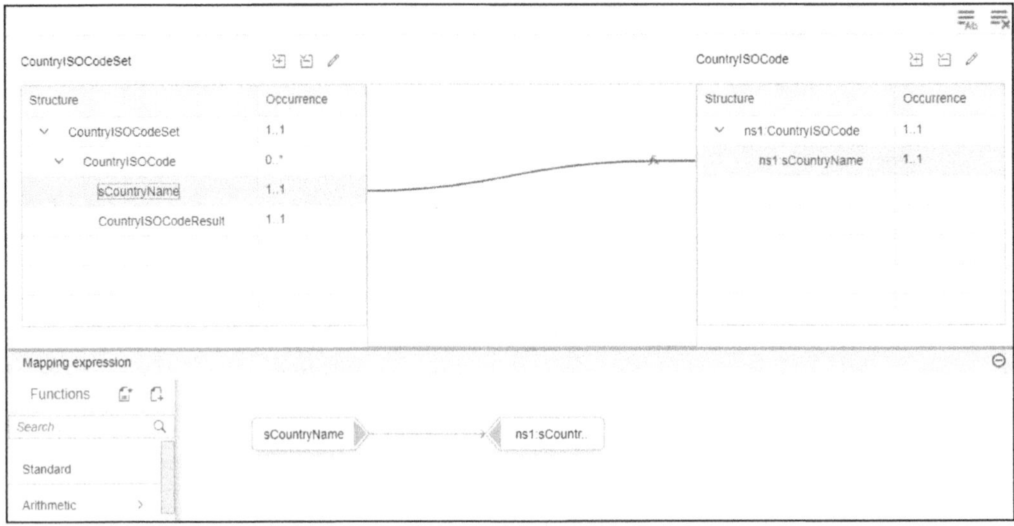

Figure 4.127 New Message Mapping

Finally, let's adjust the response mapping. As mentioned earlier, a response mapping called **Response_Mapping** (shown earlier in Figure 4.124) was included under the **Resources** tab. By default, no mapping logic is defined in this message mapping.

Figure 4.128 shows an example of the mapping logic.

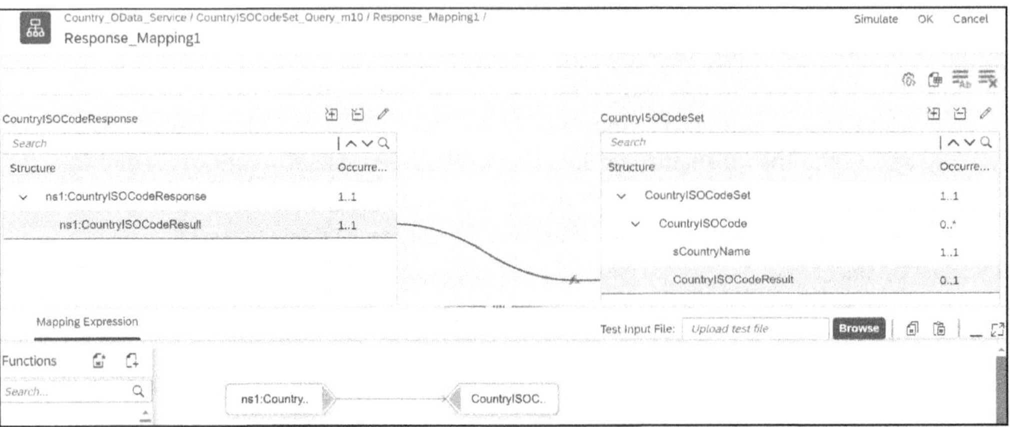

Figure 4.128 Defining the Response Mapping Logic

The iFlow is now enhanced and adjusted to suit our needs. Let's save it.

> **Note**
>
> At the time of this writing, the OData adapter only supports synchronous communication, which means that every request must have an associated response.

Deploying the OData Service

After the iFlow has been adjusted to meet your needs, the OData service can now be deployed. At this point, you'll need to return to the **Define and Provision an OData Service** view (shown earlier in Figure 4.123). Click on **Save**, and then click on **Deploy**. After a successful deployment, the OData service should now be available in the **Manage Integration Content** section of the **Monitor** page, as shown in Figure 4.129.

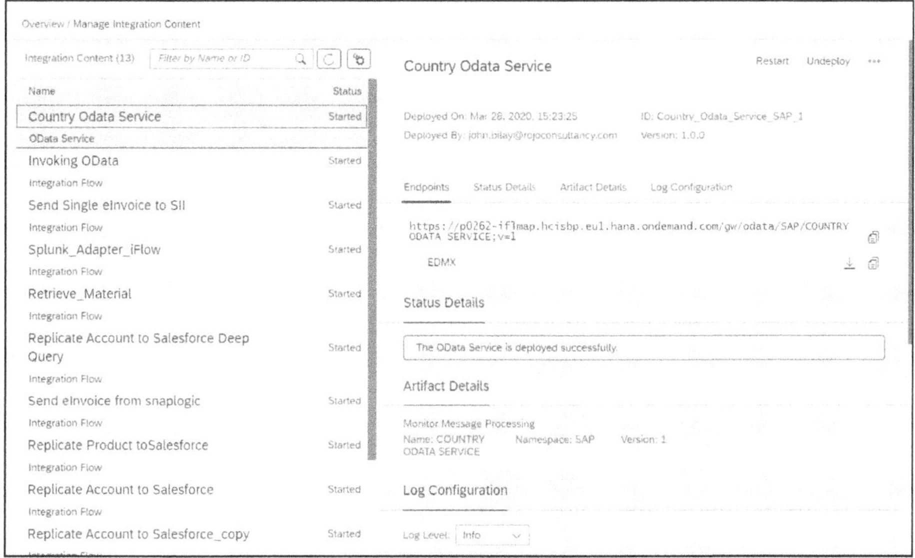

Figure 4.129 The Deployed OData Service from the Monitor

You can now call and test the newly provisioned OData service using an endpoint URL in the following format:

https://<IFLMAP_URL>/gw/odata/<OData_Service_Namespace>/<OData_Service_Name>;V=<Version>

> **Note**
>
> The spaces included in the service name (*COUNTRY ODATA SERVICE*) are replaced by *%20*.

Well done! You've successfully completed the last step in defining and provisioning an OData service.

4.5.3 Providing a SOAP Service

Cloud Integration provides an artifact type specifically designed for exposing SOAP APIs. Creation of this artifact generates a template iFlow in background that can then be edited to design your specific service logic. We'll use the web service specified in Section 4.5.1 as our basis for this SOAP API.

Let's start by creating the SOAP API artifact:

1. From the **Design** page of your Cloud Integration tenant, select the relevant package, and switch to edit mode.
2. Click the **Add** button, and then click **SOAP API** from the resulting dropdown menu, as shown in Figure 4.130.

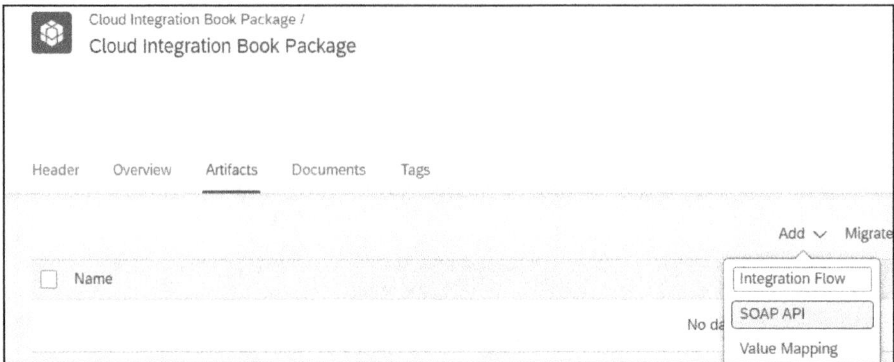

Figure 4.130 Creating a SOAP API Artifact

3. Give the artifact a suitable name, such as "Country_SOAP_Service" and leave the other fields with their default values. Note that, by default, **Product Profile** is set with the value **Cloud Integration**, as shown in Figure 4.131. Click the **OK** button.

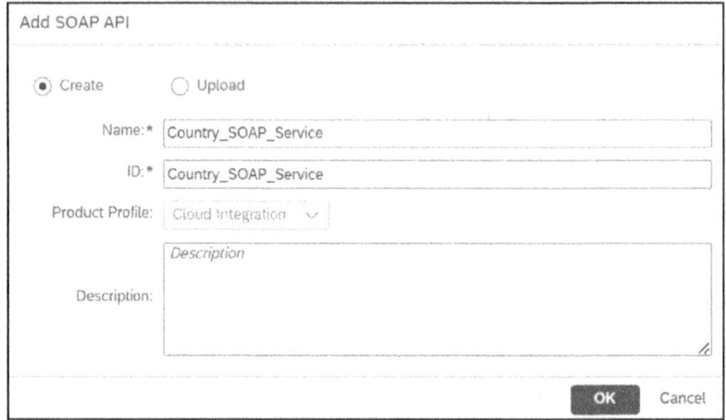

Figure 4.131 SOAP API Creation Options

You'll notice that a template iFlow is created automatically with a SOAP sender channel. This iFlow has one main process pool named **Integration Process** and one local integration process named **Handle Request**, as shown in Figure 4.132.

The purpose of the **Handle Request** process is to implement the custom service logic for the API. In our example, we want to call the Country Info SOAP service using the SOAP receiver adapter. Let's model our integration logic by editing the template iFlow as shown in Figure 4.133.

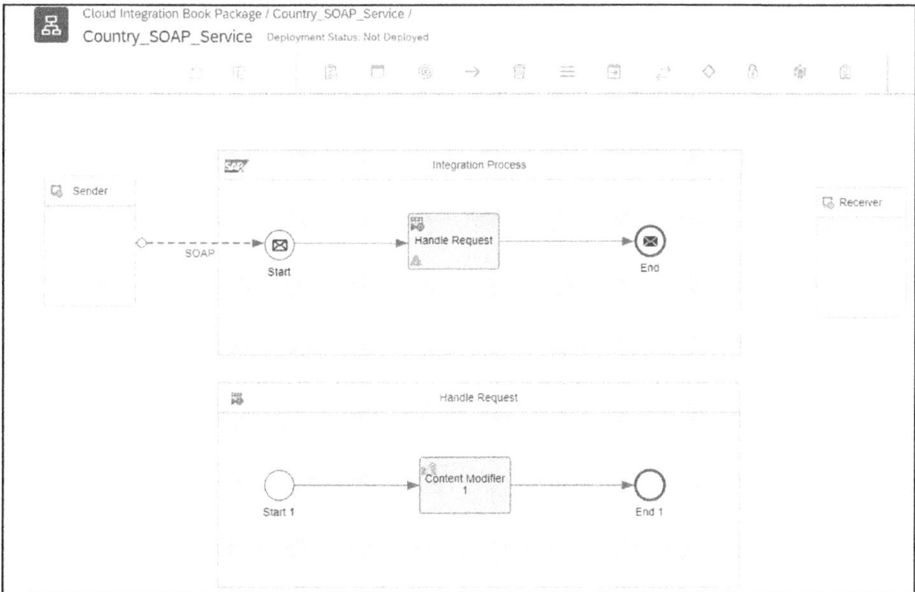

Figure 4.132 Default SOAP Service Template iFlow

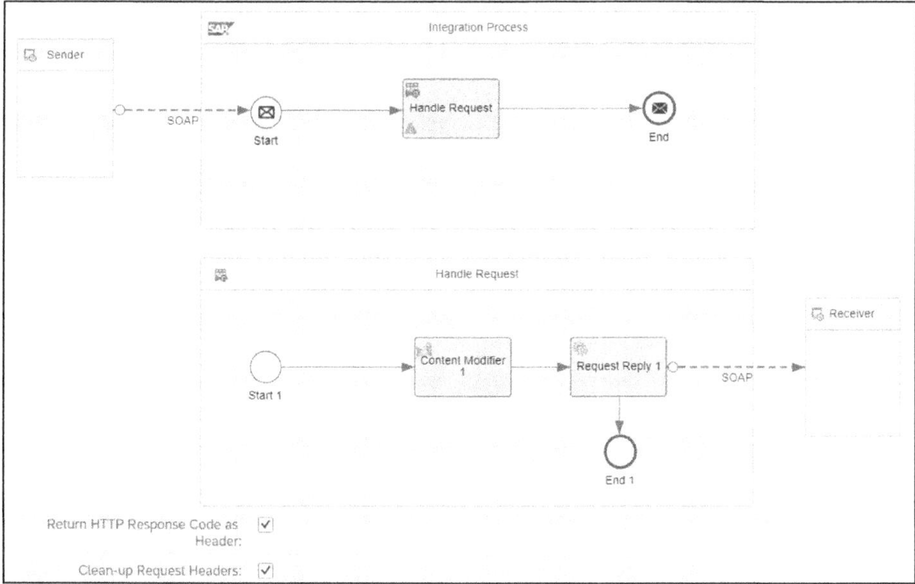

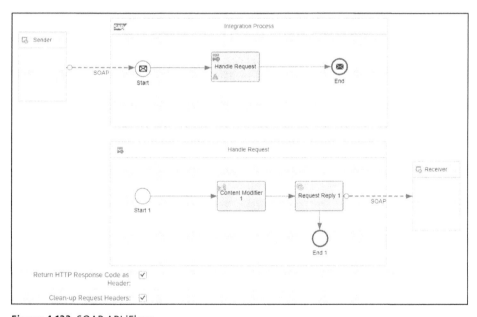

Figure 4.133 SOAP API iFlow

Let's configure the SOAP **Sender** channel by entering the **Address** as "/soapapi/Country ISOCode". Import the WSDL in the SOAP **Sender** channel, and select **CountryISOCode** as the **Service** operation. Refer to Section 4.1.3 for more details on steps to import the WSDL in the SOAP **Sender** channel. After configuration, the **Sender** channel will look as shown in Figure 4.134.

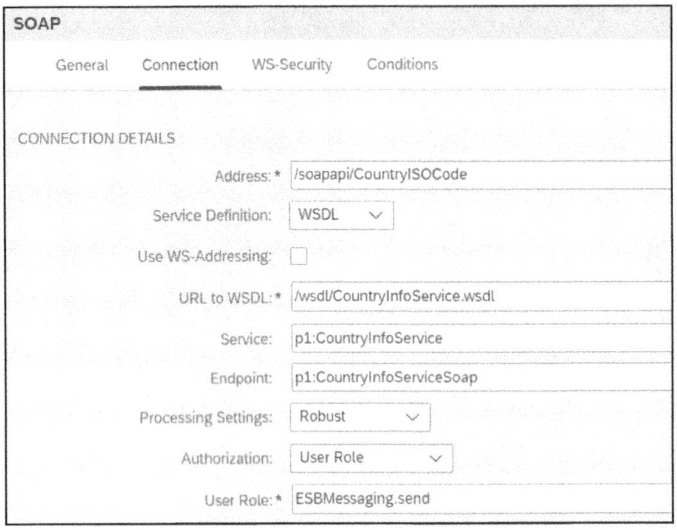

SOAP

General | Connection | WS-Security | Conditions

CONNECTION DETAILS

Address: * /soapapi/CountryISOCode
Service Definition: WSDL
Use WS-Addressing:
URL to WSDL: * /wsdl/CountryInfoService.wsdl
Service: p1:CountryInfoService
Endpoint: p1:CountryInfoServiceSoap
Processing Settings: Robust
Authorization: User Role
User Role: * ESBMessaging.send

Figure 4.134 Sender SOAP Adapter Configuration

In this iFlow, we're calling the `CountryInfoService`, so we need to configure the SOAP **Receiver** adapter to point to this service. In the **Address** text box, enter the service URL, which is "http://webservices.oorsprong.org/websamples.countryinfo/CountryInfoS-ervice.wso" for our target scenario.

Import the WSDL file and select the service operation CountryIsoCode. The SOAP Receiver Adapter configuration will look similar to the configuration in Figure 4.135.

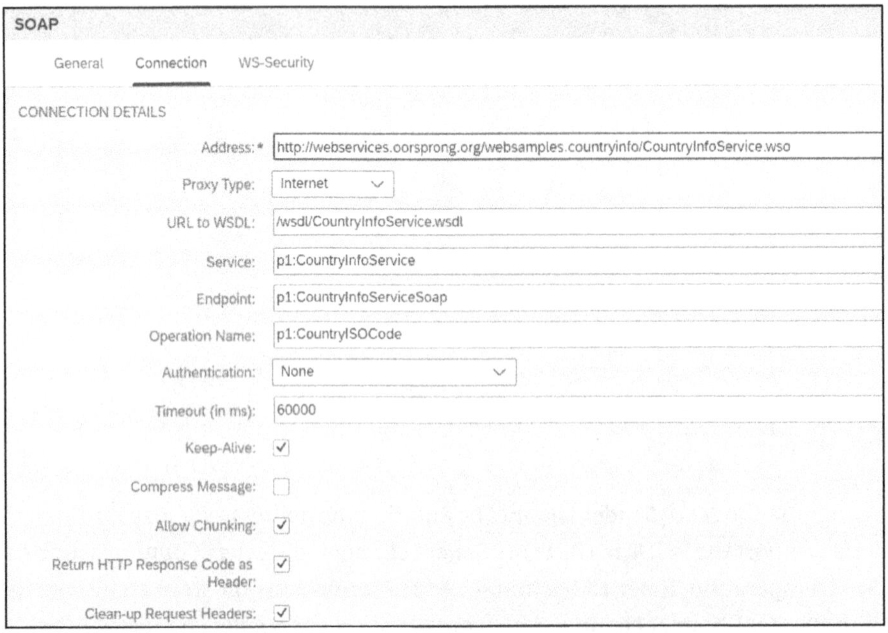

SOAP

General | Connection | WS-Security

CONNECTION DETAILS

Address: * http://webservices.oorsprong.org/websamples.countryinfo/CountryInfoService.wso
Proxy Type: Internet
URL to WSDL: /wsdl/CountryInfoService.wsdl
Service: p1:CountryInfoService
Endpoint: p1:CountryInfoServiceSoap
Operation Name: p1:CountryISOCode
Authentication: None
Timeout (in ms): 60000
Keep-Alive: ✓
Compress Message:
Allow Chunking: ✓
Return HTTP Response Code as Header: ✓
Clean-up Request Headers: ✓

Figure 4.135 SOAP Receiver Adapter Configuration

Save and deploy the iFlow as usual, and test the iFlow using the SoapUI test tool as explained in Section 4.1.6. With this, you've successfully exposed a SOAP API from Cloud Integration.

4.5.4 Providing a REST Service

Like the SOAP service, you can also expose a REST service from Cloud Integration by creating a dedicated REST API artifact in your integration package. Creating this artifact will generate a standard REST API template iFlow as shown in Figure 4.136. This template consists of a main integration process and a local integration process dedicated to the logic of the REST service. Notice that instead of a SOAP Sender channel of the SOAP API, the REST API template has an **HTTPS Sender** channel.

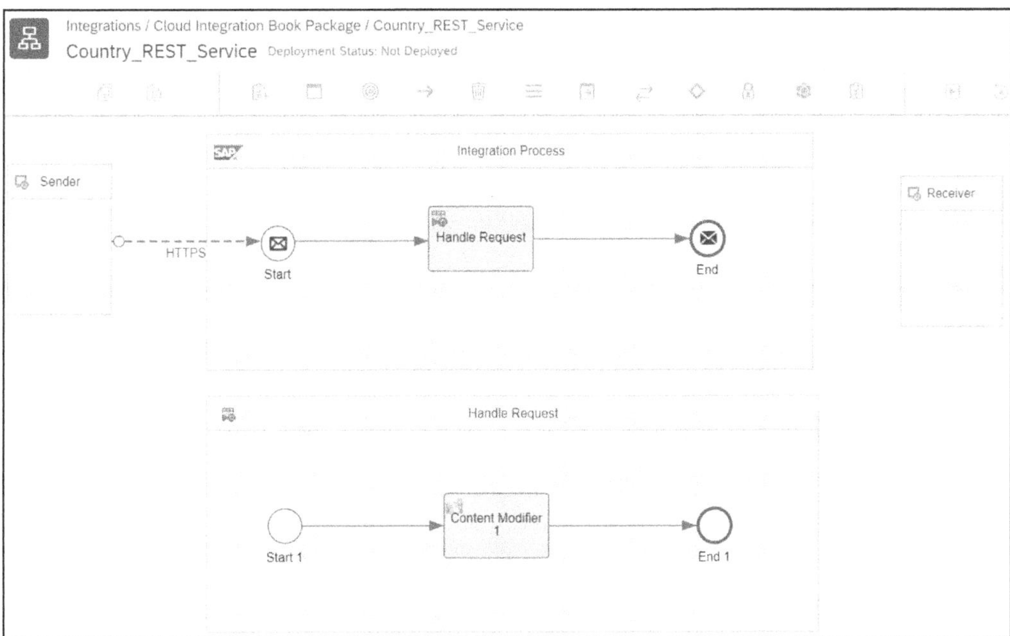

Figure 4.136 Default REST API iFlow Template

Go ahead and modify this template to call the desired target `countryISOCode` service. The final iFlow will look similar to Figure 4.137. For the SOAP **Receiver** configuration, refer to Section 4.5.3.

The main component of the REST API iFlow is the **HTTPS Sender** channel. For the **HTTPS Sender** channel configuration, enter an **Address** such as "/restapi/CountryISOCode". All other options on the communication channel can be left as is (see Figure 4.138).

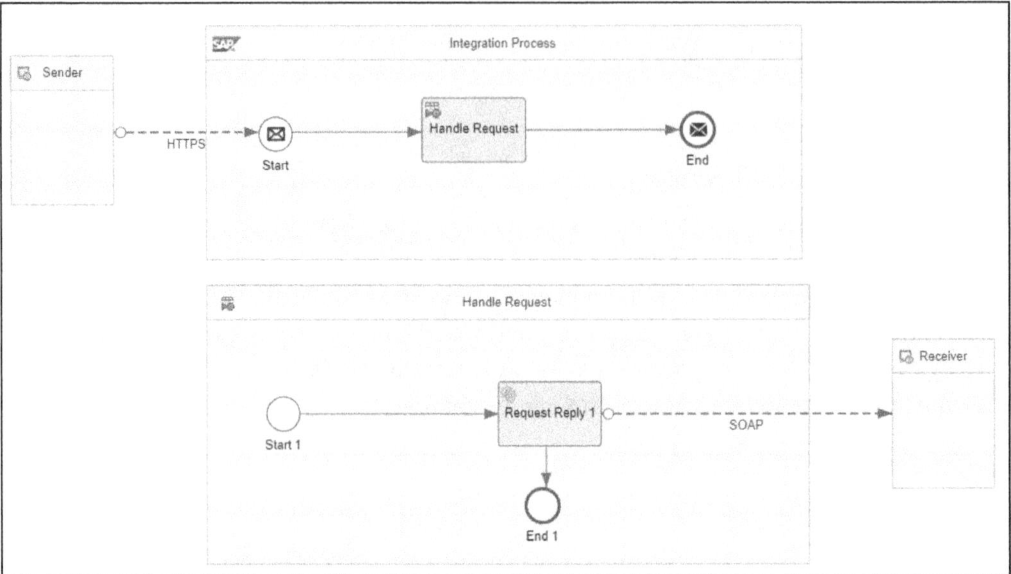

Figure 4.137 REST API iFlow

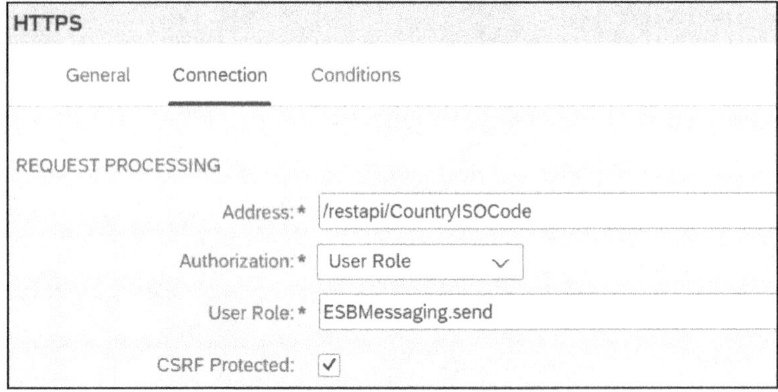

Figure 4.138 HTTPS Adapter Sender Channel Configuration

Save and deploy this iFlow as we've discussed earlier. To test this scenario, you'll need the endpoint on which this service is exposed. You can get this URL from the **Deployed Integration Flow** tile under the **Monitor** view. For testing, use the same test message as in Section 4.5.3.

4.6 Message Routing

Cloud computing is one of the most talked-about topics in the IT industry. However, this trend toward migrating to cloud computing has led to increased heterogeneity in a company's IT landscape, which itself brings an increased need for integration. Often, messages must be exchanged between on-premise and cloud-based applications. Fortunately, cloud-based integration solutions, such as Cloud Integration, can help your company solve this integration challenge.

Looking more closely at how messages are treated within Cloud Integration, one question comes up repeatedly: How can we model different message handling execution paths (i.e., routes) in a single integration scenario? This question stands in the middle of what is known as *content-based routing (CBR)*, the topic of this section. CBR takes care of forwarding messages to the right recipients depending on the content of a message. As an example, let's look at an order. Depending on the type of item, an order might require different treatment within the processing chain or by dedicated backend systems. So, depending on the message's content, the order will need to be transferred to the respective system. That's what CBR is all about.

CBR is nothing new, as one of the famous enterprise integration patterns described in Hohpe and Woolf's *Enterprise Integration Patterns* (Addison Wesley, 2003). As mentioned in previous chapters, Apache Camel is the basic integration framework on which Cloud Integration is built. One major goal of the Apache Camel project was, from the beginning, the implementation of enterprise integration patterns. Thus, we find the implementation of CBR in Cloud Integration as well. Let's see how you can apply a CBR pattern to your integration projects.

4.6.1 The Scenario

Let's start by looking at the scenario we want to build. An example iFlow using CBR is shown in Figure 4.139.

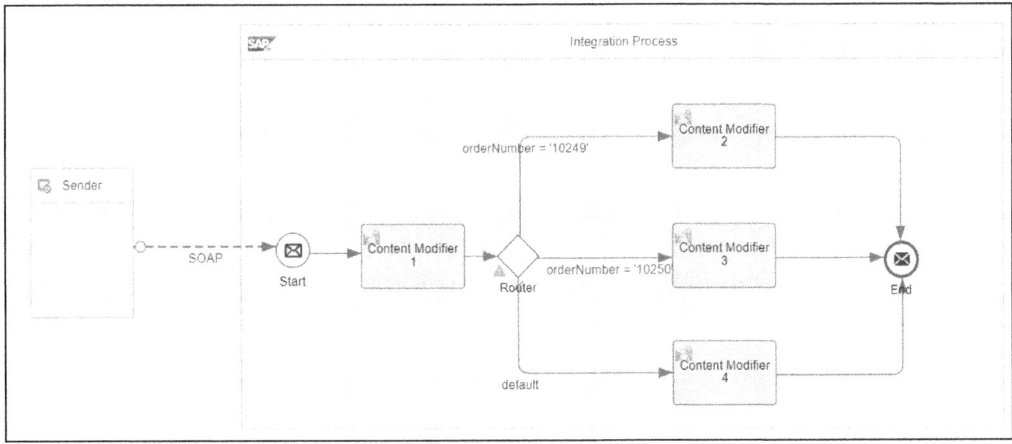

Figure 4.139 Example iFlow Using Content-Based Router

This iFlow shows different message handling execution paths after the diamond shape. The iFlow's semantical behavior can be described in this way: the sender on the left (represented by the **Sender** pool) sends a message via the **SOAP** channel to the iFlow. In this example, we'll reuse the same input message from Chapter 4. Its structure is shown in Figure 4.140.

The incoming message starts the iFlow on the Cloud Integration server. The first **Content Modifier** step, **Content Modifier 1**, takes the order number from the message and stores it in the message's header area. Figure 4.141 shows the **Content Modifier**'s configuration.

```
<soapenv:Envelope xmlns:soapenv="http://schemas
   <soapenv:Header/>
   <soapenv:Body>
      <demo:OrderNumber_MT>
         <orderNumber>10249</orderNumber>
      </demo:OrderNumber_MT>
   </soapenv:Body>
</soapenv:Envelope>
```

Figure 4.140 Example Message

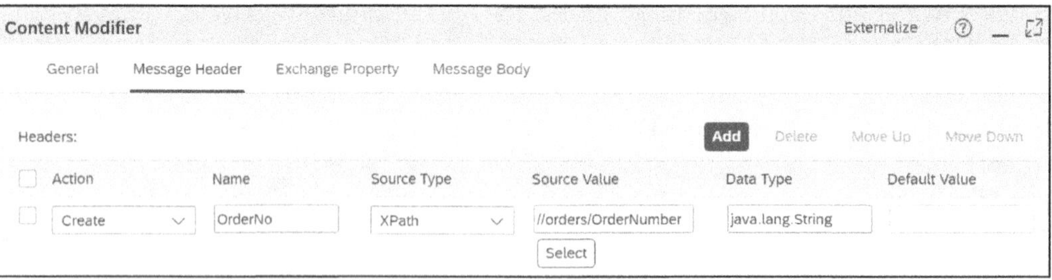

Figure 4.141 Writing Data into the Message's Header Area

The order number is stored in the newly created header variable, `OrderNo`. We can later access this value to define routing conditions. Next, CBR comes into the picture. CBR is modeled using a BPMN-exclusive gateway (the diamond shape). As described in Chapter 4, the entire modeling environment of Cloud Integration is based on BPMN. In BPMN, the exclusive gateway is used to indicate the split of the initial sequence flow into several independent execution paths. Exactly one of the paths leaving the gateway (also known as a *gate* in BPMN nomenclature) will later be executed at runtime, depending on conditions that are attached as labels to each of the outgoing sequence flows. However, looking more closely at the gates, you'll need to recognize one exception: The sequence flow leaving the gateway vertically, which is shown with the tick mark, has no condition associated with it. This gate is a default gate, which is executed during runtime if no other conditions meet the Boolean value `TRUE`. Now, we can describe the behavior of the gateway as follows:

- If the incoming order number equals 10249, the upper path will be followed.
- If the incoming order number equals 10250, the gate in the middle will be taken.
- In all other cases, the default gate will be taken.

To verify the correct behavior of the gateway during runtime, we'll set the body of the message via the respective **Content Modifier** shapes, which are connected with each of the three sequence flows leaving the gateway. The **Content Modifier** steps write the following messages as replies into the message's body:

- `orderNumber = 10249` for the upper sequence flow
- `orderNumber = 10250` for the sequence flow in the middle
- `orderNumber unknown` for the default gate

Figure 4.142 shows an example configuration for the uppermost **Content Modifier**.

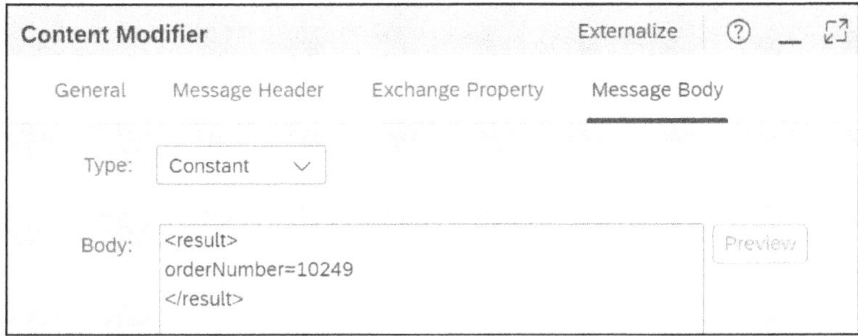

Figure 4.142 Configuration of the Content Modifier for the Uppermost Sequence Flow

4.6.2 Configuration of the Content-Based Router

Now, we know how CBR should behave during runtime, but how is this achieved during design time? Where can you find the gateway in the modeling palette of Cloud Integration's graphical editor? In the main menu of the palette shown in Figure 4.143, click on the **Router** icon ◇.

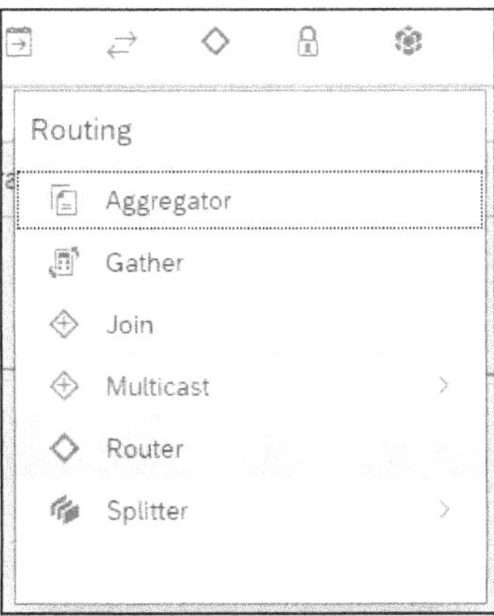

Figure 4.143 Router Shape in the Modeling Environment Palette

A submenu opens, revealing different routing options, including the **Router** symbol, shown in Figure 4.143. Click on the symbol, hover your mouse over the pool for the iFlow, and click again to position the shape. Then, model the three **Content Modifiers**, and connect them with sequence flows from the diamond shape to their respective **Content Modifier** activities. Note that you can only configure the gateway after you've connected it with the three previous steps; otherwise, you won't be able to configure the gates correctly because you won't have access to the sequence flow's properties to define its labels and evaluation conditions. So, let's configure each gate, one after another, starting with the top one. Click on the sequence flow, leaving the gateway so that its color turns to orange, as shown in Figure 4.144.

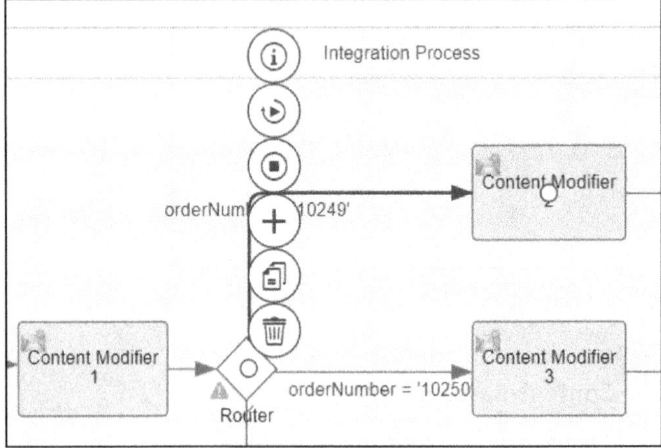

Figure 4.144 Selecting a Sequence Flow for Configuration

As always, you can configure the attributes of the selected shape in the **Properties** section, found beneath the process model. In our case, we want to tell the runtime engine that the execution of the model should be continued on the upper path of our model if the order number equals 10249. You have two options for defining such a routing condition:

- Directly access the contents of the message (in the body area of Apache Camel's message model), and retrieve the value that should be used for the decision from there.
- Use header variables that have been already been declared and set.

Note

The first option is only possible for XML-based message content. If your incoming message isn't available in XML, you'll have to convert the content into XML first.

Let's begin with the first option. In this case, you must define an XPath expression to the field you want to access. In our case, we want to access the **orderNumber** field of the incoming message (shown earlier in Figure 4.140). Therefore, the configuration looks like the screen shown in Figure 4.145.

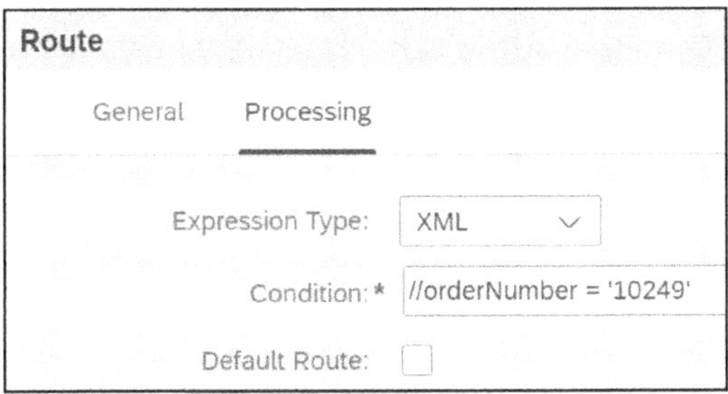

Figure 4.145 Defining the Condition for the Uppermost Sequence Flow

Under the **General** tab, the name of the sequence flow is set, but under the **Processing** tab, the configuration is defined. The **Expression Type** dropdown list, shown in Figure 4.145, contains the values **XML** and **Non-XML** and is particularly important. The selected value influences how the **Condition** field is interpreted by the execution engine during runtime. If **XML** is chosen, the **Condition** is interpreted as an XPath expression. If **Non-XML** is chosen, the **Condition** is interpreted as an expression using the Simple Expression Language. You'll see an example of the second case when we define the other gate. For now, though, stick with the XML option in this case. The **Condition** is formulated using a classic XPath expression. You can also combine several expressions using the logical operators and Routing: condition or (e.g., `//orderNumber = '10249' or //orderNumber = '10250'`) to formulate more sophisticated routing logic.

For the second gate, we'll use the header variable `OrderNo`, which we created by the invocation of the first **Content Modifier** (shown earlier in Figure 4.139), in conjunction with the configuration shown earlier in Figure 4.141. The condition can be formulated now, as shown in Figure 4.146.

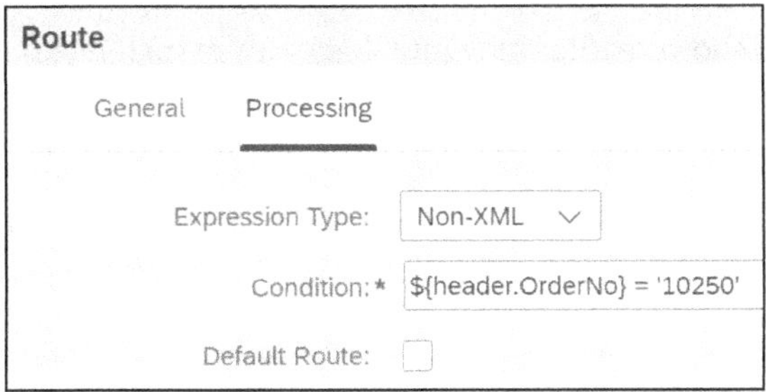

Figure 4.146 Configuring the Gate's Condition Using the Content of a Header Variable

We can easily identify the typical Apache Camel Simple Expression Language for accessing variables (e.g., $ or {}). The string header in ${header.OrderNo} indicates the area from which the value (the message's header area) should be loaded, and the OrderNo after the dot indicates the name under which we stored the value earlier. Note that the **Expression Type** dropdown list has been changed to **Non-XML**. Because you use this dropdown list to define how the **Condition** string is interpreted, you should be aware that you can't mix XML-based variables with Apache Camel–based variables. If you try to mix them, for example, ${header.OrderNo} = '10250' or //orderNumber = '10251', you'll receive a validation error, as shown in Figure 4.147.

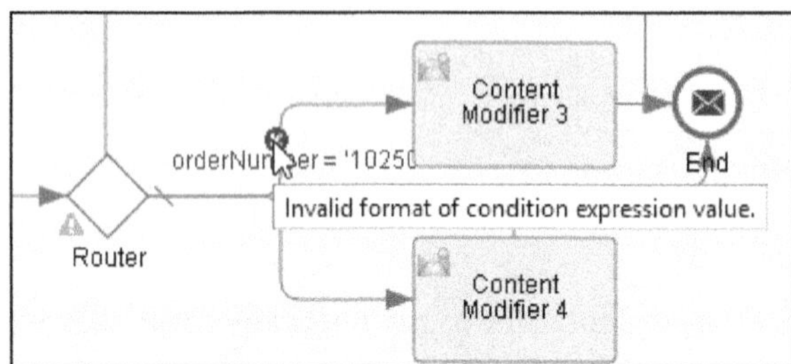

Figure 4.147 Validation Error If the Expression Mixes Both XML and Non-XML Parts

The definition of the last gate is probably the easiest part of configuring CBR. Simply select the **Default Route** checkbox, as shown in Figure 4.148, to define the gate that should be followed during runtime if none of the explicit conditions of the other gates evaluate to TRUE.

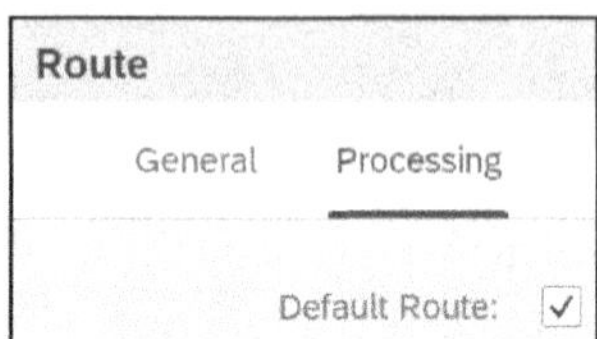

Figure 4.148 Defining the Default Route

From what you've learned so far, you know how to formulate expressions for the XML setting of the **Expression Type** field, shown earlier in Figure 4.145. Now, you'll need to apply the rules laid out in the XPath specification, as defined by the World Wide Web Consortium (W3C).

But what about non-XML expressions—which operators are allowed here? For your convenience, the table from SAP Help Portal (*http://s-prs.co/507717*) has been reproduced in Figure 4.149. As shown in Figure 4.149, several operators are allowed for formulating non-XML expressions.

Operator	Example
=	${header.SenderId} = '1'
!=	${header.SenderId} != '1'
>	${header.SenderId} > '1'
>=	${header.SenderId} >= '1'
<	${header.SenderId} < '1'
<=	${header.SenderId} <= '1'
and	${header.SenderId}= '1' and ${header.ReceiverId} = '2'
or	${header.SenderId}= '1' or ${header.ReceiverId}= '2'
contains	${header.SenderId} contains '1'
not contains	${header.SenderId} not contains '1'
in	${header.SenderId} in '1,2'
not in	${header.SenderId} not in '1,2'
regex	${header.SenderId} regex '1.*'
not regex	${header.SenderId} not regex '1.*'

Figure 4.149 Usage of Operators in Non-XML Expressions

4.6.3 Running the Content-Based Router Scenario

Now that our configuration is complete, we can finally run the scenario. Use the SOAP tool of your choosing (e.g., SoapUI as described in Section 4.1.6) and invoke the solution. We'll use the input message shown earlier in Figure 4.140. Depending on the order number's value, you'll receive specific replies from the iFlow. If your order number is 10250, the reply should look similar to the message shown in Figure 4.150.

```
<soap:Envelope xmlns:soap="http://schemas.
   <soap:Body>
      <result>orderNumber = 10250</result>
   </soap:Body>
</soap:Envelope>
```

Figure 4.150 Reply Message If the Order Number of the Input Message Was 10250

If you provide a number for which no routing rule exists, you'll see the response shown in Figure 4.151 because the default route of the gateway was followed.

```
<soap:Envelope xmlns:soap="http://schemas.xml
   <soap:Body>
      <result>orderNumber unknown</result>
   </soap:Body>
</soap:Envelope>
```

Figure 4.151 Reply Message If the Order Number Lacks a Routing Rule

At this point, we could stop with our description of CBR. However, one interesting question hasn't yet been answered: What happens if the routing rules contain overlapping conditions? Mistakes are always possible, and especially for complex routing conditions, these mistakes may sometimes result in overlapping conditions, so that potentially two or more conditions could evaluate to `true` during runtime. If this happens, more gates may be triggered. On the other hand, we know that an exclusive gateway will trigger one—and only one—gate. So, when conditions overlap, which gates should be triggered, and can we influence the sequence in which expressions are evaluated?

Let's try a little experiment. We'll change the conditions so that they overlap. Let's change the condition of the gate labeled with **orderNumber = '10250'** to **${header.OrderNo} = '10249'**. This overlaps with the gate already labeled with **orderNumber = '10249'** and its condition **//orderNumber = '10249'**. Both are checking for order number 10249.

Now, save and deploy your changes and run the scenario again using 10249 as the input value for the order number. After you run the scenario in your own environment, you'll see the result shown earlier in Figure 4.150. Thus, the changed path was executed, although if you compare our design of the scenario shown earlier in Figure 4.139, you'll see that the path is now positioned in the middle of the three gates. One might think the conditions are evaluated from top to bottom in the visual diagram, so the model's visual appearance has something to do with execution sequence. Our experiment proves that this isn't the case. (We also want to stress that *our* scenario works this way. It may be that *your* scenario is still working correctly!)

What else influences the execution sequence, then? The answer is hidden behind the gateway shape itself. Select the diamond shape of the router and look at its properties. In our example, the gateway has the properties shown in Figure 4.152.

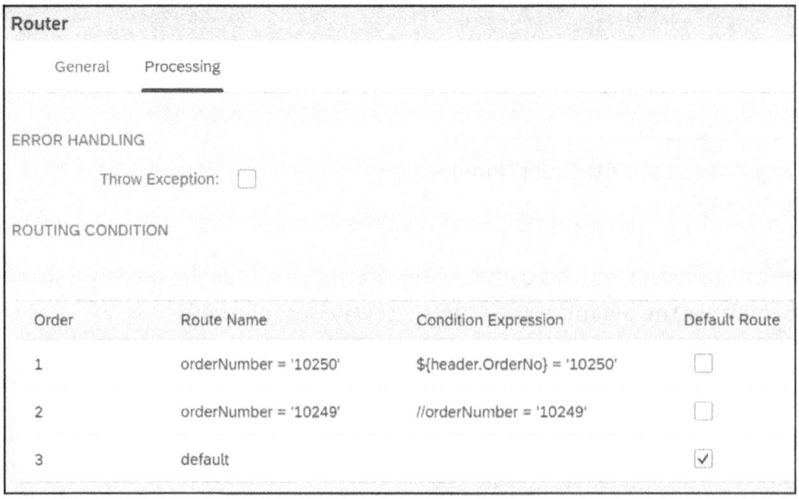

Router

General Processing

ERROR HANDLING

Throw Exception: ☐

ROUTING CONDITION

Order	Route Name	Condition Expression	Default Route
1	orderNumber = '10250'	${header.OrderNo} = '10250'	☐
2	orderNumber = '10249'	//orderNumber = '10249'	☐
3	default		☑

Figure 4.152 Configuration of the Exclusive Gateway

Take note of the **Order** column, which tells us the sequence in which the conditions will be evaluated. The route labeled with **orderNumber = 10250** will be evaluated first. Additionally, because the condition is true, you'll get the expected result. The second row will no longer be evaluated because the gateway has already found a valid gate, and no more gates are allowed to fire due to the exclusive behavior of the gateway.

This exclusivity explains the gateway's behavior. But how can we influence the evaluation's sequence? The answer is rather straightforward: the order of the rows is determined by the connection's modeling sequence. Every connection you're modeling from the gateway to any task beyond the gateway adds a new row to this table. Note that every new row will be added at the bottom of the table. You can conclude from this description how we created the process model shown earlier in Figure 4.139. We first drew the connection to the **Content Modifier** in the middle (resulting in the first row in the table), then to the one at the top (second row in the table), and finally to the **Content Modifier** at the bottom (third row in the table). If we want to change the execution sequence, what do we need to do? Look at Figure 4.152 again. We want the second row to be at the first position. So, in your process model, delete the connection responsible for the first table row: the connection labeled with **orderNumber = 10250**. The second row will move up to first place automatically, exactly as we want. Next, draw the connection that we just deleted again, add the label and the condition in its properties, and verify the condition's list at the gateway. The gateway's configuration should now look like the screen shown in Figure 4.153.

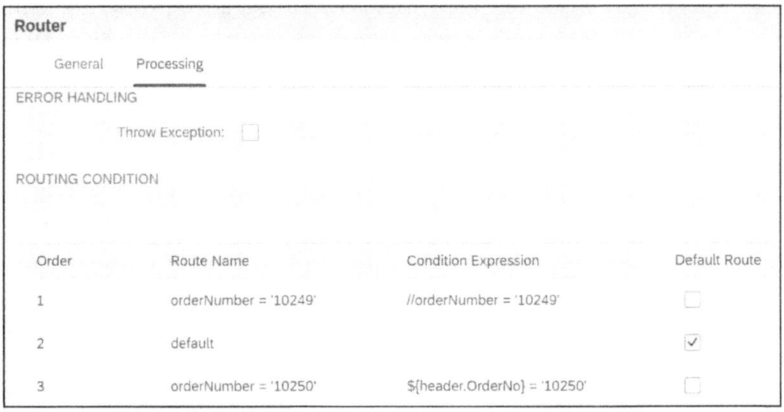

Router

General Processing

ERROR HANDLING

Throw Exception: ☐

ROUTING CONDITION

Order	Route Name	Condition Expression	Default Route
1	orderNumber = '10249'	//orderNumber = '10249'	☐
2	default		☑
3	orderNumber = '10250'	${header.OrderNo} = '10250'	☐

Figure 4.153 Evaluation Sequence after Deleting and Redrawing the Connection with the Route Name orderNumber = 10250

Note the changed order sequence in comparison to the sequence shown earlier in Figure 4.152. If you invoke the route again with order number 10249, you'll see the expected (correct) result, as shown in Figure 4.154.

```
<soap:Envelope xmlns:soap="http://schemas.xml
    <soap:Body>
        <result>orderNumber = 10249</result>
    </soap:Body>
</soap:Envelope>
```

Figure 4.154 Returned Message after Correcting the Evaluation Sequence at the Gateway

To summarize, routing messages to different message handling paths is an important aspect of every integration project. Cloud Integration is based on Apache Camel, which implements typical enterprise integration patterns. One of those patterns is CBR, whose task is to split a sequence flow into different independent execution paths, which can then be activated based on certain conditions. Exactly one of those execution paths will be selected during runtime. In this section, you learned how to model CBR in Cloud Integration's graphical modeling environment and how to configure the conditions correctly. To define the expressions, you have two options at your disposal: XML and non-XML. You learned when to use which option and how to influence the condition's evaluation sequence. Now, it's your turn to work with CBR in your own integration projects.

4.7 Summary

Congratulations! You've now mastered your first basic integration scenarios using Cloud Integration. Look back and be proud of your achievements: you now know how to work with data within Cloud Integration, how to invoke external OData services, how to provision an OData service, how to map different data structures to each other, and finally how a **Router** step works. You're now ready to tackle the next challenges: message aggregation, the handling of messages containing lists of entries, and asynchronous message handling. All of these topics will be covered in the next chapter.

Chapter 5
Advanced Integration Scenarios

So far, we've introduced you to the development environment, as well as the runtime, of Cloud Integration. The time has come to address more sophisticated, real-life integration scenarios. In this chapter, more advanced integration patterns are discussed for the integration developer.

In the previous chapter, you learned a lot about the inner workings of Cloud Integration. You've seen how to work with its data model, how to enrich messages with data retrieved from an external OData service, and how to solve mapping challenges using the built-in mapping engine. In this chapter, we'll continue our journey with topics for addressing more advanced integration scenarios, such as the following:

- Message aggregation
- Working with lists
- Asynchronous message handling
- Sending messages to multiple receivers using multicast
- Asynchronous decoupling of inbound and outbound processing
- Using event-driven messaging

Let's get started!

5.1 Working with an Aggregator

According to Gregor Hohpe and Bobby Woolf in their book *Enterprise Integration Patterns* (Addison-Wesley, 2004), an aggregator pattern answers the question of how you can combine the results of individual (but related) messages so that they can be processed as a whole.

As shown in Figure 5.1, let's say you have a scenario involving system A, which needs to send an order message to system B. However, system A is only capable of sending a message with a maximum of 1 item at a time. Thus, for system A to send an order with 10 items, it would need to send 10 different messages, each containing 1 item. For the sake of illustration, let's assume that the incoming order item message looks like the message shown in Figure 5.2.

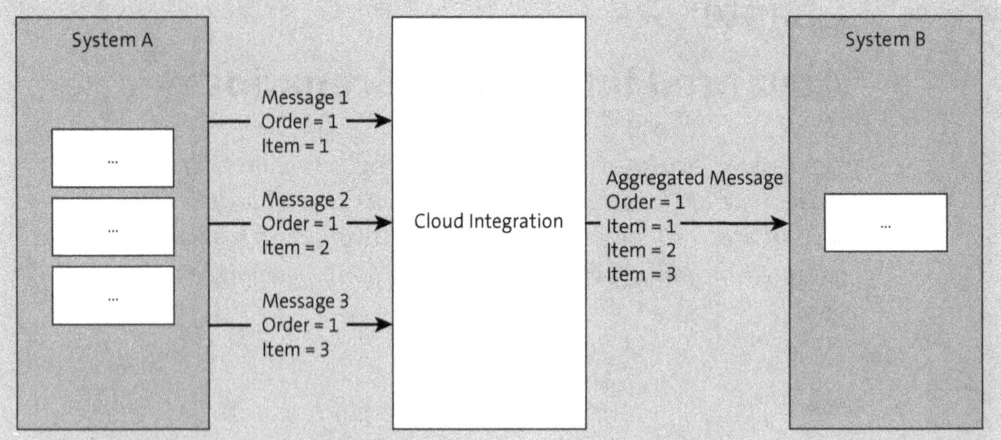

Figure 5.1 Sample Aggregator Situation

```
<OrderItem xmlns:demo="http://ci.sap.com/demo">
    <orderNumber>AA2345</orderNumber>
    <Item>
        <ItemNo>1</ItemNo>
        <Quantity>1</Quantity>
        <Unit>Kg</Unit>
        <LastStatus>false</LastStatus>
    </Item>
</OrderItem>
```

Figure 5.2 Sample Incoming Order Item Message

To solve this challenge, you'll need to use a *stateful filter*, also called an *aggregator*, to collect and store individual messages (each containing 1 item, as shown in Figure 5.2) until a complete set of related messages has been received. Then, the aggregator sends a single message (with all 10 items) extracted from the individual messages.

When dealing with an aggregator, you'll need to address the following questions:

- How do we identify that an incoming message is related to another incoming message?
- How do we identify that a complete set of messages has been received? In other words, how do we know when to stop collecting incoming messages because we've received the last one?
- What do we do if the sender system never sends the last message?

Luckily, Cloud Integration provides an **Aggregator** step to combine multiple incoming messages into a single message. This step helps you solve this challenge.

5.1.1 Sample Scenario

Let's use a sample scenario to illustrate the use of the **Aggregator** step. Figure 5.3 shows what the final integration flow (iFlow) will look like.

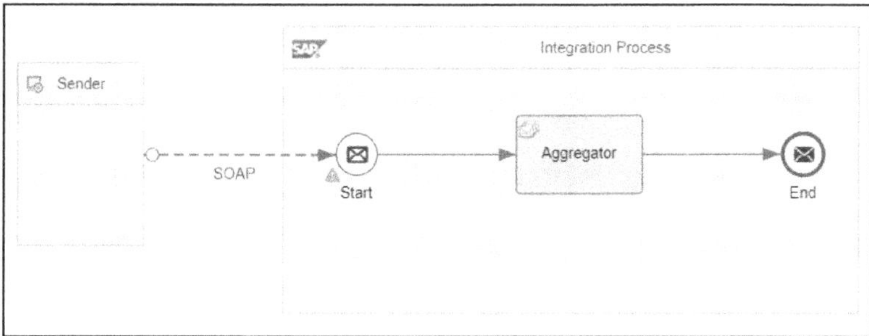

Figure 5.3 Sample Target iFlow

Note that, in the sample iFlow shown in Figure 5.3, no receiver systems exist. This omission is purely for the sake of illustration. In a real-life scenario, you'll probably send the aggregated message to a receiver system. Furthermore, the **Message Exchange Pattern** field of the Simple Object Access Protocol (SOAP) adapter is set to **One-Way** in this example, as shown in Figure 5.4. This setting ensures that the message is asynchronous. We'll show you how to deal with asynchronous processing in the following sections.

Figure 5.4 Settings of the Sender SOAP Channel

We won't spend time describing how to create the iFlow in this section, which is covered in previous chapters. Instead, we'll mainly focus on the configuration of the **Aggregator** step in Cloud Integration. Follow these steps:

1. Navigate to the **Design** page of Cloud Integration, and select the **Aggregator** step from the palette, as shown in Figure 5.5.
2. Drag the step to your iFlow.
3. Select the **Aggregator** step from the iFlow, and specify the different attribute properties, as shown in Figure 5.6 and Figure 5.7. The meanings of the attributes available in an **Aggregator** step are listed in Table 5.1.

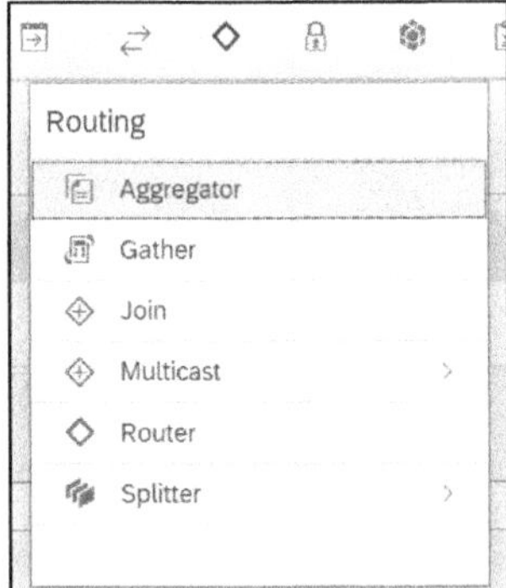

Figure 5.5 Aggregator Step in the Design Palette

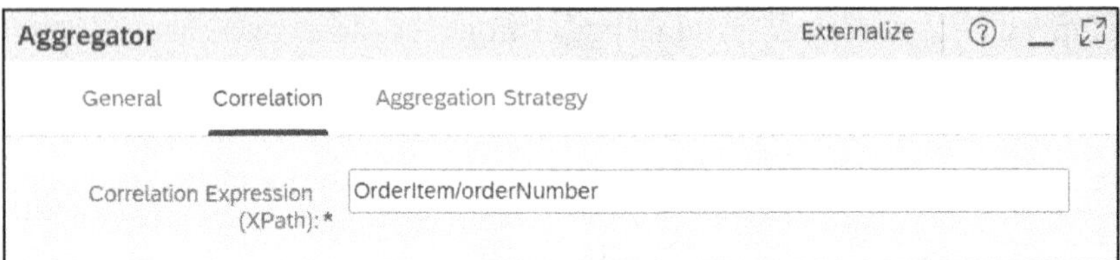

Figure 5.6 Aggregator: Correlation Tab

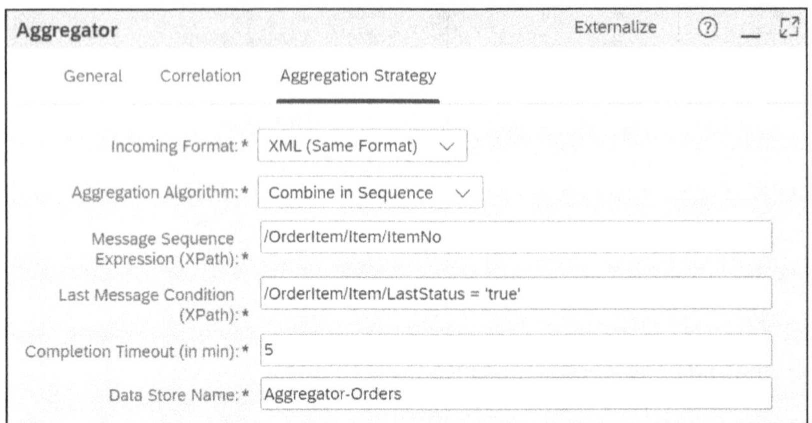

Figure 5.7 Aggregator: Aggregation Strategy Tab

Name	Description
Correlation Expression (XPath)	An XML Path Language (XPath) expression that points to an element to be used to match all correlated incoming messages. This field provides a solution to a problem we asked at the beginning of the section—how to identify that an incoming message is related to another incoming message.

Table 5.1 Attributes of the Aggregator Step

Name	Description
Incoming Format	Specifies the content type of the incoming message. At the time of this writing, **XML (Same Format)** is the only option.
Aggregation Algorithm	Specifies how the correlated messages should be aggregated. The following aggregation methods are possible: ▪ **Combine** All incoming and correlated messages are aggregated using a random order. ▪ **Combine in Sequence** All incoming and correlated messages are aggregated according to a sequence order defined by the **Message Sequence Expression (XPath)** field.
Message Sequence Expression (XPath)	Specifies the sequencing order by which messages should be sorted during the aggregation process. Note that this field is only available if the **Combine in Sequence** option was selected from the **Aggregation Algorithm** dropdown list.
Last Message Condition (XPath)	An XPath value to specify how to identify the last message to be aggregated. This field provides a solution to the problem of identifying when a complete set of messages has been received or when to stop collecting incoming messages because the last message has been received.
Completion Timeout (in min)	Specifies the maximum time between the processing of two messages before the aggregation is automatically stopped. The default value is set to 60 minutes. This field provides a solution to the problem of what happens if the sender system never sends the last message. Specifying a timeout ensures that the process doesn't wait for incoming messages forever. However, note that the value used in this field must be agreed to with the sender system. Messages arriving after the completion timeout has elapsed will start a new message processing run.
Data Store Name	Specifies the name of the temporary data store to be used for storing the aggregated message. By default, Cloud Integration specifies a randomly generated name, but this name can be changed to any unique name. Note that the solution uses only local data stores. Global data stores currently aren't supported.

Table 5.1 Attributes of the Aggregator Step (Cont.)

After you finish building the iFlow that includes the **Aggregator** step, save and deploy it.

5.1.2 Sending Messages via SoapUI

Let's now run the scenario by sending messages via SoapUI and observing how our iFlow behaves in the Cloud Integration monitor.

Sending the First Message

The first message to be triggered is shown in Figure 5.8. Note that the example message shown uses the correlation (`OrderNumber`) `AA2345` and sequence number (`ItemNo`) value `1`.

```
<soapenv:Envelope xmlns:soapenv="http://schemas.xmlsoap.org/soap/envelope/">
   <soapenv:Header/>
   <soapenv:Body>
      <OrderItem xmlns:demo="http://ci.sap.com/demo">
         <orderNumber>AA2345</orderNumber>
         <Item>
            <ItemNo>1</ItemNo>
            <Quantity>1</Quantity>
            <Unit>Kg</Unit>
            <LastStatus>false</LastStatus>
         </Item>
      </OrderItem>
   </soapenv:Body>
</soapenv:Envelope>
```

Figure 5.8 First Message for the Aggregation Scenario

After triggering the message, look in the **Monitor Message Processing** section of Cloud Integration. As shown in Figure 5.9, notice that two new log entries have been added to the monitor.

Figure 5.9 First Message Arriving in Cloud Integration

In an aggregation scenario, log entries are added in pairs:

- The first log entry represents the message received in the **Aggregator** step.
- The second log entry represents the confirmation that the message has been persisted in the data store. In our case, the data store is named `Aggregator-1`, as shown earlier in Figure 5.7. We'll discuss data stores in detail in Chapter 7, Section 7.4.

Notice also that the **Data Stores** tile in the **Manage Stores** monitoring section shows two entries, as shown in Figure 5.10.

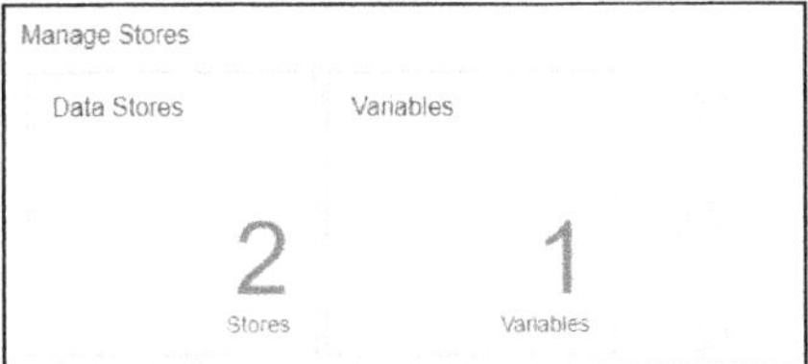

Figure 5.10 View of the Manage Stores Tiles

Click on the **Data Stores** tile to view its content, which consists of the following two entries:

- **Data Store Aggregation Repository**
  In this repository, one entry is created for each new correlation ID, as shown in Figure 5.11.
- **Data Store**
  One entry is created for each correlated message, as shown in Figure 5.12.

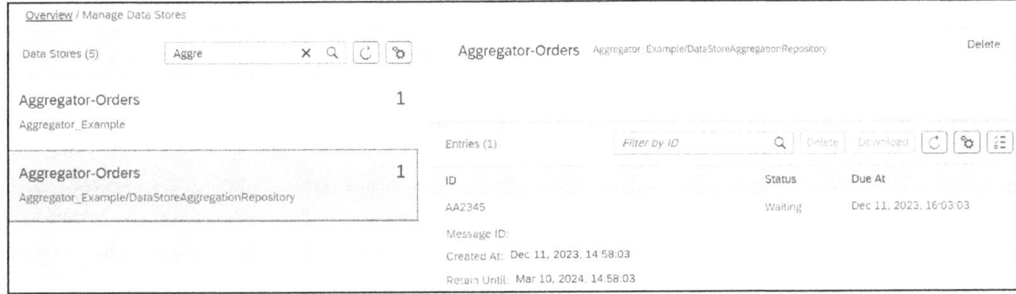

Figure 5.11 View of the Data Store Aggregation Repository Entries after the First Message

Assuming three messages are sent to Cloud Integration with the same correlation ID, you can expect to have one entry in the **Data Store Aggregation Repository** and three entries in the **Data Store**.

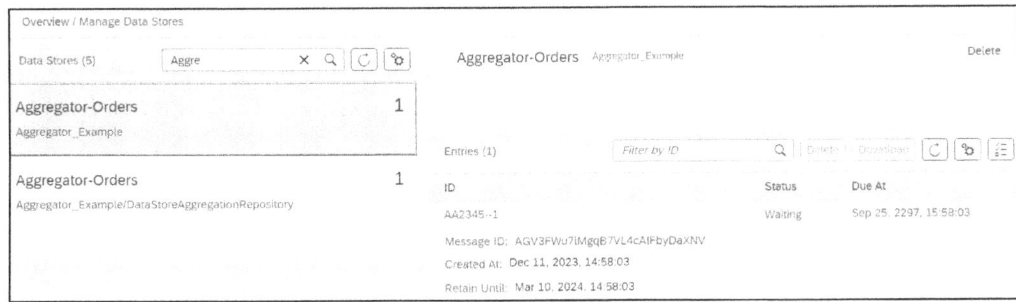

Figure 5.12 View of the Data Store Entries after the First Message

Sending the Second Message

Let's now send a second message (shown in Figure 5.13) via SoapUI.

```
<soapenv:Envelope xmlns:soapenv="http://schemas.xmlsoap.org/soap/envelope/">
   <soapenv:Header/>
   <soapenv:Body>
      <OrderItem xmlns:demo="http://ci.sap.com/demo">
         <orderNumber>AA2345</orderNumber>
         <Item>
            <ItemNo>2</ItemNo>
            <Quantity>5</Quantity>
            <Unit>Kg</Unit>
            <LastStatus>false</LastStatus>
         </Item>
      </OrderItem>
   </soapenv:Body>
</soapenv:Envelope>
```

Figure 5.13 Second Message for the Aggregation Scenario

After sending the message shown in Figure 5.13, monitor the data store one more time, as shown in Figure 5.14. Notice that, because the correlation ID of the second message is the same as the first message, no new entry has been added to the **Data Store Aggregation Repository**. As a result, the second row shown in Figure 5.14 remains unchanged with one entry. However, a new entry has been added to the **Data Store**, as shown in the first row shown in Figure 5.14.

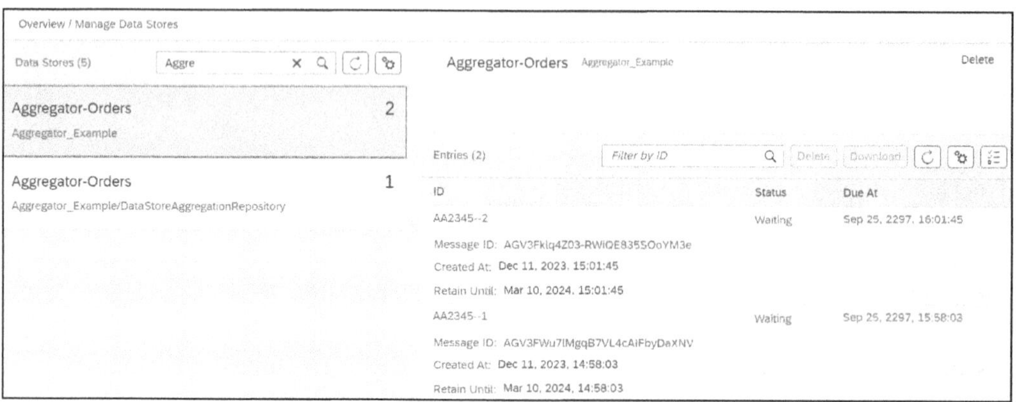

Figure 5.14 View of the Data Store Entries after the Second Message

Sending the Third Message

Let's now send a third message (shown in Figure 5.15) via SoapUI. Notice that this third message has the element `LastStatus` set to `true`. This parameter is different from the other messages we sent previously.

According to the configuration of the **Aggregator** step (shown earlier in Figure 5.7), when a message is received with the element `LastStatus` set to `true`, this message is the last. This completion condition can be seen via the **Last Message Condition (XPath)** field (refer to Figure 5.7). This condition has now been met with our last message, shown in Figure 5.15.

```
<soapenv:Envelope xmlns:soapenv="http://schemas.xmlsoap.org/soap/envelope/">
   <soapenv:Header/>
   <soapenv:Body>
      <OrderItem xmlns:demo="http://ci.sap.com/demo">
         <orderNumber>AA2345</orderNumber>
         <Item>
            <ItemNo>3</ItemNo>
            <Quantity>1</Quantity>
            <Unit>Kg</Unit>
            <LastStatus>true</LastStatus>
         </Item>
      </OrderItem>
   </soapenv:Body>
</soapenv:Envelope>
```

Figure 5.15 Third Message for the Aggregation Scenario

As the left panel of the screen shown in Figure 5.16 demonstrates, four messages exist. The first three (from the bottom) represent the messages sent via SoapUI, whereas the last message (top) is automatically created after the last message is received or after the completion timeout condition has been met.

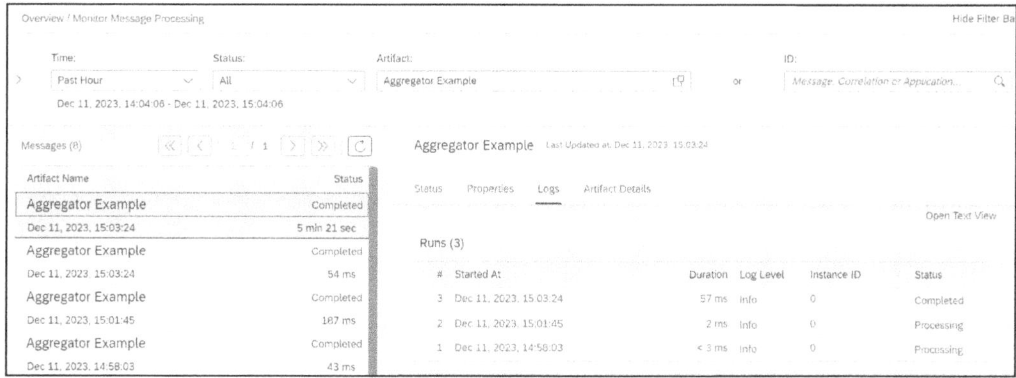

Figure 5.16 All Received Messages in the Monitor Message Processing

In addition, notice that the list of the correlated messages is displayed under the **Logs** section (shown in Figure 5.16). You can view more details by clicking on the **Open Text View** link at the top-right of the screen. The **Message Processing Log Attachments** screen will open where you'll see the **AggregateCompletedBy** field, as shown in Figure 5.17. Possible values for this field include the following:

- **Predicate**
  Indicates that the processing of the aggregator is finished because the completion condition has been fulfilled.
- **Timeout**
  Indicates that the processing of the aggregator is finished because the configured completion timeout has been reached.

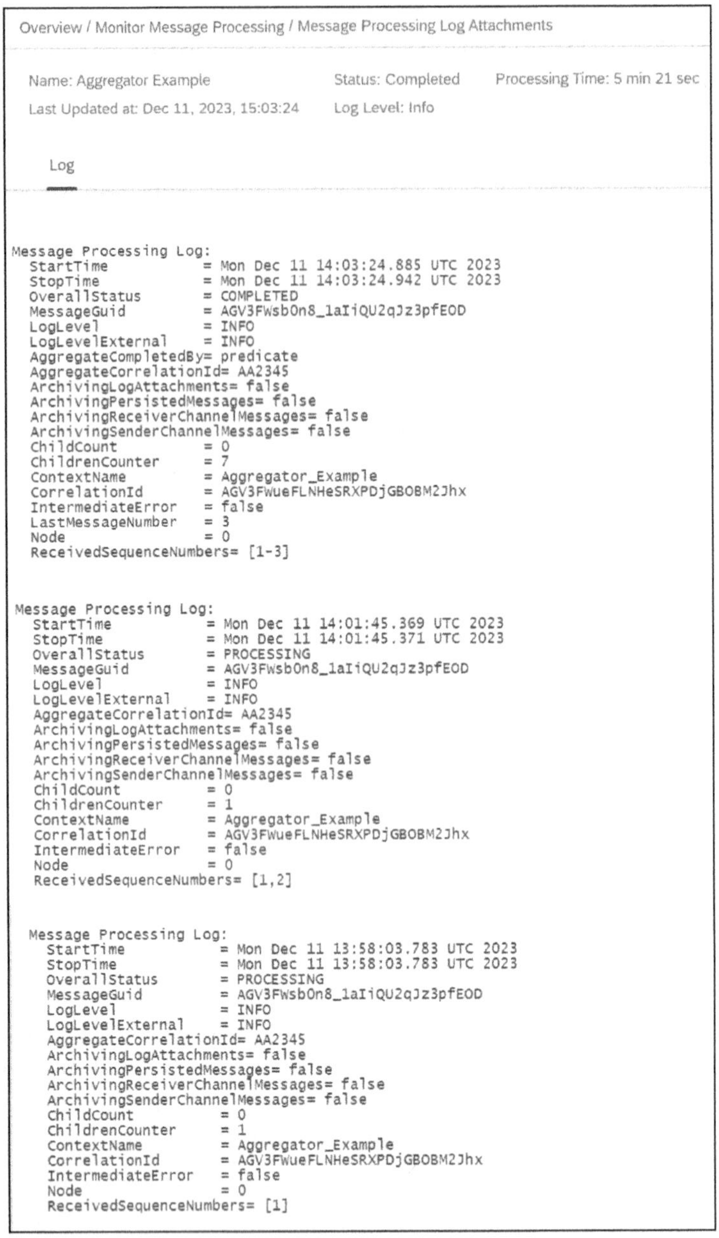

Overview / Monitor Message Processing / Message Processing Log Attachments

Name: Aggregator Example | Status: Completed | Processing Time: 5 min 21 sec
Last Updated at: Dec 11, 2023, 15:03:24 | Log Level: Info

Log

```
Message Processing Log:
  StartTime           = Mon Dec 11 14:03:24.885 UTC 2023
  StopTime            = Mon Dec 11 14:03:24.942 UTC 2023
  OverallStatus       = COMPLETED
  MessageGuid         = AGV3FWsbOn8_1aIiQU2qJz3pfEOD
  LogLevel            = INFO
  LogLevelExternal    = INFO
  AggregateCompletedBy= predicate
  AggregateCorrelationId= AA2345
  ArchivingLogAttachments= false
  ArchivingPersistedMessages= false
  ArchivingReceiverChannelMessages= false
  ArchivingSenderChannelMessages= false
  ChildCount          = 0
  ChildrenCounter     = 7
  ContextName         = Aggregator_Example
  CorrelationId       = AGV3FWueFLNHeSRXPDjGBOBM2Jhx
  IntermediateError   = false
  LastMessageNumber   = 3
  Node                = 0
  ReceivedSequenceNumbers= [1-3]

Message Processing Log:
  StartTime           = Mon Dec 11 14:01:45.369 UTC 2023
  StopTime            = Mon Dec 11 14:01:45.371 UTC 2023
  OverallStatus       = PROCESSING
  MessageGuid         = AGV3FWsbOn8_1aIiQU2qJz3pfEOD
  LogLevel            = INFO
  LogLevelExternal    = INFO
  AggregateCorrelationId= AA2345
  ArchivingLogAttachments= false
  ArchivingPersistedMessages= false
  ArchivingReceiverChannelMessages= false
  ArchivingSenderChannelMessages= false
  ChildCount          = 0
  ChildrenCounter     = 1
  ContextName         = Aggregator_Example
  CorrelationId       = AGV3FWueFLNHeSRXPDjGBOBM2Jhx
  IntermediateError   = false
  Node                = 0
  ReceivedSequenceNumbers= [1,2]

Message Processing Log:
  StartTime           = Mon Dec 11 13:58:03.783 UTC 2023
  StopTime            = Mon Dec 11 13:58:03.783 UTC 2023
  OverallStatus       = PROCESSING
  MessageGuid         = AGV3FWsbOn8_1aIiQU2qJz3pfEOD
  LogLevel            = INFO
  LogLevelExternal    = INFO
  AggregateCorrelationId= AA2345
  ArchivingLogAttachments= false
  ArchivingPersistedMessages= false
  ArchivingReceiverChannelMessages= false
  ArchivingSenderChannelMessages= false
  ChildCount          = 0
  ChildrenCounter     = 1
  ContextName         = Aggregator_Example
  CorrelationId       = AGV3FWueFLNHeSRXPDjGBOBM2Jhx
  IntermediateError   = false
  Node                = 0
  ReceivedSequenceNumbers= [1]
```

Figure 5.17 Message Processing Log Attachment

Note

Using the **Aggregator** step in combination with a Secure Shell (SSH) File Transfer Protocol (SFTP) sender adapter can generate high message volumes and consume a lot of resources. Use this step cautiously.

Now that you've learned how to use the **Aggregator** step, let's explore how you can handle use cases with lists in Cloud Integration.

5.2 Working with Lists

So far, you've learned quite a bit about Cloud Integration's functionality; the basic concepts behind it; and the various modeling techniques for solving typical integration problems, such as message enrichment, message mapping, and message routing. However, in our examples, we've focused on handling messages containing just one item, such as a single order. In this section, we'll dive more deeply into handling messages comprising a list of entries, for example, orders with multiple line items. In this section, we'll answer the following questions:

- How do I split up a message into individual pieces?
- How do I iterate over each list item?
- How do I handle the resulting single messages in the Cloud Integration message processing chain?
- How do I combine the results of each message handling sequence back into one response message?

5.2.1 The Scenario

In real-life scenarios, integrators are quite frequently confronted with input messages consisting of several items of the same message structure, grouped in a list (e.g., order line items). The integrator wants to iterate over the list: individual list items must be separated and individually managed by the iFlow. Finally, the result of each individual message handling procedure must be consolidated into one response message, which will be sent to either the sender of the message (in the case of a synchronous scenario) or to the final recipient (in the case of an asynchronous scenario). To illustrate this functionality using Cloud Integration, we'll use the input message shown in Figure 5.18 throughout this section.

Figure 5.18 is based on a Web Services Description Language (WSDL) file, which was created using the Enterprise Services Builder in SAP Process Integration. You can, of course, use any XML tool supporting the WSDL standard. We've included our WSDL file *SendOrderList_Async.wsdl* with the book's downloads at *www.sap-press.com/5760*. The message contains a list of order numbers; the other fields aren't yet relevant.

Our goal is to split the message into individual order messages, enrich each order with order details (e.g., shipping date, shipping city, shipping address, etc.), and send back the enriched message as a reply to the sender in a synchronous scenario. We'll solve this problem in two steps. The first step is to split one input message into several individual messages (splitter pattern), and then we'll join the pieces back together into one large message (gather/merge pattern). In the second step, we'll enrich the individual messages with order details (enricher pattern) and then collect those results into one large message. You can see in this example how using several smaller patterns can help you build more complex integration solutions. We encourage you to recognize and implement solutions based on common enterprise integration patterns. After you understand the basic principle, you can apply this knowledge to even more complex scenarios.

```
<soapenv:Envelope xmlns:soapenv="http://schemas.xml
   <soapenv:Header/>
   <soapenv:Body>
      <demo:OrderList_MT>
         <!--Zero or more repetitions:-->
         <orders>
            <orderNumber>10248</orderNumber>
            <customerName>?</customerName>
            <orderAmount>?</orderAmount>
            <currency>?</currency>
            <taxAmount>?</taxAmount>
         </orders>
         <orders>
            <orderNumber>10249</orderNumber>
            <customerName>?</customerName>
            <orderAmount>?</orderAmount>
            <currency>?</currency>
            <taxAmount>?</taxAmount>
         </orders>
         <orders>
            <orderNumber>10250</orderNumber>
            <customerName>?</customerName>
            <orderAmount>?</orderAmount>
            <currency>?</currency>
            <taxAmount>?</taxAmount>
         </orders>
      </demo:OrderList_MT>
   </soapenv:Body>
</soapenv:Envelope>
```

Figure 5.18 Example Message Comprising a List of Order Numbers

The key to splitting large messages into individual pieces, iterating over them, and joining them back again into one large message is the use of two new steps available in Cloud Integration's web-based graphical modeler: the **Splitter** step and the **Gather** steps. We'll show you how to position these new steps correctly in your message processing chain (i.e., route). The **Splitter** and **Gather** steps are used in the integration process model shown in Figure 5.19. In this iFlow, the steps between the **Splitter** and **Gather** steps ❶ will be repeated for every list item. This message processing chain will become the first step of the two-step implementation plan we outlined previously.

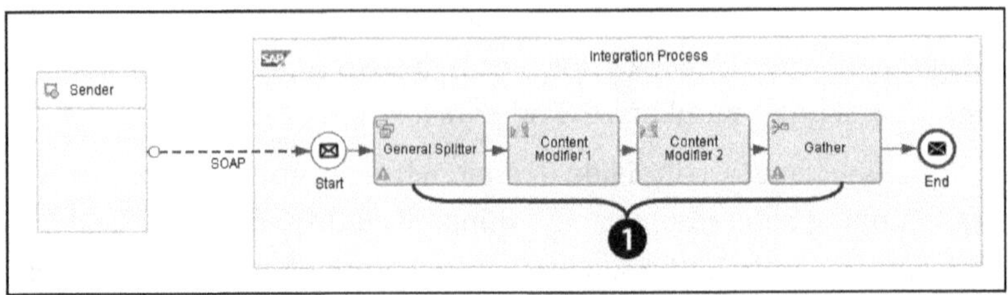

Figure 5.19 Splitting a Large Message into Individual Pieces and Collecting Them Back Using Gather

You can find the **Splitter** step at the beginning and the **Gather** step at the end of the processing chain. For your overall understanding of the entire splitter-gather construct, keep in mind the following considerations:

- The steps between the **Splitter** step and the **Gather** step (the two **Content Modifier** steps, in our case) are executed as many times as the **Splitter** creates individual messages.
- Each step within a **Splitter/Gather** pair will receive the separated individual messages that the **Splitter** has created as input messages, one after another.
- You can model a splitter scenario without a **Gather** step. In that case, however, all steps after the **Splitter** step will be executed repeatedly until an **End** event is reached. Thus, the repeated execution of steps is dependent on the **Splitter** step, not on the **Gather** step.

5.2.2 Configuring the Integration Flow

Let's look at the configuration for our scenario. As a reminder, we'll repeat the settings for the **Sender** pool and the message flow from the **Sender** pool to the **Start** message event.

When drawing the line for the message flow between the **Sender** pool and the **Start** message event, you'll select **SOAP** as the **Adapter Type** and **SOAP 1.x** as the **Message Protocol**. Figure 5.20 shows the **General** tab of the SOAP adapter's channel configuration, which opens in the **Properties** section after the creation of the message flow.

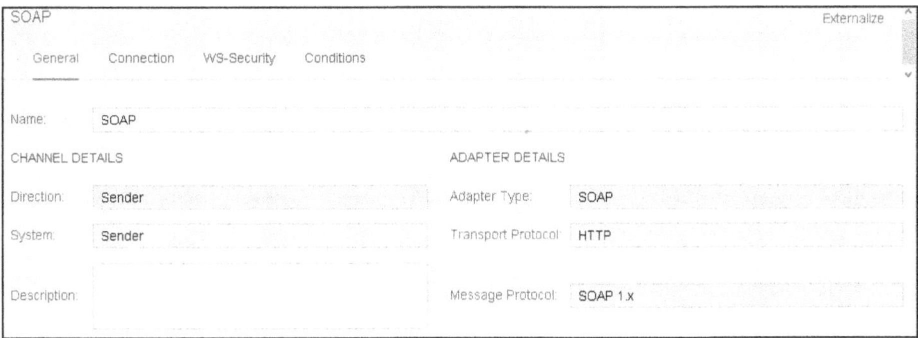

Figure 5.20 SOAP Channel: General Configuration

You can now configure the connection details in the **SOAP** adapter configuration screen, under the **Connection** tab, as shown in Figure 5.21. The **Address** field is important to note because the address entered will later be part of the URL used to call the flow.

Because we want to get a response to our SOAP requests, we'll keep the **Service Definition** dropdown list as **Manual** but select **Request-Reply** from the **Message Exchange Pattern** dropdown list. In Section 5.3.1, we'll go into more detail about message exchange patterns (MEPs), including trying out different configuration options and seeing the resulting behaviors.

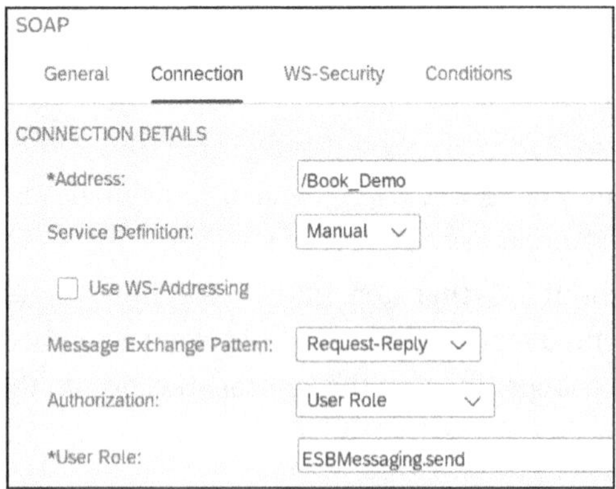

Figure 5.21 SOAP Channel: Connection Configuration

We won't select the **Use WS-Addressing** checkbox for our scenario because we don't want to use Web Services Addressing (WS-Addressing). This setting is required if you want to exchange messages following the WS-Addressing specification. In this case, the sender of a message is expected to specify additional addressing information in the SOAP header, for example, <wsa:Address> or <wsa:ReplyTo>.

Next, select **User Role** from the **Authorization** dropdown list to allow the sender to call the iFlow with user name and password credentials while invoking the iFlow. In the **User Role** field, keep the default value **ESBMessaging.send**. (The different authorization options and available user roles were described earlier in Chapter 2.)

Let's continue with the iFlow itself. The first step in the flow, after the flow is instantiated, is the **Splitter** activity. Because this step is new, we'll explain this step in more detail. During development, you can find the activity in the palette on the left of the modeling environment by following the path **Message Routing** ◇ • **Splitter** (Figure 5.22) • **General Splitter** (Figure 5.23).

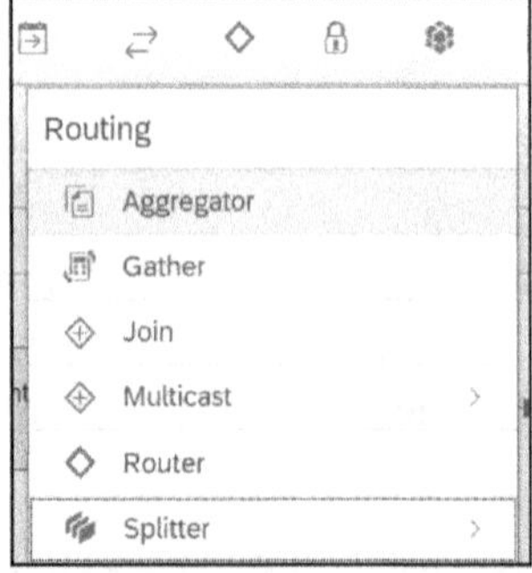

Figure 5.22 Opening the Splitter Submenu from the Palette

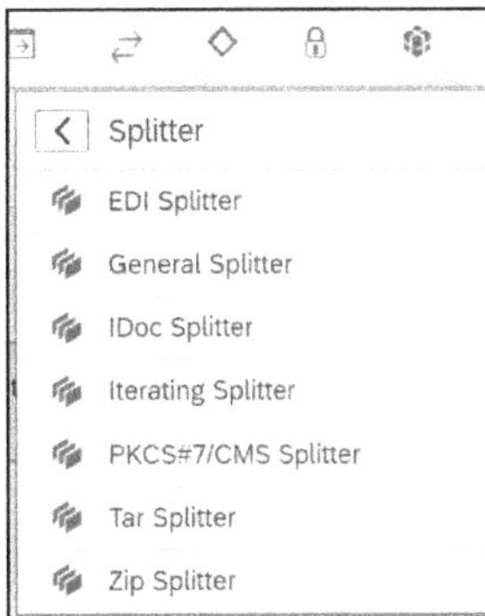

Figure 5.23 Selecting the General Splitter from the Splitter Submenu

Cloud Integration supports several different splitter types; however, in this section, we'll focus solely on the **General Splitter**.

Other Splitter Implementations in Cloud Integration

Cloud Integration provides several splitter implementations (as shown in Figure 5.23). The **General Splitter** will be described in more detail throughout this chapter, but the following splitters are also available:

- **EDI Splitter**
  You can split composite electronic data interchange (EDI) messages with this splitter, and you can configure how inbound EDI messages are validated and acknowledged. The **EDI Splitter** is generally used in business-to-business (B2B) scenarios.
- **IDoc Splitter**
  This dedicated splitter takes care of composite IDoc messages by splitting a composite IDoc into a series of individual IDoc messages, including its enveloping elements. No special configuration settings are required to use this splitter.
- **Iterating Splitter**
  This splitter behaves like the **General Splitter** in that it also splits up a composite message into a series of individual messages; however, this splitter doesn't copy the enveloping parts of a message into the individually split messages. But what are enveloping elements, exactly? These parts of the original incoming message exist above the nodes that are used for splitting. Figure 5.24 shows a visual depiction of the differences between the **General Splitter** and the **Iterating Splitter**.

  The **Iterating Splitter** simply copies the parts beginning with the splitting tag ❸ and the related subnodes, whereas the **General Splitter** also copies the nodes above the splitting tag ❶, ❷. This distinction is especially important if you want to navigate to elements in the tree structure using absolute XPath expressions.

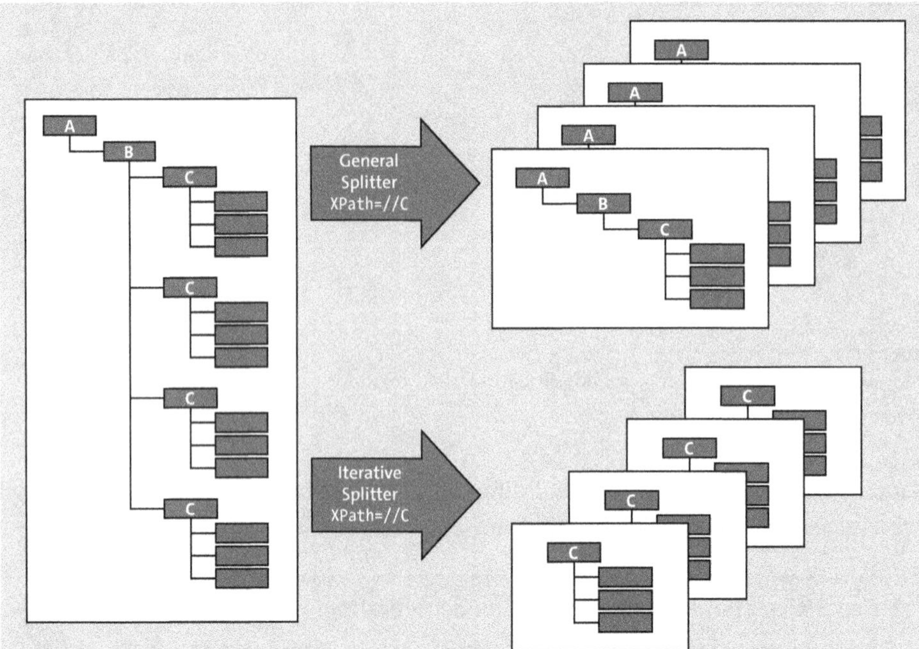

Figure 5.24 Differences between General Splitter and Iterating Splitter

- **PKCS#7/CMS Splitter**
  You can use the Public-Key Cryptography Standard (PKCS) to sign and encrypt messages. This splitter is useful if a client sends you a PKCS#7-signed message that contains both a signature and content. This splitter type breaks down the signature and the content into separate files. During configuration, you can provide the names of the files that should contain either the payload or the signature after the splitting step. You can also specify which file should be handled first after splitting (the signature or the content file), and you can decide whether the payload/signature should be Base64 encoded after splitting.
- **Tar Splitter**
  Tar Splitter is used to split and process individual files that are a part of a .tar archive.
- **Zip Splitter**
  Zip Splitter is used if you want to process individual files of a .zip archive.

After positioning the **General Splitter** shape in the main pool (**Integration Process**, shown earlier in Figure 5.19), you can set the splitter's properties according to the parameters shown in Figure 5.25.

Figure 5.25 Configuration of the Splitter Step

Let's walk through the parameters one by one:

- **Expression Type**
  In the **Expression Type** dropdown list, you'll specify how the split points should be identified in the inbound message—either via an **XPath** expression or a **Line Break**. As our inbound message is an XML message, we can easily define the split points via XPath expression. The **Line Break** option is useful for non-XML messages that have multiple lines and need to be split into smaller messages. If your inbound message is, for example, a *.csv* file containing several lines, you can use the **Line Break** option to split the message into smaller messages containing a defined number of lines or into messages containing only one line. Note that empty lines in the inbound message will be ignored; no empty messages will be created.

- **XPath Expression**
  This field directs the integration engine during runtime to search for the given tag in the input message and to use this tag as the split argument. In our example, we used the relative path **//orders**. Relative paths are indicated by the double-slash at the beginning and are quite convenient for allowing the engine to search for the tag's occurrence in your input message. The alternative would have been to use absolute paths starting with a single forward slash. With absolute paths, therefore, you must know the exact path from the root to the tag that should be used for splitting. If you wanted to extend the message later, for example, by adding tags between the root tag and the splitting tag, the absolute path would no longer be valid because the new tag would not be considered on the way from the root to the splitting tag. To summarize, absolute paths are static and quite error-prone when it comes to changes in a message's structure—errors that could be avoided by using relative paths.

  Let's see how the definition of the XPath expression influences execution during runtime. Look at our example input message shown earlier in Figure 5.18. Notice the three `<orders>` tags in our message. The splitter should generate three individual messages. An example individual message forwarded to the two **Content Modifier** steps following the **Splitter** is shown in Listing 5.1 (with different order number values).

```
<orders>
    <orderNumber>10248</orderNumber>
    <customerName>?</customerName>
    <orderAmount>?</orderAmount>
    <currency>?</currency>
    <taxAmount>?</taxAmount>
</orders>
```

Listing 5.1 Individual Message Containing Exactly One Order

Notice that the single messages will also contain the <orders> tags. Consider this while processing each of the individual messages. If you want to understand what the message produced by the splitter looks like in greater detail, read on to Section 5.2.3.

- **Grouping**
  With the **Grouping** field, you can define the number of items that should be grouped into one message for individual processing. We chose the value **1**, which means that *every* occurrence of <orders> should result in a dedicated individual message for further processing. If we had selected **2** as our value, the splitter would group the first 2 items as a single message, the next 2 items in the second message, and so on. So, if we set the **Grouping** parameter to **2**, assuming our input message contains 10 items in total, the splitter would generate five messages, each containing 2 items.
- **Streaming**
  The **Streaming** checkbox is important with regard to memory consumption. Normally, the splitter works on messages by loading them completely into the main memory. However, messages can get quite large. Think about payments sent to a bank once a day. Individual payment transactions are collected throughout the day and forwarded at night. These collected messages can become huge, so loading them entirely into the main memory before processing them doesn't make sense (and is sometimes impossible). Therefore, letting the **Splitter** start working on incoming streamed data, even though not entirely loaded, can be a useful approach. This approach is called *streaming* because you can read a chunk of data, work on it, read another chunk, and so forth until the entire message is processed.
- **Parallel Processing**
  As the name indicates, this checkbox allows you to run individual message-processing tasks in parallel by leveraging Java's concurrency features using thread pools. By parallelizing tasks, you can get more work done in less time. However, the execution sequence can't be guaranteed, as the threads run independently of each other. Once the **Parallel Processing** checkbox is selected, two additional configuration fields will be available, as shown in Figure 5.26:

- **Number of Concurrent Processes:** In this field, you can define how many split messages are processed in parallel. Although you can further influence the overall processing time of the incoming message, be careful with this parameter because setting its value too high may cause out-of-memory errors due to the high memory consumption involved in processing split messages in parallel. If the split messages are sent to a receiver system, you'll need to confirm that this system can handle so many parallel calls.
- **Timeout(in s):** In this field, you define the time after which parallel processing should be aborted and the next processing step in the processing chain, for example, the **Gather** step, is executed. In other words, if split messages are still running when the timeout interval expires, the processing of those messages will never reach the **Gather** step. Thus, you must define a timeout value higher than the expected overall processing time for the message.

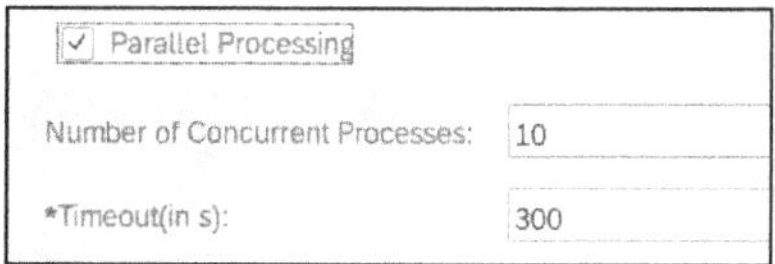

Figure 5.26 Configuration of Parallel Processing in the Splitter Step

- **Stop on Exception**
  If you select this checkbox, the route's processing will immediately stop if an error arises, and that error will be propagated back instantly. Otherwise, the splitter continues working on the individual messages and reports the error back at the end, after handling the complete input message.

Now that you understand how a splitter handles the incoming message, let's continue with our first **Content Modifier**. Although we've described its behavior several times already, let's quickly review its configuration, shown in Figure 5.27.

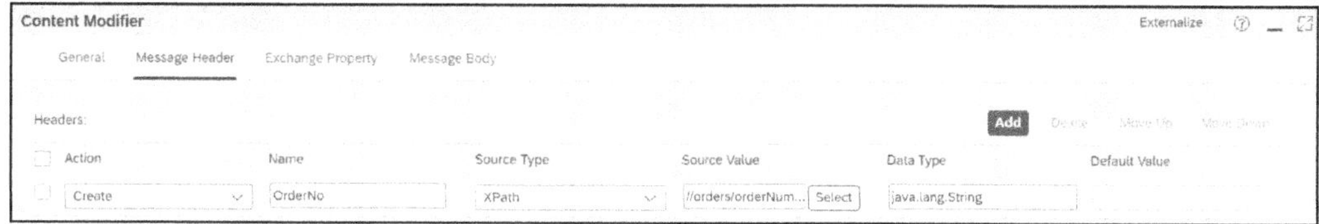

Figure 5.27 Configuration of the First Content Modifier in the Route

Note

Because this **Content Modifier** is placed after the **Splitter** step, the **Content Modifier** step is invoked for each message created by the **Splitter**, each representing one order out of the original message's order list. This distinction is crucial to understanding the entire route.

In our example, we'll set a variable named **OrderNo** in the message's header area and store the order number of the current item in that variable for later reference. We'll also enter "//orders/orderNumber" into the **Source Value** field as the path is relative and only one order number is expected in each message.

The recently stored header value will be retrieved by the second **Content Modifier** step and copied into the result message according to the configuration shown in Figure 5.28. Note that, this time, we've selected **Expression** from the **Type** dropdown menu. This selection is required because our **Body** part contains, not just text but also an Apache Camel expression. If you select **Constant** instead of **Expression**, the expression `${header.OrderNo}` would be interpreted as simple plain text during runtime, and the generated message body would not contain the order number defined in the header.

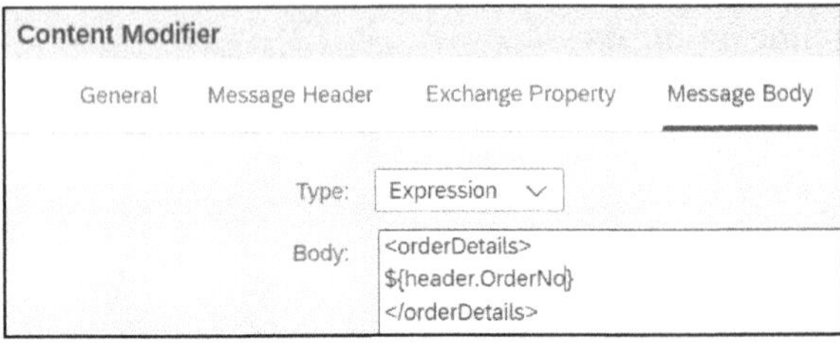

Figure 5.28 Configuration of the Second Content Modifier in the Route

Again, the second **Content Modifier** step will also be invoked for each message. The **Gather** step is the step that finally collects all the individual single messages, created for each invocation of the **Splitter**, into a single bulk message. Figure 5.29 shows the **Gather** step's configuration.

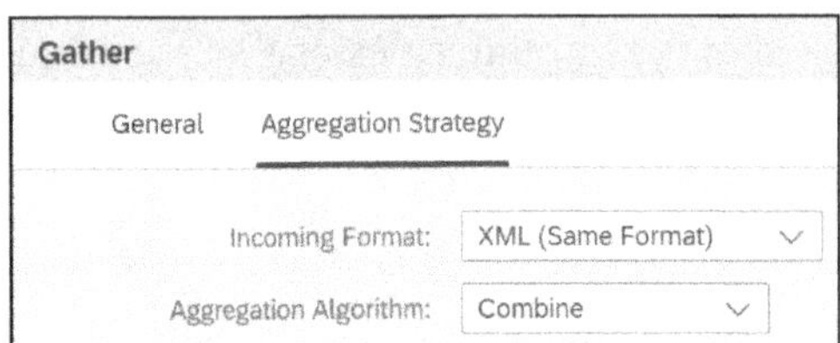

Figure 5.29 Configuration of the Gather Step

All the resulting single messages are of the same format; therefore, we'll set the **Incoming Format** dropdown menu to **XML (Same Format)**. The **Gather** step should simply put each of the individual pieces together into one result message. Consequently, we'll select **Combine** from the **Aggregation Algorithm** dropdown list.

The other configuration options provided by the **Gather** step depend on the selection made in the **Incoming Format** dropdown list, which provides the following three options:

- **Plain Text**
  For this **Aggregation Algorithm** option, only **Concatenate** is allowed. All plain text messages generated by the single messages will simply be concatenated to one large string, one after another. This result will then be returned to the caller.
- **XML (Different Format)**
  For this **Aggregation Algorithm** option, only **Combine** is allowed, which is similar to the behavior of the **Concatenate** option in the previous case. The individual XML fragments from the individual messages are brought together in one response message using a multimapping.
- **XML (Same Format)**
  If you choose this option, you can influence the construction of the response message in two ways:
  - First, you can also apply the **Combine** option: This behavior is identical to the **XML (Different Format)** option we just described.
  - Second, another option allows you to copy parts from the source message into a user-defined envelope consisting of XML tags. The XML node from which parts of the source message should be copied is formulated using an XPath expression. The XML envelope is defined using an absolute path definition, such as `/root` or `/level_1/level_2`. The associated configuration screen is shown in Figure 5.30. The behavior is pretty simple: The XPath expression of the **Combine from source (XPath)** field takes the source message (the single message created by the **Splitter**), navigates within that message to the node specified by the XPath expression, and copies the node, including all nested XML subnodes. Then, the copied XML-subtree snippet is pasted after the tags that the user has defined as the envelope. The idea behind the envelope is that every valid XML document requires one root element, which is exactly what you can define in the **Combine at target (XPath)** field: the root element (e.g., `/root`) or, if necessary, an absolute root path (e.g., `/level_1/level_2`). During runtime, the copied XML subtree will be pasted after the node(s) specified in the **Combine at target (XPath)** field. In other words, the node in the **Combine at target (XPath)** field is the parent of the snippet to be inserted. The corresponding closing tag(s) of the envelope will automatically be added after the gathering has completed (e.g., `</root>` or `</level_2></level_1>`).

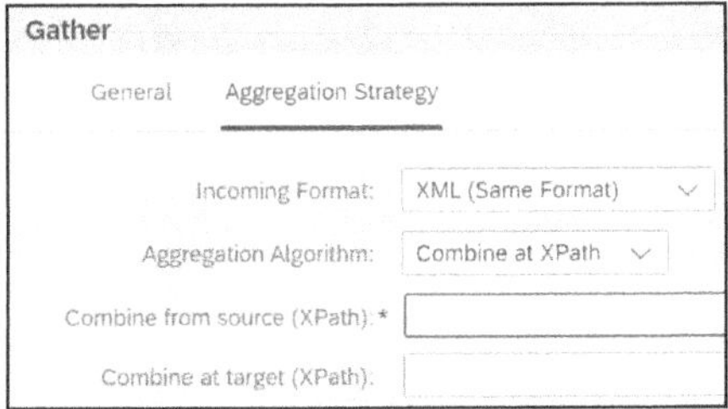

Figure 5.30 Configuration of the Gather Step to Combine Individual Messages Using XPath Expressions

Let's look at a concrete example. We'll assume the **Splitter** generates two messages, as shown in Listing 5.2 and Listing 5.3. These messages will later be the source messages in the **Gather** step's configuration.

```
<payload>
    <route>
        <multicast>Parallel</multicast>
        <branch>A</branch>
    </route>
</payload>
```

Listing 5.2 First Generated Splitter Message

```
<payload>
    <route>
        <multicast>Parallel</multicast>
        <branch>B</branch>
    </route>
</payload>
```

Listing 5.3 Second Generated Splitter Message

Next, assume the following settings for the configuration of the **Gather** step:

- **Combine from source (XPath)**: **/payload/route** (only absolute XPath expressions allowed for this field)
- **Combine at target (XPath)**: **/xyz/abc**

An example of the final resulting message is shown in Listing 5.4.

```
<xyz>
    <abc>
        <route>
            <multicast>Parallel</multicast>
            <branch>A</branch>
        </route>
        <route>
            <multicast>Parallel</multicast>
            <branch>B</branch>
        </route>
    </abc>
</xyz>
```

Listing 5.4 Combined Message Generated by the Gather Step

You can now easily understand how this result message was created: the engine copied the parts from the source messages starting at the /payload/route node, including the <route> tag and all nested nodes, and pasted this text into the target message, which starts with the <xyz><abc> nodes representing the opening part of the envelope. Remember, the same pasting process will be done for all messages resulting from the splitter. Thus, we have two <route> tags in between the envelope. Finally, we'll add the closing tags of the envelope, which can be derived from the definition of the **Combine at target (XPath)** field. Because we defined that field with the value /xyz/abc, the closing tags must be in opposite sequence, resulting in </abc></xyz>.

Note

Providing an entry for the **Combine at target (XPath)** field isn't mandatory. If you leave the field empty, the resulting message will have the same tags that are specified in the **Combine from source (XPath)** field. Referring to the preceding example, the resulting message would start with <payload><route>.

5.2.3 Running the Integration Flow

Now that we've configured the scenario completely, we can finally run it. Save your changes and deploy your iFlow. Don't forget to retrieve the URL for invoking the integration scenario from Cloud Integration's **Monitor** (refer to Chapter 2, Section 2.3.4, for instructions on how to retrieve the URL). Provide the URL in the SOAP tool of your choice (e.g., SoapUI), and invoke the iFlow. The result should look like the screen shown in Figure 5.31.

Our iFlow has successfully retrieved the order numbers from the incoming message containing the order list and has also created an appropriate response message, which is the exact result we hoped to achieve.

```
<soap:Envelope xmlns:soap="http://schemas.xmlsoap.org/soap/envelope/">
   <soap:Body>
      <multimap:Messages xmlns:multimap="http://sap.com/xi/XI/SplitAndMerge">
         <multimap:Message1>
            <orderDetails>10248</orderDetails>
            <orderDetails>10249</orderDetails>
            <orderDetails>10250</orderDetails>
         </multimap:Message1>
      </multimap:Messages>
   </soap:Body>
</soap:Envelope>
```

Figure 5.31 Final Response Message after Invoking the iFlow with a List of Order Numbers

What Is the Splitter Delivering to the Processing Chain?

In some situations, you might need to see what the individual messages produced by the **Splitter** actually look like and perhaps determine which individual messages reach the next step of the iFlow. Maybe you want to pick a concrete field by an absolute XPath expression instead of using a relative XPath due to a potential name conflict. In this case, you'll need to know exactly what the single message looks like; otherwise, your absolute path won't work. We'll take the process model shown earlier in Figure 5.19 as the basis for this task, but now, we'll configure the first **Content Modifier** with the information shown in Figure 5.32.

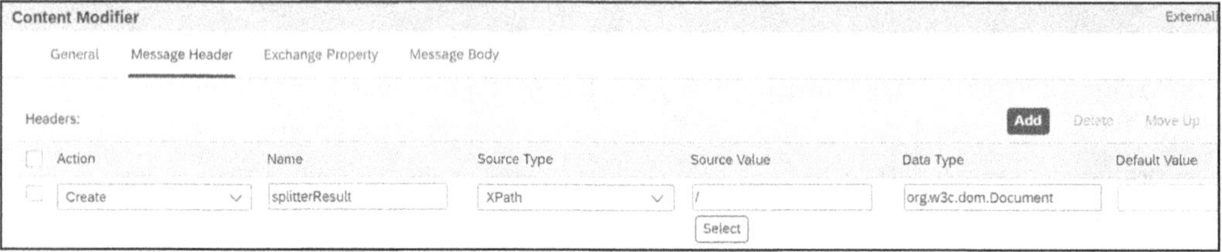

Figure 5.32 Adding the Complete Single Message into the Header Area

Now, we're using an absolute XPath expression to point to the root of the received single message. Thus, we're really putting the complete message into the header variable called **splitterResult**. For this variable, we'll enter "org.w3c.dom.Document" to represent the whole XML document in the **Data Type** field. In the second **Content Modifier** step, we'll now pick the variable's content and place this content into the body. The result of the second **Content Modifier**'s configuration is shown in Figure 5.33.

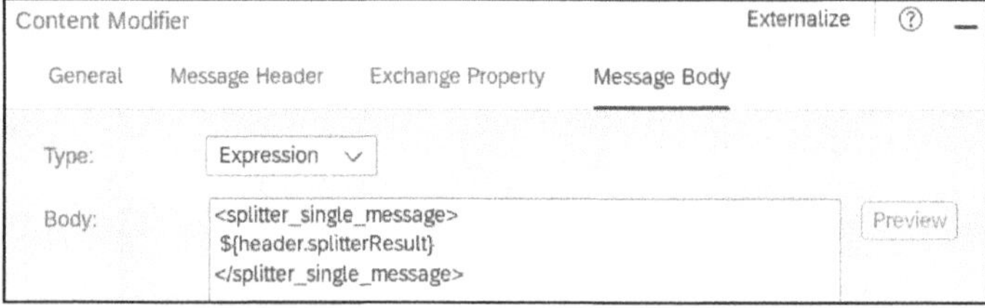

Figure 5.33 Copying the Splitter's Message into the Body

Running the scenario results in the output shown in Figure 5.34.

In between the <splitter_single_message> tags, you can now easily identify the fragment that was produced by the splitter. With this knowledge, you can formulate the absolute path within that single message to the orderNumber field: /demo:OrderList_MT/orders/orderNumber. Let's quickly verify the accuracy of this field by adjusting the two **Content Modifier** configurations. The updated properties are shown in Figure 5.35 and Figure 5.36.

```
<soap:Envelope xmlns:soap="http://schemas.xmlsoap.org/soap/envelope/">
   <soap:Header/>
   <soap:Body>
      <multimap:Messages xmlns:multimap="http://sap.com/xi/XI/SplitAndMerge">
         <multimap:Message1>
            <splitter_single_message>
               <demo:OrderList_MT xmlns:demo="http://cpi.sap.com/demo">
                  <orders>
                     <orderNumber>10248</orderNumber>
                     <customerName>?</customerName>
                     <orderAmount>?</orderAmount>
                     <currency>?</currency>
                     <taxAmount>?</taxAmount>
                  </orders>
               </demo:OrderList_MT>
            </splitter_single_message>
            <splitter_single_message>
               <demo:OrderList_MT xmlns:demo="http://cpi.sap.com/demo">
                  <orders>
                     <orderNumber>10249</orderNumber>
                     <customerName>?</customerName>
                     <orderAmount>?</orderAmount>
                     <currency>?</currency>
                     <taxAmount>?</taxAmount>
                  </orders>
               </demo:OrderList_MT>
            </splitter_single_message>
            <splitter_single_message>
               <demo:OrderList_MT xmlns:demo="http://cpi.sap.com/demo">
                  <orders>
                     <orderNumber>10250</orderNumber>
                     <customerName>?</customerName>
                     <orderAmount>?</orderAmount>
                     <currency>?</currency>
                     <taxAmount>?</taxAmount>
                  </orders>
               </demo:OrderList_MT>
            </splitter_single_message>
         </multimap:Message1>
      </multimap:Messages>
   </soap:Body>
</soap:Envelope>
```

Figure 5.34 Result Message after Invoking the iFlow

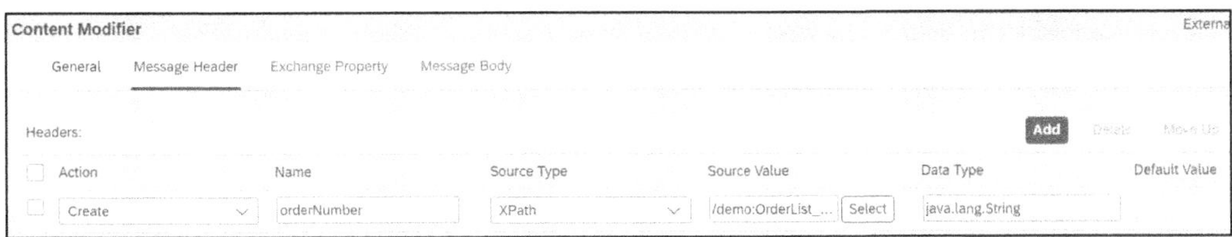

Figure 5.35 Accessing the orderNumber Field via an Absolute XPath Expression in the First Content Modifier

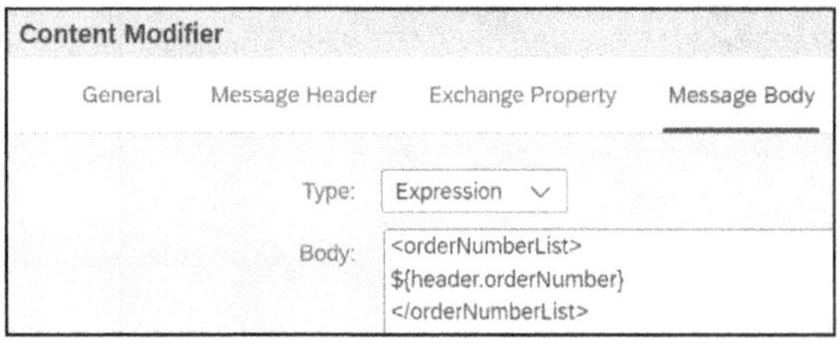

Content Modifier

General | Message Header | Exchange Property | Message Body

Type: Expression

Body:
```
<orderNumberList>
${header.orderNumber}
</orderNumberList>
```

Figure 5.36 Pasting the Copied Order Numbers into the Result Message's Body in the Second Content Modifier

We can't run this scenario quite yet because we still must consider one small, but important, detail. Look at the **Value** column shown in Figure 5.35. The XPath expression begins with **/demo:OrderList_MT**, right? The important detail is the namespace **demo**. The message handling route isn't aware of this namespace or what it means. Thus, you must explicitly declare the namespace in the route's configuration. You can define some global settings for an iFlow by clicking somewhere outside of the pools to access the route's properties beneath the process model. Reviewing the properties of the iFlow, select the **Runtime Configuration** tab, as shown in Figure 5.37.

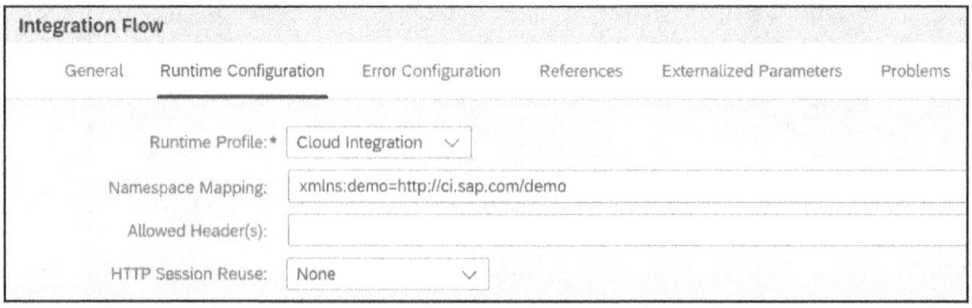

Integration Flow

General | Runtime Configuration | Error Configuration | References | Externalized Parameters | Problems

Runtime Profile:* Cloud Integration

Namespace Mapping: xmlns:demo=http://ci.sap.com/demo

Allowed Header(s):

HTTP Session Reuse: None

Figure 5.37 Global Configuration Options for an iFlow

The **Runtime Configuration** tab allows you to define the namespace mappings in a dedicated field. For our example, we'll simply copy the namespace definition shown earlier in Figure 5.34. Remember to remove the quotation marks when pasting the string into the **Namespace Mapping** field. Now, the route is aware of the namespace and can handle the XML fragment accordingly. Let's try out our modified iFlow. The result should look like the screen shown in Figure 5.38.

```
<soap:Envelope xmlns:soap="http://schemas.xmlsoap.org/soap/envelope/">
  <soap:Body>
    <multimap:Messages xmlns:multimap="http://sap.com/xi/XI/SplitAndMerge">
      <multimap:Message1>
        <orderNumberList>10248</orderNumberList>
        <orderNumberList>10249</orderNumberList>
        <orderNumberList>10250</orderNumberList>
      </multimap:Message1>
    </multimap:Messages>
  </soap:Body>
</soap:Envelope>
```

Figure 5.38 Result Message after Picking the Order Number via Absolute XPath Expression

5.2.4 Enriching Individual Messages with Additional Data

In this section, we began with a relatively simple example to concentrate on the behavior of **Splitter** and **Gather**. However, we can now extend this example to something more useful by invoking an external OData data source and enriching our result message. This example reflects a typical scenario where some basic data must be enriched by data from external sources. In our case, we want to retrieve order details for each order number extracted. In Chapter 4, Section 4.3.3, we configured an OData connection to retrieve detailed data for order numbers, which is exactly what we'll do next: replace the second **Content Modifier** (which just sets the body of the single message artificially with the extracted order number) with a **Request Reply** step invoking the OData service and providing useful data as the response for each message created by the **Splitter**. After adding the **Request Reply** step into the iFlow, finally, our final scenario should resemble the iFlow shown in Figure 5.39.

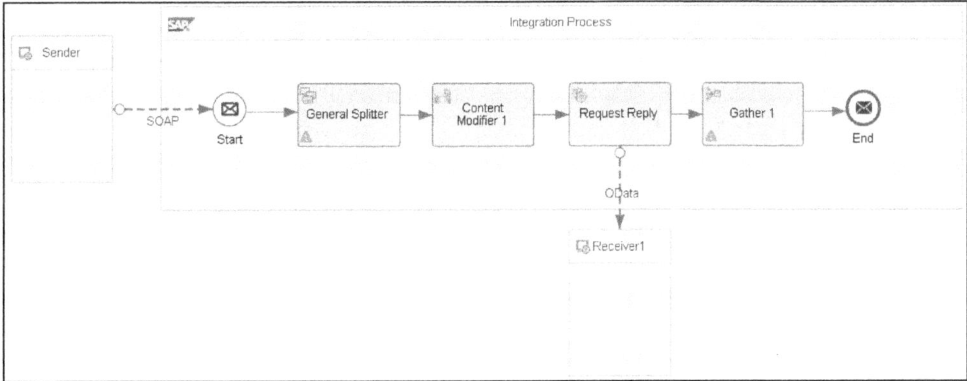

Figure 5.39 iFlow with Splitter, Gather, and the Invocation of an External OData Source

The steps for configuring the **Request Reply** step are identical to the steps described in Chapter 4, Section 4.3. For your reference, the configuration of the OData channel is shown in Figure 5.40 and Figure 5.41.

OData

General | Connection | Processing

CONNECTION DETAILS

Address:* http://services.odata.org/Northwind/Northwind.svc

Proxy Type:* Internet

Authentication:* None

CSRF Protected:

Figure 5.40 Configuration of Connection Settings in OData Adapter

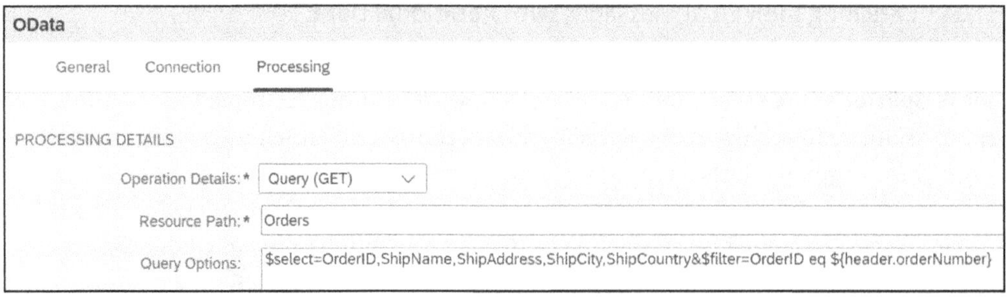

OData

General Connection Processing

PROCESSING DETAILS

Operation Details: * Query (GET)

Resource Path: * Orders

Query Options: $select=OrderID,ShipName,ShipAddress,ShipCity,ShipCountry&$filter=OrderID eq ${header.orderNumber}

Figure 5.41 Configuration of Processing Settings in OData Adapter

Note

The call of the **Request Reply** step is executed for every order number of the original incoming message. We can't stress enough the importance of this specific behavior of an iFlow making use of the **Splitter** step. All activities following the **Splitter** are invoked for each message generated by the **Splitter** until either the end of the flow or the **Gather** step is reached! The invocation of the iFlow finally results in the response message shown in Figure 5.42.


```xml
<soap:Envelope xmlns:soap="http://schemas.xmlsoap.org/soap/envelope/">
   <soap:Body>
      <multimap:Messages xmlns:multimap="http://sap.com/xi/XI/SplitAndMerge">
         <multimap:Message1>
            <Orders>
               <Order>
                  <ShipPostalCode>51100</ShipPostalCode>
                  <ShippedDate>1996-07-16T00:00:00.000</ShippedDate>
                  <OrderID>10248</OrderID>
                  <ShipCity>Reims</ShipCity>
                  <ShipAddress>59 rue de l'Abbaye</ShipAddress>
                  <ShipCountry>France</ShipCountry>
                  <ShipName>Vins et alcools Chevalier</ShipName>
               </Order>
            </Orders>
            <Orders>
               <Order>
                  <ShipPostalCode>44087</ShipPostalCode>
                  <ShippedDate>1996-07-10T00:00:00.000</ShippedDate>
                  <OrderID>10249</OrderID>
                  <ShipCity>Münster</ShipCity>
                  <ShipAddress>Luisenstr. 48</ShipAddress>
                  <ShipCountry>Germany</ShipCountry>
                  <ShipName>Toms Spezialitäten</ShipName>
               </Order>
            </Orders>
            <Orders>
               <Order>
                  <ShipPostalCode>05454-876</ShipPostalCode>
                  <ShippedDate>1996-07-12T00:00:00.000</ShippedDate>
                  <OrderID>10250</OrderID>
                  <ShipCity>Rio de Janeiro</ShipCity>
                  <ShipAddress>Rua do Paço, 67</ShipAddress>
                  <ShipCountry>Brazil</ShipCountry>
                  <ShipName>Hanari Carnes</ShipName>
               </Order>
            </Orders>
         </multimap:Message1>
      </multimap:Messages>
   </soap:Body>
</soap:Envelope>
```


Figure 5.42 Result Message, Including Order Details Retrieved from the External OData Source

To summarize, frequently, Cloud Integration solutions deal with handling messages containing lists of items. In this section, we used the **Splitter** step to split a message containing several order numbers into individual messages, each containing a single order number. The individual messages can be treated separately by Cloud Integration, which can then combine the results of each message processing chain back into a single integrated response message using the **Gather** step. In this section, you learned how to configure both the **Splitter** and the **Gather** steps correctly to set up this message handling behavior. In the next section, we'll take a close look at asynchronous message handling.

5.3 Asynchronous Message Handling

The core task of an integration solution is the routing of messages across your company's distributed IT landscape, including connectivity to partners and suppliers. Such integration scenarios can be synchronous or asynchronous in nature. *Synchronous message handling* means, in this regard, the following procedure:

1. A sender opens a connection to Cloud Integration and sends a request message.
2. After sending the request message to Cloud Integration, the sender will keep the connection open because a reply is expected.
3. Cloud Integration finds the receiver for the respective request message (e.g., by inspecting the message's content), opens a connection to the receiver, and routes the message to the receiver.
4. After sending the message to the receiver, Cloud Integration will also keep its connection open.
5. The receiver acts on the request message by creating a response message and returns the response to Cloud Integration via the still-open connection.
6. After receiving the message, Cloud Integration will close its connection to the receiver and route the received message as a reply message to the original sender.
7. The sender can now close its connection to Cloud Integration after receiving the final reply message.

The connections from the sender to Cloud Integration, as well as the connection from Cloud Integration to the receiver, are kept open as long as message processing is ongoing. The communication involves a bidirectional message transfer in one session. This message handling procedure significantly differs from *asynchronous* message handling where the procedure looks like the following:

1. A sender opens a connection to Cloud Integration and sends a message.
2. After Cloud Integration receives the message correctly, it acknowledges its receipt of the message to the sender.

3. After receiving the acknowledgment from Cloud Integration, the sender closes the connection.
4. Cloud Integration opens a connection to the receiver of the message and forwards it accordingly.
5. After receiving the message completely, the receiver also acknowledges its receipt of the message to Cloud Integration.
6. After receiving the acknowledgment from the receiver, Cloud Integration closes the connection.

The connections are immediately closed as soon as the messages have been confirmed by the receiving parties. The overall communication only involves a message transfer in one direction. In brief, these are the main differences between synchronous and asynchronous communication. But how does this knowledge affect our discussion of Cloud Integration? First, Cloud Integration absolutely must support both communication styles as a general-purpose integration infrastructure prepared for all kinds of integration requirements. However, in previous sections of this chapter, all communications were synchronous. So far, this synchronicity has been useful in seeing the immediate results of our iFlow invocations in the SOAP clients that we've been using to call our message handling chains. Now, the time has come to turn to asynchronous message handling as well, including how to influence communication styles.

5.3.1 Synchronous versus Asynchronous Communication from the Cloud Integration Perspective

Let's repeat some main aspects regarding our synchronous versus asynchronous discussion from Chapter 4, Section 4.1.1. A key term used in Chapter 4 was the word *exchange*, as shown in Figure 5.43.

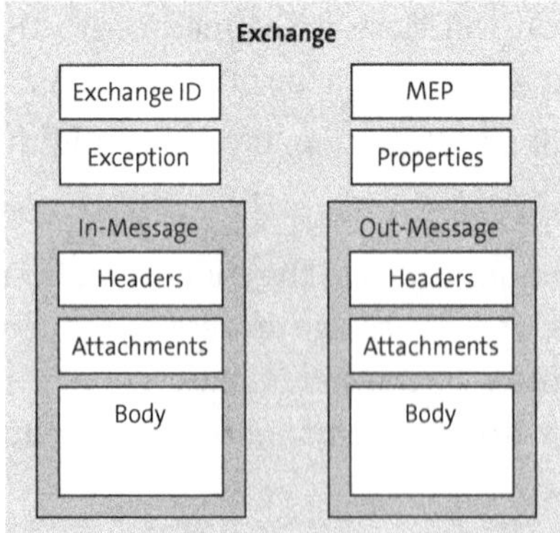

Figure 5.43 Structure of an Exchange

Exchange comes from Apache Camel terminology and represents a container for a message while the message is being processed inside the integration engine. We know so far that the exchange will be always filled with an `In` message, whereas the `Out` message in the exchange only plays a role in synchronous scenarios where the sender expects a response, as discussed in Chapter 4, Section 4.1.1. Additionally, the communication type (synchronous or asynchronous) is determined by the **Message Exchange Pattern** field (MEP) within the exchange, which can contain two potential values:

- **InOnly**
  Represents the asynchronous use case: the route handles a one-way message, and the sender doesn't expect a reply from the respective receiver. Therefore, the exchange carries an `In` message only.
- **InOut**
  Represents the synchronous communication style: the route handles a request-response message. The sender expects a reply from the route, which will be stored as an `Out` message in the exchange.

The component that determines whether a message should be handled synchronously or asynchronously is, in fact, the *channel*, which might surprise you. However, we'll show you how to influence synchronous and asynchronous message handling in Cloud Integration by using the SOAP adapter.

In our example, we'll reuse the scenario we built in Section 5.2.4. For your convenience, screenshots of the scenario are shown in Figure 5.44, and the associated input message is shown in Figure 5.45.

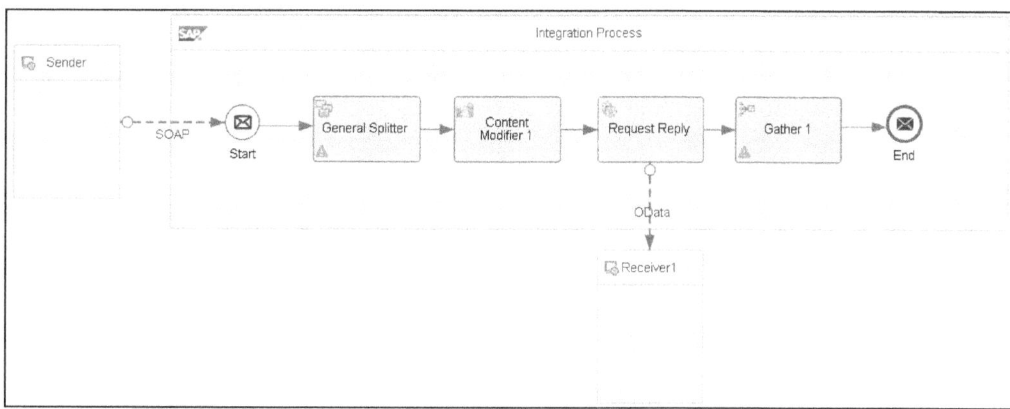

Figure 5.44 Demo Scenario for Splitting and Joining Messages

The iFlow, in essence, splits the incoming message into three individual messages. Each message contains exactly one order. The two **Content Modifier** steps are executed three times (for each of the single messages). The first **Content Modifier** extracts the order number from the original message and writes it into the message's header area, whereas the second **Content Modifier** retrieves the order number from the header area again and writes the number, embedded inside `orderDetails` tags, into the body area of the message. As this is done three times, the resulting message contains just the three order numbers, each one surrounded by `orderDetails` tags, as shown in Figure 5.46.

```
<soapenv:Envelope xmlns:soapenv="http://schemas
   <soapenv:Header/>
   <soapenv:Body>
      <demo:OrderList_MT>
         <!--Zero or more repetitions:-->
         <orders>
            <orderNumber>10248</orderNumber>
            <customerName>?</customerName>
            <orderAmount>?</orderAmount>
            <currency>?</currency>
            <taxAmount>?</taxAmount>
         </orders>
         <orders>
            <orderNumber>10249</orderNumber>
            <customerName>?</customerName>
            <orderAmount>?</orderAmount>
            <currency>?</currency>
            <taxAmount>?</taxAmount>
         </orders>
         <orders>
            <orderNumber>10250</orderNumber>
            <customerName>?</customerName>
            <orderAmount>?</orderAmount>
            <currency>?</currency>
            <taxAmount>?</taxAmount>
         </orders>
      </demo:OrderList_MT>
   </soapenv:Body>
</soapenv:Envelope>
```

Figure 5.45 Example Input Message for the Demo Scenario

```
<soap:Envelope xmlns:soap="http://schemas.xmlsoap.org/soap/envelope/">
   <soap:Body>
      <multimap:Messages xmlns:multimap="http://sap.com/xi/XI/SplitAndMerge">
         <multimap:Message1>
            <orderDetails>10248</orderDetails>
            <orderDetails>10249</orderDetails>
            <orderDetails>10250</orderDetails>
         </multimap:Message1>
      </multimap:Messages>
   </soap:Body>
</soap:Envelope>
```

Figure 5.46 Result Message after Invoking the iFlow

The screenshots for the input, as well as for the result message, are taken from a SoapUI test client. The scenario is currently synchronous; otherwise, we wouldn't have received a response. What is strange is that the incoming message was built using a WSDL file containing the description of an *asynchronous* interface. You can verify this fact by downloading the associated WSDL file, called *SendOrderList_Async.wsdl*, from *www.sap-press.com/5760*. The content of the file is shown in Figure 5.47.

```
<wsdl:portType name="SendOrderList_Async">
    <wsdl:documentation/>
    <wsdl:operation name="SendOrderList_Async">
        <wsdl:documentation/>
        <wsp:Policy>
            <wsp:PolicyReference URI="#OP_SendOrderList_Async"/>
        </wsp:Policy><wsdl:input message="p1:OrderList_MT"/>
    </wsdl:operation>
</wsdl:portType>
```

Figure 5.47 Definition of the Service's Operation

The operation consists of an input message, but no output message, which would be needed for a synchronous interface. But why, then, is Cloud Integration interpreting this message as a synchronous message exchange? Remember the setting for the **Message Exchange Pattern** we configured when creating the SOAP channel in Section 5.2.2? Let's take a closer look at the SOAP adapter's configuration, as shown in Figure 5.48.

The **Address** field is set with a string used to create the URL for invoking the iFlow. In addition, we've chosen the default configuration for the **Service Definition** and **Message Exchange Pattern** dropdown lists. These fields are where the Cloud Integration runtime finds information about synchronous or asynchronous message handling.

SOAP

General | Connection | WS-Security | Conditions

CONNECTION DETAILS

*Address:	/Book_Demo
Service Definition:	Manual
☐ Use WS-Addressing	
Message Exchange Pattern:	Request-Reply
Authorization:	User Role
*User Role:	ESBMessaging.send

Figure 5.48 Configuration of the SOAP Channel in the Demo Scenario

When the channel receives a message from a client, the channel knows nothing about the data that arrives at its address, how the data was constructed, or whether the data is based on a synchronous or asynchronous WSDL file. The channel only knows whether the received message should be treated synchronously or asynchronously because of the configured **Message Exchange Pattern** field.

Note

The WSDL file was just used in the SoapUI client to create a proper input message. However, the WSDL file was never used in any of the Cloud Integration configuration steps for that scenario. Thus, Cloud Integration knows nothing about the data it should process. This lack of knowledge is the payload-agnostic behavior of Apache Camel we've described in previous chapters. You can push anything to Cloud Integration, and processing should work as long as you don't have processing steps in your route that rely on a specific format.

We selected the **Request-Reply** option from the **Message Exchange Pattern** dropdown list; therefore, the SOAP channel set the **MEP** field in the exchange to **InOut**. This configuration explains the synchronous behavior of our scenario. So, the message walks through the steps of the iFlow, and a resulting message is created at the end of the chain at the **End** event (shown earlier in Figure 5.44). In this process, something magic happens: because no additional step exists for processing, the last status of the message's body will be copied automatically into the body of the exchange's `Out` message. Remember, synchronous messages in an exchange have both an `In` and an `Out` message, and the reply must be an `Out` message. The `Out` message (including its body, headers, and attachments) is finally returned to the caller.

The next issue is how to make the route behave asynchronously. You have two options for specifying asynchronous communication: selecting the **One-Way** option from the **Message Exchange Pattern** dropdown list or making the SOAP channel aware of the concrete messages it receives.

Let's try out both options, starting with the easier approach. Simply change the value for the **Message Exchange Pattern** dropdown list to **One-Way,** as shown in Figure 5.49.

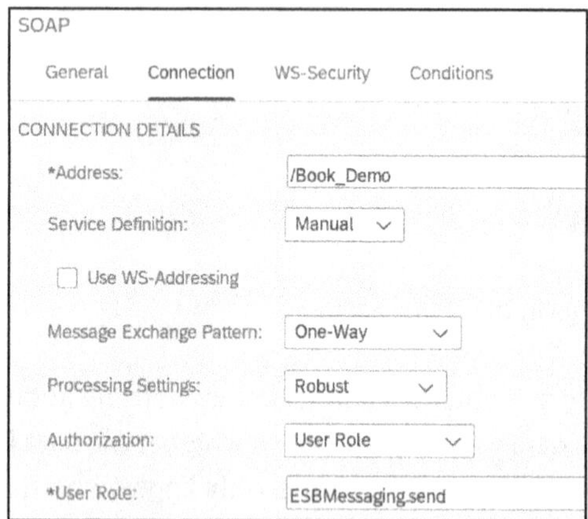

Figure 5.49 Configuration of the SOAP Channel after Changing the Message Exchange Pattern Field to One-Way

As soon as we change this setting, the **Processing Settings** dropdown will appear, where the following two configuration options are available:

- **WS Standard**
  In the Web Service Standard, one-way processing is also known as the *fire-and-forget method*. This method is useful if the sender of the message just wants to initiate a request but doesn't care if the request is processed successfully. In Cloud Integration, this behavior can be configured with the **WS Standard** option. SAP BTP will process the SOAP request received but won't report back any errors that may occur during the processing of the message.
- **Robust**
  This is the default option available in Cloud Integration and is also known as robust in-only or robust one-way. With this configuration, the SOAP adapter synchronously reports back error information to the sender if an error arises during message processing in Cloud Integration or when calling the receiver. This feature is important for reliable one-way message exchanges, where the sender of a message needs guaranteed delivery by Cloud Integration. We'll select this option because we want to know whether the message was processed in Cloud Integration.

After these changes are saved and deployed, you can invoke your iFlow again from your SOAP test client of choice. If you're using SoapUI, you'll get nothing back as a reply message. You'll only receive an acknowledgment from Cloud Integration about the successful reception of the message as HTTP response code 202, as shown in Figure 5.50.

Header	Value
date	Mon, 01 Jan 2024 10:47:58 GMT
content-length	0
server	SAP
expires	0
x-frame-options	DENY
x-vcap-request-id	0353aaeb-ae57-4a34-6756-22755e6addb7
pragma	no-cache
strict-transport-security	max-age=31536000; includeSubDomains; preload;
x-content-type-options	nosniff
x-xss-protection	1; mode=block
x-correlationid	0353aaeb-ae57-4a34-6756-22755e6addb7
#status#	HTTP/1.1 202 Accepted
cache-control	no-cache, no-store, max-age=0, must-revalidate

Headers (13) Attachments (0) SSL Info (3 certs) WSS (0) JMS (0)

Figure 5.50 Returned Header after Invoking an Asynchronous Route via SOAP Channel

Now, let's see if we correctly receive the error information back if an error arises during processing. For this capability, we'll need to change the iFlow in such a way that an error is raised. For example, perhaps you've entered an incorrect address into the **OData** channel retrieving additional information for enriching the message. For the sake of illustration, enter "http://test_error_situation" into the **Address** field, as shown in Figure 5.51. Save and deploy the iFlow.

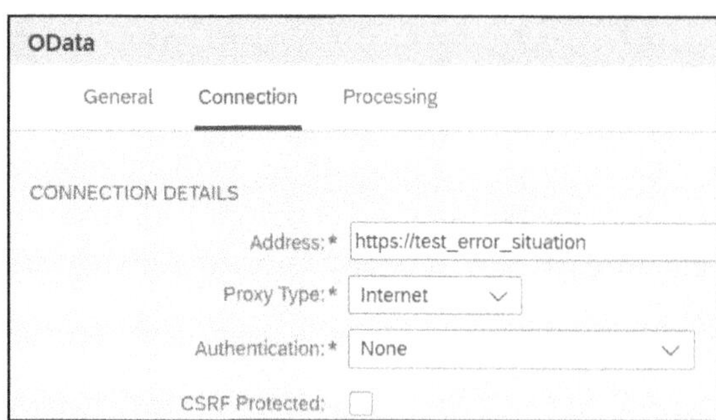

Figure 5.51 Configuration of the OData Channel after Changing the Address

Now, when you call the iFlow again from your SOAP test client, you'll receive a SOAP fault error, as shown in Figure 5.52. The SOAP fault contains `faultcode` and `faultstring`. The `faultcode` only tells you that an error has occurred in the SOAP server; details about the error can be found in `faultstring`.

```
<soap:Envelope xmlns:soap="http://schemas.xmlsoap.org/soap/envelope/">
   <soap:Header/>
   <soap:Body>
      <soap:Fault>
         <faultcode>soap:Server</faultcode>
         <faultstring>An internal error occurred. For error details check MPL ID ... in
         message monitoring or use the URL ... to directly access the error information.</faultstring>
      </soap:Fault>
   </soap:Body>
</soap:Envelope>
```

Figure 5.52 SOAP Fault Received in the SOAP Test Client

The real error, that the OData call wasn't successful, isn't provided: only a generic error containing the message processing log (MPL) ID and a direct link to the error in Cloud Integration's message monitoring are provided. You won't see the real error due to security concerns; internal details must not be provided externally to avoid attacks. Thus, you'll need to call the URL provided to access the MPL in Cloud Integration's message monitoring to investigate the real error, as shown in Figure 5.53. Calling the URL is secured by authentication in Cloud Integration so that only authorized users have access to detailed error descriptions.

```
Inbound processing in endpoint at /listHandlingScenario failed with message "Fault:Sequential processing
failed for number 0. Exchange[ID-810cb490-49dd-4660-5bce-96ff-1704093853175-525-
3]. Caused by: [com.sap.gateway.core.ip.component.odata.exception.OsciException - HTTP Request failed wit
h error : test_error_situation: Name or service not known]", caused by "UnknownHostException:test_error_s
ituation: Name or service not known"
```

Figure 5.53 Error Details Shown in Cloud Integration's Message Monitor

Let's now see what happens if we select **WS Standard** from the **Processing Settings** dropdown list in the SOAP channel. Let's change the configuration with the details shown in Figure 5.54 and then save and deploy our iFlow.

Invoke the iFlow from your SOAP test client. You should now receive the same HTTP response code 202 as in the successful scenario execution (shown earlier in Figure 5.50). Because the message was successfully delivered to Cloud Integration, the error isn't returned to the sender—the fire-and-forget behavior described earlier. You, as the sender, aren't interested in whether the message has been processed successfully or not.

Figure 5.54 Configuration of the SOAP Channel with WS Standard Selected

Now, let's try out the second option to configure asynchronous processing in the SOAP channel: making the SOAP channel aware of the concrete messages it receives. For this approach, the configuration of the SOAP channel provides an option to configure the service via WSDL. Switch the configuration for **Service Definition** to **WSDL**. Then, a dedicated field labeled **URL to WSDL**, shown in Figure 5.55, will appear below the **Service Definition** dropdown. This field allows you to point to your WSDL file.

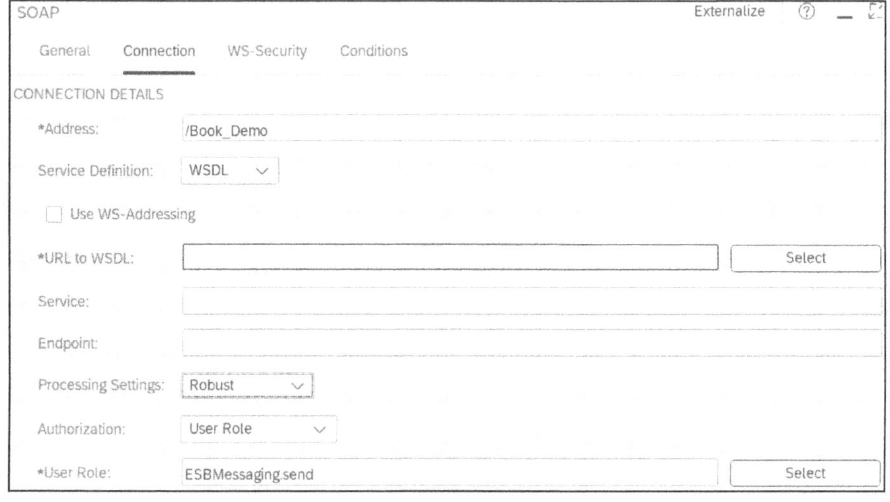

Figure 5.55 Configuration of SOAP Adapter Using Service Definition from WSDL

To assign the WSDL file, simply click on the **Select** button. In the **Select WSDL Resource** dialog box, click on **Upload from File System**, as shown in Figure 5.56.

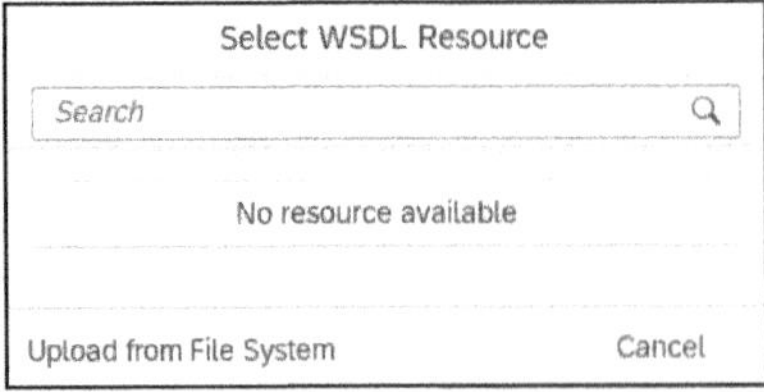

Figure 5.56 Adding a WSDL File to the SOAP Channel

A normal file picker dialog box opens. Select the *SendOrderList_Async.wsdl* file from your file system. When uploading the WSDL into the iFlow, Cloud Integration reads the services defined in the WSDL and automatically sets the service and the endpoint as defined in the WSDL. In our WSDL file, one service (SendOrderList_Async) has been defined in the service tag, as shown in Figure 5.57, with the endpoint SendOrderList_AsyncBinding.

```
<wsdl:service name="SendOrderList_Async">
    <wsdl:port name="SendOrderList_AsyncBinding" binding="p1:SendOrderList_AsyncBinding">
            <soap:address
        location="https://server:port/cxf/Book_Demo" />
    </wsdl:port>
</wsdl:service>
```

Figure 5.57 Service Definition in the WSDL

The service and the endpoint are propagated into the SOAP adapter configuration, including a link to the WSDL file. Now, the configuration should look like the screen shown in Figure 5.58.

SOAP

General | Connection | WS-Security | Conditions

CONNECTION DETAILS

*Address:	/Book_Demo
Service Definition:	WSDL
☐ Use WS-Addressing	
*URL to WSDL:	/wsdl/SendOrderList_Async.wsdl
Service:	demo:SendOrderList_Async
Endpoint:	demo:SendOrderList_AsyncBinding
Processing Settings:	Robust
Authorization:	User Role
*User Role:	ESBMessaging.send

Figure 5.58 Configuration of SOAP Adapter after Assigning the WSDL File

Notice that the namespace `demo` has been added. The namespace definition `xmlns:demo=http://ci.sap.com/demo` is automatically added into the iFlow, under the **Runtime Configuration** tab, if not configured already. In our case, the namespace definition was already available because we configured it in Section 5.2.3.

In addition to the WSDL-specific settings, the **Processing Settings** dropdown list is also available for configuration via WSDL. In this case, the same options, **Robust** and **WS Standard**, are available as described earlier. Select **Robust** to receive error information back if message processing in Cloud Integration fails.

Save and deploy your changes. By adding the WSDL file to the SOAP channel's configuration, correct asynchronous message handling can be ensured. The channel now expects to receive an asynchronous XML message, compliant with the WSDL and will set the **MEP** field of the exchange to **InOnly**. However, a validation of the incoming message against the WSDL isn't performed for the incoming data. Cloud Integration provides a dedicated processing step for that purpose: the XML validator, which requires the assignment of a WSDL file in its configuration.

Once deployed, you can invoke your iFlow again from your SOAP test client of choice. You'll receive the same HTTP response codes as for the configuration without WSDL. If you still have the incorrect address set in the OData channel, you'll receive a SOAP fault error because the **Processing Settings** are configured for robust processing (shown earlier in Figure 5.52). Correct the OData address, and then save and deploy the iFlow again. Now, you should get the HTTP response code 202 (shown earlier in Figure 5.50), which means the message processing was successful in Cloud Integration.

But what happened to our message inside Cloud Integration, and where can we track this message, now that we don't have SoapUI showing the result? In this case, simply navigate to Cloud Integration's monitoring dashboard by clicking on the three horizontal bars in the upper-left corner, and select **Monitor** from the dropdown menu, as shown in Figure 5.59.

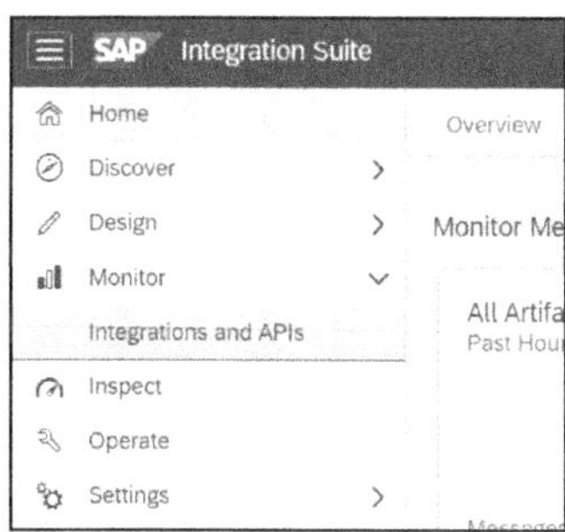

Figure 5.59 Switching to Cloud Integration's Monitoring Environment

The monitoring dashboard will open. Let's start by looking at the successfully completed iFlows by clicking on the **Completed Messages** tile in the **Monitor Message Processing** area of the screen, as shown in Figure 5.60.

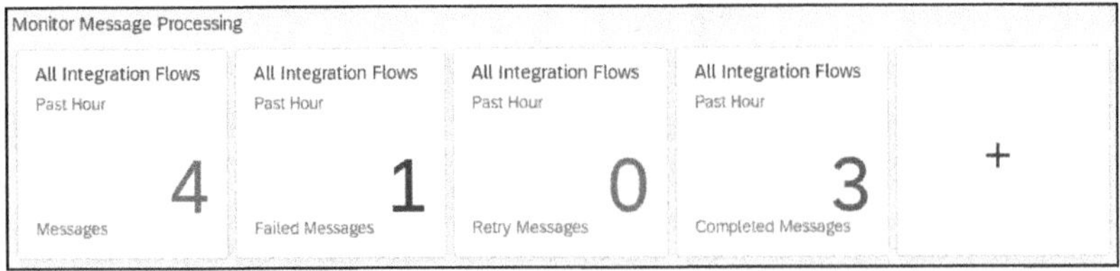

Figure 5.60 Tiles for the Monitors of Completed and Failed Messages

Once you've clicked this tile, you'll see a list of successfully completed messages sorted by date and time (as shown in Figure 5.61, on the left). Select a message, and in the right half of the screen, you'll see the status, logs, and artifact details of the message's processing.

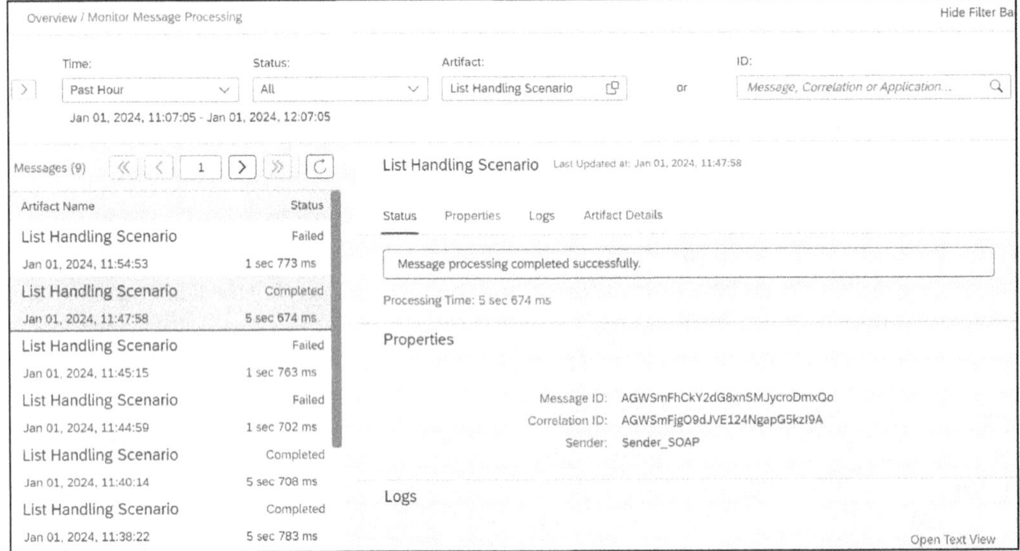

Figure 5.61 Details of a Successfully Completed Message

If errors exist, click the **Failed Messages** tile, shown earlier in Figure 5.60, to see a list of failed messages. Become familiar with the message processing monitor so you can use these tools for root cause analysis. You'll find additional information about message monitoring capabilities in Chapter 7.

> **Note**
>
> The SOAP channel supports both communication styles: synchronous and asynchronous. In this section, we've shown you how to influence its behavior. This flexibility isn't available with all adapters, however. The SFTP adapter, for example, supports asynchronous message handling only. Thus, this adapter will only support **InOnly** in the **MEP** field. Consequently, communication styles are highly dependent on the adapter used and differ from adapter to adapter.

5.3.2 Adding an Asynchronous Receiver

Now that you know how to make a SOAP invocation asynchronous, you probably also want to deliver the message to an asynchronous receiver to verify that the content of the received message is correct. For the sake of simplicity, we'll use an email receiver in this scenario. Because we introduced email receivers in Chapter 2, we won't go into detail in this section, but we've included the email adapter's configuration for your reference.

To run our scenario with an email receiver, follow these steps:

1. Add a **Receiver** to the model on the right side of the iFlow. You'll find the **Receiver** shape next to the participant's node in the palette, as shown in Figure 5.62.

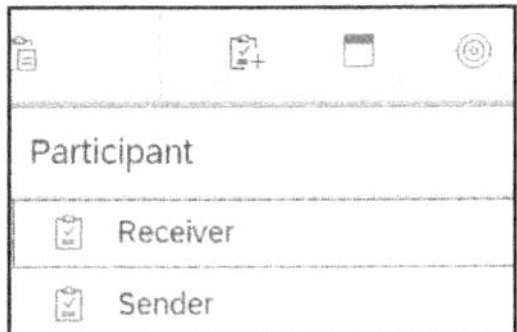

Figure 5.62 Selecting a Receiver from the Palette

2. Position the **Receiver** on the right side of the **Integration Process**, close to the message **End** event, as shown in Figure 5.63.

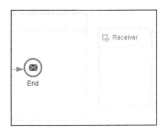

Figure 5.63 Positioning the Receiver Pool Close to the End Event

3. Connect the **End** event with the **Receiver** pool, as shown in Figure 5.64.

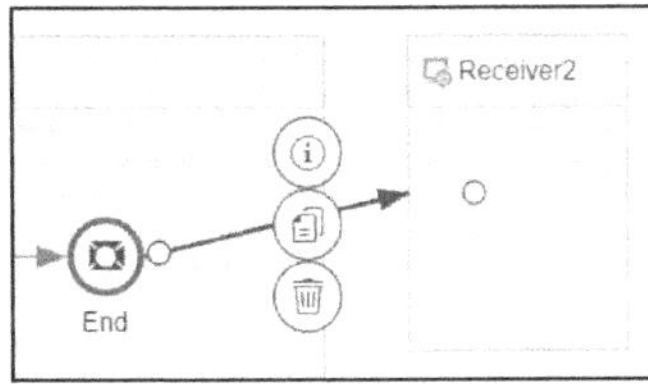

Figure 5.64 Connecting the End Event with the Receiver Pool

4. In the **Adapter Type** dialog box, select the **Mail** entry. Configure the adapter according to your email account. The values shown in Figure 5.65 and Figure 5.66 fit a Google email account.

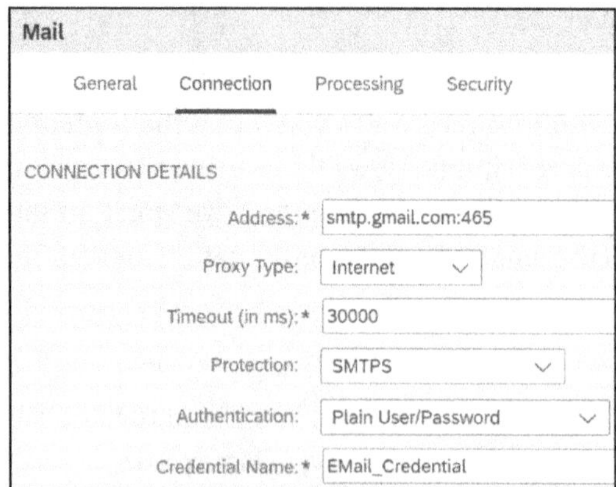

Figure 5.65 Configuring the Connection Details of the Mail Adapter

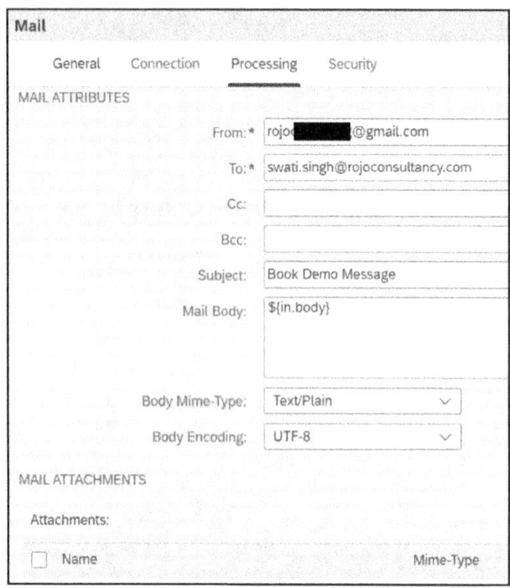

Figure 5.66 Configuring the Mail Attributes of the Mail Adapter

> **Note**
>
> For details on the configuration of the fields and the creation of the user credentials, refer to Chapter 2.

The final scenario should look similar to the iFlow shown in Figure 5.67. You can easily identify the sender on the left, the message processing steps in the middle, and the final receiver on the right. Take advantage of this graphical environment, which clearly and intuitively describes how a message arrives at the server; how it's handled within the Cloud Integration server; and to which systems, using which channels, the message is sent.

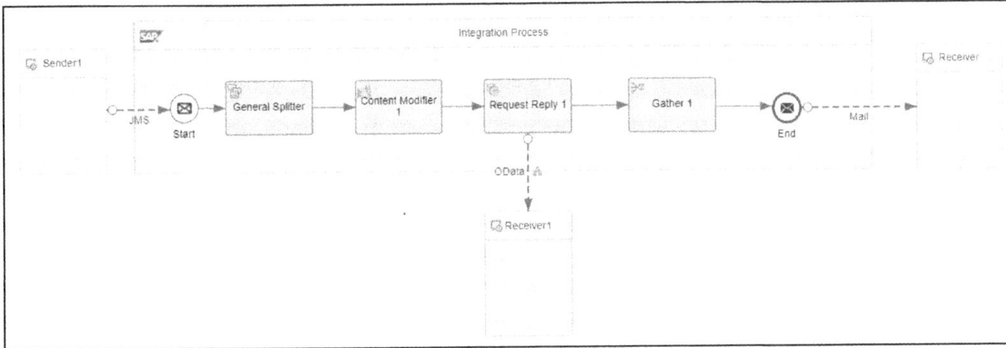

Figure 5.67 Asynchronous iFlow with Email Receiver

After finishing your configuration, run the scenario again. This time, the message will be delivered to your email account. You should receive an email containing the three order numbers. A screenshot of the email's content is shown in Figure 5.68.

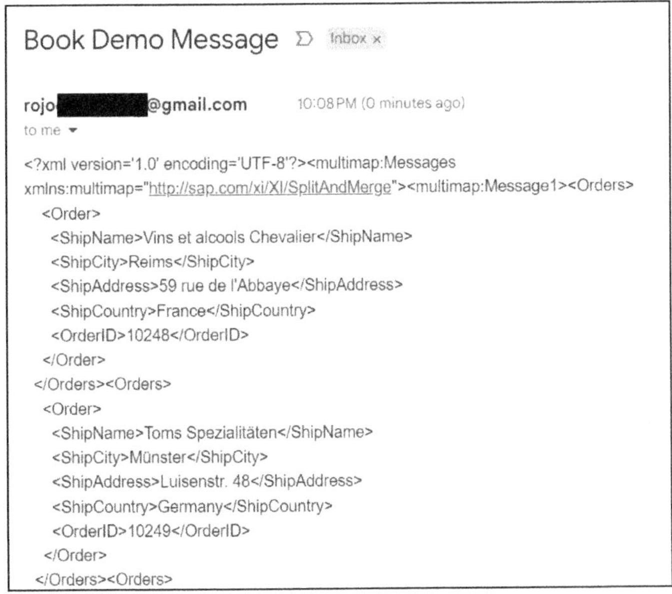

Figure 5.68 Content of Received Email

Note

For analyzing issues that may arise in connecting to the email server, refer to the troubleshooting information found in Chapter 2, Section 2.3.6.

5.3.3 Routing a Message to Multiple Receivers Using the Multicast Pattern

You've now successfully sent the message to one receiver, but some scenarios may require sending the same message to multiple receivers—either in the same format or in different formats—and maybe even only parts of a message. These options are all possible in Cloud Integration, so let's configure a multicast scenario now.

We'll use our scenario from the preceding section and add another email receiver, which will simply receive an email containing a notification that the message has been processed successfully.

We used a **Router** step to configure the routing of messages to multiple receivers. However, the message would only go to the first receiver, the one for which the routing condition is met because the **Router** is based on a Business Process Model and Notation (BPMN)-exclusive gateway. Therefore, this step doesn't meet the requirements of our use case involving sending the message to multiple receivers. To send the message to multiple receivers, you must add a flow step based on the BPMN-parallel gateway. For these use cases, Cloud Integration offers the multicast pattern.

Two options are available for the multicast pattern:

- **Parallel Multicast**
  With this option, the message is routed to the different branches in parallel. We'll start with this option.
- **Sequential Multicast**
  With this option, an order of execution can be specified. This method is especially important if the second branch shouldn't be executed if the first branch fails. We'll describe this option in more detail later.

Let's start modeling. To add the **Multicast** step, from the main menu of the palette, select the **Message Routing** ◇ shape. A submenu opens, revealing different routing options, including **Multicast**, as shown in Figure 5.69.

When you select **Multicast**, another submenu will open, with two options, **Sequential Multicast** and **Parallel Multicast**, as shown in Figure 5.70. Select the **Parallel Multicast** option for now, and place the step between the **Gather** step and the **End** event, as shown in Figure 5.71.

Figure 5.69 Multicast Shape in the Modeling Environment Palette

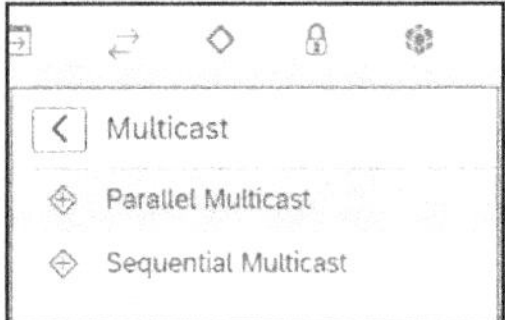

Figure 5.70 Multicast Options in the Modeling Environment Palette

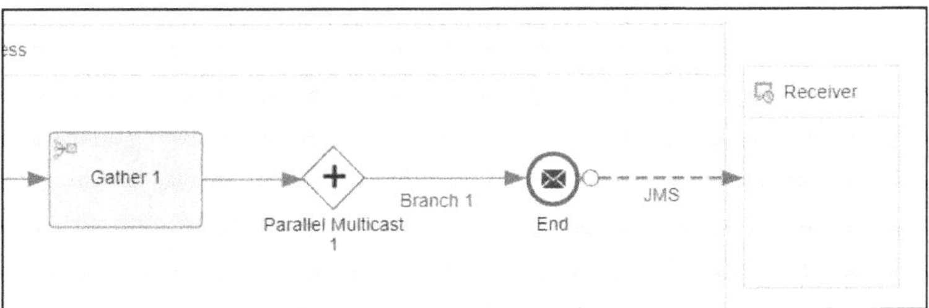

Figure 5.71 Placing a Parallel Multicast between Gather and the End Event

To send the message to a second receiver, you must add another **End Message** event and one more **Receiver**. To add another branch for the multicast processing, draw a line between the **Parallel Multicast** step and the **End** event. Then, connect the **End** event with the new **Receiver**, select the **Mail** adapter, and configure it with the same connection details as earlier, except now define a different subject and body for the mail, as shown in Figure 5.72. In this scenario, we'll enter "Status of Message Processing" into the **Subject** and add a short status text in the **Mail Body** entry field. Notice that we've added the SAP header for the MPL ID (SAP_MessageProcessingLogID) into the email's body. This value will help later when searching for the message in the Cloud Integration's message monitoring.

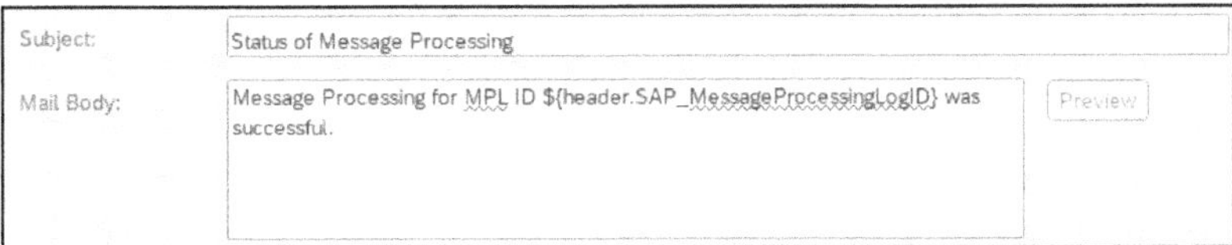

Figure 5.72 Configuring the Mail Adapter for the Second Receiver

The scenario should now look similar to the iFlow shown in Figure 5.73. Two branches leave from the **Parallel Multicast** shape: **Branch 1** leads to the first mail receiver, and **Branch 2** leads to the newly added mail receiver.

Note

In each branch leaving the multicast shape, you can configure additional flow steps, for example, mappings or conversions. Thus, you can send completely different messages or even different parts of an inbound message to specific receivers.

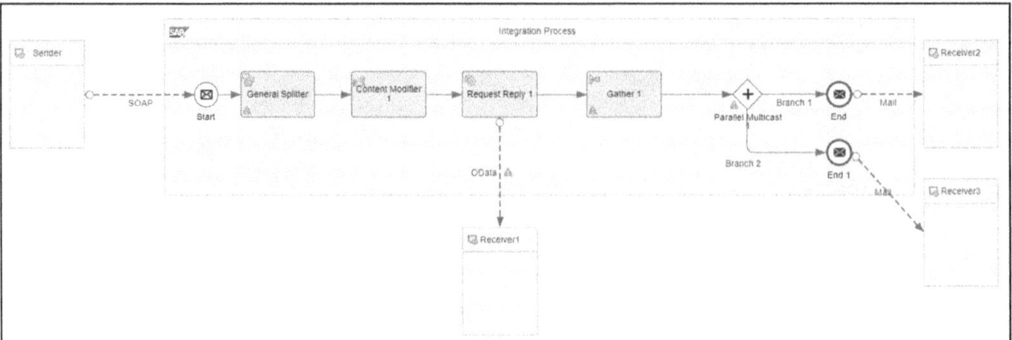

Figure 5.73 iFlow with Parallel Multicast and Two Receivers

After you've finished your configuration changes, saved, and deployed the iFlow, run the scenario again. From your SOAP test client, the request will be sent successfully to Cloud Integration, and this time, the message will be delivered twice to your email account: once with the message created by the **Gather** step and the second time with the status mail text configured in the second **Mail** adapter channel. The received email content of the status is shown in Figure 5.74.

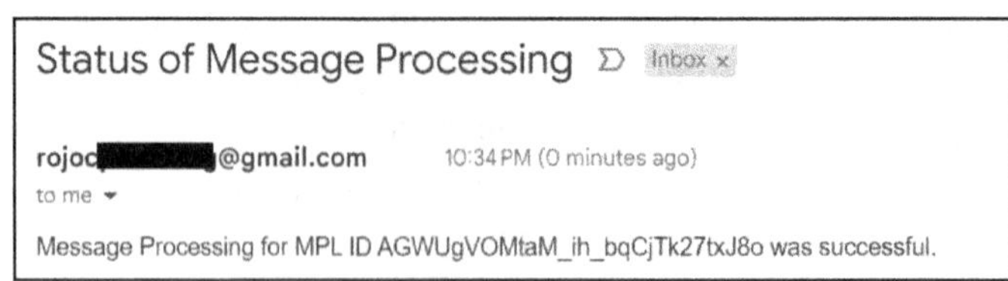

Figure 5.74 Content of Received Email Containing the Message Processing Status

In the email containing the processing status, you'll get the **MPL ID** for the message's processing in SAP BTP. With this information, you can easily check the processing and status in the message monitor by searching for the MPL ID, if required. Open the **Monitoring** page, described in the previous section, and click the **All Messages** tile. As a search criterion, paste the MPL ID from your email into the **ID** field, as shown in Figure 5.75. Press Enter or click the magnifier icon next to the added MPL ID to start the search. The search opens the **Message Processing** details of your message.

Figure 5.75 Searching for a Specific MPL ID in the Message Monitor

But what happens if **Branch 1** can't be completed because of an error? Let's find out! To produce an error in **Branch 1**, change the **Address** field in the first **Mail** adapter channel to some configuration that doesn't work, for example, to **smtp.gmail.com:444**. Save and deploy the iFlow, and run the scenario again.

Now, you'll see an HTTP 500 error in your SOAP test client because the message could not be processed successfully in Cloud Integration, as expected. However, you'll still receive an email that the message processing was successful. Let's take a detailed look at the message processing of this message in Cloud Integration. Use the MPL ID received in the email as a search criterion in the **ID** field in the message monitor, as shown in Figure 5.76. Notice that the message processing of the message has the status **Failed**. You'll also see the reason: A connection to `smtp.gmail.com:444` wasn't possible. But why do we still get the status email if message processing is failing?

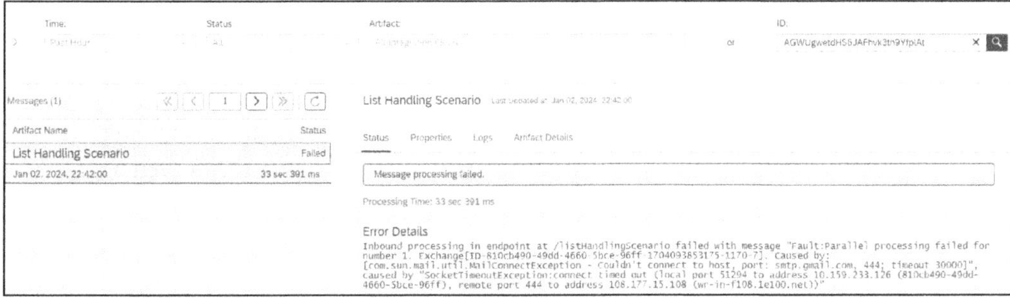

Figure 5.76 Searching for the MPL ID of the Failed Message in the Message Monitor

You'll need to understand the processing of a message in the multicast pattern in Cloud Integration. Recall our earlier discussion about inbound processing in the SOAP adapter, in which the message is processed by each of the configured flow steps one after the other. However, now, as soon as the message reaches the **Multicast** step, the message is multiplied as many times as outbound branches exist leading from the **Multicast** step. Each of these messages is processed independently, in its branch, until reaching an **End** event or a **Join** step.

For our scenario, the two branches leaving the parallel multicast are executed in parallel and are completely independent of each other. Thus, **Branch 2** is executed even if **Branch 1** fails. But this isn't desirable in our scenario; instead, we want to receive a successful status email only when the first call is successful. Thus, we'll need to make sure the branches are executed one after the other and ensure that the second branch is executed after the first branch. In Cloud Integration, in this case, you'll use the second multicast option: **Sequential Multicast**.

Combination of Multicast with Join and Gather

In this chapter, we're using the **Multicast** pattern to send messages to multiple receivers. However, in Cloud Integration, another use case for the **Multicast** pattern exists. In combination with **Join** and **Gather**, the **Multicast** step can process a message in different branches. Later, several branches can be brought together using a **Join** step, and multiple messages can be combined into a single message using a **Gather** step. This processing would look similar to the flow shown in Figure 5.77. For more details about this configuration, refer to the documentation for Cloud Integration (found at *http://s-prs.co/v576010*; search for "Define Gather and Join").

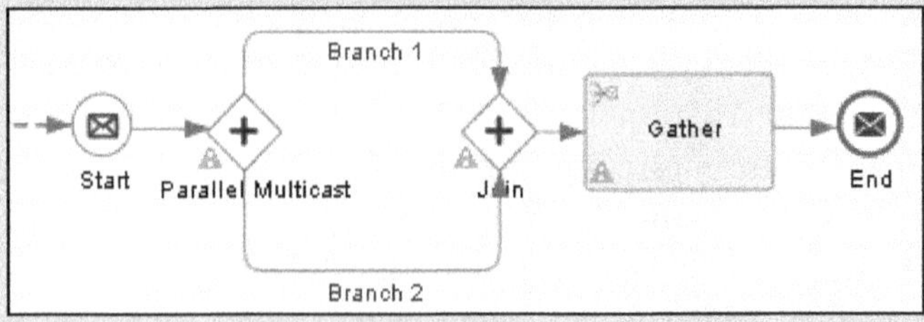

Figure 5.77 Using Multicast with Join and Gather

Now, let's change the iFlow by removing the **Parallel Multicast** step and adding the **Sequential Multicast** step instead. Afterward, we'll connect the **Gather** step with the **Sequential Multicast** and **Sequential Multicast** step with the two **End** events connected to the two **Receiver** boxes, as shown in Figure 5.78.

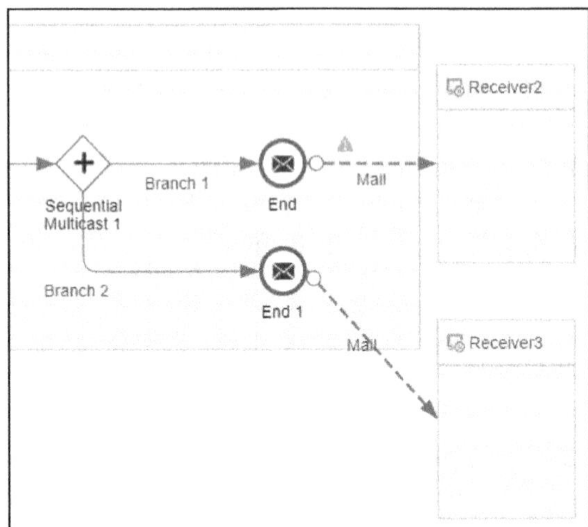

Figure 5.78 Sequential Multicast Connected with Two Receivers

You must ensure that the two branches, **Branch 1** and **Branch 2**, are executed in the correct order. First, **Branch 1** will be processed by sending out the message produced by the **Gather** step, and if this branch is executed successfully, **Branch 2** will be processed. To check and, if necessary, change the order, you can select the **Sequential Multicast** step to access its details in the **Properties** section. Under the **Routing Sequence** tab, a table with branches that have been configured is displayed, as shown in Figure 5.79. Make sure the branch to the first **Receiver** (in our iFlow, **Branch 1**) is at the top of the table so that this branch is executed first. To change the order or branches, use the **Move Up** and **Move Down** buttons.

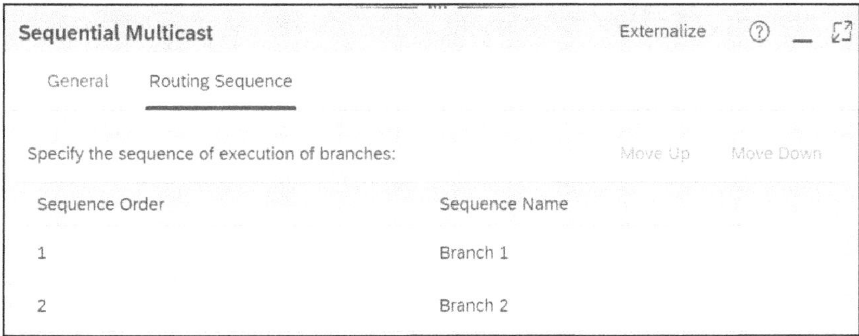

Figure 5.79 Configure Order in Sequential Multicast

When the configuration is complete, save and deploy the iFlow. Trigger the scenario again from your SOAP test client. You'll still get the HTTP 500 error, but you shouldn't receive the status email anymore.

To check the successful execution, correct the value of the **Address** field in the first **Mail** adapter channel, and then save and deploy the change. The execution should now correctly send the message produced by the **Gather** step and the status email to your email account.

At this point, you know two different configuration options for parallel gateway processing in Cloud Integration, but a third, special option is available when configuring this specific multicast scenario. If, as in our case, no additional configuration step must be executed in the first multicast branch, you can use the **Send** step instead.

Let's configure the scenario with a **Send** step by adding the **Send** step from the palette in your iFlow, after the **Gather** step. You'll find the **Send** step under the **Call** ⇄ menu item. Select the shape, and a submenu with the two options, **External Call** and **Local Call** opens, as shown in Figure 5.80. Select **External Call**, and you'll see three options for external calls from Cloud Integration: **Content Enricher**, **Request Reply**, and **Send**, as shown in Figure 5.81. **Request Reply** and **Content Enricher** have already been explained in detail in Chapter 4, so now, we'll focus only on the **Send** step.

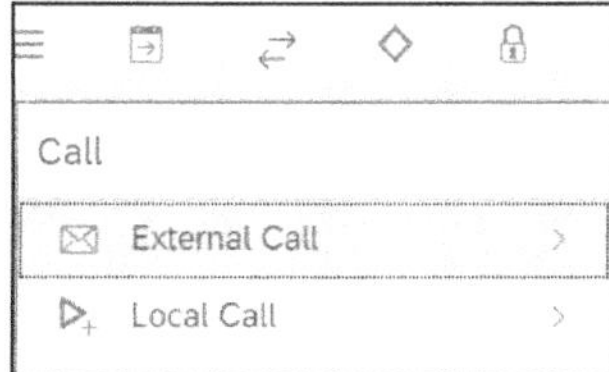

Figure 5.80 External Call Shape in the Modeling Environment Palette

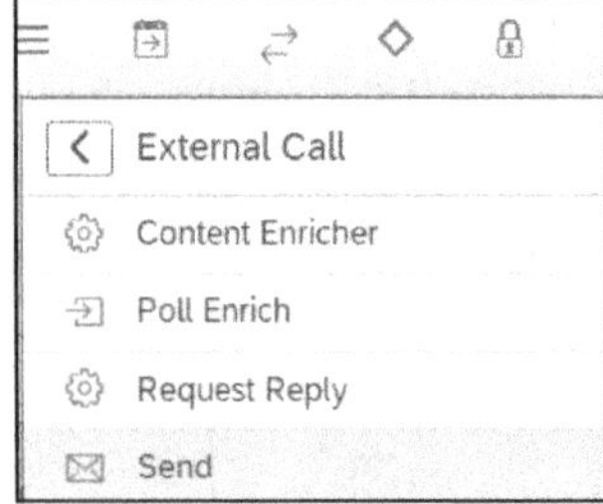

Figure 5.81 Send Shape in the Modeling Environment Palette

Connect the **Gather** step with the **Send** step, and draw a line from the **Send** step to the first **Receiver**, which is expecting the message coming from **Gather**. Select the **Mail** adapter, and reconfigure the **Mail** channel as configured in the iFlow using **Multicast** (shown earlier in Figure 5.65 and Figure 5.66). Connect the **Send** step with the **End** event. Your iFlow should now look similar to the flow shown in Figure 5.82.

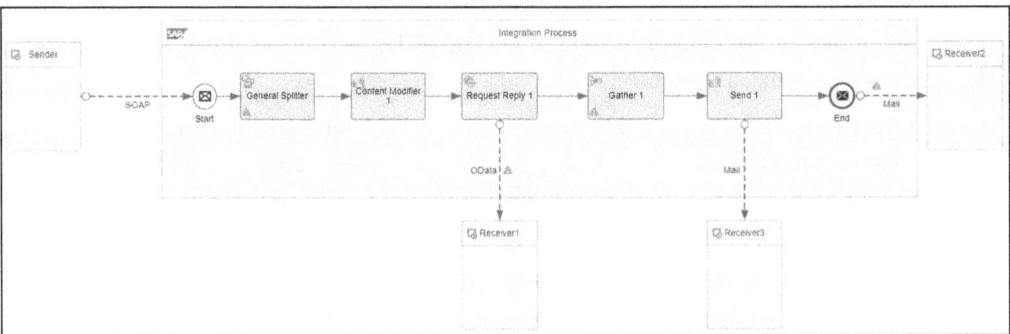

Figure 5.82 iFlow with Send Step and Additional Receiver

Save the configuration, and deploy the iFlow. Triggering the flow from your SOAP test client will produce the same result as when calling the iFlow with **Sequential Multicast**. The message will be sent successfully, and two emails, one created by the **Gather** step and the other the status email, will be received in your mailbox.

During runtime, if the sending of the email in the **Send** step fails, the processing will stop, and the status email won't be sent. Therefore, in the runtime, the **Send** step behaves like a **Sequential Multicast** step. In fact, the **Send** step is a sequential multicast with exactly two branches: the first branch goes to the connected **Receiver**, and the second branch goes to the next processing step.

Synchronous and asynchronous message handling procedures are at the core of every integration solution, and Cloud Integration is no exception to this rule. In this section, you learned more about internal message processing in Cloud Integration. You've seen how synchronous and asynchronous message handling can be controlled for the SOAP channel and how multiple asynchronous receivers can be added to your scenario using the multicast pattern. We also showed you how the message monitor can help you track message processing within Cloud Integration. In the next section, we'll go a step further and decouple the inbound and outbound processing of the iFlow to make our scenario more robust and less error-prone.

5.4 Reliable Messaging Using the JMS Adapter

In the previous section, you learned how to configure asynchronous messaging in Cloud Integration, the basic concept behind asynchronous messaging, and several modeling techniques for sending a message to multiple receivers. We used robust one-way communication to make asynchronous scenarios reliable by ensuring guaranteed message delivery and notifications to the sender about errors so that erroneous messages can be resent.

In general, such robust one-way scenarios using Cloud Integration feature the following characteristics:

- This pattern relies on a retry mechanism in the sender system. If an error arises during processing in Cloud Integration (e.g., if one of the receivers is temporarily unavailable), an error will be reported back to the sender, and the whole message processing must start from the beginning. Restarting will need to be triggered by the sender system.
- If parallel multicast is used, temporary connection issues associated with one of the receiver systems will trigger retries from the sender system and may lead to duplicate messages in the other receiver systems.
- The overall execution time of a reliable, asynchronous messaging scenario includes the whole message's processing in Cloud Integration until the message finally reaches the receiver. In a complex iFlow, execution time may become undesirably long.

This behavior isn't desirable in many scenarios; often the sender wants to deliver the message and expects an asynchronous response later—and doesn't want to care about retries. Usually, the sender wants to send the message and expects the middleware to handle temporary connection problems to receiver systems using built-in retry mechanisms. In this section, we'll extend the scenario developed in the preceding section so that retries are triggered from Cloud Integration automatically if execution errors occur.

5.4.1 Asynchronous Decoupling of Inbound Communication

To trigger retries from Cloud Integration when an error occurs during message processing, you must decouple inbound message processing in Cloud Integration from outbound processing. You'll also need to temporarily persist the message in Cloud Integration so that a message can be restarted from Cloud Integration's persistent storage if an error occurs during processing.

In the next section, we'll discuss the available Cloud Integration options for temporarily persisting messages, show you how to configure such scenarios, and describe the monitoring options you can use.

Data Store and Message Queues

Cloud Integration provides two options—data store and message queues (also known as Java Message Service [JMS] queues)—to temporarily store messages during message processing. Let's look at these two options in more detail:

- **Data store**
  Based on the database on which Cloud Integration is running, a data store is used to store messages (using a **Write** step), and subsequently data is read from the data store using a **Select** or **Get** step. Because a data store isn't designed to execute high-performance messaging, this solution isn't optimal for our scenario. The main use cases for using a data store are as follows:
  - You need to temporarily store a message during message processing because the original payload is required later in the processing of the message. With a **Write** step, the initial message is saved in the data store. Afterwards, changes to the payload are made, for example, using mappings, converters, or scripts. Later in the processing, the initial message is fetched using a **Get** step. Such persistence features are common in some integration patterns, for example, in the claim check pattern, which is described in detail at *http://s-prs.co/v576014*.
  - The data store is often used in the push-pull pattern. The sender is sending messages to Cloud Integration, where the messages are temporarily stored in the data store. In a synchronous call, the receiver actively polls the messages from the data store (using a **Select** step) and acknowledges the receipt of each message. Afterwards, these acknowledged messages are deleted from the data store (using a **Delete** step). We won't go into detail about the push-pull pattern in this chapter, but for your reference, a small sample iFlow is shown in Figure 5.83.
- **JMS queues**
  JMS queues are the second option for temporarily storing messages in Cloud Integration. Messages are stored in JMS queues using the **JMS Receiver** adapter and read from JMS queues using the **JMS sender** adapter. Because JMS supports high-speed messaging with high throughput, JMS queries are an optimal solution for reliable messaging using asynchronous decoupling. Thus, we'll choose this option in our scenario.

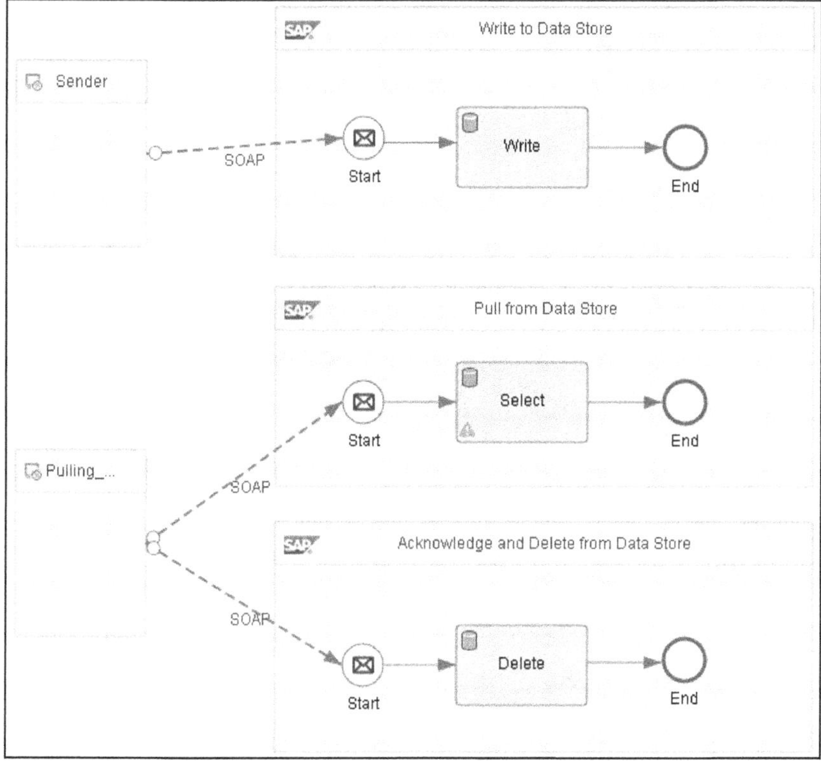

Figure 5.83 Sample iFlow for the Push-Pull Pattern

Java Message Service

Java Message Service (JMS) is a standard Java-based application programming interface (API) for sending and receiving messages. This API enables reliable asynchronous communication between different components based on a JMS message broker. The JMS message broker is a separate runtime component that ensures the handling of messages in JMS queues. Available in Cloud Integration, the JMS adapter is used to store and consume messages in the JMS queue via the JMS message broker embedded in Cloud Integration. The JMS adapter can't connect to arbitrary message brokers. To connect to external message brokers, you can use the Advanced Message Queuing Protocol (AMQP) adapter.

The processing sequence used by the JMS adapter is first-in, first-out (FIFO), which means that messages stored in the JMS queue last are also consumed last. Be aware that sequence doesn't mean that messages are processed in a guaranteed order because Cloud Integration uses several workers consuming messages from the JMS queue in parallel. Furthermore, messages that cause errors are taken out of the processing queue and are retried later according to the retry interval defined in the JMS channel.

To decouple the inbound processing of the integration scenario from its outbound processing, you must split the scenario into two processes: one for receiving the message and storing it in a JMS queue, and a second process for consuming the message from the JMS queue, further processing the message, and sending the final response to the receiver.

Prerequisites for Using the JMS Adapter

JMS messaging is available only with dedicated licenses, for example, with SAP Integration Suite, standard edition; with SAP Integration Suite, premium edition; with SAP BTP Enterprise Agreement; or if a JMS messaging license is purchased separately. If your Cloud Integration system lacks the required license, the JMS adapter won't appear in the list of available adapters.

Furthermore, you'll need a JMS message broker provisioned for your Cloud Integration tenant. The provisioning process is triggered using a self-service function in the SAP BTP cockpit. Details about provisioning a JMS message broker can be found at *http://s-prs.co/507718*.

Extending the Integration Scenario

Let's start extending the scenario we configured in the previous section. First, to decouple the inbound processing from all the other processing steps, we'll create and configure a new integration process for the inbound processing. Make the following changes to the iFlow:

1. Add a new **Integration Process** below the existing integration process by selecting it from the modeling palette under the **Process** shape. In the submenu, the **Integration Process** option is one of the process elements available, as shown in Figure 5.84.

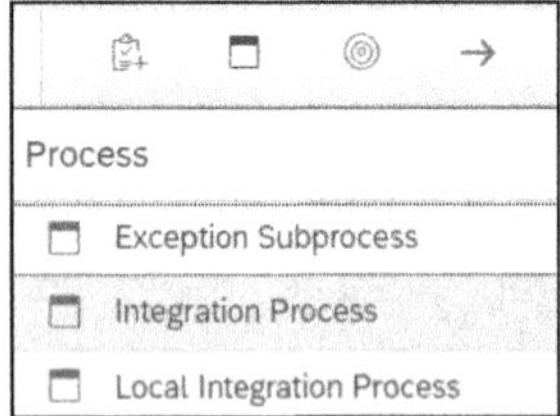

Figure 5.84 Process Shape in the Modeling Environment Palette

2. In the new integration process, add a **Start Message** event and an **End Message** event from the **Events** shape, as shown in Figure 5.85. Connect the **Start Message** event with the **End Message** event.
3. Select the dotted line representing the message flow from the **Sender** to the first integration process's **Start** event. The line will turn orange with small blue dots at the start and the end of the line. Select the blue dot appearing at the **Start** event in

the first **Integration Process**, and move the blue dot to the **Start** event in the new **Integration Process**, as shown in Figure 5.86. Now, the existing **SOAP** channel points to the new integration process, and you don't have to remodel the channel.

4. Add a **Receiver** to the model, on the right side of the new integration process. Remember, you can find the **Receiver** under the **Participant** shape in the palette.
5. Connect the **End** event of the new **Integration Process** to the new **Receiver**. In the adapter selection screen, choose the **JMS** adapter. (Note that the JMS adapter entry will only appear in the list if you're using SAP BTP Enterprise Agreement.)

Figure 5.85 Event Shapes in the Modeling Environment Palette

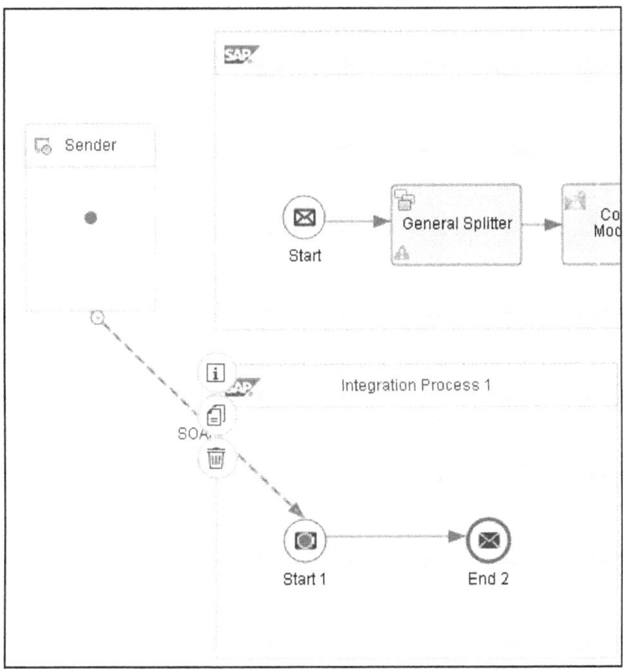

Figure 5.86 Connecting the SOAP Sender Channel to the New Integration Process

6. In the **JMS** channel, under the **Processing** tab, configure the following properties, as shown in Figure 5.87:
   - **Queue Name**: This is the most important configuration setting, in which you'll specify a unique name for the JMS queue to be used for this scenario, that is, "Inbound_Queue". The JMS queue is used by the JMS receiver adapter to store messages there and by the JMS sender adapter to consumer messages from it.
   - **Retention Threshold for Alerting (in d)**: You'll set the number of days the message should be picked up from the JMS queue and further processed. If the message stays in the JMS queue for a longer time than configured, the message appears as **Overdue** in the monitoring dashboard in Cloud Integration to indicate that some problem occurred during processing: perhaps, the consuming iFlow doesn't run anymore.
   - **Expiration Period (in d)**: Only limited resources are available on the JMS instance configured for a Cloud Integration system. Therefore, JMS queues are only allowed for temporary storage. In the **Expiration Period** field, you'll define after how many days the message is automatically deleted from the JMS queue. The default value is 90 days, and the maximum value allowed is 180 days, but keep in mind that the maximum capacity allowed in the JMS instance for all messages in all JMS queues in your Cloud Integration system. This maximum capacity is based on the number of messaging licenses purchased. The available capacity and the used capacity are shown in the queue monitor, which we'll check later when we run the scenario.
   - **Encrypt Stored Message**: This checkbox should be enabled to encrypt the messages in the JMS queue for security reasons. When you're processing messages that aren't security-sensitive, you can deselect this checkbox to improve performance.

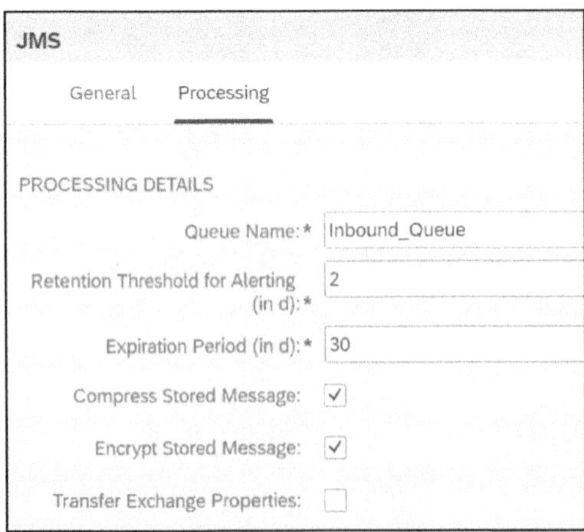

Figure 5.87 JMS Receiver Channel Configuration

- **Transfer Exchange Properties**: Exchange properties aren't usually transferred using JMS queues. If, for any scenario-specific reason, transferring exchange properties is required, select the **Transfer Exchange Properties** checkbox. However, keep in mind that there is a hard limit of 4 MB for storing headers and properties in JMS queues. If the limit is hit during runtime, the message will go into the **Failed** status with an error stating that the limit for headers and properties has been reached.

Now, the new process looks similar to the iFlow shown in Figure 5.88.

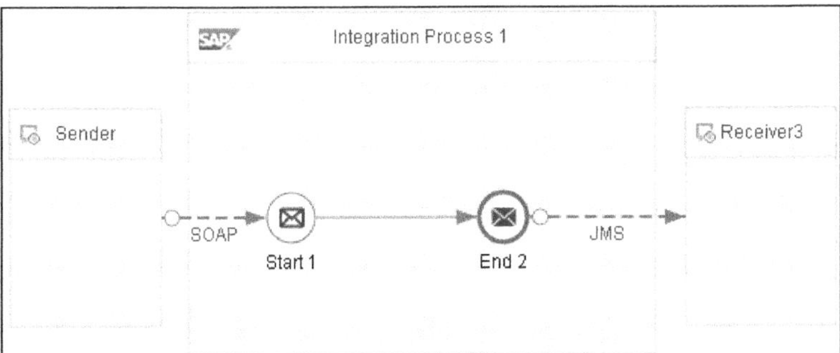

Figure 5.88 Integration Process with JMS Receiver

Limits for JMS Resources

Limited resources are available on the JMS instance connected to the Cloud Integration tenant. The JMS resources available depend on the licenses purchased.

As mentioned, one hard limit is the overall size of 4 MB for storing headers and properties in a JMS queue. This limit can neither be configured nor increased, not even by purchasing additional licenses for JMS messaging. We recommend you avoid transferring properties via JMS queues and restrict the usage of headers.

More details about JMS resources can be found at *http://s-prs.co/507719*.

We've now changed the inbound processing so that the message isn't processed by Cloud Integration and sent to the receiver. Instead, after being received, the message is directly stored in a JMS queue. Let's run the scenario before we configure the main integration process that will consume the messages from the JMS queue.

Save and deploy the iFlow. Now, trigger the iFlow from your SOAP test client. The HTTP response code 202, notifying you about the successful execution, is shown more quickly than in the executions triggered in the previous section. This added speed is the result of the change we made in the iFlow: now, the message is only stored in the JMS queue, and no further processing is executed in Cloud Integration.

The message is now stored in the JMS queue, waiting for consumption and further processing. You can monitor the JMS queues in the Cloud Integration's monitoring dashboard to locate them. Open the dashboard, and in the **Manage Stores** area of the screen, you'll find the **Message Queues** monitor, as shown in Figure 5.89.

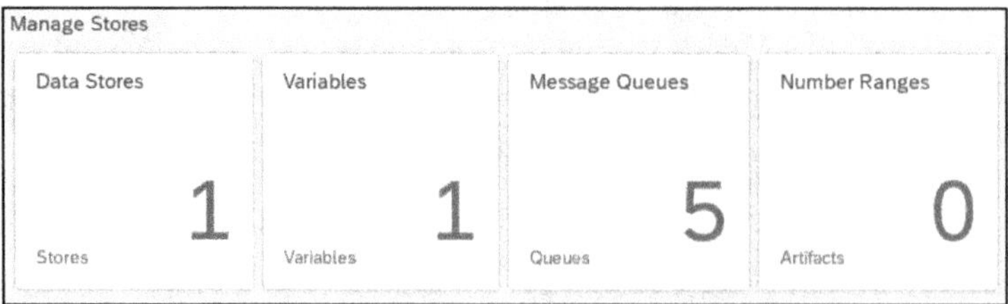

Figure 5.89 Manage Stores Section in the Monitoring Dashboard

Queue Creation during Deployment

The JMS queues are created automatically in the JMS messaging instance during the deployment of the first iFlow using a new JMS queue name. Be aware of the following two aspects:

- If the same **Queue Name** is used in multiple iFlows or integration processes, the same JMS queue is used in runtime. As a result, multiple processes may write to the same JMS queue, or multiple JMS senders may consume from the same JMS queue. The integration developer may want this behavior if the same queue will be reused by different scenarios, but this behavior may also happen by accident.
- JMS queues aren't deleted automatically when undeploying an iFlow because messages may still exist in the JMS queue, and deleting the queue would delete those messages as well, leading to data loss. Only the owner of the scenario knows if the JMS queue can be deleted with all of its content or if this data is still required. A JMS queue can be deleted in the **Manage Message Queues** monitor using the **Delete** action.

Select the **Message Queues** monitor to view a list of JMS queues created in the JMS messaging instance of your Cloud Integration system. Search for the JMS queue with the name **Inbound_Queue**, which was the queue name we defined in the JMS receiver channel. Select the queue to display the messages in this specific queue, as shown in Figure 5.90.

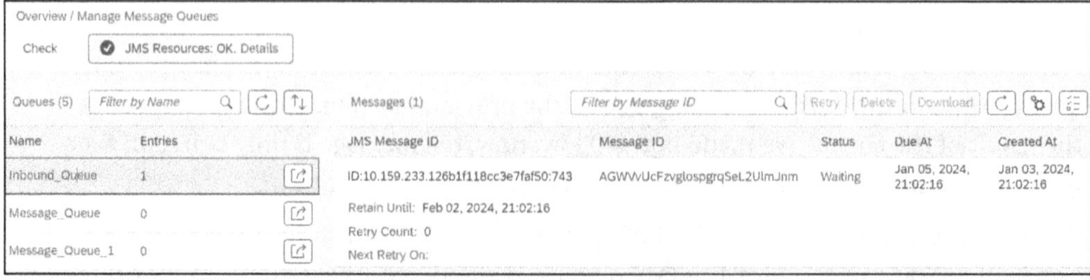

Figure 5.90 Message in Waiting Status in the Manage Message Queues Monitor

Notice that the message sent to Cloud Integration is displayed with the status **Waiting**. This status indicates that the message is waiting to be consumed by another process.

Configuring the Integration Process

Now, let's configure the integration process, which consumes and finally sends the message to the receiver. Follow these steps:

1. Add a **Sender** to the model on the left side of the integration process configuring the main processing. Remember, you'll find the **Sender** under the **Participant** shape in the palette.
2. Connect the **Sender** to the **Start** event of the integration process. In the adapter selection screen, choose the **JMS** adapter.
3. In the **JMS** channel, under the **Processing** tab, configure the following properties, as shown in Figure 5.91:
   - **Queue Name**: Define the same value as specified in the JMS receiver (**Inbound_Queue**) to consume the messages from the JMS queue that the inbound processing stores the messages in.
   - **Number of Concurrent Processes**: Messages from the JMS queue can be consumed in parallel if required for high message throughput. In the **Number of Concurrent Processes** field, specify the number of parallel processes consuming messages from the JMS queue.
   - **RETRY DETAILS**: The retry configuration is specified in this section, as follows:
     - **Retry Interval (in min)**: Define after how many minutes the first retry is executed.
     - **Exponential Backoff**: Select this checkbox to avoid lots of retries in a short time. When **Exponential Backoff** is selected, the retry interval is doubled after each unsuccessful retry. For example, if a receiver system isn't available because of maintenance, retrying the message every second doesn't make sense.
     - **Maximum Retry Interval (in min)**: Define the maximum interval between two tries to avoid an endless increase of the retry interval if the **Exponential Backoff** checkbox has been selected.
     - **Dead-Letter Queue**: Takes messages that cause outages of the runtime node, for example, by an out-of-memory error, out of processing. Messages where processing stopped unexpectedly are retried only twice when the **Dead-Letter Queue** checkbox is enabled. Further details about this feature, its usage, and its monitoring can be found at *http://s-prs.co/507720*.

An example iFlow with the two new integration processes is shown in Figure 5.92.

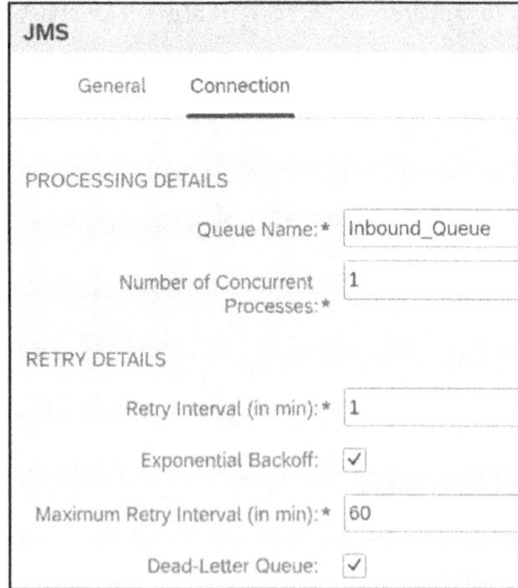

Figure 5.91 JMS Sender Channel Configuration

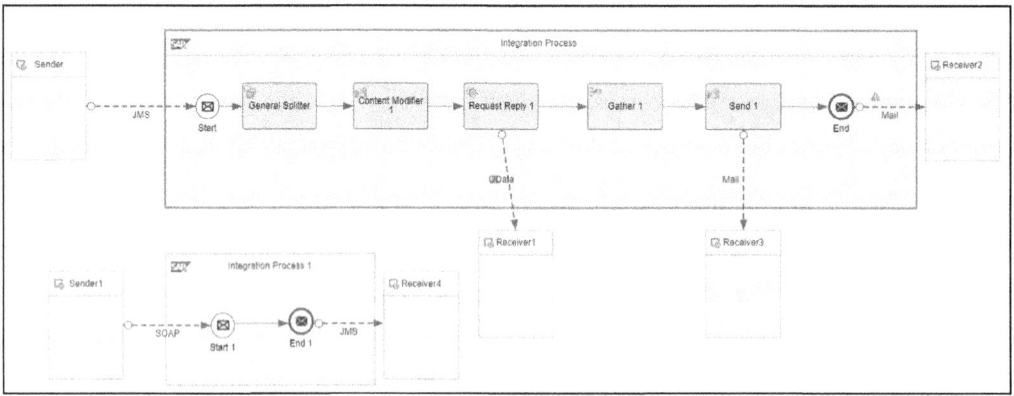

Figure 5.92 iFlow with JMS Sender and JMS Receiver Adapter

Retry from JMS Queue

Messages in JMS queues are retried as long as the messages aren't successfully processed or the expiration period is reached. As soon as the message goes to **Completed** status, the message is removed from the JMS queue. The message can either get the **Completed** status after successful execution of the scenario or if the message processing error is caught in an **Exception Subprocess**. The second option will be discussed later in this chapter.

Save your changes, and deploy the iFlow. The JMS sender channel now consumes the message from the JMS queue, and you'll get the missing emails. Triggering the iFlow again from your SOAP test client, you'll receive the emails directly because storing the message in the JMS queue and consuming it there doesn't require much time in Cloud Integration.

You've now seen that, for successfully delivered messages, not much changes from an end-to-end perspective. But how does Cloud Integration handle retries if errors occur in Cloud Integration's runtime? Let's try it out. We'll change the **Address** field in the **Mail** channel connected to the **Receiver** from the **Send** step to an address that doesn't work, for example, to **smtp.gmail.com:444**. Save and deploy the iFlow, and run the scenario again.

In your SOAP test client, you'll get an HTTP response code 202 because the message was successfully delivered to Cloud Integration, but you won't get an email. We've expected this behavior because of the incorrect **Address** configuration in the **Mail** channel. But what happens in Cloud Integration? How is the retry executed, and where do we find the processing details for the message? Let's look at the Cloud Integration's monitoring dashboard.

Open the monitoring dashboard, and select the **Message Queues** to monitor. Select the JMS queue **Inbound_Queue** that we're using in the scenario. As shown in Figure 5.93, the message in the JMS queue has the status **Failed**, and the retry count indicates the number of retries that were already executed. In addition, the time of the next retry is displayed.

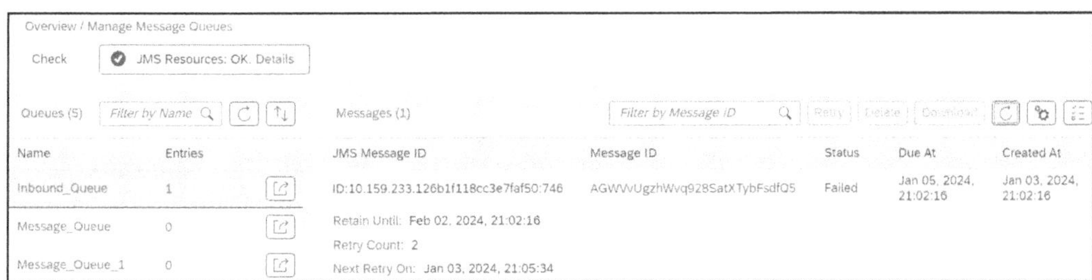

Figure 5.93 Message in Failed Status in Manage Message Queues Monitor

Message Processing Details

To access more details about the processing of this message and the error, you must check the message in the message processing monitor. To find a specific error, you can either search for the message ID shown in the message processing monitor or directly click the link for the **Message ID** that opens the **Message Processing** monitor for this specific message, as shown in Figure 5.94. Then, you'll see details about the message processing and the error information. Notice that the status of the message in the message processing monitor is **Retry**, indicating that this message isn't in a final status. In the **Error Details** for the message, details about the error from the last processing attempt are shown.

Correct the incorrect address configuration in the mail channel, and then save and deploy the iFlow. The next retry will consume the message and process it with the new configuration resulting in a successful execution. The emails finally arrive in your email account.

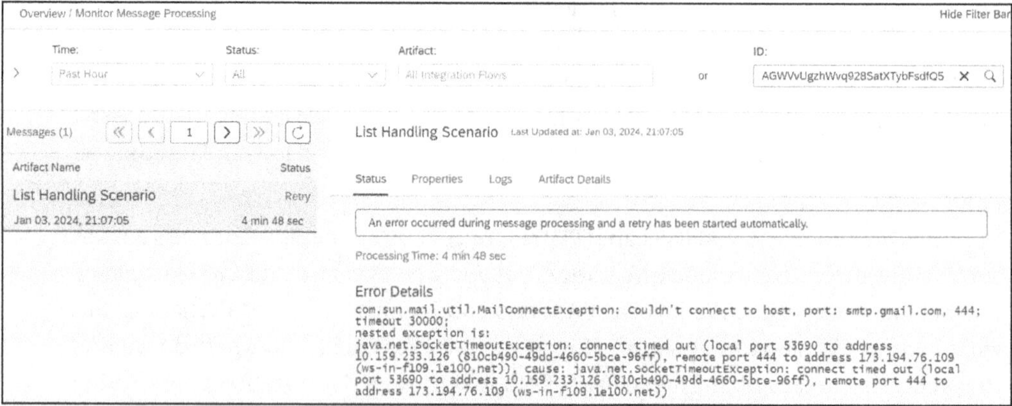

Figure 5.94 Message Processing Details for a Message in Retry Status

> **Triggering a Retry in the Manage Message Queues Monitor**
>
> If you don't want to wait for the expected next retry, you can initiate a retry in the **Manage Message Queues** monitor by selecting the **Retry** action for this message. Then, the next retry will be executed immediately, and the message will be processed.

Now, you can configure reliable messaging scenarios with decoupled inbound processing in Cloud Integration, ensuring that retries of the message are executed in Cloud Integration if errors arise during message processing. With this configuration, you've speeded up the processing time for the sender and ensured reliable messaging by using the retry functionality based on JMS queues offered by Cloud Integration.

5.4.2 Configuring Retry for Multiple Receivers

For the scenario configured in the previous section, the retry initiated directly after the inbound processing is sufficient because the message isn't sent to multiple receivers in parallel. However, in a parallel multicast scenario, where a message should be delivered to multiple receivers in parallel, you'll still have problems with some receivers getting duplicate messages if a temporary communication error occurs while sending a message to one of the receivers. To address this potential problem, we'll use separate outbound queues for each receiver to execute the retry only for the message going to the receiver that is temporarily not available, not for the other receivers.

To showcase this functionality, let's change the scenario slightly by simply sending the same message out to two receivers using the mail adapter. For ease of testing, we'll send both messages to the same email account using different subjects. Follow these steps:

1. Add another **End Message** event to the integration process configuring the main processing.

2. Select the dotted line representing the message flow from the **Send** step to the **Receiver**. The line will turn orange with small blue dots at the start and the end of the line. Select the blue dot at the **Send** step, and move it to the new **End** event. Now, the existing **Mail** channel is connected from the **End** event.
3. Reconfigure the **Mail** channel going to **Receiver2** to send the message payload instead of the status email: in the **Subject** field, enter "Message to Receiver2", and in the **Mail Body** field, include the message's payload, as shown in Figure 5.95.

Subject:	Message to Receiver2	
Mail Body:	${in.body}	Preview

Figure 5.95 Configuring the Subject and Mail Body in the Mail Adapter for Receiver2

4. Remove the **Send** step, and add a **Parallel Multicast** step instead. Draw a second line from the **Parallel Multicast** step to the new **End** event to configure the second multicast branch.

The changed part of the iFlow now looks similar to the flow shown in Figure 5.96.

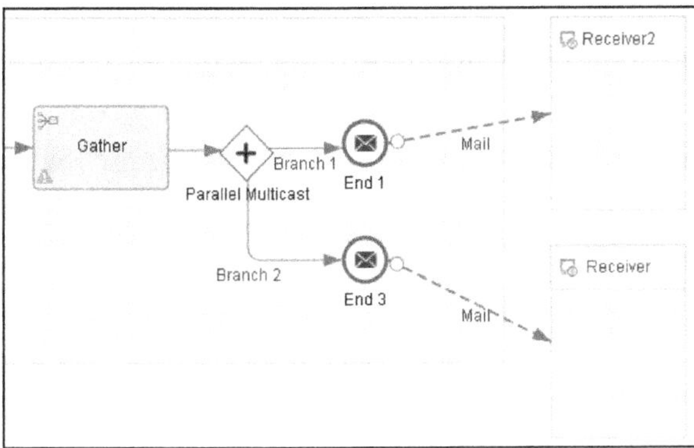

Figure 5.96 Configuration of a Parallel Multicast to Two Receivers

Save the changes, and deploy the iFlow. When triggering the iFlow from your SOAP test client, two emails will be sent to your email account—each representing the message flow in one of the two multicast branches and both containing the same message in the email's body.

To test the retry behavior triggered from the inbound JMS queue in this parallel multicast scenario, change the **Address** for one of the **Mail** channels to a configuration that doesn't work, for example, **smtp.gmail.com:444**. Save and deploy the iFlow. Call the iFlow from the SOAP test client. You now get the same email again and again, one for each retry triggered from the inbound JMS queue. Because the second **Mail** receiver can't be reached, the overall processing status of the message is **Retry**, so the message stays in the JMS queue and is retried according to the **Retry Details** configured in the **JMS** sender adapter.

The behavior of sending the message again and again in error situations may cause problems in the receiver system if the receiver can't handle duplicates. To make sure the receiver doesn't get the same message multiple times, we'll now change the scenario so that separate outbound queues are used for each of the receivers. Follow these steps:

1. Add a new **Integration Process** below the existing integration process. Remember, you'll find the **Integration Process** in the modeling palette under the **Process** shape.
2. In the new **Integration Process**, add a **Start Message** event and an **End Message** event from the **Events** shape. Connect the **Start** event with the **End** event.
3. Select the dotted line representing the message flow from the **End** event to **Receiver2** in the integration process doing the main processing. The line turns orange with small blue dots at the start and the end of the line. Select the blue dot at the **End** event and move it to the **End** event in the new integration process. Now, the existing **Mail** channel is connected from the **End** event of the new integration process.
4. Add a **Receiver** from the **Participant** shape to the model on the right side of the integration process doing the main processing.
5. Connect the **End** event of the integration process doing the main processing to the new **Receiver**. In the adapter selection screen, choose the **JMS** adapter.
6. In the **JMS** channel, under the **Processing** tab, enter "Outbound_Queue2" in the **Queue Name** field, and keep the default values for the other configuration settings, as shown in Figure 5.97.

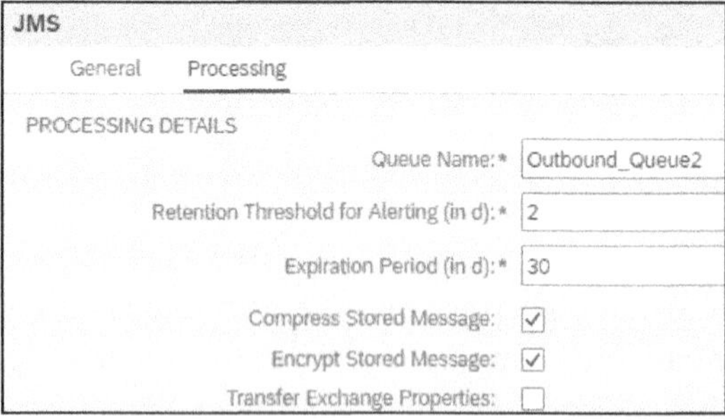

Figure 5.97 Configuration of the JMS Receiver Channel for Outbound Queue

7. Add a **Sender** from the **Participant** shape to the model on the left side of the new integration process.
8. Connect the **Sender** to the **Start** event of the new integration process. In the adapter selection screen, choose the **JMS** adapter.

9. In the **JMS** channel, under the **Processing** tab, in the **Queue Name** field, enter the same value as in the **JMS** receiver channel: "Outbound_Queue2". With the JMS outbound queue configured for the first receiver, the extended parts of the iFlow now look similar to the process shown in Figure 5.98.

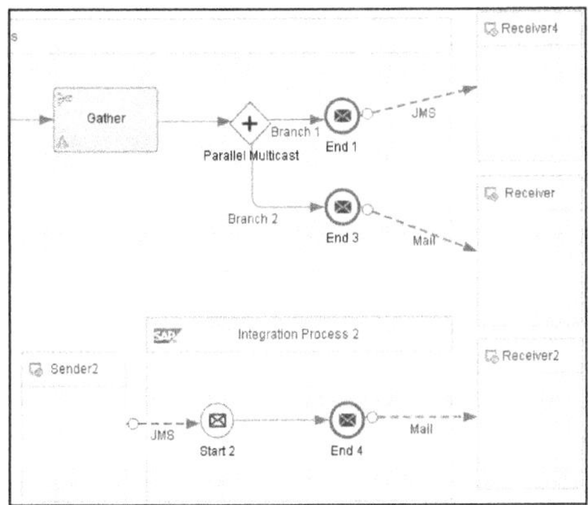

Figure 5.98 Configuration of JMS Outbound Queue for Receiver2

10. Create another **Integration Process** configuring a JMS outbound queue for **Receiver**. Execute the same configuration steps, move the existing **Mail** channel to the new integration process, and enter "Outbound_Queue1" in the **Queue Name** field in the **JMS** adapter. The configuration of the JMS outbound queues now looks similar to the process shown in Figure 5.99.

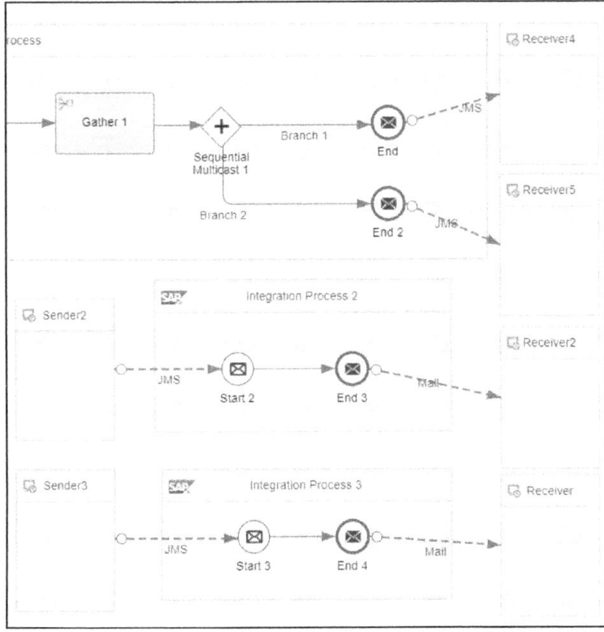

Figure 5.99 Configuration of JMS Outbound Queues for Both Receivers

11. Because we're using two **JMS** receiver channels in the same integration process, we must configure a JMS transaction handler. The transaction handler makes sure the message is either stored in both JMS queues consistently or in none of them; if an error arises, the whole transaction is rolled back. Select the integration process configuring the parallel multicast, and the properties for the integration process are shown in the **Properties** section. Under the **Processing** tab, the configuration options for transaction management are available. In the **Transaction Handling** dropdown list, you'll configure the transaction handler for the integration process, as shown in Figure 5.100, by choosing from among three available options:
    - **Required for JDBC**: Choose this option if Java Database Connectivity (JDBC)-transacted resources, such as **Data Store** steps, are used in the scenario, and you need to ensure end-to-end transactional processing in all steps accessing the database.
    - **Required for JMS**: Choose this option if, like in our scenario, JMS-transacted resources are used, and end-to-end transactional processing is required. We configured this setting for our integration process.
    - **Not Required**: Choose this option for most of the scenarios that don't use transaction resources and therefore don't require a transaction handler.

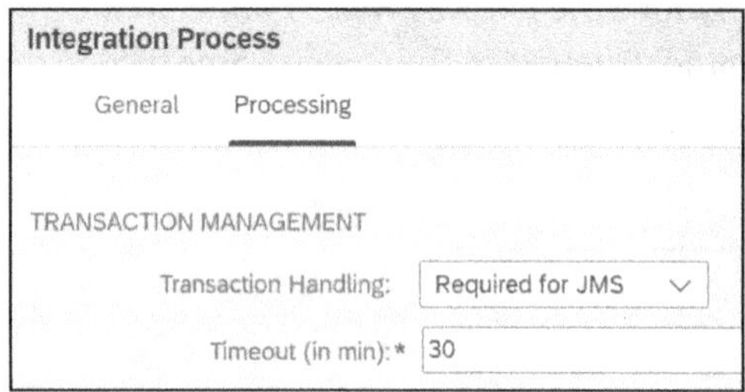

Figure 5.100 Configuration of Transaction Handling

If a transaction handler, JMS or JDBC, is configured, a **Timeout** needs to be defined. Because the number of transactions is limited in the database, in the JMS instance, this setting is required to make sure the transaction is stopped after some time and doesn't run forever. You must configure a timeout sufficient for your scenario but not too high, keeping the limit on transactions in mind. If the available number of transactions is reached in runtime, no new messages can be processed.

Configuration of Transaction Handling

In integration scenarios, you usually must ensure consistent end-to-end processing and roll back all actions in the database or in JMS queues consistently. These capabilities are ensured by a transaction handler. Cloud Integration offers two transaction handlers: one for JMS transactions and one for JDBC transactions. Distributed transactions between JMS and JDBC aren't supported in Cloud Integration. Recommendations and limitations using transaction handlers, including several sample scenarios, are explained in detail at *http://s-prs.co/507721*.

Save the changes made in the iFlow to trigger the check's execution for the iFlow. Notice that a check error is now shown for the main integration process; the error indicates that JMS transaction handling isn't allowed for parallel multicast, as shown in Figure 5.101.

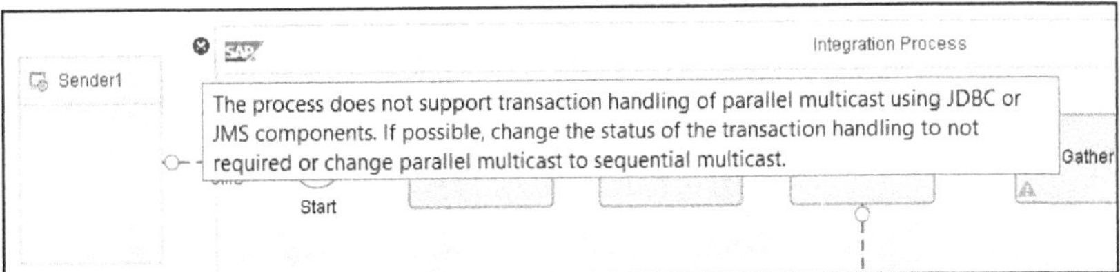

Figure 5.101 Error When Using JMS Transactions with Parallel Multicast

What is the background of this error, and what do we need to do? We already learned that the message is copied in the Cloud Integration's runtime in the parallel multicast pattern, and the different messages are processed independently in all branches leaving the multicast. The problem is that such independent requests can't be rolled back consistently. For our scenario, you must use sequential multicast and store the messages in the different JMS outbound queues one after the other. If an error happens, the whole process is rolled back, no messages are stored in the JMS outbound queues, and the processing starts again from the JMS inbound queue or the sender system if no JMS inbound queues are used. After successfully storing the messages to all the JMS outbound queues, the consumption of the messages from the JMS outbound queues is executed in parallel for each of the receivers.

Make the necessary changes by following these steps:

1. Remove the **Parallel Multicast** step, and add a **Sequential Multicast** step instead.
2. Reconnect the **Gather** to the **Parallel Multicast** step, and connect the **Parallel Multicast** to the two **End** events.

The final iFlow now looks similar to the process shown in Figure 5.102.

Save and deploy the iFlow, and trigger the integration process from your SOAP test client. Now, you'll get only one email, the one processed by the mail adapter that is configured correctly. The message for the second receiver, the one with the wrong configuration, is now available in the JMS outbound queue for this receiver, as shown in Figure 5.103, and is retried from this queue. If the message in **Failed** status from the last scenario execution is still available in the JMS inbound queue, it will be retried at the next retry time, or you can trigger an immediate retry in the **Manage Message Queues** monitor.

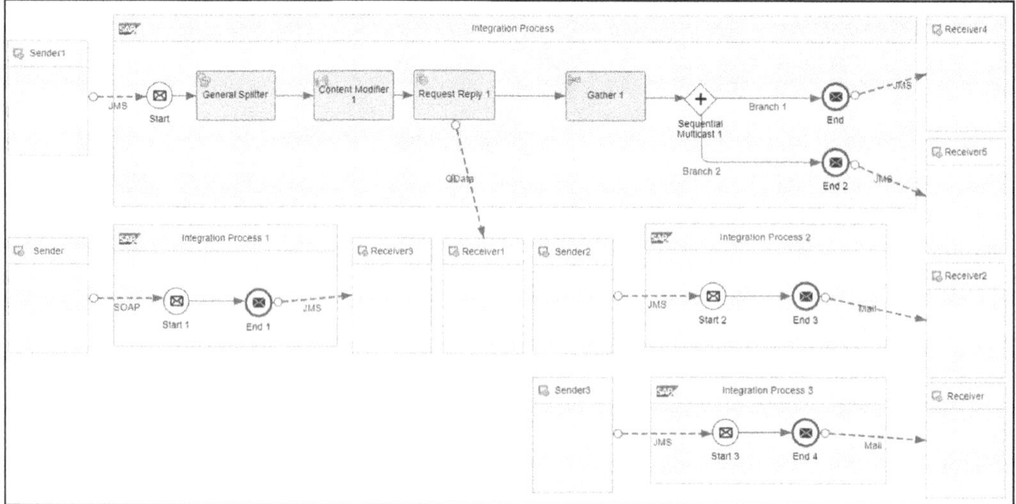

Figure 5.102 iFlow with Sequential Multicast and JMS Outbound Queues

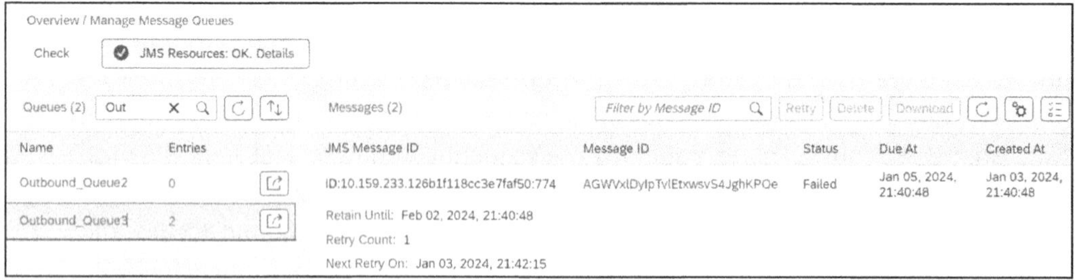

Figure 5.103 Message in the JMS Outbound Queue in Failed Status in the Manage Message Queues Monitor

Configuration Option: Use Separate Integration Flows

We configured the different integration processes for storing the messages in a JMS queue and consuming from the JMS queue in one single iFlow, but they can also be configured in different iFlows instead. When separate iFlows are used, you'll be more flexible when changes and redeployments of the iFlow are necessary.

You've now successfully set up a reliable messaging scenario using inbound and outbound JMS queues, inbound processing of your scenario is decoupled from further processing of the message in Cloud Integration, and sending to multiple receivers is executed asynchronously using a separate JMS outbound queue for each receiver. You've significantly shortened the processing time for the sender and ensured reliable messaging to multiple receivers using the retry capabilities based on JMS queues offered by Cloud Integration.

5.4.3 Configuring Explicit Retry with Alternative Processing

Depending on the scenario or the receiver system, you may want to retry the message only a few times and then perform alternative processing of the message. This scenario isn't possible with the default retry configuration offered in the JMS sender channel: the JMS sender adapter retries the message forever. However, Cloud Integration offers the option to configure explicit retry handling by using an exception subprocess. In this section, we'll extend our scenario and configure explicit retry handling in the process, sending the message to one of the receivers.

To extend the iFlow to support explicit retry configuration, you must create a local integration process that contains the configuration for the retry. More details about using local integration processes will be shared in Chapter 6. To extend the iFlow, follow these steps:

1. Add a **Local Integration Process** below the existing integration processes by choosing it from the modeling palette under the **Process** shape. Under the **General** tab, enter the name "Retry Configuration" to give the local process a meaningful name.
2. In the new **Local Integration Process**, add a **Router** from the **Message Routing** shape between the **Start** and **End** events. Add an **Error End** event from the **Events** shape below the newly added **Router** step. Connect the **Router** step to the **Error End** event, as shown in Figure 5.104.

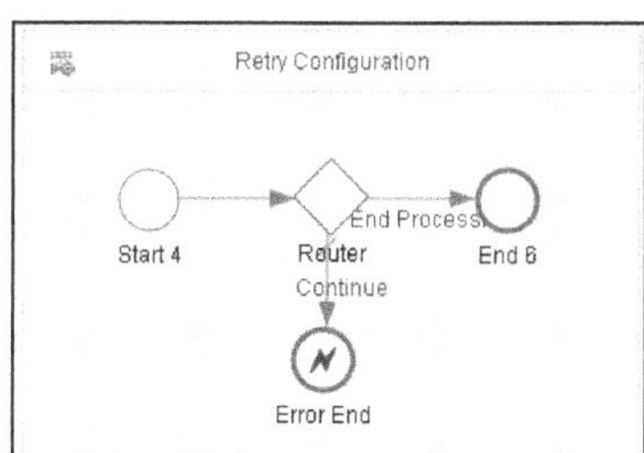

Figure 5.104 Configuration of a Local Integration Process

3. The JMS sender adapter sets the header `SAPJMSRetries` at runtime. This header allows you to configure a specific retry behavior and contains the number of retries that already are executed. Based on the value of this header, you can configure whether the message processing continues or ends. If you configure it to end, you can also configure an alternate process for the message in the **Router** step. As a simple example, let's say we want to specify that, after five retries, the message is sent via email to an administrator, and no further retries are executed from the JMS queue. We'll configure the two routes leaving the **Router** step, as shown in Figure 5.105:
   - In the route going to the **End** event, we'll define a **Non-XML** condition based on the `SAPJMSRetries` header: `${header.SAPJMSRetries} > '5'`. With this configuration, the route to the **End** event is executed as soon as the value of the `SAPJMSRetries` header is larger than `5`. Thus, with the sixth retry (`SAPJMSRetries = 6`), the

message is routed to the **End** event, which ends the processing. The message goes to the status **Completed** and is removed from the JMS queue.

– The route to the **Error End** event we'll define as the default route so that, during runtime, the message is routed to the **Error End** event as long as the value of `SAPJMSRetries` is smaller than 6. The **Error End** event raises an error and makes sure the message stays in the JMS queue, and the message gets the status **Retry**.

4. Add an **Exception Subprocess** from the **Process** shape to the outbound integration process connected to the **Receiver** for which we want to configure alternative processing. This **Exception Subprocess** is supposed to catch the error in the outbound processing.

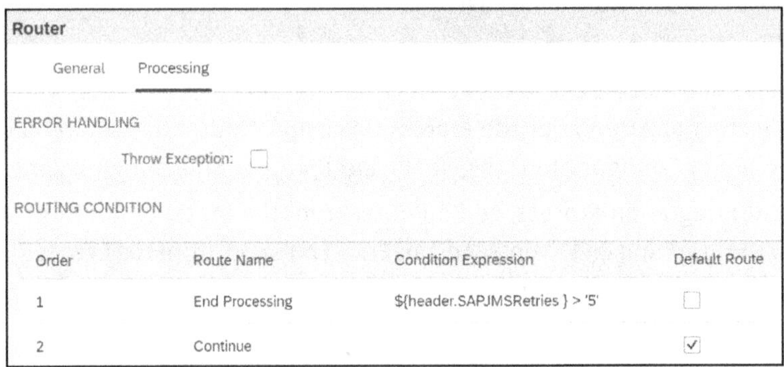

Figure 5.105 Configuration of Router Step in Local Integration Subprocess

5. Add a **Process Call** (from the **Call** shape, submenu **Local Call**), and place it between the **Error Start** event and the **End** event of the newly added **Exception Subprocess**. In the properties area for the **Process Call**, select the local integration process **Retry Configuration**, which we created before, as shown in Figure 5.106.

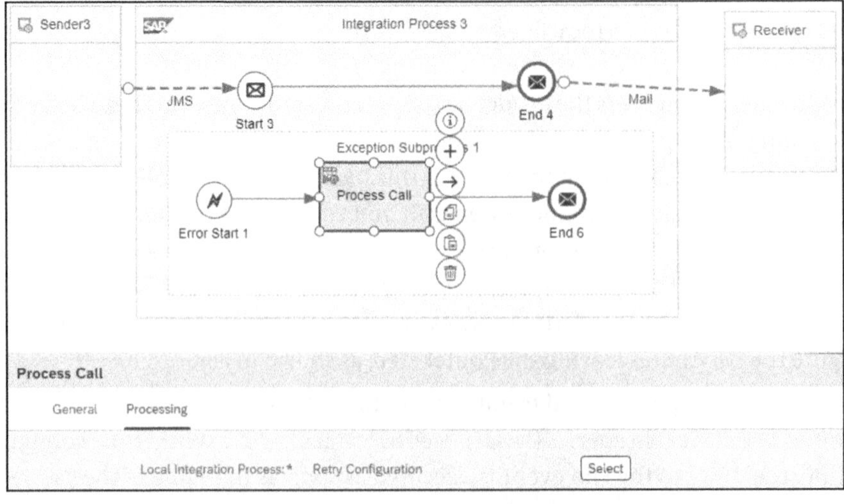

Figure 5.106 Configuration of the Process Call in the Exception Subprocess

6. Add a **Receiver**, available under the **Participant** shape, and place it on the right side of the integration process that contains the **Exception Subprocess**. In the properties for the **Receiver**, enter "Administrator" in the **Name** field. Draw a line from the **End** event of the **Exception Subprocess** to the newly added **Receiver**, and select the **Mail** adapter in the adapter selection screen.
7. Under the **Connection** tab of the **Mail** adapter, configure the **Connection Details** according to your email account and the **Mail Attributes**, as shown in Figure 5.107. For ease of testing, you can use the same email account to send the email created for the administrator too, but you'll use a different **Subject** to identify that this email is meant for the administrator.

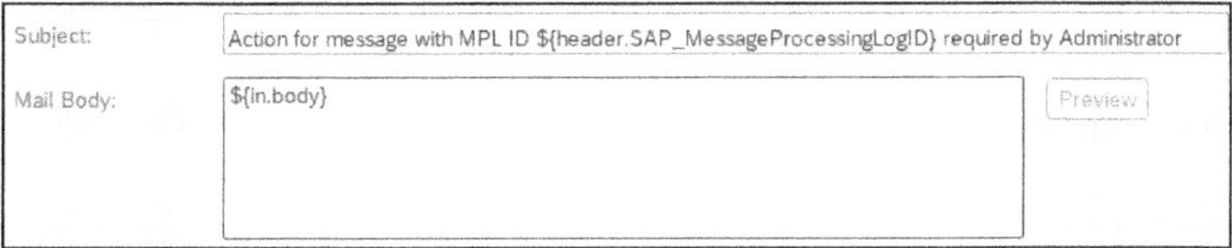

Figure 5.107 Configuring the Mail Adapter for the Administrator

The iFlow containing all of its integration processes, the local process, and the exception process should now look similar to the iFlow shown in Figure 5.108.

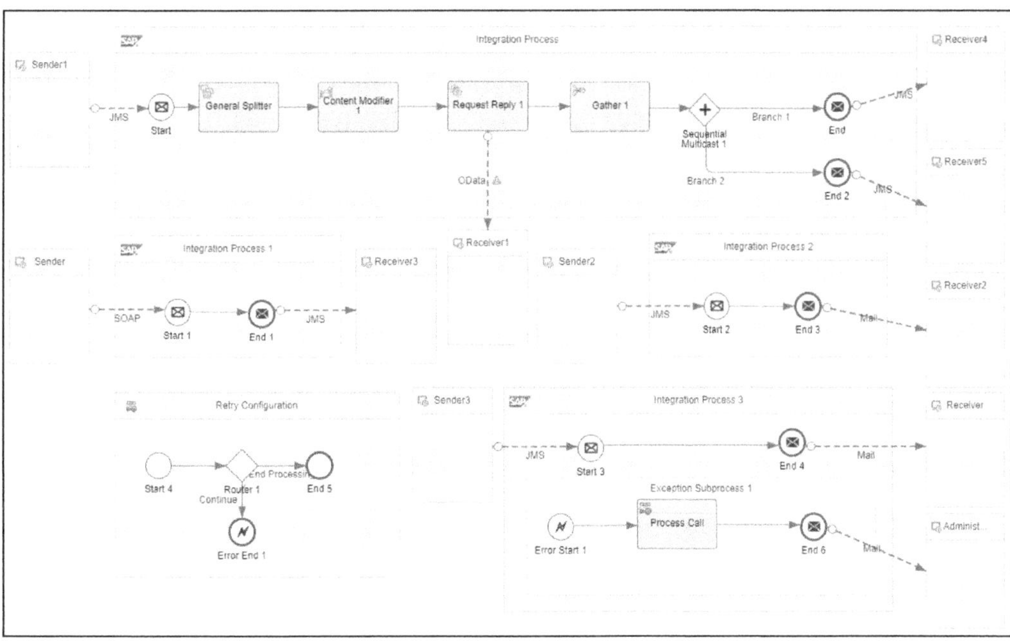

Figure 5.108 iFlow with Explicit Retry Configuration in Exception Subprocess

Save and deploy the iFlow. Now, we'll use the iFlow to test the runtime and the retry behavior by triggering the processing from the SOAP test client. Adjust the **Address** in the different **Mail** adapter channels to raise an error during runtime to trigger the retries configured.

Successful End-to-End Processing

First, we need to test a successful scenario execution. Make sure the **Address** field is correct in both **Mail** adapter channels, save and deploy the iFlow, and trigger the iFlow from your SOAP test client.

The messages are sent successfully to both receivers, and you'll receive two emails after a short time, both containing the same message in the email's body. However, the emails have different subjects: **Book Demo Msg** (for **Receiver1**) and **Message to Receiver2** (for **Receiver2**), as configured in the **Mail** adapter channels for the two receivers. These emails indicate that the end-to-end processing of the message has been executed without error, and the messages were sent asynchronously to both receivers.

Let's look at the Cloud Integration's monitoring dashboard to understand what happens during runtime. Open the **Message Processing** monitor. As shown in Figure 5.109, four entries appear for this single scenario execution, which may be surprising, but understandable when you consider the end-to-end scenario configuration and the fact that Cloud Integration writes a separate MPL for each integration process. The scenario consists of four integration processes: one integration process for inbound processing and storing the message in the JMS inbound queue, one integration process for the main processing and storing the message in the two JMS outbound queues for the two receivers, and one integration process for each of the two receivers. For each of these processes, a separate log entry is created in message monitoring.

To make end-to-end monitoring easier, the four MPLs are correlated by a **Correlation ID**, which is shown below the **Message ID** in the **Properties** of each MPL. As shown in Figure 5.109, you can search for all MPLs having the same correlation ID using the **ID** field in the search criteria.

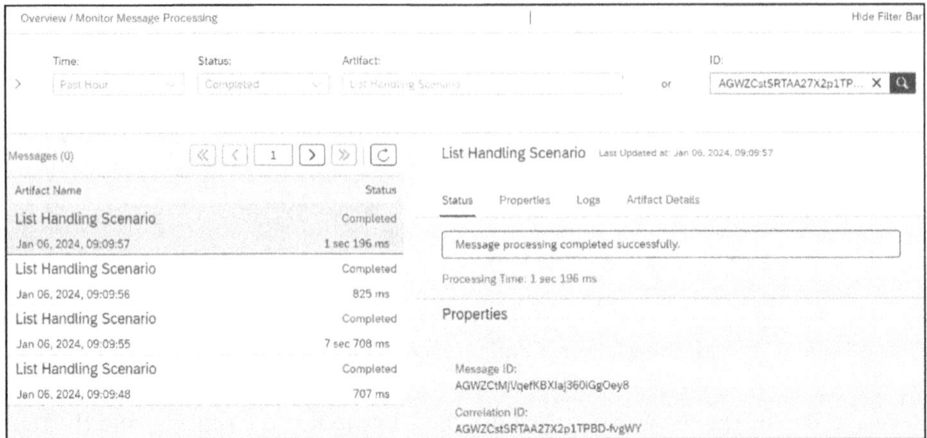

Figure 5.109 Message Processing Monitor for Successful Execution

All four MPLs have the status **Completed**, indicating that the message was executed successfully in all four integration processes.

In the **Manage Message Queues** monitor, no message should appear in any of the involved JMS queues because the messages have been consumed and successfully processed.

Error Sending Message to Receiver2

We'll now change the **Address** field in the **Mail** adapter channel connected to the **Receiver** with the name **Receiver2** to simulate processing to a broken **Receiver2**. Save and deploy the iFlow, and trigger the iFlow from your SOAP test client.

Because the message is successfully sent to the **Receiver**, you'll get one email with the subject **Book Demo Msg**. However, the other message expected to be sent to **Receiver2** remains in the JMS outbound queue **Outbound_Queue2** configured for **Receiver2** and is retried according to the retry configuration in the JMS sender channel.

In the Cloud Integration's monitoring dashboard, for this execution, you'll again see four entries in the **Message Processing** monitor, one for each process execution. The first three MPLs have the status **Completed**, but the most recent entry has the status **Retry**, as shown in Figure 5.110, which we expected because the message to **Receiver2** is being retried from the JMS queue.

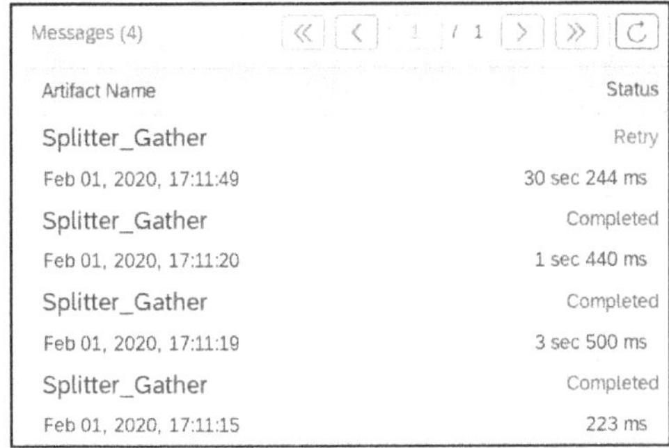

Figure 5.110 Message Processing Monitor for Erroneous Execution

As shown in Figure 5.111, the message can be found in the **Manage Message Queues** monitor in the **Outbound_Queue2** queue with the status **Failed**, providing information about the retries already executed and the time of the next retry.

To clean up the **Manage Message Queues** monitor in preparation for the next test, you have two options: First, you can correct the **Mail** adapter's **Address** configuration, redeploy the iFlow, and retry the message by using the **Retry** action in the **Manage Message Queues** monitor. Second, you can delete the message from the JMS queue using the **Delete** action in the **Manage Message Queues** monitor. Otherwise, the message is retried again and again until finally deleted after exceeding the **Retention Threshold** defined in the JMS receiver channel.

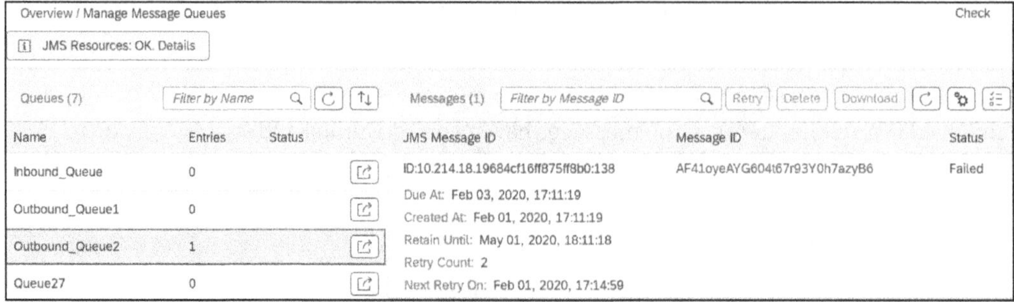

Figure 5.111 Message in Error in Outbound_Queue2 in the Manage Message Queues Monitor

Error Sending Message to Receiver

In the next test, we'll change the **Address** field in the **Mail** adapter channel connected to the **Receiver** with the name **Receiver** to a configuration that doesn't work. With this configuration, we're simulating processing to a **Receiver** that is broken. If not already done, correct the address in the **Mail** adapter channel for **Receiver2** to make sure the message to this receiver can be sent successfully. Save and deploy the iFlow, and trigger the iFlow from your SOAP test client.

Because the message is successfully sent to **Receiver2**, you'll get one email with the subject **Message to Receiver2**. About an hour later (because of the configured six retries with **Exponential Backoff**), you'll get an email with the subject indicating that the message must be processed by the administrator.

If you check the **Message Processing** monitor directly after scenario execution, you'll see the same message processing status as in the last test: three entries with the status **Completed** and the most recent entry with the status **Retry**. This time, the message that is being retried is the message to the **Receiver**. In the **Manage Message Queues** monitor, you'll see a message in the **Outbound_Queue1** with the status **Failed**, as shown in Figure 5.112.

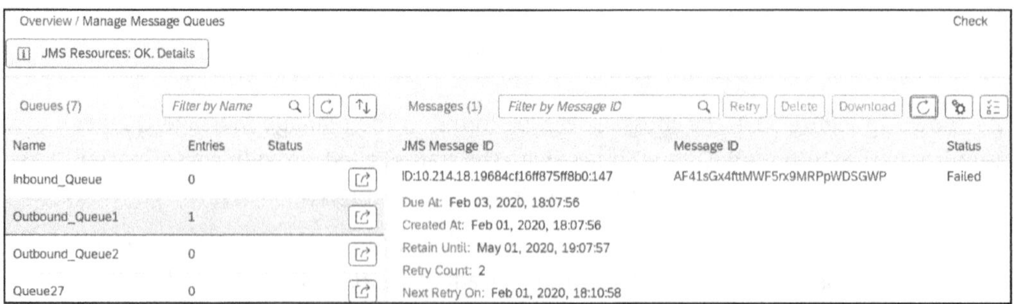

Figure 5.112 Message in Error in Outbound_Queue1 in Manage Message Queues Monitor

If you check the **Message Processing** monitor again after you receive the second email that is targeted for the administrator, you'll see that all four entries in the monitor have the status **Completed** now. All retries have been executed in the same MPL entry; no new log is created so that monitoring is easier. The sixth retry, still running in an error, triggered the alternative route and completed the message.

Error Sending to the OData Receiver

Sometimes, not only can the final connection to the receivers be broken, but errors can occur during the other message processing steps as well. In our scenario, for example, the **Request Reply** call to the OData receiver could fail. To see how the iFlow copes with this error, change the **Address** field in the **OData** adapter channel to a configuration that doesn't work. Save and deploy the iFlow, and trigger the iFlow from your SOAP test client.

For this execution, you won't get any emails because the message processing in Cloud Integration didn't even get to the outbound processing. This time, the main processing and the enrichment of the message with the additional data from the OData service could not be executed.

In the **Message Processing** monitor, you'll only see two entries this time, as shown in Figure 5.113, one with status **Completed** for the integration process storing the message in the JMS inbound queue, and one with status **Retry** for the integration process doing the main processing. So, the message in the **Manage Message Queues** monitor in the **Inbound_Queue** has the status **Failed**, as shown in Figure 5.114, and the retries are triggered from this JMS queue.

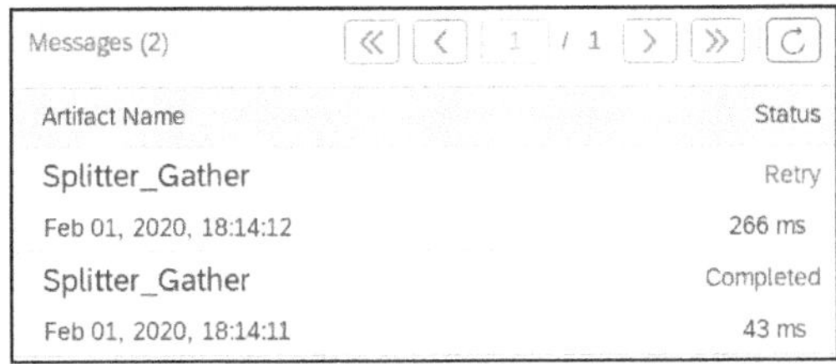

Figure 5.113 Message Processing Monitor for Errors in OData Connection

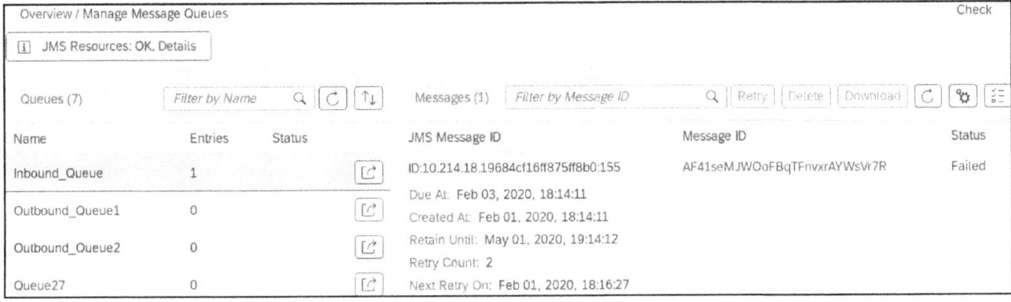

Figure 5.114 Message in Error in Inbound_Queue in Manage Message Queues Monitor

Delete the message from the JMS queue to stop the retries; otherwise, the message is retried again and again until finally deleted after exceeding the **Retention Threshold** defined in the JMS receiver channel.

At this point, you've successfully set up a reliable messaging scenario using inbound and JMS outbound queues. We showed you the different options for configuring retries from JMS queues: either defining the retry configuration in the JMS sender channel or modeling an explicit retry configuration in an exception subprocess. In the next section, you'll learn about the XI adapters.

5.5 SAP Process Integration and the XI Adapters

SAP Process Integration is one of the common protocols supported by various SAP backend applications. These backends often used proxy-based communication to exchange SAP Process Integration messages with the SAP Process Orchestration adapter engine. The message protocol is based on the W3C SOAP Message with Attachments standard. It's therefore made of three main components: SOAP header, body, and attachments.

To facilitate connection to the backend applications that support the SAP Process Integration protocol, Cloud Integration has provided the XI adapters. The XI sender adapter is used to receive messages, and the XI receiver adapter is used to send messages to backend systems such as SAP ERP.

Note

Configuring an end-to-end SAP Process Integration scenario also requires configurations in the backend systems. We won't cover these steps in this book. To learn more about setting up a scenario with XI sender adapter, refer to the SAP Blog at *http://s-prs.co/v576011*.

To learn more about setting up a scenario with the XI receiver adapter, refer to the SAP Blog at *http://s-prs.co/v576012*.

In the next section, you'll learn about the event pattern and how it can be implemented using the SAP Integration Suite, advanced event mesh adapter.

5.6 Using Event-Driven Messaging

So far in this chapter, you've learned a lot about several different message integration patterns, synchronous and asynchronous messaging, splitting and aggregating messages, and several multicast scenarios. Now, we'll introduce another integration pattern that has become increasingly important recently: *event-driven message integration*, also known as *event-based messaging*. In the scenarios we've discussed so far, a message is usually sent from a sender system to one or more receiver systems, via Cloud Integration, where message conversions, routing, and other processing steps are performed. In other words, the message is triggered by the sender of the message, and the receiver can't influence the time when message processing occurs. Furthermore, the receiver must provide an endpoint that can be called externally, which is sometimes undesirable for security reasons.

You may remember that we already mentioned one integration pattern where the receiver initiates the message processing. Recall our earlier discussion, in Section 5.4.1, on the push-pull pattern, in which messages are pushed by a sender system to Cloud Integration, where the messages are stored until pulled later by the receiver system. In this scenario, the receiver initiates the pulling of the messages, which is usually performed using a scheduler that triggers these pulls according to a predefined time schedule. You can imagine that this kind of pulling is quite inefficient because you either must pull very frequently or messages are received with a certain delay.

The much more effective way to handle receiver-initiated processing is the *publish-subscribe pattern*, where the sender publishes messages or events and the receiver consumes them. In this section, we'll build an easy, event-based publish-subscribe scenario using the AMQP adapter offered in Cloud Integration.

5.6.1 Configuring a Publish-Subscribe Scenario

To understand the publish-subscribe pattern, we'll first introduce you to some important terms used in this integration pattern. Let's use the sample publish-subscribe scenario shown in Figure 5.115 to understand how the different parties usually work together.

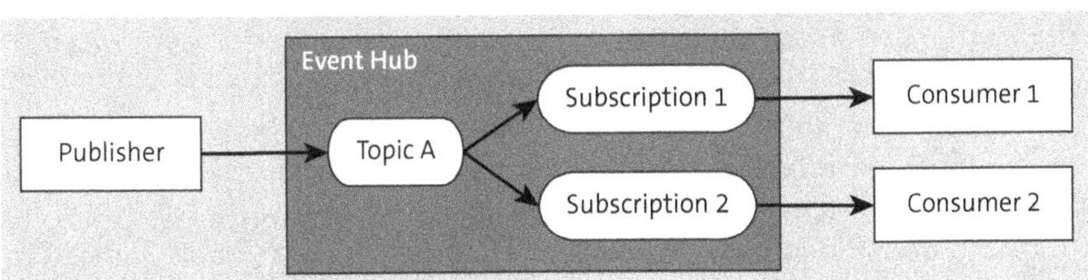

Figure 5.115 Publish-Subscribe Pattern

The publish-subscribe pattern involves the following elements:

- **Publisher/provider/producer**
  The sender of a message in a publish-subscribe pattern is called a *publisher* (aka provider or producer). This element sends the message or the event to the event hub.
- **Event**
  In publish-subscribe patterns, information—that is, messages or events—is sent by

the publisher. Whereas messages contain the whole business data, events are usually only small trigger messages to initiate follow-up actions in other systems or applications. For example, when a change to a business partner occurs in one system, other systems must be updated as well. To keep all systems in sync, the sender system publishes a `BusinessPartner.Changed` event, and whichever other systems are interested in this change can consume the event. Usually, the event only contains the ID of a change, in this case, the ID of the business partner. The real business data is fetched afterwards, directly from the sender system.

- **Event hub**
  The *event hub* (sometimes also called event bus) is an element of the infrastructure that can handle events sent by multiple publishers and allows consumers to read the events whenever they want. Whereas all messaging systems can act as event hubs, some providers offer special solutions optimized for high-speed event processing.
- **Consumer**
  The receiver of a message or event is called a *consumer*. This element consumes messages or events from the event hub.
- **Topic**
  Events are published to *topics* in the event hub. A topic is unique throughout the event hub and usually collects events with a specific pattern. The events published to a specific topic are immediately consumed by all consumers that have subscribed to the topic. If a consumer isn't available when the event is published, the consumer won't receive it.
- **Subscription**
  To consume a message or an event from a topic, a subscription to this event needs to be registered with the topic. Using this subscription, the consumer receives the message or event.
- **Queue**
  Queues can be used to store messages and events in a messaging system or event hub. A message or event is consumed from a queue by exactly one consumer. Queues are unique within the event hub and can subscribe to a topic to store the topic's messages or events for later consumption by the consumer. With this capability, the final receiver can consume the message or event even if unavailable at the time the event was published.

In the scenario shown in Figure 5.115, the publisher sends an event to **Topic A** in the event hub. Two subscriptions, **Subscription 1** and **Subscription 2**, are subscribed to this topic, so each subscription receives the same events published by the publisher. The two final receivers, **Consumer 1** and **Consumer 2**, consume the events from the two subscriptions independently of each other.

Now that you understand the basics of the publish-subscribe pattern, let's build a small sample scenario. In our scenario, the `SalesOrder.Changed` event is published by an application and consumed by Cloud Integration. You can either use a real backend to publish the event, for example, an SAP S/4HANA Cloud system, or you can simply use an HTTP client to send the event. For the sake of simplicity, we'll describe the latter option in this section.

In this section, we'll build the target scenario shown in Figure 5.116. We'll trigger the event from an HTTP client tool (e.g., Postman) to the SAP Integration Suite, advanced event mesh, where the event is stored in a queue. Cloud Integration consumes the event using the SAP integration suite, advanced event mesh sender adapter and sends a mail message to your mailbox. After successfully sending the mail, an event is sent back to the event hub using the SAP Integration Suite, advanced event mesh receiver adapter.

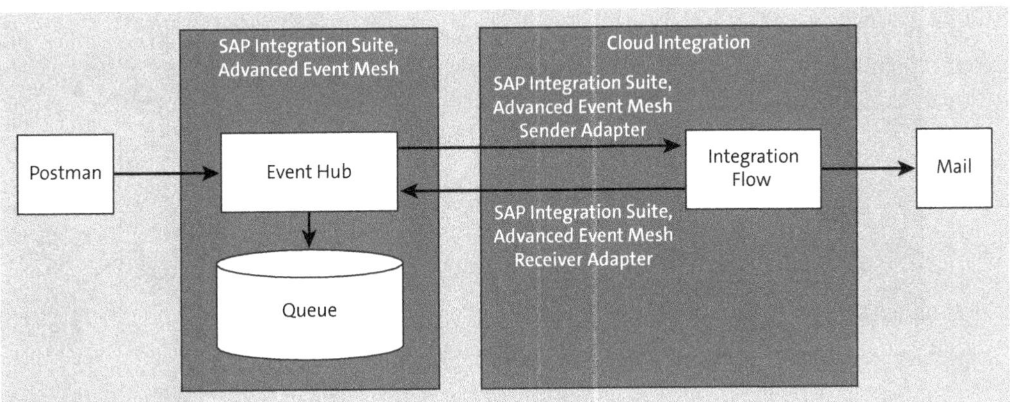

Figure 5.116 Target Scenario

Our first step is to set up an event hub that can act as the infrastructure to manage and process events.

Setting Up SAP Integration Suite, Advanced Event Mesh as an Event Hub

As described earlier, to manage the messages or events exchanged between systems, an event hub is required. The messaging system we'll use in our scenario is SAP Integration Suite, advanced event mesh . If you haven't purchased SAP Integration Suite, advanced event mesh, you're free to use any other messaging system, such as Microsoft Azure Service Bus. In this case, you'll need to execute the steps for creating queues and subscriptions in that system.

If you haven't already, create an instance of SAP Integration Suite, advanced event mesh as described under **Getting Started** at *http://s-prs.co/v576013*. The home screen of SAP Integration Suite, advanced event mesh looks similar to Figure 5.117.

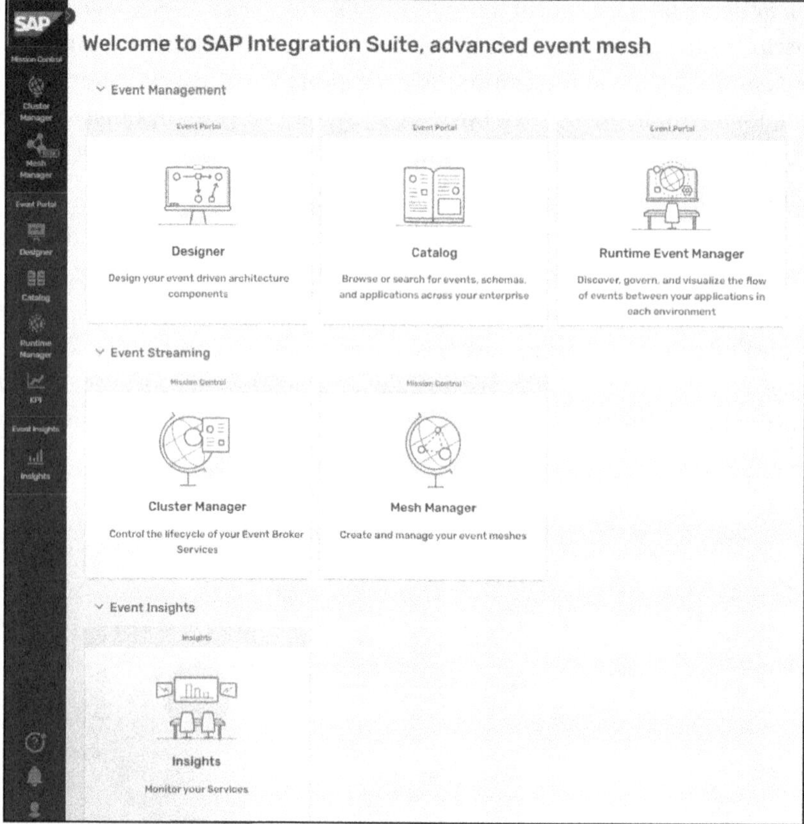

Figure 5.117 Home Screen of SAP Integration Suite, Advanced Event Mesh

Our next step is to create an event broker service by clicking on the **Cluster Manager** tile on the left side of the Cloud Console. This will open the **Cluster Manager** screen as shown in Figure 5.118. Click on the **Create Service** button on the top right of the screen.

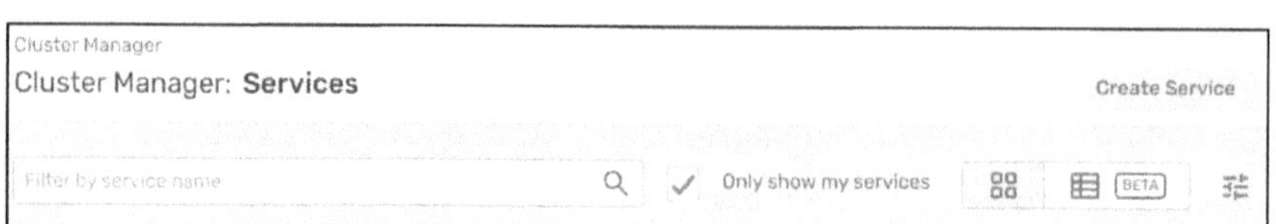

Figure 5.118 Cluster Manager screen

If you're working with a trial of SAP Integration Suite, advanced event mesh, then select **Developer** under **Service Type**; otherwise, select **Standard**. Figure 5.119 shows the selection option of **Developer**, which allows **100 Connections** and **10 GB Message Storage**.

The next step is to select a cloud service provider, region, and data center for hosting your event broker service. We've selected **EKS-EU Frankfurt** for our service, as shown in Figure 5.120.

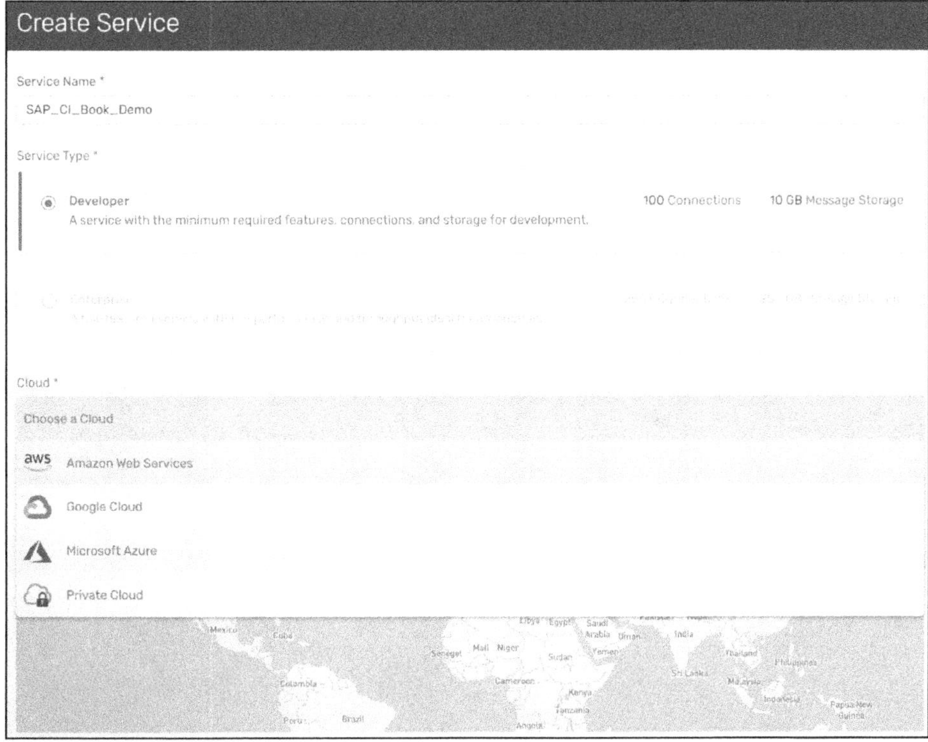

Figure 5.119 Creating a Service under the Cluster Manager Option

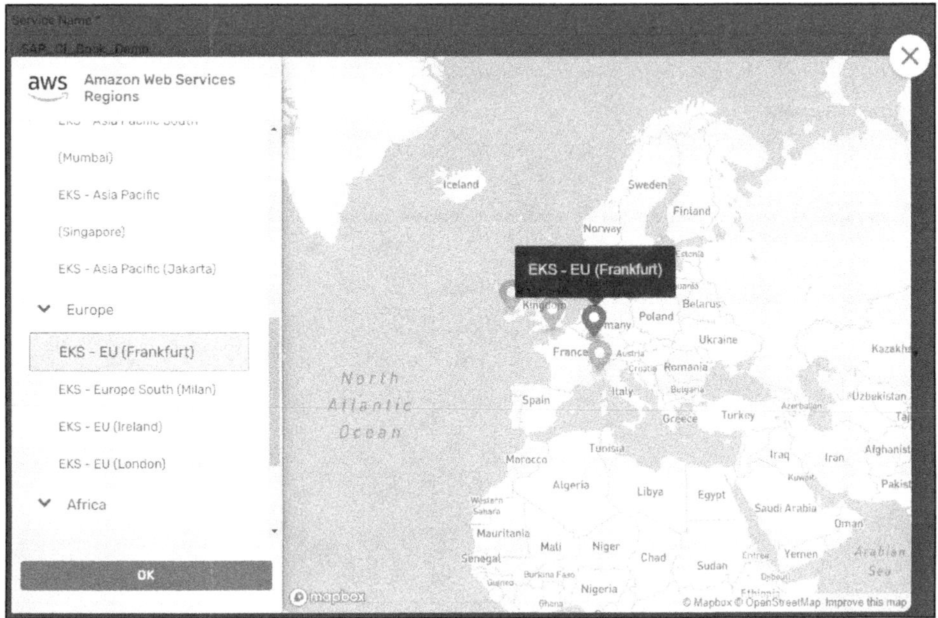

Figure 5.120 Selecting a Region and Data Center from the Map

Leave the **Broker Version** as default (see Figure 5.121).

Figure 5.121 Selecting the Default Broker Version

Click on **Create Service** on the bottom right of the page. It might take a few minutes for your event broker service to become available. Once up and running, you'll be redirected to the event broker service information page, as shown in Figure 5.122. Observe the multiple tabs on the top of the screen. The **Status** tab gives you a lot of details about the properties of the broker such as its version, availability, creation information, and so on.

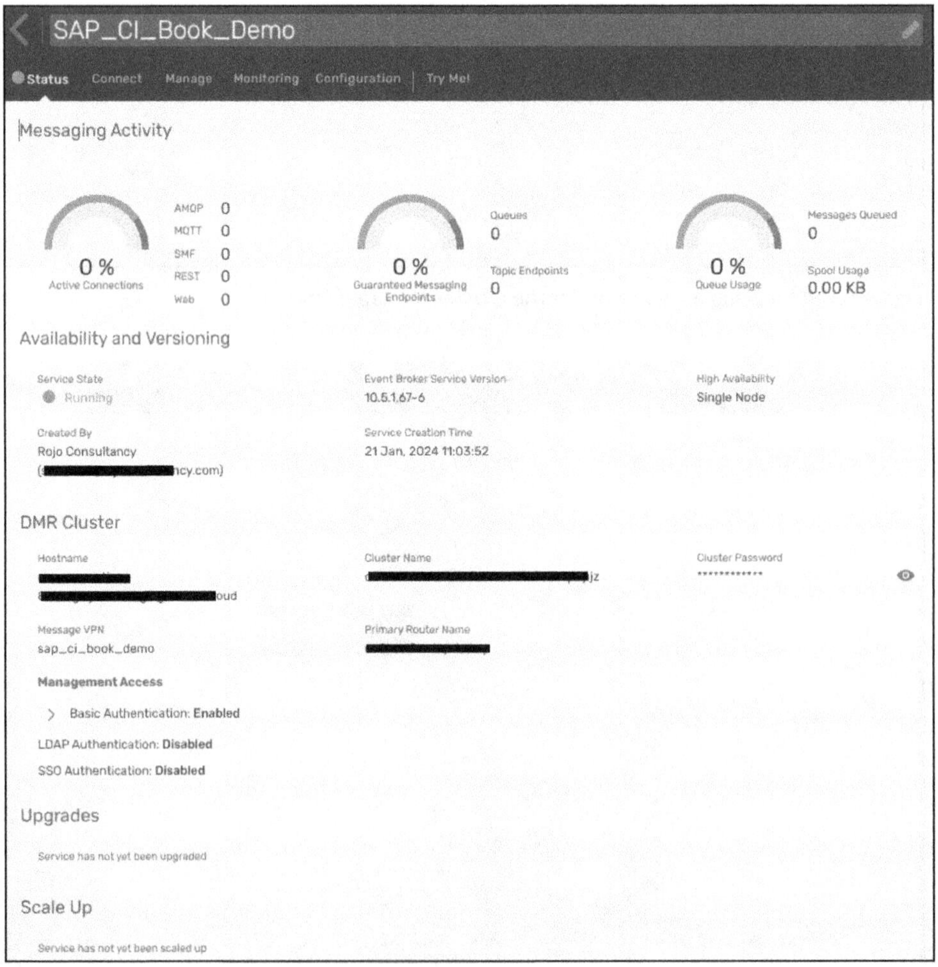

Figure 5.122 Event Broker Service Information Screen

To manage the event broker service, navigate to the **Manage** tab. From here, you can manage queues and subscriptions, authentication, clients, Message VPN, and so on.

Click the **Queues** tile to create a queue, as shown in Figure 5.123. From this queue, the iFlow will later consume events.

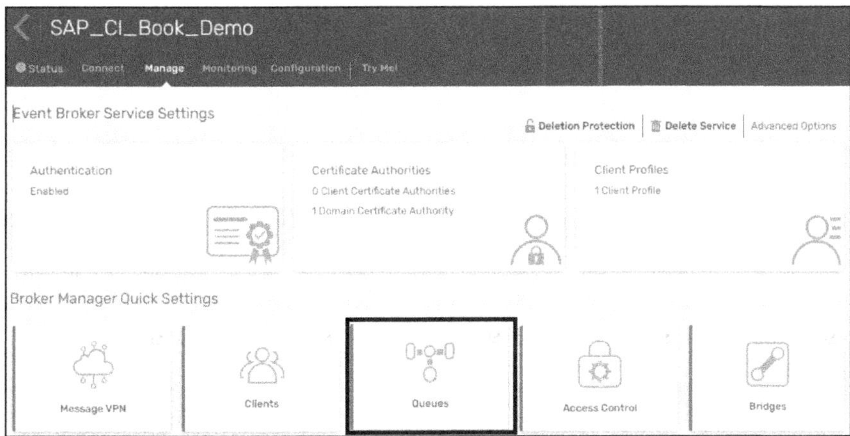

Figure 5.123 Manage Tab of Event Broker Service: Queues Tile

You'll be navigated to the broker manager interface where you can see all available queues and topic endpoints, as shown in Figure 5.124.

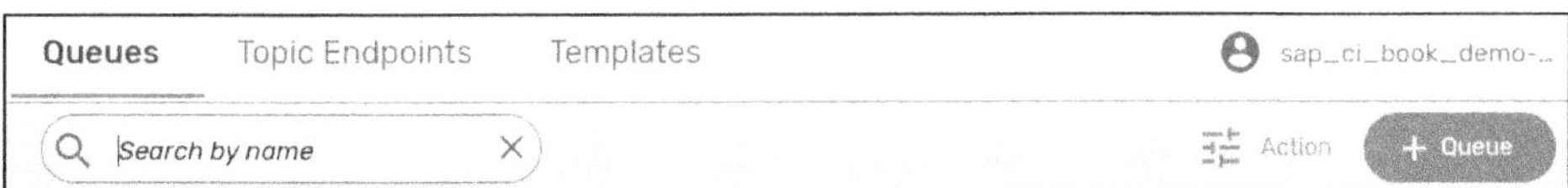

Figure 5.124 Queue Home Screen

Click on the **+Queue** button on the top right of the screen to open the **Create Queue** dialog box shown in Figure 5.125. Enter the name "SalesOrderEvents", and click **Create**.

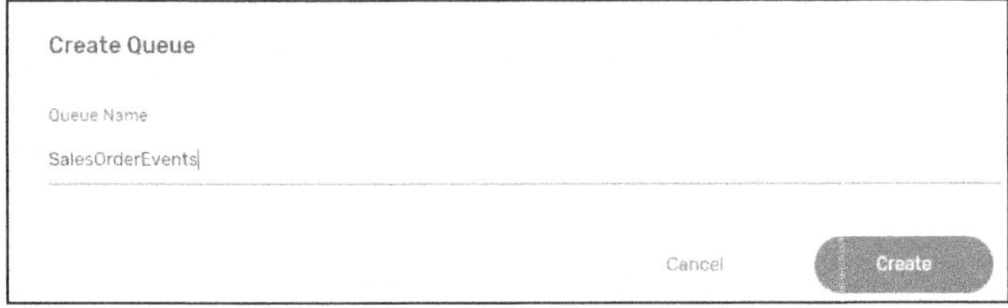

Figure 5.125 Create Queue Dialog Box

Once the queue is created, you can modify its properties from the **Edit Queue Settings** screen shown in Figure 5.126. For this exercise, leave all the queue settings as default. Keep in mind, in real-life scenarios, these settings play a crucial role in defining the usage of the queue.

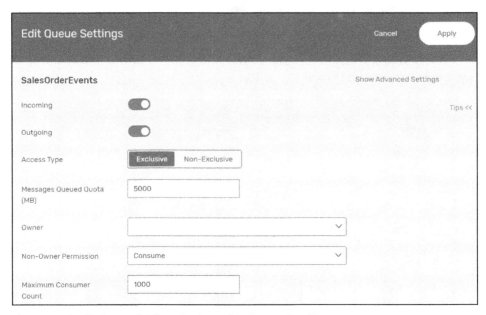

Figure 5.126 Edit Queue Settings Options after Queue Creation

Click **Apply** to finish the process of queue creation. You should see your newly created queue in the list of available queues now. Note that there are no messages in the queue yet, so the **Messages Queued (msgs)** column shows **0** (see Figure 5.127).

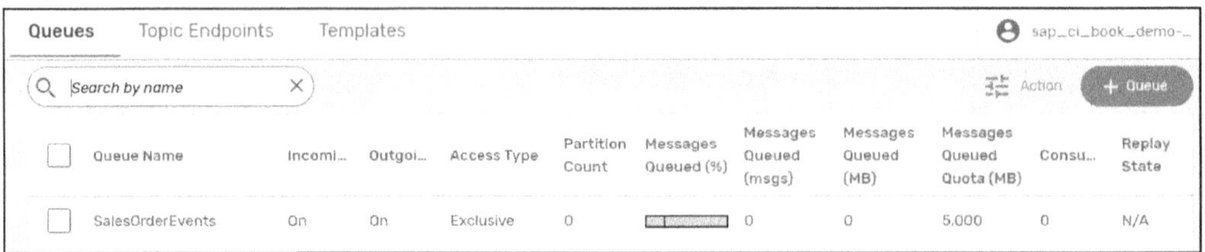

Figure 5.127 List of Available Queues

The next step is to create a topic for this queue. Click on the **SalesOrderEvents** queue, and navigate to the **Subscriptions** tab, as shown in Figure 5.128. This screen will list all available subscriptions for the selected queue. In our case, the list is empty as we don't have any subscriptions yet.

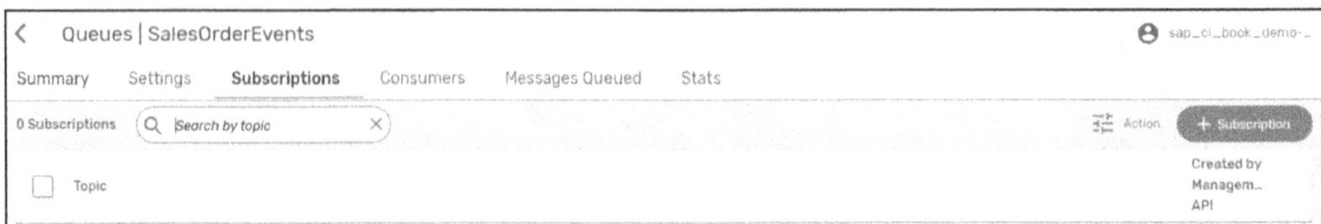

Figure 5.128 List of Available Subscriptions for a Queue

Click on the **+Subscription** button on the top right of the screen. Let's give this new subscription the name "SalesOrderTopic", as shown in Figure 5.129. Click **Create** to create the subscription.

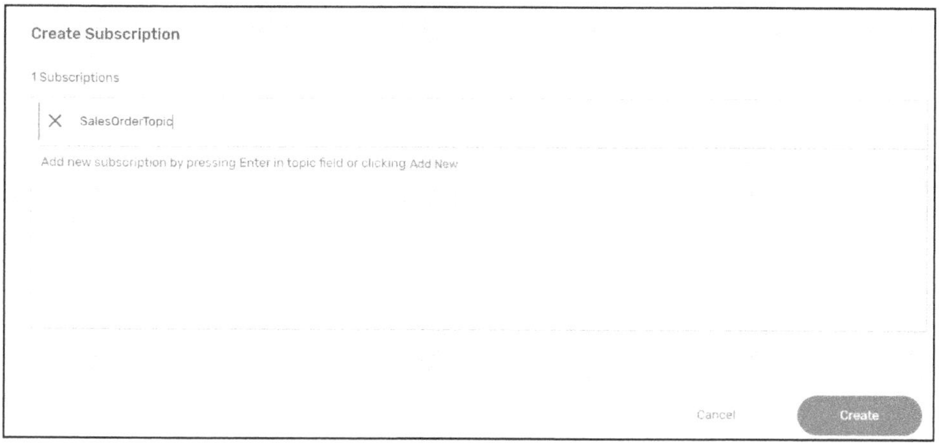

Figure 5.129 Creating a New Subscription for a Queue.

Now, SAP Integration Suite, advanced event mesh is ready to act as an event hub for our scenario, so let's trigger an event from a sender application. For simplicity, we'll use Postman to trigger an event. If you aren't using SAP Integration Suite, advanced event mesh as the event hub in this scenario, you'll need an alternative way to create an event. Check what is supported by the messaging system you're using. Either the system supports the publishing of messages or events via HTTP or a built-in test tool can be used, or you can create the event using a helper iFlow in Cloud Integration.

Sending an Event Using Postman

You might be wondering how to connect to the newly created event broker to publish messages to your queue. SAP Integration Suite, advanced event mesh provides multiple protocols to integrate with it, and the most common are AMQP, REST, and Solace messaging. For each of these options, the connection details can be found on the **Connect** tab of the event broker service. For our exercise, we'll use the REST APIs provided by SAP Integration Suite, advanced event mesh. To get the connection details, click on the **REST** option, as shown in Figure 5.130. Copy the **Username**, **Password**, and the **Secured REST Host Public Internet** endpoint.

We'll use Postman (*www.getpostman.com*) to trigger the API request. Download, install, and start Postman, and you're ready to trigger your first request.

As you can infer from these access details, we must send the request with **Username** and **Password** fields for **Basic Auth** under the **Authorization** configuration tab. The endpoint should be created by concatenating the Secured REST Host public endpoint with the topic name, that is, "SalesOrderTopic" separated by a "/".

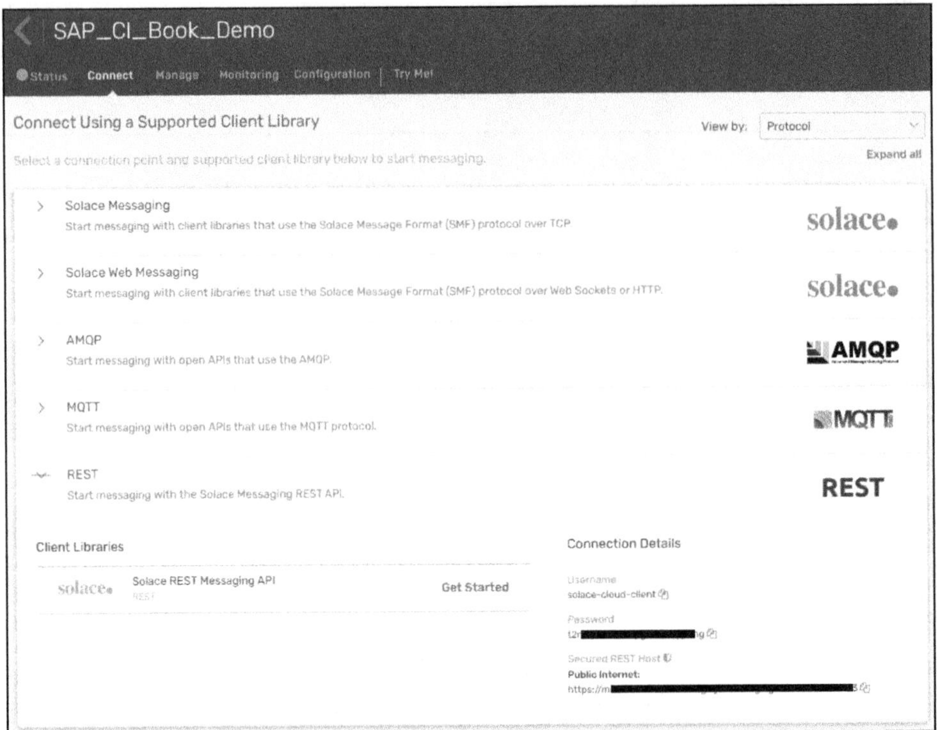

Figure 5.130 Connect Tab of the Event Broker Service

As shown in Figure 5.131 define the event to send in the **Body** tab. Select **raw** as the format of the body, and, in the content type dropdown list, select **JSON**. In the input field for the body, define the event. For easy configuration, we included the event as the *SalesOrder.json* file with the book's downloads at *www.sap-press.com/5760*.

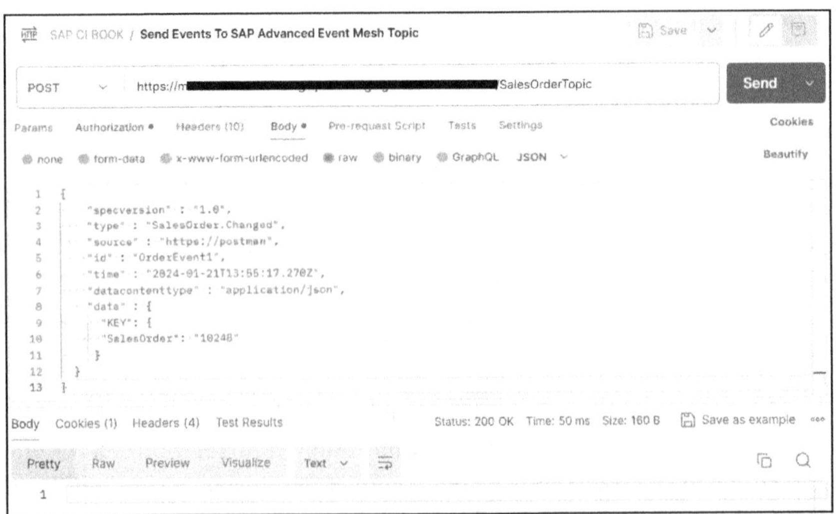

Figure 5.131 Using Postman to Send the Event to SAP Integration Suite, Advanced Event Mesh

Before we send the request, let's look more deeply at the event and its structure. Notice that our event is defined in the JSON format, one of the many options for defining events in cloud-based contexts. The standard for CloudEvents 1.0.2 was released in 2022, and the specification is available at *https://cloudevents.io/*. A standard cloud event consists of the following fields:

- `specversion`
  In this field, the version of the CloudEvents specification that the event uses is defined. This specification enables the interpretation of the context. This mandatory field is of type `string`.
- `type`
  This field defines the type of event. This property is often used for routing. The field is mandatory and must be of type `string`.
- `source`
  This describes the event producer in this field. The mandatory field is defined with type `string`.
- `id`
  The ID of the event is set in this mandatory field of type `string`.
- `time`
  In this field, the timestamp is set when the event happened. The field isn't mandatory but must be defined with type `string($date-time)`.
- `datacontenttype`
  In this option field of type `string`, the encoding format of the data field is defined. In our example, the content type is `application/json`.
- `data`
  In the `data` part of the request, the real data of the event is defined with the format defined in `datacontenttype`.

Discovering SAP Events: Using the SAP Business Accelerator Hub

To determine which events are available in the various SAP applications, use the SAP Business Accelerator Hub (*https://api.sap.com*). Search for content type **Events** to explore which events are available.

Sending a request to the topic in SAP Integration Suite, advanced event mesh creates a new message in the **SalesOrderEvents** queue, which you can view in the **Queues** monitor of SAP Integration Suite, advanced event mesh, as shown in Figure 5.132. Because we haven't created a consuming application yet, the event isn't being consumed from the queue.

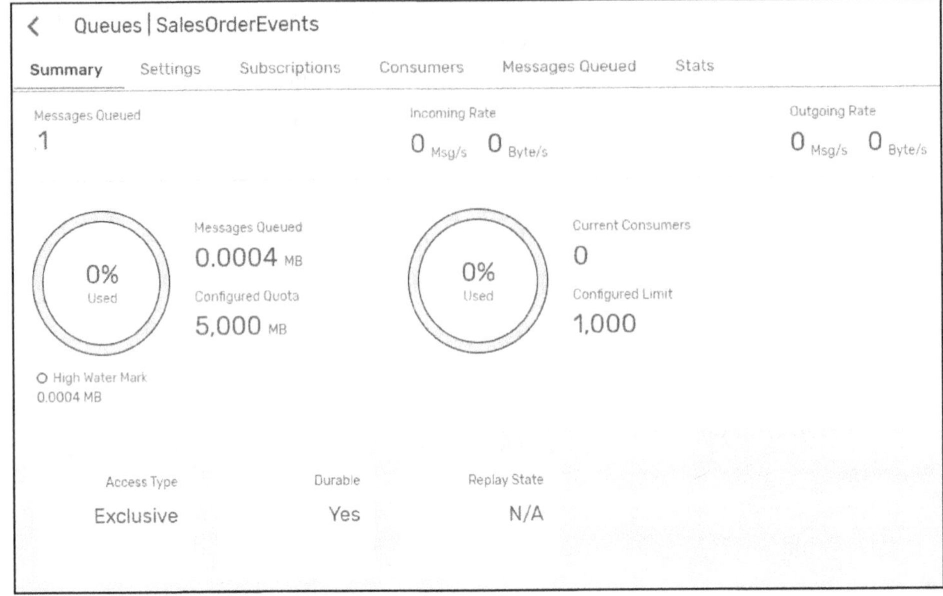

Figure 5.132 Monitoring Messages in SalesOrderEvents Queue

After we've successfully sent an event to the event hub, we can configure an iFlow to consume the event with Cloud Integration.

Consuming the Event in an Integration Flow

To consume an event in Cloud Integration, you must first retrieve the required connection details to connect to SAP Integration Suite, advanced event mesh via the Solace messaging protocol. For this information, you'll need to navigate to the **Connect** tab of the event broker service and click the **Solace Messaging** option. Copy the values of the following properties from the **Connection Details** section on the right of the page.

- **Username**
- **Password**
- **Message VPN**
- **Secured SMF Host Public Internet**

In our exercise, we're connecting via basic authentication for SAP Integration Suite, advanced event mesh broker, so we must configure user credentials in the operations view in Cloud Integration. To configure these credentials, click on the **Security Material** tile in the **Manage Security** section. Select **Create**, and choose **User Credentials** from the menu. On the **Create User Credentials** screen, enter the details noted earlier from the event broker service. Define a **Name** for the credentials object, and then click **Deploy** to activate the credentials in the runtime. The **Name** field must be maintained when configuring the iFlow.

Now, you can create the iFlow to consume the event from the queue in SAP Integration Suite, advanced event mesh. The iFlow we'll create is shown in Figure 5.133. On the inbound side, we'll configure the **AdvancedEventMesh** adapter, and on the outbound side, we'll use the already well-known **Mail** adapter.

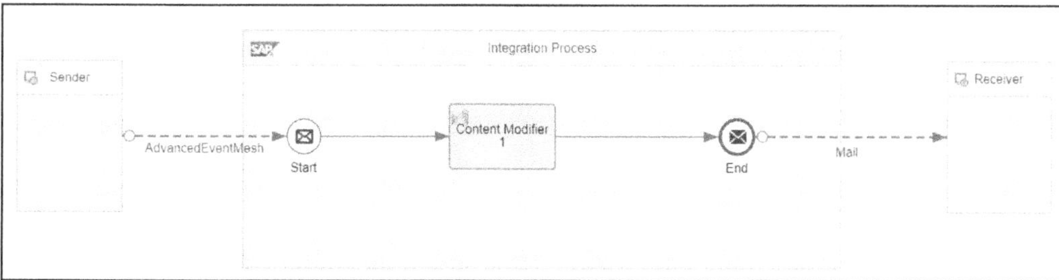

Figure 5.133 Configuring the Consuming iFlow

To create the iFlow, follow these steps:

1. Connect the **Sender** to the **Start** event of the integration process. In the adapter selection screen, choose the **Advanced Event Mesh** adapter.
2. In the **Advanced Event Mesh** adapter, under the **Connection** tab, configure the following properties, as shown in Figure 5.134:
   - **Host**: Define the hostname of the messaging system you want to connect to. For our scenario, we'll use the secured SMF host copied from the **Connect** tab of the event broker service.
   - **Message VPN**: Define the name of the message VPN to be used for connection.
   - **Username**: The user name of the SAP Integration Suite, advanced event mesh.

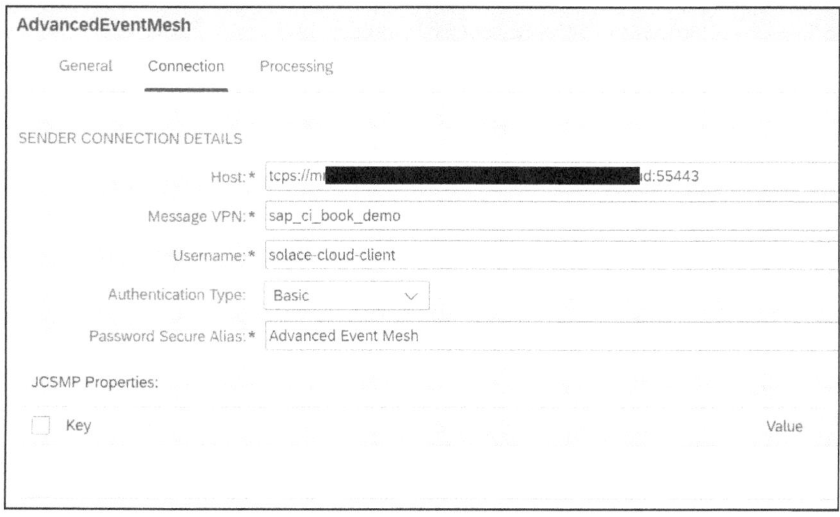

Figure 5.134 Connection Configuration in the SAP Integration Suite, Advanced Event Mesh Sender Adapter

- **Authentication Type**: Three authentication options are available: **Basic**, **OAuth2**, and **Client Certificate**. For this exercise, select **Basic**.
- **Password Secure Alias**: For basic authentication, you must provide the name of the deployed credentials. These credentials are used during message processing for authentication in the target system.

3. Next, under the **Processing** tab, configure the following properties, as shown in Figure 5.135:
   - **Consumer Mode**: The mode in which the adapter should consume events. There are two options for this setting: **Direct** and **Guaranteed**. In our exercise, select **Guaranteed** because we're reading messages from a queue and want guaranteed delivery.
   - **Parallel Consumers**: Messages from the queue can be consumed in parallel if required for high message throughput. In the **Parallel Consumers** field, you can specify the number of allowable parallel processes consuming messages from the queue. The default value is **1**.
   - **Queue Name**: Define the queue you want to consume messages from. Configure the name of the queue we've created in SAP Integration Suite, advanced event mesh: "SalessOrderEvents".
   - **Selector**: SAP Integration Suite, advanced event mesh supports the filtering of messages for consumption. Through this field, you can specify an SQL-92 selector. For our exercise, leave it empty.
   - **Acknowledgment Mode**: When a message is read from the queue, the event broker service should be notified of the successful retrieval of the message. This can be done in two modes: **Automatic Immediate** to send acknowledgment immediately after reading the event, or **Automatic On Exchange Complete** to wait till the message processing is completed successfully.
   - **Maximum Message Processing Attempts**: If an error arises during message processing, messages are kept in the queue and are retried from that queue. With this configuration, you can specify how often a message should be retried before a different delivery status is sent back to the message broker. Default value is **5**.
   - **Retry Interval (in ms)**: Time interval to delay message processing in case of an error.
   - **Maximum Retry Interval (in ms)**: Maximum time interval to delay message reprocessing.
   - **Exponential Backoff Multiplier**: In there are multiple retries, an exponential backoff mechanism can be defined to retry at an increasing time interval instead of a fixed time interval. To set a fixed time interval, leave the value of this property as **1**.

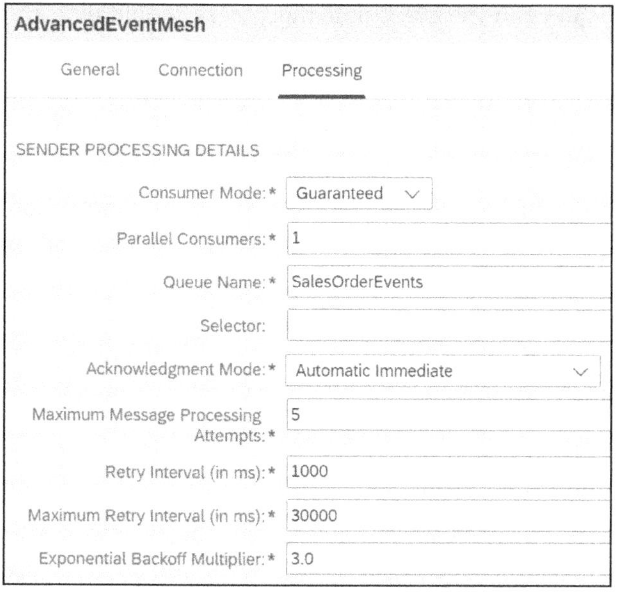

Figure 5.135 Processing Configuration in the SAP Integration Suite, Advanced Event Mesh Sender Adapter

4. Connect the **End Message** event to the **Receiver** and, in the adapter selection screen, choose the **Mail** adapter. Configure the **Mail** adapter as described in Section 5.3.2 (refer to Figure 5.65 and Figure 5.66 for configuration details). Define a meaningful subject for the email to easily identify the mail in your inbox.
5. Save and deploy the iFlow. In the operations view, on the **Integration Content** screen, check that the iFlow has started successfully as shown in Figure 5.136.

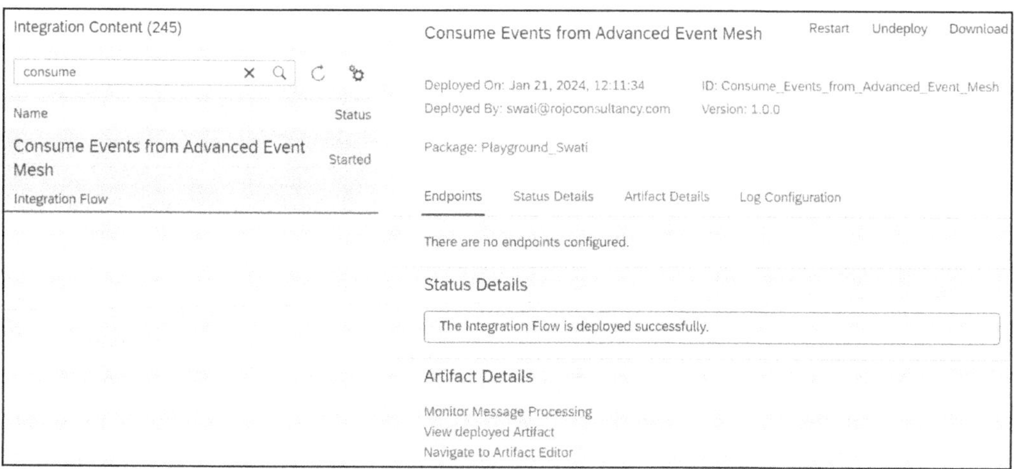

Figure 5.136 iFlow Status

If an event is available in the queue in the event hub, the system should pick it up immediately after the iFlow is started. If no event is available, this triggers a new event from Postman. After successfully publishing an event, the Cloud Integration tenant should be immediately notified about the new event and start consuming and processing the event. You'll receive an email with the event.

This scenario shows how easily events can be consumed from an event hub with Cloud Integration. However, this consumption of events is only part of the whole pattern. We've only consumed the event, not the real data the event points to. The event only provides an ID of the real data—in our scenario, the ID of a sales order that has changed. In the next step, we'll consume the event and evaluate what has changed to fetch the whole dataset directly from the sender system.

5.6.2 Reading Business Details from Providers

To fetch the whole dataset that has changed, we'll need to extend the iFlow we created earlier, as shown in Figure 5.137. We'll first convert the JSON event into an XML document so that the sales order ID can be read from the event. Then, we'll execute an OData call to fetch the whole sales order, with all of its details, and send this whole sales order to our mailbox.

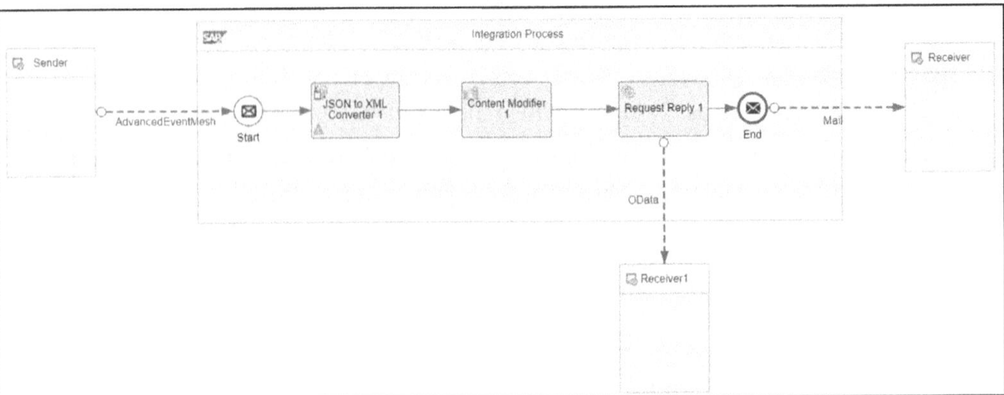

Figure 5.137 Fetching the Business Data in the Consuming iFlow

Let's start extending our iFlow. Because we need the event in XML format so that the sales order ID can be read from the document, our first step is to add the **JSON to XML Converter** next to the **Start Message** event to transform the JSON-based event into an XML document. To do so, select this event from the palette on the left of the modeling environment by following the path **Message Transformers** • **Converter** (Figure 5.138) • **JSON to XML Converter** (Figure 5.139).

Figure 5.138 Selecting the Converter from the Transformation Menu

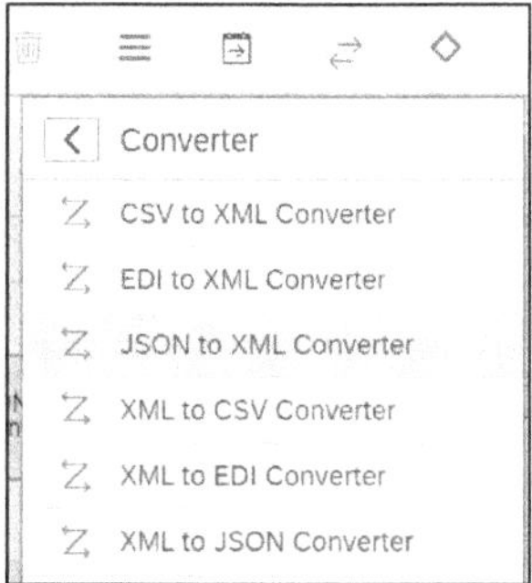

Figure 5.139 Selecting the JSON to XML Converter in the Converter Submenu

Configure the **JSON to XML Converter**, as shown in Figure 5.140. This is a new step, so we'll explain it in more detail. In this step, the following processing configurations can be defined:

- **Use Namespace Mapping**
  If you want to define a mapping between the JSON prefix and the XML namespace, select this checkbox and define the mapping. Otherwise, no namespace is defined in the XML document.
- **JSON Prefix Separator**
  Define the separator used in the JSON document to separate the prefix from the data. In most cases, a colon is used.
- **Add XML Root Element**
  Select this option to add a root node to the generated XML document. Although the JSON document we sent for the event doesn't have a root JSON member, the XML document needs a root element. Therefore, select the option to add one, and define a new root node with the following fields:

- **Name**: Define the name of the root node to be generated in this field. For simplicity, keep the default value as "root".
- **Namespace Mapping**: From the defined namespaces in the runtime configuration of the iFlow, select the namespace you want to use in the generated XML document. Because we don't require a namespace in the XML document, just leave the field empty.

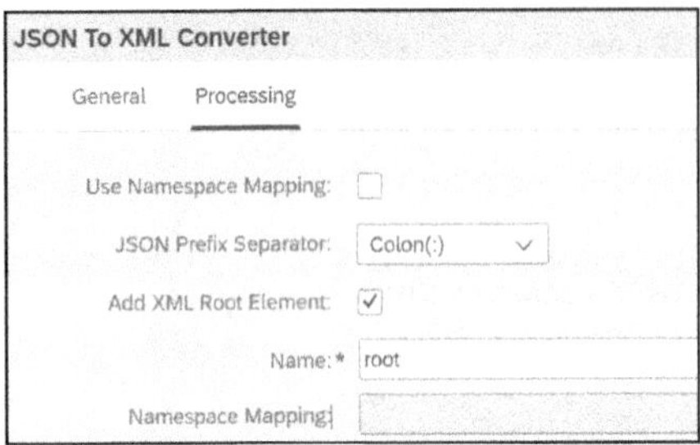

Figure 5.140 JSON to XML Converter Configuration

Now, we can run an XPath expression on the generated XML to get the order number. Add a **Content Modifier** step next to the **JSON to XML Converter** step, and configure it with the details shown in Figure 5.141. In this step, we're creating a header called **orderNumber** using the relative XPath **//SalesOrder**.

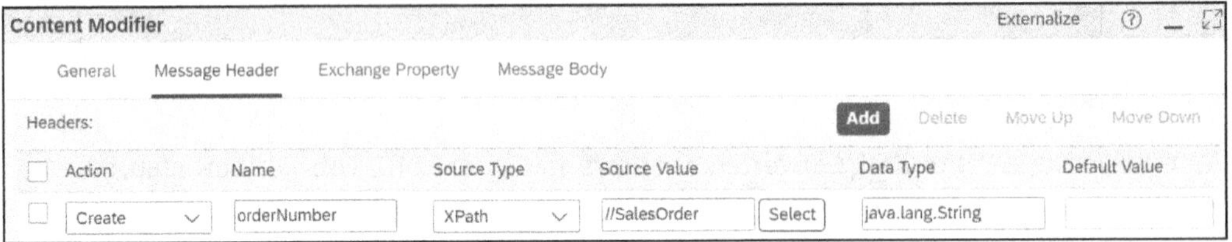

Figure 5.141 Reading the Order Number in the Content Modifier

At this point, because we have the order number, we can fetch the sales order's details from the sender system to distribute to the receiver system. Thus, we'll add a **Request Reply** step and a **Receiver** participant. The **Receiver** in this case represents the sender system from which we're fetching the sales order's details. Connect the **Request Reply** step with the **Receiver**, and then select the **OData** adapter. For simplicity, we'll use the Northwind test service to fetch the order details. The steps for configuring the **OData** adapter is identical to the steps described in Chapter 4, Section 4.3. For your reference, the configuration of the OData channel was shown in Figure 5.40 and Figure 5.41.

Save and deploy the iFlow, and trigger a new event from Postman. Now, instead of getting the event with just the sales order ID via email, you'll receive the whole sales order, with all the details fetched from the sender system—our completed event-based integration pattern. Now, you can consume an event sent by an application system in Cloud Integration, fetch the real business data, and forward this data to any receiver.

Using such an event-based integration pattern, a receiver can decide whether or not it wants to consume a specific event and trigger its related actions. The sender is never concerned about notifying the right receivers about specific changes because the receivers subscribe to the event themselves. Furthermore, the consumption of the event and the fetching of the data isn't based on the scheduler and instead run immediately the moment an event is published.

To play around a little more with events and master working with them in Cloud Integration, in the next section, we'll extend the scenario even further so that, after the successful consumption and processing of a sales order, an event is sent back to the event hub about this successful consumption event. From there, we'll then consume the response event.

5.6.3 Sending Events to SAP Integration Suite, Advanced Event Mesh

To send an event from an iFlow, we'll extend the iFlow, as shown in Figure 5.142. As described earlier in Section 5.3.3, you're already familiar with the **Sequential Multicast** pattern to send the event only after successful execution. In this scenario, the event is created in a **Content Modifier** step and sent to the event hub using the **AMQP** receiver adapter.

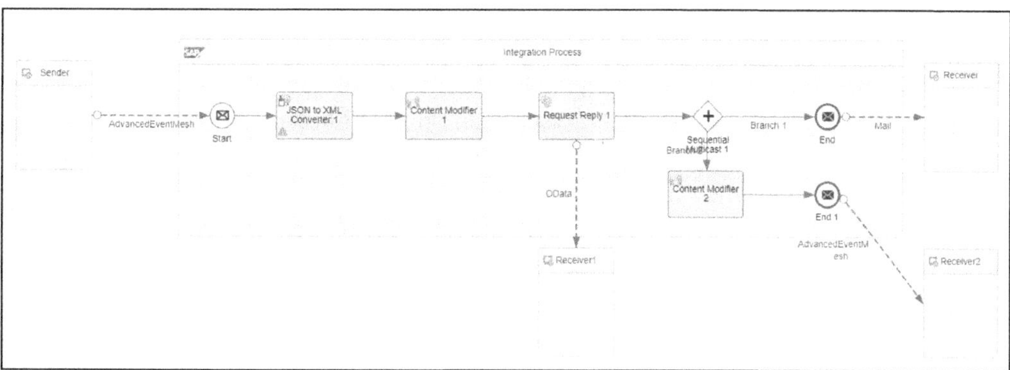

Figure 5.142 Writing the Event in the Consuming iFlow

To add the **Sequential Multicast** option, from the main menu of the palette, select the **Message Routing** ◇ shape. In the submenu, select the **Multicast** option and then **Sequential Multicast.** Place the step between the **Request Reply** step and the **End** event. Add one more **Receiver** participant and a second message **End** event. Connect the **Sequential Multicast** step with the **End** event. For a detailed description of the sequential multicast pattern, refer to Section 5.3.3.

To create the content of the event, we'll need a **Content Modifier** step. Add a **Content Modifier** step in the branch going to the new **Receiver**, as shown in Figure 5.142. When configuring the **Content Modifier** step, under the **Message Body** tab, create the payload for the event. We'll use the JSON format as the common format for events. Configure the **Content Modifier** step according to the values shown in Figure 5.143. For easy configuration, you can download the event as the *SalesOrderConsumed.json* file included with the book's downloads at *www.sap-press.com/5760*.

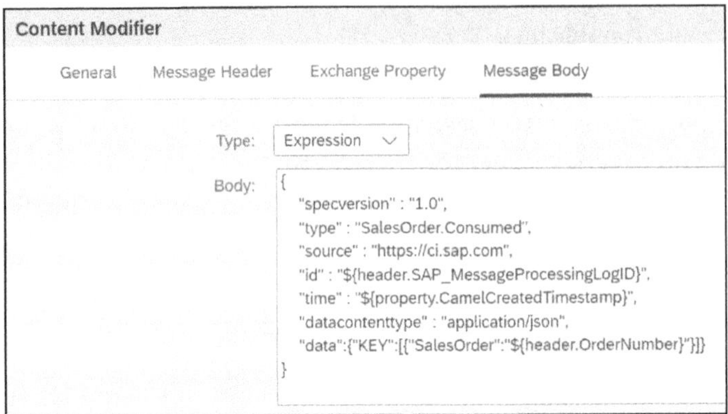

Figure 5.143 Configuring the Event in Content Modifier

When sending an event from Cloud Integration, an important step is filling in the fields in a way that the receiver of the event expects. (Refer to Section 5.6.1 for the detailed description of the fields.) In this case, we'll define the `type` of the event as `SalesOrder.Consumed` and the `source` as `https://ci.sap.com`, but you can also use different names. The important point is that the consumer of the event must understand this information. In our simple scenario, this aspect isn't relevant because we'll later simply use a test tool for consumption. As the `id` for the event, we'll set the ID of the message processing log, which, as you already learned in Section 5.3.3, can be addressed using the header `SAP_MessageProcessingLogID`. In the `time` field, we'll set the timestamp of the processing of the message, which can be read from the Camel property `CamelCreatedTimestamp`. As the `content type` for the event, we'll set `application/json` to reflect the format we're using. The real business content of the event is defined in the `data` field. In this field, we'll simply refer to the sales order number we've already consumed using the header `OrderNumber` defined earlier. Make sure you select **Expression** from the **Type** dropdown list under the **Message Body** tab to ensure that the headers and properties used in the body are interpreted as simple expressions during runtime processing.

Although we've defined the content of the event, we still must specify where to send it. Draw a line between the **End** event and the new **Receiver**, and then select the **Advanced Event Mesh** adapter. We'll connect to the same event hub from which we consumed the sales order event. Therefore, we'll use the same configuration under the **Connection** tab (shown earlier in Figure 5.134). The configuration under the **Processing** tab, as shown in Figure 5.144, differs from the configuration in the sender adapter, so let's take a deeper look now. Under the **Processing** tab, you'll maintain the following fields:

- **Delivery Mode**
  With the SAP Integration Suite, advanced event mesh receiver adapter, you can send messages and events to topics and to queues in the connected messaging system. In the **Delivery Mode** dropdown menu, select either **Direct** or **Persistent (Guaranteed)**.
- **Endpoint Type**
  Specify the destination to which you want to send the messages. It can either be a **Queue** or a **Topic**.
- **Destination Name**
  Specify the name of the receiver **Queue** or **Topic**. We'll enter a topic that we'll create later in the SAP Integration Suite, advanced event mesh system: "SalesOrderConsumed".
- **Message Type**
  You can write any type of message to the event broker service. To specify an exact type, select from the **Binary**, **Map**, or **Text**. To let the broker identify the type by itself, select **Automatic**. In our exercise, leave the setting as **Automatic**.
- **Convert Publish into Synchronous Requestor**
  If you want to use the adapter in a request reply pattern and are expecting a reply on the sent message, then you can enable this checkbox. In this exercise, leave it unchecked because we aren't expecting any reply.

Note that there is a fourth tab in the adapter configuration—**Message Properties**. This tab provides additional configuration options for the events to be sent to SAP Integration Suite, advanced event mesh. One example is passing on the Application Message ID for better tracking of event. Leave all settings of this tab as default.

By configuring the SAP Integration Suite, advanced event mesh adapter, we're done extending our iFlow. Save and deploy it by clicking **Save** and then **Deploy**.

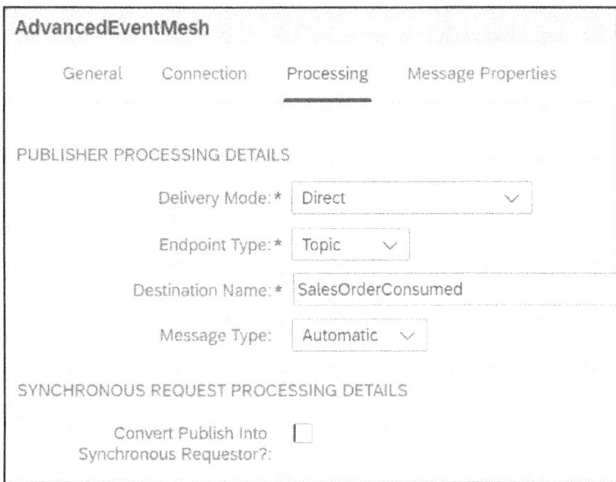

Figure 5.144 Processing Configuration in the SAP Integration Suite, Advanced Event Mesh Receiver Adapter

Before we can send the event to the configured topic in the event hub, we still need to create the topic and the subscribed queue in which the message is finally stored. As we did for the *SalesOrder.Changed* event in Section 5.6.1, we'll create a queue called `SalesOrderConsumed` for the *SalesOrder.Consumed* event and subscribe it to the topic `SalesOrderConsumed`, as shown in Figure 5.144. Make sure the name is identical to the name defined in the SAP Integration Suite, advanced event mesh receiver adapter.

Now, everything is ready to run the scenario. Trigger your event using Postman to start the scenario. You'll receive an email as before. Additionally, an event will be sent to the queue you just created in the messaging system. To check that the event has been added, use the monitoring function of the messaging system you're using. In this section, we used the familiar **Queues** monitor of the SAP Integration Suite, advanced event mesh, as shown in Figure 5.145.

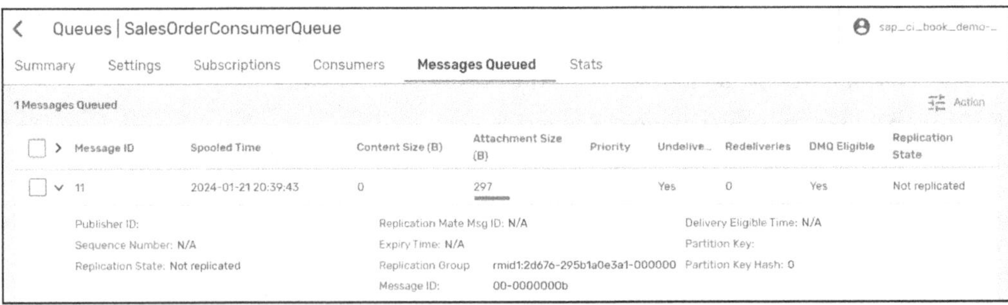

Figure 5.145 SAP Integration Suite, Advanced Event Mesh: Queues Monitor

In the SAP Integration Suite, advanced event mesh, a tool is available for consuming messages from a queue. Navigate to the **Try Me!** tab from the event broker service details page, as shown in Figure 5.146. The **Publish or Subscriber** view opens. In this view, you can publish messages to a topic or consume messages from a topic in SAP Integration Suite, advanced event mesh. Because we want to consume the *SalesOrder.Consumed* event, go to the **Subscriber** side of the tool, and click on the **Connect** button under the **Establish connection** section. In the **Subscriber** section, enter the name of the topic "SalesOrderConsumed", and click **Subscribe.** Now trigger the scenario again, and you should see the enhanced message in the **Messages** section, as shown in Figure 5.146.

We've come to the end of our discussion of event-based messaging. Now, you can configure an event-based integration scenario using the SAP Integration Suite, advanced event mesh adapter in Cloud Integration. We hope you now understand how to use the SAP Integration Suite, advanced event mesh as an event hub to manage events, consume events in Cloud Integration to read and process application data, and send events from Cloud Integration.

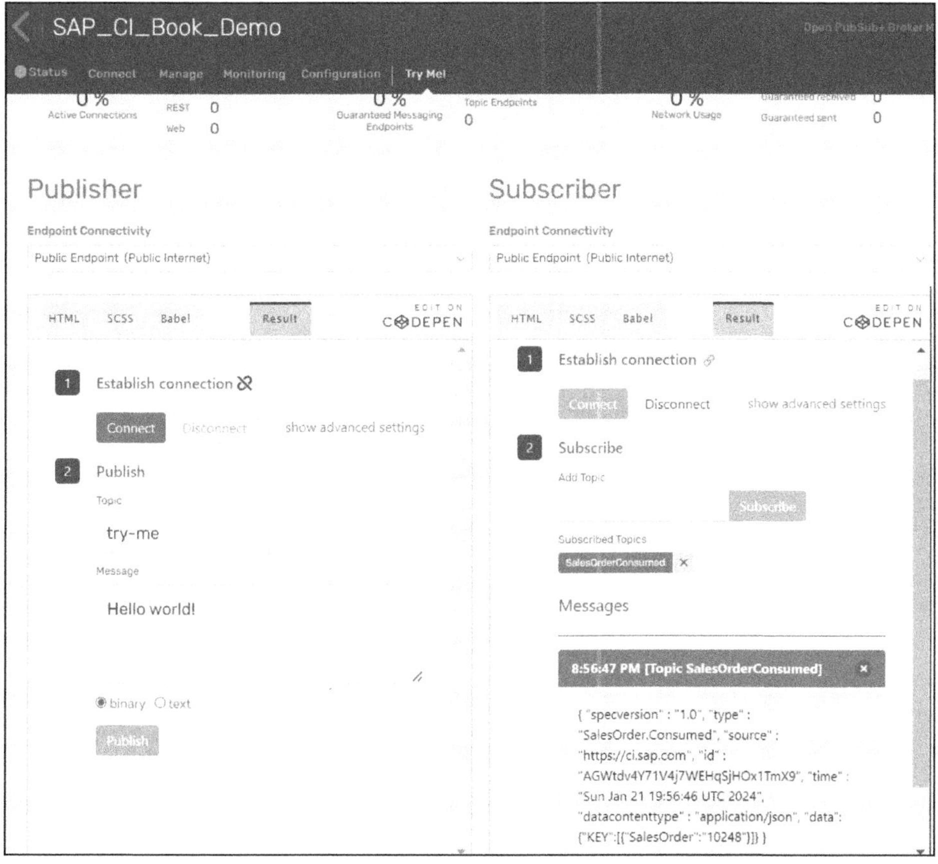

Figure 5.146 SAP Integration Suite, Advanced Event Mesh: Test Message Consumption

5.7 Summary

Congratulations! You've reached another important milestone on your journey through the world of integration using Cloud Integration. In this chapter, we started implementing more sophisticated integration scenarios, comprising steps for aggregators, and managing messages containing lists of entries. You applied the splitter pattern to create individual messages out of a list and used the gather pattern to aggregate individual messages back into a single reply message. You also learned how to influence synchronous and asynchronous message handling for the SOAP adapter and how to add asynchronous receivers to your iFlow. You used the multicast pattern to distribute the message to multiple receivers, and you used the JMS adapter to decouple inbound and outbound processing, thus ensuring that message processing is retried in Cloud Integration. At the end of this chapter, you used the SAP Integration Suite, advanced event mesh adapter to implement an event-driven integration scenario.

With this knowledge, you can play around with Cloud Integration's more advanced features. However, our journey continues: the next chapter will reveal even more capabilities, including timer-based starts for iFlows, the dynamic configuration of parameters, modularization for the structuring of large flows, and much, much more.

Chapter 6

Special Topics in Integration Development

You've learned the basic concepts behind integration development with Cloud Integration, so let's move on to a few special topics, such as timer-based message handling processes, externalizing timer configurations, structuring large integration scenarios, and using dynamic parameters. We'll also discuss integration flow (iFlow) component versioning, transport integration packages, and custom adapters, which may be required to connect to some external systems. You'll learn how to use the Java Database Connectivity (JDBC) adapter to connect your tenant to a database, how to use the AS2 adapter to connect to the AS2 server, and best practices and guidelines for good iFlow design. Finally, we'll cover script collection and advanced message mapping concepts.

In this chapter, we'll address a few typical integration scenarios that will require special attention from you. This chapter will show you how to set up the time-based triggering (Section 6.1) and dynamic configuration of iFlows (Section 6.2), as well as the slicing and dicing of complex integration logic using subprocesses (Section 6.3) and connecting different iFlows deployed on the same tenant (Section 6.4). Section 6.5 elaborates on the option to connect your tenant with a database, thus enabling you to store data permanently in a database table. Section 6.6 will demonstrate the usage of AS2 adapter, and the configurations required to connect to an AS2 server. We'll discuss versioning and simulating iFlows in Section 6.7 and Section 6.8, respectively. Furthermore, you'll learn how to transport integration packages from one tenant to another in Section 6.9 and how to develop your own custom adapters that can be integrated into the SAP BTP infrastructure in Section 6.10. Section 6.11 provides an overview of guidelines and best practices that are important when designing integrations that meet the highest quality standards. We'll discuss the creation and usage of script collections in Section 6.12. Finally, Section 6.13 will provide an overview of advanced message mapping concepts and their usage in integration scenarios.

Throughout this chapter, we'll dive into the topic of error handling on various occasions. By the end of this chapter, you'll be well equipped to handle a variety of integration challenges.

In previous chapters, you became familiar with the Simple Object Access Protocol (SOAP) sender adapter, which we used in many example iFlows. In the iFlows used in this chapter, we'll mainly use another sender adapter—the HTTPS sender adapter—that was introduced in Chapter 2. Furthermore, the scenarios shown in this chapter use the WebShop application, a public demo application provided by SAP that exposes fictitious product data. Its website, including its fictitious catalog of electronic products, is available at *http://s-prs.co/v576015*.

Throughout this chapter, we'll use this demo application to get data into the system. Based on this demo app, we'll show you how to build certain iFlows to showcase several different concepts and features. We'll use and modify one basic integration scenario to successively show each new aspect introduced with each section.

6.1 Timer-Based Message Transfers

In previous chapters, we used Cloud Integration as the cloud-based solution for facilitating reliable message transfer between on-premise and on-demand enterprise applications. So far, the integration logic executed on Cloud Integration was mainly triggered by incoming messages, such as an order request originating from a sender system, for instance, a customer relationship management (CRM) system, which needed to be routed to various backend enterprise resource planning (ERP) systems, depending on the message's content. However, not all integration scenarios require an incoming message to trigger their execution. Sometimes, you'll want to check for existing data regularly, for example, retrieving the status of a machine or related machine data in an Internet of Things (IoT) scenario to use this information in a business intelligence system for further analysis. Scenarios like this require the timely initiation of message transfers. Such scenarios are quite common in batch processing where jobs can be scheduled and run without any user interaction. In this section, we'll show you how to set up timer-based message transfers in Cloud Integration.

6.1.1 The Scenario

In this section, we'll develop an iFlow connected to the WebShop component from which product data should be read on a regular basis and further processed. Let's assume that, in this case, you're interested in getting regular updates about the products available in the WebShop, in particular, the actual price of each product.

You can design a timer-based iFlow in such a way that you'll get a list of products, including certain attributes for each product (e.g., product category, product name, and price), and send this list as an email to your email account at regular intervals. The target scenario, as shown in Figure 6.1, is quite simple.

At the start of the flow, shown on the left side of Figure 6.1, you'll see the first difference with the other iFlows we've set up so far. This iFlow begins with a new event called **Timer**, indicated by the clock ◷. This event is followed by a **Request Reply** step that is connected via an OData channel to an external component, the WebShop application. After we receive the response from the WebShop (a list of products), this information is sent to the receiver via the **Mail** adapter. With the knowledge you've acquired so far, setting up this iFlow should be no problem at all.

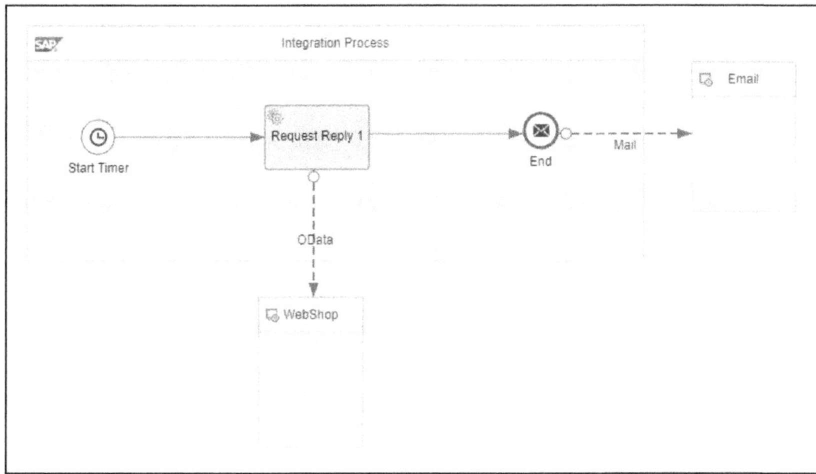

Figure 6.1 Timer-Initiated Integration Flow

6.1.2 Configuring a Timer-Based Integration Flow

The only new shape in this iFlow is the **Timer** event. We'll look more closely at its configuration in a moment. You'll find this event in the palette beneath the event's main entry ◎, as shown in Figure 6.2.

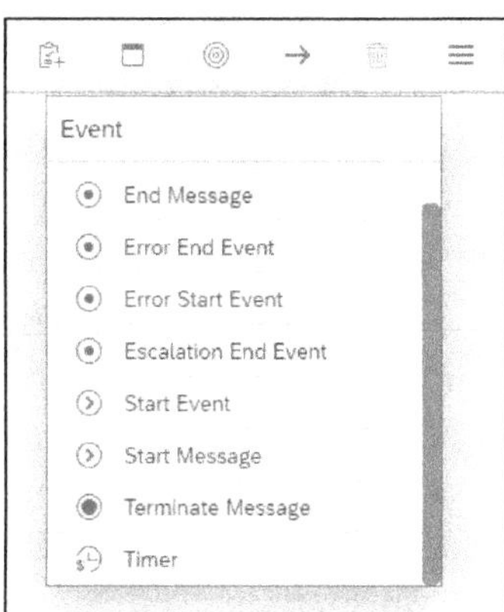

Figure 6.2 The Timer Event in the Modeling Palette

This event is responsible for initiating the flow's execution without requiring a dedicated start message. The configuration options are shown in Figure 6.3.

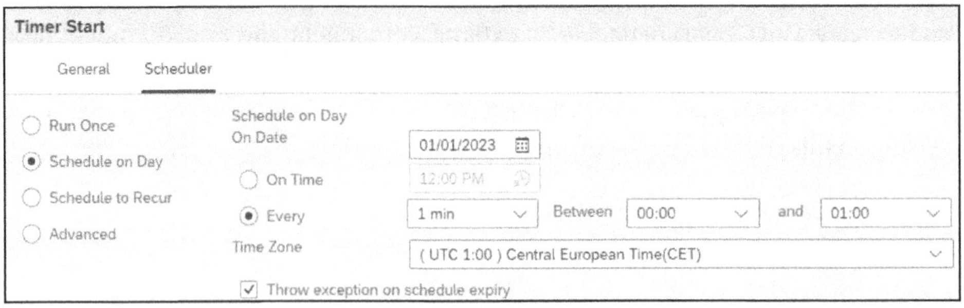

Figure 6.3 Timer Start Event Configured for Scheduled Starts on a Certain Day

You have four options at your disposal for starting the iFlow:

- **Run Once**
  The flow runs only once, immediately after deployment of the flow.
- **Schedule on Day**
  The flow is scheduled to execute on a specific day at a well-defined time (or at several well-defined times).
- **Schedule to Recur**
  A recurring schedule on a daily, weekly, or monthly basis at a well-defined time (or at several well-defined times).
- **Advanced**
  A recurring schedule on a daily, weekly, or monthly basis in a more advanced manner. The scheduling options are on a more granular level, which provides more flexibility and precision in scheduling the iFlows.

The **Run Once** option allows you to trigger the flow's execution immediately after successful deployment. This option is mostly used for testing purposes: you can try out certain integration functionalities without sending incoming messages all the time, just to get the flow started. Of course, you won't have to configure additional settings for this option because the exact point of time the iFlow runs is as soon as the flow's deployment is finalized.

The **Schedule on Day** option (shown in Figure 6.3) defines a concrete day on which the iFlow should run. In the **On Date** field, you'll enter an execution date. However, you can also specify either the one-time execution or a recurring execution on that particular date. To run the flow only once, you must set the **On Time** checkbox, accompanied by a concrete time. For the flow logic to be invoked recurrently (scheduled in intervals), select the **Every** radio button. In addition, you must define two intervals:

- **The interval after which the flow should be triggered**
  Every minute? Every hour? Other intervals are possible, such as every second minute, every 4 hours, and so on. You'll select the desired interval from the dropdown list to the right of the **Every** radio button.
- **Between which times of the day the flow should run**
  For this approach, you can define start and end times. These dropdown lists are positioned to the right of the **Between** label shown in Figure 6.3. The first dropdown list represents the start time, and the second dropdown list represents the end time.

The settings shown in Figure 6.3 represent a recurring invocation of the iFlow starting on January 1st, 2023. The flow will be called every minute during the time between midnight and 1:00 a.m. (Central European Time zone).

With these options, you can flexibly schedule the flow's execution for a certain day. Further, even for that particular day, you can define recurring execution. However, the repetition of the invocation is limited to one day. To overcome this limitation, you can use the third option, which allows you to define a more flexible period for the flow's repetition. For this purpose, select the **Schedule to Recur** radio button, as shown in . The dropdown list beneath the **Schedule to Recur** label allows you to select the period: **Currently**, **Daily**, **Weekly**, and **Monthly** repetitions are supported. Depending on your choice, you'll define additional attributes. Let's look at each of these options next:

- **Daily**
  Defines whether the flow should run only once on that day or on a recurring basis. You have the same options as described for the **Schedule on Day** selection.
- **Weekly**
  Define the days of the week on which the flow should be invoked. The chosen days will activate the flow every week. You can even pick several days, such as every Monday, Wednesday, and Friday.
- **Monthly**
  Specify the date on which the iFlow should run every month. If a chosen date isn't applicable for a certain month (e.g., 31 isn't a valid date for February, April, June, September, and November), the flow isn't executed. Only one day can be selected.

Of course, many configuration options are available for scheduling the execution of your iFlows. The **Timer** event is the method of choice for start, end, and recurring times; periods; and time spans. Returning to our initial goal of receiving order information at regular intervals, let's assume that we want to get this information into our inbox every morning at 7:00 a.m.

Therefore, a reasonable configuration is to select the **Schedule to Recur** radio button and then set the **Schedule to Recur** dropdown list to **Daily**. In addition, select the **On Time** radio button, and set the field to have the value **7:00 AM (Central European Time)**, as shown in Figure 6.4.

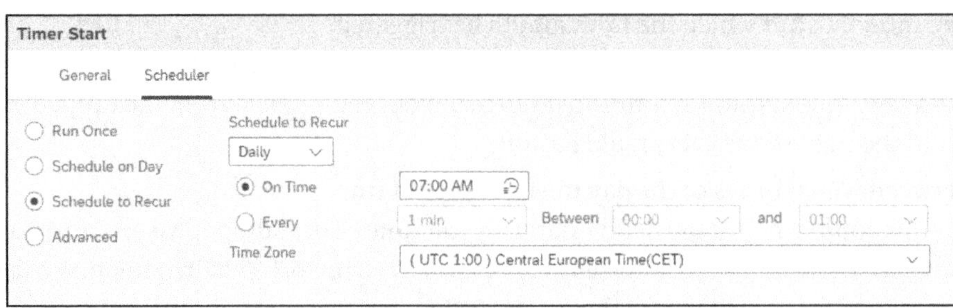

Figure 6.4 Setting the Recurrence to Every Day at 7:00 a.m.

However, another approach is possible, especially if you want to retrieve the information only for workdays. In this case, choose the **Weekly** entry from the **Schedule to Recur** dropdown list, and set the checkboxes for the required workdays (e.g., Monday to Friday), as shown in Figure 6.5.

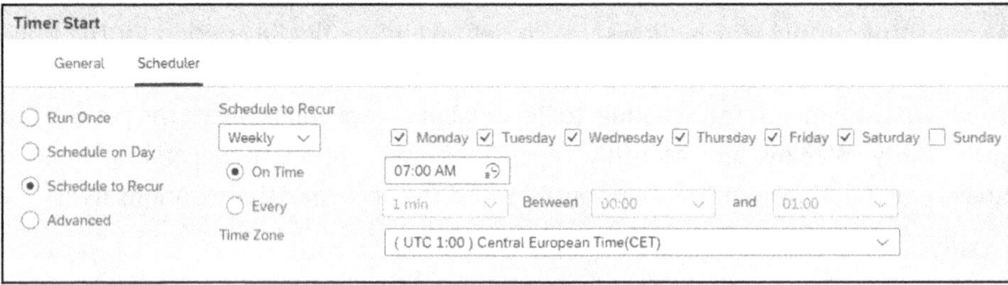

Figure 6.5 Setting the Recurrence to Workdays

What can be configured with the **Timer** event is quite impressive. You can use the many configuration options available to define your own schedule.

To continue, let's now configure the OData connection. (For more discussion on configuring an OData connection in general, refer to Chapter 4, Section 4.3.) In this scenario, we'll just modify the OData adapter by configuring it with the settings shown in Figure 6.6.

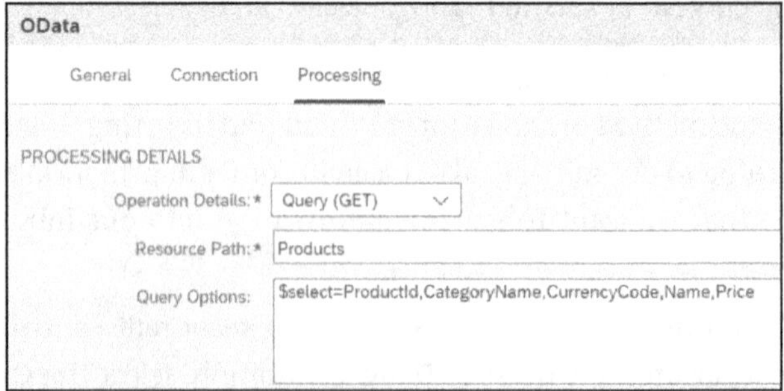

Figure 6.6 OData Adapter Processing Settings to Retrieve Products, Including Certain Attributes for Each Product, from the WebShop Component

Note that, under the **Connection** tab, the **Address** should contain the following URL: `https://refapp-espm-ui-cf.cfapps.eu10.hana.ondemand.com/espm-cloud-web/espm.svc/`

Under the **Processing** tab (shown in Figure 6.6), you'll specify that the OData entity **Products** should be retrieved. As a quick refresher on OData receiver adapters when you create the OData channel from scratch (see Chapter 4 Section 4.3.3), after you've entered the OData endpoint address on the **Connection** tab, you can use the query wizard to help you select among various OData entities on the **Processing** tab. One of these entities is the **Products** entity. We've configured the OData adapter in such a way that, in the **Query Options** field, the following expression is specified: **$select=ProductId, CategoryName, CurrencyCode, Name, Price**, which ensures that all products, including the specified elements, are retrieved.

6

Note

In Figure 6.6, we're only showing you the relevant settings to change to highlight the specific query option. For a discussion of the other OData adapter settings, see Chapter 4, Section 4.3.

Before we can test this iFlow, we must define the connection to the email server. We described this process in detail when we discussed asynchronous message handling in Chapter 5, Section 5.3. Refer to Chapter 2, Section 2.3.4, to configure the connection to the email server correctly. Let's assume that, in the **Subject** field for the **Mail** adapter, found under the **Processing** tab, you enter "Product List" (compare with Figure 6.60 later in this chapter to see the mail adapter's settings).

6.1.3 Externalizing Timer Configurations

Now that you've learned about all the configuration parameters of a timer-based iFlow, you also might want to know how these configured parameters are externalized. In this section, we'll use the same example and externalize the configuration done in the **Timer** shape. Externalizing the configuration helps in changing the schedule per the requirement without editing the iFlow.

Select the **Timer** shape in the iFlow created in the above section shown in Figure 6.1.

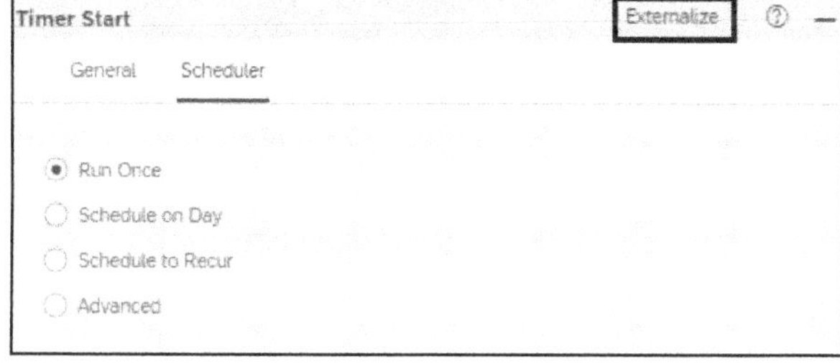

Figure 6.7 Timer Configuration

To externalize the parameters, select the **Externalize** button highlighted in Figure 6.7. Once the **Externalize** button is selected, the externalization parameters need to be defined. In Cloud Integration, the externalized parameters are defined as **{{parameter name}}**. In this example, we've defined the parameter with the name **{{Schedule}}**, as shown in Figure 6.8.

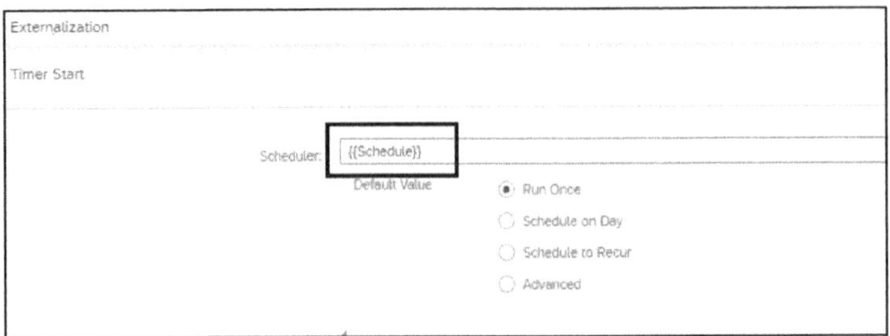

Figure 6.8 Define the Parameter to Externalize the Schedule

Now that the externalization parameter is defined, the schedule can be edited and changed without editing the iFlow. It can be done by using the **Configure** option available in the iFlow, as shown in Figure 6.9.

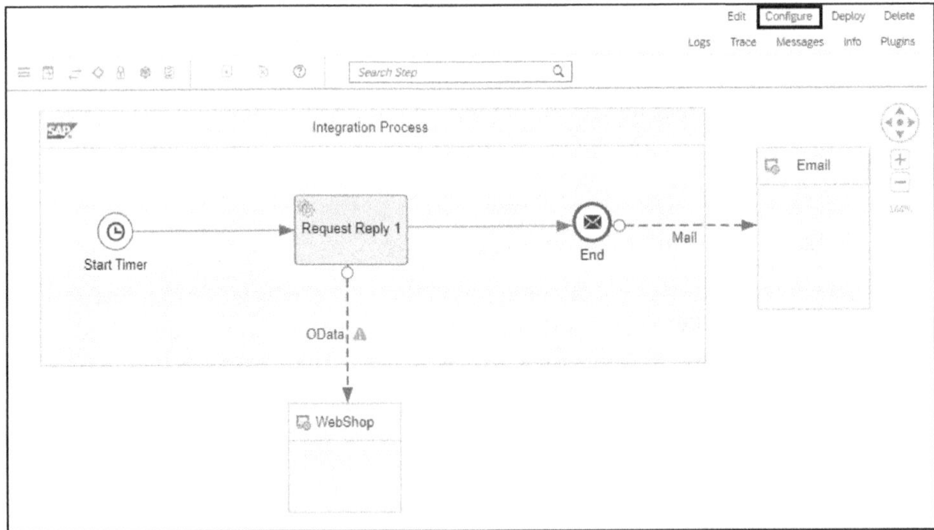

Figure 6.9 Configuration of the Externalized Parameter

Once the **Configure** option is selected as shown in Figure 6.9, a new screen with all the configuration options will be presented. The **Timer** was configured as **Run Once**. Now let's change the configuration schedule for the iFlow to run on a specific date and time. You can select the **Schedule on Day** radio button, as shown in Figure 6.10.

Once the schedule is changed, the iFlow needs to be deployed again for the changes to reflect at runtime.

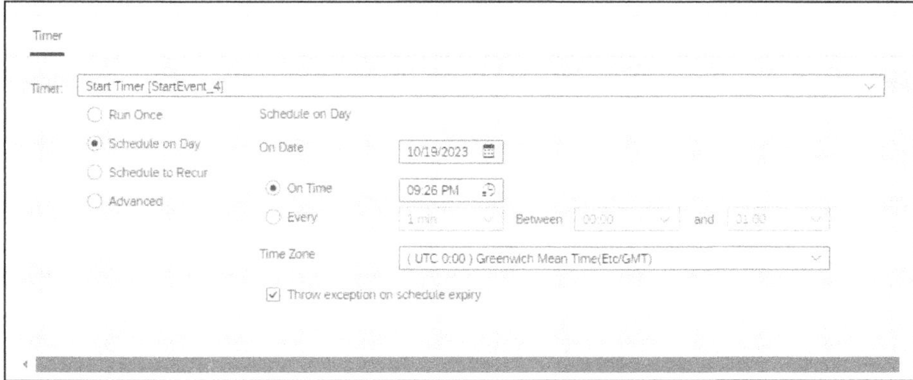

Figure 6.10 Changing the Schedule Using the Externalization Option

6.1.4 Running the Integration Flow

Now that our iFlow has been configured, let's trigger our timer-based iFlow. We recommend you set the **Timer** event to **Run Once** for the first time, just to avoid waiting for the timer to expire on the next scheduled day at 7:00 a.m. With the timer set to **Run Once**, the iFlow will begin automatically after deployment, which is exactly what we need for testing purposes. Once deployed, connect to your email provider to check for the email.

If the iFlow executes successfully, you'll receive an email like the one shown in Figure 6.11, with the subject as specified in the mail adapter ❶ and a list of products, including the elements specified in the OData adapter's **Query Options** field ❷.

Figure 6.11 Received Email Containing a List of Products (Only First Three Product Items Shown)

To summarize, regularly fetching data and forwarding messages to receiver systems are typical requirements for integration solutions such as Cloud Integration. In this part of the book, we've shown you how to prepare iFlows for this purpose. You learned how to use the **Timer** event to trigger the regular execution of an iFlow. Whether you want to run the flow only once or in a recurring fashion doesn't matter: The **Timer** event is prepared for all kinds of invocation scenarios.

We'll return to this basic scenario in Section 6.2 and Section 6.5, where we'll enhance this scenario with additional features. Therefore, we recommend that you don't delete this demo iFlow after you've finished this section. The same also applies for all of the following tutorials.

6.2 Using Dynamic Configuration via Headers or Properties

All iFlows you've learned about so far in this book have been designed under the tacit assumption that, when modeling the iFlow (during design time), you already know the values of all adapter and iFlow step attributes. However, you can easily think of scenarios where this assumption doesn't apply and where certain attribute values are only known during runtime—when the iFlow is being executed.

You might, for example, need to configure an iFlow with a mail receiver adapter, and part of the email text you'd like to send isn't known yet during design time. The email you send in response should instead depend on some actual value of an element found in the inbound message at runtime.

Cloud Integration also has a solution for use cases like this: various iFlow steps and adapter attributes that can be configured *dynamically*. To understand how this works, think again about Apache Camel's data model, introduced in Chapter 4. In that chapter, you learned that Cloud Integration provides the option to pass along certain information during the processing of a message: first in the message header and second in the exchange (as an exchange property). During message processing, this data can be used in various ways. For example, with a **Content Modifier** step, you can write data into the message header or (as a property) into the exchange container in a well-defined way. As a result, this data can be accessed at a later step during the message processing (e.g., in a routing condition). We've shown you how to use **Content Modifier** steps several times throughout this book.

The dynamic configuration of an attribute means that, instead of a concrete value, you'll enter a reference to a certain header or property for this attribute. At runtime, Cloud Integration resolves this reference by looking up the actual value of this header or property in the incoming message. The term *incoming message*, in this case, relates to the actual instance of the message that exists when message processing reaches the adapter or step that contains the dynamically configured attribute. Figure 6.12 shows the general principle.

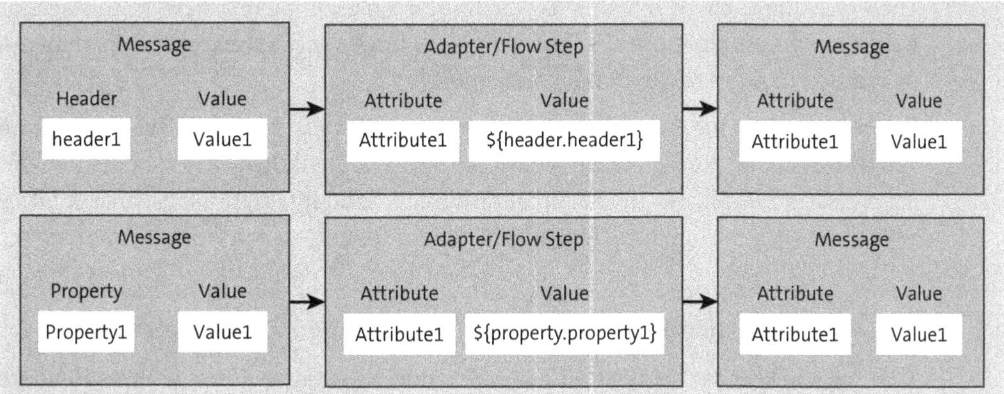

Figure 6.12 How Dynamically Configured Attributes Are Handled during Runtime Using Headers (Top) or Properties (Bottom)

The top part of Figure 6.12 shows how a dynamically configured attribute is handled when a message header is used, and the bottom part of Figure 6.12 shows the same for when a property is used. To refer to a message header or property, you'll need to apply a certain syntax, which you've already seen in this book:

- Expression `${header.header1}` points to field `header1` in the incoming message.
- Expression `${property.property1}` points to property `property1` in the message exchange container.

Note

Recall that expressions such as `${header.header1}` are from Apache Camel's Simple Expression Language (described at *http://s-prs.co/v576017*), which we introduced in Chapter 4, Section 4.1.4.

You've already seen a specific usage of dynamically configured attributes in the following sections:

- In Chapter 4, Section 4.3.4, in the context of the OData adapter, we showed you how to dynamically configure a filter condition for an OData request by referring to a specific header.
- In Chapter 5, Section 5.1.2, a specific header was used in a routing condition to allow you to configure a content-based routing scenario.
- Furthermore, in Chapter 5, Section 5.4.3, we showed you how to use a specific header (`SAPJMSRetries`) to access the number of already executed retries in a scenario when Java Message Service (JMS) queues are used.

Therefore, the topic of dynamic configuration isn't completely new. In this section, we'll show you some more simple examples of how you can use dynamic parameters, in addition to more background information.

Before going into the details, we must mention that many, but not all, iFlow attributes support dynamic configuration. For a list of iFlow attributes that support dynamic configuration, check out the documentation for Cloud Integration available at *http://s-prs.co/v576018*. Search for "Dynamically Configure Integration Flow Parameters."

6.2.1 An Integration Flow with a Dynamically Configured Attribute

To show you how to use dynamic attributes step-by-step, we'll start with a simple scenario that you can easily derive out of the iFlow we created in the previous section (refer to Figure 6.1) with a few modifications. Figure 6.13 shows the target iFlow model.

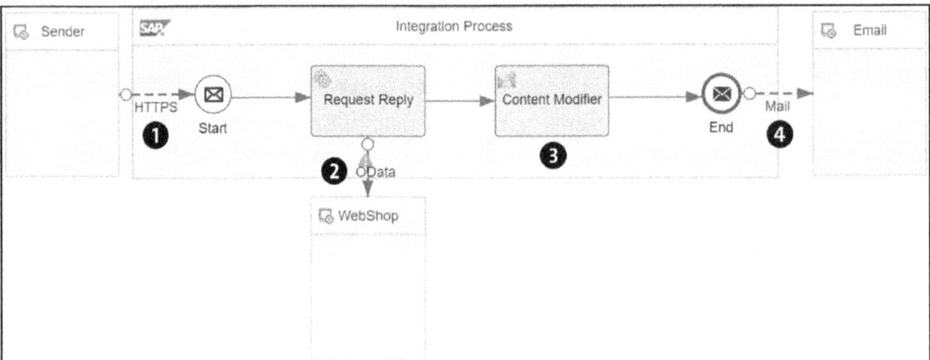

Figure 6.13 Target iFlow Reading Product Details for a Given Product Identifier

In this integration scenario, from an HTTP client (Postman), the iFlow is invoked with a dedicated product identifier (`productid`), which is provided in the HTTP message header ❶. We described setting up the connection from Postman to Cloud Integration in Chapter 2, Section 2.3. The iFlow invokes the WebShop's OData API to get details for the product associated with the given `productid` value. The **OData** adapter ❷ now contains a query condition specifying that only product details for the product identified with the product identifier are to be retrieved. This difference contrasts this scenario with the timer-based scenario we described in the previous section (refer to Figure 6.1) where a list of all products is derived. In our current scenario, only *one* product item is read from the WebShop API. In a **Content Modifier** step ❸, an exchange property is created that contains the name of the actual product, and, finally, the **Mail** adapter ❹ sends an email with the product's details to the email account, where the email subject contains the name of the actual product.

Of course, the product identifier and the product name aren't known to the integration developer when modeling the iFlow. The actual values are only known during runtime when the HTTP request has been posted. Consequently, during design time, the integration developer can only provide placeholders for these attributes, which we'll show you next.

We won't repeat every modeling step in detail because most of these steps have already been described in previous chapters. When comparing Figure 6.1 with Figure 6.13, notice that you can easily derive the new iFlow model from the iFlow we created in the previous section by following these steps:

1. Replace the **Timer Start** event by a **Start Message** event.
2. Add a **Sender** component.
3. Change the **OData** adapter query settings.
4. Add a **Content Modifier** step that sets a property for the product name, which we'll show you shortly.
5. Change the **Mail** adapter's **Subject** value by adding a dynamic expression containing the property created in the **Content Modifier** step (also shown shortly).

However, here's some important advice: Don't overwrite the iFlow developed in the previous section because you'll need a timer-based iFlow later in Section 6.5. Instead, copy the timer-based iFlow, and modify the copy as described in this section.

Designing the part of the scenario that invokes the OData service was described earlier in Chapter 4, Section 4.3, and used in Section 6.1 of this chapter. Designing a **Mail** receiver adapter (second part) was explained earlier in Chapter 2, Section 2.3.4. Therefore, in this section, we'll just show you the settings for the required iFlow elements without further elaborating on these components in detail.

When creating an HTTP connection from the **Sender** to the **Start** event, enter an address that unambiguously identifies the iFlow endpoint for the HTTP client (e.g., "/getProductDetails"), as shown in Figure 6.14.

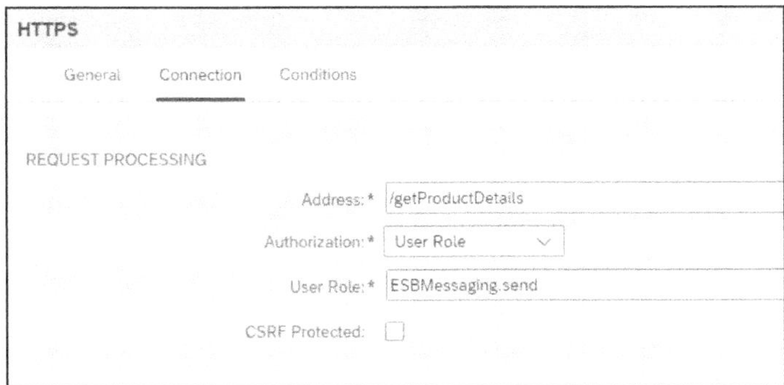

Figure 6.14 HTTP Sender Adapter Connection Settings

To ensure that the iFlow endpoint accepts the header provided from the external component (HTTP client), an additional setting is required. Click somewhere outside any shape, but inside the model area, and select the **Runtime Configuration** tab. In the **Allowed Header(s)** field, enter "productid," as shown in Figure 6.15, because this header should be retained from the incoming message. Note that, usually, the sender provides such data in the body of the message, in which case, Cloud Integration fetches the information through the XML Path Language (XPath). For the sake of simplicity, we'll provide the `productid` value in the header of the HTTP request message.

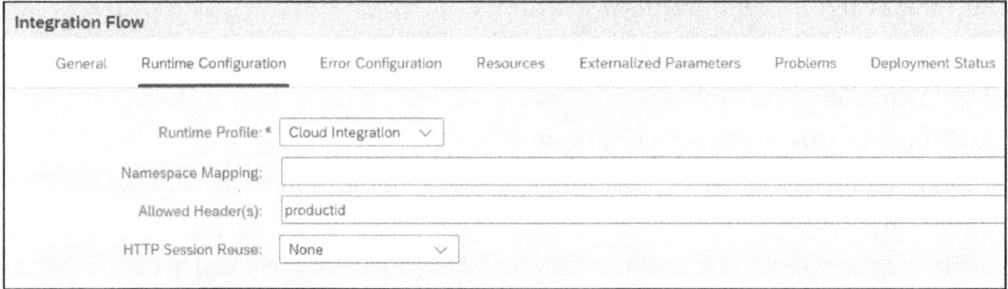

Figure 6.15 Runtime Configuration to Accept Header "productid" Sent from an External Component

Under the OData adapter's **Connection** tab, keep the same address we used in the previous scenario: `https://refapp-espm-ui-cf.cfapps.eu10.hana.ondemand.com/espm-cloud-web/espm.svc/`. Under the **Processing** tab of the adapter, make sure that the product details for the given `productid` header are queried, as shown in Figure 6.16.

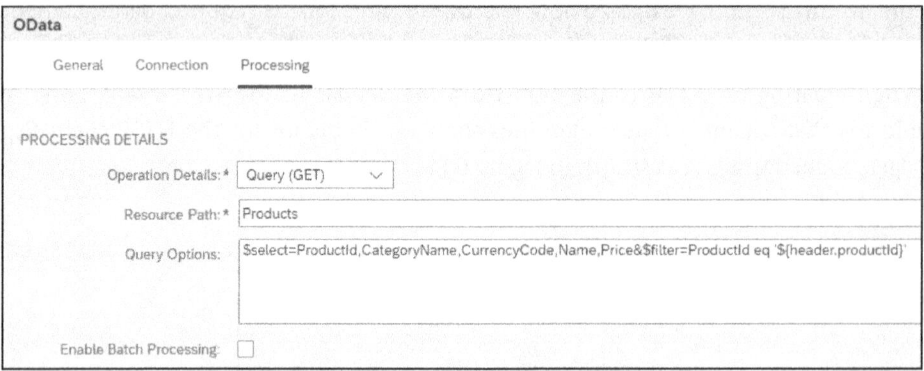

Figure 6.16 Processing Tab of the OData Adapter

Note that Figure 6.16 shows only the modified part of the settings for the current scenario. The other settings of the OData adapter can be kept (compare with Figure 6.6, shown earlier). To derive the new settings from the scenario designed throughout Section , you don't need to reinsert an OData channel again. You can simply edit the **Query Options** field and enter the expression shown in Figure 6.16. Notice that the **Query Options** field now contains a dynamic attribute that contains a placeholder for the message header provided with the inbound request: **${header.productId}**.

Notice also the difference from the iFlow created in Section 6.1 (compare Figure 6.6): in the former case, the OData adapter was configured in such a way that a list of products is derived from the WebShop API, whereas in this current scenario, the product details for only *one* dedicated product are read from the WebShop component.

In the **Content Modifier** step, under the **Exchange Properties** tab, maintain the settings shown in Figure 6.17.

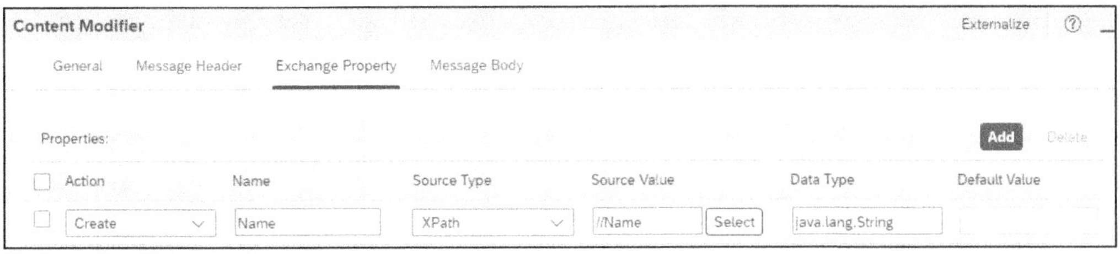

Figure 6.17 Content Modifier Settings

This step creates a property (`Name`) that contains the actual value from the `Name` field of the message. (This value is retrieved from the OData API of the WebShop.) To ensure that the indicated value is taken from the message, set the **Source Type** dropdown menu to **XPath** for the entry.

Finally, for the **Mail** adapter, you can use the same settings as in all previous scenarios using the **Mail** adapter, except for the **Subject** attribute. For the **Subject**, enter the following string:

```
Product Details for Product ${property.Name}
```

Notice again that a dynamic expression will specify this attribute:

```
${property.Name}
```

The actual value will be derived for this placeholder and written into the **Subject** field of the email only during runtime. That's it! You can now save and deploy the iFlow.

Trigger the iFlow by sending a Postman request. Start Postman, and specify a **GET** request with an address given by the iFlow endpoint address, as shown in Chapter 2, Section 2.3.4 (compare Figure 6.44). Provide a header "productId" and a **Value** (e.g., "HT-1000"). To check for reasonable values, open the WebShop's frontend, and browse through the product catalog. You'll find the product identifier (`Product ID`) when clicking for the details of a product. The WebShop's frontend can be found at the following address: *http://s-prs.co/v576020*.

If everything works, you'll get the response as shown in Figure 6.18, which also displays the settings in Postman for your reference.

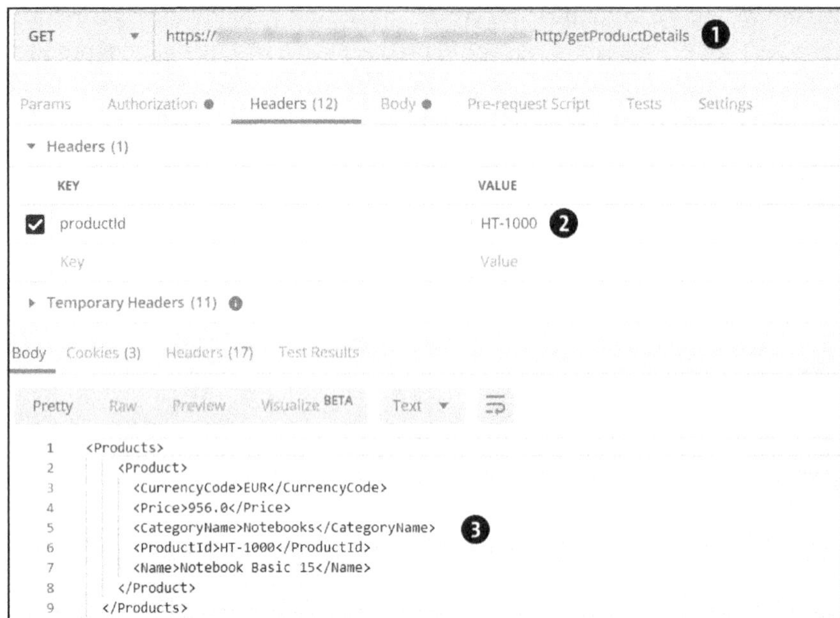

Figure 6.18 Postman Receiving a Response with Details of the Identified Product

Notice that the endpoint address ❶, as specified prior to sending the request, contains the address specified in the **HTTPS** sender adapter (compare with Figure 6.14). The header **productid** and a **Value** also must be provided for the request ❷. After the request was processed successfully, the HTTP response contains the product details for the indicated product, as expected ❸.

For now, let's open your email account and check the email you received. Figure 6.19 shows the expected result. Indeed, the email subject ❶ now contains the actual name of the product, as identified by the product identifier `HT-1000`: **Notebook Basic 15** ❷.

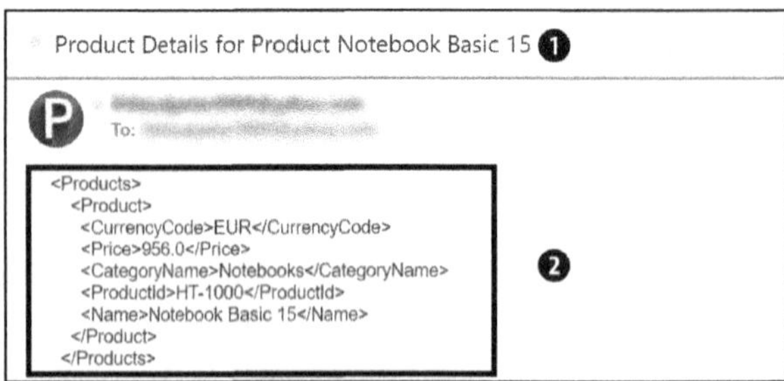

Figure 6.19 Email with Dynamically Set Subject

This specific information was completely unknown to the integration developer when designing the iFlow. The information was retrieved at runtime because of the dynamic expression `${property.Name}`. The received email confirms that our dynamic configuration of the **Mail** adapter's **Subject** attribute worked well.

6.2.2 Monitoring Dynamically Configured Attributes at Runtime

Next, we'll show you how to monitor what happens with dynamically configured attributes during message processing. For this purpose, we'll investigate the message content during message processing. As we'll describe in detail in Chapter 7, Section 7.2.2, the monitoring application provides an option to configure different log levels to specify, in what detail, processing-related information should be displayed during monitoring. For the following exercise, you must set the log level to **Trace**, which ensures payloads and headers are logged after each processing step. This log level is only activated for a short period.

In addition, you must ensure that your user has the right permissions to display the message content (as provided by this log level). In particular, role template `PI_Business_Expert` must be assigned to your user. How authorization groups or roles are assigned to a user is shown in detail in Chapter 10, Section 10.3.

To monitor dynamically configured attributes, follow these steps:

1. Go to the **Monitor** page of the Web UI, and, under **Manage Integration Content**, select your iFlow.
2. In the **Log Level** dropdown list, select **Trace.** Note that, after this activity, this log level setting is effective only for 10 minutes to save resources.
3. Run the iFlow again (use a `productid` value for which a product is available).
4. Choose a tile under **Monitor Message Processing**.
5. Select your iFlow, and click the **Trace** link in the **Logs** section.

   An overview of the message processing steps and the iFlow model will be displayed next to the list of steps, as shown in Figure 6.20.

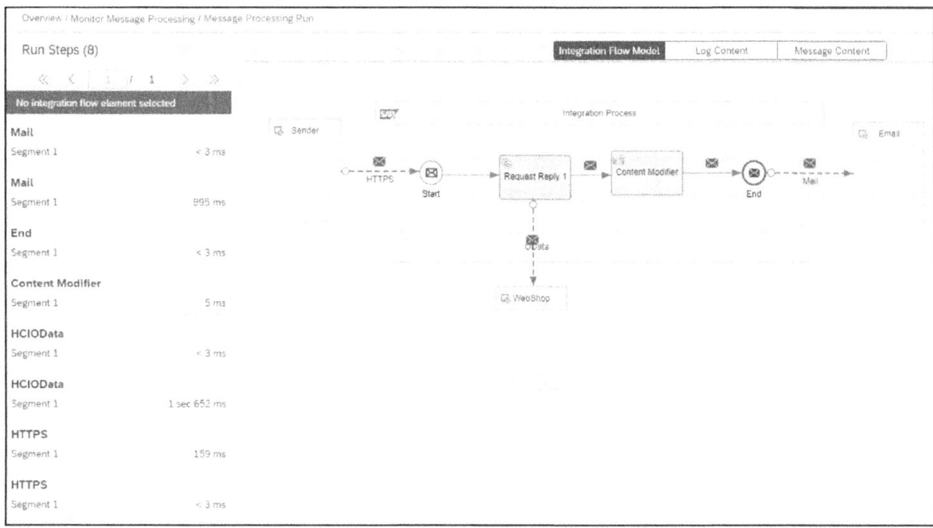

Figure 6.20 Monitoring Individual Steps during Message Processing (Log Level Trace)

6. Click the **Content Modifier** shape. The shape will be highlighted in the model as well as in the list of steps on the left.
7. Select the **Message Content** tab, which is available only when you've specified a log level of **Trace**.
8. The **Header** tile shows a list of headers and their values before the **Content Modifier** step is executed (see Figure 6.21).

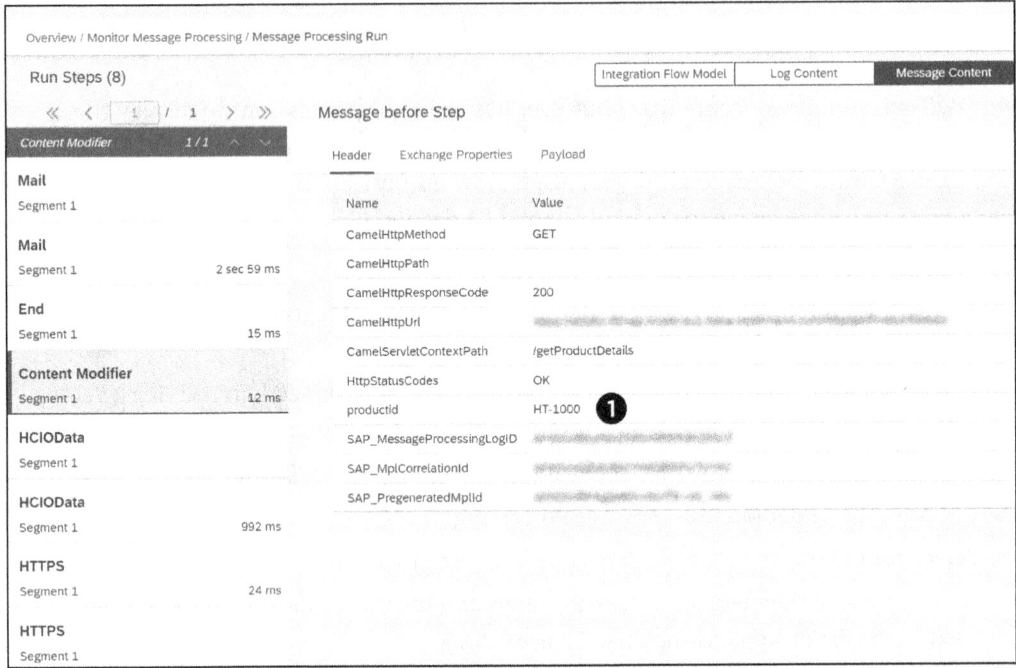

Figure 6.21 Header Tile When Content Modifier Step Is Selected

The tile displays several fields related to the message processing run, such as the request method **GET** (of the preceding OData request), the endpoint address, and other fields we won't elaborate on. What is important for our current discussion is the header **productid** with value **HT-1000** ❶. This result is expected because this value has been provided with the HTTP request.

9. Click the **Exchange Properties** tile. As shown in Figure 6.22, you'll see many properties that correspond to technical details about the actual step in the message processing run. We won't elaborate on these details. These properties are provided by the Apache Camel framework and also depend on the adapter and iFlow steps active during the message processing run. We'll elaborate more on these properties in Section 6.2.3.
10. Select the **Payload** tile. As shown in Figure 6.23, you'll see the content retrieved, during one of the preceding steps, from the WebShop application for the given **productid** value.

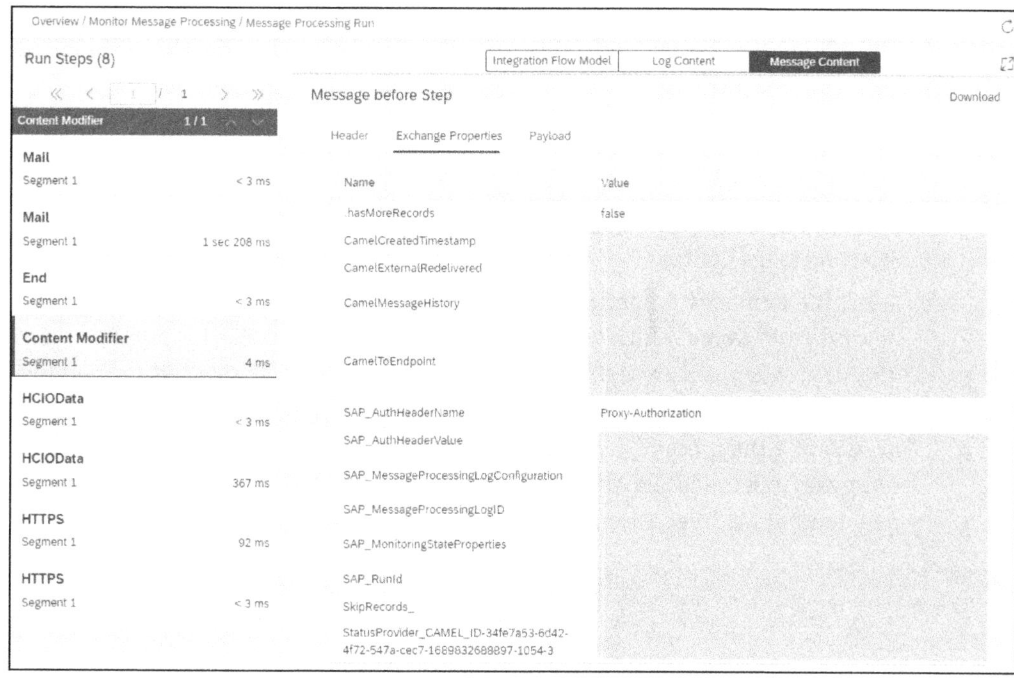

Figure 6.22 Exchange Property Tile When Content Modifier Step Is Selected

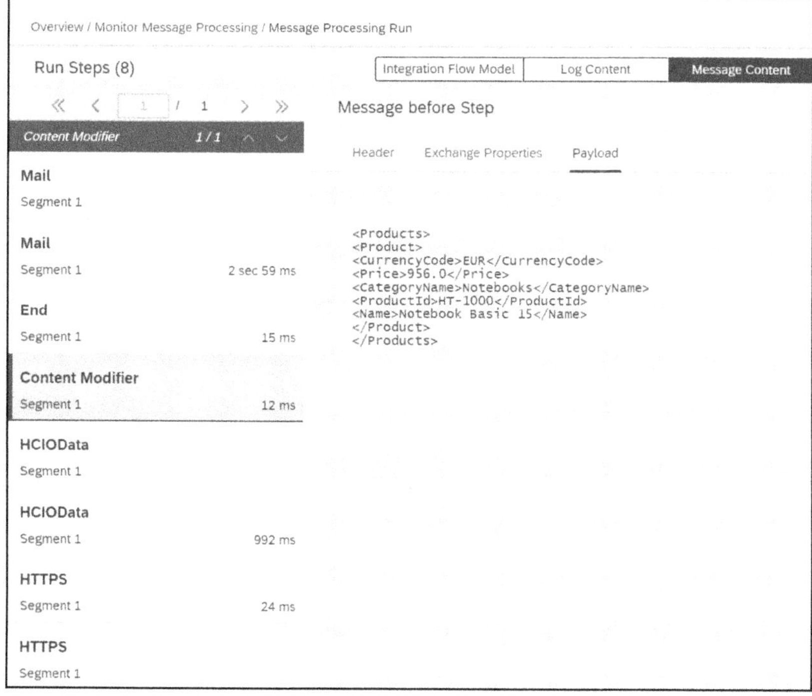

Figure 6.23 Payload Tile When the Content Modifier Step Is Selected

Now, let's see how the message has changed with the subsequent processing step. We won't walk you through all three tiles again; we'll only focus on the **Exchange Properties** tile. Follow these steps:

1. Click **Integration Flow Model** to navigate back to the model.
2. In the model, click the second **End** shape after the **Content Modifier**. The corresponding shape is highlighted in the iFlow model as well as in the list of steps on the left.
3. Select **Message Content**.
4. Select the **Exchange Properties** tile. As shown in Figure 6.24, you'll now notice the new property **Name**, which has the value **Notebook Basic 15** ❶. This property wasn't displayed when the preceding **Content Modifier** shape was selected in the model (compare with Figure 6.22). The reason for this behavior is that this property has just been set by the preceding **Content Modifier** based on the content of the message retrieved from the OData API. In other words, the property wasn't available when the first **Content Modifier** was processed.

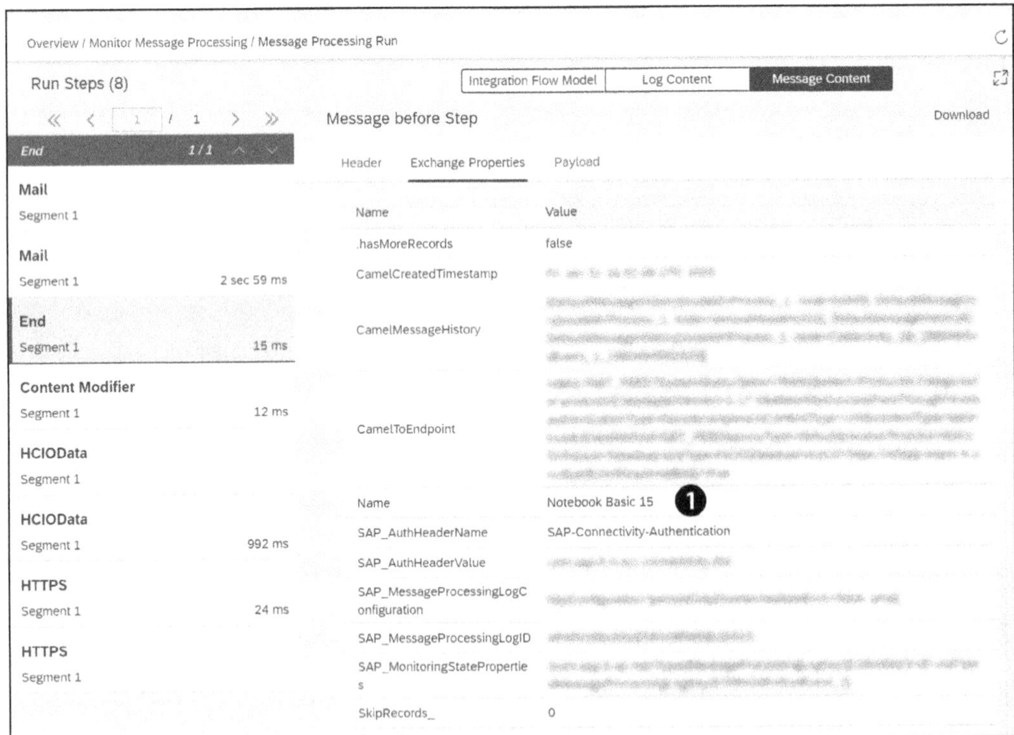

Figure 6.24 Exchange Property Tile When the End Event Is Selected

You can again click the **Header** tile to find the **productid** header, which is present throughout the whole message processing run. The **Payload** tile should also show the same content as in the previous step.

Through this simple example, you can see how to dynamically configure a certain iFlow attribute (by referring to a certain header or property) and how you can monitor the usage of this header during message processing.

In this example, you used a header provided with the inbound request (**productid**) to dynamically configure the **Query Options** attribute of the OData channel. Furthermore, a property has been created based on a value contained in the **Name** field of the message retrieved from the OData API. Based on this property, the **Mail** adapter's **Subject** attribute has been defined dynamically. The header and property values were only known at runtime.

Much could be said about dynamic parameters. In addition to using a specially created header to dynamically configure a certain iFlow attribute, you can use several *predefined* headers and exchange properties (provided by the Cloud Integration framework) to retrieve specific data during the processing of a message. You may have noticed some of these headers and properties already in the corresponding **Header** and **Exchange Properties** tile when a dedicated step in the model is selected (compare, e.g., Figure 6.21, Figure 6.22, and Figure 6.24). In the same way, as described in this section, you can also use these special headers and properties to dynamically configure iFlow attributes. We'll elaborate on these predefined headers and properties in the subsequent section.

6.2.3 Using Predefined Headers and Properties to Retrieve Specific Data Provided by the Integration Framework

In Chapter 5, Section 5.4.3, you encountered an example of a predefined header in the integration framework when using the JMS adapter. The header field `SAPJMSRetries` is automatically created by the integration framework when you use the JMS sender adapter. This field records the number of retries already executed by a JMS message. In Chapter 5, Section 5.4.3, we showed you how to use the content of this header to dynamically define a routing condition (via expression `${header.SAPJMSRetries}`).

This header is only set by adapters consuming from JMS message queues, for example, JMS sender, SAP Process Integration protocol, Applicability Statement 2 (AS2) protocol, or Applicability Statement 4 (AS4) protocol adapters. Similarly, other adapters and iFlow steps set other specific headers and properties to store data that is specific to this adapter or iFlow step.

Note

For an overview of the predefined headers and properties provided by the Cloud Integration framework, check out the documentation for Cloud Integration at *http://s-prs.co/v576021*. Search for the "Headers and Exchange Properties Provided by the Integration Framework."

In this section, we'll show you how to use another predefined header. As described in the Cloud Integration documentation, the splitter step also creates the exchange property CamelSplitSize. This property provides the total number of split items of an exchange. To learn how to use this property to dynamically configure a certain iFlow attribute, refer to the iFlow described in Chapter 5, Section 5.2 (refer to Figure 6.23).

The target iFlow is modeled as shown in Figure 6.25.

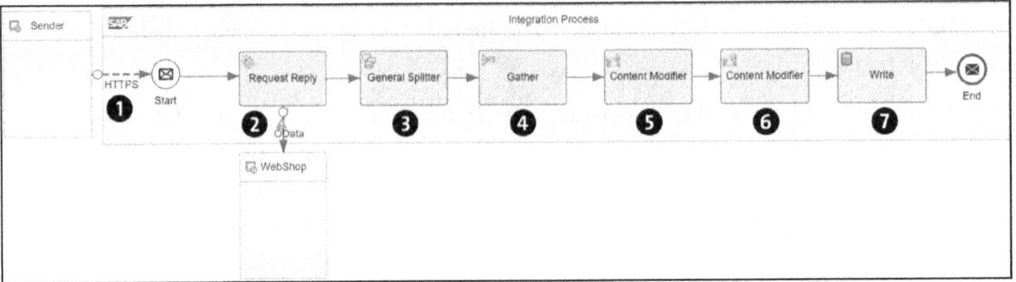

Figure 6.25 iFlow with a Message Split

As we've already discussed message splits in detail, we'll restrict the discussion in this section to a summary of the settings for each step and adapter. In this scenario, we want to retrieve again a list of products (as in the scenario shown previously in Figure 6.1), but this time, we want to filter out the products of one product category (e.g., Notebooks). For that purpose, the HTTP client provides the product category as an HTTP header together with the HTTP request, as shown in Figure 6.25 ❶. In the OData request ❷, the value of the CategoryName attribute is used to dynamically define the filter criteria. As a result, a bulk message with more than one item is likely retrieved (as more than one product might be available for a given product category). A **General Splitter** splits the message into individual ones ❸. Without further processing steps in between, we'll immediately bring together the split messages into one single message with the **Gather** step ❹.

Note

We're designing this scenario only to illustrate the usage of a predefined property. As we'll also describe later, designing such a scenario just to get the number of products isn't good practice because of its memory-intense processing.

In the first **Content Modifier** step ❺, we'll store the message payload, which is again a list of products, in an exchange property. In the second **Content Modifier** step ❻, we'll create the message body, consisting of a headline text and the payload stored in the property from the previous **Content Modifier** step. One interesting detail is that to define the headline text, we'll use a property that is provided by the framework (CamelSplitSize) and that we haven't defined in any previous step by design. This property contains the actual number of splits, which is identical to the number of products available for the given category. Finally, we won't send the result to an email inbox as you might have expected when comparing with the previous tutorials. Instead, we'll use a data store **Write** step ❼ to create a data store entry (like the entry shown in Chapter 2, Section 2.3). Because playing with dynamic attributes is fun, we'll use the category name to dynamically define the **Entry ID** of the data store.

In more detail, you'll need to specify the following settings for the iFlow steps:

1. Under the **Runtime Configuration** tab, (accessed by clicking outside any shape but still in the model pane of the iFlow), enter the following header name in the **Allowed Header(s)** field as "categoryName".
2. For the **HTTPS** sender adapter, provide again a specific address to determine the iFlow endpoint.
3. In the **OData** adapter's **Processing** tab, specify the **Query Options** parameter, as shown in Figure 6.26.

   Notice that the list of products is dynamically filtered based on the value of the header `categoryName`.

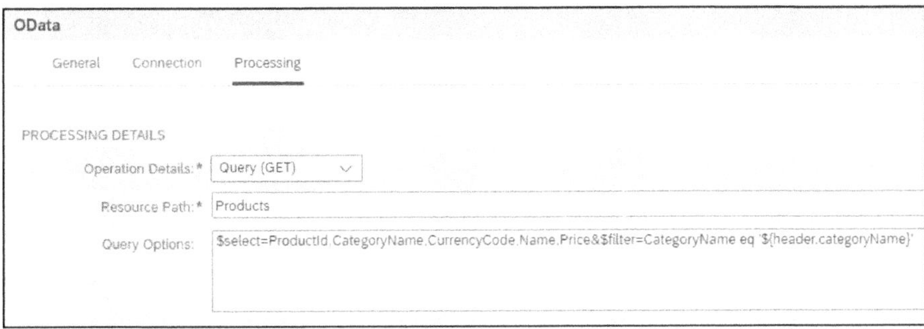

Figure 6.26 OData Adapter Processing Settings

4. In the **General Splitter**, in the **Expression Type** dropdown list, select **XPath**. In the **XPath Expression** field, enter "//Product," and make sure that the **Streaming** option has been deselected, as shown in Figure 6.27.

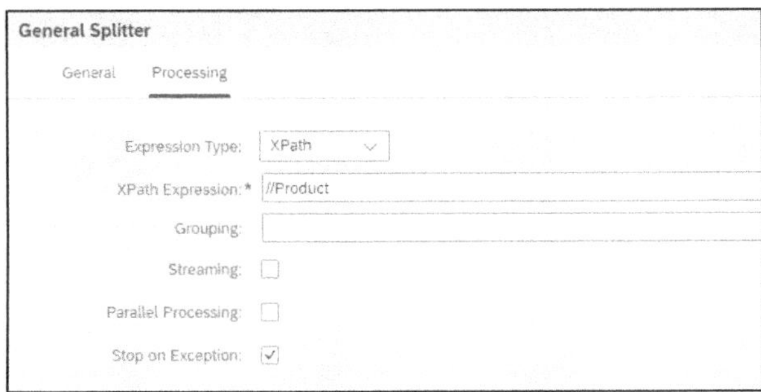

Figure 6.27 General Splitter Processing Settings

In Chapter 5, Section 5.2.1, we kept the **Streaming** option selected. However, when using the property `CamelSplitSize`, we want to disable the **Streaming** option because the property `CamelSplitSize` is only applied on the complete exchange if **Streaming** is disabled.

5. For the **Gather** step, we'll leave the default settings, as shown in Figure 6.28.

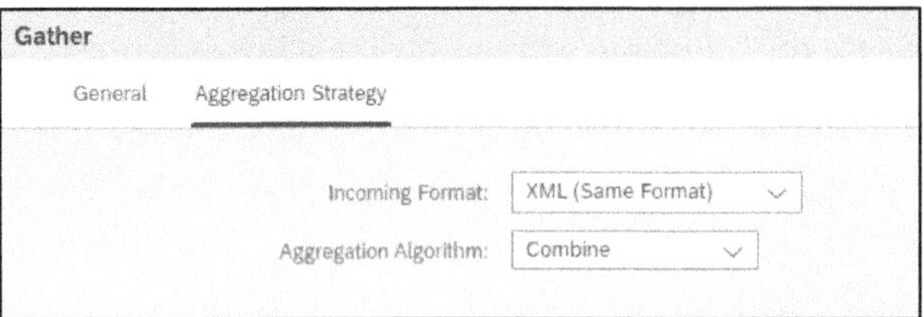

Figure 6.28 Gather Step's Aggregation Strategy Setting

6. In the first **Content Modifier** step after the **Gather** step, we only need to define a property for the message payload, as shown in Figure 6.29.

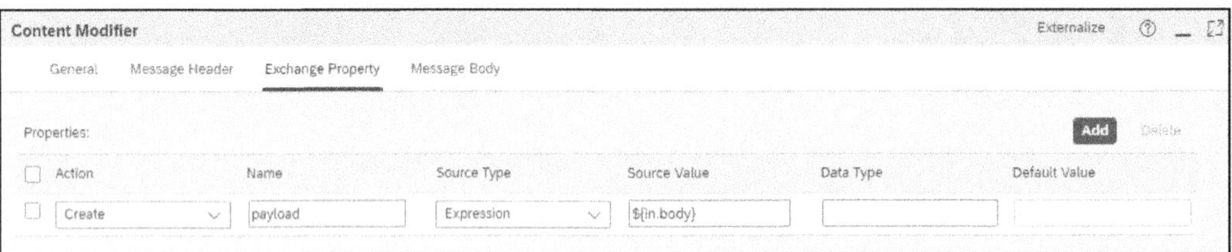

Figure 6.29 Settings of First Content Modifier

7. In the second **Content Modifier** step, under the **Message Body** tab, make sure that **Expression** has been selected in the **Type** dropdown list. Furthermore, in the **Body** field, enter the expression shown in Figure 6.30.

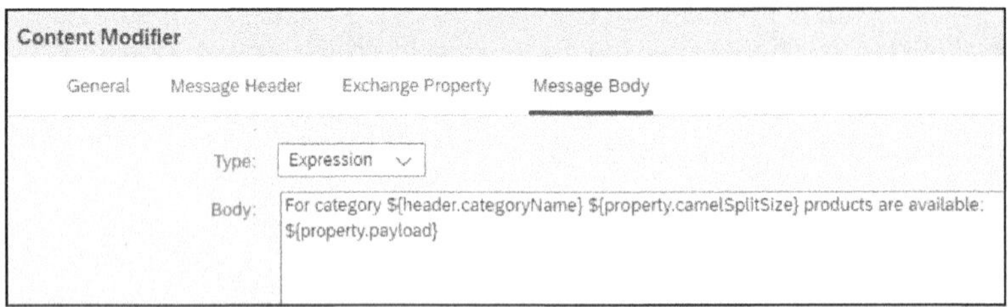

Figure 6.30 Settings of Second Content Modifier

Notice that two dynamic expressions are used to specify the message body: `${property.CamelSplitSize}` for the number of splits and `${property.payload}` for the content of the message.

8. Finally, for the **Write** step, maintain the settings as shown in Figure 6.31.

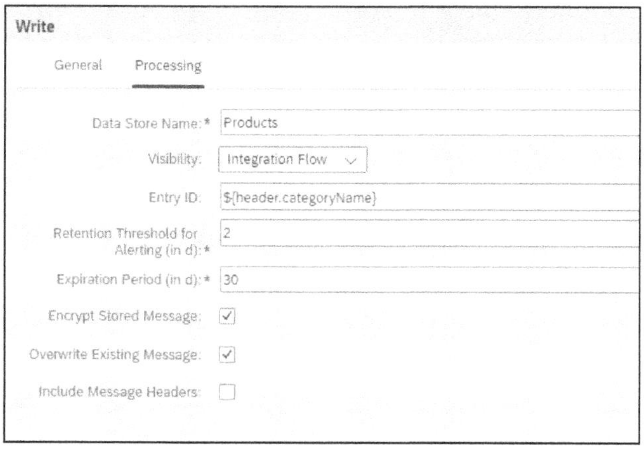

Figure 6.31 Settings of the Write Step

In the **Data Store Name** field, enter "Products" to indicate, for the message monitoring phase, that this data store contains product information.

In the **Entry ID** field, enter the following dynamic expression: "${header.categoryName}". This expression will ensure that, at runtime, an entry ID is defined based on the name of the product category relevant for the actual request at runtime. When you run the scenario with different header values for `categoryName`, you'll get different entries in the same data store.

You should select the **Overwrite Existing Message** option; otherwise, with each new message processing run (with a `categoryName` value already used in a previous message processing run), the iFlow runs into an error because an entry with the same entry ID already exists. You can keep the other default settings.

Now, run the iFlow by entering a **categoryName** value with the request (e.g., "Notebooks"). In Postman, you'll see a response like the one shown in Figure 6.32.

Figure 6.32 shows again the header provided with the request ❶ as well as the response body. Let's briefly look at the introduction text in the response (before the XML structure ❹ with the product list):

```
For category Notebooks 10 products are available:
```

When you compare with Figure 6.30, you should notice that the string `Notebooks` ❷ was dynamically derived from the expression `${header.categoryName}`, and the number `10` ❸ was derived from the expression `${property.CamelSplitSize}` at runtime. Important to note is that the `CamelSplitSize` property wasn't set by you, the integration developer, when modeling the iFlow. Instead, this property was provided by the framework automatically because a splitter step was processed.

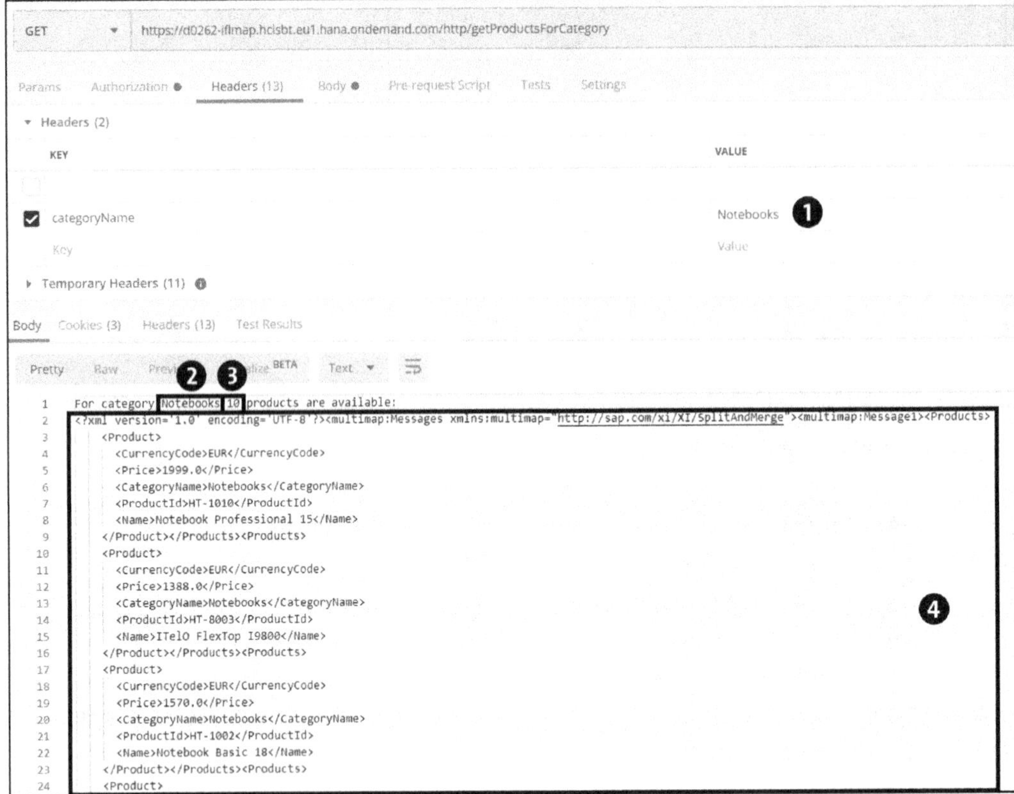

Figure 6.32 Postman Response

Let's also check the data store by going to the **Monitoring** application and clicking the **Data Stores** tile under **Manage Stores**. The data store will appear as shown in Figure 6.33.

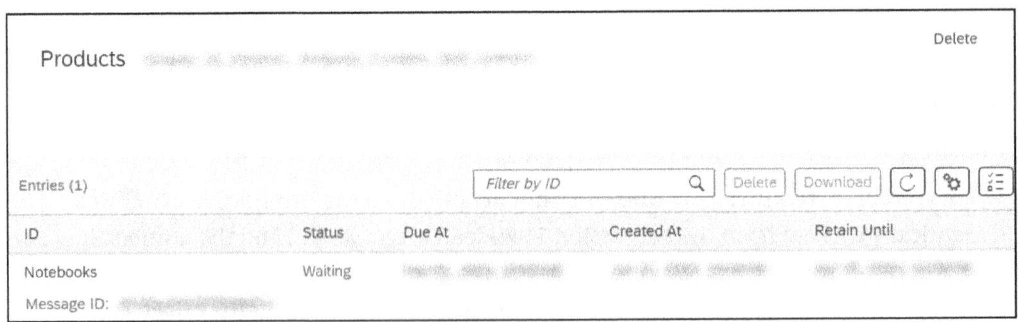

Figure 6.33 Data Store Entry

Notice that, in the previous message processing run, a data store entry (`Notebooks`) was created, based on the value of header `categoryName`. If you download the message from the data store (as explained in Chapter 2, Section 2.3), you'll see that the message contains the same introduction text and product list as the HTTP response.

Now, you can do the same exercise as we did for the previous scenario (Section 6.2.2) and analyze the headers and properties available during each step in the message processing run (with the log level set to **Trace**). We won't repeat these steps again, but leave this task to you.

We'd like to close this section with some remarks on the message split scenario used in this tutorial. A message split scenario takes quite a long time because, for each item of the message retrieved from the OData API, the message processing is repeated (compare Chapter 5, Section 5.2). Seasoned integration experts would have wrinkled their noses at the scenario we modeled earlier in Figure 6.25, all just to find out the number of items in a list retrieved from an OData service. Indeed, to use the splitter pattern to determine the number of items in a list without any further processing of the individual items is like using a sledgehammer to crack a nut. The splitter scenario we proposed in this section uses a lot of memory.

We could have received the desired result in a much smarter way. We used the message split in this case specifically to showcase the existence of the specific `CamelSplitSize` header. To round out this section, we'll show you how to get the same result with much better performance. You can just modify the previous iFlow, shown earlier in Figure 6.25, with a few steps.

As mentioned earlier, we recommend that you copy the previous iFlow and then perform the following modifications. Remove the **General Splitter** step and the **Gather** step, which should result in the iFlow model shown in Figure 6.34.

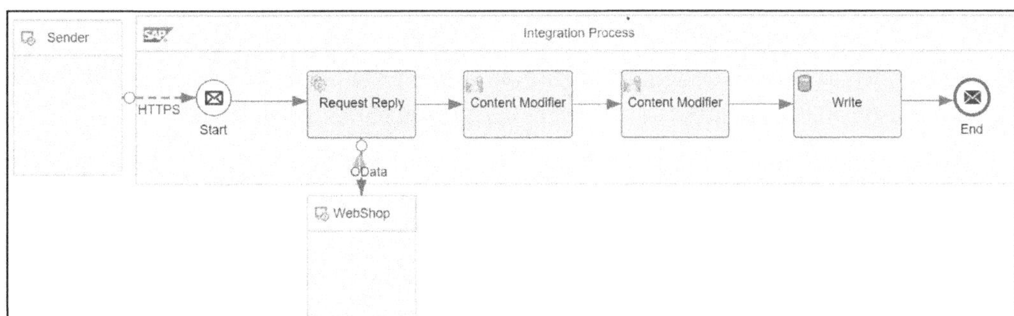

Figure 6.34 Simplified and Better Designed iFlow (without Message Split)

Configure the iFlow with the following changed settings:

- For the **HTTPS** sender adapter, specify a different address than in the previous iFlow. Otherwise, if your previous iFlow is still deployed on the tenant, and you deploy this new flow with the same endpoint address, you'll get an error.
- In the first **Content Modifier** step, define a new property like the property shown in Figure 6.35.

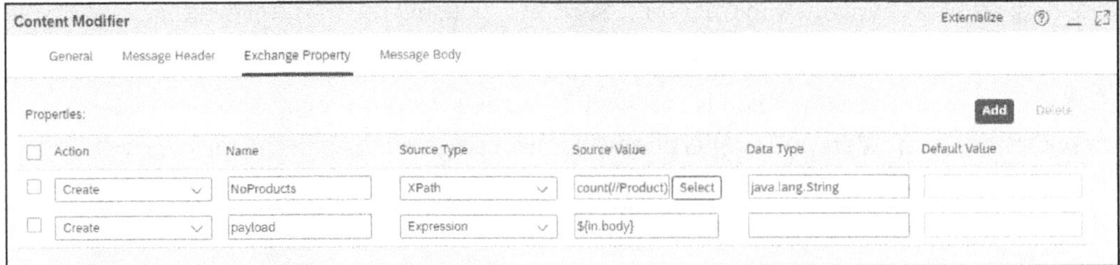

Figure 6.35 Changed Setting of First Content Modifier

The XPath expression `count(//Product)` provides the number of `Product` items in the bulk message read from the WebShop.

- In the second **Content Modifier** step, use the new property to define the entry text of the message, as shown in Figure 6.36.

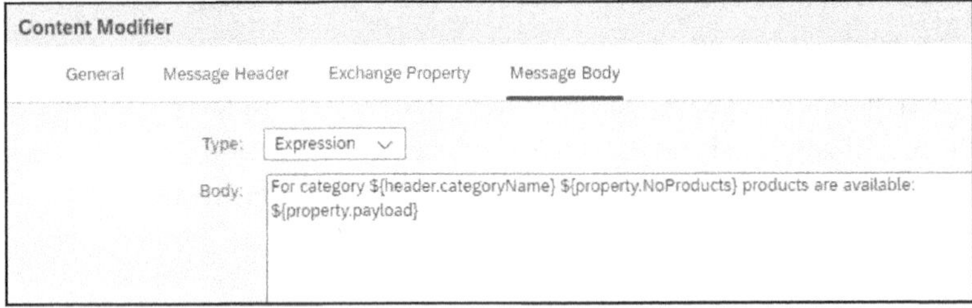

Figure 6.36 The Message Body Now Defined by the New Property

When you run this iFlow with the same request header as in the previous scenario, you should get the same result (the same message is stored in the data store).

We added this final variant to emphasize the importance of considering things such as performance when designing integration content. We'll elaborate more on this consideration and other integration content design guidelines in Section 6.11.

That's it! In this section, you've seen how to dynamically configure an iFlow attribute by using data provided by the integration framework in one of the various predefined headers.

You're now well equipped with the knowledge required for designing more sophisticated scenarios. The more creative you are when modeling even more complicated message flows, the higher the risk is that you'll lose sight of the goal of the overall iFlow. In Section 6.3, we'll show you how to manage complexity by modularizing your integration logic into smaller chunks by using subprocesses. Then, in Section 6.4, we'll introduce you to the ProcessDirect adapter, which can implement direct communications between different iFlows (on the same tenant), which is a good approach to modularizing a comprehensive integration scenario into smaller pieces.

6.2.4 Adding a Custom Header to the Message Exchange

Traceability of messages is an important aspect of integration. It helps in error detection and troubleshooting. In a complex landscape where numerous applications are interconnected, errors can occur at any time and traceability allows you to track the message and find the root cause.

Custom headers can be used to track messages in Cloud Integration using any correlation ID coming in the incoming payload. In this section, we'll explain how a custom header can be added to your iFlow.

We'll extend the iFlow used in the previous sections and add a custom header to it. The extended iFlow is shown in Figure 6.37. To extend the iFlow, add an additional **Script** step of **Add Custom Header** to it.

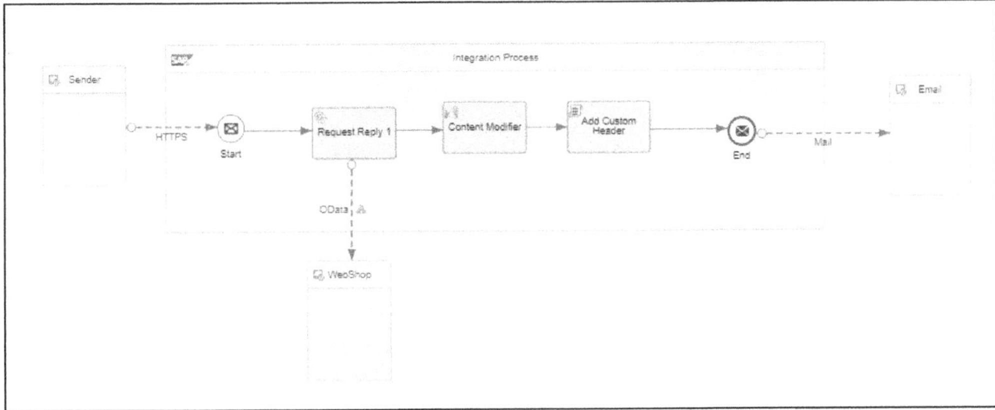

Figure 6.37 Adding Custom Header Step

In the **Content Modifier** step of the iFlow, shown in Figure 6.38, we'll add another exchange property **ProductId** to track the message, add it to the custom header, and use the same **ProductId** to search the message in message monitoring.

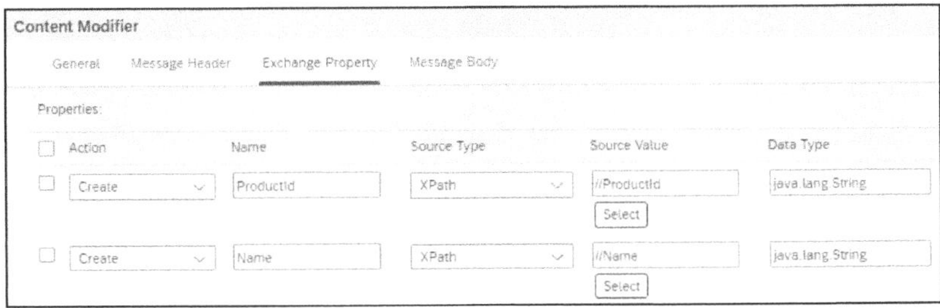

Figure 6.38 Adding Exchange Property ProductId

Now, we'll add a simple script as shown in Listing 6.1 to extract the value of the exchange property **ProductId** and create a custom header with the name **ProductId** using the method `addCustomHeaderProperty`.

```
import com.sap.gateway.ip.core.customdev.util.Message;
import java.util.HashMap;
def Message processData(Message message) {
    //Body
    def body = message.getBody();
    def messageLog = messageLogFactory.getMessageLog(message);
/*Setting the custom header*/
    map = message.getProperties();
    customHeaderValue = map.get("ProductId");
    if(messageLog != null){
    messageLog.addCustomHeaderProperty("ProductId", customHeaderValue);
}
    return message;
}
```

Listing 6.1 Script to Add Custom Headers

6.2.5 Monitoring Messages Using Custom Headers

Now that the iFlow is updated and ready to be triggered, we'll use the same Postman request as shown in Figure 6.39 that was used in the earlier section to send a message to Cloud Integration. We've used the same value in the header **productid**.

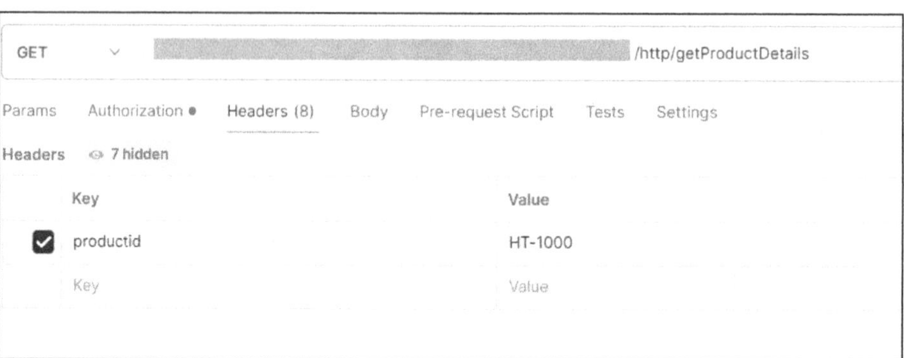

Figure 6.39 Postman Request

Once the message is successfully executed in Cloud Integration, the trace log from the execution shows that the exchange property **ProductId** was created successfully with the information returned from the webshop, as shown in Figure 6.40.

To search the same message using the custom header **PropertyId**, navigate to the monitoring view in the Cloud Integration, expand the view (Figure 6.41 ❶) to get advanced search options available, and then use the search criteria as "ProductId = HT-1000" in the **Custom Header** field ❷. Once you press Enter, the search will filter out the message based on the search criteria.

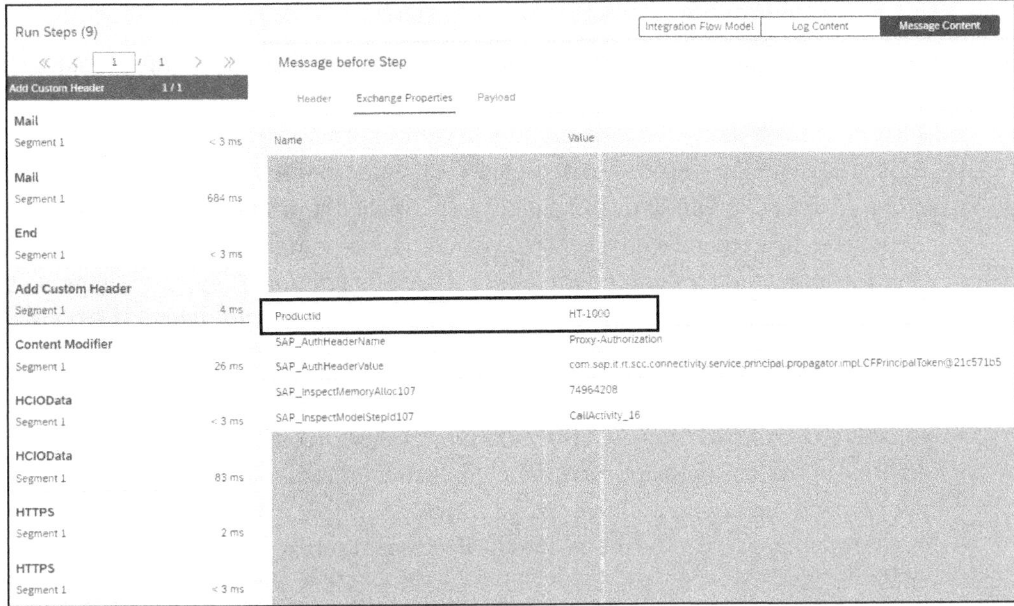

Figure 6.40 Exchange Property in the Message Trace

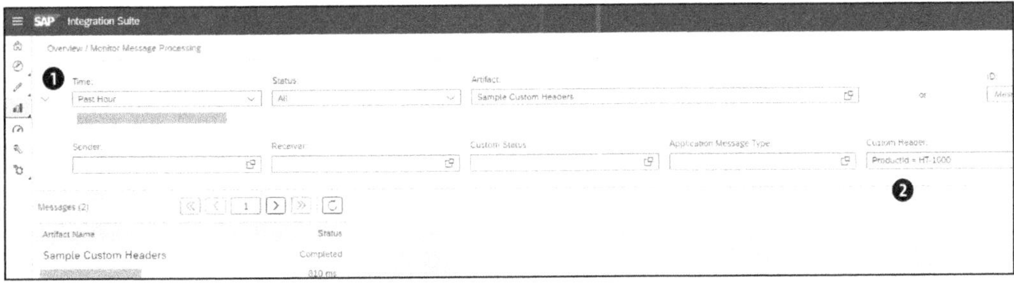

Figure 6.41 Seach Message Using Custom Headers

With this, you've learned how to add a custom header to the exchange and how to search for a message in Cloud Integration using custom headers.

6.3 Structuring Large Integration Flows Using Local Processes

With Cloud Integration, you can model fairly large integration scenarios. Due to the flexible pipeline of the underlying Apache Camel integration engine, you could potentially add as many processing steps to your route as are necessary to fulfill your integration needs. However because we're using a graphical modeler, large models can easily become confusing, which cancels out all the benefits of using a graphical notation. In this section, you'll learn how to structure large process models using subprocesses.

6.3.1 Managing Complexity through Modularization

Putting too much logic into one module is never a good idea. This warning holds true for classic programming languages, such as Java, as well as for graphical environments, such as the Web UI in Cloud Integration. In your informatics classes, you learned how to slice large programs into manageable logical units and treat them separately (*separation of concerns*). The same principles can be applied to graphically modeled iFlows. To achieve this separation of concerns in Cloud Integration, you must use subprocesses or *local processes*, as they are called in Cloud Integration. The terms "subprocess" and "local process (integration)" will be used interchangeably throughout this book.

As you'll see in this section, working with subprocesses isn't difficult. We encourage you to use subprocesses to keep your individual processes and subprocesses at a reasonable size. Note that you can also reuse subprocesses in different branches. As a general rule of thumb, a process model shouldn't contain more than 10 to 15 elements. If your models are larger, we recommend refactoring these models and reducing their size by moving parts of the model into newly created subprocesses. To apply this rule, you'll need to know how to model subprocesses and how parameters are exchanged between parent and child processes.

You may wonder whether you should define an interface for a subprocess that describes the data that a subprocess expects from its parent process and what data to return after execution. You don't have to define such an interface because the called subprocess also relies on the same exchange on which the main process is working, which is automatically handed over from step to step within the main process as well as within the subprocess. This relationship again stresses the importance of the exchange as *the* central data container within iFlows while working with Cloud Integration and its underlying Apache Camel framework.

6.3.2 Developing an Integration Flow with a Local Integration Process

In this section, we'll show you how to design the example iFlow shown in Figure 6.42. In this iFlow, we modeled the main **Integration Process** (upper shape shown in Figure 6.42) that calls a local integration process (lower shape labeled **Execute Business Logic** shown in Figure 6.42). The latter component now contains a step to call the WebShop. As in the previous scenario (shown earlier in Figure 6.34), a list of products for a dedicated product category (category name provided with the message header of HTTP request) is retrieved from the WebShop. This part of the business logic has been outsourced now. The final processing of the retrieved message, like creating the data store entry for the list of products, is again taken over by the main process.

Let's see how this scenario works in more detail. We'll look at the execution sequence first, shown in Figure 6.42, before diving into the detailed configuration of each step. The main process, modeled at the top of the diagram, is triggered by an incoming HTTP message ❶ (providing the `categoryName` header with a value as in the previous scenario;

Section 6.2.3 and compare Figure 6.34). In a **Content Modifier** step, the value of the `categoryName` header is stored as a property ❷. This step isn't necessary for our scenario, but we've introduced this step to show you how properties are handled when subprocesses are involved. With the **Process Call** step ❸, message processing is handed over to the **Execute Business Logic** component (the subprocess). In this component ❹, the WebShop is called through the OData adapter. During this call, the property created in the main process's **Content Modifier** step ❷ that contains the product category is used to filter for products for the indicated category. After having received the response from the WebShop, a **Content Modifier** step in the **Execute Business Logic** subprocess ❺ creates two properties: one property containing the payload and another property containing the number of product items contained in the message (using the XPath expression `count(//Product)` as in Section 6.2.3). Message processing is then again handed over to the main process where, in another **Content Modifier** step ❻, the message body is defined (to contain an introductory text with the number of products in the actual message and the payload). Finally, as in the previous scenario, the message is stored in a data store entry ❼ where the ID of the entry is given by the product category.

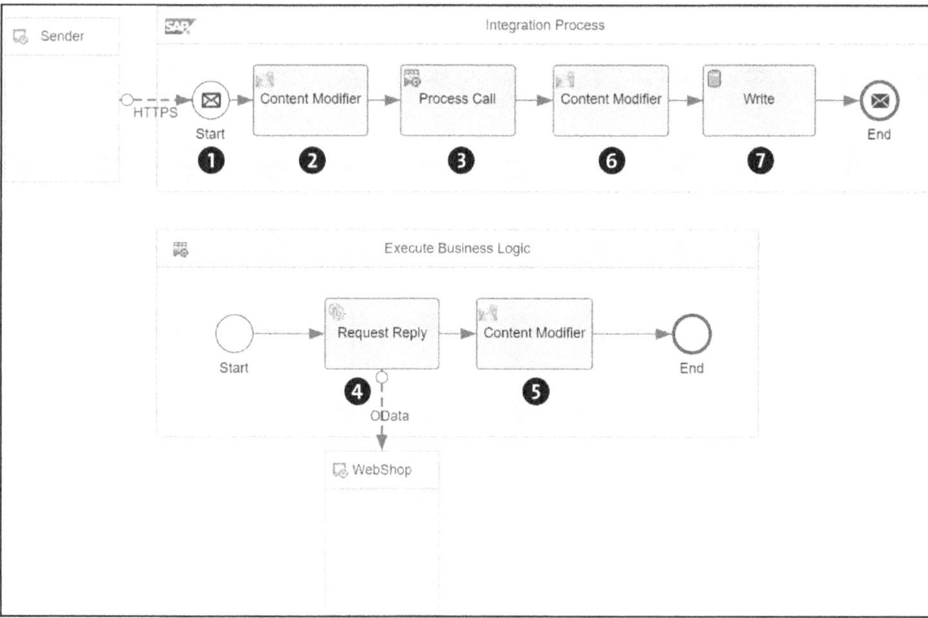

Figure 6.42 The Target iFlow

The interesting part of this scenario is the iFlow that invokes the subprocess. So, how do you model the subprocess and its invocation? We need to begin with the subprocess first, which is important because the parent process will have to reference the subprocess later. Thus, the subprocess must be in place or such a reference can't be established.

You're already familiar with most steps used in this model. As the collaboration between main process and subprocess is a new concept, we'll show you how to design the required components in detail. Because the settings of many components will be identical to the settings in the previous scenario, you can easily start with the new iFlow by copying the integration scenario shown earlier in Figure 6.34. After copying that integration scenario, follow these steps:

1. Remove the connectors between the **Start** event and the **Request Reply** step, as well as between the first **Content Modifier** step and the second **Content Modifier** step, as shown in Figure 6.43.

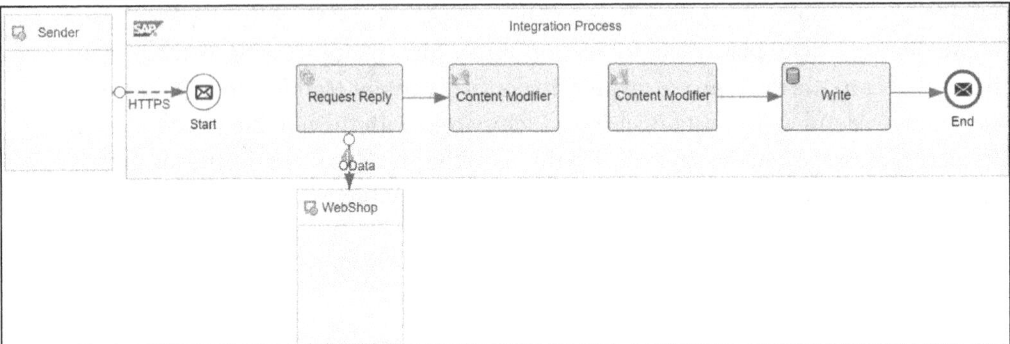

Figure 6.43 Modified iFlow with Connectors Removed

2. Create a local integration process by picking the **Local Integration Process** entry from the palette, which can be found beneath the **Process** main menu entry, as shown in Figure 6.44.

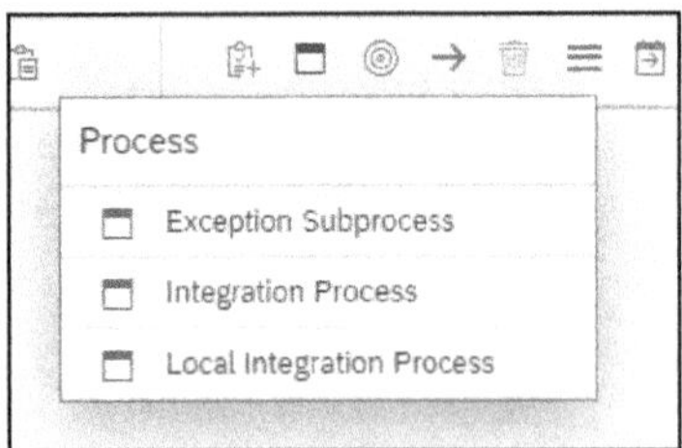

Figure 6.44 Selecting the Local Integration Process from the Palette

3. Place the **Local Integration Process** shape below the **Integration Process** shape, and change the name of the shape (under the **General** tab below the shape when selected) to the **Execute Business Logic** shape. The iFlow model now looks like the model shown in Figure 6.45.

   Note the new icon in the upper-left corner of the local process, signifying this process as a subprocess, which can't be started by an incoming message or by a **Timer Start** event. A subprocess can only be invoked from a parent process in a **Process Call** shape, which we'll explain shortly. Because of this invocation relationship with a parent process, a subprocess must start with an empty **Start** event ◯. The only attribute you can change when selecting the subprocess is its name, which you should adjust to make self-explanatory. Within the subprocess, you can model any integration logic, exactly as you would for the main process.

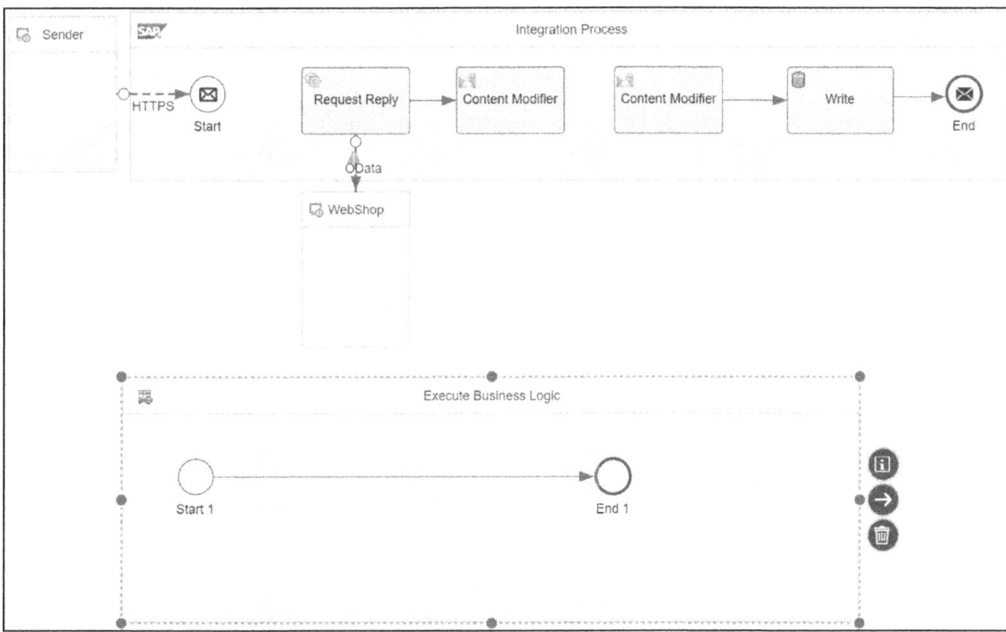

Figure 6.45 Adding the Local Integration Process Shape to the Model

Limitations of Local Integration Processes

Note that some limitations exist when using local integration processes. You can't use the following iFlow components within a local integration process:

- **Aggregator**
- **Process Call**
- **Start** message event
- **End** message event

Furthermore, using the **Splitter** step in a local integration process also requires some specific considerations because this step behaves differently from when it's used in the main process. For more information, see the SAP Community blog at *http://s-prs.co/507725*.

4. Move the **Request Reply** shape and the shape of the first **Content Modifier** step from the **Integration Process** shape into the **Execute Business Logic** shape. Before you can drag and drop the shapes accordingly, you'll need to remove the connectors between these shapes as well as the connector between the **Start 1** and **End 1** shapes.

After renaming the **Start 1** and **End 1** shapes to **Start** and **End** (only to beautify the model) and rearranging the shapes a bit, the iFlow model looks like the model shown in Figure 6.46.

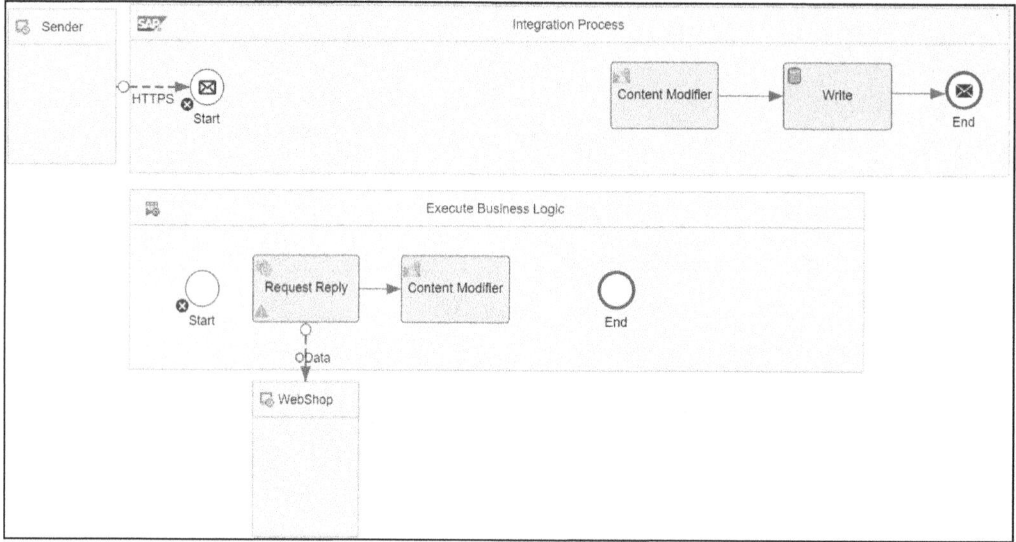

Figure 6.46 Changed iFlow Model

5. Connect the **Start** event in the **Execute Business Logic** shape with the **Request Reply** step, and then connect the **Content Modifier** step with the **End** event.
6. Insert a new **Content Modifier** step into the **Integration Process** shape after the **Start** event, and maintain the settings as shown in Figure 6.47.

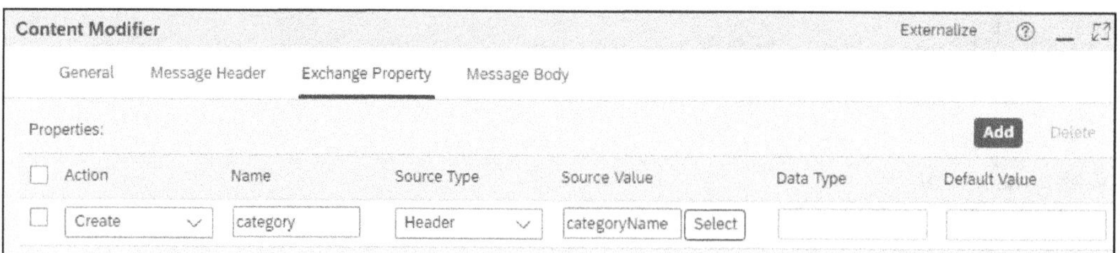

Figure 6.47 Settings for the New Content Modifier

This step will store the value of header `categoryName` (from the inbound message) in a property with name `category`. The goal is to demonstrate how variables created in the parent (main) process will also be available in the child process (**Execute Business Logic**).

Next, you'll need to model the invocation of the local integration process from the main process—the referencing of the child process from the parent process mentioned earlier. To model the invocation, follow these steps:

1. In the palette, click the **Call** icon ⇄ to open the **Call** submenu, as shown in Figure 6.48.

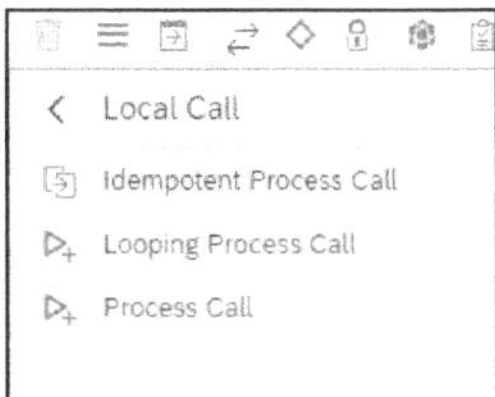

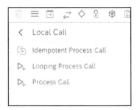

Figure 6.48 Opening the Process Call Submenu from the Palette

2. In the **Integration Process** shape, add the **Process Call** step, which will hand over message processing to the **Execute Business Logic** subprocess at runtime.
3. The last step is to connect the newly positioned **Process Call** shape with the subprocess itself. This connection is created by selecting the **Process Call** rounded rectangle in the main process and adjusting the **Local Integration Process** field in the associated properties area beneath the process model in the **Processing** tab. Click the **Select** button to open another dialog box listing all modeled local integration processes. Pick the process you want to invoke (because we've modeled only one local process only one entry should appear). The dialog box closes automatically after you've chosen an entry from the list, as shown in Figure 6.49.

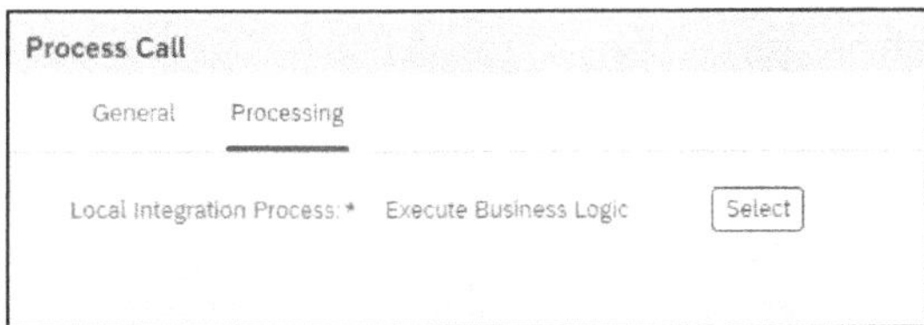

Figure 6.49 Process Call Settings

Let's look at the iFlow components and the parameters we've specified up to this point. First, inspect the OData adapter settings as well as those of the **Content Modifier** step in the **Execute Business Logic** subprocess. Note that we'll use the same settings for the OData call and for the first **Content Modifier** step as in the previous scenario, with one slight exception in the OData channel.

With the OData request, the iFlow will again retrieve a list of products for a given category (compare with Figure 6.26). But let's now slightly change the filter settings in the **Query Options** field of the **Processing** tab. Replace the expression **'${header.categoryName}'** with "'${property.category}'" so that the field has the following content:

```
$select=ProductId,CategoryName,CurrencyCode,Name,Price&$filter=CategoryName eq
'${property.category}'
```

This change isn't required to achieve the intended result of the scenario (getting a list of products for a given category). We only added this modification to show you that the property category created in the parent process will be available at runtime in the child process to resolve the OData filter condition.

The **Content Modifier** step is configured in the same way as shown earlier in Figure 6.35. Thus, two values are stored during the execution of the subprocess:

- The number of Product items in the message retrieved from the WebShop (stored in property NoProducts)
- The payload of the message (stored in property payload).

Note that we want to show that variables created in the subprocess (the two just mentioned) will be available again in the main process after the processing of the subprocess has been finished.

Note also that we didn't change the **Content Modifier** and the **Write** steps in the main process. Their configuration was described earlier, but here's a recap:

- For the **Content Modifier** settings, compare Figure 6.36. The message body (created in the main process after the subprocess has been executed) is built based on values retrieved from properties created in the subprocess (NoProducts and payload).
- For the **Write** step settings, we'll also use the same settings as specified in our original scenario (compare Figure 6.31).

When you run the scenario with a given product category provided in the HTTP request header, you should see the same result as described in Section 6.2.3 (compare Figure 6.32 and Figure 6.33). In other words, you should get an HTTP response and a new data store entry with a message, as shown in Listing 6.2.

```
For category Notebooks 10 products are available:
<Products>
    <Product>
      <CurrencyCode>EUR</CurrencyCode>
      <Price>1999.000</Price>
      <CategoryName>Notebooks</CategoryName>
      <ProductId>HT-1010</ProductId>
      <Name>Notebook Professional 15</Name>
    </Product>
    <Product>
    ...
```

Listing 6.2 HTTP Response

When designing the iFlow, we focused on the cooperation between parent and child processes, as well as how the parameter can be transferred between the two. The successful execution of the iFlow proves that data transfer between parent and child processes works. You don't need local or global variables, as you might typically find in programming languages. The only container carrying variables and their values is the exchange, which is being transferred back and forth between parent and child.

To summarize, real-life integration scenarios can grow quite large. Thus, a way to structure large process models is a pressing need. Cloud Integration supports structuring large process models by using local integration processes to keep each individual process model a reasonable size. Parameter transfer between parent and child processes is solved by the exchange, the standard container for managing data within an iFlow. As we've seen in the previous exercise, the exchange isn't only handed over from step to step, on one process level; it's also the vehicle for moving data around from parent process to child process, and vice versa, thus making the definition of global or local variables superfluous. You're now able to model, run, and monitor really complex scenarios. If you follow the recommendations given in this section, you'll also ensure manageable process sizes, making this work enjoyable.

In the next section, Section 6.4, we'll show you another concept that helps you modularize integration content by using separate iFlows deployed on the same tenant. In this setup, no common exchange relates the data used by the separate iFlows. Therefore, you'll need to take extra care to ensure that data can be shared across the different parts of an integration scenario spanning several iFlows. We'll go into more details on these considerations in Section 6.4.

But first, we want to introduce a special type of subprocess in Section 6.3.3. We'll show you how to use exception subprocesses to implement scenarios with error handling. We'll also introduce you to the topic of error handling, which we'll revisit successively in later sections as well.

6.3.3 Using Exception Subprocesses

You've already come across an exception subprocess in Chapter 5, Section 5.4.3, when we showed you how to use an exception subprocess for an explicit retry configuration in a scenario using the JMS adapter. The exception subprocess is a special kind of subprocess you can use to handle error situations that occur during message processing.

How We Introduce Error Handling in This Chapter

When designing iFlows for productive usage, as an integration developer, not only do you need to know the various features of Cloud Integration (as you're learning from this book), you also need to know how to design your scenarios so that they meet the highest security standards and use the resources provided by the cloud infrastructure in a smart way. Another guideline is that you'll need to anticipate possible error situations during design so that errors can be handled in a smart way by your scenario. In other words, integration scenarios for productive usage must meet certain qualities. At the end of this chapter, in Section 6.11, we'll introduce you to several guidelines for iFlow development.

With regard to error handling, we'd like to point out that this guideline is important because many errors can occur at runtime (e.g., the connection to a remote component breaks), but you won't want the whole scenario to stop working in each of these situations. During the design phase, you should define a behavior for your scenario explicitly for errors that can occur at runtime. In addition, in an error situation, it's important that the overall scenario is processed in a well-defined way.

The exception subprocess is one feature that supports error handling. Before going into this feature in more detail, note that many more features and aspects are associated with error handling. Therefore, later in this chapter (e.g., in at the end of Section 6.5), we'll touch again on the error handling topic. Finally, in Section 6.11, we'll return to the error handling topic in the context of other iFlow design guidelines. Error handling, although lacking an explicit section dedicated to this topic, is intrinsically handled throughout this chapter.

Now, without further delay, we'll show you how to design a simple scenario with an exception subprocess that supports basic error handling use cases.

For our simple scenario, we'll start from a copy of the iFlow developed in Section 6.2.1 (compare with Figure 6.13). Recall that our earlier scenario reads data for an individual product from the WebShop application and sends the result as an email to an email server. Many things can go wrong during the execution of an integration scenario. One typical cause of error is a failed connection to a remote system (e.g., because the remote system is temporarily unavailable). In our scenario, two systems are called, the WebShop and the email server. We'd like to enhance the iFlow now in such a way that errors, for instance, a broken connection, are handled. In particular, we'll design our scenario so that, when an exception arises, a message with specific content is generated.

For the configuration of the OData and the mail adapter, let's assume that the same settings are used as in the scenario from Section 6.2.1.

Now, we'll show you how to add an exception subprocess to the scenario. Follow these steps to modify the iFlow:

1. Rearrange the iFlow model shown earlier in Figure 6.13 so that more space is available in the **Integration Process** shape, as shown in Figure 6.50.
2. Add an exception subprocess to the iFlow by selecting **Exception Subprocess** under the **Process** root node ▭, as shown in Figure 6.51.

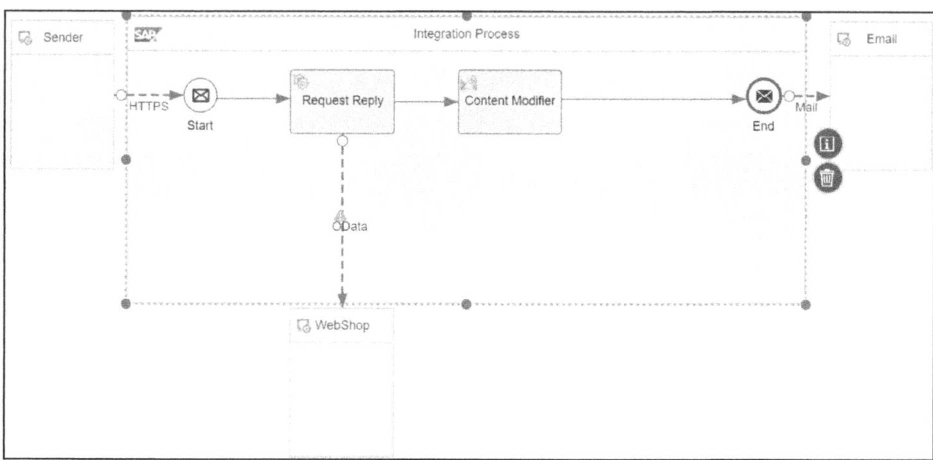

Figure 6.50 iFlow after Rearranging Shapes

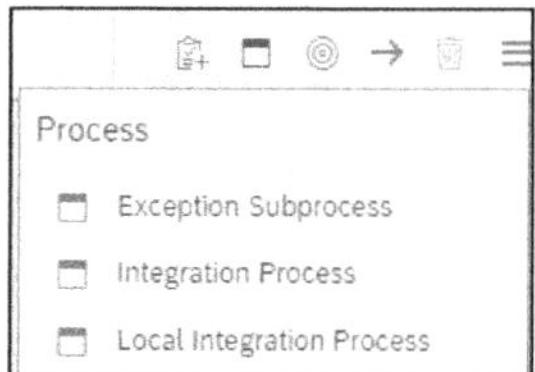

Figure 6.51 Adding an Exception Subprocess from the Palette

3. You can only place the **Exception Subprocess** in the **Integration Process** shape, which results in the change shown in Figure 6.52.

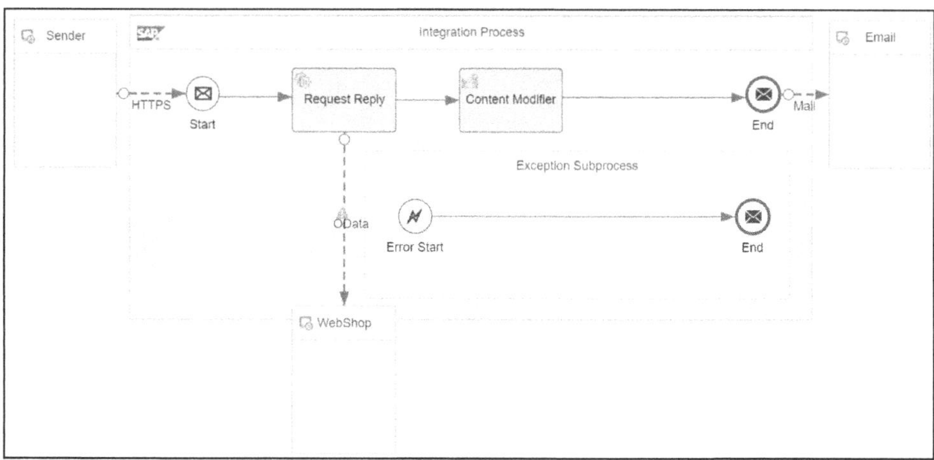

Figure 6.52 Exception Subprocess Placed within the Integration Process Shape

4. Add a **Content Modifier** step to the **Exception Subprocess**, between the **Error Start** and **End** events.

5. Under the **Message Body** tab, maintain the settings shown in Figure 6.53.

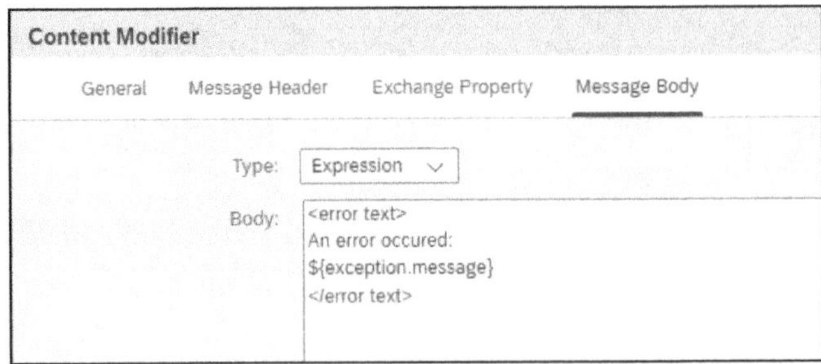

Figure 6.53 Error Message Configured in the Content Modifier in the Exception Subprocess

Notice that this step creates a message if the exception subprocess is called. The message comprises some text and a dynamic expression `exception.message` provided using Apache Camel's Simple Expression Language. Using this language allows you to access information about error situations stored in the exchange (see *http://camel.apache.org/simple.html*).

6. Connect the **Content Modifier** step with the message **End** event of the **Exception Subprocess**. The final model should look like the model shown in Figure 6.54.

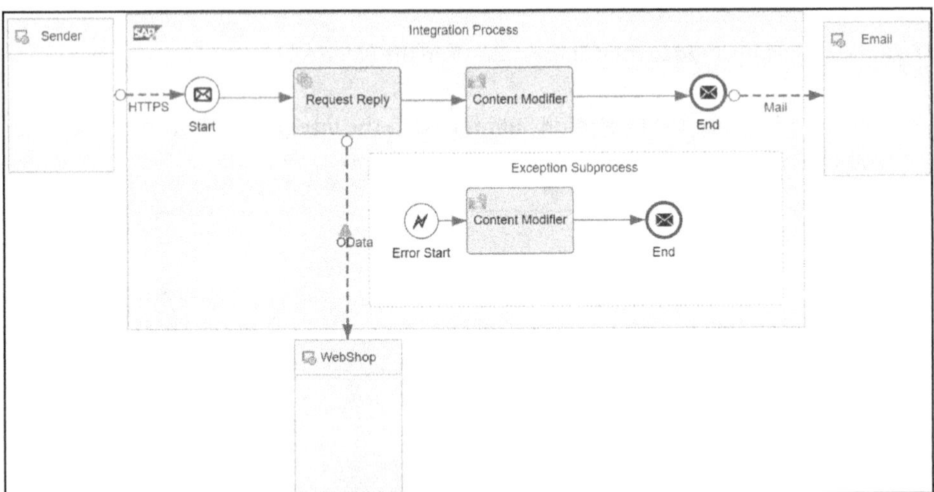

Figure 6.54 Final iFlow

Make sure that the header **productid** is listed under **Allowed Header(s)** in the **Runtime Configuration** tab of your iFlow. But if you copied the previous iFlow, this should already be the case (compare with Figure 6.15).

To initiate the scenario, you can use Postman. Make sure that the HTTP request contains header `productid` with a value for a product listed in the WebShop product catalog (e.g., `HT-1000`).

You can now run the iFlow and check your email inbox. If no error occurred, you should see an email with details of the product associated with the provided `productid` value.

Now, let's simulate an error situation. First, we'll simulate a situation where the WebShop component can't be reached. The simplest way to create this situation is to enter an incorrect address for the WebShop's API (under the **Connection** tab of the OData adapter, in the **Address** field). For instance, you could enter the following address: "https://error_refapp-espm-ui-cf.cfapps.eu10.hana.ondemand.com/espm-cloud-web/espm.svc/". Note that the correct address is as follows: `https://refapp-espm-ui-cf.cfapps.eu10.hana.ondemand.com/espm-cloud-web/espm.svc/`.

Run the iFlow again. In Postman, you should receive a response indicating that the requested resource wasn't found, such as the following example:

```
<error text>
An error occurred:
Not Found : 404 : HTTP/1.1
</error text>
```

Notice that, however, no mail has been sent because, due to the error situation after the failed OData call, the iFlow didn't process the steps after the **Request Reply** step. Instead, the exception subprocess was processed. Thus, the error message has been generated and sent back as a response to the HTTP client (as configured in the exception subprocess's **Content Modifier** step, shown earlier in Figure 6.53).

As shown in Figure 6.55, we'll quickly illustrate again the process flow in the error case. The HTTP request initiated the iFlow ❶. The OData channel tried to connect to the WebShop component, but an error occurred ❷. The remaining steps after the **Request Reply** step have therefore been skipped. Instead, the **Exception Subprocess** ❸ was processed. As a result, an error message has been created (as defined in the **Content Modifier** step of the exception subprocess). This error message was sent back to the HTTP client.

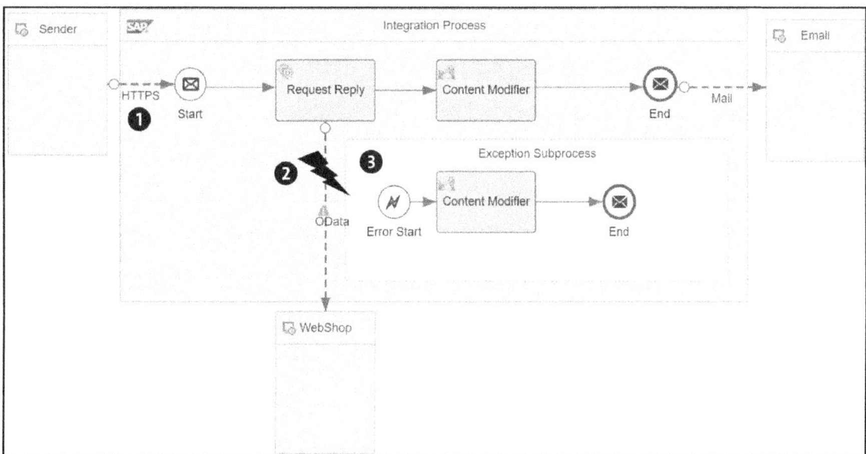

Figure 6.55 iFlow Processing in Error Case

Go to the **Monitoring** application to check the status of the executed iFlow (under **Monitor Message Processing**, compare, e.g., with Chapter 2, Section 2.3.4). Notice that the status is **Completed**. Although your iFlow has run into an error situation, this status makes sense in that, due to the encountered error situation, the exception subprocess took over message processing. This subprocess then executed successfully in that the error has been handled as designed (sending back an error message).

The observed behavior is caused by the fact that the exception subprocess in our iFlow (shown earlier in Figure 6.54) ends with an **End** event. If you modify the iFlow so that, instead of ending with an **End** event, you end the exception subprocess with an **Error End** event, the exception subprocess will fail, and errors will be handled slightly differently. We won't elaborate on this topic further. For more details, a dedicated iFlow design guideline covers this topic. You can find the corresponding iFlows and documentation on the SAP Business Accelerator Hub at *https://api.sap.com/* (integration package **Integration Flow Design Guidelines - Handle Errors Gracefully**). We'll introduce you to the iFlow design guidelines in Section 6.11.

With the iFlow, you can simulate another error situation: The email server can't be reached. To simulate this error, correct the address in the OData channel. In the **Mail** adapter, you can now refer to another **User Credential** artifact that contains wrong credentials.

When you deploy the artifact and iFlow and then run the iFlow, you should get an HTTP response like the following:

```
<error text>
An error occurred:
535 5.7.0 (#AUTH005) Too many bad auth attempts.
</error text>
```

The manually inserted message structure and text (`An error occurred`) is the same as in the error message you received when the connection to the OData API failed. However, the expression `${exception.message}` now resolves as specific error information provided by the Apache Camel framework for the encountered case:

`535 5.7.0 (#AUTH005) Too many bad auth attempts.`

This error information is provided by the Apache Camel framework to indicate that an error occurred connecting with the user specified in the credentials. When the OData connection fails, more error information is provided by the Apache Camel framework.

That's it for now! As mentioned earlier, we'll get back to the topic of error handling in later sections. In this section, you learned how to modularize integration scenarios by using subprocesses and how to handle error situations by using exception subprocesses. Next, we'll show you another option for modularizing integration content: the ProcessDirect adapter.

6.4 Connecting Integration Flows Using the ProcessDirect Adapter

In Section 6.3, we showed how you can use subprocesses to modularize larger iFlows. Another option for modularizing integration content is obvious: designing different parts of the integration logic of a complex scenario as individual, "smaller" iFlows and connecting these flows with each other. This approach is useful in situations where you must manage bigger integration projects with comprehensive integration scenarios and distributed responsibilities.

Cloud Integration comes with a variety of different adapters, so you might have already realized you could use certain adapters to connect different iFlows with each other to build a larger scenario. Of course, HTTP-based adapters might be the option of choice. So why not put parts of the integration logic into *n* different iFlows and connect them with each other; for example, iFlow 1 calls iFlow 2, iFlow 2 calls another one, and so forth. But wait—you also know that each such HTTP connection (e.g., an outbound connection from the perspective of iFlow 1 and an inbound connection from the perspective of iFlow 2) is routed through the load balancer. (Refer to Chapter 2, Section 2.1, particularly Figure 2.3, for a refresher on the place of the load balancer.) Thus, another component is involved in each communication, which increases network load and thus hurts the performance of your overall integration scenario. With many extra intra-iFlow connections, performance could be significantly and negatively impacted—even if all your connected iFlows are deployed on the same tenant.

To overcome this issue, the Cloud Integration team has developed a dedicated adapter, the *ProcessDirect* adapter, which allows you to directly connect two iFlows on the same tenant without involving the load balancer. Figure 6.56 shows a sender iFlow (left) and a receiver iFlow (right) connected through a **ProcessDirect** adapter.

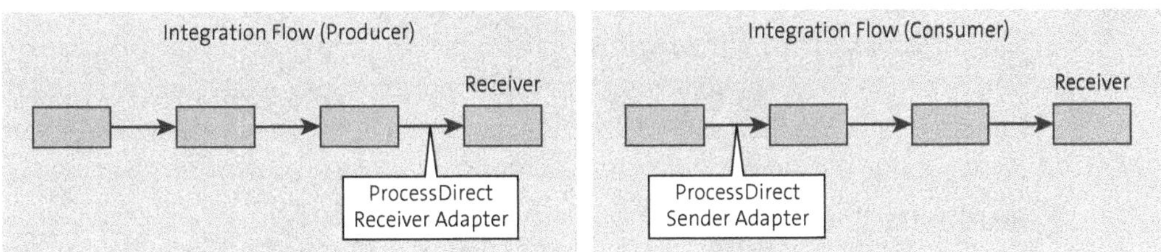

Figure 6.56 Producer and Consumer iFlow Communication over ProcessDirect Adapters

To simplify our discussion in this section, when we're talking about two iFlows connected over the ProcessDirect adapter, we'll distinguish between a *producer iFlow* and a *consumer iFlow* in the following sense:

- The producer iFlow sends the message to another iFlow over the **ProcessDirect** adapter. In the producer iFlow, you'll need to configure a **ProcessDirect** receiver adapter (to send the message to the target iFlow).

- The consumer iFlow receives a message from another iFlow over the **ProcessDirect** adapter. In the consumer iFlow, you need to configure a **ProcessDirect** sender adapter (to receive the message from the producer iFlow).

Limitations

Note the following limitations apply when using the **ProcessDirect** adapter:

- Both producer and consumer iFlows must be deployed on the same tenant.
- The cardinality of producers to consumers is restricted. Therefore, you can send messages from *N* producers to 1 consumer, but not vice versa. (The cardinality rule reads `producer:consumer = N:1`.)

However, you can use **ProcessDirect** adapters to connect iFlows from different integration packages (as long as these flows are deployed on the same tenant).

The **ProcessDirect** adapter is quite simple and has exactly one attribute, which is the **Address** of the iFlow to connect to (defining the endpoint). We'll discuss how to use this adapter shortly, but let's briefly summarize some use cases for this adapter first.

6.4.1 Use Cases for the ProcessDirect Adapter

Some of the possible use cases for the ProcessDirect adapter include the following:

- **Structuring large iFlows and separation of concerns**
  As mentioned earlier, similar to how you can use local integration processes to structure larger iFlows (refer to Section 6.3), you can use separate (smaller) iFlows and connect them through ProcessDirect adapters. Note that using separate iFlows (also, if required, within different integration packages), enables you to clearly manage different responsibilities within an integration project (also called the *separation of concerns*) in the following way: Different integration developers can work independently on that part of the integration logic they are responsible for by decomposing the overall scenario into several smaller iFlows with different owners.
- **Reusing integration logic**
  You can "source out" generic functions and parts of the integration logic that are used at many places into dedicated iFlows. Such (consumer) iFlows can be called from multiple (producer) iFlows independently. As an example of such a generic integration logic, think about error-handling strategies. If you need to make changes to a generic part of the logic, the producer iFlows wouldn't be impacted as long as you don't change the address of the consumer.

  In error-handling strategies, *N* producers can send messages to 1 consumer that contains the error-handling logic.
- **Creating multiple message processing logs (MPLs)**
  As the overall integration scenario is split into several independent iFlows, during

the operations of the scenario, several MPLs will be generated. Multiple MPLs make it easier to analyze errors and to distribute operational tasks among several people.

- **Outsourcing error handling into separate iFlows**
  Related to our earlier discussion in Section 6.3.3, you might want to separate concerns in such a way that error handling is managed by one or more separate iFlows. You can achieve such a behavior, for instance, by designing your scenario so that the exception subprocess calls another iFlow through the **ProcessDirect** adapter. The target iFlow will contain all the steps related to error handling.

  For more details, a dedicated iFlow design guideline covers this topic. You can find the corresponding iFlows and a link to the documentation on the SAP Business Accelerator Hub at *https://api.sap.com* (integration package **Integration Flow Design Guidelines - Handle Errors Gracefully**).

6.4.2 A Simple Example

Now we'll show you how to use the ProcessDirect adapter by modifying the integration scenario that we started in Section 6.3 (shown earlier in Figure 6.42) to illustrate the usage of local integration processes. We'll change the design so that the overall integration logic is split into two individual iFlows.

Recall that our earlier scenario worked in such a way that, for a given product category, a list of relevant products (including their details) was read from the WebShop application and then the message stored as a data store entry. Now, we'll source out the part of the scenario that calls the WebShop into a separate iFlow.

Figure 6.57 shows the producer (top) and consumer (bottom) iFlows next to each other so we can discuss how they interact.

We'll first summarize the message processing shown in Figure 6.57 and then describe in more detail how to develop this scenario yourself.

As in our scenario from Section 6.3.2 (shown earlier in Figure 6.42), the HTTP client calls the integration scenario. In this setup, the producer iFlow provides a product category name as header (Figure 6.57 ❶). With a **Request Reply** step, the producer iFlow now calls the consumer iFlow using the **ProcessDirect** adapter ❷. Soon, we'll show you how the **ProcessDirect** adapter has only one attribute, the **Address**. A relative address must be configured in the **ProcessDirect** adapter for both the producer iFlow and for the consumer iFlow. The address must be identical so that the message is forwarded to the desired consumer iFlow. If that requirement is fulfilled, the consumer iFlow takes over message processing from the producer iFlow through a **ProcessDirect** sender adapter (Figure 6.57 ❷ in the lower shape). Then, the same steps as in the scenario from Section 6.3.2 (shown earlier in Figure 6.42) ensures that, for the given header value, a list of products is read from the WebShop ❸, and the number of product items is now stored in a header in the **Content Modifier** step ❹. This data will be required in the subsequent steps of the producer to define the content of the final message.

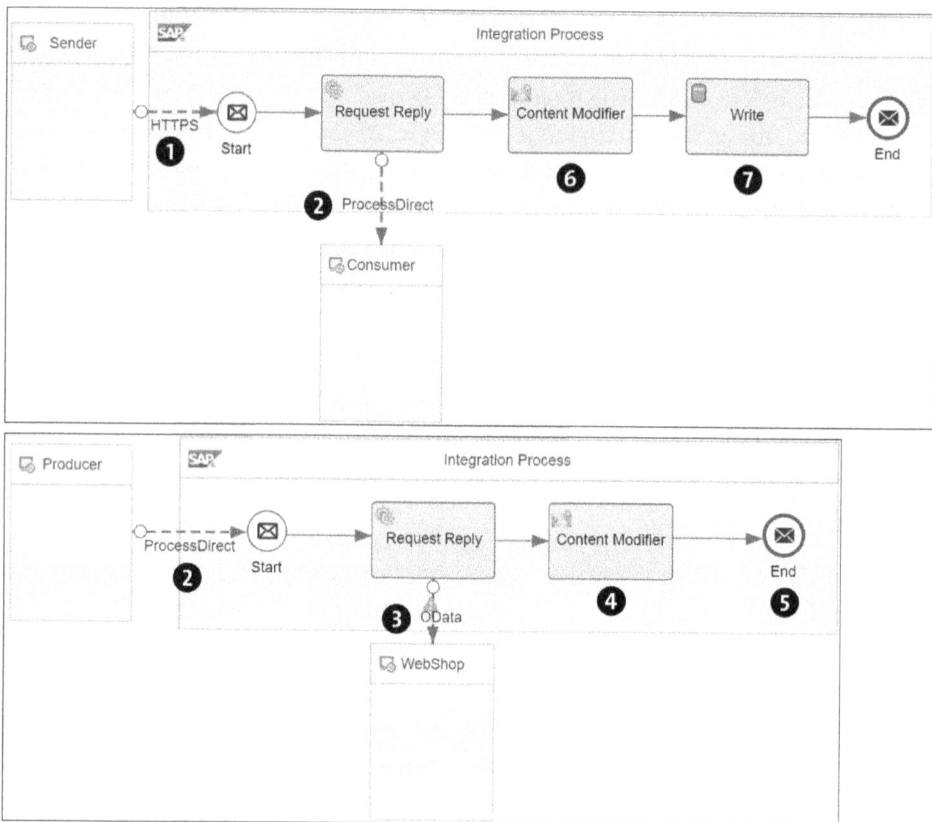

Figure 6.57 Producer and Consumer iFlow Implementing the Example Scenario

Other than in the scenario from Section 6.3.2, it's important to note that we're working with a header instead of properties. The reason to use headers is that the different parts of the scenario now don't share the same exchange container. Therefore, properties defined in the consumer iFlow aren't available for use by the producer iFlow, and vice versa. Therefore, we'll use a header to transfer data (the number of products) from one iFlow to the other. Note that the actual business data, including product details, is provided by the consumer in the message body. After the **Content Modifier** has created these headers, the consumer iFlow processing ends ❺, and the message is handed over again back to the producer. Then, in the producer iFlow, the message body is defined (using the headers transferred with the message from the consumer) in a **Content Modifier** step ❻, and finally, the message is written into the data store ❼.

Now let's discuss how to design this scenario. You can easily derive both iFlows from the flow developed in Section 6.3.2 (shown earlier in Figure 6.42) with the following steps. We recommend you create two copies of the iFlow shown earlier in Figure 6.42 and derive both iFlows (the producer and the consumer) out of these copies. We'll show you the modified settings in this section.

To create the producer iFlow, follow these steps:

1. In the first copy of the iFlow shown earlier in Figure 6.42, remove the entire **Execute Business Logic** (local integration process) shape.
2. Delete the first **Content Modifier** step in the **Integration Process** shape. (Recall that this step created a property out of the `categoryName` header, a step that isn't required anymore.)
3. Remove the **Process Call** shape and, instead, add a **Request Reply** step at the same location.
4. Add a **Receiver** shape to the model, and give it the name "Consumer". This shape represents the consumer iFlow that will be called from the producer.
5. Connect the **Request Reply** step with the **Consumer** receiver shape, and then select the **ProcessDirect** adapter from the list of available adapter types, as shown in Figure 6.58.

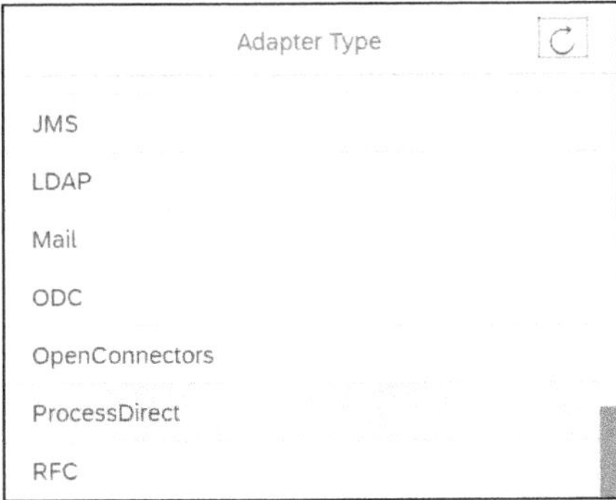

Figure 6.58 List of Available Receiver Adapter Types (Subset), Including the ProcessDirect Adapter

6. In the **Properties** section of the **ProcessDirect** adapter (below the model), select the **Connection** tab, and, in the **Address** field, enter "/getProducts," as shown in Figure 6.59.

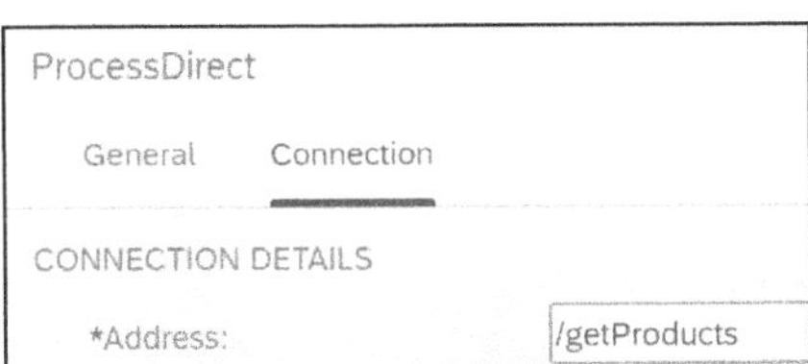

Figure 6.59 The Address: The Only Attribute of the ProcessDirect Adapter

7. Connect the **Request Reply** step with the existing **Content Modifier** step, and leave the rest of the model unchanged.

8. In the **Content Modifier** step, under the **Message Body** tab, you can see the current entry from the previous scenario, which appears as follows:

   `For category ${header.categoryName} ${property.NoProducts} products are available:`
   `${property.payload}`

   Change this entry so that, in the first dynamic expression, a header is used instead of a property, as follows:

   `For category ${header.categoryName} ${header.NoProducts} products are available:`
   `${in.body}`

   Note that the expression `${in.body}` takes the content of the message body that is transferred from the consumer.

9. Leave the **Write** step unchanged, and save and deploy your iFlow.

Now, let's create the consumer iFlow from another copy of the iFlow shown earlier in Figure 6.42. Follow these steps:

1. Remove the whole upper **Integration Process** shape but keep the **Sender** shape.
2. Rename the **Sender** shape to **Producer** because this shape will represent the producer iFlow that will call the consumer iFlow.
3. Add a new **Integration Process** shape to the model. Add a **Start Message** event and an **End Message** event to the **Integration Process** shape.
4. In the **Execute Business Logic** shape, remove the connectors between the steps. However, keep the OData channel between the **Request Reply** step and the **WebShop** receiver shape.
5. Move the **Request Reply** step and the **Content Modifier** step into the new **Integration Process** shape.
6. Remove the **Execute Business Logic** shape with the remaining **Start** and **End** steps.
7. Connect the **Producer** sender shape with the **Start Message** shape, and select **ProcessDirect** as the sender adapter type.
8. In the properties section of the **ProcessDirect** adapter, under the **Connection** tab, enter the same address as for the **ProcessDirect** receiver adapter in the producer iFlow: "/getProducts".
9. Connect the **Start** message shape with the **Request Reply** step.
10. Connect the **Request Reply** step with the **Content Modifier** step.
11. Connect the **Content Modifier** step with the **End** message event.
12. Check out the settings for the **Content Modifier** step.

    Change the settings of the **Content Modifier** so that, instead of properties, one *header* (`NoProducts`) is created. Because we're using copies of our earlier iFlow, this step should already have some settings under the **Exchange Property** tab, as shown earlier in Figure 6.35. You don't need these settings anymore. Instead of this, create an entry in the **Message Header** tab as shown in Figure 6.60.

13. Now you can delete the entries from the **Exchange Property** tab.

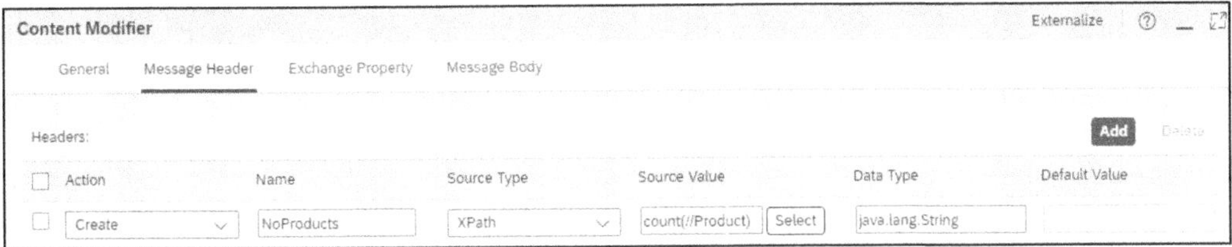

Figure 6.60 Message Header Settings

That's it! In both iFlows, you might check the settings under the **Runtime Configuration** tab. (Click any position outside the shape in the modeling area.) As our design is based on copies of the same original iFlow, you can expect that the header **categoryName** is listed in the **Allowed Header(s)** field, as shown in Figure 6.61.

Figure 6.61 Allowed Header(s) Setting

This header must be specified in both iFlows because of the following considerations:

- The producer iFlow expects this header from the HTTP client.
- The consumer iFlow expects this header from the producer iFlow.

When you run the scenario by sending an HTTP request to the producer iFlow, you should get the same result as earlier in Section 6.3.2.

Thus, you should get an HTTP response and a new data store entry with a message that starts with the text shown in Listing 6.3.

```
For category Notebooks 10 products are available:
<Products>
    <Product>
      <CurrencyCode>EUR</CurrencyCode>
      <Price>1999.000</Price>
      <CategoryName>Notebooks</CategoryName>
      <ProductId>HT-1010</ProductId>
      <Name>Notebook Professional 15</Name>
```

```
</Product>
<Product>
...
```

Listing 6.3 HTTP Response Contains Number of Products and Product Details

Notice one difference: on the **Monitoring** page of the Web UI, you'll see that the two iFlows have been processed individually and that, consequently, two MPLs have been generated.

6.4.3 Using Variables to Share Data between Different Integration Flows

In the previous section, we demonstrated that, when using different iFlows to modularize a complex integration scenario, data that dynamically resolves certain parameters at runtime can be transferred using message headers.

Other options are available for sharing data among several iFlows, such as using a **Write Variables** step. This step uses the temporary tenant storage discussed in Chapter 2, Section 2.1, in the architecture section (compare Figure 2.4 where we've denoted this data storage as the **Message Content** storage shape). You can define two different kinds of variables:

- Global variables can be shared by different iFlows deployed on the same tenant.
- Local variables can only be used in the context of one iFlow.

In the following scenario, we'll show you how to use a global variable instead of a header to share the number of `Product` items in the message processing between two iFlows.

You can easily modify the producer and consumer iFlows from the previous section to learn how to work with variables. We'll keep the description short and only focus on the key differences.

Before we get into the new setup, let's briefly discuss how the message will be processed with the modified design shown in Figure 6.62. The producer is at the top, and the consumer is at the bottom.

We won't repeat the steps already covered in Section 6.4.2. We'll only focus on aspects relevant for the usage of variables: In the consumer iFlow, the number of products for the given product category is evaluated and stored in a variable (instead of a header) in a **Write Variables** step (Figure 6.62 ❶). When the processing is again handed over to the producer iFlow, a **Content Modifier** step looks up the variable and stores its value as an exchange property ❷. When defining the message body, the second **Content Modifier** step in the producer iFlow can then use the property instead of a header to find out the number of products for the given product category.

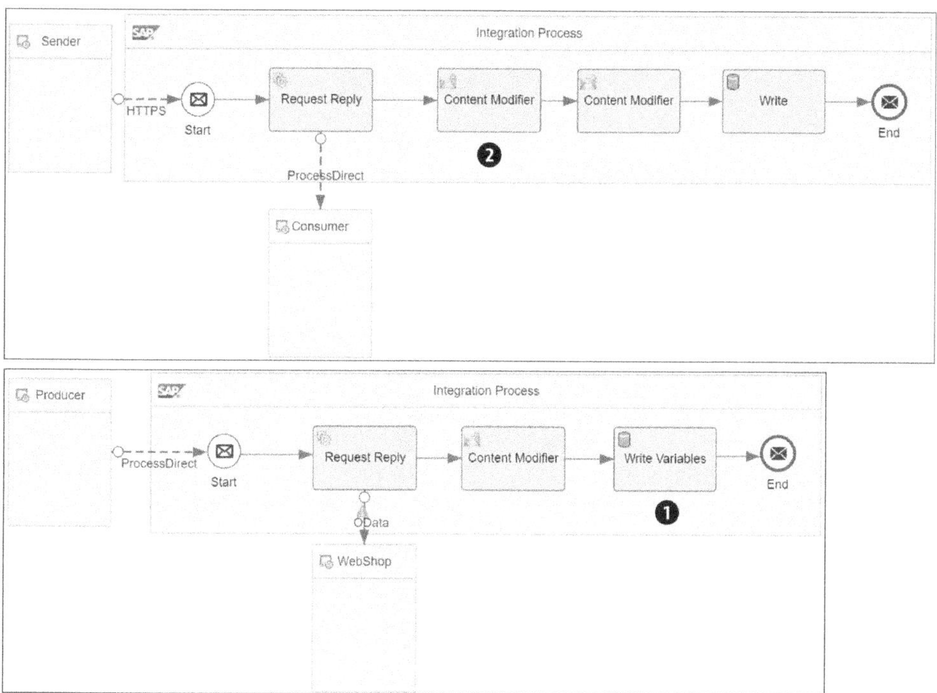

Figure 6.62 Producer and Consumer iFlows Using Global Variables

When you design this scenario, we recommend that you create a copy of both the producer and the consumer iFlows before creating any changes.

To design the producer iFlow (upper model shown in Figure 6.62), perform the following steps, which change the upper model shown earlier in Figure 6.57:

1. Between the **Request Reply** step and the **Content Modifier** step, add a new **Content Modifier** step.
2. Under the **Exchange Property** tab, specify the settings as shown in Figure 6.63.

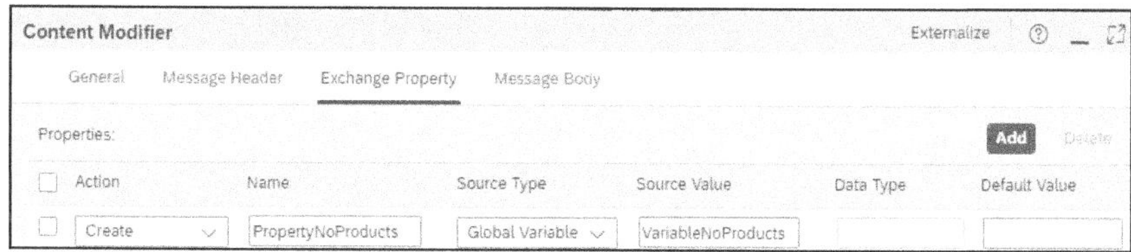

Figure 6.63 Creating an Exchange Property Based on a Global Variable

   This step will create an exchange property (with the name `PropertyNoProducts`) based on a global variable. This variable will be created during the processing of the consumer iFlow, and we'll show you how to design the associated step shortly.

3. In the other **Content Modifier** step, under the **Message Body** tab, the following entry was specified in the original scenario:

```
For category ${header.categoryName} ${header.NoProducts} products are
available:
${header.payload}
```

Change the entry so that, for the number of products, the exchange property created in the previous **Content Modifier** step is used (and not a header):

```
For category ${header.categoryName} ${property.PropertyNoProducts} products are
available:
${header.payload}
```

4. In the **ProcessDirect** adapter, specify a different address than contained in the copy we started from.
5. Save and deploy the iFlow.

To design the consumer iFlow (lower model shown previously in Figure 6.62), perform the following steps (based on the lower model shown earlier in Figure 6.57):

1. Between the **Content Modifier** step and the **End** event, add a **Write Variables** step. To find this step, in the palette, click the **Persistence** submenu, and click **Write Variables**, as shown in Figure 6.64.

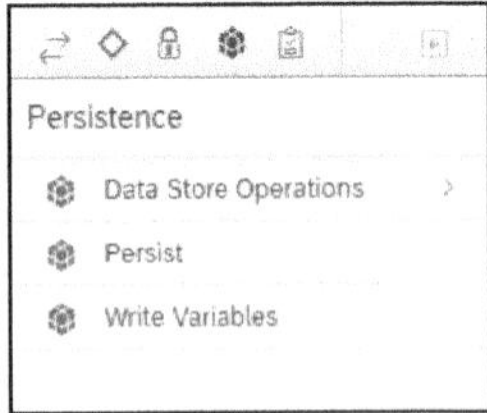

Figure 6.64 Write Variables Shape Selected in the Persistence Submenu of the Palette

2. Place the shape between the **Content Modifier** step and the **End** event.
3. Under the **Processing** tab of the **Write Variables** step, maintain the settings as shown in Figure 6.65.

   Notice that the data in the previous scenario was stored in a header but is now stored in a variable. At runtime, the variable will contain the number of products for the given category.

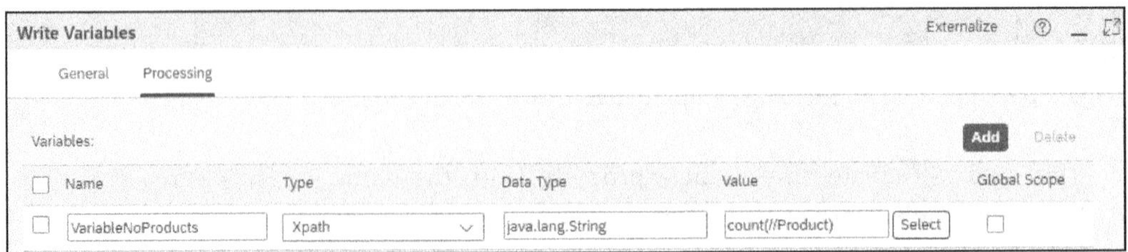

Figure 6.65 Settings for the Write Variables Step

In this step, selecting the **Global Scope** checkbox is important. Otherwise, the variable will be unavailable for other iFlows.

4. In the preceding **Content Modifier** step, under the **Message Header** tab, delete the **NoProducts** header (compare with Figure 6.60).
5. Save and deploy the iFlow.

Now, when you run the scenario (by sending an HTTP request to the producer iFlow), you should again get the same result as previously.

Be aware that you can also monitor variables. On the **Monitoring** page, under **Manage Stores**, select the **Variables** tile. You'll find the variable that was created by the consumer iFlow, as shown in Figure 6.66.

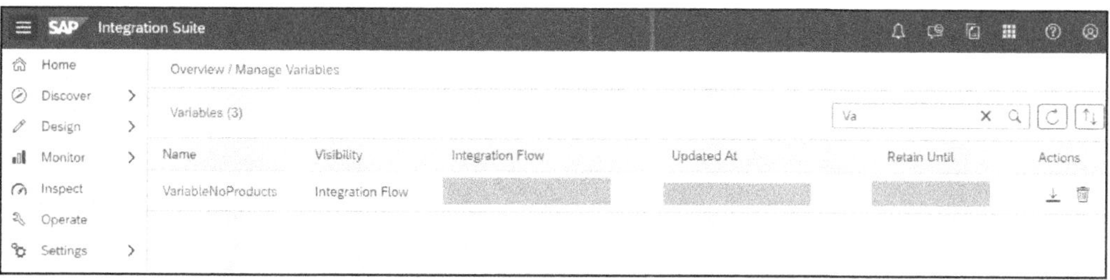

Figure 6.66 Monitoring Variables

Notice that you can also download variables (in the same way as data store entries; compare with Chapter 2, Section 2.3.4). From the entries in the **Retain Until** column, variables are only stored temporarily on the tenant, as discussed in Chapter 2. However, using a high number of variables might have a negative impact on resource consumption and the overall performance of your business scenario. We'll come back to these concerns in Section 6.11.

6.4.4 Dynamic Endpoint Configuration with the ProcessDirect Adapter

Now that you're familiar with the dynamic configuration of iFlow parameters, you'll never want to miss the chance to apply this concept. Therefore, we'll wrap up our discussion of ProcessDirect adapter with a simple example combining the ProcessDirect adapter with dynamic configuration in such a way that a target (consumer) iFlow is only called sometimes, depending on the actual value of a given header (as explained in Section 6.2).

Let's design the following scenario: The HTTP client calls Cloud Integration and provides a `productid` value. Depending on the product category associated with the product, a different processing flow is implemented. The dedicated steps (that depend on the category) are outsourced in dedicated consumer iFlows (one iFlow defined for each product category). For the sake of simplicity, we'll only define the processing for two categories: *Notebooks* and *Software*. Our example producer iFlow is modeled as shown in Figure 6.67.

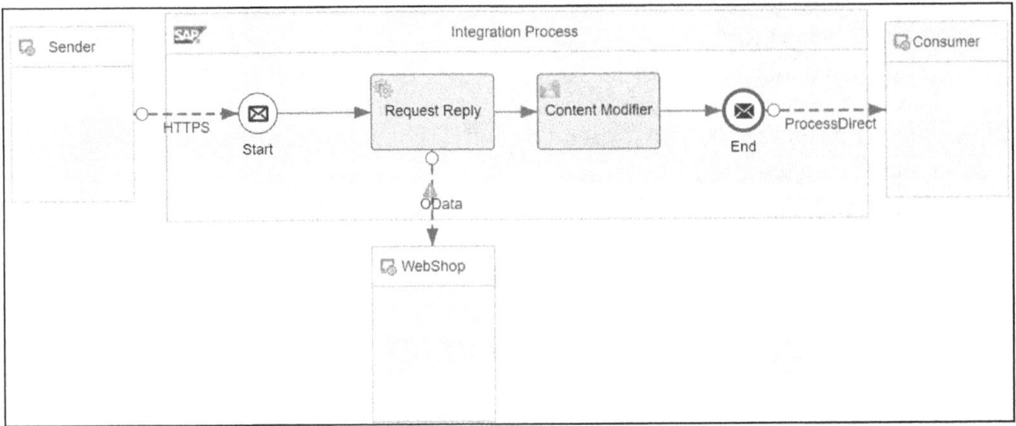

Figure 6.67 Producer iFlow

In this scenario, the producer iFlow takes an HTTP request with a `productid` value given in the header of the request. The OData channel retrieves details for one product (associated with the `productid` value). In the subsequent **Content Modifier**, an exchange property is created based on the value of the product category element contained in the response from the WebShop. The **ProcessDirect** adapter contains a dynamic expression for the address that depends on the value of the product category.

For the two different product categories, we'll define two different consumer iFlows that have the same appearance but slightly different settings, as we describe shortly.

Figure 6.68 shows the iFlow model for the notebooks consumer iFlow. (The software consumer will look the same.)

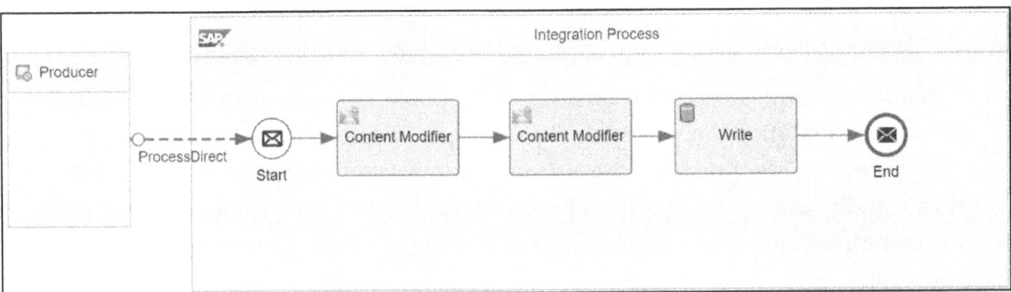

Figure 6.68 Consumer iFlow for Category Notebooks

If the product category of the derived product is `Notebooks`, this first consumer iFlow is called. Its first **Content Modifier** step creates properties for the dedicated values in the message. The second **Content Modifier** step creates the message body based on these properties. In a data store **Write** step, an entry is created in a data store with the name **Products** and an entry ID that depends (dynamically) on the product category.

To keep this integration scenario simple, we used almost the same iFlow models for the two different consumers. The only difference is that we configured the two content modifiers slightly differently so that, if the product is a notebook, only the name and price are contained in the final message. However, if the product is a software item, the name and its long description are included in the final message. In real-life scenarios, you can imagine that the iFlows might modeled in a completely different way for the two cases, which are probably also much more complex.

Let's start designing this scenario. To design the producer iFlow, create an iFlow model similar to the model shown earlier in Figure 6.67. In this iFlow, maintain the following settings:

- In the OData adapter (under the **Processing** tab), enter the following for **Query Options**:
  `$select=ProductId,Category,CategoryName,CurrencyCode,LongDescription, Name,Price,ShortDescription&$filter=ProductId eq '${header.productId}'`
- In the **Content Modifier** step (under the **Message Header** tab), create a header with the **Name** "categoryName" that is defined based on the XPath expression that points to the `CategoryName` element of the message, as shown in Figure 6.69.

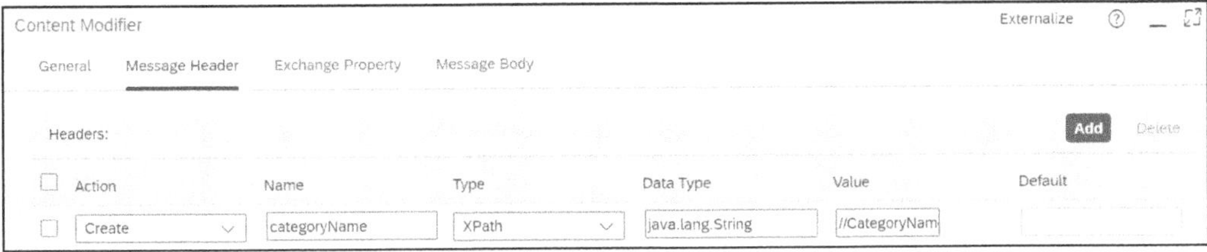

Figure 6.69 Content Modifier Settings in Producer

- In the **Address** field of the **ProcessDirect** adapter (under the **Connection** tab), as shown in Figure 6.70, enter the following expression: "${header.categoryName}"

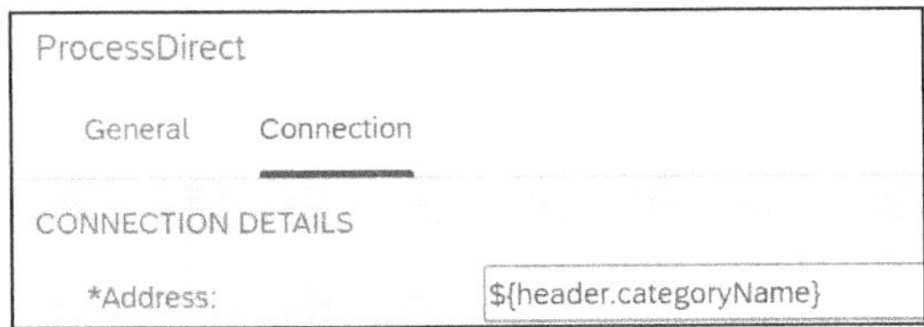

Figure 6.70 Dynamic Endpoint Address in the ProcessDirect Receiver Adapter

To define the consumer iFlow for the `Notebooks` category, design an iFlow like the one shown earlier in Figure 6.68. In this consumer iFlow, maintain the following settings:

1. In the **Address** field of the **ProcessDirect** adapter (under the **Connection** tab), enter "Notebooks".
2. In the first **Content Modifier** step, add the properties "price" (based on the `Price` element in the message) and "name" (based on the `Name` element in the message). For both entries, select **XPath** from the **Type** dropdown list, as shown in Figure 6.71.

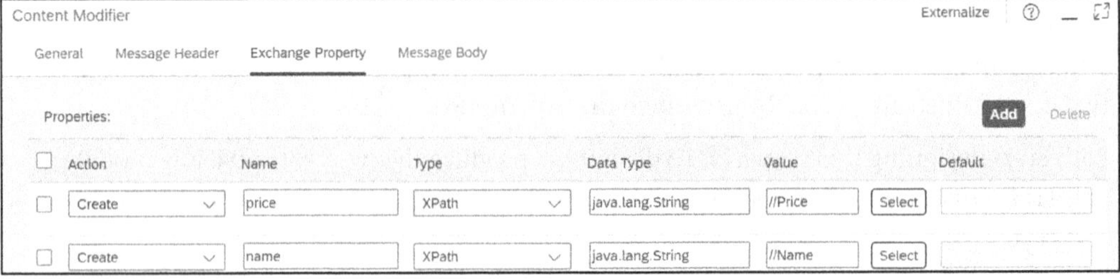

Figure 6.71 First Content Modifier in Consumer for Notebooks

3. In the second **Content Modifier** step, under the **Message Body** tab, enter the following expression, as shown in Figure 6.72:

```
${property.name} has the following price:
${property.price}
```

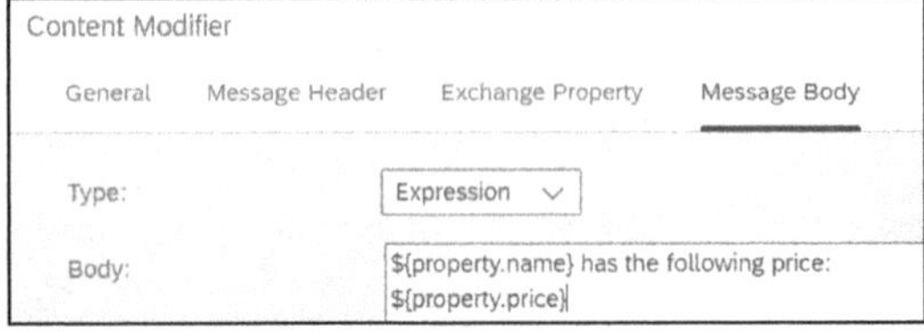

Figure 6.72 Message Body Definition in Second Content Modifier in Consumer for Notebooks

4. Configure the **Write** step with the settings shown in Figure 6.73.

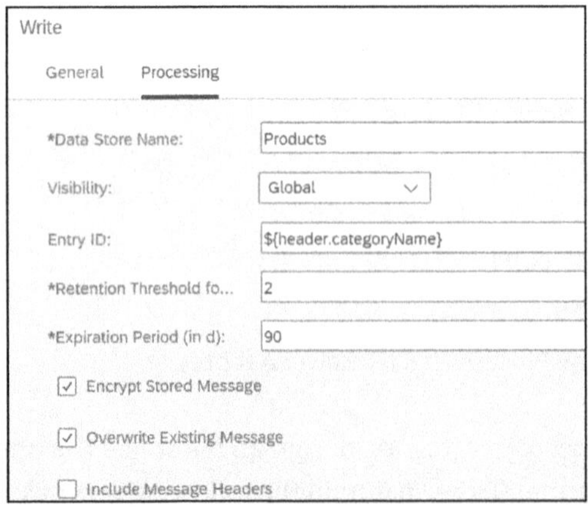

Figure 6.73 Write Step Settings in Consumer

To design the consumer integration for the `Software` category, perform the same steps, but with the following settings:

- In the **Address** field of the **ProcessDirect** adapter, enter "Software".
- In the first **Content Modifier** step, under the **Exchange Property** tab, create the two properties "longDescription" (based on message element `LongDescription`) and "name" (based on message element `Name`).
- In the first **Content Modifier** step, under the **Message Body** tab, enter the following expression:

  ```
  ${property.name} has the following features:
  ${property.longDescription}
  ```
- Use the same settings for the **Write** step, as shown in Figure 6.73.

When you run the iFlow with a `productid` value of `HT-1010` in Postman, you'll get the following response:

```
Notebook Professional 15 has the following price:
1999.000
```

Likewise, a data store entry called `Notebooks` is created in the **Products** data store with the same content.

When you run the iFlow with a `productid` value of `HT-1101` in Postman, you'll get the following response:

```
Smart Design has the following features:
Complete package, 1 User, Image editing, processing
```

Likewise, a data store entry called `Software` is created in the same **Products** data store with the same content, which is the expected result.

Although not the focus of this section, let's close this discussion with a slight enhancement that makes this scenario more robust. With this enhancement, the iFlow will anticipate our later discussion of error handling in Section 6.11.4.

What happens if you provide the request a `productid` value that doesn't correspond to either a notebook or software product? In this case, the scenario will raise an error message.

If your business case explicitly covers the handling of data for notebooks and software products (but no other product categories), you won't create a consumer iFlow for each possible product category. However, to make the scenario more robust, let's slightly enhance it by adding a routing step with an additional branch, as shown in Figure 6.74.

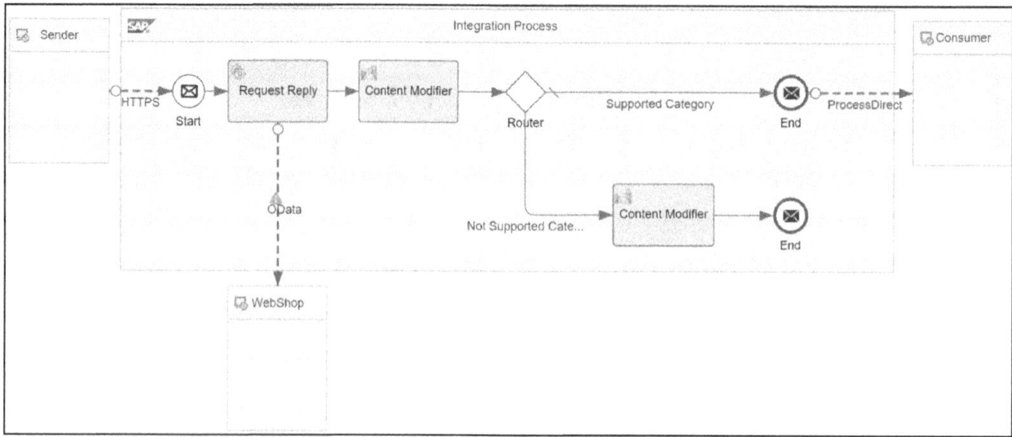

Figure 6.74 More Robust iFlow

Basically, we're adding a **Router** step, after the **Content Modifier** step, that distinguishes between two cases:

- `CategoryName` element in the inbound message has either value `Notebooks` or `Software` (upper route).
- `CategoryName` element in the inbound message has any other value than `Notebooks` or `Software` (lower route).

If the upper route is taken, everything works as described earlier in this section. If the lower route is taken, the **Content Modifier** step in the lower route creates a message, sent back to the HTTP client, that explicitly makes the sender aware that the product category associated with the product for the given `productid` isn't supported by this scenario.

We'll quickly provide the settings for this scenario:

1. Provide routing conditions as shown in Figure 6.75 (refer to Chapter 5, Section 5.1).

Router

General Processing

ERROR HANDLING

☐ Throw Exception

ROUTING CONDITION

Order	Route Name	Condition Expression	Default Route
1	Supported Category		☑
2	Not Supported Category	${header.categoryName} != 'Notebooks' and ${h...	☐

Figure 6.75 Routing Conditions

2. In the **Content Modifier** step in the lower route (associated with the second routing condition), under the **Message Body** tab, enter the following expression:

   ```
   Product associated with product ID ${header.productId} belongs to category
   ${header.categoryName}. This category is not supported by the integration
   scenario.
   ```

3. Save and deploy the iFlow. When you run the scenario with one of the two `productid` values a before, you'll get the same result. When you run the scenario, for instance, with the `productid` value set to `HT-1007`, you'll get the following response message in your HTTP client (and no new data store entry is created):

   ```
   Product associated with product ID HT-1007 belongs to category PDAs/Organizers.
   This category is not supported by the integration scenario.
   ```


At this point, you've learned how to dynamically configure your integration scenario, to modularize integration content, and to design robust and resilient scenarios anticipating error situations. You also learned how to use the temporary data storage options available on the tenant (data stores and variables) to share data across iFlows. In the next section, we'll explore a feature that allows you to permanently store data during an integration scenario in a connected cloud-based database system.

6.5 Connecting to a Database Using the JDBC Adapter

Cloud Integration is, first and foremost, a platform for exchanging data. The focus of the solution is on handling data *in transit*, rather than storing data. So far, you've become familiar with certain features that allow you to store data temporarily in a database associated with the tenant (compare Figure 2.4, in Chapter 2, Section 2.1). In particular, you can store messages in a data store, and you can also store variables that contain data at runtime to be used in a later processing step or by another iFlow (Section 6.4.3). However, these storage locations, associated with the same tenant Cloud Integration, have certain restrictions. On your tenant, an overall disk space limit of 32 GB means that you'll need to carefully consider how not to exceed the limit. A second limitation is that you can store data for a maximum of 180 days.

However, you might also need to *permanently* store data in the course of an integration scenario. You may need a mature database that allows you to store your data in various tables. For this use case, SAP provides the option of connecting your Cloud Integration tenant to a database system. For that purpose, Cloud Integration offers a dedicated adapter, the Java Database Connectivity (JDBC) adapter. We'll introduce you to this adapter in this section.

Current Supported Database and Features

Check out the documentation for Cloud Integration regularly for the most up-to-date information about enhancements to this feature. In particular, you can expect that soon you can connect other database systems hosted by non-SAP third parties (either on-premise database systems or those deployed in private clouds).

6.5.1 JDBC Adapter Concepts

Figure 6.76 shows the setup for using a permanent data storage option in the cloud. Whereas the temporary data storage areas, such as the data store, reside on the same tenant where the SAP BTP runtime is deployed (the Cloud Integration tenant, shown in Figure 6.76), the JDBC adapter allows you to connect Cloud Integration to a database system hosted in another subaccount.

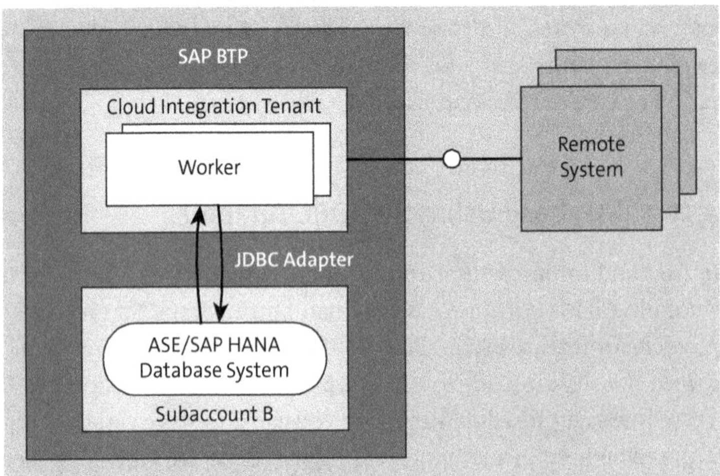

Figure 6.76 Simplified Setup with an SAP Adaptive Server Enterprise (SAP ASE)/SAP HANA Database System Connected through a JDBC Adapter

To enable the connection to the database system and the performance of read and write operations on its tables, you must give the Cloud Integration runtime dedicated permissions. As we'll describe later, access parameters (i.e., a database user, password, and access token) are deployed on the Cloud Integration tenant as dedicated artifacts (**JDBC Data Source** artifact). An iFlow can then access the database using the JDBC receiver adapter. The only parameter to be configured for the adapter is the name of the **JDBC Data Source** artifact.

So far, our story has covered how to access the database. But what about managing database tables and reading/writing table entries? On these tasks, iFlows are fully adaptive: in an iFlow, you have various options to define certain SQL commands (reading or writing operations). Alternatively, you can pass on SQL commands from sender systems to the database system through Cloud Integration. In either case, the JDBC adapter serves as a vehicle to open the database connection, to transfer commands to the database, and to receive results back from the database system. Our simple example will show you how to use this feature.

In the following sections, we'll show you in detail how to set up a database system, how to set up the connection to the Cloud Integration tenant, and how to design an iFlow that operates on the database system.

6.5.2 Setting Up a Database System

Before you can use the JDBC adapter in an iFlow to pass database operations through to a database system, first, you'll need to set up the database system/schema. Second, you'll need grant the Cloud Integration runtime access to the database system.

Performing these tasks requires certain steps that we'll only summarize in this section. You find a detailed step-by-step description of how to set up the database connection in an SAP Community blog at *http://s-prs.co/v576022*. In this section, we briefly summarize the steps. In Section 6.5.3, we'll show you how to set up a simple iFlow that performs some basic database operations.

In summary, you must perform the following tasks:

1. **Set up a database schema.**
   To set up the database schema using the SAP BTP cockpit, you'll need to create a database schema (for either an SAP HANA or an SAP ASE database system). During this step, you'll define a database user ID and a password.
2. **Give Cloud Integration the permission to access the database system.**
   To grant the SAP BTP runtime access to the database, you'll generate a database access token for the database we defined in the previous step. To generate this token, you'll need to use a command-line tool that you can download from an SAP website (as explained in detail in the blog post mentioned earlier).

When you've completed all the steps described in the blog post, you'll get an access token. With this access token (as well as the database user and password defined in the previous step when setting up the database schema), you'll define the **JDBC Data Source** artifact on the tenant.

Now that you've set up the database schema and generated the access token, you'll now deploy the **JDBC Data Source** artifact.

To deploy the artifact, perform the following steps:

1. Open the Web UI in Cloud Integration, and click on the **Monitor** menu item.
2. Under **Manage JDBC Material**, click the **JDBC Data Sources** tile.

3. Select **Add**, as shown in Figure 6.77.

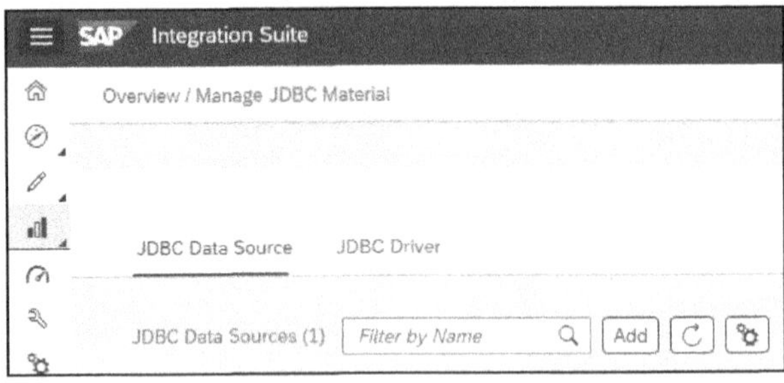

Figure 6.77 Adding a New JDBC Data Source Alias

4. Specify the settings for this artifact, as shown in Figure 6.78.

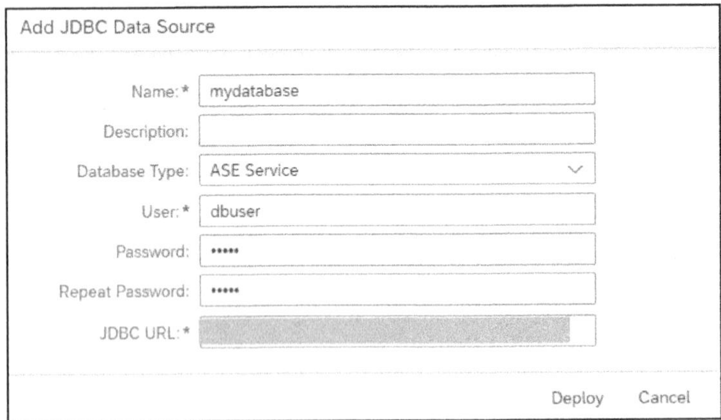

Figure 6.78 JDBC Data Source Alias Settings

Specify the settings to access the database schema:

- As **Name**, enter an alias name for the database. You'll need this alias when configuring the JDBC adapter in the next section.
- Provide a description (optional).
- Select the **Database Type**. Let's assume that you've set up an SAP ASE database system.
- For the **User** field, enter the database user you defined when setting up the database schema (with the command-line interface). In addition, enter the password for this user.
- In the **JDBC URL** field, enter the JDBC URL generated earlier.
- Click **Deploy**.

Now, let's set up your first iFlow that connects to the database.

6.5.3 Setting Up an Example Scenario

In this simple exercise, we'll show you how to use the JDBC adapter to perform some basic database operations. Now that you've set up a database system, you should be able to create tables, insert table entries, and read table entries out. The basic principle is that the JDBC adapter opens the connection to the database system, and through the iFlow, you can simply insert an SQL command. This insertion can happen either by passing an SQL command from an external client (e.g., an HTTP client) as parameter through the iFlow to the database system or by defining an SQL statement within the iFlow (e.g., in a content modifier step, as you'll see).

In this exercise, we'll use Postman as an HTTP client to inject the SQL command into the database system.

Let's first create an iFlow to create a basic connection to the database system, which is quite simple, as shown in Figure 6.79.

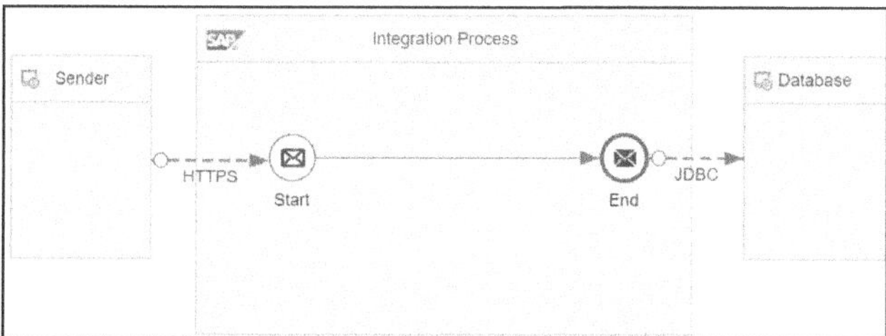

Figure 6.79 iFlow to Access Database System

Make sure that, for the HTTPS sender adapter, you specify a unique address.

The JDBC adapter configuration is simple. After a sophisticated procedure was required to set up the database system and to authorize Cloud Integration to access it, the complexity is now completely hidden while you design the integration content, which is good news!

In the JDBC adapter, for the **JDBC Data Source Alias** field, you'll just need to enter the name of the alias given when deploying the **JDBC Data Source** artifact, as shown in Figure 6.80.

JDBC

General Connection

CONNECTION DETAILS

JDBC Data Source Alias:* mydatabase

Connection Timeout (in s):* 3

Query/Response Timeout (in s):* 3

Maximum Records: 100000

Batch Mode: ☐

Figure 6.80 JDBC Adapter Settings

You can keep the default settings for the other parameters, which can be described as follows:

- **Connection Timeout (in s)**
  With this parameter, you can define a maximum time to wait for a response from the database server.
- **Query/Response Timeout (in s)**
  With this parameter, you can define a maximum time to wait for a response to a query placed on the database.
- **Maximum Records**
  With this parameter, you can specify how many data records can be fetched at maximum.

Now, open Postman, and, under the **Body** tab, enter the SQL command you want to perform on the database system. Let's first use our iFlow to create a table with the name `test`.

Therefore, enter the following SQL statement under the **Body** tab of your Postman user interface (UI), and place the `GET` request:

```
CREATE TABLE test (ColumnA varchar(255), ColumnB varchar(255))
```

This command will create a database table with two columns (`ColumnA` and `ColumnB`), where both columns can hold characters of variable length. The result in Postman should be like the screen shown in Figure 6.81.

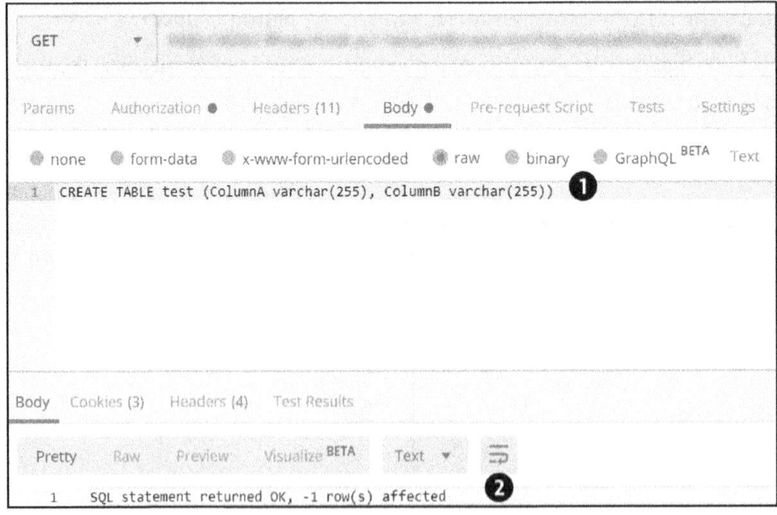

Figure 6.81 Successful iFlow Execution: Postman Success Message

As shown in Figure 6.81, you'll see the SQL statement that you entered ❶ and the success message from the database system ❷.

Now, let's insert an entry into the new table. Run another HTTP request with the following SQL command under the **Body** tab of your Postman UI:

```
INSERT INTO test (ColumnA, ColumnB) VALUES ('A1', 'B1')
```

The command adds entry `A1` into column `ColumnA` and entry `B1` into column `ColumnB`. You should again receive a success message.

To read the data from the updated table, send a request with the following command:

```
Select * From test
```

Figure 6.82 shows the request to ❶ and the response from ❷ the database system.

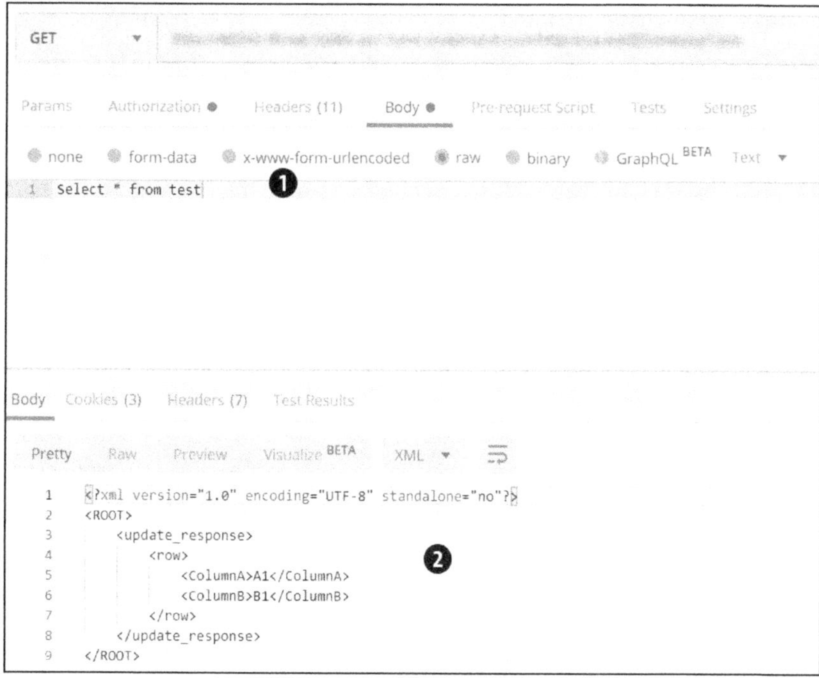

Figure 6.82 Response in Postman Shows the Content of Database Table in XML Format

Notice that the response provides the structure of the updated database table in XML format.

In this scenario, the SQL command is defined on the sender side and passed through to the database system by Cloud Integration. As mentioned earlier, you can also define the SQL command within the iFlow, which we'll demonstrate in the next tutorial.

Note that the JDBC adapter also supports SQL commands in an XML format that is also supported by SAP Process Orchestration (that has also a JDBC adapter). For more information on this, refer to the documentation for Cloud Integration at *http://s-prs.co/v576023*. Search for "JDBC Receiver Adapter."

With this simple exercise, you've seen that the connection from Cloud Integration to the database system works well.

In Section 6.3.3, we introduced you to the topic of error handling and showed you how to build a scenario that can handle certain kinds of error situations, namely, situations where the WebShop component can't be reached by Cloud Integration. Our previous business scenario involved reading a product's details as identified by product identifier.

How can you make this scenario even more robust and reliable? Let's say you'd like to further enhance the scenario from Section 6.3.3 (compare Figure 6.54) so that, if the WebShop component (with its product catalog) is temporarily unreachable, you can read out the latest details of a product (e.g., the price) from a "fallback" data source. This use case is perfect for the JDBC adapter.

Because detailed descriptions of how to design and run even more complex scenarios is beyond the scope of this book, we recommend reading the SAP Community blog at *http://s-prs.co/507726*.

In the next section, we'll introduce you to the topic of connecting to an AS2 server.

6.6 Connecting to an AS2 Server Using an AS2 Adapter

Cloud Integration plays a crucial role in seamlessly connecting various systems, applications, and data sources across the enterprise. One common integration scenario involves the use of the Applicability Statement 2 (AS2) protocol, which is widely used for secure and reliable data interchange. In this section, we'll explore the process of connecting to an AS2 server using the AS2 Adapter within Cloud Integration.

AS2 is a specification that defines the methods for secure and reliable data transmission over the internet. It provides a standardized approach for exchanging business documents such as invoices, purchase orders, and shipping notices between trading partners. AS2 uses a combination of HTTP and Secure/Multipurpose Internet Mail Extensions (S/MIME) to ensure data integrity, authentication, and confidentiality during transmission.

AS2 defines a set of rules and guidelines for transmitting structured business data, such as invoices, purchase orders, and shipping notifications, between different entities in a secure and standardized manner.

The AS2 Adapter in Cloud Integration enables organizations to connect with their trading partners, suppliers, and customers using the AS2 protocol. This adapter simplifies the configuration and management of AS2 communication, making it easier to establish secure and reliable connections. The adapter can be used to send and receive data to/from the AS2 server.

In this section, we'll take a simple example to show the usage of AS2 sender and receiver adapter. Let's take the example scenario shown in Figure 6.83, where the sender application is sending the data to Cloud Integration using the AS2 protocol, and the receiver application is receiving the data using the AS2 protocol.

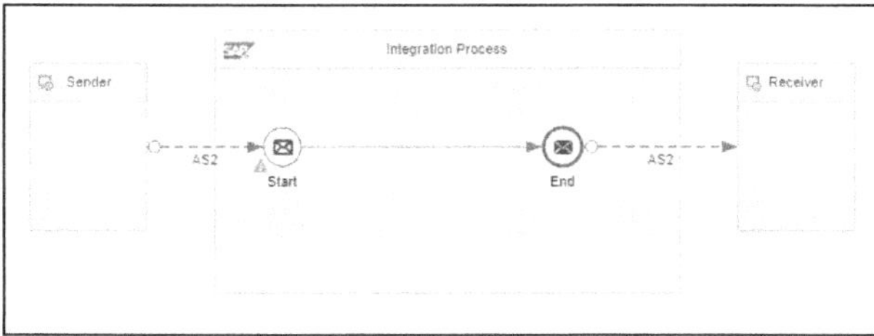

Figure 6.83 Simple Integration Scenario

6.6.1 Configuration of Sender Adapter to Receive Messages

Before configuring the sender AS2 adapter in Cloud Integration, select the sender **AS2** adapter from the list of adapters as shown in Figure 6.84.

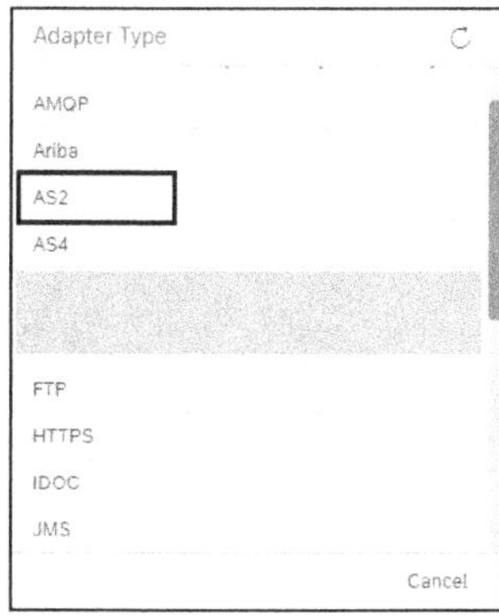

Figure 6.84 Selecting the AS2 Sender Adapter

Once the sender adapter is selected, the adapter has several tabs, as shown in Figure 6.85, that need to be configured based on the requirements.

Figure 6.85 Sections of a Sender AS2 Adapter

In the **Connection** tab of the adapter, provide the path using which the iFlow will be identified by the sender AS2 server. As shown in Figure 6.86, the address provided is "/receiveAS2Message". This endpoint gets translated into a complete AS2 endpoint point for the sender AS2 server, and the complete URL will translate into *https://{Cloud_integration host}/as2/receiveAS2Message*.

The sender application can be authorized to access the Cloud Integration endpoint and send messages to Cloud Integration in two ways:

- **User role**
  Select this option if the sender application must be authorized based on the user and the roles associated with the inbound request. The user used for the inbound request must have the `ESBMessaging.send` role assigned to it. It's recommended to have separate credentials for different partners.
- **Client Certificate**
  Select this option if the sender application must be authorized based on the certificates used in the inbound request. In this case, the client certificates must be imported into the iFlow by using the **Add** button.

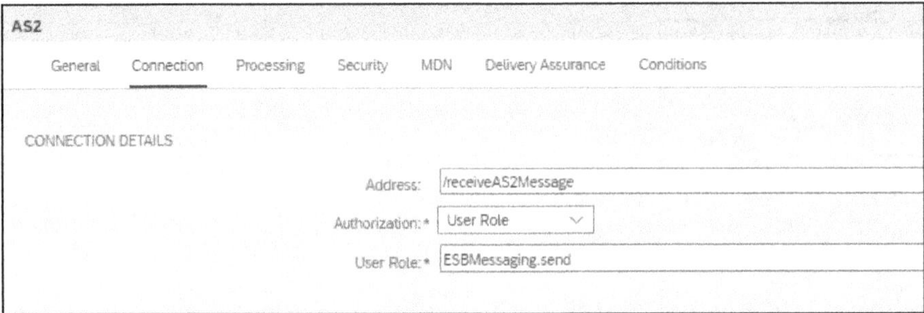

Figure 6.86 Setting Up the Connectivity with the Sender AS2 Server

Note

When connecting to the Cloud Integration endpoint from the AS2 server, if the AS2 server is unable to resolve the Secure Sockets Layer (SSL) certificate, the Cloud Integration SSL certificate must be imported into the certificate store of the AS2 server.

Once the connection configurations are done, other parameters influence the message processing in Cloud Integration. In this section, we'll discuss some of the key parameters.

In the **Processing** tab of the sender Adapter shown in Figure 6.87, the message identifiers must be defined correctly to receive the messages in Cloud Integration. These parameters define the expected inbound message. If these parameters aren't correctly defined, the messages will run into an error on the source AS2 server. The combination of parameters must be unique across all the iFlows deployed on the tenant. The parameters are as follows:

- **Message ID Left Part/Message ID Right Part**
  If a specific format is expected from the partner, configure the parameter to restrict the inbound messages to the message that follows the pattern. If no format is agreed, then wildcard ".*" can be used.
- **Partner AS2 ID**
  Specify the partner AS2 ID. Wildcard ".*" can be used to allow multiple partners to send messages to the same iFlow.
- **Own AS2 ID**
  This is a unique ID for the organization that is used by the partners to identify you as the receiver of the messages. These details must be agreed on in advance with partners.
- **Message Subject**
  The message subject refers to the subject line of the message being transmitted. It should reflect the content or the purpose of the message.

Figure 6.87 Processing Tab of AS2 Sender Adapter

The configurations in the **Security**, **MDN**, **Delivery Assurance**, and **Conditions** tabs can be left with their default settings. For our simple example scenario, we won't use signing, encryption, or asynchronous message disposition notification (MDN). A synchronous MDN is sent back to the receiver as a receipt to acknowledge that the message was successfully received. A retry will be executed every minute an error arises. Check out the documentation for Cloud Integration to get more details about the configuration options for those features.

Detailed Documentation of the AS2 Sender Adapter

Note that, for the sake of simplicity, we haven't described all the possible configuration options in the AS2 sender adapter in detail in this book. You can refer to the "Configure Communication Channel with AS2 Adapter" section in the documentation for Cloud Integration at *http://s-prs.co/v576024*.

6.6.2 Configuration of the Receiver Adapter to Send AS2 Messages

The AS2 receiver adapter in Cloud Integration is used to send AS2 messages to a receiver AS2 server. To use the AS2 receiver adapter, select **AS2** from the list of adapters on the Cloud Integration tenant, as shown in Figure 6.88.

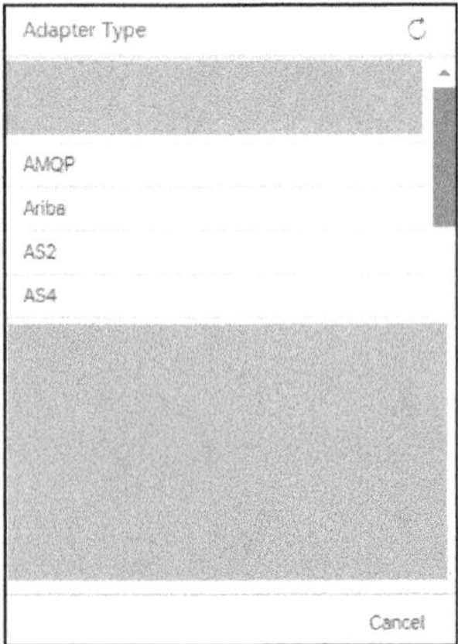

Figure 6.88 Selecting the AS2 Adapter from the List of Adapters

In the **Connection** tab of the receiver adapter, the details related to connectivity to the AS2 server need to be configured, as shown in Figure 6.89. For the sake of simplicity, we've used the Mendelson AS2 test server in this example.

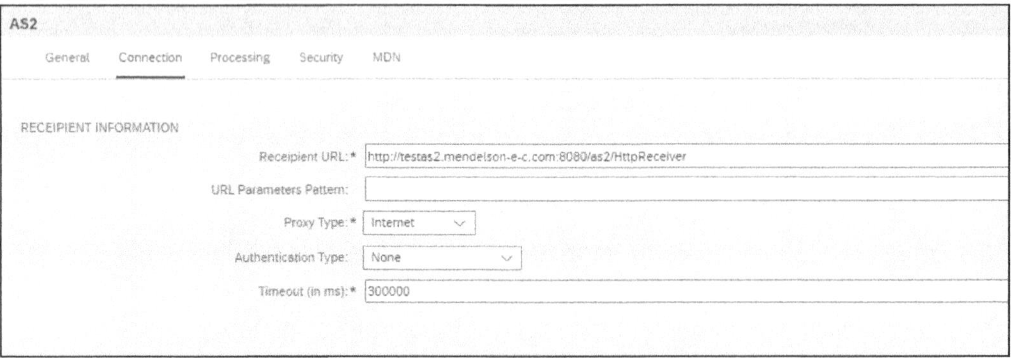

Figure 6.89 Connection Details of the AS2 Receiver Server

Select the other parameters such as **Proxy Type**, **Authentication Type**, and **Timeout (in ms)** based on your requirements:

- **Proxy Type**
  Depending on the location of the receiver AS2 server, select the appropriate option of proxy type. Select **Internet**" when the AS2 URL is publicly accessible. When the AS2 server is on-premise and can only be reached via the cloud connector, select **On-Premise**, and specify the location of the cloud connector where applicable.

- **Authentication Type**
  Based on the authentication mechanism supported by the AS2 server, select from the list of available options in the adapter.

In the **Processing** tab, configure the details related to the message, as shown in Figure 6.90. The most important settings are the configurations for the **MESSAGE INFORMATION** section, including the **Message ID Left Part**, **Message ID Right Part**, **Own AS2 ID**, **Partner AS2 ID**, **Message Subject**, **Own E-mail address**, and **Content-Type** fields because these parameters define the expected outbound message. These parameters uniquely define the message sent out of Cloud Integration to the AS2 partner application.

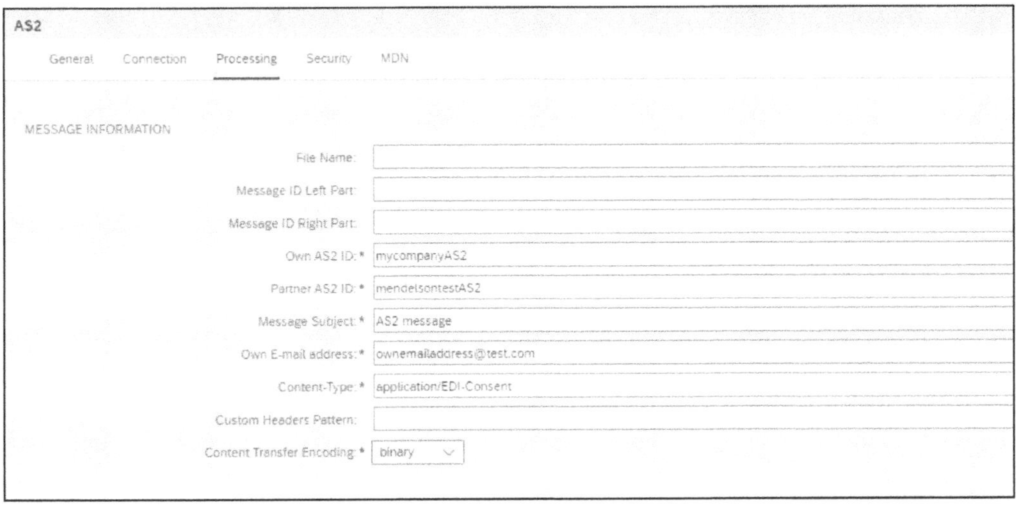

AS2

General Connection Processing Security MDN

MESSAGE INFORMATION

File Name:
Message ID Left Part:
Message ID Right Part:
Own AS2 ID: * mycompanyAS2
Partner AS2 ID: * mendelsontestAS2
Message Subject: * AS2 message
Own E-mail address: * ownemailaddress@test.com
Content-Type: * application/EDI-Consent
Custom Headers Pattern:
Content Transfer Encoding: * binary

Figure 6.90 Processing Tab of AS2 Receiver Adapter

Configure the parameters related to compression, signature, and encryption in the **Security** tab of the adapter, as shown in Figure 6.91.

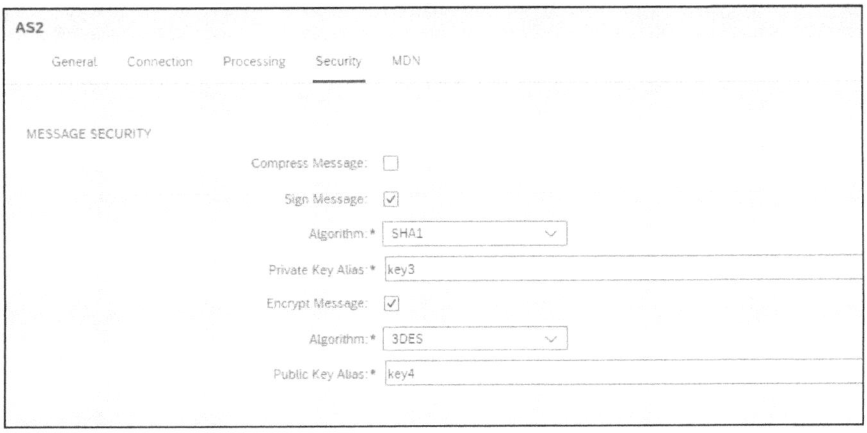

AS2

General Connection Processing Security MDN

MESSAGE SECURITY

Compress Message:
Sign Message: ☑
Algorithm: * SHA1
Private Key Alias: * key3
Encrypt Message: ☑
Algorithm: * 3DES
Public Key Alias: * key4

Figure 6.91 Security Tab of the AS2 Receiver Adapter

Select the **Compress Message** checkbox to ensure that the outbound message is compressed. In this example, we haven't selected this option. You can choose this option based on your use case. If the outgoing message has to be signed and encrypted, select the **Sign Message** and **Encrypt Message** checkboxes, as shown in Figure 6.91. If selected, the outbound AS2 message must be signed using your private key and encrypted using the AS2 partner public key. You also need to select the algorithm for signing and encryption from the **Algorithm** dropdown. In this example, we've used **SHA1** as the algorithm, **key3** as the **Private Key Alias** for signing the message, **3DES** as the other algorithm, and **key4** as the **Public Key Alias** of the Mendelson AS2 server for encryption. The public and private keys must be uploaded as security artifacts before using them in the adapter.

Now that we've looked into the configuration of the receiver AS2 adapter, we'll use a simple iFlow to send a test message to the AS2 server, as shown in Figure 6.92.

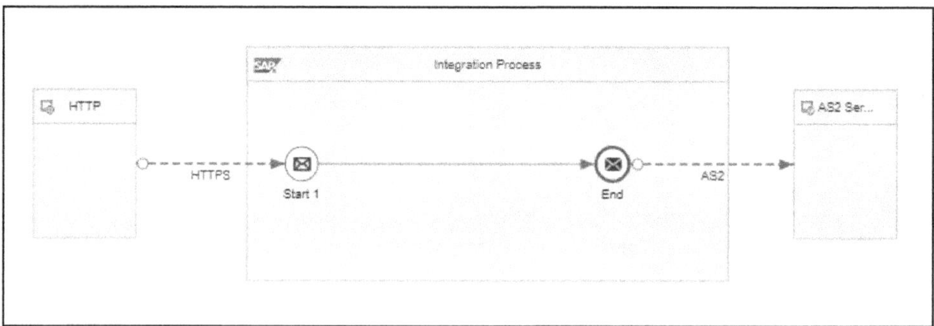

Figure 6.92 Simple iFlow to Test the AS2 Message

In this example, we're using an HTTP sender adapter to trigger the iFlow using Postman. On the receiver side is the AS2 server to receive the AS2 message.

The HTTP sender adapter is configured to receive the messages with the address "*/sendAs2Message*", as shown in Figure 6.93.

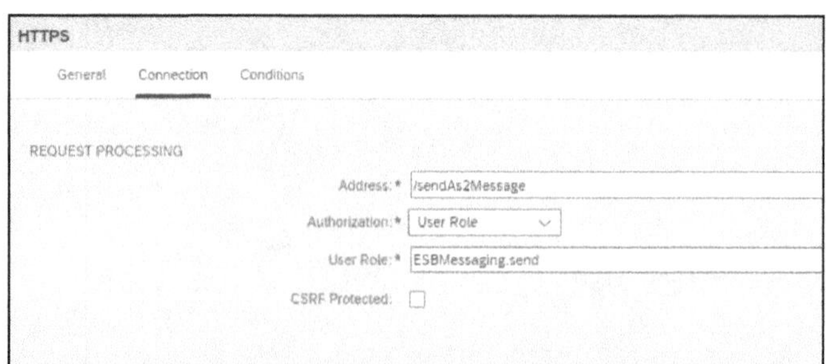

Figure 6.93 Sender HTTP Adapter Configuration

We're almost ready to run a test message and see if the AS2 server on the receiving side receives the message from Cloud Integration. You can use Postman as shown in Figure

6.94 to trigger the test message to Cloud Integration. The endpoint used in Postman can be retrieved from the deployment view of the iFlow in Cloud Integration. The URL is generated after the deployment is successful on the Cloud Integration tenant.

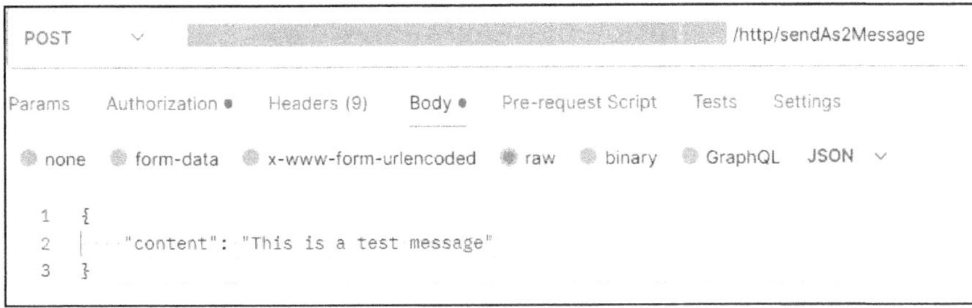

Figure 6.94 Postman Configuration to Trigger the Message to Cloud Integration

Once the Postman request is executed, the message will be received in Cloud Integration and sent to the Mendelson test AS2 server. Log in to the AS2 server to check if the message arrived there. Figure 6.95 shows the successful processing of the message in the SA2 server.

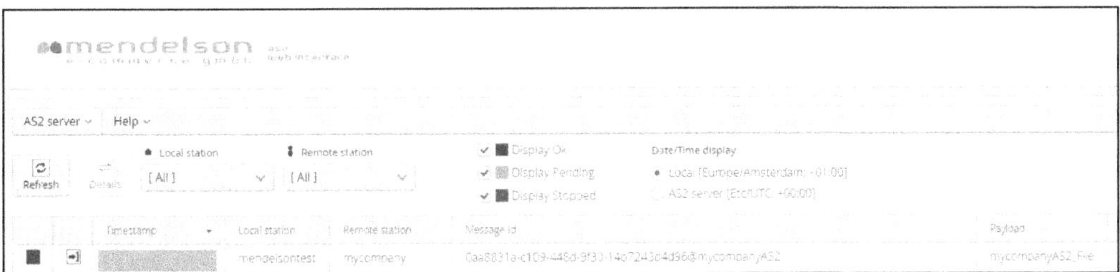

Figure 6.95 Message Processing in the AS2 Server

Figure 6.96 shows the payload information of the message received in the AS2 server. The payload received is the same as the one sent from Postman, as shown earlier in Figure 6.94.

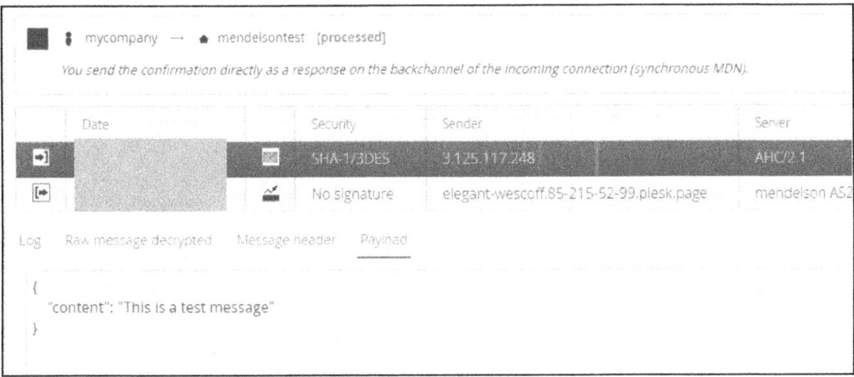

Figure 6.96 Payload Information of the Message

Congratulations, you've successfully configured the receiver adapter and tested a scenario end to end.

6.7 Versioning and Migration of Integration Flows

Cloud Integration is an on-demand software product for which SAP provides monthly updates. Thus, Cloud Integration customers work and run their scenarios on a platform that is enhanced constantly, so a critical requirement is that the software lifecycle doesn't impact any productive scenarios. SAP also must ensure that integration developers can seamlessly enhance integration content and use new features while minimizing change efforts with regard to existing iFlows.

Cloud Integration also offers a hybrid Cloud Integration content approach in which integration content designed with the Web UI can also be used on the on-premise integration bus of SAP Process Orchestration (assuming that you have a license for that product). With this hybrid approach, high demands are made on the versioning concept behind the Cloud Integration software. In this section, we'll provide an overview of versioning and integration content migration capabilities, including how to migrate iFlow components to a higher version. Finally, we'll show you how to "downgrade" iFlow components, which is required when using integration content on the SAP Process Orchestration integration bus.

Note that some of the brief exercises shown in this section might not be possible with the trial tenant. Because we expected that you set up a new trial tenant to follow along with the book, you might not have any "old" integration content on your tenant that can be migrated to a newer version.

6.7.1 Integration Flow Component Versions

With each monthly release of Cloud Integration tools, iFlow components updated with new features (e.g., new adapter or flow step attributes) are released as components with a new version (also referred to as a *component version*). In this context, *component* refers either to an adapter or an iFlow step.

To find out more, open an iFlow. To determine the version of a SOAP adapter (as one example for an iFlow component), click on the **SOAP** channel in the model, and then click on the **Information** icon, as shown in Figure 6.97.

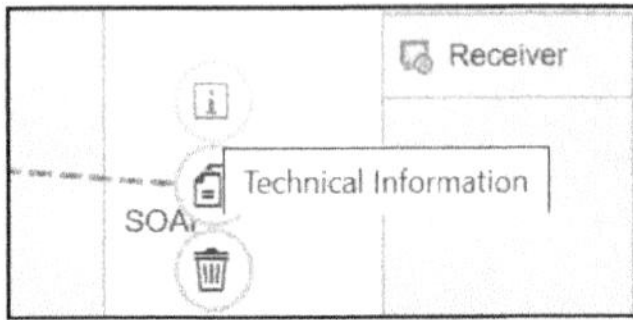

Figure 6.97 Selecting the Information Button for an Adapter

The **Technical Information** screen in this case indicates that the component version is 1.9, as shown in Figure 6.98.

Figure 6.98 Technical Information for an Adapter

The general nomenclature of a component version is **<major version>.<minor version>**, where the various parts of the version indicator have the following meaning:

- **Major version**
  The major version is usually not changed to ensure the backward compatibility of the component.
- **Minor version**
  The minor version is incremented when new features have been added to the component (e.g., when a new adapter attribute has been added).

Operating in the background and not indicated for the user is a third, additional version counter for *micro versions*, which are related to smaller improvements such as UI label changes. We won't elaborate further on this concept.

To summarize, Figure 6.98 shows how Cloud Integration software versions are related to component versions when the software is being updated.

Figure 6.99 shows the situation for the monthly software release in April 2020 (to use as an example). Components A, B, and C stand for three different iFlow components that belong to the Cloud Integration design tooling. Imagine that A, B, and C can represent adapter or iFlow step types. In a real-life scenario, we probably would need to sketch out many more components. We'll only have three components (each with just a few features) for the sake of simplicity.

In this example, the software version from March 2020 already contains the two components (A and B). With software updates to the April 2020 version, component A is enhanced by a new feature (A3), and accordingly, the component version for A is changed from 1.2 to 1.3. Component B isn't changed during this update, so the feature scope remains the same. Consequently, the component version for B isn't changed, so this version number stays 1.1. However, component C is added as a new component during this update. For C, you can imagine that SAP has added, for example, a new adapter type with a software update in April 2020. The new component gets the initial component version 1.0.

You'll more fully understand the implications and importance of this versioning concept once we introduce the concept of migrating iFlow components. We'll first explain how *upgrading* an iFlow component works, which means migrating a component to a newer version.

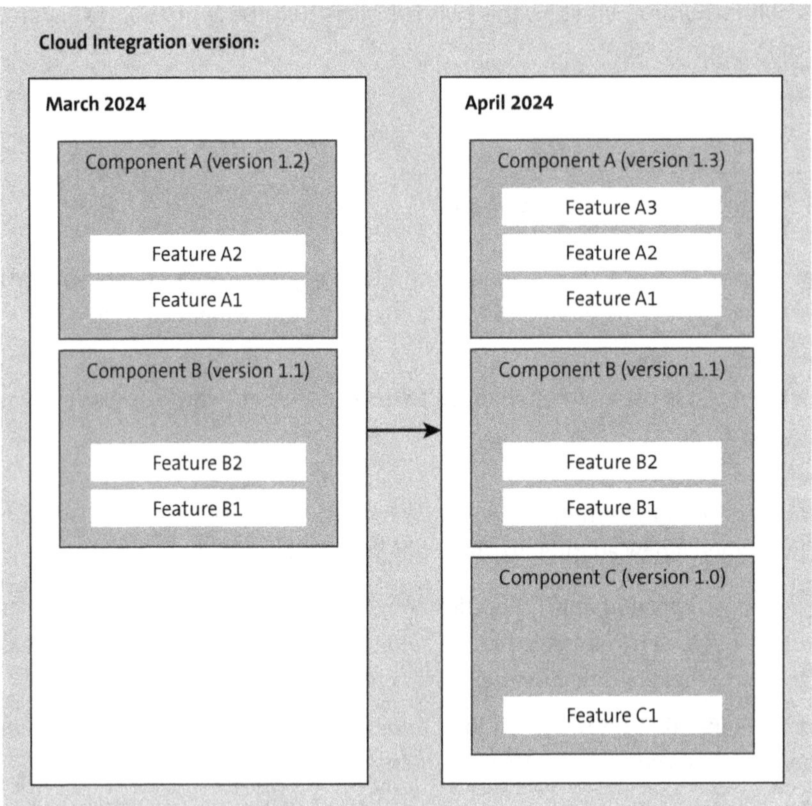

Figure 6.99 How Software Versions and Component Versions Are Related to Each Other

6.7.2 Upgrading an Integration Flow Component

Let's say that you've created, deployed, and put into operation an iFlow at a certain point in time, for example, shortly before you left for vacation. Although you're on vacation, the Cloud Integration development team never rests and provides a software update every month. When you come back from vacation a few weeks later, a new feature for a component used in your iFlow is available. Of course, your concrete iFlows, which you deployed weeks ago, don't yet reflect this new feature. As you read the new release notes for Cloud Integration, you become aware of the new feature in a certain component and want to update your specific iFlow to also support this new feature.

The best option is to migrate the iFlow component. This approach enables you to update your iFlow component to support the newest features made available by SAP without needing to re-create the component from scratch.

Save the iFlow as a Version First

After you've migrated a component to a new version, you can't undo this action to revert back to the old version. Therefore, we recommend that you save your iFlow as a version before migrating the component. Open an iFlow, and you'll see the **Save as version** option next to the **Save** option on top of the iFlow model. Using this option, you'll create a copy of the iFlow, and you can move back to the older version of your iFlow if the migration results in any issues.

To migrate a component, for example, an **Integration Process** component, follow these steps:

1. Open the iFlow, and click **Edit**.
2. Click on the component you want to migrate (in this case, the **Integration Process** shape).
3. To check the current version of the component, click on the **Information** [i] icon. The information screen shows that the version is 1.0, as shown in Figure 6.100.

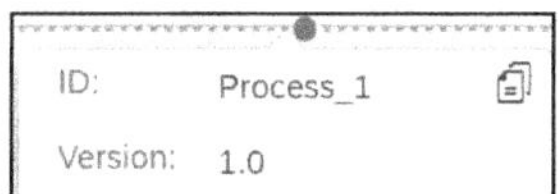

Figure 6.100 Version of the Selected Integration Process Prior to Migration

4. Click **Migrate**, as shown in Figure 6.101.

Figure 6.101 Migrating an Integration Process

   At the time of this writing, only a few iFlow components can be migrated (listed in the information box later in this section).

5. A confirmation dialog box will open displaying the source version and target version, as shown in Figure 6.102.

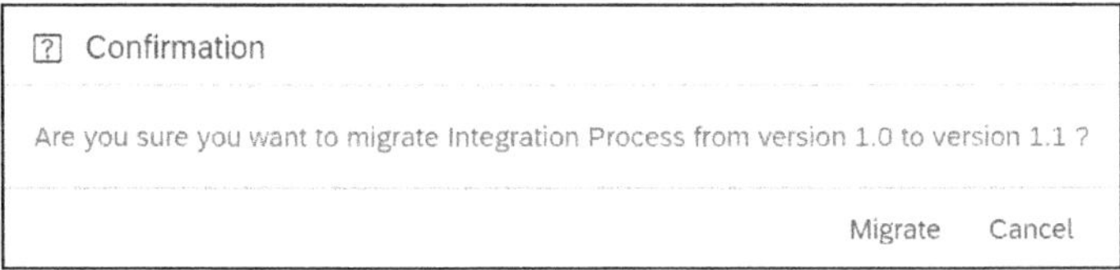

Figure 6.102 Confirmation Message

6. Choose **Migrate** to confirm your selection. The component will be migrated to the latest available version.

7. To check the version, again click the **Information** icon to display the technical information. You'll now see the new version number 1.1, as shown in Figure 6.103.

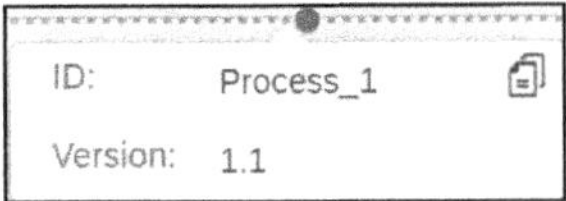

Figure 6.103 Version of Selected Component Increased to 1.1 After Migration

8. After migration, the new feature from the latest update can be consumed.

   Component version 1.1 of the **Integration Process** element has a new feature called **TRANSACTION MANAGEMENT**, as shown in Figure 6.104 (compare with Figure 6.101, which shows the **Integration Process** component prior to migration). For more information about this feature, see Chapter 5, Section 5.4.2.

9. Save the iFlow.

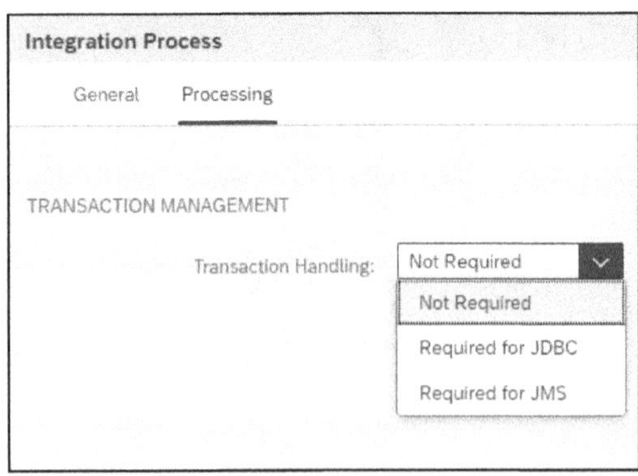

Figure 6.104 New Feature TRANSACTION MANAGEMENT in Upgraded Process

If incompatibilities exist with versions of other components within the iFlow, the iFlow model will display errors (on explicit save of the iFlow).

Alternatively, you can delete the component and re-create it. This action also updates the set of features for that component.

When Is Migration Supported?

Migrating an iFlow component is only supported when a newer version of the component is available (and your iFlow is still on an older version). When no migration option is available, no newer version is available for that component, and no **Migrate** option will be shown for the component.

Furthermore, note that the migration of iFlow components is only available for editable iFlows. In other words, for configure-only content (see Chapter 3), you can't use this feature.

At the time of this writing, SAP supports migration of the following components:

- iFlows
- Integration processes
- Local integration processes

The ability to migrate other components is listed on the Cloud Integration product roadmap, including adapters or iFlow steps that will be supported in the future. Check out the product documentation regularly to find out more.

Let's look at another example: migrating an iFlow supports consuming a newer HTTP session-handling feature for HTTP-based receiver adapters. This feature has been available since the July 2017 release of Cloud Integration.

When you edit an "old" iFlow (created before that release date) and click on the area outside the **Integration Process** shape in the iFlow modeler, you'll find these features under the **Runtime Configuration** tab, as shown in Figure 6.105.

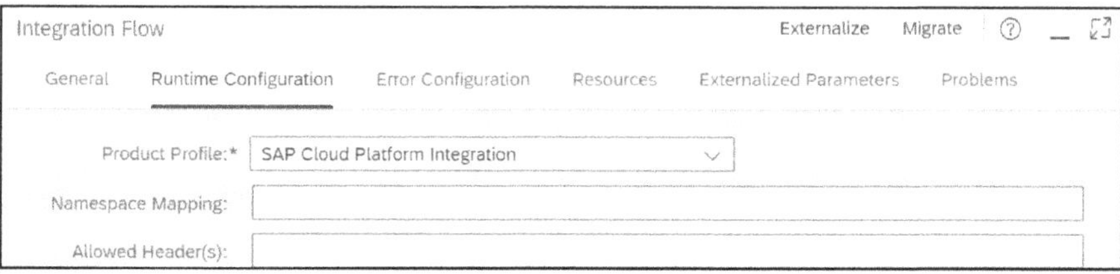

Figure 6.105 Runtime Configuration Features Before Migration

Notice the **Migrate** option in the top-right corner of the screen, indicating that this component (the iFlow) can be migrated. Now, migrate this component as described earlier. After migration, you'll notice that the **Runtime Configuration** tab now displays an additional feature, **HTTP Session Reuse**, as shown in Figure 6.106.

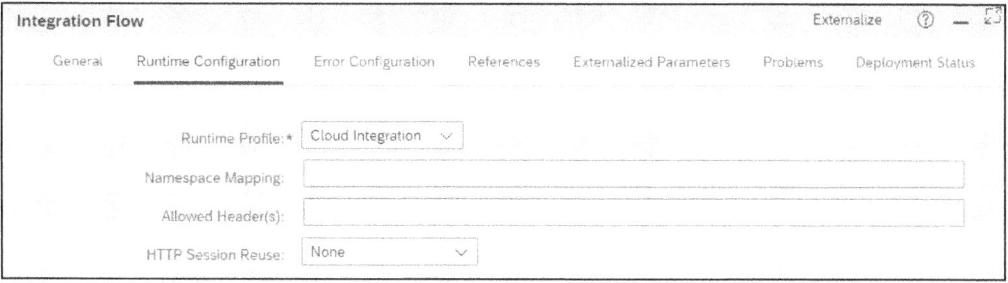

Figure 6.106 Runtime Configuration Features After Migration

Note

For more information on the HTTP session-handling feature, see *http://s-prs.co/507727*.

So far, we've discussed how you can migrate *upward* to a newer version so you can keep pace with the monthly updates of the Cloud Integration software and adapt your iFlows to use the newest available features. To complete the story, we'll now show you how Cloud Integration also supports *downward* migration to an older feature set. Check out the next section to learn more.

6.7.3 Adapting Integration Content for SAP Process Orchestration

When would it make sense to migrate iFlow components the other way around, down to an older version? Let's briefly set the context. Throughout this book, we've focused on cases where you deploy and run iFlows on your Cloud Integration tenant. In other words, all the iFlows we've developed throughout this book have been executed on a runtime node of SAP BTP. SAP provides updates for both the capabilities of the integration runtime and the integration design environment (the Web UI) on a monthly basis in the same development cycles. The development of new iFlow features and their corresponding runtime capabilities is synchronized. Thus, for each new capability released for the iFlow designer (e.g., for a new flow step offered in the palette), you can always be sure that this feature is also supported by the actual integration runtime on SAP BTP.

Product Profiles

If you're only working with Cloud Integration, that's fine, and you're happy with the migration capability we explained in the previous section. However, SAP also provides another powerful integration solution that has been already been in place for many years and has been used by many SAP customers: SAP Process Orchestration. For a comprehensive introduction of this product, check out *SAP Process Orchestration: The Comprehensive Guide* by John Mutumba Bilay and Roberto Viana Blanco (SAP PRESS, 2017, *www.sap-press.com/4431*).

As described earlier in Chapter 1, many customers use a hybrid system and process landscape where parts of the scenario run in the cloud and other parts are handled by components installed on the premises of the customer. In addition, many customers use both integration platforms in combination: both the cloud-based Cloud Integration and SAP Process Orchestration on-premise.

Therefore, a good practice is to use the Web UI as a central tool to design the following:

- iFlows that can run on Cloud Integration
- iFlows that can run on SAP Process Orchestration

When you have a license for Cloud Integration *and* SAP Process Orchestration, you can adopt this hybrid approach. To support this use case, SAP has introduced product profiles in the Web UI (which we briefly touched upon in Chapter 2, Section 2.2.1, especially Table 2.2).

What are product profiles good for? To understand this feature, note that SAP Process Orchestration and Cloud Integration are developed and updated in different cycles (we'll discuss more later). However, the features you can use in the integration content design tool (Web UI) must correspond to the capabilities of the target runtime (integration bus) where you intend to deploy the iFlow. Because the release cycles of the integration platforms—SAP Process Orchestration and Cloud Integration—also differ significantly, SAP has introduced product profiles. Choosing the right product profile ensures that the integration developer can use exactly those design and modeling features in the Web UI that are also supported by the target integration runtime corresponding to the product profile—and no more. You can choose among both the Cloud Integration product profile and recent versions of SAP Process Orchestration product profiles.

Product Profile

A product profile defines the capabilities of the Web UI design environment that are supported for a chosen target integration runtime. If you've only purchased a Cloud Integration license, you'll only need the Cloud Integration product profile. If you've purchased an SAP Process Orchestration license as well, you can choose between the following product profiles:

- Cloud Integration
- SAP PO <Support Package>

The latest available support packages of SAP Process Orchestration 7.5 are offered. Earlier releases of SAP Process Orchestration (prior to release 7.5) aren't supported; only the runtime components for the latest SAP Process Orchestration release are enhanced with regard to the runtime features of Cloud Integration.

For more detail on how product profiles are related to the topic of downgrades, let's look at the different development cycles of the two integration runtimes.

Updates for Cloud Integration (both the integration runtime components and the Web UI as the central, cloud-based design tool) are released monthly. On the other hand, updates for SAP Process Orchestration are released in "slower" cycles together with SAP NetWeaver (roughly in quarterly shipments). Therefore, the capabilities of SAP Process Orchestration (as one target integration runtime for your iFlows) lag behind the capabilities of the iFlow design tool (Web UI). When selecting a certain SAP Process Orchestration product profile, the scope of capabilities available in the Web UI is adapted so that you can only choose a feature that is also supported by the respective SAP Process Orchestration runtime. Because SAP Process Orchestration is an on-premise solution, and the features of a dedicated release aren't enhanced further, a maximum version of all components always exists for a dedicated SAP Process Orchestration product profile, whereas for the Cloud Integration product profile, the set of features is enhanced constantly each month. Only when a new release of SAP Process Orchestration is made available can you also select a new product profile, which would offer the exact updated set of design features that are also supported by the new SAP Process Orchestration release, as shown in Figure 6.107.

In our example, in SAP Process Orchestration 7.5 SP x, the SAP Process Orchestration runtime can provide maximum support for integration features developed in the Web UI prior to (and including) version *n*. In other words, the Web UI product profile SAP Process Orchestration 7.5 SP x must "filter out" all newer integration capabilities that are developed after version *n*. For the product profile SAP Process Orchestration 7.5 SP x+1, newer features can then be considered.

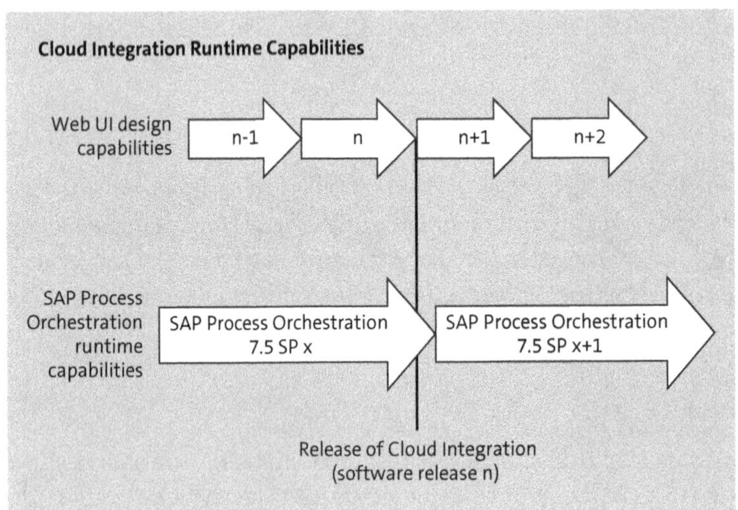

Figure 6.107 Release Cycles of Cloud Integration (with Web UI) Compared to SAP Process Orchestration

Figure 6.108 shows a visual representation of the versioning of an individual iFlow component.

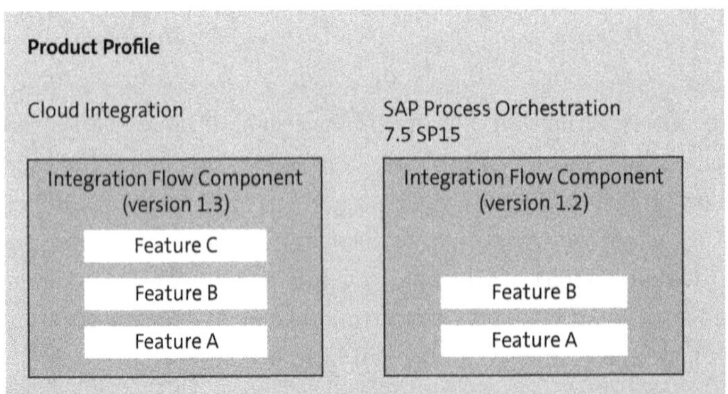

Figure 6.108 iFlow Components Showing Different Feature Sets Depending on the Chosen Product Profile

Working with Product Profiles

When you have both an SAP Process Orchestration license and an Cloud Integration license, you can choose among different product profiles in the Web UI by clicking the **Settings** menu item, as shown in Figure 6.109. Note that you'll need the role collection `PI_Administrator` (tenant administrator) assigned to your user to be able to access the tenant's settings.

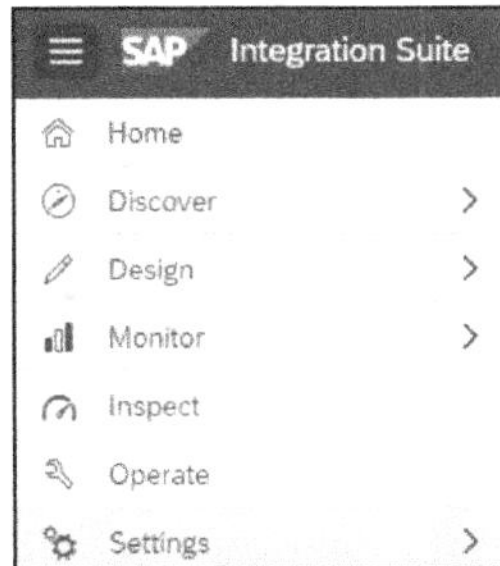

Figure 6.109 Choosing the Tenant Settings Section on the Web UI

Notice that, for this tenant, the **Cloud Integration** product profile and product profiles for recent releases of **SAP Process Orchestration** are available, as shown in Figure 6.110.

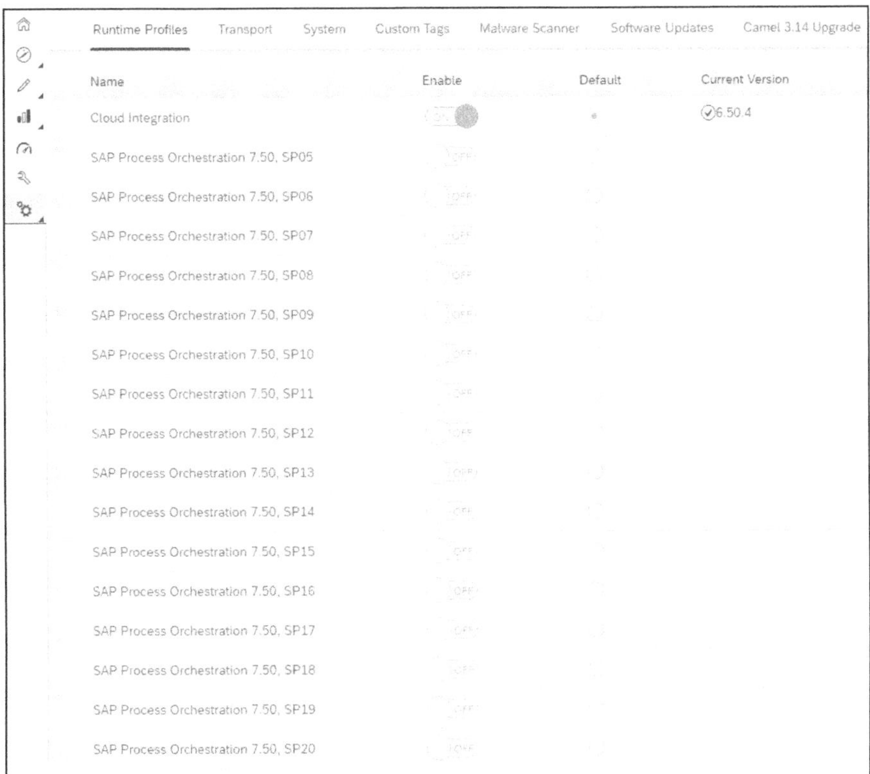

Figure 6.110 Tenant Settings Showing the Available Product Profiles

If you only see the **Cloud Integration** product profile, but also want to work with the other product profiles, create a ticket for your SAP Cloud Operations team (that provided you with the tenant). Note that, when clicking one of the product profiles, you'll get a list of component versions supported by the selected product profile.

By editing the settings, you can define a default product profile. When creating a new iFlow, the default setting will be used for this iFlow. You can also set product profiles globally for the tenant (as shown for the **Settings** section) or on an iFlow level. To illustrate, open an iFlow, click the area outside the **Integration Process** shape, and open the **Runtime Configuration** tab, as shown in Figure 6.111.

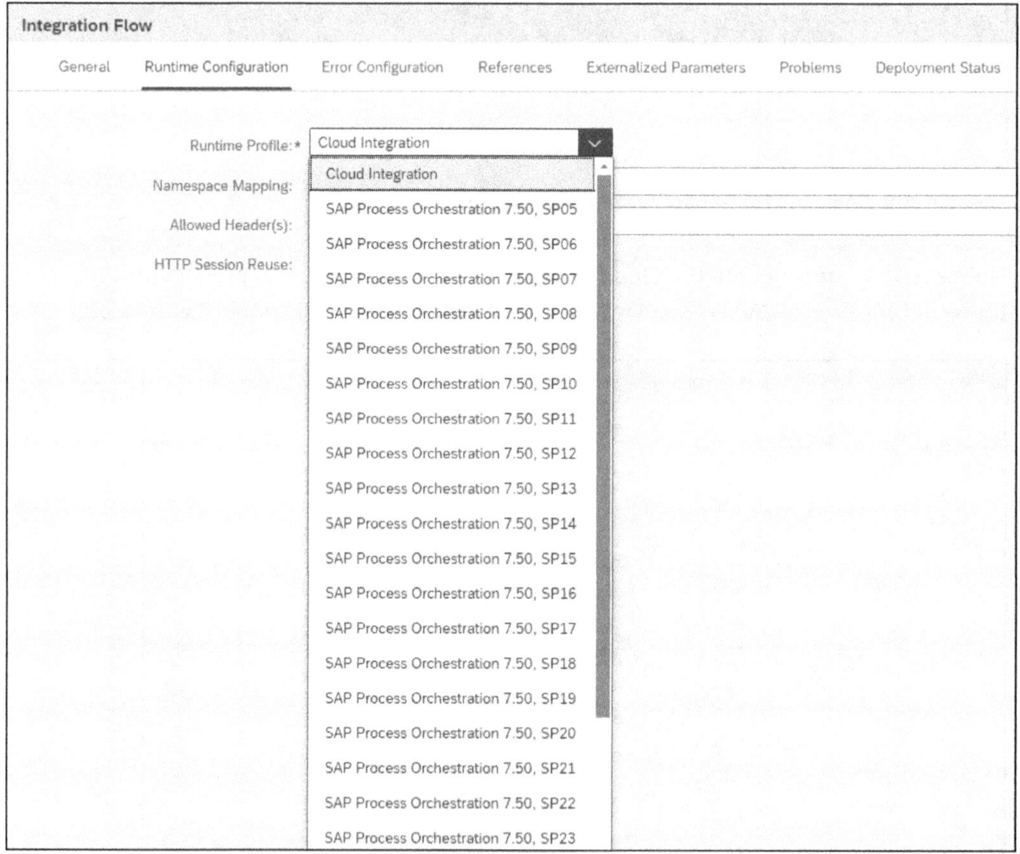

Figure 6.111 Setting a Product Profile for an iFlow

Select the **Cloud Integration** product profile, and add a new **Receiver** communication channel to your iFlow. Notice that a large number of receiver adapters are available for selection, as shown in Figure 6.112.

Cancel this activity, go back to the **Runtime Configuration** tab, and choose the product profile **SAP Process Orchestration 7.50, SP09**. Again, add a new **Receiver** channel, and you'll see a list of possible receiver adapters, as shown in Figure 6.113.

Figure 6.112 Receiver Adapter Types for the Cloud Integration Product Profile

Figure 6.113 Receiver Adapter Types for SAP Process Orchestration 7.50, SP 09 Product Profile

Notice that some adapters are missing, for example, the Facebook and Twitter adapter, because the selected SAP Process Orchestration runtime (for the chosen release 7.50 SP 09) doesn't support connectivity with these platforms. Future releases of SAP Process Orchestration might support this connectivity, however. If so, product profiles corresponding to future SAP Process Orchestration releases that are available with future releases of the Web UI might offer these additional adapter types.

The Web UI's capabilities might also differ on the detail level of each iFlow component so that certain features of an adapter or flow step are missing when an SAP Process Orchestration product profile is selected (as shown earlier in Figure 6.113). But we won't go into more detail here.

Migrating within an SAP Process Orchestration Product Profile

To conclude this section, note that the migration of iFlow components, as described earlier in Section 6.7.2, is also supported within an SAP Process Orchestration product profile. However, then, upgrading is only possible to the maximum component version supported for the chosen SAP Process Orchestration product profile. If you want to use features that were released later, you'll need to check out whether a newer SAP Process Orchestration product profile (and, thus, a newer SAP Process Orchestration release) is available.

For more information on the topic of migration, check out the SAP Community blog at *http://s-prs.co/507728*. To learn more about using integration content together with SAP Process Orchestration, check out *http://s-prs.co/507729*.

6.8 Simulation of Integration Flow Processing

When developing complex iFlows, you might need to test whether the designed iFlow works as expected before deployment in isolation from testing whether connections to the involved remote systems work without failure. Only when you know that each step does exactly what it should will you be confident enough to add more complexity and, in the end, configure connections to external systems.

Cloud Integration comes with a tool for simulating message processing without the need to deploy the iFlow. Like a debugger, this tool allows you to set a start point and an endpoint for simulated message processing. When you run the simulation, you can check the message content (headers and payload) after each step—similar to the **Trace** mode in message monitoring (see Chapter 7).

We'll show you how the tool works with a simple iFlow. Having worked up to this point in the book yourself, you're now expert enough to design the following iFlow in a few minutes, as shown in Figure 6.114. We'll only briefly explain how to configure the individual steps. The concepts used in this iFlow should be familiar to you now.

This iFlow takes an HTTP request that contains a message header (`productid`) and calls the WebShop application to get product details for the provided product identifier (as in the tutorial described earlier in Section 6.2.1, particularly Figure 6.13). A router leads to two different routes depending on the price of the retrieved product. For high-price items (e.g., over 500 euros), the upper route is taken; for low-price items, the lower route is taken. In the upper route, a data store entry is created (in a data store called

ProductCategories_HighPrice). The entry ID is defined by the product category. In the lower route, a message is created that communicates that the price of the product is lower than 500 euros, and a data store entry is created (in a data store called **Product-Categories_LowPrice**). The entry ID is again defined based on the product category.

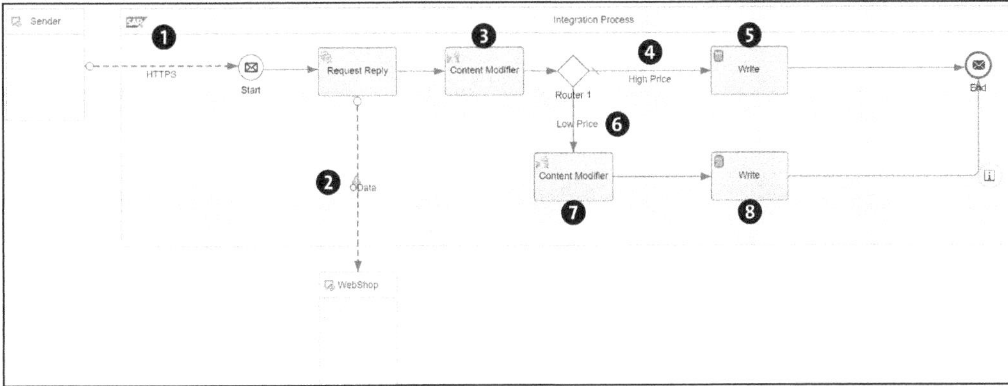

Figure 6.114 Simple Test iFlow

To implement this simple iFlow, create an iFlow model like the one shown in Figure 6.114, and configure the steps in the following way:

1. For the **Address** parameter of the HTTPS sender adapter ❶, you can enter any string as long as the address is unique across the tenant.
2. Use the same configuration of the OData receiver adapter ❷ as we used in Section 6.2.1 (and as shown earlier in Figure 6.13). In other words, for **Query Options**, specify the following:

   `$select=ProductId,CategoryName,CurrencyCode,Name,Price&$filter=ProductId eq '${header.productId}'`
3. In the first **Content Modifier** step ❸, add a message header for each element of the OData response (Figure 6.115).

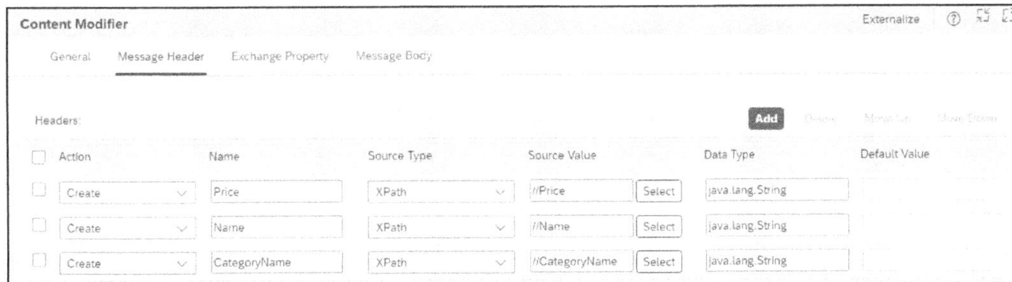

Figure 6.115 Configuration of the First Content Modifier

4. After the **Content Modifier** step, add a **Router** step, and define the upper route as the default route ❹.

5. In the upper route, add a data store **Write** step ❺ with the following parameters:
   - For the **Data Store Name** field, enter "ProductCategories_HighPrice".
   - For the **Entry ID** field, enter "${header.CategoryName}".
6. Configure the lower route ❻ using the following settings:
   - For the **Expression Type** dropdown list, select **Non-XML**.
   - For the **Condition** field, enter "${header.Price} <= '500.000'".
7. In the **Content Modifier** step in the lower route ❼, define the following message (under the **Message Body** tab):

   ```
   The price of product ${header.Name} is lower than or equal 500 Euro.
   ```
8. Configure the data store's **Write** step ❽ in the lower route with the following parameters:
   - For the **Data Store Name** field, enter "ProductCategories_LowPrice".
   - For the **Entry ID** field, enter "${header.CategoryName}".
9. Save the iFlow, but stop before deployment.

Before we go on, let's look at simulating the processing of this iFlow. The simulation menu is available on the top of the canvas, as shown in Figure 6.116.

Figure 6.116 A New Menu is Shown in Simulation Mode

Now, let's prepare the iFlow for simulation. You'll define a starting point and an endpoint. Furthermore, you'll specify the involved data to be used for simulation. If the iFlow expects an inbound message, you can define the message payload and headers. If the iFlow expects a response from an external component (as is the case in this example where data from the WebShop will be retrieved), you'll also need to specify the response payload so that the simulation tool can use the payload. Let's do these preparation steps one-by-one:

1. To define a starting point, click the connection between the **Start** event and the **Request Reply** step.

   A context menu will appear, as shown in Figure 6.117.

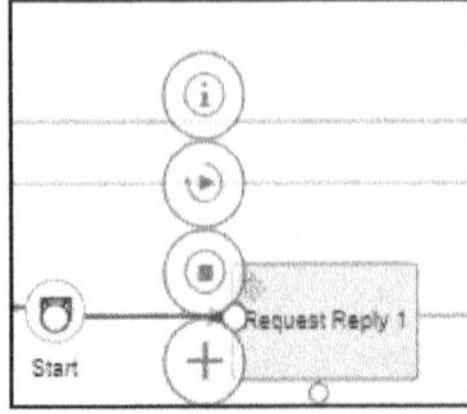

Figure 6.117 Simulation Tool Menu for the Connection between the Start Event and Request Reply Step

We mentioned the information icon [i] earlier. When you click this icon, you'll see the version number for the iFlow element.

2. Click the **Simulation Start Point** icon. This icon is attached to the connection, as shown in Figure 6.118.

Figure 6.118 Simulation Start Point Icon Attached to the Connection Shape

3. Once you click the **Simulation Start Point** icon, a new dialog box will open where you can specify headers, properties, and a message body. Because the iFlow only expects a header for the product identifier, add the header "productid" with the value "HT-1000", as shown in Figure 6.119.

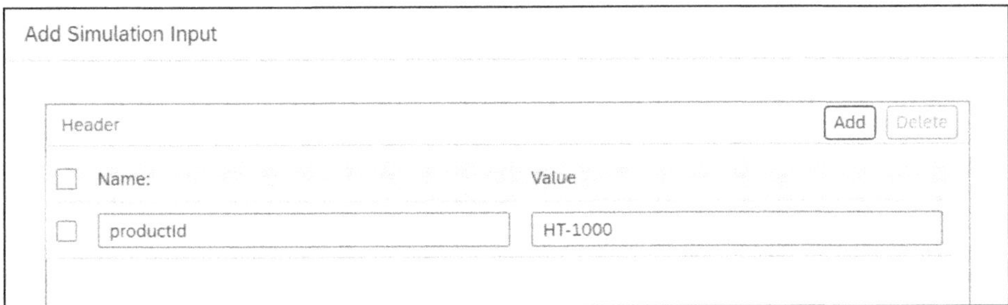

Figure 6.119 Dialog to Add Simulation Input (Only Upper Part of the Dialog Shown)

4. Click **OK** (not shown in Figure 6.119).
5. Click the connection for the OData channel, which will open a menu, as shown in Figure 6.120.

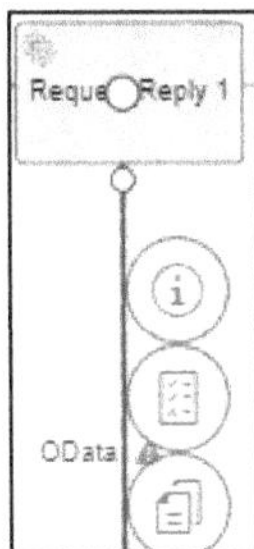

Figure 6.120 Simulation Tool Menu for the Connection between the Request Reply Step and WebShop Receiver (OData Channel)

6. Click the **Add Simulation Response** icon. The **Add Simulation Response** dialog is opened.

7. In the **Body** field, as shown in Figure 6.121, enter the XML content shown in Listing 6.4.

```
<Products>
    <Product>
        <CurrencyCode>EUR</CurrencyCode>
        <Price>956.000</Price>
        <CategoryName>Notebooks</CategoryName>
        <ProductId>HT-1000</ProductId>
        <Name>Notebook Basic 15</Name>
    </Product>
</Products>
```

Listing 6.4 Body of Expected Response Message

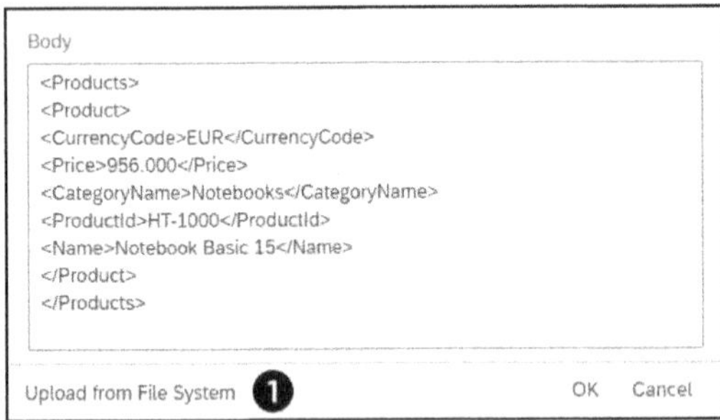

Figure 6.121 Add Simulation Response Dialog (Only Lower Part Shown)

8. Leave the fields for the header and the properties empty (not shown in Figure 6.121), and click **OK**.

   As shown in Figure 6.121 (**Upload from File System ❶**), you can also upload message content to be used for simulation from your file system. In this case, you'll need to upload a file archive (*.zip* file) that contains the message header in a file with the extension *.header*; the properties, in a file with the extension *.properties*; and the body, in a file with the extension *.body*.

9. To set a **Simulation End Point**, click one of the connectors that end at the **End** event shape. Again, a menu like the one shown in Figure 6.117 will appear.

10. Click the **Simulation End Point** icon ⊙. This icon is attached to the connection, as shown in Figure 6.122.

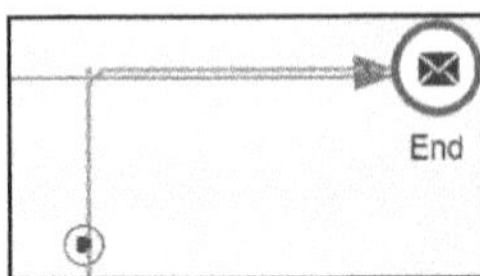

Figure 6.122 Simulation End Point Icon Attached to the Connection Shape

11. To start the simulation, from the menu on top of the iFlow model, click the **Run Simulation** icon, as shown in Figure 6.123 ❶. (The **Clear Simulation** icon ❷ is also shown in the simulation tool menu for use later.)

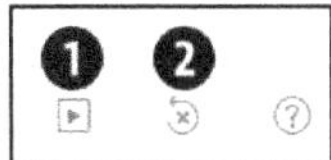

Figure 6.123 Simulation Tool Menu

12. A dialog box appears indicating that the simulation is in progress, as shown in Figure 6.124.

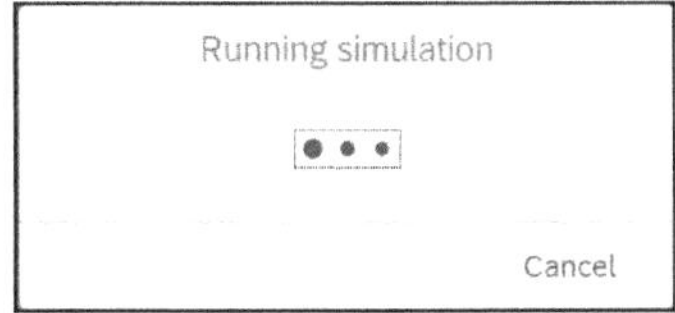

Figure 6.124 Running Simulation Dialog

Once the simulation has finished, the dialog box disappears, and in the iFlow model, the path the simulated message has taken is indicated with little message symbols, as shown in Figure 6.125.

Because the simulation ran without any errors, the **Simulation End Point** icon is shown in green.

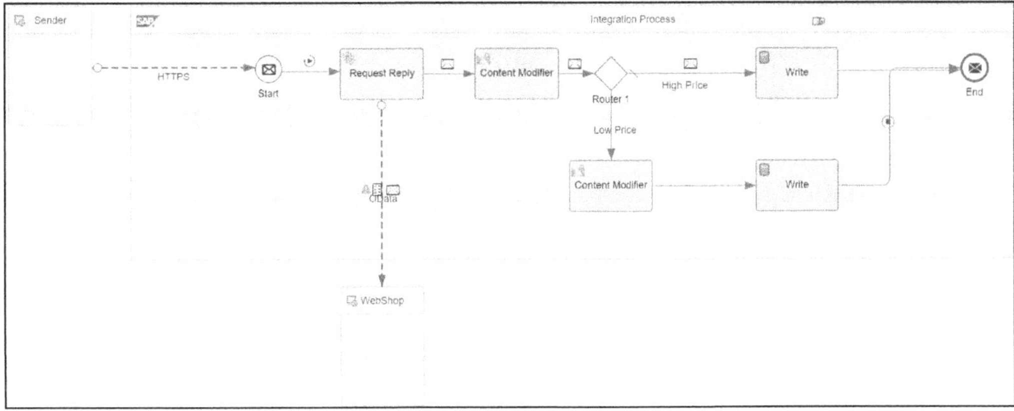

Figure 6.125 Path of the Message Indicated after Simulation

13. Click on one of the message symbols, for instance, between the **Router** step and the **Write** step in the upper route. Below the model, the **Message Content** dialog box will appear where you can inspect the message headers and the message body. Figure 6.126 shows the content of the **Headers** tab. As expected, the headers have been created based on the (simulated) response from the WebShop.

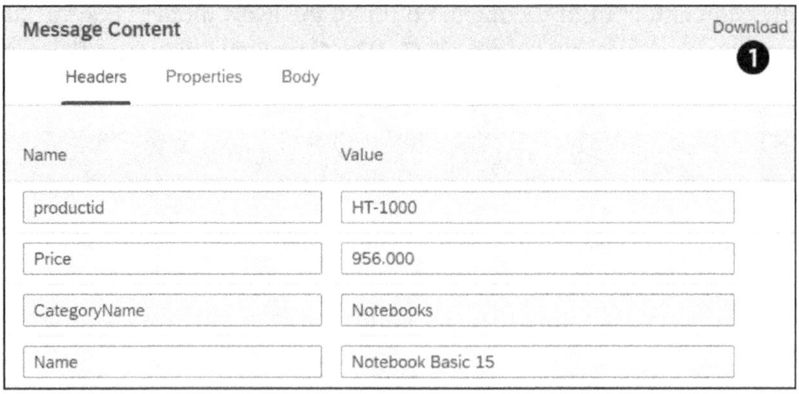

Message Content — Download ❶

Headers | Properties | Body

Name	Value
productid	HT-1000
Price	956.000
CategoryName	Notebooks
Name	Notebook Basic 15

Figure 6.126 Headers Tab of the Message Content Dialog

Under the **Body** tab in the **Message Content** dialog box (not shown), you'll find the simulated response from the WebShop because no further modifications of the message body have been accomplished.

As shown in Figure 6.126, you can click **Download** ❶ to download the message content. A file archive will be stored in your local download directory that contains files for the message body, the header, and the properties.

14. After you've inspected the simulated flow of the message, finally, you can end the simulation by clicking the **Clear Simulation** icon in the simulation tool menu (refer to Figure 6.123 ❷).

Now, you can perform another simulation with other data. For example, to simulate message processing of the lower route, at the simulation start point, add header "productid" with the value "HT-6100". In this case, as the simulation response (on the OData channel shape), you'll need to enter the body text shown in Listing 6.5.

```
<Products>
    <Product>
        <CurrencyCode>EUR</CurrencyCode>
        <Price>469.000</Price>
        <CategoryName>Beamers</CategoryName>
        <ProductId>HT-6100</ProductId>
        <Name>Beam Breaker B-1</Name>
    </Product>
</Products>
```

Listing 6.5 Body of Expected Response Message

To complete our discussion of simulations, let's inspect what happens when an error arises. For the sake of simplicity, perform the same simulation as earlier (with an inbound "productid" header "HT-1000"). However, when adding the simulation response from the WebShop (compare Figure 6.121), leave the message **Body** empty. The simulation will raise an error in this case, and an error message like the one shown in Figure 6.127 will be displayed.

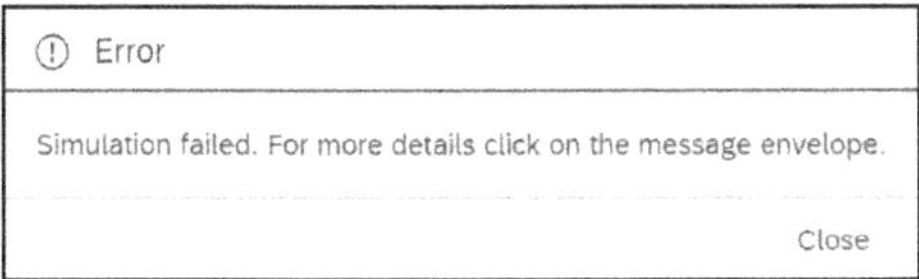

Figure 6.127 Error Message

Click **Close** so that the model is displayed again.

As expected, the error occurred after the simulated call of the WebShop. Consequently, in the iFlow model, a red message symbol is displayed at this location, as shown in Figure 6.128.

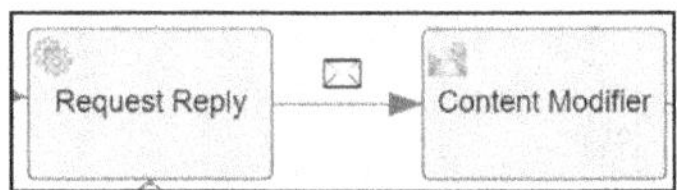

Figure 6.128 Red Message Icon Indicating an Error

Click the message icon for more details about the error. In the **Message Content** screen below the model, under the **Error Details** tab, you'll see the error cause as provided by the Apache Camel framework, as shown in Figure 6.129.

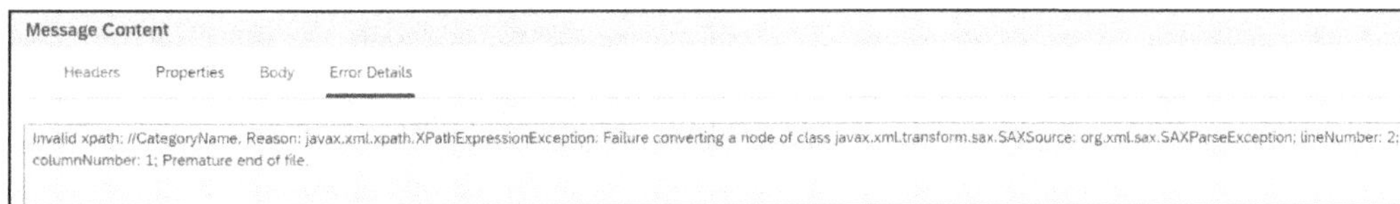

Figure 6.129 Error Details Shown on the Message Content Screen

At this point, you've learned how to use the simulation tool with a simple iFlow. For more information on this tool, check out the following information sources:

- "Integration Flow Simulation in SAP Cloud Integration": *http://s-prs.co/507730*
- "Simulation of an Integration Flow": *http://s-prs.co/507731*

6.9 Transporting Integration Packages to Another Tenant

In this section, we'll provide you an overview of the available options for transporting integration content across tenants. A typical use case is transferring integration scenarios designed in a development landscape into a test landscape after development has finished.

SAP provides the following options for transporting integration content:

- Manual transport
- Using the enhanced Change and Transport System (CTS+)
- Using the Transport Management Service

We'll provide a brief overview of these options in the following sections.

6.9.1 Manually Transporting Integration Packages

To manually transport integration packages, no prerequisites are required to set up this scenario. In the Web UI, on the **Settings** page under the **Transport** tab (shown later in Figure 6.133), you can keep the default **Transport Mode** setting as **None**.

In your source tenant, you then must open the Web UI, go to the **Design** page, and open the integration package that you want to transport. You can use the **Export** option in the upper-right corner of the screen, as shown in Figure 6.130, to store the integration package as a *.zip* file on your computer.

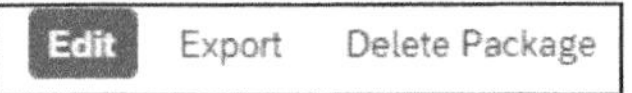

Figure 6.130 Export Function for an Integration Package (on Source Tenant)

Subsequently, you'll open the Web UI for your target tenant, go to the **Design** page, and click **Import**, as shown in Figure 6.131.

Figure 6.131 Import Function in the Web UI's Design Page (of Target Tenant)

You can now browse for and double-click the *.zip* file on your computer. Now, the integration package has been added to the target tenant.

This method is quite straightforward and is probably the best way to go when transporting content is only an occasional task. However, when productively working with many integration packages and needing to perform transports in a more coordinated way, you might consider adopting a comprehensive framework for change and transport management. In the following sections, we'll provide you more information about the available options.

6.9.2 Transporting Integration Packages Using Enhanced Change and Transport System

This option might be attractive if you already use SAP's enhanced Change and Transport System (CTS+). CTS+ is SAP's on-premise transport management system that comes with SAP NetWeaver. Note that using CTS+ as a transport management system requires a system landscape where your source tenant is connected to a CTS+ system through the SAP Connectivity services.

In this book, we won't elaborate further on this option. Instead, we recommend reading a blog series in SAP Community that provides a detailed step-by-step description of how to set up and use this transport scenario at *http://s-prs.co/507732* and *http://s-prs.co/507733*.

6.9.3 Transporting Integration Packages Using the Cloud-Based Transport Management Service

You can transport integration content across tenants with a few clicks through the cloud-based Transport Management Service. Figure 6.132 shows the landscape of a typical transport scenario where integration content is being transported from a development tenant to a test tenant.

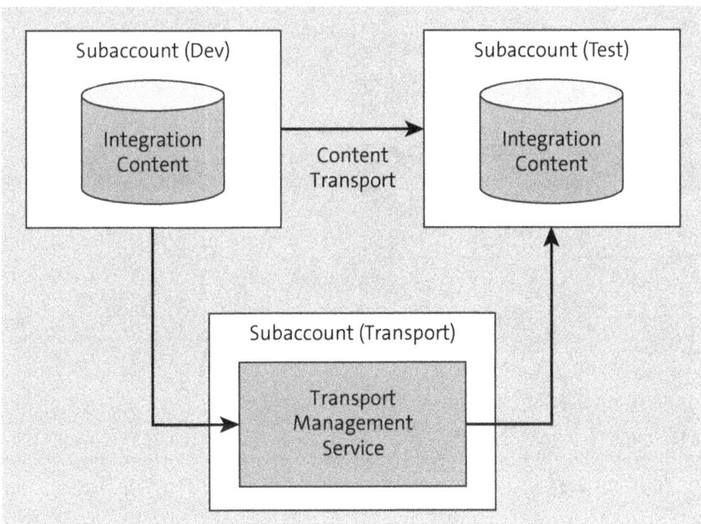

Figure 6.132 Transport Scenario

The steps for setting up such a transport landscape is described in detail at *http://s-prs.co/507734*. Therefore, we won't elaborate on the step-by-step procedure and instead only briefly summarize the process.

To enable the Transport Management Service and configure a transport landscape, the following steps are required:

1. Get access to a Transport Management Service account.
2. In the SAP BTP, Cloud Foundry environment, create a subaccount of your global account, and subscribe to Transport Management Service.

3. Enable API access to Transport Management Service.
4. To set up the transport scenario shown in Figure 6.132, in the involved subaccounts, create the required destinations that contain connection details.
5. In the Transport Management Service, create source and target nodes and a transport route to connect both.

All these tasks are described in detail in the blog mentioned earlier, with the same transport landscape used as shown in Figure 6.132, so that you can easily tie in the following description to the steps described in the blog.

Because we assume that all these steps have been performed successfully, let's now start transporting content. We'll briefly summarize the steps and refer to the blog for more details. Let's assume you want to transport an integration package from a source tenant (dev) to a target tenant (test).

1. Open the Web UI for the dev tenant, click on the **Settings** menu item, and click the **Transport** tile.
2. Click on **Edit**.
3. As shown in Figure 6.133, in the **Transport Mode** dropdown list, select **Transport Management Service** from among various options.

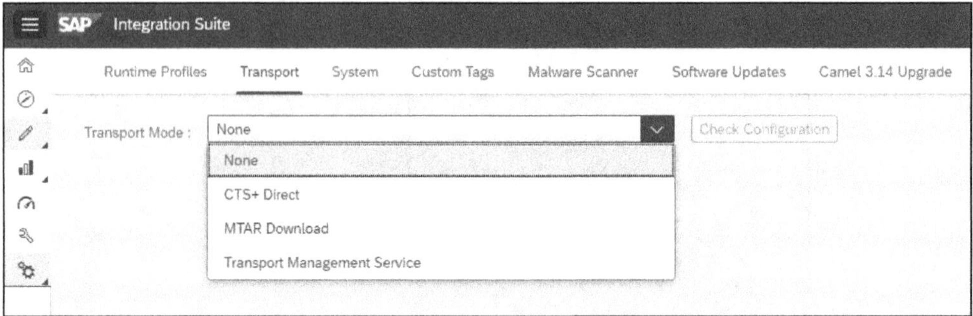

Figure 6.133 Transport Modes Selectable in the Web UI Settings Section

4. Click **Save**.

For the sake of completeness, Table 6.1 summarizes the supported transport modes.

Transport Mode	Description
None	Manually export an integration package from the source tenant to your computer, and import it to the target tenant from there.

Table 6.1 Transport Modes Available for Integration Content Development

Transport Mode	Description
CTS+ Direct	Transport an integration package directly (with one click) from a source tenant (e.g., a dev tenant) to a target tenant (e.g., a test tenant) through CTS+. *Direct* means that the integration package will be attached to your open transport request in CTS+. With this option, the integration content to transport is transferred directly as a multitarget application (MTA) archives file (MTAR file with the extension *.mtar*) to an open transport request in the configured CTS+ system. The MTA defines a file format to package a heterogeneous set of software pieces that can be created with different technologies but that all share a common lifecycle.
MTAR Download	Download an MTAR file from the tenant you want to export integration content from, and manually upload the MTAR file to a CTS+ system (or to the Transport Management Service, depending on your setup).
Transport Management Service	Transport integration content across tenants with a few clicks through the cloud-based Transport Management Service of SAP BTP.

Table 6.1 Transport Modes Available for Integration Content Development (Cont.)

You can now start transporting integration content from the dev to the test tenant by following these steps.

1. Open the **Design** page of the Web UI for the dev tenant (from which we want to transport the integration content).
2. Select the integration package you want to transport, and choose **Transport**.

   This option is only shown when you've enabled Transport Management Service, as described earlier.
3. Enter a transport comment, and choose **Transport**.

   An **Information** screen will open stating that the transport request has been created.

   Notice the name of the target transport node (TEST_NODE) configured in Transport Management Service for the target tenant (i.e., the test tenant) is part of the transport landscape defined in the Transport Management Service. In the blog mentioned earlier, you'll learn how to create this node and how it's related to the other required configuration settings in all involved accounts.
4. Check the transport import queue by opening the Transport Management Service and choosing **Transport Nodes.** (Refer to the blog mentioned earlier for more details on how to access the Transport Management Service.)
5. Select the transport node for your target account (**TEST_NODE** in our example). You should find the transport in the **IMPORT QUEUE** tab.

6. Select the queue, and choose **Import**.
7. On the confirmation screen, click **OK**.
8. Go to the test tenant (the target tenant of your transport), and check whether the package has arrived there.

For more on setting up a transport scenario for Cloud Integration source and target tenants residing in the SAP BTP, Neo environment, check out *http://s-prs.co/507735*.

6.10 Using the Adapter Development Kit

Cloud Integration can connect to a multitude of systems (in the cloud and on-premise). The solution already comes with an impressive number of adapters that allow communication with other systems on different levels, considering different technologies, security standards, and application-specific requirements. Typical examples are adapters connecting to Twitter, SAP Ariba, and SAP SuccessFactors applications or adapters connecting via protocols, such as HTTP, SOAP, IDoc, OData, or SFTP. However, SAP can't cover every single combination of applications, protocols, security standards, and versions on its own. Thus, customers and partners have the unique opportunity to fill these gaps by providing their own adapters. Note that SAP Partners have already developed various adapters and published them on the SAP Business Accelerator Hub. You can find these adapters by opening the **Discover** page of the Web UI and filtering for "adapter." Note that you'll typically find information like a description and a link to the partner's homepage for each partner adapter. When you want to use a partner adapter, you'll need to check the details provided by the partner. You can't directly copy a partner adapter from the **Discover** page of the Web UI.

In this section, we'll provide a brief introduction into the Adapter Development Kit (ADK), which enables you to develop your own adapters for Cloud Integration.

6.10.1 Overview

In previous chapters, we frequently referred to the Apache Camel engine as the central integration framework working under the hood of Cloud Integration. As such, when developing your own adapters for Cloud Integration, you're essentially developing adapters for Apache Camel. The official term in Apache Camel's nomenclature for adapters is *components*. Because Apache Camel is an open-source framework, many articles have been published describing how you can implement components to increase Camel's connectivity options. For component development, see Apache Camel's official documentation at *http://s-prs.co/v576025*, where you can also find more information about a component's implementation. We also recommend that you take a close look at the book *Camel in Action, Second Edition* (Manning Publications, 2018). Finally, to get to know Apache Camel components that are already available, we recommend checking out *http://s-prs.co/v576026*. You'll be surprised at how many Camel components are already available to simplify your life!

However, to make those components enterprise-ready, provide a configuration UI for the adapters in the Cloud Integration Web UI, and provide the integration of components within the Cloud Integration monitoring infrastructure, a lot more is involved than just writing a simple Apache Camel component. For these tasks, SAP released the ADK for Cloud Integration. The trick is, after you've developed a component following Apache Camel guidelines, as described in the various resources mentioned earlier, the ADK allows you to wrap that component up with additional code to make it compliant with the Cloud Integration infrastructure.

In this section, we'll show you how to develop a new adapter by working with the ADK and how to add a new sample adapter to your portfolio of adapters. For more detailed guidelines on adapter development, we'll also refer you to several blogs.

6.10.2 Installing the Adapter Development Kit

The development process for an adapter differs significantly from modeling and running iFlows, as we've discussed so far in this book. You can't develop an adapter using a web-based graphical modeling tool. You must use a full-blown development environment such as Eclipse, which is why the ADK comes as an Eclipse installation.

To successfully execute the steps described in this section, you'll need to fulfill the following prerequisites:

- Install Apache Maven, which you can download from *http://s-prs.co/v5760027*.
- Make sure that your Eclipse installation uses and points to a Java Development Kit (JDK) instead of a Java Runtime Environment (JRE) installed on your computer. You can specify the location of your JDK in Eclipse under **Windows • Preferences • Java • Installed JREs**.

For more details on these steps, refer to the documentation for Cloud Integration at *http://s-prs.co/v576028*. Search for "Adapter Development Process."

The current ADK was tested with Eclipse. Download the relevant release for your operating system from the Eclipse web page at *https://www.eclipse.org/downloads*. Once downloaded, you can initiate the installation procedure by double-clicking the *.exe* file. You'll be asked for an appropriate folder where Eclipse will store your project files during development. This special area is called an *Eclipse workspace*. To separate several Eclipse workspaces, we recommend you have a dedicated folder for your new installation. We've chosen the *C:\EclipseWorkspaces* folder for our example.

Click **Launch** to continue. After the Eclipse environment is up and running, install the ADK by selecting **Install New Software** from Eclipse's **Help** main menu, as shown in Figure 6.134.

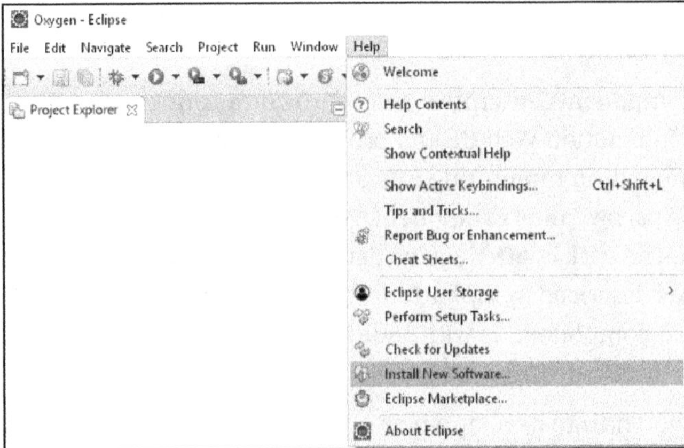

Figure 6.134 Starting the Wizard for Installing Additional Software

The installation wizard will open, asking for a location on the internet from which the new software can be downloaded. Click on the **Add** button next to the **Work with** drop-down list, as shown in Figure 6.135.

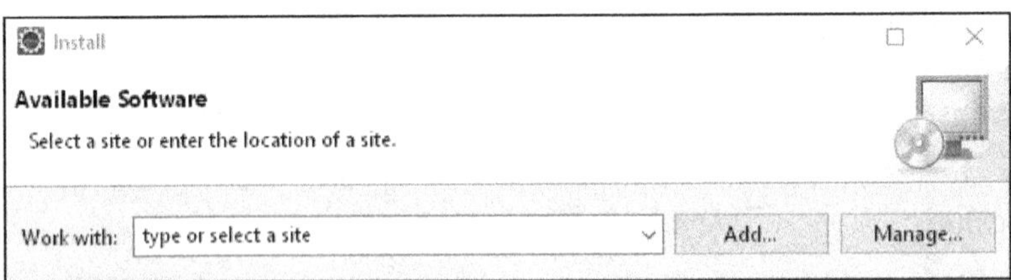

Figure 6.135 Assigning the Download Location for New Software

The **Add Repository** dialog box opens, as shown in Figure 6.136. Give your download location an appropriate name (e.g., "SAP Development Tools for Eclipse Oxygen"), and assign this name to the location URL "https://tools.hana.ondemand.com/oxygen". Click on **OK** to proceed, as shown in Figure 6.136.

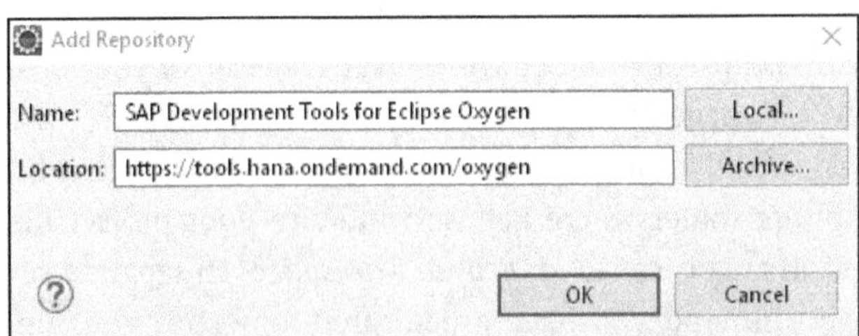

Figure 6.136 Adding the URL for Downloading the Cloud Integration Tools

On the next screen, a list of available software components will appear. Select the **Cloud Integration Tools** package. We recommend you select the complete package, as shown in Figure 6.137.

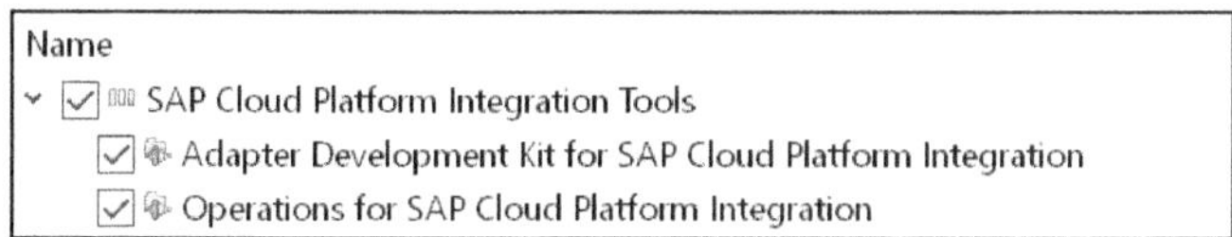

Figure 6.137 Selecting the Cloud Integration Tools for Installation

Click **Next**, confirm this selection, and all forthcoming steps without modifications. At the end of the wizard, accept the license agreement, and then click on **Finish**. The tools will be installed, and you'll need to restart Eclipse to complete the installation. After restarting, you must connect the Eclipse environment with your Cloud Integration tenant, where you'll deploy our newly developed adapter. Open the **Preferences** dialog box, shown in Figure 6.138, by selecting **Window • Preferences** from the Eclipse main menu.

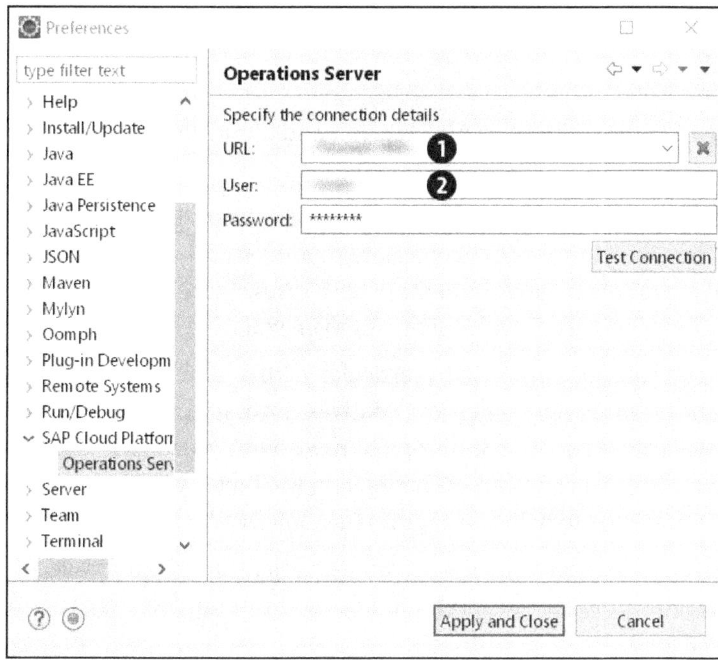

Figure 6.138 Preferences Dialog for Specifying the Connection to the Cloud Integration Tenant

The next step is only required when you use Cloud Integration in the SAP BTP, Neo environment. Expand the **Cloud Integration** node on the left of the **Preferences** dialog box, select the **Operations Server** node beneath, and enter the **URL** to your tenant ❶ and the credentials (user name and password) in the relevant fields ❷. Test the connection by clicking the **Test Connection** button to verify the validity of your entries. Once done, close the dialog box by clicking the **Apply and Close** button. We're now ready to develop the adapter.

Note that this step is required so that later, once you've finished developing the adapter project, you can deploy the adapter on the tenant. In the SAP BTP, Cloud Foundry environment, this step is performed with the Web UI (as we'll explain in Section 6.10.5).

In the next section, we'll show you how you can start developing a sample adapter with just a few clicks.

How you add the newly developed adapter to your Cloud Integration tenant depends on the environment where you use Cloud Integration:

- If you work in the SAP BTP, Cloud Foundry environment, you'll upload the files from the adapter development phase as an artifact using the Web UI. The Web UI provides various features that allow you to manage the newly developed adapter on your tenant.
- If you work in the SAP BTP, Neo environment, you'll continue using Eclipse to deploy the adapter on the tenant.

6.10.3 Developing a Sample Adapter (SAP BTP, Neo and Cloud Foundry Environments)

Let's explore how you can develop and deploy a simple sample adapter project that has been predefined by the Cloud Integration team. Note that the steps for developing an adapter are identical regardless of environment. In both cases, SAP BTP, Neo environment, and SAP BTP, Cloud Foundry environment, however, you'll need Eclipse.

People familiar with software development, in particular, with Apache Camel and OSGi (formerly known as the Open Services Gateway initiative), can easily enhance this project to define their own custom adapters. In this section, we won't go into the details of adapter development. Instead, at the end of the section, we'll refer you to the online documentation and some blogs to help you get into the topic of adapter development.

In this section, however, we'll show you how to start developing an adapter project by simply using the predefined sample adapter and how you can immediately use the sample adapter in an iFlow.

The example adapter we'll build into Cloud Integration does nothing more than either read a greeting message from a sender or send such a message to a receiver. We'll focus on the sender part and leave it to you to enhance the project as required.

To start creating an adapter project, you must first choose the appropriate perspective in Eclipse. Check whether the Java EE (default) perspective is already open. If not, perform the following steps:

1. In Eclipse, choose **Window • Perspective • Open Perspective • Other**, as shown in Figure 6.139.

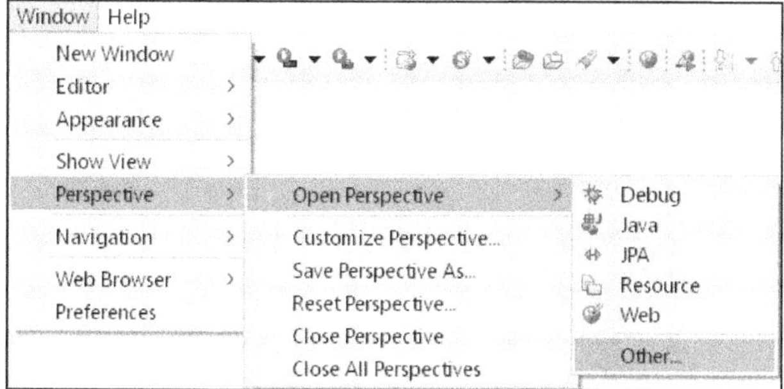

Figure 6.139 Opening a New Eclipse Perspective

2. Select **Java (default)**, as shown in Figure 6.140.

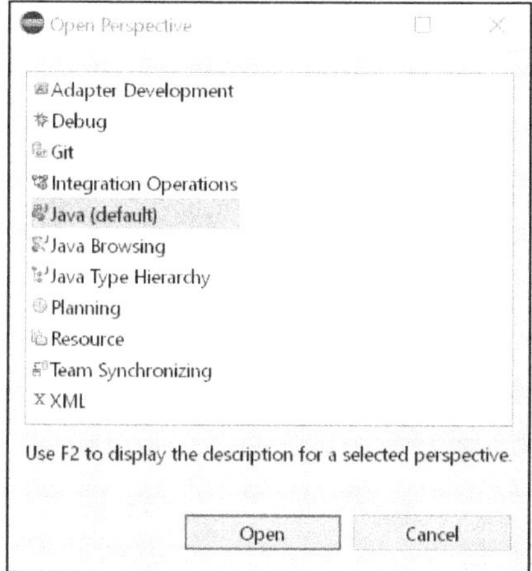

Figure 6.140 Selecting the Java Perspective

3. Click **Open**.

We'll now create an adapter project. In this example, we'll define the basic data for the new adapter type (e.g., its name). Based on our entries, the system generates a Java project structure that contains all the components required to implement the adapter's runtime and its configuration UI. Follow these steps:

1. Choose **File • New • Other**, as shown in Figure 6.141.
2. On the next screen, expand the **Cloud Integration** node, and select **Adapter Project**, as shown in Figure 6.142.
3. Click **Next**.
4. Enter meaningful basic data for the project, as shown in Figure 6.143. The next screenshot shows some proposals. Note that the sample adapter does nothing but send a greeting message, unless we further change it. Therefore, we'll simply enter "Hello" as the **Name**.

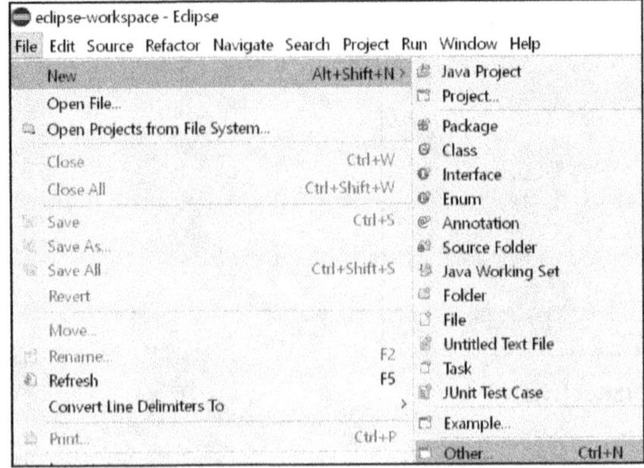

Figure 6.141 Creating a New Project in Eclipse

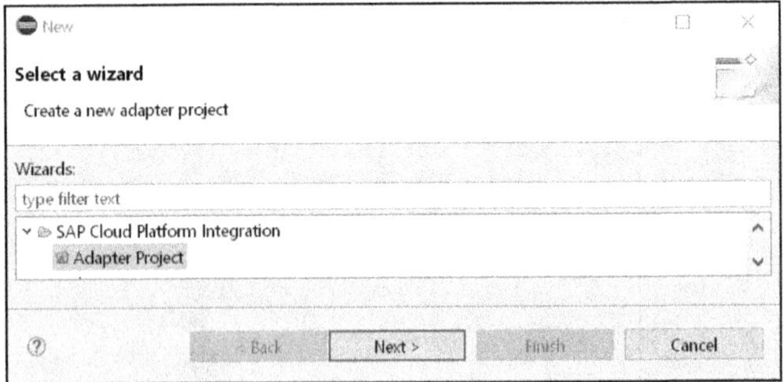

Figure 6.142 Selecting a Wizard for an Adapter Project

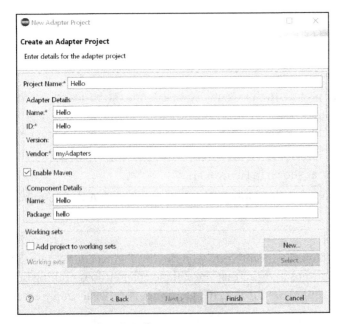

Figure 6.143 Project Details

5. Keep the **Enable Maven** checkbox selected, which is the default setting.

Maven Support for Adapter Development

Adapter development for Cloud Integration also integrates Maven support. Maven is a build management tool from the Apache Software Foundation. Selecting the **Enable Maven** checkbox ensures that the development of an Apache Camel component is integrated into your adapter project and that dependencies are automatically resolved. This option is selected by default. By keeping this default setting, you can create a sample adapter with a few clicks and modify it later. Another advantage of using Maven is that all components required for the adapter can be maintained at one place: both the runtime components that control how the adapter processes messages at runtime and the UI-related components that create the adapter's UI in the iFlow.

If you want to reuse an existing Apache Camel component (e.g., the components listed at *http://s-prs.co/v576026*), we recommend deselecting the **Enable Maven** checkbox. In this case, however, you'll need to maintain all dependencies of your software packages manually, which can sometimes be a tedious effort.

6. Click **Finish**. The project is added to the **Project Explorer** view, as shown in Figure 6.144.

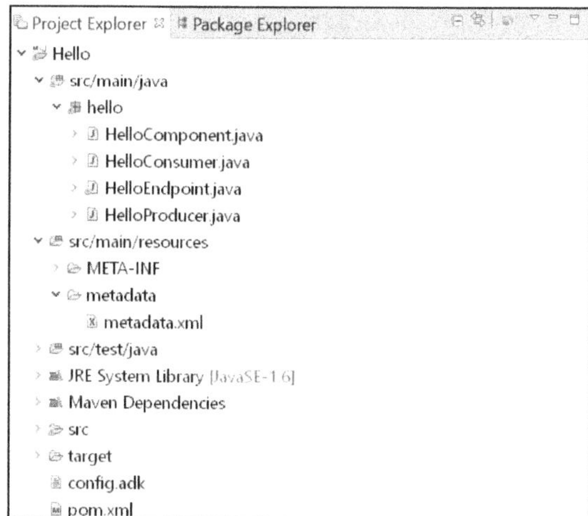

Figure 6.144 New Adapter Project Added to the Project Explorer View

As shown in Figure 6.144, we've expanded some nodes so we can briefly explain the purpose of the following nodes:

- *HelloConsumer.java*: Implements the sender adapter, which polls messages according to a certain schedule. This node generates a greeting message with the current timestamp.
- *HelloProducer.java*: Implements the receiver adapter.

- *HelloEndpoint.java*: Implements the endpoint and contains the string variable `greetingsMessage` for the message to be polled or sent (when the sample adapter has not changed). Furthermore, this component provides a logger to log data during the processing of the adapter.
- *metadata.xml*: Contains the attributes of the adapter.

7. Open the file *metadata.xml* by double-clicking on it.

Figure 6.145 shows an excerpt of the file. Note the selection of the **Source** tab at the bottom of the screen. The configurable attributes of the adapter are assembled in attribute groups. You'll find identically named XML tags throughout the metadata file.

metadata.xml d0262 metadata.xml

```
<Tab id="connection">
    <GuiLabels guid="b4c970da-a1f8-443c-b063-046773f93135">
        <Label language="EN">Connection</Label>
        <Label language="DE">Connection</Label>
    </GuiLabels>
    <AttributeGroup id="defaultUriParameter">
        <Name xsi:type="xs:string" xmlns:xs="http://www.w3.org/2001/XMLSchema"
        <GuiLabels guid="041a3129-aedb-4e5b-a351-dc8d82ae7fbc">
            <Label language="EN">URI Setting</Label>
            <Label language="DE">URI Setting</Label>
        </GuiLabels>
        <AttributeReference>
            <ReferenceName>firstUriPart</ReferenceName>
            <description>Configure First URI Part</description>
        </AttributeReference>
    </AttributeGroup>
    <AttributeGroup id="Message">
        <Name xsi:type="xs:string" xmlns:xs="http://www.w3.org/2001/XMLSchema"
        <GuiLabels guid="eaa0dc7f-e350-44ae-85bf-6a7a46853302">
            <Label language="EN">Message Details</Label>
            <Label language="DE">Message Details</Label>
        </GuiLabels>
        <AttributeReference>
            <ReferenceName>greetingsMessage</ReferenceName>
            <description>Configure Greetings Message</description>
        </AttributeReference>
    </AttributeGroup>
    <AttributeGroup id="ScheduledPollConsumer">
        <Name xsi:type="xs:string" xmlns:xs="http://www.w3.org/2001/XMLSchema"
        <GuiLabels guid="813cbd00-ea82-47a9-8302-bf16aa6727b9">
            <Label language="EN">Scheduled Poll Consumer</Label>
            <Label language="DE">Scheduled Poll Consumer</Label>
        </GuiLabels>
```

Figure 6.145 Excerpt from the Metadata.xml File

Leave everything as it is.

Next, let's build the adapter project by following these steps:

1. Right-click the adapter project **Hello**, and choose **Run As • 3 Maven build** in the context menu, as shown in Figure 6.146.
2. In the next screen, in the **Goals** field, enter "clean install" (Figure 6.147 ❶).
3. Click **Run**.

Figure 6.146 Build Adapter Project

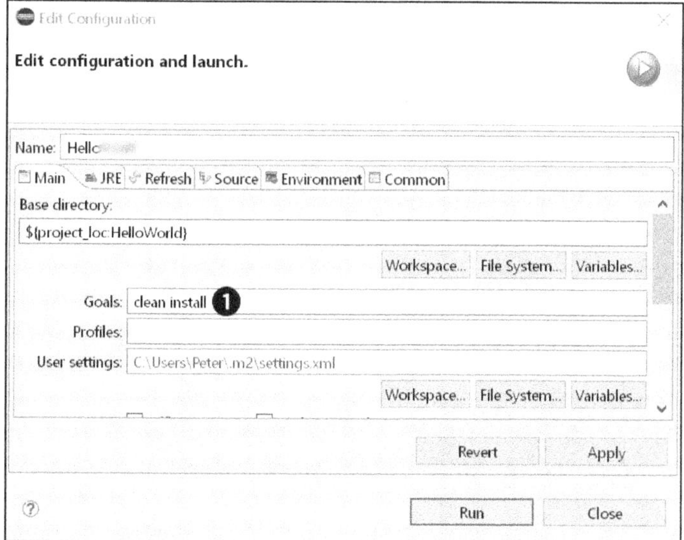

Figure 6.147 Configuration Parameters for Maven Build

After a successful build of the project, you should find additional artifacts in the project tree, under **target**.

You've now accomplished all the steps required to develop your own adapter project. To use this adapter in an iFlow, however, you still need to deploy the adapter on you tenant. How you deploy the adapter on your tenant depends on the environment where Cloud Integration is running. Keep in mind the following considerations:

- When working in the SAP BTP, Neo environment, you'll continue to use Eclipse to deploy the adapter.

- When working in the SAP BTP, Cloud Foundry environment, you'll use the Web UI to deploy the adapter.

We'll explain both procedures separately one-by-one.

6.10.4 Deploying the Adapter (SAP BTP, Neo Environment)

In the SAP BTP, Neo environment, you'll still use Eclipse to deploy the adapter on the tenant by performing the following steps:

1. After you've successfully built your adapter, in Eclipse, right-click again the root node of the project and choose **Deploy Adapter Project** in the context menu, as shown in Figure 6.148.

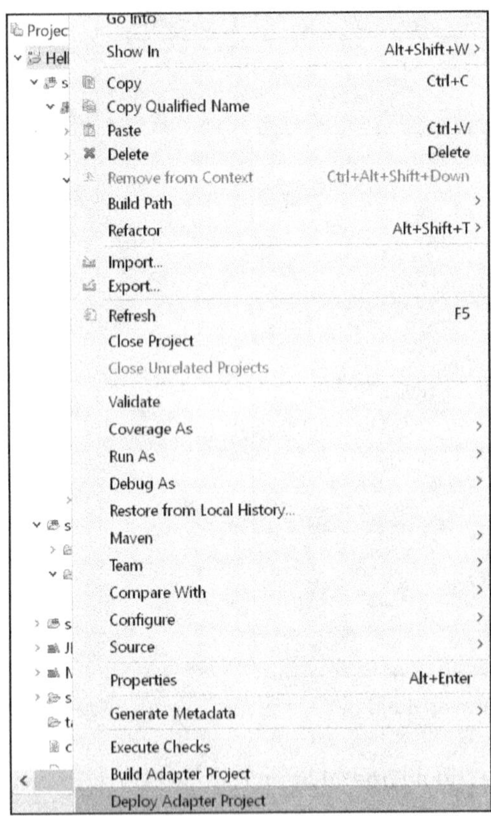

Figure 6.148 Deploy Adapter Project

2. The **Deploy Adapter Project** dialog box appears, as shown in Figure 6.149, where the tenant is displayed ❶. This tenant should be the tenant to which you're connected with Eclipse; if you have any doubts, you can check the settings under **Window • Preferences • Cloud Integration • Operations Server**.

Figure 6.149 Confirming the Tenant Where the Adapter Project Will Be Deployed

3. Choose **OK**.

Now, you can check for the deployment state of your project by following these steps:

1. Open the **Integration Operations** perspective in Eclipse. Choose **Window • Perspective • Open Perspective • Other**, and select the **Integration Operations** perspective, as shown in Figure 6.150.

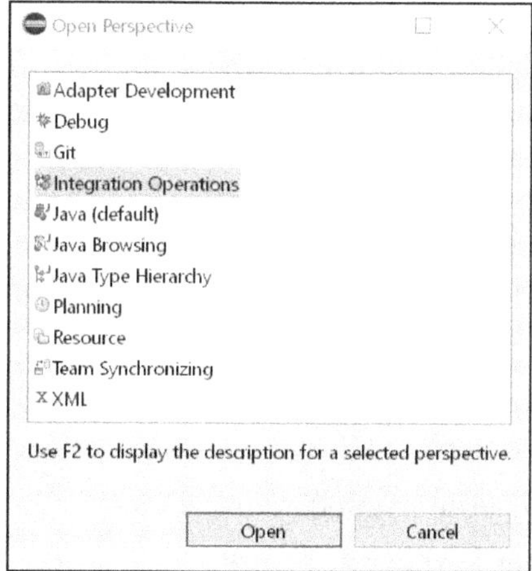

Figure 6.150 Selecting the Integration Operations Perspective in Eclipse

2. Double-click the tenant (Figure 6.151 ❶) in the **Node Explorer** view, and select the **Deployed Artifacts** editor.

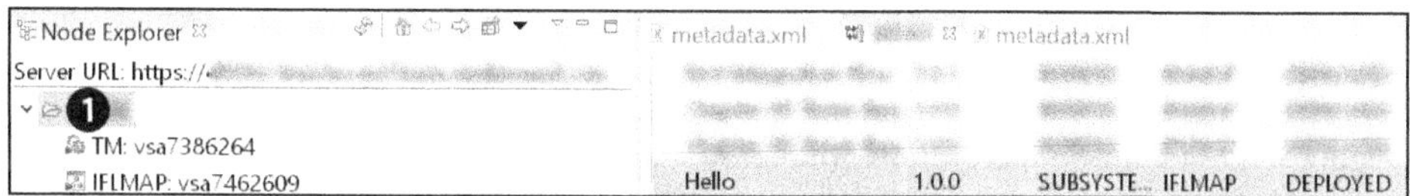

Figure 6.151 Deployed Artifacts Editor for the Tenant Selected in the Node Explorer

Notice that the adapter project is shown as a deployed artifact (with the project name, in our example, **Hello**). If everything works correctly, the **Deploy State** will be **DEPLOYED**.

6.10.5 Deploying the Adapter (SAP BTP, Cloud Foundry Environment)

When you use Cloud Integration in the SAP BTP, Cloud Foundry environment, after the successful development of an adapter project, you can use the Web UI to deploy the adapter on the tenant. In the SAP BTP, Cloud Foundry environment, the adapter is handled as a separate integration artifact (of type **Integration Adapter**) similar to iFlows and value mappings. The Web UI provides various features for managing and monitoring **Integration Adapter** artifacts.

In principle, as soon as you import an adapter project file to a tenant (as an **Integration Adapter** artifact), you can use the associated adapter type when modeling iFlows. The adapter type will appear in the adapter selection dropdown list when you create a channel. To enable the use of the adapter at runtime, similar to how you would treat an iFlow, you must deploy the **Integration Adapter** artifact on the tenant.

After you've run the Maven build for your adapter project (done in the same way regardless of environment, refer to Figure 6.147), you'll see a success message in Eclipse (among other information) with the following text:

```
.esa file will be generated at ….
```

The given file path usually points to a directory in your Eclipse workspace. At a later step, you'll need the *.esa* file to upload it to your tenant. Therefore, it's a good idea to also remember the path to the directory where this file has been stored on your computer.

To import a newly developed adapter and deploy your new adapter on your SAP BTP, Cloud Foundry environment tenant, follow these steps:

1. Open the Web UI, go to the **Design** page, and choose an integration package.
2. In **Edit** mode, choose **Add • Integration Adapter**, as shown in Figure 6.152.

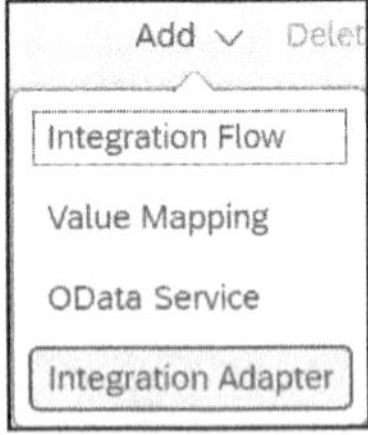

Figure 6.152 Adding an Integration Adapter Artifact

3. On the next screen, browse for the *.esa* file that was generated when you built the adapter project. Optionally, you can add a description for the adapter, as shown in Figure 6.153.
4. Choose **OK**. The deployed adapter will be shown next to the other artifacts (iFlows and value mappings) of the package (see Figure 6.154).

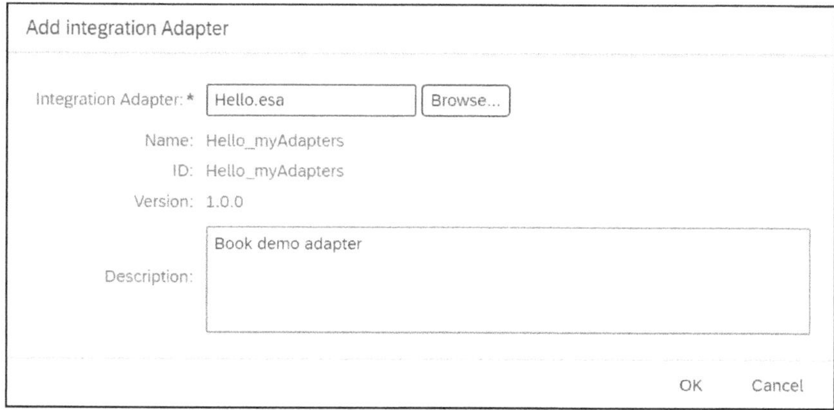

Figure 6.153 Dialog to Browse for the Adapter Project

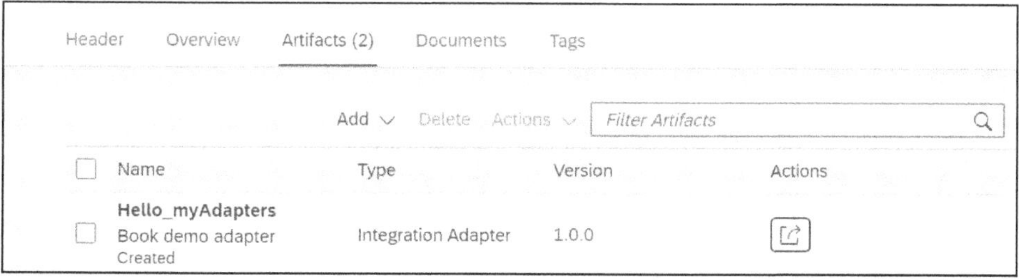

Figure 6.154 New Integration Adapter Artifact Listed for the Integration Package

5. You can now use the adapter when modeling an iFlow. The adapter will appear as an adapter type when you create a channel (as shown in Figure 6.155 when we selected a receiver adapter). You'll also this adapter when we test it later in Section 6.10.6.

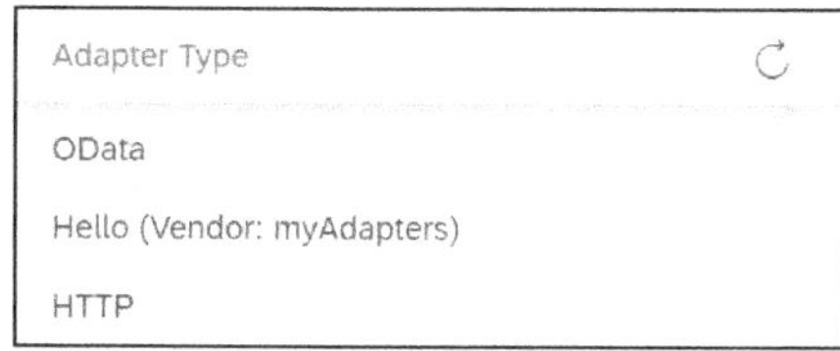

Figure 6.155 Newly Developed Adapter Type Offered When Creating a Channel (Cutout of the List of Offered Receiver Adapters)

Note that when you delete an **Integration Adapter** artifact and open an iFlow deployed on this tenant in a new browser session, the new adapter type is no longer offered when creating a channel.

6. To use the adapter at runtime, you'll also need to deploy the adapter on the tenant. Select the adapter, and choose **Deploy** (much like you do when deploying an iFlow), as shown in Figure 6.156.

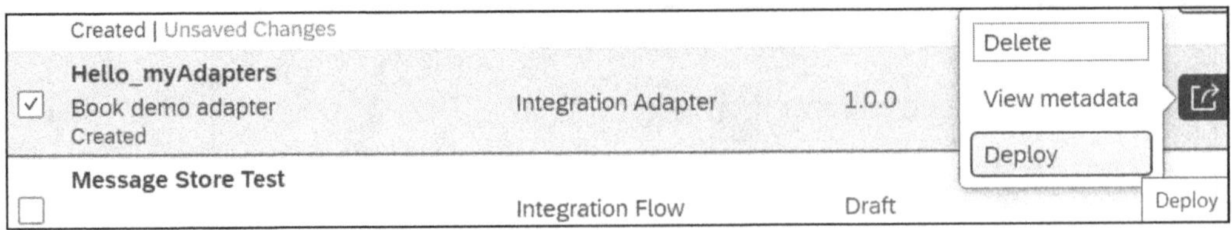

Figure 6.156 Deploy Option for the Newly Created Integration Adapter Artifact

After deployment, you can check the deployment status of the adapter.

7. Go to the **Monitor** page and, under **Manage Integration Content**, check the deployment status of the adapter, as shown in Figure 6.157 ❶.

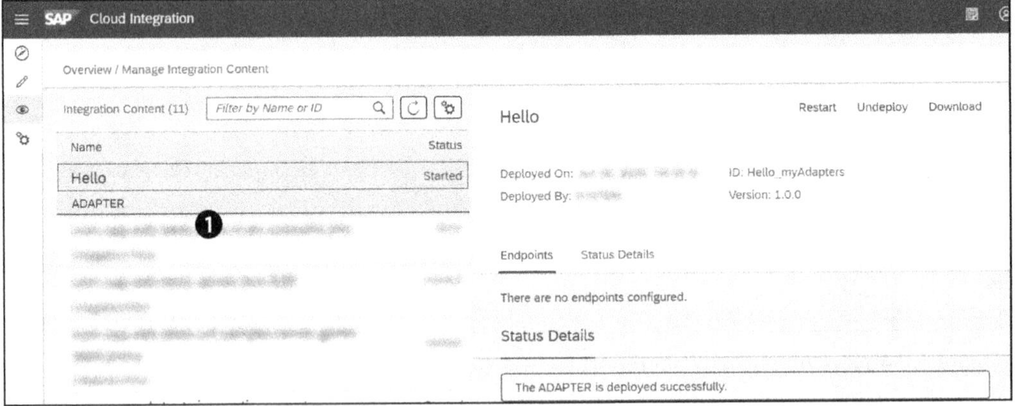

Figure 6.157 Newly Deployed Integration Adapter Artifact in the Integration Content Monitor

Before we demonstrate the new adapter in action, we'll point out some more features of managing integration adapters in the Web UI. By selecting an **Integration Adapter** artifact in the integration package and choosing the **View Metadata** option (refer to Figure 6.156), you can display the adapter name, ID, description, and version, as shown in Figure 6.158.

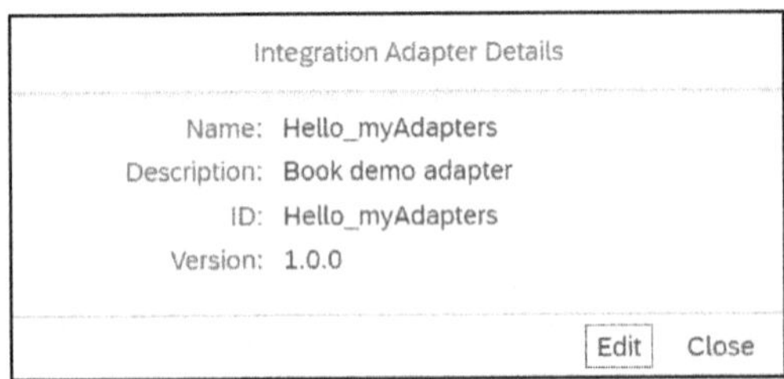

Figure 6.158 Integration Adapter Details Page

When you select **Edit**, the dialog box shown in Figure 6.159 will open.

Integration Adapter Details

Name: Hello_myAdapters
ID: Hello_myAdapters
Version: 1.0.0
Description: Book demo adapter
Integration Adapter: <Single File> Browse...
Save Cancel

Figure 6.159 Integration Adapter Details Page

From this page, you can upload a newer version of the adapter's *.esa* file to create a new version of the **Integration Adapter**.

You can update an **Integration Adapter** by a new version.

6.10.6 Testing the New Adapter

Now, we're ready to test our example adapter. To keep it simple, we propose using an iFlow with a data store **Write** step (as configured several times throughout this book). Now, let's test our new **Hello** sender adapter by following these steps:

1. Open the Web UI for the tenant, and go to the **Design** page.
2. Either create a new iFlow or reuse an existing one. We recommend that you start with the iFlow model shown in Figure 6.160.

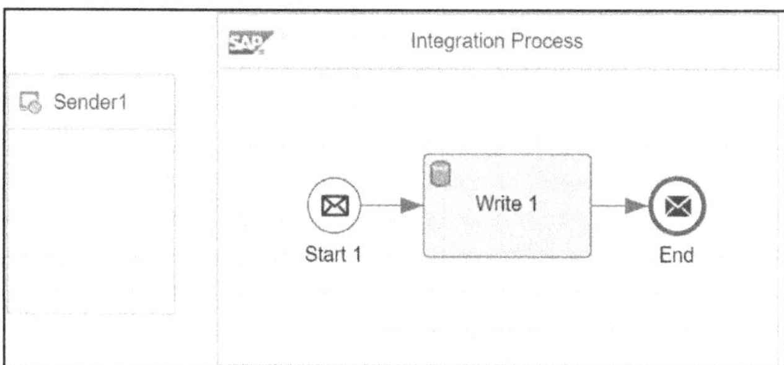

Figure 6.160 Simple iFlow to Start With

3. Add a new **Sender** channel between the **Sender** pool and the message **Start** event. Notice that the new adapter type **Hello** is available in the **Adapter Type** list, as shown in Figure 6.161.

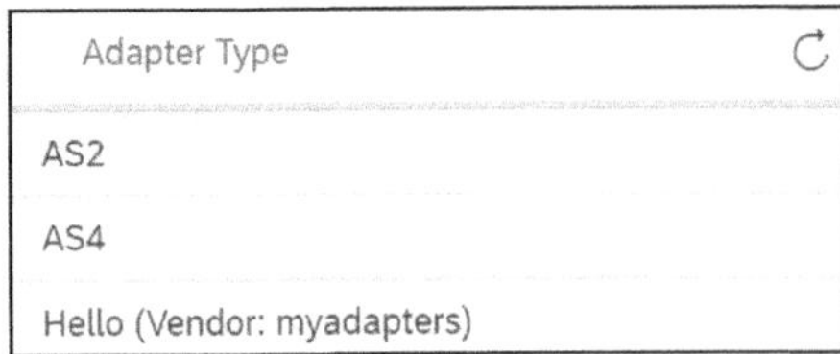

Figure 6.161 New Adapter Offered When Creating a Channel

Also notice that the vendor specified in the project is displayed to highlight that this adapter is a custom adapter and not part of the Cloud Integration portfolio provided by SAP (shown earlier in Figure 6.143).

4. Select the **Hello** adapter type, and go to the **Connection** section of the adapter. Use the settings shown in Figure 6.162.

Figure 6.162 Example Settings for the Sender Hello Adapter

Predefined Settings of the Sample Adapter

The sample adapter implements Apache Camel's polling consumer integration pattern. Similar to the **Mail** sender adapter (described in Chapter 2, Section 2.3.6), Cloud Integration polls (reads) a message from a sender before actually processing it. The settings predefined for the sample adapter are given by the scheduler component of

Apache Camel. For example, with a combination of the **Backoff Multiplier** and **Backoff Error Threshold** settings, you can control how the adapter should behave if polls result in errors. With the **Backoff Error Threshold** attribute, you can specify the number of subsequent erroneous polls before the **Backoff Multiplier** attribute becomes effective. With the **Backoff Multiplier** attribute, you can then specify the number of skipped polling attempts before polling occurs again. For example, if you enter the value "2" for **Backoff Error Threshold** and the value "3" for **Backoff Multiplier**, then after two erroneous polling attempts, the adapter waits for another three attempts before becoming active again.

For more information about all predefined attributes, check out the documentation for the scheduler component of Apache Camel at *http://s-prs.co/v576029*.

Notice that the adapter sends hello messages to Cloud Integration where they are stored as data store entries. For the settings of the data store **Write** step, we can use the setting from Chapter 2, Section 2.3.3. In the **Data Store Name** field, provide a meaningful name to facilitate monitoring the data store later.

5. Deploy the iFlow.
6. Check the data store entry (data store name is in the **Write** step).

The message body will contain a message similar to the following text (with the actual timestamp when the message has been processed):

Hello from the Book Demo! Now it is Tue May 01 14:15:19 UTC 2018

According to the settings shown in Figure 6.162, the adapter will trigger the processing of the iFlow every two minutes. Finally, don't forget to undeploy the adapter after you do this test. Otherwise, Cloud Integration will continue to trigger the iFlow and create data store entries.

We won't go into developing your own adapters further. If you're interested in developing your own adapters with more meaningful features than our example adapter, refer to the following blogs in SAP Community (*www.sap.com/community.html*):

- "SAP CPI Adapter Development - Consuming an External Jar into an Adapter": *http://s-prs.co/507736*
- "Extension of Runtime Capabilities Using Blueprint Metadata in Cloud Platform Integration SDK": *http://s-prs.co/507737*

You should also check the online documentation for Cloud Integration (*http://s-prs.co/507743*) at regular intervals for the latest news about adapter development.

For more information on available Apache Camel components, refer to the documentation at *http://camel.apache.org*.

Now, with the previous chapter, this chapter has provided you a strong and detailed foundation in integration development. So, let's round out this chapter with a summary of integration design best practices.

6.11 Guidelines for Integration Flow Development

As you work through the scenarios described in this book, you've become more and more expert at iFlow design. Successively, you learned how to apply various concepts of Cloud Integration—and you'll continue this learning journey in upcoming chapters. Furthermore, you also learned how to implement basic integration patterns such as content-based routing (Chapter 4, Section 4.6) or the splitter pattern (Chapter 5, Section 5.2), to name a few examples.

However, as soon as you become in charge of developing iFlows for productive usage, some more considerations are required. In productive cases, you'll need to understand some qualities with which you should develop your iFlows.

You must ensure, for example, that your iFlows are built in such a way that they are optimized for performance and for memory consumption. Another quality that you became familiar with earlier in this chapter is a good error handling strategy: instead of creating just a "fair weather scenario" when designing iFlow, you must anticipate error situations that can occur during runtime. The better your anticipation and the more you include strategies to handle different error situations in the scenario design, the more robust your scenario will be and the more resilient in productive usage.

Another quality is that your scenario should meet the highest security standards. When using Cloud Integration in a productive environment, more than likely, your iFlows will process business data that contain confidential information. To be clear, you should treat each kind of data processed on your Cloud Integration tenant as confidential—and make sure that this data is protected to a maximum level. In this book, we dedicated a whole chapter (Chapter 10) to the topic of security.

To help you, as an integration developer, meet such qualities, the Cloud Integration development team has published iFlow design guidelines. These guidelines include detailed documentation for each quality as well as predefined integration content that you can use out of the box to learn how to implement the guidelines.

Table 6.2 provides an overview of the integration content packages and their guidelines, which you can find on the SAP Business Accelerator Hub at *https://api.sap.com*. Note that the guidelines available at the time of publication are updated regularly, so check out the documentation for the actual list of packages.

Integration Package	Guideline
Integration Flow Design Guidelines - Run an Integration Flow Under Well-Defined Boundary Conditions	Run an iFlow under well-defined boundary conditions.
Integration Flow Design Guidelines - Relax Dependencies to External Components	Relax dependencies to external components.
Integration Flow Design Guidelines - Keep Readability in Mind	Keep readability in mind.
Integration Flow Design Guidelines - Handle Errors Gracefully	Handle errors gracefully.
Integration Flow Design Guidelines - Apply Highest Security Standards	Apply the highest security standards.
Integration Flow Design Guidelines - Enterprise Integration Patterns	Implement specific integration patterns.

Table 6.2 iFlow Design Guidelines Provided by SAP

Another way to access the guidelines is in the documentation for Cloud Integration (*http://s-prs.co/v576018*). Search for "Integration Flow Design Guidelines."

To round out this section, we'll quickly go through these guidelines and point out some rules as good examples.

6.11.1 Running an Integration Flow Under Well-Defined Boundary Conditions

This guideline deals with managing the resources on your tenant effectively when designing integration content. Some concrete rules you can adopt include the following:

- Limit the size of inbound messages. Certain sender adapters—SOAP (SOAP 1.x), SOAP (reliable messaging), and IDoc—allow you to restrict the size of incoming messages (in the **Maximum Message Size** parameter). You can restrict the size of the body and the attachments independently. The smallest value in the size limit is 1 MB in that case. The default setting for these adapters are maximum body size = 40 MB and maximum attachments size = 100 MB.
- Configure transaction handling in an appropriate way. Various adapters and iFlow steps can store data (either in the database or in a JMS queue). If an erroneous processing of the iFlow occurs, any actions that relate to persistence (storing or deleting data) must be rolled back in a consistent way (so that no data inconsistencies are generated). We recommend setting up transaction handling in Chapter 5, Section 5.4, where we discussed transaction handling in the context of the JMS adapter.

Recommendations and limitations with regard to transaction handling are explained in detail (also together with example scenarios) in the *http://s-prs.co/507738* blog in SAP Community. However, note the following recommendation concerning an optimized resource consumption: Use as few transactions as possible by "sourcing out" transactional processing to subprocesses. As every transaction consumes resources in a considerable amount, make sure that you avoid keeping a transaction open until the whole integration process is finished.

- Avoid writing large message parts or even complete messages into headers or properties. Writing so much data into headers can cause issues when sending out the message because headers are transferred along with the message to the receiver. Writing too much data into properties might also cause memory issues.
- When storing data during message processing, use properties instead of headers because properties aren't passed along with the message by the receiver adapter.
- Delete headers and properties explicitly (in particular, the large ones) if not required anymore, which helps to save memory. You can use a content modifier to perform this deletion at the end of an iFlow.
- Use HTTP session handling. Various HTTP-based adapters (e.g., the SOAP and IDoc adapters, but many more) support HTTP session handling. (You can configure this under the **Runtime Configuration** tab, after clicking outside the **Integration Process** shape; refer to Figure 6.106.) One advantage of session handling is that the client is only authenticated once with the first call, which will result in better performance. However, certain restrictions should be considered when using session handling. For more information about HTTP session handling and its restrictions, as well as to find example scenarios, check out the following SAP Community blog: *http://s-prs.co/507739*.

6.11.2 Relaxing Dependencies to External Components

This guideline helps you design integration content in such a way that Cloud Integration and the connected remote components are only loosely connected. One concrete rule you can follow was described in Chapter 5, Section 5.4—implementing the retry pattern to asynchronously decouple inbound processing.

6.11.3 Keeping Readability in Mind

This guideline helps you design integration content in such a way that your iFlows are readable by others, which improves maintenance and simplifies corrections if errors arise. In particular, in this chapter (Section 6.3 and Section 6.4), you learned several concepts and options for decomposing larger integration scenarios into smaller chunks, either using local integration processes or by distributing the integration logic over various, smaller iFlows that are connected through the ProcessDirect adapter.

Externalization was described in more detail in Chapter 4, Section 4.2.1, and is another rule you should follow in this context.

6.11.4 Handling Errors Gracefully

Error handling is a topic that we introduced as you worked your way through this section. We won't go into too much more detail and instead refer you to the related documentation. You've already applied some of this recommended rule in the tutorials described in this chapter (e.g., using exception subprocesses).

Another rule is that you might outsource error handling into separate iFlows (connected through the ProcessDirect adapter).

In Section 6.3.3, we introduced you to the exception subprocess as one component that can take over message processing when an error occurs.

6.11.5 Applying the Highest Security Standards

The topic of security is discussed in detail in Chapter 10 where you'll learn how to design iFlows that contain certain security features. In addition, security should always be your main priority when designing integration content.

To apply this guideline, we recommend the following rules:

- **Remove sensitive content before logging or forwarding data to other components.**
  With this measure, you can be sure that no confidential data is written into the MPL or forwarded to another system. Malicious parties with monitoring permissions might be able access such sensitive data if you don't follow this rule.
- **Use client certificate authentication.**
  This approach is much more secure than using authorization based on user name and password. Chapter 10 provides detailed information about this topic.
- **Use message-level security.**
  You can digitally encrypt and sign messages as described in Chapter 10, Section 10.4.6.

Note that we mention only some examples here; for a complete list, refer to the product documentation for Cloud Integration (*http://s-prs.co/v576018*). Search for "Integration Flow Design Guidelines."

6.11.6 Additional Best Practices

We'll finish this section with a few additional best practices that make for good integration design:

- Don't store payloads in the MPL. This recommendation holds true in particular for productive iFlows. Using a Script step, you can store the message payload in the

MPL, which is a convenient way to analyze the message body in the monitoring dashboard. However, relying on the MPL can cause issues with memory consumption and even cause the integration scenario to fail because the memory and CPU available on your tenant are shared by other tasks such as message processing, which should never fail, and message monitoring. Therefore, use this option with care. If, nonetheless, you still want to write the message payload into the MPL, do so in error cases only.

Use iFlow tracing by setting the **Trace** log level instead.

For more information, read the blog at *http://s-prs.co/507740*.

Note

Use the **Trace** log level only in test environments. By design, the **Trace** log level is only active for 10 minutes.

- Consider certain best practices when using JavaScript and Groovy Script (with the Script step). Certain risks with regard to memory consumption and the overall performance of your scenario may arise if you don't use these options with care. The following blogs in SAP Community can help you avoid some of these risks: *http://s-prs.co/507741* and *http://s-prs.co/507742*.
- If you enable streaming (when supported), a document will be processed in parts or segments. Use streaming whenever applicable. For example, the splitter step allows you to enable the **Streaming** option. If you deactivate this option, in the splitter case, the message is transferred fully to the memory before being split and processed further. Activating **Streaming**, on the other hand, can help you avoid this behavior. Another example of a step where streaming is supported is the XML-to-JSON converter.
- Avoid memory-intensive steps, such as mappings or accessing elements with XPath expressions, when processing large messages. Such operations will blow up the message in memory.

6.12 Working with Script Collections

In Cloud Integration, scripts refer to pieces of code written in Groovy Script or JavaScript that can be used within the iFlows to perform various tasks such as data transformation, payload logging, enrichment, validation, calling external systems or services, and so on. The reusability of these scripts is essential for efficiency, consistency, and maintainability.

In Cloud Integration, the reusability of scripts can be achieved by using a script collection. Script collections provide a centralized way to organize and manage reusable scripts that can be used across multiple iFlows. In this section, we'll walk you through the process of creating a script collection and using the script collection in multiple iFlows.

6.12.1 Creating a Script Collection

To create a new script collection, you need to add this as a new artifact from the list of available options on your Cloud Integration tenant as shown in Figure 6.163.

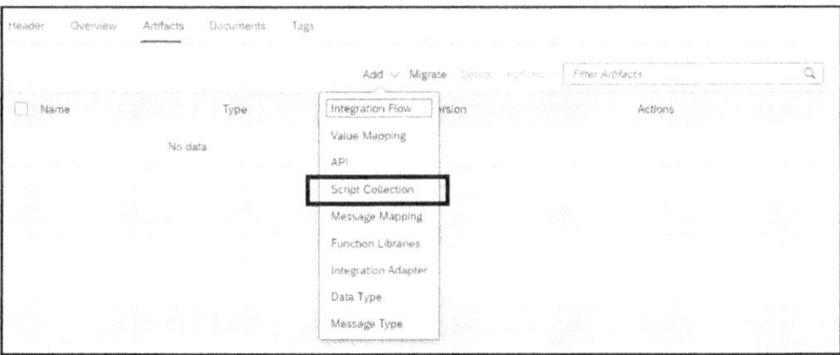

Figure 6.163 Adding a Script Collection as an Artifact

In the **Name** field, you can name the collection per your requirement, as shown in Figure 6.164. The **ID** field will be populated based on the values entered in the **Name** field, but you can edit the **ID** field. You need to ensure that the script collection has a unique ID on the tenant you're working on. The default **Runtime Profile** is selected as **Cloud Integration**. You can select the runtime profile if there are more than one runtime profile is available on the Cloud Integration tenant. You can choose to briefly describe the purpose of the script collection using the **Description** field. Even though the field is optional, it's recommended to add some context in this field for recognizing the purpose of the object.

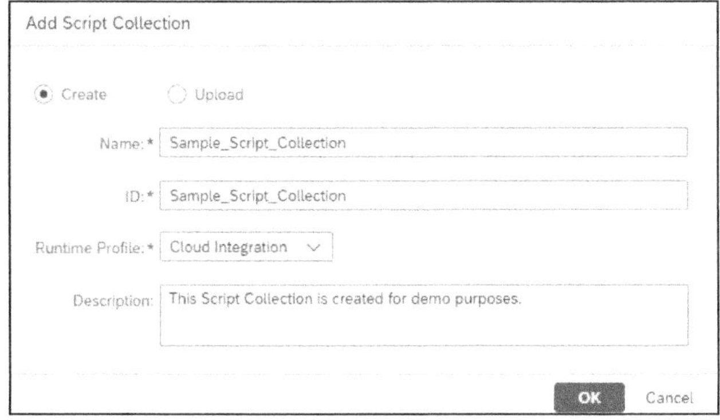

Figure 6.164 Creating a Script Collection

Once all the steps are completed, the script collection will appear as an artifact in the integration package, as shown in Figure 6.165.

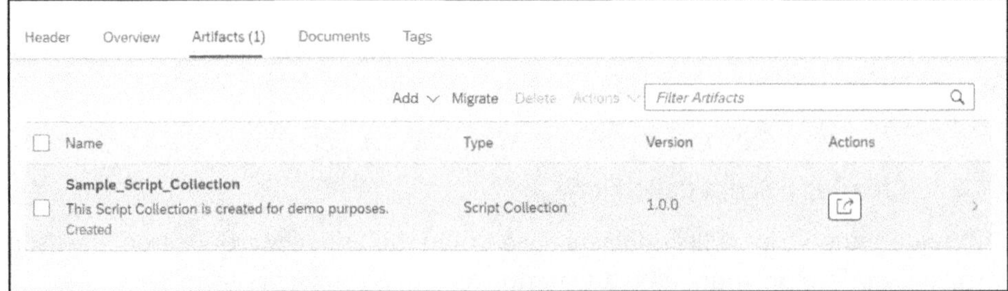

Figure 6.165 Script Collection as an Artifact in the Integration Package

Now that the script collection is created, we'll go ahead and add a Groovy script to the collection. In the example show in Figure 6.166, we'll add a simple Groovy script to log the payload by clicking **Create** and then **Groovy Script**. When creating the script, there is also an option of adding a JavaScript. In this example, we're using **Groovy Script**.

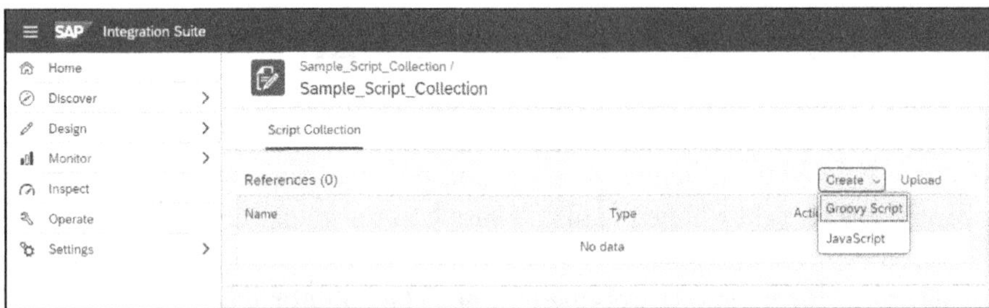

Figure 6.166 Adding a Groovy Script to the collection

You can write the script in the script editor to the right, as shown in Figure 6.167.

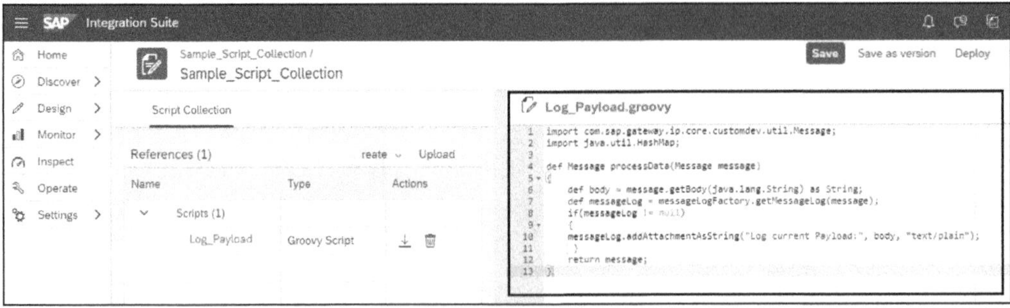

Figure 6.167 Script Editor in the Script Collection

Once the script is done, the script collection needs to be saved and deployed. Once it's deployed, the collection will appear as a deployed artifact in the **Manage Integration Content** overview, as shown in Figure 6.168.

Now that the script collection is created, the script is added to it and deployed. It's time to use the script collection in our iFlows.

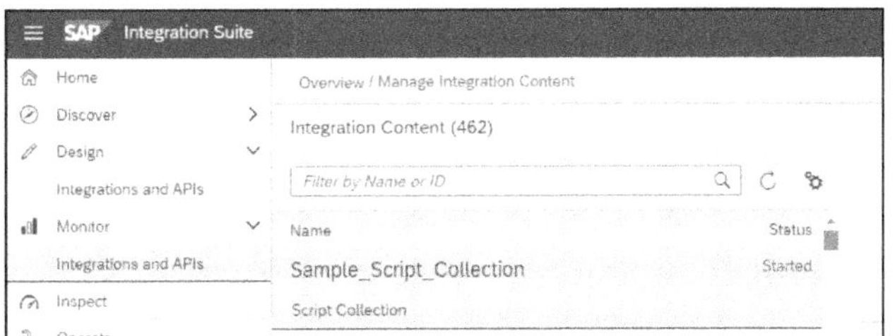

Figure 6.168 Deployment View of the Script Collection

6.12.2 Using the Script Collection in an Integration Flow

In the previous section, you learned how to create a script collection. In this section, you'll see how to use the script collection via a simple example. We'll extend the example we used in Section 6.2 while working with custom headers.

To use the script collection, the reference to the collection has to be made in the iFlow. To reference the script collection, navigate to the **References** tab of the iFlow, navigate to the **Global** tab ❶, and add a reference ❷, as shown in Figure 6.169.

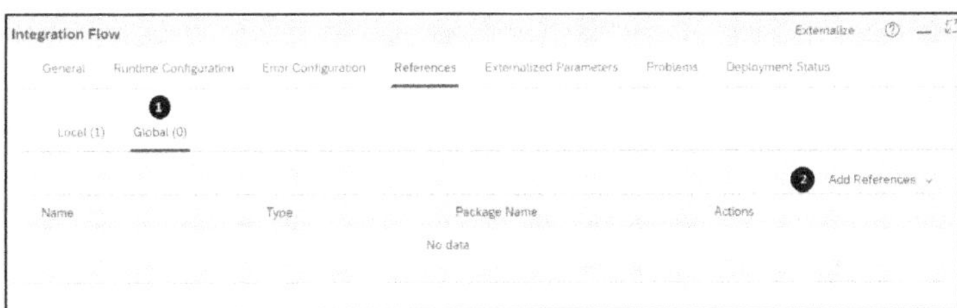

Figure 6.169 Referencing the Script Collection in an iFlow

Once the reference is added, the script collection should be available in the list of references, as shown in Figure 6.170.

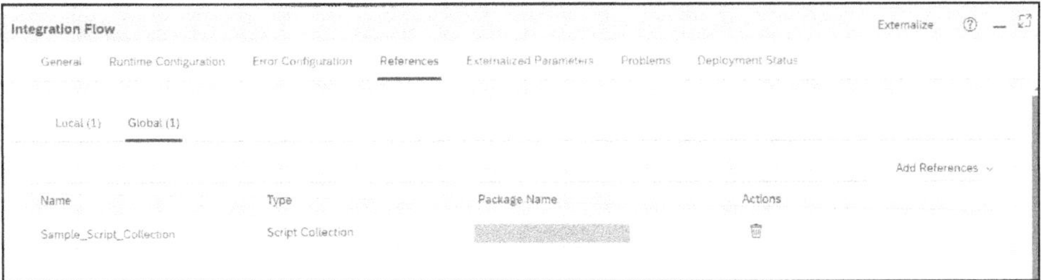

Figure 6.170 Script Collection Available in the List of References

Now we'll go ahead and extend the iFlow by adding a Script step to log the payload after the step where we've added the custom header, as shown in Figure 6.172. To add the Script step, navigate to the **Message Transformers** option in the **Design** palette (see Figure 6.171 ❶). Then, select the **Script** option ❷, and finally select **Groovy Script** ❸.

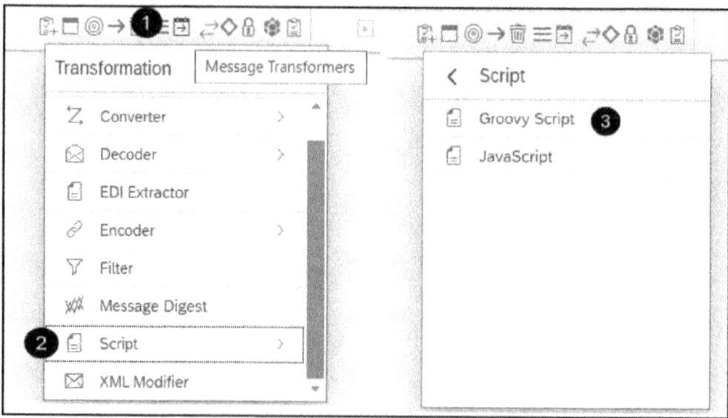

Figure 6.171 Adding the Script Step to the iFlow

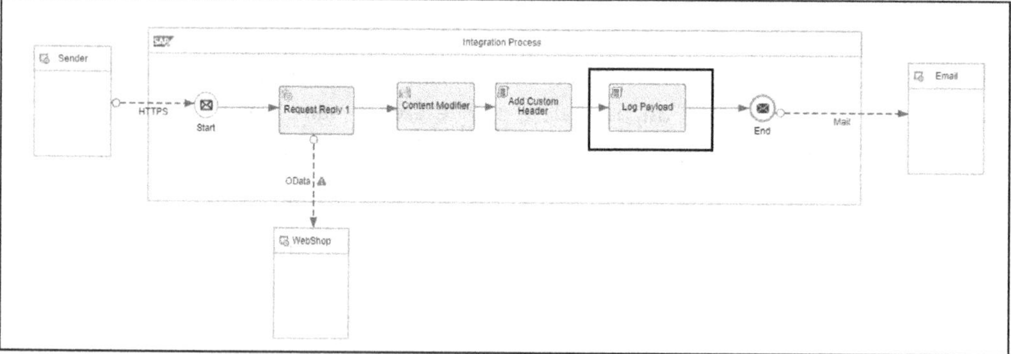

Figure 6.172 Adding the Logging Step to the iFlow

Now, assign the script to the logging step added in the previous step. To assign the script from the script collection, click on the **Assign** option, as highlighted in Figure 6.173.

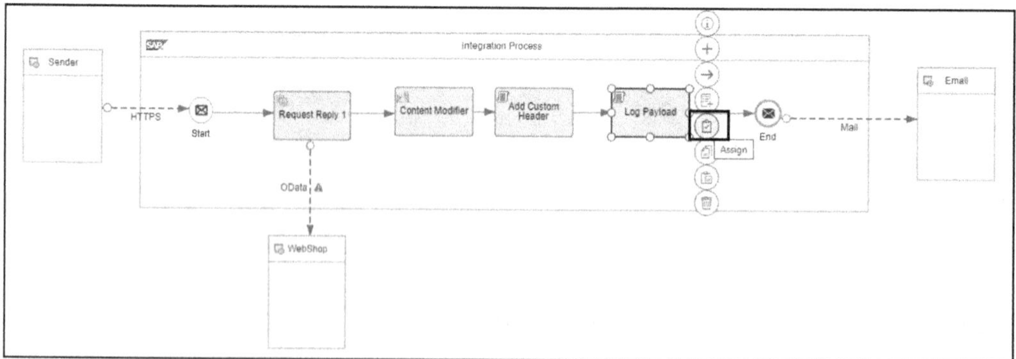

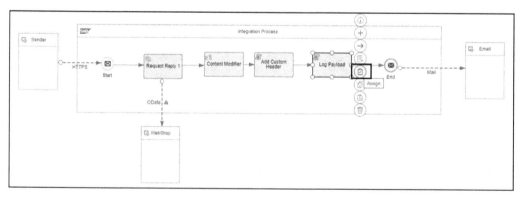

Figure 6.173 Assigning Script from the Collection

After the **Assign** option is selected, search and select the script from the list of **Global Resources**, as shown in Figure 6.174.

Select Resource

Local Resources Global Resources

List of referenced script files that are available in your Integration Flow. Select a script file to assign it to the script flow step.

Script Collection <<All Script Collection (1) >> × Sample_Script_Collection ×

Resources(1) Search

Name	Type
Log_Payload	Groovy Script

OK Cancel

Figure 6.174 Selecting the Script from the List of Global Resources

After performing all of these configurations, it's time to test the iFlow. To test the iFlow, you can use the same approach of triggering the iFlow from Postman, as shown in Figure 6.175.

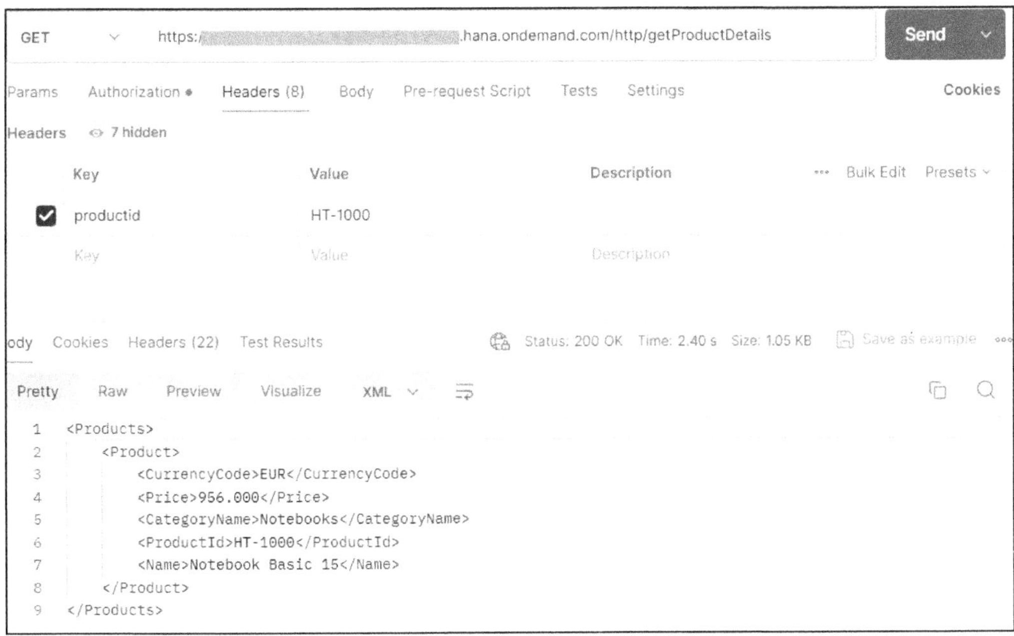

Figure 6.175 Triggering the iFlow for Testing

Let's check if the logging step was executed and the payload was logged. We could see the payload being logged in the message processing log of the iFlow, as shown in Figure 6.176.

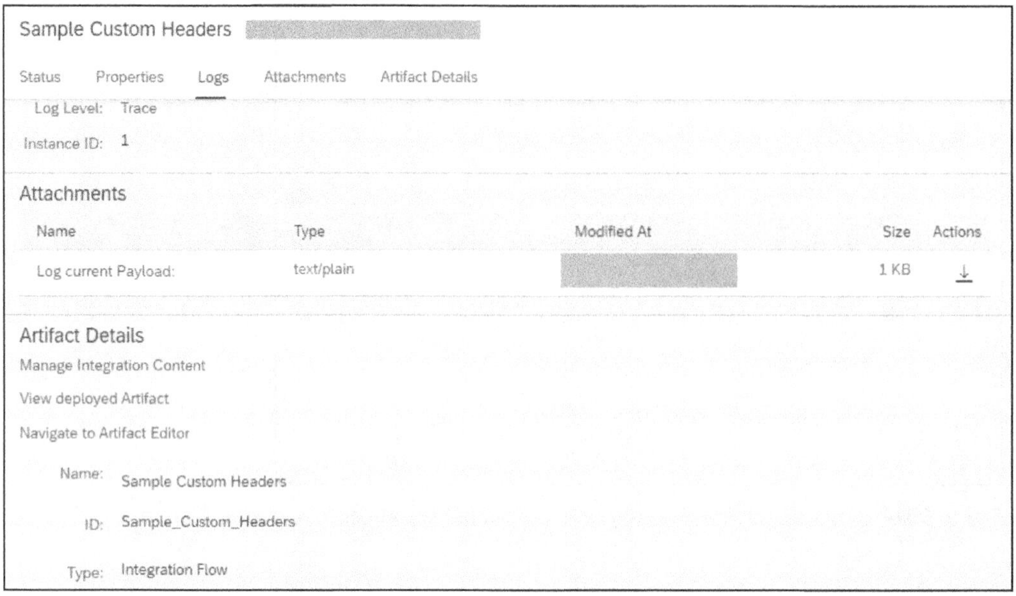

Sample Custom Headers

Status Properties Logs Attachments Artifact Details

Log Level: Trace

Instance ID: 1

Attachments

Name	Type	Modified At	Size	Actions
Log current Payload:	text/plain		1 KB	↓

Artifact Details

Manage Integration Content

View deployed Artifact

Navigate to Artifact Editor

Name: Sample Custom Headers

ID: Sample_Custom_Headers

Type: Integration Flow

Figure 6.176 Payload logged from the Script Step

6.13 Advanced Message Mapping Concepts

Message mapping is a fundamental component of Cloud Integration, enabling integration developers to map and transform data between different formats and structures. The reusability of message mapping in Cloud Integration is key to promoting efficiency, consistency, and maintainability. In this section, we'll discuss and walk you through the steps of creating a message mapping as an artifact and using it in your iFlow.

Creating message mapping as an artifact comes with some benefits. It promotes the reusability of the artifacts, which means the same message mapping can be referred to in multiple iFlows. If the same message mapping can be used in multiple iFlows, you don't need to create the mapping in individual iFlows, and the same message mapping can used if it's created as an artifact. If reduces the maintenance effort, which means if there is a change required in the message mapping, the edit needs to be done at a single place and not in all the iFlows. Because it's a single message mapping created as an artifact, it reduces the memory usage on your Cloud Integration tenant.

In the following sections, you'll see the creation of message mapping as an artifact and its usage in the iFlow. We'll be extending the example used in the previous section by adding a message mapping step to it.

6.13.1 Creating Message Mapping as an Artifact

To create a new message mapping, you need to add this as a new artifact from the list of available options on your Cloud Integration tenant, as shown in Figure 6.177.

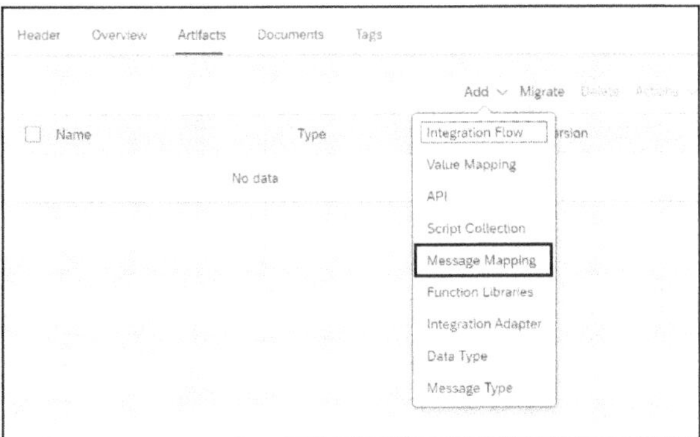

Figure 6.177 Adding Message Mapping as an Artifact

There are three options to create the message mapping as an artifact, as shown in Figure 6.178:

- **Create**
  Create the artifact.
- **Upload**
  Upload the message mapping artifact saved in your local machine.
- **ES Repository**
  Import the message mapping from the SAP Process Orchestration Enterprise Services Repository (ESR).

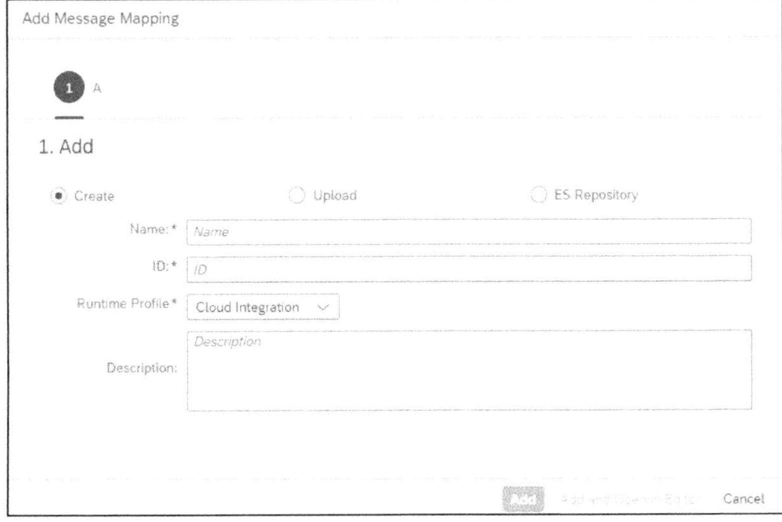

Figure 6.178 Options to Create Message Mapping

Now, we'll explore the option of creating a new message mapping. Before creating the message source and target, an XML Schema Definition (XSD) must be created to import as the source and target structure in the message mapping. In this example, we created an XSD using the response XML from the WebShop application. For the sake of simplicity, we'll use the same structure in the source and target and perform a one-to-one mapping, as shown in Figure 6.179.

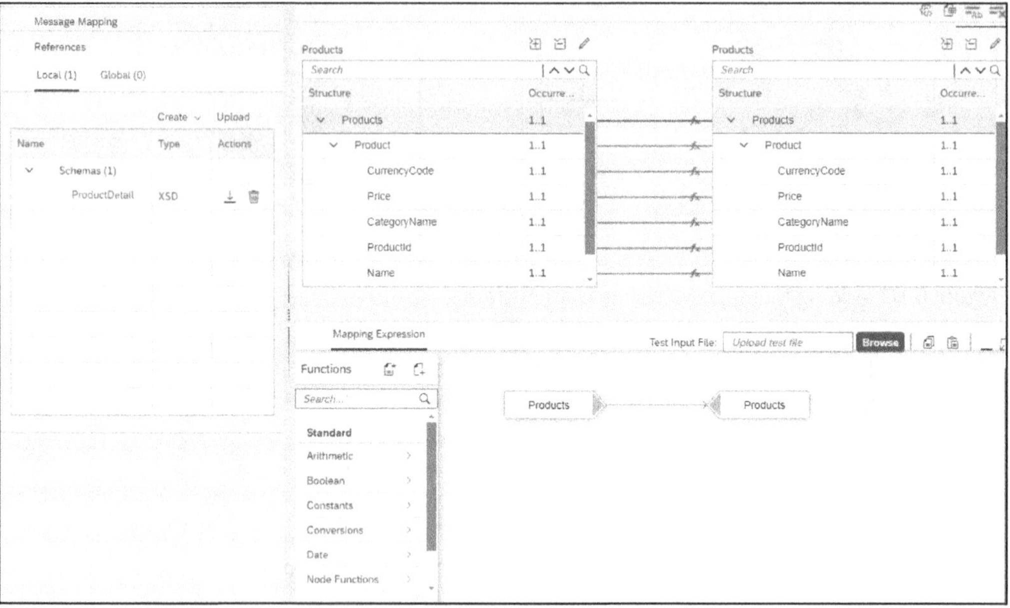

Figure 6.179 Message Mapping with Source and Target

The message mapping can be saved and deployed. With this, we've created the message mapping as an artifact. In the next section, you'll see how this can be used in the iFlow.

6.13.2 Using the Message Mapping in Integration Flow

To use the message mapping in the iFlow, we'll extend the iFlow by adding a message mapping step in the process. To add the message mapping step, navigate to the **Mapping** option in the design palette (see Figure 6.180 ❶). Then, select the **Message Mapping** option ❷. The **Message Mapping** step is added in the process, as shown in Figure 6.181.

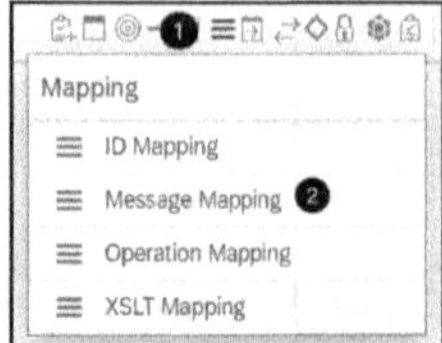

Figure 6.180 Selecting the Message Mapping Step from the Design Palette

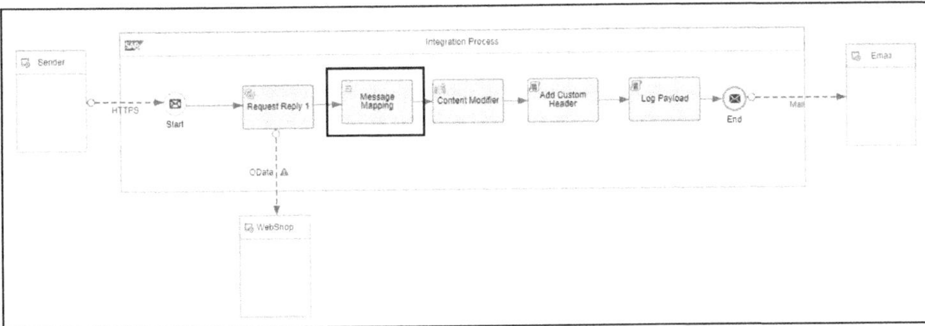

Figure 6.181 Adding the Message Mapping Step to the iFlow

The message mapping artifact also needs to be added to the references in the iFlow in the same way we added the script collection. To add the message mapping as a reference, navigate to the **References** tab of the iFlow. Because the message mapping needs to be added as a global reference, navigate to the **Global** tab in *References*, and then click on **Add References**. Once the reference is added, the message mapping should be available in the list of references, as shown in Figure 6.182.

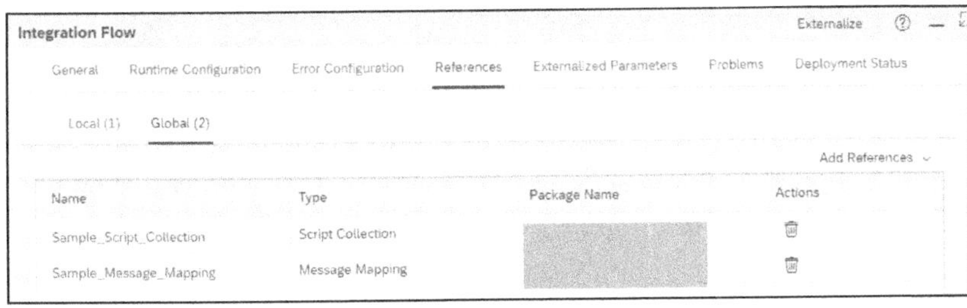

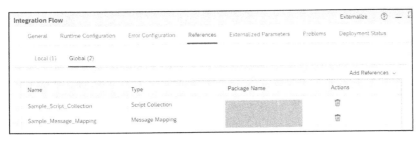

Figure 6.182 Adding Message Mapping as a Reference

With this, we're in the last step of assigning the message mapping artifact to the **Message Mapping** step we added in Figure 6.181. To do so, open the iFlow in the editor. Once you have the integration opened, click on the **Message Mapping** step. Now, you should find an **Assign** option next to the **Message Mapping** step, as shown in Figure 6.183.

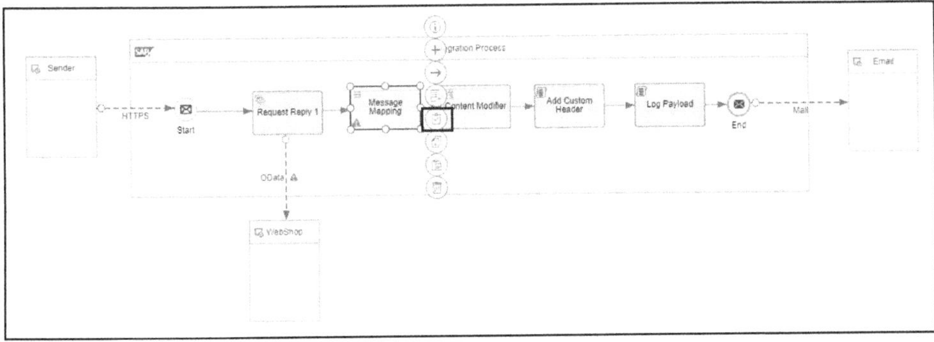

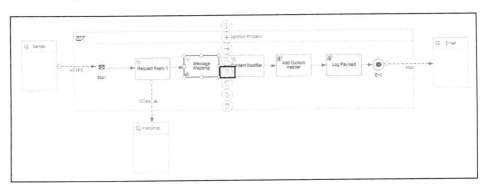

Figure 6.183 Assigning the Mapping Artifact to the Mapping Step

Select the mapping from the list of global resources, as shown in Figure 6.184

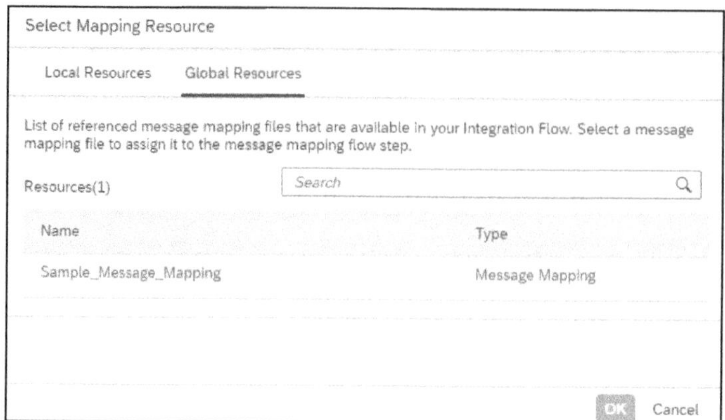

Figure 6.184 Selecting Message Mapping from the List of Global Resources

Congratulations! You've completed all the steps and learned how to use message mapping as an artifact, as well as the advantages that come along with it.

6.14 Summary

We've reached the end of our journey through the more development-oriented topics of the book. In this chapter, you learned how to trigger integration processes on time-based criteria, how to modularize complex real-life scenarios using subprocesses, and, finally, how to extend Cloud Integration's capabilities by developing your own custom adapters, allowing you to connect to a wide variety of external systems and technologies. Now your task is to play around with Cloud Integration's modeling environment to further enhance your knowledge. We come now to another important aspect in the lifecycle of integration content—monitoring. In the next chapter, we'll work you through the monitoring capabilities of Cloud Integration.

Chapter 7
Cloud Integration Operations

As an expert service provider, SAP ensures the support and maintenance of the hardware and software needed to keep Cloud Integration running optimally. However, you'll need to understand and perform a few operational tasks on your own. In this chapter, we'll explain the operational tasks that you can perform to optimize the running of your integration scenarios.

In Chapter 4 through Chapter 6, you learned how to implement both simple and complex integration scenarios using Cloud Integration. When you've successfully developed, configured, and deployed your own iFlows in Cloud Integration, your business will be ready to use and trigger them during runtime.

As integration scenarios are being used at runtime, you, as the customer, will need to maintain your integration scenarios to ensure that your organization continues to reap the benefits provided by these integration scenarios. For you, maintenance will be an ongoing job and includes regularly monitoring iFlows and temporary data as well as managing users and security artifacts.

To gain access to details about specific iFlow instances during runtime, you must use Cloud Integration's monitoring capabilities. The monitoring features provide insights into iFlows that are running so you can ensure they are correctly performing the job they were built for and are helping your business achieve its goals.

In this chapter, we'll focus on what is required to properly manage, track, and detect issues in running integration scenarios in your Cloud Integration tenant. Additionally, we'll explore the features and tools available to support ongoing maintenance and operations. Let's start by providing a big picture view on the operational activities needed for your Cloud Integration tenant.

7.1 Operations: Overview

In traditional on-premise platforms, the customer is responsible for the entire maintenance and operation of the platform, which is the case if you're running an SAP Process Orchestration installation. SAP Process Orchestration is Cloud Integration's sister on-premise integration platform. With SAP Process Orchestration, you're responsible for maintaining the hardware and software and for monitoring the integration scenarios that are built on top of it.

Cloud Integration, as a cloud-based platform, brings several benefits to you in terms of maintenance and operational aspects. As a service provider, SAP has anticipated most headaches that arise in the day-to-day support and maintenance of the Cloud Integration platform. Thus, you can focus your energy on the core business at hand: developing, running, and monitoring integration scenarios.

Although most people are aware of the operational benefits of using a cloud-based platform such as Cloud Integration, not everyone has a clear view of the demarcation line between the operational activities taken care of by SAP as a service provider and the operational activities that you'll still need to cover as a customer. Table 7.1 provides an overview of tasks involved in day-to-day operations with Cloud Integration. The table also provides a responsibility matrix covering the tasks both performed by SAP and by you, as a Cloud Integration customer.

Task	Responsibility	Description
Manage users and roles	Customer	Maintain users and assign roles to them to clearly define what actions they can perform on the Cloud Integration tenant.
Hardware and infrastructure maintenance	Infrastructure provider	The selected infrastructure provider, e.g., Amazon Web Services (AWS), Microsoft Azure, or SAP, is responsible for ensuring that infrastructure components such as networks and operating systems run properly. This responsibility area includes performing "health checks" on the operating system, memory, CPU, and more.
Software updates and maintenance	SAP Team	Software updates are performed on a regular basis by SAP while ensuring near-zero downtime. Your tenant is upgraded automatically, and the newly installed features can immediately be used by all your customers. The SAP team ensures that the updates performed do not negatively affect integration scenarios currently running.
SAP content updates	SAP Team	Updates to the prepackaged content in the content catalog are regularly performed by SAP.
Updates of consumed SAP content	Customer	Updates to the content packages in the content catalog must be consumed by you, either manually or with automation. Refer to Chapter 3 for more details.

Table 7.1 Responsibility Matrix of Operational Tasks

Task	Responsibility	Description
Monitoring of runtime messages and bug fixes	Customer	You're responsible for monitoring, fixing, and maintaining your own integration scenarios and content.
Managing SAP keys	SAP Team	SAP-owned keys are updated by SAP before they expire. We'll look at this later in Section 7.3.2.
Managing security material	Customer	Customers deploy and maintain security artifacts needed for their iFlows. Certificates are a good example of such artifacts.

Table 7.1 Responsibility Matrix of Operational Tasks (Cont.)

Cloud Integration is constantly being developed and maintained; SAP releases updates for the platform about once a month. This short update cycle ensures that you'll continually receive new features and improvements to your Cloud Integration platform. During these updates, you'll experience no downtime. Table 7.1 contains several activities regularly performed by SAP. However, in this chapter, we'll mainly focus activities that fall under your responsibility.

Now that you're aware of the activities required to maintain your Cloud Integration tenant, this section will take you through each of the tools and features available for performing operational tasks. We'll cover the following activity areas:

- Monitoring integration components and message processing
- Performing security material management
- Monitoring message stores, such as data stores and message queues
- Checking log files
- Monitoring locks created during message processing

Let's start with how to monitor your Cloud Integration tenant.

7.2 Monitoring Integration Content and Message Processing

After an iFlow has been deployed to the Cloud Integration tenant, let's monitor all our running integration artifacts to make sure that they're correctly doing the job for which they were built. In this section, we'll focus on looking at what is required to properly manage, track, and detect issues on running iFlows. Monitoring deployed artifacts is part of the ongoing job of maintaining and improving your organization's IT environment. Besides monitoring the runtime artifacts deployed on your tenant, in this section, we'll also describe monitoring the message processing in the cluster's runtime.

Open the Web UI's homepage at *http://<server>:<port>/itspaces*. The monitoring screens can be accessed via the **Monitor** menu item on the left, as shown in Figure 7.1.

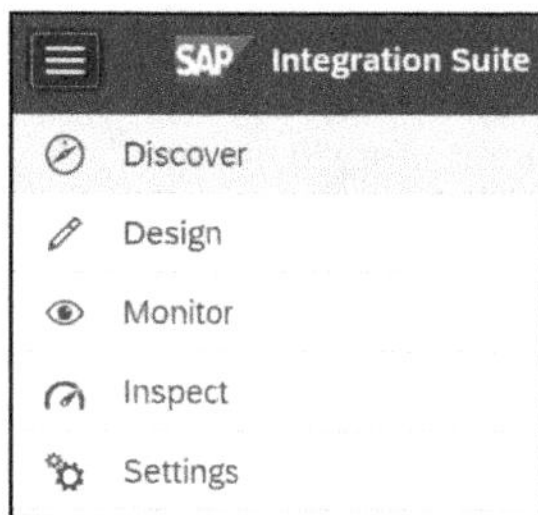

Figure 7.1 Accessing Cloud Integration's Monitoring Features

On the **Monitor** page, you'll be taken to a screen with several tiles displaying various statistics, numbers, and statuses pertaining to the messages that have been processed by the runtime engine of Cloud Integration. Figure 7.2 shows an overview of the main monitoring screens in the SAP BTP, Cloud Foundry environment. From this screen, also known as the *monitoring dashboard*, you can access the various available monitors for monitoring integration content and messages.

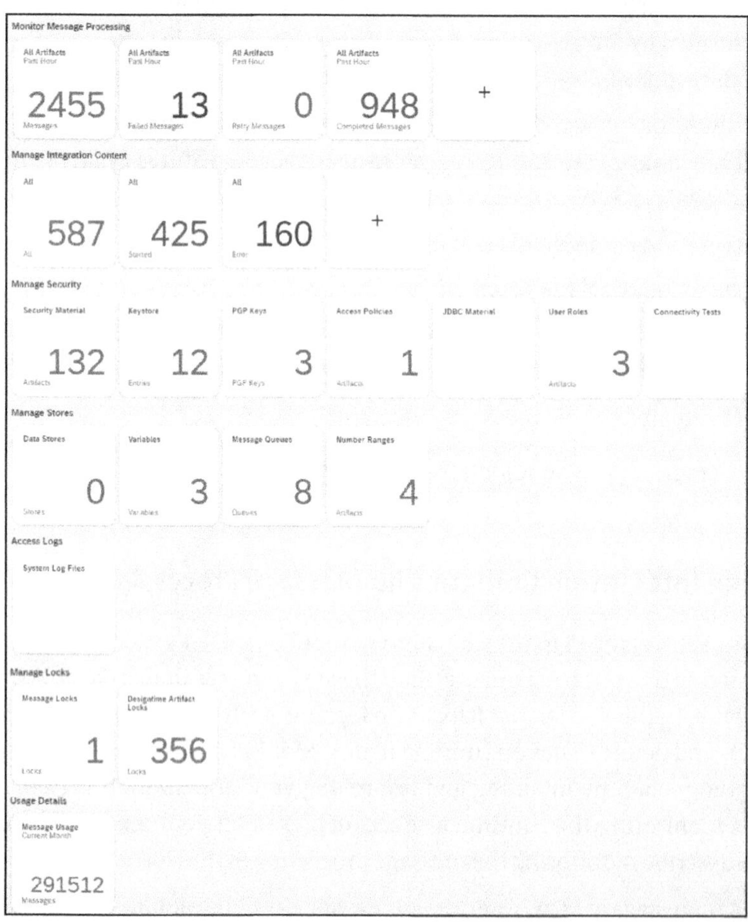

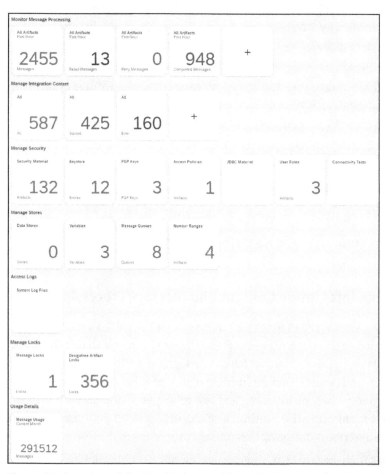

Figure 7.2 Overview of the Monitoring Dashboard in SAP BTP, Cloud Foundry Environment

The dashboards for the SAP BTP, Neo environment and SAP BTP, Cloud Foundry environment are slightly different. For example, in the SAP BTP, Neo environment, the **User Roles** tile doesn't exist; instead, the **Certificates-to-User Mappings** tile is shown in the **Manage Security** section. This book is mainly focused on the SAP BTP, Cloud Foundry environment, but we'll discuss the monitoring features in both the SAP BTP, Neo and SAP BTP, Cloud Foundry environments in this chapter.

A tile is a block on a page that filters messages or artifacts corresponding to a particular status (e.g., completed messages). As shown in Figure 7.2, the monitoring dashboard screen contains six main tile groupings:

- **Monitor Message Processing**
- **Manage Integration Content**
- **Manage Security**
- **Manage Stores**
- **Access Logs**
- **Manage Locks**
- **Usage Details**

Let's first explore the **Manage Integration Content** section's tiles because we'll need to understand the options for monitoring integration content and how these options help you monitor message processing.

7.2.1 Managing Integration Content

The tiles in the **Manage Integration Content** section of the screen display the statuses of the different integration artifacts that have been deployed on the tenant. Deployed integration artifacts include, for instance, iFlows and OData services. Referring to the screen shown in Figure 7.2, notice that a total of 1,212 integration artifacts have been deployed (first tile in the **Manage Integration Content** section). Out of those 1,212, 1,186 have successfully started (second tile), and 16 have failed (third tile). You can click on the second tile to view all integration artifacts that have been successfully deployed on your Cloud Integration tenant.

As shown in Figure 7.3, in a table on the left, the monitor presents the deployed artifacts with their statuses and artifact types. Table 7.2 contains a detailed description of these attributes and their possible values.

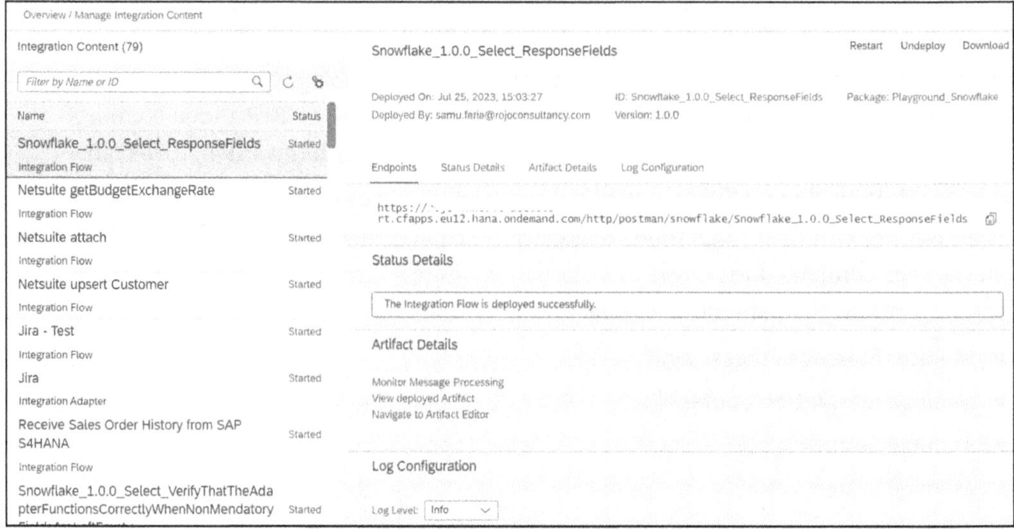

Figure 7.3 Manage Integration Content Monitor

Attribute	Description
Name	The name of the integration artifact that has been deployed. The type of integration content appears below the name, for example, **Value Mapping**, **Integration Flow**, **Integration Adapter**, or **OData service**.
Status	The deployment status of the integration artifact: ■ **Starting**: The integration artifact is starting but can't be executed yet. ■ **Started**: The integration artifact is ready to be used. ■ **Error**: The integration artifact is in an error state and needs manual action, for example, changing the artifact and then redeployment. ■ **Stopping**: The artifact is in the process of stopping, for example, during undeployment, and can't be executed anymore. An artifact in this status can't be downloaded, undeployed, or restarted.

Table 7.2 Attributes of the Integration Artifact on the Left

The content of the table is sorted by the time of the last deployment, which means that the artifact deployed most recently is shown on top. To customize the list of displayed artifacts, you can either search for specific artifacts by artifact name or ID, or you can filter the table content by attributes such as status or artifact type. To sort or filter the content of the table, select the **Table Settings** icon [icon] at the top of the table. On the subsequent screen, define how the table entries should be sorted by specifying an attribute and whether the entries should be sorted in ascending or descending order for that attribute. You can also filter the table entries to focus on certain attributes.

On the right side of the monitor, details about the selected artifact are shown. At the top, the most important details about the deployed integration artifact are provided, such as its ID, version, who deployed it when, and to which package this artifact belongs. Descriptions of these attributes are summarized in Table 7.3.

Attribute	Description
Deployed On	Specifies date and time at which the most recent deployment was performed.
Deployed By	Specifies the user who deployed the artifact.
ID	The technical ID of the integration artifact. This ID is necessary, for example, when searching for errors in log files.
Version	The version number of the deployed integration artifact.
Package	The package the integration artifact belongs to.

Table 7.3 Attributes of the Integration Artifact on the Top Right

The following actions, among others, can be performed on each artifact:

- **Restart**
  Restarts the integration artifact if a problem arises but has been solved. For instance, perhaps the necessary credentials weren't deployed on the tenant. These errors don't need a full redeployment; you just need to restart the integration artifact. If changes in the integration artifact were required to solve the error, the integration artifact must be redeployed from the **Design** view, and restarting isn't sufficient. Note that the **Restart** action isn't always available; whether this action is available depends on the status of the artifact and the type of error.
- **Undeploy**
  Remove an artifact that was previously deployed on the tenant. To undeploy an integration artifact, select the artifact in the table on the left of the monitor, and choose **Undeploy**.
- **Download**
  Download the content of an integration artifact. The artifact is then stored on the local machine in the form of a Java Archive (JAR) file. Downloading integration content can be useful as a backup method. The backed-up data can then, for instance, be reimported or transported to another Cloud Integration tenant. Note that read-only integration artifacts can't be downloaded.

The actions available on the top-right corner of the monitor depend on the status of the artifact and whether the artifact is a read-only artifact.

Below the header information, the view is divided into several sections. You can navigate between these sections using the tabs, shown on top:

- **Endpoints**
  HTTP-based sender adapters, such as the Simple Object Access Protocol (SOAP) sender adapter or the HTTP sender adapter, expose endpoints that can be called to start the runtime processing of a specific artifact. Under the **Endpoints** tab, all accessible endpoints, that is, endpoints that are exposed by the selected artifact, are listed. We used this option earlier in some of our example scenarios to retrieve the URL to be called to trigger the iFlows using a SOAP sender adapter.
- **Status Details**
  This section provides the overall status of the integration artifact. For started integration artifacts, you'll see a message that the integration artifact is deployed successfully (shown earlier in Figure 7.3). For polling (**SFTP** or **Mail** adapter) and consuming adapters (**JMS** or **AMQP** adapter), an additional section labeled **Polling Information** is shown. This section provides information about the last poll and the state of the polling or consumption.

  If the integration artifact is in an error status or an error arose during deployment of the iFlow, the error details are shown in Figure 7.4. You can also download the log by clicking the **Download** icon ⤓, for example, to attach it to a support ticket.

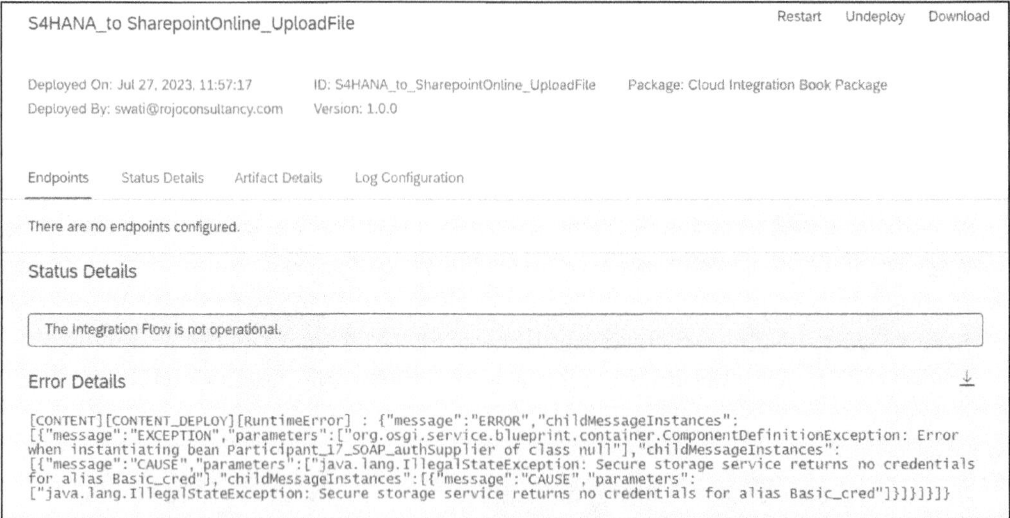

Figure 7.4 Error Details in the Manage Integration Content Monitor

- **Artifact Details**
  The information provided in this section depends on the artifact type. In general, there are three important links. When selecting the **Monitor Message Processing** link, the message monitor opens and shows all messages processed for the selected artifact in the past hour. Note that this link is only available for iFlows, and SOAP, REST, and OData APIs. The second link, **View Deployed Artifact**, opens the selected artifact in its modeler in read-only mode. You can, for example, use this view to

explore the configured steps and adapters in an iFlow and check the defined properties. You can't change the configuration and redeploy the artifact from this view. The view is meant for monitoring only. The third link, **Navigate to Artifact Editor**, opens the artifact in the editable mode. Note that none of these links are available for the artifacts of type integration adapter.

- **Log Configuration**
  You can configure different log levels for the iFlows and APIs deployed on the tenant in the **Log Configuration** section. This section isn't available for other artifact types such as value mappings or integration adapters.

Let's now look more closely at the log levels available for iFlows and the consequences of changing them.

7.2.2 Log Configuration

To monitor your iFlows efficiently in all phases of developing a new scenario, different log levels are available. With this configuration option, you can, for example, monitor iFlows during development and test phases with a high log level, which provides details about runtime execution in all steps and adapters, and observe payloads and headers after each step. Later, when the iFlow runs in a productive scenario, you won't need such detailed logs anymore.

As shown in Figure 7.5, the following **Log Levels** are provided by Cloud Integration:

- **None**
  No message processing log (MPL) is written.
- **Info**
  This log level is the default set when a new iFlow is deployed. With this log level, only the most important information about the runtime execution of a message is logged, such as start and stop times and the overall status. Nevertheless, if the message encounters an error during runtime execution, the final steps are logged in detail so you can analyze the error. You should use this log level for iFlows running in a productive scenario.
- **Error**
  When an iFlow logging is set to log level **Error**, the MPL is stored only in case of an error in processing. For all successful scenarios, no MPL is written. Be careful when using this log level for retry scenarios because only failed processing attempts are logged even though your last retry attempt is successful, and hence you can have a misleading picture of the execution.
- **Debug**
  All flow steps and adapter calls are logged in detail, even on successful execution of a message. This log level is mostly used during development and testing for a new

scenario. This log level should not be used in productive scenarios due to the negative impact on performance and the data volumes stored in the database. To prevent accidental setting of log level debug for an extended period of time, there is a fixed 24-hour expiration after which the log level is reset to the previous setting.

- **Trace**
  This log level is the most detailed log level available. With this log level, payloads, headers, and properties are logged after each processing step. **Trace** is generally activated only for a short period to analyze issues in scenario execution in detail. The maximum time the log level **Trace** can be activated for is 10 minutes to avoid overloading the database with too much data. After this time, the log level resets automatically to the log level that was configured before activating **Trace**.

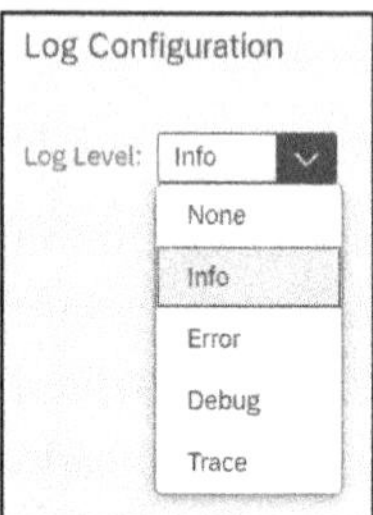

Figure 7.5 Log Levels for Log Configuration

During the first deployment of a new iFlow, the log level is set to **Info**. Then, you can configure the log level as desired in the **Manage Integration Content** monitor. Subsequent deployments of the same iFlow won't reset the log level; the setting will be kept.

As soon as you change the log level in the **Log Configuration** dropdown menu, the option is active: no additional save action is required, and you don't need to restart the iFlow. The next MPL of a message is written with the new log level.

Now, you know how to monitor your integration content and how to define the log level for deployed iFlows. With this information, let's dive more deeply into monitoring message processing in the Cloud Integration runtime.

7.2.3 Monitoring Message Processing

As shown earlier in Figure 7.2, within the monitoring dashboard, the top section of the screen includes a list of tiles that all relate to message processing. After clicking on any of the tiles in this section, you'll be taken to a new page, as shown in Figure 7.6.

By default, the screen displays two views:

- On the left, you'll see a list of messages matching the tile's configuration. You can select any of the messages listed to further view its log details, which will be displayed on the right.

- On the right, you'll see details about the entry you selected on the left. The **Status**, **Properties**, and **Logs** fields offer further navigation to the MPL, to the MPL attachments, and to the iFlow.

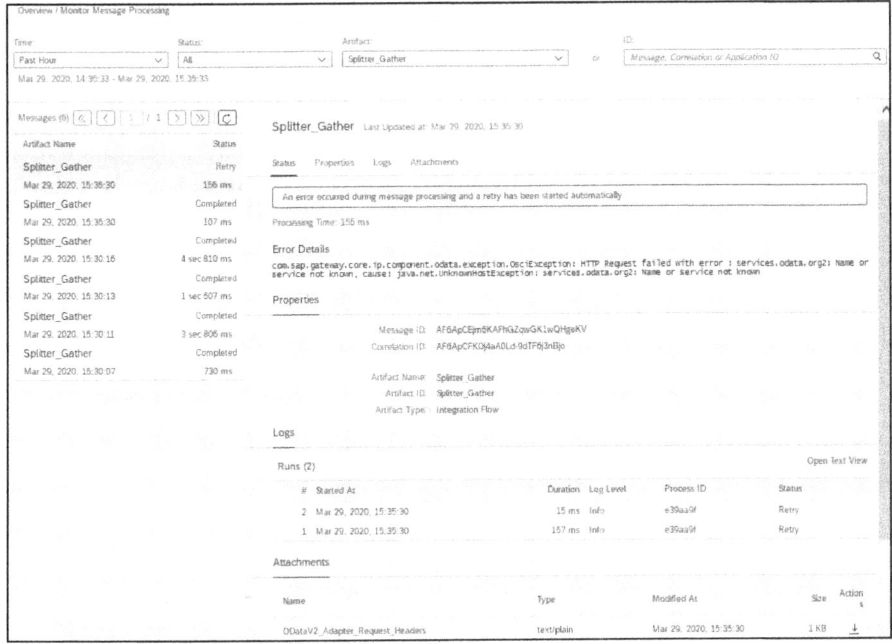

Figure 7.6 Monitor Message Processing

As shown in Figure 7.6, you can filter the list of messages by changing the filtering settings. Messages can be filtered based on **Time, Status, Artifact**, or **ID** (includes **Message**, **Correlation**, or **Application ID**). Table 7.4 provides descriptions for these filter attributes.

Filter Name	Description
Time	The date and time at which the message was triggered.
Status	The status of the MPL entry in the monitor. The following values are possible: ▪ **All** ▪ **Failed** ▪ **Retry** ▪ **Canceled** ▪ **Completed** ▪ **Processing** ▪ **Escalated** ▪ **Discarded** ▪ **Abandoned**

Table 7.4 List of Filter Attributes in the Monitor

Filter Name	Description
Artifact	The name of the iFlow or OData service as created in your design workspace.
Message ID	A unique identifier for a specific MPL across the tenant. This attribute is often used as a filter when troubleshooting a specific iFlow instance with a known message ID.
Correlation ID	A unique identifier for a specific group of messages that belong together. This attribute is relevant for scenarios where different MPLs belong to a single end-to-end process, for example, in a Java Message Service (JMS) scenario where a message is stored in a JMS queue using one MPL and consumed in a second MPL.
Application ID	Only relevant when the `SAP_ApplicationID` header element has been specified using either the Content Modifier or Script step. The header can be specified based on any message attribute the integration developer likes to search for, for example, the ID of a processed order.

Table 7.4 List of Filter Attributes in the Monitor (Cont.)

On the left side of the screen, you'll see the overall number of messages matching the selection criteria. Using the arrows at the top of the **Messages** table, you can navigate between the different pages of the monitor to check all the messages available, as shown in Figure 7.7.

Figure 7.7 Navigation in the Message Monitor

For each message entry on the left, the processing time and the status of the message are displayed. When you select any entry on the left, further details about the message are displayed on the right side of the screen:

- At the top, the time of the last update in the log for this message is shown.
- The **Status** section provides the overall status of the message processing, together with the overall processing time. If an error occurred during the processing of the message, details about the error will be displayed, as shown in Figure 7.8.
- Under the **Properties** tab, the message ID and the correlation ID along with certain custom properties of the execution are displayed.
- The **Logs** section contains information about the **Log Level** and the **Process ID** for the message processing. The **Process ID** indicates the ID of the runtime node on which the message was executed; this information is important to find the related system log if an error needs to be analyzed in detail (Section 7.5.2). The **Log Level**, for example, **Debug**, is a link, and if clicked, this option will open the detailed steps of the

message processing in a new window. In this window, the processing steps are shown in a table at the top, and the message's path is depicted in the model below. We'll discuss this view in more detail later in this section. The textual representation of the **Message Processing Log** can be accessed by clicking the **Open Text View** link.

- The **Artifact Details** section provides the details of the deployed integration artifact, including the name, the ID, the type, and the package of the artifact. You can also find the links to navigate to **Manage Integration Content**, **View Deployed Artifact**, and **Navigate to Artifact Editor**.
- If MPL attachments are created during message processing, an additional tab, **Attachments**, is available. Under this tab, the MPL attachments are listed in a table showing the name of the attachment, the type, and the time the attachment was modified last. MPL attachments can, for example, be created during message processing using the **Script** step.

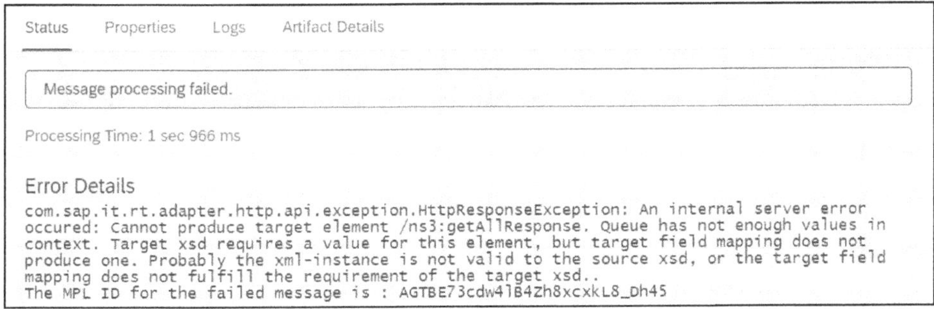

Figure 7.8 Status Details for an Erroneous Message

Let's check out the available sections in more detail.

Properties

In the **Properties** section, the message ID for this specific message processing and the properties of the deployed iFlow are listed. Table 7.5 describes each of these attributes.

Attribute	Description
Message ID	ID of the selected MPL to be used as a search criterion in message monitoring and in log files.
Correlation ID	ID of a group of MPLs that belong together, which can be used as a search criterion in message monitoring.
Sender	Name of the sender system. This property can be set by populating the standard header as "SAP_Sender".

Table 7.5 List of Attributes in the Properties Section

Attribute	Description
Receiver	Name of the receiver system. This property can be set by populating the standard header as "SAP_Receiver".
Application Message ID	ID of the application sending the information. This ID is visible by populating the standard header as "SAP_ApplicationID".
Application Message Type	Message type of the content. This attribute is populated by setting the value of the header as "SAP_MessageType".
Custom Status	User-defined status of the iFlow. This attribute is populated by setting the "SAP_MessageProcessingLogCustomStatus" property.

Table 7.5 List of Attributes in the Properties Section (Cont.)

Apart from **Message ID** and **Correlation ID**, all other attributes are optional and will only be visible if a value is assigned to their dedicated header or property.

Logs

Let's look more deeply at the **Logs** section (shown earlier in Figure 7.6). In this section, the MPL can be explored in both visual and textual representations.

The **Logs** tab may contain a table listing several message processing runs, as shown earlier in Figure 7.6. This case arises, for example, when JMS queues are used for temporary message storage, such as in the SAP Process Integration or Applicability Statement 2 (AS2) adapter, or if the message is retried by the JMS sender adapter. Then, for each message processing run, one line appears in the table. However, in most scenarios, the **Logs** tab will resemble the screen shown in Figure 7.9. Because only a single message processing run is executed, the data isn't provided in a table.

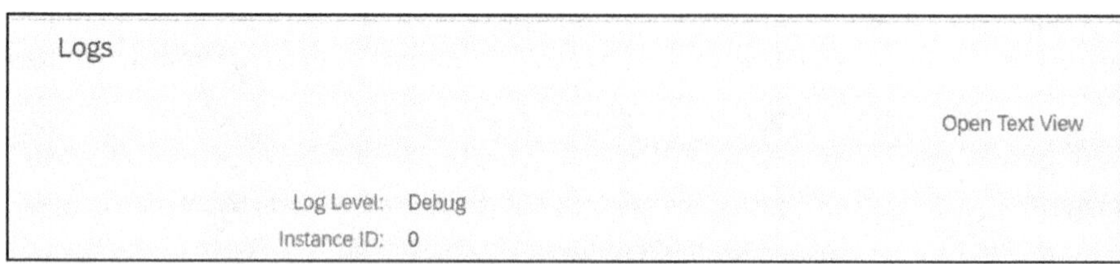

Figure 7.9 Logs Tab for a Single Message Processing Run

The log level that was used to write the MPL is displayed. Recall our earlier discussion of log levels and how to set log levels from Section 7.2.1. The log level value is a link under the **Logs** tab. As shown in Figure 7.10, selecting the link opens a new window that provides a table with all the executed processing steps on the left side and a graphical model of the iFlow on the right side of the screen. The details shown depend on the log level being used; we'll elaborate more on this in the next couple of pages. Note that, for log level **Info**, no link is available because in this case no graphical model of the processing is available.

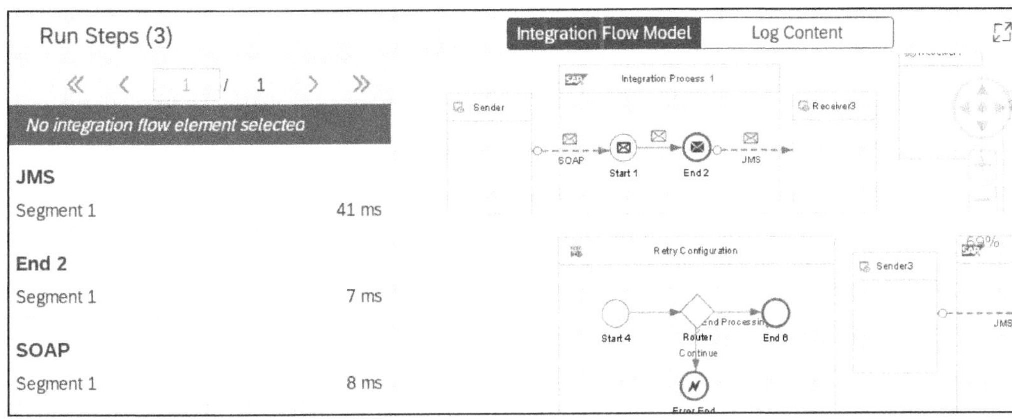

Figure 7.10 Visual Representation of the Message Processing Log

As shown in Figure 7.11, for erroneous messages, the error is highlighted in the table with an **Error** icon ⓘ, which you can click to view details about the error.

Segment 3
HCIOData
Segment 3 37 ms
com.sap.gateway.core.ip.component.odata.exception.OsciException: HTTP Request failed with error : services.odata.org2, cause: java.net.UnknownHostException: services.odata.org2

Figure 7.11 Visual Representation of the Message Processing Log for an Erroneous Message

The table on the left side of the monitor contains all executed processing steps sorted by execution time, starting with the last step executed at the top. The various attributes are listed in Table 7.6.

Attribute	Description
Name	Name of the flow step or adapter channel.
Segment	ID of the processing segment in the runtime. This value is especially interesting if multiple branches are executed for one message processing flow because, in this case, multiple processing segments are available. This case arises, for example, if splitter or multicast patterns are used.
Time	The processing time for this step.

Table 7.6 Attributes in the Message Processing Log

On the right side of the monitor, under the **iFlow Model** tab, the model of the iFlow is shown with the traversal path for the message processing. As shown earlier in Figure 7.10, envelope icons ✉ are shown in the model to indicate the path this specific message has taken during processing. For steps causing an error, the envelope is shown in red ✉.

Icons for Path Traversal Depend on the Log Level

Note that the unfilled envelopes are shown if log level **Info** or **Debug** was used for the message processing. If trace level **Trace** was used, the envelopes indicating the traversal path are filled. This indicates that also the payload data is available in the detailed log data. The blue envelope icon ✉ shows the traversal path for successfully executed steps, and the red envelope ✉ points out that there was an error executing this step.

When you select a specific step or adapter in the iFlow model, the configuration of this step is shown below the model, as shown in Figure 7.12. You can explore the defined settings in the iFlow step or adapter. The configurations for the flow steps or adapters are shown in read-only mode. As shown in Figure 7.12, you'll see two configuration tabs for the **JMS** receiver adapter: **General** and **Processing**. You can navigate between the tabs and discover all configurations defined for this flow step or adapter.

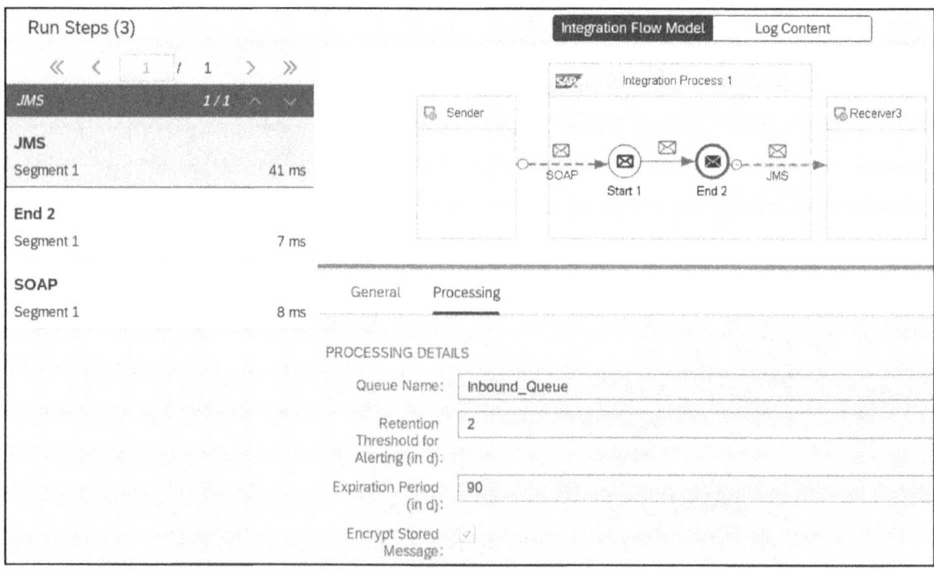

Figure 7.12 Configuration Details of a Single Processing Step

When you select the **Log Content** tab for a specific processing step in the table at the top of the monitor on the right, details for this processing step will be displayed. As shown in Figure 7.13, under the **Properties** tab, the technical details for this step are depicted, including the **Name**, **ID**, and **Type** of the step in the **Model Step** property, the **Start Time**, and the **Duration** of the processing. The **Process Step** value represents the order in which the steps are executed. The **Segment** information isn't relevant for our simple scenario but is important in multicast or splitter scenarios, where multiple processing segments are available, one for each branch. In such scenarios, you'll need the segment information to understand which steps belong to which branch or execution segment.

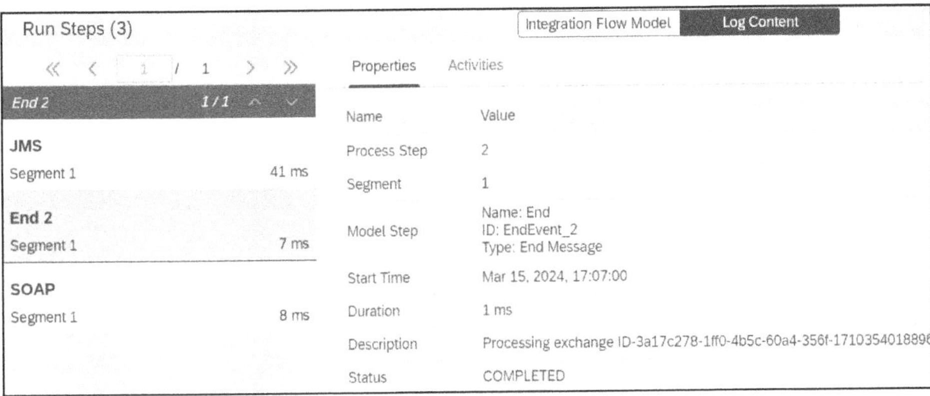

Figure 7.13 Properties of the Selected Processing Step

Under the **Activities** tab, all technical executions within this step are collected. Some simple steps will only have one entry, but others, as shown in Figure 7.14, may involve a long list of internal execution steps, including conversions, setting or deleting headers or properties, and so on. These details are quite technical and generally are only required during error analysis. As the integration developer, you won't need to understand these details. In the context of a support ticket, SAP may ask you for details found in this monitor.

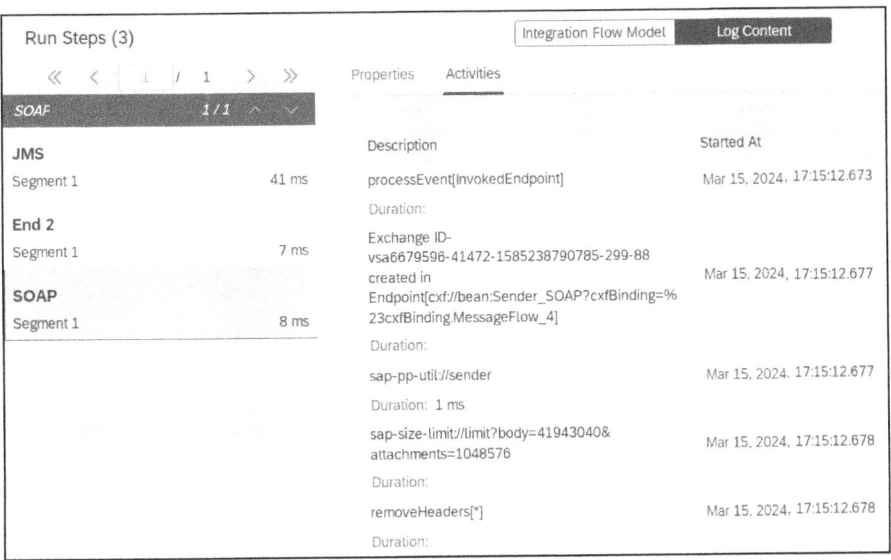

Figure 7.14 Activities of the Selected Processing Step

The **Message Content** tab, if available, provides the payload, exchange properties, and headers before the execution of the flow step or adapter. The details are shown in three different tabs: **Header**, **Exchange Properties**, and **Payload**. Under the **Header** tab, all the headers available before the execution of this step or adapter are shown. As shown in Figure 7.15, for example, you'll find the headers available before the message is sent to the JMS queue in the JMS receiver adapter.

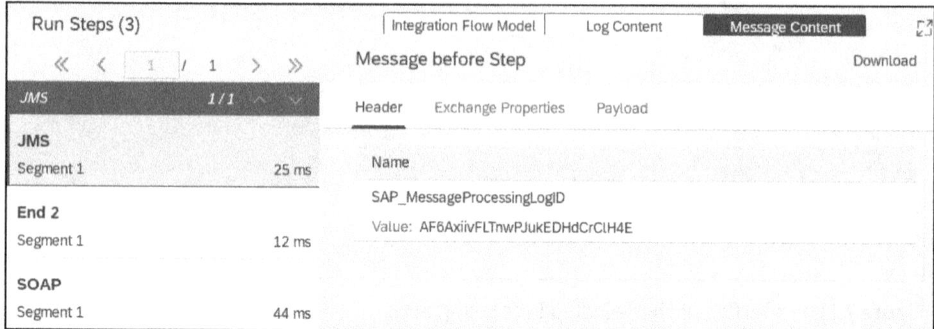

Figure 7.15 Headers Set before Message Is Stored to the JMS Queue

Under the **Exchange Properties** tab, you'll see the exchange properties available at this time, as shown in Figure 7.16. Under the **Payload** tab, you'll see the corresponding payload sent to the **JMS** queue, as shown in Figure 7.17.

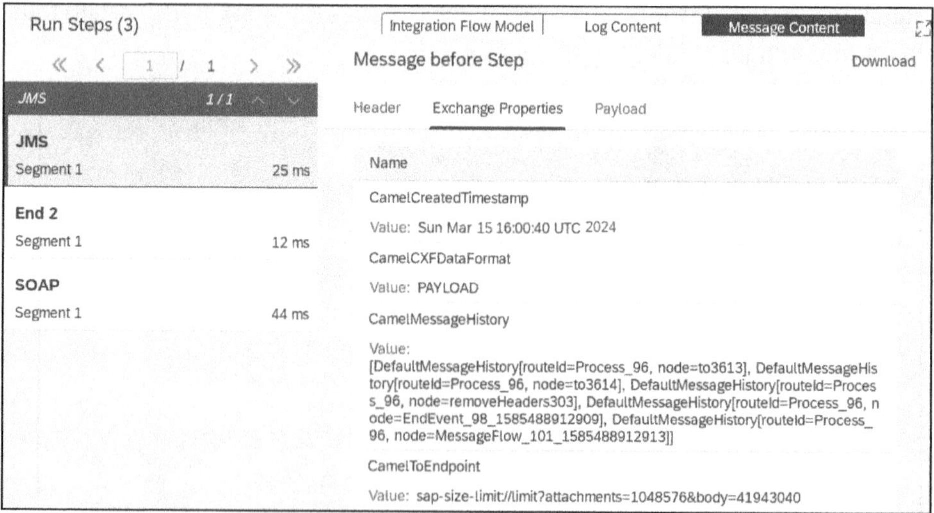

Figure 7.16 Exchange Properties Set before Message Is Stored to the JMS Queue

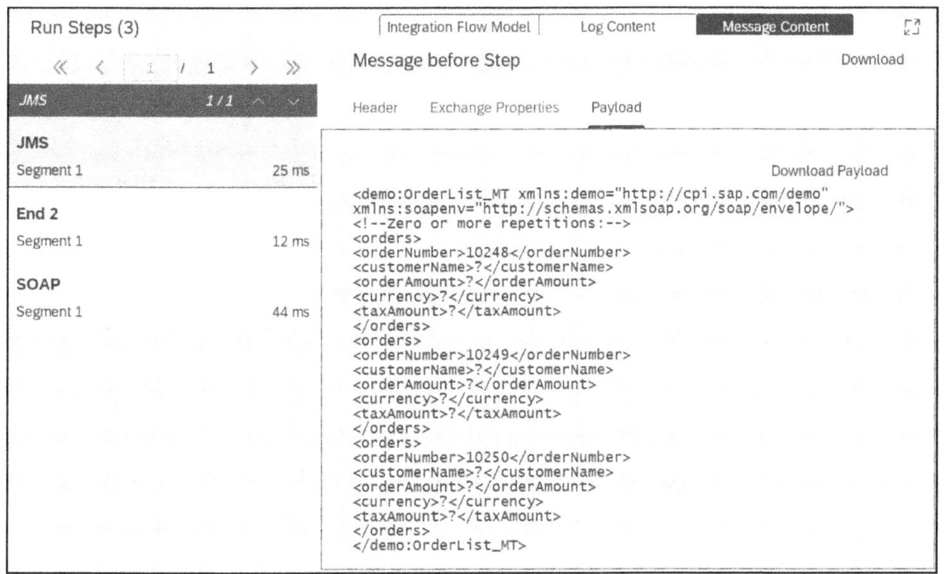

Figure 7.17 Payload before Message Is Stored to the JMS Queue

With these details, you can know exactly how the headers and payload changed during the execution of this specific step. This information can especially be useful if you need to understand a specific error situation in the scenario execution. With the **Download** link, you can download the payload, exchange properties, and the headers. Refer to Chapter 6, Section 6.2.2, for a sample scenario where tracing is used for detailed analysis.

Message Content Not Available?

Note that the message content for a specific step is only available if log level **Trace** was defined for this message processing.

Details Available Depend on the Defined Log Level

Depending on the log level set for the iFlow, different details are available in the MPL:

- **None**
  The MPL isn't available at all.
- **Info**
  For successfully processed messages with log level **Info**, no visual representation of the message processing is available. If the message processing ended with the status **Failed**, the traversal path is available in the model combined with the configuration of the iFlow steps. The final processing steps before the error occurred are listed.

- **Debug**
  The traversal path is available in the model. In addition, all processing steps are listed, and the details and configurations of the processing steps are shown with the respective data.
- **Trace**
  The traversal path is available in the model. In addition, all processing steps are listed, and the details and configurations of the processing steps are shown with the respective data. In addition, the headers, exchange properties, and payload at each execution step are available.

In addition to the graphical representation of the MPL, a textual representation is available that contains details about all steps executed during the processing of the message in one single file. You can click the **Open Text View** link in the message processing monitor (shown earlier in Figure 7.6) to open the textual log view.

As shown in Figure 7.18, the main attributes of the message processing are shown, such as the start and stop times, overall status, and message guide. If log level **Info** was set for this message processing, no additional details are shown, and the individual steps and adapters aren't logged.

If an error occurs when processing the message, a more detailed log is available for the last steps before the error occurred, shown in Figure 7.19, even for log level **Info**. This log provides integration developers enough information to easily spot problems or errors at hand. Aside from exploring the contents of the log, you can also download the log by clicking the **Download** button in the top-right corner of the page.

Figure 7.18 Log of a Completed Message

Artifact Name: Splitter_Gather Status: Retry Processing Time: 17 h 30 min
Last Updated at: Mar 30, 2020, 09:06:23 Log Level: Info

Log ODataV2_Adapter_Request_Headers ODataV2_Adapter_Request_Headers ODataV2_Adapter >

Download

```
com.sap.gateway.core.ip.component.odata.exception.OsciException: HTTP Request failed with
 error : services.odata.org2, cause: java.net.UnknownHostException: services.odata.org2

The message processing log is truncated. Only the first and the last 46 processing runs o
f this message are shown. Others are omitted.

Message Processing Log (last processing run):
  StartTime            = Mon Mar 30 07:06:23.633 UTC 2020
  StopTime             = Mon Mar 30 07:06:23.645 UTC 2020
  OverallStatus        = RETRY
  MessageGuid          = AF6ApCEjm6KAFhGZqwGK1wQHgeKV
  ChildCount           = 0
  ChildrenCounter      = 1
  ContextName          = Splitter_Gather
  CorrelationId        = AF6ApCFKDj4aA0Ld-9dTF6j3nBjo
  IntermediateError    = false
  Node                 = vsa7399851
  OriginComponentName = CPI_m6201
  PreviousComponentName= CPI_m6201
  ProcessId            = 638d4b6766a0e418d46a84949c893932dad24198
  TransactionId        = 99f3cd5b234e4745b98dc68d6478062a

Segment:
   Exchange ID-
vsa7399851-41341-1585516626766-9-627 created in Endpoint[jms://Inbound_Queue?cacheLevelNa
me=CACHE_CONNECTION&chunkReceiveTimeout=10000&chunking=true&concurrentConsumers=1&
connectionFactory=%23connectionFactory&defaultTaskExecutorType=ThreadPool&
exceptionListener=%23jms.exception.listener.MessageFlow_103&maxConcurrentConsumers=1&
maxMessagesPerTask=10&receiveTimeout=5000&transacted=true&
transactionManager=%23jmsTransactionManager]:
      StartTime             = Mon Mar 30 07:06:23.634 UTC 2020
      StopTime              = Mon Mar 30 07:06:23.645 UTC 2020
      Status                = RETRY_TRIGGERED
      ChildCount            = 1
      ModelStepId           = MessageFlow_103
```

Figure 7.19 Log of a Message in Error Status

Note that, for log level **Debug**, all steps and adapters are always logged, independent of whether the message was processed successfully or ended with an error.

As mentioned earlier, the log's details are often referred to as the *MPL*. The textual MPL represents a well-structured tree of log information. The MPL structure consists of two main components: the top and bottom sections. The top section contains the properties and metadata of the message as a whole, similar to a header section. This section is available with log level **Info**. The bottom section contains one or more branches with entries for each step of a particular iFlow. This section is only available with log level **Debug** or if an error occurred during message processing.

The MPL structure always includes a predetermined set of attributes, which are listed in Table 7.7 and Table 7.8. Becoming familiar with these attributes will help you better understand the information captured in the logs and therefore improve your ability to troubleshoot issues. Note that not all properties listed in these tables are present in every MPL. Depending on the status of a message, only a few properties might be shown in the MPL. For instance, the `Error` attribute is only present if a message is in the **Failed** status, as shown in Figure 7.19.

Property	Description
Error	Specifies the error of a particular step in the iFlow. Note that this attribute is displayed at the top of the log in red and is only available in the MPL of messages that are in a failed state.
StartTime	The time that message processing started.
StopTime	The time that message processing ended.
OverallStatus	The status of the message processing, as discussed earlier in this section in Table 7.4.
ChildCount	The serial number of the current processing step. For the overall overview at the top of the MPL, this number is always 0.
ChildrenCounter	The total number of message processing steps executed.
ContextName	The name of the iFlow.
CorrelationId	The ID that identifies correlated messages. Messages can be correlated, for example, when different iFlows on the same tenant communicate with each other, for example, using JMS queues. A correlation ID is a Base64-encoded ID that is generated in this case by the first integration process and stored in the message header. As part of the message header, the CorrelationId is then propagated across all related iFlows.
CustomHeaderProperties	Shown if you specify your own headers via the script API in a Script step.
IntermediateError	If, during message processing, an error occurred, or message processing needed more than one minute, the value of this property is set to true.
LastErrorModelStepId	ID of the step that caused the error. Note that this attribute is only available in the MPL of messages that are in a failed state.
MessageGuid	A key that identifies the message uniquely in the database.
Node	The host name of the runtime node that processed the message.
Process ID	The ID of the runtime process that executed the message. This information is useful to identify the system log file in which details of the message processing are logged.

Table 7.7 Properties Contained in the MPL Header

Property	Description
ReceiverId	The name of the receiver as configured in the iFlow using the header SAP_Receiver, for example, in a content modifier or script step.
SenderId	Specifies the name of the sender as configured in the iFlow using the header SAP_Sender, for example, in a Content Modifier or Script step.
Id	Displayed in the MPL header if the ID has been defined using the header SAP_ApplicationID in the iFlow, for example, in a Content Modifier or Script step.
MessageType	Displayed in the MPL header if the message type has been defined using the header SAP_MessageType in the iFlow, for example, in a Content Modifier or Script step.

Table 7.7 Properties Contained in the MPL Header (Cont.)

Property	Description
Segment	Indicates that the following steps have been processed in the same processing segment. If a split or multicast step is used, the steps belonging to one subroute are grouped together within one segment.
StartTime	The time that each step of the iFlow started.
StopTime	The time that each step of the iFlow stopped.
Status	The status of each step of the iFlow.
ChildCount	The serial number of the current processing step.
ModelStepId	The ID of a particular step in the iFlow. This ID is used to specify the relation between a modeled step (in the iFlow) and an MPL entry. iFlow model steps are fragmented in the Apache Camel runtime environment into several processing steps.
StepID	The ID of a particular step in the log.

Table 7.8 Properties Contained in the MPL for Each Step

Attachments

In addition to viewing the log, you can also access MPL attachments written during message processing. As shown earlier in Figure 7.6, under the **Attachments** tab, all MPL attachments are listed in a table showing the name of the MPL attachment, the type, the size, and when the attachment was last modified. The name of the attachment is a link. When you click this link, the attachment will open in a new window. As shown in Figure 7.20, for example, the MPL attachment called **My MPL Attachment** is open.

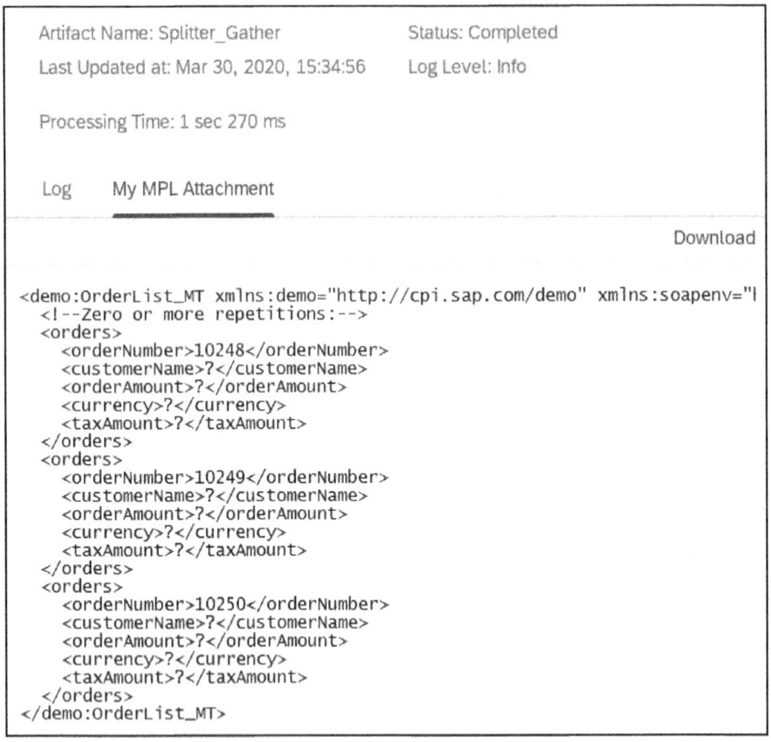

Artifact Name: Splitter_Gather   Status: Completed

Last Updated at: Mar 30, 2020, 15:34:56   Log Level: Info

Processing Time: 1 sec 270 ms

Log   My MPL Attachment

Download


```
<demo:OrderList_MT xmlns:demo="http://cpi.sap.com/demo" xmlns:soapenv="
  <!--Zero or more repetitions:-->
  <orders>
    <orderNumber>10248</orderNumber>
    <customerName>?</customerName>
    <orderAmount>?</orderAmount>
    <currency>?</currency>
    <taxAmount>?</taxAmount>
  </orders>
  <orders>
    <orderNumber>10249</orderNumber>
    <customerName>?</customerName>
    <orderAmount>?</orderAmount>
    <currency>?</currency>
    <taxAmount>?</taxAmount>
  </orders>
  <orders>
    <orderNumber>10250</orderNumber>
    <customerName>?</customerName>
    <orderAmount>?</orderAmount>
    <currency>?</currency>
    <taxAmount>?</taxAmount>
  </orders>
</demo:OrderList_MT>
```


Figure 7.20 Accessing the MPL Attachment

MPL attachments are written by some adapters, including the AS2 adapter. However, you can also create MPL attachments yourself in a Script step. Refer to Chapter 10, Section 10.4, for more details about using Java APIs in scripts.

Using MPL Attachments

MPL attachments can be created in the Script step using the `MessageLog` API. You should use this option with care and avoid writing the whole payload into an MPL attachment, which can cause out-of-memory errors in the worker node and ultimately lead to the whole scenario becoming unavailable.

Important recommendations for using MPL attachments can be found in the "Avoid Storing Payloads in the Message Processing Log, Especially in Productive Integration Flows" blog at *http://s-prs.co/507765*.

Now that you know how to monitor messages through Cloud Integration's monitoring capabilities, let's explore how you can manage and customize the tiles displayed on your monitoring dashboard.

Artifact Details

The **Artifact Details** section provides detailed information about the integration artifact to which the respective MPL belongs. It contains a set of links along with basic properties of the artifact, as shown in Figure 7.21.

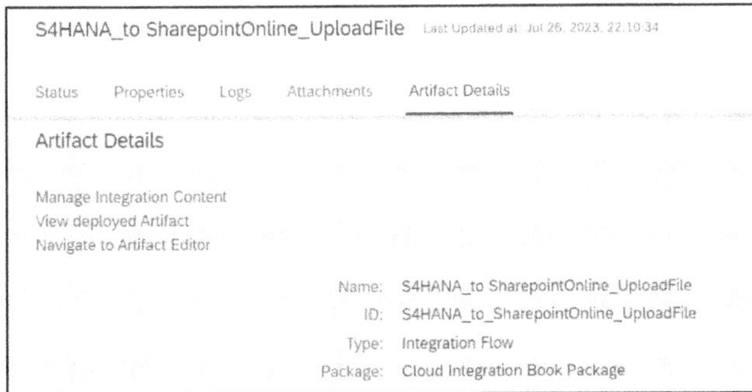

Figure 7.21 Artifact Details Section

Table 7.9 describes the quick links shown in the top part of the **Artifacts Details** section.

Link	Description
Manage Integration Content	Navigates to the integration artifact in the **Manage Integration Content** view discussed in Section 7.2.1.
View deployed Artifact	Opens a read-only view of the deployed integration artifact. Note that you can't change the configuration and redeploy the iFlow from this view. The view is meant for monitoring only.
Navigate to Artifact Editor	Navigates to the integration artifact editor in the design-time view, so you can carry out the edit, configure, and deploy or delete functions.

Table 7.9 List of Navigation Links in the Artifact Details Section

The bottom half of the **Artifact Details** section provides basic metadata information about the artifact, as described in Table 7.10.

Attribute	Description
Name	Name of the integration artifact
ID	The technical artifact ID of the integration artifact
Type	Type of artifact, which can be **Integration Flow**, **OData API**, **REST API**, or **SOAP API**
Package	Name of the package where the artifact is created

Table 7.10 List of Attributes in the Artifact Details Section

7.2.4 Managing Tiles

As mentioned earlier, a tile in the **Monitor** page is a block in a page that filters messages or artifacts corresponding to a particular status. Each tile can be clicked to display a list of messages or artifacts matching that status. The message and artifact tiles are presented and grouped by statuses. For messages, the following tiles are available by default:

- **All Messages**
- **Failed Messages**
- **Retry Messages**
- **Completed Messages**

Note

By default, all tiles in the **Monitor Message Processing** section use a one-hour period, which means, for instance, that the **Failed Messages** tile only shows failed messages of the past hour. However, you can choose another value from the **Time** dropdown menu, as shown in Figure 7.22.

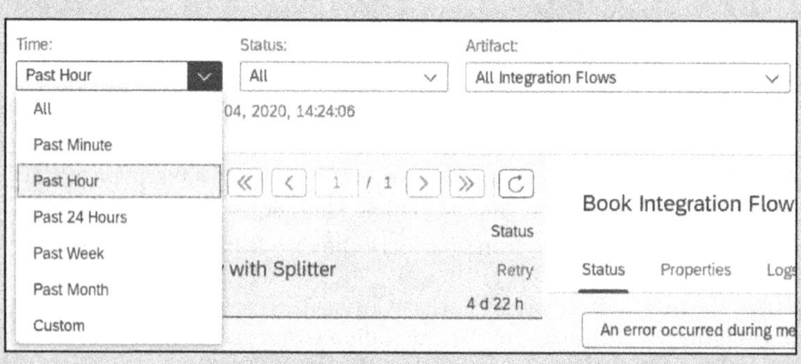

Figure 7.22 Changing Time Frame Values

You may think of these tiles as preconfigured message or artifact filters, or as shortcuts to quickly access the messages or artifacts that you're looking for. Furthermore, you can also remove or move the default tiles to suit your needs. To move a tile, follow these steps:

1. Mouse over the tile to be moved.
2. Drag and drop the tile to the desired location.

To completely delete or remove an existing tile, follow these steps:

1. Right-click the concerned tile.
2. From the resulting context menu, select the **Delete** option, as shown in Figure 7.23.

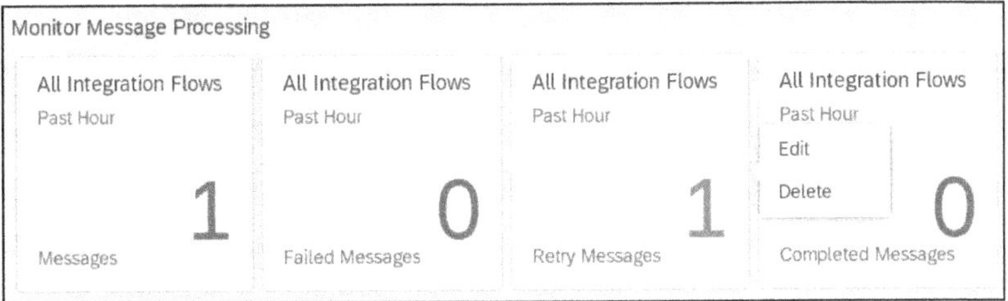

Figure 7.23 Editing and Managing Monitor Message Processing Tiles

If you often apply a particular filter to messages or artifacts, you can also create a new tile for it. For the sake of illustration, let's say you want a tile to view all escalated messages. Follow these steps:

1. Click on the empty tile, with the **+** sign, on the right side of the screen.
2. The new **Tile Settings** popup screen appears, where you can specify the filtering criteria to be applied to previous runtime messages. Figure 7.24 shows how to select the **Escalated** option from the **Status** dropdown menu.

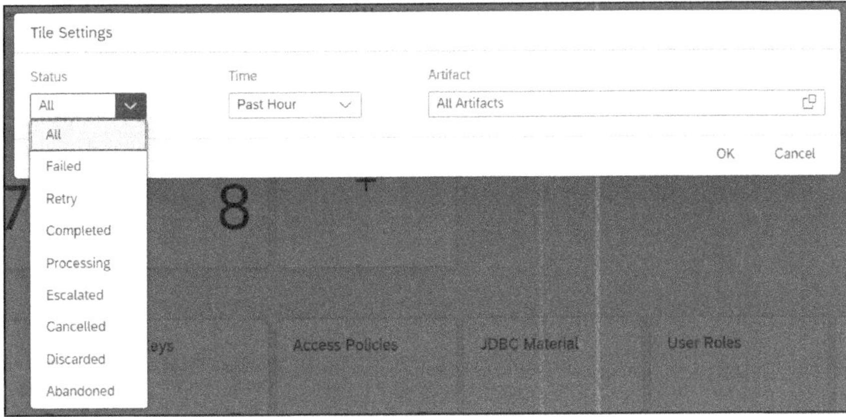

Figure 7.24 Creating a New Message Monitoring Tile

In the **Tile Settings** popup screen for messages, the following filtering options are available:

- **Status**
  Different message statuses can be selected, such as **Failed**, **Retry**, **Completed**, and so on.
- **Time**
  Different filtering time frames are available for selection, including **Past Minute**, **Past Hour**, **Past 24 Hours**, **Past Week**, and so on.
- **Artifact**
  All available iFlows and OData services on the target runtime system and tenant are

listed. By selecting a particular iFlow or OData service on your tile settings, you can further restrict the filtering of messages to entries of the selected iFlow or OData service, as shown in Figure 7.25.

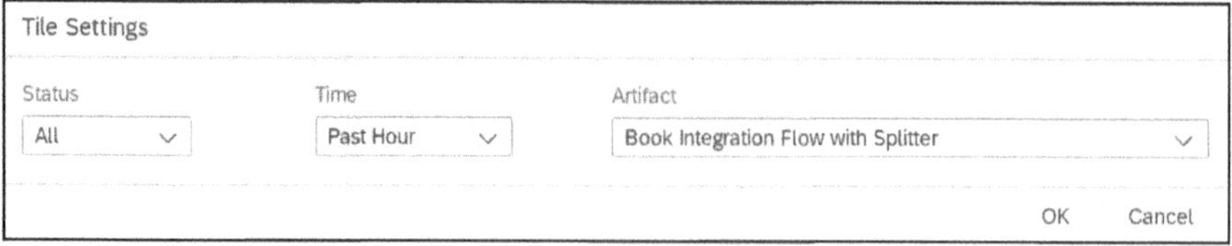

Figure 7.25 Selecting a Specific iFlow in the Tile Settings

As an administrator of your Cloud Integration tenant, you must gain a good understanding of what each message status in the monitor means. Currently, eight statuses are available, as listed in Table 7.11.

Status	Description
Failed	The message hasn't been delivered to the receiver; message processing failed and ended in a dead end. Message processing has ultimately failed, and no more retries are possible.
Escalated	The message runs into an escalation end event as configured in the iFlow. Several escalation categories are available for configuration, for example, `Receiver not reachable`, `Receiver not found`, `Not authorized to invoke the receiver`, and so on. An error is raised back to the sender.
Retry	The message processing went into **Error** status, and an automatic retry was triggered.
Processing	The message is currently being processed.
Completed	The message has been successfully delivered to the receiver.
Canceled	The message was deleted from the temporary storage (message queue or data store).
Discarded	When your Cloud Integration has multiple worker nodes and an iFlow is set up with scheduled trigger such as timer, then the message processing happens only on one node. This results in MPL being shown only one worker node, and all other message processing starts are shown with status **Discarded**.
Abandoned	Thes MPL wasn't updated for a long time due to an interruption in message processing. This status isn't final and can be reset if the scenario is set to **Retry**.

Table 7.11 Possible Message Statuses in the Message Monitor

Now that you understand how to monitor integration artifacts and messages processed by the artifacts, we'll explore how to maintain the security artifacts for your integration content.

7.3 Managing Security

When dealing with integration scenarios, security is an important topic. To consume other services, you'll most likely need to use security objects such as certificates, user names, passwords, and more. The types of objects needed to secure your interfaces are called *security artifacts*. Table 7.12 presents a complete list of security artifacts available in Cloud Integration.

Note

In this section, we'll mostly focus on managing these artifacts. For more information on the security concepts behind these artifacts, see Chapter 10.

Type	Description
Secure Shell (SSH) known hosts	Contains the trusted hosts, which must be specified when the tenant is connected with a remote component using SeSSH.
OAuth2 credentials	Contains the client ID and client secret of the client you're connecting to using Open Authentication (OAuth) 2.0, together with additional data required to specify this authentication method, for example, the URL of the authorization server.
Pretty Good Privacy (PGP) public keyring	Contains the public keys required when the exchanged messages are digitally signed or encrypted using Open Pretty Good Privacy (Open PGP). See Chapter 10, Section 10.4.
PGP secret keyring	Contains the private keys required when the exchanged messages are digitally signed or encrypted using Open PGP. See Chapter 10, Section 10.4.
Secure parameters	Contains credentials to be used together with specific authentication options, such as OAuth. To find out how to use such an artifact when setting up a scenario with OAuth authentication, see Chapter 10, Section 10.4.5.
User credentials	Contains user name and password information for basic authentication. We introduced this artifact type already with the first scenario described in this book (Chapter 2, Section 2.3.4).

Table 7.12 Integration Artifact Types Related to Secure Messaging

Type	Description
Keystore artifacts	In the keystore, the keys and certificates required to enable a secure connection of the tenant with other components based on public key certificates (type X.509) are maintained. See also Chapter 10, Section 10.5, for more details.
Certificate-to-user mapping	Client certificates mapped to users for role-based authorization. In the SAP BTP, Neo environment, client certificates for inbound authentication must be maintained on this monitor. See also Chapter 10, Section 10.4.4, for more details.
User roles	User roles for calling iFlows are configured in this monitor. See Chapter 10, Section 10.3.3, to learn how to configure user roles when setting up a secure connection.
Access policies	To restrict access to certain integration packages in the monitoring, access policies can be defined. See Chapter 10, Section 10.3.4, for more details about this option.
Java Database Connectivity (JDBC) data sources	Configure JDBC data sources to connect to a database. These data sources can then be used with the JDBC adapter. See Chapter 6, Section 6.5, for a sample scenario using JDBC data sources.

Table 7.12 Integration Artifact Types Related to Secure Messaging (Cont.)

Security-related artifacts can be maintained in the monitoring dashboard in the **Manage Security** section. As shown in Figure 7.26, multiple tiles are available in this section for the various security artifacts such as **Keystore** for certificates and key pairs, **User Roles**, **Security Material** for credentials and secure parameters, and **Access Policies**.

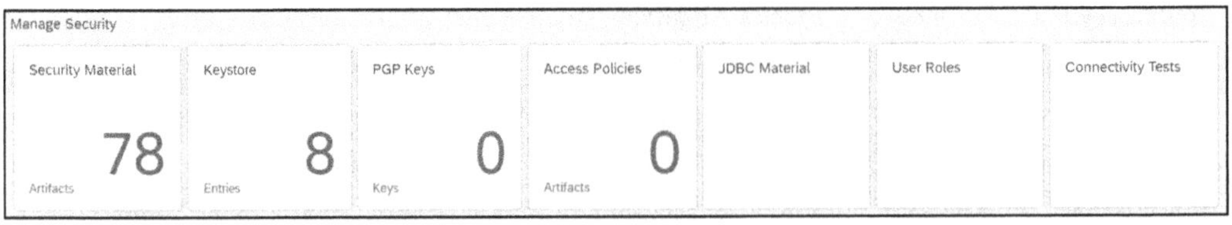

Figure 7.26 Manage Security Section in the Monitoring Dashboard in the SAP BTP, Cloud Foundry Environment

As shown in Figure 7.27, in the SAP BTP, Neo environment, the **User Roles** tile isn't available because user role management is performed in the SAP BTP configuration for that specific environment. However, notice an additional tile exists in the SAP BTP, Neo environment that isn't available in the SAP BTP, Cloud Foundry environment: **Certificate-to-User Mappings**. We'll touch upon more environment-related differences when we discuss the various monitors available.

Figure 7.27 Manage Security Section in the Monitoring Dashboard in the SAP BTP, Neo Environment

In addition to the security-related tiles, the **Connectivity Tests** tile is available in both environments. With this tile, you can execute several outbound connectivity tests to test whether the security material is maintained correctly and the connection can be executed successfully. Refer to Chapter 2, Section 2.3.6, for a sample scenario where the **Connectivity Tests** tile is used to retrieve the server certificate of a mail server.

Let's explore the different tiles in more detail. We'll start with the **Security Material** tile.

7.3.1 Maintaining Security Material

Cloud Integration provides the **Security Material** tile, shown earlier in Figure 7.26, to enable users to manage security material on the tenant. After clicking on the link, you'll be redirected to a page similar to Figure 7.28. This table displays a list of the different security materials that have been deployed on the tenant and shows details about these security artifacts in different columns. Table 7.13 provides descriptions of the columns.

If you're not satisfied with the sorting or filtering of the table shown in Figure 7.28, you can change and customize it using the **Table Settings** icon at the top-right corner.

Overview / Manage Security Material

Security Material (79) | Filter by Name or Deployed By | Create | Upload

Name	Type	Status	Deployed By	Deployed On
OAuth_SharepointOnline	OAuth2 Authorization Code (Microsoft 365)	Unauthorized	swati@rojoconsultancy.com	Jul 27, 2023, 15:14:30
Snow_AB	User Credentials	Deployed	[illegible]@rojoconsultancy.com	Jul 19, 2023, 16:07:01
Solace_Credential	User Credentials	Deployed	[illegible]@rojoconsultancy.com	Jun 26, 2023, 13:41:51

Figure 7.28 Manage Security Material

Column Name	Description
Name	Contains the name of the security artifact.

Table 7.13 Attributes of a Security Material

Column Name	Description
Type	Specifies the type of security artifact with the following values: ▪ **User Credentials**: Used for storing user credentials for basic authentication. ▪ **OAuth2 Client Credentials**: Stores security information related to OAuth2 Client Credential grant type. ▪ **OAuth2 SAML Bearer Assertion**: Stores security information related to OAuth2 SAML Bearer Assertion type. ▪ **OAuth2 Authorization Code**: Stores security information related to OAuth2 Authorization Code grant type. ▪ **Secure Parameter**: Used for storing secret keys, and so on. ▪ **SSH known hosts:** Contains the public keys of the connected Secure Shell File Transfer Protocol (SFTP) servers.
Status	Specifies the states of the deployed artifact on the Cloud Integration server with the following values: ▪ **Error**: Security artifact has an error. ▪ **Deployed**: Security artifact is successfully deployed on the worker node. ▪ **Unauthorized**: Applicable for OAuth2 Authorization Code security artifact in case the authorization is unsuccessful. ▪ **Stored**: Security artifact is stored but not yet deployed on the worker node.
Deployed By	The name of the user who performed the deployment.
Deployed On	The date and time when the deployment was performed.

Table 7.13 Attributes of a Security Material (Cont.)

OAuth 2.0 Authorization Framework

The OAuth framework defines the standard for providing third-party applications with limited access to an owner's resources hosted on servers without sharing credentials. The OAuth 2.0 framework supports multiple grant types such as client credentials and authorization code grant flows.

For detailed information on the OAuth 2.0 framework, go to *http://s-prs.co/v576030*.

Let's now explore how you can add or deploy a new security artifact to your tenant. Follow these steps:

1. In the top-right corner of the screen, click the **Create** button, as shown in Figure 7.29.
2. Select the desired type of artifact (e.g., **User Credentials**), and fill in the requested details, as shown in Figure 7.30.

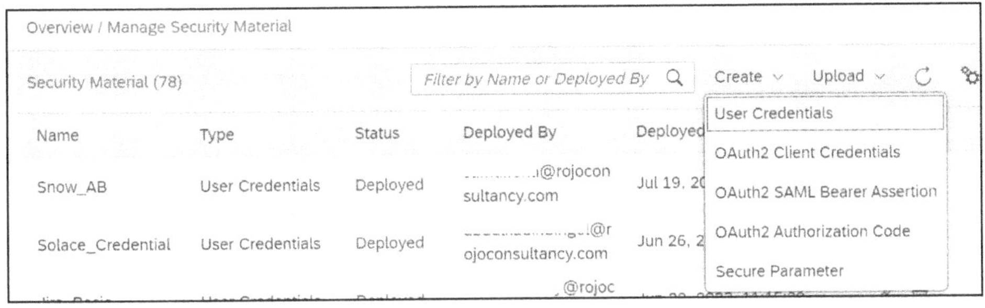

Figure 7.29 Adding a New Security Artifact

Create User Credentials

Name:* SuccessfactorsCredentials
Description: Sample Credentials
Type:* SuccessFactors
User:* MyUser
Password: •••••••
Repeat Password: •••••••
Company ID:* 1333456

Deploy Cancel

Figure 7.30 Sample Security Credentials for an SAP SuccessFactors Scenario

3. If the desired artifact is a credential to be used for an SAP SuccessFactors–related integration scenario, from the **Type** dropdown list, select **SuccessFactors**, and fill in the **Company ID** field. The **Company ID** field represents the client instance used to connect to the SAP SuccessFactors system.
4. Click **Deploy** at the bottom of the **Create User Credentials** dialog box. The new security artifact is deployed and added to the list.

Credential artifacts can be changed and edited by performing the following steps:

1. Select a credential entry from the table of security artifacts and click on the **Edit** button as shown in Figure 7.31.

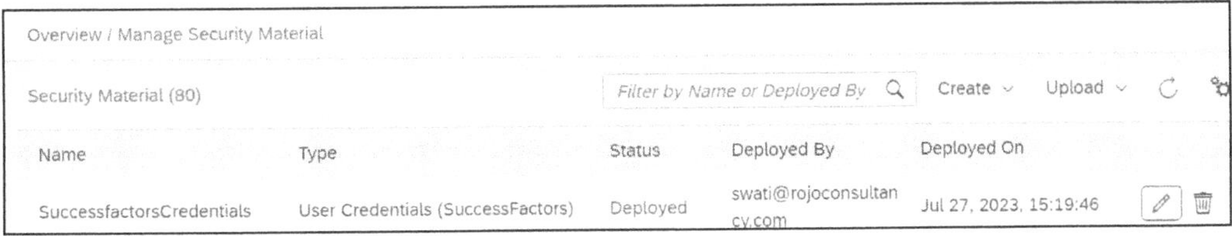

Figure 7.31 Selecting a Credential Artifact for Editing

2. Click icon to change the properties of the credential artifact. Figure 7.32 shows an example of a user credential being edited. Note that the **Password** and **Repeat Password** text boxes clear once you go into edit mode.

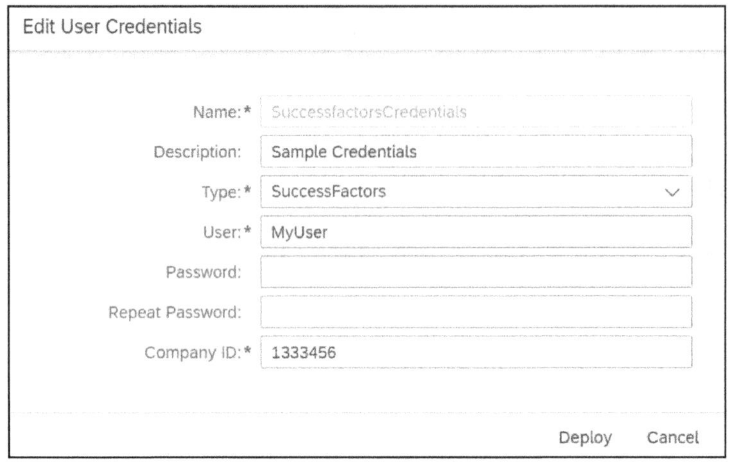

Figure 7.32 Updating Security Material of Type User Credential

SSH known hosts can be uploaded by clicking on the **Upload** menu and downloaded by clicking the icon, as shown in Figure 7.33. Furthermore, all artifact types can be removed from the tenant by clicking the icon.

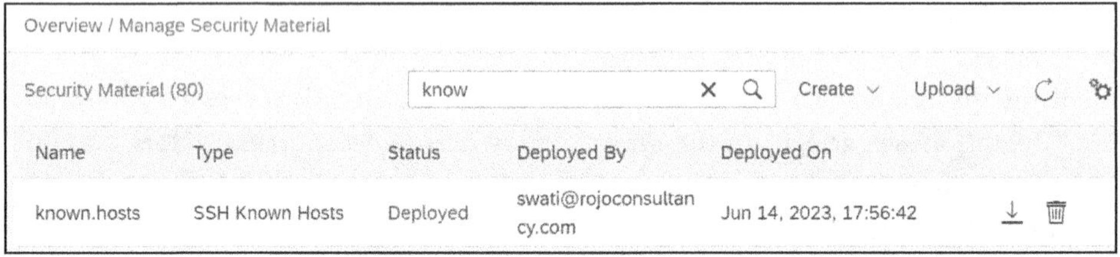

Figure 7.33 Selecting a Known Hosts File for Downloading

In case of an OAuth 2 authorization code, the artifact can be authorized by clicking on the ooo icon. Let's now discuss how to manage certificates and key pairs in the keystore monitor.

7.3.2 Managing the Keystore

Using the second tile in the **Manage Security** section—**Keystore**—you can maintain the certificates and private key pairs deployed on the tenant.

Preinstalled Artifacts in the Keystore

When provisioning a new tenant, SAP preinstalls the following artifacts in the keystore:

- One key pair with the alias `sap_cloudintegrationcertificate`. Note that, for trial account tenants in the SAP BTP, Cloud Foundry environment, no key pair is preinstalled.
- Some SAP-owned root certificates, which enable communication with other SAP cloud systems, such as SAP Ariba and SAP Customer Relationship Management (SAP CRM).

These certificates and key pairs can be used to set up secure HTTP connections to backend systems using client certificates; for scenarios using message-level security; to sign or decrypt messages using Public-Key Cryptography Standard (PKCS#7), XML, or simple signer; or in Web Services Security (WS-Security).

More details about the various security features available in Cloud Integration are provided in Chapter 10.

To open the keystore monitor, select the **Keystore** tile. As shown in Figure 7.34, four tabs are available, and the most important tab—the **Current** tab—is opened when selecting the **Keystore** tile. This tab shows all the certificates and key pairs currently deployed on the tenant in a table. Expired artifacts are highlighted in red for your attention because these artifacts usually need to be updated to for the scenario to be executed successfully.

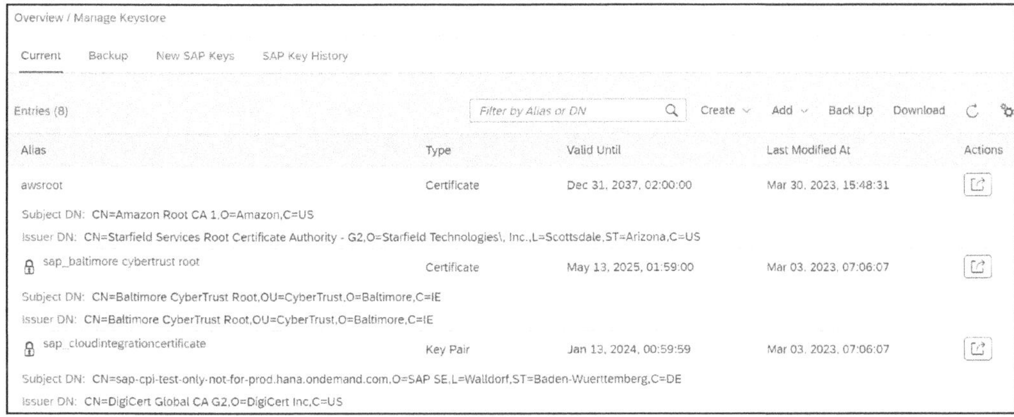

Figure 7.34 Keystore Monitor

The table on the screen provides the header details of the certificates and key pairs in different columns. Table 7.14 describes the columns.

Column Name	Description
Alias	Contains the alias name of the certificate or key pair. The alias name is a link that displays details about the certificate or key pair when clicked, as shown in Figure 7.35. SAP-owned artifacts are indicated by the **Lock** icon 🔒. Note that the prefix sap_ is reserved for SAP-owned key pairs and certificates.
Subject DN	The unique identifier for the object being secured with information about the object being certified, including common name, organization, organization unit, and country codes, among others.
Issuer DN	The name of the party that signed the certificate.
Type	The type of the keystore artifact. The following values are available: ▪ **Certificate** ▪ **Key Pair** For more details, see Chapter 10, Section 10.5.2.
Valid Until	Validity of the certificate or key pair. If the artifact is already expired, the validity timestamp is shown in red.
Last Modified At	The date and time when the artifact was changed.
Actions	The actions available differ depending on the artifact and also on the owner of the artifact: ▪ For **Certificates: Delete, Download, Rename**, and **Update** ▪ For **Key Pairs: Delete, Download Certificate, Download Certificate Chain, Download Root Certificate, Download Signing Request, Download Public OpenSSH Key, Rename, Update, Update SSH Key**, and **Update Signing Response** ▪ For **SAP-owned certificates: Download** ▪ For **SAP-owned Key Pairs: Download Certificate, Download Certificate Chain, Download Root Certificate**, and **Download Public OpenSSH Key** Detailed descriptions about these actions can be found in the "Cloud Integration - Keystore Monitor Now Available for Tenant Administrator" blog at *http://s-prs.co/507766*.

Table 7.14 Attributes of Keystore Artifacts

At the top of the table, actions that relate to the whole keystore are available. See Table 7.15 for details about these actions.

Action	Description
Filter	Filter for specific artifacts. The filter is executed for the **Alias**, the **Subject DN**, and the **Issuer DN** fields.
Create	Create key pairs or SSH keys directly in the keystore. Note that you can't create artifacts with the prefix sap_ because this prefix is reserved for SAP-owned keys.
Add	Add entries from keystore files, individual certificates, key pairs, RSA Key, keystore and SSH keys. Note that you can't add artifacts with the prefix sap_ because this prefix is reserved for SAP-owned key pairs and certificates.
Back Up	Back up all certificate and key pairs owned by the tenant administrator. Backups for SAP-owned artifacts are executed by SAP and aren't visible in the keystore monitor.
Download	Download the public content of the keystore. The downloaded keystore file is called *PublicContentKeystore.jks* and is saved without a password. This file can be opened and maintained by any external keystore editor. Note that private key pairs aren't downloaded; for security reasons, private keys never leave the tenant.
Reload icon	Reload the content of the page.
Settings icon	Define table-specific settings, such as sorting and filtering by owner and artifact type.

Table 7.15 Actions for Keystore

As shown in Figure 7.34, the alias name of the certificate or key pair is a link. When you click the link, the details about the selected entry are provided in a new window. Figure 7.35 shows, for example, details of a key pair.

On the left side of the screen, the *certificate chain*, also known as the *chain of trust*, is shown as a tree with the key pair at the bottom and one or more certificates at the top. For a signed key pair, you usually have the key pair at the bottom, one or more intermediate certificates, and then the root certificate at the top, which identifies the root certificate authority (CA). You can click each entry in the tree to see the details of all involved certificates.

On the right side of the screen, the details of the certificate or key pair are provided, such as **Subject DN**, **Issuer DN**, **Key Type**, **Signature Algorithm**, and **Valid From/Valid Until** (see also Chapter 10, Section 10.5.2). The unique fingerprint of the artifact, also known as a *thumbprint*, is provided under the **Fingerprints** tab. The fingerprint is shown in hexadecimal format and is used to verify that the key wasn't subject to an injection attack by a hacker, for instance, during key exchange.

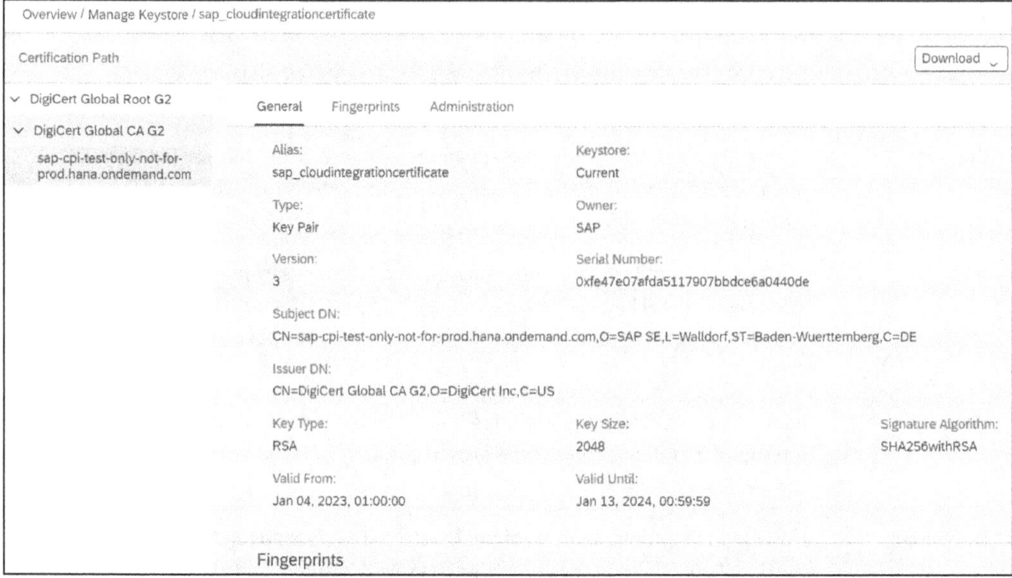

Figure 7.35 Details of a Keystore Artifact

The **Administration** tab shows the user who created and modified the artifact, as well as the time the artifact was created and changed.

> **Note**
>
> More details about security, especially about keystore artifacts, together with processes for how to handle security material, are provided in Chapter 10.

In the top-right corner of the screen, the same actions as in the table containing all certificates and key pairs are offered, such as **Delete**, **Update**, **Rename**, and **Download** if it's a non-SAP certificate.

Backup

For secure system management, you must be able to restore certificates and key pairs if problems arise. To support you in this task, Cloud Integration offers the **Backup** option in the keystore monitor. With this option, a backup can be created for all keystore artifacts owned by the tenant administrator. Note that the entries maintained by SAP aren't backed up.

> **No Backup for Single Certificates or Key Pairs**
>
> When creating a backup, *all* certificates and key pairs from the keystore are backed up; there is no option to back up individual artifacts of the keystore.

The backup functionality can be explored under the **Backup** tab in the keystore monitor. As shown in Figure 7.36, the table shown under the **Backup** tab contains all certificates and key pairs that have been backed up.

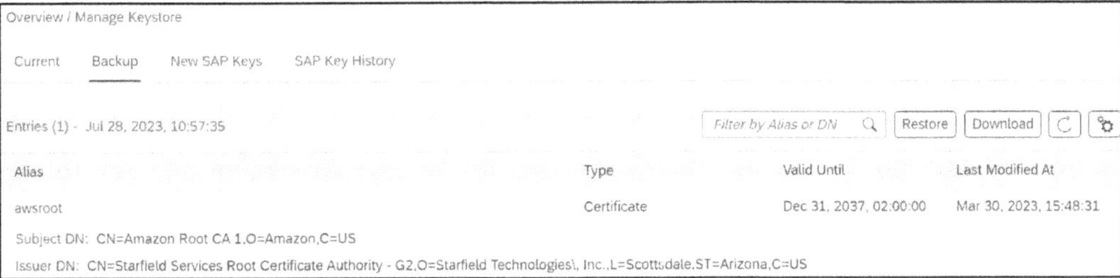

Figure 7.36 Backup Tab in Keystore Monitor

At the top of the table, the timestamp shows when the last backup wperformed. Note that only one backup is kept, which means the next backup will overwrite the backup created previously.

The **Backup** tab provides the same details for the artifacts in the backup as the **Current** tab does for currently active artifacts (as described earlier in Table 7.14), except that the **Actions** column isn't available under the **Backup** tab because backed-up artifacts can't be changed. Like it appears in the **Current** tab, the **Alias** name is a link that allows you to access details about the artifact in a new window. You can use this view to explore the content of the backup, but you can't modify artifacts in the backup.

The actions available in the **Backup** view are **Restore** and **Download**. Using **Restore**, the active keystore is overwritten by all the certificates and key pairs from the backup. This option helps you switch back to the old keystore, for example, if changes in the keystore caused communication errors in running integration scenarios.

Restore Overwrites Active Keystore with Backup

When using **Restore**, the whole keystore is replaced, meaning newly created artifacts in the active keystore that don't exist in the backup are removed. Only SAP-owned entries are kept; they aren't touched by the backup and restore operations.

We always recommend creating a backup before making any changes to keystore artifacts, for instance, renaming aliases or overwriting key pairs and certificates. Using the backup, you then have the option to switch back to the last keystore version that worked correctly.

SAP-Owned Keys

As mentioned earlier, you can't change SAP-owned key pairs and certificates, but you can use them in your integration scenarios. When such SAP-owned artifacts expire,

SAP is responsible for renewing them. The renewal process differs depending on the artifact type:

- For SAP-owned root certificates, the process is easy: SAP adds the new root certificate to the keystore, and the artifact is active immediately. You don't need to act at all for the update.
- If an SAP-owned key pair expires, the process is more complex because SAP can't just update the key pair, which would lead to errors in existing scenarios. If the Cloud Integration tenant gets a new key pair, all backend systems connected using this key pair must be updated as well.

To address the need to update the associated keys in the involved backends, the keystore monitor features the **New SAP keys** tab. As shown in Figure 7.37, the table under the **New SAP keys** tab contains the new key pairs uploaded by SAP. See Table 7.16 for a description of the columns used in this table.

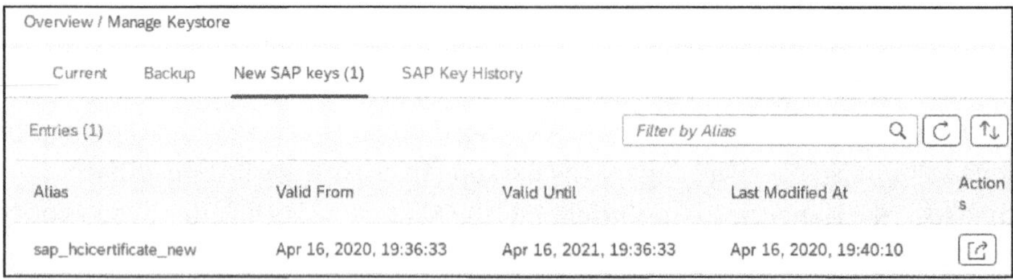

Figure 7.37 New SAP Keys Tab in the Keystore Monitor

Column Name	Description
Alias	Contains the alias name of the new SAP key pair. The alias name is a link, and clicking this link shows you details about the key pair.
Valid From	Start time the key pair is valid from.
Valid Until	Validity period of the new key pair.
Last Modified At	The date and time when the new key pair was changed.
Actions	Actions available for the new SAP key pair: ■ **Activate** ■ **Download Certificate** ■ **Download Certificate Chain** ■ **Download Root Certificate**

Table 7.16 Attributes of SAP Key Pairs under the New SAP Keys Tab

The new SAP key pair isn't active yet in the keystore but is available to trigger the update process on the customer side. The tenant administrator will need to coordinate the overall renewal process, as described in Chapter 10, Chapter 10.5.3, as well as in the "Cloud Integration - Activate SAP Keys in Keystore Monitor" blog at *http://s-prs.co/507767*.

During activation of the new SAP key pair, a backup of the old SAP key pair (with its respective alias) is stored under the **SAP Key History** tab so you can reverse the change, if necessary. The **SAP Key History** tab lists all SAP key pairs that were active in the tenant, as shown in Figure 7.38. Table 7.17 provides descriptions for the columns in the table.

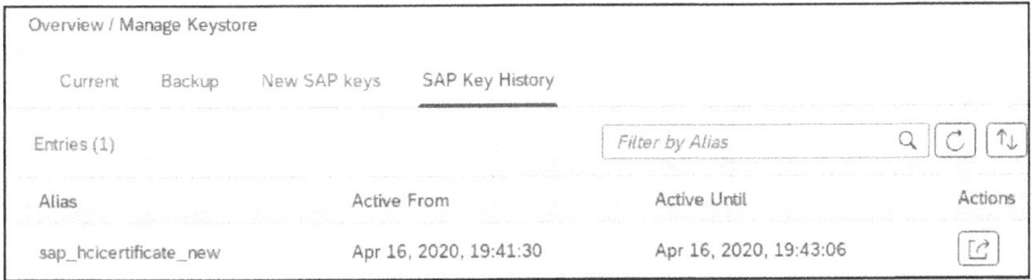

Figure 7.38 SAP Key History Tab in the Keystore Monitor

Column Name	Description
Alias	Contains the alias name of the backed-up SAP key pair. The alias name is a link, and clicking this link shows you details about the key pair.
Active From	Time the key pair was active from.
Active Until	Time the key pair was active until.
Actions	Actions available for the backed-up SAP key pair: ▪ **Add to New SAP keys** ▪ **Download Certificate** ▪ **Download Certificate Chain** ▪ **Download Root Certificate**

Table 7.17 Attributes of SAP Key Pairs in the SAP Key History Tab

The most important action under the **SAP Key History** tab is the **Add to New SAP keys** action. With this option, you can revert to the old SAP key pair. When you select this option, the SAP key pair is written back to **New SAP keys**, and you can reactivate the key pair from there. When reverting to an old SAP key pair, keep in mind that some backends may have already activated the new certificate. Therefore, use this option with care!

Automatic Activation of New SAP Key Pairs

If the new SAP key pair wasn't activated by the tenant administrator before the key pair expired, a job activates the new SAP key automatically on behalf of the tenant administrator. This automatic activation is designed to ensure that the tenant has a valid key pair in the keystore.

For more information on the lifecycle management of keys, read Chapter 10, Section 10.5.3.

Now that you know how to manage security material such as credentials, certificates, and key pairs, you'll need to understand how to assign roles to communication users so you can successfully configure inbound authentication.

7.3.3 Maintaining Pretty Good Privacy Keys

The PGP includes the following options:

- **PGP public keyring**
  Contains the public keys used for PGP encryption and signature verification.
- **PGP secret keyring**
  Contains the private and public keys used for PGP decryption and signing.

To deploy the secret key, go to the **Monitoring** page of the Web UI and, under **Manage Security**, select the **PGP Keys** tile. Select **Add • PGP Secret Keyring**, as shown in Figure 7.39.

Figure 7.39 Adding a PGP Secret Keyring

Browse for the file with the secret key (*tenantkey_secret.gpg*), enter the passphrase ("Abcd1234"), and click **Deploy**. The artifact is now shown on the **Manage Security Material** page, as shown in Figure 7.40.

The complete scenario of dealing with keyrings and a sample exercise will be covered further in Chapter 10.

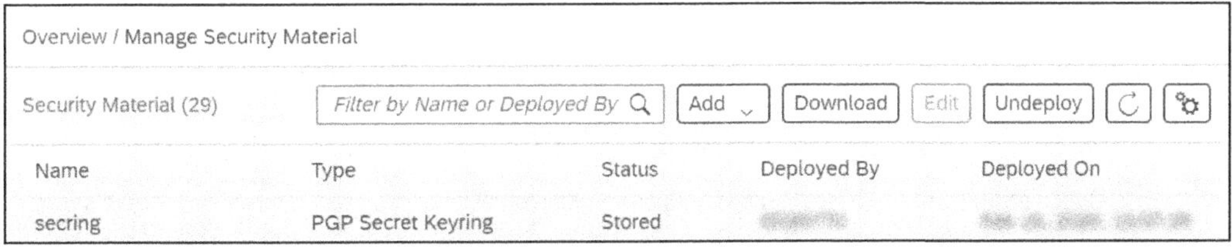

Figure 7.40 PGP Secret Keyring Artifact Added to the Security Material Deployed on the Tenant

7.3.4 Defining User Roles

We already touched upon configuring inbound authorization using different user roles in some scenarios throughout this book. You learned that you can, in addition to using the SAP-delivered role `ESBMessaging.send`, use your own role to secure the runtime of dedicated iFlows (for more technical details, refer to Chapter 10, Section 10.3.3). In the following pages, we'll explain how you can use the user roles monitor to maintain user roles.

> **User Roles Monitor: Not Available in the SAP BTP, Neo Environment**
>
> If you're already familiar with Cloud Integration in the SAP BTP, Neo environment, you know that user roles are assigned there using the SAP BTP user interfaces. However, in the SAP BTP, Cloud Foundry environment, user roles for inbound authorization are configured in a dedicated monitor in the Cloud Integration monitoring dashboard—the user roles monitor. Thus, if your tenant resides in the SAP BTP, Neo environment, this monitor doesn't appear on your monitoring dashboard.

To open the monitor for maintaining the user roles, from within the **Manage Security** section of the monitoring dashboard (shown earlier in Figure 7.26), select the **User Roles** tile. As shown in Figure 7.41, the monitor shows all user roles available in the system that are relevant for calling iFlows during runtime.

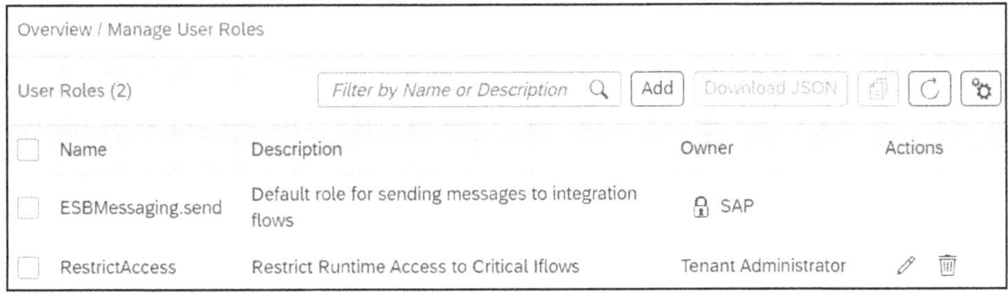

Figure 7.41 Manage User Roles

The attributes of the user roles are listed in Table 7.18.

Attribute Name	Description
Name	The user role name, which must be configured in the iFlow to restrict runtime access to this iFlow.
Description	The description of the user role.
Owner	The owner of the user role with the following values: ▪ **Tenant Administrator**: These user roles are maintained by the customer's tenant administrator. ▪ **SAP**: The user role `ESBMessaging.send` is the only user role that is delivered and maintained by SAP. This role can't be changed or deleted by you, the customer, as indicated by the **Lock** icon 🔒.
Actions	Actions available for customer-owned user roles: ▪ **Edit** ▪ **Delete**

Table 7.18 Attributes of User Roles

Using the actions buttons in the table, you can edit ✎ and delete 🗑 user roles owned by the tenant administrator. The SAP-owned user role `ESBMessaging.send` can neither be changed nor deleted.

At the top of the table, actions that relate to the whole table are available. Table 7.19 details these actions.

Action	Description
Filter	Filter for specific user roles. The filter is executed for the **Name** field and the **Description** field.
Add	Add a new user role.
Download JSON	Download the selected user roles in a JavaScript Object Notation (JSON) file that can be used for configuring the service instance in the SAP BTP cockpit. You can execute this action for one or more user roles, depending on which user roles are to be assigned to the service instance.
Copy icon	Copy the selected user roles in JSON format to the clipboard so that these roles can be used for configuring the service instance in the SAP BTP cockpit. This action can be used for one or more user roles, depending on which user roles are to be assigned to the service instance.
Reload icon	Reload the content of the page.
Settings icon	Define table-specific settings such as sorting and filtering by owner.

Table 7.19 Actions for User Roles

The user roles defined in the user roles monitor are required when creating the service instance for runtime access in the SAP BTP cockpit. For details on creating the service instance, refer to Chapter 2, Section 2.3.3, and to Chapter 10, Section 10.4.4. The user roles defined in the service instance can then be used to restrict runtime access to an iFlow in the Cloud Integration system and to specify the authorization for components connecting to Cloud Integration using the OData API (see Chapter 8). When configuring the inbound adapter of an iFlow, you'll define the user roles with which the iFlow can be called. The user roles can be used in scenarios with basic authentication or OAuth authentication as well as with client certificate-based authentication. If client certificates are used for inbound authentication, the relevant client certificate must be assigned to a service key for the service instance in which the user roles are defined. The usage and setup of user roles in scenarios using client certificate–based inbound authorization is described in detail in the "Cloud Integration on CF - How to Setup Secure HTTP Inbound Connection with Client Certificates" blog at *http://s-prs.co/507768*.

Now, you know how to configure user roles in the SAP BTP, Cloud Foundry environment and how to use these roles in basic authentication or client certificate–based authentication in the SAP BTP, Cloud Foundry environment. However, because you may still operate tenants in the SAP BTP, Neo environment, we'll also briefly cover the monitor for configuring client certificate–based inbound authentication in the SAP BTP, Neo environment next.

7.3.5 Maintaining Certificate-to-User Mappings

As mentioned in the previous section, access to iFlows during runtime can be restricted using different user roles. This feature is the same in the SAP BTP, Cloud Foundry environment and in the SAP BTP, Neo environment. As you learned in the previous section, in the SAP BTP, Cloud Foundry environment, when using client certificates for inbound authentication, the client certificate must be mapped to the service key in a service instance, and the service instance defines the user roles that are checked during runtime. In the SAP BTP, Neo environment, this mapping is completely different because of the underlying technical architecture. In the SAP BTP, Neo environment, the client certificate must be mapped to a user, which is then assigned a user role in the SAP BTP cockpit.

The usage and setup of certificate-to-user mappings in scenarios using client certificate–based authentication for inbound authorization are described in detail in the "Cloud Integration - How to Setup Secure HTTP Inbound Connection with Client Certificates" blog at *http://s-prs.co/507769*.

Now that you understand the idea behind using certificate-to-user mappings, let's look at how you can create them. From within the **Manage Security** section of the monitoring dashboard (shown earlier in Figure 7.27), one of the included tiles is labeled

Certificate-to-User Mappings. This tile provides access to all certificate-to-user mappings defined and deployed in your tenant. After clicking on this tile, you'll be redirected to a page with a list of available certificate-to-user mappings, as shown in Figure 7.42.

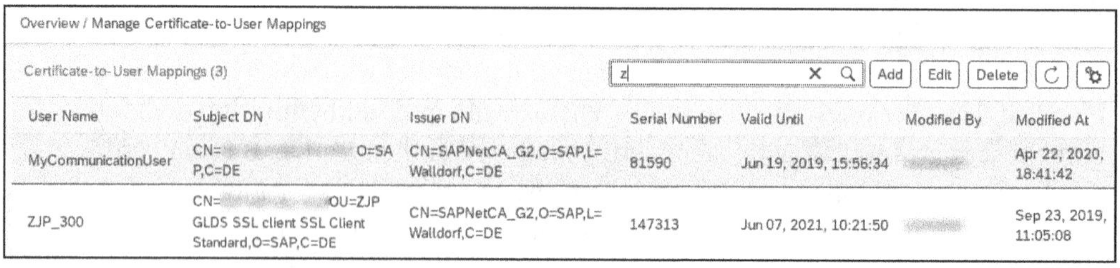

Overview / Manage Certificate-to-User Mappings

Certificate-to-User Mappings (3) z Add Edit Delete

User Name	Subject DN	Issuer DN	Serial Number	Valid Until	Modified By	Modified At
MyCommunicationUser	CN= O=SAP,C=DE	CN=SAPNetCA_G2,O=SAP,L=Walldorf,C=DE	81590	Jun 19, 2019, 15:56:34		Apr 22, 2020, 18:41:42
ZJP_300	CN= OU=ZJP GLDS SSL client SSL Client Standard,O=SAP,C=DE	CN=SAPNetCA_G2,O=SAP,L=Walldorf,C=DE	147313	Jun 07, 2021, 10:21:50		Sep 23, 2019, 11:05:08

Figure 7.42 Listing Certificate-to-User Mappings

A certificate-to-user mapping comprises several attributes, which are listed in Table 7.20.

Attribute Name	Description
User Name	The unique identifier of the user to which the certificate needs to be mapped
Subject DN	The unique identifier for the object being secured, with information about the object being certified, such as common name, organization, organization unit, and country codes, among others
Issuer DN	The name of the party that signed the certificate
Serial Number	A number that uniquely identifies the certificate, which is issued by the CA
Valid Until	The date and time the certificate expires
Modified By	The user that last changed the certificate-to-user mapping artifact
Modified At	The date and time the certificate-to-user mapping artifact was most recently changed

Table 7.20 Attributes of a Certificate-to-User Mapping

On the page shown in Figure 7.42, you can edit mappings by clicking the **Edit** button or delete them by clicking the **Delete** button. Furthermore, you can add new certificate-to-user mappings to your tenant by following these steps:

1. Click the **Add** button in the top-right corner of the screen (shown in Figure 7.42).
2. Specify the **User Name** to which the certificate must be mapped, as shown in Figure 7.43.

3. Click the **Browse** button and search for the certificate file (a **.cer* file) on your local file system. The details of the certificate, as listed in Table 7.20, are automatically populated based on the imported certificate.
4. Click **OK**.

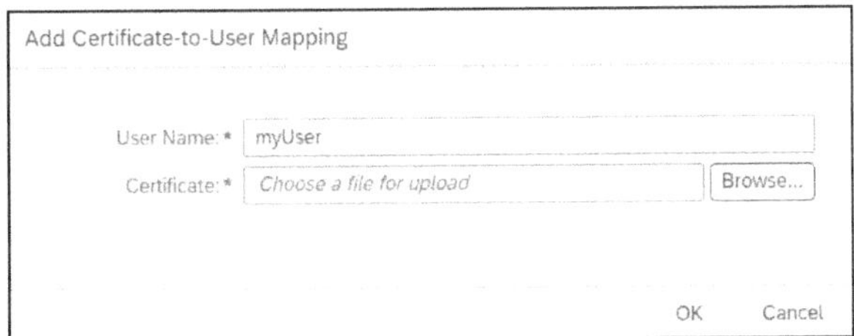

Figure 7.43 Adding a New Certificate-to-User Mapping

Now, you know how to handle users, keys, and certificates with Cloud Integration. With user roles, you learned how to restrict access to iFlows during runtime. In the next section, you'll learn how you can restrict access to the monitoring of specific scenarios.

7.3.6 Defining Access Policies

In previous sections, we worked you through the options for restricting runtime access to iFlows. However, in many scenarios, you may be required to restrict access to the monitoring of certain scenarios, in particular, to restrict access to business data collected during the execution of dedicated iFlows. In other words, using an access policy, you can protect a defined set of iFlows in such a way that only users with a certain role (associated with the access policy) can access the data processed by the specified set of iFlows. This feature is of special interest for scenarios that process confidential data, for example, when exchanging user data. Only a restricted user group should be allowed access to the monitoring of these scenarios. With the user roles predelivered by SAP for monitoring messages processed by iFlows, a user with the right role for message monitoring can monitor all messages processed by all iFlows. You can't restrict monitoring access to specific scenarios. To address this requirement, you can use custom user roles and define access policies for these user roles for dedicated sets of iFlows in the Cloud Integration dashboard. A more detailed description of this feature can be found in the security chapter of this book, specifically Chapter 10, Section 10.3.4.

Whereas custom roles are defined and assigned in the SAP BTP cockpit, access policies are maintained in the Cloud Integration monitoring dashboard. To manage access policies, from within the **Manage Security** section of the monitoring dashboard (shown earlier in Figure 7.26 and Figure 7.27), select the **Access Policies** tile. After clicking on this tile, the monitor for the access policies opens, as shown in Figure 7.44. This tile shows you all the access policies defined in the tenant.

The monitor is shown in a detail view. On the left side of the monitor, you'll find the list of defined access policies; on the right side, you'll get the details about the selected access policy. An access policy consists of the configuration artifacts for which the access should be restricted and a user role that can be assigned to the users that should be allowed to monitor the artifacts defined in the access policy.

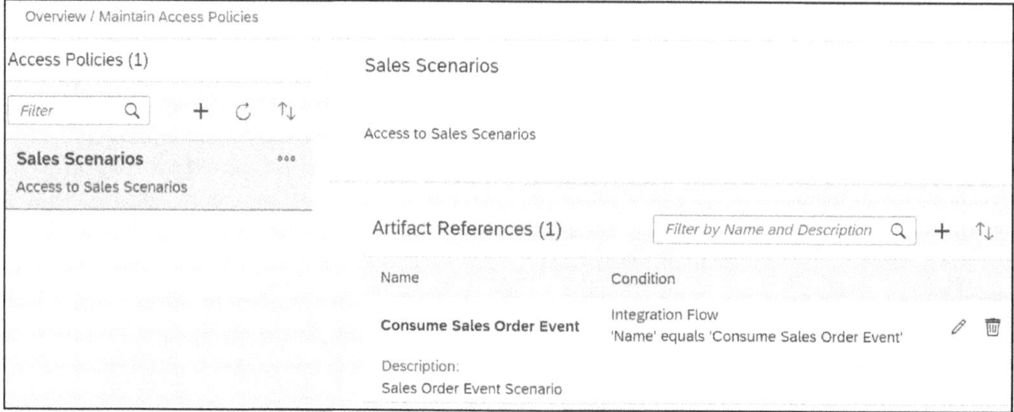

Figure 7.44 Maintain Access Policies

The view on the left, called the master view, provides a list of access policies available in the system, including the name of the user role and a description of the access policy. Click the three dots icon ∘∘∘ to open the actions menu for the selected access policy, as shown in Figure 7.45. Two actions (**Edit** and **Delete)** are always available for access policies.

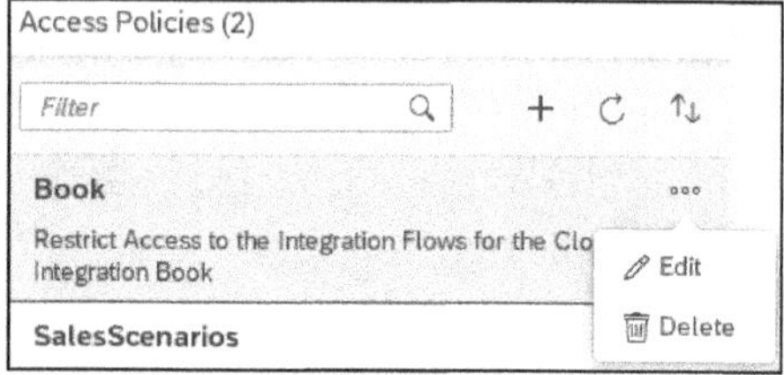

Figure 7.45 Menu for a Single Access Policy

At the top of the table on the left, the actions you can take on the list of access policies are shown; Table 7.21 details those actions.

Action	Description
Filter	Filter for specific access policies. The filter is executed for the **Name** and the **Description** of the policy.
Create icon	Create a new access policy using the + action.

Table 7.21 Actions for the Access Policies List

Action	Description
Reload icon	Reload ↻ the list of access policies.
Sort icon	Change the sorting order by using the ⇅ action.

Table 7.21 Actions for the Access Policies List (Cont.)

After selecting an access policy on the left, its configuration details will be shown on the right, in the details view. Below the name and the description of the access policy, you'll see the list of artifact references belonging to this access policy. Artifact references are references to configuration artifacts for which access will be restricted, for example, iFlows. The attributes for artifact references are listed in Table 7.22.

7

Attribute Name	Description
Name	Name and description of the artifact reference.
Condition	The configuration of the reference to the configuration artifacts. The condition consists of the artifact type, the artifact name, and the expression, for example, `Integration Flow 'Name' equals 'Consume Sales order Event'`.
Actions	The two actions **Edit** ✎ and **Delete** 🗑 are available for artifact references.

Table 7.22 Attributes of Artifact References

On the top-right of the table, the actions for the list of artifact references are shown. Table 7.23 details the actions.

Action	Description
Filter	Filter for specific artifact references. The filter is executed for the **Name** and the **Description** of the artifact reference.
Create icon	Create a new artifact reference using the + action.
Sort icon	Change the sorting order by using the ⇅ action.

Table 7.23 Actions for the Artifact References List

No predelivered access policies are available because the policies that need to be defined in the system are specific to the customer and may even differ from test system to productive system. To create new access policies in your tenant, follow these steps:

1. Click the **Add** button + at the top of the master view to create a new **Access Policy** (shown earlier in Figure 7.44).

2. On the **Create Access Policy** screen, specify the **Role Name** to be assigned to the user for the restricted access and optionally provide a **Description**, as shown in Figure 7.46.
3. Click **Create** to create the access policy.

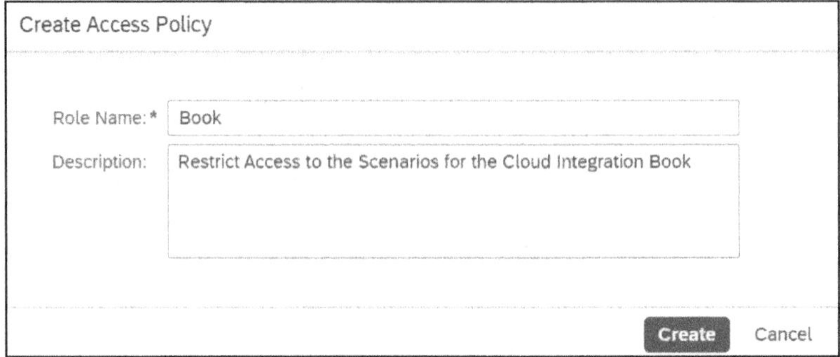

Figure 7.46 Create Access Policy

4. After creating the access policy, in the details view on the right, click the **Add** button + to add one or more artifact references to the access policy.
5. On the **Create Artifact Reference** screen, as shown in Figure 7.47, you must specify the following attributes:
   - Enter the **Name** and **Description** of the artifact reference.
   - In the **Artifact Type** dropdown, choose from values such as **Integration Flow**, **REST API**, **SOAP API**, **Global Data Store**, **Message Queue**, and so on.
   - In the **Attribute** dropdown list, select either the **Name** or **ID** of the specific artifact.
   - Select between **Equals** or **Matches** to specify that you want to reference exactly one artifact, or you can specify an expression to refer to multiple artifacts.
   - If you select the **Equals** radio button, in the **Value** field, specify the **Name** or the **ID** of the artifact. If you select the **Matches** radio button, specify a regular expression for the **Name** or the **ID** of the artifacts.
6. Click **Create** to create the artifact reference in the access policy.

Now that you've created the access policy, you can assign the user role specified in this access policy to users that should have access to the monitoring capabilities for defined configuration artifacts. Refer to the "Cloud Integration - Access Policies: Defining Roles on Artifact Level" blog at *http://s-prs.co/507770* for a sample scenario and the most recent extensions available for this feature.

After this extended discussion of various security artifacts such as users, certificates, keys, and user roles, let's now discuss how to set up the JDBC data sources required for access to databases that use the JDBC adapter.

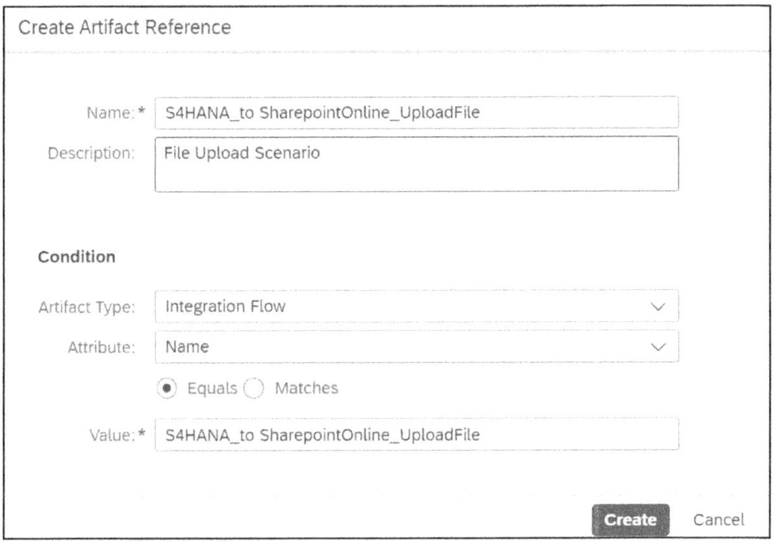

Figure 7.47 Add the iFlow to the Access Policy

7.3.7 Managing Java Database Connectivity Data Sources

In Chapter 6, Section 6.5, we showed you how to set up a scenario using the JDBC adapter and touched on the monitor for maintaining JDBC data sources. In this section, we'll return to this monitor to create JDBC data sources and to look at the available configuration options in more detail.

To manage JDBC data sources, from within the **Manage Security** section of the monitoring dashboard (shown earlier in Figure 7.27), click the **JDBC Material** tile. From this tile you can manage the JDBC data sources and JDBC drivers configured in the tenant for accessing external databases via the JDBC adapter. The following section describes both options in detail.

JDBC Data Source

When you click on the **JDBC Material** tile, the **Monitor** tab for JDBC data sources opens by default, as shown in Figure 7.48. A JDBC data source is required to make connections to an external database from Cloud Integration. It contains information such as database type, credentials and the JDBC URL. The screen is divided into a master view on the left, where configured JDBC data sources are listed, and the detail view on the right, containing details of the selected data source. In the master view, not only the **Name** of the JDBC data source is shown, but also the **Status** of the data source. The following statuses are used:

- **Deployed**
  The data source is successfully deployed on the worker node.

- **Deploying**
  The data source is currently being deployed on the worker node.
- **Failed**
  The data source is in error and can't be used in scenarios using the JDBC adapter.
- **Stored**
  The data source is stored, but not yet deployed on the worker node.
- **Undeploying**
  The data source is currently being undeployed from the worker node.

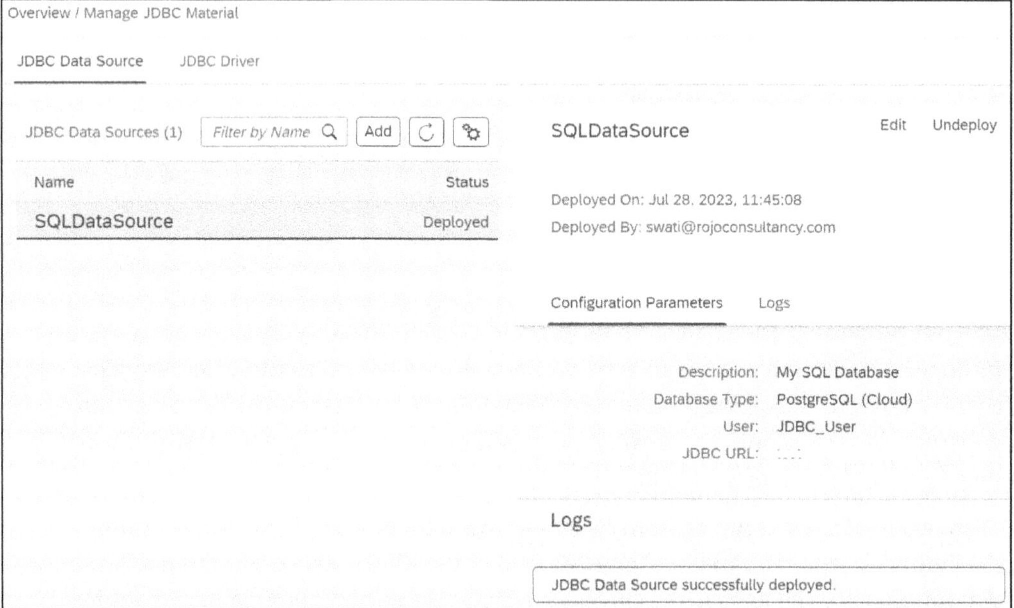

Figure 7.48 Manage JDBC Data Sources

At the top-left of the table, the actions that you can take on the list of JDBC data sources are shown. Table 7.24 details these actions.

Action	Description
Filter	Filter for specific JDBC data sources. The filter is executed for the **Name** of the data source.
Add	Create a new JDBC data source.
Reload icon	Reload the list of JDBC data sources.
Settings icon	Change the sort by field, sort order, and filter details by using the button.

Table 7.24 Actions for JDBC Data Sources

After selecting a JDBC data source on the left, its configuration details will be shown on the right. Below the name of the JDBC data source, you'll see the date of the last deployment and the user who deployed the data source. In the **Configuration Parameters** section, you'll find the following configuration details of the selected JDBC data source:

- **Description**
  Description of the JDBC data source.
- **Database Type**
  Type of the connected database. At the time of this writing, the following options are available: **ASE Service** for SAP Adaptive Server Enterprise (SAP ASE), **SAP HANA Cloud**, **SAP HANA Platform (On-Premise)**, **PostgreSQL (Cloud)**, **PostgreSQL (On-Premise)**, and **SAP ASE Platform.**
- **User**
  User to connect to the configured database.
- **JDBC URL**
  URL of the database.

In the **Logs** section, the deployment status of the JDBC data source can be found. If an error arose during the deployment of the data source, detailed error information will be shown.

In the top-right corner, two actions for the selected JDBC data source are available. By clicking the **Edit** action, the selected data source can be adjusted and deployed again. The **Undeploy** action removes the JDBC data source from the tenant.

To create a new JDBC data source in your tenant, follow these steps:

1. Click the **Add** button at the top of the master view to create a new **JDBC Data Source**, as shown in Figure 7.48.
2. On the **Add JDBC Data Source** screen, specify the following parameters, as shown in Figure 7.49:
   - Enter a **Name** and **Description** of the JDBC data source. The **Name** is required in the configuration of the JDBC adapter.
   - Select the desired **Database Type.** For the latest status, search for "Managing JDBC Data Sources" in the documentation for Cloud Integration (*http://s-prs.co/v576028*).
   - **User** and **Password**: Specify the user name and password to connect to the configured database.
   - **JDBC URL**: Configure the connection URL that will be used to access the database.
3. Click **Deploy** to deploy the data source to the tenant.

After the JDBC data source has successfully deployed, you can use it when configuring the JDBC adapter in an iFlow to connect to the configured database during runtime.

Add JDBC Data Source

Name:* DBName
Description:
Database Type: SAP HANA Cloud
User:* user
Password:
Repeat Password:
JDBC URL:* dburl

Deploy Cancel

Figure 7.49 Creating a JDBC Data Source

JDBC Driver

The second tab in the **Manage JDBC Material** tile is **JDBC Driver**, as shown in Figure 7.50. As an integration consultant, you'll come across situations where you might have to connect to third-party databases such as Microsoft SQL Server or DB2. Cloud Integration supports such use cases by providing your tenant administrator with the power to install JDBC drivers on your tenant. The **JDBC Driver** tab is identical to the **JDBC Data Source** tab: on the left pane, you have the list of deployed **JDBC Drivers** and their **Status**. The right panel provides deployment details such as when the driver was deployed, and which user was responsible for the deployment. The **Configuration Parameters** tab specifies the **Version** of the driver, and if there are any errors, the **Logs** area will show additional details of the error.

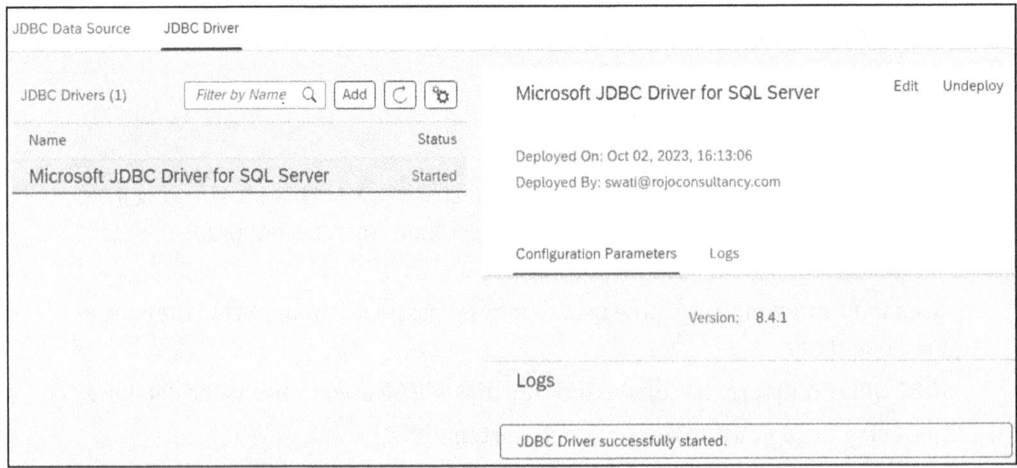

Figure 7.50 Manage JDBC Drivers

To Add a new JDBC driver, follow these steps:

1. Click the **Add** button at the top of the left pane. This will open a screen to provide the details required to deploy a new driver, as shown in Figure 7.51.
2. On the **Add JDBC Driver** screen, provide the details shown in Figure 7.51, and click **Deploy**.

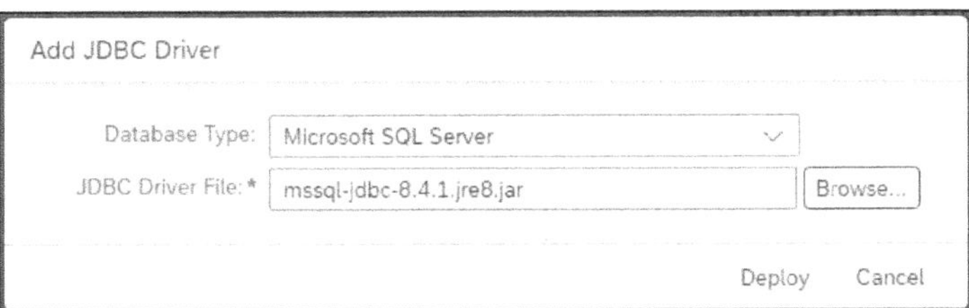

Figure 7.51 Adding a New JDBC Driver

With this discussion on maintaining JDBC material, we've finished our exploration of managing security material. However, as you may have noticed in the monitoring dashboard (shown earlier in Figure 7.26 and Figure 7.27), one more tile is available in the **Manage Security** section: the **Connectivity Tests** tile. Let's check out how this tile can help you test security material.

7.3.8 Testing Outbound Connectivity

Using the tests available in the **Connectivity Tests** tile, you can check that the security material deployed can be used successfully to establish secure connections to connected backends, mail servers, messaging brokers, and SFTP servers.

As shown in Figure 7.52, when you click the **Connectivity Tests** tile, a new window will open that features the following tabs for each connection option:

- **TLS**
  This test tries to establish an HTTPS connection via Transport Layer Security (TLS) to a backend. HTTPS is used by several receiver adapters, such as SOAP, IDoc, and HTTP, to connect to the backends.
- **SSH**
  This test tries to establish a connection via SSH to an SFTP server. The SSH protocol is used by the SFTP sender and receiver adapters to communicate with the SFTP server.
- **FTP**
  This test tries to establish a connection via File Transfer Protocol (FTP) to an FTP server. FTP is used by the FTP sender and receiver adapters to communicate with the FTP server.

- **SMTP**
  This test tries to establish a Simple Mail Transfer Protocol (SMTP) connection to a mail server. This protocol is used by the mail receiver adapter to send messages to the mail server. You used this tool already when setting up our very first iFlow in this book (refer to Chapter 2, Section 2.3.6).
- **IMAP**
  This test tries to establish a connection via Internet Message Access Protocol (IMAP) to a mail server. This protocol is one of several used by the mail sender adapter to poll messages from mail servers.
- **POP3**
  This test tries to establish a connection via Post Office Protocol version 3 (POP3) to a mail server. This protocol is the second protocol that the mail sender adapter can use to poll messages from mail servers.
- **AMQP**
  This test tries to establish a connection via the Advanced Message Queuing Protocol (AMQP) to a message broker. This protocol is used by the AMQP sender and receiver adapter to communicate with the message broker.
- **Kafka**
  Kafka Connectivity Test checks for a successful connection to the specified Kafka broker using the Kafka message protocol. The Kafka sender and receiver adapter uses the same connection mechanisms to read and write data from Kafka Topics.
- **Cloud Connector**
  This test checks the connection to the SAP Connectivity services, which can be used by different adapters to connect to on-premise systems.

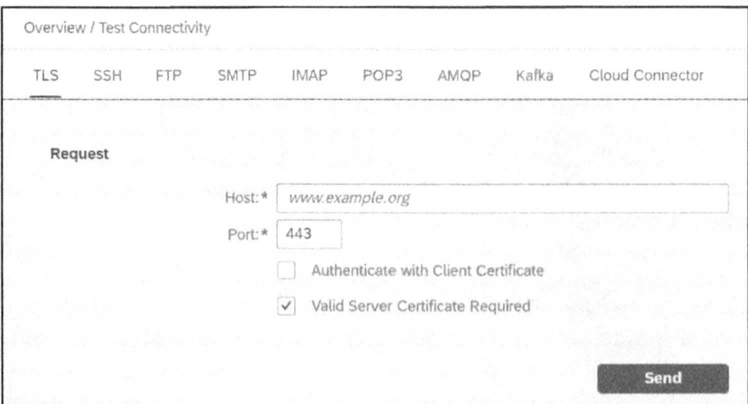

Figure 7.52 Connectivity Tests

Let's look at the different tests available in more detail.

Testing HTTPS Connections

The **TLS** test tries to establish an HTTPS connection via TLS to the server specified. For the **TLS** test, the **Host** and **Port** fields of the server to connect to must be maintained. As shown in Figure 7.53, a test has been executed against **google.com**. Notice that the response indicates an error arose during the SSL handshake because no valid certificate could be found in the keystore.

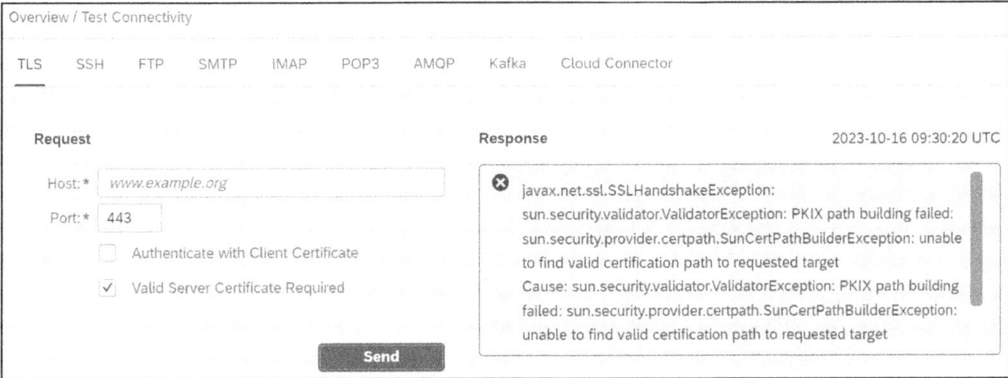

Figure 7.53 TLS Connection Test with SSL Handshake Error

Notice that the default setting is to validate the server certificate, which is always the case when a TLS connection is established during runtime. But in the connection test, you have the option of deselecting the **Valid Server Certificate Required** checkbox. By using this option, which establishes a connection without validation of the server certificate, you can determine whether the server can be reached at all, and the necessary certificates provided by the servicer for validation will be displayed. As shown in Figure 7.54, notice that the TLS test without a validation check has executed successfully, and the information that the server certificate is invalid is shown in the **Response** view. In addition, you'll receive the invalid **Server Certificate Chain** sent by the server. Open the **Server Certificate Chain** section by clicking the **Expand** icon > to see the list of certificates in the chain.

You don't need much more to get the TLS connection established successfully: You can either get a trusted root certificate from the backend server or simply download the certificates provided in the TLS connection test by clicking the **Download** link. The **Download** action creates a *certificates.zip* file in the download folder of your local PC. This file contains all certificates from the connection test. Extract the **.cer* file of the root CA, and add it to the keystore using the keystore monitor. If the server response contains a valid root CA, then you also select **Add to Keystore**. On clicking this link, the root certificate is added directly to the keystore. Let's execute the test again, but now with the **Valid Server Certificate Required** checkbox selected. The test should now pass successfully because the certificate can be validated by Cloud Integration.

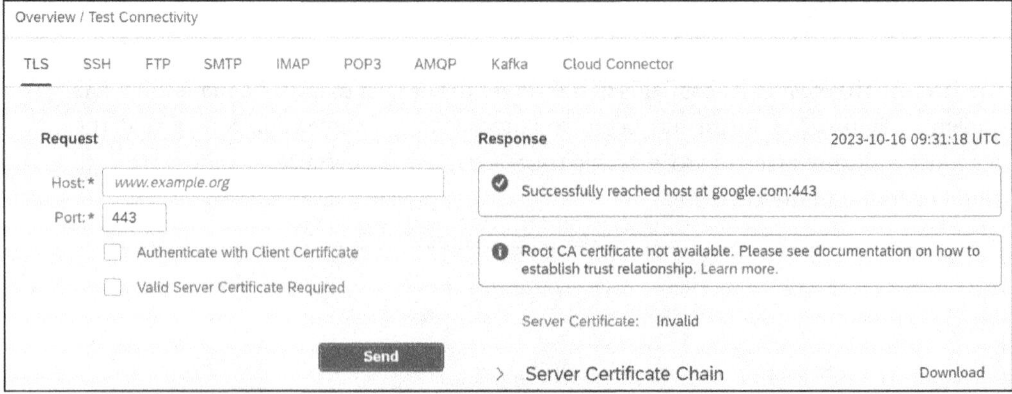

Figure 7.54 TLS Connection Test without Validating the Server Certificate

Select the other checkbox, **Authenticate with Client Certificate**, to test the client certificate-based authentication at the backend. As shown in Figure 7.55, when you select this checkbox, a new field labeled **Alias** appears, where you can enter a keystore alias for the key pair you want to use for authentication. If you want to test connectivity to the backend system using the new SAP Keys provided by SAP you can check the **Include new SAP Key** checkbox. If the **Alias** field is left empty, the system tries to find a valid key pair in the keystore and uses that key pair.

After the test has been executed, the **Response** section indicates whether the client certificate-based authentication was executed and shows the **Alias** that was used. Additionally, under **Trusted CAs for Client Certificates**, the test provides a list of all CAs that the receiver system trusts for client certificate–based authentication. This list is of interest if the client certificate you're using isn't accepted by the receiver system. In this case, the problem often is that the CA that signed the key pair isn't contained in the list of trusted CAs.

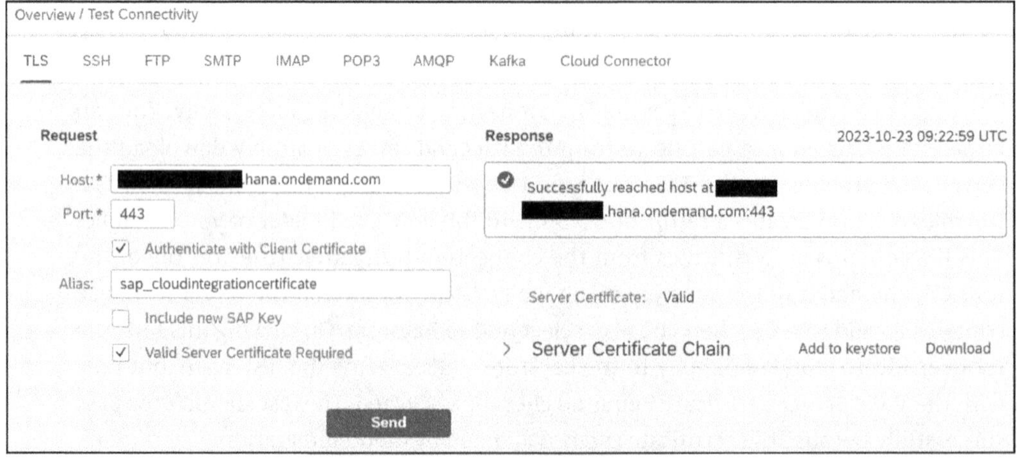

Figure 7.55 TLS Connection Test with Client Certificate Authentication

You've now learned how to use the TLS test to test the transport-level security against backends connected via HTTPS. With this approach, you have the option of testing the connection and authentication settings used in the iFlow channels of all adapters using HTTPS, such as SOAP, HTTP, IDoc, and XI.

Testing the Connection to the SFTP Server

To test the connection to an SFTP server, the **SSH** test can be used. The **Host** and **Port** fields of the SFTP server need to be entered, together with the **Authentication** option to be used when connecting to the SFTP server, as shown in Figure 7.56. When connecting to an on-premise SFTP server, select **On-Premise** as the **Proxy Type**, and specify the **Location ID** as configured in the SAP Connectivity services, as shown in Figure 7.57.

Using **Authentication** option **None**, you can test that the SFTP server can be reached at all, and you can download the host key of the SFTP server using the **Copy Host Key** button at the bottom of the **Response** screen. This host key needs to be added to the known hosts file and deployed in the **Manage Security Material** tile to be able to successfully establish an SSH connection to the SFTP server. This process is described in detail in the "Cloud Integration - How to Setup Secure Connection to sftp Server" blog at *http://s-prs.co/507772*.

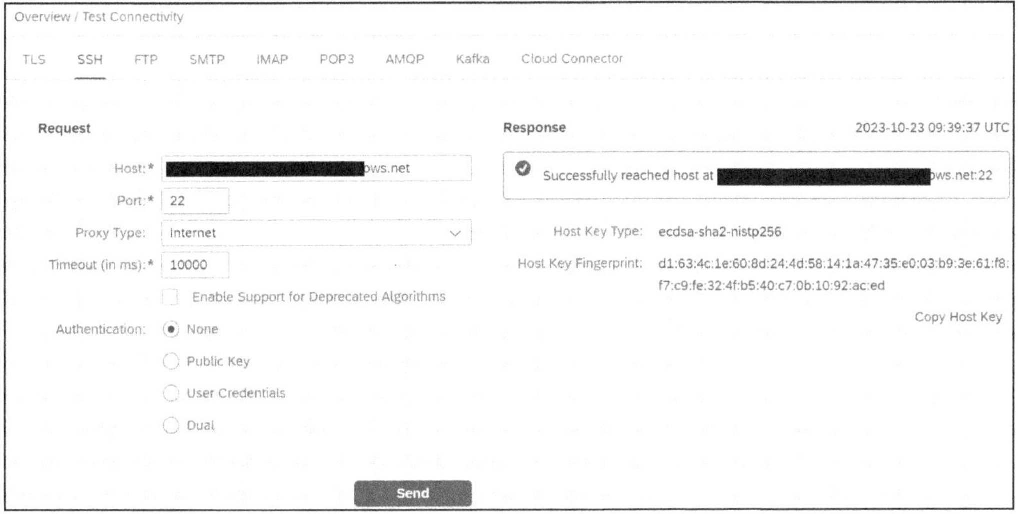

Figure 7.56 SSH Connection Test without Authentication

Request

Host:* rojostoragedatalakegen2.blob.core.windows.net

Port:* 22

Proxy Type: On-Premise

Location ID: Loc-01

Figure 7.57 Connecting to an On-Premise SFTP Server

If **Public Key**, **User Credentials**, or **Dual** is used for **Authentication**, additional checks are available, as shown later in Figure 7.59:

- **Host Key Verification**
  Using the host key verification check, it's possible to check that the host key is stored in the known hosts file and that the Cloud Integration tenant trusts the SFTP server. During runtime, this check is always executed; otherwise, messages can neither be polled from the SFTP server nor sent to the SFTP server.

  There are two places the known hosts file can be stored; either deployed on the tenant using the **Security Material** monitor or stored in the Partner Directory using the respective OData APIs. In **Host Key Verification**, select the location of the known hosts file. If **Against Partner Directory** is selected, you need to specify the **Partner Directory URI** to point to the known hosts file in the Partner Directory, as shown in Figure 7.58, by following the pattern for Partner Directory URIs: **pd:<Partner ID>:<Parameter ID>:Binary**. More details about the usage of the Partner Directory can be found in Chapter 8, Section 8.5.

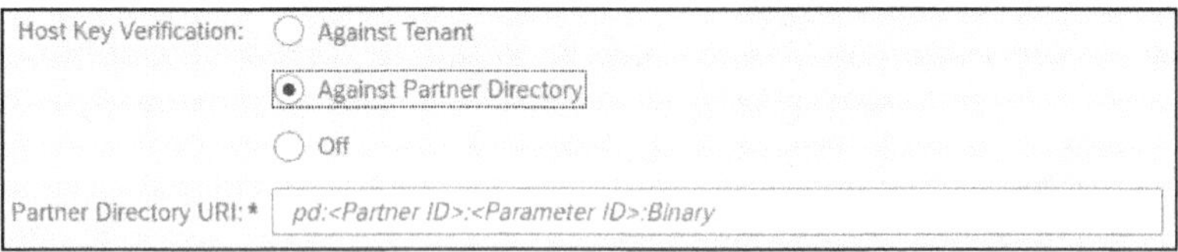

Figure 7.58 Host Key Verification

- **Check Directory Access**
  By selecting this checkbox, you can test whether the user connecting to the SFTP server has the authorization to access its directories. If you enter a specific directory in the **Directory** field, all files and folders in this directory will be listed on the **Response** screen.

Authentication: None

Note, that the **Authentication** option **None** is only available in the SSH test so that you can download the host key without authentication. This option isn't available in the SFTP adapter because either public keys or user name/password authentication is mandatory at runtime.

Now that you know how to test the connection to SFTP servers and how to download the host key, you can successfully set up and test scenarios using the SFTP sender or receiver adapter.

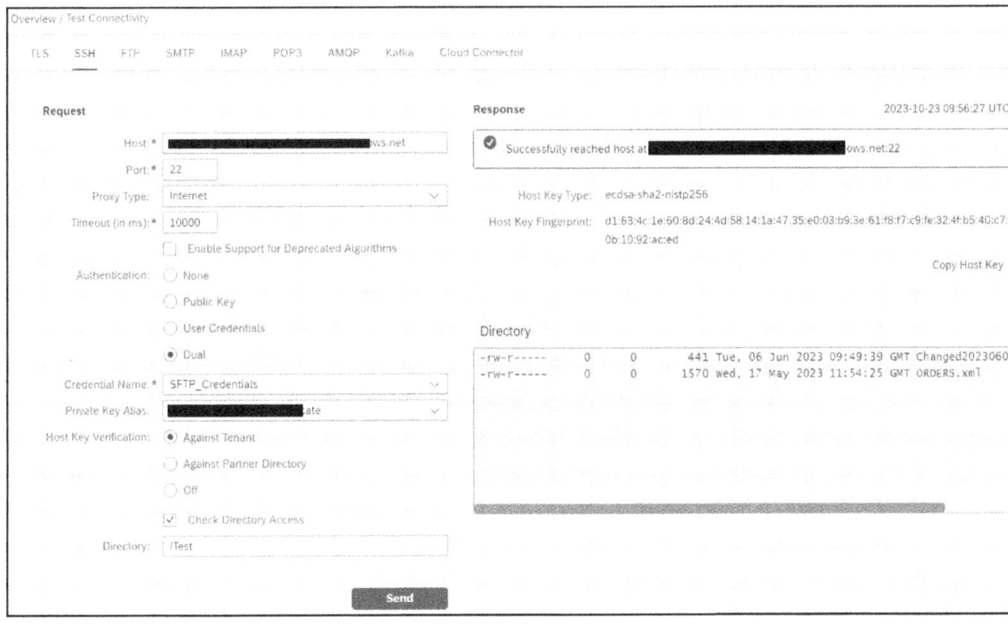

Figure 7.59 SSH Connection Test with Dual Authentication

Testing the Connection to the FTP Server

To test the connection to an FTP server, the **FTP** test can be used. The test is similar to the SSH test for testing connections to SFTP servers, but some minor changes exist because SSH and FTP are different, and not all authentication options are equal.

The **Host** and **Port** fields of the FTP server must be maintained, and a **Proxy Type** must be selected. When connecting to an on-premise FTP server, select **On-Premise** as the **Proxy Type**, and specify the **Location ID** as configured in SAP Connectivity services. Figure 7.60 shows an example FTP connection test without authentication.

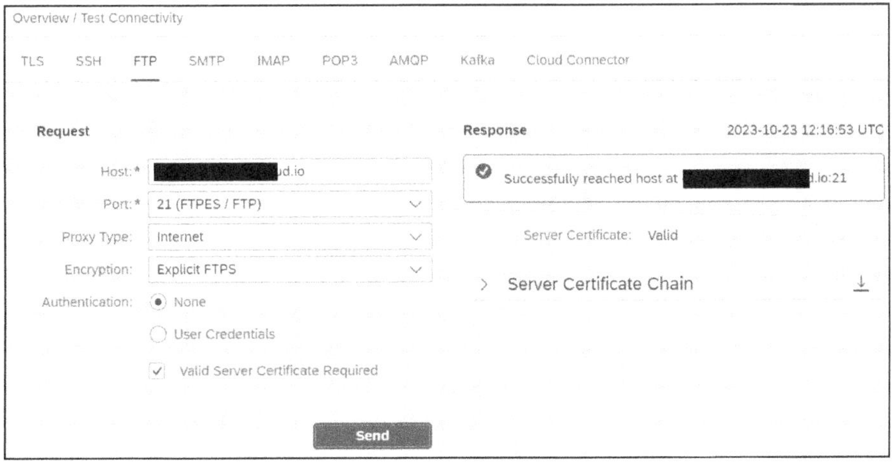

Figure 7.60 FTP Connection Test without Authentication

As in the TLS test, you can deselect the **Valid Server Certificate Required** checkbox to establish a connection without validating the server certificate. Using this option together, with the **None** radio button for the **Authentication**, you can determine whether the server can be reached at all and also download the required server certificate, if needed.

In the **Response** view, the **Server Certificate Chain** that the server provides for validation is displayed. Open the **Server Certificate Chain** by clicking the **Expand** icon > to view the list of certificates in the chain. If the connection test with the **Valid Server Certificate Required** option isn't successful, you'll need to upload the server certificate to the tenant's keystore. To manage server certificates, download the certificates provided in the FTP connection test by clicking the **Download** icon ⤓. This action creates a *certificates.zip* file in the download folder of your local PC. This file contains all certificates from the connection test. Extract the **.cer* file of the root CA, and add it to the keystore using the keystore monitor. Execute the test again, but this time with the **Valid Server Certificate Required** checkbox selected. The test should now pass successfully because the certificate can be validated by Cloud Integration.

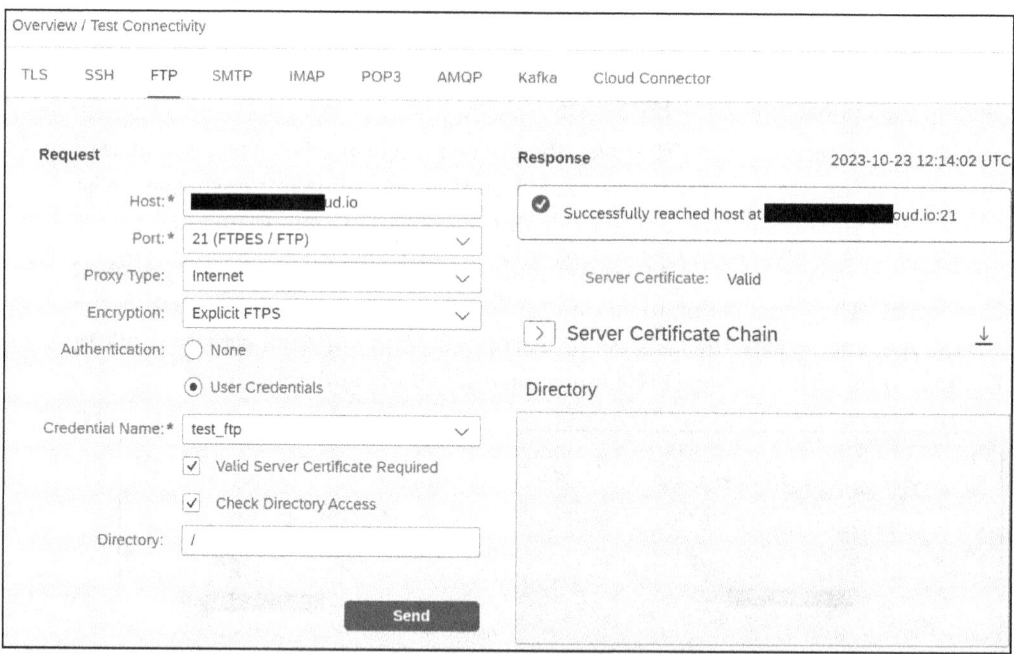

Figure 7.61 FTP Connection Test with Checked Directory Access

If you've selected the **User Credentials** radio button for **Authentication**, an additional check is available—**Check Directory Access**—as shown in Figure 7.61. By selecting this checkbox, you'll test whether the user connecting to the FTP server has the authorization to access its directories. If you enter a specific directory in the **Directory** field, you get all files in this directory listed on the **Response** screen.

Authentication: None

The **Authentication** option **None** is only available in the FTP test so that you can download the server certificate without authentication. This option isn't available in the FTP adapter because user name/password authentication is mandatory at runtime.

Now that you know how to test the connection to FTP servers and how to download the server certificate, you can successfully set up and test scenarios using the FTP sender or receiver adapter.

Testing the Connection to the Mail Server

If you need to analyze issues connecting to a mail server, either for sending messages to the mail server or for polling messages from the mail server, three different tests are available to assist you. While the **SMTP** test checks the outbound connection for sending messages to the mail server, the **IMAP** and **POP3** tests check whether messages can be polled from the mail server.

As shown in Figure 7.62, for executing the **SMTP** test to the mail server, you'll specify the **Host** and **Port** of the mail server and then select the **Protection** mechanism the mail server supports. For **Authentication**, select the **None** radio button to test whether the mail server can be reached and the secure connection can be established. Like in the SSH connectivity test, you can also test the connection to an on-premise mail server by selecting **On-Premise** from the **Proxy Type** dropdown list and specifying the correct **Location ID** as configured in SAP Connectivity services.

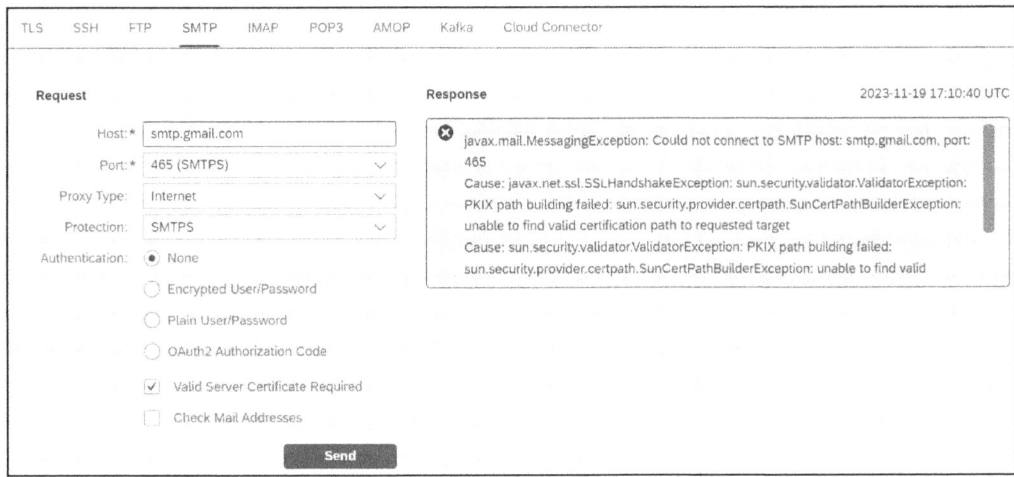

Figure 7.62 SMTP Connection Test with an Error

As shown in Figure 7.62, notice that an error occurred during the SSL handshake when connecting to the mail server. As in the TLS test, you have the option of executing the

SMTP test without validating the server certificate by deselecting the **Valid Server Certificate Required** checkbox. Then, you can use the **Download** option to get the certificates and add the root CA to the keystore using the keystore monitor. Afterwards, the **SMTP** test should pass successfully. The **Response** screen displays whether the server certificate is valid.

If **Authentication** with user and password is used—either **Encrypted User/Password**, **Plain User/Password**, or **OAuth2 Authorization Code**—a new entry field named **Credential Name** appears where the name of the deployed credential needs to be entered, as shown in Figure 7.63. The **Response** screen displays whether the authentication with the credentials was successful.

A useful option in the SMTP test is to check the email addresses used in the mail receiver channel. By selecting the **Check Mail Addresses** checkbox, two new entry fields will be displayed: **From** and **To**. In these fields, enter the mail addresses used in your iFlow in the mail receiver channel. The **SMTP** test checks whether the mail server supports these addresses and displays the check result in the **Response** screen, as shown in Figure 7.63.

The **IMAP** and **POP3** tests support similar features as the **SMTP** test, except the check for the mail addresses. This option just isn't relevant for mail sender adapters where messages are polled from a mail server. Along with the connection test, IMAP and POP3 support the possibility to list folders and check mailbox content.

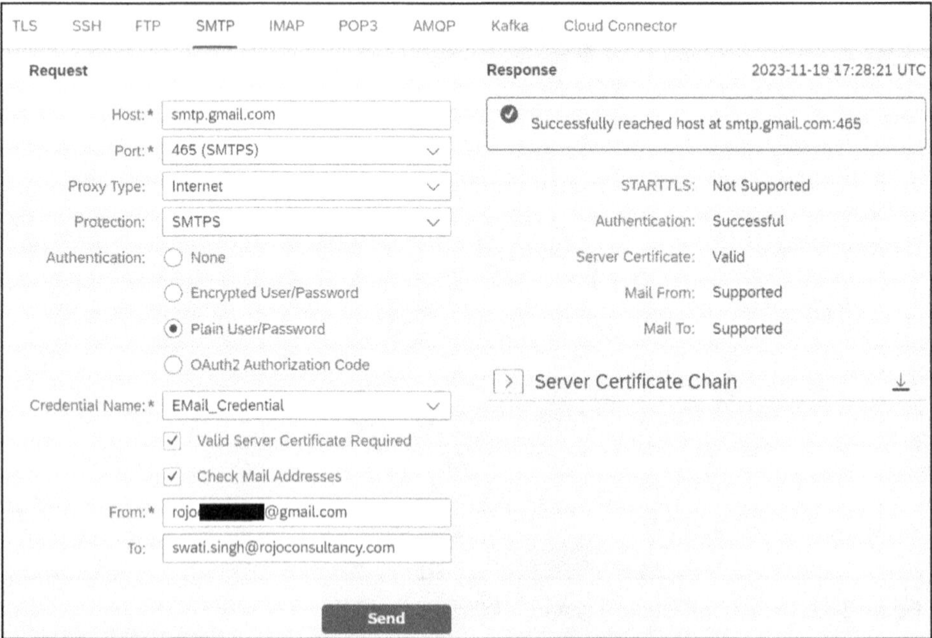

Figure 7.63 SMTP Connection Test with Checking of Mail Addresses

In Figure 7.64, the **IMAP** test to *imap.gmail.com* is shown as an example. Notice that the **Host** and **Port** of the mail server must be entered together with the **Proxy Type**, **Protection** mechanism, **Authentication**, and **Credential Name**.

For the **IMAP** test, the following check features are available:

- **Valid Server Certificate Required**
  As in the **SMTP** test, deselecting this checkbox will test whether the mail server can be reached at all. Furthermore, the provided mail server certificates can be downloaded and added to the keystore.
- **List Folders**
  If selected, the test lists all folders in the mail server for the user connected using the credentials. As shown in Figure 7.64, the **Folders** are shown at the end of the **Response** screen.
- **Check Mailbox Content**
  If selected, a new entry field named **Folder** appears, where the folder in the mail server must be entered. The test checks how many mail messages are available in the specified folder and how many of them are **Unread**. The result of the check is shown on the **Response** screen.

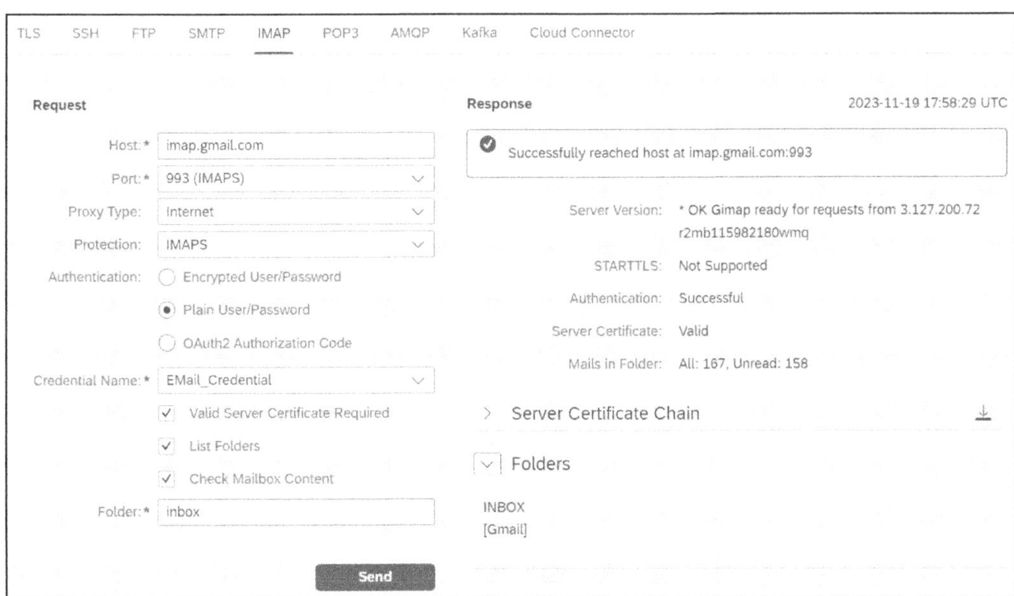

Figure 7.64 IMAP Connection Test

The **POP3** test is similar to the **IMAP** test. As shown in Figure 7.65, the **Request** and **Response** details look almost identical to the **IMAP** test.

The following check features are available for testing the POP3 connection:

- **Valid Server Certificate Required**
  As in the **SMTP** and **IMAP** tests, deselecting this checkbox will test whether the mail server can be reached at all. Furthermore, the provided mail server certificates can be downloaded and added to the keystore.
- **Check Mailbox Content**
  The test checks how many mail messages are available in the *Inbox* folder. The result of the check is shown in the **Response** screen.

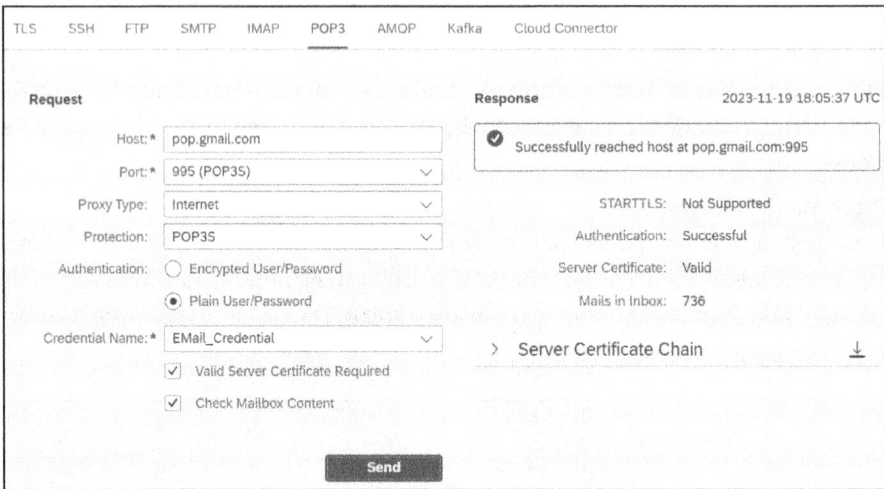

Figure 7.65 POP3 Connection Test

> **Note**
> POP3 doesn't support different folders, so only the *Inbox* folder is relevant. Because of this limitation, the check for mailbox content doesn't offer an option to specify a dedicated folder but does provide the mail messages contained in the *Inbox* folder. In addition, POP3 doesn't distinguish between read and unread mail, so all mail messages in the *Inbox* folder will be shown.

Now you know how to test the connection to the mail server and how to download server certificates. With this information, you can successfully set up and test scenarios using the mail sender adapter or mail receiver adapter.

Testing the Connection to the Messaging System

To test the connection to a messaging system via AMQP, the **AMQP** test can be used (for a sample scenario using the AMQP adapter, refer to Chapter 5, Section 5.6). First, select the **Transport Protocol** required to connect to the messaging system. Like in the AMQP adapter, **WebSocket** and **TCP** are offered. Afterwards, enter the **Host** and **Port** of the message broker. In addition, for the WebSocket protocol, enter the access path of the message broker in the **Path** field, as shown in Figure 7.66. When connecting to an on-premise messaging system using SAP Connectivity services, select **On-Premise** as the **Proxy Type**, and specify the **Location ID**, as configured in SAP Connectivity services.

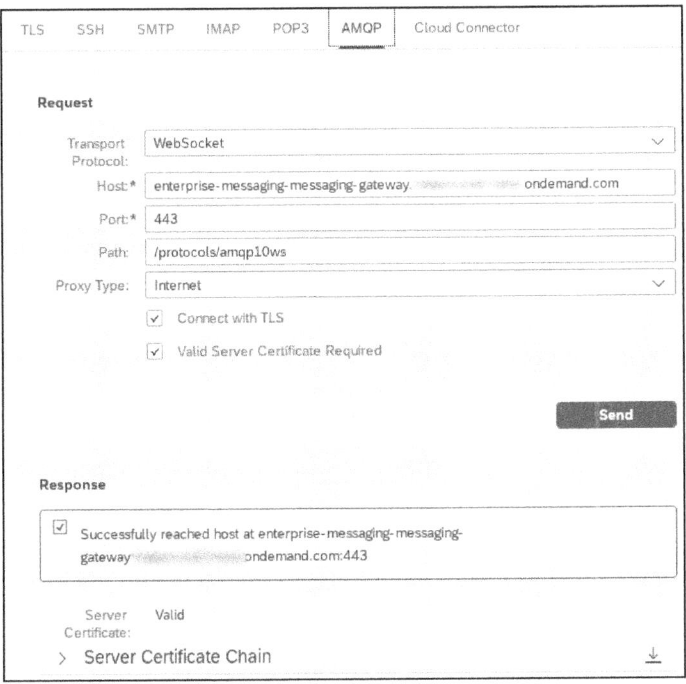

Figure 7.66 AMQP Connection Test

If you want to connect to the messaging system with TLS, select the **Connect with TLS** checkbox. In this case, during the SSL handshake, the validity of the server certificate is checked, which makes the connection more secure. For this option, a valid server certificate must be available in the tenant keystore, or the connection will fail. As in the other connectivity tests, the connection test can be executed without this certificate verification to enable the download of the required certificates. To achieve this downloading process, deselect the **Valid Server Certificate Required** checkbox. The connection will be established even if the server certificate isn't valid, and you can click the **Download** icon ⤓ in the response to receive the certificate, which you can then upload to the keystore. Afterwards, you can successfully establish the connection to the messaging system with TLS.

Testing the Connection to SAP Connectivity Services

As you've already seen in most of the connectivity tests so far, the connection to on-premise systems can be established using SAP Connectivity services. To easily test whether SAP Connectivity services is connected to the Cloud Integration tenant, the **Cloud Connector** connectivity test can be used.

As shown in Figure 7.67, only one entry field is given for configuration, the **Location ID**. Enter the location ID that is configured in SAP Connectivity services when connecting SAP Connectivity services to the Cloud Integration tenant. If SAP Connectivity services is configured without a location ID, leave the field empty.

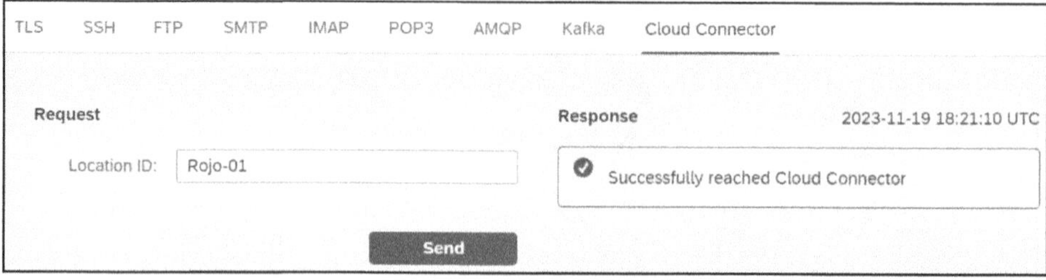

Figure 7.67 SAP Connectivity Services: Connection Test

In the response, you'll see whether or not SAP Connectivity services can be reached successfully at the given **Location ID**.

Now that you know how to manage security-relevant artifacts in your Cloud Integration tenant and how to test connections using transport-level security, let's discuss some monitors that are relevant only in specific scenarios. Let's first look into scenarios using temporary data, such as data stores and JMS queues.

7.4 Managing Temporary Data

In many scenarios, temporary data must be stored; this data can be either whole messages, parts of messages, error messages, or configuration data. The main storage options available in Cloud Integration are data stores and JMS queues.

In the **Manage Stores** section of the monitoring dashboard, you'll find several monitors for handling temporary data, as shown in Figure 7.68.

Figure 7.68 Manage Stores Section in the Monitoring Dashboard

7.4.1 Monitoring Data Stores

The **Data Stores** tile in the **Manage Stores** section shows the data stores used in the deployed iFlows. Data stores are used by the following flow steps and adapters:

- **Data Store flow steps**
  The following four flow steps work on data contained in the data store: **Write**, **Get**, **Select**, and **Delete.** Refer to Chapter 5, Section 5.4.1, for more information about use cases for the data store.
- **AS4 adapter**
  The Applicability Statement 4 (AS4) sender adapter temporarily stores messages for exactly-once (EO) scenarios, either in a data store or in a JMS queue. If storage in a data store is configured in the AS4 adapter, these messages will appear in the **Manage Data Stores** monitor.
- **XI adapter**
  The XI adapter temporarily stores messages for EO scenarios, either in a data store or in a JMS queue. If storage in a data store is configured in the XI adapter, these messages will appear in the **Manage Data Stores** monitor.

As shown in Figure 7.69 and Figure 7.70, the data store monitor consists of two sections: the master table on the left and the details table on the right. The master table on the left shows all data stores on the Cloud Integration tenant that contain messages. Table 7.25 provides detailed descriptions of the attributes in the master table.

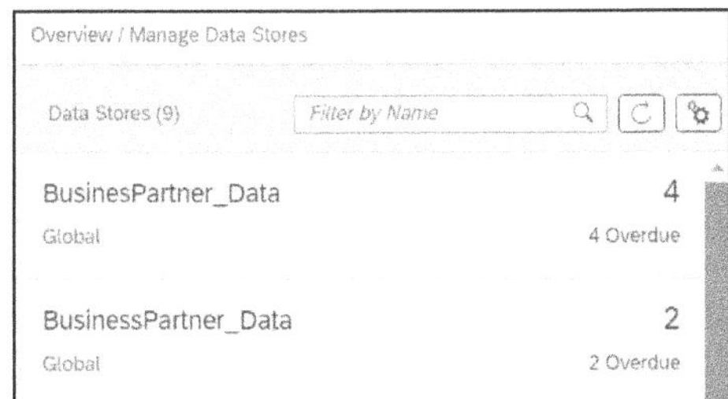

Figure 7.69 Manage Data Stores Monitor: Master Table

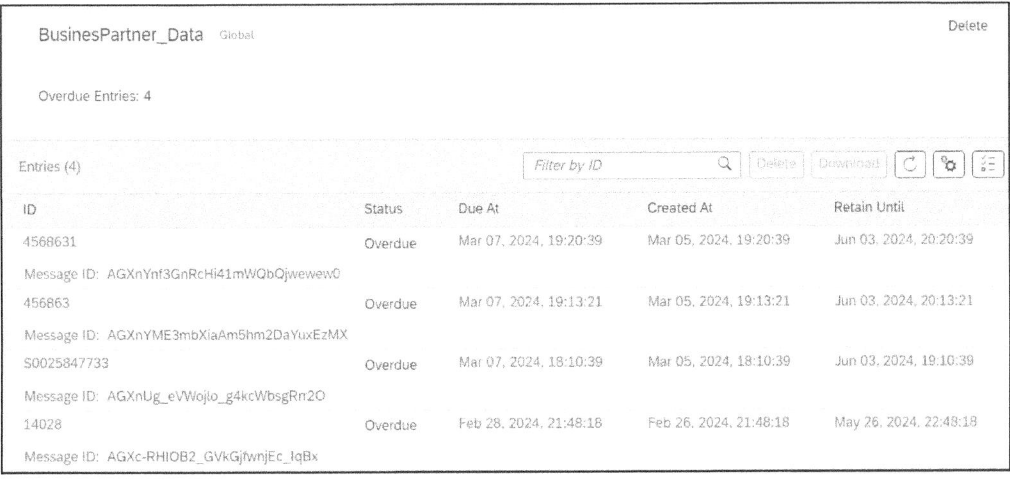

Figure 7.70 Manage Data Stores Monitor: Details

Data Stores without Messages Aren't Visible

Only data stores containing data are shown in the monitor because a data store is only created and kept in runtime as long as entries exist in that specific data store. As soon as all data/messages are consumed from the data store, the data store is removed.

Attribute	Description
Name	The name of the data store, as configured in the data store flow step. If the data store is used by an XI or AS4 adapter, the data store name is generated according to the following pattern: ■ **<participant>_<channel name>**
Visibility	The visibility of the data store, as configured in the data store flow steps with the following values: ■ **Global**: The data store can be used globally by all iFlows deployed on the tenant. ■ **Integration Flow Name**: The data store is used by the specified iFlow only. If the data store is used by an XI or AS4 adapter, the iFlow name shown has the following pattern: ■ **<integration flow>/XI** ■ **<integration flow>/AS4**
Number of Entries	The number of entries currently contained in the data store.
Number of Overdue Entries	The number of entries that already should have been processed but are still stored in the data store. This value is shown in red.

Table 7.25 Attributes of Data Stores in the Master Table

When you select a data store on the left, all entries in this specific data store will be shown on the right, in the details table. Table 7.26 describes the attributes of individual data store entries and their possible values.

Column	Description
ID	The ID of the entry in the data store. The entry ID can be specified in one of the following ways: ■ The entry ID can be specified in the data store **Write** step (e.g., by using a specific unique ID from the message payload). ■ If not specified in the data store **Write** step, a unique ID is generated by the runtime when the entry is written to the data store. ■ The XI and AS4 adapter generates a unique ID when the message is written to the data store.
Message ID	The ID of the message that wrote the message to the data store. The **Message ID** is a link. Clicking the link opens the message in the message processing monitor. This approach can be useful if you need to analyze why this message wasn't consumed.
Status	The status of the data store entry with the following statuses: ■ **Waiting**: This status applies after the entry has been written to the data store, but the message/data is waiting to be consumed by another process or iFlow. ■ **Overdue**: If the message wasn't consumed in the due time specified in the data store's **Write** step, the message will get the status **Overdue**. For such entries, the tenant administrator should check why the data isn't consumed (e.g., maybe the consuming iFlow doesn't run anymore) and solve the problem.
Due At	The date and time the entry is expected to be consumed next. This time is configured in the data store's **Write** step in the **Retention Threshold for Alerting** field. If the message is processed by the XI or AS4 adapter, the due time is automatically set by the adapter to 2 days.
Created At	The date and time the entry was created in the data store.
Retain Until	The date and time the entry will be deleted. This time is configured in the data store's **Write** step in the **Expiration Period** field , which is 90 days per default. If the message is processed by the XI or AS4 adapter, the expiration period is automatically set by the adapter to 90 days.

Table 7.26 Attributes of Data Store Entries

For entries in data stores, Cloud Integration offers the following actions at the top of the details table:

- **Filter by ID**
  Filter for a specific ID. This action can be especially useful if the ID specified in the **Write** step should be set by a unique ID from the incoming message payload. In this case, you can filter for this ID.

- **Delete**
  Remove the selected entries from the data store if not needed anymore.
- **Download**
  Download the selected entries. An *<ID>.zip* file is created in the download folder of your local PC containing the payload stored in the data store.
- **Reload** [C]
  Reload the content of the details table.
- **Table Settings** [⚙]
  Sort the entries and filter by the **Status** column.
- **Multi-select Mode** [☰]
  Select multiple entries at once. This option is useful when you need to delete multiple entries. Note that the **Download** action isn't available for multiple entries.

Now that you understand the data store monitor, let's look at the variables monitor. You'll notice that several attributes are identical because the variables are technically also stored in the same data store table.

7.4.2 Monitoring Variables

In some scenarios, variables are used to store configuration data, which is read and updated during message processing. Refer to Chapter 6, Section 6.5, where we introduced variables as part of a JDBC scenario. Variables are used by the following flow steps:

- **Write Variables**
  The **Write Variables** flow step is used to write or update variables in the runtime. Variables can have local or global visibility, which means that a variable can be read and updated only by the same iFlow or by all iFlows deployed on this tenant.
- **Content Modifier**
  The **Content Modifier** flow step can read the value of a global or local variable and use it to set headers or properties.

The second tile in the **Manage Stores** section provides monitoring options for variables used in runtime. When you select the **Variables** tile, a table containing all variables defined in the Cloud Integration tenant appears, as shown in Figure 7.71. Table 7.27 provides detailed descriptions of all the columns of the table.

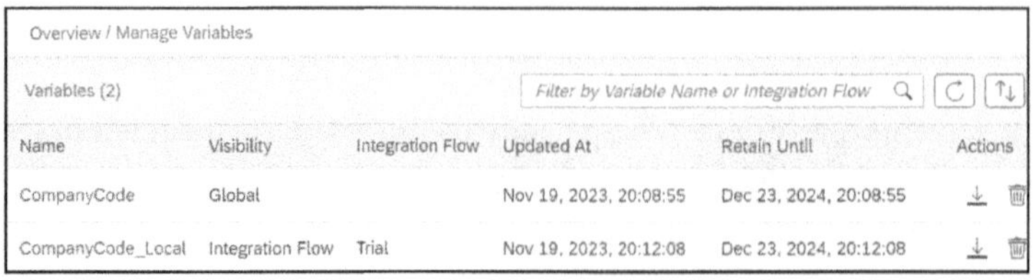

Overview / Manage Variables

Variables (2) — *Filter by Variable Name or Integration Flow*

Name	Visibility	Integration Flow	Updated At	Retain Until	Actions
CompanyCode	Global		Nov 19, 2023, 20:08:55	Dec 23, 2024, 20:08:55	
CompanyCode_Local	Integration Flow	Trial	Nov 19, 2023, 20:12:08	Dec 23, 2024, 20:12:08	

Figure 7.71 Manage Variables Monitor

Column	Description
Name	The name of the variable as defined in the **Write Variables** flow step. The name is a link. Clicking the link opens the variable in text format.
Visibility	The visibility of the variable as defined in the **Write Variables** step with the following values: ■ **Global:** The variable can be used globally by all iFlows deployed on the tenant. ■ **Integration Flow:** The variable is used by the iFlow only.
Integration Flow	If the **Visibility** is **Integration Flow**, in this column, the iFlow using this variable is shown.
Updated At	The date and time the variable was last changed.
Retain Until	The date and time the variable will be deleted. This time is set to 400 days after the creation of the variable, but this timer is reset by any update of the variable.
Actions	Actions available for variables include the following: ■ **Download** ⤓ : This option downloads the variable as a *<variable>_<integration flow>.zip* file, which contains the variable in a *headers.prop* file, to the download folder of your local PC. ■ **Delete** 🗑 : This option deletes the variable.

Table 7.27 Attributes of Variables

When you select the name of the variable, which is a link, a popup window will open displaying the content of the variable in text format, as shown in Figure 7.72. You can also download the variable's content using the **Download** button.

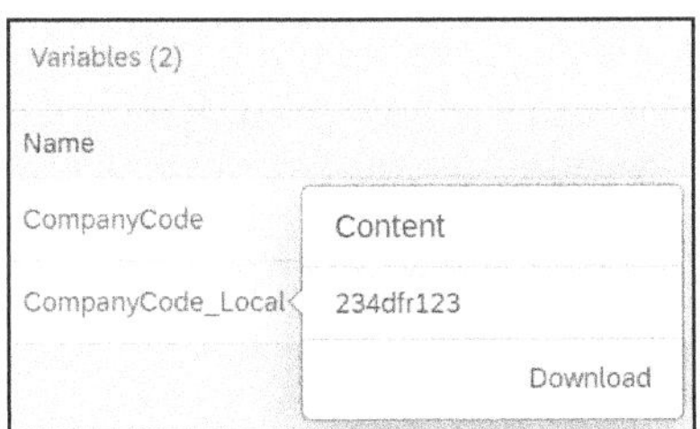

Figure 7.72 Content of a Variable

The two storage options described, data stores and variables, are based on the database of the Cloud Integration tenant. The third storage option for temporary data is a JMS queue based on a JMS message broker connected to the Cloud Integration tenant. For this option, the third tile in the **Manage Stores** section is most important.

7.4.3 Maintaining Message Queues

The **Message Queues** tile in the **Manage Stores** section shows the JMS queues used in the deployed iFlows. JMS queues are used by the following adapters:

- **JMS adapter**
  The JMS adapter can directly process messages to and from JMS queues: the **JMS** receiver adapter writes messages to JMS queues, and the **JMS** sender adapter polls messages from JMS queues. Refer to Chapter 5, Section 5.6, where we introduced reliable messaging using JMS queues.
- **AS2 adapter**
  The **AS2** sender adapter temporarily stores messages during runtime processing in JMS queues.
- **AS4 adapter**
  The **AS4** sender adapter temporarily stores messages for EO scenarios, either in a data store or in a JMS queue. If storage in a JMS queue is configured in the **AS4** adapter, these messages appear in the **Manage Message Queues** monitor.
- **XI adapter**
  The **XI** sender and receiver adapters temporarily store messages for EO scenarios, either in a data store or in a JMS queue. If storage in a JMS queue is configured in the **XI** adapter, these messages appear in the **Manage Message Queues** monitor.

Manage Message Queues Monitor Not Visible?

JMS messaging is available with SAP Integration Suite; with SAP BTP Enterprise Agreement; or if a separate JMS messaging license was purchased. If your Cloud Integration system isn't running with the correct license, and no JMS messaging license has been purchased, the JMS adapter won't appear in the list of available adapters.

Furthermore, you'll need to get a JMS message broker provisioned for your Cloud Integration tenant. The provisioning is triggered using a self-service in the SAP BTP cockpit. Details about the provisioning of a JMS message broker can be found in the documentation for Cloud Integration (*http://s-prs.co/v576028*) and in the "Cloud Integration - Activating and Managing Enterprise Messaging Capabilities (AS2, JMS, and XI Adapters) in Neo" blog at *http://s-prs.co/507773*.

The **Message Queues** tile is visible in the monitoring dashboard only after a JMS message broker has been successfully provisioned.

As shown in Figure 7.73 and Figure 7.74, the **Manage Message Queues** screen consists of two sections: the main table on the left and the details table on the right. The main table on the left shows all the JMS queues available in the JMS message broker. Table 7.28 provides detailed descriptions of the attributes of the JMS queues.

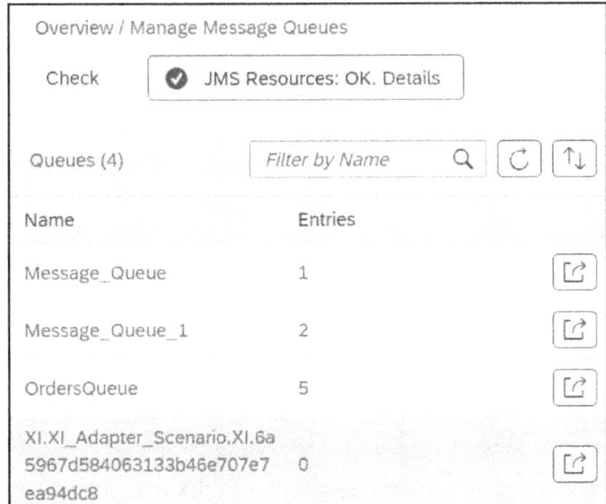

Figure 7.73 Manage Message Queue: Master Table

Messages (2)

Filter by Message ID

JMS Message ID	Message ID	Status	Due At	Created At	Retain Until	Retry Count	Next Retry On
ID:10.134.152.186aacd18c293c923d0:9	AGVq0qbFYHql3fx8JywdekWaRlqv	Failed	Dec 04, 2023, 07:45:58	Dec 02, 2023, 07:45:58	Jan 01, 2024, 07:45:58	1	Dec 02, 2023, 07:46:28
ID:10.134.152.186aacd18c293c923d0:6	AGVq0p3x7xSq1NsVGx_wi676U38N	Failed	Dec 04, 2023, 07:45:49	Dec 02, 2023, 07:45:49	Jan 01, 2024, 07:45:49	1	Dec 02, 2023, 07:46:19

Figure 7.74 Manage Message Queue: Details for Selected Message Queue

Attribute	Description
Name	The name of the JMS queue as configured in the JMS adapter. If the JMS queue is used by an AS2, AS4, or XI adapter, the queue name is generated automatically per the following pattern: ■ **AS2.<Integration Flow Name>.<Channel Name>.<Guid>** ■ **AS4.<Integration Flow Name>.<Channel Name>.<Guid>** ■ **XI.<Integration Flow Name>.<Channel Name>.<Guid>**
Entries	The number of entries currently contained in the JMS queue.
Actions	The actions for the JMS queue, as shown in Figure 7.75. The following actions are available: ■ **Retry** Restarts all messages in the selected queue. ■ **Status** Shows the storage status of the selected queue, as shown in Figure 7.76. As shown, three subqueues are available for the JMS queue: – **Processing Queue**:Messages are waiting to be consumed.

Table 7.28 Attributes of JMS Queues in the Master Table

<table>
<tr><th>Attribute</th><th>Description</th></tr>
<tr><td>Actions
(Cont.)</td><td>
– Error Queue: Contains messages with an error status that are waiting for the next retry. From this queue, messages aren't consumed; instead, the messages are put back to the Processing Queue when the configured retry interval is reached.
– Chunking Queue: Because the message broker doesn't support messages over a certain size, messages larger than 5 MB are split into one 5 MB parent message and multiple chunks. Parent messages still have a size limit of a maximum of 5 MB. The parent message is stored in the Processing Queue while the multiple related chunks are stored in the Chunking Queue.
If the storage of one of these subqueues reaches a certain limit, a warning ⚠ icon or error ⓘ icon will be shown for the subqueue. Click the Configure Size button to directly open the configuration screen for managing queue size.
▪ Configure Size
Opens the screen for configuring the storage sizes for the three subqueues, as shown in Figure 7.77. For an explanation of the three subqueues, refer to the Status action. You can enter storage sizes for the subqueues independently because this configuration heavily depends on the message sizes and the load you process in the specific scenario. The default for each queue is 95% of the total queue capacity on the broker. The size for each subqueue can be configured to any value between 100 MB and 95% of the total queue capacity.
▪ Where-Used
Shows the iFlows using the selected queue. This action is important if one queue runs full, and you need to find the iFlow that is expected to consume from the queue.
▪ Move
Moves all messages from the selected queue to another queue. This option may be required in the context of changing participant or channel names in iFlows using the AS2, AS4, or XI adapter because, for these adapters, the participant and channel name are part of the autogenerated queue name. Changing one of these names thus leads to a new queue name, and consequently, messages from the old queue aren't consumed anymore. Using the Move option, messages from the old queue can be moved to the new queue.
▪ Delete
Deletes the selected queue. Be careful with this option, which deletes the queue with all the messages in the queue. To re-create the queue, the iFlow must be redeployed.
</td></tr>
</table>

Table 7.28 Attributes of JMS Queues in the Master Table (Cont.)

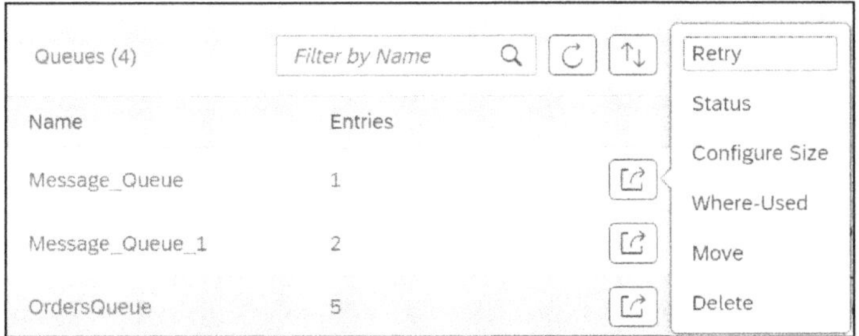

Figure 7.75 Actions for the Selected Queue

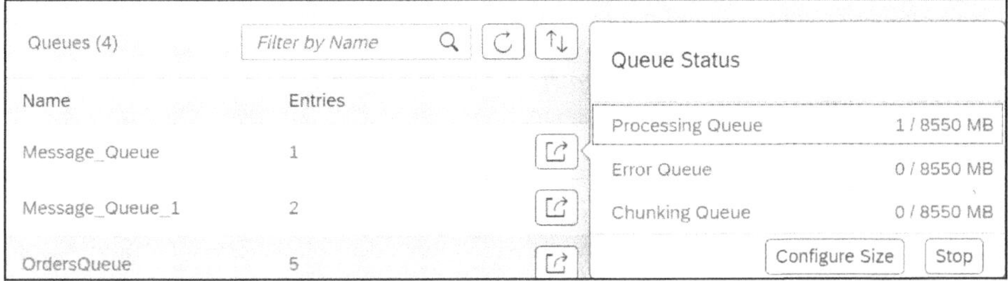

Figure 7.76 Queue Status for the Selected Queue

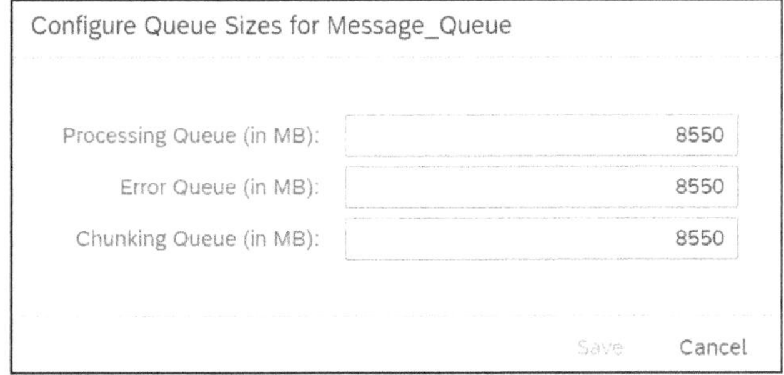

Figure 7.77 Configure Size for the Selected Queue

Automatic Queue Creation

JMS queues are created automatically in the JMS messaging instance during deployment of the first iFlow using a new JMS queue name. Unlike the data store monitor, JMS queues show up in the monitor even if no messages are available in the queue.

The actions available for all queues are shown at the top of the master table. The following actions are available:

- **Filter by Name**
  Filters the list of queues based on the name of the queue.

- **Reload** [C]
  Reloads the content of the table containing the JMS queues.
- **Sort** [⇅]
  Offers sorting options for the available columns.

Queues Aren't Deleted Automatically

JMS queues aren't deleted automatically during undeployment of the iFlow. Why not? Some messages may still exist in the JMS queue, and deleting the queue would delete these messages as well, thus leading to data loss. Only the owner of the scenario knows whether the JMS queue can be deleted with all its content or if its content is still required.

Queues without messages are deleted by a background job if no iFlow using this queue is deployed. This cleanup job runs every 12 hours.

When you select a specific queue on the left, all the messages in this specific queue will be displayed on the right, in the details table. Table 7.29 describes the attributes of individual messages in JMS queues and their possible values.

Column	Description
JMS Message ID	The ID of the entry in the JMS queue. The **JMS Message ID** is a unique ID generated by the runtime when the entry is written to the JMS queue.
Message ID	The ID of the MPL. The **Message ID** is a link, and clicking the link opens the MPL in the message processing monitor.
Status	The status of the message with the following values: ▪ **Waiting**: This status applies after the entry was written to the JMS queue. The message is waiting to be consumed by another process or iFlow. ▪ **Failed**: The last processing of the message ended with an error. Click the link to the MPL to see details about the error. ▪ **Blocked**: The message caused several runtime node outages and isn't being processed anymore. The dead letter queue feature is described in detail in the "Cloud Integration - Configure Dead Letter Handling in JMS Adapter" blog at *http://s-prs.co/507774*. ▪ **Overdue**: The message will receive this status if it wasn't consumed by the due date/time. For these entries, the tenant administrator should check why the message hasn't been consumed (e.g., maybe the consuming iFlow doesn't run anymore) and solve the problem.

Table 7.29 Attributes of JMS Queue Entries

Column	Description
Due At	The date and time the message is expected to be consumed latest. This time is configured in the **JMS** receiver adapter in the **Retention Threshold for Alerting field.** If the message is processed by the **AS2**, **AS4**, or **XI** adapter, the due time is set to 2 days by the adapter.
Created At	The date and time the entry was created in the JMS queue.
Retain Until	The date and time the message will be deleted. This time is configured in the **JMS** receiver adapter in the **Expiration Period field**, which is 30 days per default. If the message is processed by the **AS2**, **AS4**, or **XI** adapter, the expiration period is automatically set to 30 days by the adapter.
Retry Count	The numbers of retries executed for this message.
Next Retry On	The date and time the message will be retried next.

Table 7.29 Attributes of JMS Queue Entries (Cont.)

The following actions are available on the top of the details table for messages stored in JMS queues:

- **Filter by Message ID**
  Filters for a specific message ID, which can be either the JMS message ID or the MPL ID.
- **Retry**
  Restarts the selected messages.
- **Delete**
  Deletes the selected messages from the JMS queue. Only use this option if the messages aren't needed anymore.
- **Download**
  Downloads the selected entries. A *<ID>.zip* file is created in the download folder of your local PC containing the message stored in the JMS queue.
- **Reload**
  Reloads the content of the details table.
- **Table Settings**
  Allows sorting of the entries and filtering by the **Status** column.
- **Multi-select Mode**
  Allows you to select multiple entries at once. This option is useful when you need to delete multiple entries. Note that the **Download** action isn't available for multiple entries.

In addition to the actions located on top of the details table, a **Check** action is available at the very top of the monitor (shown earlier in Figure 7.74). Some consistency checks for JMS queue usage are executed, for example, whether queues aren't used by any iFlows anymore. A detailed description of the available checks and their results can be found in the "Cloud Integration - Checks in JMS Message Queue Monitor" blog at *http://s-prs.co/507775*.

Retry of Blocked Messages

When triggering a retry for messages with the **Blocked** status, keep in mind that messages with the **Blocked** status could not be processed because the runtime node crashed multiple times. In this case, it's highly likely that the message caused the crash. Retrying again may cause another runtime node crash.

JMS Resource Check

JMS resources in the connected JMS message broker instance are limited. Therefore, you must monitor the use of these resources carefully, especially if the load for scenarios using JMS queues increases. If JMS resources are exhausted, you'll encounter errors during runtime processing, which must be avoided. Details about the JMS resources available with the Cloud Integration licenses can be found in the "Cloud Integration - JMS Resource and Size Limits" blog at *http://s-prs.co/507776*.

To monitor JMS resources, keep an eye on the info bar at the top of the **Manage Message Queues** monitor screen, which shows the result of the JMS resource check (shown earlier in Figure 7.73). The following three severity levels are available in the info bar:

- **Info** ✓
  The green message tells you that the use of JMS resources falls within the purchased limits. No action is necessary in this case.
- **Warning** ⚠
  The orange message indicates that at least one JMS resource is in a critical state.
- **Error** (!)
  If at least one JMS resource is exhausted, a red error message is shown.

When you click the **Details** link, the different JMS resources with their current statuses are shown (see Figure 7.78). If dedicated resources are critical, the tenant administrator, together with the scenario owner, should take actions to bring the resources back to normal. If JMS resources are exhausted, message processing is affected, and immediate action is required.

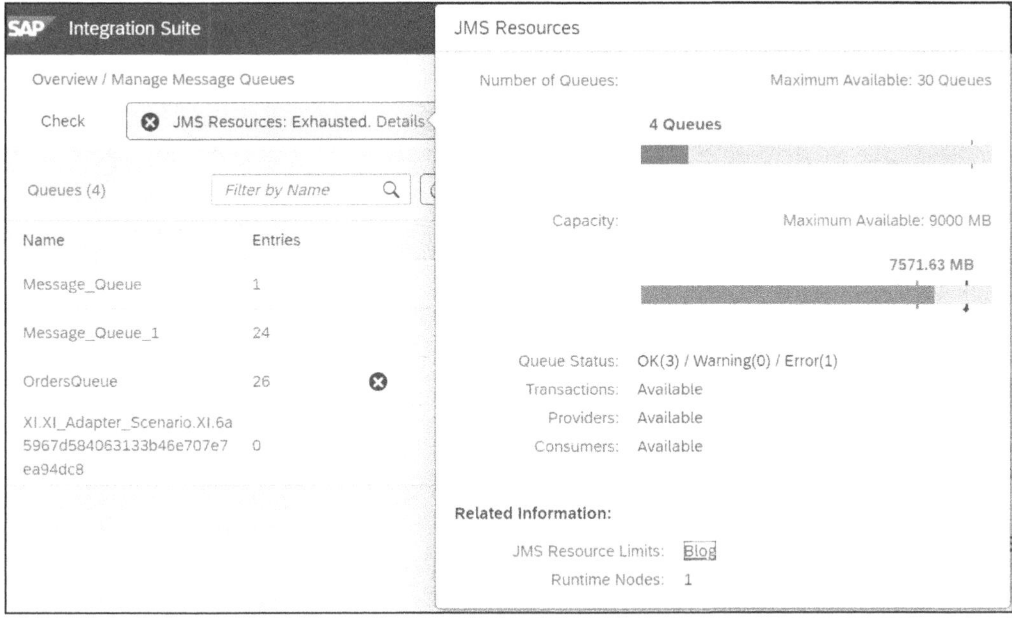

Figure 7.78 Details of JMS Resources

Let's look more closely at the **JMS Resources** screen, as shown in Figure 7.78, to explore what the options mean and what must be done if JMS resources are in a critical state or exhausted:

- **Number of Queues**
  This number is the number of JMS queues created on the JMS message broker during iFlow deployment. If the limit is reached on the JMS message broker, deployments of iFlows using new JMS queues will fail because the new JMS queue can't be created on the JMS message broker. How can you fix this problem? Simply clean up the JMS queues if new queues are required. Use the **Check** action (shown earlier in Figure 7.74) to find unused queues and delete them. Furthermore, you can check whether all iFlows using JMS queues are still required; if not, undeploy these iFlows, and delete their corresponding queues.
- **Capacity**
  An overall storage capacity is available in the JMS message broker instance connected to your tenant for all queues. If 100% of the available capacity is used, no messages can be stored in the JMS queues anymore, and the processing of messages will end in a runtime error. To avoid this problem, check why so many messages exist in JMS queues and why these messages aren't being consumed. For example, a consuming iFlow might not be running, or some dedicated queues might not be needed anymore because they only contain messages from an old scenario. Check and correct the problem as soon as the **Critical** limit is reached to avoid downtime in your deployed scenarios.

- **Queue Status**
  As described earlier when explaining the columns listed in Table 7.28, in addition to the overall storage capacity, each queue has a storage capacity. If 100% of the assigned queue capacity is used, no messages can be stored in this specific JMS queue anymore, and the processing of messages will end in a runtime error. The **Queue Status** shows how many queues have the statuses **OK**, **Warning**, and **Error**. To avoid errors in runtime, check for queues with a **Warning** or **Error** status. This status is shown for each queue in the master table in the **Status** column. Check and correct the problem as soon as a queue receives the status **Warning** to avoid downtime in your deployed scenarios.
- **Transactions**
  To consistently process messages in Cloud Integration, JMS transactions are required in the JMS message broker to roll back processing if errors arise (see Chapter 5, Section 5.4.2, for detailed information). Many transactions are created in the JMS message broker as consumers and providers are under processing in parallel. If the limit for transactions gets **Critical**, you'll need to reduce the parallelism for the consumer and/or provider connections.
- **Providers**
  Providers are created by the **JMS** receiver adapter in the JMS message broker to store messages in a JMS queue. The number of providers created matches the number of messages sent to the JMS queue in parallel. If the value of providers reaches the **Critical** limit, the parallelism of the inbound processing is too high. You'll need to reduce the number of parallel inbound calls from sender systems sending messages to scenarios using JMS queues.
- **Consumers**
  Consumers are created in the JMS message broker from **JMS** sender adapters to consume messages from the JMS queue. For each JMS queue used in a JMS sender channel, as many consumers are created as concurrent processes are configured in the JMS sender channel in the **Number of Concurrent Processes** parameter (see Chapter 5, Section 5.4.1). If several runtime nodes are started in the Cloud Integration cluster, those many consumers are created from each runtime node. If the number of consumers gets **Critical**, you'll need to reduce the parallelism, either by reducing the **Number of Concurrent Processes** in the **JMS** sender channels or by reducing the number of runtime nodes started in the cluster.

If the actions we've described don't solve your JMS resource shortage, you may need to purchase more JMS messaging units and add them to the JMS message broker instance connected to the tenant to increase the available JMS resources in the JMS message broker.

The last tile in this section is **Number Ranges**, which will be explained in the next section.

7.4.4 Maintaining Number Ranges

Number ranges are required to define unique interchange numbers for each document to facilitate Electronic Data Interchange (EDI) processing. A number range object (NRO) can be used to define the length of the number and its minimum and maximum values. The NRO is defined and monitored in the **Number Ranges** monitor and used during runtime when an iFlow is executed.

Clicking the **Number Ranges** tile opens the list of defined NROs in a table, as shown in Figure 7.79. Table 7.30 provides detailed descriptions of the available attributes of NROs.

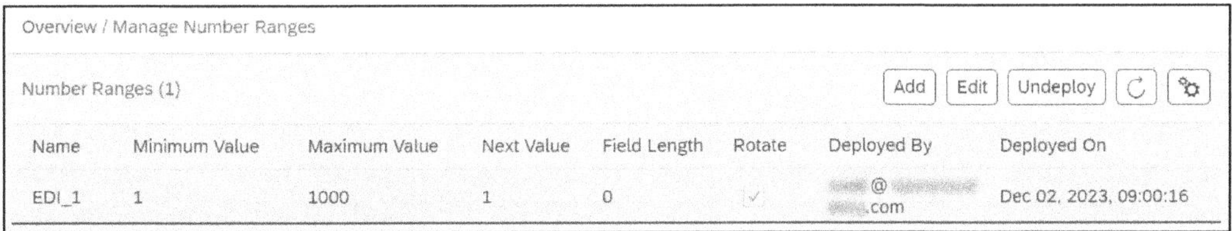

Figure 7.79 Number Ranges Monitor

Column	Description
Name	Name of the NRO. This name is used in the iFlow configuration to refer to the NRO.
Minimum Value	Minimum value allowed, which should be greater than or equal to 0.
Maximum Value	Maximum value allowed in this NRO.
Next Value	The next value used in runtime when invoking the NRO.
Field Length	Field length of the number. Leading zeros are added to the current value to achieve a fixed field length in runtime. Thus, if the current value is 5, the unique number used in runtime is 0005 to achieve a field length of 4. If the **Field Length** field is set to 0, no leading zeros are added. The maximum value allowed for this field is "99".
Rotate	If this flag is set, and the number range reaches the specified maximum value, the current value resets to the specified minimum value.
Deployed By	The user who deployed the NRO.
Deployed On	Date and time the NRO was deployed.

Table 7.30 Attributes of Number Range Objects

The following actions are available for NROs and can be accessed at the top of the table:

- **Add**
  Opens the **Add Number Range** dialog box where you can define and deploy new NROs, as shown in Figure 7.80.
- **Edit**
  Opens the **Edit** dialog box to adjust the definitions of a selected NRO.
- **Undeploy**
  Removes an NRO from the tenant.
- **Reload**
  Reloads the content of the table.
- **Table Settings**
  Allows sorting of the entries and filtering by the name of the NRO or by the user who deployed the NRO.

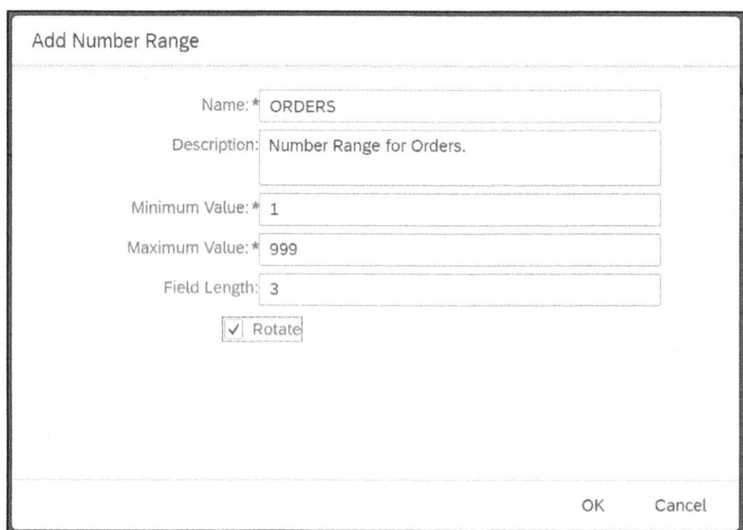

Figure 7.80 Add Number Range Dialog Box

With this discussion of NROs, we've completed the **Manage Stores** section and can start exploring the **Access Logs** section of the monitoring dashboard where access to different logs is provided.

7.5 Accessing Logs

The **Access Logs** section in the **Monitoring Overview** screen (see Figure 7.81) offers access to different logs created in Cloud Integration. Logs are important, for example, when specific errors that occur during runtime processing need to be analyzed. Often, detailed logs are requested by SAP support to analyze specific error situations. Therefore, you must know which logs are available and what they contain.

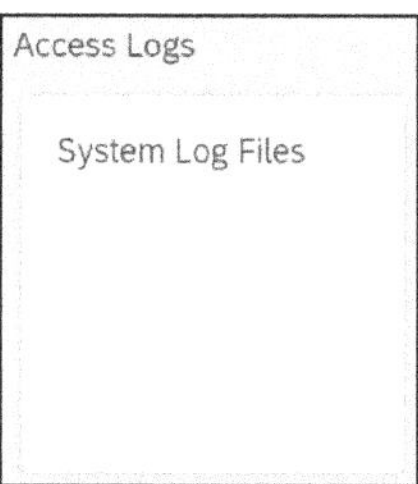

Figure 7.81 Access Logs Section in Monitoring Dashboard

In the **Access Logs** section of the monitoring dashboard, SAP BTP, Cloud Foundry environments have **System Log Files** tile. SAP BTP, Neo environments have an additional tile, named **Audit**. An audit log is more relevant for auditing purposes, and the system logs are mainly required for error analysis.

7.5.1 Monitoring Audit Logs

Audit logs are security-relevant records. Cloud Integration needs to log all system changes on the Cloud Integration tenant. The changes that are logged include configuration changes, deployments, or deletions of security artifacts; log-level changes; and more. All these changes are logged in the audit log. The monitoring dashboard offers access to the audit log via the **Audit Log** tile in the SAP BTP, Neo environment.

Audit Logs in the SAP BTP, Cloud Foundry Environment

In the SAP BTP, Cloud Foundry environment, the audit log is currently not available in the Cloud Integration monitoring dashboard. Instead, you can access audit logs from the SAP BTP cockpit. Refer to the "Audit Logging in the Cloud Foundry Environment" chapter in the SAP BTP documentation, available at *https://help.sap.com/docs/btp*.

In the future, the audit log will also be available in the monitoring dashboard in Cloud Integration for the SAP BTP, Cloud Foundry environment.

Clicking the **Audit Log** tile opens a table in a new screen showing all audit logs from the past hour, as shown in Figure 7.82.

Retention Time

The retention time of an audit log is 30 days, after which the audit log is automatically deleted.

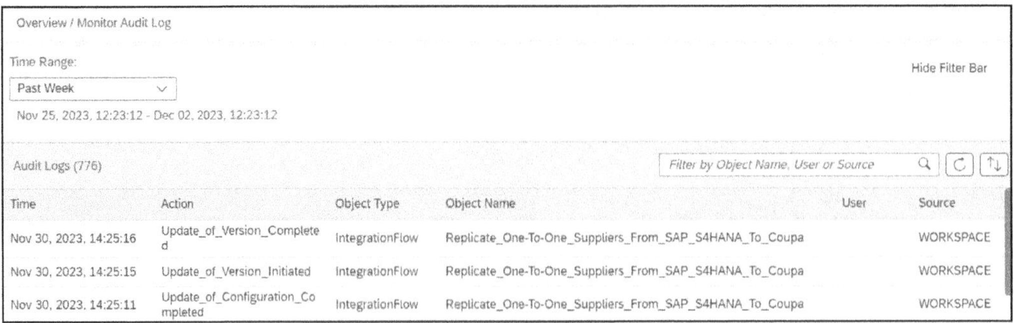

Figure 7.82 Audit Log Monitor

However, you can adjust the **Time Range** at the top of the table to see audit logs for a longer time period. As shown in Figure 7.82, for example, you can view the audit logs for the **Past Week**. Table 7.31 provides detailed descriptions of the attributes found in audit log entries.

Column	Description
Time	The date and time the audit log entry was created.
Action	The action performed on the system with the following values: ■ **Create**: Creation of artifacts or configurations, for example, certificates in the keystore. ■ **Change**: Changing of configuration parameters, for example, log levels of an iFlow. ■ **Delete:** Deletion of artifacts, for example, certificates, variables, or messages. ■ **Read**: Read access to artifacts, for example, to message payloads using the trace feature or to messages or variables in temporary storages.
Object Type	Type of the object that was changed, for example, **Message Store Entries**, **Message**, **Variable**, **Configuration Parameter**, or **X.509 Certificate**.
Object Name	Name or ID of the object that was changed, for example, the ID of a message, the name of an X.509 certificate, or the name of a variable.
User	User who triggered the change. If an SAP user triggered the change, **SAP** is displayed.
Source	IP address the change was triggered from. If an SAP user triggered the change, **SAP** is displayed.

Table 7.31 Attributes of Audit Log Entries

You can sort the entries by clicking the **Sort** icon ↑↓ or filtering by the **Object Name**, **User**, or **Source** using the **Filter** fields located at the top of the table.

Now, let's look at the second tile in the **Access Logs** section, which provides access to system logs.

7.5.2 Checking System Log Files

Sometimes, the error messages shown in the MPL aren't sufficient to fully understand the root cause of an error. Other times, SAP support will require detailed information for analyzing an error. In these cases, you'll need to investigate the system logs written during message processing on the runtime node. The **System Log Files** tile provides access to these technical system logs.

Clicking the **System Log Files** tile opens a table containing the most important log files of the runtime nodes running in your cluster, as shown in Figure 7.83, under the **Log Files** tab. Table 7.32 provides detailed descriptions of the attributes of the system log files.

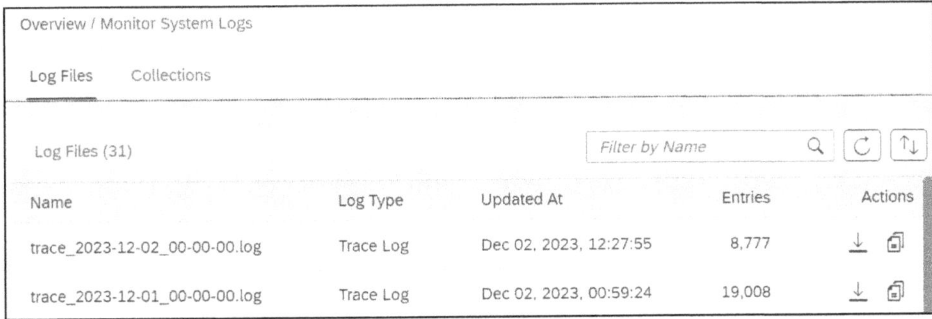

Figure 7.83 Monitor System Logs Screen

Column	Description
Name	Name of the log file. The name has the following pattern: **<log type>_<date>.log**. The process ID is shown in the message processing monitor, so that you can easily identify the system log in which details about message processing are logged.
Log Type	Type of log file with the following values: ▪ **Trace Log**: System trace file. ▪ **HTTP Access Log**: Log file containing the HTTP inbound requests. One log file is available for each runtime node.
Updated At	Date and time the log file was updated.
Entries	Number of entries in the log file.

Table 7.32 Attributes of Log Files

Column	Description
Actions	Actions available for the log file include the following: ▪ **Download** ⤓ : Downloads the log file. ▪ **Copy Download URL** ⎘ : Copies the download URL to the clipboard.

Table 7.32 Attributes of Log Files (Cont.)

Retention Time

The retention time of the system log files is seven days. After seven days, the system logs are automatically deleted.

You can sort the entries using the **Sort** icon ⇅ or filter by **Name** using the **Filter** field at the top of the table.

Under the **Collections** tab, you can access collections of the system log files, as shown in Figure 7.84. You can download the collections as an archive by clicking the **Download** icon ⤓ , or you can copy the URL by clicking the **Copy** icon ⎘ . When downloading the collection, you'll receive a **.zip* archive containing the latest log files.

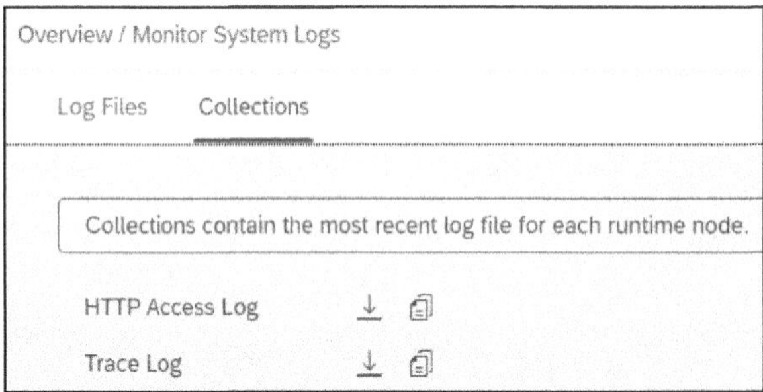

Figure 7.84 Collections Tab in System Logs

With this step, we've completed our review of the **Access Logs** section. Let's continue with the next, rather specific, section, which handles locks created during message processing.

7.6 Managing Locks

On the Cloud Integration tenant, locks are written by some components to maintain integrity and consistency in the way these components are handled by multiple processes or users. There are two types of locks supported by the Cloud Integration environment:

- **Runtime**
  Message locks are required for efficient and consistent processing of messages. To monitor these message processing locks, click the **Message Locks** tile in the **Manage Locks** section of the monitoring dashboard, as shown in Figure 7.85.
- **Design time**
  Design time locks ensure that integration artifacts such as packages and iFlows aren't updated by multiple users at the same time. To monitor these locks, click on the **Designtime Artifact Locks** tile, as shown in Figure 7.85.

Figure 7.85 Manage Locks Section in the Monitoring Dashboard

In this section, we'll cover both locks in more detail.

7.6.1 Dealing with Message Locks

During message processing in Cloud Integration, some adapters write entries into an in-progress repository to avoid the same message being processed multiple times in parallel, for example, by different runtime nodes, or to avoid large messages leading to out-of-memory issues on runtime nodes again and again.

The following adapters write message processing locks:

- **SFTP and FTP sender adapters**
  To prevent double processing of files by the SFTP and FTP sender adapter, a lock entry is written to the in-progress repository each time a file is processed by a worker. As long as this lock entry exists, no other runtime node can access the file. After message processing, independent of whether the processing ended in the **Completed** or **Failed** status, the lock is removed by the runtime. If the worker crashes during processing of the message, for example, because of an out-of-memory error, the message processing lock isn't removed. Upon restart of the worker, the message is retried by the adapter. If the worker crashes two more times during the processing of this message, the message is taken out from processing, and the message lock remains in the in-progress repository. Manual action is required by the tenant administrator, together with the scenario owner, to check why this file could not be processed. For example, maybe the file is too large to be processed by the iFlow. In

this case, the file should be removed from the polling directory and be split into smaller files. The lock can then be released.

- **Mail sender adapter**
  To prevent double processing of emails by the mail sender adapter, a lock entry is written each time mails are polled from a folder on the mail server by a runtime node. As long as this lock entry exists, no other runtime nodes can poll from this folder. After message processing, independent of whether the processing ended in the **Completed** or **Failed** status, the lock is removed by the runtime. If the runtime node crashes during processing of the message, the lock is removed after the lock timeout configured in the mail sender adapter.
- **JMS sender adapter**
  The JMS sender adapter uses the in-progress repository only if **Dead Letter Queue** handling is switched on (for more details, refer to Chapter 5, Section 5.4.1). If the runtime node crashes during the processing of the message, for example, because of an out-of-memory error, the message processing lock isn't removed, and upon restart of the runtime node, the message is retried by the JMS sender adapter. If the runtime node crashes two more times during processing of this message, the message is taken out from processing and marked as **Blocked** in the queue monitor (described earlier in Section 7.4.3). The message lock in the message lock monitor is removed.
- **AS2 sender adapter**
  Because the AS2 sender adapters use JMS queues to store the message during processing, the same behavior as described for the JMS sender adapter applies for the AS2 sender adapter. The in-progress repository is only used if **Dead Letter Queue** handling is switched on. The message is marked as **Blocked** in the queue monitor, and the message lock is removed from the message lock monitor if the runtime node crashed multiple times during the processing of this message.
- **AS4 sender and XI sender and receiver adapters**
  The AS4 sender adapter and the XI adapters, both sender and receiver, can use either JMS queues or data stores for temporary storage of the messages during processing:
  - If JMS queues are used, the same behavior as described for the JMS and AS2 sender adapters holds true for the AS4 sender adapter and the XI adapters as well. The in-progress repository is only used if **Dead Letter Queue** handling is switched on. The message is marked as **Blocked** in the queue monitor, and the message lock is removed from the message lock monitor if the runtime node crashed multiple times during processing of this message.
  - If the data store is used as temporary storage, the in-progress repository is always used to avoid a message crashing the runtime node again and again; no configuration option is available. If the runtime node crashes three times during processing of this message, the message is taken out of processing, and the message lock remains in the in-progress repository. These entries stay in the message locks monitor until you manually release them. Before releasing the lock, check the

corresponding message in the data store monitor, for example, to see if the message is too large to be processed by the iFlow. In this case, you'll need to request that the sender of this message split the message and send smaller messages instead. The message in the data store can then be removed, and the lock in the lock monitor can be released.

You can monitor entries in the in-progress repository in the **Message Locks** tile. When you click the **Message Locks** tile, a table containing all currently set message processing locks will be displayed, as shown in Figure 7.86. Table 7.33 provides detailed descriptions of the available attributes of message processing locks.

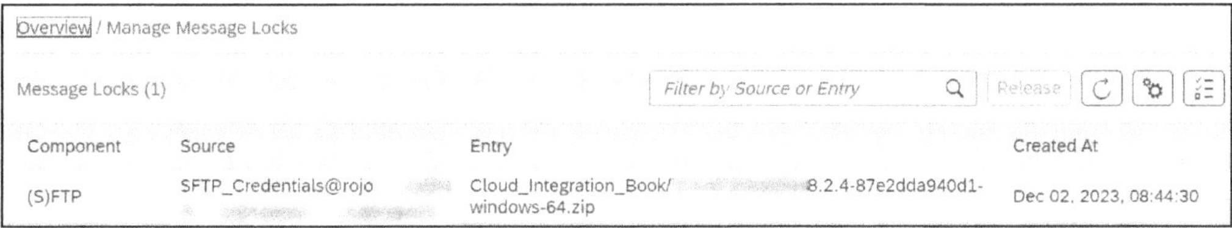

Figure 7.86 Message Locks Monitor

Column	Description
Component	Component that set the lock and has the following values: ■ **SFTP**: The lock was set by the **SFTP** sender adapter. ■ **FTP**: The lock was set by the **FTP** sender adapter. ■ **Mail**: The lock was set by the **Mail** sender adapter. ■ **JMS**: The lock was set by the JMS component, which is the case for the **JMS** adapter, **AS2** adapter, **AS4** adapter, and **XI** adapter when JMS queues are used for temporary storage. ■ **XI**: The lock was set by the **XI** adapter when using the data store for temporary storage. ■ **AS4**: The lock was set by the **AS4** adapter when using the data store for temporary storage.
Source	Identifies the source of the lock. The following values are possible: ■ For SFTP: **<sftp user>@<sftp server>** ■ For FTP: **<ftp user>@<ftp server>** ■ For Mail: **<mail server>:<mail user>** ■ For JMS: **JMS:<queue name>** ■ For XI: **XI_<integration flow name>.<participant name>_<channel name>** ■ For AS4: **DA_<integration flow name>.<participant name>_<channel name**

Table 7.33 Attributes of Message Locks

Column	Description
Entry	Identifies the locked object, for example, the message or file name: ■ For SFTP and FTP: **<directory/filename>** ■ For Mail: **<mailbox>** ■ For JMS: **ID:<JMS message ID>** (clicking the link opens the JMS message in the queue monitor) ■ For XI: **<Entry ID from data store>** ■ For AS4: **<Entry ID from data store>**
Created At	Date and time the lock was set.

Table 7.33 Attributes of Message Locks (Cont.)

The following actions at the top of the screen are available for message processing locks:

- **Filter**
  Filters the table by specifying values for the **Source** or the **Entry** column. Using this option, you can, for example, search for a specific message ID or a file name.
- **Release**
  Releases the lock and thus triggers another retry of the message or file.
- **Reload**
  Reloads the content of the table.
- **Table Settings**
  Allows the sorting of the entries and filtering by the **Component** column.
- **Multi-select Mode**
  Allows you to select multiple entries at once. This option is useful when you need to delete multiple entries.

Releasing Locks Can Lead to a Runtime Node Crash

When releasing locks, keep in mind that messages received the lock because they could not be processed due to multiple runtime node crashes. Thus, it's likely that the message caused the crash. Releasing the lock triggers another retry of the file or message and thus may cause another runtime node crash.

7.6.2 Managing Design Time Artifact Locks

As you've seen so far, Cloud Integration design time is used to create various integration objects. Every user of Cloud Integration can create or modify these objects. To ensure that an object can only be modified by one user at a time the platform provides the design time artifact locks. The lifetime of the lock starts when the user starts editing an object and stays until the user saves the object, even if the session of Cloud

Integration becomes invalid. The user who was modifying the object can always restore unsaved changes. There can be a situation when an object needs to be modified but the user who locked it is unavailable. In these cases, the tenant administrator can unlock the objects using the **Designtime Artifacts Locks** tile of the Monitoring Overview, as shown earlier in Figure 7.85.

All available design time locks are visible in the **Locked Designtime Artifacts** table shown in Figure 7.87. Table 7.34 provides detailed descriptions of the available attributes of design time locks,

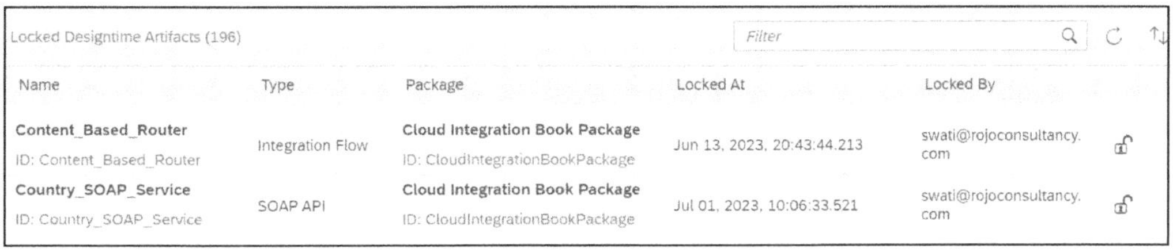

Locked Designtime Artifacts (196) — Filter

Name	Type	Package	Locked At	Locked By	
Content_Based_Router ID: Content_Based_Router	Integration Flow	**Cloud Integration Book Package** ID: CloudIntegrationBookPackage	Jun 13, 2023, 20:43:44.213	swati@rojoconsultancy.com	
Country_SOAP_Service ID: Country_SOAP_Service	SOAP API	**Cloud Integration Book Package** ID: CloudIntegrationBookPackage	Jul 01, 2023, 10:06:33.521	swati@rojoconsultancy.com	

Figure 7.87 Overview of Locked Designtime Artifacts

Column	Description
Name	Name and ID of the locked object.
Type	Type of the integration object, for example, **Integration Flow, Value Mapping, SOAP API**, and so on.
Package	Name and ID of the package in which the object exists.
Locked At	Date and time the lock was set.
Locked By	The user who was editing the object.

Table 7.34 Attributes of Design Time Artifact Locks

To unlock a specific object, click on the unlock icon available in the end of each entry in the **Locked Designtime Artifacts** table. Unlocking an object will revert it to its last saved state, and any unsaved changes will be lost. You can also the **Filter**, **Reload**, and **Sort** actions on the table that appear above the table.

With this discussion, we've completed this section about message processing locks. In the next section, let's discuss how you can analyze the message load running through your Cloud Integration environment.

7.7 Monitoring Message Usage

As mentioned in Chapter 2, the SAP Integration Suite capabilities also support a Pay per Message model. Therefore, as an integration consultant, you would most likely want to be on top of the usage statistics of your Cloud Integration tenant. The **Message Usage** tile in the **Usage Details** section provides high-level statistics about the messages processed by your tenant. By default, the tile shows the usage statistic of the current month, as shown in Figure 7.88.

Figure 7.88 Message Usage Tile under Usage Details

Click this tile to see the detailed statistic dashboard as shown in Figure 7.89. The dashboard is divided into three sections. On the top left of the dashboard, you can select the date range for which you want to see the usage throughput. Keep in mind that at one point, a maximum window of 31 days can be selected. Once you select the date range you're interested in, the dashboard refreshes with the data based on your selection. The left part of the dashboard provides the total message count for the **Total Cloud Integration messages** and **Total SAP to SAP Integration Messages (Excluded)**. The third metric derived using these two statistics is the **Total Chargeable Messages**. For more details on what constitutes a chargeable message, see the following boxed note.

Message Metering: How Are Cloud Integration Messages Counted?

Like many software as a service (SaaS) applications, Cloud Integration also has a licensing model based on Pay per Use. This model requires a clear definition of what constitutes a message. In Cloud Integration, a message is determined by calculating the total size of all outbound messages that pass through all the receiver adapters configured in the iFlow. Now this total size in kilobytes is divided by 250 to determine the number of messages. To explain further, if an iFlow has one receiver adapter that processes a message of 50 KB, then it constitutes as one message, but if the same iFlow processes a message of 300 KB, then the message count constitutes two messages.

Note that SAP to SAP out-of-the-box prepackaged contents that are listed on the SAP Business Accelerator Hub are exempt from metering. For more details of all possibilities and details on message metering, refer to SAP Note 2942344.

On the right half of the dashboard, you see a bar chart visualization of messages spread over the date range with each bar representing a single date, as shown in Figure 7.89.

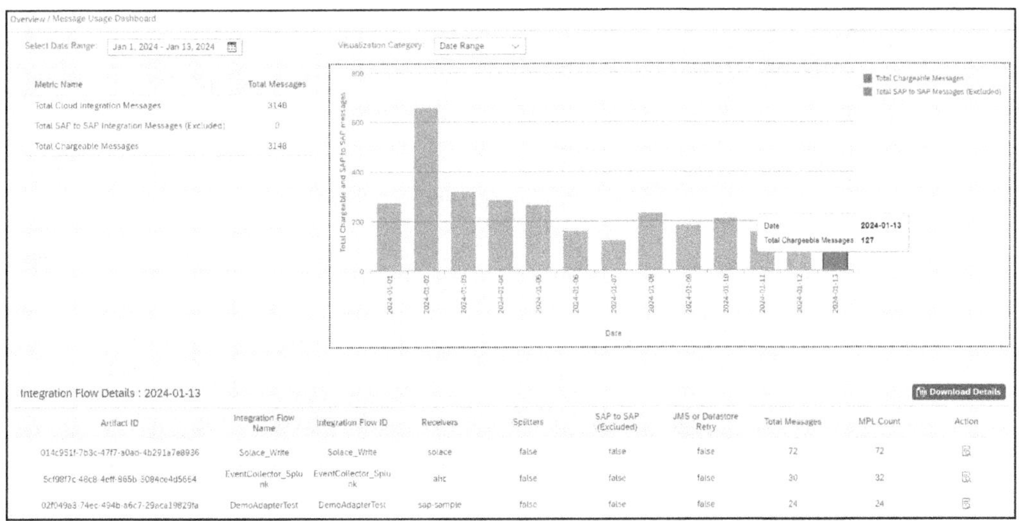

Figure 7.89 Message Usage Dashboard for the Date Range Visualization Category

The **Visualization Category** dropdown at the top of the dashboard can be used to visualize the same data as an area chart based on the deployed iFlow artifact ID and the message count, as shown in Figure 7.90.

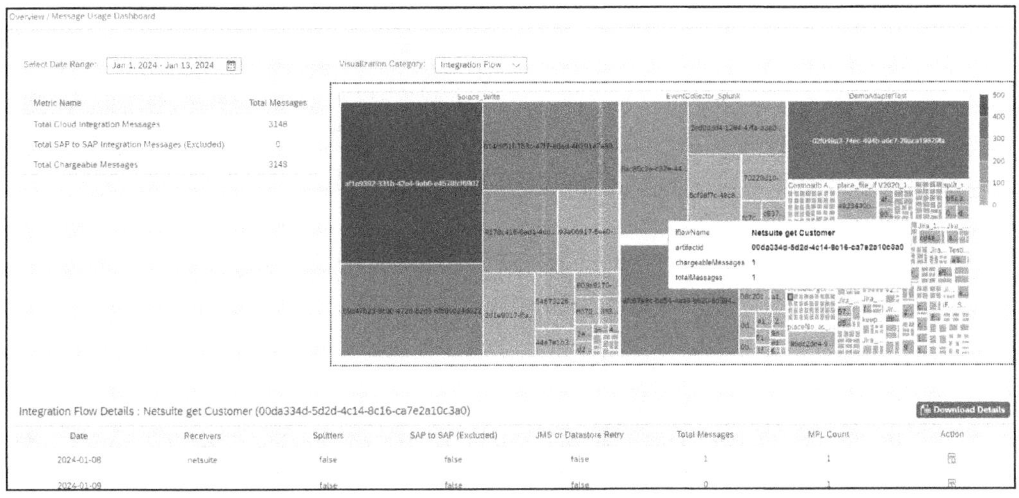

Figure 7.90 Message Usage Dashboard for iFlow Visualization Category

On the bottom part of the dashboard, you can find a more detailed breakdown of the message count by clicking on a specific bar or rectangular block on the visualization. Table 7.35 lists the attributes of the iFlows that are part of the selection.

Attribute	Description
Artifact ID	The GUID of the deployed iFlow. This column is part of the table when the **Visualization Category** is **Date Range**.
Integration Flow Name	Name of the iFlow. This column is part of the table when the **Visualization Category** is **Date Range**.
Integration Flow ID	ID of the iFlow. This column is part of the table when the **Visualization Category** is **Date Range**.
Date	Date for which the statistics are displayed. This column is part of the table when the **Visualization Category** is **Integration Flow**.
Receivers	List of all the receivers that are part of the iFlow.
Splitters	If the iFlow contains a splitter, the value of this attribute is **true**.
SAP to SAP (Excluded)	If the iFlow belongs to the SAP to SAP prepackaged content, which isn't part of metering, then this attribute is **true**.
JMS or Data Store Retry	If the iFlow has a retry mechanism setup using JMS or datastore, then the value of this attribute is set to **true**.
Total Messages	Total message count for the specific artifact ID.
MPL Count	Total number of MPL count for the specific artifact id.
Action	The actions icon provides more granular detail for a selected row. You can also download the report as an Excel file by clicking on the **Download Details** button.

Table 7.35 Attributes of the iFlow Details Section of the Message Usage Dashboard

Now that we've covered all the tiles available in the monitoring view, you should feel confident enough to operate your own Cloud Integration tenant using all the available monitoring options.

7.8 Integrating Cloud Integration with Enterprise Monitoring Tools

Enterprise monitoring solutions help operations teams monitor all mission-critical applications from one application. You might ask why we would need such an application when we already have excellent monitoring capabilities in Cloud Integration itself. An enterprise's IT landscape in general is quite complex with multiple applications working in harmony to run a business process. We're talking about ERPs, CRM systems, file shares, databases and don't forget integration platforms such as Cloud Integration that are responsible for the smooth integration of these applications. Although each of these applications provides its own monitoring console, monitoring these distributed, heterogeneous applications is a humongous task. The solution to this problem is bringing in an enterprise monitoring application that would add the following benefits for an organization:

- Use one application to monitor all mission-critical applications throughout the enterprise, hence breaking the silos. Look at business process performance, health of infrastructure, security, and various other organization key performance indicators (KPIs) from one view.
- Connect, combine, and correlate logs, metrics, and traces quickly in a matter of minutes rather than hours or days.
- Prevent and predict outages to minimize business downtime.
- Store logs for a longer time frame for analysis and compliance purposes.
- Use the power of artificial intelligence (AI)/machine learning (ML) on the gold mine of data to derive smart statistics and make data-driven decisions.

Some of the most used enterprise monitoring solutions are SAP Cloud ALM, Splunk, Microsoft Azure Monitoring, and so on. Cloud Integration provides the following ways to extract the logs from your tenant and monitor those through any enterprise application of your choice:

- **Cloud Integration OData APIs**
  These are publicly available OData APIs that can be used to connect to your Cloud Integration tenant and retrieve various types of logs such as HTTP, trace logs, and MPLs.
- **External logging**
  Cloud Integration also allows MPLs to be offloaded to an external system. At the time of writing this book, external logging is only supported for Splunk.

In the following sections, we'll follow a step-by-step guide to setting up external logging for your Cloud Integration tenant.

7.8.1 Configuring Splunk to Receive Data from Cloud Integration

Splunk is a unified security and observability platform available in both cloud and on-premise offerings. You can ingest any format of data to it and store it for as long as you like. In this exercise, we'll point our Cloud Integration tenant to a Splunk Cloud Trial environment. If you don't have access to a Splunk environment in your organization, you can open a trial from the official website: *http://s-prs.co/v576040*.

To receive MPLs from the Cloud Integration tenant, we need to create a data input in Splunk. Splunk supports numerous data inputs such as files and directories, network events, operating system information, and so on. In our case, we need to create a data input of type HTTP Event Collector (HEC). HEC enables applications to send logs to a

Splunk HTTP/HTTPS endpoint by using a token for authentication and correct ingestion of data. To create an HEC token, click on **Settings** from the top menu, and select **Data inputs** under the **DATA** section, as shown in Figure 7.91.

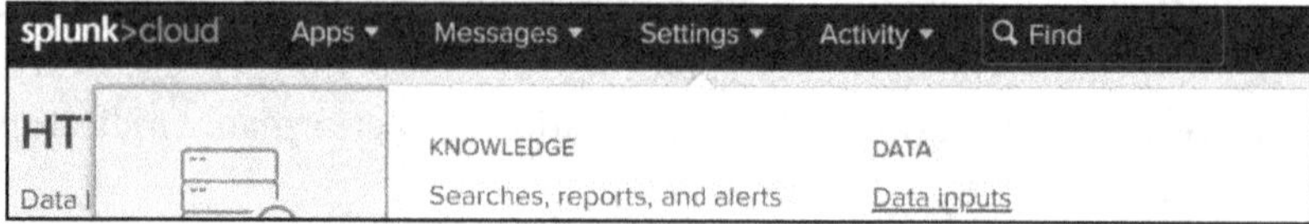

Figure 7.91 Creating a New Data Input in Splunk

This opens a list of all possible data inputs supported by your Splunk tenant. Click on the **Add new** button in the same row of the **HTTP Event Collector** input type, as shown in Figure 7.92.

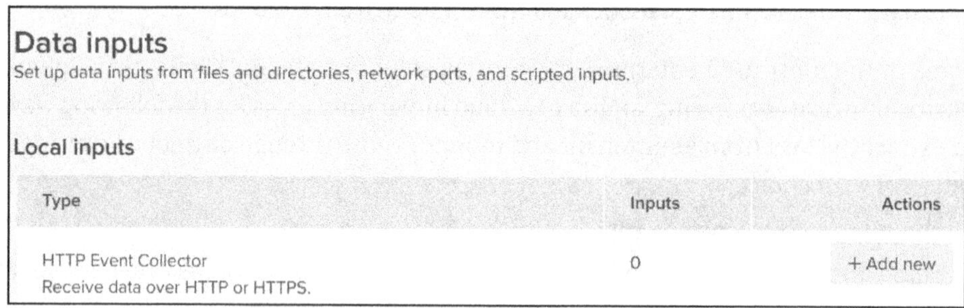

Figure 7.92 Creating a Data Input of Type HTTP Event Collector

Now we need to provide additional details about the type of data to make it more meaningful and easier to find. In Splunk, there are a few metadata fields associated with each event as listed here:

- **Select Source**
  This parameter is reserved to identify the source of data input. By default, all events ingested via this endpoint will have the source as **http:<input name>**. In our case, we'll provide a specific value for **Source** by setting the optional parameter **Source name override**, as shown in Figure 7.93.

  Provide a meaningful name and description for the source, and click **Next**.
- **Source Type**
  Specifies the type of data being ingested. It can be structured or unstructured. The source type also specifies rules for data interpretation, for example, the time stamp of the event, line breaks, truncation rules, and so on. The MPLs are JSON events, so we'll select the **Source Type Category** as **Structured** and give it a meaningful name, as shown in Figure 7.94. Note that if you don't provide this information while creating the HEC token, Splunk will assign a default value while ingesting data.

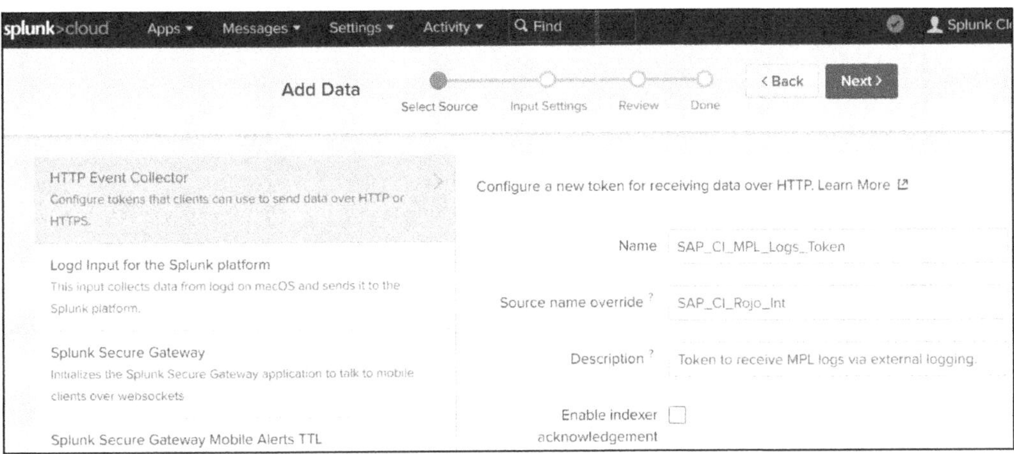

Figure 7.93 Select Source Configuration for HEC Add Data

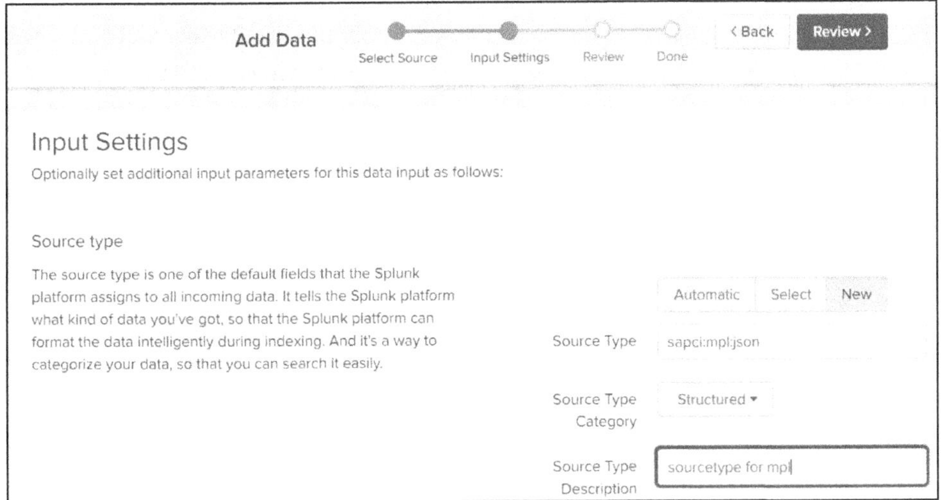

Figure 7.94 Source Type Configuration for HEC Add Data

- **Index**
  Index specifies the bucket/folder in which the data resides. **Index** is one of the most important parameters in Splunk as it provides the logical separation of data, which in turn helps with retention and access control features. For the sake of simplicity, we'll select the index **main** from the list of default indexes, as shown in Figure 7.95. Ideally, your Splunk admin should create a dedicated index based on the organization's best practices for data retention.

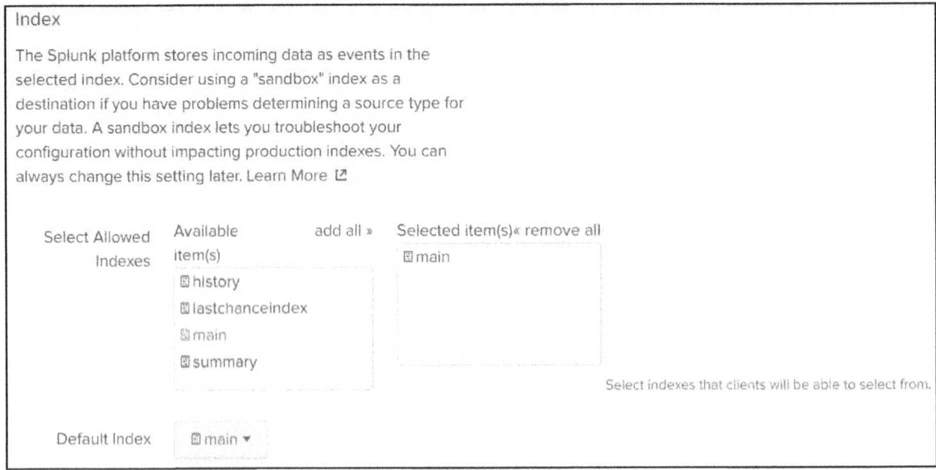

Figure 7.95 Index Configuration for HEC Add Data

Once you've provided all the parameters as expected, click on **Review** and verify that your input configuration looks similar to the screen shown in Figure 7.96.

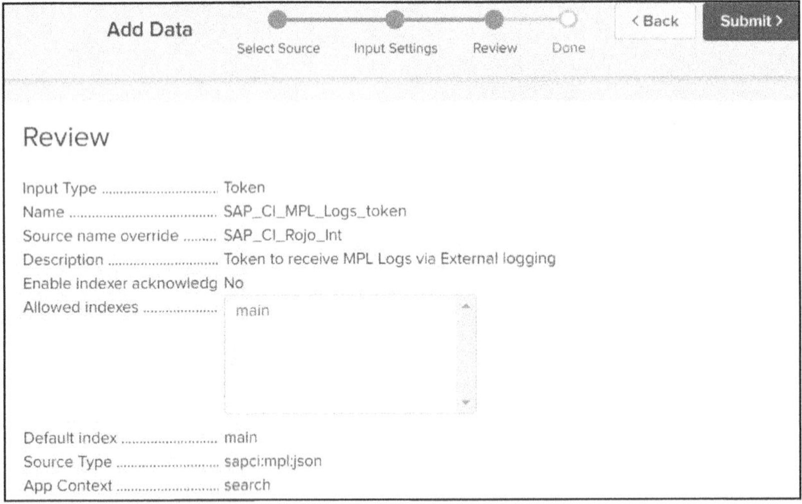

Figure 7.96 Review Configured Details for HEC Add Data

Click on **Submit** to create your token. After successful creation of the HEC data input, you'll get the token, as shown in Figure 7.97. Copy and save it, as you'll need to reference it in later steps, as explained in the following section.

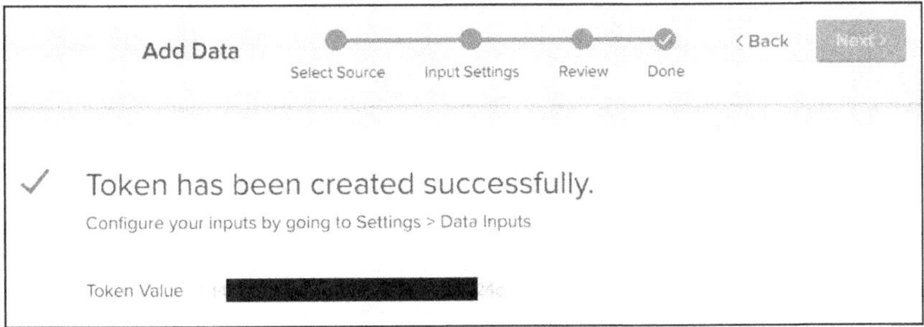

Figure 7.97 Confirmation of Successful HEC Token Creation

7.8.2 Enabling External Logging from SAP BTP Cockpit

To enable external logging for your tenant, you need to create a new HTTP destination in your SAP BTP Cockpit. You need to have the following roles to be able to activate external logging:

- `AuthGroup_Administrator`
- `ExternalLoggingActivate`

Navigate to your subaccount, and select **Destinations** under the **Connectivity** option. Click on **Create Destination** to add a new destination, as shown in Figure 7.98.

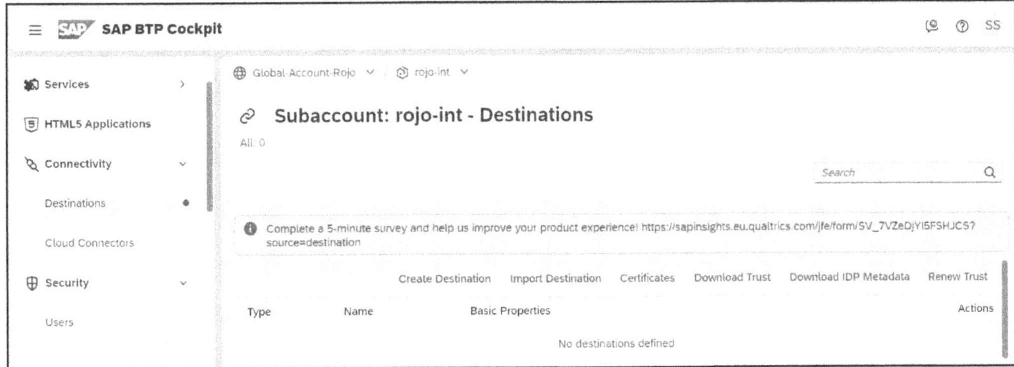

Figure 7.98 Connectivity Destinations for Your Subaccount in SAP BTP Cockpit

Configure the destination by defining the parameters listed in Table 7.36.

Parameter Name	Value
Name	Enter “CloudIntegration_MonitoringDataConsumer”.
Type	Select **HTTP**.
Description	Give a meaningful description for the destination.

Table 7.36 HTTP Destination Parameters for External Logging

Parameter Name	Value
URL	Provide the URL of the HEC without the endpoint path. For the Splunk Cloud trial, it's "https://http-inputs-splunkhost.splunkcloud.com".
Proxy Type	Select **Internet** (because we're connecting to Splunk Cloud).
Authentication	Select **BasicAuthentication**.
User	Enter "Splunk".
Password	Enter the HEC token that was generated in the previous step.
TargetSystem	Enter "Splunk".
Host	Give the name of your Cloud Integration tenant. This isn't a mandatory field, but it's good to have this information in the setting as it helps with searching the MPL logs in Splunk.
index	Provide the name of the index configured in HEC. In our exercise, it's "main".

Table 7.36 HTTP Destination Parameters for External Logging (Cont.)

After correct configuration, your destination should look like Figure 7.99.

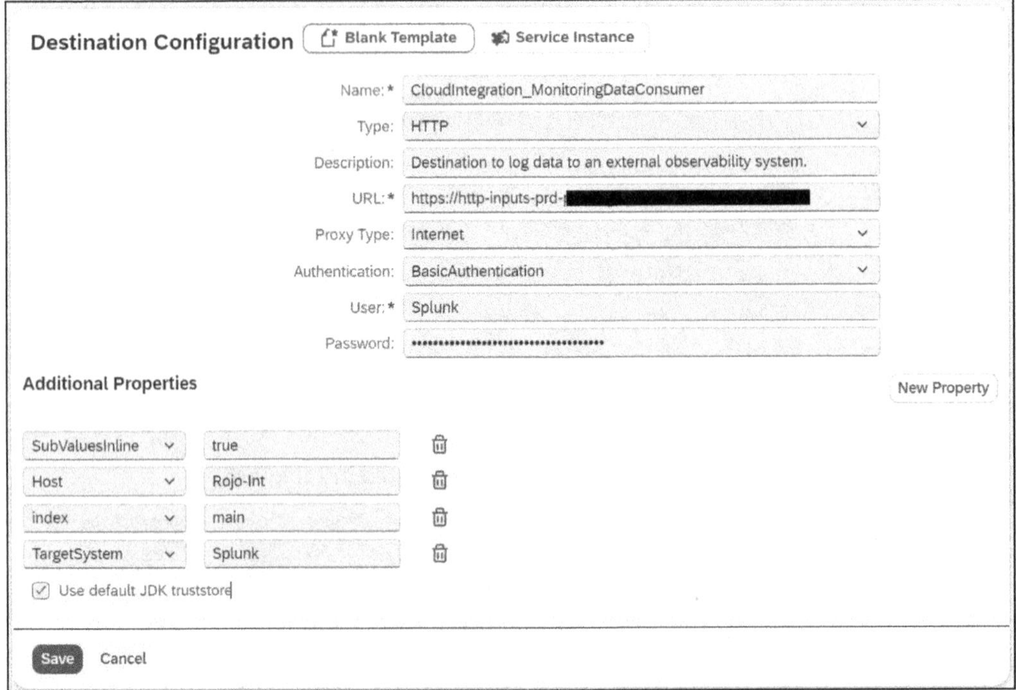

Figure 7.99 Destination Configuration for Splunk External Logging

Now that the destination is created successfully, we need to activate external logging by calling the Cloud Integration OData endpoint. You can use any HTTP client of your choice for this operation. In this exercise, we'll use the Postman HTTP client. Set the request by using the following parameters, as shown in Figure 7.100:

- **HTTP Operation: POST**
- **Endpoint:** "https://path-to-odata-api/api/v1/activateExternalLogging"
- **Query Params: defaultLogLevel** with possible values of **NONE**, **INFO**, or **ERROR**

To call this endpoint, your user should have the `ExternalLoggingActivate` role. On the successful activation, you'll get a 200 OK response from the API with a message that **ExternalLogging successfully enabled for tenant**, as shown in Figure 7.100.

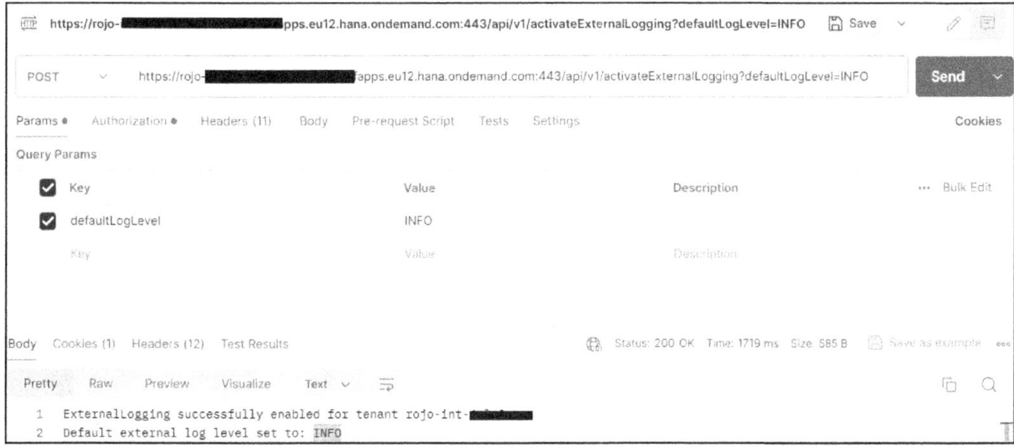

Figure 7.100 Activating External Logging via HTTP Client

Once external logging is enabled, all your deployed iFlows will get an extra dropdown in the **Log Configuration** section, as shown in Figure 7.101. The possible values for **External Log Level** is **None**, **Info**, and **Error**. As shown in Figure 7.100, we called the OData API with the value of **defaultLogLevel** query parameter as **INFO**, so all the iFlows deployed in our tenant have the default **External Log Level** as **Info**.

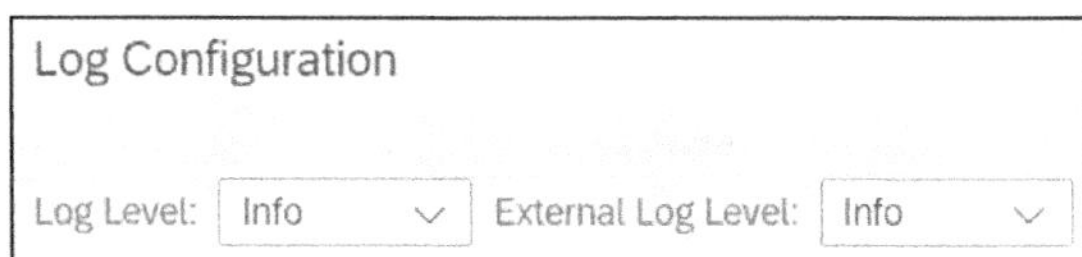

Figure 7.101 External Log Level Selection in the Log Configuration Section of Deployed Integration Content

Now let's log in to our Splunk environment and check if we're receiving the MPLs from our Cloud Integration tenant. Open Splunk's default Search and Reporting app, and navigate to the **Search** tab. In the search bar, and enter the following query: "index=<your index name> host=<your host name>".

You should see the MPLs flowing into Splunk, as shown in the Figure 7.102. Note that the values of source and source type are exactly what you provided while configuring the HEC.

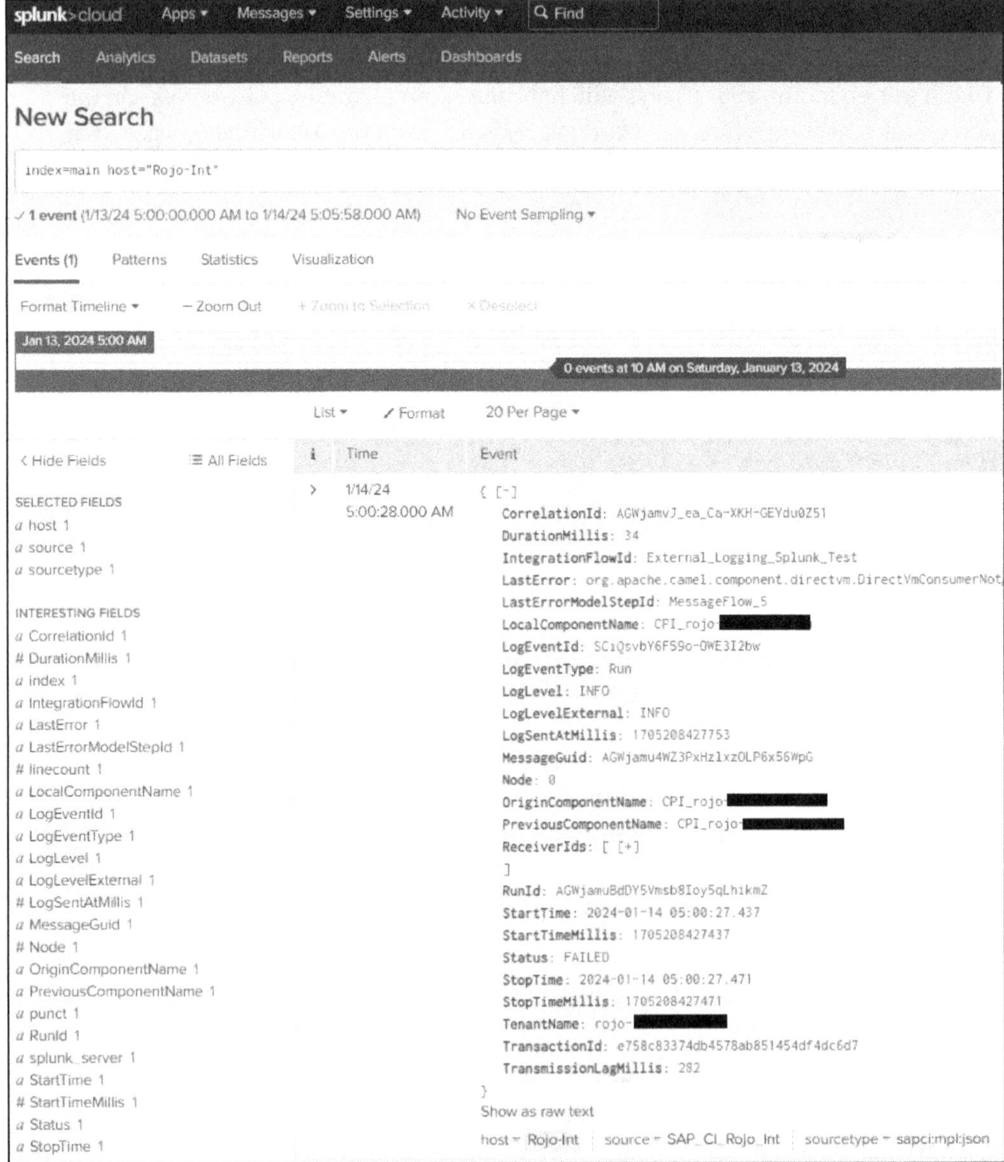

Figure 7.102 MPL visible in Splunk Event Search

As shown in Figure 7.103, these logs can be used to create various interesting dashboards in Splunk.

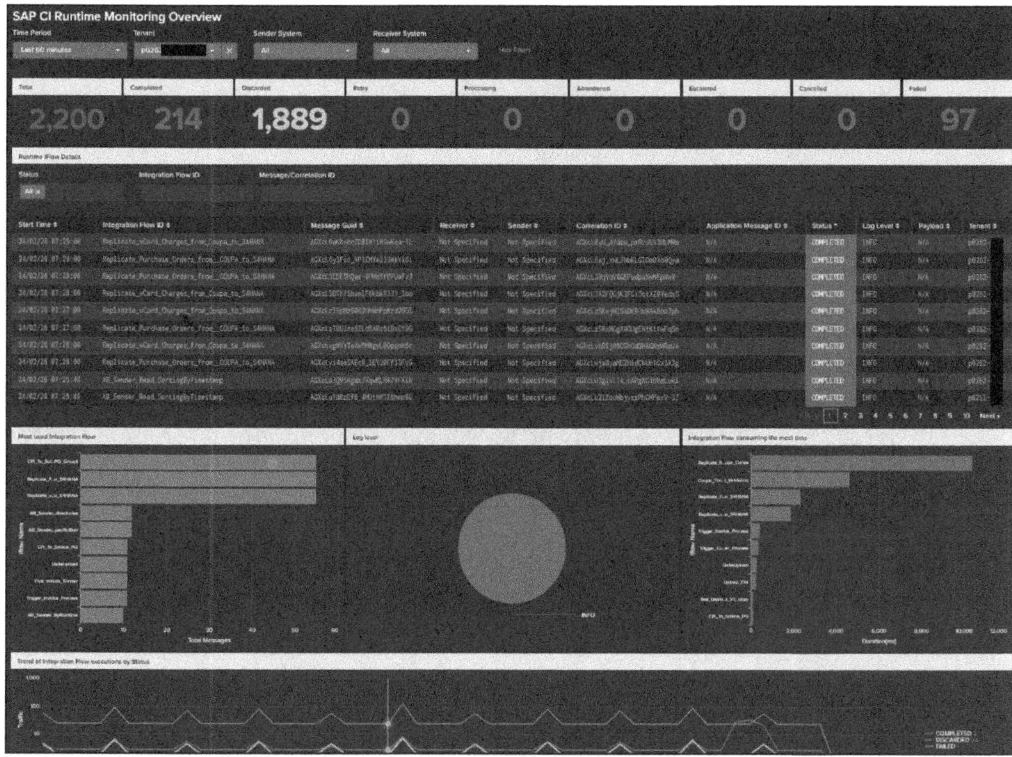

Figure 7.103 Sample Splunk Dashboard Based on MPL Data Obtained by External Logging

With this exercise, you're now an expert in offloading MPLs to an external system. You're now better equipped to facilitate use cases such as business monitoring by populating custom headers, system load monitoring, and long-term analytics over your Cloud Integration data.

7.9 Summary

No one wants to build a castle that only stands one day. After spending all this time building integration scenarios to help your business meet its integration goals, you'll want to ensure that the business continues to enjoy their benefits for a long time. Your castle, as such, requires regular checks and maintenance work to stay in optimal condition. The same applies for your Cloud Integration platform, which requires maintenance by monitoring the iFlows that are running and the data that is stored temporarily.

Given that Cloud Integration is a cloud-based platform, most operational tasks (e.g., health checks) are performed by SAP, as the service provider. Thus, this chapter focused on operational activities performed by you, as the customer. In the chapter, we explored the various features and monitors in Cloud Integration that you can use for monitoring and operational purposes. The monitors were discussed in detail, with concrete scenarios outlined as well.

After reading this chapter, you should be able to monitor all iFlows deployed in your tenant and use the logging and tracing features to analyze the runtimes of your iFlows. You're now well equipped to manage the various security artifacts, such as certificates and JDBC data sources, that are needed for your iFlows. In addition, you now know how to monitor temporary data, such as messages and variables, stored in the Cloud Integration tenant's database or in JMS queues.

With this, we've covered the complete lifecycle of developing integration scenarios in the web designer of Cloud Integration and monitoring your integration scenarios in the monitoring dashboard. In the next chapter, we'll take you into the wide world of APIs offered by Cloud Integration for developing and monitoring integration content.

Chapter 8
Application Programming Interfaces

SAP enables the consumption and provision of application programming interfaces (APIs) to expose different functionalities to the outside world. This chapter dives into the specifics of using APIs in the context of Cloud Integration, presents available features, and explores the APIs currently available for customers.

In today's connected world, almost everything is a click away. From traditional desktops and mobile phones to connected devices such as smartwatches, you can purchase goods, write articles, and book flight tickets. But how does data move from application A to B when, for instance, booking a flight or a car? The hidden enablers in most cases are known as application programming interfaces (APIs).

An API within the context of integration is an interface through which data exchange is made possible between applications. APIs are used to expose functionalities (or programmable interfaces) to the outside world through a service path or URL.

Simply put, an API takes a request from the caller, performs a task on a server application, and returns a response to the caller. The application providing the API is known as a *service provider*, and the application or user using the API is generally called a *service consumer*.

In this chapter, we'll introduce you to the Java and Open Data Protocol (OData) APIs provided by Cloud Integration and explain how to use them. This chapter further explores API Management and how to use it together with Cloud Integration.

8.1 Introduction

Much can be said about APIs—a topic that deserves its own book. This descriptive introduction is only intended to provide a brief overview.

If you're familiar with the topic of integration, you might be wondering what the difference is between an API and a traditional web service. Table 8.1 points out some differences between the two.

Aspects	Web Service	API
Network	Needs a network connection for its operation	Can also operate offline
Protocols	Simple Object Access Protocol (SOAP), Representational State Transfer (REST), and XML-RPC. XML-RPC enables the calling of remote procedure using XML as the encoding and HTTP as the transport protocol	SOAP and REST but can also communicate via cURL
Exposed via	XML over HTTP	Java Archive (JAR), Dynamic Link Library (DLL), XML, or JavaScript Object Notation (JSON) over HTTP

Table 8.1 Comparing Web Services to APIs

Furthermore, besides the differences listed in Table 8.1, all web services can be considered APIs, but not all APIs can be considered web services.

A *web service* is a type of API that almost always operates over HTTP (hence the "web" in the name). However, some protocols such as SOAP can use alternate transports, for example, Simple Mail Transfer Protocol (SMTP). The official World Wide Web Consortium (W3C) definition specifies that web services don't necessarily use HTTP, but this is almost always the case and is usually assumed unless mentioned otherwise.

On the other hand, one could argue that every bit of every function ever created—whether DLL, JAR, web service, or plain code—is an API. APIs can use any type of communication protocol and aren't limited to HTTP like web services are.

Now that you have a good, high-level understanding of what APIs are, let's explore the Java APIs currently provided by Cloud Integration.

8.2 Java APIs Provided by Cloud Integration

Cloud Integration provides some Java-based APIs to access and control the processing of messages on your tenant. At the time of this writing, you can use Groovy or JavaScript as the programming language to access these APIs. Accessing the functionality provided by these APIs in a script step or while creating a user-defined function (UDF) for mapping can be handy, which we'll describe in detail in Section 8.3.

Furthermore, you can use APIs when developing custom Cloud Integration adapters using the Adapter Development Kit (ADK). Note, however, that for a custom adapter, Java is used as a development language. We discussed the ADK in Chapter 6, Section 6.10.

Existing APIs can be classified under the following categories:

- **Generic APIs**
  Complete and parent set of APIs covering various features. These APIs are kept in the package `com.sap.it.api`. Table 8.2 provides a list of interfaces contained in this package.
- **Message APIs**
  Provides APIs to access properties of a message. These APIs are kept in the package `com.sap.it.api.msg`. Table 8.2 provides a list of interfaces contained in this package.
- **Script APIs**
  Provides APIs to control scripts.
- **Mapping APIs**
  Provides APIs to control mappings. These APIs are contained under the package `com.sap.it.api.mapping`. Table 8.2 lists a few commonly used packages and their corresponding interfaces.

Package	Interface	Description
com.sap.it.api.msg	ExchangePropertyProvider	Provides access to the properties of a message exchange.
com.sap.it.api.msg	MessageSizeInformation	Provides information about the size of a message.
com.sap.it.api.mapping	MappingContext	Mapping context object to be provided to mapping UDFs.
com.sap.it.api.mapping	Output	Class used in advanced UDFs (execution type All values of Context or All values of a Queue) to return the result of a function.
com.sap.it.api.mapping	ValueMappingApi	Used to execute value mappings with the given parameters.
com.sap.gateway.ip.core.customdev.util	Message	Accesses the exchanged message. The API provides an extensive set of functionalities, including manipulating attachments; reading and changing payloads; and retrieving message properties such as size, header, and so on.

Table 8.2 API Packages and Interfaces

Package	Interface	Description
com.sap.it.script.logging	ILogger	Performs different operations on the logs (e.g., writing message logs).
com.sap.it.public.generic.api	ITApiException, KeystoreService, SecureStoreService, UserCredential	Global API covering a wide range of functionalities, including access to key storage services, access to deployed user credentials, and access to exception objects.
com.sap.it.api.pd	PartnerDirectoryService	Performs different operations on Partner Directory parameter values, the partner IDs, the alternative partner IDs, and the authorized users of a partner.
com.sap.it.api.pd	BinaryData	Container for binary data relevant for Partner Directory binary parameters.

Table 8.2 API Packages and Interfaces (Cont.)

For a full list of interfaces and classes, refer to the JavaDocs at *http://s-prs.co/5077150*.

Note

Note that the summary of API packages listed in Table 8.2 relates to API version 2.22.0.

To illustrate the usage of the APIs, let's next look at UDFs in a mapping.

8.3 Using the Java API in a User-Defined Function

Let's say you need a message mapping to perform a complex transformation between a source and target message. In Chapter 4, Section 4.4, you learned how to work with mappings. Furthermore, imagine that none of the existing standard functions can fulfill the needed logic. Luckily, a UDF can come to the rescue.

A UDF is a custom function built for special mapping needs that can't be expressed by the predefined mapping functions in the mapping editor. In Cloud Integration, a UDF can be built using Groovy or JavaScript. A UDF generally uses the mapping-related APIs listed in Table 8.2 to transform the messages. (To see an illustration of a UDF in use, go to the example in Chapter 4, Section 4.4.)

In this section, we've built an iFlow that consumes an external OData service. After invoking the OData service, we received the response shown in Figure 8.1.

```
<soap:Envelope xmlns:soap="http://schemas.xmlsoap.org/soap/envelope/">
   <soap:Header/>
   <soap:Body>
      <ns1:OrderShippingDetails_MT xmlns:ns1="http://hci.sap.com/demo">
         <orderNumber>10249</orderNumber>
         <customerName>Toms Spezialitäten</customerName>
         <shipCity>Münster</shipCity>
         <shipStreet>Luisenstr. 48</shipStreet>
         <shipPostalCode>44087</shipPostalCode>
         <shipCountry>DE</shipCountry>
         <shipDate>1996-07-10T00:00:00.000</shipDate>
      </ns1:OrderShippingDetails_MT>
   </soap:Body>
</soap:Envelope>
```


Figure 8.1 Response of the iFlow from Chapter 4

Let's imagine that, with regard to the consumer application, you would prefer not to have the empty spaces in the element `shipStreet` between the street name and the house number. Furthermore, let's say the consumer requires that the street field to be appended with the order number as a suffix, and the entire field should be returned in uppercase. Looking at the example shown in Figure 8.1, the value `Luisenstr. 48` should be transformed into `LUISENSTR.48_10249`.

You can implement this requirement by using a combination of predefined functions in the mapping. However, for the sake of illustration, let's try to achieve this requirement using a UDF by following these steps:

1. On the **Design** page of the Cloud Integration Web UI, navigate to the concerned package, and open the iFlow.
2. Click the **Edit** button.
3. Select the **Message Mapping** step to be enhanced with the UDF, as shown in Figure 8.2.

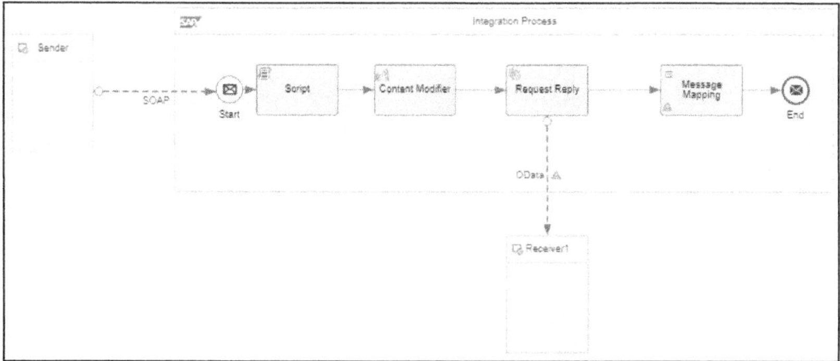

Figure 8.2 Selecting the Message Mapping Step to Be Enhanced with a UDF

4. Under the **Processing** tab, click on the **/ODate2XML.mmap** link. This will open the mapping editor as shown in Figure 8.2.

5. Select an element on the target message structure (e.g., the **shipStreet** field shown in Figure 8.3). Notice that a section called **Functions** appears in the bottom-left corner of the mapping editor, as shown in Figure 8.3.

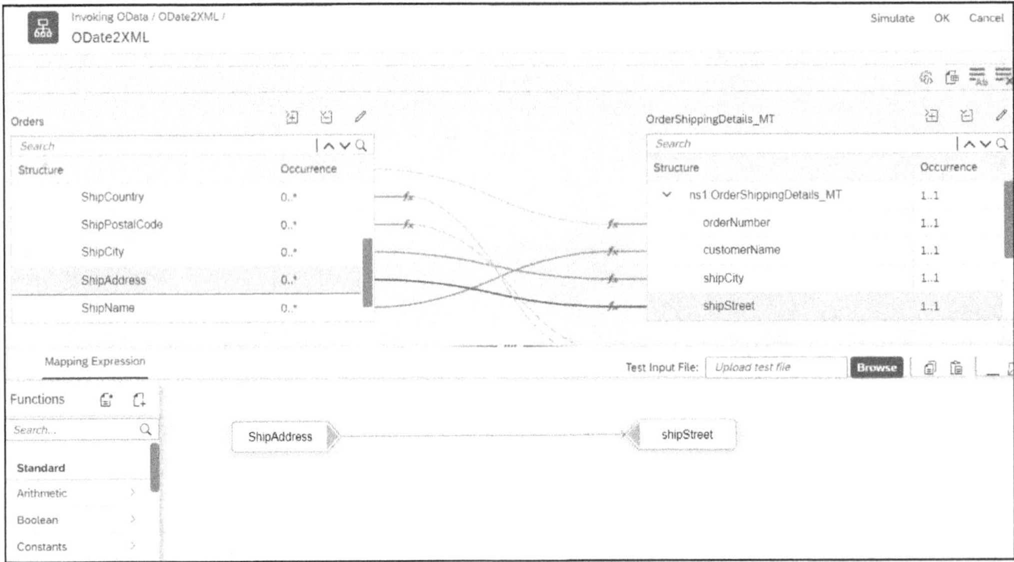

Figure 8.3 Mapping Editor with the Details of the Mapping to Be Enhanced

6. Let's now create a new UDF by clicking the **Create** icon next to the **Functions** box in the mapping editor.
7. Specify a name for the UDF to be created, as shown in Figure 8.4.

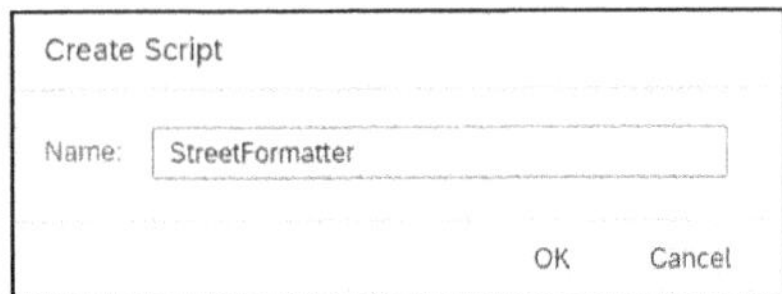

Figure 8.4 Providing a Name for the UDF

You're redirected to the UDF editor, which will contain some standard code, as shown in Figure 8.5.

Note

As shown at the top of Figure 8.5, the mapping API has been imported by the statement `import com.sap.it.api.mapping.*;`, which is the same package described earlier in Table 8.2.

Note that Figure 8.5 also shows some sample source code to showcase what is possible. The sample code is included between the /* and */ characters

Design / Playground_John_Cloud Integration Book Package / Invoking OData / ODate2XML / StreetFormatter.groovy /

StreetFormatter.groovy

```
import com.sap.it.api.mapping.*;

/*Add MappingContext parameter to read or set headers and properties
def String customFunc1(String P1,String P2,MappingContext context) {
        String value1 = context.getHeader(P1);
        String value2 = context.getProperty(P2);
        return value1+value2;
}

Add Output parameter to assign the output value.
def void custFunc2(String[] is,String[] ps, Output output, MappingContext context) {
        String value1 = context.getHeader(is[0]);
        String value2 = context.getProperty(ps[0]);
        output.addValue(value1);
        output.addValue(value2);
}*/


def String customFunc(String arg1){
    return arg1;
}
```

Figure 8.5 Standard Groovy Script Code Provided When Creating a UDF

8. Rename the Groovy method (e.g., "streetFormatterFunc"), and adapt the source code to suit your needs, for example, with the code shown in Figure 8.6. In line 5, this code removes all extra spaces and converts the result to uppercase. Then, line 6 of the code shown indicates that the code provided is using the Java API to retrieve the `OrderNo` from the message header. Furthermore, line 8 concatenates the input with the retrieved `OrderNo` from the message header.

Design / Playground_John_Cloud Integration Book Package / Invoking OData / ODate2XML / StreetFormatter.groovy /

StreetFormatter.groovy

```
1  import com.sap.it.api.mapping.*;
2
3
4  def String streetFormatterFunc(String arg1,MappingContext context){
5      String newInput = arg1.replace(" ","").toUpperCase();//remove empty space and make upper case.
6      String order = context.getHeader("OrderNo");//Retrieve order ID for the message header
7
8      return newInput + "_" + order;
9  }
```

Figure 8.6 Code Adapted to Remove Empty Spaces, Retrieve Message Header Attributes, and Perform a Concatenation

9. Click the **OK** button in the top-right corner of the screen.
10. Return to the mapping editor, and find the newly created **StreetFormatter** UDF under the **Custom** section, as shown in Figure 8.7.

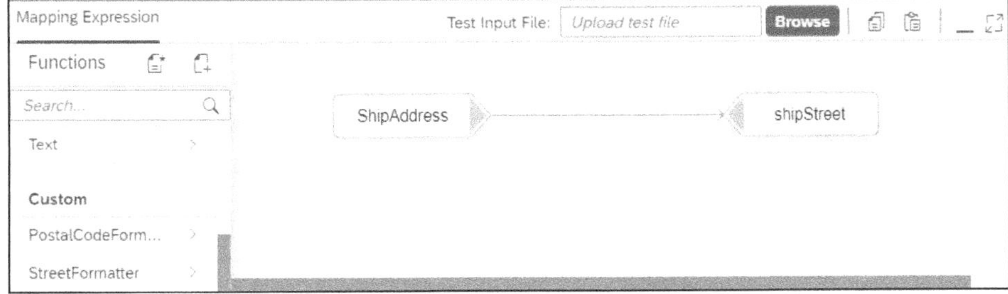

Figure 8.7 The Newly Created UDF Now Available in the Mapping

11. Click on the **StreetFormatter** UDF to see its method name. In our example, the method is called **streetFormatterFunc**, as shown in Figure 8.8. Note that **streetFormatterFunc** comes from the name that we provided for the Groovy method shown earlier in Figure 8.6.
12. Let's now use our new function by dragging and dropping it between **ShipAddress** and **shipStreet**, as shown in Figure 8.8.

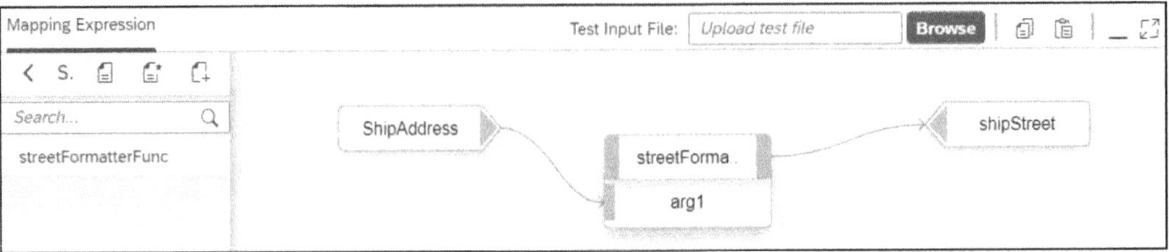

Figure 8.8 Inserting the UDF into Your Mapping Logic

13. Save and deploy the iFlow.
14. Test the service using SoapUI. You'll get a response in the field `shipStreet` without spaces, in uppercase, and suffixed with the order number, as shown in Figure 8.9.

```
<soap:Envelope xmlns:soap="http://schemas.xmlsoap.org/soap/envelope/">
   <soap:Header/>
   <soap:Body>
      <ns1:OrderShippingDetails_MT xmlns:ns1="http://hci.sap.com/demo">
         <orderNumber>10249</orderNumber>
         <customerName>Toms Spezialitäten</customerName>
         <shipCity>Münster</shipCity>
         <shipStreet>LUISENSTR.48_10249</shipStreet>
         <shipPostalCode>44087</shipPostalCode>
         <shipCountry>DE</shipCountry>
         <shipDate>1996-07-10T00:00:00.000</shipDate>
      </ns1:OrderShippingDetails_MT>
   </soap:Body>
</soap:Envelope>
```

Figure 8.9 Response Returned by the iFlow after Adding the UDF

You now know how to create a UDF that uses Cloud Integration Java APIs to perform transformation logic in a mapping. Let's now move to the next section, where we'll show you how to use a script step in Cloud Integration.

8.4 Using the Script Step

Cloud Integration provides a script step that enables you to write different custom scripts to perform a wide range of activities and use the Java APIs we explored earlier in Section 8.2. The scripting feature opens the door to your development imagination so you can do almost anything. Note, however, that scripting should be used with due diligence and caution to avoid unnecessary overhead and performance issues.

At the time of this writing, the script step supports Groovy and JavaScript:

- Groovy is a Java syntax-compatible, object-oriented programming language for Java platforms. To learn more about Groovy, go to *http://groovy-lang.org*.
- JavaScript is a dynamic, weakly typed, prototype-based, and multiparadigm programming language for the web. Many websites use JavaScript. To learn more about JavaScript, go to *www.w3schools.com/js*.

Both languages are relatively easy to learn, and plenty of resources are available on the internet that you can use as references.

Cloud Integration provides a Script API in a form of a JAR file. Using this JAR file, a Java developer can easily import a library into his development tool of preference and inspect the provided methods. The Script API JAR file can be downloaded from *http://s-prs.co/v576032*. On that page, search for the **Using Script API** section, as shown in Figure 8.10. Then, click on the **Download** link to save the JAR file to your local file system.

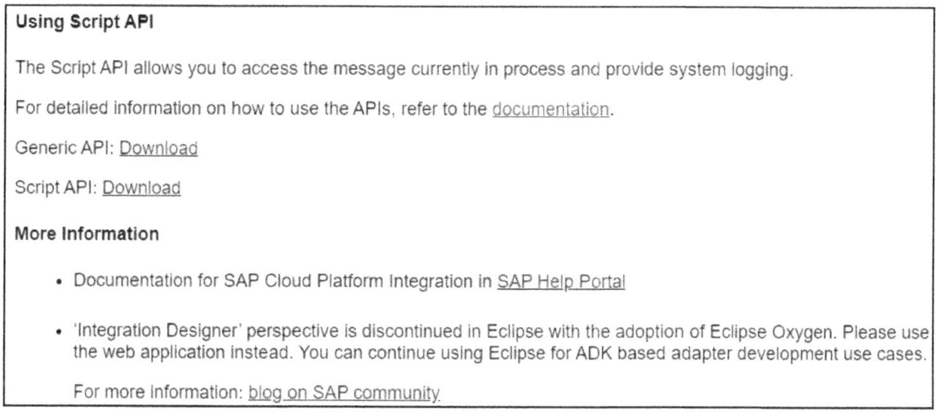

Using Script API

The Script API allows you to access the message currently in process and provide system logging.

For detailed information on how to use the APIs, refer to the documentation.

Generic API: Download

Script API: Download

More Information

- Documentation for SAP Cloud Platform Integration in SAP Help Portal
- 'Integration Designer' perspective is discontinued in Eclipse with the adoption of Eclipse Oxygen. Please use the web application instead. You can continue using Eclipse for ADK based adapter development use cases.

  For more information: blog on SAP community

Figure 8.10 Downloading the Script API JAR File

At the time of this writing, the JAR file is called *cloud.integration.script.apis-2.7.1.jar*.

To better illustrate the usage of the Script API, we'll use a sample scenario in the next section.

8.4.1 Target Scenario

Let's reuse the example from Chapter 4, Section 4.3, to illustrate the use of the Script step. In that example, we invoked an external OData service from our iFlow. Figure 8.11 shows the iFlow that we built for it.

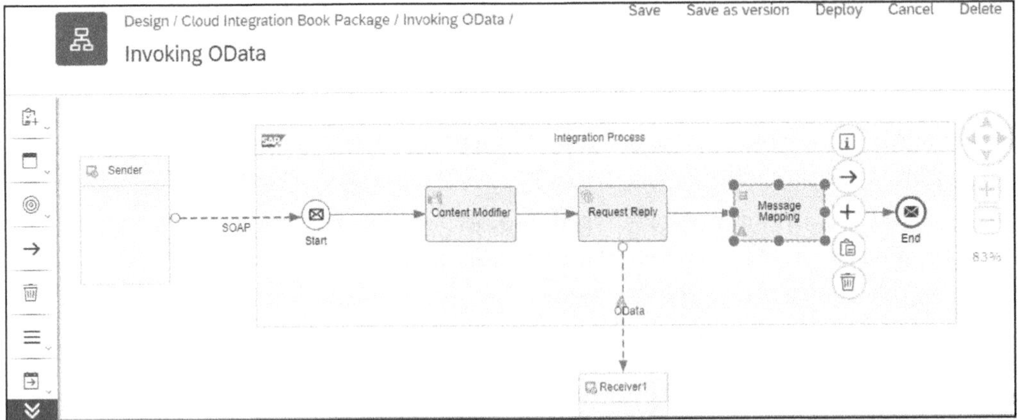

Figure 8.11 Invoking an OData Service

Imagine that the organization providing this iFlow is currently running a lottery on every incoming message. The sender of one randomly selected message will win a prize. As an integration developer, you've been asked to change the iFlow by generating a random number to be associated with each call. This random number will be used by your organization later to pick the lucky winner.

Keeping the solution simple, you can create a script that generates a random number and uses the API to save this value as a message header.

8.4.2 Enhancing the Integration Flow

Let's now change our iFlow. Note that we won't describe every step because, at this point, you should already be familiar with editing iFlows. Follow these steps:

1. On the **Design** page of the Cloud Integration Web UI, navigate to the correct package and iFlow.
2. In the opened iFlow, click the **Edit** button.
3. Select a **Script** step from the palette, as shown in Figure 8.12. You'll find this shape in the palette under **Message Transformers** .
4. Another menu appears from the palette with a choice of **JavaScript** or **GroovyScript**. Click on **GroovyScript**, as shown in Figure 8.13.
5. Place the shape in your iFlow, right after the **Start** icon .
6. The **Script Editor** automatically opens with some sample script, as shown in Figure 8.14. Note that this editor is the same toll we used when we created a UDF in Section 8.3.

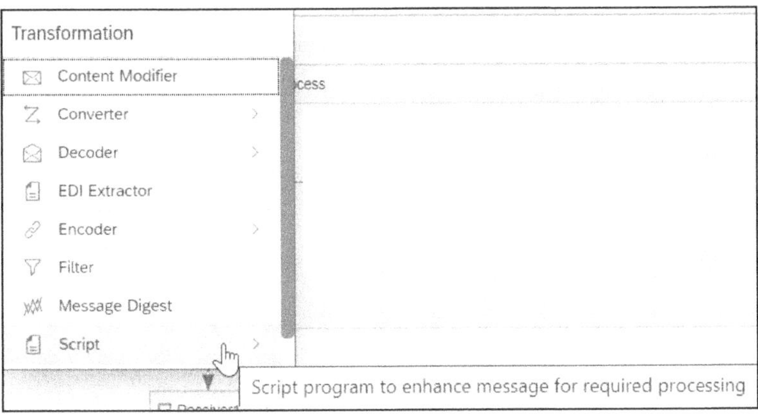

Figure 8.12 Adding the Script Step to the iFlow

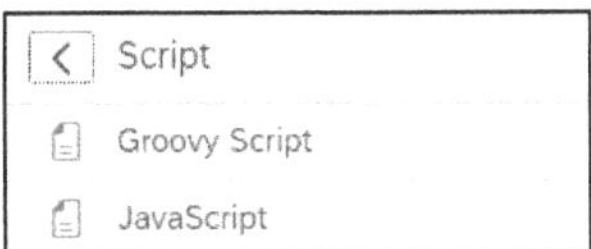

Figure 8.13 Selecting Groovy Script from the Palette

Design / Playground_John_Cloud Integration Book Package / SampleIntegrationFlow / script1.groovy /

script1.groovy

```
/* Refer the link below to learn more about the use cases of script.
https://help.sap.com/viewer/368c481cd6954bdfa5d0435479fd4eaf/Cloud/en/148851bf8192412cba1f9d2c17f4bd25.html

If you want to know more about the SCRIPT APIs, refer the link below
https://help.sap.com/doc/a56f52e1a58e4e2bac7f7adbf45b2e26/Cloud/en/index.html */
import com.sap.gateway.ip.core.customdev.util.Message;
import java.util.HashMap;
def Message processData(Message message) {
    //Body
    def body = message.getBody();
/*To set the body, you can use the following method. Refer SCRIPT APIs document for more detail*/
    //message.setBody(body + " Body is modified");
    //Headers
    def headers = message.getHeaders();
    def value = headers.get("oldHeader");
    message.setHeader("oldHeader", value + " modified");
    message.setHeader("newHeader", "newHeader");
    //Properties
    def properties = message.getProperties();
    value = properties.get("oldProperty");
    message.setProperty("oldProperty", value + " modified");
    message.setProperty("newProperty", "newProperty");
    return message;
}
```

Figure 8.14 Sample Code Included in the Groovy Script Editor

7. Change the `processData` method part of the script shown in Figure 8.14 to adapt the script to meet your requirements. In our case, we used the code shown in Figure 8.15. Note that the `processData` method takes a `Message` object as input and also returns a `Message` object as an output. If you're a programmer, the script shown in Figure 8.15 is self-explanatory. The code generates a random number between 0 and 1000. The generated random number is then added as a message header named `LuckyNumber`.

The code also includes comments in plain English for those less familiar with Groovy. The Groovy script shown in Figure 8.15 is included with the book's downloads at *www.sap-press.com/5760*.

Invoking OData / script2.groovy /

script2.groovy

```
/*
 The integration developer needs to create the method processData
 This method takes Message object of package com.sap.gateway.ip.core.customdev.util
which includes helper methods useful for the content developer:
The methods available are:
    public java.lang.Object getBody()
    public void setBody(java.lang.Object exchangeBody)
    public java.util.Map<java.lang.String,java.lang.Object> getHeaders()
    public void setHeaders(java.util.Map<java.lang.String,java.lang.Object> exchangeHeaders)
    public void setHeader(java.lang.String name, java.lang.Object value)
    public java.util.Map<java.lang.String,java.lang.Object> getProperties()
    public void setProperties(java.util.Map<java.lang.String,java.lang.Object> exchangeProperties)
       public void setProperty(java.lang.String name, java.lang.Object value)
 */
import com.sap.gateway.ip.core.customdev.util.Message;
import java.util.HashMap;
def Message processData(Message message) {

       //Generate a random Number
       int max = 1000;
       int min = 0;
       Random r = new Random();
       def value = r.nextInt((max - min) + 1) + min;
       //Properties
       map = message.getProperties();
       message.setHeader("LuckyNumber", value);

       return message;
}
```

Figure 8.15 Final Result of the Groovy Script

8. Click the **OK** button in the top-right corner of Figure 8.15 (not shown) to return to the iFlow. Figure 8.16 shows the final look of the iFlow extended with the **Script** step.

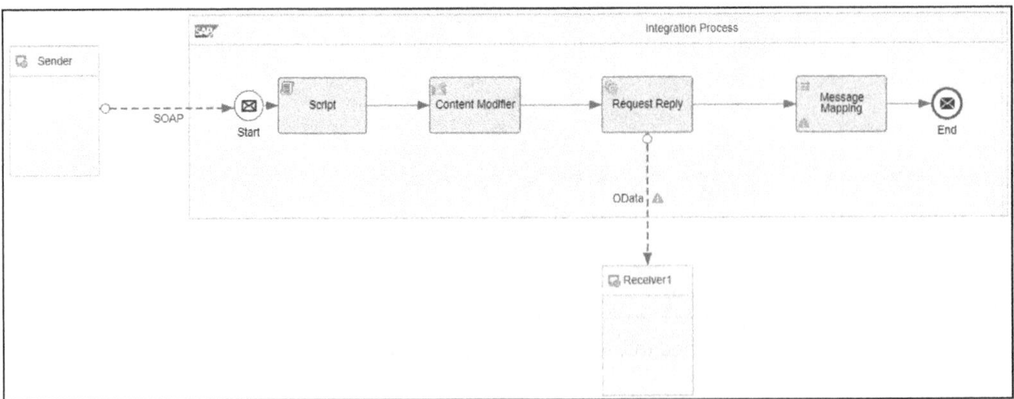

Figure 8.16 Enhanced Overview of the iFlow

9. Save and deploy the iFlow.

You're now ready to send a message via SoapUI. After you've triggered the message, the randomly generated number is returned in the header of the response message (Figure 8.17). Notice the `LuckyNumber` in the header section of the response shown in Figure 8.18.

This result is exactly what we asked the script to do (see line 15 of the code shown in Figure 8.15).

```
<soapenv:Envelope xmlns:soapenv="http://schemas.xmlsoap.org/soap/envelope/" xmlns:demo="http://cpi.sap.com/demo">
   <soapenv:Header/>
   <soapenv:Body>
      <demo:OrderNumber_MT>
         <orderNumber>10249</orderNumber>
      </demo:OrderNumber_MT>
   </soapenv:Body>
</soapenv:Envelope>
```

Figure 8.17 Returned Response Headers A

Body Cookies (4) Headers (21) Test Results Status: 200 OK Time: 3.48s Size: 1.04 KB Save Response

KEY	VALUE
Set-Cookie	JSESSIONID=11696AE7D64F68045F9AD20892401CDF; Path=/; Secure; HttpOnly
Address	http://services.odata.org/Northwind
AutheticationType	None
clientSidePageSize	200
ComponentContentType	xml
destinationAlias	IGNORE
destinationManagerImpl	com.sap.it.rt.adapter.odata.destination.HCIDestinationManagerImpl@6858bc27
HttpStatusCodes	OK
LuckyNumber	516

Figure 8.18 Returned Response Headers B

Congratulations! You can now use the **Script** step to perform different tasks using the APIs. Let's now move on to discuss the OData API.

8.5 Open Data Protocol API

Besides the Java APIs, Cloud Integration also allows you to access various aspects of the platform using an OData API. These are REST APIs that use the OData as a technical protocol. As a result, these APIs use the well-known HTTP methods of GET, POST, PUT, FETCH, and DELETE. The concept of OData isn't completely new; you already came across OData in Chapter 5, Section 5.2.4.

> **Note**
>
> At the time of this writing, OData specification version 2.0 is supported by the Cloud Integration OData APIs. To read more about the OData V2 specification, go to *http://s-prs.co/v576033*.

The OData APIs can be accessed using an HTTP URL in the following format:

https://<host>/api/v1/<resource>?$<property1>=<property1_value>&$<property2>=<property2_value>

In this URL, note the following:

- ***<host>***
  Represents the URL address of the service instance in SAP BTP, Cloud Foundry environment, also called the Cloud Integration Management Host Address. We introduced this service in Chapter 2, Section 2.1.3. In the SAP BTP, Neo environment, you'll need to use the URL address of the tenant management node.
- ***<resource>***
  Represents the path of the entity types to be called. Some entity resources are listed later in Table 8.5. For example, you can use the resource `MessageProcessingLogs` to address the message processing log (MPL).
- ***<property1>***
  Represents the name of the property to be queried. For example, you can use the property `count` to return the total number of MPLs. This property is always prefixed by a dollar sign ($). Note that the property field is optional. Furthermore, you're can add as many properties as you need by using an ampersand (&) between them.

OData APIs are protected by OAuth in SAP BTP, Cloud Foundry environment, whereas in the SAP BTP, Neo environment, these same OData APIs are protected by basic authentication (user name and password) and require the API client to enable HTTP cookies. Furthermore, to use an API, you must have the correct role collection assigned to your user. Table 8.3 lists the role collections required for the various API actions in SAP BTP, Cloud Foundry environment. Similarly, Table 8.4 lists the authorization groups required for different API actions in the SAP BTP, Neo environment.

Role Collection	Description
`PI_Business_Expert`	Enables a business expert to perform tasks such as monitoring iFlows and monitoring message content stored in temporary storage
`PI_Administrator`	Enables the tenant administrator to perform administrative tasks on the tenant cluster, for example, deploying security content and iFlows
`PI_Integration_Developer`	Enables an integration developer to display, download, and deploy artifacts (e.g., iFlows)
`PI_Read_Only`	Enables a user to display integration content and to monitor messages

Table 8.3 Required Authorization Groups for SAP BTP, Cloud Foundry Environment

Authorization Group	Description
AuthGroup.Administrator or AuthGroup.IntegrationDeveloper	Display message overview
AuthGroup.IntegrationDeveloper	Undeploy integration content
AuthGroup.BusinessExpert	Download a message

Table 8.4 Required Authorization Groups for SAP BTP, Neo Environment

Cloud Integration's OData APIs are structured around entity types or resources. Every entity type contains a number of properties. A property can also refer to another entity type, which means you can start with one entity type and navigate to another entity type. Therefore, you must fully understand the various entity types, their tasks, and their relationships with each other. Table 8.5 lists all available entity types and describes their use.

Entity Types	Task Description
MessageProcessingLog	Reads an MPL
MessagePropcessingLogCustom HeaderProperty	Reads custom header properties of the MPL
MessageProcessingLogErrorInformation	Reads error information for a message
MessageProcessingLogAdapterAttribute	Reads adapter-specific attributes
MessageProcessingLogAttachment	Reads an MPL attachment
MessageStoreEntry	Reads a message from the message store
MessageStoreEntryProperty	Reads a header property of a message from the message store
MessageStoreEntryAttachment	Reads an attachment of a message from the message store
MessageStoreEntryAttachmentProperties	Reads properties of message attachments from the message store
IntegrationRuntimeArtifact	Reads properties of deployed integration content
PartnerDirectory	Accesses the Partner Directory, creates entries, and helps manage them
LogFile	Accesses all current (nonarchived) log files
LogFileArchives	Accesses all archived log files

Table 8.5 Entity Types and Their Tasks

To illustrate how entity types relate to each other, Figure 8.19 shows an entity model around the `MessageProcessingLogs` entity type to help you better grasp how to use the APIs related to the monitoring of message flows.

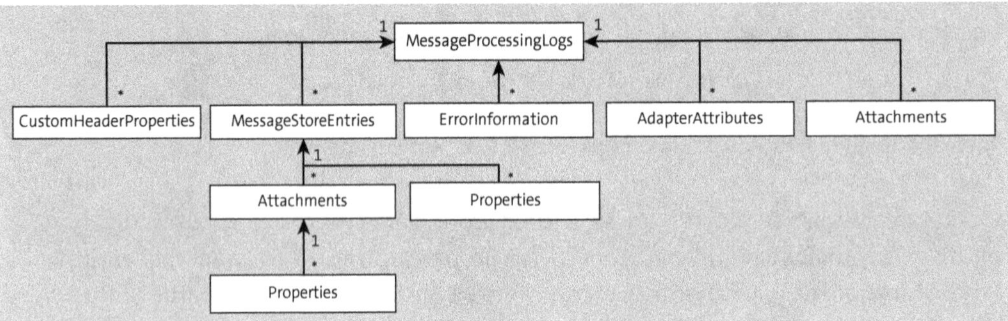

Figure 8.19 Entity Model Diagram for MessageProcessingLogs

As specified by the SAP documentation (shown in Figure 8.19), the `MessageProcessingLogs` entity contains several subentities, including `CustomHeaderProperties`, `MessageStoreEntries`, `ErrorInformation`, `AdapterAttributes`, and `Attachments`. Descriptions of each subentity's function are listed in Table 8.5.

Additionally, the OData APIs provided by Cloud Integration make use of common query options. These query options can be used on different entity types to perform specific actions on them. However, not all options are supported by each entity type. Table 8.6 lists some common query options.

Option	Description
`$filter`	Retrieves a set of entries based on the resource entity and the filter expression used in the Uniform Resource Identifier (URI)
`$metadata`	Retrieves the data model and structure of all resources
`$select`	Retrieves a subset of information on the entities identified by the resource path section of the URI
`$top`	Returns a subset of *n* top records from the resource used in the URI
`$count`	Returns the number of entries that matches the resource specified in the URI or the filter-specified criteria
`$inlinecount`	Indicates that the response contains a count of the number of entries in the collection of records identified by the resource path section of the URI
`$value`	Retrieves specific values of an entity resource specified by a Global Unique Identifier (GUID)

Table 8.6 Commonly Used Query Options

Option	Description
`$skip`	Skips *n* records in the collection returned according to the resource path section of the URI
`$expand`	Retrieves related and correlated entities for a given navigation property in line with the entities being retrieved
`$orderby`	Specifies the sorting of the returned collection by one or more values

Table 8.6 Commonly Used Query Options (Cont.)

Note

The OData APIs provided by Cloud Integration limit the number of entries in a response to a maximum of 1,000 entries for each call. This limitation protects against negative impact in the performance of the Cloud Integration runtime environment and potential problems from queries returning huge amounts of data.

Queries with more than 1,000 entries are capped, and a **Next** link element is added to the response, which can be used to initiate the return of the additional entries.

Later in this chapter, we'll explore APIs and entities related to the following aspects:

- Monitoring MPLs
- Deployed integration content
- Log files
- Message store
- Security material
- Partner Directory

These APIs can easily be tested and explored using the SAP Business Accelerator Hub, which we'll discuss next.

8.5.1 SAP Business Accelerator Hub

The available OData APIs are exposed and documented in the SAP Business Accelerator Hub, which represents the central catalog of all SAP-provided and partner-developed APIs for developers to build sample apps, extensions, and open integrations with SAP. The SAP Business Accelerator Hub landing page can be found at *https://api.sap.com*, as shown in Figure 8.20.

Scroll down in the middle of the page, and click on the **APIs** tile to open a view similar to that shown in Figure 8.21. From this page, enter the keyword "Cloud Integration" in the search bar to find tiles with different packages related to Cloud Integration, as shown in Figure 8.22.

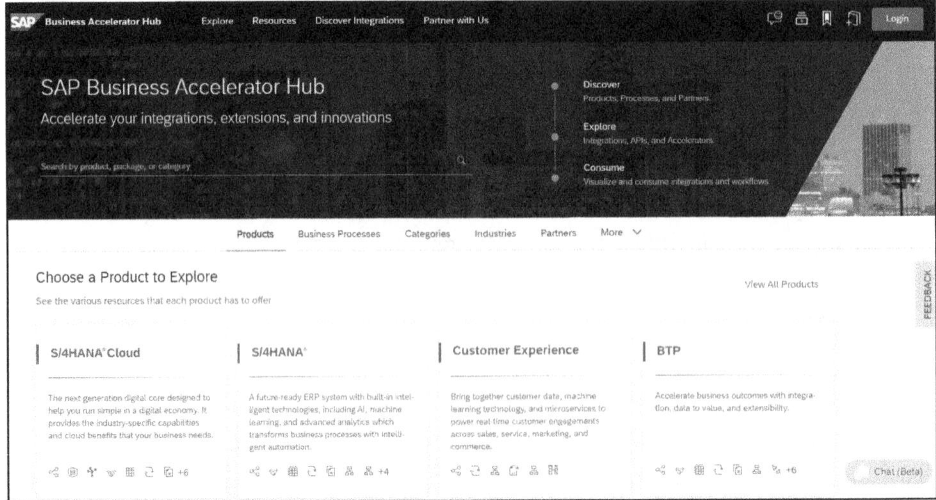

Figure 8.20 SAP Business Accelerator Hub Landing Page

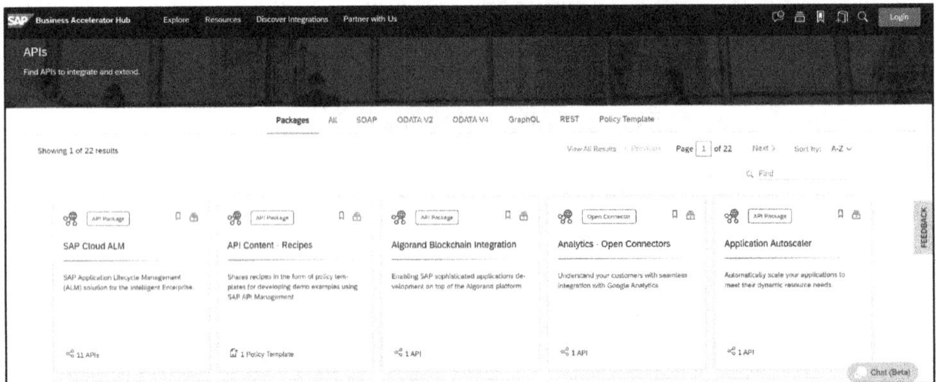

Figure 8.21 SAP Business Accelerator Hub Landing Page: APIs Section

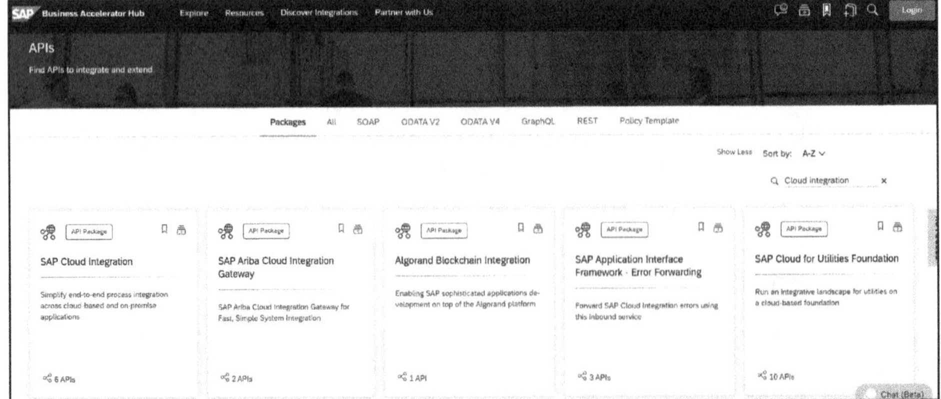

Figure 8.22 List of Available API Packages

Select the package called **Cloud Integration**. If you can't find this package, filter the list of packages by searching one of the keywords of the tiles, as shown in Figure 8.23.

Figure 8.23 Artifacts of the OData APIs in the Cloud Integration Package

From the page shown in Figure 8.23, you can explore many APIs. Using the SAP Business Accelerator Hub, you can try out and test APIs directly without having to implement any code or using a third-party REST client such as Postman (*www.getpostman.com*). For APIs implementing the HTTP GET method, you can also use a simple browser.

SAP Business Accelerator Hub has two different approaches to performing tests:

- An API sandbox
- Your Cloud Integration tenant

Each of these testing approaches will be explored next.

API Sandbox

If you don't have access to a Cloud Integration tenant to use for testing, you can always use the API sandbox, which is provided by SAP. The API sandbox is filled with test data and presents a quick way to get a feel for the way the APIs operate. Note that only operations using the GET method are supported in the API sandbox. Operations needing write access are forbidden because you need to log on before you can call operations requiring write access in the API sandbox.

For instance, let's use the Log Files API to illustrate testing using the API sandbox approach. Note that the Log Files API isn't yet available in the SAP BTP, Cloud Foundry environment, at the time of writing. But we can still use the Log Files API to illustrate how to test an API against a sandbox machine, which is still in a SAP BTP, Neo environment. You're already familiar with the Log Files API because we discussed how to access log files in the Web UI on the **Monitor** page. For that, follow these steps:

1. Click on **Log Files** from the page shown earlier in Figure 8.23.
2. The resulting page lists all operations of the API. Note that the **API Endpoint** field is automatically assigned with a sandbox-related URL.

3. Assuming we want to test the **LogFileArchives** API, we'll need to click on the **Log File Archives** link, as shown in Figure 8.24.

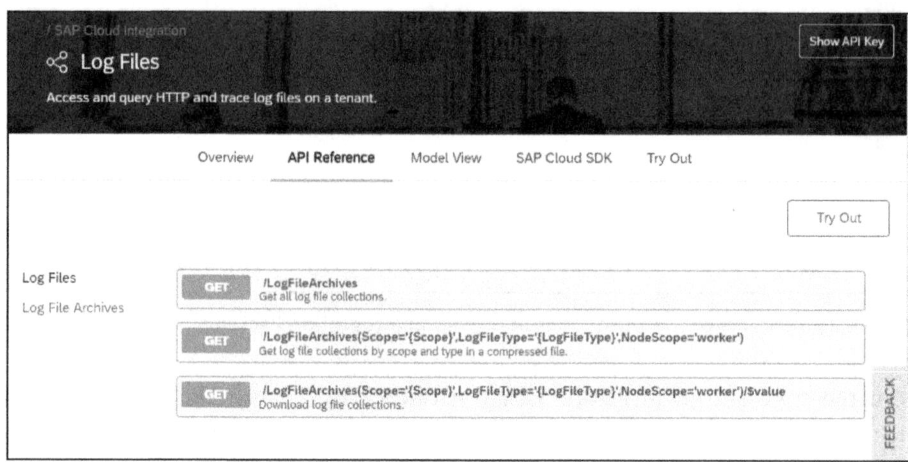

Figure 8.24 List of Entity Types Available for the Log Files API

4. From the resulting page, click the **GET** button to the left of **/LogFileArchives**.
5. A page similar to the page shown in Figure 8.25 will open. Click the **Try Out** button. Note that if your API requires input parameters, these parameters will be listed on this page. You'll need to fill in the required parameters at a minimum.

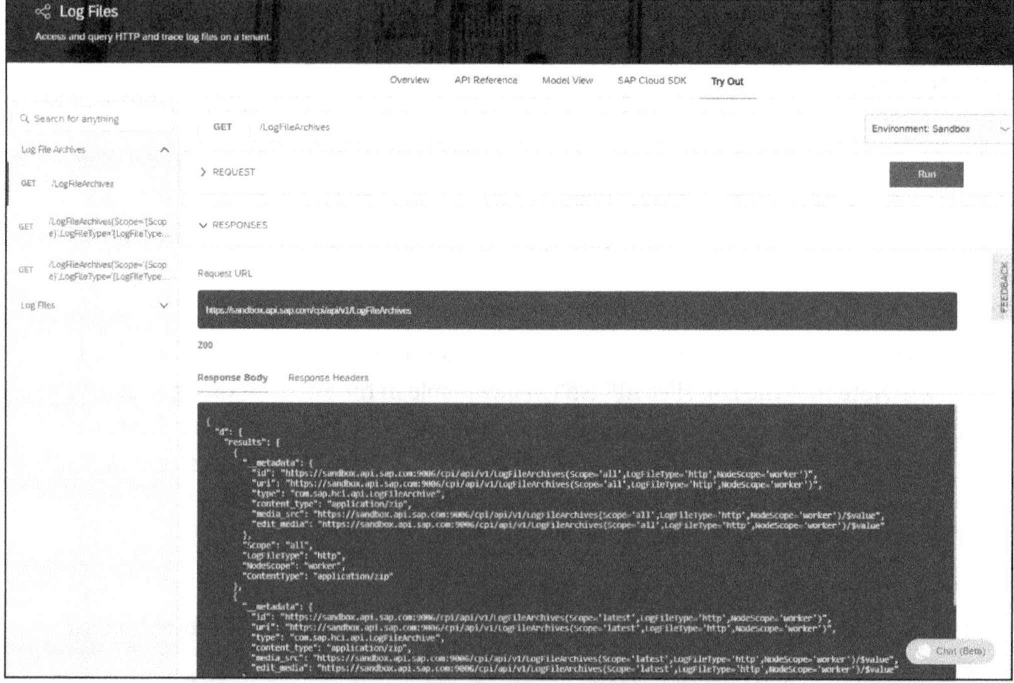

Figure 8.25 The SAP Business Accelerator Hub Try Out Page

6. After clicking on the **Try Out** and **Run** buttons, a response header and body will be returned on the page, as shown in Figure 8.26.

Javascript Java Swift Curl SAPUI5 ABAP SAP BTP, ABAP environment

```
var data = null;

var xhr = new XMLHttpRequest();
xhr.withCredentials = false;

xhr.addEventListener("readystatechange", function () {
  if (this.readyState === this.DONE) {
    console.log(this.responseText);
  }
});

//setting request method
//API endpoint for API sandbox
xhr.open("GET", "https://sandbox.api.sap.com/cpi/api/v1/LogFileArchives");


//adding request headers
//API Key for API Sandbox
xhr.setRequestHeader("APIKey", "dLzljSl00HWjdon1CI4mxtNB2EG2zfAu");
xhr.setRequestHeader("DataServiceVersion", "2.0");
xhr.setRequestHeader("Accept", "application/json");


//sending request
xhr.send(data);
```

Figure 8.26 Code Snippet to Consume the API in Different Languages

Let's look at how to configure SAP Business Accelerator Hub to test against your own Cloud Integration SAP BTP, Cloud Foundry environment tenant next.

Your Cloud Integration Tenant for SAP BTP, Cloud Foundry Environment

As mentioned earlier, SAP Business Accelerator Hub also makes it possible to test against your tenant. For this approach, you'll need to configure SAP Business Accelerator Hub to point to your tenant by changing the API endpoint. Follow these steps:

1. Click on the **Environment: Sandbox** link in the top-right corner of the page shown earlier in Figure 8.25.
2. If you're not already logged in, the **Login Required** popup window, shown in Figure 8.27, will open. Click the **Log On** button, and provide your credentials. If you're already logged in, proceed to step 4.

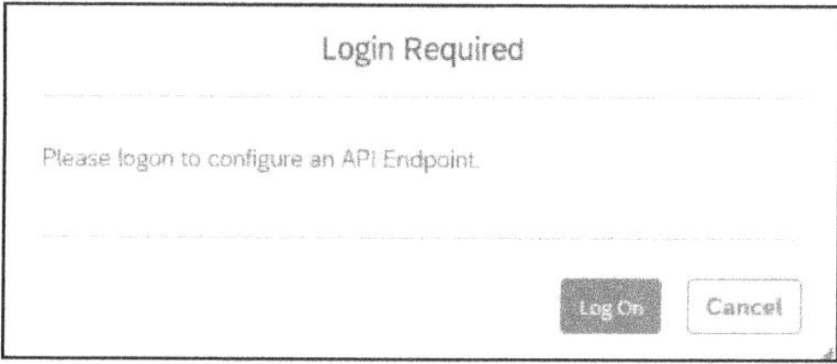

Figure 8.27 Login Page When Configuring the API Endpoint

3. You're redirected back to the main page (shown earlier in Figure 8.24). Click on the **Configure Environments** link one more time. You'll then presented with the popup window shown in Figure 8.28.

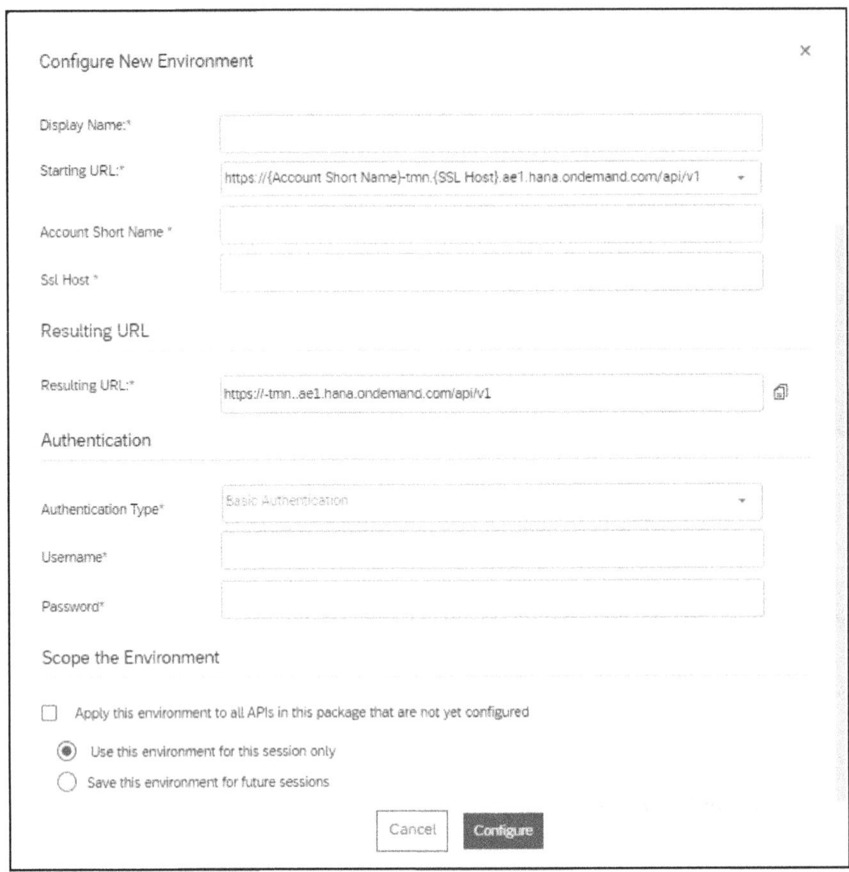

Figure 8.28 Filling in Environment Details for Your Cloud Integration Tenant

4. For the SAP BTP, Cloud Foundry environment, you'll need to select **https://{Custom Name}{Domain}/api/v1** from the **Starting URL** dropdown menu.
5. You'll then need to fill in the fields on the screen shown in Figure 8.28 according to the details listed in Table 8.7, which lists and describes all the relevant fields.

Column	Description
Display Name	Enter a human-readable alias name, for example, "Development", "Test", or "Acceptance".

Table 8.7 Attributes of the Configure API Endpoint Page for SAP BTP, Cloud Foundry Environment

Column	Description
Custom Name	Based on the URL of your SAP BTP, Cloud Foundry environment tenant, the custom name is the part of the URL found between the double slashes (//) and the first dot (.).
Ssl Host	If an SSL host is relevant, fill in the URL.
Resulting URL	The resulting URL is automatically built for you. Ensure that this URL is the same as your SAP BTP, Cloud Foundry environment tenant URL.
Username	The username of your Cloud Integration tenant account.
Password	The password of your Cloud Integration tenant account.

Table 8.7 Attributes of the Configure API Endpoint Page for SAP BTP, Cloud Foundry Environment (Cont.)

Voilà! From this point, you can perform the API calls against your own tenant. As mentioned earlier, SAP BTP, Cloud Foundry environment requires OAuth to connect to its APIs. (We'll discuss OAuth in more detail in Chapter 10, Section 10.4.3.). Additionally, you'll need to add specific authorization groups, listed earlier in Table 8.3, relevant to the operation to be performed. To enable OAuth, first, you must perform the following activities:

- Define a service instance, which represents the technical user to be used when calling the API later. Within the context of OAuth, a service instance represents an OAuth client.
- Define a service key for the API client, which contains the OAuth credential values, including **client id**, **client secret**, **token URL**, and **url**.

You already came across these entities (the service instance and the service key) in Chapter 2, Section 2.3.3, when we defined authorization enabling a user to call and access an iFlow's endpoint. (We'll also further discuss these entities in Chapter 10, Section 10.4.4.) For now, let's discuss the steps required for each of the activities listed earlier.

To define a service instance, follow these steps:

1. From the SAP BTP cockpit, navigate to your subaccount, and select the **Entitlements** menu item on the left, as shown in Figure 8.29. Then, verify that the API **Plan** under the **Process Integration on Runtime** service is available and enabled.
2. Scroll on the top-left pane, and then navigate to the space management page by clicking on **Overview • Spaces**, as shown in Figure 8.30.

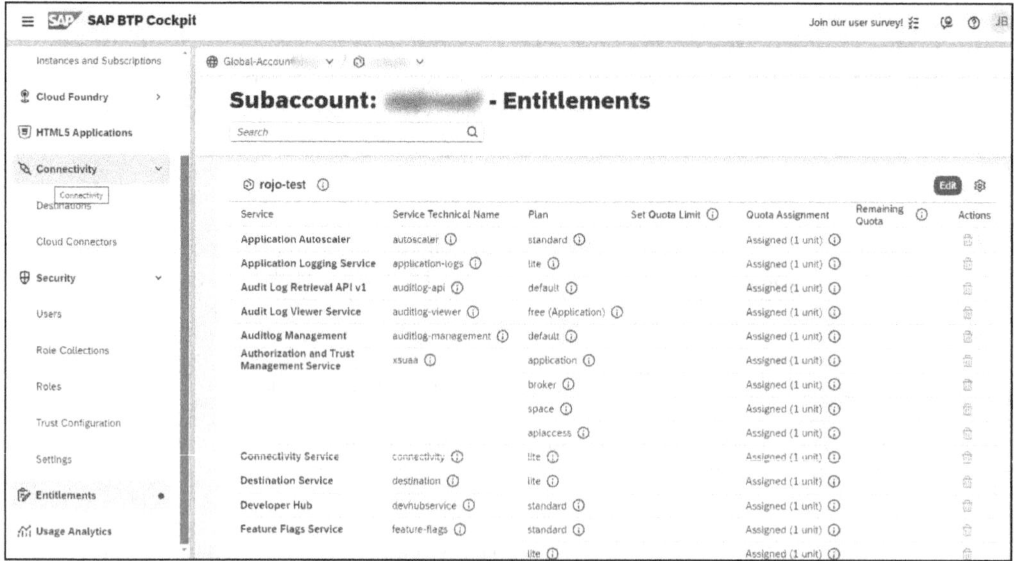

Figure 8.29 Checking That the API Plan Is Enabled

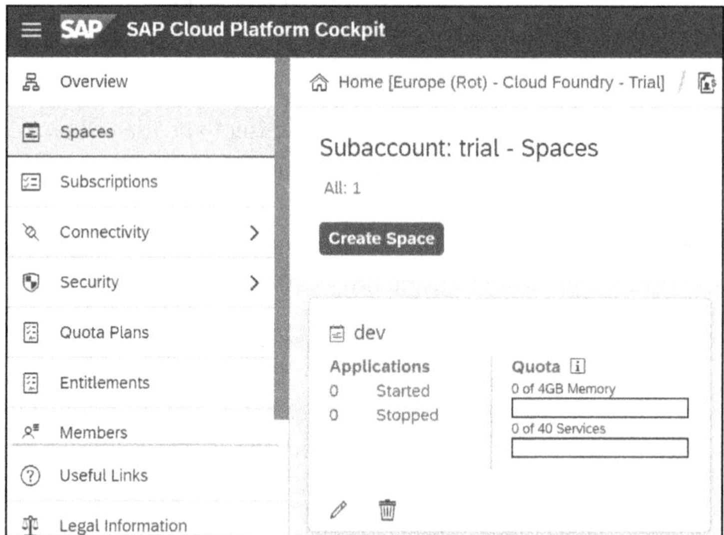

Figure 8.30 Selecting the Space to Hold the API Client

3. Select the space under which the API client should be created. For our example, as shown in Figure 8.30, you'll need to select the **dev** tile.
4. Under the **Services** menu item on the left, select **Service Marketplace**, as shown in Figure 8.31.

5. On the **Service Marketplace** page, search for the "process integration" keyword, as shown in Figure 8.31.

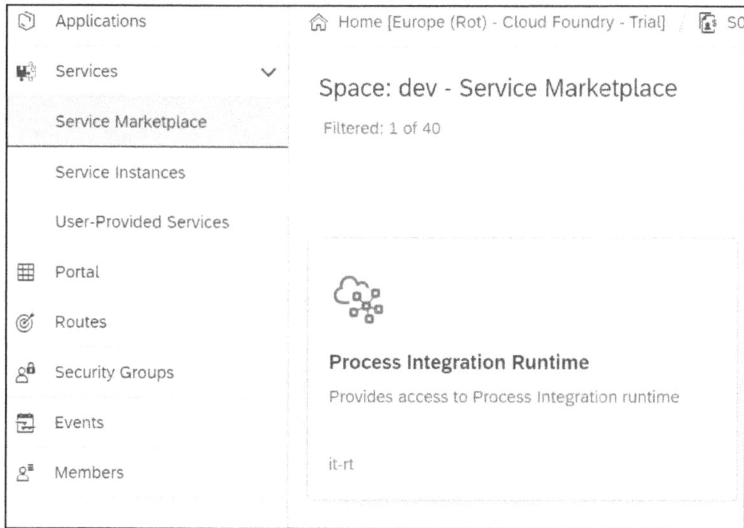

Figure 8.31 Selecting a Service from the Service Marketplace

6. In the returned results, select the **Process Integration Runtime** service.
7. Click on the **Instances** menu item on the left to view a list of existing instances, as shown in Figure 8.32.

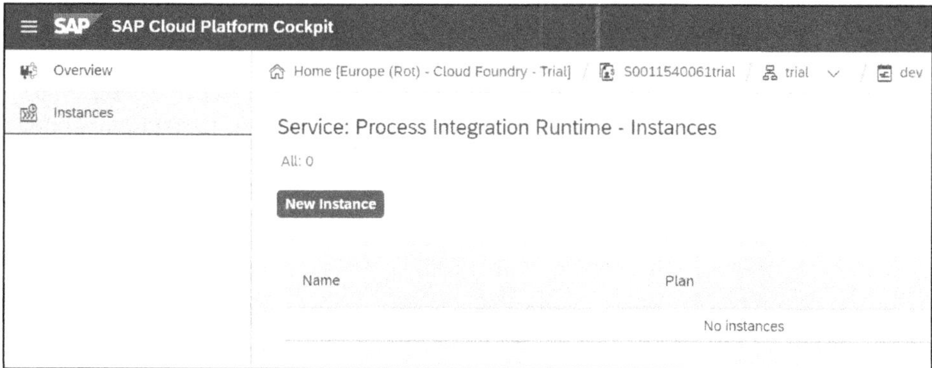

Figure 8.32 Creating a Process Integration Runtime Instance

8. To create an API client, click the **New instance** button, as shown in Figure 8.32. A new creation wizard will open.
9. On the next page, for the **Choose Service Plan** step, select **api** from the **Plan** drop-down list, as shown in Figure 8.33, and then click **Next**.

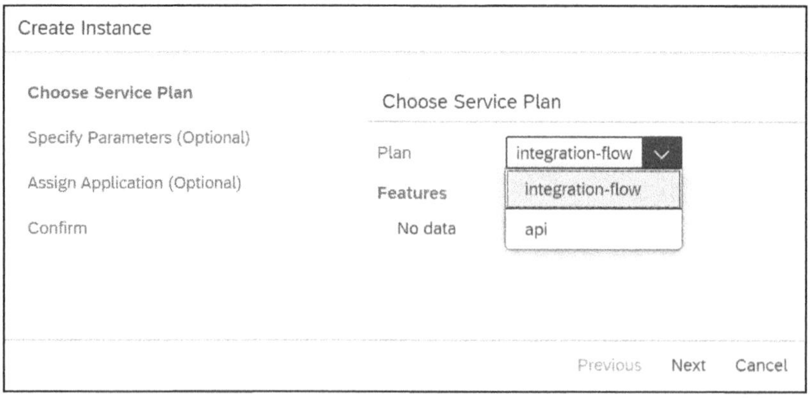

Create Instance

Choose Service Plan	Choose Service Plan
Specify Parameters (Optional)	Plan: integration-flow
Assign Application (Optional)	Features: integration-flow
Confirm	No data: api

Previous Next Cancel

Figure 8.33 Selecting the API Service Plan

10. On the next page, you must enter a role assignment. Assuming that we're trying to access the MPLs in our Cloud Integration on the SAP BTP, Cloud Foundry environment, you'll need to paste the sample JSON code shown in Listing 8.1.

```
{
    "roles": [
        "MonitoringDataRead"
    ]
}
```

Listing 8.1 Example JSON for Role Assignment

Note

A role assigned enables you to specify the type of action a user can perform on an API. The `MonitoringDataRead` role, used in Listing 8.1, enables a user to read monitoring data, including MPLs. For a full list of roles for both SAP BTP, Neo environment and SAP BTP, Cloud Foundry environment, refer to the documentation for Cloud Integration at *http://s-prs.co/v576028* and search for "Tasks and Permissions." To specify multiple roles for a user, separate the roles with a comma, for example, `MonitoringDataRead`, `WorkspaceArtifactsDeploy`.

11. Click the **Next** button, and then click **Next** again on the page that follows.
12. Then, enter an instance name of your choice, and click **Finish**.

Now, create a service key by following these steps:

1. Select our newly created service instance to open a screen similar to the screen shown in Figure 8.34.
2. Click the **Create Service Key** button.
3. Provide a name for the service key, and click **Save**.

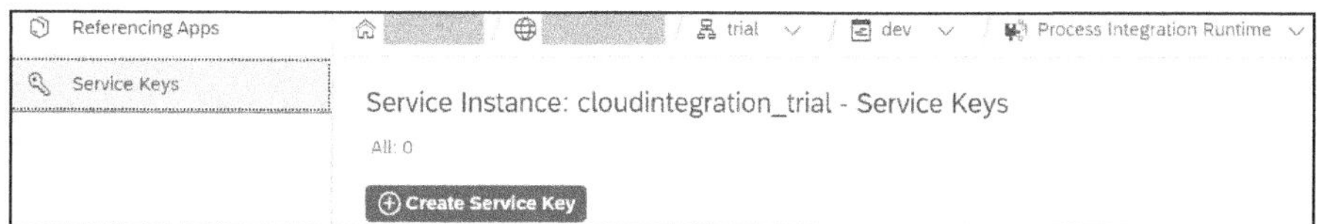

Figure 8.34 Creating a Service Key from a Service Instance

You're then presented with parameter values of your service key. Note that the service key contains few security parameters, including `clientid`, `clientsecret`, `tokenurl`, and `url`, as shown in Figure 8.35. A description of each parameter field is provided in Table 8.8.

Service Instance: api_messagepayloadsread - Service Keys

All: 1

Create Service Key

Search

api_messagepayloadsread_key


```
{
    "oauth": {
        "clientid": "",
        "clientsecret": "",
        "tokenurl": "",
        "url": "",
        "roles": [
            "MessagePayloadsRead"
        ],
        "grant-types": [
            "refresh_token",
            "urn:ietf:params:oauth:grant-type:saml2-bearer",
            "client_credentials",
            "password",
            "authorization_code",
            "user_token",
            "urn:ietf:params:oauth:grant-type:jwt-bearer"
        ]
    }
}
```


Figure 8.35 List of Generated Service Key Parameters to Be Used for OAuth Authentication

Parameter	Description
`clientid`	Represents the user name to be used by the API client to call the API
`clientsecret`	Represents the password to be used by the API client to call the API
`tokenurl`	Represents the authorization server URL, which is responsible for issuing the OAuth token
`url`	Represents the base URL of the OData API

Table 8.8 Service Key Parameters

Voilà! You now have the details you need to perform an OAuth OData API call to your Cloud Integration in SAP BTP, Cloud Foundry environment. Let's now explore how to use the service key parameters we obtained earlier, as shown in Figure 8.35, to connect to an OData API using OAuth 2.0.

You can use any API client of your choice, but for illustration, we'll use Postman (*www.getpostman.com/*) because you already used Postman for a scenario in Chapter 7. You'll first need to retrieve an OAuth token with the OAuth credentials by following these steps:

1. Perform an HTTP `POST` request on a request URL, which follows the format *https://<tokenurl>?grant_type=client_credentials*.
2. Select **Basic Auth** from the **Type** dropdown list, as shown in Figure 8.36.

> **Note**
>
> For the URL, the *<tokenurl>* can be retrieved from the screen shown in Figure 8.35. With the basic authentication, enter "clientid" in the **Username** field and "clientsecret" in the **Password** field. Both `clientid` and `clientsecret` values can be retrieved from the service key shown in Figure 8.35.

3. Trigger the call by clicking the **Send** button.

As a result of the call, an `access_token` is returned in the response. You'll need to append the `access_token` to any subsequent OData API calls.

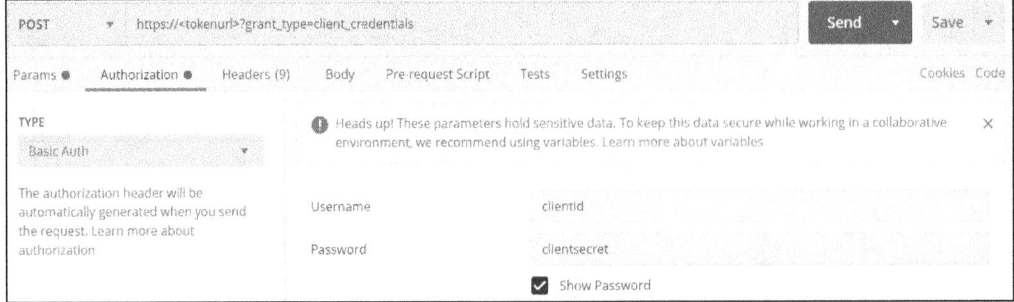

Figure 8.36 Postman Set Up to Retrieve the OAuth Token

Assuming that you intended to retrieve MPL data in your subsequent API call, you'll need to use a URL in the following format:

https://<tokenurl>/api/v1/MessageProcessingLogs?access_token=< access_token_value>

Note that, for the `<access_token_value>`, use the `access_token` value returned from the previous call.

If you're using Cloud Integration in the SAP BTP, Neo environment, you can explore how to configure your tenant in the next section.

Your Cloud Integration Tenant for SAP BTP, Neo Environment

When using the SAP BTP, Neo environment, you must select the region-specific host of your Cloud Integration tenant from the **Starting url** dropdown list, which is shown in Figure 8.37. Compare your tenant URL with one of the entries shown in Figure 8.37 to find the right match.

Then, maintain the **Display Name for Environment**, **Account Short Name**, and **SSL Host** fields and your user credentials. Refer to Table 8.9 for more details about these attributes.

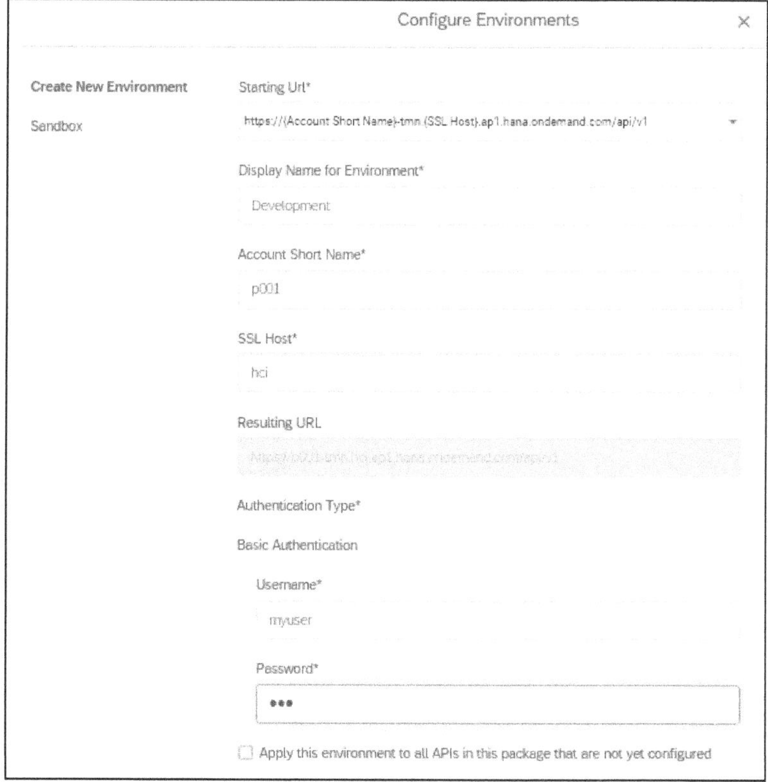

Figure 8.37 Selecting the Region of Your Tenant for SAP BTP, Neo Environment

Column	Description
Display Name for Environment	Enter a human-readable alias name, for example, "Development", "Test", or "Acceptance".

Table 8.9 Attributes of the Configure API Endpoint Page for SAP BTP, Neo Environment

Column	Description
Account Short Name	This value is your tenant ID, which can be found between the // and -tmn in your tenant URL. The tenant URL is always of the format: *https://{Account Short Name}-tmn.{SSLHost}.{Region}.hana.ondemand.com.*
SSL Host	This value can be retrieved from your tenant URL. The tenant URL is always of the format: *https://{Account Short Name}-tmn.{SSLHost}.{Region}.hana.ondemand.com.* Example: For *{SSL Host}*, use hci.
User name	The user name of your Cloud Integration tenant account.
Password	The password of your Cloud Integration tenant account.

Table 8.9 Attributes of the Configure API Endpoint Page for SAP BTP, Neo Environment (Cont.)

For those using the SAP BTP, Neo environment, let's now discuss the cross-site request forgery (CSRF) token handling in the next section. If you're using SAP BTP, Cloud Foundry environment, you can skip the next section.

8.5.2 Cross-Site Request Forgery Token Handling for SAP BTP, Neo Environment

Because APIs on the SAP BTP, Neo environment use basic authentication, they are vulnerable for cross-site request forgery (CSRF) attacks. This type of security attack or malicious exploit occurs when unauthorized commands are transmitted from a user that the web application trusts. CSRF exploits the trust that a site has in a user's browser. One example is a banking website that uses cookies to identify you in the future.

Within the context of APIs, a CSRF attacker can execute an action on the target application via an API without the knowledge or permission of the consumer application. In general, CSRF attacks have the following characteristics:

- Generally, involve sites that rely on a user's identity
- Exploit the site's trust in that identity
- Trick the consumer application into sending HTTP requests to a target site
- Involve HTTP requests that change application data

To prevent CSRF attacks, some OData APIs provided by Cloud Integration require X-CSRF token validation. An X-CSRF token is mostly required for APIs that need permission to write and change objects via the POST, PUT, and DELETE HTTP operations. We don't have the time to go into how X-CSRF tokens work, so for further reference, you can consult the many resources available online, including *http://s-prs.co/507754*.

When an API uses an X-CSRF token, calls made to the API without an X-CSRF token are rejected. As a result, you must retrieve an X-CSRF token first, before invoking such an API. Let's now explore how you can fetch an X-CSRF token.

Let's use Postman as our API client because we already used it back in Chapter 7. To retrieve the X-CSRF token, you'll need to use the following endpoint:

- *https//<TMN-host>/api/v1* for SAP BTP, Neo environment
- *https//<tokenurl>/api/v1* for SAP BTP, Cloud Foundry environment

For the remaining sections in this chapter, whenever an OData endpoint is presented with *https//<tokenurl>/...*, you can assume that this represents a SAP BTP, Cloud Foundry environment URL. The equivalent SAP BTP, Neo environment URL can be constructed by replacing *<tokenurl>* with *<TMN-host>*.

In this context, *<TMN-host>* represents the tenant host of Cloud Integration. As shown in Figure 8.38, select **GET** as the HTTP method, and specify the OData API endpoint. For SAP BTP, Neo environment, you'll also need to select **Basic Auth** and enter your credentials. For SAP BTP, Cloud Foundry environment, you'll need to select **No Auth** and extend the URL with the `access_token` query parameter, as discussed in Section 8.5.1.

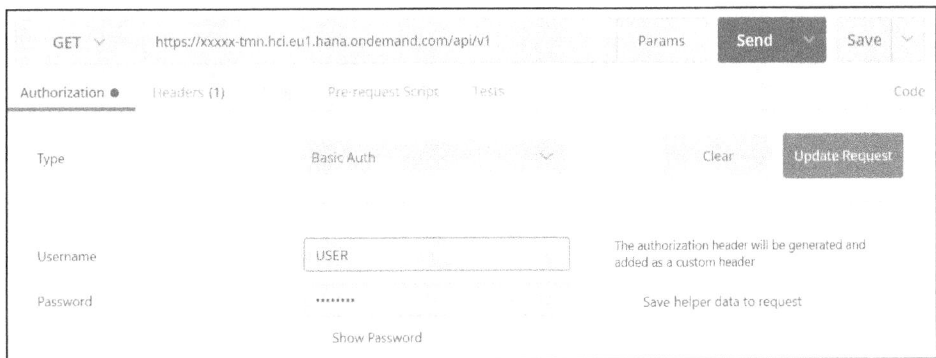

Figure 8.38 Configuring Endpoint and Authorization in Postman for SAP BTP, Neo Environment

Under the **Headers** tab, add a new key named **X-CSRF-Token** with the value **Fetch** to request an X-CSRF token, as shown in Figure 8.39.

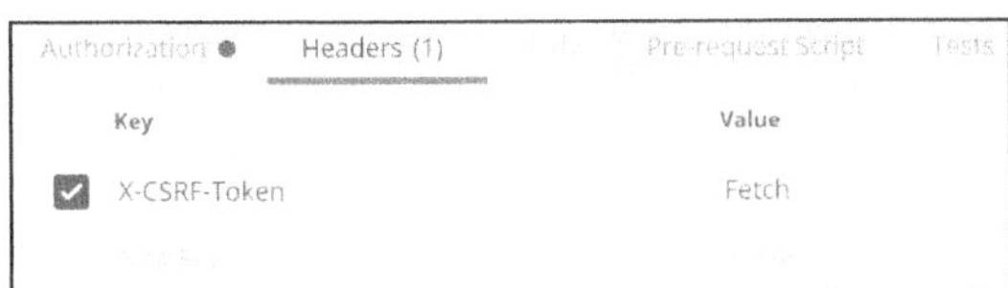

Figure 8.39 Adding the X-CSRF-Token Header

Click the **Send** button (shown earlier in Figure 8.38 in the top right) to trigger the request. The response message includes a number of headers, including the X-CSRF token, which can be identified by the label **x-csrf-token** under the **Headers** tab, as shown in Figure 8.40.

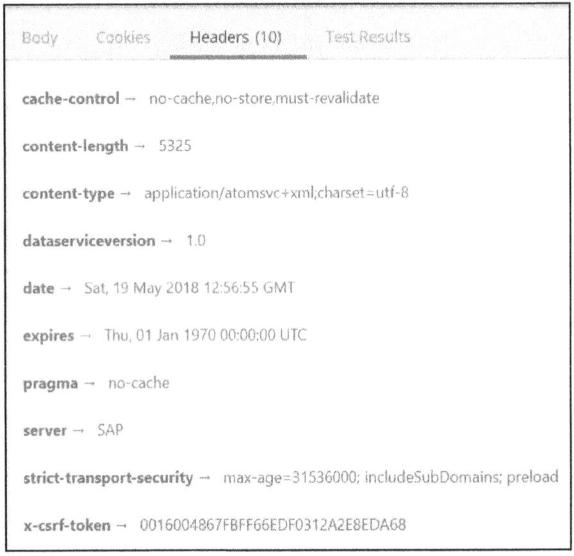

Figure 8.40 X-CSRF-Token in the Headers Tab

You can now use the value of the X-CSRF token in the header of your next OData API request. Furthermore, the body of the response message is filled with a list of entity types that the X-CSRF token can be used with. In other words, the scope of the X-CSRF token is limited to the entity types listed in the response, as shown in Figure 8.41.

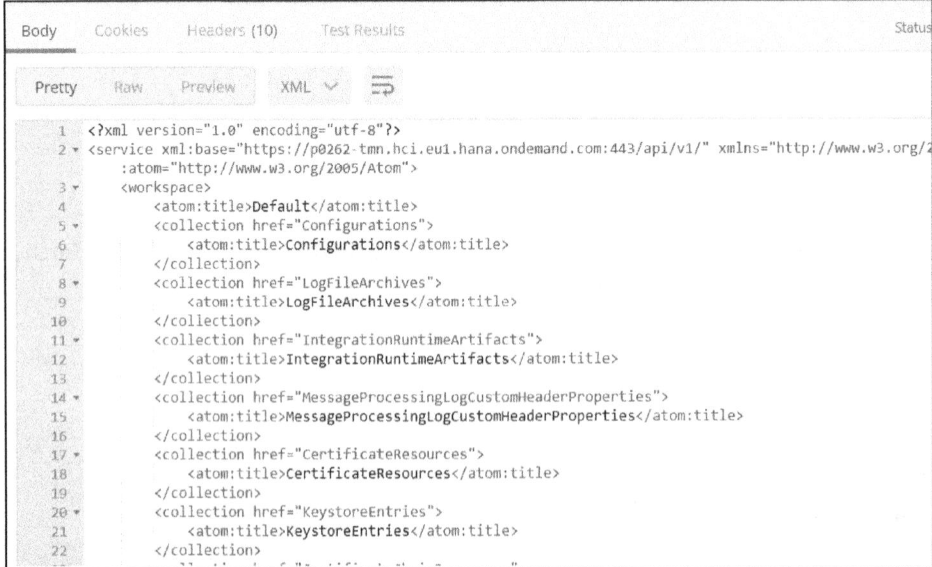

Figure 8.41 Response Body Associated with the X-CSRF Token

In the following sections, we'll explore the following different API categories:

- Monitoring message flows using the API
- Managing deployed integration content using the API
- Managing log files using the API
- Managing the message store using the API
- Managing security material using the API
- Managing the Partner Directory using the API

Let's start with message flow APIs.

8.5.3 Monitoring Message Flows Using the API

In Chapter 7, Section 7.2.3, we described how you can monitor message processing. In APIs related to monitoring message flows, the following entity types play key roles:

- `MessageProcessingLogs`
  Maintains responsible for MPLs. This entity is the main and parent entity of the API. From this entity, you can navigate to all other entities.
- `MessageProcessingLogAdapterAttributes`
  Encapsulates the adapter attributes of the MPL of a specified message entry. This entity includes details such as the type of adapter used in the related iFlow.
- `MessageProcessingLogAttachments`
  Contains attachments of the MPL related to a specified message entry.
- `MessageProcessingLogCustomHeaderProperties`
  Contains custom header properties of MPLs related to a specified message entry.
- `MessageProcessingLogErrorInformation`
  Contains error information for the message related to a specified message entry.

Many APIs are included in these entities. Describing all of these APIs in detail is beyond the scope of this chapter. However, you can find extensive details and examples in the SAP documentation at *http://s-prs.co/507755*. You can also explore these APIs via the SAP Business Accelerator Hub at *https://api.sap.com/*.

Figure 8.42 shows the entities and APIs available for MPLs. You can test and explore each API using one of the testing approaches we explored in Section 8.5.1.

Let's walk through an example scenario to illustrate some functionalities and the usage of APIs related to the monitoring of message flows. We'll assume that your organization uses many integration platforms, including SAP Process Orchestration, Cloud Integration, and other third-party platforms. You've been asked to build a custom dashboard monitoring solution so that users can see at a glance, statistics and lists of messages failing in the various integration platforms. The advantage of this dashboard is that the user won't need to log on to each of these platforms individually. Instead, after logging on to the custom dashboard, the user will see errors as they occur on all integration platforms.

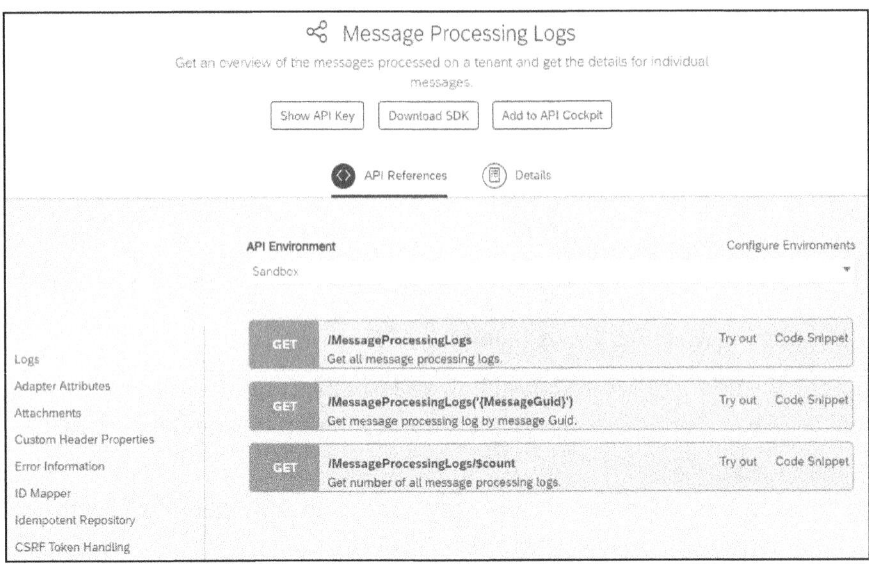

Figure 8.42 Entity Types and APIs in the MPLs

How can you programmatically retrieve the relevant information from the MPLs in Cloud Integration and find the entries with errors? Monitoring message flows APIs come to the rescue.

To solve this challenge, you'll need an API that retrieves all MPLs in an error state from the last hour, which will require the use of the `MessageProcessingLogs` entity. One potential solution is to use the following OData endpoint:

```
https://<tokenurl>/api/v1/MessageProcessingLogs?$inlinecount=allpages&$filter=
Status eq 'FAILED ' and LogStart gt datetime '2023-05-24T12:00:00 ' and LogEnd
lt datetime '2023-05-24T13:00:00 '&$expand=AdapterAttributes
```

Let's examine this OData endpoint with the help of the attributes listed in Table 8.10 to understand what's happening. (Note that some attributes described in Table 8.10 were also previously explained in Table 8.6.)

API Endpoint Element	Description	Example
`MessageProcessingLogs`	Retrieves MPL entries.	`MessageProcessingLogs`
`inlinecount`	Indicates that the response should contain a count of the number of entries in the returned collection.	`allpages`

Table 8.10 Attributes Included in the OData Endpoint to Retrieve Entries with Errors

API Endpoint Element	Description	Example
filter	Filters the result based on various criteria. In the example column, we're filtering for all messages that have the status **Failed**. Additionally, we're filtering for all message logs that have been created between 29/04/2023 at 12:00:00 and 29/04/2023 at 13:00:00.	Status eq ‘FAILED’ and LogStart gt datetime’2023-04-29T12:00:00’ and LogEnd lt datetime’2023-04-29T13:00:00’
expand	Retrieves correlated entities for a given navigation. In our case, we also want to retrieve adapter-specific attributes.	AdapterAttributes

Table 8.10 Attributes Included in the OData Endpoint to Retrieve Entries with Errors (Cont.)

After calling the OData endpoint that solves our challenge, you'll get the response message shown in Listing 8.2.

```
<feed xmlns="http://www.w3.org/2005/Atom" xmlns:m="http://
schemas.microsoft.com/ado/2007/08/dataservices/metadata" xmlns:d="http://
schemas.microsoft.com/ado/2007/08/dataservices" xml:base="https://xxx-
tmn.hci.eu1.hana.ondemand.com:443/api/v1/">
<id>
https://xxxxx.hci.eu1.hana.ondemand.com:443/api/v1/MessageProcessingLogs
</id>
<title type="text">MessageProcessingLogs</title>
<updated>2023-04-29T12:58:12.413Z</updated>
<author>
<name/>
</author>
<link href="MessageProcessingLogs" rel="self" title="MessageProcessingLogs"/>
<m:count>1</m:count>
<entry>
<id>
https://xxxx2-tmn.hci.eu1.hana.ondemand.com:443/api/v1/
MessageProcessingLogs('AGYBvMjkXEldf5exOQVi-6sVMo5Q')
</id>
<title type="text">MessageProcessingLogs</title>
<updated>2023-04-29T12:58:12.413Z</updated>
<category term="com.sap.hci.api.MessageProcessingLog" scheme="http://
schemas.microsoft.com/ado/2007/08/dataservices/scheme"/>
<link href="MessageProcessingLogs('AGYBvMjkXEldf5exOQVi-6sVMo5Q')" rel="edit"
```

```
title="MessageProcessingLog"/>
<link href="MessageProcessingLogs('AFr1v7POJUYGSI2bXJAGRQ74tiHyP')/
CustomHeaderProperties" rel="http://schemas.microsoft.com/ado/2007/08/
dataservices/related/CustomHeaderProperties" title="CustomHeaderProperties"
type="application/atom+xml;type=feed"/>
<link href="MessageProcessingLogs('AFr1v7POJUYGSI2bXJAGRQ74HMyP')/
MessageStoreEntries" rel="http://schemas.microsoft.com/ado/2007/08/
dataservices/related/MessageStoreEntries" title="MessageStoreEntries" type=
"application/atom+xml;type=feed"/>
<link href="MessageProcessingLogs('AFrlv7POJUYGSI2bXJAGRQ74tiHyP')/
ErrorInformation" rel="http://schemas.microsoft.com/ado/2007/08/dataservices/
related/Errorinformation" title="Errorinformation" type="application/
atom+xml;type=entry"/>
<link href="MessageProcessingLogs('AGYBvMjkXEldf5exOQVi-6sVMo5Q')/
AdapterAttributes" rel="http://schemas.microsoft.com/ado/2007/08/dataservices/
related/AdapterAttributes" title="AdapterAttributes" type="application/
atom+xml;type=feed">
<m:inline>...</m:inline>
</link>
<link href="MessageProcessingLogs('AFrlv7POJUYGSI2bXJAGRQ74tiHyP')/Attachments"
rel="http://schemas.microsoft.com/ado/2007/08/dataservices/related/Attachments"
title="Attachments" type="application/atom+xml;type=feed"/>
<link href="MessageProcessingLogs('AGYBvMjkXEldf5exOQVi-6sVMo5Q')/Runs"
rel="http://schemas.microsoft.com/ado/2007/08/dataservices/related/Runs"
title="Runs" type="application/atom+xml;type=feed"/>
<content type="application/xml">
    <m:properties>
                <d:MessageGuid>AFr1v7POJUYGSI2bXJAGRQ74HMyP</d:MessageGuid>
         <d:CorrelationId>AFr1v7MGmzLrpFrOxqOolvAcig5Y</d:CorrelationId>
        <d:ApplicationMessageId m:null="true"/>
        <d:ApplicationMessageType m:null="true"/>
        <d:LogStart>2023-04-29T12:50:59.723</d:LogStart>
        <d:LogEnd>2023-04-29T12:51:00.12</d:LogEnd>
        <d:Sender>Sender_SOAP</d:Sender>
        <d:Receiver m:null="true"/>
         <d:IntegrationFlowName>Invoking_OData</d:IntegrationFlowName>
        <d:Status>FAILED</d:Status>
        <d:AlternateWeblink>...</d:AlternateWeblink>
        <d:IntegrationArtifact m:type="com.sap.hci.api.IntegrationArtifact">
            <d:Id>Invoking_OData</d:Id>
            <d:Name>Invoking OData</d:Name>
            <d:Type>INTEGRATION_FLOW</d:Type>
        </d:IntegrationArtifact>
        <d:LogLevel>INFO</d:LogLevel>
```

```
        <d:CustomStatus>FAILED</d:CustomStatus>
</m:properties>
</content>
</entry>
</feed>
```

Listing 8.2 Response of the OData Endpoint Call

When examining the response message shown in Listing 8.2, you'll notice an element named entry, which represents a log entry in the message monitor. Note that if multiple entries are returned, the entries are sorted in descending order (with the oldest entry on the top) by default. The entries returned in this response can also be found on the **Monitor** page in the Cloud Integration Web UI.

In addition, you'll see that the entry shown in Listing 8.2 has a MessageGuid with a value AGYBvMjkXEldf5exOQVi-6sVMo5Q. The same entry can also be found in the **Monitor Message Processing** section of Cloud Integration, shown in Figure 8.43, next to the **Message ID** field. Also note that the response message has a field labeled count, which specifies the number of returned entries. Furthermore, note that the field IntegrationFlowName has the value Invoking_OData, which will be of use later in Section 8.5.4.

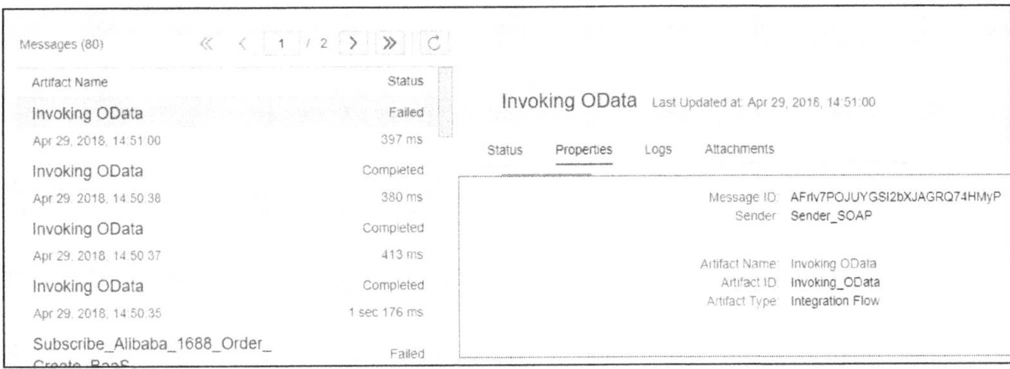

Figure 8.43 MPLs in Cloud Integration

The entry returned in the OData API call contains a number of properties, as shown earlier in Listing 8.2. Table 8.11 lists the MessageProcessingLogs properties and their descriptions.

Property	Description
MessageGuid	GUID of the message that the processing log concerns.
CorrelationId	GUID of the correlated messages.

Table 8.11 Properties of the MessageProcessingLogs

Property	Description
ApplicationMessageId	GUID specific to a particular application. Think about this value as an identifier set for the sake of identification by an external application. This value can be set using a **Content Modifier** step and assigning a value to the SAP_ApplicationID header element.
ApplicationMessageType	Property to represent a type of message as known by a business application. Use a **Script** step in the iFlow to set this property.
LogStart	Date and time that the writing of the log started.
LogEnd	Date and time that the writing of the log ended.
Sender	Identifier of the sender system.
Receiver	Identifier of the receiver system.
IntegrationFlowName	Name of the iFlow.
Status	Status of the message processing. Currently, the following statuses are possible: **Completed**, **Processing**, **Retry**, **Error**, **Escalated**, and **Failed**.
AlternateWebLink	Link used to directly open the MPL on this monitoring entry.
IntegrationArtifact/Id	Technical name or ID of the iFlow.
IntegrationArtifact/Name	Name of the iFlow. This value is identical to the IntegrationFlowName property.
IntegrationArtifact/Type	Type of artifact that this message processing concerns, for example, INTEGRATION_FLOW.

Table 8.11 Properties of the MessageProcessingLogs (Cont.)

In the following sections, we'll continue with our OData API journey by exploring APIs that relate to deployed integration content.

8.5.4 Managing Deployed Integration Content Using the API

Using the OData APIs provided by Cloud Integration, you can query the content of integration artifacts deployed on a tenant. The APIs that access the deployed integration content revolve around the following entity types:

- **IntegrationRuntimeArtifact**
  Manages all deployed integration artifacts in the tenant. It's also possible to use the POST method to deploy an artifact from the file system. Additionally, an already deployed artifact can be undeployed using the DELETE method.

- `IntegrationRuntimeArtifactsErrorInformation`
  Holds error information of a specific deployed integration artifact.
- `CSRF Token Handling`
  Holds the X-CSRF token for this session. The X-CSRF token is only required for write access (as discussed in Section 8.5.2).

Too many APIs use these entities to discuss them all in this chapter. However, you can find extensive details and examples in the SAP documentation at *http://s-prs.co/507757*. You can also explore these APIs via the SAP Business Accelerator Hub (*http://s-prs.co/v576034*).

Figure 8.44 shows the entities and APIs available. You can test and explore each API using one of the testing approaches we explored in Section 8.5.1.

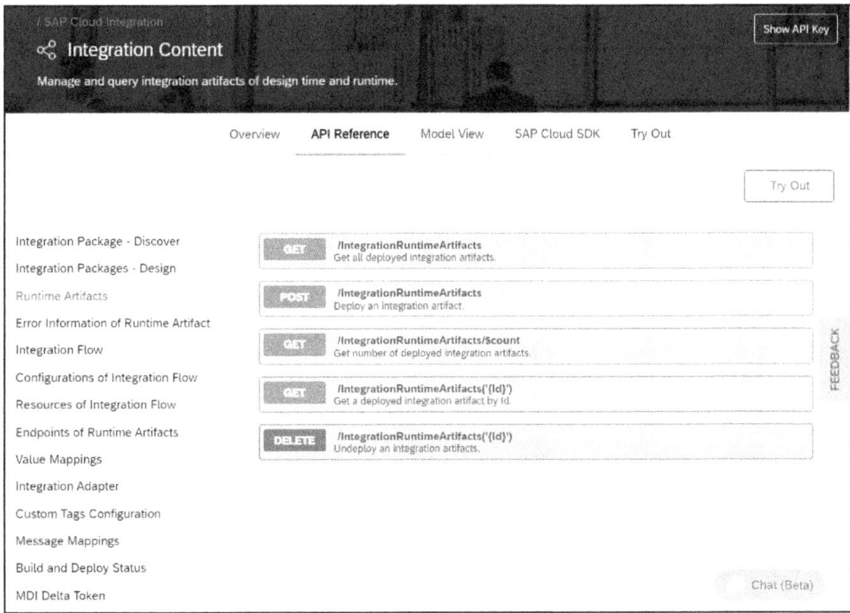

Figure 8.44 Entity Types and APIs Related to Deployed Integration Content

Let's further enhance the example scenario from Section 8.5.3 to illustrate the usage and functionalities for managing deployed integration content. In the previous section, we retrieved an entry with an error using the APIs for MPLs. Imagine that after retrieving and displaying an entry with an error in your custom dashboard, you now also want to see details about the related deployed integration content. Perhaps, you're interested to know the name, status, and version of the deployed content, as well as the user who deployed it and when.

To solve this challenge, you'll need to use the `IntegrationRuntimeArtifact` entity. One solution is to use the following OData endpoint:

https://< tokenurl>/api/v1/IntegrationRuntimeArtifacts('Invoking_OData')

Note the value `Invoking_OData` was retrieved from the field `IntegrationFlowName` within the `content` node, as shown in Listing 8.2.

The resulting response of the preceding OData endpoint is shown in Figure 8.45.


```
▼<entry xmlns="http://www.w3.org/2005/Atom" xmlns:m="http://schemas.microsoft.com/ado/2007/08/dataservices/metadata"
 xmlns:d="http://schemas.microsoft.com/ado/2007/08/dataservices" xml:base="https://p0262-tmn.hci.eu1.hana.ondemand.com:443/api/v1/">
 ▼<id>
    https://p0262-tmn.hci.eu1.hana.ondemand.com:443/api/v1/IntegrationRuntimeArtifacts('Invoking_OData')
  </id>
  <title type="text">IntegrationRuntimeArtifacts</title>
  <updated>2018-04-29T15:49:08.406Z</updated>
  <category term="com.sap.hci.api.IntegrationRuntimeArtifact" scheme="http://schemas.microsoft.com/ado/2007/08/dataservices/scheme"/>
  <link href="IntegrationRuntimeArtifacts('Invoking_OData')" rel="edit" title="IntegrationRuntimeArtifact"/>
  <link href="IntegrationRuntimeArtifacts('Invoking_OData')/$value" rel="edit-media" type="application/octet-stream"/>
  <link href="IntegrationRuntimeArtifacts('Invoking_OData')/ErrorInformation"
  rel="http://schemas.microsoft.com/ado/2007/08/dataservices/related/ErrorInformation" title="ErrorInformation"
  type="application/atom+xml;type=entry"/>
  <content type="application/octet-stream" src="IntegrationRuntimeArtifacts('Invoking_OData')/$value"/>
 ▼<m:properties>
    <d:Id>Invoking_OData</d:Id>
    <d:Version>1.0.0</d:Version>
    <d:Name>Invoking OData</d:Name>
    <d:Type>INTEGRATION_FLOW</d:Type>
    <d:DeployedBy>S0011540061</d:DeployedBy>
    <d:DeployedOn>2018-04-28T21:11:25.951</d:DeployedOn>
    <d:Status>STARTED</d:Status>
  </m:properties>
</entry>
```


Figure 8.45 Response of the OData Endpoint Call

Every <entry> element returned in the response shown in Figure 8.45, represents an artifact in Cloud Integration. In our case, we only have one entry returned. The `properties` element of the response message shown in Figure 8.45 includes a number of attributes to describe the deployed integration content. These properties are listed in Table 8.12.

Attributes	Description
`Id`	Technical identification of the integration content.
`Version`	Latest version of the integration content when deployed.
`Name`	Name of the integration
`Type`	Type of artifact that this message processing concerns. Possible values include `INTEGRATION_FLOW`, `VALUE_MAPPING`, `DATA_INTEGRATION`, and `ODATA_SERVICE`.
`DeployedBy`	Name of the user who deployed the content.
`DeployedOn`	Date and time that the integration content was last deployed.
`Status`	Current status of deployed integration content. Possible values include `STARTED`, `STARTING`, and `ERROR`.

Table 8.12 Properties Available for the Deployed Integration Content OData API

In the next section, we'll explore APIs that relate to log files.

8.5.5 Managing Log Files Using the APIs

Using the OData APIs provided by Cloud Integration, you can query log files on a tenant. Note that, at the time of this writing, the Log Files API is only available in the SAP BTP, Neo environment and not yet in the SAP BTP, Cloud Foundry environment.

Log files come in two types:

- **Default trace**
  These log files include processing information of a technical nature.
- **HTTP access logs**
  These log files include information about all inbound HTTP requests arriving in Cloud Integration.

The APIs that facilitate the access to log files revolve around two main entity types:

- `LogFileArchives`
  Used for all archived log files.
- `LogFiles`
  Used for all current (nonarchived) log files.

These entities include a number of APIs. We won't explore them all in this section, but we'll look at a scenario to showcase what's possible. To get a full description of the different APIs, refer to the SAP documentation at *http://s-prs.co/507759*. You can also explore these APIs via the SAP Business Accelerator Hub at *http://s-prs.co/v576035*.

Figure 8.46 shows the available entities and APIs. You can test and explore each API using one of the testing approaches we explored in Section 8.5.3.

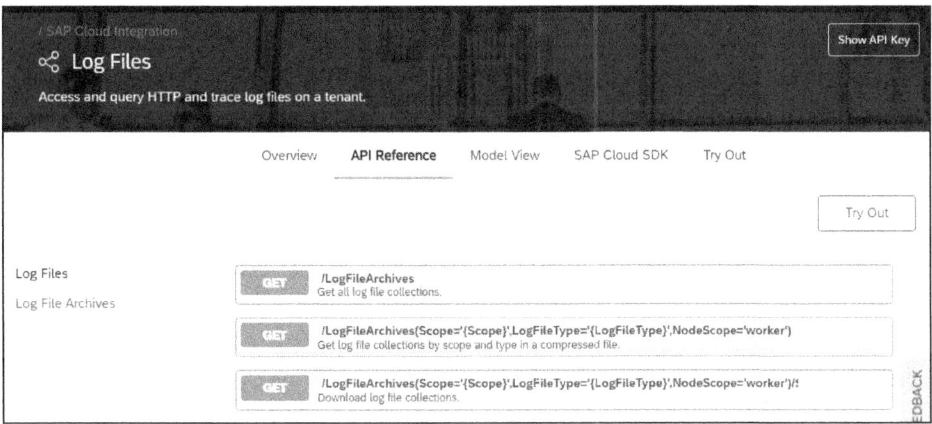

Figure 8.46 Entity Types and APIs Related to Log Files

Let's return to our example scenario to illustrate the usage and functionalities of APIs relating to log files. In Section 8.5.3, we retrieved an entry with an error using the MPL

API. Imagine that you want to further troubleshoot the error from your custom dashboard. For this task, you want to download a copy of all log files of type HTTP around the time that the error occurred. Note that the error occurred around 12:51, as indicated by the `LogStart` field shown earlier in Listing 8.2.

To solve this challenge, we can use the `LogFileArchives` entity by invoking the following OData endpoint:

https://<tokenurl>/api/v1/LogFileArchives(Scope='all',LogFileType='http',NodeScope='worker')/$value?modifiedAfter=2023-04-29T12:50:00Z

Let's now examine this OData endpoint in detail to understand what is happening, referring to the details listed in Table 8.13.

Endpoint Attribute	Description
`LogFileArchives`	Entity used to retrieve an archived log file.
`Scope`	Indicates which scope/type of log files you want to download. Possible values include `all` (to download all existing HTTP log files) and `latest` (to only retrieve the latest HTTP log files).
`LogFileType`	Filters the result based on the type of log file. Possible values include `http` and `Trace`.
`NodeScope`	Specifies that we're only interested in retrieving log files from runtime nodes (also referred to as worker nodes).
`value`	Specifies that the next parameter in the URL will contain parameter values.
`modifiedAfter`	Specifies the time after which the filtered log file was changed.

Table 8.13 Attributes Included in the OData Endpoint to Log Archive Entries

Note that you must have the role `IntegrationOperationServer.read` assigned to your user to call log file APIs.

In the next section, we'll explore APIs that relate to the message store.

8.5.6 Managing Message Store Entries Using APIs

Using the OData APIs provided by Cloud Integration, you can access the tenant's message store entries. In scenarios with the requirement to persist messages, message content can be written and saved in the message store using the **Persist Message** step of an iFlow. You can then access the stored message and analyze it later. However, note that a message is stored on the runtime for a maximum of 90 days. After this time, the message is automatically deleted.

Note

At the time of this writing, no user interface is available for the message store. The OData API is the only option for accessing the content of a message store.

For each entry in a message store, you can retrieve its properties, headers, payload, and attachments. The APIs that access message stores revolve around the following four main entity types:

- `MessageStoreEntries`
  Used to manage message store entries.
- `MessageStoreEntryProperties`
  Used to manage properties of message store entries.
- `MessageStoreEntryAttachments`
  Used to manage attachments from a specific message store entry.
- `MessageStoreEntryAttachmentProperties`
  Used to manage properties of an attachment in the message store.

Referring to the entity model diagram shown earlier in Figure 8.19, a direct relationship exists between a message store entry (represented by the entity type `MessageStoreEntries`) and `MessageProcessingLogs`. This relationship means that for every entry in the processing log with an attachment, you can try to retrieve its related message store entries (if available).

In this section, we won't explore all APIs involving in the entities listed earlier, but we'll look at a scenario to showcase what is possible. To get a full description of the different APIs, refer to the SAP documentation at *http://s-prs.co/507761*. You can also explore these APIs via the SAP Business Accelerator Hub at *http://s-prs.co/v576036*.

Figure 8.47 shows the entities and APIs available. You can test and explore each one of these APIs using the testing approaches we explored in Section 8.5.1.

Figure 8.47 Entity Types and APIs Related to the Message Store

Note that you must have the role `esbmessagestorage.read` assigned to your user to call Message Store APIs.

Consider the message aggregation scenario we explored in Chapter 4, Section 4.6, in which we aggregated correlated messages. Imagine that, after the aggregation process is finished, we want to persist the final aggregated payload in the message store. We can write the payload to the message store using the **Persist** step to our iFlow.

To start developing this iFlow, follow these steps:

1. On the **Design** page of Cloud Integration, open the iFlow that we created in Chapter 4, Section 4.6.
2. Switch to edit mode by clicking the **Edit** button in the top-right corner of the iFlow screen.
3. Add the **Persist** step to the iFlow. The **Persist** step can be found in the palette on the left, as shown in Figure 8.48.

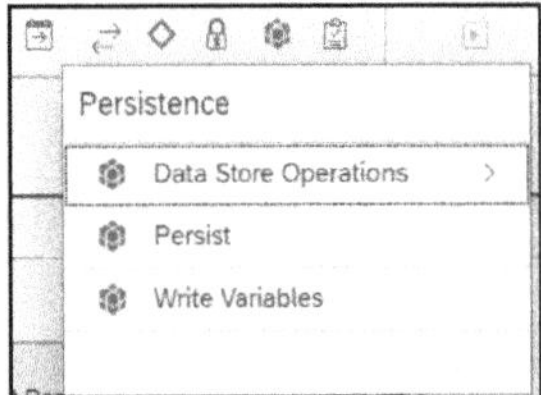

Figure 8.48 Selecting the Persist Step from the Palette

4. Ensure that the **Step ID** of the newly added step is unique. The final iFlow should be similar to the processes shown in Figure 8.49 and Figure 8.50. According to our iFlow, the message store is only populated after all messages have been collected because the **Persist** step comes after the **Aggregator** step.

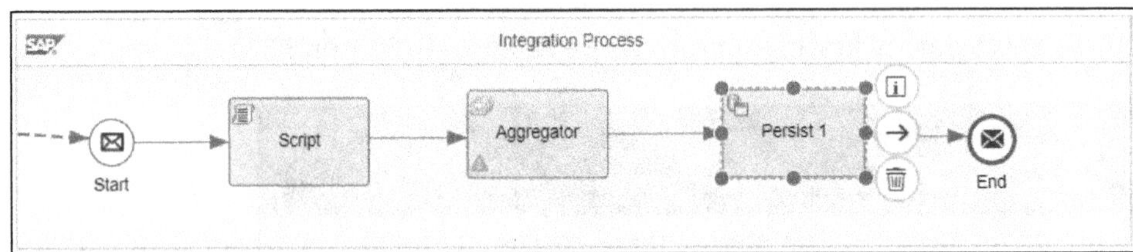

Figure 8.49 Overview of the iFlow Extended with a Persist (Step A)

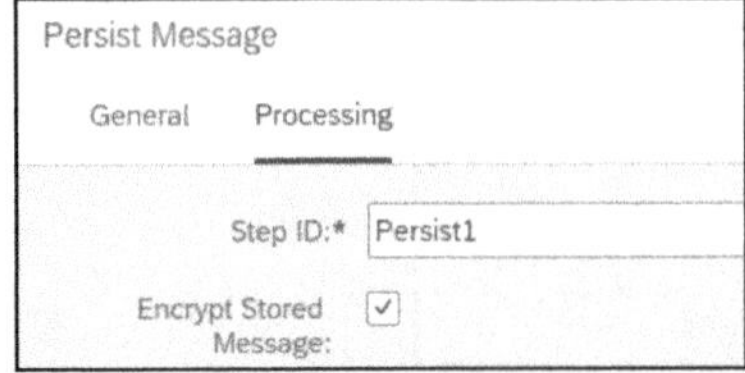

Figure 8.50 Overview of the iFlow Extended with a Persist (Step B)

5. Save and deploy the iFlow.

Now, let's assume that in our custom dashboard application that we started building in Section 8.5.3, we want to be warned if a failed message flow contains entries in the message store. In this case, you'll retrieve the payload of the entry in the message store.

To retrieve the payload of the entry in the message store, you'll need to call several OData APIs in the following sequence:

1. Use `MessageProcessingLogs` to retrieve the list of failing messages. You already know how to query for failed messages from our discussion in Section 8.5.3.
2. Use the message `Guid` of the message retrieved from the first call to make a second call to query if there are message store entries for messages with the specified message `Guid`. In this step, you can use the following endpoint:

   https://<tenant>/api/v1/MessageProcessingLogs('<Guid>')/MessageStoreEntries

   The response of the API call is shown in Listing 8.3.

   ```
   <content type="application/octet-stream" src="MessageStoreEntries("sap-it-
   res%3Amsg%3Aac965bd8f%3Abe694f69-73a5-4430-b681-1673c963fd4c")/$value"/>
   ```

   Listing 8.3 Response of the OData API Call

3. Retrieve the payload of the entry in the message store. Looking at the entry returned in Listing 8.3, notice the `src` attribute of the `content` element. The value of this attribute provides details regarding how to retrieve the payload. In this example, use the following link to retrieve the payload:

   ```
   https://<tokenurl>/api/v1/MessageStoreEntries('sap-it-res%3Amsg%3Aac965bd8f
   %3Abe694f69-73a5-4430-b681-1673c963fd4c')/$value
   ```

In this URL, the value between */v1/* and */$value* is copied from the `src` attribute of Listing 8.3. The API returns the aggregated payload, as shown in Figure 8.51.


```
<?xml version="1.0" encoding="UTF-8"?><multimap:Messages xmlns:multimap="http://sap.com/xi/XI/SplitAndMerge"><multimap:Message1>
<OrderItem xmlns:demo="http://hci.sap.com/demo" xmlns:soapenv="http://schemas.xmlsoap.org/soap/envelope/">
        <orderNumber>AA2345</orderNumber>
        <Item>
           <ItemNo>1</ItemNo>
           <Quantity>1</Quantity>
           <Unit>1</Unit>
           <LastStatus>false</LastStatus>
        </Item>
     </OrderItem><OrderItem xmlns:demo="http://hci.sap.com/demo" xmlns:soapenv="http://schemas.xmlsoap.org/soap/envelope/">
        <orderNumber>AA2345</orderNumber>
        <Item>
           <ItemNo>2</ItemNo>
           <Quantity>5</Quantity>
           <Unit>1</Unit>
           <LastStatus>false</LastStatus>
        </Item>
     </OrderItem><OrderItem xmlns:demo="http://hci.sap.com/demo" xmlns:soapenv="http://schemas.xmlsoap.org/soap/envelope/">
        <orderNumber>AA2345</orderNumber>
        <Item>
           <ItemNo>3</ItemNo>
           <Quantity>25</Quantity>
           <Unit>1</Unit>
           <LastStatus>true</LastStatus>
        </Item>
     </OrderItem></multimap:Message1></multimap:Messages>
```


Figure 8.51 Aggregated Payload Returned by the Message Store API

Now that you know how to use the Message Store API, let's explore the OData APIs related to security materials.

8.5.7 Managing Security Material Using the API

Using the OData APIs provided by Cloud Integration, we can access keystore content and other security-related artifacts, for example, **User Credentials** artifacts.

Note

This API contains a lot of features that can't all be explored in this section. For a full description of the different APIs available for managing security material, refer to the SAP documentation via *http://s-prs.co/507763*.

To give you an idea of how to use these APIs, let's work through an example scenario to illustrate its usage. Let's assume that you want your keystore entries to be automatically backed up at the end of each month. Given that you don't want to perform this activity manually every month, you're looking for some way to automate the process via your custom dashboard application. (Note that we discussed the topic of keystores in detail in Chapter 10, Section 10.4.1.)

You can easily achieve this automation task by getting your custom application to call the Security Material API. More specifically, you can use an API that enables backs up all keystore entries via the endpoint:

https://<tokenurl>/api/v1/KeystoreResources

Note that you'll need to use a POST method for this request. Listing 8.4 shows an example request. You can also include, in the request, the query option indicated in Table 8.14.

```
{"Name":"backup_admin_system"}
```

Listing 8.4 Example Request Body to Back Up Keystore Entries

Query Option	Description
returnKeystoreEntries	Possible values include true and false. When set to true, the KeystoreEntry instances that have been backed up are returned in the response. Note that this query is optional and defaults to false.

Table 8.14 Possible Query Option for Renaming an Alias

Because the keystore OData API is protected against CSRF attacks, you must first fetch an X-CSRF token before you can make this API call. (We explored how to fetch X-CSRF tokens in Section 8.5.2.)

Let's now explore APIs that relate to managing the Partner Directory in the next section.

8.5.8 Managing the Partner Directory Using the API

The Partner Directory tenant is a component is part of the business-to-business (B2B) component of SAP Integration suite. A Cloud Integration owner might decide to build an application where partners involved in the scenario can maintain their own configuration data. For such a scenario, the Partner Directory can be used.

At the time of this writing, Partner Directory information can only be maintained via an OData API. The HTTP addresses required to make outbound calls to the partner systems are examples of the type of data stored in the Partner Directory.

Assuming that the purpose of the Partner Directory is clear to you, we'll now focus on using the Partner Directory OData APIs provided by Cloud Integration. These APIs access the Partner Directory, create entries, and help manage them. These APIs revolve around the following entity types:

- `AlternativePartners`
- `AuthorizedUsers`
- `BinaryParameters`
- `Partners`
- `StringParameters`
- `UserCredentialParameters`
- `CSRF Token Handling`

Updated details about these APIs can be found via the SAP Business Accelerator Hub at *http://s-prs.co/v576037*.

Figure 8.52 shows the entities and APIs available. You can test and explore each of these APIs using one of the testing approaches we explored in Section 8.5.1.

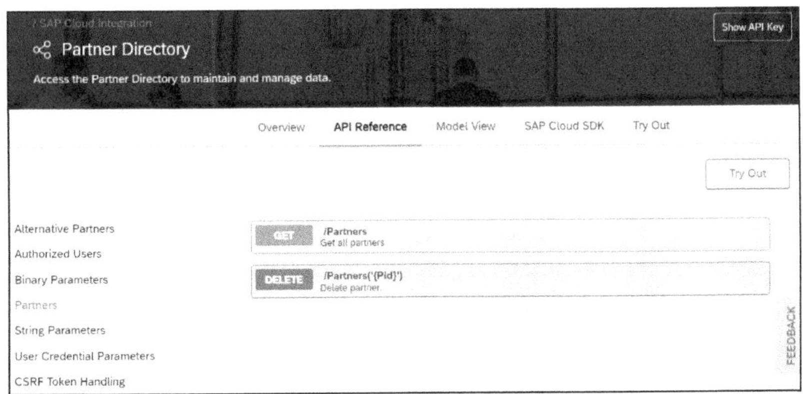

Figure 8.52 Entity Types and APIs Related to the Partner Directory

Note

Be aware of the following Partner Directory limitations:

- The number of `AlternativePartners` in the tenant is limited to a maximum of 1,000,000.
- The number of `AuthorizedUsers` in the tenant is limited to a maximum of 500,000.
- The number of `BinaryParameters` in the tenant is limited to a maximum of 400,000.
- The number of `StringParameters` in the tenant is limited to a maximum of 3,000,000.

8.6 Using Cloud Integration with API Management

In the past, APIs were mostly only known to programmers, but in today's digital era, even business executives are aware of APIs and their potential financial impacts. In a digitized world, many companies are generating revenue by exposing their APIs to business partners, suppliers, and customers as they would for any other service offering.

Companies such as Amazon, Facebook, Twitter, Netflix, Uber, and Google are generating huge revenues based on their APIs. So, chances are high that APIs will play a key role in the digital transformation journey of your organization. Today, APIs are managed like traditional products!

API Management is, next to Cloud Integration, a key constituent of SAP Integration Suite. The API Management solution can help you in your digital transformation journey by providing simple, scalable, and secure access to your organization's digital assets through APIs. API Management enables developer communities to consume and discover your organization's APIs. Refer to *http://s-prs.co/5077119* to read more about API Management.

Some key capabilities of API Management include the following features, just to name a few:

- The ability to provision APIs via REST, OData, and SOAP in a standardized and consistent way
- Real-time and historic analytics on API usage, errors, monitoring, and traffic
- High security standards for the APIs to prevent against attacks such as denial-of-service (DoS) attacks, cross-site scripting (XSS), CSRF, and so on
- Robust traffic management of APIs
- Full API lifecycle management

- Management, discovery, testing, subscription, and consumption of APIs by the developer community
- Monetization of APIs

Figure 8.53 shows the positioning of API Management within your landscape. Different applications can consume APIs via API Management, which is acting as a gateway. API Management also proxies the calls to the backend systems (either on-premise or cloud-based systems). API Management connects to these backend systems via various protocols, such as SOAP, REST, OData, and so on.

Figure 8.53 shows the different personas involved with API Management, such as the following:

- **External applications (mobile, web, etc.)**
  These applications consume the APIs provided by API Management.
- **App developer**
  This developer is responsible for making external applications that consume APIs. This developer must be able to discover existing APIs and easily figure out how to consume them.
- **API developer**
  This person is responsible for designing and implementing APIs via API Management.
- **API admins and owners**
  These people are responsible for administering and managing APIs via monitoring, analyzing, and monetizing processes.

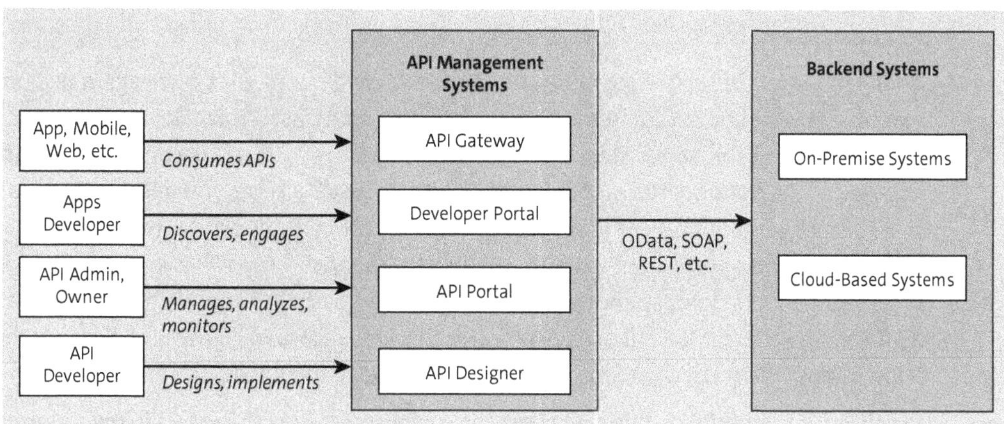

Figure 8.53 Positioning of API Management and Its Personas

The positioning of API Management, as shown in Figure 8.53, also means that API Management can proxy services provided by Cloud Integration, which is the main subject of this section.

API Management is a big topic that deserves its own book. In the following sections, we'll briefly explore how you can use API Management to publish APIs from services provided by Cloud Integration in a secure manner.

Note

To find out more about API Management, follow the tutorials available at SAP Community (*www.sap.com/community.html*).

Note that API Management also sits on top of SAP Integration Suite. You can also register for a free trial account at *http://s-prs.co/v576038*.

You might be wondering how API Management and SAP Business Accelerator Hub are different. API Management enables any organization to expose its own APIs. This solution also allows their business partners to discover and consume these APIs in a secure manner. In contrast, SAP Business Accelerator Hub allows you to discover, explore, and test the APIs offered by SAP.

After obtaining your API Management tenant, one of your first tasks will be to establish a connection to your Cloud Integration tenant. Let's explore how this next.

8.6.1 Establishing a Connection between Cloud Integration and API Management

Much could be said about the topic of provisioning APIs through API Management. Our intention isn't to provide a guide for API Management in this section, but rather to give you a glimpse of what it can do and how it can work in combination with Cloud Integration to create APIs.

To illustrate the provisioning of an API via API Management, let's once again use our example iFlow built in Chapter 4, Section 4.3. We already used this iFlow in Section 8.3 when exploring the **Script** step (shown earlier in Figure 8.11). This scenario currently exposes a SOAP endpoint. Our goal is to provide this SOAP service as a REST-based API in API Management and apply restrictions to the API by limiting the number of calls per minute. This approach of wrapping an existing service as an API is known as an *API proxy*. REST APIs can accept both JSON or XML as payloads. For simplicity, we'll stick to XML for our scenario. The final end-to-end scenario is shown in Figure 8.54. Because the iFlow already exists in Cloud Integration, we only need to expose it as an API.

Recall from Chapter 4, Section 4.3, that the endpoint of the concerned iFlow followed this format:

https://<tenant>/cxf/CPI_Book_Demo_OData

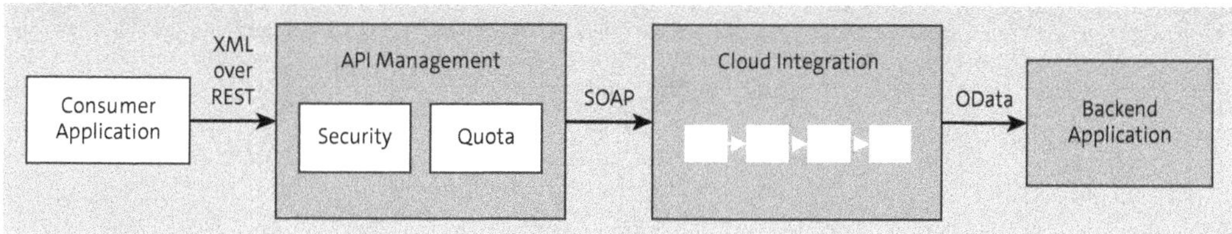

Figure 8.54 End-to-End Overview of Scenario

We can now start the offsetting up our API Management from SAP BTP cockpit. To access the main page of your API Management, follow these steps:

1. Log on to your API Management tenant via the following URL (if you have a trial account): *http://s-prs.co/v576039*. The link to the productive account is given in the tenant provisioning email you received from SAP when getting a new tenant.
2. Navigate to the **Instance and Subscriptions** section from the menu on the left, as shown in Figure 8.55.
3. Click on the **Integration Suite CD3** link under the **Subscriptions** section, as shown in Figure 8.55, in the right panel.

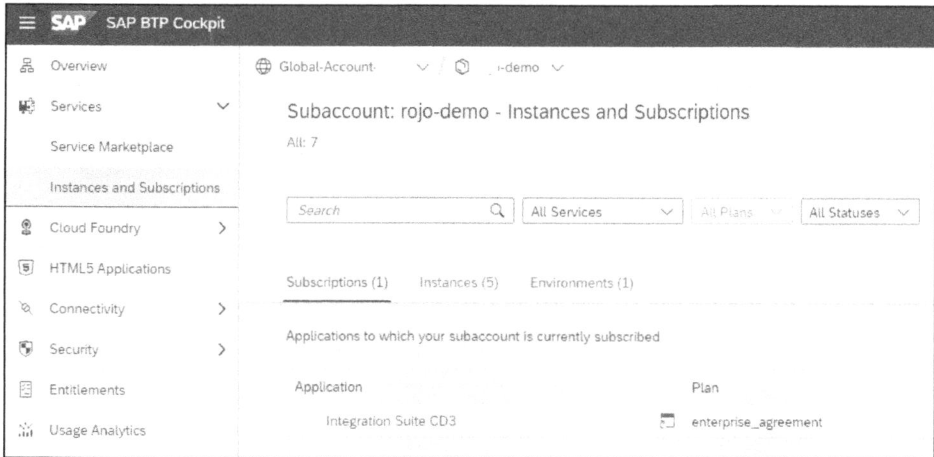

Figure 8.55 Navigating to the API Management Service

4. A new tab will open with different capabilities of SAP Integration Suite. This is the landing page of SAP Integration Suite. From here, select the **Design APIs** link inside the **Manage APIs** tile, as shown in Figure 8.56.
5. The next screen presents a page from where the API can be created and configured. From this page, select **Configure** from the menu on the left, as shown in Figure 8.57.

Let's now create our first API in the next section.

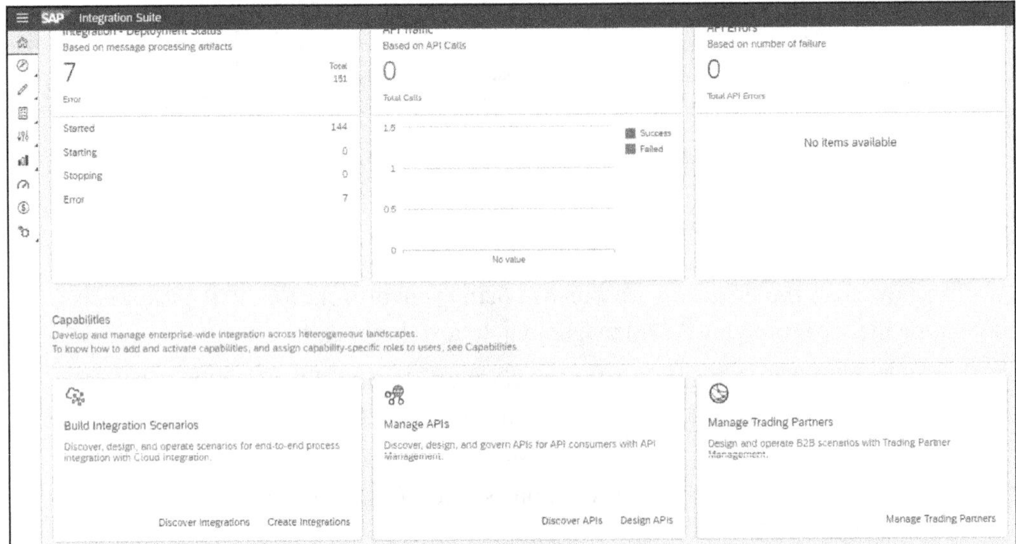

Figure 8.56 SAP Integration Suite Landing Page with an Overview of Its Capabilities

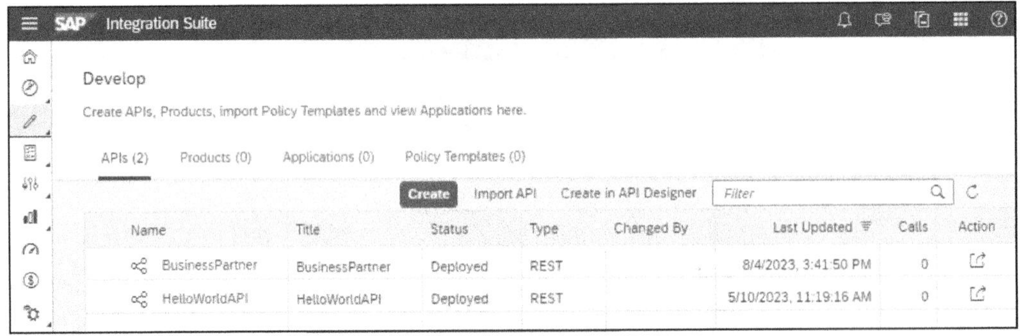

Figure 8.57 Overview of the API Portal

8.6.2 Provisioning APIs

To start creating an API, click on the **Create** button, which can be found in the middle of the screen shown in Figure 8.57. A page will open where you'll fill in the details about the API proxy. The API proxy must point to the iFlow in Cloud Integration. Specify the endpoint of Cloud Integration in the **URL** field as shown in Figure 8.58 and Figure 8.59. (Note that both figures are parts of the same page.)

Click on the **Create** button at the bottom-right corner, as shown in Figure 8.58. You then see a page similar to Figure 8.59.

Figure 8.58 Adding Details of the API Proxy to Be Created: Top of Screen

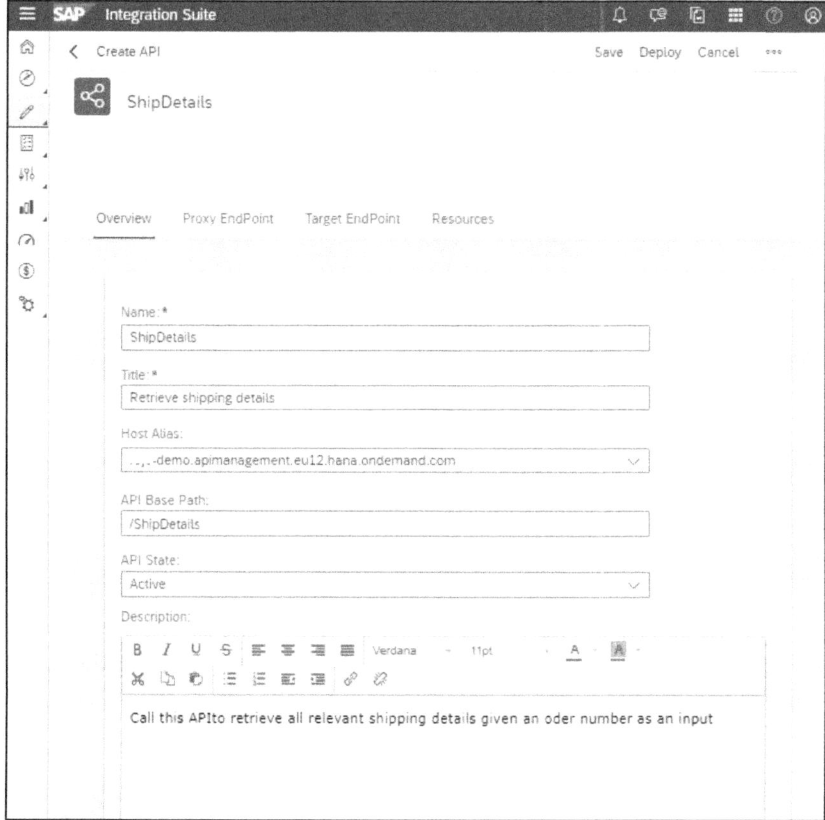

Figure 8.59 Adding Details of the API Proxy to Be Created: Bottom of Screen

Table 8.15 provides descriptions of the fields used in the screen shown in Figure 8.58 and Figure 8.59.

Field	Description
URL	Specifies the full iFlow's endpoint, which can be found from integration artifact monitoring, as discussed in Chapter 4, Section 4.1.
Name	Meaningful name for the API.
Title	Title for the API.
Description	Description for the API.
Host Alias	Automatically populated with the host details of our API Management tenant. Leave this field with its default value.
API Base Path	Specifies the base path to be used as part of the endpoint for the API.
Service Type	Possible values include **REST**, **SOAP**, and **ODATA**.

Table 8.15 API Proxy Fields

It's also possible to add a resource by clicking the **Add** button under the **Resources** tab, as shown in Figure 8.60. An API can have multiple resources, and each resource represents an endpoint.

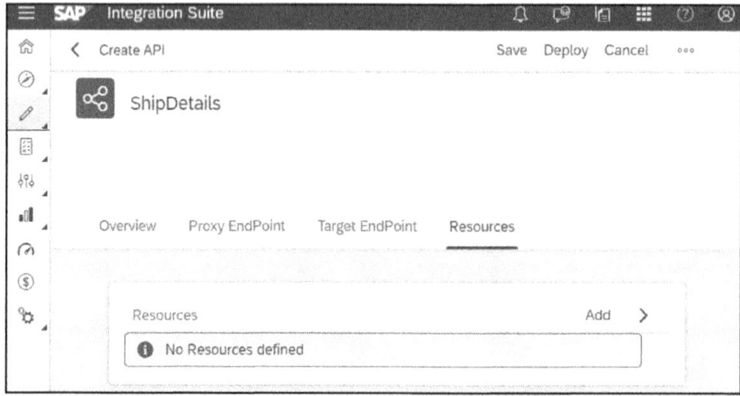

Figure 8.60 Resource Tab of the API Proxy

On the next screen, as shown in Figure 8.61, enter "RetrieveShipment" in the **Tag** field, and enter "Shipment" in the **Path Prefix** field of the resource. Remove all other HTTP methods, and only select **POST** as the supported HTTP method. Then, specify a description, and click the **Add** button.

Figure 8.61 Adding a Resource to an API

Let's now add some policies to our API. An *API policy* is a module that implements a specific API behavior. API policies are designed to let you add common management capabilities to an API, such as security, rate-limiting, transformation, and mediation. You can access the policy editor by clicking the **Policies** button in the top-right corner of the screen, as shown in Figure 8.62.

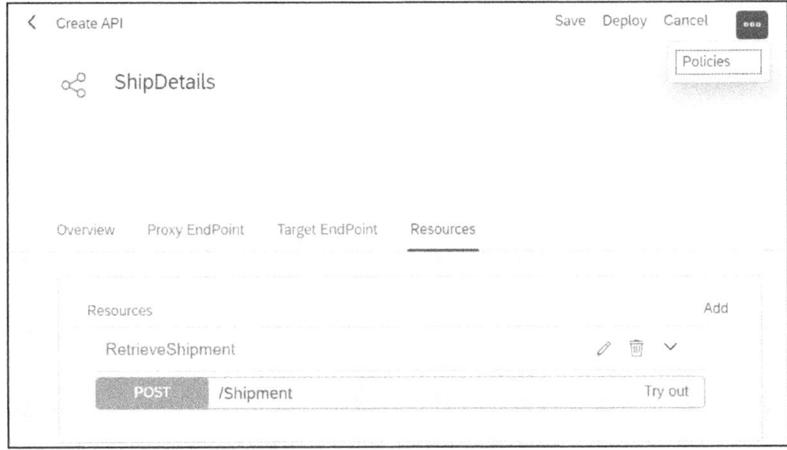

Figure 8.62 Navigating to the Policy Editor

You're redirected to the policy editor page from which a wide variety of policies can be added to fulfill your requirements, as shown in Figure 8.63.

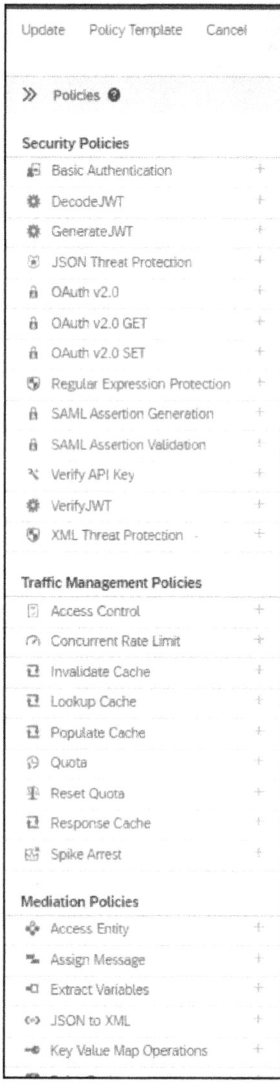

Figure 8.63 An Overview of the Policy Editor Page and Available Policies

At the time of this writing, the following categories of API policies are included in the policy editor:

- **Security**
  Includes various policies aimed at protecting your API. You can add basic authentication; use different versions of OAuth, Security Assertion Markup Language (SAML), and XML thread protection; verify API keys; and so on.
- **Traffic management**
  Helps you regulate your API traffic using techniques such as caching, quotas, access control, concurrent rate limit, and so on.

- **Mediation**
  Provides actions and scripts, such as for the extraction of variables and conversion of JSON to XML (and vice versa).

Any number of policies included in this editor can be mixed together and used in any combination to fulfill your desired requirements.

The rectangular image shown in the middle of Figure 8.64 represents a policy flow in API Management. This policy flow defines a processing pipeline and the order of execution of the included policies.

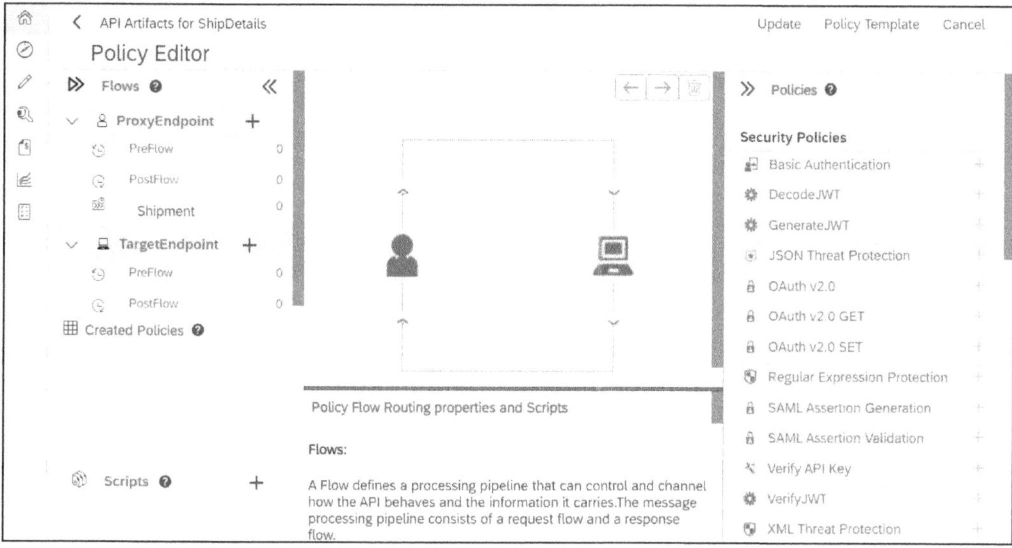

Figure 8.64 API Artifacts View

The flow has two main execution paths: **PreFlow** and **PostFlow**. The **PreFlow** path, the top part of the rectangle, represents the actions to be executed first before the control is passed to the API provider (Cloud Integration, in our case). On the other hand, the **PostFlow** path, the bottom part of the rectangle, represents the actions to be performed after the API provider has been called, that is, the actions to be performed before sending the response back to the API consumer.

For simplicity, let's add a policy to check the quotas on API calls. Assuming that our backend system can only accept a limited number of calls per minute, let's use API Management to limit API consumption to a maximum of two API calls per minute. This approach is a good way to regulate traffic by preventing your backend system from being flooded with calls. Adding a quota policy in the **PreFlow** path makes sense and prevents calls to Cloud Integration if a quota violation occurs.

Let's start by selecting **PreFlow** in the top-left corner under the **Flows** section (refer to Figure 8.63). Then, click on the plus icon + next to **Quota** on the right panel, under the **Traffic Management Policies** section. You're then presented with a popup window where you'll provide the name of the policy, as shown in Figure 8.65.

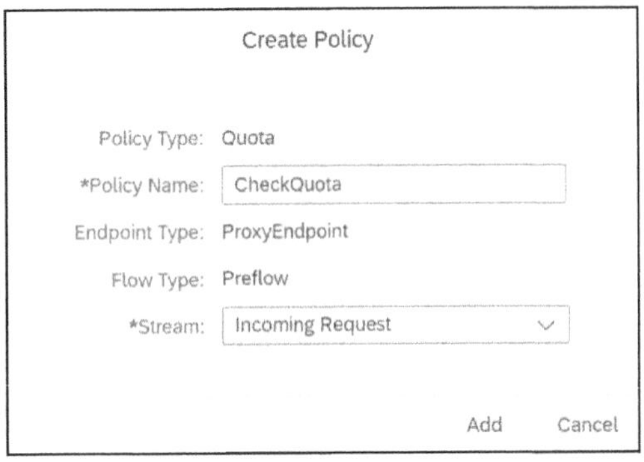

Figure 8.65 Adding the Quota Policy

Besides providing a name for the policy, select the **Incoming Request** value for the **Stream** dropdown, as shown in Figure 8.65. Then, click the **Add** button. On the next screen, specify the maximum number of allowed API calls per minute in the tag element `Allow count`, as shown in Figure 8.66. In our case, we used the value 2 to fulfill our requirement, as described previously.

```
<!-- can be used to configure the number of request messages that an app is allowed to submit to an API over a course of unit time -->
<Quota async="false" continueOnError="false" enabled="true" type="calendar" xmlns="http://www.sap.com/apimgmt">
    <!-- specifies the number of requests allowed for the API Proxy -->
        <Allow count="2"/>
    <!-- the interval of time for which the quota should be applied -->
    <Interval>1</Interval>
    <!-- used to specify if a central counter should be maintained and continuously synchronized across all message processors -->
    <Distributed>true</Distributed>
    <!-- Use to specify the date and time when the quota counter will begin counting,
        regardless of whether any requests have been received from any apps -->
    <StartTime>2015-2-11 12:00:00</StartTime>
    <!-- if set to true, the distributed quota counter is updated synchronously. This means that
        the update to the counter will be made at the same time the API call is quota-checked -->
    <Synchronous>true</Synchronous>
    <!-- Use to specify the unit of time applicable to the quota. Can be second, minute, hour, day, or month -->
    <TimeUnit>minute</TimeUnit>
</Quota>
```

Figure 8.66 Configuration of CheckQuota

Click the **Update** button, located in the top-right corner, as shown in Figure 8.67, to update the API with the added policies.

To find more information about any policy, refer to the SAP Documentation at *http://s-prs.co/576074*. Search for "SAP Integration Suite API Management."

On the next screen, click the **Save** button. Well done! You're now ready to consume the API, which we'll do in the next section.

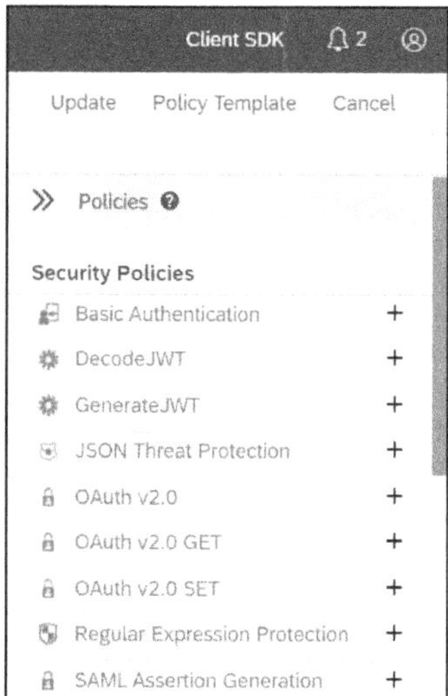

Figure 8.67 Updating the API with the Flow of Policies

8.6.3 Consuming APIs

Now that the API is ready, you can test it using any REST client of your choice (e.g., Postman). You can also perform a test directly in API Management by navigating to the test tool via the **Test** icon in the menu on the left, as shown in Figure 8.68.

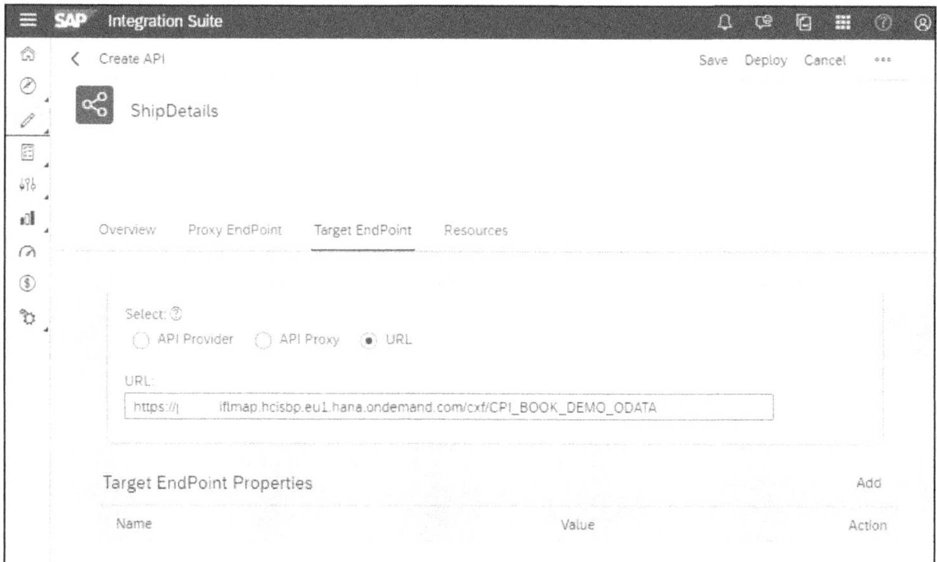

Figure 8.68 Overview of the Created API

You're then redirected to a new test page where you should select **ShipDetails** on the left side of the screen shown in Figure 8.69. By default, an endpoint ending with **/SWAGGER_JSON** is selected, as shown in Figure 8.69. You'll need to select the other endpoint from the dropdown list. The correct endpoint will end with the prefix used while creating the resource (in our scenario, **/Shipment**).

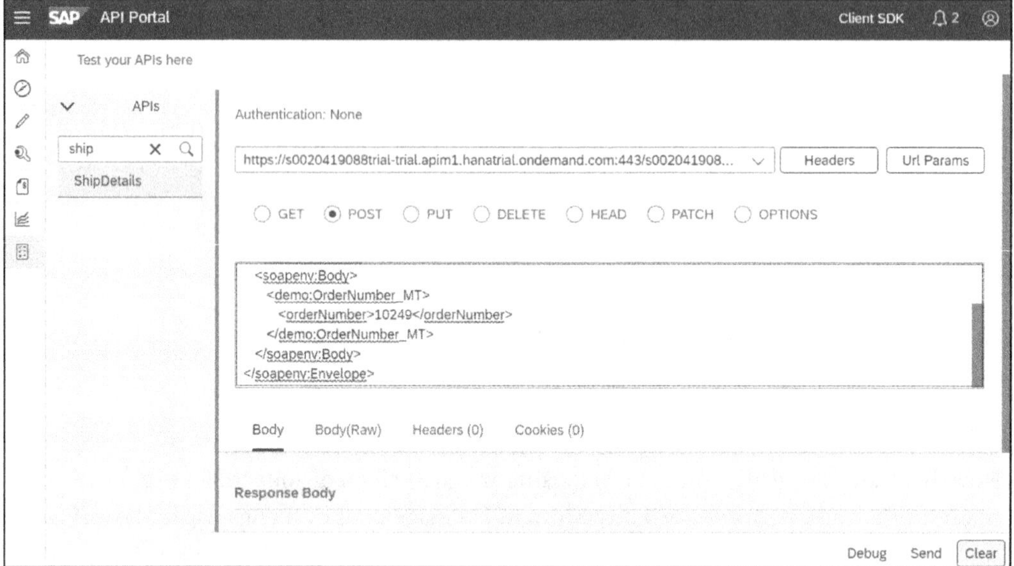

Figure 8.69 Setting Up the API Test Tool

> **Note**
> If you're using an external REST client such as Postman, you'll need an endpoint to post the API call to. The endpoint of the newly created API can be obtained via the dropdown menu, as shown in Figure 8.69.

After selecting the correct endpoint, specify the HTTP method as **POST** by selecting its radio button, provide the desired request XML payload, and change the authentication method to basic authentication. The authentication can be changed by clicking the **Authentication** link in the top-left corner of the screen shown in Figure 8.69.

You can now trigger the call by clicking on the **Send** button at the bottom-right corner of the screen. In the background, API Management performs a check to validate whether we're still within our quota limits. Because this message is the first message, the call is accepted and sent to Cloud Integration, which in turn returns a valid response, as shown in the **Response Body** section shown in Figure 8.70.

Quickly perform the same call two more times to exceed our quota limit. You'll then see a quota violation error, as shown in Figure 8.71. This error indicates that we've exceeded the quota of two calls within the same minute.

Figure 8.70 The Test Result of Our API Call

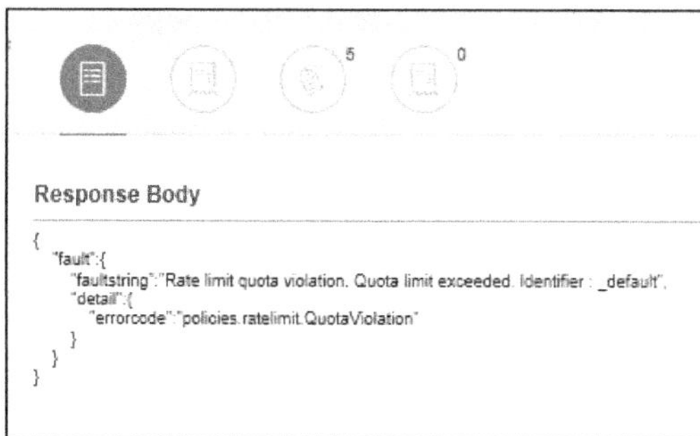

Figure 8.71 Response When Quota Is Exceeded

Congratulations, you've successfully provided, called, and consumed the API. Be aware that our scenario was quite simplistic. In a real-life scenario, you should consider the following additional aspects:

- **Authentication in API Management**
  By default, the API exposed can be consumed without authentication. If you want to protect the API, you'll need to add the relevant policy (e.g., OAuth, API key, etc.).
- **Authentication in Cloud Integration**
  In our scenario, we're simply passing along to Cloud Integration whatever header was provided during the API call. Thus, the user name/password details used while calling the API are also forwarded and used for authentication in Cloud Integration. You could decide to use the basic authentication security policy to provide the logon details for Cloud Integration.
- **Payload**
  Note that the sample request message shown in Figure 8.69 includes the entire SOAP message. Given that we're exposing a REST API, we could decide to only use the SOAP body as input. This option, however, will require you to perform some logic to extract the relevant data from the incoming message and construct the SOAP message to send to Cloud Integration. This step is necessary because the service that we're consuming in Cloud Integration is of type SOAP.
- **Error message**
  Note that the error response returned by the API when the quota was exceeded (as shown in Figure 8.71) is in JSON format. In a real-life scenario, you'll want to convert the response to XML before returning this data to the consumer. (Hint: consider the JSON2XML policy.)

This chapter didn't tackle these points, which are beyond the scope of this chapter. For more insights on the subject of API Management, refer to *SAP API Management* (SAP PRESS, 2019) written by Carsten Bönnen, Harsh Jegadeesan, Divya Mary, and Shilpa Vij (*www.sap-press.com/4928*).

You now understand how to use API Management to wrap services available in Cloud Integration and expose them as APIs, as well as how to enforce different policies.

8.7 Summary

This chapter introduced you to the API-related capabilities and features of Cloud Integration. An overview of Java-based APIs was provided, and you also learned how to use APIs in UDFs. This chapter then explored a number of OData APIs available in Cloud Integration and walked you through some examples to illustrate their usage.

Finally, this chapter explored how to use Cloud Integration, in combination with API Management, to provision APIs. Even though this chapter wasn't intended to be a chapter on API Management, you also learned how to add policies to APIs through a scenario.

In the next chapter, we'll explore Open Connectors.

Chapter 9
Connecting to External Third-Party Systems

The chapter dives into the specifics of the Open Connectors and showcases how you can use this solution together with Cloud Integration to connect to various third-party applications.

SAP Integration Suite comes with Open Connectors, which extends the connectivity capabilities and options available in Cloud Integration, ultimately enabling it to connect to more than 160 software as a service (SaaS) applications in a uniform and simplified manner.

As cloud adoption accelerates across the business landscape, recent years have seen a rapid increase in the number of cloud applications offered. Many organizations seek a best-of-breed approach instead of a monolithic one. Each organization can select the combination of SaaS and on-premise applications that suit their needs. Further, each SaaS application generally operates in a silo and is particularly good at what it does.

To help your organization achieve its business goals and optimize its processes, the involved SaaS and on-premise applications must be integrated and enabled to exchange data with each other, which is where the Open Connectors can come to the rescue. As discussed in Chapter 1, Open Connectors is, next to Cloud Integration, a key constituent of SAP Integration Suite.

9.1 Introduction

Open Connectors is a unified application programming interface (API) layer and standards-based implementation that includes many connectors. With a catalog of more than 160 connectors for non-SAP cloud applications, Open Connectors can easily connect to most popular SaaS applications, such as Salesforce, Jira, Google, and so on. A connector in Open Connectors plays the same role as an adapter in Cloud Integration.

Cloud Integration can leverage the connectivity options made possibly by Open Connectors, thus enabling you to extend the connectivity options available in Cloud Integration. Recall the summary of the Open Connectors we provided in Chapter 1, Section 1.3.3, when we discussed the various connectivity options available. Note that Open

Connectors is included in Cloud Integration, Standard Edition, and Cloud Integration, Premium Edition.

Note that Open Connectors is available both for the SAP BTP, Neo environment and the SAP BTP, Cloud Foundry environments. We'll mostly focus on the SAP BTP, Cloud Foundry environment in this chapter.

To get started with Open Connectors, you can open a trial account by following the steps described in this tutorial: *http://s-prs.co/507777*. Additionally, you can also follow the steps described in this tutorial: *http://s-prs.co/v576072*.

Note

To set up your trial account for Open Connectors for SAP BTP, Neo environment, follow the steps described in this SAP Community blog: *http://s-prs.co/507779*.

After creating a trial account for Open Connectors, log on, and you'll be redirected to the main page, as shown in Figure 9.1.

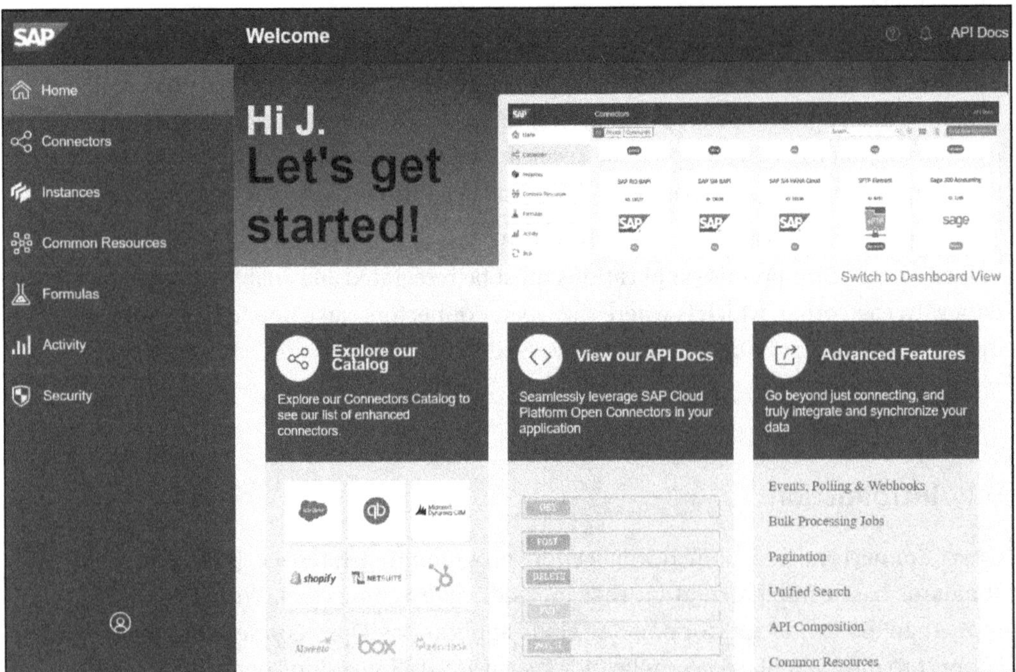

Figure 9.1 Open Connectors Landing Page

In the menu on the left of the landing page shown in Figure 9.1, you'll see that the Open Connectors has the following components:

- **Connectors**
  Contains a catalog of more than 160 available connectors. We'll further discuss connectors in Section 9.3.
- **Instances**
  Represents connections toward third-party applications. Once created, you can use an instance to make API requests to the provider.
- **Common Resources**
  Represents common data models or canonical views of your company's business data objects.
- **Formulas**
  User-defined workflows that have a trigger (incoming event, API request, timer, etc.). When triggered, a series of steps is executed in Open Connectors.
- **Activities**
  Keeps log entries of all API activities performed in Open Connectors. This is used as a monitoring tool.
- **Security**
  Enables you to perform security tasks such as adding members to your Open Connectors tenant, assigning roles, and so on.

Note that, in this chapter, we'll only explore some of these components. We hope to give you enough background to build an integration flow (iFlow) in Cloud Integration that will leverage Open Connectors' capabilities.

Now that you have some awareness of the role Open Connectors can play in your landscape and have a trial account, let's further explore Open Connectors in more detail in the following sections.

9.2 Open Connectors: Connectors Catalog

With a list of more than 160 (and counting!) prebuilt connectors, Open Connectors enables users to simplify and accelerate connectivity to various popular third-party and non-SAP cloud applications. This robust, feature-rich platform can help you reduce the time required for integrating with these third-party applications.

You don't need to understand the technologies behind the APIs exposed by these third-party applications. Open Connectors enables you to connect to these applications by simply configuring the relevant connectors. Most of these third-party applications use Representational State Transfer (REST)-based APIs. Open Connectors has consolidated various connectivity aspects, including ways to discover API resources, configure authentication, handle errors, search, pagination (handling a response which includes multiple pages), and bulk support without regard to the architecture of the concerned third-party applications.

To access the repository or catalog of existing prebuilt connectors, select the **Connectors** menu item on the left. This link can be accessed from the landing page shown in Figure 9.1. You'll then see a page listing the available connectors, as shown in Figure 9.2.

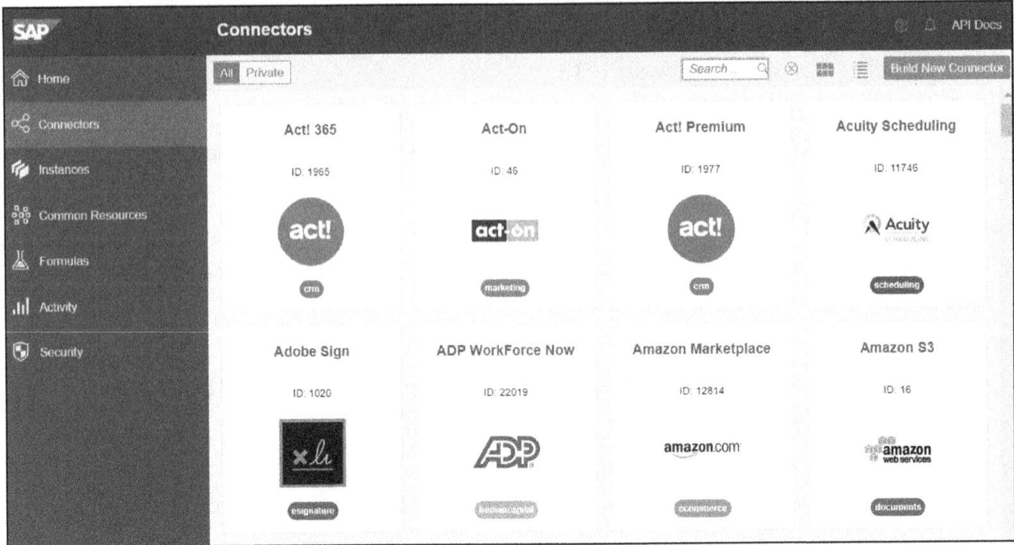

Figure 9.2 Accessing the Connectors Catalog

From the menu at the top of Figure 9.2, you can access the following functionalities:

- **All/Private**
  Choose between private connectors and all connectors. Clicking the **Private** button in the top-left corner enables you to list your own (private) custom-built connectors. As the name suggests, the connectors in this list are only available for your tenant. Similarly, clicking the **All** button lists all the available prebuilt connectors, as shown in Figure 9.3.
- **Search**
  Enables free-text search and filtering of results to find the desired third-party application to connect with.
- **Layout**
  Changes the layout of the displayed third-party applications as tiles or simply a list.
- **Build New Connector**
  Create your own connectors and extend the existing catalog of applications (customers and SAP partners).

From the listed connectors, you can click on the **Settings** icon to open a popup menu, shown in Figure 9.4, with several options: **Overview**, **Resources**, and **API Docs**.

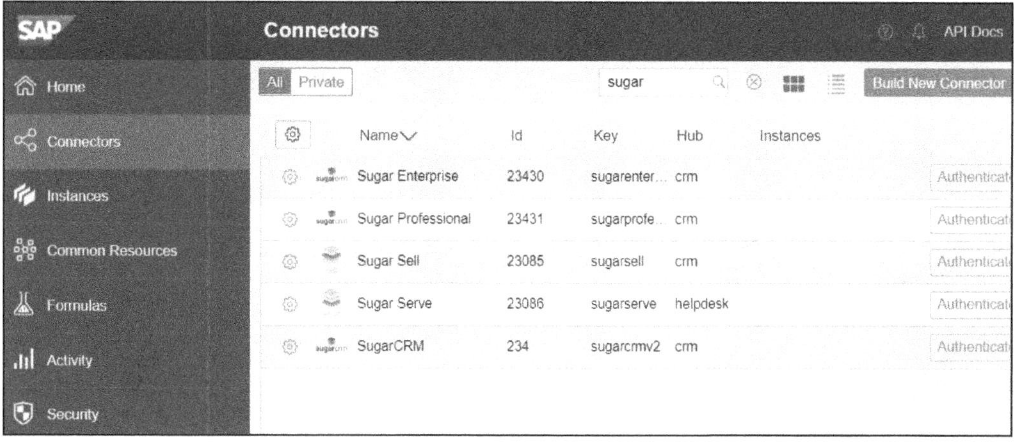

Figure 9.3 Search and List of Connectors

Figure 9.4 Menu Option for More Details about a Connector

When you select one of these options, as shown in Figure 9.4, you'll be redirected to a page with all necessary information about the connector.

For the sake of illustration, Figure 9.5 shows the connector for SugarCRM, which is a cloud-based application that focuses on customer relationship management (CRM). As shown in Figure 9.5, from the top, you can access the following information about each connector:

- **Overview**
- **Information**
- **Setup**
- **Resources**
- **Validation**
- **API Docs**

Each of these information tabs will be discussed in the following sections. Additionally, you can find more information on each connector, including tips, answers to FAQs, best practices, and suggestions for working with connectors, in the documentation at *http://s-prs.co/507780*.

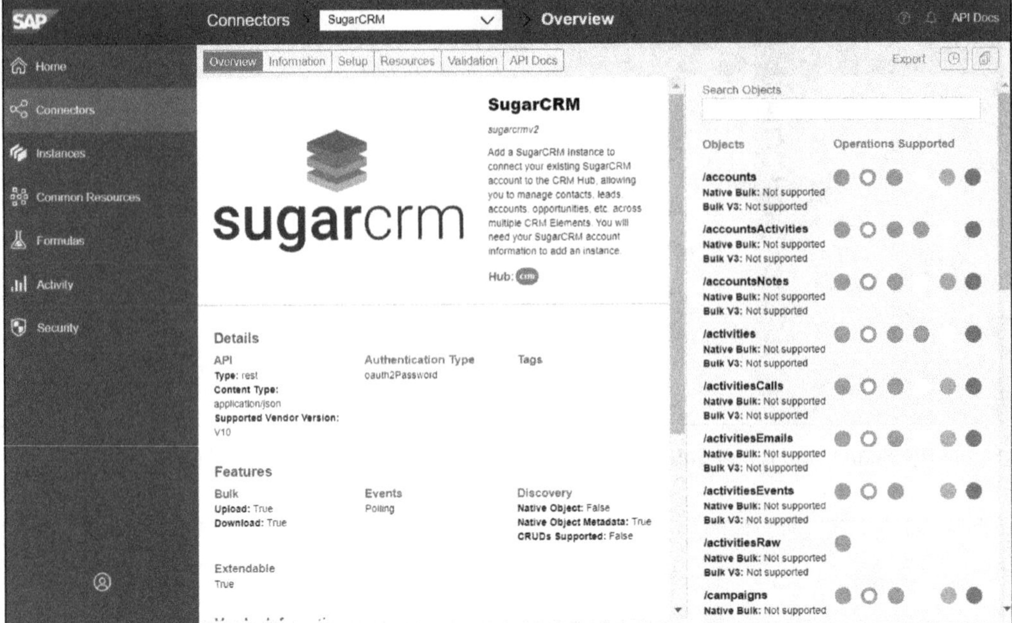

Figure 9.5 Detailed View of Connector Information and Documentation

> **Note**
>
> Given that Open Connectors makes extensive use of the OpenAPI standard for documenting the APIs of various third-party systems, some terms we use later in this chapter relate to the OpenAPI standard. The OpenAPI standard is a rich enough topic to deserve a chapter of its own, but we won't try to explain its concepts in this book. Instead, we recommend referring to the OpenAPI specification at *https://swagger.io/resources/open-api/*.

9.2.1 Overview Tab

In this section, we'll provide a high-level summary of all the features available for the selected connector. This information also includes the type of supported authentication, the content type, supported vendor's version, vendor's information special notes, and so on. The overview page looks like the screenshot shown in Figure 9.6. On the right side, a panel lists all the business objects or entities supported. Most third-party applications have several business objects available. Not all business objects are always supported for every version of the connector. Therefore, looking up the information on the panel on the right is important for keeping up with objects that are supported.

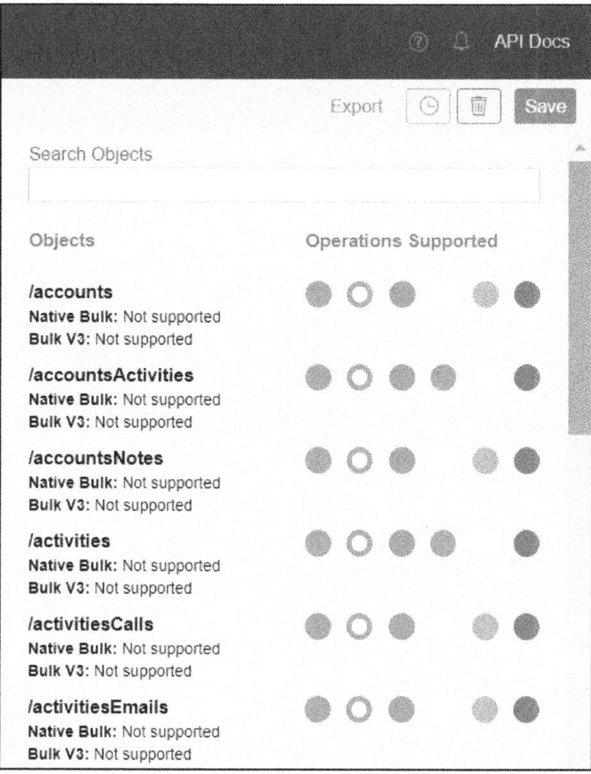

Figure 9.6 Objects and Operations Supported by the Connector

For illustration, the example shown in Figure 9.6 relates to the SugarCRM connector. As a CRM system, SugarCRM has business objects such as accounts, leads, opportunities, and so on. The SugarCRM enables users to interact with any of these objects.

Because most third-party applications expose their functionalities via REST-based APIs, the following HTTP methods, shown in Figure 9.6, are often used:

- GET
  Reads and retrieves objects or resource details from the third-party application.
- GET by ID
  Reads and retrieves a specific object or resource details from the third-party application. The unique identifier of the concerned object must be provided in the request.
- POST
  Creates objects or resources in the third-party application.
- PUT
  Updates the data of an existing object or resource in the third-party application using a unique identifier.

- DELETE
  Deletes an existing object or resource in the third-party application using a unique identifier.
- PATCH
  Makes a partial update on a resource. This is not to be confused with PUT requests, which modify or replace the entirety of the business object in the third-party application using a unique identifier.

As shown in Figure 9.6, detailed information about what operations are supported is organized into six columns; for each supported operation, its availability is represented with different colored bullets. Table 9.1 lists each bullet and its meaning.

Bullet Type	Meaning
(White)	The operation in question isn't supported.
(Blue)	The GET operation is supported.
(Blue ring)	The GET BY ID operation is supported.
(Green)	The POST operation is supported.
(Blue)	The PUT operation is supported.
(Light-green)	The PATCH operation is supported.
(Red)	The DELETE operation is supported.

Table 9.1 Meaning of the Colored Bullets

Let's next look at the information tab.

9.2.2 Information Tab

Under this tab, you'll see general information about the connector, including its logo, a description, and the type of service used. You can also export the connector's metadata by clicking the **Export** button in the top-right corner of the page shown in Figure 9.7. The metadata will be exported as a JavaScript Object Notation (JSON) file. This file can be used to move connectors that you build to different environments or to make copies of public connectors.

This JSON file can be imported into different environments, but the topic of importing or modifying connectors is beyond the scope of this chapter. For more information, check out the documentation for Open Connectors (*http://s-prs.co/v576041*) and search for "Import Connectors."

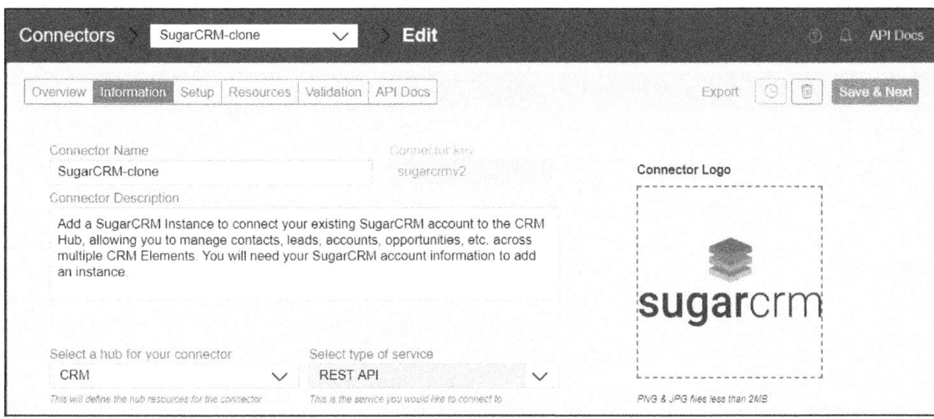

Figure 9.7 General Connector Information

9.2.3 Setup Tab

The **Setup** tab contains details about configuration attributes to enable the connection with the third-party system. Note that the details on this page are mostly in display mode only and can't be edited. Only cloned, imported, or newly created connectors can be edited. The **Setup** tab contains the following main sections:

- **Properties**
  Properties relates to the connectivity to the third-party system, such as host name, port name, content type, and so on.
- **Authentication**
  Details needed to authenticate to the third-party system. Depending on the supported authentication type, details such as API key, API secret, OAuth Callback, OAuth Token Url, OAuth Scope, user name, password, and so on will be listed. This list will indicate which fields are mandatory with a flag.
- **Configurations**
  Represents the storage place for any data needed for parameters and hooks. If the API provider requires specific information with each request, these requirements can be added to the configuration, and then you'll define a parameter to pass that data with each request. This configuration can be exposed to a user who can then supply the information when they authenticate. You can also store default values in the configuration for later use.
- **Parameters**
  Connector parameters allow you to pass various properties with each request. You can create parameters that require user input or that get their values from other sources. Use the connector parameters to configure required query parameters, searches, pagination, IDs, and required fields.

- **Hooks**
  Hooks are used to programmatically manipulate requests made to the connector or responses coming from the connector. If you apply a hook to a connector under this tab, the hook will be applied to every request going through this connector. If you only want to manipulate a specific request, add a hook to that endpoint.
- **Events**
  An event is an outbound call from the third-party system that this connector relates to. An event is generally sent asynchronously from the third-party system to Open Connectors when specific actions occur in the third-party system. The event contains information about what happened.

An example of a configured **Setup** tab is shown in Figure 9.8.

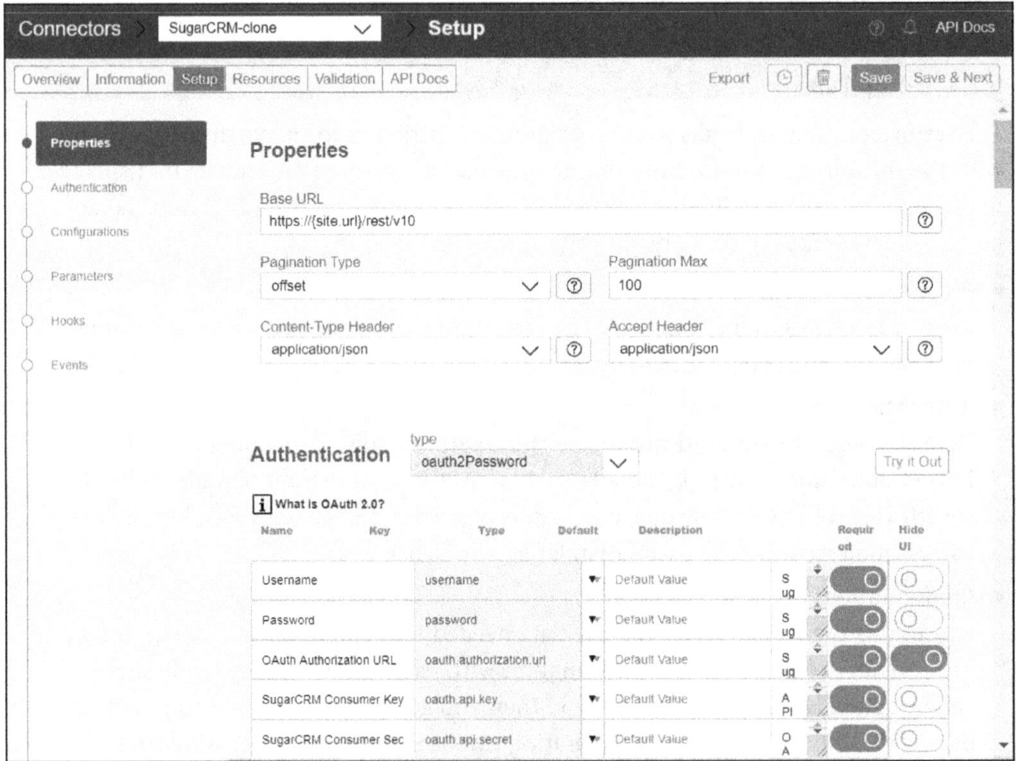

Figure 9.8 Connector Setup Page

9.2.4 Resources Tab

This tab lists all the API resources available for the third-party system. A *resource* represents a dedicated data set that can be accessed to (read or write) through the API. For example, the **accounts** resource lets you manage a SugarCRM account through the API.

A resource has a set of operations or methods that can be used to manipulate it. Typical operation objects provide the ability to perform create, read, update, and delete (CRUD) operations (among others). If you're familiar with a modern programming language, you can compare a resource to an object instance in object-oriented programming. As shown in Figure 9.9, typically, resources support the HTTP methods we discussed in Section 9.2.1.

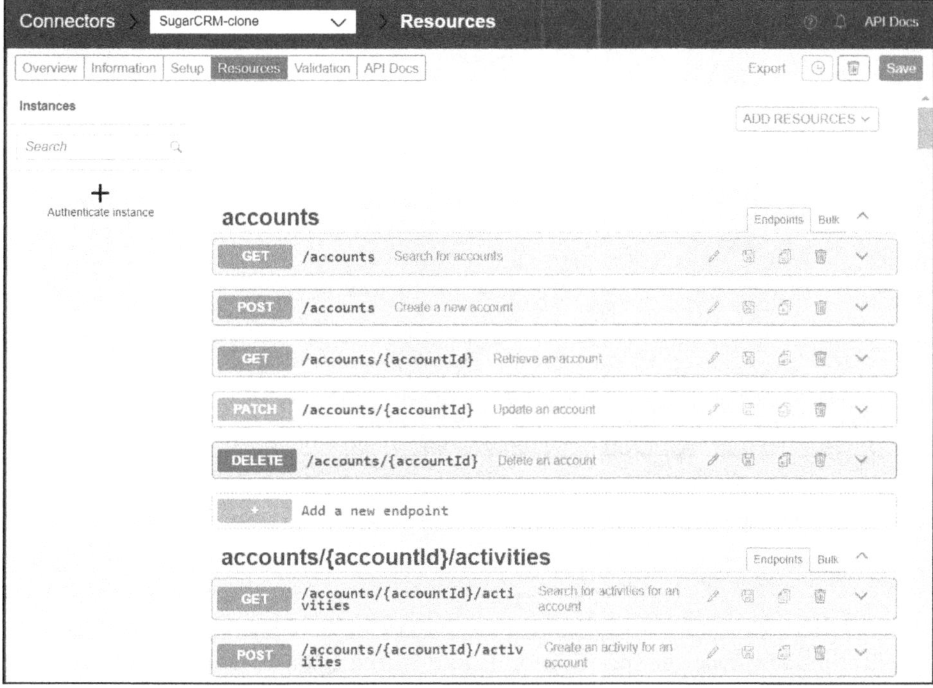

Figure 9.9 Connector Resources Page

9.2.5 Validation Tab

This tab enables users to determine whether the configuration of the connector is correct. As shown in Figure 9.10, click on the **Validate Connector** button to run different consistency checks on the connector. The result of the validation is displayed on the right side of the page. As shown in Figure 9.10, warnings will be indicated by the ● (yellow) icon. A full description of the warning is available to the right of the icon. Errors will be indicated by the ● (red) icon.

Furthermore, the Open Connectors provides tips on resolving errors and warnings. You can see these tips by hovering over the 💡 icon to the right of an error or warning.

Finally, you can also directly navigate to the problem area by first selecting the error or warning line, and then clicking on the **Go To** button in the top-right corner of the page.

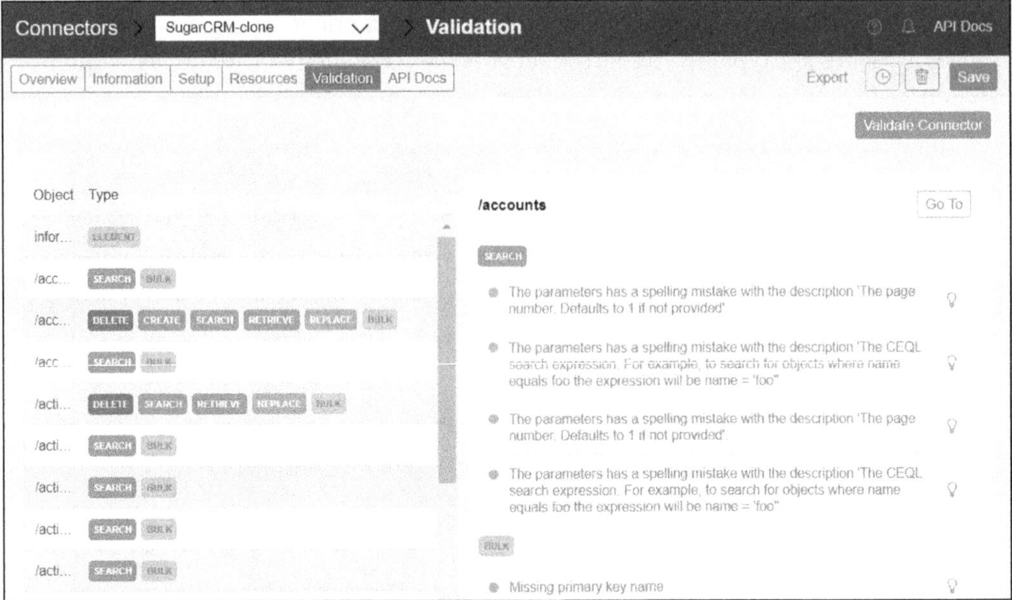

Figure 9.10 Validation Tab of a Connector

9.2.6 API Docs Tab

The **API Docs** tab provides a Swagger definition of all included APIs of the third-party application. The Swagger specification is part of the OpenAPI specification, which is used to describe and document RESTful APIs. Multiple versions of the OpenAPI specification exist. However, Swagger especially refers to version 2.0.

Much can be said about the Swagger specification; however, in this chapter, we won't attempt to explain Swagger in detail. We'll just mention a few pointers to enable you to follow along with our description of the Open Connectors.

The Swagger specification allows you to describe the structure of your APIs so that machines can read them. Therefore, the **API Docs** tab of Open Connectors, shown in Figure 9.11, enables the developer to look into the details of the provided APIs, the different entities (and their HTTP methods), and a data model representation of the request and response message. The model specifies aspects such as the field name, data type, and description of each element. You can also see example values for each field. As shown in Figure 9.11, the page displays the list of possible HTTP methods for each entity.

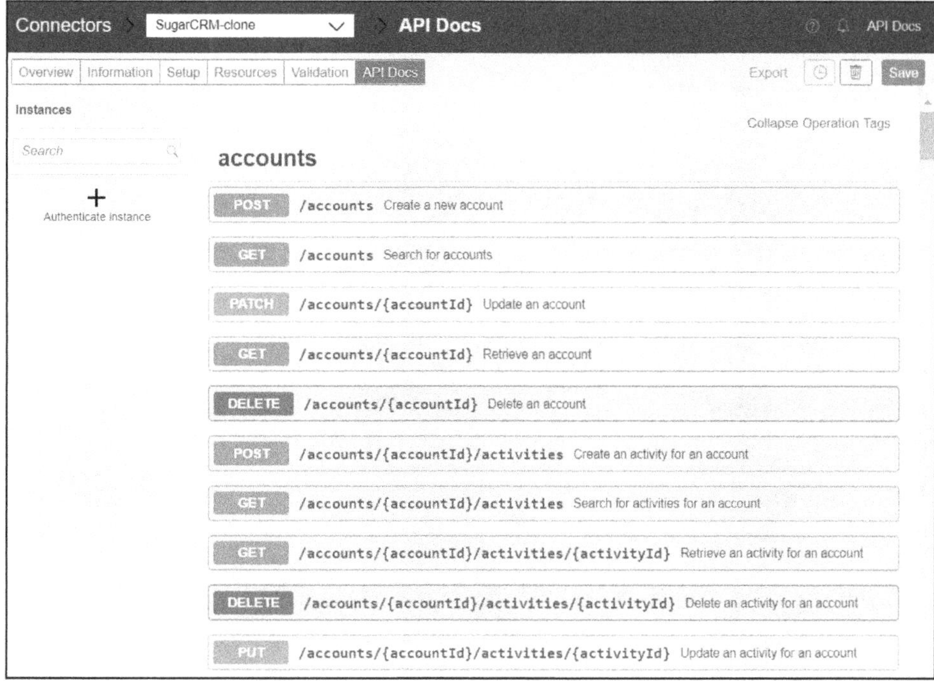

Figure 9.11 API Docs Tab of the Connector's Page

You can collapse each of these entities to see the list of all entities associated with the application. As shown in Figure 9.12, at the top, entities such as **accounts**, **activities**, and **activities-calls** are listed. Additionally, you can click on any of the HTTP methods to see more details about the operation. As shown at the bottom of Figure 9.12, when you click on an HTTP method (e.g., **POST**), a list of related parameters ❶ will be displayed. Each parameter contains the following information:

- **Name**
  A descriptive name for the parameter.
- **Description**
  A description of what the parameter is used for and its semantic framework. Sometimes, example values for these parameters will also be displayed.
- **Data type**
  As indicated by ❷ in Figure 9.12, the data type represents the data type of a schema's element. Examples of commonly used data types include `string`, `number`, `integer`, `boolean`, `array`, and `object`. For a full list of available Swagger data types, refer to the Swagger website at *http://s-prs.co/v576042*.
- **Required**
  If the parameter is mandatory and required to perform the API call, this parameter will be flagged with a red **Required** tag. An example of a required parameter is shown

in Figure 9.12 (the **Authorization** field and **call** field). Note the presence of the *** required** icon to indicate the parameter is required.

- **Parameter type**
  As indicated by ❷ and ❸ in Figure 9.12, OpenAPI distinguishes between several different parameter types, including **header**, **path**, **body**, and **query**. Table 9.2 lists each parameter type and provides descriptions of each.

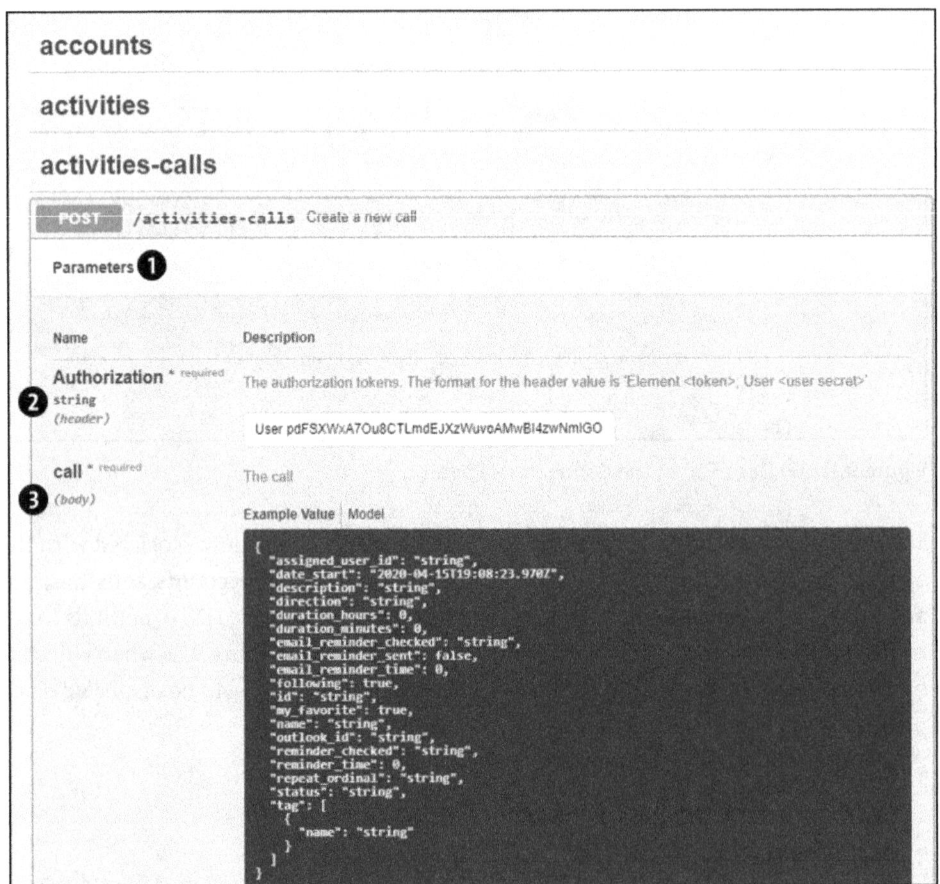

Figure 9.12 List of Entities and Details of an Operation

Name	Description	Example
Header	An API call might require that custom headers be sent along within the HTTP request. The OpenAPI enables you to define custom request headers.	`X-Request-ID: ded580b2-766b-4993-94c6-5baa55e35c00`

Table 9.2 List of Possible Parameter Types

Name	Description	Example
Path	A path parameter is part of a URL path for invoking an API. This value is typically used to point to a specific resource within an API. For instance, a unique identifier for a customer (e.g., to identify a customer by ID) could be used. A URL can contain several path parameters, each indicated by curly braces { }. If multiple path parameters must be used, you can stack them sequentially.	`/customers/{id}`
Query	Query parameters are the most common type of parameters. These parameters are found at the end of the API URL. The beginning of a set of query parameters is marked by a question mark (?) and followed by a series of different name-value pairs, each separated by an ampersand (&).	`/customers?offset=200&limit=50`
Body	Indicates the structure of the message body to be sent as part of the API's request or to be returned as part of the API's response.	See the body section shown in Figure 9.12.

Table 9.2 List of Possible Parameter Types (Cont.)

Parameters of type body must be further explained. In Open Connectors, the body parameter section generally includes the following:

- **Example Value**
  Based on the definition of a data model, an example message of the structure to be sent or received is automatically generated. This example is useful to indicate how a sample message might look like.
- **Model**
  This section represents the data model or schema. The schema object helps us specify the definition of the input or output data types. These data types can be primitives, arrays, or objects. The example shown in Figure 9.12 represents an object.

The example shown in Figure 9.12 comes from the `POST` method, which represents an operation to create an instance of the **activities-calls** entity.

9.3 Open Connectors: Understanding Connectors

In Section 9.2, you learned some general attributes and functions of a connector in Open Connectors. Now, let's get a bit more practical and work with a ServiceNow tenant. ServiceNow is a SaaS application to help with incident management. You can use ServiceNow to create and maintain incidents for your organization. You can easily create a trial account for ServiceNow at *http://s-prs.co/v576043*.

From the trial page, you'll need to register and request an instance. Once you've received the details of your new ServiceNow instance, including the URL, user name, and password, as shown in Figure 9.13, keep these details because you'll need this information later.

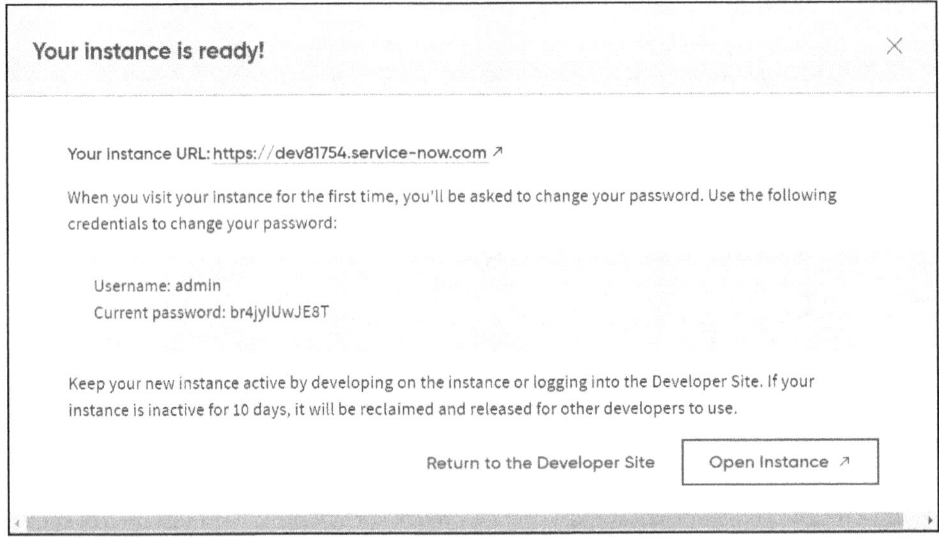

Figure 9.13 Details of ServiceNow Instance

Open Connectors has a special connector for ServiceNow among its existing 160 prebuilt connectors. Let's use the ServiceNow connector to help you better understand how the connectors work! The following sections will guide you through the steps required to connect to ServiceNow. In the process of helping you better grasp how connectors work, we'll perform the following steps:

1. Authenticate connections with API providers.
2. Inspect authenticated connector instances.
3. Test the API docs.

We're only using ServiceNow in our next tutorial for the sake of simplicity. You can use these same steps with any other SaaS application of your choice. You can use a SaaS application that you already use, or you can open trial accounts in any of the applications listed in Table 9.3. Note that these applications are listed because, at the time of this writing, they provided easy access to a trial account.

Name	Link for Trial or Sandbox Account
Shopify Sandbox	*http://s-prs.co/v576044*
Dynamics 365 Operations Sandbox	*http://s-prs.co/v576045*

Table 9.3 Some SaaS Applications Offering Trial Accounts or Sandboxes

Name	Link for Trial or Sandbox Account
SugarCRM Sandbox	*http://s-prs.co/v576046*
Magento 2.0 Sandbox	*http://s-prs.co/v576047*
Amazon Marketplace	*http://s-prs.co/v576048*

Table 9.3 Some SaaS Applications Offering Trial Accounts or Sandboxes (Cont.)

9.3.1 Authenticate Connections with API Providers

Connecting to an API provider is the core functionality of Open Connectors. After creating a connection, a connector instance will be generated. This connector instance has an ID and a connector token, which you'll use when making API requests to an API provider through Open Connectors.

The first step in connecting to any SaaS application is to find its corresponding connectors. In our case, you'll need to find the ServiceNow connector by following these steps:

1. From the main page of Open Connectors, click on the **Connectors** menu item to go the Connectors Catalog.
2. Use the search box in the top-right corner of the page to search with the "ServiceNow" keyword, as shown in Figure 9.14.

Figure 9.14 Selecting the ServiceNow Connectors from the Connectors Catalog

3. Hover over the **ServiceNow** connector card, and then click **Authenticate**, as shown in Figure 9.15.

   You'll be redirected to another page where you can provide your ServiceNow login credentials and server details.

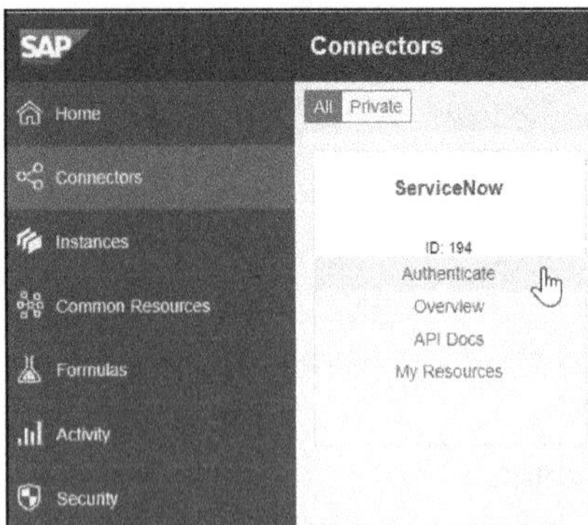

Figure 9.15 Authenticating with the ServiceNow Connector

4. Enter your ServiceNow tenant and credentials, and then click on **Create Instance,** as shown in Figure 9.16.

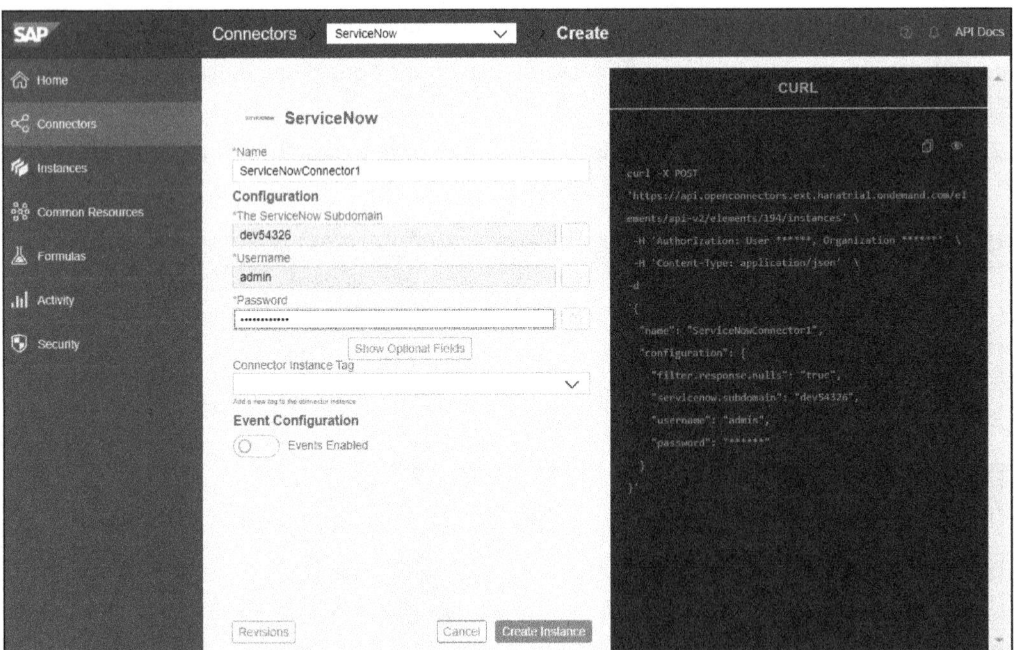

Figure 9.16 Creating a ServiceNow Instance

The details populated into the screen shown in Figure 9.17 were provided when opening the ServiceNow trial instance. **The ServiceNow Subdomain** field can be filled with the first part of your ServiceNow instance URL (the masked section shown earlier in Figure 9.13).

If the credentials you enter are incorrect, you'll see an error while trying to create an instance. Otherwise, you'll be redirected to a success page like the page shown in Figure 9.17.

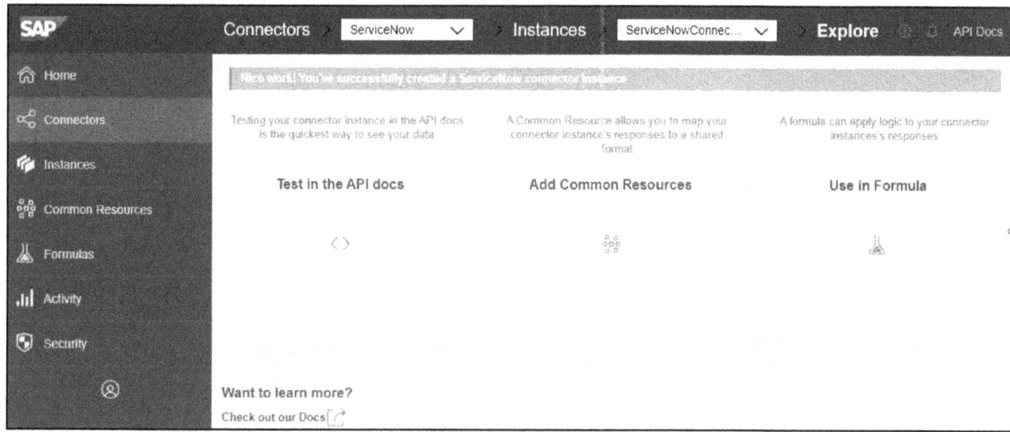

Figure 9.17 A Successfully Created Connector Instance

Note that being redirected to this success message also means that an instance of this connection has been created. In other words, an instance entry has been added to the **Instances** section (from the menu on the left of Figure 9.17). As shown in Figure 9.17, you can now test the API docs (by clicking **Test in the API docs**) and add common resources. These topics will be further discussed in Section 9.3.3 and Section 9.4, respectively.

Note

If you're facing issues when creating your instance, refer to a more detailed description of how to create and troubleshoot your ServiceNow connector instance available at the following link: *http://s-prs.co/507781*.

Now that you've created an instance of a ServiceNow connector, you'll see it in the list of available connectors. Confirm this fact by clicking on the **Connectors** menu option and searching for the keyword "ServiceNow" in the search textbox.

The search results shown in Figure 9.18 feature an icon 1 on the right side of the ServiceNow tile. This number indicates that one instance of a connector is available in this Open Connectors tenant. These results are a good way to identify whether an existing connection to the SaaS application is available for reuse, instead of creating a new connector instance.

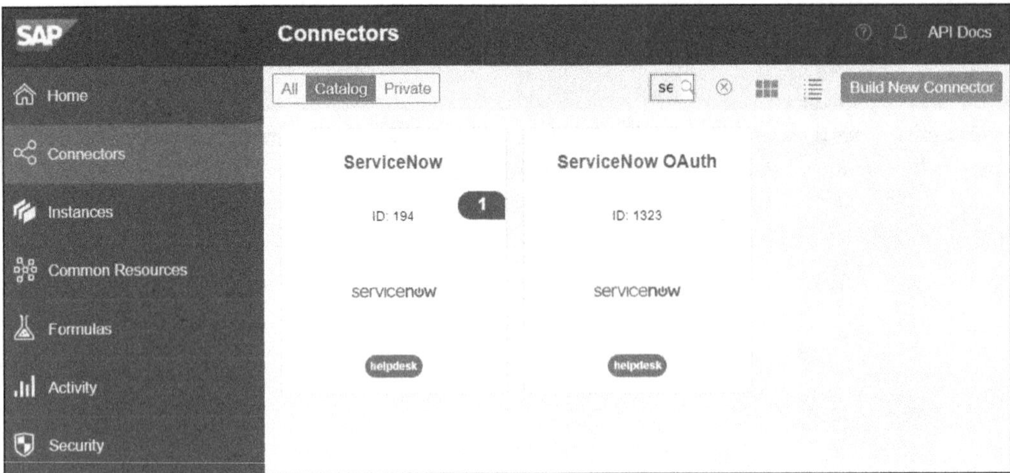

Figure 9.18 Search Results of the Connector Catalog

9.3.2 Inspect Authenticated Connector Instances

An authenticated connector instance is a representation of a unique connection to an API provider. Note that what makes a connection unique is generally a combination of user name and SaaS application host/tenant/subdomain.

Thus, if you have two users who must authenticate to a single API provider (e.g., ServiceNow), you'll need to create two instances of the ServiceNow connector. Similarly, if you need to connect to two different ServiceNow subdomains or tenants, you'll also need to create two different ServiceNow connector instances. By authenticating with an API provider, you're effectively creating a connector instance in Open Connectors.

An authenticated connector instance authorizes Open Connectors to access your data at the API provider (in this case, ServiceNow). An authenticated connector instance can be used to perform the following activities:

- Apply logic to a connector instance with formulas.
- Map your connector instance to a common resource.
- Test your instance (under the **API Docs** tab).

In Section 9.3.1, we successfully created a ServiceNow instance. To view the list of created instances, click on the **Instances** menu item (shown earlier in Figure 9.17). You're then redirected to a page that lists all available connector instances, as shown in Figure 9.19.

The **Instances** page allows you to manage your authenticated connections to different API providers (connector instances) and any executed workflows (formula instances). We won't discuss formula instances further in this book, but you can learn more at the following link: *http://s-prs.co/507782*.

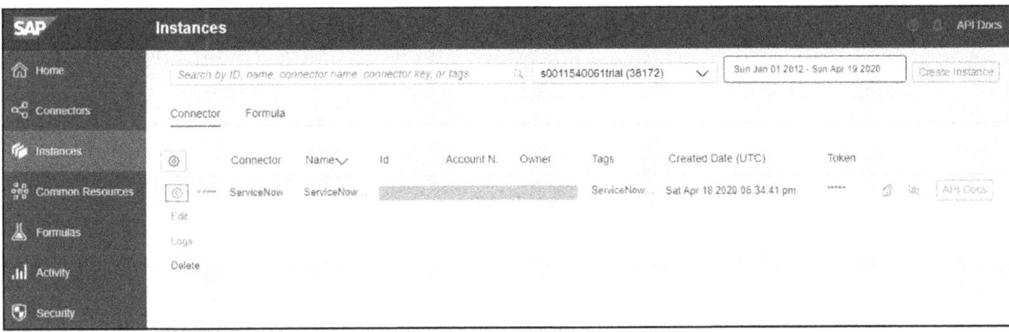

Figure 9.19 List of Existing Connector Instances

An existing connector instance has several attributes, which are described in Table 9.4.

Name	Description
Connector	This attribute indicates the type of connector, for example, a ServiceNow connector.
Name	A descriptive name for this specific connector instance. This name is entered while performing the authentication, as discussed in Section 9.3.1.
Id	A unique connector instance ID.
Account Name	This name is the name of the SAP BTP subaccount ID to which the Open Connectors is attached.
Owner	Name of the user responsible for creating the connector instance.
Tags	For categorizing the instance. You can add multiple tags.
Created Date	The creation date of the connector instance.
Token	An automatically generated token for the connector instance. Note that a connector token is used to make API requests available to the provider through Open Connectors.

Table 9.4 List of Connector Instance Attributes

Additionally, from the **Instance** page, the following actions can be performed:

- You can view different instance options by clicking the ⚙ icon. This menu gives you the options for editing, deleting, and logging. Viewing the logs of an instance is also possible. These options are shown in Figure 9.19. The logs option takes the user to a page that lists all activities performed on the connector instance, as shown in Figure 9.20.

- You can copy the connector instance's token to your clipboard by clicking the icon. Note that this token is important later when connecting from Cloud Integration to the application through Open Connectors.
- You can show/hide a token's details by clicking the icon.
- You can view API documents by clicking the **API Docs** button. This option redirects you to a page that we'll discuss in Section 9.3.3.

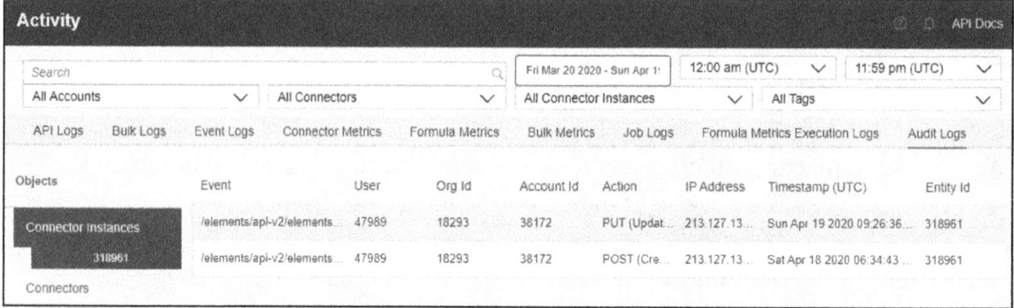

Figure 9.20 Activity Logs View of a Connector Instance

Next, we'll discuss how to test the APIs and verify whether we can retrieve data from the API providers.

9.3.3 Testing in the API Docs

After successfully creating a connector instance, you can test the API of the third-party application by retrieving its data. This test can be conducted in one of the following ways:

- By clicking on the **Test in the API docs**, shown earlier in Figure 9.17. To get back to this page, open the connector again (under **Connectors**) and then click the number (in the round shape) under the **Instances** column (when the connector is shown in the list view). Then, you see the connector as a tile from which you can click **Explore**, which finally leads you to the screen with the **Test in the API docs** functions.
- From the list of connector instances, shown earlier in Figure 9.19.

Both approaches lead you to an **API Docs** page similar to the page shown in Figure 9.21. The **API Docs** page provides you with a list of all entities and their supported CRUD operations. In addition, notice the **Instance Token** field at the top of the page. This token uniquely identifies a connection instance (as listed in Table 9.4). Thus, we can test all operations below using the connection details of the connector instance represented by the token.

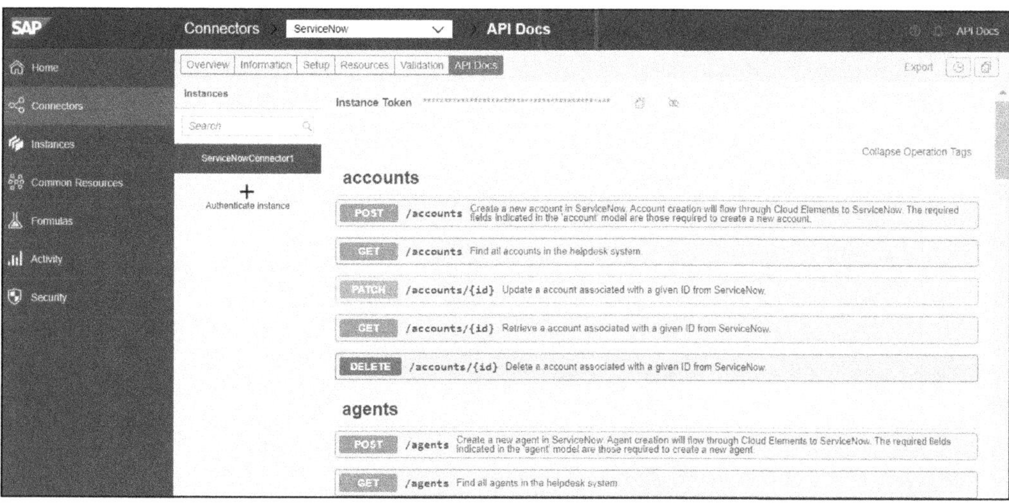

Figure 9.21 API Docs Page with the List of APIs

> **Note**
>
> If you have multiple connector instances for the same connector type, you'll be presented with a list at the top of the page shown in Figure 9.21.

Let's now test our connector instance by performing the following steps:

1. Click on the desired operation from the list of operations presented on the **API Docs** page. For our example, as shown in Figure 9.22, we clicked on **Get /incidents**. You'll then see a page with information about the API and a **Try it out** button, which enables you to interact with the third-party system and perform different operations.
2. Click on the **Try it out** button and fill in the attributes shown in Figure 9.22. You can, for instance, choose to fill in the `pageSize` attribute with the value `10`. In this case, a maximum of 10 incident records will be returned on each page of the result set. Note, however, that for simplicity's sake, we've left all the attributes empty, as shown in Figure 9.22.
3. Now, click the **Execute** button to trigger a call to ServiceNow, as shown at the bottom of Figure 9.23.

> **Note**
>
> You can also specify the content type (or format) of the response message via the **Response content type** dropdown list. Typical content type choices include `application/xml` and `application/json`. This parameter specifies whether the response sent by the third-party system will be returned in the JSON format or the XML format. In the case of ServiceNow, only the content type `application/json` is supported.

You can also reset the **API Docs** page by clicking the **Cancel** button. This action will disable the **Execute** button as well as the input text boxes for all the attributes.

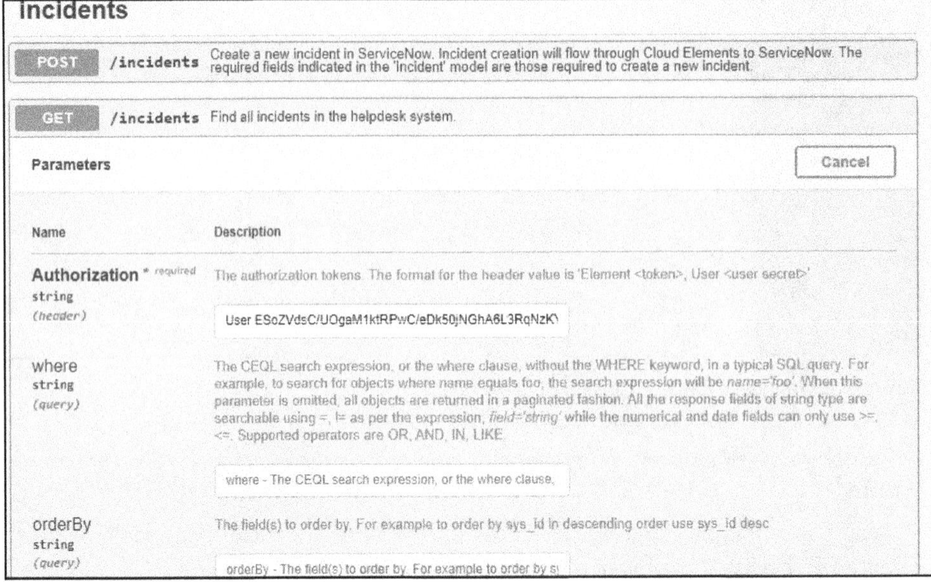

Figure 9.22 Details of the API Operation to Be Tested

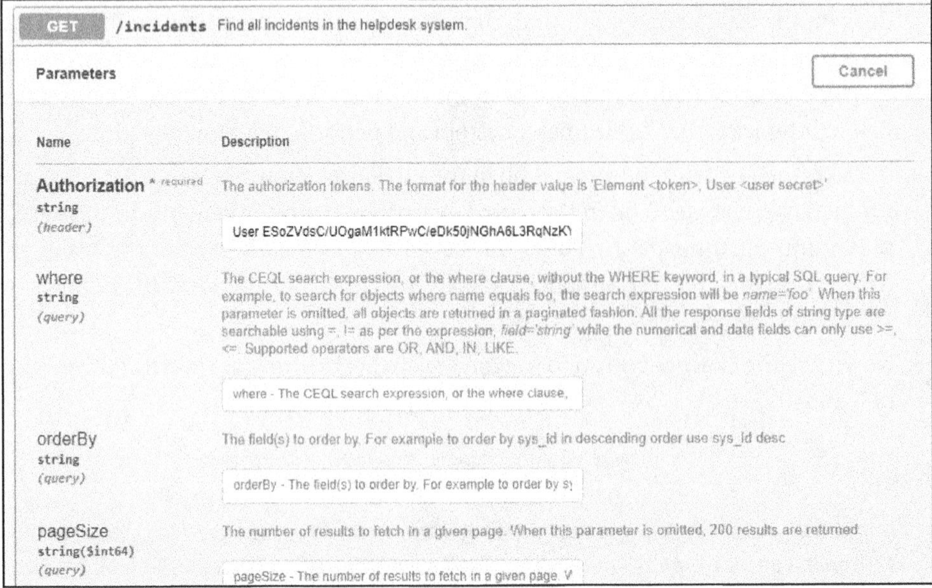

Figure 9.23 Performing a Call to ServiceNow to Retrieve Incidents

After you click the **Execute** button in the previous step, a call is performed toward the third-party system, and its response is returned in the XML or JSON format depending on the choice made in the **Response content type** dropdown list.

Figure 9.24 shows an example ServiceNow response listing incident details. The following information is displayed on the response page:

- **Curl**
  Represents the cURL command, which can be used to send a request to ServiceNow and retrieve the desired data. cURL is a tool to transfer data to a server using the HTTP or HTTPS protocols. cURL is commonly used to perform API calls using the command-line tool. To learn more about cURL, refer to *https://curl.haxx.se*.
- **Request URL**
  Represents the URL used to send a request to ServiceNow and retrieve the desired data. This URL can be used, for instance, to perform a test on ServiceNow via Postman.
- **Code (server response code)**
  Contains the HTTP response status code returned by the third-party system (e.g., ServiceNow). The returned code generally follows a well-defined, standard list of HTTP response status codes. To learn more about HTTP response status codes and their meanings, go to *http://s-prs.co/v576049*.
- **Response body (server response body)**
  Contains the returned response message.

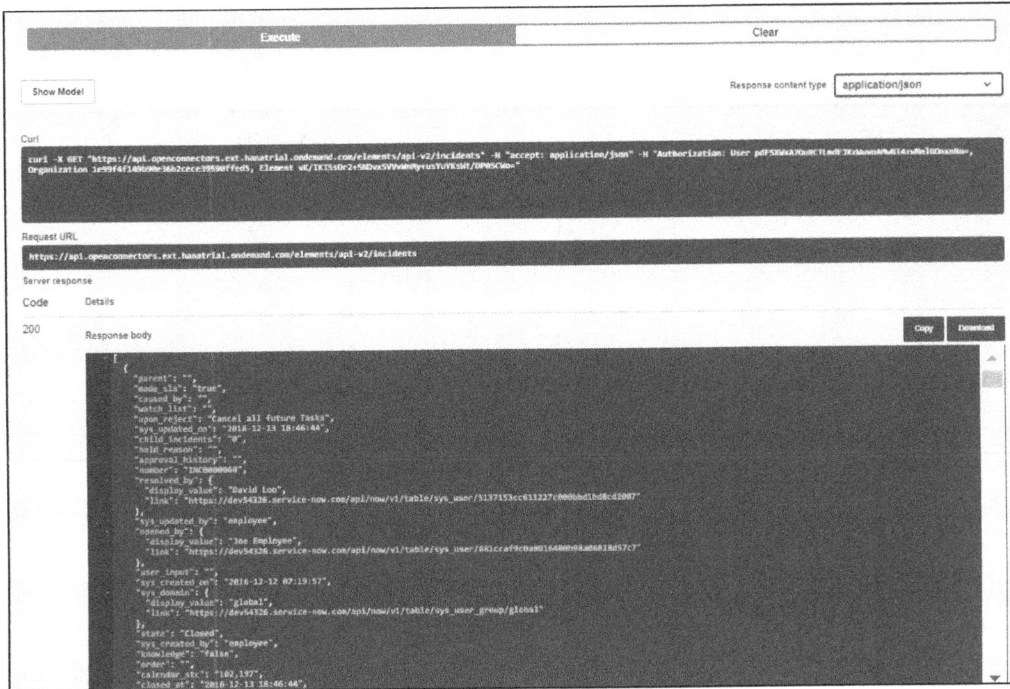

Figure 9.24 Example Response Message from the ServiceNow Instance

- **Copy button**
  Copies the returned response message to your clipboard.
- **Download button**
  Downloads the returned response message to your computer.

Save the values included in the **Curl** section, shown at the top of Figure 9.24, because you'll need this information later in Section 9.5. Now that we've successfully tested an operation on the **API Docs** page, as demonstrated by the list of incidents we received, let's explore the next feature of Open Connectors—common resources.

9.4 Open Connectors: Understanding Common Resources

If you've ever had to retrieve data from multiple sources and third-party systems, you probably know how tedious and time-consuming this task can be. Without a shared definition and common understanding of the same data, you'll need to create custom structures and mappings for each application and data source. A common data model can usually handle these situations by providing a shared data definition for specific business objects.

This need for a common language is exactly where common resources come to the rescue. In Open Connectors, common resources represent common data models or canonical views of your company's business data objects. Some examples of business data objects (or common resources) include an invoice, order, employee, or product. Common resources define how your organization views these objects, including what type of attributes and fields represent such common resources.

Using a canonical view as part of your integration enables you to avoid the need to map or transform source data into target data using a point-to-point approach. Thus, you'll only need to map data toward the common resource. Open Connectors takes care of the mapping between your requests to different types of endpoints, including Simple Object Access Protocol (SOAP), Representational State Transfer (REST), files, databases, and more. Therefore, you can easily achieve a one-to-many relationships experience for developers. Figure 9.25 shows how common resources are used when mapping any other objects. In our example scenario in Section 9.5, you'll also see how you can consume a common resource from Cloud Integration.

Common resources from Open Connectors enable you to map any third-party-specific structure to your organization's common data model. In Open Connectors, two types of common resources are available:

- **Templated resources**
  These resources are prebuilt resources in Open Connectors. They normally exist for frequently integrated resources and mappings to popular API providers. You can use these resources as templates for common mappings to connectors.

- **Custom resources**
  Represent your organization's resources that you've built. You can leverage prebuilt resources by cloning them and customizing them to meet your organization's needs. You can also add or remove fields, connectors, and mappings.

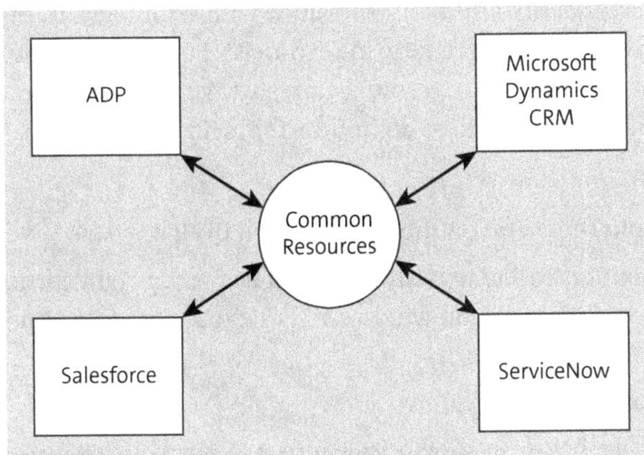

Figure 9.25 Common Resources Mapping to Third-Party Objects

All the fields and mappings created for a common resource are defined within a four-level hierarchy. This hierarchy defines which users can change which attributes and whether these attributes belong to the entire organization or not. The different levels are listed in Table 9.5 in order of ascending priority.

Level	Description
System	Represents the highest level of the hierarchy. This level is reserved for prebuilt resources. Thus, custom common resources don't have fields at this level.
Organization	Represents the second-highest level available for Open Connectors users. When a resource is built at this level, default mappings are also created and made available for all accounts within the organization.
Account	Represents the third-highest level available for Open Connectors users. Accounts generally represent your organization's customers. Transformations created at the account level are also available to all users associated with a specific account.
Instance	Represents the lowest level available for Open Connectors. Transformations created at this level are only relevant to a specific connector instance.

Table 9.5 Resource Field Hierarchy Levels

Now that you have a high-level understanding of what common resources are used for, let's discuss how to create them next.

9.4.1 Creating a Common Resource

Note that a common resource isn't always required to consume and leverage Open Connectors in Cloud Integration. However, in some cases, exposing a common resource to Cloud Integration might be better than directly exposing the resource exposed by the connector. We'll demonstrate how you can use Cloud Integration to leverage a common resource in our example scenario in Section 9.5. For now, let's practice what you've learned by creating a common resource named `MyIncident`. This common resource will be our common data model, or definition, for incidents.

To create a common resource, follow these steps:

1. Select **Common Resources** from the menu on the left, as shown in Figure 9.26.
2. Then, click the **Build new Common Resource** button, located in the top-right corner of the page, as shown in Figure 9.26. A popup window will ask you to choose either **Build New Resource** or **Build from JSON object**.
3. Select the **Build New Resource** option.
4. On the next page, you can add fields, as shown in Figure 9.27, for your resource. Notice that the resulting page has two sections: one section for organization-level fields and one section for account-level fields (described earlier in Table 9.5). For the sake of simplicity, let's use the account level in this example.

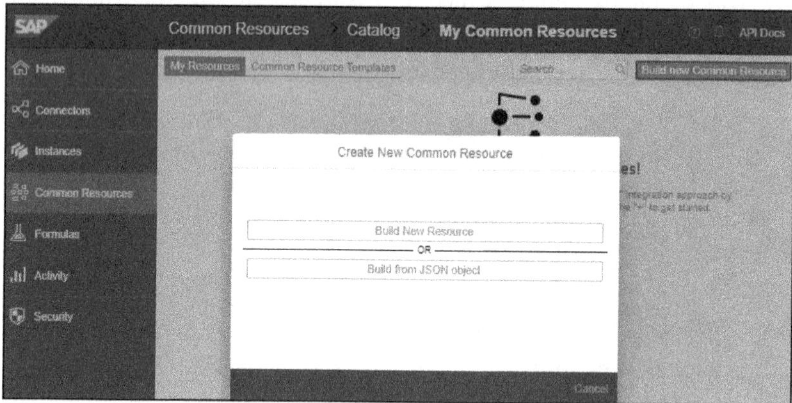

Figure 9.26 Creating a New Common Resource

5. Provide a name for your resource. For simplicity, let's create a custom resource to represent an incident. Enter "MyIncident" in the textbox next to the **Save** button, as shown in Figure 9.27.
6. Create the structure of the common resource. Add fields to your custom resource by clicking the + icon in the **Account Level Fields** section on the right. For each field, you'll provide a **Field Name**, data **Type**, and **Display Name**. Follow the example shown in Figure 9.27 to build a complete set of fields for the resource. To keep things simple, we only created a limited number of fields for an incident.

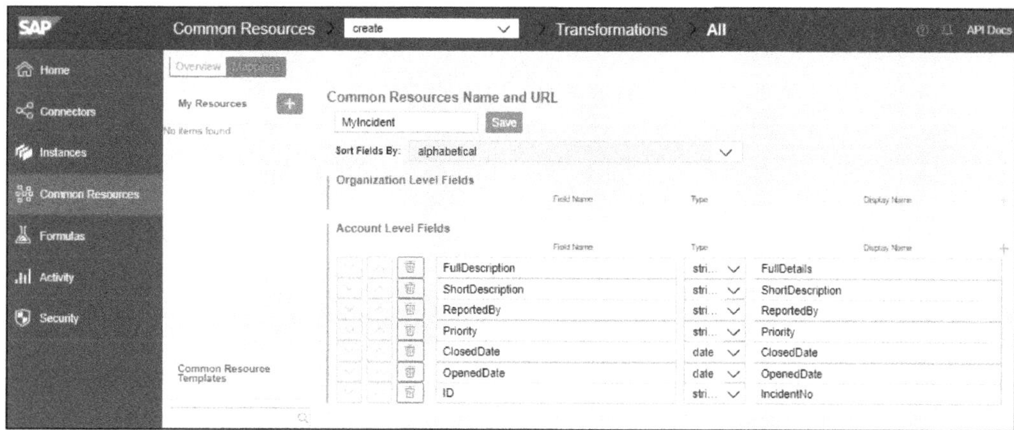

Figure 9.27 Adding Fields to a Resource

7. Click the **Save** button at the top of the page, next to the name of the resource. After the resource is successfully saved, you'll see the resource listed under the **My Resources** panel on the left side of the screen, as shown in Figure 9.28. You'll also be presented with the ability to create a new transformation for the newly created resource (e.g., **MyIncident**). This newly created common resource will be used later in our example scenario described in Section 9.5. We discussed transformations in Section 9.5.1.

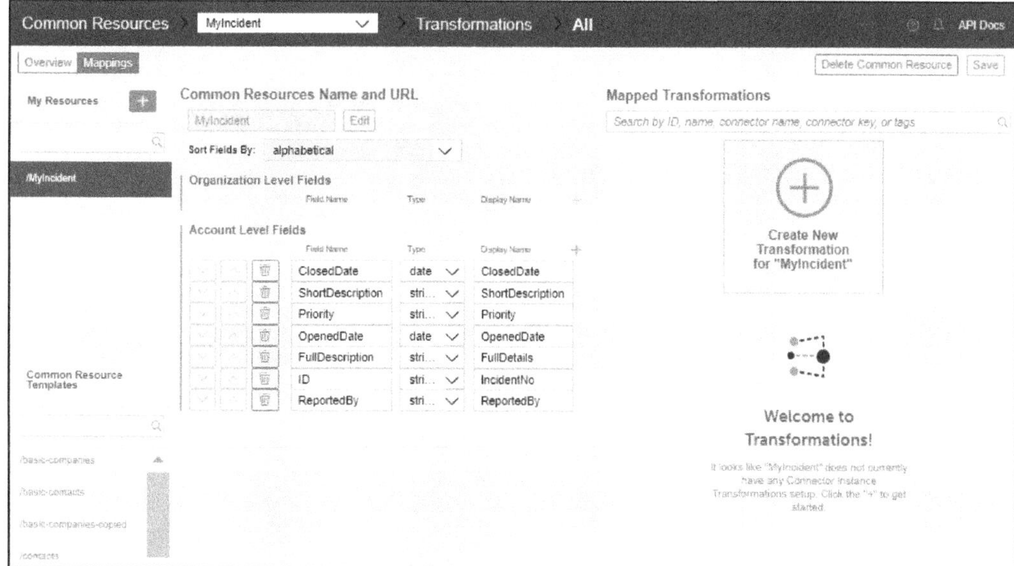

Figure 9.28 View of a Created Custom Resource

Note

You can also create a common resource via an API or by importing a JSON payload. As shown earlier in Figure 9.26, recall that when creating a common resource, you had the option of building a common resource using a JSON object. If you selected this option, you must provide a JSON definition.

To keep things simple, we won't discuss how to create common resources via an API or a JSON object in this book. Instead, refer to the Open Connectors help page at *http://s-prs.co/v576041*.

9.4.2 Cloning Common Resources

As mentioned in the previous section, templated common resources are prebuilt resources that provide fields for frequently integrated resources and mappings to popular API providers. Open Connectors gives you the ability to clone a template and leverage existing default mappings to the API providers. After cloning a template, the related fields and mappings become available at the account level, and you can add, delete, or adjust any of its related fields.

To clone an existing common resource, follow these steps:

1. From the **Common Resources** page, select the resource that you want to clone from the **Common Resource Templates** section. Note that you can also search for a template by entering keywords in the text box in the bottom-left corner, as shown in Figure 9.29.

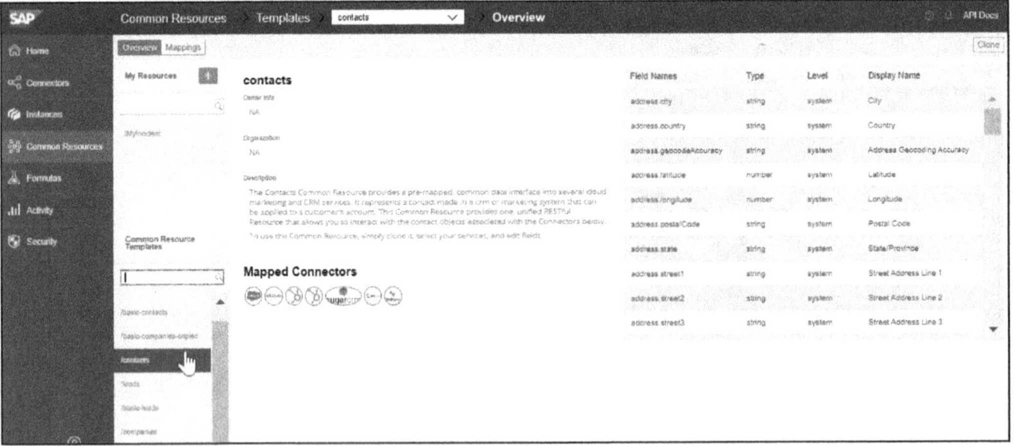

Figure 9.29 Cloning a Common Resource Template

2. After selecting a common resource template (e.g., **contacts**), its details will be displayed on the right.

3. Click the **Clone** button, located in the top-right corner of the page. You'll be presented with a popup window, shown in Figure 9.30, where you'll select the account(s) into which the resource template should be cloned.

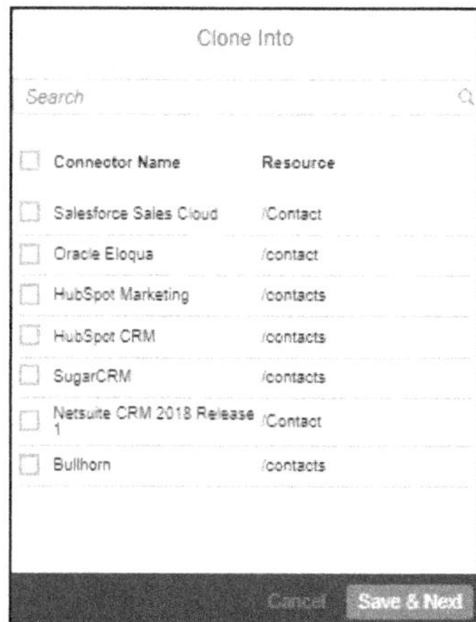

Figure 9.30 Selecting the Target Account Where the Template Should Be Cloned

4. After selecting the concerned account(s), click the **Save & Next** button. You'll be asked to choose to which level the fields/mapping should be placed. You'll choose either **Organization** or **Account**.
5. Next, provide a new name for your cloned resource, for example, "MyContact." Then, click on the **Save & Exit** button.

Voilà! Your cloned resource is now available for use. Let's next explore how to perform mappings and transformations on our resources.

9.4.3 Transforming Resources

Now that you've created a resource to represent your organization's shared definition and understanding of some data, the next step is to convert the data fields of an API provider's resource (e.g., ServiceNow) to match the fields in the common resource (e.g., the `MyIncident` resource that we just created). In other words, we need to perform a mapping between the connector instance resources and our common resource. To perform these field mappings, follow these steps:

1. Open your resource, for example, **MyIncident**. You'll see a page like the one shown earlier in Figure 9.28.
2. Click on the **Create New Transformation for "MyIncident"** tile. Note that this tile is available under the **Mapped Transformations** pane on the right side of the page.
3. Select the connector instance, in our case, the ServiceNow instance that we created in Section 9.3. Then, select the desired instance resource, in our case **incidents**, as shown in Figure 9.31. You're then redirected to a transformation page.

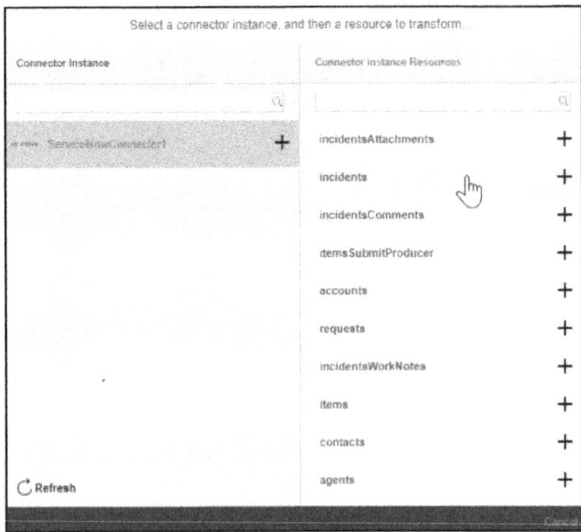

Figure 9.31 Selecting the Connector's Instance Resource

4. On the mapping or transformation page, the common resource is displayed to the left of the mapping (as a source). The connector instance resource is on the right side of the page. You'll need to select a target field from the dropdown menu, as shown in Figure 9.32. For simplicity, we've already mapped out all the relevant fields, as shown in Figure 9.32. Feel free to map these field to suit your specific business scenario.

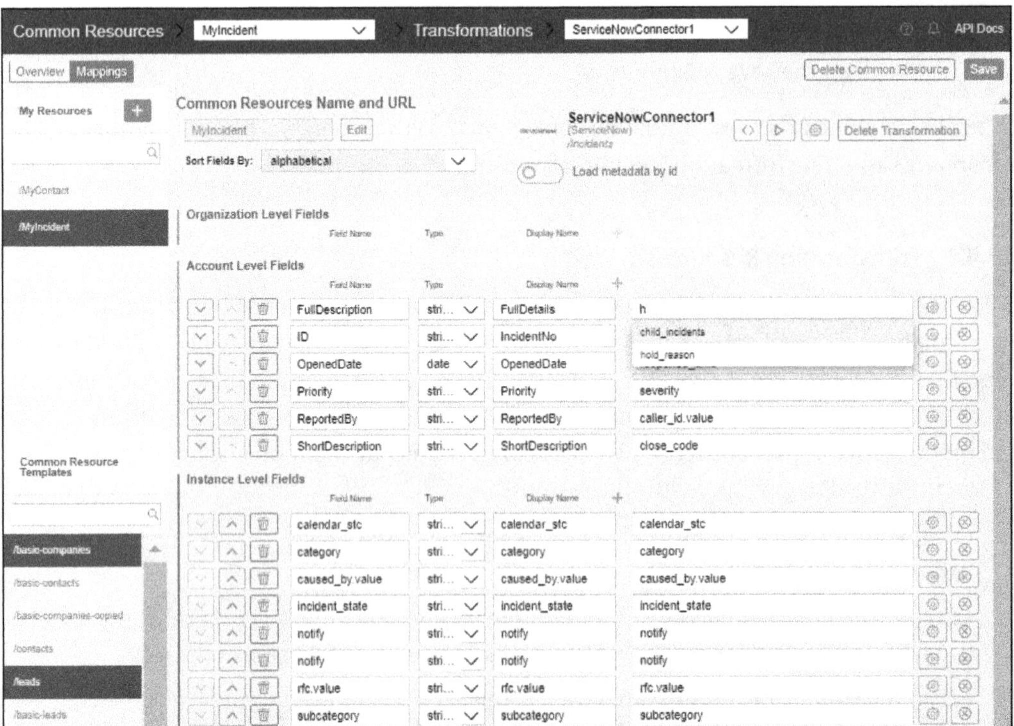

Figure 9.32 Mapping a Common Resource to a Connector's Instance Resource

Note that you can further specify the settings of any specific field in the mapping shown in Figure 9.32, by clicking the **Field Settings** icon. You'll then get a popup window, shown in Figure 9.33, where you can perform the following activities:

- **Type**
  Specify the data type of the field (e.g., **string**, **Boolean**, etc.).
- **Set Vendor True Value**
  Specify whether to convert Boolean TRUE values to either a specific value (e.g., 1) or a null value.
- **Remove Field on Requests**
  Specify whether the label of the field will be included/excluded from the request message. Note that, by default, the fields are always passed through and included in the request.
- **Remove Field on Responses**
  Specify whether the label of the field will be included/excluded from the response message. Note that, by default, fields are always passed through and included in the response.
- **Default Request Value**
  Specify a default value in case the field is empty.
- **Default Response Value**
  Specify a default value in case the field is empty.

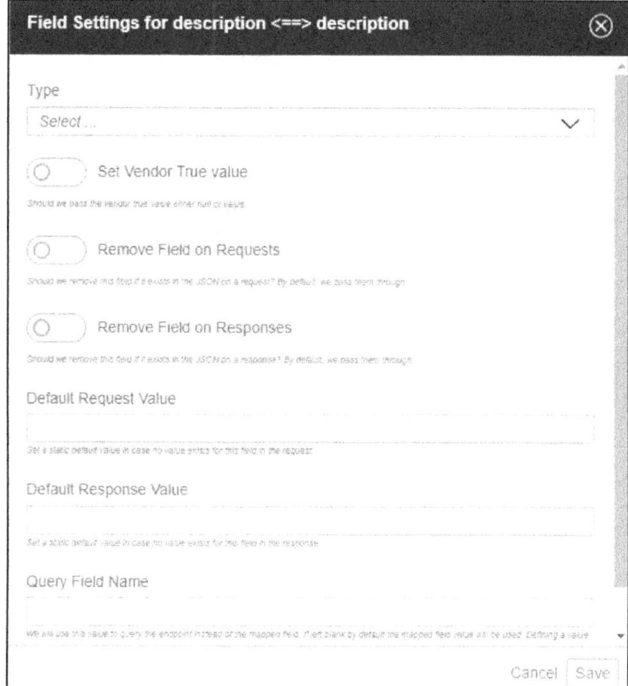

Figure 9.33 Specifying Details Field Settings in the Transformation

Finally, you can verify that the mapping is correct by testing it. On the **Transformations** page, click the ▷ icon, as shown in the top-right corner of Figure 9.32. A new page appears, enabling you to specify input parameters for your test. In our example, we simply want to retrieve incident data. Click the **Send** button to retrieve the data and see the output of your transformation, as shown in Figure 9.34.

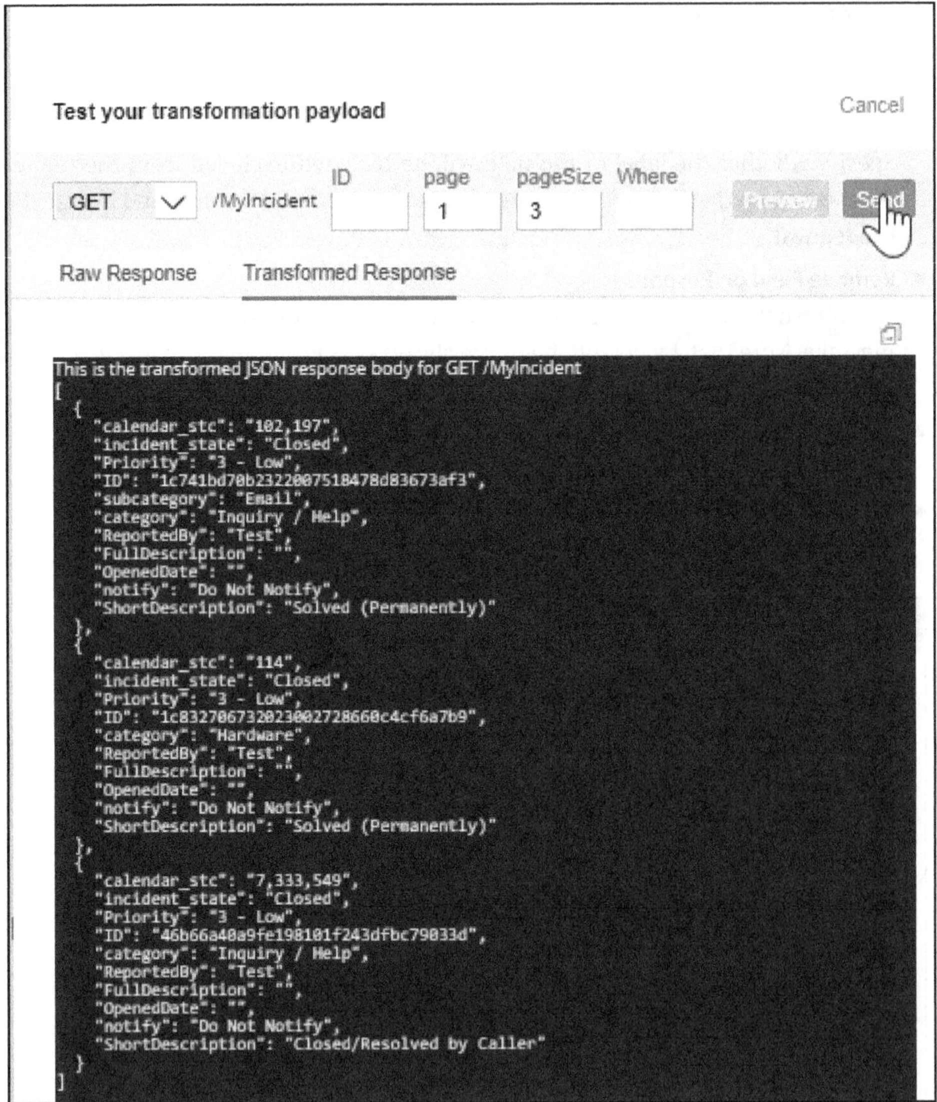

Figure 9.34 Testing Our Transformation Payload

This transformation will be automatically executed when Open Connectors receives the */MyIncident* common resource with the ServiceNow instance.

Congratulations! You've successfully tested your first transformation. Let's now explore how to call this ServiceNow instance in Cloud Integration.

9.5 Using Cloud Integration with Open Connectors

In this section, you'll learn how to leverage the connection instance created in Open Connectors for use in a Cloud Integration's iFlow. We'll start by describing the integration scenario that we'll build in this section.

9.5.1 Scenario

For simplicity's sake, let's assume that you want to expose a SOAP service in Cloud Integration. This service enables its consumers to retrieve a list of incidents from ServiceNow, as shown in Figure 9.35.

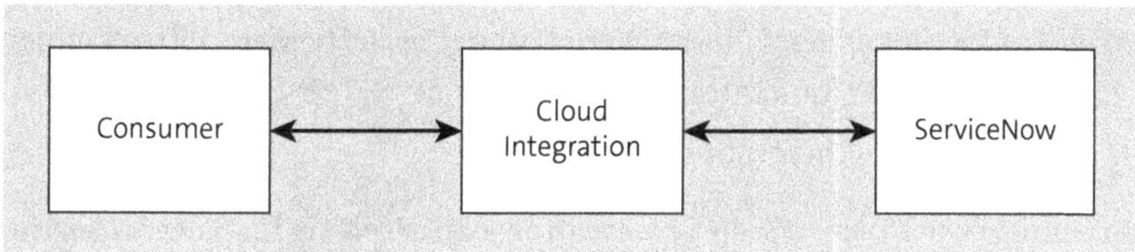

Figure 9.35 Scenario to Retrieve ServiceNow Incidents

As the time of this writing, no standard ServiceNow adapter is available in Cloud Integration. To achieve this scenario and communicate with ServiceNow, the following options are available:

- **Using an HTTP adapter**
  This option involves the tedious task of becoming familiar with the relevant ServiceNow REST APIs and building some authentication scripts.
- **Using an SAP partner-provided adapter for ServiceNow**
  You can find the available SAP partner adapters in Cloud Integration on the **Discover** page.
- **Using Open Connectors**
  This approach is what we'll explore in the following sections.

When using Open Connectors together with Cloud Integration, you must use the Open Connectors adapter in Cloud Integration. This adapter was briefly mentioned in Chapter 1, Section 1.3. The Open Connectors adapter enables Cloud Integration to connect to Open Connectors and reuse its connector instances.

As shown in Figure 9.36, Open Connectors will act as a receiver system in the Cloud Integration's iFlow. The Open Connectors adapter will need to authenticate itself with Open Connectors using a security credential especially created for this purpose. Let's next explore how you can build an iFlow to solve this challenge and achieve the connections shown in Figure 9.36.

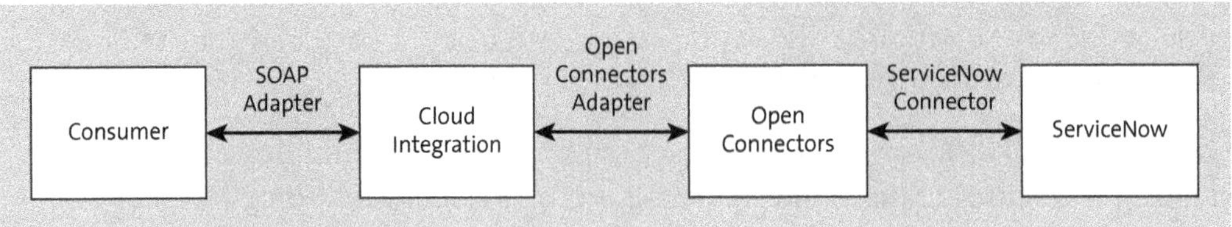

Figure 9.36 Connecting Cloud Integration and Open Connectors

9.5.2 The Solution

To enable Cloud Integration to interact with Open Connectors, you'll need to perform the following high-level steps:

1. Add a receiver system for Open Connectors, and use the Open Connectors adapter.
2. Create a **User Credentials** artifact (in the Web UI under **Security Material**) to connect to Open Connectors from Cloud Integration.
3. Create your iFlow in Cloud Integration and deploy it.

Because we've already performed step 1 by creating a ServiceNow instance in Section 9.3, let's now discuss steps 2 and 3 in the following sections.

Creating a User Credentials Artifact

An important step for our solution involves creating a **User Credentials** artifact to authenticate to Open Connectors from Cloud Integration. (We discussed security materials in detail in Chapter 7, Section 7.3.)

To create a **User Credentials** artifact of type `openConnectors`, follow these steps:

1. From the landing page of Cloud Integration, click on the **Monitor** menu item on the left.
2. Click on the **Security Material** tile, under the **Manage Security** section.
3. In the top-right corner of the page, click the **Add • User Credentials**, as shown in Figure 9.37.

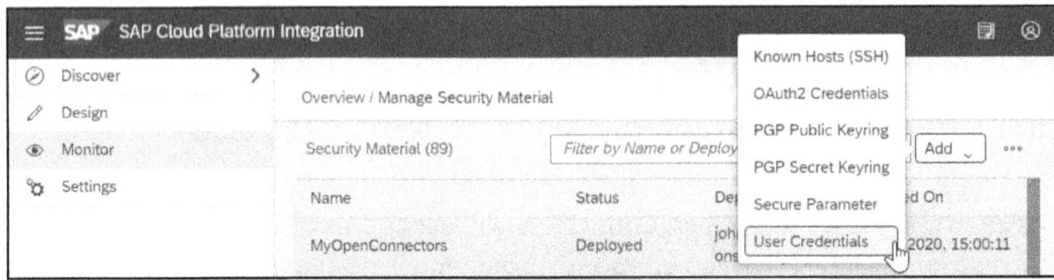

Figure 9.37 Adding User Credentials for Open Connectors

4. Fill in the details of your connection to Open Connectors. Make sure you select **OpenConnectors** from the **Type** dropdown menu, as shown in Figure 9.38.

Add User Credentials

Name: * MyOpenConnectors
Description: Credential to my OpenConnectors
Type: * OpenConnectors
User: * ••
Organization: * ••••••••••••••••••••••••••••••
Element: * ••

Deploy Cancel

Figure 9.38 User Credentials Details Needed to Connect to Open Connectors

Note

To fill in details of the **User**, **Organization**, and **Element** fields shown in Figure 9.38, refer to the details you saved in Section 9.3.3, as shown earlier in Figure 9.24. Alternatively, you'll need to retrieve these details from your Open Connectors. To retrieve the required details, follow these steps:

1. Go to the **API Docs** page, reached by selecting the **Instances** menu item and then clicking on the **API Docs** of the relevant instance. We previously demonstrated this process in Section 9.3.3.
2. Select the concerned resources (e.g., an incident), and click on **Try it Out**, as described earlier in Section 9.3.3 and shown in Figure 9.22.
3. Click the **Execute** button to trigger a call to ServiceNow, as described earlier in Section 9.3.3 and shown at the bottom of Figure 9.23. You'll get a page with the results of your call, as shown in Figure 9.39. From this screen, relevant details such as the **User**, **Organization**, and **Element** fields can be found in the **Curl** section of the page, inside the `Authorization` tag.

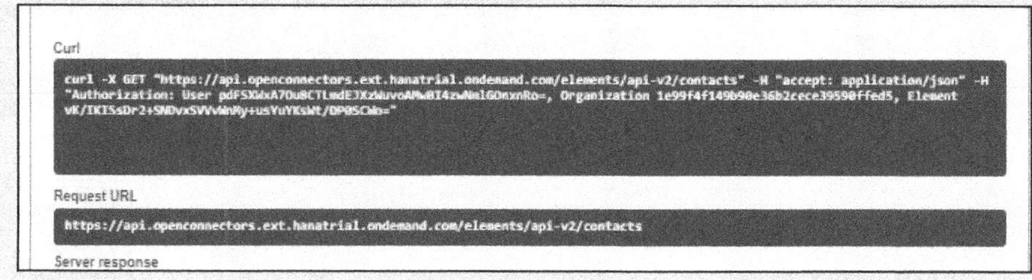

Figure 9.39 View of the Curl Command with Authorization Details Needed in Cloud Integration

4. Click the **Deploy** button of the user credential that you created earlier, as shown in Figure 9.38.

After creating the **User Credentials** artifact, let's create the iFlow in Cloud Integration.

Creating an Integration Flow in Cloud Integration

It's now time to build our iFlow and call Open Connectors. Follow these steps:

1. Select the **Design** menu item in Cloud Integration.
2. Navigate to your desired integration package, and add an iFlow under the **Artifacts** section. You learned how to create an iFlow in previous chapters, so we won't repeat all these steps in detail.
3. Name your iFlow "RetrieveSnowIncidents", and open it. Now, use the SOAP adapter between the sender participant and the **Start** event in the **Integration Process** area, as shown in Figure 9.40. Note that we've set the **address** of the SOAP adapter to be **/listIncidents**. Furthermore, ensure that the adapter **Message Exchange Pattern** is set to **Request-Reply**.
4. Rename the receiver system to "Open Connectors", add a **Request Reply** step in the **Integration Process** area, and link this new step to the **Receiver** system using the **OpenConnectors** adapter. The result is shown in Figure 9.41.

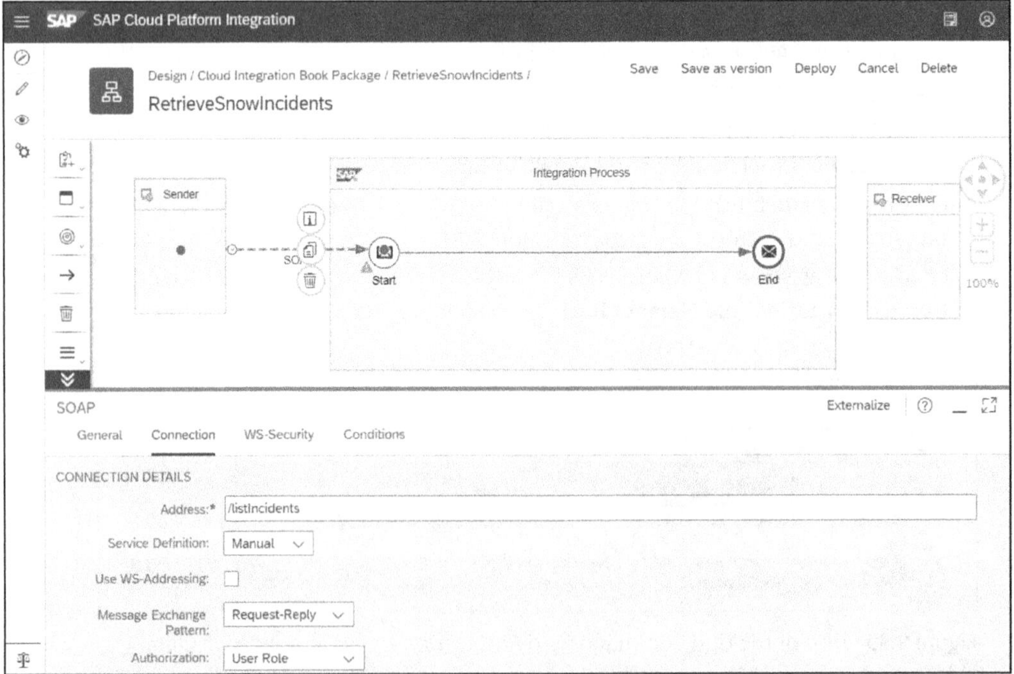

Figure 9.40 An iFlow to List Incidents from ServiceNow

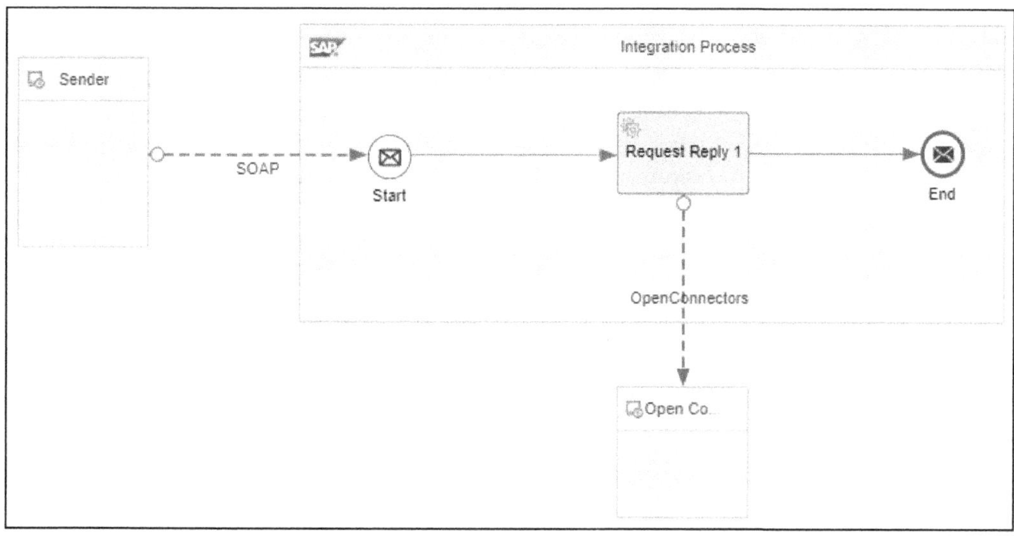

Figure 9.41 Adding a Request Reply Step to Call Open Connectors

5. Select the connector line between the **Request Reply** step and **Open Connectors**. Under the **Connection** tab, set the values of the various attributes according to the screen shown in Figure 9.42.

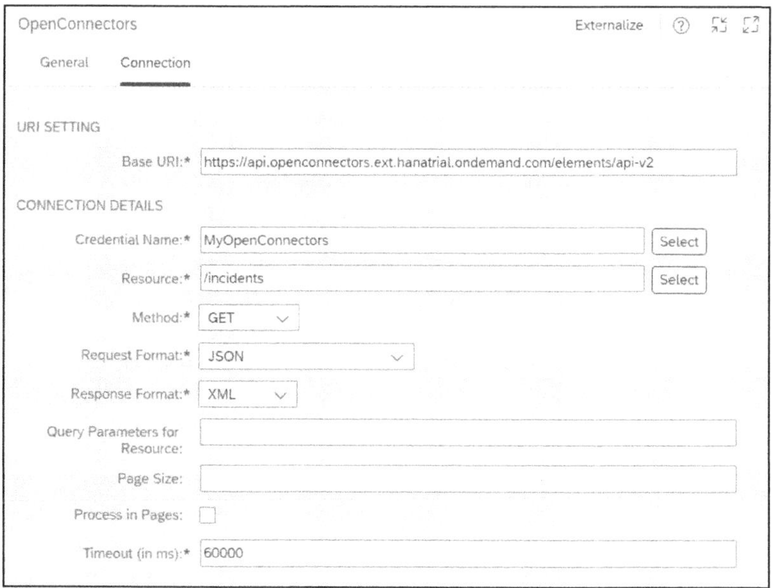

Figure 9.42 Maintaining Attributes of the Open Connectors Adapter

To better understand how to maintain the attributes for the Open Connectors adapter, see Table 9.6.

Attribute	Description
Base URI	This field represents the Open Connectors' base URI, which is a URI to your Open Connectors tenant. This URI can be obtained from the **API Docs** page and by clicking on the **Try it Out** button. When you click the **Execute** button, you'll be presented with the response. The Base URI can be obtained from the **Request URL** section, as shown earlier in Figure 9.39. Note that the entire URL must be copied until the `/api-v2` value. Ultimately, the URI will follow the format *https://<open connectors service url>/elements/api-v2.*
Credential Name	This field represents the name of the user credential (created in the previous section, as shown earlier in Figure 9.38). Note that you can also find this value by clicking the Select icon.
Resource	This field is the name of the Open Connectors common resource that you want to interact with within the Open Connectors ' instance. Note that you can also find this value by clicking the Select icon. A popup window will open similar to the window shown in Figure 9.43. In our case, we selected **/incidents** because we want to retrieve the list of incidents in ServiceNow.
Method	Given that we want to retrieve the list of incidents, we'll need to select the **GET** method. HTTP methods and their meanings were discussed in Section 9.2.1.
Request Format	Specify the format to be used to send a message to Open Connectors. Two possible values include **XML** and **JSON**. For example, if the request message produced is a result of any previous step (**Mapping** or **Message Modifier**) and is in the XML format, then select **XML**. In our example shown earlier in Figure 9.42, we're not using any request message, so we'll keep the default value **JSON**, for simplicity's sake.
Response Format	Specify the format that Open Connectors should use to return the response message. You can choose between **XML** or **JSON**. To keep things simple, keep the default value **XML**. The XML format is the easiest to use because Cloud Integration works with XML. If **JSON** is selected, depending on the scenario, it might be necessary to add a JSON to XML Convertor step in the iFlow to convert the returned JSON back to XML.
Query Parameters for Resource	Query parameters for resources are used to define a set of parameters to be added at the end of a URL. Query parameters are used as extensions of the URL to help define specific content or actions based on the data passed to Open Connectors. For example, you can limit the number of incident fields returned by ServiceNow using the value **fields= number, sys_updated_on**. In this case, ServiceNow will only return two fields in each record (`number` and `sys_updated_on`).

Table 9.6 Attributes of the Open Connectors Adapter

Attribute	Description
Page Size	Used to specify the maximum number of records to be returned on each page, for example, 10 records per page.
Progress in Pages	Messages are processed in batches of the size specified in the page size. This attribute should only be used in combination with the looping process call. We discussed the topic of Process Call in Chapter 6, Section 6.3.2. By default, this field is unchecked.
Timeout (in ms)	Maximum time the system will wait before terminating the operation. By default, this field's value is set to **60000**.

Table 9.6 Attributes of the Open Connectors Adapter (Cont.)

6. Click on **Select** next to **Resource** to open a screen similar to the screen shown in Figure 9.43.

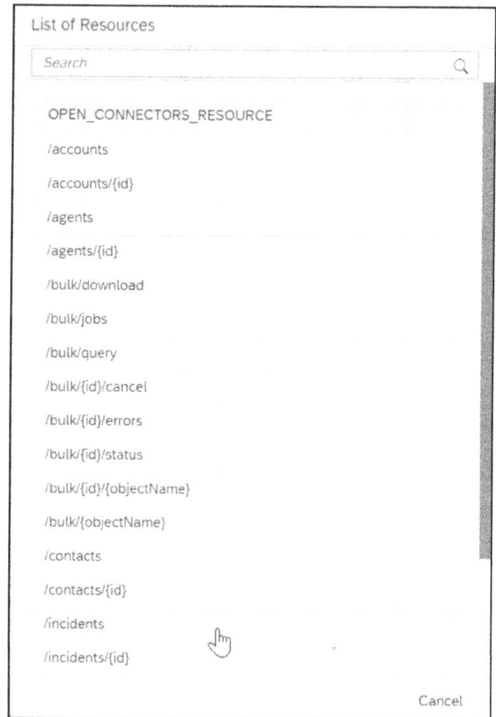

Figure 9.43 Selecting a Resource from the Open Connectors Adapter

As shown in Figure 9.43, we selected **/incidents** in the **Resource** field, which is a resource of ServiceNow. Now that you've finished setting up your iFlow and connecting it to Open Connectors, it's time to deploy and test it. Based on the knowledge you've acquired in previous chapters, deploying iFlows and finding their endpoints on the **Monitor** page of Cloud Integration should be easy.

Test the deployed iFlow using Postman. The response should be similar to the output shown in Figure 9.44, which contains many incidents returned from ServiceNow.

Note that the response shown in Figure 9.44 is a representation of the incident resource as that resource is known in ServiceNow. The response is the XML representation of the test that we performed earlier, as described in Section 9.3.3 and shown earlier in Figure 9.24.

Pretty Raw Preview Visualize XML


```
<soap:Envelope xmlns:soap="http://schemas.xmlsoap.org/soap/envelope/">
    <soap:Header/>
    <soap:Body>
        <OCRESPONSE>
            <incidents>
                <parent/>
                <made_sla>true</made_sla>
                <caused_by/>
                <watch_list/>
                <upon_reject>Cancel all future Tasks</upon_reject>
                <sys_updated_on>2016-12-13 18:46:44</sys_updated_on>
                <child_incidents>0</child_incidents>
                <hold_reason/>
                <approval_history/>
                <number>INC0000060</number>
                <resolved_by>
                    <display_value>David Loo</display_value>
                    <link>https://dev54326.service-now.com/api/now/v1/table/sys_user/5137153cc611227c000bbd1bd8cd2007</link>
                </resolved_by>
                <sys_updated_by>employee</sys_updated_by>
                <opened_by>
                    <display_value>Joe Employee</display_value>
                    <link>https://dev54326.service-now.com/api/now/v1/table/sys_user/681ccaf9c0a8016400b98a06818d57c7</link>
                </opened_by>
                <user_input/>
```


Figure 9.44 Result of the iFlow in Postman

Congratulations! You've successfully called Open Connectors from Cloud Integration.

Let's now extend our scenario by introducing a common resource. In Section 9.4.1, we created a common resource called **MyIncident**, which we'll now use. To use this common resource, we'll need to implement the solution shown in Figure 9.45.

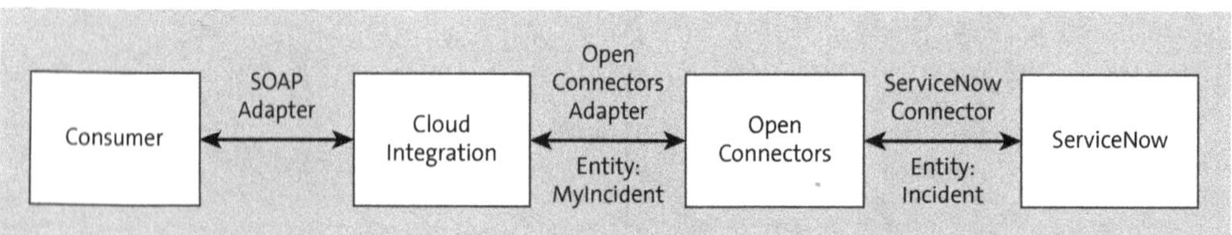

Figure 9.45 Calling Open Connectors from Cloud Integration via Common Resources

In the scenario shown in Figure 9.46, we'll need to call Open Connectors using the resource named **/MyIncident**, which we created in Section 9.4.1. To extend the scenario, follow these steps:

1. Go to Cloud Integration, and open the iFlow that we created earlier (Figure 9.41).
2. Select the connecting line between **Request Reply 1** and the receiver system. You're then presented with the **OpenConnectors** detail screen.
3. You can change the value of the **Resource** field to **/MyIncident**, which is the name of the common resource we created in Section 9.4.1.
4. Now that you've finished setting up your iFlow connected to Open Connectors using a common resource, you're ready to deploy the flow.

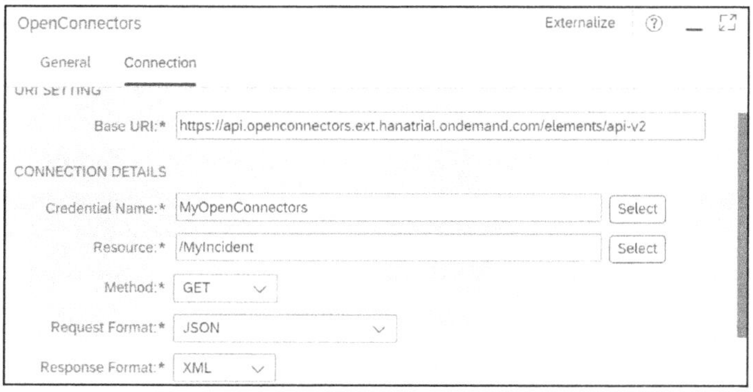

OpenConnectors — Externalize

General | Connection

URI SETTING

Base URI:* https://api.openconnectors.ext.hanatrial.ondemand.com/elements/api-v2

CONNECTION DETAILS

Credential Name:* MyOpenConnectors [Select]

Resource:* /MyIncident [Select]

Method:* GET

Request Format:* JSON

Response Format:* XML

Figure 9.46 Cloud Integration with a Resource Pointing to a Common Resource

But first, let's test the deployed iFlow using Postman one more time. The response should be similar to the output shown in Figure 9.47, which contains many incidents returned from ServiceNow.

```
<soap:Envelope xmlns:soap="http://schemas.xmlsoap.org/soap/envelope/">
    <soap:Header/>
    <soap:Body>
        <OCRESPONSE>
            <MyIncident>
                <calendar_stc>102,197</calendar_stc>
                <incident_state>Closed</incident_state>
                <Priority>3 - Low</Priority>
                <ID>1c741bd70b2322007518478d83673af3</ID>
                <subcategory>Email</subcategory>
                <category>Inquiry / Help</category>
                <ReportedBy>Test</ReportedBy>
                <FullDescription/>
                <OpenedDate/>
                <notify>Do Not Notify</notify>
                <ShortDescription>Solved (Permanently)</ShortDescription>
            </MyIncident>
            <MyIncident>
                <calendar_stc>114</calendar_stc>
                <incident_state>Closed</incident_state>
                <Priority>3 - Low</Priority>
                <ID>1c83270673202300272866 0c4cf6a7b9</ID>
                <category>Hardware</category>
                <ReportedBy>Test</ReportedBy>
```

Figure 9.47 Result of the iFlow Using a Common Resource in Postman

Note that the structure of the returned incidents follows the defined **/MyIncident** common resource. How is that possible? The transformation we defined in Section 9.4.3 performs a mapping between the ServiceNow structure `/Incident` and the common resource `/MyIncident`. This transformation is automatically performed by Open Connectors as soon as it receives the `/MyIncident` common resource.

9.6 Using Cloud Integration to Connect to Third-Party Systems without Open Connectors

In the past three years, Cloud Integration has been introducing capabilities and features to connect to third-party systems without to need to use Open Connectors. A third party represents any non-SAP System. This means that developers and integrators who are well versed in Cloud Integration can connect to third-party CRM systems such as Salesforce using the same techniques that they are already familiar with. From an architectural point of view, using the Open Connectors approach is depicted in Figure 9.48.

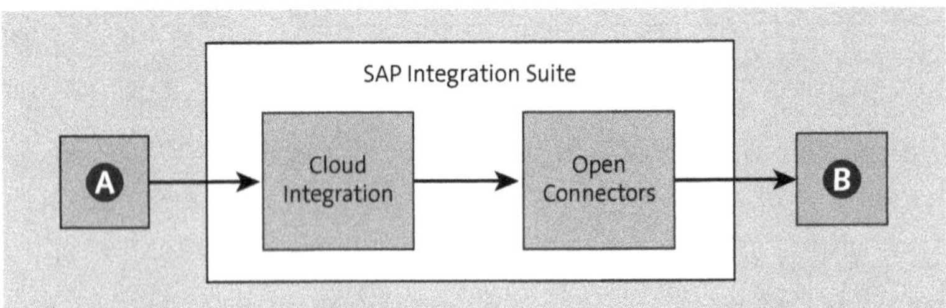

Figure 9.48 Integration Using Both Cloud Integration and Open Connectors

As shown in Figure 9.48, all connections from Cloud Integration are first routed to Open Connectors. The Open Connectors in turn then routes the connection to the third-party system (**B**). Observe that this is a longer router from System **A** to System **B** because the route includes two hop stations—**Cloud Integration** and **Open Connectors**.

If we were to only use Cloud Integration connectors, our approach would look like Figure 9.49.

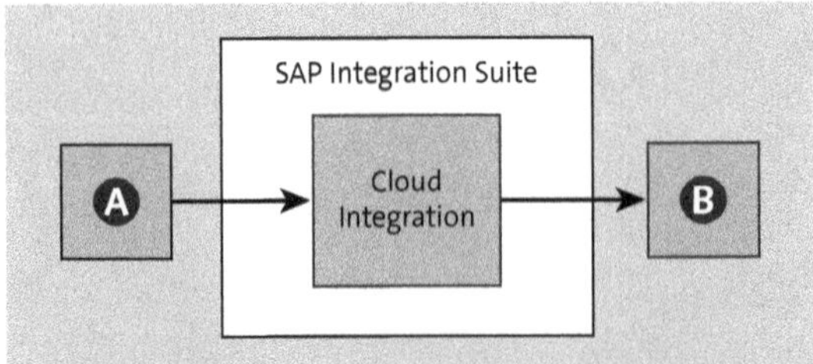

Figure 9.49 Integration Using Only Cloud Integration

As shown in Figure 9.49, all connections from Cloud Integration are directly routed to the third-party system (**B**). Observe that this is a shorter router from System **A** to System **B**.

Some advantages of connecting directly from Cloud integration include the following:

- More cost-effective because the customer only needs the Cloud Integration license.
- No need to learn two different systems and approaches.
- Reduced connectivity overhead and leaner iFlow.
- Simplified monitoring. With the former approach, if things go wrong in the chain, you need to potentially monitor and troubleshoot both in Cloud Integration and Open Connectors. With this new direct connection, all monitoring and troubleshooting can centrally happen in Cloud Integration.

To find out the current and up-to-date list of available adapters or connectors, go to *http://s-prs.co/v576050*. In the list, note that there are some new connectors:

- AmazonWebServices
- SugarCRM
- Salesforce
- Microsoft Dynamics CRM
- Workday
- ServiceNow
- AdvancedEventMesh
- Dropbox
- AzureStorage
- Microsoft SharePoint

In the next section, we'll explore two of these adapters: Salesforce and AmazonWebServices.

9.6.1 Connecting to Salesforce

Salesforce is a cloud-based software that provides CRM service and enterprise applications focused on customer service, marketing automation, analytics, and application development. If a customer needs to exchange data between their SAP landscape and Salesforce, Cloud Integration can be used as the IPaaS of choice. Let's explore some of the high-level features of the Salesforce Adapter for SAP Integration Suite:

- **Support for multiple API versions**
  Salesforce releases a few versions of its API every year. The adapter supports various versions of the Salesforce API.
- **Secure authentication with OAuth 2.0**
  Every REST call between Salesforce and Cloud Integration is secured by OAuth 2.0.
- **Support for multiple Salesforce operations**
  This includes all of the CRUD operations.
- **Querying and searching**
  In addition to all the operations that the Salesforce adapter offers, the adapter allows the querying of data from a Salesforce system using Salesforce Object Query Language (SOQL) and Salesforce Object Search Language (SOSL) queries.

- **Dynamic configuration with headers and properties**
  The Salesforce adapter provides the freedom to assign dynamic values to its different properties. It allows referring to dynamic parameters using Cloud Integration exchange headers and properties.
- **Processing large sets of data**
  With support for the bulk operation, the Salesforce adapter is optimized for loading or deleting large sets of data. Using batches, numerous records can be processed asynchronously.
- **Support for XML and JSON**
  XML and JSON are fully incorporated in the adapter, while the REST Bulk API additionally supports CSV and ZIP files. Furthermore, the Salesforce adapter also processes binary content from a Salesforce system. For example, the REST – Get Blob operation supports documents and attachment objects.
- **Query and XSD Eclipse plug-in**
  The Eclipse Query plug-in enables the creation of SOQL and SOSL queries. The Eclipse XSD plug-in helps in generating all necessary up-to-date messages XSDs for the specific Salesforce version and custom objects.
- **Full integration support for custom objects and fields**
  In addition to supporting all the standard Salesforce objects, the adapter integrates with all the custom objects in Salesforce.
- **Support for creation/upsert of aggregated structures**
  The Salesforce adapter supports a composite Salesforce call where the request body can contain a combination of different operations (e.g., `Upsert` and `Read`) on multiple `sObjects` at the same time.
- **Support nested structures in the CRUD operations**
  This feature supports the references that link nested `sObjects` to a main `sObject` in the XSD Generation plug-in. This allows the mapping of referenced `sObjects` in the structure. For example, the Account XSD contains the referenced `sObjects` `Account`, `ReportsTo`, and `Owner`.
- **Suport for Apex Call and APIs**
  This feature enable customers to interact with Apex-provided APIs. Apex is a strongly typed, object-oriented programming language that allows Salesforce developers to execute flow and transaction control statements on the Salesforce Lightning platform.
- **Event processing**
  The event processing feature enables Cloud Integration to subscribe (for the sender adapter) and poll (for the receiver adapter) events from Salesforce. The following event types are currently supported in the adapter: PushTopic, Platform, Generic, and Change Data Capture.

To illustrate the use of the adapter, let's use a simple scenario that includes the development of an iFlow to query the details of a few customers (accounts) in Salesforce. Given that you're already familiar with creating iFlows in Cloud Integration, we'll focus this discussion on showcasing how to configure the Salesforce adapter. The Scenario to be built is depicted in Figure 9.50.

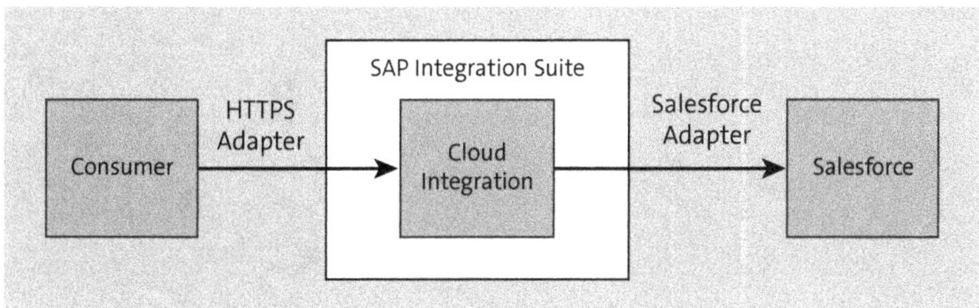

Figure 9.50 Connection Cloud Integration to Salesforce.

As shown in Figure 9.50, for this example, we'll use the HTTPS sender adapter to expose the integration over HTTPS. Furthermore, a Salesforce receiver adapter needs to be used in the iFlow to query Salesforce for the last two accounts (or customers).

Notes

The Salesforce adapter for SAP Integration Suite might not be available by default on your tenant. However, you can make it available by downloading it on SAP Service Marketplace via *http://s-prs.co/v576051*.

The package of the adapter includes the documentation explaining how to deploy the adapter.

Build the iFlow in Cloud Integration, similar to the one presented in Figure 9.51. Note that the **Request Reply** step is used for the Salesforce adapter.

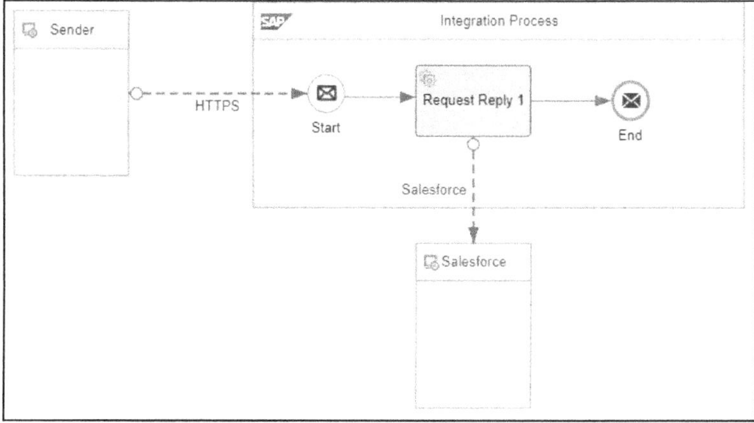

Figure 9.51 Example iFlow

After selecting the Salesforce adapter on your iFlow, several parameters need to be configured to connect to your specific Salesforce instance. Figure 9.52 shows an example configuration.

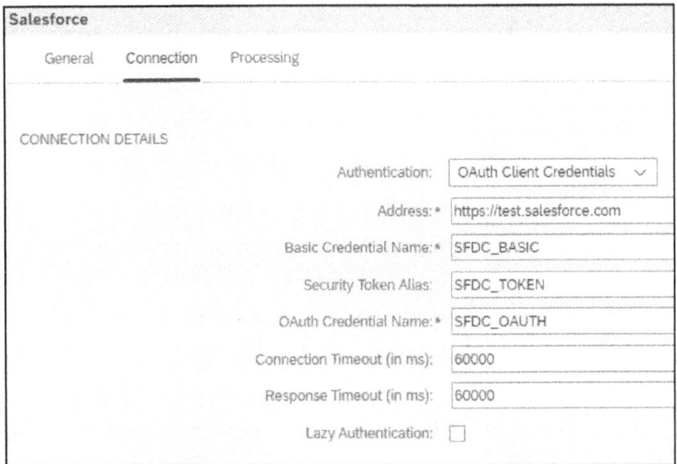

Figure 9.52 Configuration of the Connection Tab

Table 9.7 explains each of the parameters on the **Connection** tab.

Field Name	Description
Authentication	Select your preferred authentication method: OAuth or JWT.
Address	Specifies the recipient's endpoint URL. By default, the URL **https://login.salesforce.com** is used. This can be changed according to a scenario.
Basic Credential Name	This field specifies the name of the?User Credentials?artifact that contains the credentials for basic authentication. This refers to the user name-password pair used to log in to Salesforce. This pair must be created as a security artifact of User Credential type and subsequently referred to in the adapter.
Security Token Alias	This field specifies the name of the Secure Parameter artifact that contains the security token needed to connect to Salesforce. This property enables the system to fetch the security token from the keystore for authentication. This field can be omitted if the IP has been whitelisted in Salesforce. To whitelist an IP address, add the IP range in the **Network Access** section in the **Security Control** menu in Salesforce.

Table 9.7 Fields in the Connection Tab

Field Name	Description
OAuth Credential Name	Specifies the name of the User Credentials?artifact that contains the Salesforce's OAuth Consumer Key-Consumer Secret pair. Configure the **Consumer Key** as **User** and the **Consumer Secret** as the password in the security artifact of type **User Credential**. Then refer to it in the adapter's **Connection** tab.
Connection Timeout (in ms)	Specifies the connection timeout in milliseconds. The timeout allows control of the wait time until the connection is established.
Response Timeout (in ms)	Specifies the response timeout in milliseconds. The timeout allows control of the wait time until the message is received.
Lazy Authentication	Enables OAuth token retrieval or generation until the first API call. Note that when using a splitter with parallel processing, it's important to disable **Lazy Authentication** as this feature isn't supported with parallel processing.

Table 9.7 Fields in the Connection Tab (Cont.)

Now that the connectivity toward the Salesforce instance has been configured, it's time to configure the **Processing** tab. The Processing tab enables the developer to specify the details of the operation to be performed in Salesforce. In our case, we want to perform a SOQL query. SOQL is the query language that powers our interactions with the Salesforce database. See Table 9.8 for more details on the semantics of the fields available in Figure 9.53.

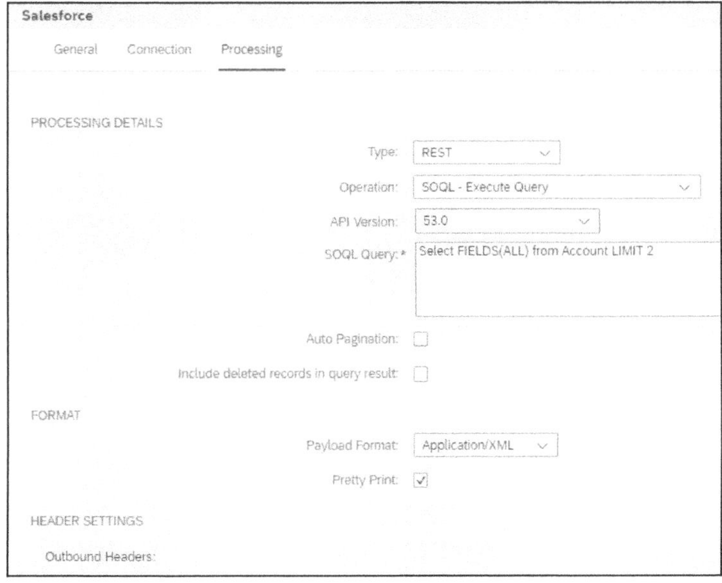

Figure 9.53 Configuration of the Processing Tab

Field Name	Description
Type	Specifies the category of the API to be used to interact with Salesforce. Possible values include **REST**, **REST Bulk**, and **REST Place Order**.
Operation	Specifies the type of action desired to be executed in Salesforce.
API Version	Specifies the version of the Salesforce API. Note that the Salesforce API version can be overwritten by manually entering the Salesforce API version.
SOQL Query	Specifies the SOQL query to be executed in Salesforce. SOQL is an adaptation of the well-known SQL query language. A simple `SELECT ID, Name FROM Account` provides all the ID and names for all account records in Salesforce.
Payload Format	Specifies the format of the request message to be sent to and the response to be returned from Salesforce. Possible values include **Application/XML** and **Application/JSON**. Note that the default value is **Application/XML**.
Pretty Print	Nicely formats the XML payload and improves its readability.

Table 9.8 Fields of the Processing Tab

After successfully configuring the **Processing** tab, you're ready to deploy your iFlow. When the iFlow is deployed, it can now be called externally using a client such as Postman. Figure 9.54 showcases the results after calling the iFlow from Postman.

Figure 9.54 Calling the iFlow via Postman

You've now called Salesforce from Cloud Integration to retrieve a few customers' (accounts) records. Let's next explore how to connect to Amazon Web Services using the AmazonWebService adapter.

9.6.2 Connecting to Amazon Web Services

Amazon Web Services (AWS) is a comprehensive and broadly adopted cloud that offers various services from data centers globally. Some of the most used services in AWS include the following:

- **Amazon Simple Storage Service (S3)**
  S3 is an object storage service that offers industry-leading scalability, data availability, security, and performance. Customers of all sizes and industries can use Amazon S3 to store and protect any amount of data for a range of use cases, such as data lakes, enterprise applications, and big data analytics.
- **Amazon Simple Queue Service (SQS)**
  SQS is a service that lets you send, store, and receive messages between software components at any volume, without losing messages or requiring other services to be available. As the name suggests, it uses queues.
- **Amazon Simple Notification Service (SNS)**
  SNS is a managed service that provides message delivery from publishers to subscribers (also known as producers and consumers). Publishers communicate asynchronously with subscribers by sending messages to a topic, which is a logical access point and communication channel. Clients can subscribe to the SNS topic and receive published messages using a supported endpoint type, such as Amazon Data, Amazon SQS, HTTP, email, mobile push notifications, and mobile text messages (SMS).
- **Amazon Simple Workflow Service (Amazon SWF)**
  Amazon SWF provides a way to build, run, and scale background jobs that have parallel or sequential steps. With Amazon SWF, you can coordinate work across distributed components, tracking the state of tasks.
- If a customer needs to exchange data between their SAP landscape and any of the preceding services (S3, SQS, SNS, or SWF), Cloud Integration can be used as the IPaaS of choice. Let's explore some of the high-level features of the AmazonWebServices adapter for SAP Integration Suite:
- Availability of the AWS S3 protocol to poll files from AWS S3 service:
  - Support for patterns in the file name
  - Possibility to archive processed files to the same bucket as part of the post-processing step
  - Possibility to archive processed files to a different bucket as part of the post-processing step

  - Possibility to sort files based on file name, file size, and timestamp
  - Capability to retrieve additional metadata maintained for the file on the S3 bucket with multiple attributes able to be retrieved at the same time
  - Support for server-side decryption
  - Dynamic properties and headers support for most properties
  - Functionality to generate pre-signed URLs
- Availability of the AWS SQS protocol to receive a message from an AWS SQS queue:
  - Support for standard and FIFO queues
  - Possibility to keep or delete the message from the queue after reading as part of the post-processing step
  - Possibility to keep a message in the queue after processing.
  - Capability to retrieve additional metadata maintained for a message on the SQS queue with multiple attributes able to be retrieved at the same time
- Availability of the AWS S3 protocol to push files into AWS S3 service:
  - Option to append timestamp and message ID to the file name during the creation process
  - Option to select a storage class
  - Different handling options for existing S3 bucket files
  - Option to upload attachments to the S3 bucket
  - Server-side encryption
  - Possibility to add multiple custom metadata to the file while storing it
  - Capability to read a particular file from the S3 bucket using the Read operation of the receiver adapter
- Availability of the AWS SQS protocol to send a message to the AWS SQS queue:
  - Support for standard and FIFO queues
  - Option to add multiple message attributes while writing a message to the queue
  - For the standard queue, the option to provide delay seconds to avoid subsequent processing by any other consumer
  - For the FIFO queue, the option to provide message deduplication ID and message group ID
- Availability of the AWS SNS protocol to push real-time notification messages to interested subscribers over multiple delivery protocols:
  - Support for standard topics
  - Option to provide identical payload for all consumers
  - Option to provide custom payload for different consumers

- Option to format the response in XML and JSON formats
- Option to provide multiple message attributes
- Availability of the AWS SWF protocol to provide full control over implementing tasks and coordinating them:
  - Support for multiple operations that can be selected from a predefined list
  - Option to determine request and response format; currently with support for JSON

To illustrate the use of the adapter, let's use a simple scenario that includes the development of an iFlow to read a file from an S3 bucket and write it to a SQS queue. Given that you're already familiar with creating iFlows in Cloud Integration, we'll focus this discussion on showcasing how to configure the AmazonWebServices adapter. The scenario to be built is depicted in Figure 9.55.

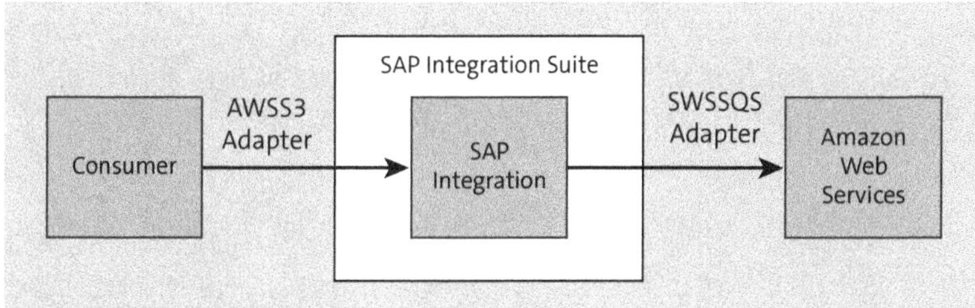

Figure 9.55 Connection of Cloud Integration to Amazon Web Services

As shown in Figure 9.55, for this example, we'll use the Amazon Web Service S3 (**AWS S3**) sender adapter to read files from an S3 Bucket. Furthermore, an Amazon Web Service (SQS) receiver adapter needs to be used in the iFlow to write the file content to an SQS queue.

Notes

The AmazonWebService adapter for SAP Integration Suite might not be available by default on your tenant. However, you can make it available by downloading it on SAP Service Marketplace via *http://s-prs.co/v576052*.

The package of the adapter includes the documentation explaining how to deploy the adapter.

Build the iFlow in Cloud Integration, similar to the one presented in Figure 9.56. Note that we used both the sender (to pick up files from an S3 bucket) and receiver adapters (to write the file into an SQS queue).

Figure 9.57 shows more configuration details of the sender adapter. It specifies how the connection part of the adapter can be filled in.

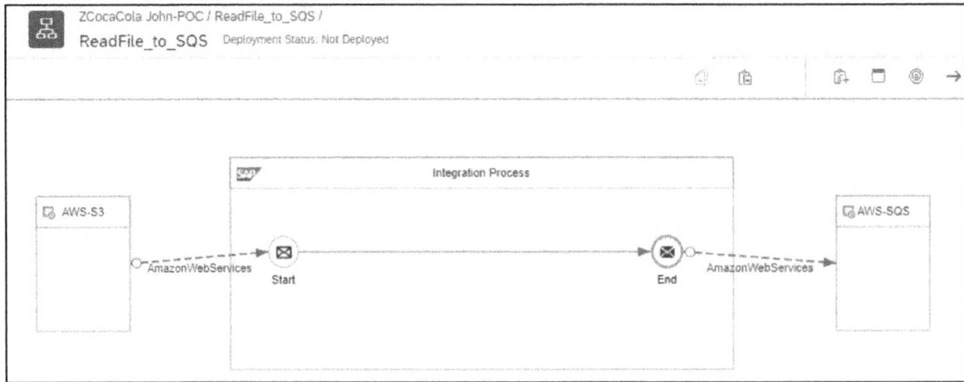

Figure 9.56 Example iFlow

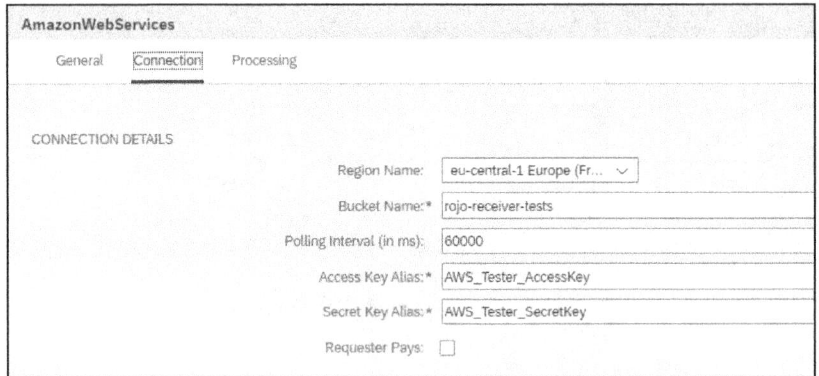

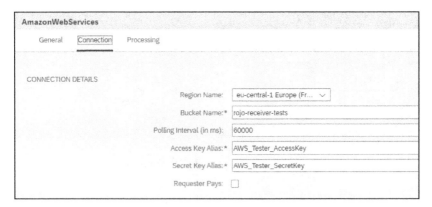

Figure 9.57 Configuration of the Sender Connection Tab (S3)

Table 9.9 explains each of the parameters on the **Connection** tab.

Field Name	Description
Region Name	AWS region where the bucket resides. Select the region from the preconfigured list. If the region doesn't exist in the preconfigured list, then you can manually enter the region name.
Bucket Name	Name of the bucket on AWS where the sender adapter should poll files from. Example: AWS-Sender-Bucket. Note: The bucket name should not contain "." characters.
Polling Interval (in ms)	Polling interval in milliseconds. Default value: **60000**

Table 9.9 Fields of the Connection Tab

Field Name	Description
Access Key Alias	Name of the secured parameter that stores the AWS Access Key. The values can be read dynamically.
Secret Key Alias	Name of the secured parameter that stores the AWS Secret Key. The values can be read dynamically.
Requester Pays	Select this option if the request should pay for data transfer and the request. Note: To use this feature, the **Requestor Pay** option should be enabled in the AWS bucket. If the **Requestor Pay** option is enabled in the bucket, then it's mandatory to select the checkbox in the adapter.

Table 9.9 Fields of the Connection Tab (Cont.)

Let's now proceed to configure the **Processing** tab of the AmazonWebServices adapter. This section enables you to specify the details of the type of files to be selected from the S3 bucket. As shown in Figure 9.58, we've configured the adapter to pick any files ending with the extension **.txt** from a directory named **myDirectory** in the S3 Bucket.

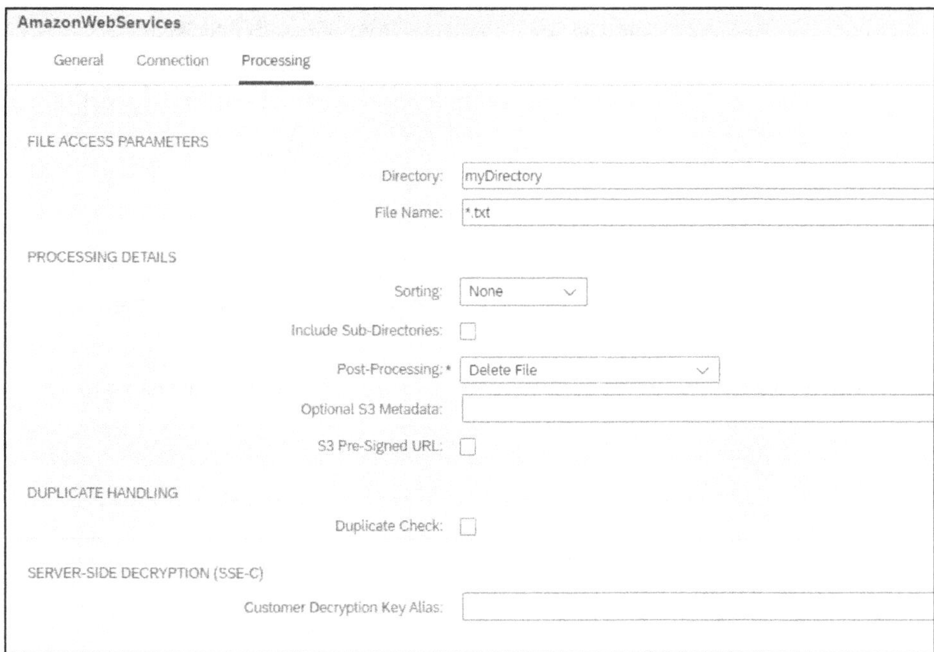

Figure 9.58 Configuration of the Sender Processing Tab (S3)

See Table 9.10 for more details on the semantics of the fields available in Figure 9.58.

Field Name	Description
Directory	The path on the AWS bucket from where the file should be read. Example: Directory/SubDirectory The value can also be read dynamically using a header or property. If left blank, then the adapter will read the root directory.
File Name	The file name to be read. Example: Filename.txt Other supported values include wild card characters: asterisk (*) and question mark (?). An asterisk (*) represents zero or more characters in a string of characters, and a question mark (?) represents any one character. Example: *.xml. The adapter will read all the files where the file name ends with *.xml* or *abc?.xml* and will read all the file names such as *abcd.xml* or *abc1.xml*. When left blank, the adapter will read all the files present in the *S3* directory.
Sorting	The property on which sorting should be done while polling files. The sorting will be done in ascending order of the option selected. Available options include the following: ▪ **File Name**: The sorting is performed based on the file name. ▪ **File Size**: Sorting is performed based on file size. ▪ **Time Stamp**: Sorting is performed based on the timestamp. ▪ **None (default)**: No sorting is performed. This is the default option for sorting.
Include Sub-Directories	Select this checkbox to read all the files in the directory and subdirectory.
Execute Post-Processing When Message Successfully Processed	Select this checkbox to execute the post-processing step only when the file is successfully processed by the exchange.
Post-Processing	Specify the action that should be taken after the file has been processed. Available options include the following: ▪ **Delete File**: Select this option to delete the file after processing. This is the default option. ▪ **Keep File and Process Again**: Select this option to keep the file in the source directory and process again. ▪ **Move File to an Archive Directory**: Select this option to move the file to an archive directory. After selecting this option, specify the archive directory. It's also possible to add a timestamp in the archived file.

Table 9.10 Fields of the Sender Processing Tab for S3

Field Name	Description
Post-Processing (Cont.)	■ **Copy file to an Archive Bucket**: Select this option to copy the file to another bucket. After selecting this option, specify the archive bucket and archive directory. It's also possible to add a timestamp in the archived file. ■ **Move the file to an Archive Bucket**: Select this option to move the file to another bucket. After selecting this option, specify the archive bucket and archive directory. It's also possible to add a timestamp in the archived file.
Optional S3 Metadata	Specify the metadata to be populated from S3 object metadata. Multiple metadata can be specified and separated by a comma (,). If specified, then a property with the same name will be created in Cloud Integration. Example: If the file in the S3 bucket has metadata named "MyMetadata" associated with it, to retrieve the metadata in the iFlow, "MyMetadata" has to be specified in the adapter. During execution, a property with the name "MyMetadata" will be created in Cloud Integration and can be accessed using the expression `${property.MyMetadata}`.
S3 Pre-Signed URL	Select this option to generate a pre-signed URL. Select the HTTP method and the expiration duration of the pre-signed URL. The pre-signed URL is attached to a property with the name `S3PreSignedURL`. The value of the pre-signed URL can be accessed using the expression `${property. S3PreSignedURL}`.
HTTP Method of Pre-Signed URL	Select the HTTP method that should be used for the pre-signed URL. Choose from the following options: ■ GET ■ DELETE ■ HEAD ■ PATCH ■ POST ■ PUT
Expired Duration of Pre-Signed URL (secs)	Specify the duration in seconds for the pre-signed URL to expire. The default value is **86400**.
Duplicate Check	Enable this option to avoid duplicate message processing for the period, which will be specified by the **Message Expiration Period** field.

Table 9.10 Fields of the Sender Processing Tab for S3 (Cont.)

Field Name	Description
Duplication Key	Select the key on which the duplication check should be performed from the following options: ■ **S3 Object Key** ■ **S3 File Name**
Message Expiration Period (in seconds)	Specify the time (in seconds) for which the message key will be stored for the duplicate check.
Customer Decryption Key Alias	Specify the name of the secured parameter that contains the decryption key for Amazon S3 to decrypt data.

Table 9.10 Fields of the Sender Processing Tab for S3 (Cont.)

Now that we're ready with the sender adapter, let's configure the SQS queue on the receiver adapter to write the file to the queue. Figure 9.59 shows the configuration of the **Connection** tab of the receiver adapter. In our case, we've configured the adapter to write the file in a queue named **TestQueue**.

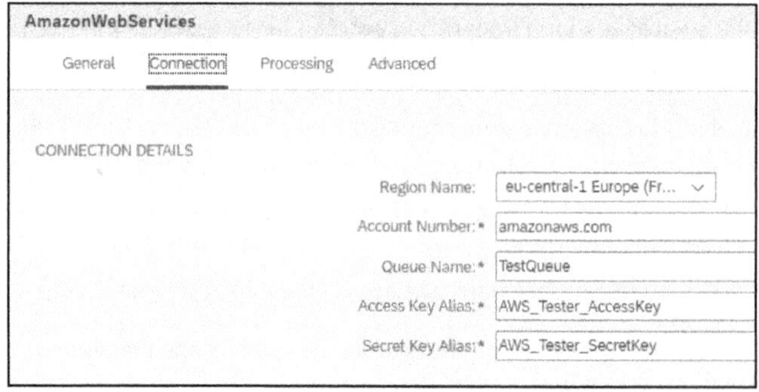

Figure 9.59 Configuration of the Receiver Connection Tab (SQS)

For more details on the semantics of the fields available in Figure 9.59, see Table 9.11.

Field name	Description
Region Name	AWS region where the bucket resides. Select the region from the preconfigured list. If the region doesn't exist in the preconfigured list, you can manually enter the region name.
Account Number	The 12-digit AWS account number for the queue. Example: 123456789012
Queue Name	The AWS SQS queue name where the adapter should poll.

Table 9.11 Fields of the Receiver Connection Tab for SQS

Field name	Description
Polling Interval (in ms)	The polling interval time (in ms).
Access Key Alias	Name of the secured parameter that stores the AWS Access Key. The values can be read dynamically.
Secret Key Alias	Name of the secured parameter that stores the AWS Secret Key. The values can be read dynamically.

Table 9.11 Fields of the Receiver Connection Tab for SQS (Cont.)

Congratulations, you can now deploy the iFlow and will start picking up all files with the extension *.txt* from the specified bucket and folder.

9.7 Summary

In this chapter, we introduced you to the capabilities and features available with Open Connectors. You learned about the connectors catalog, how connectors work, and how to use them. The chapter then explored common resources.

This chapter also explained how to use Cloud Integration in combination with Open Connectors to connect to a variety of third-party applications easily and consistently. We also walked through a practical example to illustrate how to use Cloud Integration and Open Connectors together.

Some topics related to Open Connectors haven't been discussed in the chapter (e.g., formulas, query language, events, etc.). But we've covered enough for the main focus of this book: Cloud Integration.

Finally, we introduced some new adapters enabling Cloud Integration to easily connect with some third-party systems. We've showcased both the Salesforce and AmazonWeb-Services adapters using two simple scenarios.

With the information you've learned in this chapter, you can now easily tackle those other subjects on your own. In the next chapter, we'll explore different security topics in Cloud Integration.

Chapter 10
Cloud Integration Security

Using an integration platform in the cloud implies that your data is processed on servers outside the boundaries of your organization and thus beyond your influence. This assumption raises questions about how secure the data hosted by the software provider actually is and how this data can be protected. In this chapter, we'll summarize the measures undertaken by SAP to protect your data at the highest level and show you what you can do to maximize the security level of your integration scenarios.

A fundamental characteristic of using cloud software, in contrast to on-premise software, is the fact that you, the customer, hand over some of the responsibility for your data to the software provider—in this context, SAP. In particular, using an integration platform as a service (iPaaS) implies that your data is processed on servers outside your organization. Your data is also potentially stored on servers hosted by your cloud infrastructure provider. Therefore, the topic of security is of a fundamental and existential importance.

This chapter will show you that your data is in safe hands by answering two questions: How secure is your data passing through Cloud Integration during the execution of an integration scenario, and what measures has SAP implemented to reduce the risk of malicious actions taken on your data?

In Section 10.1 and Section 10.2, we'll cover the following:

- Security mechanisms that are already in place (i.e., inherently provided by the technical infrastructure)
- Security levels that are guaranteed by the processes associated with the development and use of Cloud Integration

Section 10.3 covers the topic of user management, which will be your first task when you start working with Cloud Integration. In this section, you'll learn how to set up dedicated permissions for people involved in an integration project.

Section 10.4 shows how you can use the tools provided by Cloud Integration to configure integration scenarios with the highest possible protection for the involved data. Finally, Section 10.5 explains how to manage the lifecycle of keys in the tenant keystore, a central component required to set up secure integration scenarios.

The tutorials provided in this chapter focus on the security-related aspects of the described integration scenarios. We won't repeat each step required to set up the scenario because, after walking through the previous chapters, you're now an integration expert who knows how to design various kinds of integration flows (iFlows). An exception will be tutorials where we introduce certain security-related iFlow steps (Section 10.4.7) or adapters that we haven't introduced yet (e.g., the Twitter adapter in Section 10.4.5).

10.1 Technical System Landscape

In this section, we'll discuss the security level that is imposed by the technical system landscape. We'll first cover the security of the software architecture and the network design. Then, we'll quickly glance at physical data security, which is provided by the fact that the workers that process your messages operate out of data centers run by the cloud infrastructure provider, which is either SAP, in which case you would use Cloud Integration in the SAP BTP, Neo environment, or companies such as Amazon or Microsoft, in which case, you would use Cloud Integration in the SAP BTP, Cloud Foundry environment (see Chapter 2, Section 2.1). Next, we'll discuss how *data at rest*—that is, data stored at various steps during the processing of a message—is protected by the infrastructure. Finally, we'll close this section by showing you how data protection and privacy are ensured when using Cloud Integration.

10.1.1 Architecture

In this section, we'll focus on aspects of the architecture that make Cloud Integration a secure cloud-based integration platform. In Chapter 2, Section 2.1, we showed how a clustered, containerized design establishes Cloud Integration as an integration platform shared by many participants that allows the flexible allocation of resources for different participants. We also introduced the basic concept of tenant isolation, which ensures that the platform resources assigned to different participants are strictly isolated from each other. Each participant has an SAP Business Technology Platform (SAP BTP) subaccount and tenant assigned to it. On each tenant, an individual (containerized) integration runtime is installed, which is strictly separated from those of the other tenants.

In other words, the data and processes for each customer are kept apart. Further, in a more general sense, a customer like you can use different tenants for different purposes (e.g., test and production). The architecture of Cloud Integration makes sure that the processes and data belonging to those different use cases are strictly isolated from each other.

We'll now take a closer look at the architecture and show how tenant isolation is achieved. We'll also introduce you to the concepts behind the secure communication between the involved participants and technical components.

In Chapter 2, Section 2.1, we introduced the architecture of Cloud Integration and glanced at the internal structure of the integration platform. We'll now address the following additional questions:

- How is user access to Cloud Integration restricted, and how is the platform protected against unauthorized access?
- How is *data at rest* (stored data) protected?
- How is *data in transit* (data exchanged between the participants and Cloud Integration) protected?
- How is secure communication implemented between the participants and the involved components of the cluster?

Figure 10.1 shows a high-level view of the architecture from Chapter 2, enriched with information on the security protocols used for the involved communication paths.

Let's walk through Figure 10.1 and discuss the security-related aspects of the architecture.

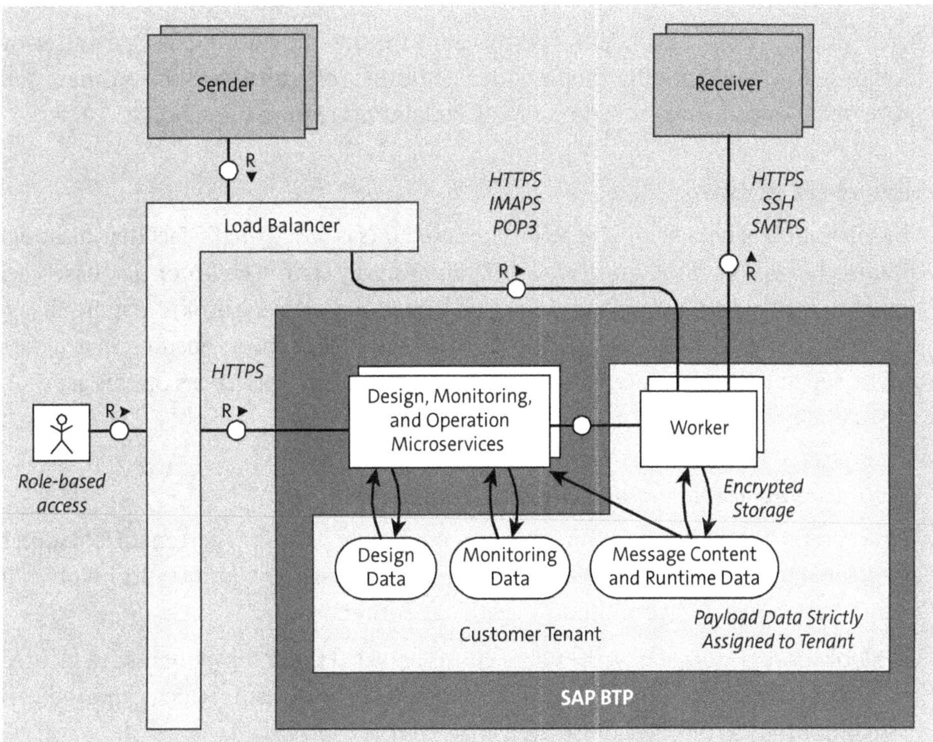

Figure 10.1 High-Level Architecture with Technical Connections, Transport-Level Security Options, and Persistence Steps

Role-Based User Access and User Management

Let's begin with the interaction points for dialog users. Access to Cloud Integration in the context of specific tasks (e.g., deploying integration content on a tenant) is always controlled by authorizations based on user-to-role assignments. User-to-role assignments are accomplished through the SAP BTP cockpit, which we introduced in Chapter 2, Section 2.2, and Figure 2.8.

With regard to user management and authorization, all platform resources are strictly isolated: in other words, a user with specific permissions on a test cluster might not have the same permissions on a productive cluster.

Each customer is given access to one or more subaccounts (by default, to one test and one productive account). The clustered design of Cloud Integration and the role-based access to the platform ensure that, first, each subaccount is reserved for a dedicated set of users who are completely isolated from the user setup associated with other subaccounts of the platform. In larger companies, users assigned to a test subaccount will be associated with persons other than those assigned to the productive subaccount.

Second, the SAP BTP user management capabilities allow you to assign to the users of each subaccount granular role templates or role collections (specific groups of roles) that are tailored to the different sets of tasks that come into play in an integration project. We'll cover this topic in more detail in Section 10.3.

Furthermore, you can also define permissions on the integration package and iFlow level in such a way that only people with a dedicated role can access the business data processed by a defined set of iFlows. We'll explain this feature in Section 10.3.4.

Secure Data Storage

The separation of data belonging to different tenants is based on the fact that, although different tenants of Cloud Integration might physically share a common database, each tenant stores its data in a separate logical database or a message broker instance if Java Message Service (JMS) queues are used. This logical separation ensures that data is strictly separated and isolated per tenant. In Section 10.1.3, we'll focus on this aspect in more detail.

Secure Communication among Technical Components

The separation of platform resources covers more than data storage; tenant isolation is also related to the processing of data and the way the various components involved in an integration scenario communicate with each other.

Let's look more closely at how the connections between these components are secured. The Cloud Integration runtime is established as a set of workers, which can have various connections to remote components.

A common protocol that can be used for both inbound communication (when Cloud Integration is addressed by an incoming request) and outbound communication (when Cloud Integration sends a message to a receiver) is HTTPS. This protocol comes with Transport Layer Security (TLS).

For inbound HTTPS requests, we first need to differentiate between requests from the user interfaces (UIs) to the **Design, Monitoring, and Operation Microservices** (e.g., when a user connects to the tenant using the Web UI, as shown in Figure 10.1), and, second, requests from external sender systems (to get messages processed). In both cases, inbound communication is forwarded to the runtime component of Cloud Integration (worker) by a load balancer. As a result, the load balancer terminates incoming TLS requests and establishes new ones.

The **Design, Monitoring, and Operation Microservices** shape was described in detail in Chapter 2, Section 2.1.2. See also the Note box about microservices in Chapter 2, Section 2.1.6. In Section 10.4.2, we'll describe how HTTPS based on TLS works in more detail.

Additional Protocols Supported

Note that additional protocols are supported by Cloud Integration. For a summary of supported protocols, check out Table 10.3 later in Section 10.4.2.

10.1.2 Network Infrastructure

In this section, we'll cover the security aspects of the *network design*. Let's consider that a *network* is a setup of physical machines or virtual machines (VMs) that communicate with each other in a well-defined and controlled way. A network comprises different *network segments*, and all components within one network segment are on the same trust level. The trust level determines the kind of communication allowed, based on the implemented protocols and security settings. As such, the specific design of the network determines how the various components of the Cloud Integration infrastructure are arranged in the network and how these components are protected by various measures, such as firewalls.

Figure 10.2 shows the network design of Cloud Integration from a bird's-eye view. For simplicity, we omitted use cases using protocols such as Secure Shell File Transfer Protocol (SFTP), Java Database Connectivity (JDBC), and Advanced Message Queuing Protocol (AMQP), which aren't connected via the load balancer.

As shown earlier in Figure 10.1, external components (sender and receiver systems as well as dialog users on the customer side) access the Cloud Integration platform from the internet. In terms of the network view, the internet is a large and untrusted network. The components of Cloud Integration that process sensitive customer data can't directly be called by components from the internet. (The intervening load balancer terminates each inbound TLS request.) After the load balancer has established a new TLS request, the external call is forwarded to the **Design, Monitoring, and Operation Microservices** or a worker (assigned to the tenant) that actually processes the request. As described earlier in Section 10.1.1, this pattern applies both for sender components that call Cloud Integration from the internet and for dialog users that connect to Cloud Integration through a web browser (when, e.g., a user designs iFlows with the Web UI). In terms of the network design, the load balancer resides in the demilitarized zone (DMZ). A common practice is for organizations to avoid exposing their external-facing services directly to the internet and instead locate these services in a DMZ.

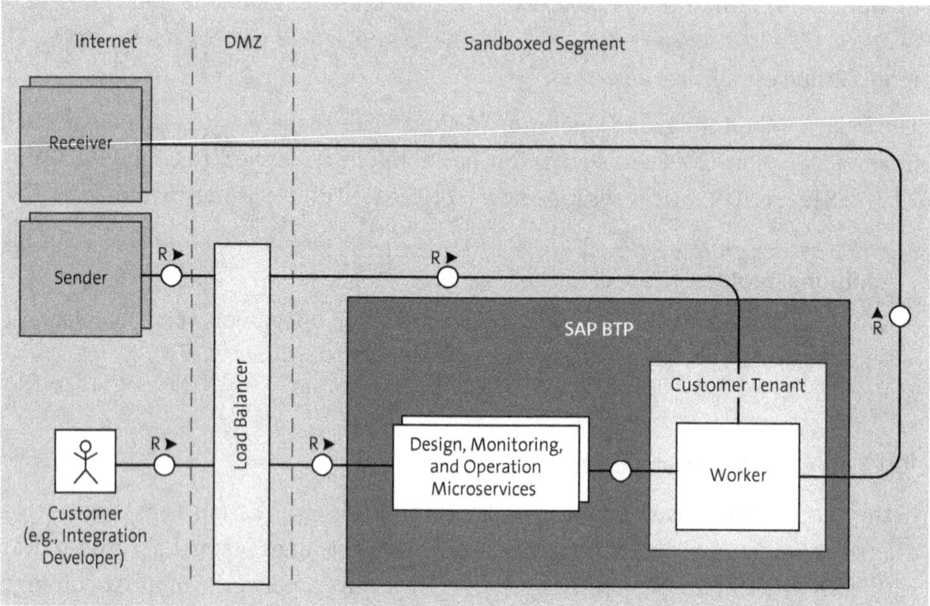

Figure 10.2 High-Level Network Design of Cloud Integration

The workers that process customer data aren't only shielded from the outside world. As shown in Figure 10.2, the workers in a Cloud Integration cluster reside in a separate network segment: the *sandboxed segment*. Sandboxing means, in its most general sense, separating IT processes from each other. In terms of Cloud Integration, *sandboxed* means that, to a certain extent, each worker, in its own sandbox or micro-network, runs in isolation from other workers. In other words, each worker is shielded from other workers in the same network segment because sandboxes can't interfere with or even "see" each other. This design ensures that all components in the sandboxed segment are strictly isolated from components in other sandboxes.

We've restricted our discussion so far by saying "to a certain extent": to be more precise, let's limit and refine our discussion with the fact that a microservice (as indicated by the **Design, Monitoring, and Operation Microservices** shape in Figure 10.2) can interfere with other workers assigned to the same tenant ID. For example, when a user requests monitoring data through the Web UI, the associated monitoring microservice must communicate with the worker overseeing the processing of the message to retrieve the relevant data. However, workers themselves can't interfere with other workers, and workers assigned to different tenants are strictly isolated from each other, as mentioned earlier.

10.1.3 Data Storage Security

As an integration platform, Cloud Integration acts like a *transit place* for data, as its task is essentially to receive, process, and forward messages. However, different kinds of data associated with message processing can also be stored at various steps during message processing. In this section, we summarize by which measures *data at rest* is protected at a maximum level.

As described in Chapter 2, Section 2.1.2, and Table 2.2, the following types of data can be stored during runtime:

- **Message content**
  Integration developers can configure dedicated steps of an iFlow to store message content temporarily (by default, 90 days). The message can either be stored using the **Persist** step to make it available after the message processing run, for instance, for auditing purposes. Other options for temporary data storage can be achieved by using the data store **Write** step or by using JMS queues. In contrast to data stored with the **Persist** step, data stored in the data store or JMS queues is available for subsequent processing steps.
- **Monitoring data**
  The message processing log (MPL) records the overall status of the message processing run. MPLs can be accessed on the **Monitor** page of the Web UI by users that have the appropriate permission.

The tenant isolation concept ensures that data belonging to different participants is strictly isolated from each other.

Message content stored in a database can be encrypted with an encryption key, which is generated automatically and is unique for each tenant using Advanced Encryption Standard (AES) and a key length of 256 bits. Encryption keys are stored in a different database than the encrypted data.

In addition, with regard to access permissions, data stored in different tenants is strictly isolated: an administrator on tenant A won't have the permissions to access data stored on tenant B. This rule also applies to employees of your cloud infrastructure provider. Furthermore, those people will have no access to data stored in customer tenants.

In any case, the principle of *least privilege* is always applied, which means that users are limited to the minimum set of privileges (permissions) required to perform a necessary task.

Using the JDBC adapter, you can connect an iFlow with a database system on SAP BTP and store data permanently in this database. Two databases are supported: SAP Adaptive Server Enterprise (SAP ASE) or SAP HANA. These database systems can be connected and reside either in the same subaccount or in different subaccounts other than the subaccount assigned to the Cloud Integration tenant. In these cases, access to the database is protected through an authentication mechanism. We showed you in Chapter 6 how to set up the connection from the Cloud Integration tenant to such a database system.

10.1.4 Data Protection and Privacy

Data protection is always related to legal requirements and privacy concerns. In this section, we'll first briefly summarize how and when data sensitivity should be considered in an integration project. Second, we'll provide information on the specific measures taken to protect such data within Cloud Integration.

Generally, customer data processed by and stored within the Cloud Integration infrastructure is classified as *confidential*, in the sense that it requires (and receives) the highest level of protection.

What Data Must Be Protected

Table 10.1 provides examples of kinds of sensitive data to consider at various steps in the Cloud Integration lifecycle.

Phase	Kind of Data
Message processing	Data contained in customer messages and processed on a Cloud Integration component at runtime is usually business data that can contain personal information, such as names or addresses. The measures to protect this data have been explained in Section 10.1.3.
Monitoring	The MPL records the executed processing steps for a message. Therefore, information about customer activities can be derived out of it (e.g., through the frequency of message processing). This data is only accessible per tenant (as subject to tenant isolation) and for users with dedicated permissions.
Audit log	Certain events and system changes (e.g., deletion of temporarily stored data or the undeployment of integration artifacts) are logged during the operation of Cloud Integration. Audit logs are generated for tenant administrators. Access to audit log data is protected by specific roles. For more information, see the following section.

Table 10.1 Examples of Customer Data Stored during the Cloud Integration Lifecycle

Phase	Kind of Data
Dialog user logs in to the Cloud Integration Web UI	When customers log on to their tenant through the Web UI, they'll register to the SAP ID service. In this case, certain data is collected, and personal data (names and email addresses) also comes into play. The SAP ID service is a special SAP BTP tenant (managed by SAP) that is used as a default identity provider for SAP Cloud applications (see also Section 10.3). Note that you can also use another identity provider.

Table 10.1 Examples of Customer Data Stored during the Cloud Integration Lifecycle (Cont.)

We'll now provide an overview of measures that are taken by SAP to protect this data.

Audit Logs

To increase data protection, access to data and other incidents are recorded in an audit log. Audit logs are generated, first, for administrators at SAP to enable them to monitor these incidents and prevent malicious actions. These audit logs provide a chronological record of events, for example, configuration changes to the system (namely, iFlow changes or content deployment tasks). Logging such data enables SAP to perform regular audits to meet the regulatory compliance requirements.

Audit logs are generated for each tenant, which means that log data related to different customers is separated. In addition, strict access control is imposed, and no log modifications by malicious users are possible.

When you use Cloud Integration in the SAP BTP, Neo environment, audit logs are displayed in the **Monitor** page of the Web UI. Such information is retained for 30 days and then deleted automatically. To view audit logs, the user must have the right roles assigned. In a future version of Cloud Integration, these audit logs might also become available in the SAP BTP, Cloud Foundry environment. More information on how you can access these audit logs can be found in Chapter 7, Section 7.5.1.

European General Data Protection Regulation

Cloud Integration has established the necessary processes and the infrastructure to comply with the *General Data Protection Regulation* (*GDPR*), which came into effect in the European Union (EU) on May 25, 2018. For more information, check out the documentation for SAP BTP at *http://s-prs.co/v576053*.

Data Protection in the EU

More information about data protection in the EU can be found at the following:

- EUR-Lex, "General Data Protection Regulation" (*http://s-prs.co/507783*)
- European Commission, "Data Protection" (*http://s-prs.co/507784*)

10.1.5 Malware Scanner

As an integration developer, you can upload various design time artifacts to your Cloud Integration tenant. These include integration artifacts such as iFlows and supporting resources such as Web Services Description Language (WSDL) definitions, scripts, XML Schema Definitions (XSDs). A file affected by malware can compromise the security of the entire platform. To prevent this vulnerability Cloud Integration provides a Malware Scanner to scan any uploaded file. Note that, by default, the Malware Scanner is switched off.

To switch on this feature, navigate to the **Integrations** option under the **Settings** menu as shown in Figure 10.3.

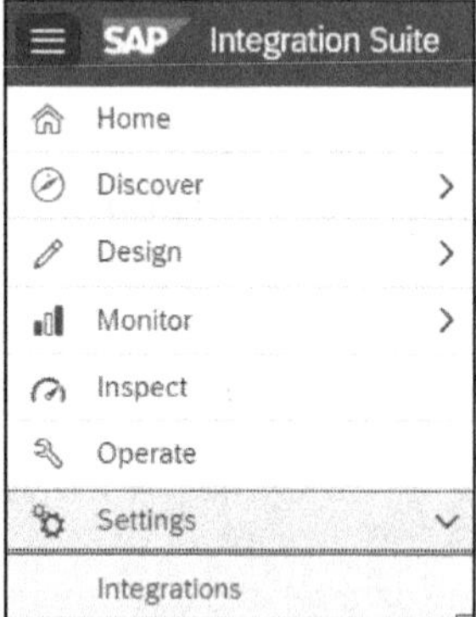

Figure 10.3 Settings Menu for Cloud Integration

From the **Settings** menu, navigate to the **Malware Scanner** tab, as shown in Figure 10.4. Notice that, by default, the **Malware Scan** checkbox is unchecked.

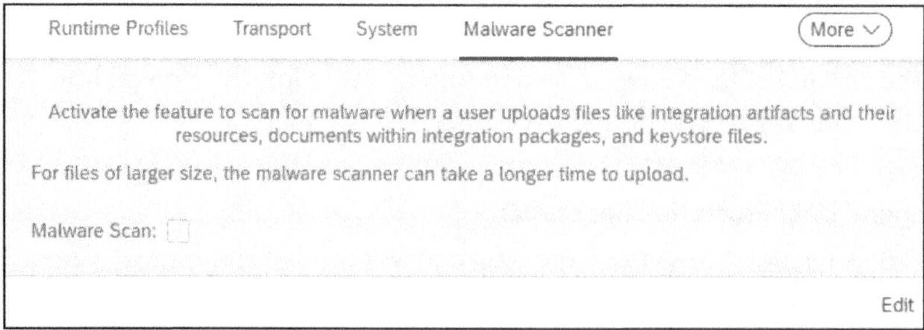

Figure 10.4 Malware Scanner Tab in the Settings Menu

To enable the scanning, click **Edit** in the bottom right of the screen, check the checkbox, and click **Save**. From now on, any file uploaded to the tenant will be scanned for malware. As you can imagine, this would add latency to the upload time if you have large file sizes.

Note

At the time of writing this book, the Malware scanner doesn't scan JDBC drivers.

10.1.6 Physical Data Security

Now that you understand the security inherently provided by the architecture, the network infrastructure, and data protection guidelines, let's look more closely at *physical data security*. Then, we'll look at how processes related to an integration project are protected.

The workers that process customer messages run on servers located in various regions worldwide. Cloud Integration runs in the SAP BTP, Cloud Foundry environment and in the SAP BTP, Neo environment (refer to Chapter 1). Data exchanged in the course of integration scenarios is technically stored and processed within an infrastructure of an organization such as Microsoft or Amazon (if the SAP BTP, Cloud Foundry environment is used) or on servers located in SAP data centers (if the SAP BTP, Neo environment is used). Customer data is also stored in the cloud provider's infrastructure for a certain time.

These world-class data centers meet the highest security standards. For example, SAP data centers rely on redundant power supplies, physical access is protected by biometric-access control mechanisms, and there is 24-hour surveillance. A security and facility support team is onsite 24/7, and locations are monitored by hundreds of surveillance cameras with digital recording capabilities. Buildings are protected against fire by ceilings, walls, and doors that provide 90 minutes of fire resistance. All these measures are checked and audited on a regular basis.

10.2 Processes

In this section, we'll focus on various processes around the development, provisioning, and usage of Cloud Integration. We'll demonstrate how these processes fulfill the highest security standards.

First, SAP has certified that the development, maintenance, and operations of Cloud Integration comply with many standards, including but not limited to the following:

- SAP Business Technology Platform ISO/IEC 27001:2013
- SAP Business Technology Platform C5 Audit Report 2023 H1
- SAP Business Technology Platform SOC 1 (ISAE3402) Audit Report 2023 H2
- SAP Business Technology Platform SOC 2 (ISAE3000) Audit Report 2023 H2
- SAP Business Technology Platform ISO/IEC 22301:2019
- SAP Business Technology Platform TISAX

You can find these certificates at *http://s-prs.co/507785*. On this page, click the **Offering Name** filter, and select **SAP Business Technology Platform** from the list of offerings. This list of certifications is renewed annually or half yearly depending on the certification requirements.

We'll now walk you through the security-relevant aspects of the processes that are in place.

10.2.1 Software Development Process

Cloud Integration software, like all SAP software, is developed in compliance with the SAP Security Development Lifecycle (SDLC), which helps build security into the software from the beginning and includes the following features:

- Test-driven development, including source code reviews, architecture audits, and security scans. In addition, quality gates must be passed through on a monthly basis. An example quality gate is scanning the source code for security issues (checking the source code, identifying possible security issues and gaps, and helping developers fix any issues that may arise).
- Threat modeling techniques are selectively applied, which means that possible security gaps in individual components of the architecture are identified and modeled in advance. In this way, possible vulnerabilities in the system can be anticipated and taken into consideration when designing the software.
- Open-source components being used are scanned for security vulnerabilities based on a risk assessment process.

The requirements imposed by the SDLC on the software development process are dynamically adapted and updated regularly based on publicly accessible sources that provide information on known software vulnerabilities (e.g., *Common Weakness Enumeration* or *Common Vulnerabilities and Exposures*). For more details on this topic, go to *http://s-prs.co/v576054*.

10.2.2 Operating the Cloud Infrastructure and Providing and Updating the Software

Providing and operating cloud software has two aspects: first, operating and managing the cloud infrastructure, and, second, providing and updating the software that is deployed on this infrastructure.

In the case of Cloud Integration, the cloud infrastructure is operated by SAP (when we talk about the SAP BTP, Neo environment) or another infrastructure provider (when we talk about the SAP BTP, Cloud Foundry environment). The software, however, is always provided and updated by SAP.

In other words, when Cloud Integration is operated in the SAP BTP, Cloud Foundry environment, SAP (as the software provider) and the infrastructure provider (e.g., Amazon) share responsibilities for tasks related to the provisioning of the software and the management of the underlying cloud infrastructure. This topic is beyond the scope of this book because the detailed setup depends on the infrastructure provider. Nevertheless, in general, you can assume that security responsibilities are shared between software and infrastructure provider in the following way:

- The infrastructure provider operates and controls the host operating system, which involves the virtual system landscape where Cloud Integration is deployed. Additionally, the infrastructure provider, of course, also owns the physical facilities where the operating system is installed, that is, server farms in the data centers. You can expect state-of-the-art security level with regard to the operations and management of these technological layers because SAP collaborates with world-class organizations such as Amazon or Microsoft.

  You can also assume that the infrastructure provider takes certain measures to minimize the risk of malicious actions on the part of personnel who have access to the Cloud Integration platform.
- As the software provider, SAP is responsible for provisioning and updating the Cloud Integration software. As mentioned in Section 10.2.1, the software development process at SAP meets the highest security standards.

When Cloud Integration runs in the SAP BTP, Neo environment, both the infrastructure and the software provisioning processes are managed by one party: SAP. In this case, Cloud Integration is managed and administered by software as a service (SaaS) administrators in a dedicated team at SAP.

When talking about the SAP BTP, Neo environment, we can state that these SAP teams are on duty around the clock. Team members act in the role of SaaS administrator. Although the team oversees administering and operating the infrastructure that backs the integration platform, the permissions granted to these persons are reduced to the bare minimum needed to perform operational tasks—the principle of least privilege. Operations team members, for example, have no permissions to access the content of messages processed on a customer tenant. Monthly audits of the process make sure that the access rights of the involved persons are constantly monitored, reviewed, and strictly controlled. All system-related activities of the team members are logged and can be checked.

When Cloud Integration is operated in the SAP BTP, Cloud Foundry environment, you can assume that comparable measures are taken because we're dealing with world-class cloud infrastructure providers.

Availability of Cloud Integration

To find out on which infrastructure Cloud Integration is available, choose the documentation for SAP BTP at *http://s-prs.co/v576073*, and search for topic "SAP Business Technology Platform Regions" to find the availability of Cloud Integration. At the time of this writing, Cloud Integration is available on the following infrastructures. The list also contains the corresponding website URLs so that you can inform yourself about the infrastructure providers:

- **SAP (SAP BTP, Neo environment)**
  www.sap.com
- **Amazon Web Services (SAP BTP, Cloud Foundry environment)**
  https://aws.amazon.com
- **Microsoft Azure (SAP BTP, Cloud Foundry environment)**
  https://azure.microsoft.com
- **Google Cloud (SAP BTP, Cloud Foundry environment)**
  https://cloud.google.com/?hl=en
- **Alibaba Cloud (SAP BTP, Cloud Foundry environment)**
  www.alibabacloud.com

Finally, providing the tenant is performed by the customer in a self-service function in SAP BTP. To learn more, read the "Self-Service Enablement of Cloud Integration Service on Cloud Foundry Environment" SAP Community blog at *http://s-prs.co/507786*.

10.2.3 Setting Up Secure Connections between the Tenant and Remote Systems

One prerequisite to reliably operating an integration scenario is to set up secure connections between the sender and receiver systems and the Cloud Integration tenant. A core task is the implementation of the required technical trust relationships between the remote systems (sender and receiver) and the tenant. In most cases, this task includes the generation of digital keys and the associated configuration of the keystores of the remote systems and the tenant. Usage of public key technology always requires the exchange of public keys between the administrators of the connected sender and receiver systems and the tenant administrator (as explained in Section 10.4.1).

The tenant administrator is responsible for setting up processes and communication channels that guarantee a reliable way of exchanging security-related material with the administrators of the associated systems.

In other words, the tenant administrator is mainly responsible for managing the required security material for the tenant. However, one private key is still provided by

SAP. Because keys have a limited validity period, this SAP-owned key must be updated on a regular basis by SAP. Note, however, that each change or renewal of a key pair entails the update of the associated public keys implemented in the keystores of the connected remote systems. Therefore, the keystore management functions provided by Cloud Integration ensure that the tenant administrator still keeps control over the activation of updated SAP keys on the tenant (as explained in Section 10.5). To learn more, read the SAP Community blog "Cloud Integration - Activate SAP Keys in Keystore Monitor" (*http://s-prs.co/507787*).

The individual key renewal processes for the different use cases are documented in detail in the documentation for Cloud Integration at *http://s-prs.co/507788*.

10.3 User Administration and Authorization

In the architecture overview of Section 10.1.1, we showed where user management and authorization come into play in the lifecycle of a Cloud Integration project. In this section, you'll learn the basic concepts of user management and authorizations related to Cloud Integration. We'll show you how to manage authorizations for persons involved in an integration project.

User Management and Authorization in the SAP BTP, Neo Environment

Before continuing with this topic, we'd like to point out that user administration and authorization management works quite differently when working in the SAP BTP, Neo environment. This difference is also evident in the UI of the SAP BTP cockpit and in a slight change in the following terminology:

- *Role collections* used in the SAP BTP, Cloud Foundry environment (to tailor groups of individual roles along the needs of typical personas) correspond to *authorization groups* in the SAP BTP, Neo environment. For example, in the SAP BTP, Cloud Foundry environment, all roles required for typical integration developer tasks are grouped in the predefined role collection `PI_Integration_Developer`. In the SAP BTP, Neo environment, the required roles are grouped in the authorization group `AuthGroup.IntegrationDeveloper`.
- The individual roles to define permissions for individual tasks are named differently in both environments, and different sets of roles are required to define a dedicated permission when comparing both environments. For example, to grant the permission to view monitoring data, in the SAP BTP, Cloud Foundry environment, you need the `MonitoringDataRead` role, whereas in the SAP BTP, Neo environment, you need the `IntegrationOperationServer.read` and `NodeManager.read` roles.

To find out how to manage users and roles and how to create custom roles, check out the documentation for Cloud Integration at *http://s-prs.co/v576028*. Search for "Managing Users and Role Assignments in the Neo Environment." To determine the names and descriptions of the authorization groups and roles required when dealing with user and roles management in the SAP BTP, Neo environment, go to the documentation for Cloud Integration at *http://s-prs.co/507789*, and click on **Security in the Neo Environment** (the tasks and role collections are documented in detail in topic **Tasks and Permissions**).

10.3.1 Technical Aspects of User Management

Users and authorizations for integration project teams are managed separately for each customer account within SAP BTP. However, note that SAP BTP has no built-in user management component (as compared, e.g., to the User Management Engine that comes with the Java stack of SAP Process Orchestration). Instead, SAP BTP delegates authentication and user management to another system dedicated to managing information about user identities, also referred to as an *identity provider*.

By default, SAP BTP uses the SAP ID service, which is a tenant that exposes an SAP-operated identity provider. The connection and trust relationship of your subaccount with the SAP ID service is preconfigured when you register with SAP BTP. The SAP ID service also supports Single Sign-On (SSO), which allows users to log on once and then receive seamless access to all deployed applications. You can also use another identity provider to manage user access.

When you initially access SAP BTP, you'll register with the SAP ID service. This service manages users for different SAP websites, such as SAP Community. Note that, for example, if you register for an SAP BTP trial account (see Chapter 2, Section 2.3.2), you're automatically given a user in the SAP ID service. Therefore, when you have such a user (e.g., an S-user), you're already registered with the SAP ID service, and no further actions are required. You can also use a custom identity provider (using an SAP BTP tenant with the SAP BTP Identity Authentication service).

For more information, check out the documentation for SAP BTP at *http://s-prs.co/507790*.

10.3.2 Personas, Roles, and Permissions

To manage authorizations for users involved in integration projects, SAP BTP provides predefined roles that allow you to give subaccount users permissions related to their tasks. According to the main tasks for integration projects, these roles are grouped in the role collections described in Table 10.2.

Role Collection	Description
PI_Business_Expert	Enables a business expert to perform tasks such as monitoring iFlows and monitoring message content stored in temporary storage
PI_Administrator	Enables the tenant administrator to perform administrative tasks on the tenant cluster, for example, deploying security content and iFlows
PI_Integration_Developer	Enables an integration developer to display, download, and deploy artifacts (e.g., iFlows)
PI_Read_Only	Enables a user to display integration content and to monitor messages

Table 10.2 Role Collections for Integration Team Members

The tenant administrator (who is the first to access the tenant and perform user and authorization management tasks) assigns the relevant role collections to the users that are associated with people involved in integration projects and oversee specific tasks (e.g., developing integration content).

In addition to assigning role collections to users, you can also define permissions on a more detailed level by assigning individual roles. For example, to view the MPL (as explained in Chapter 7, Section 7.5.1), role template `MonitoringDataRead` must be assigned to the user.

For a detailed documentation of the roles available for the various tasks associated with an integration project, go to the documentation for Cloud Integration at *http://s-prs.co/507791*. Note that this topic summarizes and compares the roles and role templates used in both SAP BTP, Neo environment and SAP BTP, Cloud Foundry environment.

So far, we've only considered users associated to persons involved in an integration project. However, you'll also need to define authorizations for certain technical users associated with components or systems that need to be connected to Cloud Integration. For these technical users, a specific role needs to be assigned: `ESBMessaging.send`. You can also define custom roles for this purpose, as we'll describe in Section 10.3.3.

In Section 10.3.3, we'll show you step-by-step how to assign one or more role templates to a user. We'll show, first, how to assign a certain set of role templates to a human user (who is to be granted certain monitoring permissions). Second, we'll recap the steps required to assign role template `ESBMessaging.send` to grant permission to a sender application to call the Cloud Integration runtime. In Section 10.3.4, we'll show you step-by-step how to use a custom role for that purpose instead of using the predefined role `ESBMessaging.send`.

10.3.3 Managing Users and Authorizations for a Cloud Integration Subaccount

Note that the procedure described in this section is different depending on whether you work in the SAP BTP, Cloud Foundry environment or the SAP BTP, Neo environment. In this section, we'll mainly describe the procedure for the SAP BTP, Cloud Foundry environment and, at the end of this section, point to the documentation where the procedure is described for the SAP BTP, Neo environment.

The first step after you've finished tenant provisioning (as already shown in Chapter 2, Section 2.3.3) is to define the authorizations for all the people in your organization that will work on your integration project.

After you've logged on to the SAP BTP cockpit, navigate to your global account, and then your subaccount. From the menu on the left, click **Security • Role Collections**, which will open the UI shown in Figure 10.5.

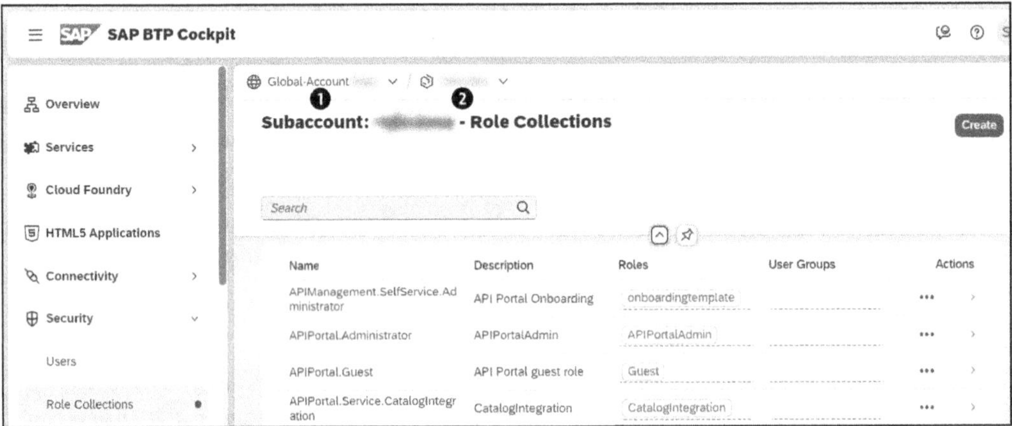

Figure 10.5 Selecting a Subaccount in the Role Collection Section of the SAP BTP Cockpit

Figure 10.5 shows in the breadcrumb link the global account ❶, and the subaccount ❷. As the tenant administrator, you can now start managing users and authorizations for the account. This process comprises two steps:

1. Define the members of the account. These users are all the people who are supposed to work as tenant administrators.
2. Assign authorization groups to the users of all (additional) persons that are supposed to perform tasks related to the tenant (e.g., integration developers).

Adding Members to the Account

To add additional users to your Cloud Integration tenant, follow these steps:

1. In the SAP BTP cockpit navigation area for your subaccount, shown in Figure 10.5, click **Security • Users**.

If you're logged on to your trial account, you'll only see the email address associated with your user. You can now add additional users as members of the account.

2. Click on the **Create** button on the top right of the page, enter the corresponding **User Name** and **E-Mail** address of an additional user, as shown in Figure 10.6. Click on the **Create** button to create a user.

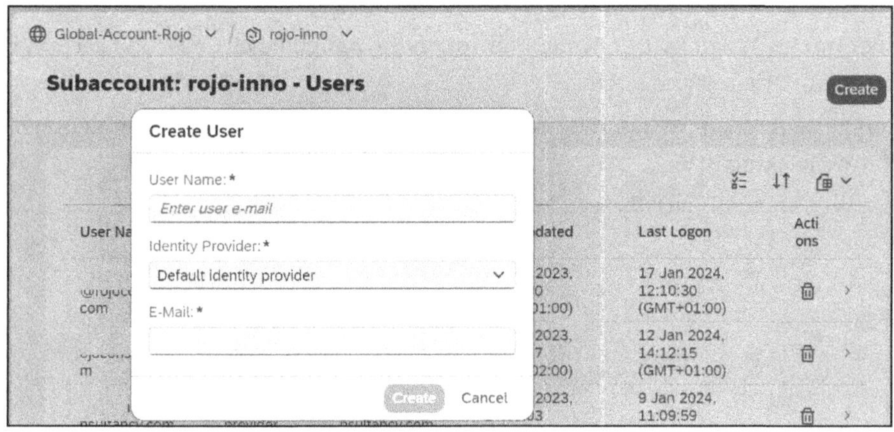

Figure 10.6 Adding Members to a Subaccount

3. Once the user is added, click on it to view the details of this newly added user, as shown in Figure 10.7.

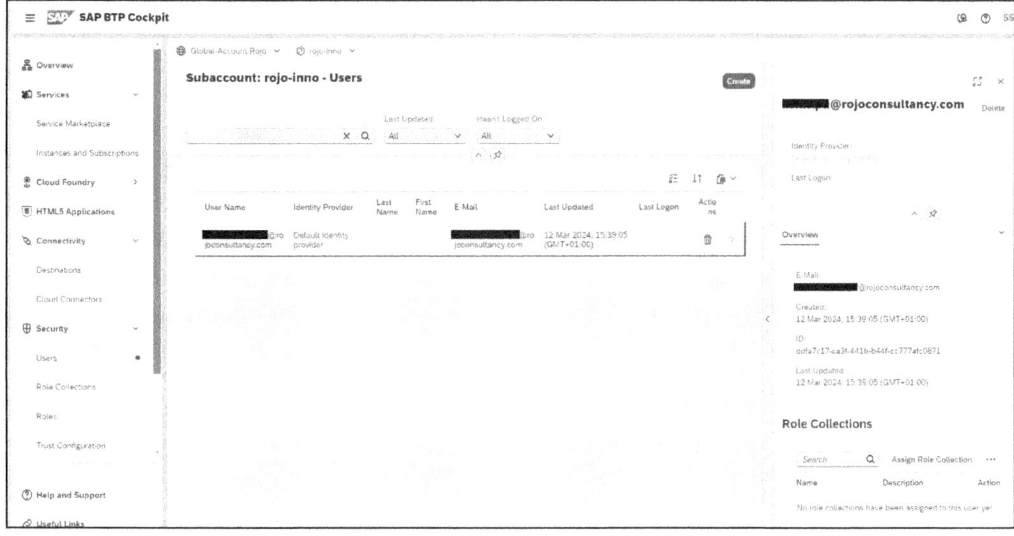

Figure 10.7 View User Details in the SAP BTP Cockpit

4. See that there is no roll collection assigned to this user under the **Roles Collections** section.

Defining Authorizations for Integration Team Members

After you've defined the subaccount members (tenant administrators), you'll assign role collections or roles to users associated with the people who are supposed to work in an integration project (e.g., for integration developers). Follow these steps:

1. From the menu, choose **Security • Users**, and navigate to the user for which you want to assign a roles collection, as shown in Figure 10.7.
2. Click on the **Assign Role Collection** button in the **Assign Roles Collection** section in the bottom right of the screen.
3. On the next screen, assign the available role collections (or a subset) to the user, as shown in Figure 10.8.

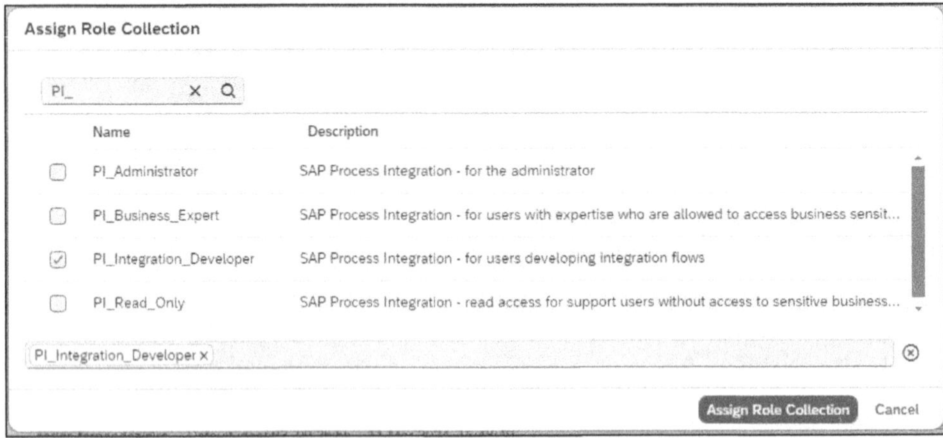

Figure 10.8 Assign Role Collections Dialog

With these steps, you can assign role collections that have already been defined to users. As mentioned earlier (see Table 10.2), predefined role collections each contain a set of roles tailored along the needs of the most important persona. If you want to grant permissions on a more granular level, for example, for individual tasks such as only monitoring message processing, you can achieve this granularity by creating a new role collection that contains a dedicated set of such roles. For information about these roles, go to the documentation for Cloud Integration at *http://s-prs.co/507792*.

To create a new role collection, follow these steps:

1. Go to the **Role Collections** page (refer to Figure 10.5).
2. Click **Create**.
3. On the next screen, specify a name for the new role collection, as shown in Figure 10.9.
4. Click **Create** to complete the process of role collection creation. Keep in mind that this role collection doesn't have any roles assigned to it.

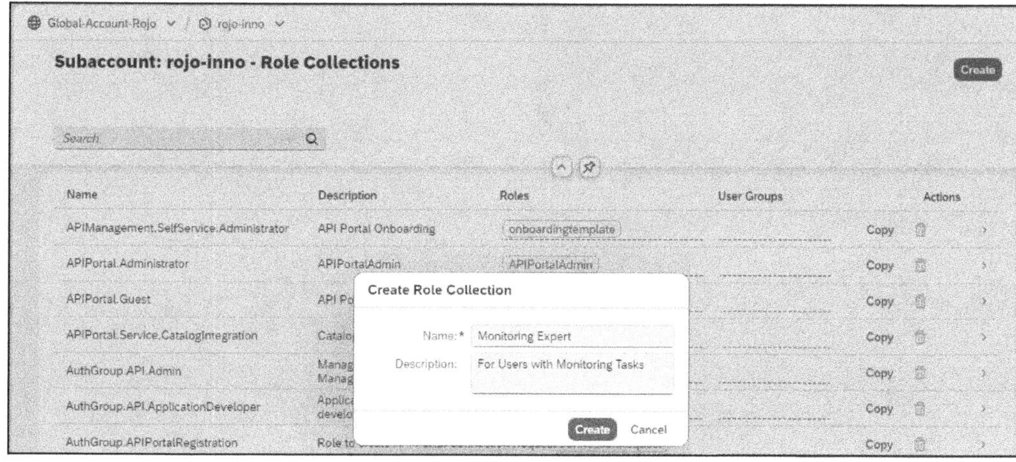

Figure 10.9 Creating a New Role Collection

5. Open your newly created role collection by giving the correct name in the search box and clicking on the collection.
6. On the next screen, click **Edit**, as shown in Figure 10.10.

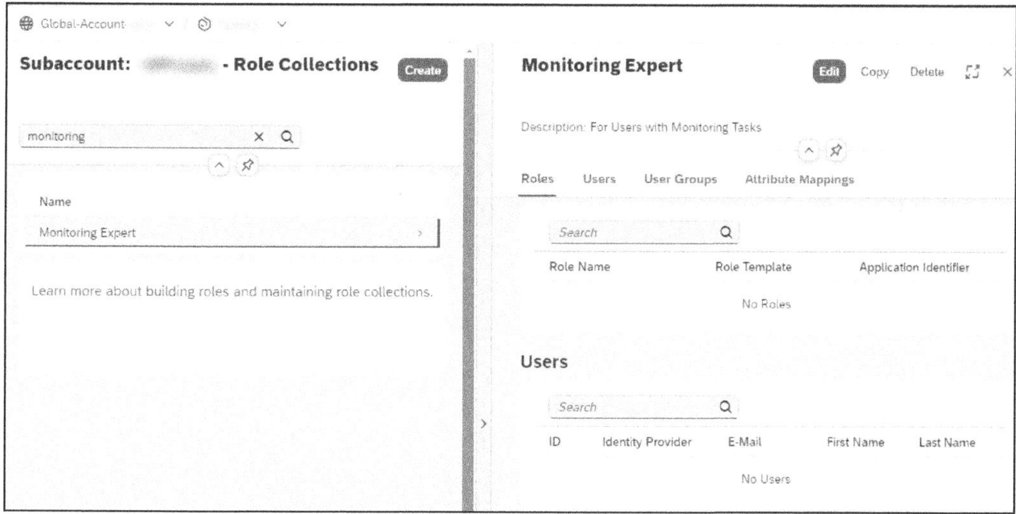

Figure 10.10 Adding a Role to the New Role Collection

7. Under the **Roles** section click on the icon to open a window with all the available roles in the tenant, as shown in Figure 10.11.
8. You can filter the roles based on **Role Template**, **Role Name**, or **Application Identifier**. Click on the checkbox to select the roles, as shown in Figure 10.12. Once you've selected all the roles you want to add to this roles collection, click on **Add**.

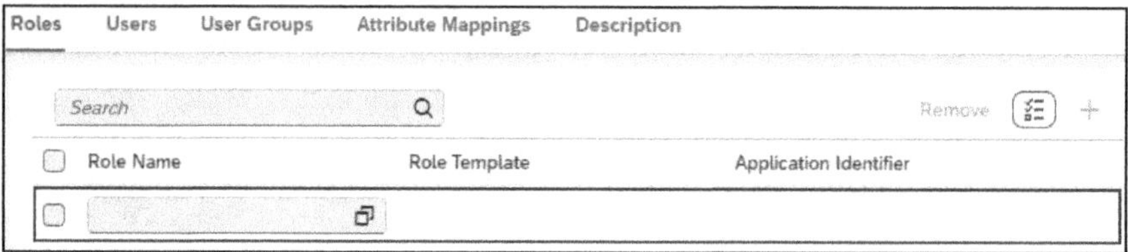

Figure 10.11 Add a Role to the Role Collection

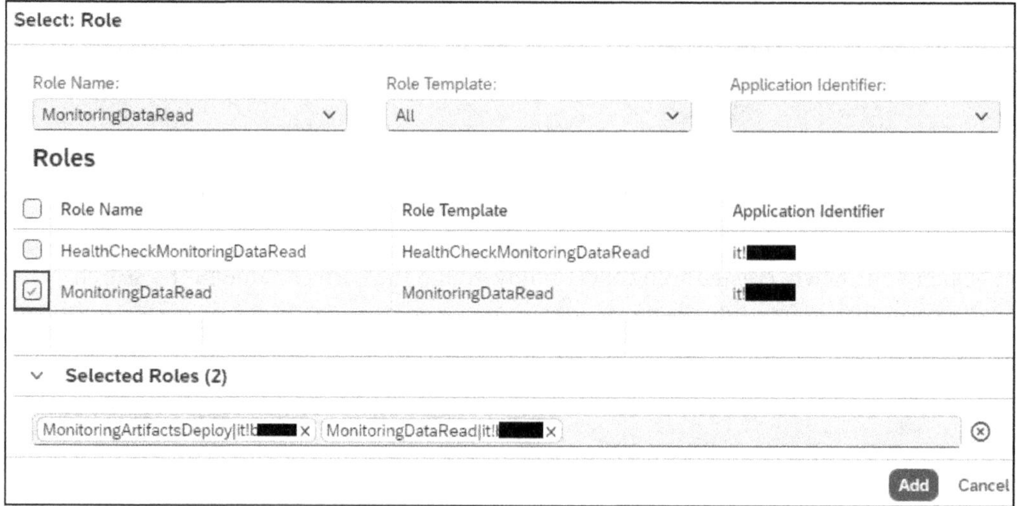

Figure 10.12 Adding an Individual Role Template to the Role Collection

9. Let's assume that you're assigning two roles (`MonitoringDataRead` and `MonitoringArtifactsDeploy`) to the `MonitoringExpert` role collection (to grant permissions to view information on processed messages in the Web UI on the **Monitor** page and to download certain artifacts from there). The resulting role collection is shown in Figure 10.13.

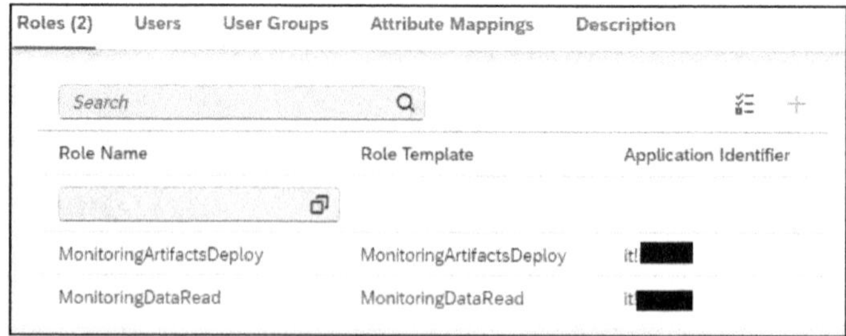

Figure 10.13 The Finally Defined Role Collection

10. Finally, assign the role collection to a user (email address). In the **Users** section of the same screen, shown in Figure 10.14, type the email address of the user, select the

respective **Identity Provider**, and click on **+** icon to add the user. Click **Save** to save the role collection.

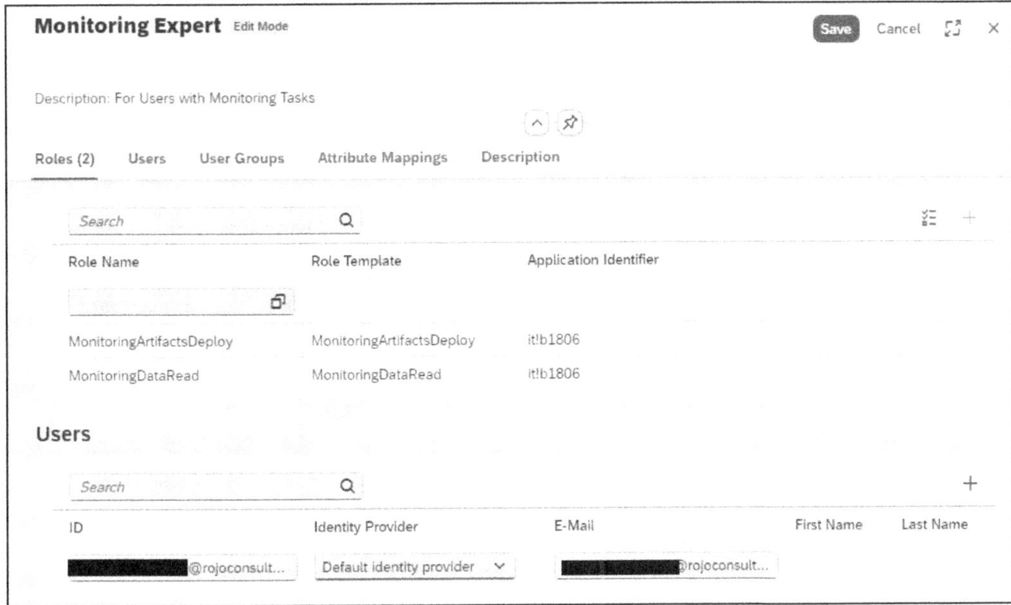

Figure 10.14 Assigning the New Role Collection to the User (Email Address)

Creating and Assigning Roles to Grant Permission for Sender Components to Process Messages

In the previous section, you learned how to define permissions for human users to perform certain tasks when connected to SAP BTP integration through the Web UI. However, technical systems that communicate with each other using Cloud Integration will also need to be securely connected to the platform. To configure such secure inbound communication paths, you'll need to define permissions for a sending application to process an iFlow deployed on a worker. This topic is the focus of this section.

As shown earlier in Figure 10.1 (and also in Chapter 2, Section 2.1), technical systems are connected to the *workers* of a Cloud Integration tenant. Therefore, the relevant permissions in such a case are to be on the level of the workers.

For a detailed description of the concepts related to this procedure, check out the documentation for Cloud Integration on the SAP Help Portal at *http://s-prs.co/507794*.

We won't reproduce all the details but we'll summarize the important facts. We'll first explain how to set up inbound communication using basic authentication. This option is the easiest, so we'll use this option to run the tutorials in this book. For productive scenarios, however, we recommend that you apply a more secure option based on client certificates. We'll come back to the topic of client certificates in Section 10.4.4.

Figure 10.15 shows the entities required for defining inbound authorization with basic authentication.

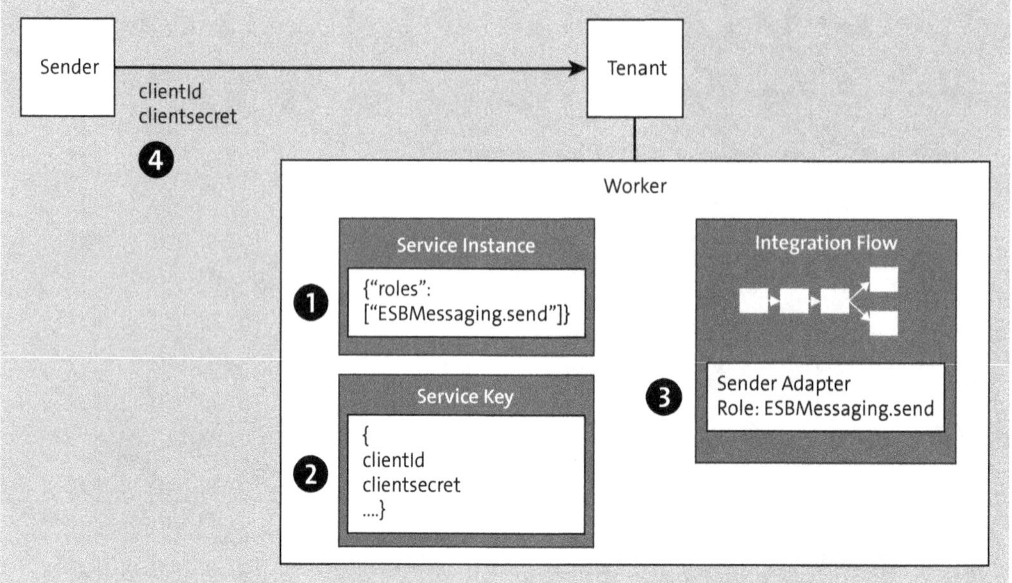

Figure 10.15 Summary of Entities Required to Define Inbound Authorization (Based on User Credentials)

When setting up a secure inbound connection to Cloud Integration, the following aspects are important:

- For inbound authorization of technical components calling iFlow endpoints, SAP provides one predefined role: `ESBMessaging.send`.

  However, using this predefined role might not be sufficient when you deal with a more complex setup of integration scenarios managed by your tenant. For security reasons, all inbound requests (to any iFlow endpoint) should not be handled by the same role `ESBMessaging.send`. Instead, you'll want to define permissions for inbound requests on the level of individual iFlow endpoints. Assume that, for example, you want to give sender 1 the permission to call iFlow 1 and sender 2 the permission to call iFlow 2, but sender 1 should not be authorized to call iFlow 2 and, correspondingly, sender 2 should not be authorized to call iFlow 1. To meet this requirement, Cloud Integration provides the option of defining your own, custom roles for inbound calls.

  In this section, we'll briefly recap the steps using the predefined role `ESBMessaging.send` to define permissions for inbound calls. In Section 10.3.4, we'll show you how to define a custom role. In Section 10.4.4, in the context of setting up an inbound communication, we'll show you how to use either the predefined role or a custom role to define a secure inbound connection.

- Using the SAP BTP cockpit, you'll define a service instance, as shown in Figure 10.15 ❶. Back in Chapter 2, we associated the role `ESBMessaging.send` with the *service instance*. In many integration scenarios developed throughout this book, you'll either use SoapUI as the SOAP client or Postman as the HTTP client to implement the sending application.

  A service instance defines how a certain service of SAP BTP can be accessed (by a remote component). In the context of Cloud Integration, a service instance is the definition of an OAuth client. A service instance is associated with one or more roles (to define permissions for the calling entity). You can define a service instance to do the following:

  - Authorize a sender to call an iFlow endpoint (service plan **integration-flow**), which is the focus in this section.
  - Authorize an application programming interface (API) client to call the Cloud Integration OData API (service plan **api**). This topic is covered in Chapter 8, Section 8.5 (compare Figure 10.33).

  We'll provide more information on the OAuth authentication mechanism in Section 10.4.3.

- For the service instance, you'll generate a *service key* ❷. The service key contains the credentials (more precisely, the OAuth credentials) that are required by the sending application to call the iFlow endpoint. Cloud Integration offers various authentication options, which we'll describe in more detail in Section 10.4.3 (see Table 10.5). In the tutorials described in this book, we always used basic authentication, which meant that the sending application connected to the endpoint with user credentials. The service key in this case contained the required credentials (given by the values of the parameters `clientId` and `clientsecret`).
- To configure the corresponding inbound authorization in the iFlow, the role `ESBMessaging.send` is specified in the sender adapter configuration ❸.
- Consequently, every sending application (e.g., Postman) sending a request to the corresponding iFlow endpoint and provides with the request the credentials contained in the service key (defined for the service instance that relates the role `ESBMessaging.send`) is authorized to process the iFlow ❹.

Note that we don't recommend using basic authentication for productive scenarios. We're only using it now to simplify the setup of example scenarios. In Section 10.4.4, however, we'll show you how to define service instances and service keys so that the sender is authenticated against Cloud Integration based on a client certificate.

Defining Custom Roles for the Authorization of Inbound Calls

As mentioned earlier, you can also define custom roles to authorize a sending application on the iFlow or integration package level. In this section, we'll show you how to define a new user-to-role assignment for this use case. To use custom roles to define permissions for inbound calls, follow these steps:

1. Open the **Monitoring** page of the Web UI, and click the **User Roles** tile under **Manage Security**, as shown in Figure 10.16.

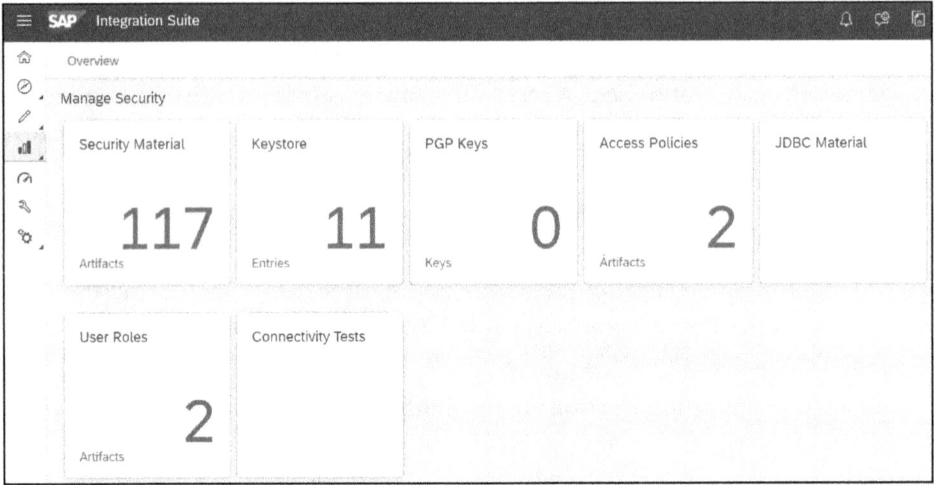

Figure 10.16 User Roles Tile in Monitoring Section of Web UI

2. On the next screen, you'll see the predefined role **ESBMessaging.send**, as shown in Figure 10.17.

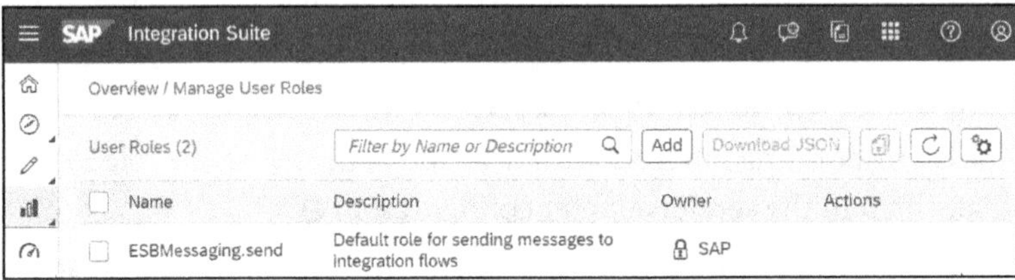

Figure 10.17 Managing User Roles Section

3. Click **Add Role**, and, on the next screen, specify a name and description of the new roles, as shown in Figure 10.18.

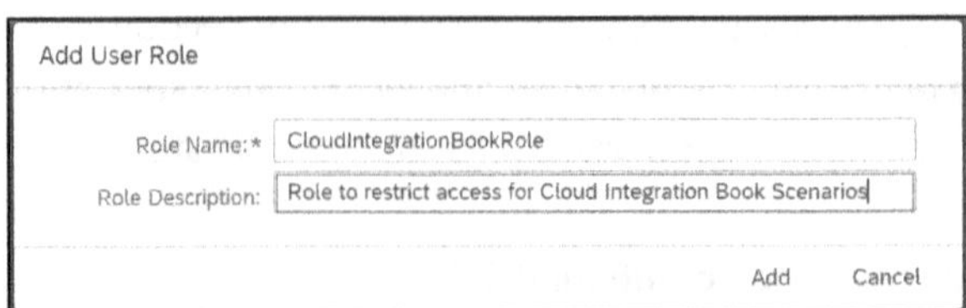

Figure 10.18 Editor to Define the New Role

4. Click **Save**.

The new role is added to the list of roles, as shown in Figure 10.19.

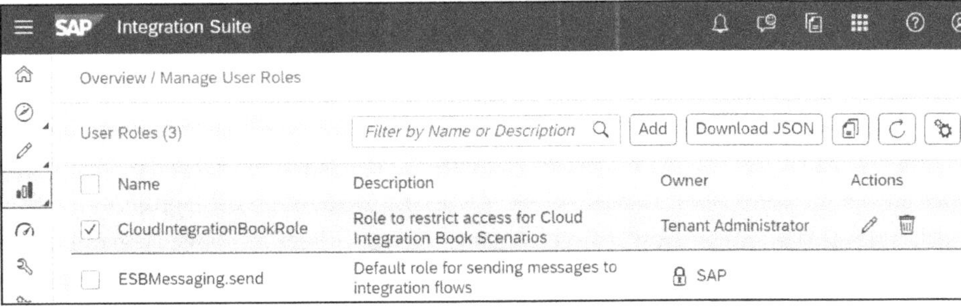

Figure 10.19 New Role Added to the List of Available User Roles

You can learn more in the documentation at *http://s-prs.co/507795*. You can now download the JavaScript Object Notation (JSON) representation of the new role (by clicking **Download JSON**, shown in Figure 10.19). The JSON content can then be used in the definition of a new service key to define inbound authorization for sending applications with users assigned only to this role. In the corresponding sender adapter (of the iFlows in question), you can then select the new role instead of the predefined `ESBMessaging.send` role.

The JSON representation of the newly created role is as follows:

```
{"roles":["CloudIntegrationBookRole"]}
```

As shown in Figure 10.20, when defining the service instance using this role (instead of the predefined role), enter this JSON expression.

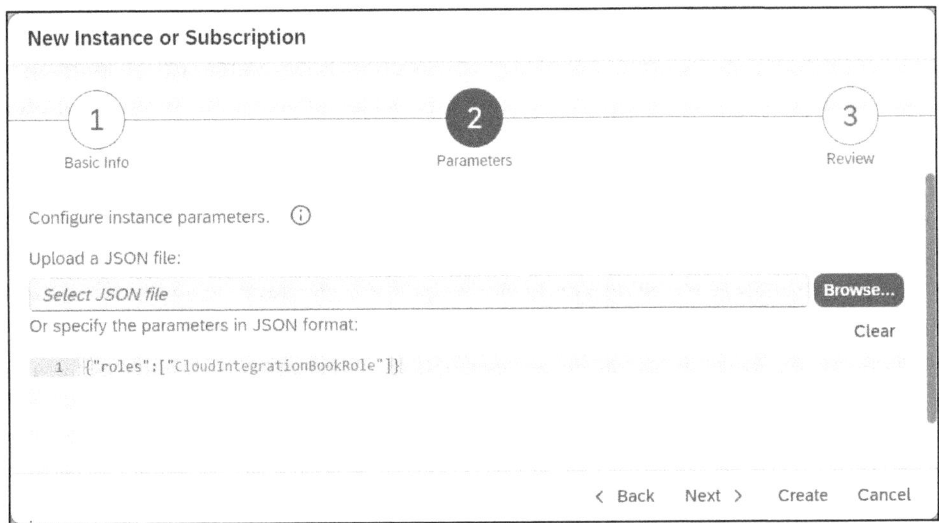

Figure 10.20 JSON Representation of a Custom Role

10.3.4 Authorization on the Package and Integration Flow Level

In the previous section, we showed you how to manage users and permissions both for human users working with the Web UI and for technical components calling the Cloud Integration runtime components to initiate an iFlow.

For human users, dedicated roles and role collections are available that grant permissions to perform dedicated tasks. As explained earlier, in this context, we're talking specifically about users associated with people working in an integration project and using tasks relevant for integration projects. Predefined role collections have been tailored to fit the needs of the integration project persona, as summarized in Table 10.2.

Cloud Integration is a message hub for business messages that, in many cases, might contain confidential data. When monitoring an integration scenario, certain options allow you to access data that has passed through the integration platform, assuming that you have the right permissions. For example, when switching on the **Trace** log level before operating an iFlow, during monitoring, you can analyze the message content that has passed through each iFlow step (for more information on the supported log levels, go to Chapter 7, Section 7.2.2).

Permissions to access business data in the monitoring trace is granted, for example, by the `PI_Business_Expert` role collection (in SAP BTP, Neo environment, by the `AuthGroup.BusinessExpert` authorization group). All people who have the role collection `PI_Business_Expert` assigned can access the business data processed by all iFlows of the respective tenant. However, this policy might not be desired in productive environments.

As shown in Chapter 6, Section 6.4, comprehensive integration scenarios are usually designed in a modularized way so that the business logic is distributed over multiple iFlows (connected through the ProcessDirect adapter). In such a scenario, certain iFlows likely process confidential data, whereas other flows aren't critical concerning data privacy. Therefore, you probably don't want all the people in the same integration team to have the same permissions to access business data processed and stored by all iFlows in the same way. The "critical" iFlows that process and store confidential data must be protected at a higher level. As the tenant administrator, you might want to grant permissions to access business data processed by these critical iFlows to only selected members of the integration team.

Cloud Integration offers a feature—access policies—to configure such a security measure: using access policies, you can protect an iFlow (or a defined set of iFlows) in such a way that only people with an additional role can access the business data processed by the iFlow (or the set of iFlows). More precisely, access policies restrict access to MPL attachments and the trace data. In the future, you'll also be able to access specific data stores, and JMS queue entries can be restricted. This statement applies both for data that is accessed through the **Monitor** page of the Web UI or the OData API.

Each access policy defines a set of iFlows and is uniquely associated with a custom role. All iFlows referenced in an access policy are protected in such a way that only users that have assigned the associated custom role (that corresponds to the access policy) can access the data processed by these iFlows. Figure 10.21 shows how access policies work.

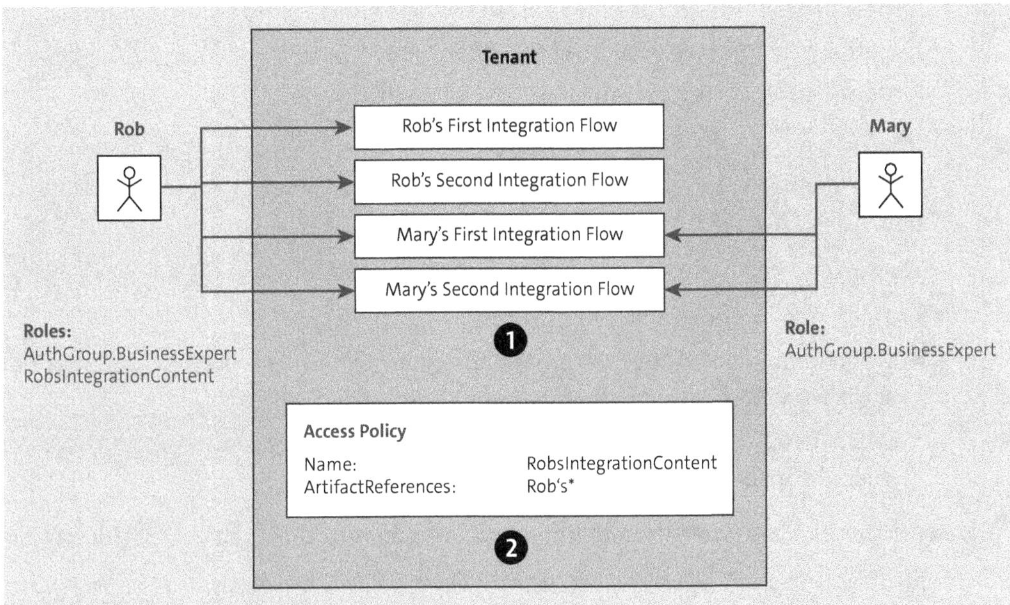

Figure 10.21 Access Policies in Cloud Integration

Let's assume Rob and Mary are integration experts learning how to use Cloud Integration. Both are using the same tenant and have already started to build their first iFlows, as shown in Figure 10.21 ❶. Both users have the role collection `PI_Business_Expert` assigned (alternatively, when testing the feature in the SAP BTP, Neo environment, authorization group `AuthGroup.BusinessExpert`).

If no further actions are taken, all users with this authorization group assigned can access the business data processed by all iFlows deployed on the tenant. However, let's assume that Rob likes to protect his content. For security, he can define an access policy ❷. The name of the access policy (`RobsIntegrationContent`) is associated with a custom role (of the same name), and the access policy contains an artifact reference. The artifact reference defines a set of iFlows: in particular, the reference `Rob's*` defines all iFlows with a name that starts with `Rob's`.

We assume that Rob has the custom role `RobsIntegrationContent` assigned to his user, whereas Mary doesn't. Once the access policy has been defined, access to business data processed by the iFlows is restricted as shown in Figure 10.21. Notice that Mary can no longer access the data processed and stored by Rob's iFlows, but, in contrast, Rob can access his iFlows as well as Mary's (as long as Mary doesn't protect her iFlows by another access policy).

To show you how to define access policies and to test this feature, we'll use a slightly modified example: Let's say you've created your first iFlow as described in Chapter 2. As proposed, this iFlow has the name **My First Integration Flow**. In this example, you'd like to define an access policy that protects access to data processed by this iFlow.

Defining an access policy is performed in two tasks:

1. Define a custom role using the SAP BTP cockpit.
2. Define an access policy using the Web UI (**Monitor** page).

How to define a custom role (first task) is explained in detail in the documentation for Cloud Integration at *http://s-prs.co/507796* under **User Management for Cloud Integration**.

We won't go into these steps in detail but would like to point out the following facts:

- These steps are accomplished using the SAP BTP cockpit.
- When defining a custom role, make sure you select an application identifier that starts with `it!` (compare with the screen shown in Figure 10.11).

  When defining a custom role in the SAP BTP, Neo environment, make sure that you select an application identifier that ends with `.tmn`.

For this exercise, you'll be defining a custom role with the name `MyFirstIntegrationFlow`.

To define the access policy (second task), follow these steps:

1. Open the Web UI, and select the **Monitor** menu item.
2. Select the **Access Policies** tile in the **Manage Security** section, as shown in Figure 10.22.

Figure 10.22 Access Policies Tile in the Web UI Monitor Section

3. To define a new access policy, click the + icon (**Create new Access Policy**), as shown in Figure 10.23.
4. As shown in Figure 10.24, in the **Role Name** field, enter the name of the custom role we just defined in the previous task. Optionally, you can provide a description. After you've entered the data, click **Create**.
5. To specify the access policy, on the next screen, shown in Figure 10.25, you can now start adding artifact references. To add an artifact reference, click the + icon.

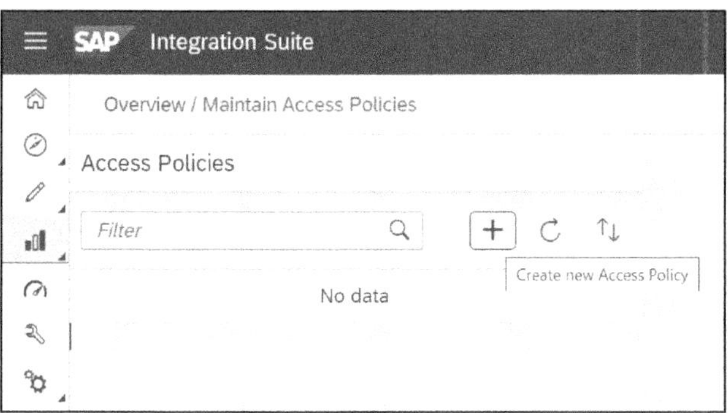

Figure 10.23 The + Button to Create a New Access Policy

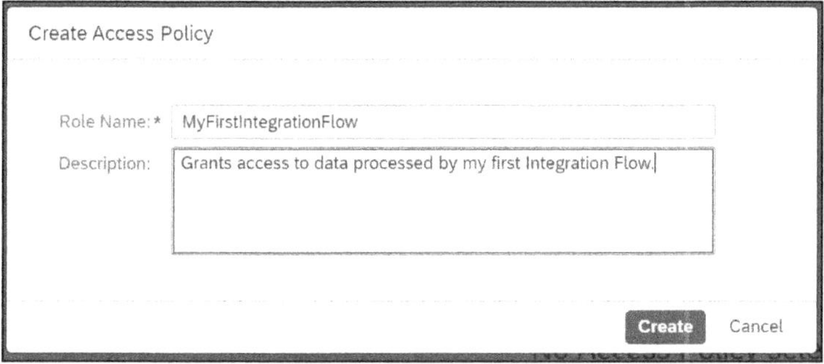

Figure 10.24 Defining the Name and Description for Access Policy

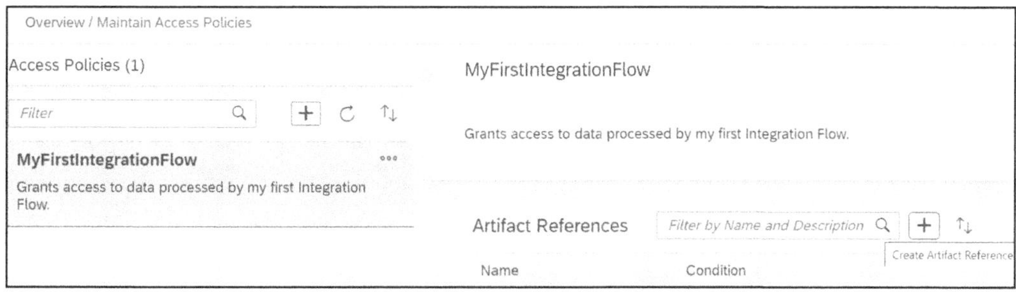

Figure 10.25 Adding an Artifact Reference to an Access Policy

6. To specify the artifact reference, provide the settings as shown, for example, in Figure 10.26.
7. Make reasonable entries in the **Name** and **Description** fields. For the **Condition** section, specify the following parameters:
   - **Artifact Type**: Select the kind of artifact for which you want to grant access. Currently, the **Integration Flow** option is preselected. In future versions of Cloud Integration, data stores and JMS queues will be supported by this feature.
   - **Attribute**: You can define whether you refer the artifact by its **Name** or **ID**.

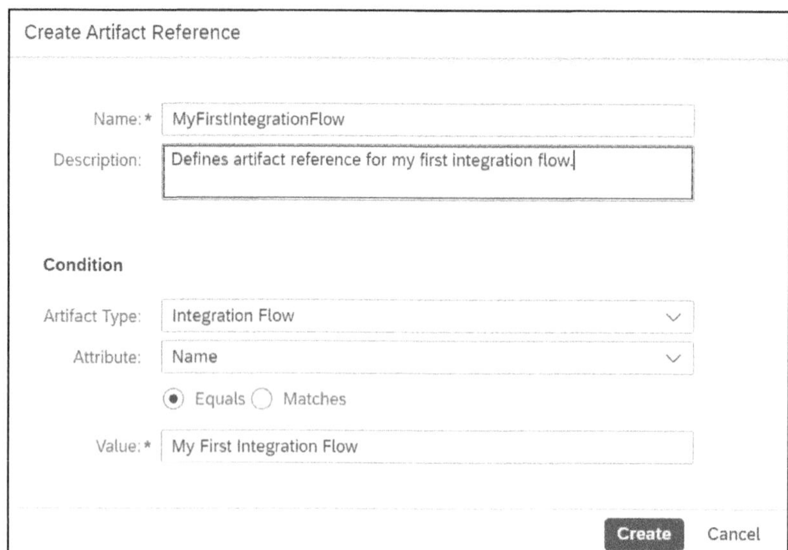

Figure 10.26 Definition of an Artifact Reference

8. Select **Equals** if you want to provide a name or ID of exactly one artifact. In the **Value** field, enter the name of the iFlow, as shown in Figure 10.26.
9. Alternatively, you can select **Matches** if you want to enter an expression to specify multiple iFlows whose name or ID matches a certain pattern. For example, to implement the use case shown in Figure 10.21, in the **Value** field, you can enter an expression such as "Rob's*" to indicate that you want all iFlows with names starting with **Rob's**.
10. Choose **Create**.

The newly defined artifact reference is shown in the list of your access policies, as shown in Figure 10.27.

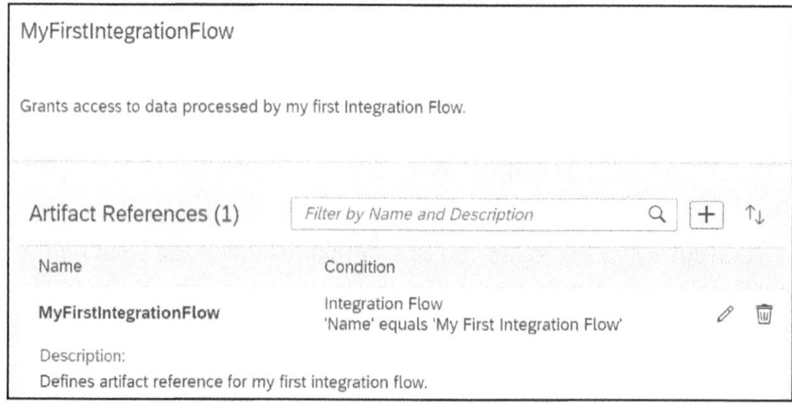

Figure 10.27 Artifact Reference Shown in the List for the Access Policy

You have the option of adding other artifact references, but we'll leave these settings as they are.

You can now test your settings by trying to access the iFlow with the name **My First Integration Flow**. However, note that a browser restart is required before a newly defined access policy becomes active. Test these settings by following these steps:

1. Reopen the Web UI in a new browser session, and deploy the iFlow with the name **My First Integration Flow** (from Chapter 2).
2. Set the log level for this iFlow to **Trace** (on the **Monitor** page of the Web UI, under **Managing Integration Content**).
3. Run the iFlow (as explained in Chapter 2, Section 2.3), and, in the Web UI, go to **Monitor Message Processing**.
4. Select the iFlow, and click **Trace**. You'll see the iFlow model. Select any step, and click **Message Content**.
5. As shown in Figure 10.28, you'll see an information message that you're not authorized to view the trace data.

10

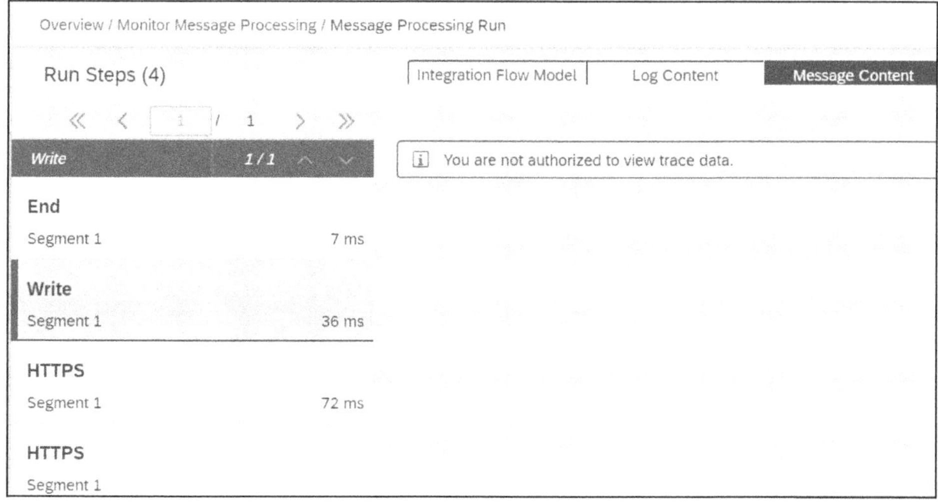

Figure 10.28 Message Monitor Indicating You're Not Authorized to Display Trace Data

6. Using the SAP BTP cockpit, assign your user the role `MyFirstIntegrationFlow`.
7. Close the browser, and open the Web UI again.
8. Run the iFlow again, and check the trace. You should now be able to view the message content for any step selected in the model (as explained, e.g., in Chapter 7).

You've now learned how to manage users and authorizations. We first showed you how to define permissions for human users (integration team members). Then, we showed you how to define permissions for sender applications to call an iFlow endpoint.

Finally, we showed you how to protect iFlows in such a way that only people with an additional role can access the business data processed by these iFlows.

Now, from a security perspective, you can start working with Cloud Integration. In the following sections, we show you all options for data and data flow security and how your integration team members can use the tools in Cloud Integration to set up scenarios with a high-security level. In the course of this section, we also showed you another authentication option attractive for productive scenarios: user role authorization with client certificate authentication. You can't use this option with a trial tenant, however, because client certificates aren't supported in trial accounts. However, in Section 10.4.4, we'll show you nevertheless how to configure secure inbound communication with client certificates. To set up a scenario with client certificate authentication, you'll need a licensed account.

You can find more information on this feature in the "Cloud Integration - Access Policies: Defining Roles on Artifact Level" SAP Community blog: *http://s-prs.co/507797*.

As mentioned earlier, the procedures related to user and authorization management are different in the SAP BTP, Cloud Foundry environment and the SAP BTP, Neo environment. In this section, we've focused on the SAP BTP, Cloud Foundry environment.

To learn more on the procedures for the SAP BTP, Neo environment, check out the documentation for Cloud Integration at *http://s-prs.co/507798* and search for the section **Security** in the documentation for the SAP BTP, Neo environment.

10.4 Data and Data Flow Security

In Section 10.1 and Section 10.2, you learned about the security measures that are already in place when you begin working with Cloud Integration—given by the architecture, the network design, the processes associated with Cloud Integration, and other aspects. Section 10.3 introduced you to the topic of user management.

In this section, we'll discuss the options available to you, as the customer, for maximizing the security of the solution by configuring the way data is exchanged between the components in the customer landscape and Cloud Integration. In other words, we'll focus on how *data in transit* (i.e., on its way between the involved parties) can be protected.

Cloud Integration provides a variety of options for protecting data in transit on the following levels:

- **On the transport protocol level**
  Establish a secure communication channel between remote systems and the involved Cloud Integration components
- **On the message level**
  Further protect the exchanged messages via digital encryption and signing

This topic, which deals with concepts of secure communication and protecting digital data, is known as *cryptography*. In Section 10.4.1, we'll provide a brief overview of the basic terms and concepts of cryptography. Note that this is general knowledge, not exclusively related to Cloud Integration. If you're familiar with the topic of cryptography, you can skip Section 10.4.1 and start with Section 10.4.2.

In Section 10.4.2 and Section 10.4.3, respectively, we'll provide an overview of the transport-level security options and the authorization and authentication options supported by Cloud Integration. In Section 10.4.4 and Section 10.4.5, two tutorials will follow to show you how to establish secure connections between your tenant and remote systems and how to develop a simple iFlow with a specific authentication option, OAuth. In Section 10.4.6, we'll discuss the message-level security options provided by Cloud Integration. In Section 10.4.7, finally, we'll explain how message-level security can be implemented using Cloud Integration (including a step-by-step tutorial that you can easily reproduce).

10.4.1 Basic Cryptography in a Nutshell

Cryptography, in the broadest sense, deals with methods and techniques that help protect data against unauthorized access. One basic measure of protecting data against unauthorized access is to encrypt it. Encrypting means to transform a *clear text* (readable by everyone) into a *secret text*, prior to sending it to a communication partner. This transformation is done on the sender side by a mathematical operation (based on an *encryption key*). The dedicated receiver needs to know the inverse operation (the *decryption key*) to transform the secret text back into the clear text.

Another measure to protect a message on its way between a sender and receiver is to apply a *digital signature* so that the receiver can be sure that the message has been sent by the trusted sender (also known as *data integrity*).

The simplest and most obvious approach (also referred to as *symmetric key technology*) is that sender and receiver use the same key.

A Brief History of Cryptography

The topic of cryptography isn't reserved exclusively to the digital age. As a child, you might already have applied cryptography on a basic level. When exchanging secret notes with your classmates, perhaps you replaced each alphabetic character in the text by the next letter in the alphabet. (Or, for "top-secret" notes, a letter *n* positions after the intended plain text letter.) In this simple example, the encryption key is the operation that shifts each letter in the text by a defined number in the alphabet, while the decryption key defines the inverse operation. In other words, this example from your childhood is a simple scenario using symmetric keys in a simple substitution cipher.

We're just scratching the surface. The rich and exciting history of encryption has been told by Simon Singh in his excellent book *The Code Book* (HarperCollinsPublishers,

1999). For a concise and entertaining introduction to cryptography, we warmly recommend reading this book.

Coming back to the topic of symmetric key technology, a critical requirement to ensuring the seamless and protected communication between sender and receiver is that the key is exchanged securely between both parties prior to the actual message exchange. Of course, this requirement can't always be met in the digital age because the number of potential communication partners and communication paths for a given channel (e.g., email) is huge and changes dynamically on short notice.

To overcome this challenge, *asymmetric* (or *public*) *key technologies* have been developed, which always require two different key types: a public key and a private (or secret) key. Both key types are generated together and are related to each other based on a mathematical operation such that the public key can be easily calculated from the private key. However, the reverse operation is impossible, and you can't derive the private key from the public key (at least, when considering the computing capacities available today). Mathematically, this approach is based on one-way functions, which we won't explain further here. For more information, refer to *Cryptography and Public Key Infrastructure on the Internet* (Wiley, 2003).

For the encryption use case, the asymmetric approach works in the following way: The intended receiver of a message generates a public-private key pair and shares the public key with the sender. The sender then uses the public key to encrypt the message. The receiver then uses its private key, which is always kept with the receiver and never shared with any other party, to decrypt the message.

For digital signatures (data integrity), the inverse pattern is applied. The sender signs a message using its private key, which is always kept with the sender, and the receiver (and many other potential receivers) can verify the signature by using the public key, which has been provided by the sender. We'll show you how this works in detail in Section 10.4.6.

Obviously, the private key must never be shared, or others would be able to sign messages in your name or to decrypt content intended solely for you.

Because of its inherent mathematical concepts (one-way functions), public keys can potentially be shared through unsecure channels (e.g., email). Any malicious party that receives the public key by mistake has no ability to decrypt or sign any message with that public key. Note, however, that certain additional measures should be undertaken to enable the receiver of a public key to validate the authenticity of that public key, as we'll describe later. If those measures aren't taken, there's space left for a *man-in-the-middle attack* where a malicious third party can intercept a message and gain control over the private conversation between two other partners. One measure is to get public keys signed by an authority trusted by all communication partners. To build a trust relationship, all parties involved must ensure their identity based on a trusted certificate, which is a signed key. As a result, a malicious party can't intercept the communication. We'll elaborate more on the topic of certificates and certificate chains later (e.g., see the Note on digital certificates).

Hybrid Approaches

Symmetric methods typically use simple bit operations to transform a clear text bit sequence into a secret text bit sequence. In asymmetric methods, however, sophisticated mathematical operations come into play, which use modulo mathematics. Because of this distinction, asymmetric methods are computationally intensive and, therefore, not well-suited to operate on the larger bit sequences that characterize large business messages exchanged in integration scenarios.

To overcome this issue, a more feasible approach is to apply hybrid approaches that combine asymmetric and symmetric methods. In encryption scenarios, the most common pattern for this approach is shown in Figure 10.29.

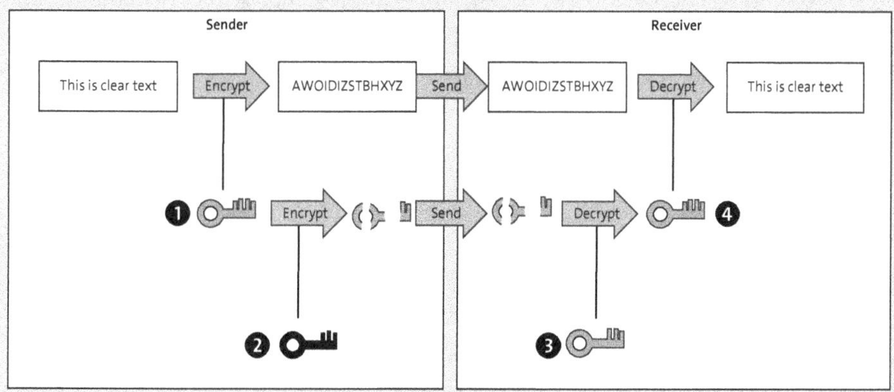

Figure 10.29 Hybrid Usage of Symmetric and Asymmetric Key Technology When Encrypting and Decrypting Message Content

The sender encrypts the (potentially voluminous) content of a message using a *symmetric* encryption key ❶. This encryption key is also referred to as *secret* key. Thereafter, the sender encrypts the symmetric encryption key with a public key ❷ and sends the encrypted symmetric key (along with the encrypted message content) to the receiver. Before the message exchange between the sender and receiver has been initiated, the public key has been generated by the receiver as part of an *asymmetric* key pair and shared with the sender without risk. With the associated private key ❸, the receiver decrypts the encrypted symmetric key as soon as the key is received and, finally, uses the revealed secret key to decrypt the message content ❹.

In this way, we can avoid applying asymmetric key operations to the whole message content.

Hybrid approaches are applied in the transport-level security option TLS, described in Section 10.4.2, as well as in the message-level security options described in Section 10.4.6. In these sections, we'll show you in more detail how these approaches work.

Keystores

To introduce another important term, note that keys (public and private keys) are stored in *keystores* owned by the involved parties. How a keystore is implemented and its characteristics depends on the type of system that implements the services of the sender and receiver.

Figure 10.30 shows how to set up components for two parties exchanging encrypted messages based on public key technology. In this general setup, the sender and the receiver each generate their own public-private key pair separately and import the key pairs into their respective keystores. In a subsequent step, both participants share the corresponding *public* key with the communication partner. Both partners also import the corresponding foreign public key into their keystores.

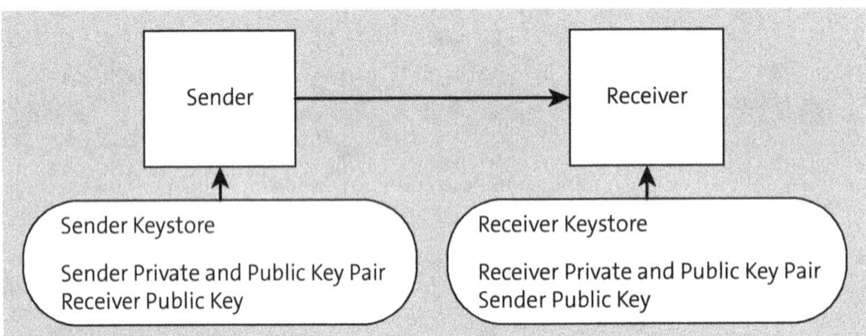

Figure 10.30 Keystores Containing the Required Key Material

Because no common term applies for the key storage of all possible kinds of systems, for simplicity, we'll always talk about *keystores* throughout this book. We'll also shorten the term *public and private key pair* to *private key pair* or *key pair.*

Keystore Types for Cloud Integration

In scenarios described in this book, the tenant is always one of the communication partners. Therefore, a keystore must be deployed on the tenant that contains the required key material. The characteristics of the keystore also depend on the security standard you've chosen (as we'll see later in Section 10.4.2 and Section 10.4.6).

For example, if you use X.509 certificates, you'll need a Java keystore, but if you use OpenPGP, you'll need two different "keystore" types: a Pretty Good Privacy (PGP) public keyring and a PGP secret keyring (Section 10.4.6 and Section 10.4.7). You already met this keystore in the beginner's tutorial in Chapter 2. In that tutorial, you needed to upload certain certificates to the keystore of your SAP BTP tenant so that the tenant could communicate with a mail server.

As an example of a remote system that can be connected to a tenant, let's say you have an SAP system based on Application Server ABAP (AS ABAP). In this case, the required keys are maintained with the Trust Manager in the Personal Security Environment, which takes over the role as the keystore.

Although we've stated that public keys can potentially be exchanged on unsecured channels (whereas private keys must never be shared with another party), a malicious party can nevertheless misuse this fact and send a public key to another party, thus pretending to be the owner of the public key (the man-in-the-middle attack we mentioned earlier). So, the question is, how can the authenticity of a public key be guaranteed to further increase security?

To answer this question, we'll briefly discuss digital certificates. As certificates are important for the whole topic of security, let's pause to define this term and explore its underlying concepts.

Digital Certificate

A *digital certificate* is a public key that is signed by a trusted authority—usually referred to as a certificate authority (CA). In this way, the identity and trustworthiness of the public key owner can be confirmed. In short, a certificate couples an identity with a public key. Using certificates to enforce a communication party to authenticate itself against another one helps to prevent situations like the man-in-the-middle attack described earlier.

Many options are available for building trust based on certificates. One example is the X.509 standard, which comes into play, for example, when two communication partners protect a communication channel using TLS (Section 10.4.2). X.509 supports the usage of Public Key Infrastructure X.509 (PKIX) certificates, which allow you to build up certificate chains. These hierarchical trust models can include many CAs on different levels, where the CA on the higher level signs the certificate of the corresponding lower level, and so forth. The CA on the top level is referred to as the *root CA*. This model is called a *certificate chain*.

An example of a CA is GeoTrust (*www.geotrust.com*). One root certificate issued by GeoTrust and supported by the load balancer is *GeoTrust Global CA*.

Another alternative trust model is the *Web of Trust*. In this model, communication partners must mutually confirm the authenticity of each other's public keys, building a network of partners rather than a hierarchical structure. The Web of Trust model can be used in conjunction with the OpenPGP security standard. Figure 10.31 shows the difference between the two trust models.

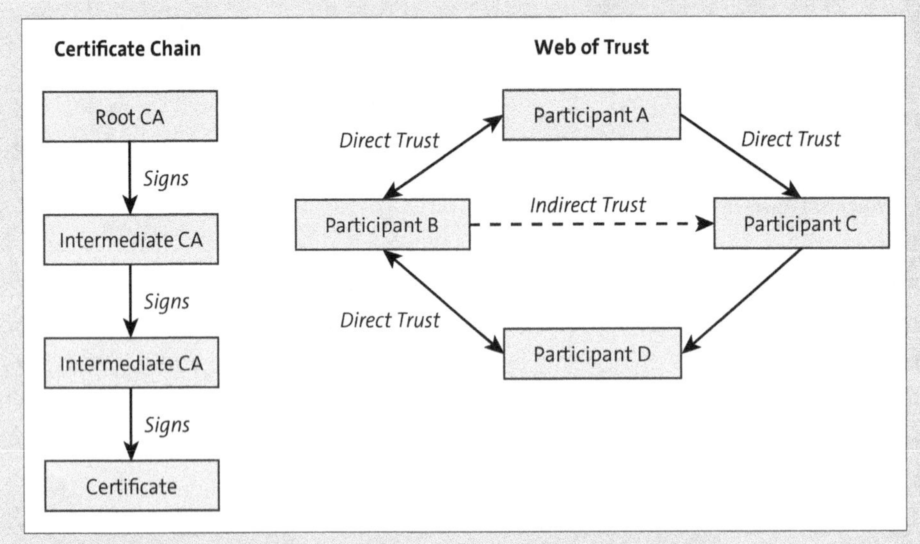

Figure 10.31 Certificate Chain (Left) Compared to a Web of Trust (Right)

X.509 Certificates

Because this certificate type is the most commonly used for transport-level security, we'd like to discuss a few basic concepts and terms. X.509 certificates allow you to implement trust models based on certificate chains. A set of elements is required to specify an X.509 certificate, although we won't go into these details in this book. We do want to point out the **Issuer** and the **Subject** field, which are required to understand the following discussion on X.509 certificates:

- **Issuer**
  Specifies the CA that issued and signed the certificate.
- **Subject**
  Specifies the entity associated with the public key of the certificate. If the certificate is used to authenticate a client calling a server, the subject usually identifies the client.

Both entries, **Issuer** and **Subject**, are uniquely defined by a distinguished name (DN), which is composed of a set of attributes such as company name, country identification, and so on. The format of DNs is defined by the Request for Comments (RFC) 5280 specification by the Network Working Group (see *https://tools.ietf.org/html/rfc5280*). In this way, DNs are guaranteed to be unique, and using them ensures two things: first, the certificate issuer can uniquely be identified (to ensure the certificate isn't tampered with by a malicious party), and second, the entity associated with the certificate certainly can be considered to be the one it should be. Certificates and their management are discussed in more detail in Section 10.5.

You're now equipped with the basic concepts and terms for understanding cryptography. In Section 10.4.2 and Section 10.4.6, we'll explain in detail how to apply cryptographic concepts to set up secure message exchange scenarios based on certain security standards.

10.4.2 Transport-Level Security Options

Cloud Integration provides various connectivity options—methods of connecting remote systems with different technical characteristics to Cloud Integration. The available adapters imply one of the transport protocols listed in Table 10.3, each with different options to secure the communication channel.

Adapter Type(s)	Communication Based on ...
SAP Ariba Applicability Statement 2 (AS2) Applicability Statement 4 (AS4) Elektronische Steuererklärung (ELSTER) Facebook HTTP Simple Object Access Protocol (SOAP) IDoc OData OData Channel (ODC) Open Connectors SAP SuccessFactors Twitter (now called XI) SAP Process Integration	Hypertext Transfer Protocol (HTTP) over Transport Layer Security (TLS) (HTTPS) TLS is a protocol for secure communication over a computer network that is widely used on the internet. As TLS is the enhancement of SSL, these terms are often used synonymously.
File Transfer Protocol (FTP)	Secure Shell File Transfer Protocol (SFTP) This protocol is used to transfer files from and to file servers. This is an extension of FTP. This option is also based on TLS and X.509 certificates.

Table 10.3 Communication Options (Adapters) and Underlying Protocols or APIs

Adapter Type(s)	Communication Based on ...
Mail receiver	Simple Mail Transfer Protocol Secure (SMTPS) This protocol enables a computer to exchange emails with a mail server. With SMTPS, SMTP connections can be secured by SSL or TLS.
Mail sender	The mail sender adapter can be used with one of the following protocols: ■ Post Office Protocol version 3 over TLS/SSL (POP3S) This option enables email clients to retrieve emails from an email server using the Internet Protocol (IP). ■ Internet Message Access Protocol over TLS/SSL (IMAPS) This option enables email clients to retrieve emails from an email server using a TCP/IP connection.
Secure Shell File Transfer Protocol (SFTP)	This protocol has been developed for the Secure Shell (SSH) and allows secure transfer of files. SSH is a network protocol that allows you to set up a secure connection to a remote computer, namely an SFTP server.
Java Message Service (JMS)	JMS is an API that supports reliable asynchronous communication based on a JMS message broker.
Java Database Connectivity (JDBC)	JDBC is an API that defines how a client accesses a database.
Remote function call (RFC)	RFC is an SAP-proprietary protocol that is used as standard for the communication of SAP systems.
AMQP (TCP)	Transmission Control Protocol (TCP) TCP is one of the main communication protocols used on the internet. TLS, mentioned earlier, often (but not always) runs on top of TCP.
Lightweight Directory Access Protocol (LDAP)	
Advanced Message Queuing Protocol (AMQP)/WebSocket	WebSocket is a protocol that supports simultaneous communication in both directions (full-duplex). Full-duplex refers to communication modes that allow the communication partners to communicate with each other simultaneously. An example known to everyone is the telephone that allows both connected partners to speak simultaneously. Cloud Integration offers this protocol for setting up connections with messaging systems.

Table 10.3 Communication Options (Adapters) and Underlying Protocols or APIs (Cont.)

Note that SAP updates Cloud Integration monthly. For an up-to-date list of connectivity options, check out the **Feature Scope Description for Cloud Integration** that you can find on the Cloud Integration page on the SAP Help Portal at *http://s-prs.co/507799*.

Because TLS is by far the most commonly used transport-level security option, we'll include a few remarks on this protocol specifically.

Transport Layer Security

TLS uses a hybrid approach of asymmetric and symmetric key technology: the asymmetrical approach is used to encrypt a symmetric session key at the beginning of the connection setup, while the latter approach is then used to actually encrypt and decrypt the data as long as the TLS connection (session) is active.

TLS uses a hierarchical trust model (based on X.509 certificates). During the connection setup, certificates between the client and server are exchanged, and the authenticity of these certificates is validated based on the provided signatures by certification authorities.

With TLS, Cloud Integration offers different options for how a client authenticates itself against the server. We'll discuss the authentication options in Section 10.4.3.

10.4.3 Authentication and Authorization

Next to measures to protect the exchanged messages by digital encryption and signatures, another important aspect that impacts the security of a system of components that communicate with each other are authentication and authorization.

Before presenting the options offered by Cloud Integration, we'll briefly clarify and distinguish between the terms *authentication* and *authorization*.

Authentication and Authorization

Authentication verifies the identity of something (or someone) in a communication workflow. This process checks, for example, if the person associated with a user (that connects to a server) is who he or she claims to be.

In IT, authentication workflows typically relate to scenarios in which a client (to be authenticated) requests access to some kind of protected resource hosted on a server. In the context of Cloud Integration, the term *protected resource* covers not only data but also message processing capabilities (e.g., implemented on a runtime component of Cloud Integration).

After authentication, an *authorization* check verifies what the authenticated entity is allowed to do in the connected server system.

In many cases, in an authorization check, user-to-role assignments of the (authenticated) user are investigated in the server system. For inbound communication (where Cloud Integration acts as server), the user-to-role assignments are defined by the tenant administrator (as shown earlier in Section 10.3).

Basic Authentication

This option is the simplest one, where authentication is based on user credentials (user name and password). When you configure basic authentication for inbound communication (where a client sends messages to Cloud Integration), the credentials of the technical user associated with the client are forwarded to Cloud Integration in the message header (through a secure channel, e.g., using HTTPS). The identity of the client is then verified based on the credentials stored at SAP.

SAP doesn't recommend using basic authentication for productive scenarios, which is less secure than using client certificates.

Client Certificate Authentication

For this option, the authentication step is accomplished based on digital certificates. Instead of credentials, the client forwards a digital certificate to the server. The authentication of the client is then achieved by checking the certificate.

Client certificate authentication is always the option of choice for productive scenarios, as certificates guarantee a higher level of security. (This kind of authentication relies on a trust relationship, which is difficult to break, as shown in Section 10.4.1.)

OAuth

Up to this point, we've only talked about authentication workflows that include two parties: a client (requesting access to a protected resource) and a server (that hosts the resource). In these scenarios, the protected resource is owned by either the client or the server.

Let's now talk about a different, more sophisticated authentication pattern, where the owner of the protected resource isn't necessarily identical to either client or server. In this scenario, the following three parties (or roles) come into play:

- A user who owns the protected resources
- A client, which is typically an application
- A server (or resource server), which is typically a service provider that hosts the protected resources

Figure 10.32 shows the basic, simplified setup for this OAuth scenario.

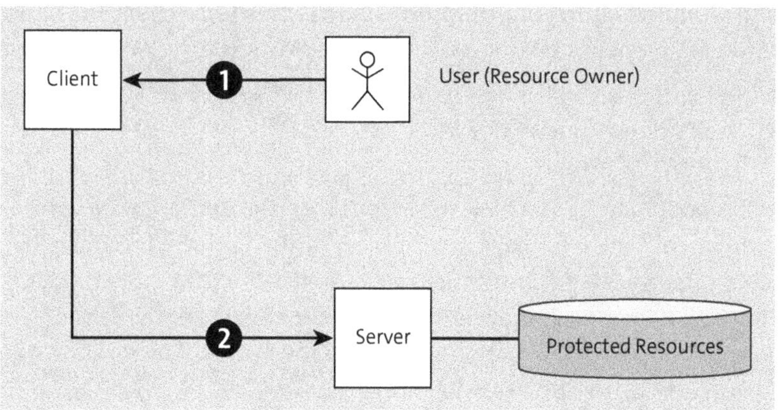

Figure 10.32 OAuth Scenario: Resource Owner Delegates Access to Protected Resources (Hosted on a Server) to a Client

10

That scenario is what OAuth is all about. The user ❶, as the owner of the *protected resource*, grants the *client* access to the protected resource (hosted by the *resource server*). The access granted to the client ❷ is typically *restricted*—no full access rights will be given. In this setup, you, the resource owner, can keep your credentials private.

Using OAuth in Cloud Integration

Before we go into more detail, let's point out that you came across this authentication method already on various occasions in this book. When setting up an inbound authentication for your very first iFlow, you created a service instance to configure a scenario where a sender calls Cloud Integration with user credentials. A service instance on SAP BTP is, in technical terms, nothing more than the definition of an OAuth client (see Chapter 2, Section 2.3.3). We'll elaborate more on how OAuth is used for client certificate–based inbound communication in Section 10.4.4.

In this section, we'll cover the OAuth topic even more:

- By showing the various options for using OAuth to define authentication for inbound and outbound communication (Section 10.4.3)
- By showing you how to set up a scenario where Cloud Integration connects to Twitter (now called X) using another variant of OAuth (Section 10.4.5)

Note

In 2023, the Twitter platform rebranded to X. For the purposes of this book, we'll refer to this platform as Twitter, as the Cloud Integration adaptor still uses the original Twitter brand name.

As an example of a simple OAuth setup, think of Twitter as a resource server and a Twitter user as the owner of his or her Twitter stream, which is the resource. We'll show you, in Section 10.4.5, how Cloud Integration (as the client application) can be granted access to Twitter content on behalf of a Twitter user. For that purpose, the corresponding iFlow uses a Twitter receiver adapter.

In OAuth 2.0, an additional role is added to the picture—the *authorization server*—which is the component that will finally grant access to the protected resource (and that issues the required access tokens, which we'll discuss in detail later). So far, as shown in Figure 10.32, the authorization server wasn't identified. For the sake of simplicity, we'll assume that the authorization server and the resource server (hosts the resource) are identical, which is also a possible scenario.

To enable client access to the protected resource, the owner doesn't need to share his own credentials with the client. However, OAuth comes with a more complex setup of credentials than the credentials used in the other authentication scenarios we discussed earlier. In addition to the resource owner's own credentials (necessary to access his or her own resource), two additional kinds of credentials come into play. Table 10.4 lists the relevant credentials.

Credential Type	Description
Resource owner's credentials	Enable the resource owner to log on to the resource server to access and manage his protected resources.
Client credentials	Identify the client (at the resource server's side). Client credentials are composed of a *consumer key* and a *consumer secret*. In OAuth 2.0 terminology, client credentials are a specific implementation of an *authorization grant*. An authorization grant is a credential used by the client to obtain an access token (see the next entry).
Token credentials	Authorize the client (on behalf of the resource owner) to access the resource. Token credentials identify the resource owner on the server's side. These credentials can be revoked by the resource owner at any time. Token credentials are composed of *access tokens* and *access token secrets*.

Table 10.4 Credential Types Used with OAuth

In the sets of credentials summarized in Table 10.4, a secret is a piece of information exclusively shared between the client and server. Using the two parts of a credential pair in combination helps to protect those credentials from being compromised.

A characteristic of the token credentials (as compared to the client credentials) is that they can be revoked by the resource owner at any time. As a result, you can adapt authorization workflows flexibly to meet changing requirements without the need to reconfigure sets of client credentials or to renew the resource owner's own credentials.

With these terms in mind, a typical OAuth authentication workflow comprises the following steps, now considering that resource server and authentication server are separate components. Figure 10.33 shows a general description of a workflow that follows the OAuth 2.0 specification, which you can find at *https://tools.ietf.org/html/rfc6749*.

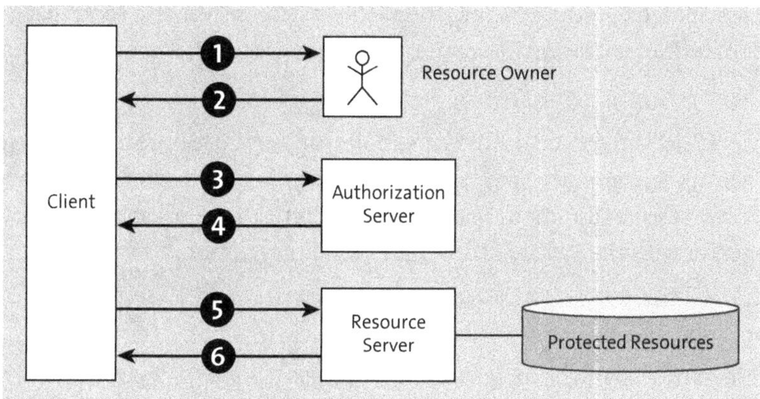

Figure 10.33 OAuth 2.0 Authentication Workflow (with Client Credentials)

The workflow comprises the following sequence of steps:

❶ The client requests authorization from the resource owner to access his protected resource.

❷ The resource owner provides the client with client credentials (a specific type of authorization grant, as indicated earlier in Table 10.4).

❸ The client connects to the authorization server and presents the client credentials.

❹ The authorization server authenticates the client; validates the client credentials; and, if the credentials are valid, provides the client with an access token.

❺ Authenticating itself against the resource server with the access token, the client requests the protected resource from the resource server.

❻ The resource server validates the access token and, if valid, grants the client access to the protected resource.

An important aspect of this workflow is that the resource owner doesn't have to share his credentials with anyone at any point in time.

Much more could be said about OAuth because this rich framework allows you to flexibly implement various authentication use cases. Before finishing this brief introduction to the topic, however, we need to introduce a term that you'll see later in this chapter. The OAuth framework specifies a number of *grant types*, each representing a specific authentication use case. We won't provide a complete description of this topic, which is beyond the scope of this book. For more information, refer to the OAuth 2.0 specification mentioned in the upcoming next information box.

We do, however, want to briefly mention two examples:

- The *client credentials grant type* specifies a workflow that we've explained earlier (Figure 10.33). A client receives an access token by sending its client credentials to an authorization server.
- The *refresh token grant type* takes into consideration that access tokens eventually expire. In the associated OAuth workflow, the authorization server also sends back a refresh token that the client can use to request a new access token when the original token expires.

This high-level workflow is the OAuth authentication workflow. In Section 10.4.3, we'll show you how OAuth comes into play when configuring secure communications between Cloud Integration and remote systems. In Section 10.4.5, we'll show you how OAuth works together with the Twitter adapter for Cloud Integration.

Adapters Supporting OAuth

Many Cloud Integration adapters support OAuth. First, social media (Facebook and Twitter) adapters are available. Further adapters that support OAuth include the AMQP sender and receiver adapter (with the WebSocket transport protocol), the OData receiver adapter, the SAP SuccessFactors (OData) receiver adapter, and the HTTP receiver adapter. (Refer also to Table 10.7.)

When using the Open Connectors adapter with connectors offered by SAP BTP, many connectors support OAuth. For more information on Open Connectors in SAP BTP, see Chapter 9.

For an overview of the various (OAuth) authentication options and their supporting adapter types, refer to Table 10.5 for inbound communication options and Table 10.7 for outbound communication options.

OAuth Terminology

OAuth is available in two versions:

- OAuth 1.0 (*https://tools.ietf.org/html/rfc5849*)
- OAuth 2.0 (*https://tools.ietf.org/html/rfc6749*)

Version 1.0 uses slightly different terminology than version 2.0 for credentials: *consumer key* and *consumer secret* (in version 1.0) are called *client credentials* in version 2.0. In addition, the *access token* and *access token secret* (in version 1.0) are referred to as *token credentials* in version 2.0. In other words, the terms *consumer* and *client* are used synonymously.

Note that the social media adapters for Cloud Integration (Twitter and Facebook adapters), which we'll discuss in Section 10.4.5, use the terms associated with OAuth version 1.0. To help you understand how these adapters work, we'll return both versions of the terms and set them into their proper context in Table 10.4.

Principal Propagation

With this authentication option, the identity of a user is transferred along all relevant communication paths of an integration scenario—from the sender to the receiver.

Inbound Authentication and Authorization (for HTTPS Communication)

We'll show you now which authentication options are supported for HTTPS-based communications for both inbound and outbound communication. In particular, we'll also explain which combinations of authentication and authorization are supported by a Cloud Integration system when acting as server (for inbound communication).

When configuring inbound HTTPS communication (where Cloud Integration is to receive messages from a sender system), note that certain sender adapters that support this protocol (e.g., the SOAP, IDoc, and HTTPS adapters) provide the option to choose an **Authorization** option (rather than an **Authentication** option). You can confirm this fact by creating, for example, a sender HTTPS channel, as in our first tutorial in the book in Chapter 2, Section 2.3.4. For your convenience, the related UI property is shown in Figure 10.34. Two authorization options are available: **User Role** and **Client Certificate**.

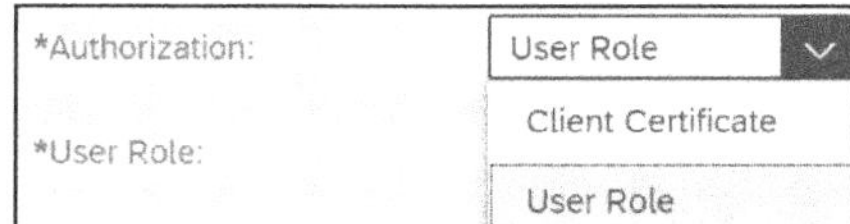

Figure 10.34 Authorization Options Offered for Certain Sender Adapters That Support HTTPS

Because we're talking about Cloud Integration as the server that is requested by a sender (client) system, you (as integration developer defining an integration scenario) can specify how the user associated with the sender is authorized to "do things" on the Cloud Integration platform. The possible options depend on the technical capabilities of the Cloud Integration platform, as follows:

- **User Role**
  For the credentials or certificates provided by the sending component, authorizations are checked based on the user-to-role assignments defined for the tenant using the SAP BTP cockpit. This *authorization* option can be used with the different *authentication* options listed in Table 10.5. (For more on the difference between authorization and authentication, Section 10.4.3.)

- **Client Certificate**
  Using this option, you'll specify the required certificate in the iFlow, in particular, in the sender adapter.
  In this case, the tenant checks whether the sender is authorized to call the tenant by comparing subject and issuer DN of the certificate forwarded by the load balancer with the one specified in the relevant iFlow.
  This option has certain disadvantages:
  - Each time the client certificate is renewed, the iFlow must be redeployed, resulting in downtime.
  - Security level is decreased because the whole certificate isn't checked, only the DNs.

  Due to these disadvantages, SAP recommends that you avoid this option. We won't, therefore, further elaborate on this option in this book.

With the selection of an *authorization* option for inbound communication, you determine already which *authentication* option can be used along with the selected authorization option.

When you select **Client Certificate** from the **Authorization** dropdown list, you'll automatically determine as the *authentication* method the option *client certificate*. In contrast, the alternative **Authorization** option, **User Role**, can be combined with different authentication options. Table 10.5 highlights the differences among the authentication options for the **User Role** authorization. A prerequisite to setting up such an authentication option is that you, the integration developer, must create an iFlow with the sender adapter's **Authorization** parameter set to **User Role**.

Authentication Option	Description
Basic authentication for technical user with client credentials from service key	The sender is authenticated based on user credentials that are generated together with an SAP BTP service key. To set up this option, using the SAP BTP cockpit, you'll create a service instance and associate a role (either a custom role or predefined role `ESBMessaging.send`) with it. For this service instance, you'll also generate a service key. The sender uses the client credentials (`clientid` and `clientsecret`) contained in the service key definition to directly call the iFlow endpoint. We assume that you're using this option when working on the tutorials in this book for the sake of simplicity (see also Section 10.3.3, Figure 10.15). For productive scenarios, however, SAP recommends using client certificate authentication or OAuth as explained at the end of this table.

Table 10.5 Authentication Options for Inbound HTTPS Communication (Service Plan Integration-Flow)

Authentication Option	Description
Basic authentication for identity provider user	The sender is authenticated based on user credentials associated with a user registered at an identity provider (Section 10.3.1). To set up this option, using the SAP BTP cockpit, you'll create a role collection that uses the predefined role `MessagingSend` (for the application with an application identifier starting with `it-rt`). In the **Trust Configuration** section of the SAP BTP cockpit, you'll assign the new role collection to the email address that is associated with the user registered at an identity provider. For more information, check out the documentation for Cloud Integration at *http://s-prs.co/5077100*.
Client certificate	The sender is authenticated based on a client certificate. To set up this option, using the SAP BTP cockpit, you create a service instance with grant type `client_x509` and associate a role (either a custom role or role `ESBMessaging.send`) with it. When creating a service key for this service instance, you enter a client certificate. The sender authenticates itself against Cloud Integration based on the client certificate. We'll describe the configuration of this authentication option in more detail in Section 10.4.4. Using this setup, the system maps a certificate to an OAuth client (for which the parameters are stored in a service key). When the sender calls Cloud Integration, it authenticates itself against Cloud Integration based on the client certificate specified in a service key. A subsequent step checks whether the sender is authorized to call the iFlow endpoint based on the role specified for the service key, which can either be the predefined role `ESBMessaging.send` or a custom role (refer to Section 10.3.3). For certain reasons (explained in Section 10.4.4), this option, together with OAuth, is a recommended option for productive scenarios.
OAuth with `client_credentials` grant type (and various other grant types)	The sender is authenticated based on an access token retrieved through an OAuth workflow. As mentioned in Section 10.4.2, for OAuth, different use cases (or variants) are specified by grant types. Cloud Integration supports various such grant types, which we won't cover in detail in this book. You can learn more from resources such as the SAP BTP product documentation.

Table 10.5 Authentication Options for Inbound HTTPS Communication (Service Plan Integration-Flow) (Cont.)

Authentication Option	Description
OAuth with `client_credentials` grant type (and various other grant types) (Cont.)	To illustrate this topic, we'll discuss only one, grant type scenario involving `client_credentials` where the sender, in the first step, gets an access token from an authorization server. In a second step, the sender uses the access token (granted by an authorization server) to call the iFlow endpoint. This option implements the OAuth workflow, as shown earlier in Figure 10.33. To set up this option, you'll create a service instance and associate a role (either a custom role or role `ESBMessaging.send`) with it. For this service instance, you'll also generate a service key. In a first call, the sender uses the `clientid` and `clientsecret` from the service key to get an access token from an authorization server. The address of the authorization server is provided by the `tokenurl` value contained in the service key. As a result, an access token is provided by the authorization server. In a second call, the sender uses the access token to call the iFlow endpoint. For more information on how to set up a scenario with such an inbound authentication option, check out the documentation for Cloud Integration at *http://s-prs.co/5077101*. Notice that, in the first option of this table (basic authentication with client credentials from service key), OAuth client credentials are also used. However, in that case, the client credentials are directly used to get access to the iFlow endpoint without going through a complete OAuth workflow to receive an access token first (as shown earlier in Figure 10.33). Using an access token is the more secure option as the token is valid only for a certain time. Therefore, this option (together with client certificate authentication) is a recommended security setup.

Table 10.5 Authentication Options for Inbound HTTPS Communication (Service Plan Integration-Flow) (Cont.)

Note that, to create a service instance for the related options mentioned in Table 10.5, as the service plan, you'll need to choose **integration-flow**. (The other service plan option, **api**, is relevant when configuring inbound authentication for API clients; see Table 10.6.)

To find out more about the supported options, check out the documentation for Cloud Integration at *http://s-prs.co/5077102*.

Table 10.5 lists the authentication options for senders to call iFlow endpoints on the tenant. This topic is relevant when—as in this section—you need to set up connections between remote systems and Cloud Integration. However, other kinds of inbound communication are also possible. As you learned from Chapter 8, Section 8.5, you can also provide access to resources in Cloud Integration for API clients. To round out the topic of inbound authentication, as listed in Table 10.6, review the inbound authentication options for API clients accessing Cloud Integration through the OData API.

Authentication Option	Description
Basic authentication for identity provider user	The API client is authenticated based on user credentials associated with a user registered at an identity provider (by default, the SAP ID service, Section 10.3.1). To set up this option, using the SAP BTP cockpit, you'll create a role collection that uses one or more roles. Note that you can assign roles depending on the use case. If you want to access monitoring data through the API, you can, e.g., assign the predefined role `MonitoringDataRead`. For a list of predefined roles, check out the documentation for Cloud Integration at *http://s-prs.co/5077103*. For the application with an application identifier starting with `it!`, in the **User** section of the SAP BTP cockpit, you assign the new role collection to an email address that is associated with a user registered at an identity provider. The API client can connect to the API directly through basic authentication using the user name and password for the registered identity provider user. For more information, check out the documentation for Cloud Integration at *http://s-prs.co/5077104*.
OAuth with the `client_credentials` grant type	The API client is authenticated based on an access token retrieved through an OAuth workflow. The corresponding OAuth workflow is the same as explained for the OAuth with the `client_credentials` grant type option for senders accessing iFlow endpoints (Table 10.5). Therefore, we won't repeat the steps. You can set up this option in the same way as explained for the iFlow endpoint with the exception that when creating the service instance, you need to choose service plan **api** instead of **integration-flow**. You can find a detailed description of how to set up this authentication option in Chapter 8, Section 8.5. You can also implement scenarios with OAuth and other grant types. However, we won't cover in detail the various grant types that are supported. For more information, check out the documentation for Cloud Integration at *http://s-prs.co/5077105*.

Table 10.6 Authentication Options for Inbound HTTPS Communication (Service Plan API)

Note that to set create a service instance for the related options listed in Table 10.6 as the service plan, you must choose **api** (instead of **integration-flow**).

10

Outbound Authentication (for HTTPS Communication)

When we talk about outbound communication where Cloud Integration acts as client, we must mention that Cloud Integration doesn't offer any choices about how the user associated with the outbound request should be authorized to execute certain actions in the receiver system. Therefore, as integration developer, you can't specify any authorization options. This situation is plausible for the following reason: how the permissions of a calling entity are checked can only be defined by the technical capabilities of the server (in the outbound communication case, the receiver system). Because Cloud Integration (as a client in this case) can't decide which technical capabilities are offered by the receiver system, Cloud Integration can't allow you to specify any authorization options in a receiver adapter.

However, in a receiver adapter, you can specify the **Authentication** option supported by the client (Cloud Integration, in this case). You can easily verify this fact by creating a receiver channel that supports HTTP communication (e.g., a receiver HTTP adapter), as shown in Figure 10.35.

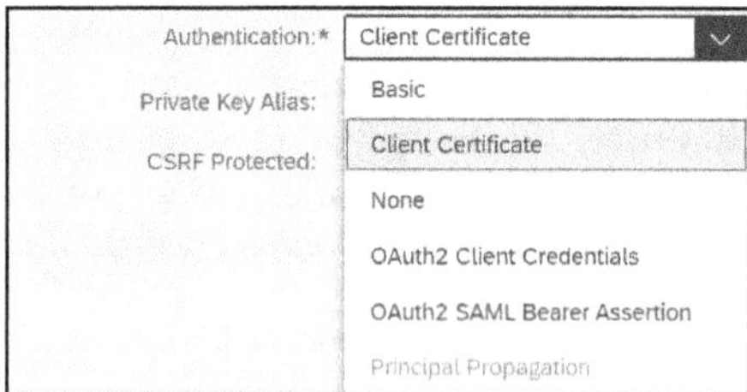

Figure 10.35 Authentication Options Offered for Receiver Adapters That Support HTTPS

Specifying an **Authentication** option makes sense because Cloud Integration can provide the required artifacts for each authentication option.

Table 10.7 summarizes the different options available and provides information on the related integration artifacts to considering when configuring each communication option.

Authentication Option	Description
Basic	Cloud Integration is authenticated against a receiver system based on user credentials (user name and password). When you configure basic authentication for outbound communication, you need to complement the related receiver adapter setting by defining a security artifact that contains the credentials (a **User Credentials** artifact as shown, e.g., in Chapter 2, Section 2.3.5). This option is supported by the following receiver adapter types: AS2, AS4, OData V2, OData V4, HTTP, IDoc, ODC, SOAP SAP RM, SOAP 1.x, SuccessFactors OData V2, and XI.

Table 10.7 Outbound Authentication Options (for HTTPS-Based Communication)

Authentication Option	Description
Client Certificate	Cloud Integration is authenticated against a receiver system based on a client certificate. A client certificate (including public and private key) and a receiver server root certificate, which is accepted by the receiver, need to be part of the **Keystore** deployed on the tenant. In the receiver adapter settings of the iFlow, the private key alias of the certificate can be modified to indicate a specific key pair must be used for this step. If you don't specify a private key alias, any appropriate key in the keystore is used. For the whole setup, refer to Section 10.4.4. This option is supported by the following receiver adapter types: Ariba, AS2, AS4, OData V2, HTTP, IDoc, SOAP SAP RM, SOAP 1.x, and XI.
Principal Propagation	Cloud Integration is authenticated against a receiver system by forwarding the identity (principal) of the user (associated with the inbound request) to the SAP Connectivity services and from there to the receiver system, which can be, e.g., an on-premise SAP system. Consequently, this option can only be selected when you've chosen **On-Premise** for the **Proxy Type** option, meaning you've configured outbound connectivity to an on-premise system through the SAP Connectivity services (see the upcoming information box). Setting up a scenario with this authentication option requires comprehensive configuration steps at the inbound and outbound side of Cloud Integration, as well as in SAP Connectivity Services and the receiver backend system. A detailed step-by-step tutorial would go beyond the scope of this book. This option is supported by the following receiver adapter types: OData V2, HTTP, IDoc, ODC, SOAP (1.x), and XI.
OAuth (when using Twitter or Facebook adapter)	Cloud Integration calls Twitter or Facebook using OAuth authentication mechanisms. A **Secure Parameter** artifact is required to store the OAuth credentials. For more information, refer to Section 10.4.5. This authentication option is supported by the Twitter and Facebook receiver adapter types. This option isn't offered for the other HTTP-based adapters.

Table 10.7 Outbound Authentication Options (for HTTPS-Based Communication) (Cont.)

Authentication Option	Description
▪ **OAuth2 SAML Bearer Assertion** ▪ **OAuth2 Client Credentials**	Cloud Integration is authenticated against a receiver system based on an access token retrieved through an OAuth workflow. Certain receiver adapters also offer the following OAuth variants: **OAuth2 SAML Bearer Assertion** and **OAuth2 Client Credentials**. To set up a scenario with such an authentication option, you also need to deploy an **OAuth2 Credentials** artifact to further specify the details for the OAuth outbound authentication (e.g., the address of the authentication server) in the **Monitor** section of the Web UI under **Manage Security (Security Material** tile). The following receiver adapter types support the **OAuth2 Client Credentials** option: AMQP/WebSocket, OData V2, OData V4, and HTTP. The following receiver adapter types support the **OAuth2 SAML Bearer Assertion** option: OData V2, HTTP, and SAP SuccessFactors OData V2.
None	If this option is selected, no authentication is required for the tenant when calling a receiver system.

Table 10.7 Outbound Authentication Options (for HTTPS-Based Communication) (Cont.)

To have permission to deploy security-related artifacts, your user must have been assigned the required roles, for example, the authorization group `AuthGroup.Administrator`. (We covered the topic of roles and authorization groups in detail in Section 10.3.)

Proxy Type

The following adapter settings are relevant in the context of configuring the **Authentication** setting **Principal Propagation**.

In most HTTP-based adapters (e.g., the SOAP and IDoc adapters), you'll find the attribute **Proxy Type**. In the scenarios we cover in this book, we always kept the default setting of this attribute (**Internet**), which ensures that the tenant can connect to another system through the internet (e.g., over HTTP).

The other option for the **Proxy Type** attribute is **On-Premise**. Using this option, the tenant can connect to an on-premise system through SAP Connectivity services.

When setting up such a scenario, you'll also need to install an additional component, The SAP Connectivity services, referred to as the *cloud connector*, in your on-premise landscape, that acts as proxy for requests that try to access your on-premise system coming from the internet.

If you use multiple cloud connector instances in your system landscape, you'll also need to specify a **Location ID**. With this attribute, you can identify the cloud connector instance you want to use for your connection.

You might have noticed that when you select **On-Premise** from the **Proxy Type** drop-down list, **Authentication** option **Client Certificate** is deactivated. This shows that when using SAP Connectivity services, this authentication option isn't supported in the respective receiver adapter. If client certificate authentication is nevertheless required for such a connection, you'll need to configure this authentication option when setting up SAP Connectivity services.

For more information, consult the documentation for SAP BTP at *https://help.sap.com/docs/btp* in the **Cloud Connector** section and at *http://s-prs.co/5077106*.

10.4.4 Securely Connecting a Customer System to Cloud Integration through HTTPS

Having introduced transport-level security options in Section 10.4.2 and authorization and authentication options in Section 10.4.3, we can now discuss how to establish a secure connection between a remote system and Cloud Integration. For simplicity, we'll focus on the most common option: using HTTPS over TLS and client certificate authentication. We'll discuss this topic separately for inbound communication (when a sender sends a request to Cloud Integration) and for outbound communication (when Cloud Integration sends a request to a receiver) because the setup of components and the sequence of tasks differ considerably, depending on the communication direction.

For inbound communication, we'll show you how to set up **User Role** authorization in combination with client certificate authentication (compare Table 10.5). For both directions, we'll first outline the target picture (setup of components and keystores) and then explain the steps required to achieve this setup.

Note that we won't provide an end-to-end tutorial on setting up a specific iFlow. Instead, we'll focus on the steps relevant to setting up a secure connection both for inbound and outbound direction, namely, the configuration of the required keys and certificates as well as certain steps in the configuration of the sender and receiver adapter. We also won't show you how to configure certain sender or receiver systems in detail, which would require a complete integration scenario and a specific technical landscape (for specific kinds of sender and receiver systems). For more information on the complete setup of integration packages offered by SAP and published on SAP Business Accelerator Hub, including the configuration of certain SAP systems at the sender and receiver side, refer to the integration guides available in the **Documents** section for certain integration packages (see Chapter 3).

When showing the connection setup steps for the sender and receiver adapters, we'll show (as an example) how to use a SOAP 1.x adapter. However, these steps work for most other adapters that support HTTP communication.

Inbound Communication

For inbound communication, the recommended option is client certificate authentication. We already briefly introduced this topic earlier in Table 10.5.

Figure 10.36 shows how the components interact with each other at runtime (on top) and the required security setup to realize this behavior (bottom).

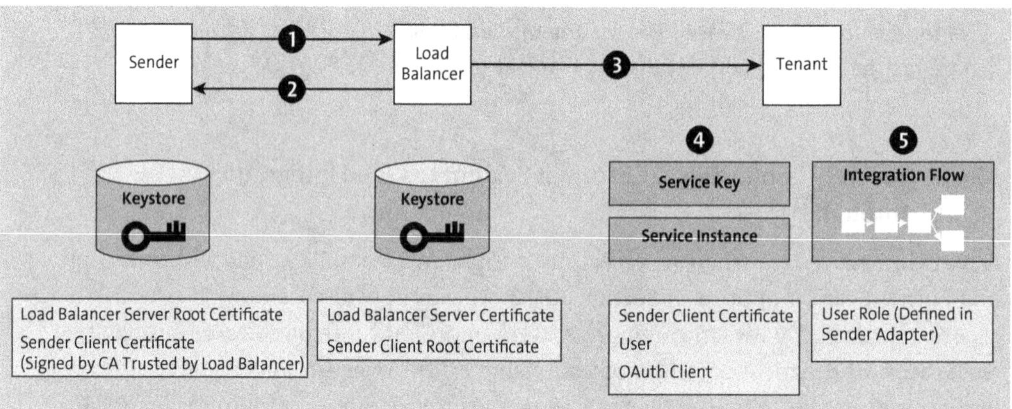

Figure 10.36 Component Setup for a Secure Inbound Connection Using Client Certificate Authentication

To begin the target setup, a characteristic feature of inbound HTTP connections is that the load balancer terminates each TLS request from the sender and establishes a new TLS connection to the tenant, which is then processing the request (shown earlier in Figure 10.1). The process is then as follows (steps in the text correspond to the numbers shown in Figure 10.36):

❶ The sender system connects to the load balancer via TLS and verifies the load balancer certificate.

❷ In the other direction, the load balancer verifies whether the certificate sent by the sender system is valid. Note that we've chosen client certificate authentication of the sender system. For this security option, certificates are stored in a keystore on the load balancer component, which is a component maintained by SAP. The client certificate installed on the sender system must be signed by one of the CAs supported by the load balancer. SAP has published a list of supported CAs in the documentation.

❸ If the validation is successful, the load balancer forwards the client certificate (as part of the message header) to the tenant.

❹ In a subsequent step, the system checks if a service key is available that contains the sender's client certificate. If this service key exists, the role specified for the associated service instance is checked.

Note that, in this setup, the service instance is an OAuth client with the following associations:

- With a dedicated role that allows the sending application to process the iFlow deployed on the worker of a Cloud Integration tenant
- With OAuth grant type `client_x509` to indicate that a client certificate is expected in the related service key definition

❺ If this role is identical to the one configured for the sender adapter of the iFlow endpoint (addressed by the sender's request), the message is processed on the worker according to the iFlow settings.

We'll show you in a minute the definition of a service instance for client certificate authentication. But let's just mention that the service instance refers to a role (e.g., `ESB-Messaging.send` or a custom role) and, thus, associates the sender (authenticated through a certificate) with the permission to call those iFlows for which in the sender adapter this role is specified.

When you go back to the setup of an inbound communication based on credentials (compare Figure 10.15 and also in Chapter 2, Section 2.3.4, especially Figure 2.30), notice that the service key definition in that case contained the client credentials (the `clientId` and `clientsecret` that correspond to user name and password of the sending application). When setting up client certificate inbound authentication, the service key contains a certificate instead. We'll show you a service key definition in a minute.

A service instance represents an SAP BTP entity that defines how a dedicated platform service can be accessed. In our scenario, this access method is via an OAuth client with grant type `client_x509`.

Note that you can create multiple service keys for one service instance. However, a client certificate can be assigned to one service instance only once.

You can find a step-by-step description of the required steps for this connection at *http://s-prs.co/5077107*. This blog outlines the necessary steps in detail. In the following subsections, we'll only summarize key aspects.

Furthermore, the iFlow design guidelines provided by SAP (see Chapter 6, Section 6.11) provide example iFlows that illustrate client certificate–based authentication. You'll find the relevant documentation and example iFlows on the SAP Business Accelerator Hub (*https://api.sap.com/*) in integration package **Integration Flow Design Guidelines - Apply Highest Security Standards**. The names of the related iFlows are **Apply Security - Use Client Certificate Authentication - Sender Channel** and **Apply Security - Use Client Certificate Authentication - Receiver Channel**.

A Note Regarding the SAP BTP, Neo Environment

In the SAP BTP, Neo environment, the steps for setting up secure inbound connections using client certificates are a bit different. We won't go into the details here, but you can refer instead to *http://s-prs.co/5077108*. You can also check out the documentation for Cloud Integration at *http://s-prs.co/5077109*.

In the SAP BTP, Neo environment, the concepts of service instance and service key don't apply. To grant permissions to process an iFlow for a sender (that authenticates itself with a client certificate), the client certificate must be related to a user in a **Certificate-to-User Mapping**, which is a dedicated artifact deployed on the tenant. Furthermore, for the user, the dedicated role (that grants the permission) must be assigned. At runtime, the system checks whether such an artifact exists that relates the certificate (provided by the sender) to a user for which the required permission is granted (as defined in a user-to-role assignment).

Configuring the Sender System

Sender system configuration includes generating a client certificate and sending the corresponding certificate signing request (CSR) to a CA for a signature. The administrator of the sender system needs to make sure that the client certificate is signed by a CA that is also supported by the load balancer. Afterwards, the administrator applies the CA's reply and imports the signed certificate into the sender keystore.

Note

How certificates are installed and the type of keystore used on the sender side depends on the kind of sender system, which we won't cover here.

Because the load balancer is controlled centrally and administered by SAP, no configuration actions are required for this component. The administrator of the sender system must make sure that the certificates installed on the sender system are compatible with those installed on the load balancer in terms of the hierarchical trust model.

You'll find a list of root certificates supported by the load balancer in the documentation for Cloud Integration at *http://s-prs.co/5077110*.

Furthermore, the sender keystore must contain the load balancer root certificate (so that the sender system can trust the load balancer). A smart way to get the load balancer root certificate is using the outbound connectivity test tool that we used earlier in Chapter 2, Section 2.3.6, and Figure 2.58. to get the certificate of an email server. In the previous case, we used this tool to find a certificate offered by a receiver system (the email server) to which Cloud Integration connected as a client. In our present case, we need to find a certificate offered by the load balancer which represents (for external sender applications) the worker of Cloud Integration. Therefore, to get the required certificate, the administrator of the sender system can use Cloud Integration, go to the **Monitor** page of the Web UI, and select the **Connectivity Tests** tile (under **Manage Security**). On the UI of the connectivity test tool, select the **TLS** tile, and, in the **Host** field, enter the URL of the worker.

You can find this URL by clicking a tile under **Manage Integration Content** and checking out a deployed iFlow with an endpoint (e.g., with an HTTPS sender adapter; compare Chapter 2, Section 2.3.4). Copy the URL (but without the iFlow-specific relative endpoint address; compare Figure 10.41, shown later) to the clipboard. The URL must contain the string *cfapps* and end with *hana.ondemand.com*. Deselect the **Validate Server Certificate** option, and click **Send**. Figure 10.37 shows the result.

You'll enter the worker URL in the **Host** field as shown in Figure 10.37 ❶. To download the certificates, click the **Download** button ❷. You'll get a compressed (*.zip*) file. Unzip this archive, select the *.cer* file that corresponds to the root certificate, and import this file into the sender system's keystore.

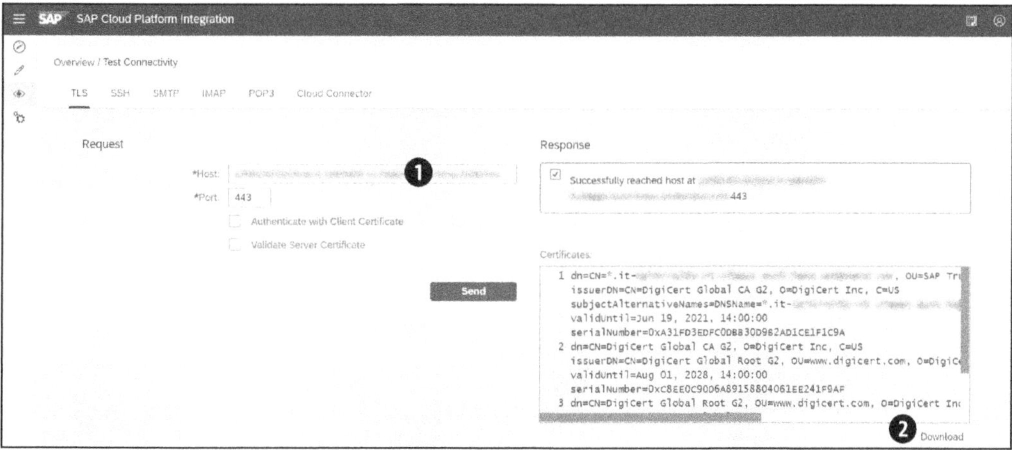

Figure 10.37 Getting the Load Balancer Root Certificate Using the Connectivity Test Tool

Configuring the Inbound Authorization in the Related Integration Flow

We assume that, as the integration developer, you're using an HTTPS sender adapter (see Chapter 2, Section 2.3.4, Figure 2.24). For **Authorization**, keep the setting **User Role** to ensure that, for the user associated with the calling sender, the permissions are checked based on certificate-to-service key mappings by the Cloud Integration framework. In the **User Role** field, you can keep the entry **ESBMessaging.send**. This role is predefined by SAP to authorize a sender (the SOAP client) to call your tenant. Alternatively, you can specify a custom role in this field. With this option, you can restrict access to Cloud Integration on the level of individual iFlows (e.g., in case certain iFlows are only to be called by specific senders). To use custom roles, you'll also need to define this custom role for the runtime node and configure the custom role in the relevant service instance in the SAP BTP cockpit (as explained earlier in Section 10.3.3).

When you've finished the iFlow design, deploy the iFlow on the tenant.

Defining the Service Instance and the Service Key

Let's first assume that you want to authorize the sender system to call the iFlow based on the predefined role `ESBMessaging.send`. Alternatively, you can create a custom role. In any case, you'll need to get the JSON representation of the role. Open the **Monitor** page of the Web UI (as explained in Section 10.3.3, compare Figure 10.16). You can either download the JSON representation of the predefined role `ESBMessaging.send` or of a different custom role. The predefined role has the following format:

```
{"roles":["ESBMessaging.send"]}
```

As mentioned earlier (refer to Figure 10.36), you must define a service instance and generate a service key for it. As described in Chapter 2, Section 2.3.3, we recommended that you to set up inbound authentication based on user credentials, which is also referred to as basic authentication. In that case, when creating the service instance, you uploaded the JSON content from the source role directly into the service instance definition (as shown earlier in Figure 10.20).

Now that the sender system authenticates itself against Cloud Integration using a client certificate, the service instance definition on SAP BTP must contain the following, modified entry (as shown in Figure 10.38):

```
{
    "roles": ["ESBMessaging.send"],
    "grant-types": ["client_x509"]
}
```

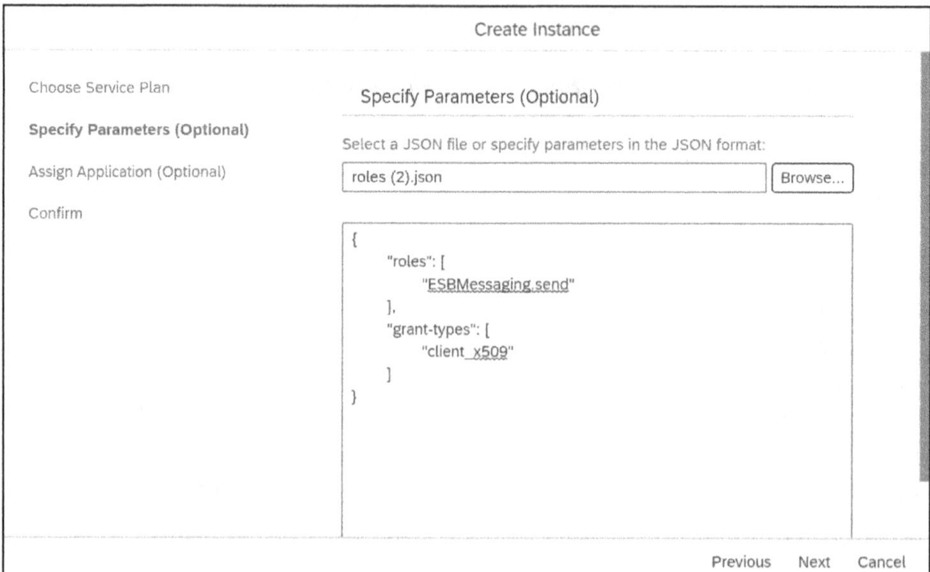

Figure 10.38 Service Instance Definition for Client Certificate-Based Inbound Authentication

In other words, you're extending the JSON representation of the role downloaded from the **Monitor** page of the Web UI by adding the grant type `client_x509`.

Using a Custom Role

Let's assume you want to define a custom role called **ProcessBookIntegrationFlow** for the worker (as explained in Section 10.3.4, compare Figure 10.20) and assign this custom role to the service instance (associated with the service key that defines the credentials associated with the inbound call).

In the sender adapter (e.g., the HTTPS sender channel), you'll define a few settings differently: in the **Authorization** dropdown list, specify **User Role**, and, in the **User Role** dropdown list, select **ProcessBookIntegrationFlow**.

In the service instance definition (compare Figure 10.38), the JSON entry has the following form:

```
{
    "roles": ["ProcessBookIntegrationFlow"],
    "grant-types": ["client_x509"]
}
```

Having configured these settings, the iFlow can only be processed when the certificate associated with the inbound call is related to role `ProcessBookIntegrationFlow`.

Notice that grant type `client_x509` tells the system that authentication is now based on client certificates (based on standard X.509). Likewise, when you create a service key for this service instance, as shown in Figure 10.39, you'll add the client certificate of the sender system, which you just stored on your computer) and enter it in Base64-encoded format under **Configuration Parameters (JSON)**.

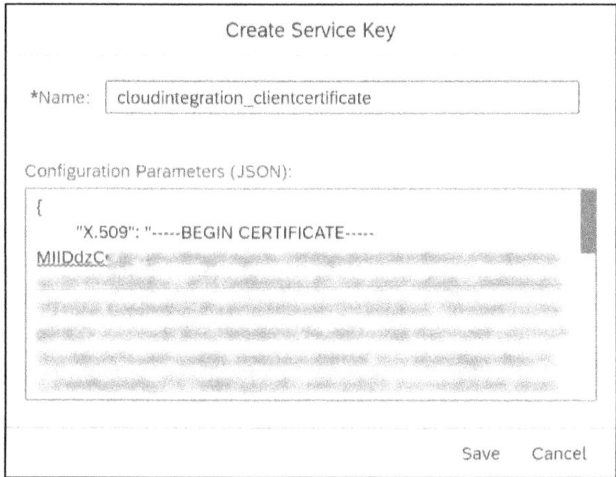

Figure 10.39 Adding the Certificate as JSON Content to the Service Key Definition

After the service key has been generated, the OAuth artifacts are displayed, as shown in Figure 10.40.

Notice that the service key relates authorization (represented by the role `ESBMessaging.send`) with authentication (the JSON representation of the service key containing the Base64-encoded client certificate).

Recall that, when using a SAP BTP, Cloud Foundry environment trial account, client certificate–based authentication of inbound calls isn't supported. Therefore, to implement the scenario we've described in this section, you must have access to a licensed SAP BTP, Cloud Foundry environment account.

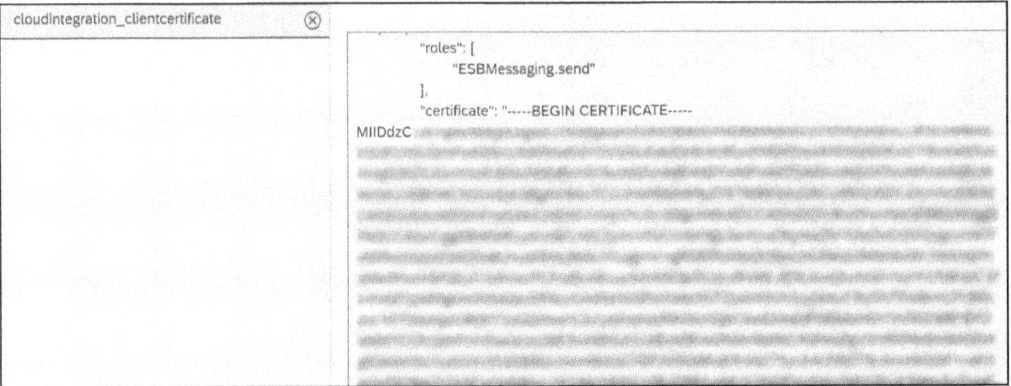

Figure 10.40 Service Key Definition (Subset of Entries) Relates Role with Certificate

> **Client Certificate Authorization**
>
> In an alternative setup, inbound communication can be defined so that the permissions of the sender are checked based on the subject/issuer DN of a client certificate, which is specified directly in the iFlow. As mentioned earlier in Section 10.4.3, SAP doesn't recommend using this option.

Outbound Communication

Let's now consider the outbound side where the tenant sends a message to a remote receiver system using an HTTP connection. Figure 10.41 shows how the components interact with each other at runtime (on top) and the required security setup to realize this behavior (bottom).

To begin the target setup, the tenant connects to the receiver via TLS and verifies the receiver certificate as shown in Figure 10.40 ❶. In the other direction, the receiver verifies whether the certificate sent by the tenant is valid ❷. These steps are performed based on the installed certificates, both on the tenant and in the receiver system. For the discussed security option, the certificates of the tenant are stored in the tenant keystore. Similar to the inbound communication case, the identity and permissions of the tenant are checked in the receiver system (based on the settings in the receiver system).

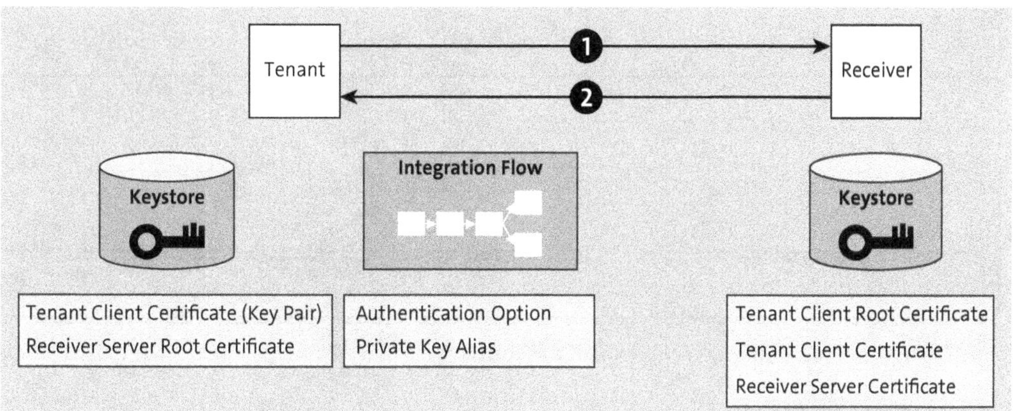

Figure 10.41 Setup of Components Required to Establish a Secure Outbound Connection Using HTTPS and Client Certificate Authentication

Configuring the Receiver System

Configuring the receiver system requires first creating a server certificate (private key pair) and then importing it into the receiver keystore. The server certificate can be a certificate chain where the top-level certificate is a root certificate issued by a dedicated CA. The administrator of the receiver system needs to download the root certificate from the receiver keystore and make it available to the tenant administrator.

Additionally, the receiver keystore must contain the tenant client certificate and the tenant client root certificate. To enable the receiver administrator to perform the necessary steps, the tenant administrator will export the certificate chain of the tenant client certificate from the tenant keystore, extract the root certificate and the client certificate out of it, and hand both over to the receiver system administrator.

Configuring the Tenant Keystore

To enable the tenant to trust the receiver system, the tenant administrator needs to import the (server) root certificate of the receiver, which is to be provided by the administrator of the receiver system, into the tenant keystore.

Before going into the configuration details, let's quickly review what we know already about the keystore. With the provisioning of your tenant cluster, SAP has already provided a tenant keystore with a number of preinstalled certificates. You can find the content of the keystore by opening the **Monitor** page of the Web UI and selecting the **Keystore** tile (under **Manage Security**) (see also Chapter 7, Section 7.3.2, and Section 10.5 in this chapter).

Figure 10.42 shows the content of a tenant keystore (example) for a licensed SAP BTP, Cloud Foundry environment account.

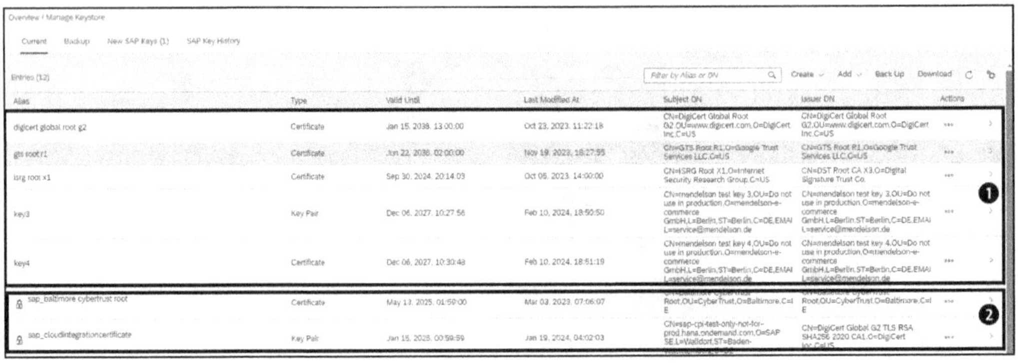

Figure 10.42 Content of the Tenant Keystore

You became familiar with the keystore in Chapter 2, Section 2.3.6 (compare Figure 2.61 when setting up the first iFlow of this book). You also learned that, to set up a secure connection to an email *receiver*, you needed to add additional certificates to the keystore. The newly imported certificate is then owned by the tenant administrator. Figure 10.42 shows a certificate and a key pair owned by SAP ❶ and certificates owned by the tenant administrator ❷, which have been added later by the tenant administrator (in other words, by you).

In an analogous way, as in the tutorial in Chapter 2 for connecting to the email receiver, you'll need to import the server certificate of any receiver system to set up certificate-based outbound communication.

To enable trust the other way around (so that the receiver trusts the tenant), a client certificate is also required as part of the tenant keystore (private public key pair). All licensed tenants provided by SAP contain already a key pair (trial tenants don't). You can use this certificate to configure this step.

Section 10.5 will provide more details on certificate management for the tenant and on all features of the keystore.

Configuring and Deploying the Integration Flow

In addition to the previous steps, you'll need to specify the required security settings in the related iFlow and the associated receiver adapter.

If you use an HTTP receiver adapter to connect the tenant to the receiver system, specify the following settings:

- **Authentication**
  Select the **Client Certificate** option.
- **Private Key Alias**
  Enter the alias of the signed tenant client certificate that you intend to use for

authentication when connecting to the associated receiver. The alias is used to point to a specific key pair in the tenant keystore. If you leave this field empty, any valid key pair will be used for this step.

As shown earlier in Figure 10.35 for the UI of the HTTP receiver adapter, under the **Connection** tab, several authentication options are available among the HTTP-based receiver adapters.

Finally, deploy the iFlow on the tenant.

Outbound Connectivity Test Tool

To test your security configuration, Cloud Integration provides an outbound connectivity test tool for the various protocols, including for HTTP connections using TLS.

When setting up the first iFlow described in this book (Chapter 2, Section 2.3.6), you were introduced to this tool, in that case, for SMTP. This tool is described in detail in Chapter 7, Section 7.3.8.

10.4.5 Setting Up a Scenario Using OAuth with the Twitter Adapter

In Section 10.4.3, we introduced the concept of OAuth, which allows a resource owner to grant client applications restricted access to his resources. Social networks, such as Facebook or Twitter, provide APIs for client applications that support OAuth.

Cloud Integration offers adapters to connect a tenant with Facebook and Twitter to write data to these platforms or to read data from them. Both adapter types work in the same way. In this section, we'll show you how to set up a simple integration scenario using the Twitter adapter.

The Twitter receiver adapter allows a Cloud Integration tenant (in terms of OAuth, this tenant is the *client*) to access Twitter (the *resource server*) on behalf of a Twitter user (the *resource owner*). After gaining access, the tenant can either read or post tweets on Twitter (via the resource owner's account). You can use this adapter, for example, to implement market analysis scenarios.

Technically, the tenant calls the Twitter API. As a prerequisite, the integration developer must prepare the tenant so that the tenant can call Twitter on behalf of a specific Twitter user. For this task, the integration developer obtains a set of client credentials from Twitter that will be used to authenticate the client (tenant) in the Twitter API.

In Section 10.4.3, we described a common OAuth authentication scenario in which, every time the client requests access to the server, the resource owner is asked by the server to grant the client access to the protected resources. A user dialog box will open for the resource owner who needs to log on to the server with credentials. For Cloud Integration scenarios, this workflow isn't feasible because, each time message processing is triggered, a resource owner must log on to Twitter and confirm that the required token credentials are being generated for the client.

To address this aspect, the Twitter adapter uses OAuth in a more system-centric way. The integration developer (who is identical to the resource owner, i.e., the Twitter account user) provides the tenant with all credentials (client and token credentials) when defining the Twitter adapter settings in the iFlow.

Figure 10.43, derived from Figure 10.32, shows the general OAuth setup adapted to the Twitter adapter scenario. On a high level, OAuth is being used in the following way in this scenario: The Twitter account owner creates a Twitter app and during this step gets client and token credentials ❶. The integration developer uses these credentials when defining the connection from Cloud Integration to Twitter ❷. To be more precise, the client and token credentials must be made known to the tenant in **Secure Parameter** artifacts. When the iFlow is processed (at runtime), the tenant can access Twitter resources and read tweets ❸. We'll explain all these steps in detail now when setting up the scenario.

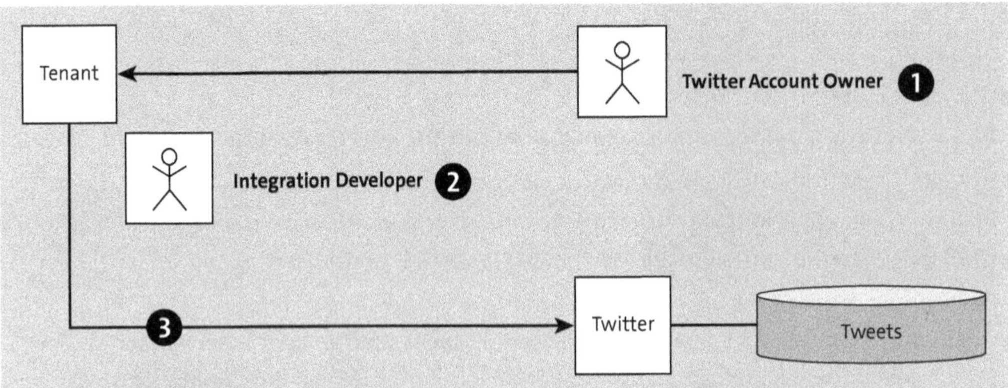

Figure 10.43 OAuth Setup of Components When Using the Twitter Adapter

Different Usage of OAuth with Cloud Integration Adapters

As you'll see in the following tutorial, when configuring a connection to Twitter using the Twitter adapter, you generate the OAuth client and access tokens (including secrets) when configuring a Twitter app for the Twitter API access. To enable the Cloud Integration tenant to access Twitter resources, the relevant iFlow needs to know the client and token credentials. The iFlow developer, for this purpose, deploys all associated OAuth credentials as **Secure Parameter** artifacts and points to these artifacts in the Twitter adapter configuration.

As mentioned earlier, other adapters (than the Twitter and Facebook adapters) also support OAuth (compare also Table 10.7). Note, however, that when using these other adapters (AMQP adapter, OData adapter, the SAP SuccessFactors [OData] adapter, and the HTTP receiver adapter), OAuth is used and must be configured in a different way.

In these cases, the integration developer only specifies client credentials when designing the integration scenario. Other than in the Twitter scenario, OAuth tokens aren't declared as part of the integration design. Instead, to make the OAuth setup work, the integration developer must specify the address of the authorization server when designing the integration scenario. Compare Figure 10.32 and Figure 10.33 and recall that the authorization server generates access token credentials for dedicated client credentials. For that purpose, to configure a proper OAuth setup, you must specify OAuth client credentials and the authorization's server address. To fulfill this requirement, you'll use another artifact type: the **OAuth2 Credentials** artifact.

To recap, in the Twitter scenario, you've generated the access token credentials when configuring the Twitter app. Furthermore, you provided both client credentials and token credentials as part of the integration design (in **Secure Parameter** artifacts). When using other HTTP-based adapters that support OAuth (and use **OAuth2 Credentials** artifacts), you leave it to the authorization server to generate the token credentials.

Designing an Integration Flow Using the Twitter Adapter

Figure 10.44 shows the target iFlow, which we'll describe briefly before explaining how to set it up step-by-step.

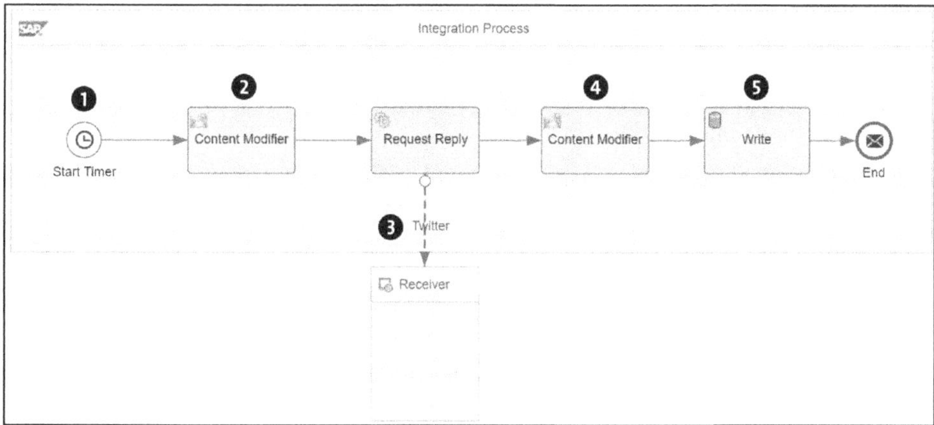

Figure 10.44 Target iFlow with the Twitter Adapter

We'll briefly explain how the iFlow works and describe the settings for its steps and channels. For the Twitter adapter, we'll provide more detailed explanations. The iFlow works in the following way (numbers correspond to those shown in Figure 10.44):

❶ A **Start Timer** event (introduced in Chapter 6, Section 6.1.2) starts the message flow.

❷ A **Content Modifier** step creates a property that contains the actual timestamp (to be used later to make transparent when data from Twitter has been read).

❸ A **Request Reply** step (see Chapter 4, Section 4.3) calls a receiver (**Receiver**, which represents Twitter) through the Twitter adapter and reads data from it.

❹ Another **Content Modifier** step defines the message body, which consists of an introductory sentence and the response received from Twitter in the previous step.

❺ Finally, the message is written to the tenant database using a data store **Write** step. The **Data Store Name** is statically defined (`TwitterContent`), whereas the **Entry ID** is defined by the timestamp.

Because we'll show you how to set up this iFlow soon, we'll keep our descriptions short and focus on aspects specific to how Twitter and OAuth come into play in this scenario.

Tasks Related to the Twitter API

Let's assume that you (the resource owner) are using your own Twitter account for this scenario. To prepare the Twitter account for a Cloud Integration scenario, follow these steps:

1. Go to *https://dev.twitter.com/apps*, and create an app by choosing **Create an app**.
2. On the next screen, you'll be prompted to apply for a Twitter developer account. Click **Apply**.
3. Select some reasons for why you want to use the Twitter API, and click **Next**.
4. Confirm your phone number.
5. You'll receive a verification code on your mobile phone, which you need to confirm on the next screen.
6. You'll be prompted for some more information, such as your country. After you've specified this information, click **Next**.
7. On the next screen, you'll be asked to explain why and to what extent you plan to use the Twitter API. Answer these questions in as much detail as you can, and click **Next**.
8. A summary of your answers will be displayed. If your answers are consistent with Twitter's guidelines, you can click on the **Looks good!** button.
9. You'll be asked to confirm the Developer Agreement. When you're ready to confirm, click **Submit Application**.
10. Finally, you'll need to verify your Twitter developer account in an email received from Twitter.
11. Now, you can start creating an app. Click **Create an app**.
12. Provide a **Name** and a **Description**. For the **Website URL** field, enter any test URL.
13. You'll be prompted again for some reasons expressing the purpose for this app. Answer these questions in as much detail as you can; leave the other fields (in particular, under **Callback URLs**) empty, and click **Create**.

    On the following page, shown in Figure 10.45, certain information will be displayed.
14. Choose the **Keys and tokens** tab.

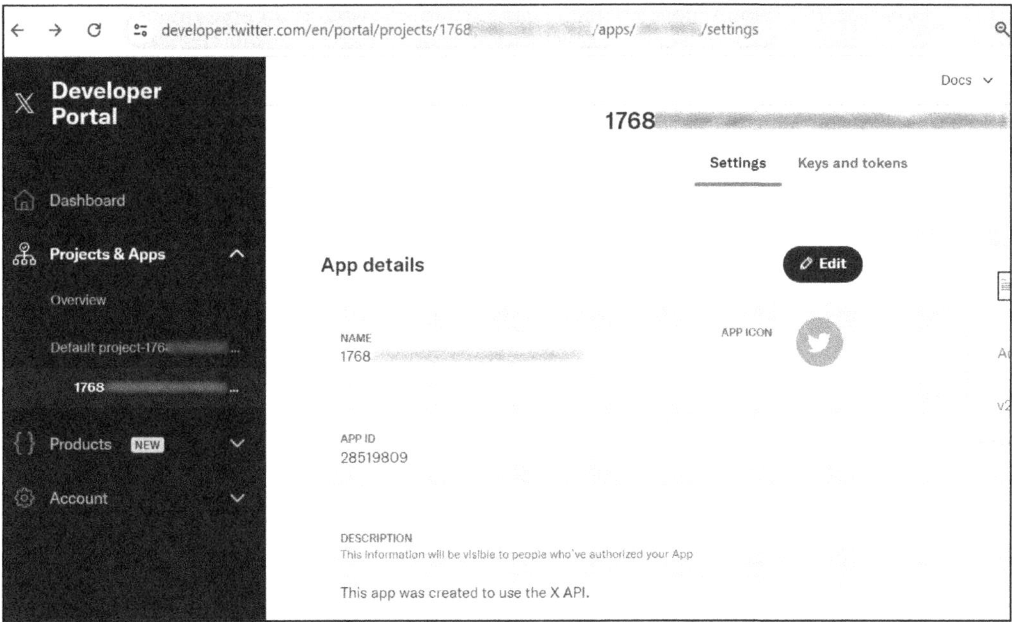

Figure 10.45 UI of the Twitter App

15. Make a note of the information displayed under **Consumer API keys**.
16. Under **Access token & access token secret**, click **Create**.

The access tokens will be displayed.

Note

Twitter will use the access token and access token secret only when you first generate these artifacts for security reasons. If you need access to this information later, you'll need to regenerate the keys, which will invalidate your current keys and tokens that you'll need in the iFlow configuration described in the following steps.

Now, you have the two credentials you need to further configure our scenario. In the next step, you'll define a separate security artifact for both the key and the secret of each of the two credentials (in total, four artifacts) and deploy them on the tenant. When configuring the iFlow, you'll refer to these artifacts in the Twitter adapter configuration UI.

Creating and Deploying the Required Security Artifacts

To provide the tenant with the credentials, you must create and deploy an individual **Secure Parameter** artifact for each of the four credential artifacts. During this step, only you, the resource owner, can see the actual values of the keys and access tokens (when creating and deploying the artifacts). As when creating and deploying a **User Credentials** artifact (see Chapter 2, Section 2.3.4), you'll give each of these entities an alias, and the alias will be used during the subsequent iFlow configuration to complete the Twitter adapter settings. In this one, only you, the resource owner, knows the keys and access tokens. Others who use the Web UI on the same tenant will only see the credential names (aliases), thus keeping confidential information protected.

For our example, we'll use the aliases listed in Table 10.8 for the four credential types.

Artifact	Alias
API key	Twitter_ConsumerKey
API secret key	Twitter_Secret
Access token	Twitter_AccessToken
Access token secret	Twitter_TokenSecret

Table 10.8 Proposed Aliases for the OAuth Credentials

Repeat the following steps for each of the four artifacts—**Consumer Key**, **Consumer Secret**, **Access Token**, and **Token Secret**:

1. Connect to your tenant using the Web UI, and choose **Monitor**.
2. Click the **Security Material** tile in the **Manage Security** section.
3. Choose **Add • Secure Parameter**.
4. For the **Name** field, enter an alias, which later you must enter into the corresponding field of the Twitter adapter. We recommend that you use the aliases listed in Table 10.8.
5. Paste the corresponding credential artifact from your Twitter app into the **Secure Parameter** and **Repeat Secure Parameter** fields.
6. Click **Deploy**.

The **Secure Parameter** artifact has now been deployed and is displayed in the table under **Manage Security Material**.

Configuring the Integration Flow with the Twitter Adapter

To create a receiver communication channel with the Twitter adapter, follow these steps:

1. Using the Web UI, create an iFlow with the elements shown earlier in Figure 10.44.
2. For the **Start** step, use a **Timer** event. You can leave the **Run Once** checkbox selected.
3. Add the first **Content Modifier** step, which will create a property to contain the timestamp of the actual message processing run. Under the **Exchange Property** tab, specify the following parameters:

- **Name**: "timestamp"
- **Type**: **Expression**
- **Value**: "${date:now:yyyy-MM-dd HH:mm:ss}"

4. Add a **Request Reply** step that connects to the **Receiver** shape using the **Twitter** channel.

   This channel connects to the Twitter API using the OAuth credentials generated when creating the Twitter app and reads Twitter content for a dedicated keyword.

5. Configure the Twitter adapter with the details shown in Figure 10.46.

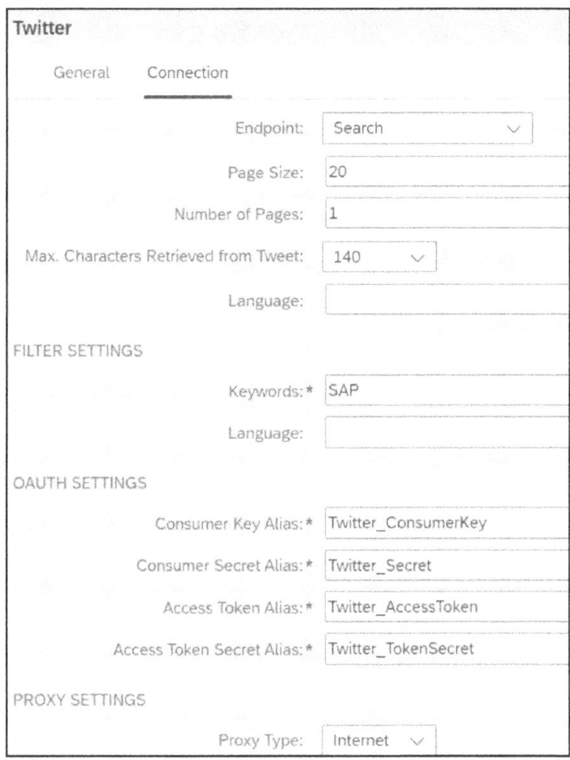

Figure 10.46 Twitter Adapter Settings: Connection Tab

For the **Endpoint** dropdown list, select **Search**, which enables the tenant to extract information from Twitter (based on certain criteria).

Two other options are available in the **Endpoint** dropdown list:

- **Send Tweet**: Enables the tenant to send a message to Twitter (to the account of the resource owner associated with the credentials configured under **OAuth Settings**).
- **Send Direct Message**: Enables the tenant to send a message to a user who doesn't necessarily have to be identical to the resource owner. When choosing the **Send Direct Message** option, you'll specify this user in an additional **User** field that is hidden when one of the other two options for **Endpoint** is selected.

Select **Search** because our iFlow starts with a timer. (Sending an empty message to Twitter makes no sense.)

6. The **Page Size** field allows you to specify the maximum number of tweets per page, and the **Number of Pages** field allows you to specify the number of pages that the tenant is supposed to consume.
7. In the **Keywords** field, you can either enter keywords or Twitter queries to filter Twitter content (queries are explained at *https://dev.twitter.com/rest/public/search*).
8. With the **Language** field, you can specify the search language (e.g., **EN** for English).
9. Under **OAUTH SETTINGS**, enter the aliases of the **Secure Parameter** artifacts we deployed in the previous step (see also Table 10.8).
10. The second **Content Modifier** step creates a message payload that contains a headline and the actual content received from Twitter. Maintain the following settings under the **Message Body** tab:
    - **Type: Expression**
    - Entry field for the body:

    ```
    This content is extracted from Twitter:
    ${in.body}
    ```

    Note that the expression `${in.body}` gets the actual message content received from Twitter.

    This detour must be made to provide a message body to be written into the database with the following data store **Write** step.
11. Add the data store **Write** step with the settings shown in Figure 10.47.
12. Save and deploy the iFlow.

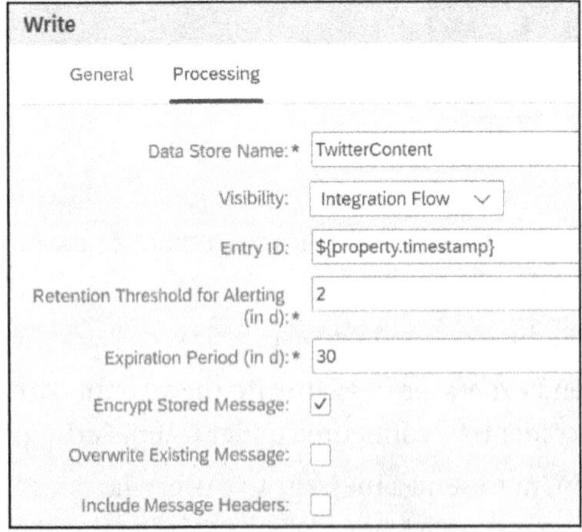

Figure 10.47 Data Store Write Step Attributes

Once you've deployed the iFlow, message processing is triggered (according to the settings in the timer **Start** event).

Download the data store entry (as shown in Chapter 2, Section 2.3.4).

Notice that, for each new deployment (for each new message processing run), a new data store entry with a new timestamp (**Entry ID**) is created. Figure 10.48 shows the content of the data store after three message processing runs.

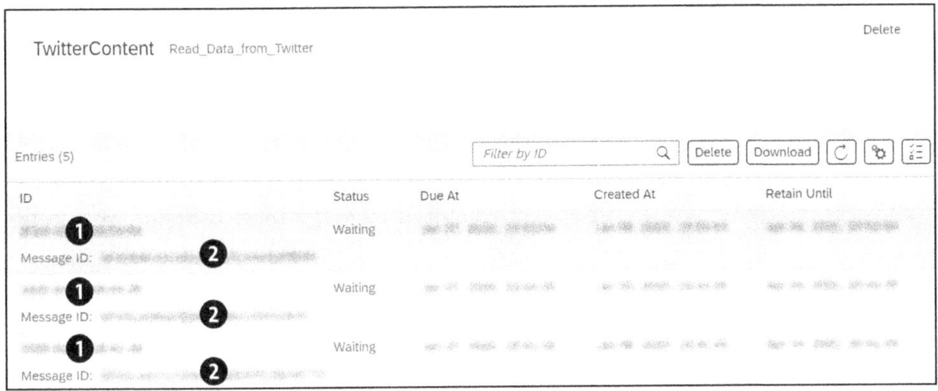

Figure 10.48 Data Store Entries after Three Different Messaging Processing Runs (Three Different Timestamps)

Notice that, for each message processing run an entry has been created, each with a timestamp ❶. Each entry also shows the actual message ID ❷ of the actual message processing run.

When you open the *body* text file contained in the downloaded *.zip* file, you'll find Twitter content for the specified settings.

You can easily enhance this iFlow in a way similar to the third part of the tutorial described in Chapter 2, for instance, by adding an email receiver so that the Twitter content is sent to an email account. You can also consider changing the timer scheduler settings so that such an email is sent on a regular basis (maybe once a day containing all top tweets for a given keyword).

10.4.6 Message-Level Security Options

On top of establishing a secure transport channel as explained in Section 10.4.2, you can further protect the messages to be exchanged with digital encryption and digital signatures. Applying these options increases the security level of your scenario because even if the transport channel is compromised, the messages still can't be read by malicious parties. Signing a message allows a recipient to validate whether the message has been received from the expected sender, increasing data integrity.

Why Decrypt Messages on the Cloud Integration Tenant?

You might ask yourself why not always pass encrypted messages through Cloud Integration and thus keep the exchanged message a *black box* for the integration middleware (unreadable for anyone in the unlikely case that any malicious party receives unauthorized access to the infrastructure at the software provider's side). Why is there any need to decrypt a message on the tenant at all? The reason is that various integration patterns require the runtime components to access the message content to process the message correctly.

One example for this is content-based routing (CBR) (see Chapter 4, Section 4.6). Consider a scenario where a message sent from one company is routed to one, or many, possible banks (receivers), and the actual receiver depends on the value of the bank identifier code (BIC) in the message. To process the routing step in the intended way, the message must be decrypted on the tenant prior to the routing step to reveal the BIC.

How Digitally Encrypting and Decrypting a Message Works

Cloud Integration supports various message-level security standards that each work in different ways. However, there is a general pattern. All these options use a hybrid approach of asymmetric and symmetric key technologies (Section 10.4.1). We'll briefly show this pattern for both use cases: encryption/decryption and signing/verifying.

For encryption/decryption, the process was already explained in the information box in Section 10.4.1 and shown in , so we'll only briefly repeat the steps.

The sender uses a symmetric key (typically randomly generated) to encrypt the message content. Additionally, the sender uses the public key of the receiver, which has been provided by the receiver in advance, to encrypt the symmetric key. The encrypted symmetric key along with the encrypted message content is sent to the receiver. The receiver then uses its private key, which is associated with the public key that was used by the sender, to decrypt the symmetric key. With the recovered symmetric key, the receiver decrypts the message content.

How Digitally Signing/Verifying a Message Works

When signing/verifying a message, the usage of public and private keys is inverted in the following way: the sender uses its private key to generate a signature out of the message content, and the receiver uses the associated public key, which has been provided by the sender in advance, to verify the signature.

As mentioned in Section 10.4.1, the usage of asymmetric keys is, in general, computationally intensive. Therefore, applying the digital signing process on the complete content of a message can have a negative impact on overall performance because message sizes can vary from a few kilobytes to several megabytes. To overcome this problem, a *hash function* is applied to the message content prior to the signing process.

A hash function allows you to calculate an expression of fixed size from an input, which can be of any size. The input, in our case, is the message content. The output is referred to as a *hash value* (other, synonyms include *digest*, *footprint*, and *fingerprint*). The calculation is accomplished in a fully reproducible way, which means performing the same hash algorithm on the same data will lead to the same hash value. However, the inverse operation isn't possible, which means the data can't be reproduced out of the hash value (this makes a difference to compression algorithms that allow recovery of the uncompressed original, based on the compressed data). The resulting small size hash value is then subject to the signing process, as shown in Figure 10.49.

As mentioned earlier, on the sender side, a hash value is calculated from the message content ❶. The asymmetric key pair of the sender comes into play in the following way: the sender's private key is used to encrypt the hash value ❷. The transferred hash value can be considered the digital signature and is sent along with the message content to the receiver. On the receiver side, the public key (associated to the sender's private key) is used to decrypt the hash value ❸. In a separate step that is independent from the decryption of the hash value, the receiver uses the hash algorithm to calculate the hash value directly out of the message content ❹ and compares the result with the hash value that has been decrypted using the public key ❺. If both values are identical, the signature is verified.

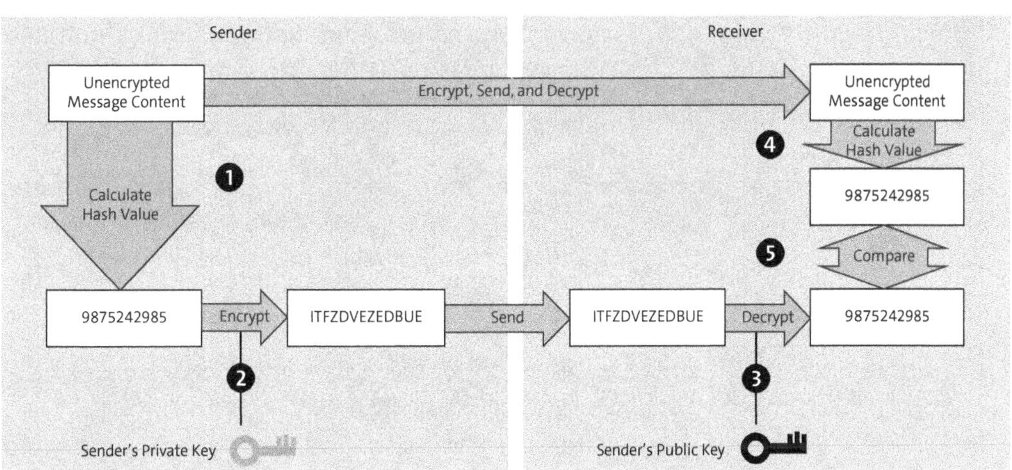

Figure 10.49 Combining Hash Functions with Asymmetric Key Usage When Signing and Verifying a Message

Overview of Supported Standards

Table 10.9 summarizes the message-level security standards supported by Cloud Integration and lists the supported options.

Standard	Options and References
PKCS#7/CMS Enveloped Data and Signed Data	PKCS stands for *Public Key Cryptography Standard*, and CMS stands for *Cryptographic Message Syntax* (see *https://tools.ietf.org/html/rfc2315*). This standard provides the following options: ▪ Encrypting the message content (and, vice versa, decrypting it) ▪ Signing a message (and, vice versa, verifying it) ▪ A combination of encrypting and signing a message (and, vice versa, the combination of decrypting and verifying it)
OpenPGP	OpenPGP stands for *Open Pretty Good Privacy* (see *https://tools.ietf.org/html/rfc4880*). This standard provides the following options: ▪ Encrypting the message content (and decrypting it) ▪ A combination of encrypting and signing a message (and the combination of decrypting and verifying it)
XML Signature	XML Signature is also referred to as *XMLDSig*, *XML-DSig*, or *XML-Sig*. This option is defined by a W3C recommendation (see *www.w3.org/TR/xmldsig-core/*). This standard allows for signing a message and verifying it.
XAdES	XML Advanced Electronic Signatures (XAdES) is an enhancement of XML Signature, which can be used in the context of the European Union Directive 1999/93/EC. This option allows you to use signatures in electronic contracts within the European Union (see *www.w3.org/TR/XAdES/*). This standard allows for signing a message.
WS-Security	Web Services Security (WS-Security) is an extension to SOAP that allows you to apply security to web services (see *http://s-prs.co/v576055*). This standard provides the following: ▪ Signing a SOAP body and verifying it ▪ Encrypting the message content and decrypting it The following adapters support WS-Security: ▪ SOAP 1.x sender and receiver adapter ▪ AS4 receiver adapter

Table 10.9 Message-Level Security Options Supported by Cloud Integration

Standard	Options and References
S/MIME	S/MIME allows you to securely transfer Multipurpose Internet Mail Extensions (MIME) data—in other words, emails. This option is used with most common email programs (see *https://tools.ietf.org/html/rfc5751*). This standard allows you to use digital signatures and to decrypt emails using the mail sender adapter.

Table 10.9 Message-Level Security Options Supported by Cloud Integration (Cont.)

Now, you know which security options are supported by Cloud Integration at the transport level and the message level. In Section 10.4.4, we showed you how to set up a secure connection with Cloud Integration based on TLS; in Section 10.4.5, we showed you how to set up a scenario using OAuth with the Twitter adapter; and in Section 10.4.7, we'll show you how to set up a scenario that includes digital encryption (using the OpenPGP standard).

10.4.7 Designing Message-Level Security Options in an Integration Flow

In this section, we'll show you how a message can be protected on the message level by digital encryption and signatures. We've provided an overview of these options and concepts in Section 10.4.6.

As for the transport-level security in Section 10.4.4, we'll also distinguish between two communication directions (from the perspective of the tenant):

- **Inbound communication**
  The sender sends an encrypted or signed message to Cloud Integration, and this message needs to be decrypted or verified on the tenant.
- **Outbound communication**
  The tenant encrypts or signs a message and sends it to a receiver where it's decrypted or verified.

We'll summarize the key tasks for setting up message-level security scenarios for both use cases. We'll then finish this section with a tutorial on setting up a simple iFlow that includes decrypting and encrypting a message.

Before we discuss the two use cases, there are a few things to consider. As for transport-level security, you'll also need to create digital keys and establish the corresponding key storages. You learned in Section 10.4.4 that SAP already provides the tenant with a Java keystore deployed on it and that, to implement certain transport-level security options, this keystore needs to contain dedicated keys.

The key material for the different message-level security options must be stored in different types of key storages. Accordingly, different security artifact types must be deployed on the tenant. As listed in Table 10.10, several artifact types are relevant for storing keys for message-level security.

Security Standard	Related Artifact Types
▪ PKCS#7 ▪ WS-Security ▪ XML Signature ▪ S/MIME	You can use X.509 keys (like when setting up secure communication using TLS). Therefore, you can import additional keys for message-level security into the same Java keystore used for transport-level security (accessible on the **Monitor** page under **Manage Security** in the **Keystore** tile; see Chapter 7, Section 7.3.2, and Section 10.5 in this chapter). However, make sure that you use separate keys for message-level security and for securing the transport channel. Keys for message-level security don't need to be signed by a CA; they can be self-signed.
OpenPGP	You can use a specific kind of key that we'll refer to as *PGP keys*. Note that this terminology is slightly different from other security standards. For example, in the context of PGP, *private keys* are referred to as *secret keys*. You also need dedicated key storages: ▪ Use a **PGP Public Keyring** to store one or more PGP public keys (associated with sender or receiver systems connected to the tenant). ▪ Use a **PGP Secret Keyring** to store one or more private keys associated with the tenant. You can access the corresponding artifacts on the **Monitor** page, under **Manage Security** in the **Security Material** tile.

Table 10.10 Security Artifacts Required to Store Keys for Certain Message-Level Security Scenarios

Most importantly, to configure message-level security options, you must add dedicated steps to the iFlow, which we'll discuss next.

Inbound Communication

Figure 10.50 shows how the components interact with each other at runtime (top) and the required security setup to realize this behavior (bottom).

In this use case, the components interact with each other in the following way:

- The sender does the following:
  - Encrypts the message content ❶ using the tenant's public key, which is associated with the tenant's private key
  - Signs a message ❷ using its own private key

- The tenant receives the message and then does the following:
  - Decrypts the message content ❸ using its own private key
  - Verifies the message ❹ using the sender's public key, which is associated with the sender's private key

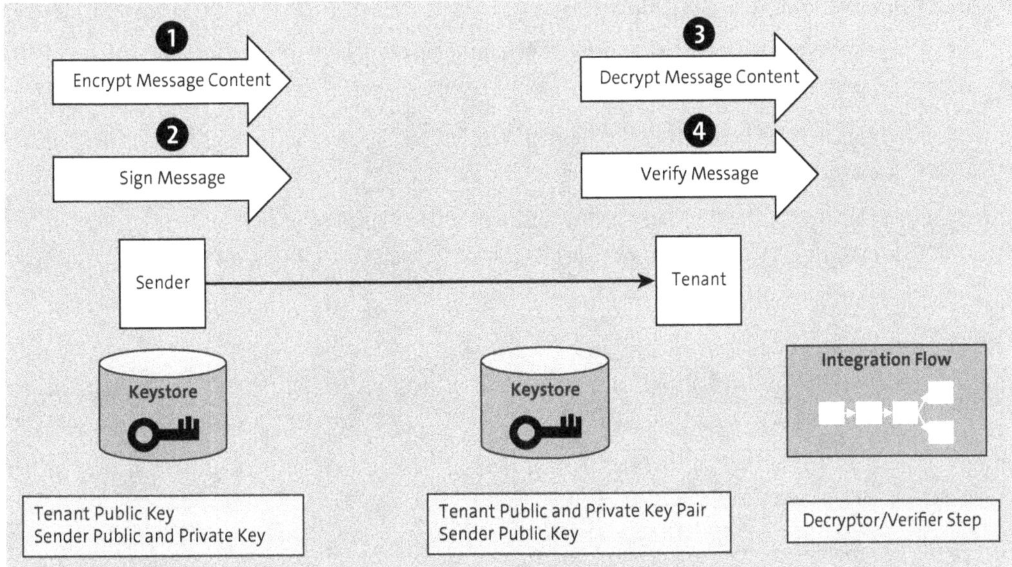

Figure 10.50 Configuring Message-Level Security for Inbound Communication

Notice that, other than in the transport-level security case, the load balancer isn't shown in Figure 10.50. The load balancer doesn't play a role because we focused on the application level (or message level), not the transport level. The termination and reestablishment of the TLS request takes place only on the transport level. The message is encrypted on its way between the sender and tenant (across the load balancer).

To implement this setup, on both the sender system side and the Cloud Integration platform side, perform the following tasks:

1. Generate key pairs for both the tenant and the sender system, and set up the keystores, as shown in Figure 10.50.
2. Import the tenant's public key into the sender's keystore.
3. Import the sender's public key into the tenant's keystore.
4. Configure the decryptor and verifier steps in the iFlow.

Note that you can also configure a combination of decryption and verification steps into one decryptor step for certain security standards. However, we won't cover this use case.

Outbound Communication

Figure 10.51 shows how the components interact with each other at runtime (top) and the required security setup to realize this behavior (bottom).

In this use case, the components interact with each other in the following way:

- The tenant does the following:
  - Encrypts the message content ❶ using a public key associated with the receiver's private key
  - Signs a message ❷ using its own private key
- The receiver does the following:
  - Decrypts the message content ❸ using its own private key
  - Verifies the message ❹ using the public key associated with the tenant's private key

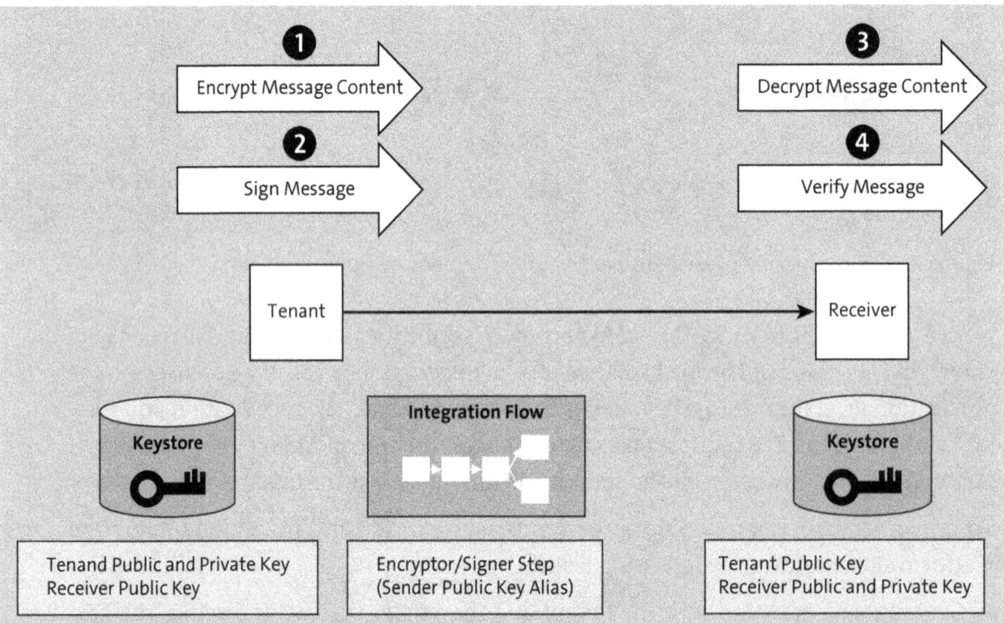

Figure 10.51 Configuring Message-Level Security for Outbound Communication

To set up this scenario, you must generate key pairs for the tenant and for the receiver, and you must configure the relevant iFlow steps on the tenant's side.

Note that the encryptor also provides the option to combine encryption/signing.

Setting Up a Simple Integration Flow with a PGP Decryption Step

To complete our section on message-level security, we'll show you how to set up an iFlow that decrypts an encrypted message.

For the sake of simplicity, we'll only take the perspective of the tenant in this tutorial and restrict ourselves to inbound communication, as shown in Figure 10.50. Again, to keep it simple, the message body with the secret text is created in a timer-initiated iFlow in a **Content Modifier** step. We'll demonstrate how this works by using the Open PGP standard. To enable you to set up and run this scenario easily, without needing to install any additional key management software, with the book's downloads (*www.sap-press.com/5760*), you'll find the following resources:

- An encrypted text in a text file (file *secrettext.txt*)
- A key pair we generated (*tenantkey_secret.gpg*)

  However, note that this scenario is a demo scenario. In a productive scenario, you should never even consider sharing any private key, not to mention, on any public website. This file has been provided by the authors to help you quickly run through this tutorial. This key will be valid for about 10 years (from the year this book is published).

  We generated the key using the open-source software Kleopatra, which is publicly available software that is easy to install. Kleopatra allows you to manage PGP keys and to sign and encrypt (as well as verify and decrypt) files and text strings. After executing our following simple tutorial, you might like to play around with the PGP keys yourself. In that case, follow the tutorial in the next section.
- The passphrase for the key (*secretkey_passphrase.txt*)

For simplicity, we also won't consider message signing/verifying.

OpenPGP

When used in the context of Cloud Integration, OpenPGP not only uses different key storages from the other security standards often used for message-level security (i.e., PKCS#7; see Table 10.10), but OpenPGP also uses a slightly different terminology. In the context of Open PGP, instead of *private key*, the term *secret key* is used. For more information, refer to the documentation for Cloud Integration at *http://s-prs.co/5077111*.

Now, we'll show how to set up an iFlow that decrypts an encrypted message and stores the resulting clear text in a data store. After this exercise, we'll show you a more sophisticated enhancement of this scenario so you can follow the end-to-end process and see how encryption and decryption work.

Figure 10.52 shows the iFlow and the related components.

Let's look at how this scenario works. Started by a **Timer** event, in the first **Content Modifier** step ❶, the message body is created. In this step, you can simply enter the secret text (*secrettext.txt*), as we'll show you in a minute. Before designing the iFlow, you must have uploaded the PGP secret key (*tenantkey_secret.gpg*) as a **PGP Secret Keyring** artifact. Using the secret key, the **PGPDecryptor** step ❷ decrypts the message and, finally, uses the **Write** step ❸ to store the message with the clear text in a data store (from which you can download the clear text for further inspection).

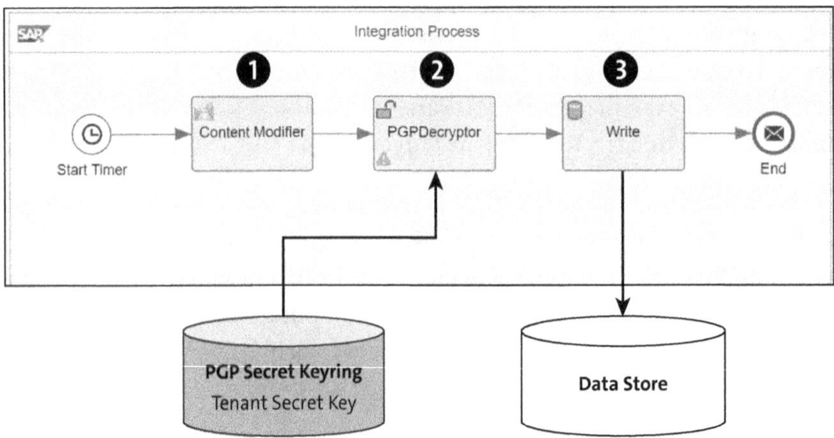

Figure 10.52 Target iFlow to Decrypt an Encrypted Message

Let's set up this scenario now step-by-step. First, you'll need to deploy the secret key on the tenant by following these steps:

1. Download the *tenantkey_secret.gpg* file from the book's downloads (supplement for Chapter 10).

   Let's again emphasize that sharing secret keys is a terrible idea, so terrible that you shouldn't even consider doing so when working in a productive scenario. The basic benefit of public key technology is that you can set up secure communications between communication partners without the need to share any private or secret keys (refer to Section 10.4.1). Therefore, sharing a secret key with a communication partner defeats the purpose of using a public key infrastructure. In this example, we're only sharing the secret key with you so you can set up a first message-level security scenario. As long as you don't use this practice in the context of a productive scenario, you should be safe.

   Furthermore, in a productive IT environment, the storage of secret keys within an organization is a critical topic. For that purpose, IT teams also don't use normal file systems. Instead, secure environments, such as a password manager, are used.

2. To deploy the secret key, go to the **Monitoring** page of the Web UI, and, under **Manage Security**, select the **PGP Keys** tile.
3. Select **Add • Secret Keys**, as shown in Figure 10.53.
4. Browse for the file with the secret key (*tenantkey_secret.gpg*), enter the passphrase ("Abcd1234"), and click **Deploy**.

Note that the passphrase is also contained in the *secretkey_passphrase.txt* file, which is included with the book's downloads (*www.sap-press.com/5760*).

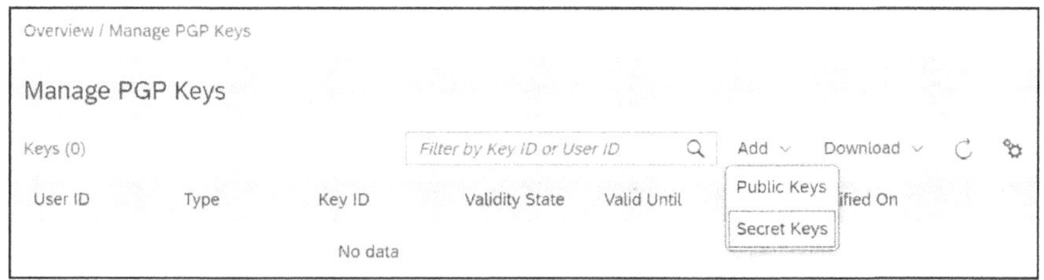

Figure 10.53 Adding a PGP Secret Keyring

Again, let's point out that this passphrase isn't a good one. We're just using something simple to show you to create keys for the sake of illustration. For productive scenarios, you should remember that any increase in the security level implies more effort.

The artifact is now shown on the **Manage PGP Keys** page, as shown in Figure 10.54.

Overview / Manage PGP Keys

Manage PGP Keys

Keys (1) Filter by Key ID or User ID | Add | Download

User ID	Type	Key ID	Validity State	Valid Until	Modified On
tenant <tenantadmin@myorg.com>	Secret	DB80 9434 D8A8 4059	Valid	Oct 10, 2030, 12:00:00	Feb 16, 2020, 14:33:20

Figure 10.54 PGP Secret Keyring Artifact Added to the Security Material Deployed on the Tenant

Now, let's design the iFlow shown earlier in Figure 10.52. We won't elaborate on adding each individual step, which we've discussed throughout the previous chapters. For more information on how to add a **Write** step, see Chapter 2, Section 2.3.4, especially Figure 2.30.

For the settings of the **Timer** step, select **Run Once** (see Chapter 6, Section 6.1).

As shown in Figure 10.55, in the **Content Modifier** step, under the **Message Body** tab, paste the secret text, which you can download from the book's downloads at *www.sap-press.com/5760* (the text file *secrettext.txt*).

Figure 10.55 Defining the Message Body by Pasting the Secret Text

To add the **PGP Decryptor** step, select the **Security** section of the palette, and open the **Decryptor** submenu, as shown in Figure 10.56.

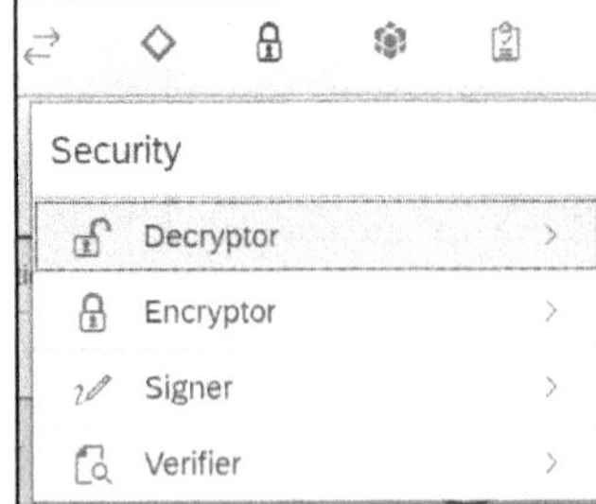

Figure 10.56 Selecting the Decryptor Submenu in the Palette

In the following submenu, choose **PGP Decryptor**, as shown in Figure 10.57.

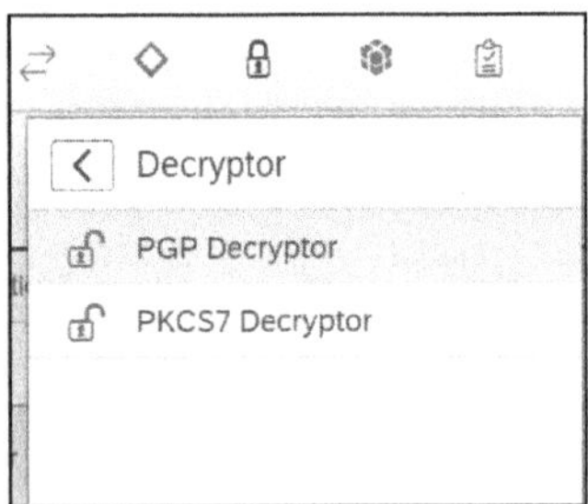

Figure 10.57 Selecting the PGP Decryptor Step Type

Leave the **Signatures** dropdown list with its default value, **None Expected**. When you keep the default setting **None Expected** in the **Signatures** dropdown list, as shown in Figure 10.58, no other parameters are shown. In this particular case, you won't need to specify any decryption key because the encrypted inbound message contains a reference that enables the system to identify, without doubt, the right key for decryption.

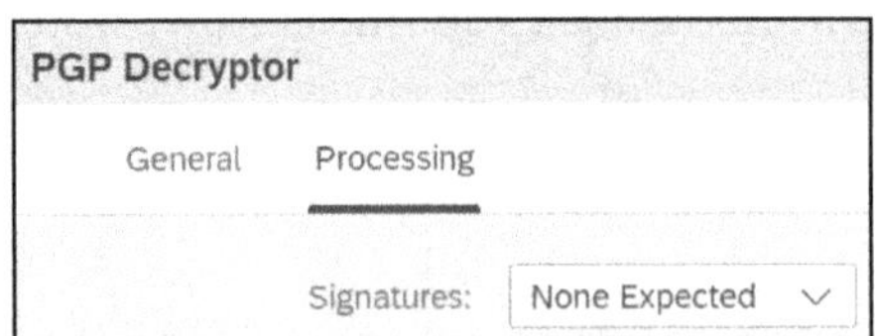

Figure 10.58 Settings of the PGP Decryptor

Note that, for the **Signatures** parameter, several other options are available (not shown in Figure 10.58 and not used in our scenario):

- **Optional**
  Select this option if you're not sure whether the inbound message contains a signature.

- **Required**
  Select this option if you're sure that the inbound message contains a signature.

In both cases, you'll need to specify an entry for **Signer User ID of Key(s) from Public Keyring**. This necessary step tells the tenant which public key to use to verify the signature. However, we don't need to select one of these options now because we know that our example inbound message will contain no signatures.

For the data store **Write** step (compare Chapter 2, Section 2.3.4), in the **Data Store Name** field, enter "DecryptedMessage."

Once deployed, the iFlow is started. After the message has been processed successfully, check for the data store entry (as described in Chapter 2), and download the data store entry. Open the *body* file to view the clear text.

To see whether you've done everything right, check out the downloadable content for this chapter at *www.sap-press.com/5760*.

Setting Up an End-to-End Scenario with Pretty Good Privacy Decryption and Encryption

The following scenario is a bit more sophisticated, but you'll get a better idea of an end-to-end cryptography process. You'll also understand why messages are decrypted on the tenant and why the content must be processed there (compare to our discussion in the "Why Decrypt Messages on the Cloud Integration Tenant?" information box in Section 10.4.6).

We'll show you how to set up an iFlow that decrypts an incoming (encrypted) message, modifies the content, encrypts the modified message, and stores the newly encrypted message as data store entry.

We'll demonstrate how this works again using the OpenPGP standard. For the management of PGP keys and the manual encryption/decryption steps in this scenario, we recommend you use Kleopatra, which is a publicly available software that is easy to install. Kleopatra allows you to manage PGP keys and to sign and encrypt (as well as verify and decrypt) files and text strings. You can download Kleopatra from *www.gpg4win.de/index.html*.

For the following tutorial, you don't need to download any content from the book's website; however, you'll need to install Kleopatra as a software for managing PGP keys.

In this tutorial, you'll successively take over the roles of all participants: the sender, who encrypts the message; the integration developer, who creates the iFlow and deploys it on the tenant; and, finally, the receiver, who decrypts the message manually.

Figure 10.59 shows the involved components and keys. As mentioned earlier, when using OpenPGP, the required keys for the tenant are to be stored separately in a PGP secret keyring and a PGP public keyring, respectively. Both entities must be separately deployed on the tenant. Although we won't deal with any keystores on the sender and receiver side, to get an understanding on the principles of public key technology, we've illustrated those components, together with the three involved personas.

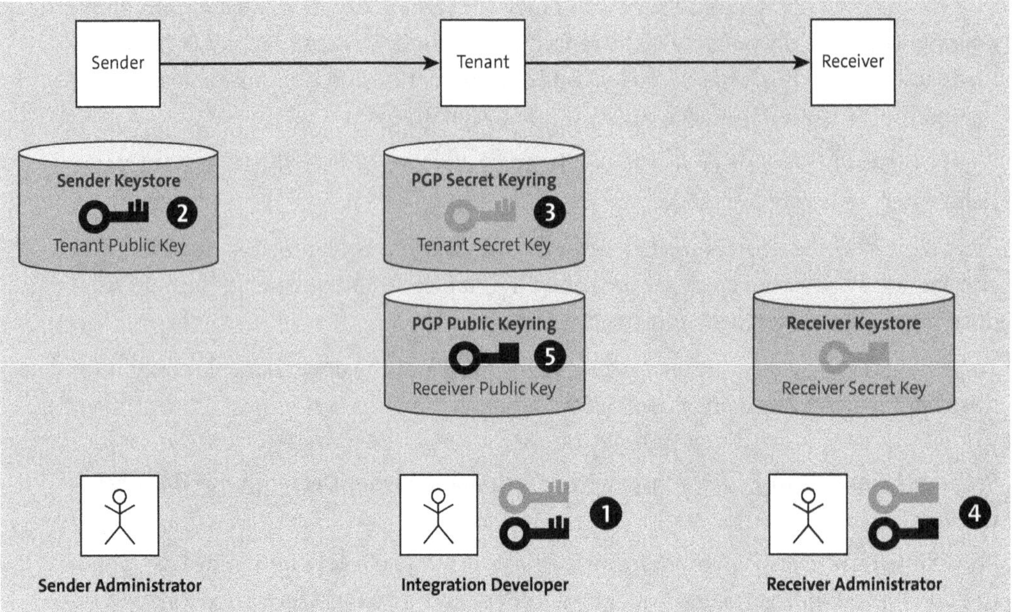

Figure 10.59 Keys and Personas Involved in the Scenario

Note that during the following tutorial, you'll slip successively into the different roles.

For the setup of keys, these personas come into the game in the following way:

- The integration developer generates a secret/public key pair for the tenant ❶ and shares the public key of the tenant key pair with the sender administrator. The sender administrator uploads the public key (of the tenant's key pair) into its keystore ❷. This key is used to encrypt the message that is to be sent to the tenant. In our dedicated tutorial, you take the role of the sender administrator and manually encrypt the message (and provide the encrypted text as HTTP request body with Postman).
- The integration developer deploys the secret key of the tenant key pair (with a **PGP Secret Keyring**) on tenant ❸.
- The receiver administrator generates a secret/public key pair ❹ and shares the public key of the receiver key pair with the integration developer. The receiver administrator uploads the secret key (of the receiver's key pair) into its keystore ❷. This key is used to decrypt the message received from the tenant. In our tutorial, you'll take the role of the receiver administrator and manually decrypt the message.
- The integration developer deploys the public key of the receiver key pair (with a **PGP Public Keyring**) on tenant ❺.

Figure 10.60 shows the iFlow. Notice that the sender is realized by an HTTP client (Postman), whereas the receiver is simulated (for the sake of illustration) by a data store.

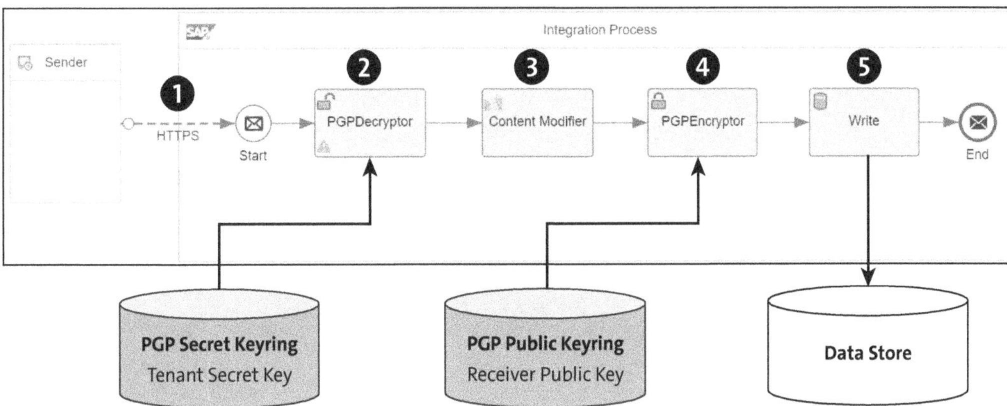

Figure 10.60 Target iFlow

10

Let's briefly summarize how the iFlow works.

The message is sent from an HTTP client through the HTTPS sender adapter ❶. Using Postman, you can provide the encrypted message, which was encrypted using the tenant's public key (shown earlier in Figure 10.59), as the request body. The encrypted message is decrypted by the **PGPDecryptor** step ❷ using the tenant's secret key (from the **PGP Secret Keyring**, shown earlier in Figure 10.59). In the following **Content Modifier** step ❸, the decrypted message (clear text) is enhanced. In the **PGPEncryptor** step ❹, the enhanced message is again encrypted (using the receiver's public key from the **PGP Public Keyring**) and, finally, stored as data store entry by the **Write** step ❺.

In the role of the receiver administrator, you can then use the receiver's secret key to decrypt the final message.

As a prerequisite, install the free software Kleopatra, which is designed for key management. You can download the software at *www.gpg4win.de/index.html*. When prompted, make sure that the software package to download includes Kleopatra.

Let's start with creating the sender key and encrypting the sender's message:

1. Open Kleopatra.
2. Under **File**, choose **New Key Pair**, as shown in Figure 10.61.

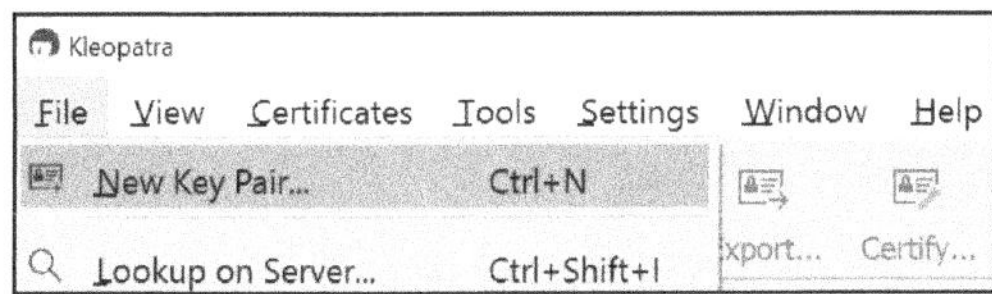

Figure 10.61 Creating a New Key Pair with Kleopatra

3. In the following dialog box, click **Create a Personal OpenPGP Key Pair.**
4. Enter a name (e.g., "Tenant" to indicate that this is the tenant's key pair) and a (fictitious) email address, and click **Next.**
5. Select **Create.**
6. Enter a passphrase to protect the key. You'll need to remember this passphrase for a later step when deploying the PGP secret keyring on the tenant.
7. Click **Finish.** The newly created key pair appears in a list, as shown in Figure 10.62.

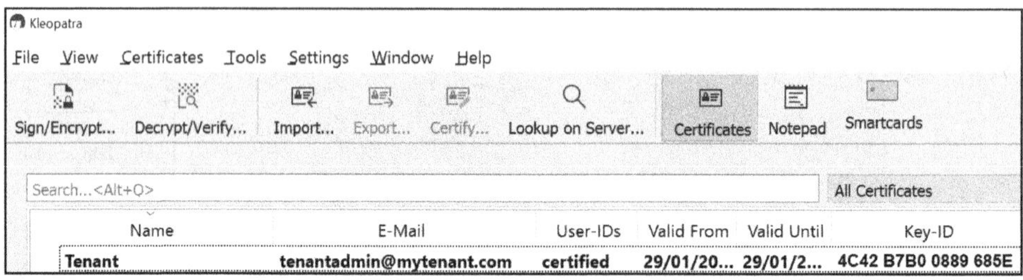

Figure 10.62 Tenant Key Pair Shown in List

8. Select the key (**Tenant**), choose **Export Secret Keys** in the context menu, as shown in Figure 10.63.
9. Save the key on your computer (as a *.gpg* file).

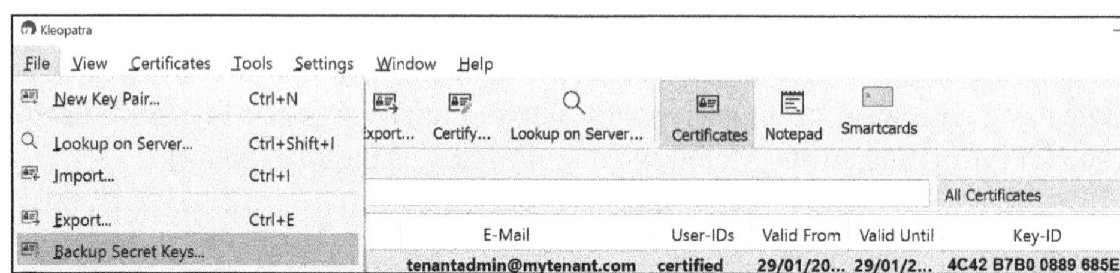

Figure 10.63 Exporting Secret Keys from Kleopatra

Now, deploy the secret key on the tenant by following these steps:

1. Open the **Monitor** page of the Web UI, and, under **Manage Security**, click the **Security Material** tile.
2. Select **Add • Secret Keys**, and click **Next**, as shown in Figure 10.64.
3. Browse for the secret key *.gpg* file on your local disk, enter the secret key passphrase, and click **Deploy**, as shown in Figure 10.65.

The newly deployed artifact will be listed on the **Manage PGP Keys** page, as shown in Figure 10.66.

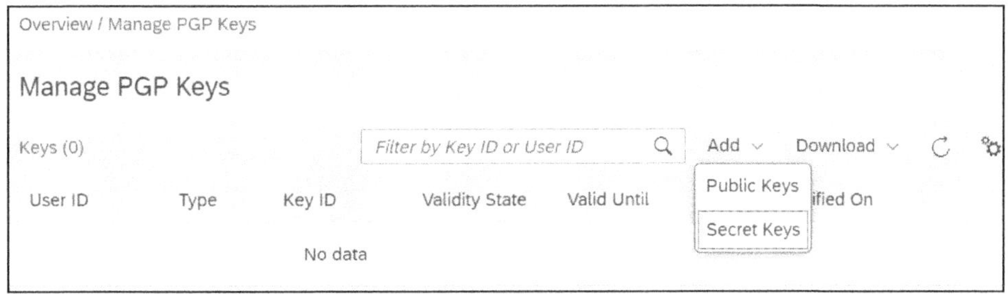

Figure 10.64 Adding a PGP Secret Keyring Artifact

Add PGP Secret Key

Keyring File: * Tenant_SECRET.gpg Browse...

Passphrase: * ••••••••

Action: Add

Overwrite Existing Keys

Deploy Cancel

Figure 10.65 Browsing for Secret Keyring File and Adding Passphrase

Overview / Manage PGP Keys

Manage PGP Keys

Keys (1) mytenant Add Download

User ID	Type	Key ID	Validity State	Valid Until	Modified On
Tenant <tenantadmin@mytenant.com>	Secret	4C42 B7B0 0889 685E	Valid	Jan 29, 2026, 12:00:00	Jan 29, 2024, 07:30:11

Figure 10.66 The Newly Deployed Artifact Displayed in the Artifact Overview

Now, switch to the role of the sender to manually encrypt the clear text with the tenant's public key. In real-life scenarios, this encryption process is usually performed automatically by the software deployed on the sender system (typically using a keystore component that contains the required keys). To manually encrypt clear text for our example, follow these steps:

1. To encrypt your text, start Kleopatra and then enter some text (e.g., "Let the great plot") into a text editor.

   When you've successfully accomplished the previous exercise, you might have an idea why entering this text is appropriate.
2. Copy the text to the clipboard.
3. In Kleopatra, choose **Tools • Clipboard • Encrypt**, as shown in Figure 10.67.

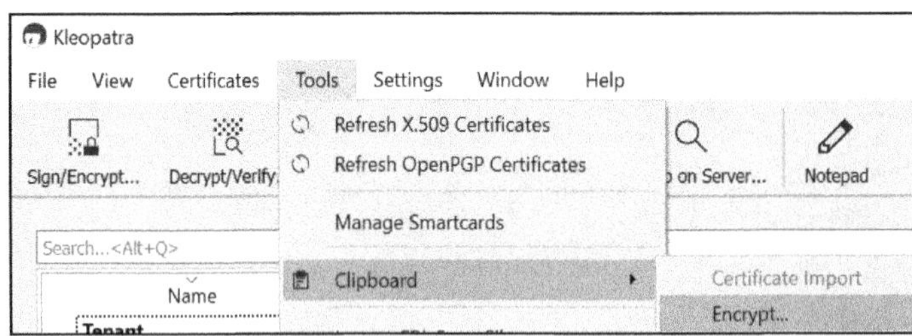

Figure 10.67 Choosing the Clipboard Encrypt Option in Kleopatra

4. Keep the **OpenPGP** option selected, and click **Add Recipient**.
5. Imagine that you, as a sender, communicate with many recipients who have shared their public keys with you. In this step, you'll select the (public) key from that recipient (the tenant, in our case) to whom you'd like to send an encrypted message, as shown in Figure 10.68.

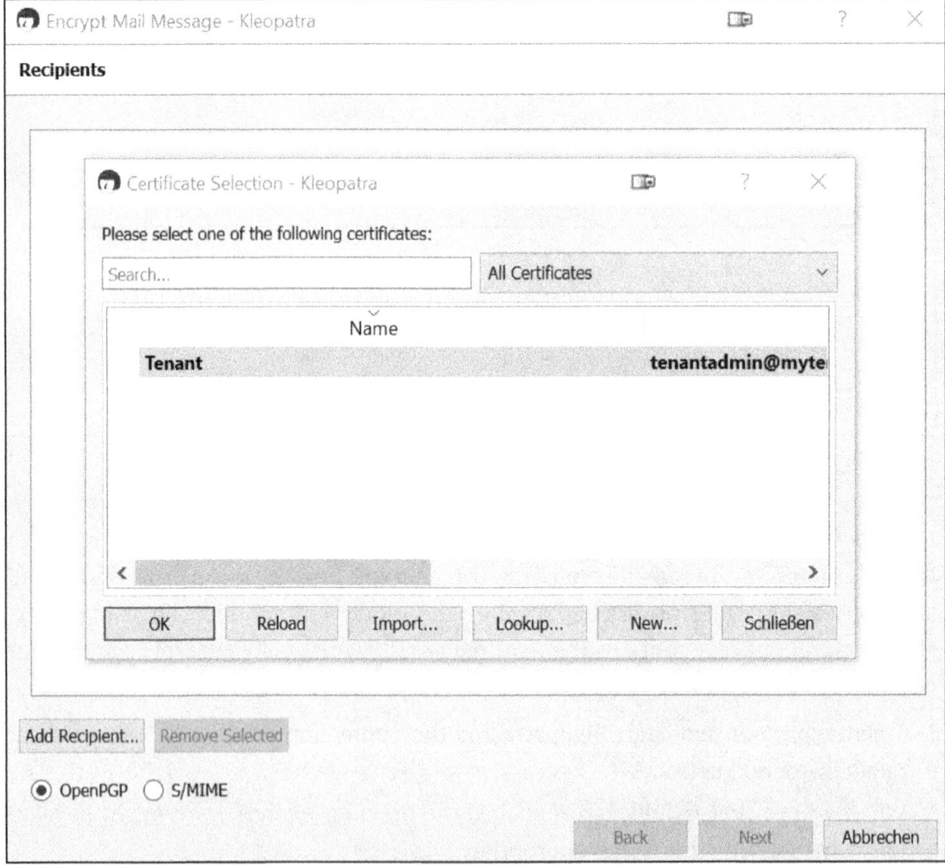

Figure 10.68 Selecting the Key That Encrypts the Clear Text

6. Select the recipient (**Tenant**), and click **OK**.
7. When the message **Encryption Succeeded** is displayed, as shown in Figure 10.69, click **OK**.
8. Paste the text from the clipboard into a text editor. The encrypted message will look the message shown in Figure 10.70.

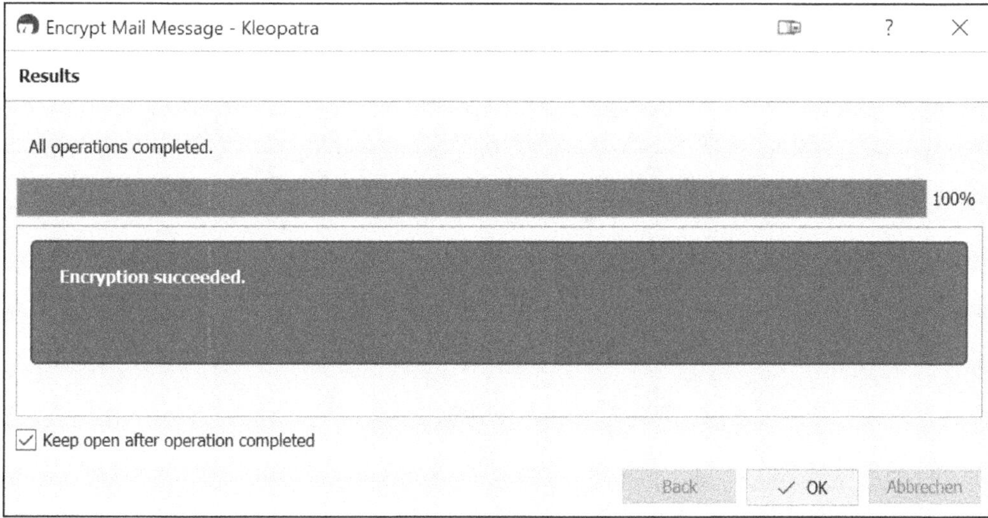

Figure 10.69 Success Message: Kleopatra Has Encrypted the Clear Text


```
-----BEGIN PGP MESSAGE-----

hQEMA1cCBsrhU31rAQgAkwHWvbrS3kTbYIjCjjX/BFZHp4GXaqlyV0jX+EVTcB2u
0H63KfVZdP3zNX7CyDXtOYwMGUEvqz7EdxFqRswWoGZswFgoUF4SF6YRdszJYtCS
KfAKChXYIet+/r6/kt3iH/exsXdNQEty0yf9YE6VBYpSw+2+gTjVONyYfQAbNKPl
uoSohbfJFOcDbAyM25OV7YwgyN/bFdHbKXpmCkiLpBSdJwTx5BZitL4e+W9K8dWI
IowgzKmkdNY+2hGAstFMhOjslVMFhdpUEVOFGpeL/NJIhKjJ664PeMVmxxMapyWT
rnyKJXCNUNNc/nU9dLniWKMmT54yWo/q/Tqp+ONHO9JNAVjNDK/8hrlnALdIbwYy
+r6CUbYbG+JJw7GiZMMUm5AeMRN+ztYigZkjJMZaKOslKZ1q/dC6OZIi4elbBtVf
9Ov3MUHgplGltmam82c=
=l+sK
-----END PGP MESSAGE-----
```


Figure 10.70 Example Encrypted Message

Store the encrypted text in a text file. You'll need this information later in the role of the sender when calling the iFlow.

Let's take the role of receiver. First, we'll need to create another key pair: the receiver's key pair. Recall that the tenant needs the receiver's public key to encrypt a message. To generate the key pair, use Kleopatra as described earlier for creating the tenant's key pair, but this time, enter "Receiver" into the **Name** field. Then, follow these steps:

1. In Kleopatra, select the newly created key pair (**Receiver**), as shown in Figure 10.71.

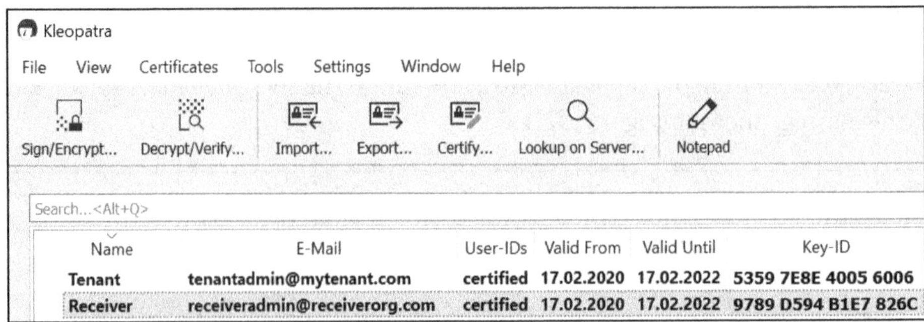

Figure 10.71 Kleopatra Key List Showing the Newly Created Receiver Key Pair

2. Choose **Export** from the context menu, as shown in Figure 10.72.

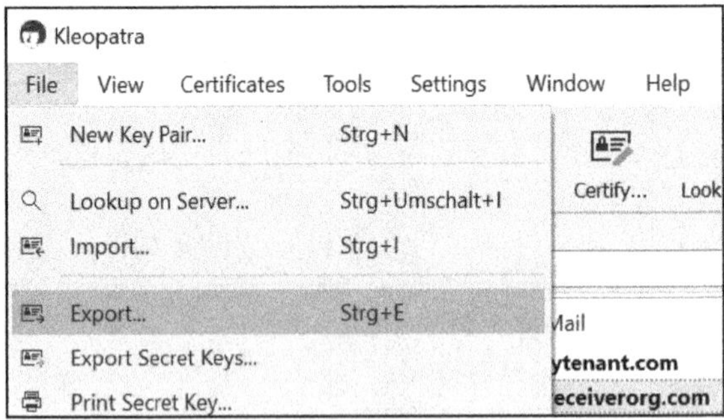

Figure 10.72 Exporting the Receiver's Public Key

As shown earlier in Figure 10.63, you now export a *public* key of the newly generated **Receiver** key pair.

3. Save the key on your computer (change the file extension to *.gpg*).

Switch to the role of the integration developer, and follow these steps:

1. Deploy the new public key on the tenant as the **PGP Public Keyring** artifact.
2. Open the **Monitor** page of the Web UI, and, under **Manage Security**, click the **Security Material** tile.
3. Choose **Add • Public Keysg**, as shown in Figure 10.73.

Figure 10.73 Adding a PGP Public Keyring Artifact

4. Browse for the public key *.gpg* file on your local disk, and click **Deploy**.

Add PGP Public Key

Keyring File:* Receiver_0x6901F14A_SECRET.asc Browse...

Action: Add

Overwrite Existing Keys

Deploy Cancel

Figure 10.74 Browsing for the Public Key File

As shown in Figure 10.75, the artifact (with the name **Receiver**) has been added to the list of deployed artifacts.

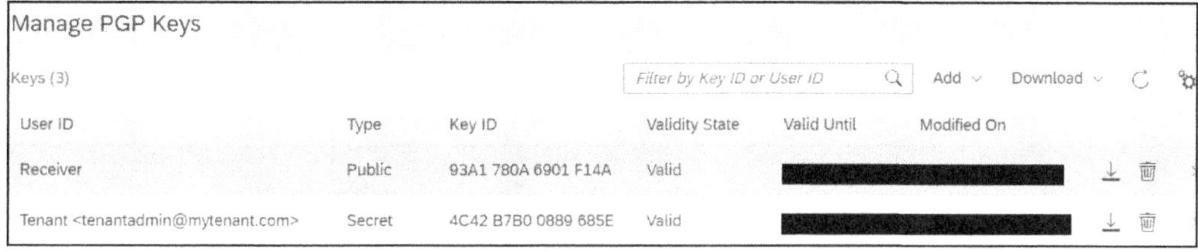

Figure 10.75 The Newly Deployed PGP Public Keyring

Now, let's move back to role of the integration developer and create the simple iFlow shown earlier in Figure 10.60.

As you've progressed through the chapters of this book, you've become an integration development expert, so we won't go into the minute details again. We'll only briefly summarize the required steps specific to this demo example.

For this example, follow these steps:

1. For the sender adapter type, choose **HTTPS**, and, in the **Address** field, enter a unique relative endpoint address (e.g., "/DecryptEncrypt").
2. Add a **PGP Decryptor** step, and, under the **Processing** tab for the parameter, in the **Signatures** field, leave the **None Expected** option (refer to Figure 10.58).
3. Add a **Content Modifier** step, and, as shown in Figure 10.76, under the **Message Body** tab, enter the following expression:

   ```
   ${in.body} commence. Signed Mary
   ```

   You'll get the joke.

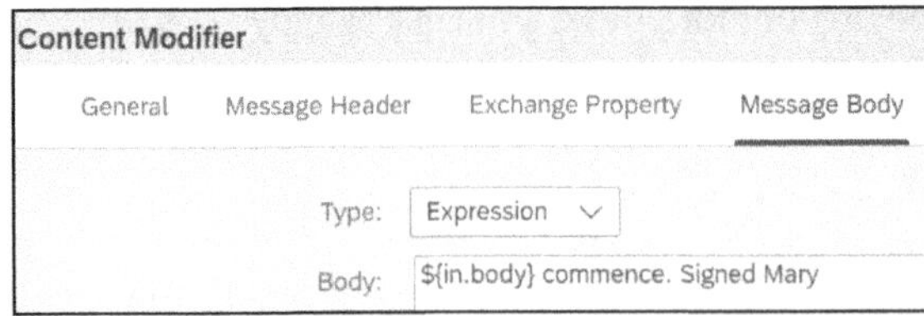

Figure 10.76 Message Body Definition in Content Modifier

4. Add a **PGP Encryptor** step by clicking the **Security Elements** icon in the palette and choosing **Encryptor**, as shown in Figure 10.77.

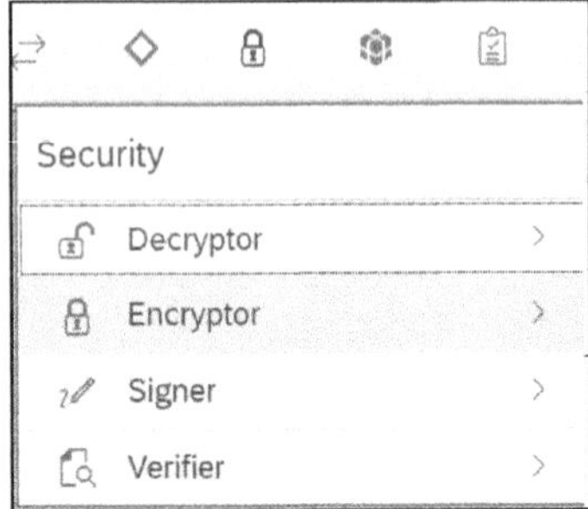

Figure 10.77 Submenu of Security Elements

5. As shown in Figure 10.78, select **PGP Encryptor**, and place your cursor to the right of **Content Modifier** shape (refer to Figure 10.60).

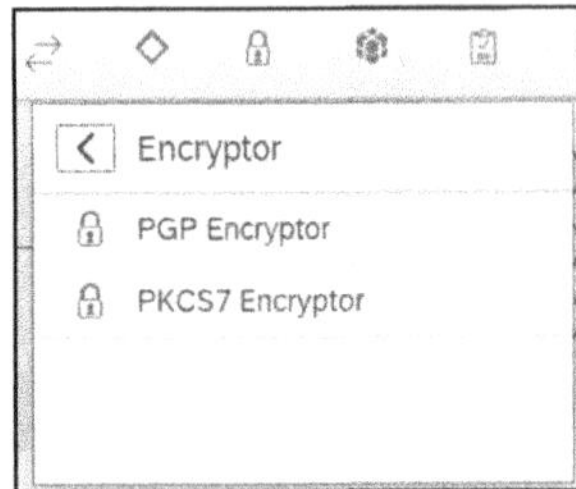

Figure 10.78 Encryptor Submenu

6. Specify the properties of the **Encryptor** step, as shown in Figure 10.79. In the **Encryption User ID of Key(s) from Public Keyring** field, enter the user ID of the related key. (To find the user ID, open Kleopatra, select the relevant key used for encryption, and look for the **Name** field of the key.) In our example, this ID is the **Receiver** key (to indicate that the receiver's public key we generated earlier is to be used to encrypt the message). For the other parameters, you can leave the default settings.
7. Finally, add the data store **Write** step, and, in the **Data Store Name** field, enter "FinalEncryptedMessage".

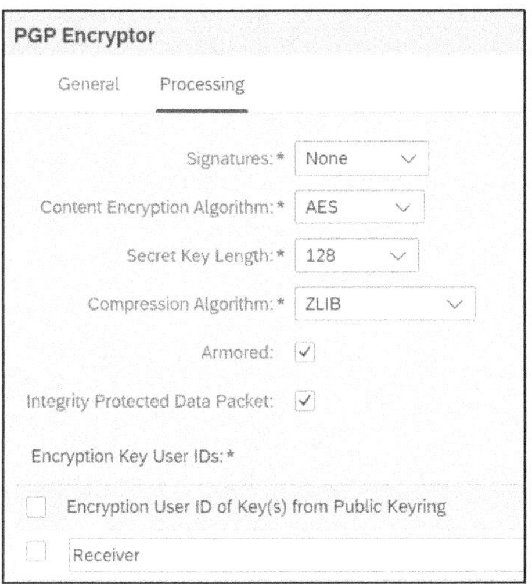

Figure 10.79 Processing Parameters of Encryptor Step

To run the iFlow, follow these steps:

1. As shown in Figure 10.80, configure Postman so that it calls the iFlow endpoint. Under the **Body** tab, choose **raw**, and paste the encrypted text that you've stored in a text file before (refer to Figure 10.70). This encrypted text has been generated with Kleopatra using the tenant public key.

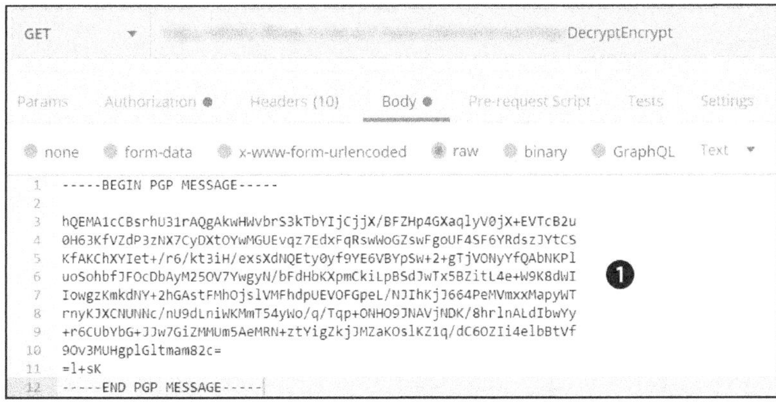

Figure 10.80 Encrypted Text Sent as Postman Request Body

2. Send the request, and, after the message has been processed successfully, download the relevant data store entry. (You'll find the data stores on the **Monitor** page by clicking the **Data Stores** tile under **Manage Stores**.) When opening the *body* part, you'll see the content shown in Figure 10.81.

```
-----BEGIN PGP MESSAGE-----

wcBMA36Kw0frDFswAQf/YVCDphW2B8OIdV1AT0lc88+0LxctTIUIOG8H2nUEt8F0
FB3c/Xxeu+N7h954wb4zgmHUTmjJN/iXjXs1p6zZgzek10Q95xWjs1Swq6WsZ9gU
Gm+V3jqwbYZx6M4OrfzWhqXJE+oSnnusM3pxR8H0sfHDpnogecrWkB/1RJrLb9h5
Hs0X3kXgUNvZ2HNzRg7c7sVoTKod5pgLr+pzjvXoqvpfwVCBk+M+4FmIPJkuujbd
pBxlVSrk+61m+DkOmRWnBc6/6lbk1lsf2Ehwh2m6KqIHMtKrCVuQvv+4lH1zsPOi
KbjmMmg6ReAkXQIIGdP40TmQ/AEJ1KVO0vvSvtoOW9JjAZgBru1k4Gh/t9psnx70
XdHsP//aY2jilqP0bNm6AiGTGMLl193W7LiRoVujGqbYVdygGOiMKjbBg7kHf4i3
gL7kS+GxN6XEdCYJX7K4f/V/BSCslDt9eQqVIRNTbqvM46IZ
=ZBT/
-----END PGP MESSAGE-----
```


Figure 10.81 Data Store Entry Containing Encrypted Text

Now, slip again into the role of the receiver (who in real life would have received the encrypted message), and follow these steps:

1. Copy the Postman response to the clipboard.
2. Go to Kleopatra, and select **Tools • Clipboard • Decrypt/Verify**, as shown in Figure 10.82.

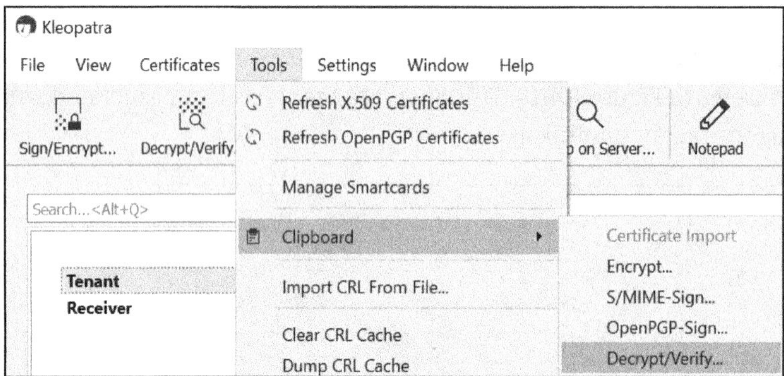

Figure 10.82 Decrypt/Verify Function of Kleopatra

3. Enter the passphrase of the keystore, and click **Finish**.
4. Paste the content of your clipboard to a text file to obtain the following content:

```
Let the great plot commence. Signed Mary
```

Voilà! You've successfully gone through an end-to-end process of message encryption and decryption. You also learned why, in certain cases, decrypting messages on the tenant is important, for instance, to modify messages or apply processing steps such as CBR or mappings.

In this tutorial, we showed you how to use OpenPGP keys to implement a scenario with message encryption. Note that these keys are stored in dedicated artifacts called the **PGP Secret Keyring** and the **PGP Public Keyring**.

However, you can also use keys from the keystore (described in more detail in Section 10.5) to implement message-level security. To find a predefined, easy-to-run scenario that uses keys from the tenant keystore, refer to the product documentation for Cloud Integration (*http://s-prs.co/v576028*) and search for "Apply Message-Level Security" under "Apply the Highest Security Standards." You can find the corresponding iFlows on the SAP Business Accelerator Hub at *https://api.sap.com/* (integration package **Integration Flow Design Guidelines - Apply Highest Security Standards**).

10.5 Keystore Management

Throughout this book and this chapter, you've become familiar with various kinds of security artifacts. We've described when you need to define **User Credentials** artifacts (Chapter 2, Section 2.3.5), **Secure Parameter** artifacts (Section 10.4.5), and **PGP Secret Keyring/PGP Public Keyring** artifacts (Section 10.4.6).

Aspects of managing these artifacts during the operation of an integration scenario were explained in detail in Chapter 7, Section 7.3.1.

We'll now elaborate on the **Keystore** artifact, introduced earlier in Section 10.4.4, where we described setting up secure connections based on HTTP.

10.5.1 Using X.509 Security Material for Cloud Integration

The **Keystore** artifact allows you to manage the content of the tenant keystore. This keystore can contain key material (private/public key pairs and certificates) based on the X.509 standard (Section 10.4.1) as well as SSH keys.

SSH Keys

You can also use the tenant keystore to manage and store the SSH keys required when configuring secure connections using SSH with the SFTP adapter, a topic which we don't describe further in this book. For more information, read *http://s-prs.co/5077112*.

Let's focus on X.509 keys. Table 10.11 lists several situations in which you would use X.509 keys, which will require you manage the tenant keystore.

Usage	Description
Certificates for TLS	To secure HTTP-based communication, connections between Cloud Integration and remote components are secured using TLS. For outbound communications, this connection includes a step where the receiver system authenticates itself as a server against Cloud Integration, which is the client in that case. To establish such TLS connections, X.509 certificates are needed.
Certificate-based authentication of communication partners when communicating over HTTPS (transport-level security)	To increase security, a client can use client certificates to authenticate itself against a server. When talking about outbound communications where Cloud Integration connects to a receiver system, the keystore must contain a client certificate. Furthermore, the client certificate should be signed by a CA that is also trusted by the receiver. We've described this concept earlier in Section 10.4.1.
Signing/verifying and encrypting/decrypting messages using the PKCS#7 standard (message-level security)	You can use dedicated iFlow steps to implement scenarios with digitally signed and encrypted messages. The following steps are available: **PKCS7 Signer**, **PKCS7 Encryptor**, **PKCS7 Signature Verifier**, and **PKCS7 Decryptor** (Section 10.4.6).
S/MIME signature and encryption when using the mail receiver adapter	You can configure the mail receiver adapter so that it signs or encrypts outbound messages (or both). For encryption, a public key is required, whereas for signing, a private key is required. Certificates used in these scenarios can be self-signed.
XML Signature	You can use an **XML Signer** iFlow step to sign a message using the XML Signature standard. For signing, you'll need a private key from the keystore.
Signing/verifying a SOAP body, encrypting/decrypting message content using WS-Security	Certain adapters support dedicated options to sign/verify messages or to encrypt/decrypt message content based on the WS-Security standard, which is an extension to SOAP. The following adapters support these options: ■ SOAP 1.x sender and receiver adapter ■ AS2 sender and receiver adapter To implement these scenarios, X.509 keys are also required in the tenant keystore.

Table 10.11 Using X.509 Keys in Cloud Integration

X.509 Keys for Transport-Level Security and Client Certificate Authentication

Secure HTTP-based communication at the transport level is based on the certificates listed in Table 10.11. Furthermore, as explained in Section 10.4.3, Cloud Integration supports various authentication options, including client certificate authentication. When you choose this authentication option for outbound connections, the tenant keystore needs to contain a client certificate, which is a signed private key pair. When you've purchased a licensed Cloud Integration tenant, SAP provides you initially with a keystore that contains one such private key pair, which has the alias `sap_cloudintegrationcertificate` (see the information box). You can use this key pair to set up an outbound HTTP connection immediately.

Limitation When Using Trial Tenants

For most of the tutorials of this book, using a Cloud Integration trial tenant is sufficient, but one limitation applies with regard to the tenant keystore. When using the trial tenant, you won't receive key pairs provided by SAP as mentioned earlier. Therefore, you won't be able to set up certificate-based inbound authentication.

Managing the lifecycle of keys *provided by SAP* (discussed in more detail in Section 10.5.3) is therefore quite restricted when using the trial tenant. Thus, in this section, we're showing you how to perform the relevant tasks based on a licensed Cloud Integration tenant.

As shown in your first iFlow in Chapter 2, the mail receiver adapter doesn't offer any client certificate authentication option. Instead, authentication is accomplished based on user credentials.

Recall that you had to create and deploy a **User Credentials** artifact to specify these credentials. At the same time, you still need to import certain certificates into the tenant keystore because the connection also needs to be protected *the other way around*: the email server must set up a trust relationship to the tenant. Therefore, we had to import a root certificate, depending on the requirements of the email server. We referred to this certificate as the *receiver server root certificate*. When discussing the setup to establish a secure outbound connection from the tenant to a receiver system, we described earlier in Section 10.4.4 how the different security artifacts come into play in the whole picture. This example demonstrated that the tenant keystore isn't only required to specify key pairs for client certificate authentication in outbound connections.

To learn more about the keystore content in different security setups, check out the documentation for Cloud Integration at *http://s-prs.co/5077113*.

X.509 Keys for Message-Level Security (PKCS#7 Standard)

As listed in Table 10.11, the keystore can also contain keys to set up scenarios that include message-level security based on the PKCS#7, XML security, or WS-Security standards. As described in Section 10.4.1, different keys are required to sign and encrypt and to verify and decrypt a message. Let's briefly review this requirement from the perspective of the tenant:

- To enable a tenant to encrypt a message (e.g., using the **PKCS7 Encryptor** step) and, correspondingly, to enable the receiver to decrypt the message, the receiver of the message must generate an X.509 private-public key pair and share the public key with the tenant administrator. The tenant administrator then imports the public key into the tenant keystore. At runtime, the tenant encrypts the message using the public key, and the receiver uses the private key to decrypt the message.
- To enable a tenant to decrypt a message encrypted by a sender system (e.g., using the **PKCS7 Decryptor** step), the tenant administrator must generate an X.509 private key pair and share the public part of it with the administrator of the sender system. At runtime, the sender system uses the public key to encrypt the message, and the tenant uses the private key to decrypt the message.

For signing and verifying messages using the **PKCS7 Signer** and **PKCS7 Signature Verifier** steps, the situation is inverted.

In Section 10.4.6, we showed you how to set up a scenario with encryption and decryption using PGP keys. The keys owned by the tenant in this case must be stored in dedicated key storage locations, namely, the **PGP Public Keyring** and the **PGP Secret Keyring**. To set up the same kind of scenario using PKCS#7, you'll need to use the tenant keystore (**Keystore** artifact) to store both the private and the public keys. Other than this difference, the same principles apply.

To set up the scenario shown earlier in Figure 10.59, but now using PKCS#7 keys, you must establish the security configuration shown in Figure 10.83.

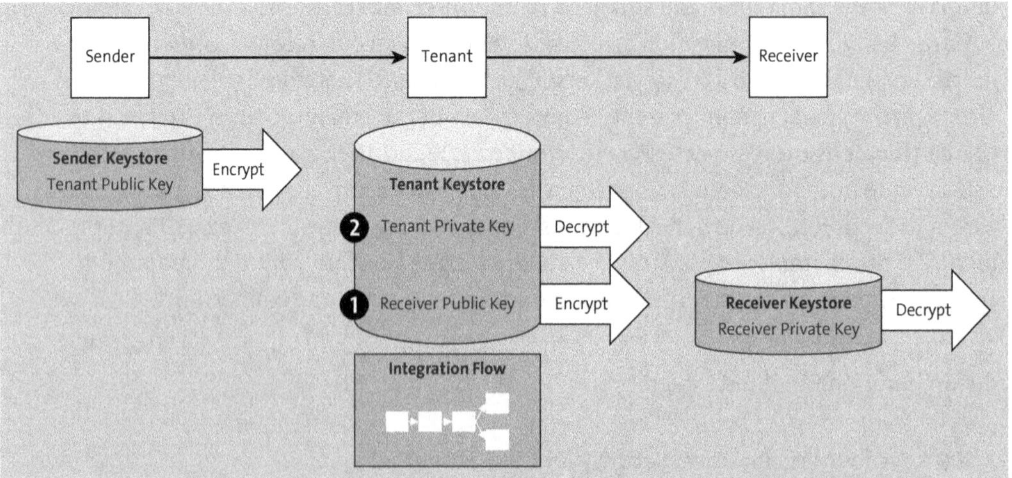

Figure 10.83 Key Setup for Encryption/Decryption Scenario Using the PKCS#7 Security Standard

To set up this scenario, the tenant keystore must contain the following elements:

- One private key pair (**Key Pair** entry)
- One **Certificate** entry ❶ that contains the public key of the receiver system (shared by the receiver administrator)

Furthermore, the iFlow uses the following steps:

- **PKCS7 Decryptor**
  This step uses the private key of the tenant ❷ to decrypt the message obtained from the sender.
- **PKCS7 Encryptor**
  This step uses the public key of the receiver system ❶ as specified by the **Receiver Public Key Alias** in the step.

10

Initial Content of the Tenant Keystore

When you get a tenant from SAP the first time, SAP also provides you with a tenant keystore that contains, as initial content, the following SAP-owned entries:

- Some SAP-owned CA root certificates that enable you to set up communications with SAP cloud systems, such as SAP Ariba and SAP SuccessFactors (e.g., with the alias `sap_baltimore cybertrust root` and `sap_digicert global root ca`)
- One signed private key pair (with the alias `sap_cloudintegrationcertificate`)

In Section 10.5.2, you'll learn more about managing keystore entries, and in Section 10.5.3, you'll learn in particular how to deal with the lifecycle of SAP-owned keystore entries.

10.5.2 Managing Security Material in the Tenant Keystore

You can access the tenant keystore on the **Monitor** page of the Web UI (**Keystore** tile under **Manage Security**). The basic functions have already been explained in Chapter 7, Section 7.3.2, in the context of Cloud Integration operations, so we won't repeat this information here. However, as a refresher, we'll briefly summarize the most important aspects and provide additional details on the content of the keystore. In Section 10.5.3, we'll then show you how to manage the lifecycle of keystore entries.

Figure 10.84 shows an excerpt of the tenant keystore (as mentioned earlier, of a licensed Cloud Integration tenant).

The keystore can contain entries owned by SAP and those owned by the tenant administrator. Those owned by SAP are indicated by a lock icon 🔒 in front of the alias and can't be changed by the tenant administrator. As shown in Figure 10.84, you'll see one key pair with alias `sap_cloudintegrationcertificate`, which has been initially provided by SAP as mentioned previously, and a certificate with alias sap_baltimore cybertrust root owned by SAP.

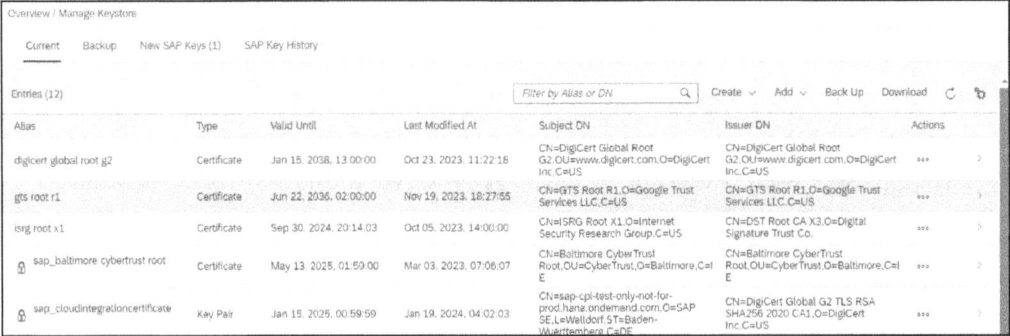

Figure 10.84 Keystore Entries

Note that, when you use Cloud Integration on a trial tenant, no SAP-owned keys will be available (compare Chapter 2, Figure 2.60).

The keystore contains entries of two different types:

- **Key Pair**
  Consists of a private key pair and (commonly) an X.509 certificate chain unless the key is an SSH key, which is used for connections to an SFTP server.
- **Certificate**
  Represents an X.509 certificate (in many cases, a root certificate).

As an example of a **Key Pair** entry, let's look at the SAP-owned key pair with the alias **sap_cloudintegrationcertificate**. You can access the details of a keystore entry by clicking its link in the **Alias** column, as shown in Figure 10.85 (compare also Chapter 7, Figure 7.36).

The left side of Figure 10.85 shows the certificate chain. Note that **Key Pair** entries are usually defined as part of a certificate chain. On top of the certificate chain of the key pair provided by SAP, you'll see the root certificate of the CA **SAPNetCA_G2**.

The details of the **Key Pair** entry are shown on the right. Note that you can navigate to the details of the intermediate or root certificate by clicking on the corresponding nodes in the certificate chain on the left; the details area on the right will change accordingly.

Note

To find more information on the constituents of an X.509 certificate, check out the X.509 standard as documented in the *Request for Comments 4158* at *https://tools.ietf.org/html/rfc4158*.

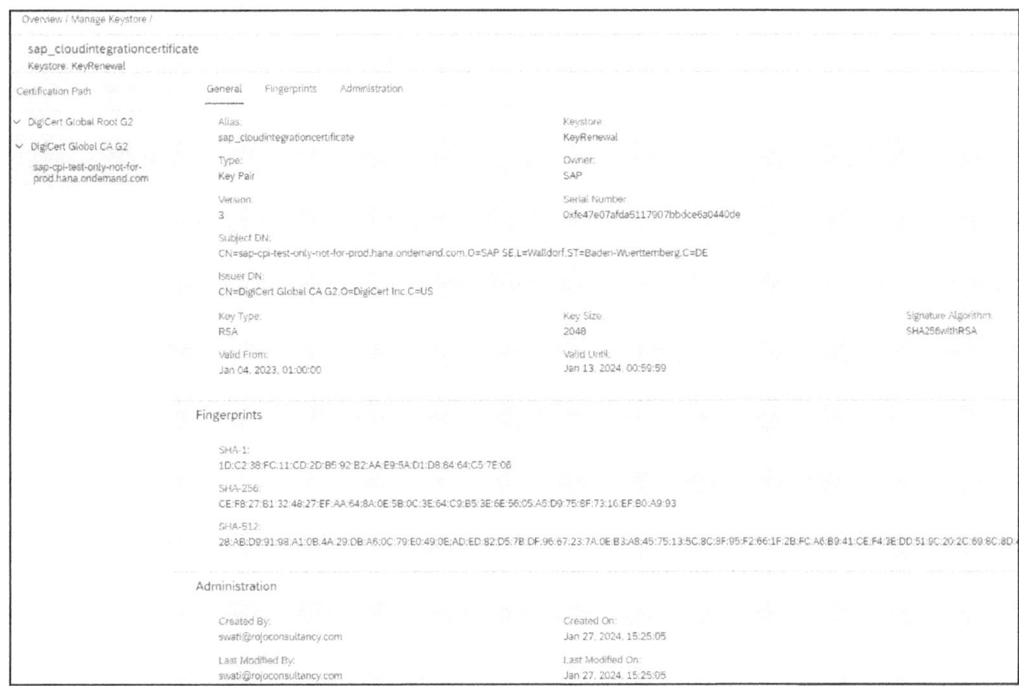

Figure 10.85 SAP-Owned Key Pair Entry

The following list describes a few of the attributes here:

- **Alias**
  The alias is the name by which you can uniquely identify a keystore entry.

When to Refer to an Alias (Examples)

In many cases, you'll need to specify the alias to tell the system which dedicated keystore entry to use for a certain iFlow step or adapter. We provide two examples:

- When configuring a **PKCS7 Encryptor**, you'll need to specify the **Receiver Public Key** alias to select the public key to be used to encrypt the message for a certain receiver.
- When you configure an **HTTP** receiver adapter and choose **Client Certificate** from the **Authentication** dropdown list, you have the option of specifying a **Private Key Alias** to point to the private key pair to be used to authenticate the tenant when calling a receiver.

- **Serial Number**
  This entry is used by the CA to uniquely identify the certificate (within the CA's organization).

- **Subject DN**
  The DN of the subject uniquely identifies the entity that is associated with the keystore entry. The DN is composed of a number of attributes that you'll need to specify when generating the key pair. These attributes comprise the common name (CN), which typically contains the server name of the VM associated with the tenant, and further information to identify the organization associated with the key pair such as **Organization (O)**, **Organizational Unit (OU)**, **Country (C)**, and other attributes (in the example shown in Figure 10.85, information about the SAP location in Germany).
- **Issuer DN**
  The DN of the issuer of the certificate identifies the authority that issued and signed the certificate (also consisting of several entries such as a **Common Name**, **Organizational Unit**, etc.).
- **Signature Algorithm**
  This algorithm is used by the issuer to sign the certificate.

The validity period is also displayed (see also Section 10.5.3).

Note that, as an SAP-owned entry, so you can only download the public key for this key pair, not the whole entry (by clicking the **Download** button at the top); no further (changing) actions are possible.

Under **Fingerprints**, you'll find hexadecimal expressions of hash values calculated out of the public key (using different hash algorithms, e.g., Secure Hash Algorithm 1 [SHA-1] or SHA-256). The tenant administrator can use the fingerprint to verify the trustworthiness of a keystore entry by sharing the fingerprint with the related communication partner (e.g., the administrator of the connected sender or receiver system) via an independent secure communication channel such as encrypted email.

Figure 10.86 shows a **Certificate** entry owned by the tenant administrator. On the left, notice that this root certificate is only one node of a larger certificate chain. The attributes have the same meaning as discussed for the **Key Pair** entry shown earlier in Figure 10.85. Note, however, that **Subject DN** and **Issuer DN** (grayed out in Figure 10.85) are identical in this case because the CA is acting both as the certificate issuer and as the entity associated with the certificate.

Figure 10.86 shows a keystore entry owned by the tenant administrator. Therefore, further actions are supported, such as renaming (changing the alias) or deleting the entity, using the **Rename** and **Delete** buttons at the top. You can also update the keystore entry. When you click the **Update** button, you can upload a new certificate to the keystore (for the same alias).

We'll now focus on the lifecycle management of security material.

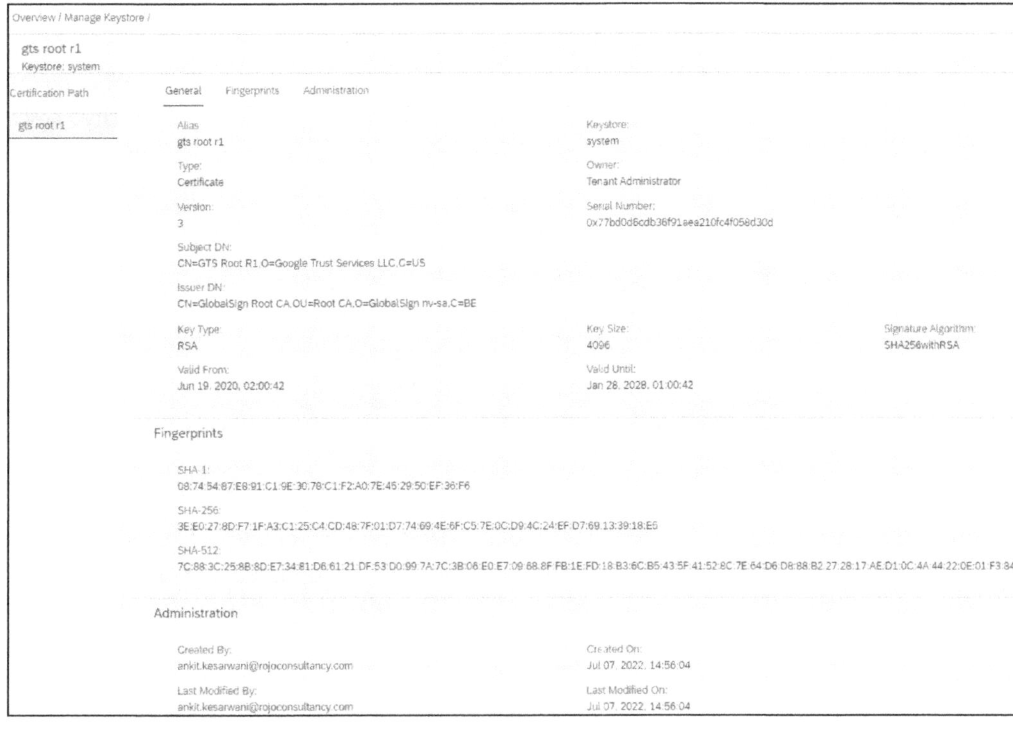

Figure 10.86 Certificate Entry Owned by the Tenant Administrator

10.5.3 Managing the Lifecycle of Keys Provided by SAP

To increase the security level of integration scenarios, digital certificates used to protect connections have a restricted validity period. Therefore, expiring certificates must be renewed at regular intervals—in the same way that changing passwords from time to time is a good idea.

However, keys are a fundamental part of the setup of each integration scenario, and each change in the setup of security material might require certain adaptations in the scenario setup and might disrupt the scenario operations if not done in a well-defined and orchestrated manner.

Therefore, managing the lifecycle of keys in a smart way is of critical importance. As the tenant administrator, you'll need to take certain actions when a key is about to expire and replace the key with a new one. You should organize this task to avoid downtime or for minimal downtime in your integration scenarios. General guidelines on renewing security material for the various use cases supported by Cloud Integration are provided in the documentation for Cloud Integration at *http://s-prs.co/5077114*.

We'll now focus on the special case when SAP-owned key material is renewed by SAP. SAP renews key pairs regularly (by default, the validity period is two years), and to enable the tenant administrator to manage renewal of SAP-owned keys, several options are available. The tenant administrator will need to activate the updated key in the tenant keystore. However, this step must be done in a coordinated manner because other components (i.e., the remote systems connected to the tenant that use the public part of the SAP key pair in their keystores) are affected by this step.

Renewal of SAP-Owned Root Certificates

As described in Chapter 7, Section 7.3.2, another option is that SAP updates root certificates that it owns. In this situation, the tenant administrator doesn't need to take any action. After the certificate has been updated, the new certificate is active immediately in the keystore.

The **Monitor** page of the Web UI provides several options for giving the tenant administrator full control over the activation of keys that are updated by SAP. In particular, described earlier in Chapter 7, Section 7.3.2, the **Monitor** page features four tabs for managing the tenant keystore:

- **Current**
  Shows the content of the keystore as currently deployed on the tenant (and actively used in your integration scenarios).
- **Backup**
  Shows backed-up keystore entries (see Chapter 7, Section 7.3.2).
- **New SAP Keys**
  Shows new keys provided by SAP in case a dedicated SAP-owned key is due to expire (see upcoming discussion).
- **SAP Key History**
  Shows recently renewed SAP keys and provides the option of moving a key back to the **New SAP Keys** store.

We won't go through all options for keystore management in this chapter, but you can refer to Chapter 7, Section 7.3.2. Instead, we'll focus on the topic of key activation and show you how the tenant administrator deals with a situation where SAP updates an SAP-owned key pair. Furthermore, to illustrate that some other components are affected by key renewal, we'll assume (as an example) that the SAP key pair is used in a scenario where a sender sends an encrypted message to Cloud Integration, and the message is decrypted by a **PKCS7 Decryptor** step on the tenant. Figure 10.87 shows an example where the SAP key pair (the tenant private key pair) is involved.

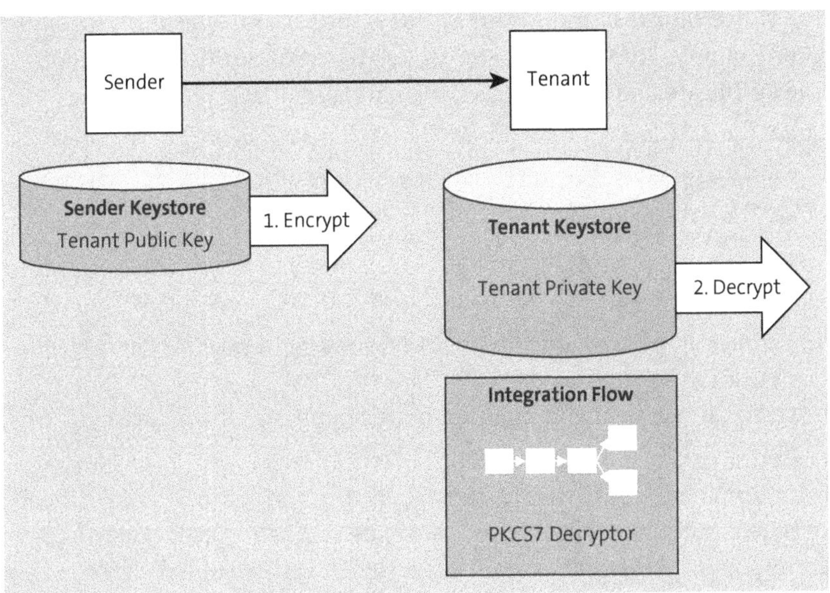

Figure 10.87 Using a Tenant Private Key Provided by SAP in a PKCS#7 Decryptor Step

Such a situation requires a coordinated procedure. Let's walk through the steps for activating the new key:

1. SAP provides a new key pair for a key pair that is due to expire soon.
2. As tenant administrator, you'll find the new key pair on the **Monitor** page of the Web UI. Under **Manage Keystore**, click on the **Keystore** tile, and then click on the **New SAP keys** tab, as shown in Figure 10.88.

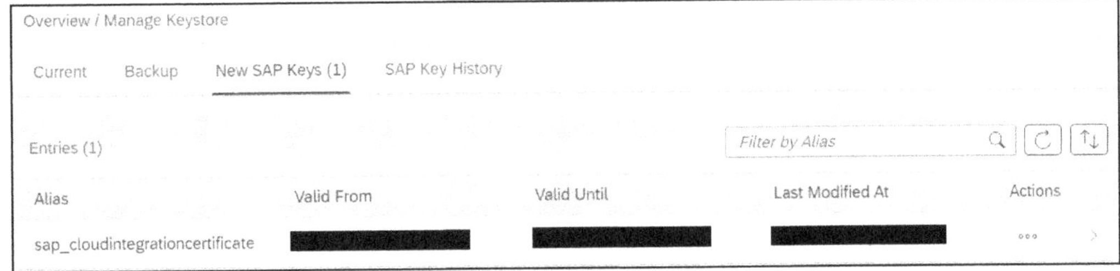

Figure 10.88 New Key Provided by SAP Shown in the New SAP Keys Tab of the Manage Keystore Monitor

3. Analyze the active iFlows and remote connections. Let's assume one of your integration scenarios uses a **PKCS7 Signer** step, which uses this key pair. Therefore, before activating the new key pair, you'll need to make sure the receiver system expects a corresponding signed message and has the public key for the newly provided SAP key pair.

4. Download the certificate from the **New SAP Keys** monitor by selecting the new SAP key (in our example, with the alias **sap_cloudintegrationcertificate**) and choosing **Download Certificate** under **Actions**, as shown in Figure 10.89.

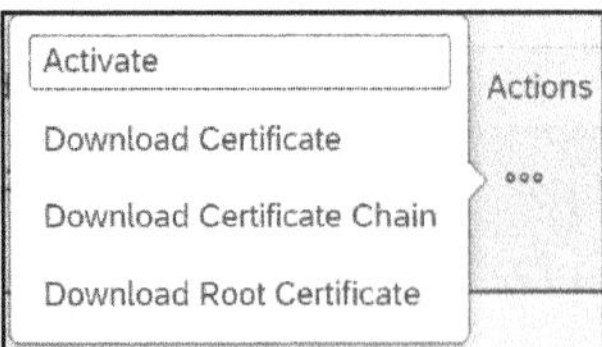

Figure 10.89 Downloading a Certificate from a Key Provided in the New SAP Keys Monitor

5. Save the certificate on your computer (in our example, as a file named *sap_cloud integrationcertificate.cer*).
6. Provide the administrator of the sender system with the certificate file through a protected channel (e.g., encrypted email), and request that the certificate be updated in the corresponding keystore of the sender system (to enable the sender to encrypt messages using the new certificate).

Key Renewal without Any Downtime

Note that, until now, we've kept quiet about a critical aspect of key renewal. In the example discussed in this section, we didn't consider downtime under certain conditions when renewing keys in all affected systems involved in a secure communication setup.

Therefore, the tenant administrator should find out, prior to the activities related to key renewal, whether the sender system is capable of encrypting messages with the old and the new SAP key at the same time. In this case, the process of key renewal can be organized so that no downtime is required for the integration scenario. The administrator of the sender system can just import the public key provided by the tenant administrator into the keystore of the sender system and inform the tenant administrator when he has finished this task. The tenant administrator can then activate the new key as shown in the next step.

In the documentation for Cloud Integration (*http://s-prs.co/5077115*), you'll find extensive information on this topic, including use cases and conditions under which a key renewal task can be set up without any downtime.

7. After the sender administrator has confirmed these actions, proceed to activate the new SAP key in the tenant keystore. Go to the **New SAP Keys** monitor, select the new SAP key (in our example, with the alias **sap_cloudintegrationcertificate**), and choose **Activate** under **Actions**, as shown in Figure 10.90.
8. A warning message is shown making sure you've completed the preparatory steps we described earlier, as shown in Figure 10.90.

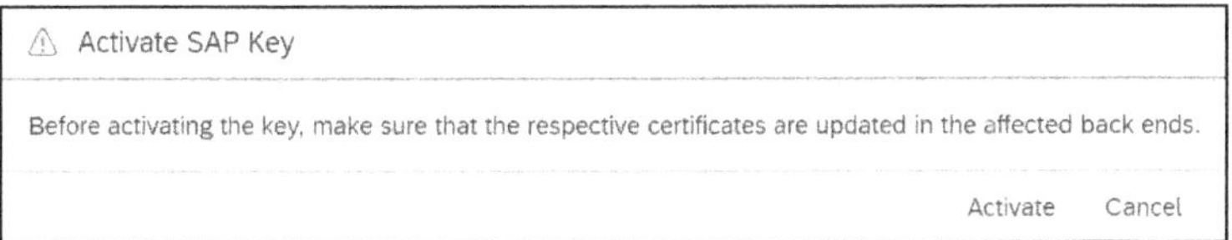

Figure 10.90 Warning Message Reminding You to Update Corresponding Keys in the Connected Remote Systems

9. Because you've already taken care of the required actions regarding the sender system, click **Activate**.

   Now, behind the scenes, the old key pair (with alias `sap_cloudintegrationcertificate`) is copied from the active keystore (**Current** tab) to the **Key History** keystore. Then, the new key pair (from the **New SAP Keys** keystore) is copied to the active keystore (**Current** tab) and overwrites the old key pair there. Finally, the new key pair is removed from the **New SAP Keys** keystore.

Note

For a detailed description of the process, check out the documentation for Cloud Integration at *http://s-prs.co/5077116*.

10. Under the **SAP Key History** tab, check to see whether the old key pair has been added, as shown in Figure 10.91.

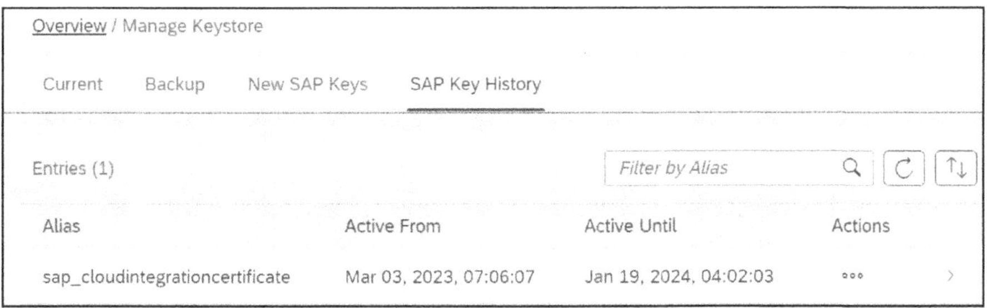

Figure 10.91 Key History Showing the Old Key Pair Replaced by the New One in the Current Keystore

The **SAP Key History** tab provides an important option, **Add to New SAP Keys**, which you can use to withdraw the activation of a new key and revert back to the previous SAP key pair (as explained in Chapter 7, Section 7.3.2, Table 7.14). Such a measure might be necessary if an error arises after key activation. One possible cause of an error is that required actions such as certificate renewal weren't undertaken in the keystore of the connected system. In this situation, the best option is to withdraw the key activation to get time until the problem is solved.

11. Finally, under the **New SAP Keys** tab, verify that the newly activated key pair has disappeared as expected, as shown in Figure 10.92.

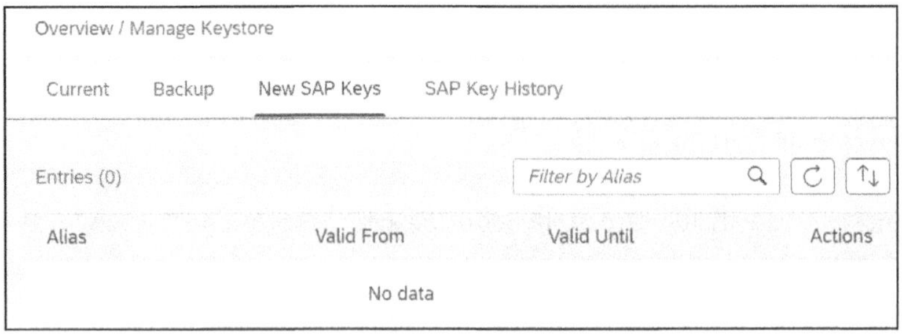

Figure 10.92 Newly Activated Key Pair Finally Removed from the New SAP Keys Monitor

To finish this discussion, let's assume that the key pair to renew is also used in an outbound HTTP connection to implement client certificate authentication (during setup, as shown earlier in Figure 10.41). In this case, prior to activating the new key, download the certificate chain of the SAP key from the **New SAP Keys** keystore (select **Download Certificate Chain** from the **Action** dropdown list), and save it as a file (in our example, with the name *sap_cloudintegrationcertificate.p7b*) to your computer. From the certificate chain, you'll finally need to extract the client root certificate and the client certificate and make both available to the administrator of the receiver system. The receiver administrator needs to import these items into the receiver keystore prior to the tenant administrator activating the new key pair.

We've only provided a simple example of a situation where a key pair renewed by SAP was used in an existing integration setup. In real-life scenarios, you must assume that expired keys will need to be removed in many more places in an integration scenario.

In this section, we only provided a glimpse into the lifecycle management of keys. Depending on the integration scenario, different processes will be in place to ensure you execute key renewal on all sides of the communication to avoid or minimize downtimes.

We'll close this section by mentioning that, if the tenant administrator hasn't activated an SAP key pair before the key pair expires, a system job activates the key pair automatically (see Chapter 7, Section 7.3.2). For a good introduction into how to organize key renewal, read *http://s-prs.co/5077117*.

10.6 Summary

Security considerations often come first when businesses consider sourcing out parts of their IT processes into the cloud. This chapter provided an overview of the various measures undertaken to protect customer data processed by Cloud Integration at the highest level. Several security features are already built-in and available via the architecture, the network design, and the way sensitive data is protected at SAP. Furthermore, you've seen how security is taken seriously by the way processes are performed during the lifecycle of an integration project. We showed you how to manage users and authorizations for your SAP BTP subaccount. Finally, you learned how you, as the customer, can configure secure message exchange between your landscape and Cloud Integration. We showed you, step-by-step, how to set up a secure connection between remote components and Cloud Integration and how to build iFlows that implement basic security features. We closed this chapter by providing a glimpse at managing the lifecycle of security material in the tenant keystore.

In the next chapter, we'll provide you with an overview of some productive scenarios that use Cloud Integration.

Chapter 11
Productive Scenarios Using Cloud Integration

Now that you've undertaken a journey through the world of Cloud Integration, you should be familiar with its foundational principles and concepts and can now begin working with it seriously. You also know that Cloud Integration enables you to build networks of IT applications flexibly on any scale. In this chapter, we'll show you a few examples of how this product can be used productively in real-life scenarios.

In Chapter 1, Section 1.2, we introduced Cloud Integration as a cloud-based integration solution that supports cloud-to-cloud integration and cloud-to-on-premise integration. We also showed you that Cloud Integration can be used in combination with on-premise integration solutions (e.g., SAP Process Orchestration) or with the Edge Integration Cell. In this chapter, we'll describe a few productive scenarios that each demonstrate one of the cloud-to-cloud and cloud-to-on-premise use cases. Additionally, we'll show you how these scenarios work in real life, in existing landscapes, and with actual applications that are connected with each other.

For most of these scenarios, predefined integration content is available in the Integration content catalog, which you can use out of the box. Thus, Chapter 3, which deals with the publication of predefined integration content by SAP, also contains information about these scenarios. Therefore, we'll keep our descriptions of these scenarios short in this chapter.

11.1 Integration of SAP Cloud for Customer and SAP ERP

SAP Cloud for Customer is SAP's cloud-based customer relationship management (CRM) solution that helps you, as an SAP customer, improve your interactions with your customers.

Using a cloud-based CRM solution often requires that you replicate master data (e.g., account, product, or employee) or transactional data from a connected on-premise SAP ERP application. Transactional data may be replicated, for example, with sales orders or may be referenced synchronously for the latest updates, such as the latest figures for a customer-specific price. Obviously, both the cloud-based application and the on-premise system must be kept in sync, so integration scenarios must be implemented.

Figure 11.1 shows the general setup of the integration of SAP ERP with SAP Cloud for Customer.

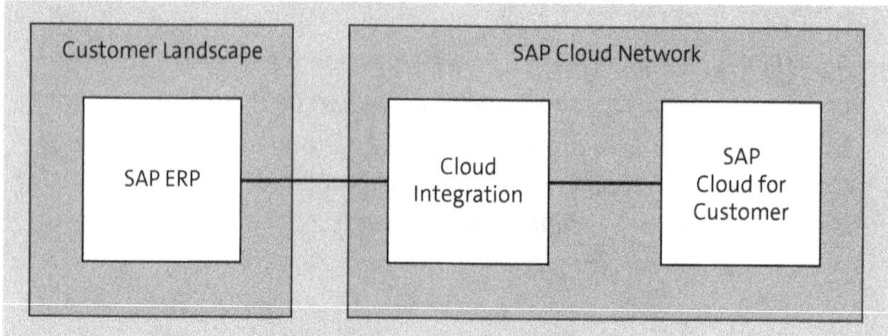

Figure 11.1 Integration of SAP ERP with SAP Cloud for Customer

SAP provides predefined integration content for the integration of SAP Cloud for Customer with SAP ERP in the integration content catalog. An overview of the content and more details on the business use case of this scenario were provided earlier in Chapter 3, Section 3.4.2.

11.1.1 Technical Landscape

The integration of SAP Cloud for Customer with SAP ERP is an example of a cloud-to-on-premise integration. Figure 11.2 shows the commonly used technical landscape for the scenario. As always, many options are available, but we'll briefly describe only a common setup.

In the proposed setup, the SAP Cloud for Customer application and the integration middleware (Cloud Integration) run in the SAP cloud network, whereas the connected on-premise application (SAP ERP) runs in the customer landscape.

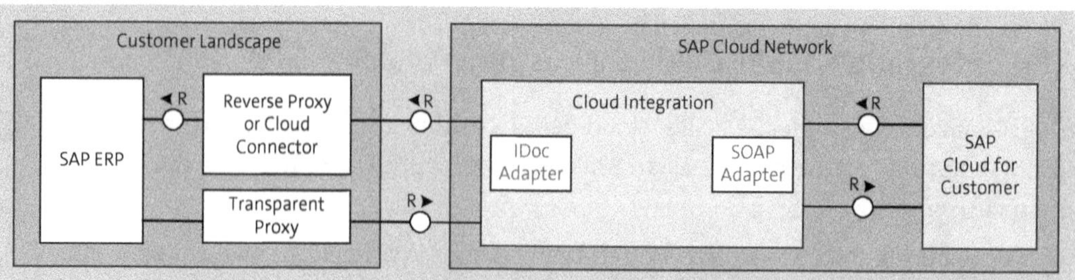

Figure 11.2 Technical Landscape for Integration of SAP Cloud for Customer with SAP ERP (Example Setup)

All components communicate with each other using HTTPS. However, note that connections between the SAP cloud network and components located in the customer landscape require particular security measures: You must ensure that the components in the customer landscape aren't directly accessible from the internet. Thus, for this communication direction, when messages are sent from the SAP cloud network to the customer-based SAP ERP system, a component in the customer landscape (either a reverse proxy or SAP Connectivity services) terminates Transport Layer Security (TLS) requests and reestablishes new requests.

The other way around, a proxy server (or transparent proxy) routes the request from the SAP ERP system to the target component (Cloud Integration) without terminating any TLS request.

Cloud Integration, as the message broker interconnected between SAP Cloud for Customer and SAP ERP, typically uses the following connectivity options:

- Simple Object Access Protocol (SOAP) adapter or IDoc adapter (also uses the SOAP protocol) for connections between SAP ERP and Cloud Integration
- SOAP adapter for connections between Cloud Integration and SAP Cloud for Customer

11.1.2 Example Adapter Configurations

To round out this section, we'll briefly show you how the connections of the scenario shown in Figure 11.2 can be configured in a productive use case on the Cloud Integration side of the communication. In this section, we've provided screenshots of the four adapters that come into play on the Cloud Integration system side.

Figure 11.3 shows an example of an IDoc adapter used for the connection between SAP ERP and Cloud Integration (messages sent from SAP ERP to Cloud Integration).

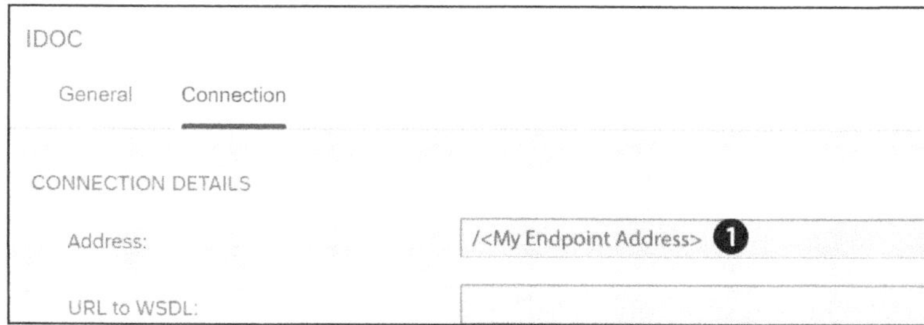

Figure 11.3 IDoc Adapter for Messages Sent from SAP ERP to Cloud Integration

As in your first integration flow (iFlow), in Chapter 2, for the **HTTPS** sender adapter, the **Address** field (Figure 11.3 ❶) should define an endpoint address so that SAP ERP can call the iFlow deployed on the Cloud Integration tenant. The final destination, which is to be configured in the SAP ERP system, is then composed of the URL, the runtime component (assigned to the tenant), and this endpoint address (see Chapter 2, Section 2.3.4). The **URL to WSDL** field was explained in the context of the SOAP adapter in Chapter 5, Section 5.3.1.

Figure 11.4 shows an example of an IDoc adapter for the connection between SAP ERP and Cloud Integration for the opposite communication direction (messages sent from Cloud Integration to SAP ERP).

In the **Address** field (Figure 11.4 ❶), you must specify the host and port of the SAP ERP system, as well as the SAP client. The string **/sap/bc/srt/idoc** is a fixed part of the address to point to the IDoc service of an SAP system.

In the **Proxy Type** field ❷, the **Internet** option is selected by default, which means that the connection is done via a reverse proxy infrastructure (an option used by many customers for such integration scenarios). As an alternative, you can select **On Premise** if you want to use SAP Connectivity services to connect to SAP ERP. For more information about this attribute, check out the "Proxy Type" information box at the end of Chapter 10, Section 10.4.3.

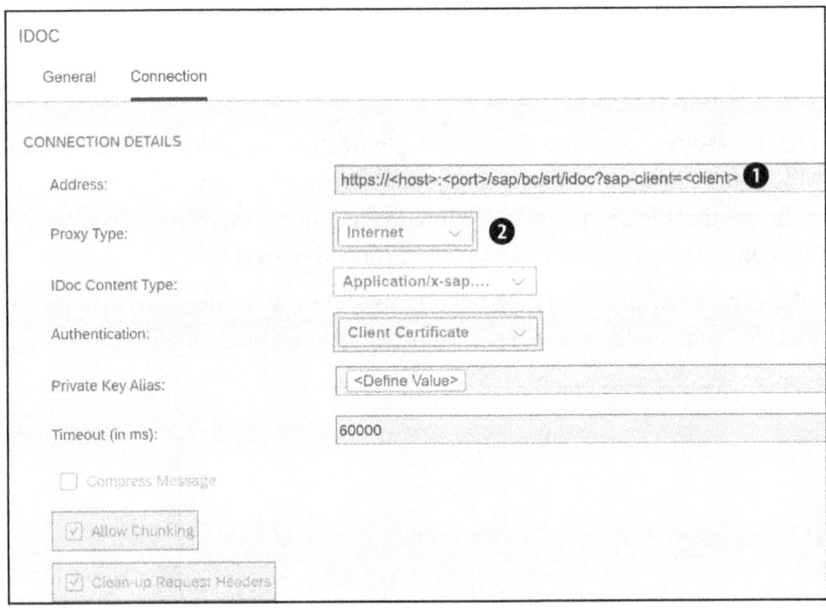

Figure 11.4 IDoc Adapter for Messages Sent from Cloud Integration to SAP ERP

Figure 11.5 shows an example of a SOAP (1.x) sender adapter for the connection between Cloud Integration and SAP Cloud for Customer (messages sent from SAP Cloud for Customer to Cloud Integration).

In the **Address** field (Figure 11.5 ❶), you'll need to define an endpoint address so that SAP Cloud for Customer can call the iFlow deployed on the Cloud Integration tenant.

In this example, in the **URL to WSDL** field ❷, a Web Services Description Language (WSDL) file is also specified, allowing Cloud Integration to access information contained in the WSDL file to process the message (as described in Chapter 5, Section 5.3.1, in our example of an asynchronous message).

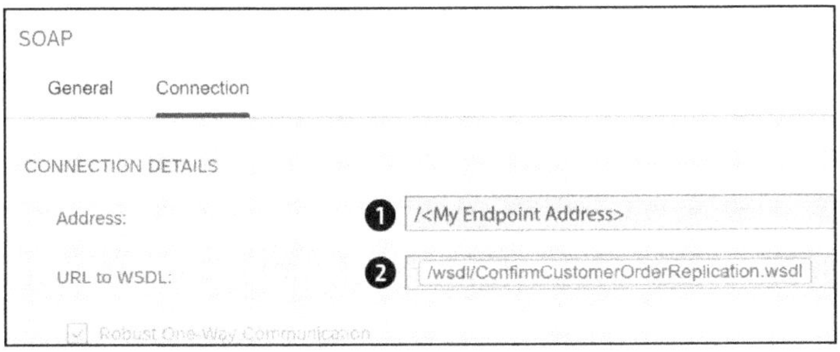

Figure 11.5 SOAP Adapter for Messages Sent from SAP Cloud for Customer to Cloud Integration

Figure 11.6 shows an example of a SOAP (1.x) receiver adapter establishing the connection between Cloud Integration and SAP Cloud for Customer for the opposite communication direction (messages sent from Cloud Integration to SAP Cloud for Customer).

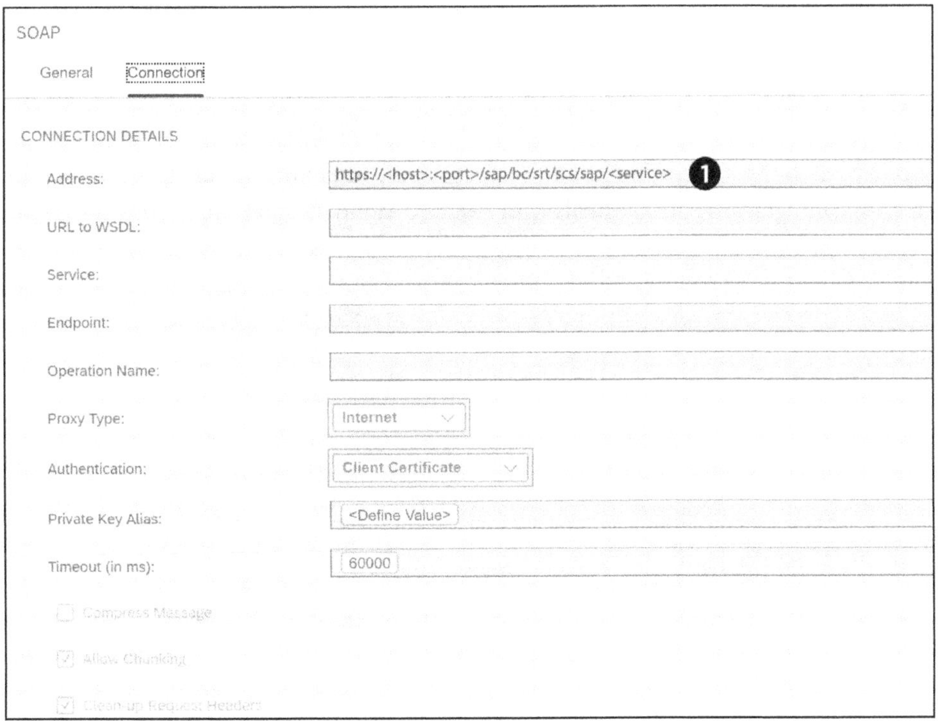

Figure 11.6 SOAP Adapter for Messages Sent from Cloud Integration to SAP Cloud for Customer

In the **Address** field (Figure 11.6 ❶), you must specify the service address in the SAP Cloud for Customer system.

Note that the examples shown in Figure 11.5 and Figure 11.6 were retrieved from content published by SAP on the SAP Business Accelerator Hub and reflect earlier versions of the SOAP adapter. In the meantime, updates to this adapter type have been provided. When you create a new SOAP adapter, you'll get a slightly different user interface (UI). For more information on the versioning concept for iFlow components, see Chapter 6, Section 6.7.

11.2 Integration of SAP Cloud for Customer with SAP S/4HANA Cloud

SAP S/4HANA is SAP's next-generation business suite, built on SAP HANA database technology, and providing SAP Fiori UIs. SAP Fiori is a modern UI technology that enables customers to extend the use of SAP applications to tablet computers and smartphones. You can install SAP S/4HANA in your own landscape (on-premise) or use it in the public cloud (owned by SAP).

Customers who prefer to run their enterprise IT processes in the cloud can choose SAP S/4HANA Cloud, which covers the areas of logistics, accounting and finance, and sales. The integration package for SAP Cloud for Customer Integration with SAP S/4HANA Cloud, available in the integration content catalog, provides a set of predefined iFlows and value mappings that facilitate the replication of objects, such as business partner and material, between SAP S/4HANA Cloud and SAP Cloud for Customer.

Compared to the integration of SAP Cloud for Customer and SAP ERP (refer to Section 11.1), this integration package deals with cloud-to-cloud integration, as shown in Figure 11.7.

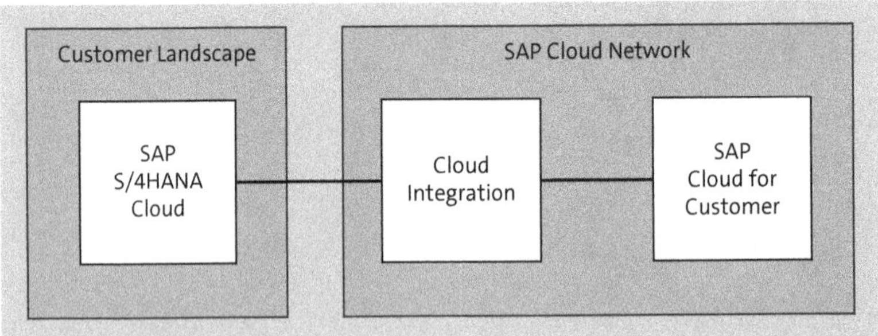

Figure 11.7 Integration of SAP S/4HANA Cloud with SAP Cloud for Customer

11.3 Integration of SAP Marketing Cloud and Various Applications

SAP Customer Experience is an on-demand product family that includes SAP Cloud for Customer (discussed in Section 11.1), SAP Commerce Cloud, SAP Customer Data Cloud, and SAP Marketing Cloud. The available integration packages were already presented in Chapter 3, Section 3.4.3, which briefly introduces these solutions.

SAP Marketing Cloud is a cloud solution offered by SAP to help customers optimize their marketing activities (e.g., by developing and executing successful marketing campaigns). As already mentioned in Chapter 3, Section 3.4.3, SAP Marketing Cloud can be integrated with other components and applications such as the following:

- SAP Cloud for Customer (e.g., for master data replication)
- On-premise SAP S/4HANA Enterprise Management, SAP Customer Relationship Management (SAP CRM), SAP Cloud for Customer, and SAP ERP
- Social media platforms, such as Twitter (now called X) or Facebook

Let's focus on the integration of SAP Marketing Cloud with Twitter (now called X) as one example of a scenario involving a social media platform.

Note

In 2023, the Twitter platform rebranded to X. For the purposes of this book, we'll refer to this platform as Twitter, as the SAP Marketing Cloud integration still uses the original Twitter brand name.

Of course, analyzing social media content can be invaluable when trying to get to know what customers or potential customers think about certain topics. Integrating SAP Marketing Cloud with Twitter allows SAP customers to load data from Twitter into SAP Marketing Cloud for further analysis. For example, SAP Marketing Cloud allows you to perform sentiment analysis on Twitter content. In this context, *sentiment analysis*, in short, is a methodology to analyze social media content (Tweets) related to a certain topic to determine the attitude of users on this topic. SAP Marketing Cloud can then use the results of this analysis to adapt and improve your marketing campaigns. Figure 11.8 shows the components integrated with this scenario.

In Chapter 10, Section 10.4.5, you became familiar with the Twitter adapter. The mentioned integration package uses the Twitter adapter to connect Twitter with Cloud Integration. On the other side of the communication, the HTTP adapter is used to connect Cloud Integration with SAP Marketing Cloud.

You can find the package **Twitter Integration with SAP Marketing Cloud** on the SAP Business Accelerator Hub (*https://api.sap.com/*). When you've copied the integration package to your workspace (see Chapter 3, Section 3.2.2), you can configure the iFlow. The available integration content has been designed in such a way that you'll only need to configure a few parameters to set the integration scenario into operation—without any further editing and adapting of any iFlow (see Chapter 4, Section 4.2, for more details on configuring externalized iFlow parameters). To finish the communication between Twitter and Cloud Integration, the only thing you need to do is to configure your Twitter application programming interface (API) and deploy the required OAuth credentials as **Secure Parameter** artifacts (shown in detail in Chapter 10, Section 10.4.5 and outlined in Figure 11.8).

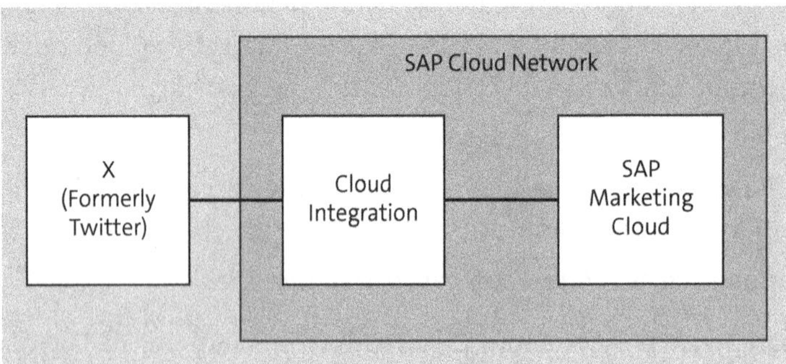

Figure 11.8 Integration of Twitter with SAP Marketing Cloud

11.4 Integration of SAP SuccessFactors and SAP ERP

SAP SuccessFactors is cloud-based human capital management (HCM) software that provides tools for recruiting, performance management, talent management, and other employee-centric solutions. This solution also provides core employee management capabilities (in the Employee Central module).

In many cases, when companies plan to move parts of their HCM processes to the cloud, a phased approach might be the solution of choice. Either the company first moves only parts of the HCM processes to the cloud (e.g., recruitment) and keeps the core functions located in the on-premise landscape, or they may prefer to migrate their HCM solution successively to the cloud, based on certain locations. In any case, seamless and tight integration between the processes running in the cloud and in the on-premise environment is critical.

As an example of the separation of processes between the on-premise landscape and the cloud, imagine your company runs its recruitment processes using SAP SuccessFactors in the cloud, whereas core employee management functions are kept in the on-premise SAP ERP Human Capital Management (SAP ERP HCM) application. Figure 11.9 shows the involved components in a high-level overview.

The integration of SAP SuccessFactors with SAP ERP is a cloud-to-on-premise integration. On the SAP Business Accelerator Hub, you can find various integration packages that facilitate the integration of SAP ERP–based processes with the cloud-based HCM processes of SAP SuccessFactors. An overview of the content and more details on the business use case of such scenarios was provided in Chapter 3, Section 3.4. In this section, we'll cover some additional aspects such as the typical technical landscape setup for such scenarios.

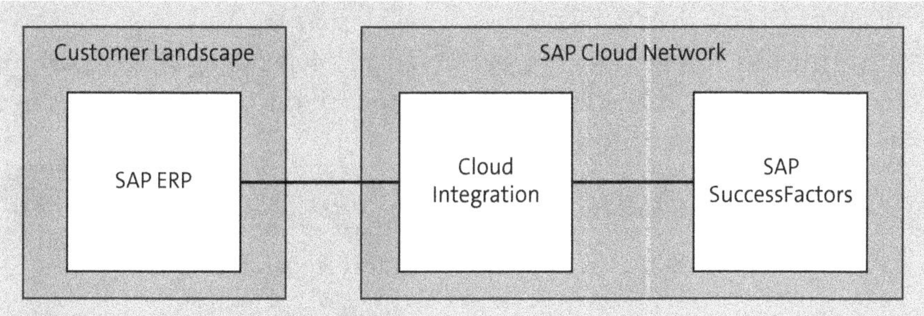

Figure 11.9 Integration of SAP ERP with SAP SuccessFactors

11.4.1 Technical Landscape

Figure 11.10 shows a common setup of SAP SuccessFactors and SAP ERP integration scenario. An obvious option is to connect the SAP ERP with Cloud Integration using web services communication (through the SOAP adapter).

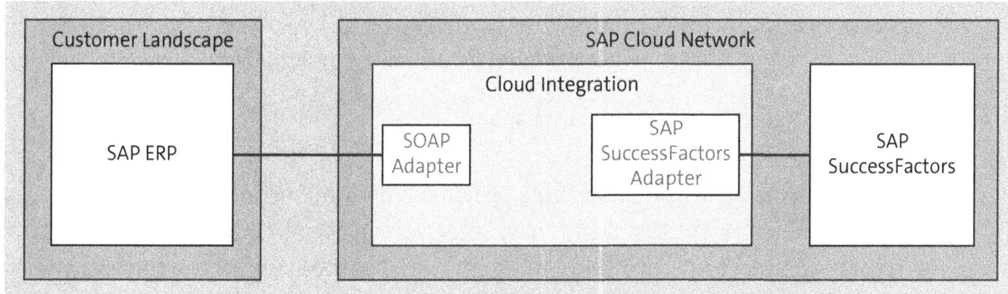

Figure 11.10 Integrating SAP ERP with SAP SuccessFactors through Cloud Integration

For the other side of the communication, SAP SuccessFactors offers various API options to technically integrate with and connect to other systems, including the following:

- **SFAPI**
  A SOAP API designed to import or export data to and from SAP SuccessFactors, this API allows you to perform create, read, update, and delete (CRUD) operations on SAP SuccessFactors entities.
- **OData API**
  This API allows you to access SAP SuccessFactors content using OData.

Cloud Integration provides an option to use these APIs in an intuitive and convenient way: the SAP SuccessFactors adapter, which is part of the standard Cloud Integration adapter offering.

11.4.2 SAP SuccessFactors Adapter

The SAP SuccessFactors adapter comes in several variants, depending on which API you want to connect the SAP SuccessFactors system with (and the communication direction). Table 11.1 provides a list of these variants.

Adapter Variant	Allows You To ...
Sender SOAP	Connect to an SAP SuccessFactors sender and read data from it using web services.
Sender REST	Connect to an SAP SuccessFactors learning management system (as the sender system) and read data from it through a Representational State Transfer (REST) API.
Receiver SOAP	Connect to an SAP SuccessFactors receiver to perform read or write operations on the content using web services.
Receiver REST	Connect to an SAP SuccessFactors receiver to perform read or write operations on the content using a REST API.
Receiver OData V2/V4	Connect to an SAP SuccessFactors receiver to perform read or write operations on the content using OData.

Table 11.1 SAP SuccessFactors Adapter Variants

Each SAP SuccessFactors adapter type provides a dedicated configuration UI to access SAP SuccessFactors entities intuitively. After you've specified an SAP SuccessFactors system to connect to, through the configuration UI of the adapter, you can easily select the entities and define certain operations on them without the need to write any line of code. When you add an SAP SuccessFactors adapter to an iFlow, you'll choose the corresponding variant by selecting a **Message Protocol**, as shown in Figure 11.11, for a SAP SuccessFactors receiver adapter.

Message Protocol
ODата V2
OData V4
REST
SOAP

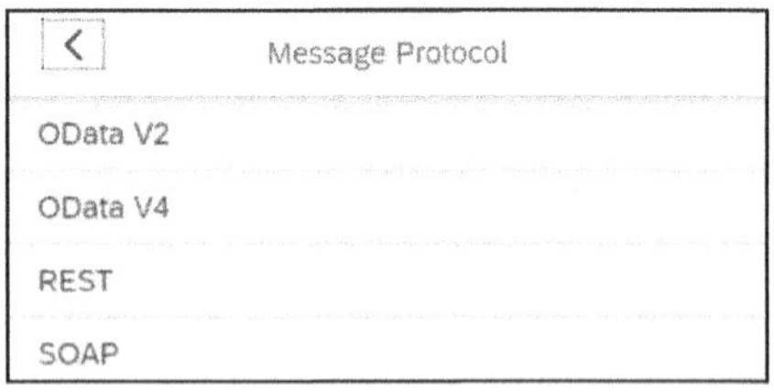

Figure 11.11 Selecting the Message Protocol to Decide Which Adapter Variant to Add (for the SAP SuccessFactors Receiver Adapter)

The detailed properties of the adapter's configuration UI depend on the chosen message protocol. Figure 11.12 shows an example of an SAP SuccessFactors adapter configuration UI for a receiver adapter when you've selected **OData V2** as the **Message Protocol**. Some key properties include the URL to the SAP SuccessFactors system ❶, the alias of

User Credentials artifact (to be deployed on the tenant) ❷, and, finally, the SAP SuccessFactors entity and the supported operations ❸.

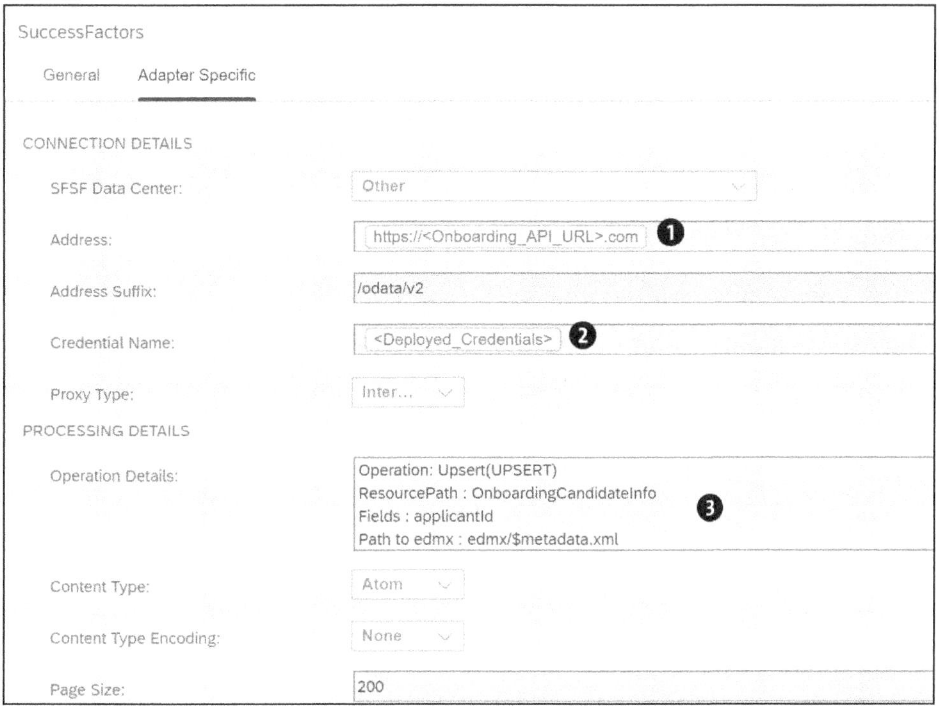

Figure 11.12 SAP SuccessFactors Adapter (Example) from SAP Business Accelerator Hub

Note that this example is retrieved from the SAP Business Accelerator Hub and reflects the component version 1.0 of the SAP SuccessFactors adapter. In the meantime, updates to this adapter type have been provided so that when you create a new SAP SuccessFactors receiver adapter (with the **OData V2** message protocol), you'll get a slightly different UI (with the settings now spread out over two different tabs, **Connection** and **Processing**). (For more information on the versioning concept for iFlow components, see Chapter 6, Section 6.7.)

When you configure an SAP SuccessFactors sender adapter (to connect to an SAP SuccessFactors sender system), you can only select between the **REST** and **SOAP** message protocols. Furthermore, you can specify only query operations. This limitation exists because the SAP SuccessFactors adapter acts as a polling adapter, reading information at scheduled intervals from the SAP SuccessFactors system (similar to how the mail sender adapter reads emails from an email server; see Chapter 2, Section 2.3.6).

The SAP SuccessFactors sender adapters offer a **Scheduler** tab that allows you to specify certain time intervals when the adapter should read data from the SAP SuccessFactors (sender) system.

For receiver adapters, all standard CRUD operations of SFAPI (query, insert, upsert, update) are supported and can be configured.

To configure a secure connection between Cloud Integration and an SAP SuccessFactors sender or receiver system, you'll use the **User Credentials** artifact type, which comprises a user name, password, and, specific to SAP SuccessFactors, a company ID (to indicate the SAP SuccessFactors system you're connecting to). When configuring the connection, you'll first define a **User Credentials** artifact and deploy it on the tenant; second, you'll refer to the alias of the artifact in the SAP SuccessFactors adapter (in the **Credential Name** field). Compare this process to the process we used for the mail adapter in Chapter 2, Section 2.3.5. When deploying a **User Credentials** artifact, make sure you select **SuccessFactors** from the **Type** dropdown list.

Figure 11.13 shows the properties of the **User Credentials** artifact to be deployed on the tenant to configure a secure connection between the tenant and an SAP SuccessFactors system.

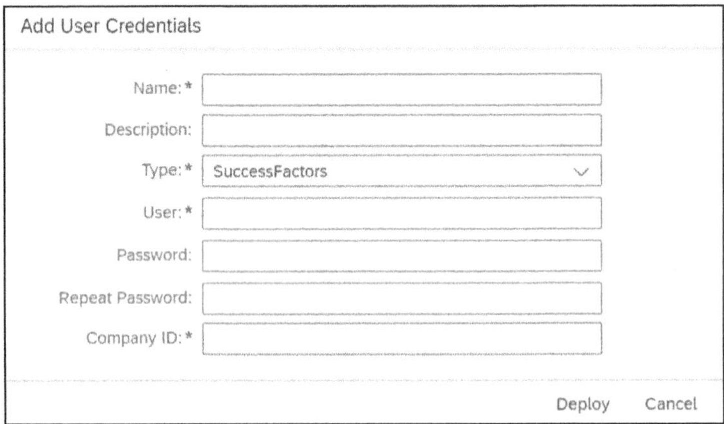

Figure 11.13 User Credentials Artifact for SAP SuccessFactors

11.5 Integration of SAP Applications with SAP Business Network

SAP Business Network provides access to a worldwide online marketplace that brings buyers and suppliers together via the internet and facilitates procurement processes. Interacting in this network, companies can streamline and accelerate their procurement processes, which include buying, selling, and cash management.

In the recent past, the majority of these processes still relied on the exchange of information on paper. Moving these processes to the network and automating them helps accelerate operations greatly and considerably reduces manual errors. Both buyers and their suppliers can benefit from such a shift. For example, buyers can pay earlier and may benefit from discounts because they are paying faster, while suppliers are receiving their money earlier.

In a basic scenario, a buyer (who uses an SAP ERP system to manage the procurement process) interacts with many suppliers through SAP Business Network. Each supplier is a registered member of SAP Business Network.

SAP Business Network supports different options for buyers to manage the procurement process:

- The buyer's SAP ERP system manages the ordering process, whereas the invoicing process is sourced out to and automated via SAP Business Network.
- The entire procure-to-pay process (including the ordering process) is automated using SAP Business Network, and the buyer's SAP ERP system only acts as a system of records.

Let's briefly focus on the first option, where the ordering process is managed by the SAP ERP system. Once set up, a typical scenario comprises the following steps on both the buyer and supplier sides:

1. The buyer creates a purchase order to order a product from the supplier's catalog and sends the purchase order to the supplier.
2. The supplier receives the purchase order in its inbox, creates an order confirmation, and sends that confirmation to the buyer.
3. The buyer receives the order confirmation.
4. After the article ships, the supplier creates an advanced shipping notification (ASN) and sends it to the buyer indicating that the article is on its way.
5. As soon as the product arrives, the buyer posts a goods receipt and sends it to the supplier.
6. After the goods receipt arrives, the supplier creates an invoice and forwards it to the buyer.

To integrate the buyer's SAP ERP systems with SAP Business Network, SAP provides an SAP Business Network Integration for SAP Business Suite Add-On 1.0, which supports the following integration options:

- Setting up a point-to-point connection with SAP Business Network (based on web services)
- Using SAP Process Orchestration as the on-premise integration platform
- Using Cloud Integration as the cloud integration solution

For integration using Cloud Integration, SAP provides predefined integration content in the integration content catalog. An overview of the content and more details on the business use case of this scenario have already been provided in Chapter 3, Section 3.4.

Figure 11.14 shows the technical landscape for integrating a buyer with the SAP Business Network based on Cloud Integration.

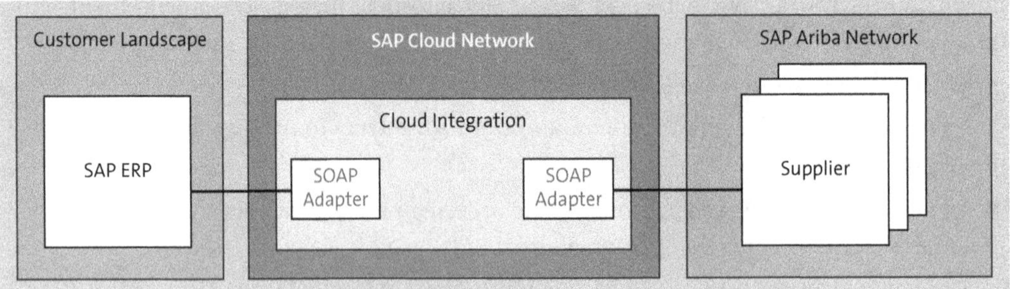

Figure 11.14 Technical Landscape for the Integration of SAP ERP with SAP Business Network

As shown in Figure 11.14, the connectivity both for the buyer's SAP ERP system and for SAP Business Network is based on the SOAP adapter.

Note that suppliers registered in SAP Business Network can use either their own proprietary applications or an SAP application to manage the procurement process from their side. Alternatively, suppliers can use a UI provided by the SAP Business Network itself.

11.6 Integration with German Tax Authorities Using the ELSTER Adapter

Digitization didn't stop with taxes. For communications with tax authorities in Germany, customers can use the *Elektronische Steuererklärung* (ELSTER; in English: electronic tax return) system. When operating ELSTER, the involved tax data is processed centrally on a server farm run by the German tax authorities located in Nuremberg, Germany, which is called the *Zentrale Produktions- und Service-Stelle* (ZPS Elster) or clearinghouse. We'll refer to this server farm as the ELSTER server.

Each client to be connected to the ELSTER server to transfer tax data must use the ELSTER Rich Client (ERiC) software (also owned by the German tax authorities). The associated libraries are usually installed on the client side.

To facilitate this kind of data transfer, SAP, as part of Cloud Integration, offers a dedicated adapter, the ELSTER adapter. When a company uses the ELSTER adapter, there's no need to install any ERiC library at the company's location. In such a scenario, the related business application of the company (usually a human resources [HR] or finance [FI] application) sends the tax data to Cloud Integration. The data is then further processed on the integration middleware, and the communication with the ELSTER server is accomplished by the ELSTER adapter. Organizations using the Cloud Integration's ELSTER adapter also won't need to manage future updates of ERiC libraries, which occur twice a year, because updates are done automatically by Cloud Integration.

On SAP Business Accelerator Hub, you can find integration packages that contain predefined integration scenarios that connect business applications with the German tax authorities through the ELSTER adapter, as shown in Figure 11.15.

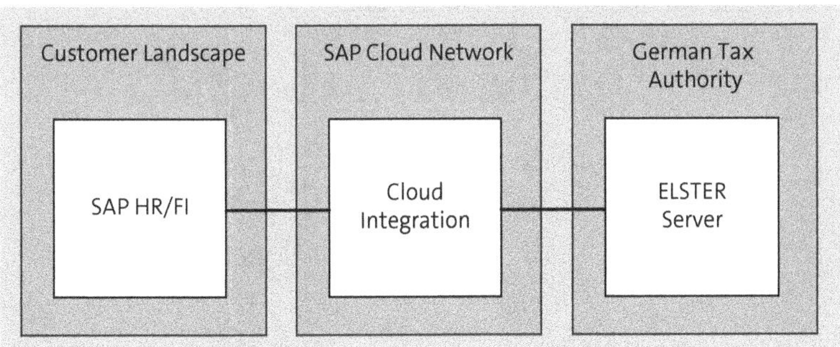

Figure 11.15 ELSTER Integration

On a more technical level, ELSTER integration works typically, as shown in Figure 11.16.

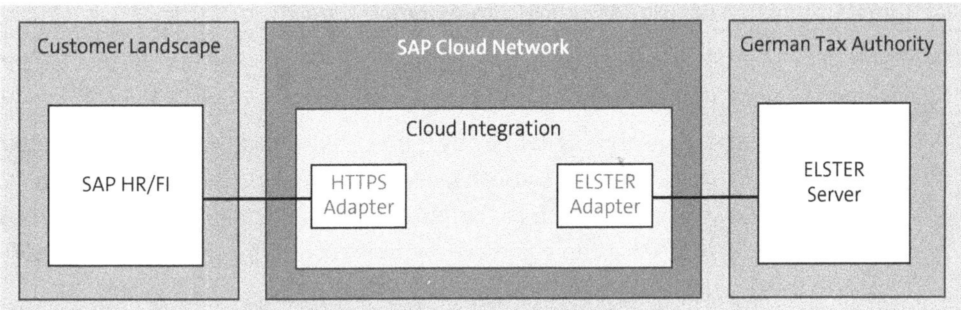

Figure 11.16 Technical Landscape for the ELSTER Integration

As shown in Figure 11.16, the SAP HR or FI system sends the tax data (as an XML document) to Cloud Integration through an HTTP connection. On the side of the SAP HR/FI system, the corresponding HTTP destination needs to be maintained. When, as shown in Figure 11.16, the HR or FI application is implemented on an SAP system, this configuration is done using Transaction SM59. The iFlow deployed on the Cloud Integration tenant receives the tax message and does further, scenario-specific processing steps.

The ELSTER receiver adapter first validates the message. Note that the ELSTER adapter can only process tax documents that adhere to certain guidelines as given by the German tax authorities. Furthermore, the ELSTER adapter signs and encrypts the message before sending it to the ELSTER server.

After Cloud Integration has received the response from the ELSTER server, it verifies and decrypts the content and sends it back to the SAP HR/FI system.

Figure 11.17 shows a screenshot of the ELSTER adapter from the iFlow **Send Finance Tax Data** (integration package **SAP Finance Applications Integration with ELSTER**). Note that the **Operation** dropdown list ❶ is set to **Validate and Send**.

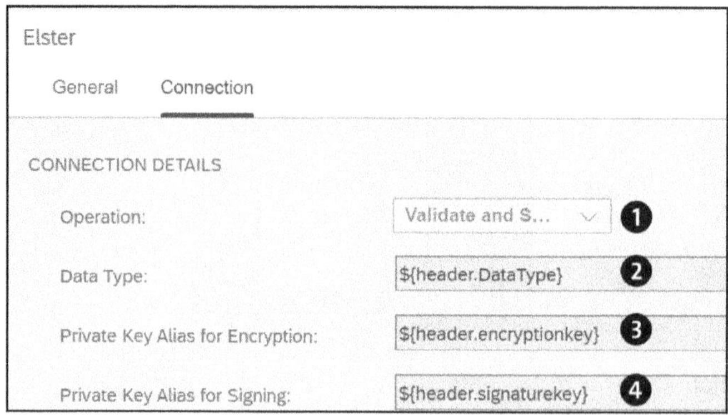

Figure 11.17 ELSTER Adapter When Operation Is Set to Validate and Send

Notice also the following additional parameters:

- The **Data Type** parameter (Figure 11.17 ❷) specifies the type of tax document provided as payload (required for the validation step).

  The list of possible data types is defined by the German tax authorities. For example, data type `UStVA_2019` stands for *Umsatzsteuer-Voranmeldung* (advance turnover tax return) for the year 2019, which is the information about the already generated value-added tax (VAT) that the organization must report on a monthly or quarterly basis to the German tax authorities.
- The **Private Key Alias for Encryption** parameter ❸ specifies the alias of the private key to be used for message encryption.
- The **Private Key Alias for Signing** parameter ❹ specifies the key pair that contains the private key to be used for message signing.

In our example, all three parameters are defined dynamically through a header (refer to Chapter 6, Section 6.2).

Note that, to set up message encryption and signing, an X.509 key pair must be uploaded to the Cloud Integration tenant keystore (see Chapter 10, Section 10.4.6). To accomplish this step, your company's tenant administrator gets the related certificate (a *.pfx* file that contains a public key and an associated, password-protected private key) from the tax authority at the ELSTER Online Portal (*www.elster.de*).

Other options for the **Operation** parameter include the following:

- **Validate**
  When this parameter is selected, the adapter only validates the tax document without sending it to the ELSTER server. In this case, you only need to specify the **Data Type**.

- **Get Version**
  In this case, no other parameter is available. The adapter retrieves the ERiC version from the ELSTER server.

  Usually, the HR/FI application needs to get the actual version information because the payload to send to the ELSTER server depends on the version. Therefore, before actually validating the payload and sending it to the ELSTER server (with an ELSTER adapter and the **Operation** parameter set to **Validate and Send**), Cloud Integration needs to get the version with an upstream communication step where the ELSTER adapter **Operation** parameter is set to **Get Version**.

For more details on the ELSTER adapter, including technical background on the ERiC libraries and steps for configuring and running the iFlows in the predefined package **SAP HR Integration with ELSTER ERiC for Germany**, read the "Cloud Integration – Usage of the Elster Adapter" SAP Community blog at *http://s-prs.co/5077118*.

11.7 SAP S/4HANA Integration with Salesforce

Salesforce is a cloud-based software that provides CRM service and enterprise applications focused on customer service, marketing automation, analytics, and application development. In their landscape, chances are high that there will be the need to synchronize different data sets between these applications. The data to be synchronized will generally include both master and transactional data.

As an example of the separation of processes between SAP S/4HANA and Salesforce, imagine your company runs its finance processes using SAP S/4HANA, whereas core CRM functions are kept in Salesforce.

On the SAP Business Accelerator Hub, you can find an integration package that contains predefined integration scenarios that connect SAP S/4HANA with Salesforce through the Salesforce adapter, as shown in Figure 11.18.

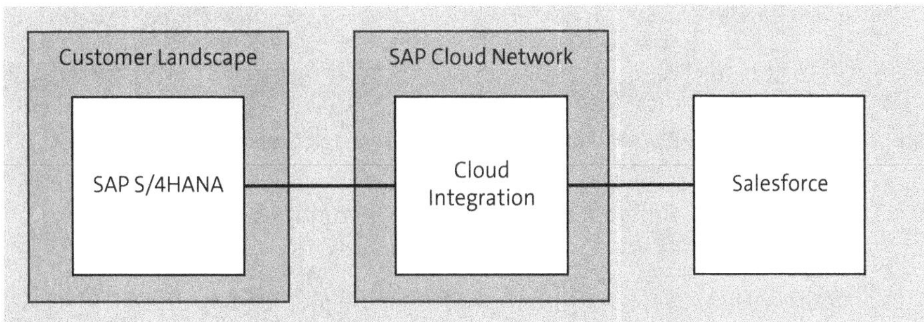

Figure 11.18 Integration of SAP S/4HANA Integration with Salesforce

The package includes iFlows that can be used as a starting point to accelerate your integration journey between SAP S/4HANA and Salesforce. These iFlows can be modified and extended to cater to customer-specific processes. There is, for instance, a high chance that the customers have added their custom fields in Salesforce. These fields can be added to the different mapping of the iFlows. At the time of this writing, the package includes the following iFlows:

- Replicate sales orders from Salesforce to SAP S/4HANA
- Replicate sales contract from Salesforce to SAP S/4HANA
- Receive sales order history from SAP S/4HANA
- Update account from Salesforce to SAP S/4HANA
- Receive sales pricing from SAP S/4HANA
- Receive availability information from SAP S/4HANA
- Replicate sales orders from SAP S/4HANA to Salesforce
- Replicate account from SAP S/4HANA to Salesforce
- Replicate product master data from SAP S/4HANA to Salesforce

11.7.1 Technical Landscape

For illustration purposes, Figure 11.19 shows the technical landscape for synchronizing business partners from SAP S/4HANA to a Salesforce account entity based on Cloud Integration. In the proposed setup, SAP S/4HANA sits on the customer's landscape. The integration middleware (Cloud Integration) runs in the SAP cloud network, whereas the connected Salesforce tenant runs on the cloud.

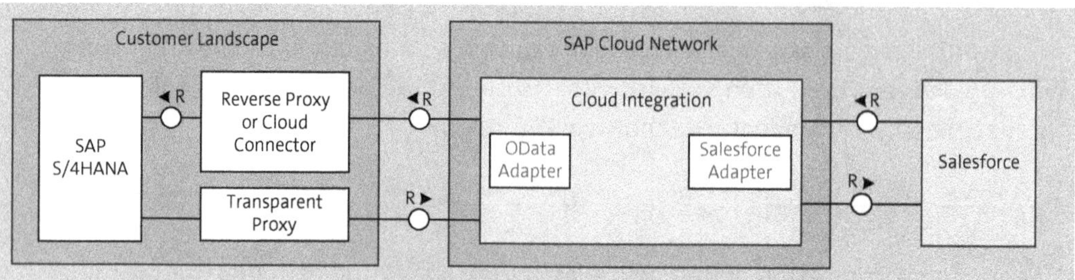

Figure 11.19 Integrating SAP S/4HANA with Salesforce through Cloud Integration

Figure 11.19 describes the different adapters used to communicate both applications:

- **OData adapter**
  This adapter is used to interact with the APIs that are provided by the SAP S/4HANA system. These APIs are used to retrieve the latest changes on the business partners. Note that in case one connects directly from Cloud Integration, the cloud connector is needed to connect to the customer's private network or landscape.

- **Salesforce adapter**
  Cloud Integration has a Salesforce adapter that is used in these flows to exchange data with Salesforce. For the preceding flows, the Salesforce adapter is used to upsert (create or update) entity records in Salesforce. The adapter automatically creates or updates in case the record already exists. In this flow, the business partner ID is used as the unique identifier both on the SAP and Salesforce side.

11.7.2 Example Adapter Configurations

The flows included in the package are configurable and come equipped with a number of externalized parameters. To round out this section, we'll briefly show you how the connections of the scenario shown in Figure 11.19 can be configured in a productive use case on the Cloud Integration side of the communication.

In this section, we've provided screenshots of the four adapters that come into play on the Cloud Integration system side. Figure 11.20 shows an example of an OData adapter used for the connection between SAP S/4HANA and Cloud Integration (messages sent synchronously from Cloud Integration to SAP S/4HANA).

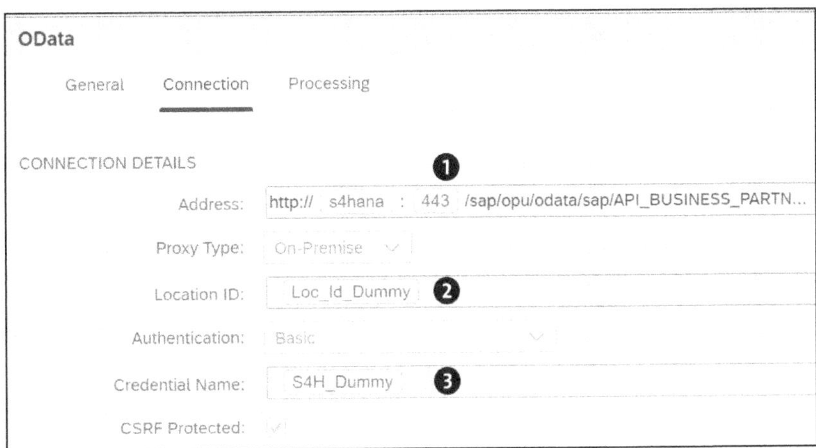

Figure 11.20 OData Adapter (Example) from SAP Business Accelerator Hub

As we discussed in Chapter 4, which described an iFlow with the OData adapter, the **Address** field (Figure 11.20 ❶) should define an endpoint address of SAP S/4HANA. This address will be used by Cloud Integration to call your SAP S/4HANA instance. From this flow, it's possible to replace the hostname and port number.

Additionally, because Cloud Integration isn't sitting in the customer's network, it's important to specify the **Location ID** ❷ of the cloud connector that sits on the same landscape as the SAP S/4HANA instance. Lastly, the OData adapter needs the credentials (user name and password) to connect to the SAP S/4HANA instance. For this, a reference to the security parameter needs to be specified in the **Credential Name** field ❸.

The iFlow also uses the Salesforce adapter to send business partner's data to Salesforce. As shown in Figure 11.21, the following additional parameters will need to be configured:

- The **Address** parameter ❶ specifies Salesforce's endpoint URL. By default, the URL **https://login.salesforce.com** is used. This can be changed according to a scenario. Typically, for Salesforce production environments, it's **https://login.salesforce.com**. For sandbox environments, it's **https://test.salesforce.com**. If MyDomain is enabled in the organization, then **https://<MyDomain>.my.salesforce.com** can be used.
- The **Basic Credential Name** parameter ❷ specifies the alias name of the **User Credentials** artifact that contains the credentials for basic authentication. This refers to the user name-password pair used to log in to Salesforce. This pair must be created as a security artifact of **User Credential** type and subsequently referred to in the adapter.
- The **Security Token Alias** parameter ❸ specifies the **Secure Parameter** artifact that contains the security token needed to connect to Salesforce. This property enables the system to fetch the security token from the keystore for authentication. This field can be omitted if the IP has been whitelisted in Salesforce. To whitelist an IP address, add the IP range in the **Network Access** section in the **Security Control** menu in Salesforce.
- The **OAuth Credential Name** parameter ❹ specifies the name of the **User Credentials** artifact that contains the Salesforce's OAuth Consumer Key-Consumer Secret pair. Configure the **Consumer Key** as **User** and the **Consumer Secret** as the password in the security artifact of type **User Credential**.

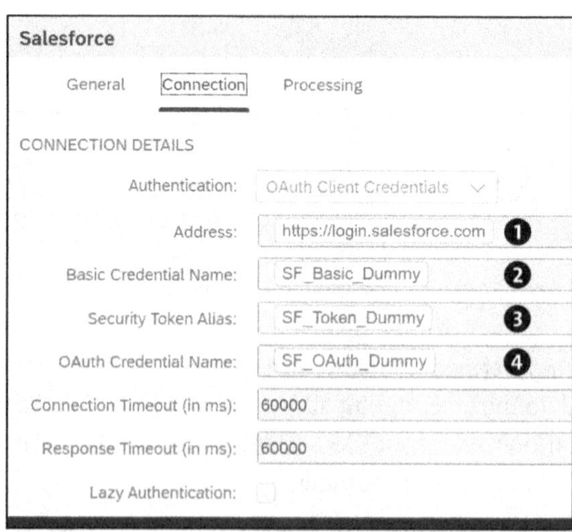

Figure 11.21 Salesforce Adapter (Example) from SAP Business Accelerator Hub

After configuring the parameters of the OData and Salesforce adapters that we've previously covered, the integration can be deployed and executed.

11.8 Summary

In this chapter, we provide you with a high-level overview of a few productive scenarios that can be implemented using Cloud Integration. We quickly walked you through a few scenarios that allow you to integrate SAP solutions in both cloud-to-cloud landscapes and hybrid cloud-to-on-premise landscapes. We closed this chapter by briefly touching on SAP Business Network integration based on Cloud Integration and by introducing the ELSTER adapter in the context of predefined scenarios that integrate SAP HR or FI systems with the German tax authorities. We've also touched on Salesforce integration based on Cloud Integration and introduced the Salesforce adapter.

With this discussion, we'll close our introduction to Cloud Integration. In the next chapter, we'll discuss general special topics in Cloud Integration, including migration aspects and the Edge Integration Cell.

Chapter 12
Special Topics in Cloud Integration

This chapter covers general special topics in Cloud Integration, as part of SAP Integration Suite. It includes various migration aspects, including from SAP Process Orchestration to Cloud Integration. The chapter also dives deep into the topic of the Edge Integration Cell.

It's not a secret anymore that SAP will discontinue the maintenance of SAP Process Integration in 2027. You can refer to SAP Note 1648480, which covers the maintenance strategy for SAP Process Orchestration, for more details on the topic. The subject is also covered in an SAP Community Topic page at *http://s-prs.co/v576056*.

Cloud Integration is the future solution of choice not only for cloud-based integrations but also for on-premise-to-on-premise integrations. The capability to cover on-premise-to-on-premise integration scenarios has been made possible by the introduction of the Edge Integration Cell, which is now generally available. We'll cover the Edge Integration Cell in detail in this chapter, before moving on to the migration process from SAP BTP, Neo Environment to SAP BTP Cloud Foundry Environment, as well migrating from SAP Process Orchestration to Cloud Integration.

12.1 Edge Integration Cell: Overview

The Edge Integration Cell extends Cloud Integration by providing a new flexible hybrid integration containerized runtime, offered as an optional extension to SAP Integration Suite. It enables customers to run integration scenarios and manage APIs within the boundaries of their managed private landscapes, including both customer-managed data centers and private clouds.

This new essential capability of SAP Integration Suite enables hybrid integrations to complete the puzzle and makes it possible to finally fully replace SAP Process Orchestration.

Figure 12.1 depicts such a setup. This is a hybrid integration strategy that uses Cloud Integration for the following integration scenarios:

- Cloud-to-cloud integration
- On-premise-to-on-premise integration
- Cloud-to-on-premise integration

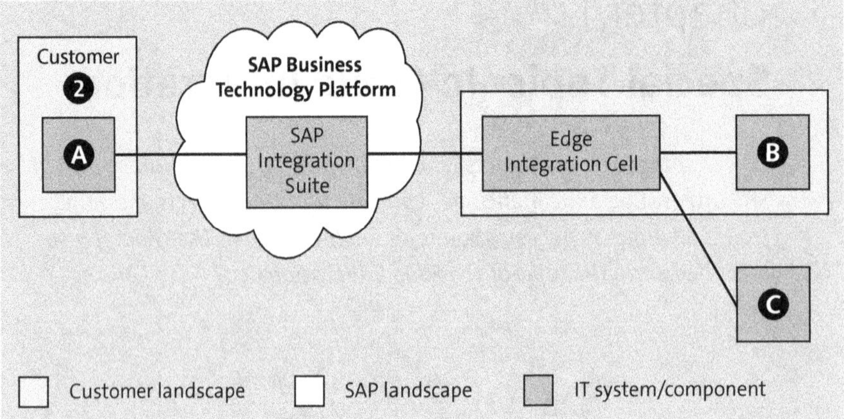

Figure 12.1 Hybrid Use Case Only Using Cloud Integration

Both SAP Integration Suite standard and premium edition licenses can enable Edge Integration Call. For relevant pricing, see *http://s-prs.co/v576057.*

Note that, at the time of this writing, the standard edition of SAP Integration Suite comes equipped with one node of Edge Integration Cell. Furthermore, the messages/transactions processed on an Edge Integration Cell runtime node are only charged at 50% of the normal costs.

The many advantages of the Edge Integration Cell include the following:

- Run APIs and integrations locally in customers' private landscapes.
- Connect remote network locations (factories) without stable internet connectivity.
- Centrally create and design all your integration artifacts from the cloud design time.
- Manage and monitor all integrations and APIs from a central cloud SAP Integration Suite.
- From the cloud, deploy integrations and API content to different local networks and private landscapes.
- Use a single integration platform instead of combining SAP Process Orchestration for premise integration scenarios and Cloud Integration for cloud-based integration scenarios.
- Enjoy greater support for security or compliance use cases. For some customers, sensitive data must strictly remain within the boundary of their network and firewall. Edge Integration Call makes this possible with the context of SAP Integration Suite.

Given that the Edge Integration Cell runs on the customers' private landscape, it's expected that the customer has more responsibilities for its maintenance compared to the cloud-based component of SAP Integration Suite, where SAP is mostly responsible. The Edge Integration Cell has been designed and developed with the knowledge that specific processes and tasks fall under the responsibility of the customer. However, it's important to note that for cloud components that are part of SAP Integration Suite and have therefore been extended to support Edge Integration Cell, the operating model remains unchanged.

Table 12.1 specifies processes and tasks within those processes that are to be performed by the customer.

Process	Customer Task
Provisioning and setup	Provisioning and setting up the Kubernetes resources and relevant systems, including network, storage, compute units, configuration, and so on
Maintenance	Regular product updates and patches, including the infrastructure, system, and services
User and access management	Maintenance and management of user's access, permission, roles, and configuration of the subaccount
System monitoring	Monitoring and management of resources such as memory, CPU, storage, network, and so on
Application management	Design, develop, deploy, configure, maintain, and operate the application within the subaccount, including application monitoring
Costs	All costs related to local infrastructure

Table 12.1 List of Customer Tasks when using the Edge Integration Cell

Now that we understand the positioning and role of the Edge Integration Cell, let's turn now to its high-level architecture.

12.2 Edge Integration Cell: High-Level Architecture

Because the Edge Integration Cell runs on a containerized runtime, it's important to first understand what type of containers are supported. A container cluster is a set of nodes that run containerized applications.

When an application is containerized, this application is packaged with all its dependencies and necessary services. As a result, the containerized application is more lightweight and flexible than virtual machines, and such clusters allow for applications to be more easily developed, moved, and managed. Typically, these clusters allow containers to run across multiple machines and environments, including virtual, physical, cloud-based, and on-premises. They also have the advantage of being operating system agnostic and can therefore be portable.

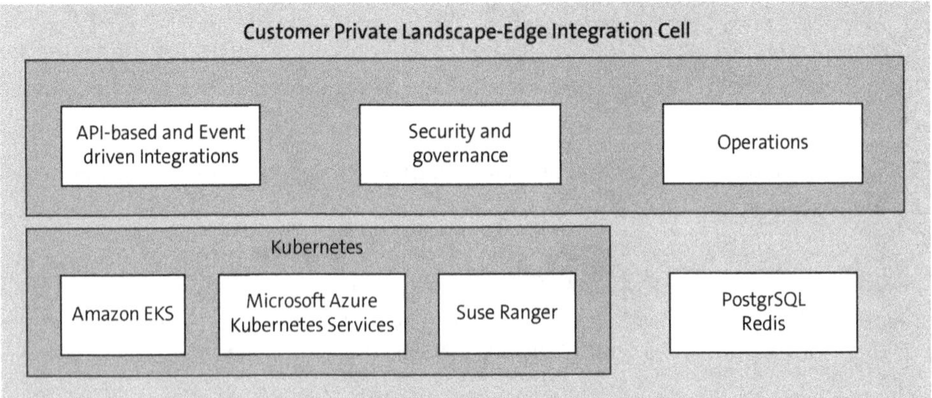

Figure 12.2 Edge Integration Cell in a Kubernetes Environment

As Figure 12.2 shows, at the time of this writing, the Edge Integration Cell supports the following customer-managed private Kubernetes environments:

- Microsoft Azure Kubernetes Service (AKS) with Kubernetes 1.25, 1.26 on Microsoft Azure
- Amazon Elastic Kubernetes Service (EKS) with Kubernetes 1.25, 1.26 on Amazon Web Services
- SUSE Rancher Kubernetes Engine (RKE), specifically RKE2 with Kubernetes 1.24, 1.25, 1.26 and RKE1 with Kubernetes 1.24, 1.25, 1.26 (at the time of this writing)

In general, SAP plans to support newer Kubernetes (also called K8s) versions as time passes by. Currently, only container images for operating system architecture Linux/amd64 are supported.

Notes

At the time of writing, Red Hat OpenShift isn't yet supported but is part of the road-map for future releases.

For more details on the sizing of each of these components, refer to SAP Note 3247839 (http://s-prs.co/v576058). To learn more about how to create a Kubernetes environment, refer to the documentation of the concerned vendors. Table 12.2 provides a high-level overview of the reference guides to follow.

Name	References
Microsoft Kubernetes Service	*http://s-prs.co/v576059*
Amazon EKS	*http://s-prs.co/v576060*
Suse Rancher	*http://s-prs.co/v576061*

Table 12.2 References to Create Kubernetes Environments

From an architecture perspective, Figure 12.3 describes the technical landscape of the Edge Integration Cell.

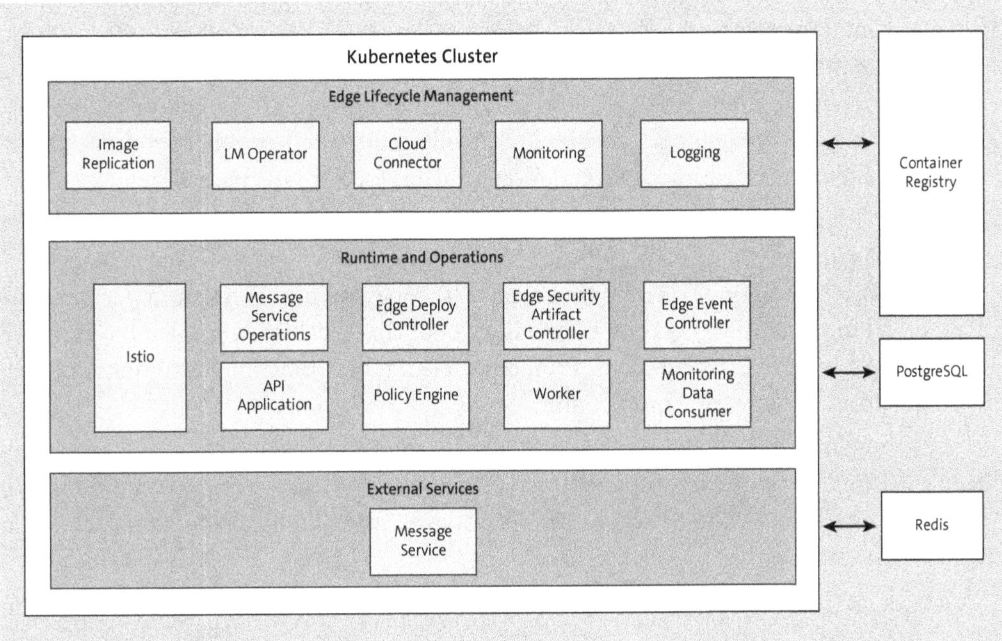

Figure 12.3 High-Level Architecture for Kubernetes Cluster

Each one of the components in this figure is described in the next sections.

12.2.1 Edge Lifecycle Management

Edge Lifecycle Management (also known as Edge LM) provides a channel and a way for products from SAP Business Technology Platform (SAP BTP) to be shipped to the on-premises or edge computing sites. These products are shipped, delivered, and managed in the form of containerized workloads. Edge Lifecycle Management includes initial setup, onboarding, deployment, continuous lifecycle management operations, monitoring, and logging.

The shipments are sent centrally based on the SAP repository-based shipment channel (RBSC). The Edge Integration Cell delivery is made up of images that are retrieved from the RBSC. Edge Lifecycle Management is responsible for performing the deployment. As can be seen in Figure 12.1, it involves the following components:

- **Image replication service**
  This optional component is used to help with mirroring container images from RBSC to a local (on-premise) container registry.

- **LM operator**
  This component is responsible for organizing the lifecycle of solutions represented as Kubernetes custom resources following the Kubernetes operator pattern.
- **Cloud connector**
  Cloud connector is an application that can be installed on a Windows and Linux operating system. It establishes a secure connection to SAP Integration Suite (on the cloud) and by doing so, enables SAP cloud products to securely communicate with systems in a customer's on-premises/private cloud landscape. It's therefore used to create a secure tunnel between cloud and edge environments.
- **Monitoring**
  This is an optional component that can be used to push system monitoring data from the Edge Integration Cell to the cloud. This is achieved using an open-source tool known as Prometheus. Prometheus is a monitoring application that collects, stores, and presents metrics efficiently.
- **Logging**
  This is an optional component that can be used to push logging data from the Edge Integration Cell to the cloud. This is achieved using an open-source tool known as Fluentd.

Notes

The customer is in control of when the Edge Integration Cell can be updated. As a result, a feature such as the Delay Software Update feature isn't available for Edge Integration Cell because customers manage the edge nodes themselves.

Next, we'll discuss the components that relate to the runtime and operations of the Edge Integration Cell.

12.2.2 Runtime and Operations

The Edge Integration Cell already has components to enable it to execute iFlows and API proxies. On top of these components, the Edge Integration Cell also comes equipped with management components for operations on the edge itself. These additional operations components need to securely communicate and connect to some services on SAP Integration Suite and SAP BTP services. As shown earlier in Figure 12.1, the following components are used to facilitate runtime and operations:

- **Istio**
  Open-source service mesh that helps in running, connecting, and monitoring distributed, microservices-based apps anywhere. It manages secure traffic flows between services.

- **Edge deploy controller**
  Supports by handling the lifecycle of contents to be deployed.
- **Edge security artifact controller**
  Enables the handling and management of security materials (user credentials, secure parameters, certificates, etc.) on the Edge Integration Cell.
- **Edge event controller**
  Distributes system events internally on the Edge Integration Cell.
- **API application**
  Provides various APIs related to the monitoring and operations of the Edge Integration Cell.
- **Policy engine**
  Provides features to enforce API traffic policies on the Edge Integration Cell. These policies mostly cover API security or traffic management.
- **Worker**
  Executes iFlow models and services on the Edge Integration Cell.
- **Message service operations**
  Manages the local Message Service.
- **Monitoring data consumer**
  Stores and processes monitoring events on the Edge Integration Cell.

Next, we'll discuss the components that relate to the external services of the Edge Integration Cell.

12.2.3 External Services

As shown earlier in Figure 12.1, Edge Integration Cell also uses an external service named Message Service. This service is used for asynchronous messaging and system internal event integration. Furthermore, besides the Kubernetes Engines, Edge Integration Cell uses both PostgreSQL and Redis as persistence layers:

- **Redis**
  Redis is an open-source (BSD licensed), in-memory data structure store used as a database, cache, message broker, and streaming engine. Redis has built-in replication, Lua scripting, LRU eviction, transactions, and different levels of on-disk persistence, as well as providing high availability via Redis Sentinel and automatic partitioning with Redis Cluster.
- **PostgreSQL**
  PostgreSQL is a free and open-source relational database management system (RDBMS) emphasizing extensibility and SQL compliance. It features transactions with atomicity, consistency, isolation, durability (ACID) properties; automatically updatable views; materialized views; triggers; foreign keys; and stored procedures.

Notes

You can also use an internal persistence of Edge Integration Cell (PostgreSQL and Redis) for test and demo purposes. As these built-in services aren't highly available nor scalable, it's not recommended to use such an internal setup for a production environment. For a production environment, it's recommended to use an external PostgreSQL database and a Redis data store outside the Edge Integration Cell deployment, as depicted earlier in Figure 12.3.

Now that we understand some high-level concepts about the Edge Integration Cell, let's discuss its setup in the customer's landscape.

12.3 Edge Integration Cell: Setup and Installation

In this section, we'll describe in a high-level manner how to install your own Edge Integration Cell. Let's start with a high-level positioning of the Edge Integration Cell.

To set up your brand-new Edge Integration Cell, several high-level steps need to be performed from the SAP BTP cockpit. The Global Account Administrator needs to perform the following steps:

1. Verify the entitlements.
2. Create subaccount.
3. Assign a quota to the subaccount.

These actions are prerequisites. Assuming that you already have SAP Integration Suite, you already have created a subaccount. In this section, we'll showcase how you can verify that you have the required entitlement to use The Edge Integration Cell. To do so, follow these steps:

1. Log in to the SAP Integration Suite homepage as a global administrator.
2. From the left side of the menu, select **Service Assignments** (see Figure 12.4).
3. On the middle of the page, enter "edge" in the search box. If you have the entitlement to use Edge Integration Cell, you see a **Plan** named **edge_integration_cell,** as shown in Figure 12.4.

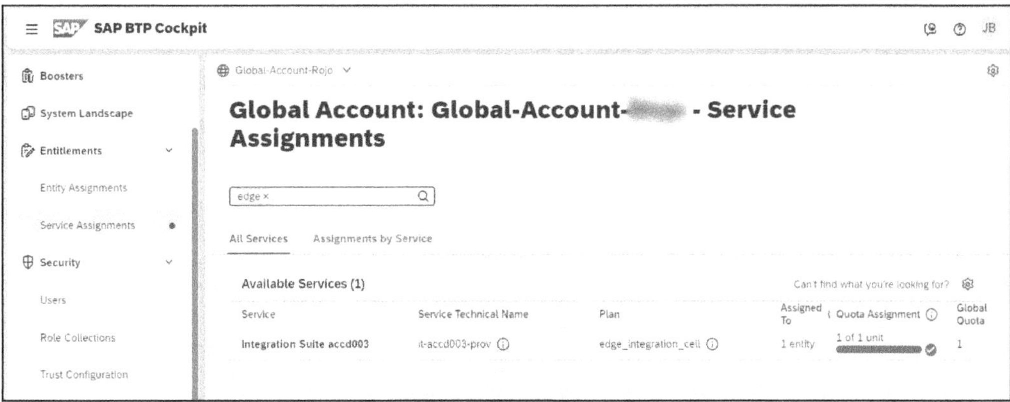

Figure 12.4 Checking for the Edge Integration Cell Entitlement

The next step in our provisioning is to assign the `Integration_Provisioner` role to users for accessing the service. Follow these steps:

1. Log in to the SAP Integration Suite homepage as a subaccount or tenant administrator.
2. You'll need to select the subaccount that has the SAP Integration Suite tenant.
3. Assign roles required to access the capabilities by selecting users in the left menu (see Figure 12.5 ❶).
4. Search for your user, and select the returned user name ❷.
5. Select **Assign Role Collection** ❸.
6. Assign it to the **Role Collection** named **Integration_Provisioner**.

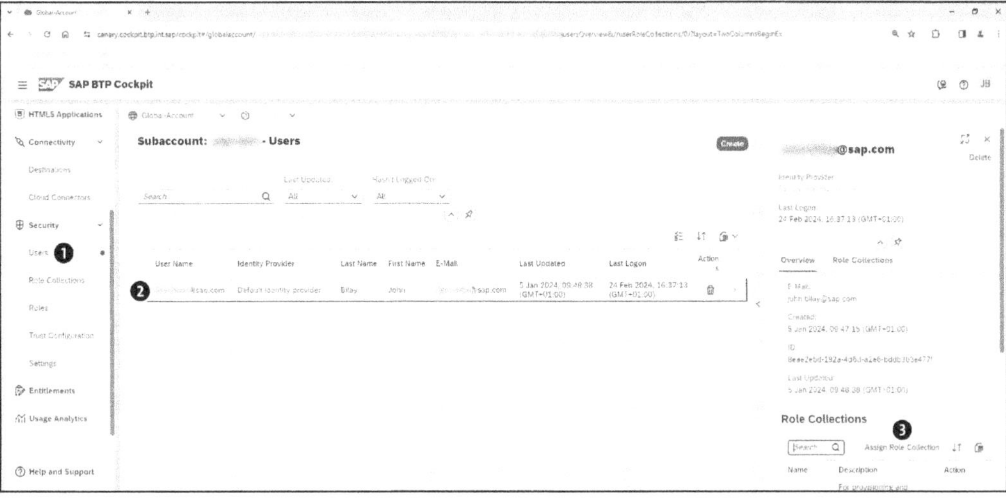

Figure 12.5 Assign a Role Collection to the User

The next step in our provisioning is to assign the entitlement to the subaccount. This is now possible because we've made sure that we're entitled (from the global account) to use the Edge Integration Cell, as shown earlier in Figure 12.4. To achieve that, go back to the main page of the subaccount, and click on the **Entitlements** link, as shown in Figure 12.6.

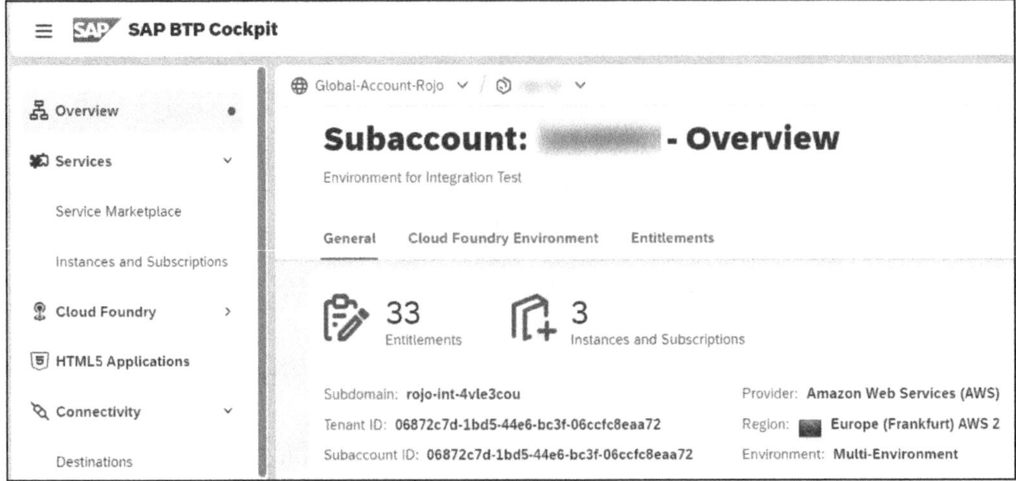

Figure 12.6 Entitlement of the Subaccount

The next step is to add the service plan by selecting **Edit**, and then clicking on the **Add Service Plans** button (see Figure 12.7 ❶). A new screen pops up allowing you to search for the **edge_integration_cell** service plan.

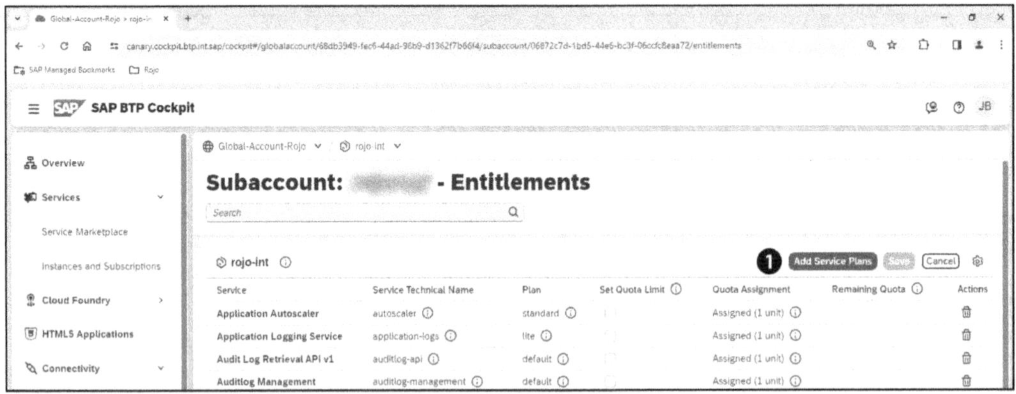

Figure 12.7 Adding a Service Plan

After selecting the **edge_integration_cell** service plan, the configuration looks as shown in Figure 12.8.

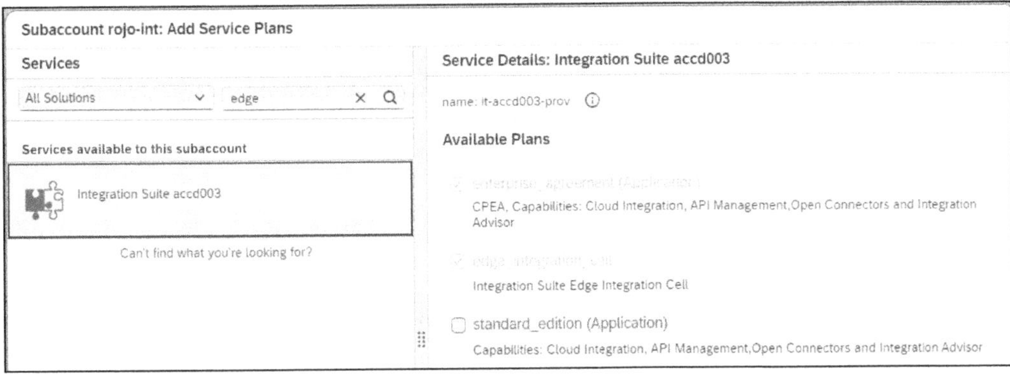

Figure 12.8 View after Adding the edge_integration_cell Service Plan

You're now able to activate the Edge Integration Cell, add an edge node, run the Edge Lifecycle Management Bridge, and deploy the Edge Integration Cell Solution. To do all that, follow the detailed steps described in the SAP Integration Suite documentation at the following URL: *http://s-prs.co/v576062*.

12

You can also perform various operations tasks of the Edge Integration Cell by following the detailed documentation provided at this URL: *http://s-prs.co/v576063*.

After all the relevant setup activities described in the previous sections have been performed, it's possible to access the Edge Integration Cell features. For instance, you can access Edge Lifecycle Management, which we discussed in Section 12.2.1, from the main page of the SAP Integration Suite homepage. From the SAP Integration Suite homepage, choose **Settings • Runtime** from the left navigation pane.

From the resulting page, you're presented with the URL to access Edge Lifecycle Management (see Figure 12.9).

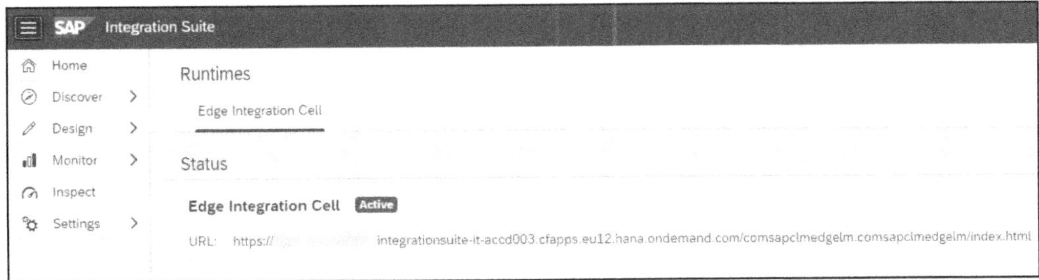

Figure 12.9 Accessing Link for Edge Lifecycle Management

Once you click the link presented in Figure 12.9, you're redirected to a page of the Edge Lifecycle Management, which looks like Figure 12.10.

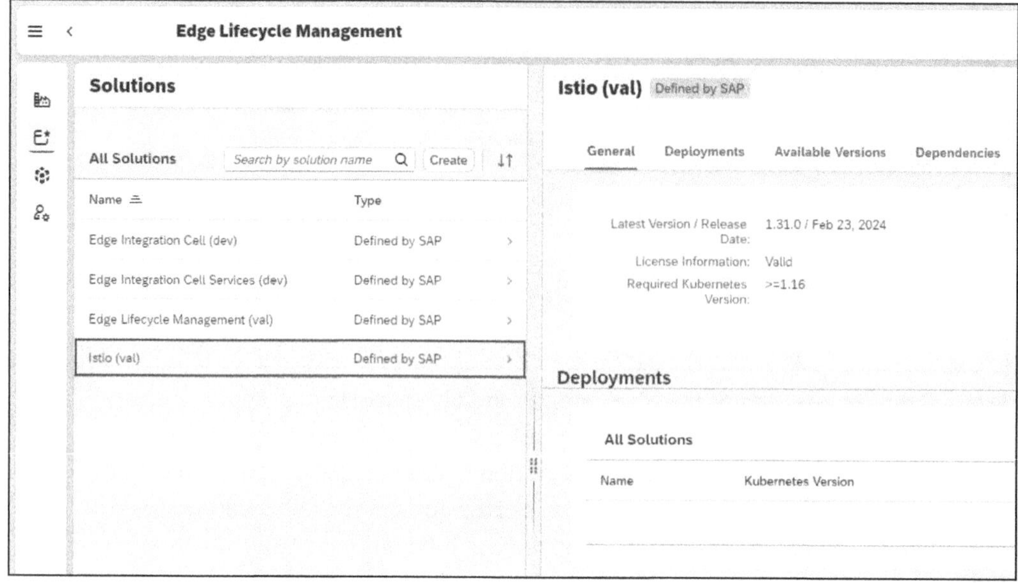

Figure 12.10 Edge Lifecycle Management View

For a more detailed step-by-step guide on setting up your Edge Integration Cell, go to the SAP Community blog at *http://s-prs.co/v576064*.

After the Edge Integration Cell has been successfully installed, you'll be able to see a new entry in your runtime profiles. To confirm that the runtime profile is available, proceed as follows:

1. Click on the Settings link on the landing page of Cloud Integration.
2. Select the **Integrations** link shown in Figure 12.11.

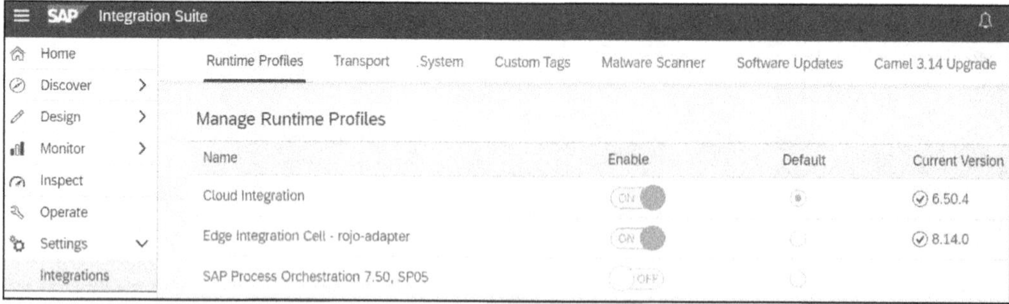

Figure 12.11 Runtime Profiles List in Cloud Integration

A new runtime profile for the Edge Integration Cell is visible here. Note that this runtime profile always starts with the prefix "Edge Integration Cell" and has the name format **Edge Integration Cell - <name of your edge node>**. In our case, the Edge Integration Cell runtime has version 8.14.0.

This runtime profile should be used to design, deploy, and monitor integrations and APIs. It's also possible to verify the list of adapters, flow steps, processes, technical capabilities, and their versions supported by this runtime by clicking on this runtime profile (see Figure 12.12).

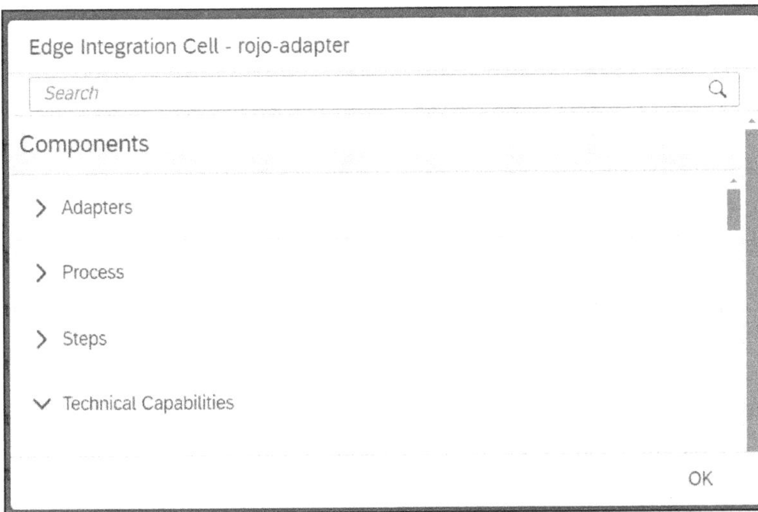

Figure 12.12 List of Adapters, Flow Steps, and Technical Capabilities

Next, we'll briefly discuss how you can deploy and run your iFlows in the Edge in the next sections.

12.4 Develop, Deploy, and Monitor Your Integrations in the Edge Integration Cell

In earlier chapters, you've mastered how to create and deploy integrations in Cloud Integration. Assuming you've installed an Edge Integration Cell in your landscape, how should you develop an iFlow which will later be deployed in the Edge Integration Cell? The most important aspect is to ensure that you select the **Runtime Profile** of your Edge Integration Cell after you've created the iFlow. You can see an example in Figure 12.13. Selecting a profile of the Edge Integration Cell limits the type of steps that can be used in the iFlow to the ones that are supported by the version of your Edge Integration Cell. Because the customer is responsible for upgrading the version of their own Edge Integration Cell, not all steps may be available to be used in iFlows. The steps, components, and capabilities are limited to the ones available in the profile, as shown earlier in Figure 12.12.

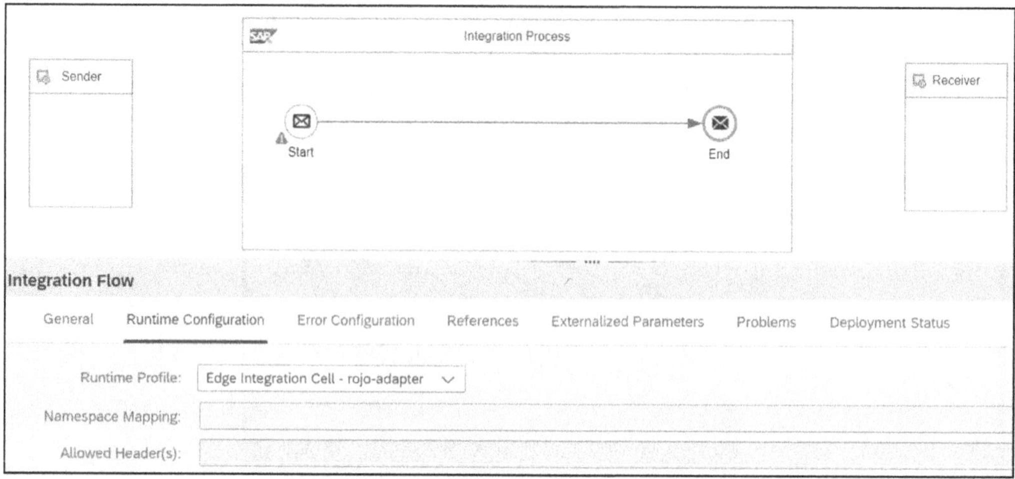

Figure 12.13 Developing a New iFlow for the Edge Integration Cell

Now that we've developed an iFlow, the next question should be how should you run the integration in your Edge Integration Cell.

There are no differences between the way you build an iFlow to be deployed in the cloud or into your Edge Integration Cell. The iFlow is centrally created on the cloud and deployed to different target runtime engines, as shown in Figure 12.14.

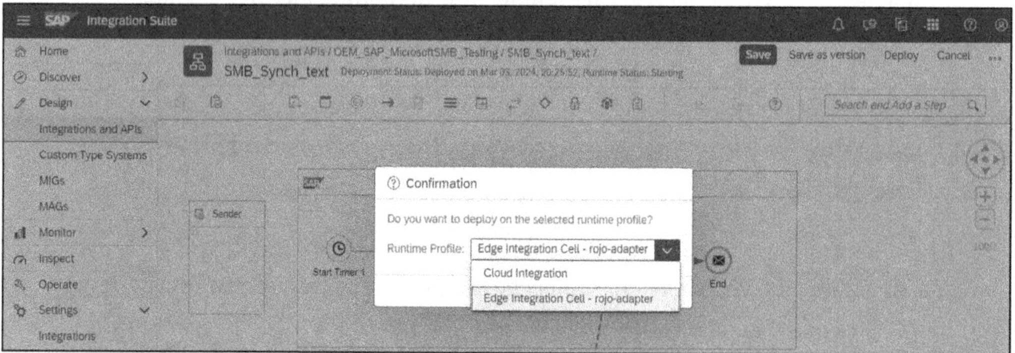

Figure 12.14 Deploying an iFlow into an Edge Integration Cell

A lot of new capabilities are expected to be added to the Edge Integration Cell in the coming months. To keep up with future developments and view the Edge Integration Cell roadmap, go to *http://s-prs.co/v576065*.

In the next section, we'll explore how you can migrate from SAP BTP, Neo environment to a SAP BTP, Cloud Foundry environment.

12.5 Migration from SAP BTP, Neo Environment to SAP BTP, Cloud Foundry Environment

Now let's discuss the migration from SAP BTP, Neo environment to SAP BTP, Cloud Foundry environment, including why this move is needed and the benefits of this migration. Following its core principles of openness and freedom of choice, SAP partners with hyperscalers such as Amazon Web Services (AWS), Google Cloud Platform (GCP), Alibaba Cloud, and Microsoft Azure. As these infrastructures come with considerable benefits compared to the SAP BTP, Neo environment, you may consider moving to the multicloud foundation. In addition, the SAP BTP, Neo environment will reach the end of life on December 31, 2028 (details in the article at *http://s-prs.co/v576066*). In preparation for the sunset, SAP has already limited new SAP BTP, Neo environment sales and won't extend or renew contracts beyond December 31, 2028.

12.5.1 Benefits of Migration to SAP BTP, Cloud Foundry Environment

SAP BTP, Cloud Foundry environment is a multicloud environment that offers multiple benefits. It opens the way for customers and partners to get the benefits of SAP BTP on their cloud infrastructure of choice, which in turn offers more flexibility, reliability, and agility to customers and partners. Moreover, new services and enhancements will only be provided to support the multicloud-first strategy. New customers and partners will be deployed on the multicloud infrastructure by default.

SAP BTP, Cloud Foundry environment provides the flexibility to choose the hyperscaler of choice to deploy the services. The available infrastructure as a service (IaaS) providers are AWS, GCP, Alibaba Cloud, and Microsoft Azure. Depending on your IT strategy, you can choose the infrastructure provider of your choice.

Table 12.3 shows a comparison between SAP BTP, Neo environment and SAP BTP, Cloud Foundry environment.

Parameters	SAP BTP, Neo Environment	SAP BTP, Cloud Foundry Environment
Regional coverage and high availability	▪ Runs in SAP data centers ▪ Uses redundancy within one data center only	▪ Includes environments that run in various data centers from different IaaS providers ▪ Uses the availability zones (AZ) concept for improved availability
Runtimes and programming languages	Supports a fixed set of runtimes and programming languages	▪ Supports a fixed set of runtimes and programming languages ▪ Provides own language support

Table 12.3 Comparison between SAP BTP, Neo Environment and SAP BTP, Cloud Foundry Environment

Parameters	SAP BTP, Neo Environment	SAP BTP, Cloud Foundry Environment
Backing services	Supports SAP-proprietary services only	Supports SAP-proprietary services as well as various backing services managed by your respective IaaS provider

Table 12.3 Comparison between SAP BTP, Neo Environment and SAP BTP, Cloud Foundry Environment (Cont.)

12.5.2 Availability Zones and Regions

Availability zones (AZs) are single-failure domains within a single geographical region and are separate physical locations with independent power, network, and cooling. These are distinct locations within a region that are designed to be isolated from each other in terms of infrastructure and power supply. Multiple AZs exist in one region and are connected through a low-latency network. To achieve high fault tolerance, it's recommended to deploy the Cloud Integration services in multiple availability zones. Figure 12.15 shows the basic setup of multiple availability zones in a region.

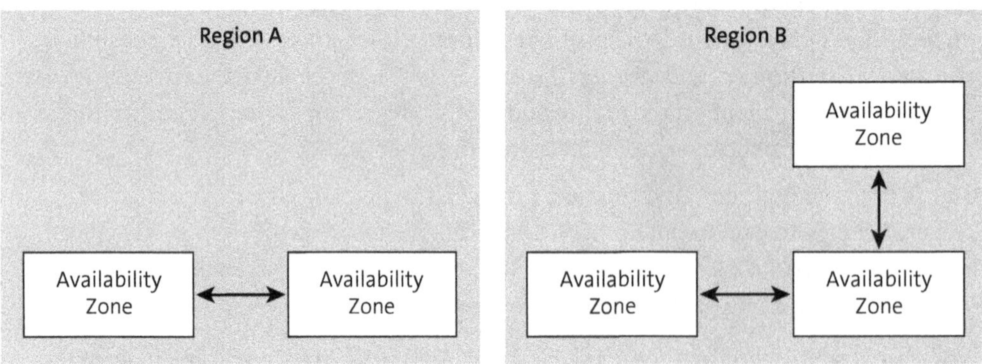

Figure 12.15 Regions with Multiple Availability Zones

In Figure 12.15, a region refers to the geographical location where the infrastructure is deployed. You can choose the region on a subaccount level, which sets up the Cloud Integration tenant. You have the option to select one region per subaccount. Depending on your IT strategy, governance, and use cases, you can also have different subaccounts in different regions. To learn more about the available regions and the corresponding API endpoints, go to the SAP BTP documentation at *http://s-prs.co/v576067*.

12.5.3 Migration Approach

In the previous section, we looked at the benefits of moving to the SAP BTP, Cloud Foundry environment. While considering the migration from SAP BTP, Neo environment to the SAP BTP, Cloud Foundry environment, you should have a well-defined approach and planning. The migration approach mainly comprises four broad stages, as shown in Figure 12.16.

Figure 12.16 Migration Phases

In this section, we'll discuss the different stages of the migration process at a high level. The detailed step-by-step guide to migration can be found at *http://s-prs.co/v576068*.

The four stages are described in the following list:

- **Assessment**
During the assessment phase, a detailed evaluation of the existing SAP BTP, Neo environment must be performed, including the iFlows that are to be migrated, configurations, and dependencies. List all the artifacts that are being used in the iFlows on the SAP BTP, Neo environment Cloud Integration tenant. This will help you define a clear strategy for the different types of objects used. You should also understand security-related contexts, assigned users, and role setup configured in the existing tenant. This information comes in handy when configuring a new tenant in the multicloud foundation.

- **Planning**
In this phase, you prepare to onboard a tenant in the SAP BTP, Cloud Foundry environment; activate the required services; and onboard the users. You should also plan a communication to all the applications that are communicating with Cloud Integration and notify them about the change. A close alignment with them is required to have a smooth migration.

- **Migration execution**
Once you have the environment ready, during this phase, you move the integration packages and the dependent objects from the SAP BTP, Neo environment to the SAP BTP, Cloud Foundry environment Cloud Integration tenant. Remember that the artifacts moved to the SAP BTP, Cloud Foundry environment Cloud Integration tenants have to be reconfigured and deployed. For example, the security artifacts such as user credentials have to be updated with the old password and deployed.

- **Validation**
Once the migration is complete and successful, test the tenant with the migrated iFlows. It's recommended to perform system integration tests and validations before using the iFlows in the productive environment.

You now know the benefits of migrating to the SAP BTP, Cloud Foundry environment. The migration process requires careful planning, assessment, and execution. The assessment stage serves as a crucial foundation for the migration process.

12.6 Migration from SAP Process Orchestration to Cloud Integration

With the end of life of SAP Process Orchestration on the horizon, a lot of organizations are contemplating the move to Cloud Integration. The task of migration can appear daunting and complex as your SAP Process Orchestration system acts as a backbone of your organization's data integration landscape. Replacing such a business-critical system from one day to another is impossible and needs careful planning and some key considerations. SAP has provided you with tools to make your migration process smooth and efficient. In this section, we'll look at the high-level approach to migrating from SAP Process Orchestration to Cloud Integration.

The whole journey of migration can be divided at a high level into three stages with main attention points in each stage. Figure 12.17 shows an overview of each of these stages.

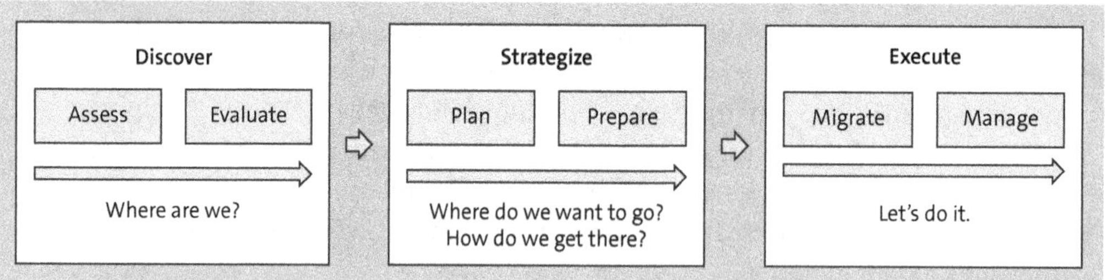

Figure 12.17 Stages of a SAP Process Orchestration to Cloud Integration Migration Project

In the following sections, we'll dive into each of these stages to address the considerations.

12.6.1 Assessment and Evaluation

The first step in any migration is to understand where you are currently. Hence, mapping out the current landscape and architecture is the key to a successful migration. Information collected as part of this exercise guides the route you need to take to plan and execute your SAP Process Orchestration to Cloud Integration migration. When it comes to the assessment of your current integration landscape, SAP has you covered. You can use the migration assessment tool to connect to your SAP Process Orchestration environment and evaluate the interfaces available in your SAP Process Orchestration tenants. The assessment tool can be set up by following these guidelines:

1. Activate the migration assessment capability in SAP Integration Suite. Once activated, the home screen of the assessment tool looks like Figure 12.18.
2. Connect your SAP Process Orchestration system to the migration assessment tool.
3. Check the **Configuration Rules** and **Effort Estimations** provided in the migration assessment tool.

4. Create a **Data Extraction** by using the connection created in step 2.
5. Generate a scenario evaluation report on the data extracted from your SAP Process Orchestration environment.

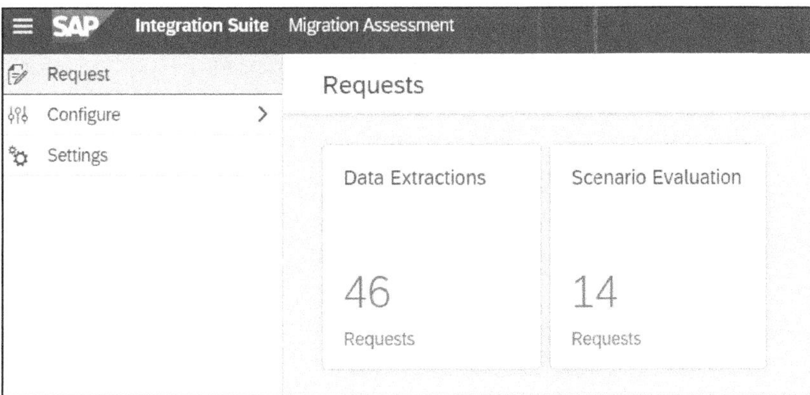

Figure 12.18 Migration Assessment Application Home Screen

You can follow the tutorial at *http://s-prs.co/v576069* step-by-step to set up the migration assessment tool.

To get a good idea of your current landscape, look at the reports generated in the scenario evaluation. As shown in Figure 12.19, the report presents two major information categories:

- **Scenarios by assessment category**
  All the interfaces available in your SAP Process Orchestration environment are categorized into **Evaluation Required**, **Adjustment Required**, and **Ready to Migrate**.
- **Scenario by effort estimation**
  The tool categorizes the **Effort Estimation** by simple sizes: S, M, L, and XL.

Along with the preceding information, you also get an overview of the sender and receiver adapters in use.

The assessment tool gives you a pretty good idea of where your landscape stands, but you should still do your due diligence to evaluate the scope and effort when determining what you should you migrate. Consider the following when making this decision:

- **Landscape overview**
  Create a high-level architectural overview of your landscape with respect to applications, adapters, and data models. Categorize your interfaces into cloud-only, cloud-to-on-premise, or on-premise-only deployment strategies. This will help you in the next step to plan the setup of Edge Integration Cell or cloud connector.
- **Prepackaged content availability**
  You should see if you have standard prepackaged content available in SAP Business Accelerator Hub for the integration scenario you're trying to upgrade. If you find it,

it's advisable to use this prepackaged content instead of redesigning or performing a one-on-one migration.

- **Native connectivity**
  Check if Cloud Integration offers native connectivity for the applications in your landscape. For example, there was no SAP standard Salesforce or ServiceNow adapter in SAP Process Orchestration, so you might have used the REST adapter to connect to these systems with complex logic to handle sessions, and so on implemented via adapter modules or additional complex steps. Cloud Integration on the other hand provides a dedicated adapter for Salesforce, which takes away all technical complexities. In these scenarios, it's advisable to modify the iFlow to use an appropriate adapter instead of a basic lift and shift.
- **Interface usage in production**
  Before migration, also check if there are interfaces that aren't used anymore but haven't been decommissioned. If you do find such interfaces, discuss with the business if you need to take them to your brand-new Cloud Integration environment or simply decommission them.

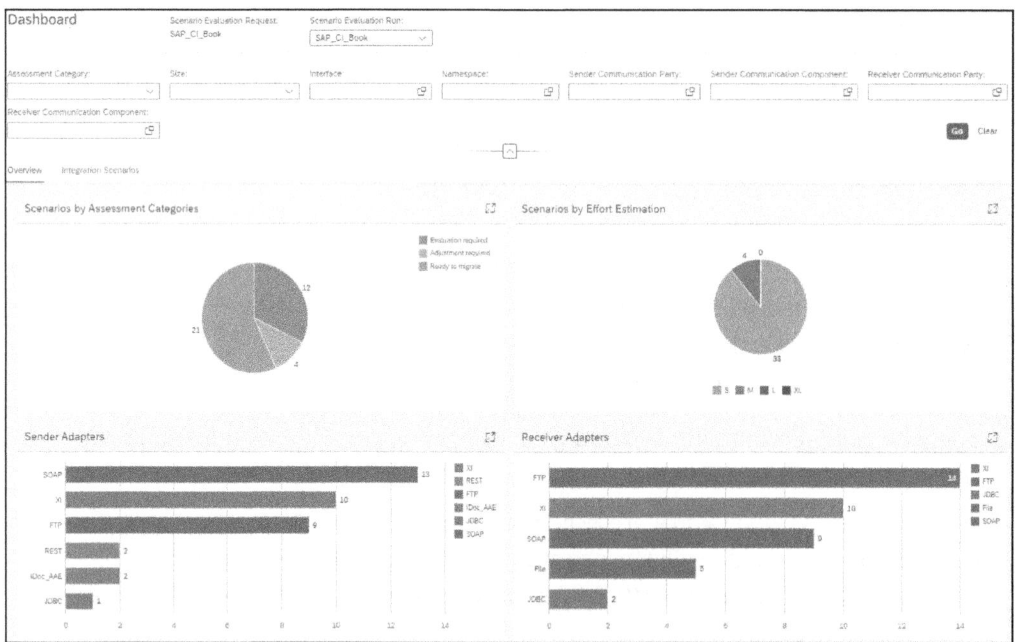

Figure 12.19 Dashboard View of a Scenario Evaluation

With these points in mind, you can collect all the information required to plan and prepare for the actual migration.

12.6.2 Planning and Preparation

Now that you have all the information about your landscape and architecture, let's see how we can leverage it to better plan and prepare for the migration. Behind any flawless execution goes a huge amount of planning and preparation. Here as well, we would have to develop a migration strategy to cover the following aspects:

- **Interface migration path**
  Consider using the assessment report to divide your scenarios into the categories of automated migration, semiautomatic automation where some manual intervention is required, and complete redesign or replacement. It's also very important to do a feature mapping exercise between SAP Process Orchestration and Cloud Integration; for example, adapters such as WebSphere MQ, X.400, and Server Message Block (SMB) aren't yet part of Cloud Integrations but are planned in the future. Your planning should reflect the availability timelines for such features.
- **Security artifacts**
  Reserve time for collecting and evaluating the security material for your interfaces. Evaluate that all applications can work with one of the supported security methodologies of Cloud Integration. In addition, connect with your application owners to inform them of changes in endpoints, credentials, or certificates required for connecting to Cloud Integration.
- **Test data collection**
  Once you've migrated a scenario successfully, you'll need to execute unit tests and integration tests to ensure that all functionalities are covered. Therefore, it's paramount that you have enough test data for each interface to simulate not only positive but negative scenarios as well.
- **Go-live strategy**
  You should also think of a go-live cutover strategy to ensure that there is the least amount of impact on the business. The migration exercise isn't only technical in nature, it also comes with the involvement of business and application owners. Account for additional testing time in case of a complete redesign or a change in integration pattern.

So far, we've spoken about the preparations with the aspect of SAP Process Orchestration, but preparation should also account for the setup of your Cloud Integration environment. This should include the following steps:

1. **Provisioning the environment**
   Setting up and provisioning your Cloud Integration and SAP BTP, Cloud Foundry environment, transport landscape, roles, authorizations, user onboarding, and security should be the first step. Look at the architectural overview, and determine if you should set up the Edge Integration Cell or cloud connector as well.
2. **Governance**
   You have an excellent opportunity with the migration project to wipe the slate clean

and start fresh, so setting up good governance in your Cloud Integration platform from the very beginning is extremely important. Having good governance will reduce redundancies and act as a guiding principle for the developers and operations engineers. Think about the most common integration patterns in your organization, standard error handling, monitoring, and troubleshooting requirements, and define standard templates for these as much as possible.

3. **Security practices**
   Outline the inbound and outbound communication guidelines. Think about OAuth, JSON web tokens (JWT), or certificate-based authentication, and outline the scenarios where each one of these is preferred.
4. **Quality assurance**
   Think about automation and regression testing for your iFlows once they are migrated.

Once you've covered the preceding points, you're ready to start with the actual migration itself.

12.6.3 Migrate and Manage

The migration option is very well integrated with the Cloud Integration tenant. From within an integration package, you can easily click on the **Migrate** button, as shown in Figure 12.20. This lets you connect to your SAP Process Orchestration and import a specific iFlow. Based on a predefined template, your iFlow is generated from your interface information.

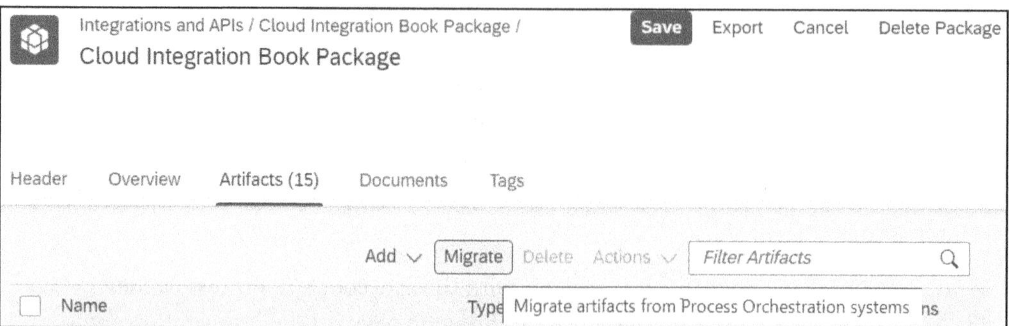

Figure 12.20 Migrate Button in the Integration Package Artifacts Tab

Once the iFlow is created in Cloud Integration, the following steps should be carried out to ensure smooth operations:

1. **Enhance.**
   The process of migration looks simple and straightforward, but you should be careful about the error handling, logging, alerting, and any additional features that

should be included in your iFlow as defined in the governance document. If possible, automate these tasks as they are common across your landscape.

2. **Deploy.**
   Based on the interface category, deploy the iFlow on the Cloud Integration runtime or the Edge Integration Cell.
3. **Communicate with stakeholders.**
   Notify the stakeholders of the new endpoints, credentials, and so on so they can adjust their development environment and connect to your Cloud Integration development environment.
4. **Test.**
   Test the iFlow stand-alone and along with the stakeholders using the test data collected in the planning phase. Use the automated continuous integration/continuous delivery (CI/CD) processes to move your integrations from the development environment to quality assurance (QA) or User Acceptance Testing (UAT), depending on your landscape.
5. **Go live.**
   Plan and execute the go-live and cutover for your interface, and move to a hypercare phase where the productive interfaces are monitored very closely.
6. **Decommission.**
   Once the interface is up and running in Cloud Integration, then kick off the decommissioning activity, which will stop the interface in SAP Process Orchestration.

As discussed in this section, migration projects are complex and can be long-running. With careful assessment. detailed planning, and incorporation of smart automation, you can have better control over the quality, timeline, and delivery of the project.

12.7 Summary

In this chapter, we introduced the Edge Integration Cell that can be used to extend Cloud Integration by providing a new flexible hybrid integration containerized runtime. It also enables customers to run integration scenarios and manage APIs within the boundaries of their managed private landscapes, including both customer-managed data centers and private clouds.

The chapter then explored how you can migrate existing SAP BTP, Neo environment–based Cloud Integration to a SAP BTP, Cloud Foundry environment–based Cloud Integration. Lastly, the chapter explored the high-level steps of how to migrate from an SAP Process Orchestration installation to a Cloud Integration tenant.

The next chapter provides a brief final look at the evolution of Cloud Integration and what you can expect to see in the future.

Chapter 13
Summary and Outlook

In this final chapter, we'll briefly wrap up what you've learned throughout this book and walk you through some of the enhancements to the Cloud Integration portfolio that you should expect to see in the coming months and years.

Congratulations! We've reached the end of the book, and you're now equipped with all the knowledge required to productively begin your own integration project. But this isn't the end of your journey into the world of cloud integration: Cloud Integration, now part of SAP Integration Suite, is updated on a monthly basis, which means that you can expect continuous product improvements. In this chapter, after a brief summary of what you've learned in this book, we'll walk you through several key enhancements you can expect to see in the future.

In Chapter 1, we introduced you to the main topic of this book by showing you how Cloud Integration is embedded into SAP Integration Suite—SAP's open and modular integration platform as a service (iPaaS) to facilitates enterprise integration. We further showed you how Cloud Integration fits into the overall cloud strategy of SAP. By outlining various use cases, we showed you how you can embed Cloud Integration into your own company's digital strategy. We also explained how, in the meantime, you can use Cloud Integration in different cloud environments, which also includes the hyperscale infrastructures offered by the likes of Amazon and Microsoft. In Chapter 2, we brought you up to speed with Cloud Integration's basic terms and concepts and followed up with a description of Cloud Integration's architecture. In that chapter, you also learned how to set up and run your first simple iFlow. Chapter 3 introduced you to the predefined integration content provided by SAP on SAP API Business Hub. That chapter also introduced you to the Web UI of Cloud Integration. Chapters 4 through 6 showed you how to use the Web UI to build your own integration scenarios, starting with the simplest integration pattern and, bit by bit, progressing to more complex integration scenarios. Each of these chapters provided a rich variety of tutorials that showed you, in detail, how to work with the tool by yourself.

Chapter 7 introduced you to another phase of the lifecycle of an integration project: the operations phase of an integration scenario. In that chapter, you learned how to use the Web UI to monitor messages and integration artifacts.

Chapter 8 provided you with detailed information on how to access Cloud Integration through application programming interfaces (APIs). We also showed you how to use Cloud Integration together with API Management, another key component of SAP Integration Suite. Chapter 9 introduced you to another component of the SAP Integration Suite to help you extend the connectivity options of your integration scenarios: Open Connectors.

To accommodate the fact that security is a key consideration when moving to the cloud, Chapter 10 introduces you to this topic in detail. You were also provided with several tutorials on how to use the Web UI to configure secure scenarios, including the digital encryption of messages.

Chapter 11 shared some examples of how Cloud Integration can be used productively in real-life scenarios. Chapter 12 introduced you to the Edge Integration Cell, which is the new flexible hybrid integration runtime, offered as an optional extension to SAP Integration Suite, enabling customers to manage APIs and run their integration scenarios within customer-managed private landscapes. The chapter also looked at aspects related to the migration from SAP Process Orchestration (of which the maintenance will discontinue) to SAP Integration Suite. And, finally, you arrived here: Chapter 13.

In this chapter, we would like to provide an overview of areas where you can expect to see major enhancements to Cloud Integration in the coming months and years. However, we ask that you view the following statements as a general roadmap based on today's assumptions, without any claim to completeness. We can't guarantee that the enhancements we mention will be available at a certain point in time, as SAP might change development plans without notice. For more reliable information to plan for your own projects and strategies, check the Cloud Integration online documentation or contact SAP directly. You can check the roadmap at *www.sap.com/products/roadmaps.html*. If you select **Business Technology Platform** and choose **Integration**, you'll find the up-to-date roadmap for Cloud Integration. On this page, you can also find roadmap information for the other capabilities in SAP Integration Suite. However, in this chapter, we'll focus on Cloud Integration.

13.1 Integration Content Design

Having gone through this book, you've learned that integration content design is the key task when dealing with Cloud Integration. In each chapter, you learned successively more complex integration content design features.

The following new features are planned to make the life of an integration developer easier and to improve productivity:

- More granular access policies will be available on the package level. Integration developers will benefit from a new feature that gives the option to restrict maintenance of artifacts in certain packages in the Cloud Integration capability of SAP

Integration Suite. You will, for instance, be able to define the authorization required to maintain the package; while it will remain possible to be able to read all packages. This extra granularity will enable organizations to isolate sensitive data for different lines of business in a tenant.

- Features will enable customers to inspect the tenant health of the Cloud Integration capability locally in SAP Integration Suite. It will bring awareness of problems affecting the tenant's health status for Java Message Service (JMS) resources. It will also provide guidance for issue resolution and will substantially reduce time to resolution.
- A "Where-used" functionality in SAP Integration Suite will be available for identifying the integration artifacts in credentials, key pairs, certificates, reusable artifacts, and resources.
- Advanced checks will be offered against the guidelines in the iFlow designer of the Cloud Integration capability within SAP Integration Suite. It will be able to check custom iFlows against iFlow design guidelines provided by SAP.
- In Chapter 6, we introduced you to the design guidelines for integration content development. You can expect that the Cloud Integration team will continuously update design guidelines with new sample iFlows and updated documentation (published on SAP API Business Hub).
- Support will be provided for exactly once in order (EOIO) processing functionality. The EOIO quality of service will improve the robustness of asynchronous integration scenarios, assuring the same sequence of messages is sent from the sender system.

13.2 Connectivity

The connectivity options of Cloud Integration will be improved by new or enhanced adapters, such as the following:

- **Exactly once (EO) quality of service**
  Support will be provided for EO quality of service as a configuration option in the Cloud Integration. This feature will also be offered to additional adapters, allowing EO according to the protocol: IDoc adapter and SAP Reliable Messaging (SAP RM) adapter.
- **A number of adapters for Cloud Integration**
  There are a number of adapters planned in the coming periods, including Coupa, Snowflake, Microsoft SMB, X.400, NetSuite, and Salesforce Marketing. The number of adapters is expected to increase in the coming years.
- **File adapter**
  A lot of customers are extensively using the file adapter in their existing SAP Process

Orchestration platform. Today, such capability doesn't yet exist on Cloud Integration. The file adapter will provide the capability to send and receive files from a Network File System (NFS) on the Edge Integration Cell.

- **OFTP2 adapter**
  The Odette File Transfer Protocol (OFTP2) was established by Odette, the European automotive standards body. OFTP is a widely used protocol in Europe for the exchange of EDI data, in particular for the automotive industry, and was initially designed to work over an X.25 network. This adapter for OFTP version 2 (OFTP2) will enable customers to send and receive messages on the Edge Integration Cell.
- **RFC sender adapter**
  The Remote Function Call (RFC) is the standard SAP interface for communication between SAP systems. RFC calls a function to be executed in a remote system. It's currently still used by customers in SAP Process Orchestration. The RFC sender adapter will enable customers to receive messages on the Edge Integration Cell through the RFC protocol.

13.3 Edge Integration Cell

As we discussed in Chapter 12, the Edge Integration Cell added the capability to have SAP Integration Suite within the customer's network. In the coming periods, the Edge Integration Cell of Cloud Integration will be enhanced with more capabilities, including the following:

- **Connectivity and adapters**
  Today, Integration Suite has a number of adapters that aren't yet available in the Edge Integration Cell. Some of these adapters will also become available on the Edge Integration Cell runtime profile, including adapters such as Amazon Web Services, Microsoft Dynamics 365 CRM, Salesforce, SugarCRM, ServiceNow, and Workday.
- **Support for Edge Integration Cell in Google Cloud Platform**
  Today, the Edge Integration Cell can't yet be deployed to all hyperscalers. The enablement of SAP Integration Suite tenants on the Google Cloud Platform to activate the Edge Integration Cell runtime in SAP Integration Suite is planned for 2024.
- **Availability in partner-managed Alibaba Cloud**
  SAP Integration Suite customers will soon be able to deploy in partner-managed Alibaba Cloud to consume Edge Integration Cell.
- **Local authentication and authorization**
  Support for local authentication and authorization as a fallback to the default cloud-based authentication and authorization in SAP Business Technology Platform (SAP BTP).

- **Local OData API access**
  It's planned to enable the Edge Integration Cell to access remote OData APIs for monitoring and operations through the Edge Integration Cell instance within the customer network.
- **Support for the container application platform Red Hat OpenShift**
  At the time of writing this book, the Edge Integration Cell can't yet be deployed on Red Hat OpenShift. This new capability will change that and enable customers to deploy the Edge Integration Cell in the Kubernetes container application platform of their choice–including Red Hat OpenShift.
- **Support for principal propagation**
  This capability will enable supporting principal propagation for the Edge Integration Cell runtime profile. It will enable forwarding of the principal (identity of a user) from the sending system to the receiving system.
- **Support for user-defined function (UDF) libraries with imported archives in message mapping**
  This feature will support importing user-defined functions (UDFs) into the Cloud Integration capability of SAP Integration Suite, which has reference to imported archives in the Enterprise Services Repository (ES Repository). It will include the following:
  - Import a function library from the ES Repository
  - Import archived UDFs
  - Consume in message mapping

13

13.4 Migration from SAP Process Orchestration to Cloud Integration

As explained in Chapter 1 and outlined in more detail in Chapter 2, Cloud Integration can either run on an infrastructure provided by SAP (when using the SAP BTP, Neo environment) or by an organization such as Microsoft or Amazon (when using the SAP BTP, Cloud Foundry environment). Recently, Cloud Integration has gained the capability to run on your company network using the Edge Integration Cell.

Customers who started by using Cloud Integration on SAP BTP, Neo environment have been offered paths and tools to support migrating their existing integration scenarios to SAP BTP, Cloud Foundry environment.

13.5 Summary

Cloud Integration is already a mature integration solution with a rich feature portfolio. However, as we've tried to show in this chapter, we're not at the end of our journey together. Cloud Integration is updated every month, and with each update, many more features are added to its portfolio one by one. Stay tuned, check out the available online resources on a regular basis to stay informed about new innovations, and—most importantly—keep enjoying your integration journey with Cloud Integration!

The Authors

John Mutumba Bilay studied computer engineering and finance at the University of Cape Town, South Africa. After completing his studies, he started his career as a software engineer. He currently works as a senior software engineer and enterprise integration consultant at Rojo Consultancy B.V. in the Netherlands. With more than 14 years of international experience in information technology, he has spent the last years primarily focused on integration technologies. His SAP specialties include SAP integration- and process-related technologies, including SAP Process Orchestration and SAP Cloud Platform Integration.

In addition to his daily integration work, he provides integration-related training for SAP and for Rojo Consultancy B.V. John is the author of *SAP Process Orchestration: The Comprehensive Guide* (SAP PRESS, 2017) and one of the co-authors of *Getting Started with SAP HANA Cloud Platform* (SAP PRESS, 2016).

Shashank Singh is an enterprise integration architect at Rojo Consultancy B.V. in the Netherlands. He holds a bachelor's degree in computer science and engineering from India. He has been working in the integration domain for more than 12 years. He is passionate about integration and likes solving integration challenges for customers and colleagues. Over the years, he has helped multiple customers define their integration strategy and governance through modern integration techniques and best practices. He has expertise in multiple integration platforms and vast experience in both SAP and non-SAP integrations.

Swati Singh holds a degree in computer engineering and has been working in the domain of software engineering for more than 10 years. She currently works as an enterprise integration architect at Rojo Consultancy B.V. in the Netherlands. She is passionate about enterprise integration and bringing transparency and observability to complex IT landscapes. In her daily work, she supports global organizations in solving modern integration challenges of A2A, B2B, event, device, and API-based integrations. She takes system integration one step further by unleashing the power of integration data through machine learning methodologies to derive patterns and add value. She specializes in multiple integration tools and platforms, including SAP Process Orchestration and SAP Integration Suite.

Dr. Peter Gutsche studied physics at Heidelberg University, Ruperto Carola. After completing his Ph.D, he joined SAP in 1999. As a technical author, Peter was involved in many knowledge management projects related to SAP's interface and integration technologies. Today, as a knowledge architect, he is responsible for the product documentation of SAP Cloud Platform Integration and works on documentation concepts for cloud software.

Peter is a seasoned technical author with wide-ranging experience in the fields of SAP Process Integration and SAP Cloud Platform Integration.

Mandy Krimmel studied engineering at Humboldt University, Berlin, Germany. In 1998, she started her professional career at a research institute of the German state of Baden-Württemberg, where she was responsible for the technical evaluation of various EU research projects. In 2001, Mandy joined SAP, working on various integration-related projects, including SAP Process Integration and SAP Cloud Platform Integration. In her current role as product owner, she is responsible for the design, architecture, and development of various cloud integration components, helping to shape the development of the SAP Cloud Platform Integration product portfolio.

Mandy is a valued mentor and an active blogger in the SAP Community on various cloud integration-related topics. She is one of the co-authors of *SAP NetWeaver Process Integration* (SAP PRESS, 2010).

Index

A

D

E

F

G

H

I

J

K

L

M

N

O

R

S

T

U

V

W

X

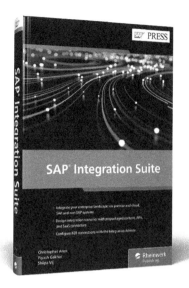

- Learn about the SAP Integration Suite certification test structure and how to prepare for the exam
- Review key topics covered in each portion of the exam
- Test your knowledge with practice questions and answers

Jaspreet Bagga

SAP Integration Suite Certification Guide

Development Associate Exam

Preparing for your C_CPI_14 exam? Make the grade with this SAP Integration Suite certification study guide! From API Management to the Integration Advisor, this guide will review the key technical and functional knowledge you need to pass the test. Explore test methodology, key concepts for each topic area, and practice questions and answers. Your path to SAP Integration Suite certification begins here!

417 pages, pub. 08/2023
E-Book: $74.99 | **Print:** $79.95 | **Bundle:** $89.99

www.sap-press.com/5735

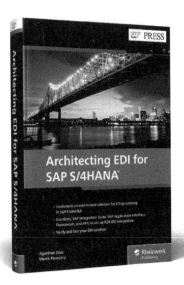